D1376360

To John

Merry Christmas 1969

Mom and Dad

GRANT LEWI

HEAVEN KNOWS WHAT

GRANT LEWI

1968
LLEWELLYN PUBLICATIONS
P.O. Box 3383
Saint Paul, Minnesota 55101
U.S.A.

Copyright and published 1935
by Doubleday Doran and Co., Inc.

Reissued 1937
by the Sun Dial Press

Copyright 1947
by Grant Lewi

Reprinted 1949

Copyright 1962
by
Llewellyn Publications

Copyright 1967
by
Llewellyn Publications

Reprinted 1968

Printed in the United States of America

1902 GRANT LEWI 1951

By Carl Payne Tobey

GRANT LEWI has become a legend. He was the lad who quit teaching English at Dartmouth and became an astrologer. He was not surprised when his *Heaven Knows What* became the best selling astrological book of the twentieth century. He expected it to be. Yet, he didn't even sign his name to it. He signed it *Scorpio,* despite the fact that he had no planets in Scorpio. This has confused some people. He said, it was the first thing that came to his mind, and he dismissed it there.

When he first courted Carolyn Wallace, his curiosity was aroused, when he discovered that her mother was an astrologer, for she was Atlene Gayle Wallace. What was this all about? He had to find out for himself. All this was before there was an astrology magazine on a newsstand, and few people knew the difference between astrology and astronomy. While he was working on the manuscript of *Heaven Knows What,* Grant was also writing for the early issues of the first astrology magazine to appear on newsstands and stay there. Two earlier ones had failed. The magazine and its founder, Paul G. Clancy, are credited with making America astrology conscious. All this at a time when well-known Joanne Clancy, the current publisher, was in her early teens. Serving as Research Editor of American Astrology at the same time when Grant Lewi was on the staff, the writer first came to know Grant at the same time he was preparing *Heaven Knows What.*

Heaven Knows What was originally published in 1935 by Doubleday Doran and Co. It was re-published in 1937 by the Sun Dial Press, and republished again in 1947 by the Morris Press. Since about 1953, it has been out of print. Rare book shops have been combed for it. Librarians assert that library copies have been stolen. For nine years, the writer has had to answer letters explaining that he does not know any secret place where there might be a copy at any price.

Grant left the staff of *American Astrology Magazine* to become editor of Dell Publications' *Horoscope.* Many other astrology magazines also came into the field, but under his editorship, *Horoscope* came to lead the field in two years with a monthly circulation of nearly 200,000 copies. He remained in this position for a decade. Although there was a desk at Dell with Grant's name on it, you would not be likely to find him there. He was a restless Sun-in-Gemini conjunct the node of Uranus, with Leo on the Ascendent, and he was usually in motion. The Sun was also in opposition to Uranus to increase his rating as a rebel. He was a true intellectual. He believed that man should have a better destiny. It bothered him to see people living in slums. He liked people, and he met them wherever he found them. Money nearly always seemed to come his way to the extent that he needed it, but he wasn't much interested in money. Although Grant was usually moving around somewhere, by some miracle he always seemed to arrive in time to meet deadlines. He never stood up those presses, but the moment they were rolling, he was gone again.

He didn't believe in paying for life insurance, because he said he had no intention of dying right away. When he was 48-1/2, he changed his mind and bought life insurance. Right after his 49th birthday, he died of a cerebral hemorrhage. At least that's what the doctors said it was. I'm not sure they knew. Anyway, he saved himself thirty years of life insurance premiums. He finally paid one premium and the insurance company had to pay off.

Grant and the writer were neighbors in Westchester County in New York State. We saw a good deal of each other. We constantly exchanged astrological ideas and experiences. He would tell people he was not a "joiner." He didn't like to belong to organizations, particularly astrological organizations. He finally did join the American Federation of Astrologers, but he told me that was because he liked Ernest Grant. He didn't go along with the orthodox ideas of a lot of the astrologers, and he didn't want to bother arguing with the orthodox astrologers. He didn't use progressions, but when asked about this he would tell other astrologers, "If progressions work for you, you use them. I don't use them." He did not employ astrology as a causal phenomenon. To him, as to some other astrologers, it was an algebra of life. He used planetary nodes and Arabic points. Many astrologers ignore these factors because they can't see how a mathematical point can have an "effect", but they use house cusps, unaware that these are mere mathematical points. Even the Zodiac is a matter of mathematical points. Grant believed that a person's life is something very individual and personal. He didn't want to intrude into the personal part of the other fellow's life, and he didn't want anybody intruding too far into his. He felt the same way about a horoscope. It was something very individual and personal that was only for its owner. He would be glad to help with it if someone needed help, but one should learn all about it for one's self.

He was a good story teller. His sense of humor was always working. There was a gleam of laughter in his eyes, and his personality was full of charm. He enjoyed talking to small groups more than talking to large groups. He liked Greenwich Village and he liked its people. He lived there for a while. He approached his work as a scientist, but he thought there was room for the poet and the artist too. One of his own prose poems, a tribute to Franklin D. Roosevelt, filled two columns on the editorial page of the New York Evening Post. He selected a great many of his friends from the arts rather than from astrology. He didn't have too many intimate friends among the astrologers. Few people knew history as well as Grant. He was interested in the principles that were hidden behind life itself. Sometimes he wrote novels.

I never really knew Grant well when we were both on the staff of American Astrology Magazine. It was later when I lived in Westchester that he spent many weekends at my home. It was just that Grant was fun to have around. His conversation was always stimulating. He made a good guest because you didn't have to worry about him or wait on him. He made himself one of the family and took care of himself.

It takes 84 years from the moment of birth for Uranus to go around the circle of the heavens, or the ellipse of the heavens if you like it that way better. It is always a turning point in a life when it gets half way around, and in the case of Grant, when it got half way 'round it was on its own node, and it was on the Sun in his chart. This isn't an easy aspect to experience if you want to stay in one place. Grant never did like to stay too long in one place.

It was a pleasant summer morning when he stopped off to see me on his way to Manhattan. It was so nice that we just sat out on the grass and talked.

"I've got to have a change. I can't stand it. I'd like to quit my job."

In surprise, I asked, "Why?" After all, he had the best paying job in the business. He seldom went near the office. Why did he want to give up his job?

"There's nothing wrong with the job. George Delacorte is a swell guy to work for. They don't come any better. I just don't want to stay any longer. I must go on to something else. I know I have to do it. If I knew where to get the capital, I'd start my own magazine."

Excusing himself, the writer went to a telephone. He wanted to see how difficult it would be to get the money for Grant to start his own magazine. After an official of the American News Company had listened to the story on the phone, he said, "Tell Mr. Lewi to come down and have lunch with me today."

That was how the magazine *The Astrologer* was born.

This was not the end of the restlessness. The family had seen Arizona. Carolyn and two of the children were already out there. I was seeing much of Grant, and he was talking about Arizona. I was interested too. I had never been to Arizona. Because of western movies, my six-year-old son was also interested in Arizona, wanting me to take him there to live. My curiosity was causing me to ask many questions about Arizona. One day, Grant left New York to meet his wife and family in Arizona. He located up in the mountains near Prescott, the old mining town from frontier days, which hadn't changed much. The name of one of its main streets was, and still is, "Whiskey Row."

His children were reaching university age, and Grant was concerned about their education. You can't get much of a college education up in those mountains. So, Grant and his family moved to the university town of Tucson. Everything was going great. Early in 1951, Grant wrote me a long letter. He wanted me to quit, come to Arizona, and go in business with him. He loved every inch of Arizona. There wasn't much in the entire state that he and his whole family had not explored. Weekends, they explored Arizona, and after Alaska and Texas, it is the third largest state in area. There were only two towns of consequence in the whole state. Although the university is in what is now the center of town, back in frontier days its site was selected by a group of gamblers who bought the land and gave it to the university free to get education out of town, where it wouldn't cause people to want to limit gambling houses.

I was interested in Grant's proposal, but being Taurus, I had to think it over. I thought it over for six months, and then I wrote Grant and agreed to his proposition but said it would be a year before I could move to Arizona myself. It was a late Saturday afternoon when my special delivery was handed to him. He was about to have dinner. He was very cheerful at dinner, but perhaps Grant was getting restless again. Early the next morning, I received a telegram from his daughter, Jan, saying he had passed away before daylight. I took a train for Arizona. I never came back.

Tucson folks were awed. They told me many stories. If you are an astrologer, some people are apt to think you are a bit mystic and different from other people. They thought Grant knew he was about to go. There was that story about the life insurance company. There were other stories. He died before dawn on the morning of July 14th, 1951. He had refused to make any appointments for the month of August. He told some people, "I'll consider it if I am still here." He joked about not knowing whether he would even be around in August. People wondered about him, and when news of his passing came they were sure that he had been ready, that he had planned on heading off on another journey.

Upon arriving in Tucson, I had to help Carolyn read the mail that was arriving. I was a little surprised to learn the number of prominent people in all walks of life who had been followers of Grant Lewi's *The Astrologer*. During the next year, I met many interesting and prominent people who came to Arizona because they wanted a few inside words about Grant. At least a half dozen of these people wound up moving to Tucson. We thought about it as a small town then, a little place of 40,000 people, not the quarter million population that we find ten years later. In Grant's Tucson days, it was known as a cow town.

Grant's children graduated, and left Tucson to carve out their own careers. There was Jan, her husband, Troy, and there was Carol and Bill. Carolyn, their mother, has moved on to Los Gatos, California. But, Tucson is still filled with friends of the Lewi's.

As for the old saying that deaths come in threes, first it was Grant Lewi. Shortly thereafter, came the word of the passing of Llewellyn George, soon followed by the news of the death of Elbert Benjamine, three of the most prominent astrologers of the first half of the twentieth century. They all died in 1951, although George and Benjamine were much older men.

Grant could be the last word in informality. Conventions had no interest for him. He believed in living and making decisions intellectually instead of following any outmoded rules or regulations. He didn't like schedules. He didn't gear himself too much to either time nor society. In many ways, he was a very free person. He knew freedom. He liked freedom for others. He was casual. He dressed casually. He was a handsome lad, but it was the charm of his personality that warmed and captured people. He always carried a gleam in his eye that indicated something was secretly amusing. He was as interested in the horoscope of a beggar as in that of a millionaire or a president.

The writer leaped at an opportunity to write an introduction to the republication of Grant's first astrology book, because Grant Lewi was an important influence in the lives of a lot of people. He was an important influence in the writer's life. One afternoon at a cocktail party, a Tucson newspaperman singled me out. "Before he died, Grant Lewi told me I would never have to work after this year if I didn't want to. I didn't take stock in that sort of thing, but I just became the recipient of a trust fund that will support me for the rest of my life."

Grant Lewi did not use progressions. He did not use fixed stars. He found everything he wanted in the solar system. He was a practical rather than a theoretical astrologer. He wasn't concerned with why astrology works. He was more concerned with the fact that it does. This was no more unexpected or mysterious to him than the fact that trees grow. We don't know how nor why. He was more concerned with astrology as the only real key to psychological understanding of self than with any of its other phases. His novels included "The Gods Arrive" and "The Star of Empire."

He didn't speak about it out loud, because he didn't want to hurt the feelings of others, but there was much of the orthodox astrology that Grant considered mere superstition. He didn't want to hurt anybody nor did he want to see anybody hurt. He was a liberal in his political thinking, and he was horrified when the first atomic bomb was dropped. Soon thereafter, he sent me a gift. It was a book entitled, "Modern Man is Obsolete." He would go far out of his way to help people. He was very loyal to his friends. He could earn money but he never bothered protecting it after he earned it. He was not an insecure person. When he lived in New Rochelle, he spoke his piece on all public matters.

Heaven Knows What has been popular for its simplicity. It takes a part of astrology and makes it possible for you to use it in your own life, without the necessity of knowing all the technicalities of the construction of a horoscope. It makes a great starting point for the beginner. Yet most professional astrologers want a copy of it near. His interpretations were different. Llewellyn George once told a friend that

Grant's interpretations must be intuitive because they were unlike any that had been written before him. All you need do is follow Grant Lewi's own instructions. It won't tell you everything you may want to know about either yourself or astrology. The book that will do that has not been written, but you will find no superstitious quotations from the dark ages. It will get you on your way. It supplies interpretations that will not be found elsewhere, because they are a part of the personality of Grant Lewi himself. He was strictly original. He didn't borrow ideas from others. He had more of his own than he could use.

Grant Lewi has departed but he left us a heritage. Grant is gone, but *Heaven Knows What* lives on. It is one of his brain children. It is the intention of the publisher to revive and republish his other brain children. The writer has met many people who are good astrologers themselves today. Their first introduction to the subject was reading *Heaven Knows What,* which was followed by *Astrology For The Millions.* These are both human documents. Grant Lewi was human himself and he liked humanity. He thought he saw a way to help and improve it. I neglected to say that he was also born with the Sun conjunct Pluto. When the writer first wrote an article introducing Pluto as the ruler of Aries instead of ruler of Scorpio, pointing out that people born with the Sun conjunct Pluto had the same pioneering characteristics as people born with Sun in Aries, Grant read the article, and with his customary amused expression said, "You can say that again. You overlooked the fact that I am one of those people."

It has been a source of great satisfaction to the writer that Carl L. Weschcke, the new owner of Llewellyn Publications selected the books of Grant Lewi for republication, and I know it would be a great source of satisfaction to Llewellyn George if he were still alive, but perhaps he and Grant are still carrying the ball in another sphere. Perhaps they found another place to pioneer. Perhaps they have reached a new frontier.

In his "Preface to Limited Edition" — not this edition — which follows, Grant Lewi talks about the progress in astrology since HEAVEN KNOWS WHAT first made its appearance. Let us bring his remarks up to date. First. I would like to go back a bit. I would like to consider what Charles Fort called a fairytale — astronomy. When I first read Mr. Fort's statement, I thought he was joking. Many years of experience have taught me he was not. Allegedly, astronomy is a science, and in some countries it has been somewhat as alleged. As generally described, astronomy is a physical study of whatever may be beyond the earth and in space. It was originally called natural astrology. There have been accomplishments by some astronomers, but most of the accomplishments for which astronomers claim credit came about as the work of non-astronomers and were opposed and ridiculed by the astronomers of that time.

Originally, all was astrology. It is the world's oldest science. There came a time when a particular Pope in Rome, unfamiliar with astrology but believing that it was a doctrine of fatalism, declared himself against it, with the result that a new word was coined to satisfy the Church. Astronomy was to be purely physical and materialistic in such a way that it would not be working the same side of the street as the church and could not be looked upon as a competitor. Up until the time of Ptolemy, it was always recognized that the Sun was the center of the solar system, but the Bible said that God made the earth first and built all these other objects in space around it, so everything had to be changed to conform to the Bible, and whether he liked it or not, Ptolemy had to teach that the earth is the center of the solar system. For all we know, he may have spoken in relative terms. You can employ anything as a center using it as a particular frame of reference, and when we draw a horoscope today we place the earth in the center, *because that is where we are, and we want to see things from where we are.* The astronomers all accepted Ptolemy, and they all accepted the earth as the center. This is as we should expect it, because astronomers always accept what they are told to accept. They are a very obedient people. When it is to their purpose, the astronomers call Ptolemy an astronomer, and when they find it convenient for some ulterior purpose, they call him an astrologer. Actually, it was about 500 years after the birth of Christ that the word astronomy first came into being.

There was no such word as astronomy at the time of Plato, and yet the copies of Plato sold to students in some universities today have been rewritten, and the word astronomy has been substituted for astrology, to give the impression that Plato's interest was in astronomy and not astrology, which is impossible because in the days of Plato, there was no such word as astronomy. As we proceed, you will see the thorough job of brainwashing that was attempted.

Along came an astrologer named Copernicus. His is one of the greatest names honored by astronomers today. They now classify him as an astronomer, because they find it convenient to misappropriate credit for his accomplishments. Copernicus wrote a paper under the title *de Revolutionibis.* Addressing himself to the Pope, he mildly suggested that the astronomers were wrong, that perhaps the earth was not the center of the solar system. Copernicus was a mathematician, which most astronomers are not, and he demonstrated that if we considered the Sun as the center of the solar system, it would explain the motion of the planets. They would always be going on their way, while when observed from the earth, they sometimes appear to be moving backward. He pointed out that the heliocentric system employed by the ancient Greek astrologer, Aristarchus, a pupil of Pythagoras and dating back to about 500 B.C., was more perfect and valid than the geocentric system of Ptolemy and the church, the system of the astronomers.

Although they are now attempting to call him one of them, there was great opposition to both Copernicus and his paper by the astronomers of his day and by the church. Publication of his book was forbidden. Yes, they had censorship in those days. However, his paper was finally published, and now various astronomers glorify him as one of them, fail to mention that he was an astrologer, so declare in classrooms, "Copernicus disproved astrology by proving that the sun and not the earth is the center of the solar system."

It has always been a characteristic of astronomy that astronomers oppose and deny a new discovery until their position is no longer possible, and then they claim credit for the discovery. Meteors had been falling from the sky for a long time. They had been seen to fall by vast numbers of people, but astronomers explained them away. Somebody down the street threw them. Finally, so many meteors fell on one town in France, that the astronomers decided to accept them. They have made no attempt to explain how, when the earth was turning on its axis, all the meteors were falling on the same town. Such discrepancies never bother an astronomer. If a student points out the disturbing facts, an astronomer can always say, "I don't want to argue with you." After all, what right has a student to argue with an astronomer? Isn't it right there in the book? Are you going to believe what you or other people see or experience, or are you going to believe what is in the book and what the astronomer says?

Kepler was an astrologer. He followed Copernicus, and because he was considering the sun as the center of the solar system, he was able to write the three laws of planetary motion. Now, the astronomers point with pride to Kepler, call him one of their own and say, "Look what we accomplished!" They now forget that he was an astrologer and put him down in their history books as an astronomer. The work of Kepler, a very poor man, was financed by another astrologer, Tycho Brahe, who had an "in" with the king and thereby was able to live in pretty good style. The king wanted better predictions, and to make the king happy, Brahe called on Kepler, because Kepler was a mathematician, while Brahe wasn't. Kepler had the mathematical knowledge to do the job and did it. Now, the astronomers have nominated him to their club. After all, he is dead and that makes it safe, because he can no longer make any discoveries which might upset textbooks, classrooms, ivory towers or tranquility. New discoveries are very hard on an astronomer's nerves. When you live in a dream world and you like it, you dislike people who wake you and request that you face reality. Astronomers live in the past. They look far out into space where they see things as they were many millions of years ago. The present or future is very annoying to them.

Astronomy was born as a form of religious bigotry, and in academic circles it has never changed. Over in England, they had a different kind of a church, but they still had fancy-robed men who set up standards to be certain that all new discoveries would conform with their conception of the Bible, as they had written it. A mathematician named Sir Isaac Newton discovered that gravity seemed to obey a mathematical formula. He was investigating for his own amusement and knowledge, but an astronomer named William Lilly offered to have a book on the subject printed if Newton would write it. Newton wrote the book in Latin and it was published in Latin. There was, as usual, great astronomical opposition to Newton's conception. It was said that gravity and levitation (and both words are to be found in Newton's book) were occult. Anything that was occult belonged to God, and if any mathematician knew what was good for him, he better not go fussing around with any of God's fancy occult forces.

As always happens in these matters, Newton was an astrologer, and it has been said that this displeased William Lilly a great deal and caused him to chide Newton about it, but we have never been able to find any verification for the story. Anyway, we find that the discoveries were made by a man who was a combination astrologer and mathematician, and all the great astrologers of the old days were also the leading mathematicians of those days. We don't seem to find much progress that we can attribute to the brain-washing teachers of astronomy. It would seem that they teach and lecture for pay to brain-wash others in identical manner to their own original brainwashing. Newton was an interesting man. How interesting we do not know, because most of his writings have never been published. Their publication has been forbidden in England. They have not been burned, but they are locked up in a museum to conceal his real beliefs. One of his secrets was that he did not believe in the holy trinity. He was head of the Royal Society, principal "scientific" organization in England, and no man was allowed to head this organization unless he believed in the holy trinity. This was sort of fraudulent in a way because he really put it over on the king, the church, his brother "scientists" and all those high and brilliantly robed powers of the church. He never allowed them to look into his mind or real beliefs. He turned out to be a good politician, because he also obtained a good-paying job from the king himself. The king made him Exchequer of the whole kingdom.

Anyway, Newton wrote a book in Latin, and in 1937, it was finally published in the United States in English. In time the astronomers took over Newton's gravitation, invented a story about Newton sleeping under an apple tree and being bopped by an apple, whereupon he woke up and said, "Well, what do you know. I just discovered gravitation!" This story is in complete disagreement with Newton's theory of gravity.

From this point on, astronomers taught the theory of gravitation, but what they taught as Newton's theory had little resemblance to Newton's theory. It seems quite possible that none of the astronomers ever read Newton's book, because they didn't appear to know what was in it.

Astronomers appear to like apples but somebody is always upsetting the applecart. This time it was two mathematicians in two different countries, one named Leverier and one named Adams. They noted that Uranus didn't behave very well. They did much calculating, and although neither knew of the other, they covered the same ground, and came up with the same answer. They said that if astronomers would point a telescope at a certain mathematical point in space, they'd be looking at a newly discovered planet. Adams, who finished his calculations first sent them to the Astronomer Royal in all of his holiness. That was a presumptuous thing to do, and he didn't seem to know that the Astronomer Royal was too royal and too holy to read that kind of trash. The Astronomer Royal glanced at the content of the letter to see what the fellow wanted, didn't bother to look at the calculations, but threw them into a drawer where they were to remain for some time.

Later, Leverrier finished his calculations and sent them to an astronomical observatory in France. *New planet discovered!*

FLASH! ! The Astronomer Royal remembered something. It was — a letter. What was it that fellow was talking about? Didn't he say something about a new planet? Sure enough. It wasn't France that made the discovery. It was England. Here was a letter from Adams. Here were the same figures. The Astronomer Royal claimed the discovery for his holy office. This led to a bit of conflict, but it was ultimately patched up, probably with the help of a few special ambassadors, and no war between England and France resulted. Now we have a discovery which is claimed by the astronomers although Adams was not an astronomer. He was a mathematician.

Astronomer Perciful Lowell at Flagstaff, Arizona, decided we might as well continue discovering planets, so he calculated a planet beyond Neptune, but never found one. After his death, a young lad with no rating as an astronomer happened to be working at Flagstaff and in between studied pictures of the sky. He noted an object which had moved between one photograph and another. He showed the pictures to his superiors, who were skeptical, but they were thinking about Lowell, a real astronomer belonging to their club. He was dead. They decided to name the planet Lowell. The young lad who discovered it was named Clyde Tombaugh. Nobody suggested naming it after Tombaugh. After all, he didn't have a Ph.D. and without a Ph.D., no astronomer has been properly brainwashed. Not all astronomers wanted the planet named after Lowell, so they picked Pluto, a Greek God, but they compromised on the symbol. They combined two letters of the alphabet P and L into ♇ , and this made anti-Lowell astronomers happy because they said it was the first two letters of PLUTO, the name agreed upon, while the pro-Lowell astronomers said the PL stood for Perciful Lowell. Another astronomical war was avoided. One thing still bothers the astronomers. They should never have admitted Tombaugh discovered the planet, because some years later the superior eyesight of Tombaugh embarrassed them further. One day, he saw a flying saucer and happened to mention it to the press. This was bad because it is part of the present dogma and religious bigotry of astronomy to claim there are no flying saucers, as years back there were no meteors. Meteors have been accepted into the club, and anything that looks like a flying saucer is a meteor. If near enough to the sun, it might be a sunspot that slipped off but sunspots were not always respectable either. The first sunspot was discovered by a Catholic priest, who was told that if there was anything such as a sunspot, Socrates would have written about it. He knew better than to do that again, and it was six months before he dared again look through a telescope. He probably had to pray that long to atone for his sin. However, if we wait long enough astronomers always accept what they deny today, and claim they discovered it.

After both meteors and sunspots were accepted into the mystic fraternity of astronomers, RCA Communications Inc., a subsidiary of Radio Corporation of America wanted to know what caused interference with shortwave radio. The astronomers said it was sunspots, so RCA tossed a few million dollars to the astronomers and in effect said, "Find out how sunspots affect shortwave radio transmission." The astronomers supposedly did research and told RCA about beautiful sunspots. Sometimes when there was more than the usual frequency of sunspots there would be shortwave radio interference. At other times, there would be a high ratio of sunspots but no radio interference. Again there would be no sunspots but much radio interference. This was very confusing to RCA. It was suggested that the astronomers use some of the money RCA was handing out to find whether planetary aspects might have some connection with magnetic storms, but this horrified the astronomers who said, "Why that would be astrology." The astronomers knew that if planets could have any connection with radio, Socrates or Harlow Shapley would have written about it in their books. The astronomers dropped the matter and never came back to it. RCA wasn't convinced. They were a troublesome lot, and probably didn't know their Socrates. They didn't say anything more to the astronomers but selected a radio engineer named John H. Nelson, bought him a telescope, set it up on the roof of a building near Wall Street, and began their own research program. Within two years, they made an announcement. They had found they could predict magnetic storms and consequent radio weather by studying planetary aspects.

Here was a typical American business firm doing things in a typical business way. About this time, I interviewed John H. Nelson. A big magnetic storm was under way. It was interfering with the teletype machines receiving messages coming across the North Atlantic route from Europe. The machines were printing gibberish. This would mean no messages coming from Europe. No news coming either. News must come by radio. However, all was well. It had been possible to predict this storm far in advance. An extra staff had been flown to Tunisia. Messages were coming in from Europe. They were going around the storm. They were being beamed to Tunisia and rebeamed from Tunisia to New York. Thousands and thousands of dollars were being saved. Engineers had solved the problem that astronomers could not or would not solve. I had to leave this meeting because I had a luncheon appointment at the Engineers Club uptown.

Here, we have an odd coincidence. My luncheon date was with the astronomer who was in charge of the original research program of the astronomers being financed by money donated by RCA. He was a personal friend of mine. We had visited back and forth at each other's homes. He was secretly interested in astrology, studied it, had his own secret astrological library, but could not openly admit anything because of the academic pressure exerted on him by organized astronomy in the United States and England. If he dared admit his astrological interest, he would be excommunicated. Despite his interest in astrology, he dared not go beyond sunspots. When I met him, he was a sad man. His work was over. His university research funds had been cut off. His work would have to stop. He did not know why they had been cut off, but it was pretty clear when he informed me that his university's whole research program had been financed by RCA. Without giving any reason, RCA had, in effect, said, "That's all there is. There isn't any more."

Because of its very inborn bigoted nature, astronomy had failed to do the job it was paid to do. Impatient with delays and lack of results, a big American corporation had called in its own engineers and had done the job itself. It didn't need the astronomers. They were too impractical. It had been giving them handouts in the form of millions of dollars long enough. Astronomy is not only a fairytale; it is a disease.

What was the reaction of the world of astronomers to all of this?

The story of the discovery of RCA was on the front pages of the newspapers. It was in the news and other magazines. It did not appear in any astronomical journal. Astronomers held their heads high, looked the other way and chose to ignore the matter. For more than two decades, RCA has been saving millions of dollars by employing the planets to predict magnetic storms so they know how to beam messages to go around such storms.

Over in England, a British astronomer wrote an article in which he said the RCA work was a gross misuse of statistics. He had never seen the statistics. He had never interviewed anyone connected with RCA. He had no access to any data. He was 3000 miles away. Yet he was able to write an article and say that the RCA work was a gross misuse of statistics.

In February 1962, I was in a debate concerning astrology with Dr. George Abel of U.C.L.A., an astronomer. Another astrologer, Sydney Omarr and a psychologist named Paul Bindram were the other participants. It was the Ben Hunter program over KTTV in Los Angeles. Sydney brought up the RCA work. Dr. Abel sneered, quoted the British astronomer mentioned above and referring to Engineer Nelson of RCA as "that guy" said, "Why he's only an amateur astronomer." In other words, he doesn't teach school and he hasn't been accepted into the cult. Astronomers appear to live in a little isolated world of their own where they recognize neither the outside world nor any form of reality. Their beliefs have to come from textbooks having no relation to what may be in the sky, and all scientific evidence that is contrary to their cultist beliefs is excluded. There is a definite parallel in the way an astronomer thinks of himself as a "professional" and the manner in which a prostitute considers herself a "professional." Each is getting paid. The girl merely sells her body, while the astronomer sells his soul. When he becomes an astronomer, he joins a more-or-less secret fraternity that is based on hypocricy, and forever after he must be intellectually dishonest. At least, that has been the way astronomy has been up through the ages since its origin and until the beginning of the space age.

In the '30s, Harvard had an astronomer named Dr. Bart J. Bok. They brought him over from Holland. Bok was an inoffensive sort of a fellow, but the job they gave him was less inoffensive. He was to go forth and destroy astrology. First, he wrote an article purporting to investigate astrology. The investigation consisted of interviewing enemies of astrology and publishing their vindictive assertions. In no case did they interview a person who had studied or tested astrology. To qualify to be interviewed you had to be against astrology. The article did tell a cute story about how the astronomers had pulled a fast one and used their influence to have the Federal Communications Commission bar astrology from the air unless someone was to condemn the subject. Free speech? Paul Clancy was publisher of *American Astrology Magazine.* He re-printed the Bok report in *American Astrology Magazine.* He made no comment, but there was something he did do. Next to the Bok report he published another astronomical report coming out of Harvard College Observatory in the 1890's. It was a "scientific" report proving conclusively that it would never be possible to fly a heavier-than-air machine with a gasoline motor. The motor itself would be so heavy that it would hold the vehicle to earth. The report was very "scientific." It contained a lot of mathematics and was heavy with gravitation.

Dr. Bok marched on. He called at university after university and made speech after speech condemning astrology. In the writer's presence, he once said that it bothered his conscience, but he was working under Dr. Harlow Shapley at Harvard and this was his bread and butter. He was singing for his supper. On one occasion, he spoke at the Museum of Natural History in New York City, and discovered that his audience was composed principally of astrologers. This time, Dr. Bok was conciliatory. His theme was, "Why can't the astronomers and the astrologers get together? Why should there be this animosity? Yes, why? He made reference to the writer's statistical work, stated that he was familiar with it, praised it, and in effect said that's what we should be doing. He criticized the astrologers from one viewpoint. He said they had no basic hypothesis to show how planets affected people. Ernest A. Grant, then Executive Secretary of the American Federation of Astrologers asked him to explain what hypothesis the astronomers had that would explain their conception of gravitation. This upset Bok no end, because, they didn't have any either.

Astronomers do have some other hypotheses, however. They have a conception of an expanding universe where everything goes out from the center. Everything is going away from everything else, but this isn't exactly consistent with their other idea where everything is pulling everything else toward it. This is no problem in astronomy, where no degree of consistency is regarded as necessary once you have been taken into the mystic fold and granted a Ph.D., Bok finally disappeared and went to Australia.

It was a grey day at Harvard Observatory when word of Dr. Bok's kind words for astrologers reached there. Things went from grey to black when it was learned that Bok's speech had been recorded by the astrologers who were about to publish it. A representative was sent to call on all astrology magazine editors. They were told that if they published Bok's speech they would be sued. The American Federation of Astrologers published the speech, but nobody sued them. The writer also published it and publicly dared them to sue him, but they didn't. SKY Magazine, published by the astronomers, printed an entirely different speech and said it was the one Bok delivered. It wasn't. There were some conferences and it was decided that the astrology picture was getting too hot to handle and that opposition to astrology should go more underground.

The next epidemic broke out in Philadelphia. Dr. Roy K. Marshall was head of the Fels Planetarium and he hated astrologers. He entered into a debate with Sydney Omarr. It was pretty hot. The owners of the TV station were watching and became so interested that they phoned the station and ordered all other programs cancelled for the evening to allow the debate to continue so long as the station was on the air. This was one of the last attacks on astrology Dr. Marshall ever made. He was later indicted by Federal authorities for sending obscene literature through the mails to teenage girls. He was placed in a mental institution for a while. He pleaded "no defense" to the indictment, and the judge suspended the sentence on the agreement that the astronomer would take psychiatric treatments. It would appear that the treatment Sydney Omarr gave him wasn't psychiatric enough. Interesting to note what finally happens to these astronomers.

It wasn't until February 1962 that another astronomer went looking for an argument about astrology. We have already mentioned that he was Dr. George Abel of U.C.L.A. With a psychologist named Paul Bindram, he appeared on the Ben Hunter program over KTTV, Los Angeles, against Sydney Omarr and the writer.

Dr. Abel proudly announced that the astronomers brought about the space program. Because of the record to the contrary, this was a very embarrassing assertion for him to make. Sydney told him that the reason why the United States fell behind Russia in the space program was because of the incompetency of the American astronomers. The writer had made this same charge over the KTX radio station of CBS a month earlier, but now Dr. Abel blew up. He charged this was false information, and accused Omarr of publicizing false information about the astronomers. The writer interrupted to address Ben Hunter and offered to produce statistics to prove Sydney's assertion. Almost hysterical, Dr. Abel screamed at the writer, "Now, you stop. You're trying to protect him!"

Ben Hunter allowed the writer to read from the record. The record showed that out of 800 professional astronomers in the United States at the beginning of the space age, less than six knew enough about celestial mechanics to teach the subject. To get the space age off the ground, governmental agencies, space and aircraft companies had to find people to teach celestial mechanics. One aircraft company wanted ten such persons immediately. Thus, nearly all the people chosen to teach celestial mechanics to space engineers were imported from other countries. With a sneer on his face, Dr. Abel had to listen to the report as it was being read publicly. He couldn't refute the figures, so he adopted what we might term a "SO-WHAT?" attitude. From there on, most of Dr. Abel's attacks were confined to his religious objections. Only the astrologers were able to confine themselves to a scientific and intellectual discussion.

It is doubtful whether we will hear further astrological comment from Dr. Abel. In fact, it is doubtful whether he will ever be quite the same man again.

More information about the incompetency of American astronomers will be found in an article of the writer published in the July 1962 issue of HOROSCOPE Magazine. The important item to remember is that astronomy was born of religious bigotry and up until the current publication of this book, it has never been anything else in either the United States or England. Astronomers now claim to be responsible for discovering the sun as the center of the solar system, the laws of planetary motion, gravitation, meteors and the space age, and yet none of these things came about because of astronomers but in spite of astronomers, who originally opposed and fought all these ideas. Astronomers have always been motivated by religious bigotry rather than by science, and yet, they have been given a place of "respectability" in our academic world, but that is the way politics works, and our educational system has developed into a series of bureaucracies. Funds donated for research purposes by well-intentioned people are used for political and propaganda purposes. We have had astrologers who may not have been as scientific as they might have been, but when compared to astronomers, they are quite scientific. They are also sincere, which the astronomers as a group are not. One British astronomer condemned the opening of the space age as extravagant and said the money should be spent to buy him a new telescope. The space age is being run, not by astronomers but by engineers, and as this is being written these engineers are at work designing a telescope that will orbit the earth in a satellite. Its speed will be the same as the earth's rotation. It will remain in one position over the earth, 22,000 miles up over Kitt Peak near Tucson, Arizona, from where it will be possible to point the telescope in any desired direction, and where whatever the telescope sees will appear on a television screen. We will no longer have to view the heavens through the earth's atmosphere. The British astronomer mentioned above can continue to use his old telescope, through which he probably never saw anything that wasn't first in a textbook.

Many astrologers predicted that 1962 would be an important and progressive year for astrology. The year opened with newspaper stories coming out of India to the effect that Hindu astrologers were predicting the end of the world to come in February. These stories were a hoax. The predictions were never put forth by astrologers but by religious fanatics. The whole story of this hoax was told in the June 1962 issue of HOROSCOPE Magazine in an article by the writer entitled, "*The Great Neptunian Hoax of February 1962.*" The astronomers, including Dr. Abel, tried to blame the predictions on the astrologers, but they knew better, and after Dr. Abel's first attempt to lay blame on the astrologers, when the writer again offered to produce the record, Dr. Abel withdrew and said he would concede that it was a hoax, but later he again tried to blame it on the astrologers.

Astrology has made terrific forward strides in 1962. One eastern university is employing IBM electronic computers to check relationships between weather and the planets, but since the work has not yet been made public, the writer can mention no details at this time. In the April issue of CYCLES Magazine, published by the Foundation for the Study of Cycles, affiliated with the University of Pittsburgh, appeared a very significant editorial announcing a new research program to determine any connection between planetary motion and weather, economics and the stock market. The editorial stated that this would be called astrology and that some claimed astrology to be discredited. The editorial added that astrology had been discredited WITHOUT INVESTIGATION and that such prejudice was not going to influence or alter their policies.

During the year, the writer was invited to speak at a banquet of the Denver Astrological Club, which was attended by many state and Denver officials who later conferred with the writer, because they had been investigating astrology and wanted to pass laws that would recognize, regulate and protect it in that state. The opposition of astronomers to astrology is of little consequence. They have been defeated and frustrated at every turn except in bureaucratic academic circles. Astronomy has never been able to support an astronomical magazine in the United States without subsidization. At the most, a few thousand people buy or read any publication dealing with astronomy, while more and more people turn to astrology. Until the first 31 years of this century were over, there was never an astrology magazine on the newsstands. Today, monthly astrology magazines sell a half million copies in this country alone. In addition, there are many other types of astrological publications sold on the newsstands. The annuals have a very big sale. While astrology is self-supporting, astronomy has never been. Astronomers and their families have to be supported by gifts made to universities. The more its enemies attack astrology, the more people become interested and the more it grows. Neither psychology nor psychiatry can do the things that can be done with astrology. Astrology was the first psychology. It was a study of psychology thousands of years ago, and it is the only science that will reveal a mathematical pattern of either group or individual psychology. It is advancing very rapidly today. Since 1956, the writer has taught astrology to over 600 people who included psychologists, psychiatrists, mathematicians, about every kind of an engineer, housewives, business men, doctors, surgeons, and those in many other walks of life. Astrology is spreading. It is reaching out. It is overcoming religious bigotry. Grant Lewi was one of the more important people who helped to get it off the ground. It has had its enemies, but they have not dented it. During 1962, the writer also spoke on astrology at the Minneapolis Press Club and the Minnesota Historical Society. Lack of time made it necessary to turn down invitations to speak in many other places. Several years back when the Open Forum at Tucson invited an astronomer, to speak before that body, they made sure to balance it by having the writer, as an astrologer, speak the following week.

Like astronomy, the practice of medicine grew out of astrology. Savage tribes often know more about the use of some herbs than we do. We have to standardize. The ancient Egyptians had some form of surgery. Hippocrates is known as the father of medicine. He was an astrologer of ancient Greece, living somewhere between 460 and 377 B.C. Paracelsus is known as the father of *modern* medicine. He was an astrologer and alchemist living in Europe from 1493 to 1541. Although he is honored by the medical profession of today, so long as he is dead, he was persecuted by the medical profession of his own day.

Although we say that modern chemistry grew out of alchemy, the alchemists were also occultists who belonged to secret orders deemed necessary to oppose the dogma of their own day. Nevertheless, in the time of Paracelsus, physicians did not treat patients without first casting their horoscopes, and they made definite associations between illness and human characteristics. Paracelsus opposed fatalism and said he did not use astrology to predict the future but to determine characteristics and associated ailments to better understand and treat them. In our own century, Dr. Carl Jung, the psychiatrist stated that he never treated a patient without first studying his horoscope.

In various parts of the United States today, we have small organized groups of physicians employing astrology in their work, but it is assumed that they would be persecuted if this were too widely known. During most of his life, Ernest A. Grant, a former president of the American Federation of Astrologers and long its executive secretary, has specialized in teaching medical astrology to physicians in Washington, D.C. A good many physicians have taken the writer's correspondence course in astrology. Dr. William Davidson of Chicago has long taught medical astrology. It was an ancient claim that surgery should never be performed on a part of the body when the Moon was in the sign ruling that part of the body. Although never dealing in medical astrology, the writer has observed violations to this rule over 35 years with unfortunate consequences. The ancients claimed that there was excessive bleeding and failure of nature's healing process when this law was violated. The sincere physician would do well to investigate the rule.

Although we have had progress in the cure of some ailments by the medical profession, we have fadism. We have big drug companies, and we have television to sell their products. We have the American Medical Association and we have expensive prescriptions. If a physician cannot cure your ailment he can at least give it a name that is hard to pronounce. One of the new drugs went haywire in Europe during the summer of 1962. Thalidomide given to pregnant women resulted in thousands of deformed children. The drug did not get into the United States, although it reached Canada and one Phoenix woman managed to take the drug. All this happened with Saturn square to Neptune. From this square, the 1962 *Moon Sign Book* had warned of serious health problems. Meanwhile, doctors in Saskatchewan went on strike and refused to treat sick people or deliver babies, while in the United States, private insurance companies and the American Medical Association employed their powerhouse of influence to temporarily defeat passage of government health insurance for the aged. Had physicians and drug companies known a little about astrology, they would have been less likely to put thalidomide on the market until they knew more about it, and had the public known more about astrology, it would have been more cautious in accepting the authority of the medical world.

Bigotry and various "interests" have long opposed astrology. This is why a secrecy about its practice has existed for 2000 years. This secrecy is becoming less necessary, but men like Dr. William Petersen of the University of Illinois, who maintained that indirectly the Moon affects the patient because it affects ionization, have feared use of the word astrology. Sir Isaac Newton maintained that the Moon affects mental illness, and most anyone who works in a mental institution will secretly admit this. Writing in the magazine *Analog,* Joseph Goodavage states, "Even the staid *Journal of Mental Disease* claims that the solar-lunar or synodic cycle of the 29-1/2 days has a marked 'effect' on mental illness.....Dr. Harold S. Burr of Yale has found correlations between lunar influence and micro-potentials in trees and plants. Drs. Leinex and Gibbs report in the *Journal of Heredity* that brain waves actually do correlate with phases of the Moon. And Dr. Leonard J. Ravitz of the Veterans Bureau in Downey, Ill., detected mood changes in people analogous to the Moon's phases. On the distaff side, Dr. Hannah Hendrick of the United States Naval Observatory, in her study of mental institutions, noticed that women were more likely to enter a mental hospital during a full moon; men on the second day after the new moon."

Yet, none of these people dare openly use the word astrology because of the bigotry that exists in both the medical and astronomical worlds. Nevertheless, their work is the first indication of a breakthrough that will allow us to get beyond the iron curtain of medical, astronomical and academic bigotry. The progress of science has always been retarded by these factors of bigotry. The space age is changing many things, but it was brought about by practical men, mainly engineers in private corporations, not by the academicians and certainly not by astronomers who now like to steal credit for everything they originally opposed.

HEAVEN KNOWS WHAT will not only introduce astrology to the layman, it will allow him to employ it in a limited way. You won't learn astrology by reading this book, but it will start you on your way. The tables have been brought up to date, while the last edition carried them only to 1935. Thirty years of tables have been added. You will enjoy employing this book to understand and entertain your friends better. You can have a lot of fun with it, while simultaneously you will be learning something new. Astrology can be a road to your own freedom and security. Should you choose to do so, you can go further. You can study astrology yourself, and we will be glad to tell you how to go about that when you are ready.

Enjoy *Heaven Knows What.* If it is your first introduction into astrology, you have a long, interesting road ahead of you. In any event, you will find it an important addition to your library. You will find yourself employing it a great deal once you have mastered the simple rules that Grant Lewi presents.

SINCE *Heaven Knows What* was first published in 1937, a great deal has happened in the world of astrology.

Widened interest on the part of the public has supported numerous magazines until the leader reached a monthly circulation of nearly 200,000 per month. The type of mail received from readers in the offices of the leading astrology magazines has proved that people of education, high intelligence, and broad general interests are the main supporters of these magazines. The type of stationery on which the letters are written, the typing or the handwriting, the grade of stationery used, and the questions raised bear out the conviction that those interested in astrology are in the main men and women of intellectual curiosity and a desire to better themselves individually. Analysis of a questionnaire inserted in the magazine of highest circulation further supports these findings. From my own experiences and contacts over a period of 13 years as author of astrology books, editor of astrology magazines, lecturer, and occasionally individual advisor I know that the men and women who are actively interested in astrology stand at an extremely high moral and intellectual level.

This is as it should be in an age which is painfully and with difficulty, awakening into a world that is changing at a sometimes alarming rate of speed. We are discovering new values, and rediscovering older ones that have been preserved from ages less materialistic than our own. Physical science has tended since the Middle Ages to replace moral science. The science of man's comfort has tended to supercede the science of man himself. Astrology belongs in the latter class, and men of science are beginning to open their eyes on its vistas to which, till now, they have been voluntarily blind.

Thus John J. O'Neill, science editor of a leading New York daily and a Pulitzer prize winner, wrote a year ago in HOROSCOPE magazine, when I was editor of it, "It is my belief that some of the most important discoveries in the not far distant future will be made in the field now covered by astrology."

Study and research continues quietly and unobtrusively. For many years Carl Payne Tobey published privately a pamphlet called *Astro-statistics,* which won the serious attention of statisticians and men of science. By rigid statistical methods, he demonstrated the validity of the chief premise of astrology, that men are products of, among other things, the time of their birth. His work is noted by Dr. Ellsworth Huntingdon of Yale in his book *Season of Birth* (Yale University Press) in which he reproduces some of Mr. Tobey's graphs and makes them a part of his own study.

Charles A. Jayne Jr. has done considerable study of eclipse paths and historical cycles. A recent book, *Cycles: The Science of Prediction,* by Edward R. Dewey and Edwin S. Dakin (Henry Holt) came to Mr. Jayne's attention. The authors had plotted the curves of recurring historical cycles, from the records of history without benefit of astrology.

Mr. Jayne discovered that these historic cycles correspond to planetary cycles. He has also pointed out the correspondence of sunspot cycles (supposed to influence business trends) with cyclic movements of the major planets.

In 1940, my book *Astrology for the Millions* (Doubleday Doran and Co., Inc.) detailed the laws of transits and the extent to which the movements of the planets correspond to developments in individual lives. Later, in a series of articles in HOROSCOPE magazine, *Preventive uses of Astrology,* I outlined the extent to which astrology can be valuable to the practising psychiatrist, as an aid in the diagnosis of personality conflict.

The renaissance of astrology is in full swing; it continues, despite some of the purely commercial enterprises that flourish in its name, to reach an always widening, more alert, more intelligent, more scientifically trained audience; and is becoming with the years a greater and greater force for social and individual betterment.

HEAVEN KNOWS WHAT has met with a hearty response from both the general public, and from students and teachers of astrology. You can amuse yourself and your friends with it, and you can also use it as a definitive text-book covering the meaning of the aspects, and the interpretation of the 144 solar-lunar polarities.

A word on how the book is constructed may answer some questions that have been the subject of considerable correspondence.

This book is constructed so that the aspects — the angular relations between the planets — will emerge. For this reason, a planet may appear in *Heaven Knows What* to be in a sign adjacent to the one it actually occupies at birth. This is necessary in some cases to bring out an important aspect which would not otherwise appear. For example, if Saturn is at 29° Libra and Mars at 0° Leo, they are 89° apart, in close square aspect. But, if these positions were accurately recorded, Saturn would appear in space 21, and Mars in space 13. When you point the arrow at Mars, in space 13, the square will not fall on Saturn in space 21, but will fall in space 22. For this reason, so that the important square will emerge, Saturn is "moved" into space 22. This does not matter for purposes of this book, which deals only with aspects, and not with the meaning of planets in the signs. Do not, therefore, take the sign-positions from this book, but check them elsewhere before you conclude that you have, let us say, Saturn in Scorpio, and look up somewhere what that means. Use this book exclusively for aspects.

The Sun and Moon are not moved out of their signs for any purpose, since the solar-lunar polarities (paragraphs 1-144) depend on sign positions of the Sun and Moon.

In *Astrology for the Millions,* the Tables are accurate for sign positions, and the readings given there are for the meaning of the planets in the signs, without respect to aspects.

Heaven Knows What is accurate for aspects; *Astrology for the Millions* is accurate for sign positions and their meanings.

THE WHEEL uses only two symbols, the triangle and the square. The triangle is used to signify both the trine (120°) and the sextile (60°) aspects. The square is used to symbolize both the square (90°) and the opposition (180°) aspects. To have used four symbols, and to have doubled the number of paragraphs, would have made the book unwieldly without accomplishing anything of importance.

The trine and the sextile, though subtle differences have been adduced between them, are of very similar meaning. Both represent smooth interaction between the planets; they are aspects of harmony and relaxation.

Similarly, the square and the opposition are of similar effect, though some minor differences do exist. Both are aspects of tention, of stress, and therefore of either conflict or power, depending on the total individual set-up and the uses to which the individual puts it.

THE CHIEF use of the horoscope is its aid in self-discovery, or in your discovery of what makes your friends tick. The horoscope shows the basic underlying psychological and emotional drives of the individual; and through using this book with this in mind, you may be able to discover some hitherto unsuspected facts about yourself and others.

This is, among other things, The Age of Psychiatry. More people have more problems than ever before, and the world is becoming increasingly aware of the existence of complexes, phobias, fixations, and the like. Some of these need professional — that is, psychiatric — aid. Some can find themselves otherwise. Clues to hidden disturbances can be found in the horoscope.

For example, if you find an individual with the Moon square (or opposition) Saturn, or in the same space with it, you are pretty sure to find an individual in whose life the mother has been of extreme importance, for better or for worse. The same is true of the Moon and Mars; though the effect is different and the individual behaves differently, the underlying effect of the female principle is of the utmost importance in determining the personality and behavior pattern.

With Sun square (or opposition) Saturn in a man's chart, expect the psychological drive toward success, which is very strong, to derive from some complicated interaction of the father and the mother. With Sun conjunct (in same space with), Saturn, in either a man's chart or a woman's chart, the influence of the father is dominant, and often emotionally disturbing. In a woman's chart especially, the square, opposition, or conjunction is likely to indicate some emotional confusion, stemming from some real or imagined influence of the father.

With Venus square, opposition, or conjunction Saturn, emotional caution rising from early influences tends to slow up the life.

All these Saturnian influences tend toward anxiety — over-caution — over-protectiveness — resulting from early influences that have gone deeply into the nature and have become embedded, probably far below the level of consciousness.

MARS INFLUENCES, on the other hand, while they make people appear bold and even reckless, indicate a psychological base in either fear or a sense of guilt, sometimes largely unrelated to real experience. Among these influences are those indicated by Sun or Moon square, opposition, or conjunct Mars; and Mars square, opposition, or conjunct Saturn. Here the interaction between the male principles (Sun and Mars) and the female principles (Saturn and Moon) produce effects in the personality that may be baffling to the individual and his friends until the psychological basis for them is recognized, and the unproductive emotional habits brought into the light of consciousness for re-evaluation. The horoscope can help in this uncovering process; if psychiatrists could be induced to learn astrology and to use it as an aid to diagnosis, it is my conviction that the often lengthy process of analysis could be materially shortened, and a satisfactory result produced in much less time than analysis is now supposed to take.

A PRIME use of astrology in this connection with basic psychology has to do with the recognizing in children, at an early age, of a basis for later personality difficulty. The horoscope is the only device that can reveal this while the child is still in infancy. If parents might know from the beginning where the seeds of difficulty lie in the child (and also in themselves, for the horoscope will show the effect that each parent has on the individual child, from the child's viewpoint) then early care and training might eliminate much later unhappiness.

Because this is a main use of astrology, and because the tables in this book have been brought up only to 1935,* I will be glad to supply parents of small children with the planetary numbers for the date of the child's birth. If you have a child born after 1935* whose horoscope you want to learn, send me the birth date, and I will send you back the numbers to use in reading the child's horoscope from this book.

I WANT to thank all those whose orders and purchases made this book possible, and to thank the early subscribers for their patience during the unavoidable delays in production.

GRANT LEWI

* Note that Mr. Lewi's reference here goes with the Limited Edition and has nothing to do with this edition, where tables run through 1964 instead of 1935.

March 27, 1947

HOROSCOPE BLANK

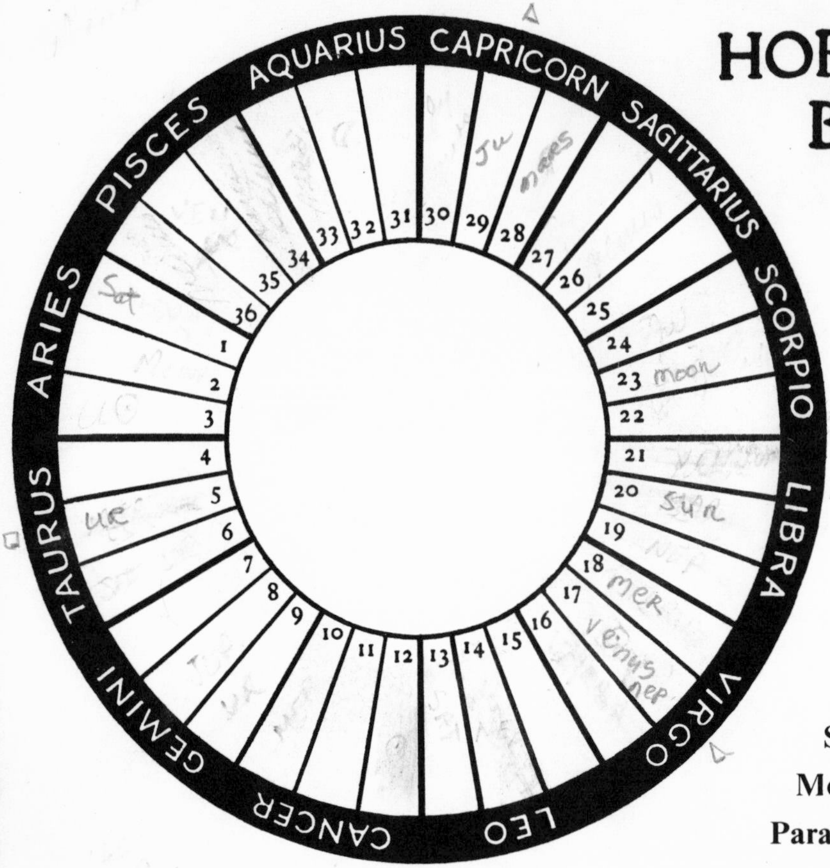

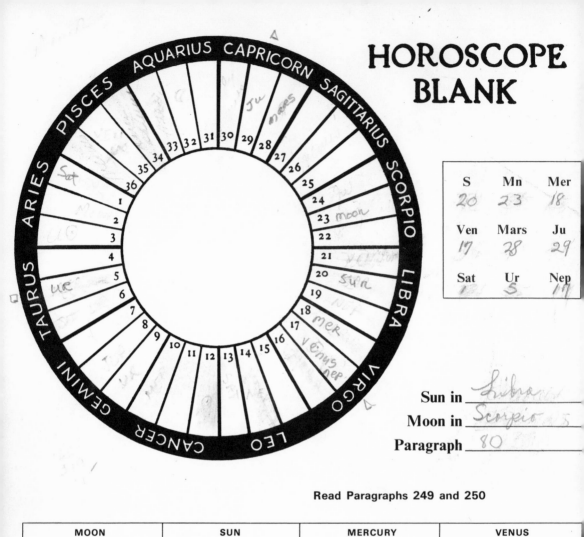

S	Mn	Mer
20	23	18
Ven	**Mars**	**Ju**
17	28	29
Sat	**Ur**	**Nep**
[illegible]	5	17

Sun in Libra

Moon in Scorpio

Paragraph 80

Read Paragraphs 249 and 250

MOON

in same space with

Sun	245	Jupiter	148*
Mercury	145	Saturn	149*
Venus	146*	Uranus	150*
Mars	147*	Neptune	151

MOON △

Sun	246	Jupiter	155
Mercury	152	Saturn	156
Venus	153	Uranus	157
Mars	154	Neptune	158

MOON □

Sun	247	Jupiter	162
Mercury	159	Saturn	163*
Venus	160	Uranus	164
Mars	161*	Neptune	165

SUN

in same space with

Mercury	166*	Jupiter	169*
Venus	167*	Saturn	170*
Mars	168*	Uranus	171*
		Neptune	172*

SUN △

Mercury	—	Jupiter	174
Venus	248	Saturn	175
Mars	173	Uranus	176
		Neptune	177

SUN □

Mercury	—	Jupiter	179
Venus	—	Saturn	180*
Mars	178*	Uranus	181*
		Neptune	182*

MERCURY

in same space with

Venus	183*	Saturn	186*
Mars	184*	Uranus	187*
Jupiter	185	Neptune	188*

MERCURY △

Venus	189*	Saturn	192
Mars	190	Uranus	193
Jupiter	191	Neptune	194

MERCURY □

Venus	—	Saturn	197
Mars	195	Uranus	198
Jupiter	196	Neptune	199

VENUS

in same space with

Mars	200*	Saturn	202*
Jupiter	201	Uranus	203*
		Neptune	204*

VENUS △

Mars	205	Saturn	207
Jupiter	206	Uranus	208
		Neptune	209

VENUS □

Mars	210*	Saturn	212*
Jupiter	211	Uranus	213*
		Neptune	214

NOTE:–

When you have finished underlining all the paragraph numbers on this sheet, look them up in the book, reading the *basic numbers* first (this is the number you wrote on the paragraph line in the upper half of this blank) the underlined numbers with the asterisks next and the other underlined numbers last. **Heaven Knows What Horoscope Blanks in pads of 100 may be obtained for $2.00 from Llewellyn Publications, P.O. Box 3383, Saint Paul, Minnesota 55101, U.S.A.**

SATURN

in same space with

Uranus 236* Neptune 237*

SATURN △

Uranus 238 Neptune 239

SATURN □

Uranus 240 Neptune 241

URANUS

in same space with

Neptune 242 } △Neptune 243, □Neptune 244

MARS

in same space with

Jupiter	215*	Uranus	217*
Saturn	216*	Neptune	218*

MARS △

Jupiter	219	Uranus	221
Saturn	220	Neptune	222

MARS □

Jupiter	223	Uranus	225
Saturn	224*	Neptune	226*

JUPITER

in same space with

Saturn 227* Uranus 228*
Neptune 229*

JUPITER △

Saturn 230 Uranus 231
Neptune 232

JUPITER □

Saturn 233 Uranus 234
Neptune 235

HOW TO CAST YOUR OWN HOROSCOPE

HEAVEN KNOWS WHAT is the first and only book to enable you to cast a detailed horoscope in ten or fifteen minutes without the slightest study or knowledge of astrology. In this book all the laborious and difficult work has been done for you, and every day of every year from 1876 to 1921 inclusive is carefully tabulated so that you can be sure of absolutely accurate results. You don't need to know anything at all about horoscopes or astrology to cast a long, thorough, accurate, and professional horoscope all by yourself. All you need do is follow the simple directions carefully, step by step, and you can't go wrong. Everything is clearly explained, and after you have finished doing the sample horoscope given here, you will find your own so easy, so fascinating, and so accurate that you will be at it all the time, casting all your friends' and acquaintances'. Don't attempt to cast a horoscope until you understand how the sample horoscope is done.

The first thing is to clip from the back of the book one of the Horoscope Blanks, also cut out one of the wheels printed on the last page. Don't do anything with the cardboard wheel at present—just put it aside to be used later. The Horoscope Blank is the sheet on which you will set up the chart. A reproduction of this Horoscope Blank is shown on the opposite page.

Notice the abbreviations in the box in the upper right-hand corner of the Horoscope Blank. These are the abbreviations for the nine heavenly bodies as follows:

S	— Sun	Ju	— Jupiter
Mn	— Moon	Sat	— Saturn
Mer	— Mercury	Ur	— Uranus
Ven	— Venus	Nep	— Neptune
Mars	— Mars		

Now, with this Horoscope Blank in front of you, turn to the TABLE OF YEARS in the back of the book. Each page in the section represents a year (the year is indicated at the bottom of the second column). Turn to the birth date of the person whose horoscope you wish to do and note the nine numbers which you find there. We are going to cast the horoscope of a person whose birth date is May 10, 1908, as an example, so be sure to follow *step by step* everything that we do and apply it later to your own birthday.

On the page for 1908 (Tables) find May in the vertical column and run down the column until you come to the date — the 10th. In this space—May 10, 1908—you will find nine numbers in two rows as follows:

5 17 5 11 9

14 2 29 11

Write these numbers *exactly as you find them*—in the order given and in two rows—in the box mentioned above, each number to be directly under its corresponding abbreviation. When you have done this the box will look like this:

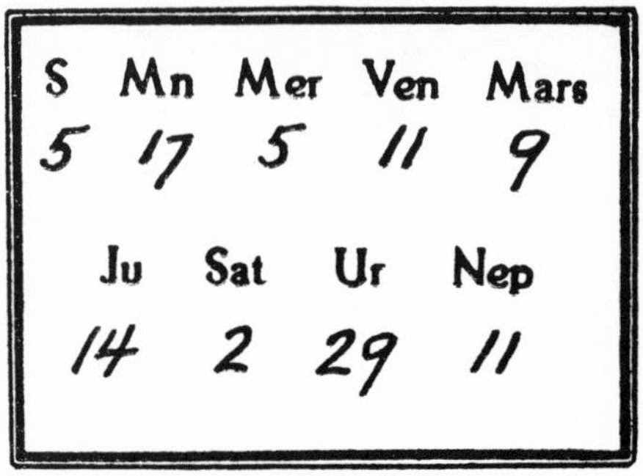

S Mn Mer Ven Mars
5 17 5 11 9
Ju Sat Ur Nep
14 2 29 11

Now you have finished with the tables and have all the data on the Horoscope Blank.

Now look at the circle on the Horoscope Blank. Note that it is divided into 36 numbered spaces. The numbers which you have just written in the box correspond to these numbered spaces. The number 5 (under S) tells you to write S in space 5 of the circle.

17 (under Mn) tells you to write Mn in space 17 of the circle.

5 (under Mer) tells you to write Mer in space 5 of the circle.

Note: Don't worry about having two or more abbreviations in one space—go ahead and put them in.

9 (under Mars) tells you to write Mars in space 9 of the circle.

Write in the other planets exactly as described, taking care to write as small as you can and as lightly as you can, because you may want to use the chart again for another casting, and if you write too heavily you won't be able to erase. Your chart will now look like Fig. 1.

If you care to, you can substitute symbols for the abbreviations. The abbreviations have been given because they are simpler. If you want to learn these planets by their symbols it will give a more professional touch to the horoscope, and at the same time you will get to know the astrology signs much better. These symbols are given below:

☉ ☽ ☿ ♀ ♂

♃ ♄ ♅ ♆

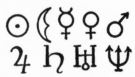

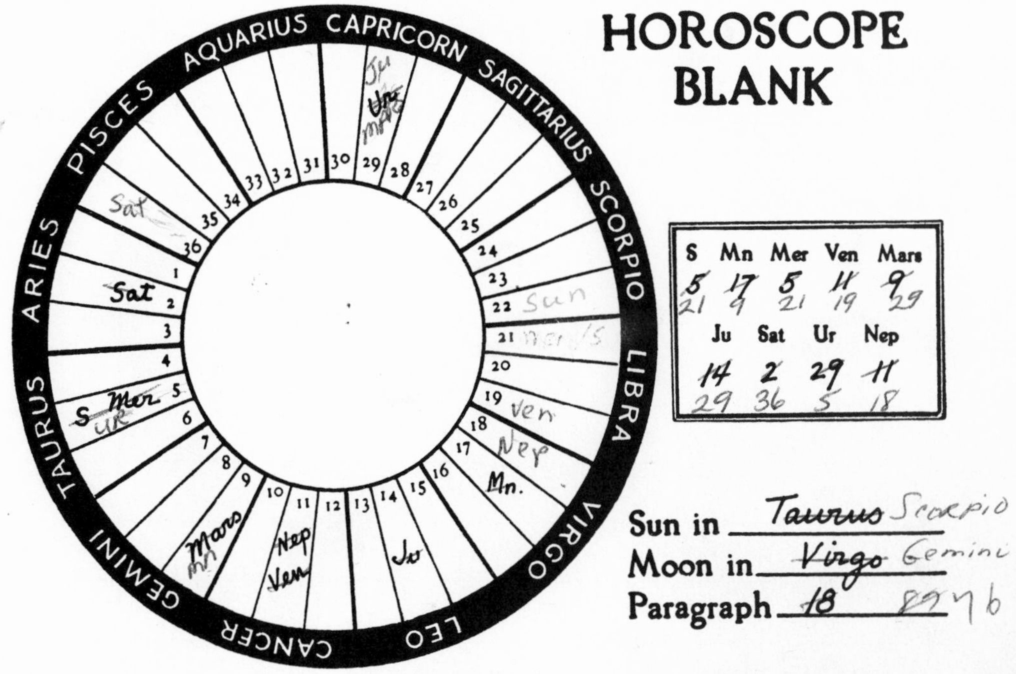

Fig 1

The horoscope is now set up. All you have to do is read it.

READING THE HOROSCOPE

Around the edge of the circle in white letters on a black background you will find the twelve zodiac names. Find under which name the Sun, S, appears. In this case it is TAURUS so write TAURUS in the space where it says SUN IN ——————.

Now find the Zodiac name that the Moon, Mn, comes under. In this case it is VIRGO—so write VIRGO in the space where it says MOON IN ———————.

Now, in Table I, on the next page, find the number which corresponds to S IN TAURUS and Mn IN VIRGO. This number is evidently 18. Write it in the space where it says PARAGRAPH ———————. This is an extremely important paragraph, because it forms the basis of your horoscope. We will refer to it later.

Now let us look at the reading matter in the lower half of the Horoscope Blank. Here you will see the Sun, Moon, and seven planets in combination with one another. For instance, you will see "Moon in the same space with Mercury," "Moon in the same space with Venus," etc.

TABLE I

	Moon in ARIES	Moon in TAURUS	Moon in GEMINI	Moon in CANCER	Moon in LEO	Moon in VIRGO	Moon in LIBRA	Moon in SCORPIO	Moon in SAGGITARIUS	Moon in CAPRICORN	Moon in AQUARIUS	Moon in PISCES
S in ARIES	1	2	3	4	5	6	7	8	9	10	11	12
S in TAURUS	13	14	15	16	17	18	19	20	21	22	23	24
S in GEMINI	25	26	27	28	29	30	31	32	33	34	35	36
S in CANCER	37	38	39	40	41	42	43	44	45	46	47	48
S in LEO	49	50	51	52	53	54	55	56	57	58	59	60
S in VIRGO	61	62	63	64	65	66	67	68	69	70	71	72
S in LIBRA	73	74	75	76	77	78	79	80	81	82	83	84
S in SCORPIO	85	86	87	88	89	90	91	92	93	94	95	96
S in SAGGITARIUS	97	98	99	100	101	102	103	104	105	106	107	108
S in CAPRICORN	109	110	111	112	113	114	115	116	117	118	119	120
S in AQUARIUS	121	122	123	124	125	126	127	128	129	130	131	132
S in PISCES	133	134	135	136	137	138	139	140	141	142	143	144

A note on the Basic Paragraphs.

The second number in the space of your birth date indicates the position of the Moon by sign, on the date of your birth. Owing to the rapid motion of the Moon, on some days she will be in two signs, passing from one to the other during the day. The sign in which the Moon is placed on your birth date is the sign in which the Moon was located for the *majority of the hours* on that date. If your basic paragraph reading very patently does not fit you, it is because you were born on one of those days when the Moon was changing signs. If this is your case, you can find the correct reading to apply to you by following the rule given in the summary on page XLI.

Similarly you will see the Sun in the same space with the other planets, Mercury in the same space with the other planets, etc. This means that if you have (as we have in this particular case) the Sun, or the Moon, or any of the planets in the same space with any other planet, you merely read the number opposite the particular reading which applies. For example: In our case, the Sun (S) is in the same space with Mercury (Mer) (space 5). You therefore look for the number following "Sun in same space with Mercury" and underline it. It is number 166. This is the number of a paragraph in your horoscope.

You now look around for other "conjunctions" and find that Venus (Ven) is in the same space with Neptune (Nep). Referring to Venus you read "Venus in same space with Neptune" number 204. Underline 204 for this is another paragraph in the horoscope. If you had other planets in the same space with one another you would continue along this line, always getting a paragraph number which should be underlined.*

Now you are ready for the last part of the horoscope. Take the small cardboard wheel which you put aside a little while ago and fasten it with a pin point or paper fastener to the center of the circle on the horoscope chart.

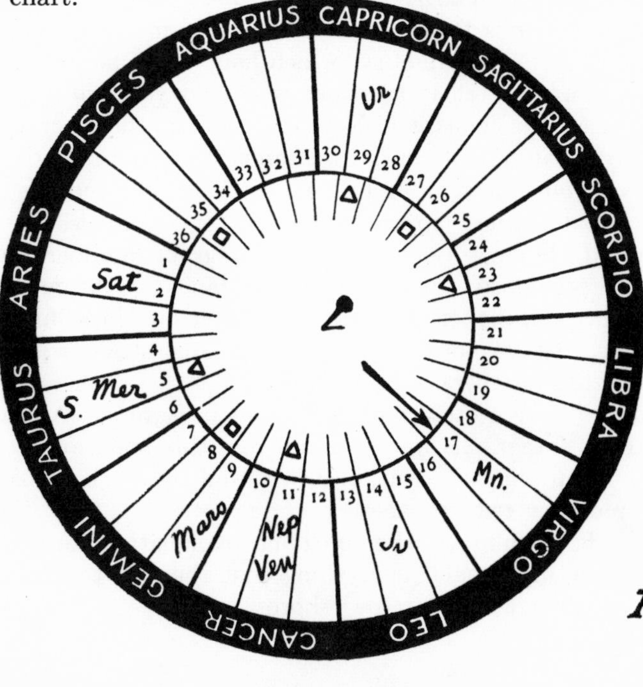

Fig 2

*If three planets happened to be in the same space, get all three combinations; for example: Venus, Mars, and Mercury in the same space, look under "Venus in same space with Mars," "Venus in same space with Mercury," and "Mars in the same space with Mercury."

Note that this small wheel contains four triangles and three squares. Point the arrow first to the Moon (in our case the Moon is in space 17, so point the arrow to space 17 as shown in Figure 2.), and note where the triangles and squares come. You will see triangles opposite Uranus (space 29), opposite the Sun and Mercury (space 5), and opposite Venus and Neptune (space 11). This will give quite a number of "aspects" or readings, as you can readily see. Since these are all triangles, you now refer to the section "Moon △" and look at the numbers next to Sun, Mercury, Venus, Uranus, and Neptune. This gives paragraph numbers 246, 152, 153, 158, and 157. These paragraphs should be underlined because they are all paragraphs in the horoscope.

Note that none of the squares appeared opposite any of the planets, so ignore them.

Now turn the wheel, placing the arrow to the Sun, and see where the triangles and squares come.

Here we have a triangle on Uranus, a triangle on the Moon, a triangle on Venus and Neptune, and a square on Jupiter. Referring now to the "Sun △" section we see Uranus, paragraph 176, Neptune, paragraph 177, and Venus, paragraph 248. These paragraphs, of course, should be underlined. We also have Sun □ Jupiter, which gives paragraph 179 in the "Sun □" section. You don't need to look up the Sun △ Moon, since it is the same as Moon △ Sun. Now turn the wheel and put the pointer to Mercury (which happens to be in the same space as the Sun) and proceed in the same way, and you will see triangles on Uranus, the Moon, Venus, and Neptune. Look up these paragraphs under the Mercury heading (Mercury △ Uranus, etc.) and underline the paragraphs. Now put the pointer to Venus (space 11) and we see squares on Saturn and Uranus (spaces 2 and 29) and triangles on the Moon, the Sun, and Mercury. Look up these paragraph numbers under Venus as you did previously under the other planets. Continue this process through the seven planets, setting the pointer on Mars, Jupiter, Saturn, and Uranus, in turn noticing where the triangles and squares fall and underlining the numbers.

You now have quite a few underlined paragraphs. All you need do is look these paragraphs up by number in this book and read what it says. The result will be a true, accurate, and thorough horoscope, sometimes as much as twelve pages.

If you have followed the foregoing explanation carefully, step by step, you now understand everything that there is to it and can proceed immediately with your own horoscope.

SUMMARY

1. Tear a Horoscope Blank from the back of the book.
2. Look up your birth date in the correct table and write the numbers you find in the exact order that you find them, under the corresponding abbreviations in the box provided on the Horoscope Blank.
3. Write each abbreviation in its corresponding numbered space on the circle on the Horoscope Blank.
4. Note the Zodiac names in which the Sun and Moon appear. Look these up in Table I and record this with the paragraph number in the space provided on the Horoscope Blank.
5. Note what planets appear in the same space with one another or the Sun or Moon and refer to the bottom of the sheet for the correct paragraph number and underline for future reference.
6. Place the wheel (cut from last printed page in the back of the book) on the chart, pointing the arrow to the space where the Moon appears. Note where the triangles and squares come and look them up at the bottom of the sheet under "Moon △ this" and "Moon □ that." Underline these paragraph numbers for future reference.
7. Place the arrow at the Sun and note where the triangles and squares appear, proceeding as before.
8. Continue this through the seven planets, placing the arrow to each planet in turn and noting where the triangles and squares appear. Always refer to the bottom of the sheet for the correct paragraph numbers.
9. Collect all these paragraph numbers and look them up in the book—reading the basic number (the paragraph number on the Horoscope Blank) first, then the numbers with the asterisk, and lastly the underlined numbers.

Rule.

1. If you were born *early in the day,* read the basic paragraph *preceding* the one you obtained from table of Solar-Lunar polarity.
2. If you were *born late in the day,* read the basic paragraph *following* the one you found in the Solar-Lunar table.
3. *If you do not know the hour* of your birth, and the basic paragraph does not fit you, it is probable that the Moon had moved on another sign, or was not yet advanced to that sign, at the hour of your birth. In that case, you will find that either the paragraph following or the one preceding will fit your case.

VERY IMPORTANT: Regardless of the above consideration, *do not move the Moon* in your horoscope from the place it is given on your birth date; the aspects there indicated are yours and must not be tampered with!

THE FOLLOWING BASIC INTERPRETIVE PARAGRAPHS REFER TO SUN AND MOON. THE REGULAR PARAGRAPHS INTERPRETING PLANETARY ASPECTS BEGIN ON PAGE 159.

1

SUN IN ARIES—MOON IN ARIES

(You belong to the positive or executive group)

WHATEVER ANYONE ELSE can say about you, it will never be that you don't know your own mind. In fact, it's far more likely that they will say you know your own mind too well and are too ready to express whatever comes into it; for independence is the outstanding trait of your nature—independence in both intellectual and material matters. You are an individualist, first, last, and always; you believe in Yourself, and in your own ability to overcome the forces of heaven and earth, man and God, in order to arrive at that goal of personal ambition which is so clearly defined in your mind as to be already an actuality. You are likely to be somewhat intolerant of divergent opinions on the part of others. Not only are you intolerant of them, but you may just plain not understand them, for Understanding is not your strong point. The troubles of other people are not especially interesting to you, although by a paradoxical twist you frequently expect other people to listen to your troubles, at some considerable length. Not because you want or need or expect or would be likely to use advice, but just because you are so absorbed by your own problems that you expect everyone else to be willing and even anxious to listen to them. You express readily and forcefully and with considerable dramatic effect. All in all, you are a rather impressive person and more likely than not to go places and do things with that excellent quick intelligence and that absorption in your own life, your own problems, and your own ambitions. Even if you haven't had a college education—and you are so energetic and ambitious that it's likely you would leave formal schooling behind, out of sheer impatience—your mind is always active: reading, talking, discussing. You are not a student in the profound sense of the word, but you get things readily and will keep on getting them as long as you live. There's nothing the matter with your head—nor with your heart either, as far as that goes. But despite an affectionate nature which craves understanding, you are not likely to get it until you have learned to be more interested in other people. You have to overcome a tendency to appear hard-boiled through being too matter of fact. You see the intellectual and sensible solution to personal problems so readily that you don't quite get the emotional turmoil of less intellectual people who feel more and analyze less. Try to see things from the other fellow's viewpoint. Learn to temper your independence with coöperation and tact and with consideration for the wishes and feelings of others, and there is nothing you cannot do.

This is one of the best combinations of Sun and Moon and leads far upward, once you have mastered the more self-centered leanings of your nature and learned to objectify.

With 163 or 180, you will rise from obscurity and early responsibility to some position of success or importance in your own sphere, whatever it may be, achieving a type of personal success that will be very gratifying. With 149 or 180, tendency to introversion must be watched and fought down. Objectify! Forget yourself and do not rebel against what comes your way. With 147, 161, 168, or 178, quarrelsome. Learn to hold your tongue, and do not think there is any special virtue in telling people unpleasant things about themselves. You will catch more flies with sugar than with vinegar... and they will stick around longer, too.

2

SUN IN ARIES—MOON IN TAURUS

(You belong to the positive or executive group)

YOU ARE one of those tactful and forceful people who manage to do pretty much as they please and get away with it. Your energy, vitality, independence, and magnetism operate under the ægis of a certain charm, reserve, and poise that stabilizes your position, even in the face of enmity and opposition. You can hardly go through life without making enemies, and perhaps very important and powerful enemies at that, but unless other things are very bad in your horoscope, you will always manage to come out at the right end of a quarrel, or at least be able to go on and leave your enemies trailing in the dust. You are not exactly magnanimous: you are a strong and implacable fighter and give no quarter; but you are too intent on your own problems and ambitions to worry about revenge. You have an acute business sense, and although your artistic and intellectual leanings may lead you into pursuits that are not ordinarily supposed to be remunerative, you are more likely than not to feather your nest pretty well even in the service of the muses. Your best place in life would be an executive one, in charge of some artistic or intellectual project, for you are a manager as well as a creator. You have a curious way of appearing tactful even when you are laying down the law or insisting on your own way, and you are pretty likely to get what you want out of people and make them like it. If they don't like it, that's too bad. You are somewhat considerate of others, but, more than this, you have a way of making people think you are being considerate of them when you are doing exactly as you jolly well please. To more dependent sorts of people, this makes you seem not exactly hardboiled but a little detached from ordinary human frailty; even your weaknesses have a sort of air about them, as if you could overcome them if you wanted to but don't think it's worth the trouble. You have an "I can take it or I can leave it alone" attitude about pleasure, indulgence, and other off-the-routine matters, which is the despair of people who have consciences or acute sense of the value of time. The truth of the matter is that you don't waste time at all but do what you have to do in a clipped, efficient, and scheduled manner, so that you have time left over after you have accomplished more than most people do with all their time. You are likely to think pretty well of yourself, although you may be quiet about it and not cram it down people's throats; but a pervading sense of your own abilities is the foundation of your life—few people with this position will be found with any vestige of an inferiority complex, and the reverse is likely to be more nearly their story. You have to learn to rule without dominating and to adjust your desires not only to your own needs but to the happiness of those around you.

In a man's horoscope, this position usually indicates a splendid, helpful, and possibly a wealthy wife who stabilizes him, adds to his prestige, and in every way contributes to his success. If in a woman's horoscope, she is likely to wear the trousers of the family to pretty good purpose.

With 147, tremendous ability, probably artistic; a sort of inspirational and magnetic person of artistic leanings which do not interfere with business. With 149 or 170, danger that knowledge of worth will never find expression; a sort of relaxed-tense condition, in which you know you're good but don't seem to be able to do anything about it. With 181, unconventional ideas—and probably they don't stay merely ideas either. You know your own mind and let others know it. Trouble through being too outspoken and too quick to take action. With 148, material well-being; also 146. With both 148 and 149, nothing stops you; power and position are secure.

3

SUN IN ARIES—MOON IN GEMINI

(You belong to the positive or executive group)

THIS IS one of the talkiest positions in the entire Zodiac. You have to learn to keep things to yourself at least until you've made up your own mind, which you don't find easy to do. Concentration is not your strong point, and you seem to feel that by sitting down and talking about it everything will be made manifest and clear and your course of action laid out for you. This somehow fails to work. Your best way to success is to learn, and practice, the art of secrecy; go off in a corner with your problems, and fight them out with yourself before you take the world and his wife into your confidence. And speaking of the world and his wife, you are extremely fond of the details of their lives and like to talk them over with all and sundry. You have a keen sense of news values—which may not be so pleasant to those of your friends who want to keep certain matters in the dark. This is all well and good so long as no one is hurt, but you are likely to have a pretty sharp tongue in spite of your good intentions, and to barb your quips and rumors so that they stick. Just be careful that they don't turn around on you and come back flying in your face.

Naturally, with your keen intellectual endowments, your facile manner of expression, and your delight in drama, news, and romance, you should make your career along one of these lines: writer, speaker, actor, advertising—anything that deals with the written or spoken word. You have a sort of hankering to be an executive, but this isn't precisely your forte. You have a pretty shrewd business head which, applied in the literary world, ought to get you well paid for whatever you produce; for in spite of your sometimes jittery inability to make up your mind (which would hurt you as an executive) you have no trouble making up your mind about what you are worth in dollars and cents, and in getting it by hook or crook. You are not exactly tactful, but you're able to get what you want by a rapid flow of argument, logic, and reasons pro and con—you know all the answers and know also how to use them to your own advantage. You will talk (and write) your way through the world and make a lot of friends who will admire your glibness, your quickness, your wit, and your insight, which you are able so aptly to express. Not a deep student, you are none the less likely to be, or to appear to be, the best informed person around, for you pick things up readily and glean odds and ends of knowledge as you go along, being able to haul them out at impressive moments. If you would apply this mental ability to concentrated study there is nothing in an intellectual way that you could not accomplish, but restlessness is likely to take you away from books and formal study and plunge you early into the active life of the world. You should try to overcome a certain superficiality with respect both to intellectual and emotional matters, for unless Venus or Mercury, or both, are in Taurus, you're likely to appear in both these respects a little flighty.

In a male horoscope this is likely to indicate either no marriage at all or more than one marriage. It rarely accompanies one marriage only unless with Venus in Taurus. It indicates a clever and witty wife and a lot of fun and happiness through women.

With 195, a gossip—look out for the tongue! With 147 or 151, artistic intellectual gifts. With 181, erratic emotional nature; neurosis. With 163 or 180, concentrative powers are helped; you go far through intellectual training and effort. This also cuts down the talkiness and puts the energy to better uses.

4

SUN IN ARIES—MOON IN CANCER

(You belong to the positive or executive group)

WELL, THERE'S no doubt about it—you are sensitive—extremely sensitive, and extremely capable. You have a good deal of pride in your own ability, a sort of determination to live up to the best that is in you in a personal and artistic way. This is one of the positions that makes for both artists and executives, students and doers at the same time, for your intellectual powers are strong and are bolstered up still further by an intuitive understanding of both people and things. You know how to catch the imagination of your audience, however broad or narrow it may be, without giving up any least iota of your own individualism, which is peculiarly precious to you. You have a keen social sense and a sense of the dramatic, which makes you lively company—when you're in the mood. But you are much subject to moods and can change from sprightly gayety to pretty heavy dejection, all in the twinkling of an eyelash. You know how to manage people to your own ends, which, if the truth can be known, do not always coincide with the ends of other people. There's a good deal of selfishness here—perhaps not selfishness so much as self-centeredness. You know well enough what will make other people happy, but you are more likely than not to give your own whims precedence over the needs of other people—at the same time that you are able to make them think that you are really the best and most considerate of souls. You wouldn't willfully hurt a fly, but, on the other hand, it seems as if you frequently do hurt people without understanding that you are doing so. You have a keen sense of the dramatic and could therefore be successful either directly on the stage, as an actor, or in related arts and crafts that deal with drama through the spoken or written word. You are extremely fluent both in speech and writing, with a wit and charm to your manner of expression that make you popular. You give the impression of independence, originality, and dash, even when you're internally quavering at your own daring and wondering how you are mustering up the courage to appear so exciting. You love your home and all things connected with it despite the fact that this position often brings obligations from family ties that are far from appealing. You are able, through will power, to work out your intimate personal problems, but in the working out there may be a good deal of self-dramatization which impedes the progress of your rational solution. You should learn, for your greatest success, not to take yourself too seriously in your personal life; and to transfer your dramatic sense and your energy into the outer world where your natural talents will find a public, and a just reward.

With 163 and 181, talent amounting to genius when personal problems are overcome and mastered; sensitivity to a high degree must be fought down; objectivity must be sought. With 147, explosive nature, much talent, and probably great success; some difficulty with or through parents or home, but huge powers! With 149, danger of introversion and wasting of talents through a moody disposition and temperament. With 180, powerful nature, magnetic, determined—going places! With 161 or 168, dissipation of energies through anger, confusion, or self-indulgence. Quarrels are destructive; touchiness needs to be guarded. If you have these, you are precocious, and will need to guard your talents so that they will not disappear in later life.

5

SUN IN ARIES—MOON IN LEO

(You belong to the positive or executive group)

ROMANCE and adventuresomeness combine to make your life interesting. You have a keen sense of both of these, and a certain loyalty and fixity of devotion and purpose that make you a good friend, a good sweetheart, and a good business man—despite the fact that you want your own way and pretty generally manage to get it. You love not only individuals but people as a whole, and people, feeling this, flock around you and fill your life with the pleasant contacts of friendship. This intense social sense and social magnetism may in extreme cases (for example, with 147, 171, 200 or 210) make for a Great Lover sort of person—a Don Juan, or whatever the female of that is—and in any case the love element plays an important part in your life. You need love and affection and generally manage to get it.

This is furthermore a fine executive position, and you are able to manage affairs, both your own and those of others, to excellent advantage. You are expressive, even eloquent, and may have an exceptionally fine speaking voice. Ambition is keenly marked and assumes a personal form. You *need* success for the gratification of your inner regard for your own ability quite as much as for the plaudits of the world. This makes the truly creative spirit, for you create out of a combination of the head and the heart which touches your work, whatever it may be, with fire, at the same time that its intellectual content loses nothing. You have a way of making your emotions and your instincts appear plausible and even inevitable, not only to yourself but to your world, with the satisfying result that people take you seriously, sensing the underlying soundness of your nature.

But despite all these good influences, if this position occurs in a horoscope this is largely composed of triangles, especially if there is no square □ to the Sun or Moon, you may be lucky without ever having to develop the great abilities in you. In this case, there is a high degree of inertia. Things come to you. There is plenty to occupy you—and the Manifest Destiny lies dormant without ever finding adequate expression. Under these circumstances you may appear a little smug, a little too well pleased with yourself, a little inclined to take things and people and luck for granted, as your right and due.

With 170, this introversion will be especially dangerous, and you will have to make a serious effort to overcome the inertia of your nature and to organize and unleash your energies. With 147, the energies will be unleashed right enough, and you will be lucky almost to a fault, but something will not be developed that ought to be, and you may live and die unsatisfied with your own development, despite economic security.

The best results will accrue from this polarity of the Sun and Moon under 163 or 180; while if you have the combination with 147 and 180 together, there is no limit to the success you may achieve. With 171, outer appearance of nervousness is controlled and made constructive by internal poise and calm and by sheer force of will. Will power is your great asset—and it's up to you to see that it takes its aggressive form and doesn't degenerate into mere Won't power.

6

SUN IN ARIES—MOON IN VIRGO

(You belong to the positive or executive group)

YOU HAVE A FINE critical and analytical mind, scientific in its bent rather than creative or executive, but capable through the exercise of mental powers of rising to great heights which may give you the appearance of executive power and authority. Your best road to success, however, is along lines where studious application to details, scientific analysis, and a respect for the known and knowable facts will reap their reward. A lawyer, a doctor, a judge, a scientist—or a business man depending on his own powers of analysis to create his business and success—these are the fields in which you can hope to excel. But underlying all must be a strong intellectual training—formal schooling if possible, and if this is not possible, continued study on your own, which because of your deep-seated curiosity will be congenial to you. This is the position under which you never stop learning and wanting to learn; you are continually on the search for facts, knowledge, information, and details, and the piecing together all of these facts gives you a grip not only on the details but also on the broader and more general viewpoints which are merely products of a multitude of facts. You don't take very much for granted; you expect to do your best yourself, and you brook no slipshod methods in those who work around you, or with you, or for you. You are a stern but just judge. You are likely to sit in judgment on your friends and neighbors for you're a good deal of a Puritan at heart and have little use for human frailty and weakness. A certain dash to your manner is deceptive in this respect, and makes you appear to be quite a gay person while you are more likely than not to stay strictly within the bounds of convention. With 150, 154, 171, 178, 200, or 210 this may be altered, but if you ever do step off the beaten track under stress of circumstances, you do it with a consciousness of sinning, and not from any inner conviction that you have a right to transgress the codes and laws of society. You are willing and eager to be yourself, but being yourself does not impel you to do things that are likely to make you criticized... Thus, with some or all of the above mentioned numbers, you can get away with murder. Your transgressions will have a sort of humble and apologetic note, and you will get yourself readily forgiven.

You have to be careful of being too harsh with the frailties of other people, for the judicial note is strong, and there is danger that it will degenerate into a holier-than-thou attitude which is aggravating to more earthbound mortals. You have to remember that people must be judged by their own standards as well as by yours. You can get to the truth of the matter well enough, and it's up to you to select a matter where the truth is of some consequence.

With 162 or 163 or both, admirable career, respected, honored, and honorable. With 195 or 215, financial wizardry and likelihood of considerable wealth. With 185, mind needs training and is likely to be too critical without being constructive. With 188, remarkable mental powers, both analytical and intuitive, capable of the extremes of progress through intellectual development and aptness of thought and expression. With 159, careless mind, quick enough but inaccurate, and much in need of training. With 178 or 181, impulses can be curbed by intellectual effort and should be; develop tact and avoid anger or hastiness of action. As the palmists say, let the Head rule the Heart.

7

SUN IN ARIES—MOON IN LIBRA

THIS IS a curiously difficult position, presenting a problem between the emotional and mental natures. You are ambitious, eager to get ahead and anxious to please people, with a sort of personality that seems to reach out to others as if you are in need of support and guidance and affection from someone or from many people. Despite a nature which in many ways is highly individualized, you are strangely dependent on others—can be thrown off your balance by lack of sympathy, or by coldness, or hardness, or lack of consideration in those around you. This is odd of you because you are perfectly capable of ignoring the feelings, opinions, and wishes of others when you get a set idea in your head. You go ahead in spite of man, God, and the devil, let the chips fall where they may—and like as not they fall right back on you, to your great confusion. You will undoubtedly be found in a professional or artistic, rather than in an executive career, but you have a hard time concentrating (unless with 163 or 180) and a tendency to daydream is your besetting evil. You can give the appearance of concentration and of working to beat all get-out, at the same time that your mind is millions of miles away. You are likely to resort to all kinds of devices to accomplish concentration—and when you get it, be unable to do anything anyway. You have to bear in mind, in all things, that the solution to your problems is not to be found in other people or in your surroundings, but in yourself. Until such a time as you cease to look to the outer world for support, sympathy, and guidance and take yourself gently but firmly by the scruff of the neck and (to mix metaphors) look yourself squarely in the face, you are likely to waste your energies woefully. Whether you're merely a daydreamer, or think yourself inspired, or a medium, your surest recipe for success is to plant your feet solidly on terra firma, look into your own nature with infinite detachment, and determine how you and the world in which you find yourself may be brought realistically and constructively into contact with each other. A sort of romantic belief in yourself, unaccompanied by action, makes it likely that you will not develop to the highest point, while romantic matters tending to go awry further confuse your mind by introducing a note of frustration. You'll do best to avoid romance as much as possible. Get your love life settled early and then forget it; learn to take these matters more for granted, less dramatically —for if you don't your life is likely to be one continuous drama in which you, as the leading character, will not be able to find time for anything of material consequence. A certain facility for poetry accompanies this position but only in the presence of rigid intellectual training can this be made constructive and progressive. Though your tendency is to the arts, you will make greater progress along more material lines, such as business, in which you will have to force yourself to think things out straight and true, and where perforce you will have to swallow that inspirational lump that keeps rising in your throat. Stick to the facts, and the Great Principles will take care of themselves.

With 161, precocity and early brilliance that needs careful nursing later; emotional forces descend at adolescence to the confusion of your mental powers. With 163 or 180, powerful personality, great ability, but danger from inertia—get going! With 149, too great dependence on others, probably on one other in particular. You look and appear independent but in reality are not very.

8

SUN IN ARIES—MOON IN SCORPIO

WELL, WHATEVER may happen to you, good or bad, life is never going to be dull. Between your own aggressiveness and vitality, your conviction of your own worth, and the way you are able to make the world believe in it, you will have your ups and downs, but you will never lose that zest for living which fills you with energy and inner drive. Although not by any means always happy (you have a way of brooding over secret matters, real or imagined, of which even those closest to you have little knowledge), you none the less give the impression of competence, ability—of holding the strands of your life firmly in your hands and of doing with them pretty much as you please. Even in adversity, you are undismayed; for a combination of faith in yourself, and in some higher power which you may or may not call God, or Luck, surrounds you with a kind of aura of invulnerability. You seem so competent and capable that you are likely not to get nearly as much sympathy from the world as others do—and you don't want sympathy; you scorn it. Ready enough to give it to others (though in a rather detached and impersonal manner), you would consider yourself humiliated if sympathy were offered to you. You are able to take care of yourself, and do, and are proud of it, and resent any implication that you can't. This justifies your pride both to yourself and to the world. You have a turbulent nature, and in many ways lead a turbulent life. If you are born low, you go high; if you're born high and secure, you're likely to go low and jump back again. There's a steel spring in you that stays wound up, waiting for the emergencies of life, for you are not really ambitious in a worldly sense. You want security, comfort, activity, excitement, perhaps, but you are content with these. You like recognition, but for its own sake rather than for wealth. Your rewards in life are deeply intimate and personal, and the conviction of your own worth, is of more value to you than all the money or property in the world. Thus, as an artist, though you may, through your vitality and your ability to magnetize the public, achieve some degree of fame and recognition, you pursue your art from a truly inner sense of well-being in a task well done, in a Self properly realized and expressed. But at the same time that you are expressing yourself in this or in some other way, there are deep wells of secret things that you do not express at all—ideas, ideals, dreams, imaginings, that never come to the surface and would surprise your friends if they knew of them if they were not prepared never to be surprised by anything you may do. This great fund of secret ideology provides inspiration if you are an artist of any kind, and magnetic force to your personality, either in business or in social matters. You are pretty set in your ways, very inflexible when your mind is made up—determined without the appearance of being stubborn (though of course you *are* stubborn!), and able to convince people peaceably even against their wills. You are exceptionally loyal and devoted in matters of love and stick to your friends through years and years. You are capable of demanding little and giving much; but you won't be imposed on, and you have a sure instinct for the chiseler, the sycophant, or the fawner who may seek your friendship merely to be helped by your money or your influence. Him you detect and scorn. But you will give the shirt off your back for a worthy person, though you have in general little interest in causes. You will help individuals and let the causes take care of themselves. A high temper is compensated for by deeply sincere emotions, which, with 147, 161, 168, 178, 200 or 210, may get you into trouble. Even without these you have to watch out that emotional impulses don't involve you treacherously.

With 202, 212, disappointment in some early love matter warps your emotional nature; your genius of never forgetting rebounds on you embitteringly and needs rooting out. You must learn to forget if not to forgive, for dislikes and hatreds can eat the heart out of your energies and powers, and prove boomerangs if you let them. With 149, danger of introversion. With 171, unconventionality makes trouble. With 163, possibility of genius or anyway great ability and concentrative powers. Success through highly personal lines of endeavor. Slow rise and swift fall, if emotional impulses are not curbed.

9

SUN IN ARIES—MOON IN SAGITTARIUS

(You belong to the positive or executive group)

INDEPENDENCE of thought, action, and speech—that's you! You believe in the truth with an almost pious devotion—not so much the technical truth of scientific investigation as the fundamental truths of large doctrines, philosophies, abstractions. You are more a speculator than a seeker—details irk you. You look for truth along larger lines. This is likely to lead into the errors of inspirationalism, and unless you temper these grandiose mental tendencies with the scientific method, you're likely to lapse into obscure generalities, large phrases insufficiently defined. With your extreme honorableness and insistence on honor in your own life, you can be a tremendous force for good in the world *if* you give yourself that rigid mental training which will bring your generalizations down to earth and make them realistically significant. You are in many ways a pioneer, a fighter, a doer, a pleader of new doctrines and lost causes; you are strongly individualistic, with a powerful desire to bring your world, whether it be great or small, to your way of thinking. Your executive powers are strongly marked, taking the form of controlling others with an idea, a thought, a principle, rather than with the power of position or authority. You derive your greatest satisfaction not from power over the bodies of men, but over their minds. You might be the man who said, "Let me write the songs (or the editorials) of the nations, and I care not who makes its laws (or leads its armies)." You have terrific force of expression—maybe (with 161, 168, 184, 195 or 196) too terrific and forceful for your own good; for you are in no case likely to be too tactful. The truth is so evident to you that you see no use in mincing words. Intense emotionally, you are capable of achieving that much-to-be-desired state in which "the intellect is a passion and the passions are cold"—for there is a sort of detachment to your emotional nature which, though ardent, tends to become sublimated in ideas, rather than in human beings. You are not especially aware of the feelings of other people but are likely to be acutely aware of your own, which is tough on those around you. You have to cultivate understanding of people as well as of ideas; and in both fields regard for details is the quality of mental and emotional activity that needs attention. While keeping your wagon hitched to a star, you're likely to drive it into the ditch. You are capable of spouting idealistically about love at the very moment when you've forgotten to bring home that pack of cigarettes your wife wanted. Your best field of activity is definitely professional—though you are so active physically that you are likely to choose some profession that requires a lot of moving around. You have little capacity or desire for staying in one place. You will achieve your greatest satisfaction through your appeal to other people, and whether you're a lawyer, an actor, a doctor, or a divine, your self-gratification comes not so much through power or through wealth as it does through Influence.

With 170, more self-centered and worldly; with 180, powerful personality; with 161, 168, 184 or 195, quarrelsome, contentious. With 215 or 229, likelihood of great wealth and influence. With 200 or 210, strongly marked love-nature, passionate but not exactly warm-hearted, and a danger of hurting those you love and who love you.

10

SUN IN ARIES—MOON IN CAPRICORN

(You belong to the positive or executive group)

YOU HAVE that inner drive of ambition that makes almost inevitably for success. You're a hard person to get the better of, for you know your own mind and have definite ideas of where you're going and how you're going to get there; and you let nothing stand in your way. No matter how sweet and gracious you may be—and there's every chance that you are, at least when you want to be—there's a hard underlying foundation of rock in your nature that does not get shaken and does not yield to blandishment. You're an excellent business person, an executive capable of ruling men, and if other things concur (such as 163, or 180, or 147 or 168) you may find yourself at the top of the heap—or rather not *find* yourself there so much as *force* yourself there. You seem to know the laws of the conservation of energy and to be able to take all the pep, energy, enthusiasm, and magnetism of your makeup and put it into constructive action through the power of a rigidly controlled personality. Your manner of expression is forceful without being offensive; you seem to know instinctively the right way to say the right thing at the right time and powerful people will help you at the beginning of your life as you will help others at the end. One or both parents is likely to mean a great deal to you both psychologically and materially. With 163 and 181, or with 150 and 181, there is some danger that early impressions either through the home or the parents may set up psychological bogies that will need overcoming. But even with these initial handicaps you will be able to go far under your own power, especially after you have shaken loose from family ties and got out on your own. You should do this early in life and not allow family complications to hold you back. Independence is your crying need, and only when freed of the ties of your mother's or father's home will you achieve your maximum success. Fame is important to you—recognition the lodestar of your life; you are extremely worldly; your idealism is of a practical and hard-boiled variety, and you are capable of sacrificing a good deal to success—and of getting it. Although this is a position for a happy marriage, it is not one in which marriage is likely to be the beginning and the end of existence by any means. It is more an incident, and as often as not people with this configuration are found in marriages of convenience rather than of romance—which doesn't mean, of course, that they don't make excellent husbands and wives. There's a practical common sense about you that makes up for a lack of demonstrativeness.

You have a good sound intellectual equipment which you put to practical use. Abstract knowledge or knowledge for its own sake is of no especial importance to you, though you are an apt, even exceptional student. But your bent is too practical for the abstractions of intellect, and your mind serves the purposes of the world rather than any detached purposes of its own. This leads to various types of careers according to other indications, but in any case the career's the thing, to which emotional and mental matters become subordinated. You are an opportunist and can take advantage of things as they arise as well as create your own opportunities.

All in all, this is a very powerful and dynamic position, and with 146, 147, 148, 149, 155, 162, 163, 168, 169, 174, 180, 215, 216, 218, 227, 228, 229 or 230 can take you almost anywhere you want to go. Any one of the above number paragraphs in your horoscope will bring great success; with two you don't even think about it.

11

SUN IN ARIES—MOON IN AQUARIUS

(You belong to the positive or executive group)

YOUR INTEREST in people pays large dividends, whether it takes the form of dealing with people in business, in public life or in the remoter forms of public contact. You are highly social and magnetic, and likely in some way or other to be well paid for anything you undertake that depends on your popularity with, or purchasing power of, the masses. You'd make a good salesman, either of merchandise, of yourself, or of any ideas you may have. You give a great impression of being interested in what goes on around you at the same time that you don't lose sight of the main chance. This combination of assets makes it possible for you to analyze situations pretty accurately where either people or business matters are concerned. Very little grass grows under your feet. Your life moves at a rapid pace. You're romantic, courageous, and adventurous; large ventures appeal to you. You have little use for the trifling or the picayune. You probably have had the advantages of a good family background and the education that goes with it, for a certain aristocracy of breeding is denoted by this position, of which you know how to take advantage. Democratic notions are not marked, for you are an extreme individualist, believing in yourself, and those in your financial and social strata; and despite your success in dealing with people, you have no particular faith in them. Politically, you are more likely to be a reactionary than a liberal. Economically, you believe in capitalism and its perquisites— for the very sufficient reason that this system has in all probability been very good to you. Realizing, however, that success in any system derives from the masses, you are able to conceal your inner feeling that most people are sheep or worse, and to make the most of public and private opportunity. You are not wanting in self-esteem and it's likely that your good opinion of yourself, your ideas, and your mode of life contributes to your lack of sympathy with those who think differently, or pursue different modes of life, or dwell on a lower economic scale. You go with the right people, live in the right part of town, belong to the right clubs, and send your children to the right schools. Intellectually you are sound and thorough; emotionally you are romantic and highly idealistic, ardent, but probably not impulsive, unless with 168, 178, 181, 200, or 210. This is a good position for material success and well-being, and also for some degree of public recognition, either in political, business, or intellectual pursuits.

12

SUN IN ARIES—MOON IN PISCES

YOU BROOD and you worry; you're moody and temperamental. You give a great impression of force, but internally you're a little timid, a little afraid of the world and even of your own opinions. You're likely to be imposed upon through this lack of inner conviction, although you bitterly resent being imposed upon. You express readily, having a facile flow of language, and you have a conviction that you know the truth of many matters which for some reason or other you cannot get across to your associates. This is a Cassandra-like position—a prophet who is very likely to be right but can't make anyone believe him. Despite your apparent vitality, you're likely to worry about your health far more than it warrants—and by worry you run the risk of actually producing, through nerves, the sort of physical difficulties you fear. Bold as a lion on the surface, you aren't nearly so bold underneath, for you're highly sensitive and afraid of saying or doing the wrong thing. Solitude is periodically necessary to you, and you can regain strength and self-confidence in private. Large gatherings of people are more likely than not to irritate and annoy you; and you are capable of going into a brown (or black) study in the midst of a laughing throng. There's a liberal dose of introspection here, and also of self-pity—and many of your troubles are self-created. You have some difficulty concentrating, and even when environmental conditions are of the best may find yourself not devoted to the task in hand but brooding or dreaming. Emotionally you are impressionable and run to odd people. You're likely to bestow your affections quite foolishly, or on some unworthy person, and then to be sorry for yourself instead of making the best of it. In a man's horoscope this may give a wife chronically ill; in a woman's horoscope it is not good for her health and warns her against trying to live up to the maximum of what she thinks her vitality to be—also against creating physical trouble through nerves and worry.

Your best and most congenial career will be found in something of a highly personal nature such as music, art, poetry, writing—the creative arts—in which your inspirational and brooding tendencies may be harnessed to your energy. You have a broad and deep understanding of many complex matters, and once you have mastered a medium of expression, can catch the hearer's, or the reader's, imagination with the somewhat unusual quality of your viewpoint and style. You are not likely to be happy in business though you might be successful, especially with 148 or 169.

With 163, ability to concentrate is helped and can lead to ability along intellectual and artistic lines amounting to genius; with 180, perseverance in material matters gives self-confidence and success, but health needs watching, as also with 147, which brings a liberal supply of the world's goods. With 147, 148, and 215, great wealth. In any case, this is a highly charitable position, and if you have money under it, you are a philanthropist in the true sense of the word. Even if you haven't much, you tend to give a good deal of it away.

13

SUN IN TAURUS—MOON IN ARIES

(You belong to the positive or executive group)

YOU HAVE a powerful personality. There is a certain fixity of purpose in you which your highly expressive nature may conceal, and a certain ruthlessness in getting what you want—though the skies fall—that may not be apparent except to those who know you intimately. Your intellectual and emotional natures, each powerful in its own right, are not closely allied, and you frequently express thoughts which bear no least relation to your emotions. Since you have deep wells of unprobed consciousness (subconsciousness), you may not even be aware of your own inconsistencies, but for all that, what you say when you are on guard and what you do when you are off guard often bear no discernible relationship to each other. You will express the most tolerant and broad-minded of viewpoints at one moment and then, when an emotion is touched, be as biased and unreasonable as the very people you were flaying as bigots ten seconds before. You have a truly remarkable mental equipment which is capable of mastering anything however abstruse or realistic it may be. But unless supported by powerful aspects to the Sun or Mercury (such as 178, 180, 186 or 192) these mental powers are more likely than not to get you into difficulty. Even with the most powerful of supporting aspects, you will have to exercise a high degree of self-control to submerge the tendency to dominate your environment and those in it, for you are capable of making both yourself and those around you unhappy by getting your own way. Even when you aren't overtly insisting on something, you have a way of making your wishes known by a manner, a gesture, or a lack of enthusiasm of which you may not even be conscious but which your environmental associates may crumble under. When you are arguing directly for your point, you have a way of being so plausible and so apparently reasonable that you wear down resistance. This is all very well if you do not reduce your associates to the status of dependents—which is the danger of this position. You're so sure of yourself, so confident of what you think and believe and want, that you're likely to take the starch out of other people who aren't so sure. You should learn to let other people alone, to allow them to lead their own lives in their own ways, and to put your great mental and physical energies into a wholly impersonal type of pursuit, whether it be business, artistic, or professional. If you do this your success is assured, for your best medium of expression is the impersonal. Put your energy, your passion, your determination, into that and you will go far. But set your mind on other people, either with a subconscious desire to dominate them or with a feeling of dependence on them, and you will get what you want—but after you get it, it won't please you. This is truly a position of "Beware your desire for assuredly you will have it." It is also a position in which you should dispassionately view yourself—develop introspection—and find what hidden recesses of consciousness need a housecleaning. You'll find plenty there—and once you bring the debris to light, you'll lead a more fluent, happy, contented, and successful life.

With 151, shallow mind, unless also with 163, 186 or 197. With 178 or 180, persistence increased, aggressiveness marked, and likely to be successful. With 145, the mental qualities will follow the indications of that aspect and of the aspects of the Sun. With 145 and 146, creative urge strong and likely to be successful when you have depersonalized your outlook and approached the world on a purely objective basis.

In any case, this position of Sun and Moon cries aloud for depersonalization, and sensitiveness, touchiness, quarrelsomeness, arrogance, dominance are all anathema to your highest development.

14

SUN IN TAURUS—MOON IN TAURUS

(You belong to the positive or executive group)

THE STUBBORNNESS that made you a highly difficult child changes as you grow older into great determination and reasonableness, which gives you an irresistible power both over people and over your own environment. You assume responsibility readily, and your shoulders are broad and capable of carrying almost any load. You have a fine insight into all manner of things: people, the arts, business; and a fixed idea of your own worth and ability that impresses other people strongly. Superiors and those in authority over you are impressed by it at the beginning, and when you yourself get into a position of authority those under you are impressed by it. You know how to take orders, but only because of your long-headed conviction that the way to become an order-giver is first, and cheerfully, to be an order-taker. Your respect for authority is based on the determination to become the authority yourself. Thus you make a good subordinate—except for the fact that if the boss doesn't look out you'll eventually have his job. You are not unscrupulous, but you are hard-headed, and though you are loyal, you are not likely to have any loyalties that will interfere with your progress. You are an ardent and passionate lover as well as a very imperious one. You'll rule your own home or know the reason why. Where your personal pride or emotions are in any way touched you are capable of stubbornness, temper, and anger of a truly childish nature—though in impersonal matters you can be patient, calm, reasonable with an almost Machiavellian detachment. You have a tongue-in-cheek diplomacy which humors your opponents until in the end you have your own way, and you don't mind waiting a long time to get it. Thus by patience, worldliness, and great energy, you're pretty likely to be successful in whatever field you choose to make your life work.

With 148 or 169, business; with 145, 146, 151, 166, 167 or 172, intellectual, artistic, musical; with 155, 156, 174 or 175, public life; with 227, unlimited success, possibility of world fame. If no aspects to Sun or Moon, great ability, but difficulty in getting wide recognition. Your great gifts and magnetism will have their best chance for expression when you are acting, thinking, and speaking from a detached and objective viewpoint, for under the stimulus of emotional or personal excitement, your energies disappear in anger, stubbornness, and fretfulness. Don't hold grudges—they eat you out from within. Scorn your enemies but don't hate them or try to think up ways to get even. Cultivate magnanimity, objectivity, and dispassionate logic and there are few heights to which you cannot go.

15

SUN IN TAURUS—MOON IN GEMINI

PERSONAL DISCONTENT will run away with you and make a muddle of your life if you don't learn to control your critical attitude toward other people. You think yourself loyal, devoted, persistent, and capable, but as a matter of fact, you have a tendency to fly, emotionally, from one thing to another and especially from one person (sweetheart, friend) to another. You start out a personal relationship all fire and love and devotion, and before you know it you're finding something the matter with the loved one. Like as not you think that he (or she) has become unworthy of the great love you have to offer, or you find some flaw in his (her) character, manner of speech, or brand of hair tonic (or lipstick). You have an aggressive and adventurous spirit, and in both a figurative and geographic sense are likely to wander a good deal during your years on earth. Your emotional and business stability will develop directly in proportion to your intellectual training. Get as much schooling as you can, and if you can't get formal schooling, satisfy that curious mentality of yours with facts and figures rather than with mere idle talk and speculation. Study will steady you down. You'll find yourself more contented, less restless, more constant in love, and more successful in business in proportion as you occupy your mind with some set course of study. Study by correspondence—learn how to play the piano or draw the plans for a bridge, in seventeen easy lessons—and you'll be surprised how everything straightens out as you give your mind something tangible and concrete to bite on. At the same time that you do this stay in one spot and don't allow yourself to gossip or listen to idle talk. People are always coming to you with wild yarns about your friends, and you're impressionable and likely to be swayed, though at heart you are loyal. But what you are at heart doesn't make much difference if you don't put it into practise. Study, read, and if you don't create, get into some occupation that keeps your mind busy—secretarial or the like; salesmanship is good—this gives you a chance to express yourself with cash advantages.

With 168, 178, 181, 200 or 210, ardent, impulsive, and disappointing love experiences; with 202, 203, or 212, hurt through the opposite sex, the mother, or both; with 204 or 214, very impressionable and sensational nature; 161, early mental promise yields scattered results—high temper disintegrating. With 163 or 180, you are able to concentrate and so achieve success in a personal or worldly way, though with these positions there is some unhappiness through romance.

16

SUN IN TAURUS—MOON IN CANCER

(You belong to the positive or executive group)

YOU HAVE a highly sensitive nature, are easily hurt, and likely to become very resentful of real or imagined slights or offenses. You are an ardent lover and a permanent hater, though you can conceal your dislikes very well and have a sort of protective diplomacy about you that makes it difficult for others to know just where you stand or what you are thinking about, in either personal or business matters. You are a dangerous enemy or opponent, changing your position and tactics to suit your purposes, and popping up on the flank without warning while your victim is busy protecting his vanguard. Your ambition is of a deep-seated, personal nature, closely allied with your vanity. Your apparent self-assurance is only skin deep, and underneath (unless with 163) you're jittery and nervous as a schoolgirl on her first date. But despite all this you are likely to arrive, by diplomacy and the judicious using of influence, at some position of authority—though you are not (unless with 163, 147, 168, 169, or 180) a real executive, and even with these aspects or one of them there are flaws in your executive procedure. Your capacity for conciliating all parties makes you appear weak, even when you know your own mind and what you want. Learn to take a stand, even if you antagonize someone or some faction, for otherwise your success, though possibly great on the surface, will rest on shifting sands. You need security and, even if a man and noted for your *affaires du cœur* (which you probably are), require the stabilizing influence of a home. Both male and female of this combination do best after marriage, even though they are frequently late in settling down. You must develop determination rather than stubbornness; forthrightness rather than diplomacy. Excess diplomacy can amount to weakness, and agreeableness to unreliability; just as hedging on important issues can amount to having no convictions at all. Take a stand and be damned for it; a good knockdown and drag-out argument is what you need once in a while. Learn, when you know you're right, to give no quarter. You can so easily see the other fellow's viewpoint that it disrupts your own. Let the other fellow give ground once in a while, or eventually he'll push you to the wall—and that'll be that.

With 151 and 164, neurosis, impressionability, emotionalism dangerous; learn calm, poise, and concentration. With 172, mystic and confused. With 168, 178, 180, 169 or 174, executive talent; success through powerful people. With 163, artistic talent marked. With 200 or 210, explosive love-nature needs the check rein. With 202 or 212, disappointments in love go hard. With 183 or 189, and 188, idealistic mind; if also with 163, creative artist.

17

SUN IN TAURUS—MOON IN LEO

(You belong to the positive or executive group)

THERE'S NOTHING wishy-washy about *you!* A strong determined will, well-defined opinions, and a complete willingness to let anyone know what they are make you a forthright, honest, and fearless person with a fine scorn and contempt for those people whom for any reason you don't like. Your dislikes are not necessarily founded on abstract or logical grounds, but arise from an instinctive feeling about people which rarely is changed or shaken—when you don't like 'em, you don't like 'em, and that's that. On the other hand, you're an equally loyal friend and stick to people through thick and thin if you have any reason at all to believe in their worth. You have an excellent mind, both creative and executive. If on the creative side, you will excel in the constructive or mathematical arts, such as sculpture, music, or achitecture. You're a powerful executive though not financially minded, and while your magnetism, forthrightness, and directness can make you excel in business activity if you want to, your real genius is not for money but for people, so that you will be found in the social-executive positions—army, navy, social work. You tend to dominate any group you may be in or any individual you may come in contact with, and since you aren't long on tact, you can get yourself disliked. You understand people but you haven't any special hankering to be understood by them; there is something a little lonely and proud and aloof about you that holds people at a distance even when you may want them closer. You are ardent and devoted in love, somewhat romantic in an abstract and idealistic way, likely to be disappointed in the foibles of less idealistic people, and to withdraw into yourself for contemplation of your own worth. This doesn't draw people to you emotionally, though they do respect and admire and like you, and if you can relax a certain stiffness of approach, you can be extremely popular. But you find this relaxation difficult, and you give the impression of pride even when you don't want to. For all this you're likely to have a wide circle of friends and be well liked by them; you can grapple them to your heart with hoops of steel if you will express your emotions with the same force that you put into your opinions.

With 180, very forceful person, successful in executive work; if also with 181, unconventional but a trifle cold. Erratic emotional nature in early life, stabilizing later. With 168, tactlessness very harmful; with 163, creative; with 186, 187 scientific and critical genius; with 217 or 218, high order of ability, aggressive, magnetic, versatile; with 224, high-flying and quick-falling.

18

SUN IN TAURUS—MOON IN VIRGO

YOU HAVE charm, poise, balance, and admirable common sense and the extent to which you develop these qualities to your own intellectual and economic advantage will depend on other things. *If there are no conjunctions or squares* to the Sun or Moon you're likely to coast through life in a sort of gracious and relaxed condition, being lucky in material matters without having to give much thought to them. You always seem in some way provided for, and if put to it can provide for yourself, for this is one of the lucky material positions. *If there are* conjunctions and squares to the Sun or Moon or both, your boundless energy, intelligence, and above all common sense, will carry you far, in either an intellectual or an artistic career. Your executive qualities are not well marked, but in mental undertakings, or when carrying out the instructions of a superior, you are excellent. Your strong Taurean independence, however, makes it hard for you to take orders for long, and thus you'll do best in an independent career that depends neither on giving nor on taking orders—art, letters—or housekeeping. You have a good intelligence, and though not precocious mentally (your emotions get ahead of your intellectual development), you learn steadily and keep it up for a long time, once you start. You will always be reading, studying, and absorbing what other people have to give you. And above all you have grace and charm of manner, especially pleasant in a woman's horoscope. You're sure to be popular with both men and women. In a man's horoscope this position gives a fine intellect, and brings success in a career that depends on this gift. The chief danger is that general good luck and protection from worry will swamp its possibilities for development, for an inclination to relax and go to sleep intellectually is very strong, especially when the emotional wants (which are very strong) are satisfied. A little adversity is good for you and tends to wake you up, for you are extremely conscientious and will not fall down on a job when it's put up to you. Thus, such aspects as 163, 147, 161, 180, 181, 210, 212, 213 or 224, though they bring you hardships and disappointments and hurts, are really blessings in disguise since they stimulate you, open your eyes, and set a pace for you to follow.

With 202, 212 or 213, emotional disappointments, love frustrations, cause hurt and are stimulating. With 180 or 181, nervous tension finds a constructive and progressive outlet; with 161, quick mentality, perhaps a little lazy; with 147, extraordinary financial luck; with 167, 163 or 166, creative talents; with 188, confusion; with 204, dangerously impressionable; with 213, hurt through bad friends.

19

SUN IN TAURUS—MOON IN LIBRA

YOU ARE a confirmed romantic, and whatever your station or occupation may be, your success, your failure, your happiness, and your disappointments come directly through your emotional nature. You may be an actor and derive success and satisfaction through the emotional stimulus from your audience; a poet and express your feelings and those of the world in particularly appealing form; a husband or wife and get your greatest satisfaction from your spouse; but wherever you go it is your heart-interest in one form or another that counts to you. No matter how powerful your intellect may be, nor how detached and intellectual you may seem; no matter how impersonal your aggressiveness may appear, you have a real need for sympathy and affection. You are basically constant and fix your devotion in one person or in your family, though if with 163, 164, 150, 181, 200, 202, 203, 204, 210, 212 or 213 there may be a continuous search for the sympathetic soul which will lead you into many and varied love affairs.

In any case this is a position of high nervous tension. If with 224, temperament is emphasized, as well as a likelihood of great rise and fall in life, in which some frustration of the affections plays an important part. Nerves also will be induced in this highly sensitive position by 216, 217, 225, 218, 226, 184, 187, 188, 195, 198 or 199. You are capable of having an important and popular career in anything which deals either with the public or with young people, for the double influence of Venus (both Sun and Moon being in one of Venus's signs) gives you a great deal of charm which even high nervousness cannot dissipate; and when your energies are controlled by such an aspect as 180, 181, or 166; or your magnetism and dash heightened by 215, 218, or 161, great popularity and success are likely. If a man, you will be a favorite with women—and love it! If a woman you will never lack for admirers and sweethearts although the ramifications of your love life (whichever gender you belong to) will generally lead at some time or other to hurt and disappointment. Self-dependence is what you chiefly need—the ability to feel that you are in yourself complete, for the devotion to another, though fine and romantic, can leave you bewildered and confused if the proper person is not forthcoming, or if in some way your love is forced to come to an end. Eventually you will have to learn the lesson of self-reliance, and if you learn it early you will be spared a good deal of unhappiness and readjustment in later life.

20
SUN IN TAURUS—MOON IN SCORPIO

YOU HAVE a strong, impulsive, passionate nature. You know what you want and, for good or bad, get it. You are self-willed, headstrong, independent, usually getting under way early in life and contriving to resist or break any chains which anyone tries to throw around you. You are capable of rearing up on your hind legs, kicking over the traces, taking the bit in your teeth, and running away at a moment's notice—or without any notice at all. Needless to add, you are not an easy person to deal with and anyone who marries you has his (her) work cut out. You'll keep your spouse locked up (or would if you could) at the same time that you're ranging the land in search of more worlds to conquer—which you generally succeed in finding and subjugating. You think with one part of your brain and feel with another and therefore reason doesn't have any effect on your emotions of love, jealousy, or hatred—any one of which is capable of swamping you so that you aren't good for anything else. Intensely dramatic, you can be successful as an actor or a speaker, for your charm is instantaneous. But unless you watch out, all your dramatic ability will be used up strutting the stage of whatever little world you move in. You're not critical of your audiences, and get quite as much satisfaction out of a ham audience as out of a metropolitan first night. This doesn't mean that you're by any means a ham actor for you're not—you have the gift, if you'll only develop ambition to the point of using it properly. But, though eager for personal acclaim, you're not ambitious in the climbing sense and you have continuously to overcome tension which tries to drive you back to simply getting away from it all and relaxing utterly. A curious twist causes tension to turn into inertia instead of into action, and with 163 you're prone to resort to artificial means of releasing tension and getting away from it all. Alcohol, drugs, stimulants, are dangerous to you; stay away from them. They're merely helping you to forget what you really want, which you are willing to forget because it takes effort.

With 163 or 180, and *not* with 149 or 170, your drive will be terrific and success assured. With 149 or 170, introspection, introversion, and inertia overcome you. With 200, 202, 203, 210, 212 or 213, emotional turmoil takes up too much time and energy; with 204, great abilities and magnetism but impressionable to romance; with 218 or 215, lots of luck and a kind of halo of charm and energy. With 150, erratic and unreliable emotional nature; trouble through women. With 175, 174 or 173, so much luck you don't have to worry. With 168 or 147, explosive temper, destructive rages and bursts of temperament.... You have extraordinary mental gifts—an insight into things almost without study—and the extent of your intellectual attainments is limited only by your application. With 183, exceptionally fine mentality, scientific and inspirational as well.

21

SUN IN TAURUS—MOON IN SAGITTARIUS

YOU HAVE a highly developed social sense. You are fond of people who must, however, be the *right* people. You'd rather stay home alone with a good book than be bored by dullards or surrounded by people you think uninteresting or déclassé. You are able to get on well enough with all classes for you know how to say the right thing at the right time, and this quality of tact in human relations contributes much to your success, which frequently will have to do with a good many people. You make a good executive, teacher, or lecturer; your manner of expression is forthright and direct and you make your sincerity and decisiveness felt. Your extremely stubborn nature expresses in a flexible manner, and you are able to talk all around Robin Hood's barn at the same time that you are sticking to your point and eventually driving it home exactly as you wish. You have very high principles and will stick to them despite everything. A keen moral sense, both in your own personal conduct and in the abstract for truth in its own right, makes you something of a moralist, and you're likely to sit in judgment on your friends and neighbors—though you may never let them know what you think about them. But your thoughts are your own just the same, and for those who transgress the laws of right conduct or fair dealing as you understand them, you have scant tolerance. You're something of a gossip; you love a good yarn and will tell one at the drop of a hat. You are also a good listener, especially if the story being told has a touch of personal interest. A good deal of your sinning is likely to be done vicariously, in talking about, and probably condemning, the horrible actions of someone else. You yourself, are pretty likely to walk the straight and narrow and find it rather pleasant—and a good deal easier than the harrowing excitement of the Primrose Path. You should cultivate precision of thinking and speaking, for a tendency to spin yarns in one way or another is very strong, especially if with 145, 159, 188, 199, 184 or 195. This story-telling quality, with 163, 180, 186, 197, 183 or 189, or any triangle to the Moon or Sun, may be developed into creative ability as a writer of fiction, for then the artistic and expressive notes of your nature are brought together. Whether you actually create or not you have nice taste in a bold sort of way, and are fond of bright colors and brave new combinations which you manage to put together artistically, perhaps against all the established rules of color and design. You are in all ways a courageous person and despite your tact, when it comes to points of principle, will not mince matters even with the Judge himself. Here you stick to your guns admirably and tell the world in no uncertain terms what is what. You are reasonable in argument and a fair debater. You can see the other fellow's viewpoint, answering it logically point for point, without losing sight of your own. Your qualities of magnetism, fair-mindedness, and imagination will lead you to success in either business or the arts and professions, depending on the aspects to the Sun, Moon, and Mercury.

22

SUN IN TAURUS—MOON IN CAPRICORN

(You belong to the positive or executive group)

SECURITY IS of the utmost importance to you—not wealth, perhaps, but security of home, of position, and of prestige. You are proud, and a sweet and gracious exterior conceals an inner sense of your own worth which you like to see made manifest in the material things of the world—your accomplishments or your surroundings. You are idealistic, but more than this, you are a realist; you would rather have dignity and comfort in this life than all the fame in the world after death. You will "take the cash, and let the credit go." This leads to an appearance of materialism which is not entirely justified, for you're the most honorable of human beings and your idealism is of a practical work-a-day variety that counts for most in the world of things as they are. You believe in fair dealing and practise it; yours are the virtues of earth rather than the virtues of heaven. Your bent is critical and executive for, despite a deeply underlying sentimentality, you are a good analyst of people and of situations—a shrewd judge of the public consciousness and also of the consciousness of your intimates. You have an instinct for knowing what people are thinking and what they are going to be thinking in a little while. An ability to gauge the public temperament, and what it will take, is your greatest asset toward worldly success. Though needful of security, your real yen is for influence. You like to control and direct, and feel that *you* are responsible for the thoughts and actions of your public, whether it be great or small, and in extreme cases (with 163, 180 or 224) this leads to uninhibited lust for power and authority which (if also with 146, 148, 168 or 169) may well be gratified, for then your power for sensing public sentiment goes into action in a big way and you come out on top. Without any of these stimulating influences or without other squares to your Sun or Moon, you are likely to rest on your oars and accept the security that comes to you; but even here your mind keeps working, if only to worry, for your mental vigor is so great that if it doesn't find a positive outlet it finds a negative one.

With 200, 202 or 210, powerful passions need checking; with 181 or 171, danger of neurosis from worry or health; with 180 and 181, hectic emotional nature, ups and downs both material and emotional, and opportunities for power that have a way of collapsing before, or just after, realization. With 163, executive or creative genius; with 159, facility of expression can be made to produce success—writers, speakers, etc.

23

SUN IN TAURUS—MOON IN AQUARIUS

YOUR AFFABILITY, sunniness, good looks, and generally easy and gracious manner conceal a core of hard purpose which will amaze your friends when they run into it. You give ground with a smile, you yield (up to a point), you back and fill and sashay around tactfully and charmingly, but you never forget for a single instant what you want. You have taken the advice of St. Paul: "Be ye therefore wise as serpents and harmless as doves." Only rarely do you have to put your foot down in open conflict for you've learned the art of getting around things, instead of crashing through them, and though you don't waste much energy or time in the circumnavigation, you'd rather win people over than force them to your will. This makes you a sure bet for success along any one of a dozen lines, for you're versatile and capable of controlling either others, as in a business or political career, or yourself, as in an artistic or professional career. Deeply romantic and even sentimental, you've learned to translate your emotional energies into practical use. Genuinely interested in people, you are able to understand them because you understand yourself, and you seem to realize instinctively that loving your neighbor as yourself means little if you don't love yourself somewhat. An inferiority complex is something you simply haven't got. You are independent, a self-starter capable of going far under your own power, and you'll rarely ask help from the outside, though your many and influential friends stand ready to help you. But your pride keeps you plugging along on your own, and your ability justifies your efforts. You'll probably marry early in life, for you have an ardent and romantic love-nature together with a high degree of conventionality (unless with 181, 200 or 210), and there are some rocks and reefs in store for your idealism as you learn that the world does not have the same clear and high-minded outlook that you have. With 202, 212, 204 or 214, you will have some major, and perhaps embittering, love experience from which, however, you will rebound with your ideals unshaken, for so strong are your convictions, they are not likely to be permanently disturbed. People are attracted to you as flies to sugar; they sense both your idealism and your sympathy, and your underlying conviction that humanity is very frail doesn't come to the surface to distress them. You are a lover of peace, both for your own personal uses and for the benefit of the world; in fact, all your convictions and thoughts pass swiftly from the personal to the broad and general. If the education is strong this will make you a leader politically, or place you in a position of authority over others in some public way. Though a shrewd business man, your honor never deserts you. You scorn to get by foul means what you can so easily find out how to get by fair, and if you can't get it by fair, you skip it.

This is a very magnanimous position, and though you can be deeply hurt and may never forget an injury, you will forgive, according to your code of fair dealing. With 163, professional career or artistic; with 180, business or political. With both, look out that psychological complexes do not produce inertia.

24
SUN IN TAURUS—MOON IN PISCES

YOU HAVE deep wells of hidden consciousness that even your best friends don't know about. You lead a private dream-life of your own that may have no discernible relationship with reality and that serves to isolate you somewhat from intimate human contact, though you have a great need for affection and sympathy. If this exists with 145 or 159, you may be a great and voluble talker, but for all that you say and all the confidences you apparently give out, you none the less keep the important things to yourself. In a horoscope with conjunction and squares dominating, you will be able to translate this into creative and artistic power, for your powers of reserve and restraint are remarkable, and if your energies are controlled by such aspects as 167, 166, 147, 163 or 180, or even possibly 170 or 149, you will succeed in a career of personal gratification—writing, music, or the like. This is primarily the position of the artist, for the executive gifts are not strong, and though you're protected from material want and worry and therefore may be said to have some material luck in life, money is not important to you, except in so far as it brings security for the pursuit of your more personal and idealistic aims. You are highly sensitive to emotional matters, impressionable to love and flattery, and have to be careful that you don't fall in with the wrong people, for there is a chance that you will be imposed upon by your friends. If this occurs with 200, 202, 212, 210, 170, 180 or 181 in a woman's horoscope, or with 200, 210, 202, 212, 161 or 147 in a man's horoscope, some major disappointment in love leaves a sharp imprint in the early life that has a lingering influence. You have an innately solemn outlook on life, unless with 148, 169 or 174, and even with these your mental bent is serious and sober. Life is real, life is earnest to you, and if the grave is not its goal, you have metaphysical rather than religious ideas of what happens after death. Occult, mysterious, hidden things appeal to you. Out-of-the-way studies and pleasures fascinate you. Magic and spiritualism can get a hold on you, and you have a belief in the doctrines of mind over matter, thought processes, and the like. This is a good thing, for there's a tendency to illness derived from nerves and worry, and thought-control will do a good deal to eliminate a tendency to hypochondria. You are pretty self-sufficient, and there's a tendency to introversion that will be emphasized with 149 or 170. You should cultivate objectivity and expressiveness and try not to take yourself and your problems too seriously—or at least, if you do take yourself seriously, to talk things over with a sympathetic friend rather than keep them bottled up. You'll have to do this voluntarily, for no one can draw you out if you don't wish to be drawn. You shut up like a clam and stay shut, resenting the intrusion on your privacy and bringing all your stubbornness to bear on the intended intruder. You are tractable enough under ordinary circumstances, but not when you are being quizzed nor when you've made up your mind and someone opposes you. Then you can balk!

25

SUN IN GEMINI—MOON IN ARIES

(You belong to the positive or executive group)

YOU ARE QUICK as a cat, witty, versatile, mobile, both in mind and in body. You are a witty companion, a dangerous opponent, especially in a battle of words, for your retorts have a lightning-like speed and a sharpness of intention that can get through the thickest skin. Not a profound thinker or a careful student, you none the less have a vast fund of information, stories, and quips. Something is always reminding you of something, and the result is likely to be the delight of the assembled multitude. You are the life of the party. Your aptness in human relations makes you popular, and you are likely to reach some important position through popularity. You will rely on wit to replace hard work or justice, and quickness to replace serious application. Wherever you may be, you are a sort of soldier of fortune, romantic, individualistic, versatile, a fighter who wins the battle of life less by combat than by being in so many places at once that blows cannot hit him. Though you make friends readily, slap people on the back intimately, and leave them pretty much set up over their own importance and your own goodfellowship, you are pretty hard-headed underneath. A certain selfishness marks you, and in the middle of your good humor you are looking out for number one. Shrewd in business matters, you will accumulate a competence not by saving, which very thought is foreign to you, but by slapdash methods. You have such infinite faith in your own powers that so long as you have your health you can't imagine not being secure, and momentary worries such as you may be induced by 163, 180, 186 or 197 you throw off with your fundamentally high spirits. You are pretty likely to slide through life easily, without too much harm or trouble, for your emotional nature is inclined to be happy-go-lucky. You're ardent—for a while—but it takes a persistent and tolerant sweetheart to get along with you for very long, for your mind (and heart) wanders and perhaps even forgets to come back. Two marriages at least are generally indicated by this position. Intellectually of great possibilities, the danger of this position is that glibness and facility will make it unnecessary for you ever to develop your mental or personal powers past the elementary stages, though with 163, 180, 183, 186, 197 or 224 you may become a remarkably capable person in the artistic or literary field. In any case, physical activity will be marked, and whatever field you may be in you will be on the move all the time, not only mentally, but also physically and geographically. This is a restless combination, and you will move around from place to place, from study to study, from occupation to occupation, or from sweetheart to sweetheart, as if by second nature.

26

SUN IN GEMINI—MOON IN TAURUS

(You belong to the positive or executive group)

YOU ARE one of the most popular people you know. Your cleverness makes friends and your stability keeps them. For, underlying the fluency and facility of Gemini, is the solid rock of Taurus, and though the circumstances of your world may bring you disappointment and unhappiness through separations from, or unreliability in, those you love, you yourself remain untouched and loyal to your ideals and your friends. You are romantic without being fickle; you will rarely let go of a firmly established relationship. You make a good executive, having persistence and determination that may surprise those who see only the surface glitter and charm of your nature. You also have marked intellectual and artistic gifts and, with 163, 180, 181, 183, 189 or 188, will have creative talents; with 163, 180, 181, 184, 186, 187, 195 or 198, critical and analytical nature is marked. You are likely to see through people pretty thoroughly at the same time that you are tolerant of them. But you aren't fooled. The simpleton, the rogue, and the fourflusher appear to you in their true colors, no matter what mask they wear, and you have your own capable way of seeing that they don't hurt you, at the same time that you don't hurt them. This is a good combination for worldly progress, giving you sound business judgment and common sense as well as an aptitude for business intricacies.

With 169, 180, 166, 167 or 168, you can have a very successful business career; with 163 or 181, more likelihood of an artistic or professional occupation. With 163 and 164, trouble through women if a man and through health if a woman, but in either case marked concentrative ability and determination to succeed which will generally bear fruit.

27

SUN IN GEMINI–MOON IN GEMINI

(You belong to the positive or executive group)

NERVES ARE your bête noir and a kind of continuous high-voltage runs through you restlessly affecting both your mental and emotional natures. You are quick to enter into and quick to jump out of romances, and before you marry you are pretty sure to know from experience what you are up to. At least no one will ever say you jumped at the first chance you had. You will rarely admit that you are fickle, for you have some plausible explanation to offer for all the variations in your heart-life. What the cause really is you only know—probably a critical approach to other people that brings their flaws to the surface and causes you to tire of or become disappointed in them. You exhaust their possibilities quickly, and your variety is so infinite that while they are still trying to catch on to you, you are off to some place or someone else. You have a searching, quick mind which, unless with 163, 180, 183, 185, 186 or 197, doesn't get far beneath the surface of things. You are an omnivorous reader even when you aren't a deep student. You are also a great talker—glib, facile, witty, and clever—but unless with some of the above paragraphs, are likely to rattle on at a great rate. There's more than a little of the gossip here. You have tremendous intellectual and artistic possibilities once you have learned to concentrate, which is the chief lesson you have to learn, and if put to it you can be successful in business, for you are extremely adaptable. You are independent but know how to yield opportunistically when the occasion arises; with 170 or 180, 149 or 163, this makes you an admirable politician, and if Mars adds its fire by an aspect to either the Sun, Moon, or Mercury, you are a fighter to be reckoned with.

With 164 or 181, high nervous tension jeopardizes health; if also with either 161 or 178, 151 or 172, health needs attention: the mental powers wear out the physical stamina, and you should let intellectual matters alone and build up your body. With 188 and 183 or 189, artistic and creative gifts are likely, especially if also with 163 or 180. You are popular and a great traveler, loving to be on the go and to have lots of people around you. To you even strangers are preferable to solitude, for you haven't a great deal of self-sufficiency and require people around you. Having lots of friends and probably also lots of relatives, you don't have much trouble accomplishing this, but you have to be careful that people, parties, and gatherings aren't wearing you out even when you think you are having the best of times. You need rest, relaxation, and quiet and should train yourself to get plenty of them, despite your wish to be always on the move.

28

SUN IN GEMINI—MOON IN CANCER

(You belong to the positive or executive group)

YOU RECEIVE impressions like a wax plate, remember them well, and give them off readily. Thus, if this combination exists with 163 or 180, there's a fine chance for intellectual and literary achievement. Under these conditions your sensitiveness finds a constructive outlet, you learn to overcome personal touchiness and to concentrate. If without these concentrating influences you are just as sensitive, your memory is good (for personal matters), and you give off what you feel and think volubly but more in personal ways. You talk a lot about people and have many grievances that you don't hesitate to air. You are nervous anyway, and have to fight nerves all your life, and the success of your fight depends in large measure on your mental training. If you concentrate on some study or pursuit, putting your mind on it and keeping it there, you'll find your nerves disappearing as if by magic. But if you allow the intimate, personal side of your life and all the petty little problems to which your sensitive nature is heir to absorb your thoughts, you will find yourself becoming progressively more nervous. You have a great need for peace, quiet, and stability around you and should therefore establish yourself in your own home as early as you can and stick to it, though you'll probably be able to think up thousands of reasons why you shouldn't do this. But you have a real need for domestic stability, and this should be in your own home rather than in that of your parents. Until the emotional side of your nature is dominated either by intellectual training or by favorable domestic environment or both, you are likely to flounder. Once these matters are settled and you don't have to think so much about personal troubles, you will be amazed at the depths of contentment you are capable of.

With 151, 172, 164 or 181, high nervousness and tension; confusion and internal discord. You are self-reliant with a kind of defensive insistence on independence, and if need arise you can take care of yourself in the business world through some independent type of work, or something that requires quickness, aptitude, and a sense of people or words rather than strenuous concentrated effort. You have a peculiarly sure conviction that your own opinions are right, and once you think you have sensed the inner core of a subject, a person, or a problem, nothing can sway you from that conviction. It's almost as if you had, or believed you had, a magic power of divination in which you have the utmost faith. Thus you are a hard person to fool, having a curious knack for ferreting out the other fellow's purposes. You would make a good detective if you could stand the detailed ground work, for you can be very subtle when the need arises, and are on to all the curves with which human beings fool one another.

The possibilities of this combination of Sun and Moon are limitless, and if your horoscope shows 163 or 180; 183, 185, 186 or 197; 188 with 183 or 189; 184 with 197, 191, 192 or 193; 187 with 190, 191 or 192, you may expect to go far through concentration and mental development.

29

SUN IN GEMINI—MOON IN LEO

AN APPARENTLY happy-go-lucky nature conceals a good deal of sound good sense in you, just as the apparent fickleness of your romantic life conceals a deep-seated loyalty and fidelity. On the way to stability in love you go through a lot of indecision, wavering, and probably vocal lamenting of the difficulty you have in making up your mind. But when you do make it up and get married, you stick. You are clever and quick intellectually, with a ready grasp of facts, information, and people. You have great staying powers and can master anything that you set your mind on. Early in life you are so sociable that you may not give much attention to studies, skimming the surface and getting by with your quickness rather than because of any strict application to work. But as you grow older you become more serious minded and are likely to go on studying and learning all your life. Your love-life is extremely important to you, and you will give up anything in the world to have peace and security and love around you. You hate quarrels and, though you won't allow yourself to be imposed on, will keep the peace for a long time even under pretty trying circumstances. When aroused, you are capable of high temper and of speaking your mind in no uncertain terms. You are ardent and demonstrative and, because of your sunny disposition and lively witty speech, popular and sought after socially. If in a woman's horoscope, this may make you a leader socially or even politically, for you are able to use your popularity to good practical advantage.

With 163, 180, 183, 188 or 189, some creative ability is shown; with 184, 186 or 187, the mind is more critical and analytical, and you are likely to be found in the intellectual pursuits that don't require actual creation.

With 147, a very brilliant career is likely in a man's horoscope; also if with 215, 216 or 218. Considerable luck in life attends this position, and if with 219, 230, 231, 232, 229, 155 or 174, you are protected from want and worry—although this protection may not keep you from worrying, for a certain brooding spirit underlies your good nature, and you see the woes of the world and your own woes pretty clearly, sometimes too clearly for your own good. With 186 or 197, 178, 180 or 181, this leads to profound periods of dejection and depression which have to be looked out for; with 149 or 170, nerves and worry make for bad health, or you worry about your health. You are blessed with a "personality" and with a good level head, and you should fight down as unworthy the dejected states you fall into. You are lucky and, if you put your energies to constructive use, can do a good deal in the world through ability and popularity.

30

SUN IN GEMINI—MOON IN VIRGO

YOU'RE MOODY and temperamental. Under a sprightly and gay exterior you hide a world of woe and may look upon yourself as a Pagliacci sort of person—laugh, clown, laugh—or the smile that hides the breaking heart. There's a good deal of self-dramatization here, with a tendency to feel misunderstood or unappreciated. Your romanticism is highly colored by a worship of the mind, and your constant aim is mental affinity—with a contradictory inclination for thinking yourself intellectually above your circle, your sweetheart, your husband, or your wife. This is part of your tendency to discontent, for in some way or another the grass is always greener on the other side of the fence. You have a hard time settling yourself for long, and this carried into intellectual and employment matters causes you to jump from one thing to another, always finding a good reason for doing so, but at the same time not getting deeply into anything. You have a hard time completing jobs, tiring even of the things you start with great enthusiasm and you are similarly capable of dropping people who have been in their day grand passions. With 165, 181 or 172, the jumpiness is increased, amounting to a neurosis and an almost physical inability to hold yourself to anything or anyone; with 149, 163, 170 or 180, circumstances cause discontent, your stability is increased, but while you stick, you are unhappy about it with a sort of brooding and involving sort of feeling that makes your troubles, real or imagined, additionally burdensome.

Although this position gives the creative flair, or rather a desire *to be* an artist or writer, it rarely gives the concentrative ability necessary for success along these lines. The urge is less creative than it is an admiration for intellectual people and a desire to belong in their circle. Thus you are likely to be imitative rather than original and to take Stevenson's injunction "to play the sedulous ape" too seriously and too absolutely. You succeed best in business if you can bring yourself to stick to it, for you have quickness and adaptability, and putting these to constructive use will make you a valuable asset to some executive or organization. In order for the creative urge to show forth here it is necessary to have 147, 168, 180, 171, 224, 215, 218, 237, 183, 193, 188 or 194, and usually more than one will be required for any considerable accomplishment. Seek first contentment—an ability to relax and be happy in your world as you find it—and second, purpose and stick-to-it-ive-ness, after which your mental facility and business sense will show forth to good advantage.

31
SUN IN GEMINI—MOON IN LIBRA

YOU ARE an active, imaginative, romantic person—clever, sociable, and idealistic—and you lead an active life in which you combine business and pleasure to good advantage. A good amount of luck in material matters eases your way of life, and you are able, through influential friends and your own efforts, to rebound from the varied experiences that come your way. You have a good deal of optimism and elasticity and don't stay down in the depths for long. You take advantage of things as you find them, for you have no wish to mold people or the world to your will, but rather make it your practice to adapt yourself. Thus you are able to find something to interest you or something with which to earn your living wherever you pop up—and being a restless and active person, you're likely to pop up almost anywhere on a moment's notice. You like to travel and would be a Nellie Bly, the World Traveler, if you could be. This failing, you travel when and as you can or else take out your restlessness in the variety of your friends, sweethearts, books, or studies. You are nervous and voluble, a good conversationalist—maybe too good—for your stories are likely to become detailed, complex, and long. You're a yarn spinner, delighting in anything that smacks of the personal or the romantic, but an absence of malice removes you from the gossip category. In matters of the affections you are passive rather than ardent, and you quickly wear out the possibilities of your sweethearts and go on to new fields. You'll stand for no fooling, and will leave a sweetheart (or wife or husband) rather than tolerate any personal or financial injustice from him. This position inclines to two marriages in the horoscope of either sex, the tendency being emphasized in a woman's horoscope by 172, 180, 181, 168 or 178; in a man's horoscope by 149, 150, 151, 163, 164, 165 or 161; and in both sexes by 200, 201, 202, 212, 203, 204, 213 or 214. You survive emotional turmoil and change well, rebounding from disappointment and going on.

With 184, 195, 198 or 188, mental facility emphasized; the creative talent present in some degree, but this requires 163 or 180 to be brought out constructively. This is a good position for dealing with large groups of people, and in social work, personnel work, or executive duties involving many individuals, you can be successful.

32
SUN IN GEMINI—MOON IN SCORPIO

(You belong to the positive or executive group)

YOUR INTELLECTUAL QUICKNESS and your emotional depth can combine to make you a forceful, magnetic, and versatile person if you can ever get them working together. The danger of your nature is that sensationalism, over-emphasis on the personal and self-indulgent pleasures of life, will absorb your vitality and your energy. You can so easily become a playboy (or playgirl!). You are sensitive to the impressions you receive from other people, intuitive, and magnetic, and your power over others is your strength and your weakness. When you are living on the cold, detached, intellectual, and analytical plane you control others through a sort of impelling diplomacy. But when you are pleasure- or sensation-seeking, others control you. Of considerable brilliance and promise, you tend to fall in with evil companions and to be attracted to the waifs and strays of the world. You have to be continuously careful of your associates not only because "a man is known by the company he keeps" but also because you're prone to take on the color of your surroundings and therefore, the better the surroundings, the better color you take on. Without caution, you can be like the chameleon which, being put on a Scotch plaid, went crazy trying to make good. You will rise when the tide is rising and sink when it sinks, if you aren't always vigilant in keeping alive your driving force. Ambition is not natural to you for you prefer ease and pleasure to other things, and, especially if with 161, 164, 165, 149 or 150, early brilliance and promise are likely to peter out very disappointingly. All manner of self-indulgence is dangerous to you: watch out for it. Emotionally you are ardent —while the emotion lasts—but unlikely to find happiness through your emotional life. The objective, detached approach is best for you in all things. The hard streak applied to the world makes for progress, but applied to love makes for unhappiness.

Both men and women with this position have their major trouble through the opposite sex. You are better equipped for an artistic or professional career than for business, for your highly personalized nature demands a personal rather than a routine recognition. Through expression of your own ego in the arts and professions you tend to build constructively on your need for acclaim and to turn your pride to good account. Look out for a tendency to drift and daydream. And look out that ability to plan and visualize does not turn into mere opportunistic scheming over petty matters off the beaten track of progressive living.

33

SUN IN GEMINI—MOON IN SAGITTARIUS

YOU'RE A ROMANTIC: you believe in the far away and long ago. Things at a distance make an appeal to you with the result that you are always on the move. Either you are actually traveling or you are getting the satisfaction of mobility in stories and yarns, real and imagined, of out-of-the-way places such as you read of in romances. This is O. K. so long as your yarn-spinning stays in the realm of the imagination purely, but when you apply that imagination of yours to your friends and start to tell tall tales about them—look out! You love to hold the center of the stage and to appear to know the inside dope on any and all subjects—with the result that what you say is frequently unreliable. Not that you mean to tell untruths, but your imagination is so vivid that you really believe what you say and can make others believe it. You must cultivate mental accuracy, for the analytical and scientifically critical bent is not native to you, and you're gullible as well as inventive where stories are concerned. With any encouragement at all you will believe in ghosts, witches and warlocks, spiritualism, and the weird products of séances. Stay away from things like this, for they only feed your imagination with trouble-making imagery. A tendency to tell all you know and to invent what you don't know is likely to get you into trouble. There isn't an ounce of malice in your nature, but you can set whole neighborhoods by the ears with a carelessly dropped hint of scandal. You are romantic as well as adventurous and not very constant in love, though when you fall you generally stay put for some time. You are restless, however, and tire of people, and this position frequently leads to more than one marriage. You need mental training and should forego the reading of novels and romances for some definite, set line of study, which will do much to overcome restlessness. You are popular, lively and gay in company, very expressive, and a pretty good listener. Your facility in speech and movement makes you a good actor while your peculiar brand of tact makes it possible for you to succeed in a business or political career. You are a hard person to pin down and can get around a good many situations that would stump others. But you aren't invulnerable and are likely to meet your match some day, unless you train yourself strictly in logical mental processes, when your quickness, shrewdness, and insight into people will carry you far.

34

SUN IN GEMINI—MOON IN CAPRICORN

(You belong to the positive or executive group)

YOU HIDE a world of determination under a very genial and apparently "easy" exterior. You are a source of surprise to friends and associates who may think they can put things over on you. They find out. You are affable, courteous, social, generous, but no one can impose on you, and your business judgment is amazingly shrewd. You are likely to get pretty much what you want in the world by taking people unawares, for you chat gayly, talk volubly, get apparently sidetracked from the business in hand—and before you know it your vis-à-vis has agreed to something that maybe he doesn't want to. You have a fine sense of justice and, despite a show of independence and individuality, are strictly conventional. You bargain shrewdly, but you are fair and utterly honorable. You are intensely ambitious, and when you settle yourself into a career, after early casting around, you go far, for your nervousness and restlessness are well controlled. Your intellectual grasp of matters, including yourself, replaces an early, highly personal attitude, and a sort of intellectual detachment lends direction and force to your life. Emotionally, though you are a good fellow, you are somewhat cold —with 147, 161, 149 or 163, even hard—in personal dealings, though a sense of justice is likely to prevent any overt unkindness. You are highly sensitive and also conscious of other people's sensitive points, though it may suit your purposes to ignore them, when you can be unkind, with a wide-eyed astonishment at the other fellow's bewilderment and harm. You are analytical rather than creative, and rarely go in for the arts; professional and business life are your best media. You are somewhat selfish, especially where your career is concerned, and capable of the utmost in diplomacy where it seems called for. But you don't think it good policy to antagonize people, however insignificant. "Good policy" is your constant aim, and through your capable mentality, your determination to succeed, and your ability to pick your way carefully in human relationships, you can carry yourself a long way up the ladder. A little more of the personal touch, a little more susceptibility to romance, lend warmth to the character, and with 168, 148, 155, 162, 169, 174, 179, 146 or 153, make you a very unusual person, reserved and at the same time warm-hearted and affectionate. A just, dependable, and loyal friend. Without these, you are a little cold, but your very detachment is your strength and your foundation.

35

SUN IN GEMINI—MOON IN AQUARIUS

(You belong to the positive or executive group)

YOU HAVE extraordinary gifts of foresight and insight—a kind of visionary intellectual quality that makes the potentialities of the future clear to you in terms of the present. You have a ready intuition for things and for people and through ability to organize and express what you understand so clearly can achieve success either in the sciences, the arts, or in any branch of activity that requires control over the minds of men, such as politics, law, or religion. You see through things and, being at heart a Romantic, you express what you see in terms that have a universal appeal to your circle, whatever it may be. You are genuinely humanitarian in your outlook, generous-minded and desirous of helping others—probably through improving them intellectually or æsthetically. This is therefore an excellent position for a teacher, and whatever walk of life you may be in, you will in some way lead and teach those whom you contact. In romance your idealism leads you far and wide in search of perfection and complete sympathy, so that you may appear fickle and unstable. If, without conjunctions or squares to the Sun or Moon, this may be a relaxed and unprogressive position, for daydreams and imaginings absorb you and vitiate action. But if there are squares or conjunctions, you will go far through your expression of what you intuitively know, and wind up with considerable influence and perhaps authority.

With 183, this position is greatly helped and the magnetism and creative gifts are helpfully accentuated; with 186, profound mind; with 187 or 188, inspirational; with 184, quick, scientific, alert, analytical. With 200, 210, 203 or 213, erratic love-life makes trouble; with 202 or 212, some major disappointment hurts the love-nature and you also tend to hurt others. With 172, magnetic control of others, when you have controlled your own sensational tendencies. With 216 or 217, political power; with 215 or 218, business success in financial executive capacity. The artistic qualities of this position are helped by such paragraphs as 180, 163, 184, 195, 187, 188, 186, 183, 215, 218, 229 or 227.

36

SUN IN GEMINI—MOON IN PISCES

INTUITION is your best friend and your worst enemy. It is your best friend at the times when it is accurate, and your worst enemy when it is wrong—because, right or wrong, you have a sense of its being right—and it can lead you into very profitless paths. You are sensitive and impressionable to other people and highly protective in getting your emotions into a place where they can't be hurt. This makes you at times more voluble in defense of your rights, your loves, or your opinions than you have to be. You have a habit of explaining your motives at considerable length, as if the entire world cared about the whys and wherefores of your mental and emotional processes. You are highly introspective and capable of holding fixed ideas about yourself which may be completely at variance with the facts. You believe yourself misunderstood and nurse an image of yourself as you really are, in the firm and somewhat hurt conviction that the rest of the world doesn't see or appreciate the real you. Your emotional life is tortured by your mental processes, for in addition to being very affectionate you are also very critical, and you have a hard time reconciling the two. You crave sympathy, understanding, and love, but this doesn't prevent details from interfering with the course of love and diverting you from it. You'll seek an intellectual, or an æsthetic, affinity, and perhaps leave out, or be totally ignorant of, realistic considerations. You have a quick, perceptive mind when you aren't daydreaming or absorbed in your own woes. You make a good shrewd business man, being able to detach your ideals from matters of business and act according to the routine and motives around you.

With 147 or 172, introspection carried to dangerous length, danger of introversion through real or imagined woes. With 163, 180, 148 or 169, objectivity and good spirits helped and luck improved. With 197 or 198, erratic and irascible mind, highly nervous, tending to much gloom and depression. You tend, under any circumstances, to fall into periods of dejection and depression varying in intensity and length, and your constant aims should be objectivity, detachment from your woes and problems, and optimism. Most of the troubles in the world never happen, but in your mind they all happen very vividly, plus a lot of woes that never were on land or sea. Build up a sense of your own worth, step out into the middle of life, and your internal troubles will take care of themselves.

37

SUN IN CANCER—MOON IN ARIES

THERE'S LITTLE that you aren't capable of intellectually, for you have a quick mind and a remarkable memory. You are sensitive, intuitive, understanding of the feelings of other people, and considerate of them because you know how much consideration means to you. You have a "Do unto others as you would be done by" attitude toward life which makes you popular and respected. You have a keen sense of your own worth and a determination to make it known to the world. You are most likely to succeed in the arts and the professions. In business you are well liked, courteous, and affable, but you don't have the sense of business that is needed to highest advancement. People, ideas, and creations mean more to you than money; thus you make good in any humanistic science such as medicine, law, sociology, or in creative artistic work. You are devoted to your home, and in either male or female horoscope this indicates a good spouse and considerable contentment in the married life through mutual respect and devotion. You are somewhat romantic, affectionate rather than ardent, but capable of a good deal of jealousy, with or without cause. For you are sensitive and suspicious and cannot endure the idea of being fooled. This is tough on people who are trying to get away with something, for you are a detective at heart, especially when you think that you, personally, are having something put over on you. You'll harry your wife (or husband) about what went on at the soda store, but wouldn't bother to arrest Public Enemy Number One if he came up and rested on your doorstep. You are sociable and like parties, gatherings, and groups of people. You also like to hold the center of the stage and do it in so engaging a manner that others like it too; you are sensitive enough to other people to know when they've had enough of you, and you aren't likely to wear out your welcome.

With 168, 178, 147 or 161, you are contentious and quarrelsome;

with 170, 180 or 163, energetic and ambitious but moody, a shrewd business man. With 149, dejection is periodically dangerous to your peace of mind. With 181 or 172, confusion, sensationalism; with 181 or 172 and 149, involving and introverted nature, sensationalist, and impressionable.

38

SUN IN CANCER—MOON IN TAURUS

YOU ARE a person of considerable charm and talent, versatile, sensitive, and adaptable, but with a certain core of determination and hard purpose that is very close to your heart. If it weren't for this you might be called "sweet," because there are about you a graciousness and ease of manner that endear you to people and make you popular. You understand what people want in their friends and sweethearts and manage to give it without giving up any of your individuality. You don't take yourself very seriously, but you know what you are after. You tend to be objective because you have been introspective in your day and know yourself and your purposes well enough to understand that you must work for what you want. The only magic you believe in is the magic of your own ability. You are a realist, but you frequently work in romantic creative mediums. You are capable of writing or thinking allegory, and you like to spin yarns of fairies or paint pictures with a slightly eerie overtone. Everything you do—emotional, structural, creative—has a touch of the magnificent or the unusual, for you are strongly original, and you bring to your originality enough of a knowledge of your public to make it acceptable to them. It's unusual without being bizarre; it plays up their own dreams at the same time that it satisfies yours. In romance you are impressionable but have a good sense of balance and proportion; you don't get swept off your feet even when you are greatly impressed mentally or emotionally. You are a well organized and well-controlled person. This is a position of good luck in material matters. You can be successful in business where your qualities of imagination and foresight are turned to good account, and if you are in a professional or artistic career, your feeling for the public makes your work popular.

With 147, 148, 151, 168, 169, 174, 200, 204, 215, 218, 227, 229 or 237, material luck is greatly increased, even up to wealth. With 200, 210, 213, 204 or 214, emotional impressionability not under such good control and trouble through love matters. With 202 or 212, material worries as well as hurt through misplaced affections. With 216, too adaptable; with 224, timidity and indecision hampers success till it is overcome. This is an excellent domestic indication for either a man or a woman and shows the likelihood of a good wife (husband) and a happy home which means much in the life-progress; it also increases the number of children.

39

SUN IN CANCER—MOON IN GEMINI

SENSITIVITY, flexibility, and adaptability are your strengths— and your weaknesses. You feel the world around you, people, facts, situations, with an almost too-acute sensitiveness. In a man's horoscope this makes you trusting, eager, anxious to please, susceptible, and teachable; it also makes you a little wavering, a little indecisive, a little too ready to agree. You are internally not sure of yourself despite your glibness and facility. You express too readily, inclining to agree and tell all your plans before they are complete. You can cultivate self-confidence by cultivating reserve, for in life, as in poker, you stand a better chance of winning the pot if you don't tip your hand before the draw.

In a woman's horoscope this is considerably better than in a man's. Here it is the arch-type of the well-known woman's intuition. Your indecision is made to appear tact, your quality of saying yes, which is weak in a man, becomes feminine and appealing, and because you conceal a considerable amount of purpose, like a stiletto under your femininely trailing skirts, you are pretty likely to be a success in business. Circumstances, or your own restlessness, are likely to take you into a career; you don't care for housekeeping and would rather work ten hours a day in business than boil an egg. Your very manner is flattering to the bosses, and you are pushed ahead. In either sex this is a highly emotional position, and erratic early years, with their share of love affairs, should teach you a good deal about the way of the world. Here, again, the women of this sign learn more readily than the men. The women continue romantic and impressionable to the end, to be sure, and are independent in matters of their emotions; but they know what they're up to. They have been hurt and know how to avoid being hurt again without giving up anything. If you're a man with this combination, your youth may have been stormy, and indecision may have been costly to you, but you tend to maintain a glowing optimism; everything is going to be all right, and something will turn up. You believe in luck, whether good or bad. Also in Justice, Truth, and the eventual reward of the righteous. What you have to cultivate is push, integration of purpose, and a goal, an objective, a set ambition.

With 147, 163, 168 or 180, this is assisted; with 164, 161, 165, 172 or 181, confusion is likely to interfere with progress— you become mentally muddled by adversity and lapse into periods of inertia and dejection. Whether male or female, this position calls for an early conquering of the restless, touchy, and romantic sensitiveness and a firm integration of purpose, after which your qualities of good-fellowship and understanding of people, coupled with your quick and facile mind, will bring you the goods of the world that are so important to you.

40

SUN IN CANCER—MOON IN CANCER

(You belong to the positive or executive group)

YOU ARE tremendously sensitive and self-protective. You have a shell which you crawl into periodically, or permanently, as a defense against the intrusions of the world. In personal matters you are touchy with a keen sense of injury and hurt at real or imagined offenses. Thus you are likely to become suspicious of other people and very cagey in all your dealings with them, either business or personal. You are highly affectionate and naturally demonstrative, but so afraid of being hurt and rebuffed that you may appear unapproachable. It takes a long time to win your confidence, and even when it's apparently won, you're likely to turn tail at some harsh word or uncongenial thought and put on your armor again. Thus, though you're intensely domestic and love your home, you may not marry till late in life, and after marriage you may be, or may imagine yourself to be, unhappy in it because most other people in the world won't satisfy your deep sense of sympathy and your need for it. You absorb all that it gives and then find hidden places of your soul that have not been saturated in it and brood. This sensitiveness, if turned to objective matters, can make you a very powerful artist along inspirationally creative lines. If turned to business, your caution and suspiciousness make you a shrewd trader, and although you're not really an executive, you may find yourself in executive positions where you will be able to outguess your subordinates or keep them on the hot seat with your taciturnity and periods of aloofness. You are a clever diplomat, your stock in trade being to let the other fellow talk till he's worn himself out when you can trip him up. You fight by indirection and by outguessing your antagonist, rather than by frontal attack. Sometimes this will succeed in tripping yourself up but not often, for you can move quickly and in any direction. There are always likely to be flaws in your management and your best way to success is to leave the executive duties to someone else while you do the head work, for your timidity gets in the way of your management. You can be muddled and muddle everyone around you by your shifting tactics. Women with this position are good homemakers, loving wives and mothers, but difficult for their husbands, who never get to really know them in a life time of living together. This elusive quality is common to men and women of this combination, and though you crave society, companionship, and sympathy, you frequently fail to get it in sufficient quantity to satisfy you because of your fear of being hurt by it in the end. Courage! Let the world in, even if it does hurt: a little hurt is better than continual loneliness.

With 161, 163 or 180, rise to authority and danger of fall therefrom;

with 151, sensational and introverted nature; if also with 164, erratic quality, conventionality, and unconventionality fighting for precedence, and a love-nature that needs watching. With 202 or 212, withdrawal due to hurt in love; with 168, 147, 161 or 178, a fighter to be watched out for, shifting and cagey.

41

SUN IN CANCER—MOON IN LEO

YOU HAVE a great feeling for other people, and you cover up your independence under a coöperative spirit which really isn't more than skin-deep, for you are deeply an individualist and, if it comes to a showdown, will have your own way and make the world like it. But you know that you catch more flies with sugar than you do with vinegar, and so you are able to give the illusion of tractability. You compromise by appearing to understand what the other fellow is driving at, but you get your own way in the end. In the presence of constituted authority you will take orders, but it is your constant aim to work yourself into a position where you can give orders. You are proud, honorable, and highly self-respecting. When your apparent good-nature is imposed upon you are capable of simply walking off in cold blood rather than in anger or resentment. You haven't a great deal of faith in people, but you have a good deal of faith that you can get things out of them that no one else can. You believe that although people are fundamentally deceptive, treacherous, or stupid they will be loyal to you personally when they might not be to someone else. As a matter of fact you are right in this, for your sense of justice and fair play makes people stick to you, and even those who have no especial sense of right and wrong for its own sake will do right by you. You take yourself rather seriously, and others are willing to accept your own estimate of yourself, which is rarely low. You give the appearance of pride and hauteur and your associates are ready to assume that there must be something behind it. You are good at analysis, detail, and business organization and frequently will be found in executive capacity in the business or professional world. Emotionally you are loyal without being constant, if you know what I mean, which you will. You understand the "I have been true to thee, Cynara, *in my fashion*" sophistry only too well. You are tolerant of the foibles of the world, not excluding your own, but you are capable of the inconsistency of "Do as I say, not as I do" where matters of love-loyalty are concerned.

With 200, 210, 204, 213 or 214, hectic emotional life; with 163, 180, considerable depth, concentrative ability and trouble through the affections; with 172, 181 and/or 180, impressionable nature, alternately hot and cold, with some danger of sensationalism absorbing the personality and its energies.

42

SUN IN CANCER—MOON IN VIRGO

(You belong to the positive or executive group)

YOU HAVE COME a long way from the child who was sensitive, timid, and afraid of his own shadow; for though you are still sensitive, and to some extent timid, you have rationalized yourself out of these traits and by sheer will-power and mental force taken your place in the world as a person to be reckoned with. You are still conscious of an inner quaver when you try to make important decisions, and especially when you try to make others do your bidding; but so strong is your need for success, and so completely have you developed reserve and poise beneath your protective armor, that you are likely to find yourself in some place of importance, with people hanging on your word and doing as you tell them. You are not an easy master, for being fundamentally unsure of yourself, you reverse this into being even more of an autocrat than is necessary and insist on absolute adherence to the letter of the law—and especially to your word. You are utterly conventional, and although you may think along advanced social lines, you are a strict believer in authority—especially your own authority. Your power over people arises from your sensitiveness to what they are thinking and feeling and your ability to put yourself in their places without giving up your own individuality. Your tact can be either constructive, contributing to your progress, or it can be weak and subservient; but in either case it is dictated by your feeling for policy and expediency. You will rarely be found fighting a losing cause; you, like the God of Battles, will be found on the side of the greatest numbers. You are a sweet and tractable person, highly amenable to sympathy, affection, and understanding; thrown off your balance and confused by hardness or unkindness but capable of striking back if your opponent is not too big for you. You develop fearlessness and courage out of a feeling of shame over being the reverse. You are a loyal and understanding sweetheart (husband, wife) though you can drive your spouse crazy with your sensitiveness. And as an employer you can muddle those under you by changing your mind all the time. You must cultivate real self-confidence in order that your truly great abilities may meet with adequate recognition in the world.

With 163, fine executive capabilities; with 161, erratic mental processes; with 224, bad judgment due to timidity—a dangerous position for security. With 215 or 218, high success; with 147, great authority; courage develops marvelously, bringing with it leadership. With 166, appeal to the general public brings success.

43
SUN IN CANCER—MOON IN LIBRA

YOU HAVE a curious combination of independence and dependence, self-sufficiency, and a kind of reaching into the world in search of companionship. You don't give a great deal of yourself, being sensitive and a trifle introverted; but you like to absorb other people. You have a charm of manner that makes other people respond to you readily. You are romantic, love flattery and attention, and also love to have people around you; but your satisfaction is derived from watching other people, their reactions, moods, and temperaments, rather than from your own emotions. You are a little afraid of your own emotions—afraid of being hurt, afraid of being fooled, for you are somewhat suspicious. Once you have been disappointed by being too trusting (as you have been) you develop a high degree of self-protectiveness. This is all right, as far as it goes, but it makes you an elusive person in romance; and your admirer is likely to feel like a fly under a microscope, having his reactions analyzed, while you yourself are untouched. If this analytical caginess can be broken down and your confidence won, you are sweet, loving, and affectionate. Your delight in observation and the detachment with which you are capable of watching things make you well fitted for an artistic or scientific career, as a writer or investigator, where by sitting on the side lines you can find grist for your mill in the world around you. Your loyalty is to abstractions rather than to individuals; and though you are very sensitive yourself, you can have a pretty cavalier disregard for the feelings of others—which surprises them, because you look as if you wouldn't hurt a flea. You're a prize exponent of the "that's different" school of argument. You are a social asset, though more satisfactory in a large gathering than in a twosome. You are not especially constant in love and for one reason or another (which you're able to explain) will have an active career of romance before you settle down. But your whole development will change, stabilize, and mature when you are settled in a home of your own.

With 147, 161, 168 or 178, dangerously changeable in love; with 172, 181, sensationalist, impressionable to a fault; with 149, 180, concentrative powers helped; with 181, independence marked, highly idealistic; with 200, 210, 204 or 213, overexpansive and sensational love-nature, and trouble through it; with 202 or 212, disappointment warps the nature but provides drive to success.

44

SUN IN CANCER—MOON IN SCORPIO

YOUR STRONG personal magnetism and keen sense of dramatic values makes you a person to be reckoned with; wherever you are, people will know you are around for some reason or other, for yours is a personality that attracts attention. In horoscopes of men this will assist you in drama, the arts, or medicine; in women's horoscopes the business bent is strong, and through energy, insight, and magnetic control over others (who may or may not like it, but have to mind anyway) these women gain considerable influence. You are not so popular as you are impelling; there is a certain dignity about you that stands up under all circumstances where your emotions are not involved and demands recognition. You are very proud, jealous of your authority when you have it, eager to get it if you haven't it. When you aren't involved in some romance (which isn't often) you are capable of the extremes of concentration on a purpose. You have a self-protective ruthlessness although you don't like to hurt people, for you are not unkind or cruel; but if there's a choice between hurting yourself and hurting someone else, let the other fellow look out! You are not an idealist. Practical dollars and sense, earthly love, worldly ambition, and worldly goods are the tenets of your creed. You've never sworn to abhor the World, the Flesh, and the Devil for there is a liberal share of all of them in you. You are lavish in your affections, demonstrative and ardent, but not especially faithful, though you're likely to return from your escapades to the one and only who more than likely is more constant than you merit. Men with this position usually select vital girls who lead them a merry chase—but no merrier than they deserve. You can succeed in the arts when you have learned to use your dramatic and magnetic gifts constructively, and when you have settled the personal, romantic side of your life.

With 147, 148, 215, 218, 227 or 237, lots of material good luck; with 200, 210, 204, 213, 172, 181, 147 or 161, dangerously intense emotional nature; with 163, 168 or 180, artistic powers increased, ability to depersonalize helps to success.

45

SUN IN CANCER—MOON IN SAGITTARIUS

(You belong to the positive or executive group)

YOUR IDEALISM finds good practical expression. You have translated your very intimate type of ambition into large symbols and set yourself a high goal at which to aim. There's a wide streak of sentimentality in you. You are something of a hero-worshiper and usually select some individual as your ideal whom you strive to emulate and imitate. You believe in the conventional virtues so far as personal conduct is concerned—that is, you believe in them for other people. Where your own emotions come into play, you do pretty much as you please, feeling that your philosophy in some way justifies what would be mere fickleness or sensationalism in someone else. You have a wide view of things and through imagination, vision, and foresight, (which take into consideration the temper of your associates) you are able to organize your life on a long-range basis and stick to your plan of action. You want to be rich, not secure; famous, not popular; adored, not merely loved. You are not one for halfway measures, and you despise low aims, petty ideals, insignificant ambitions. Earth may be your home, but heaven's your destination. You are philosophic, speculative, a bit mystical, and probably also superstitious, with some pet theory, belief, or symbol that stands for your luck and your success. In human relations you are warm-hearted, affectionate, sensitive to the needs of others, genial and courteous. You have a forceful manner of speech and, despite your diplomacy, people know where you stand. The beautiful has a great appeal for you, and no matter how much of a man of the world you may be, there's something of the poet, the æsthete, about you. Your philosophy and your intellect go deeper into things than do your emotions. You express yourself romantically and sentimentally, but your ardor gives the impression of being the product of an ideal rather than a spontaneous emotional expression. You are very sensitive and easily hurt, but you forgive readily and don't hold grudges, except when you have reason to suspect duplicity, when you are capable of never trusting that individual again.

With 215, 218, 227, 229, 237, 148, 162, 168, 169, 173 or 174, great driving force, magnetism, and luck in life; rise from original station to power, authority, and possibly wealth. With 202 or 212, hardened love-nature, early disappointments and restrictions depersonalize you, lend drive and force to the nature, but do not increase the milk of human kindness. With 163 or 180, creative powers manifest. With 172 or 181, dreamy, erratic, imaginative; difficulty in getting down to brass tacks; with 183 or 188, poetic, musical; with 200, 210, 204 or 213, sensational love-life with plenty of variety. Both men and women with this position are likely to "marry well."

46
SUN IN CANCER—MOON IN CAPRICORN

YOU ARE a good executive, your sensitive nature knowing how to reach out into the world and draw to itself the recognition that is so precious to you. You are a nice blend of the strictly personal, sensitive, protective spirit, and the calculating, shrewd, business man looking out for the main chance: thus you are able to accomplish your purposes without hurting any feelings and are likely to make many warm friends among business associates. You can drive a hard bargain with a smile on your face, and make the other fellow like and respect you even when he's giving you the shirt off his back. You have keen insight into people. You are good at recognizing underlying motives, for you have a deep knowledge of yourself, and by judging the world according to your own intricate and varied processes, you are able to know most of your fellow men pretty well. You need affection and generally get plenty of it, for if you are a man you are a favorite with women; and if a woman, you have, over a distinct and appealing femininity, a masculine approach, a sense of good sportsmanship and fair play, that makes a strong appeal to men.

You may (with 163 or 181, 183, 187, 188, 166, 215 or 218) have creative literary talent, for your innate understanding makes you able to appeal strongly to the public. With 216 or 224, business and executive talent marked. In any case, you need a home of your own and will be happiest and most successful when established in it. With 149 or 170 marriage may be delayed till later in life, but when it comes you will know how to derive a high degree of contentment through it. You know how to coöperate, have a generous regard for the rights of others—just as you expect them to have a regard for your rights—and this quality makes human relationships, in private or public life, easy and satisfactory.

47

SUN IN CANCER—MOON IN AQUARIUS

YOU ARE able to translate your knowledge of yourself into terms of the people around you and, in whatever circle you may move, thus gain considerable prestige for being understanding, sympathetic, and considerate. You have a fine objective intellect, capable of large viewpoints, especially in social matters. This, combined with a critical, scientific, and accurate mind, can win you almost any amount of acclaim you want to look for. You will do best in public life of the sort which takes you before large groups of people. Your splendid voice, magnetic personality, and quick, accurate mind will bring you acclaim in politics or on the stage. There is a certain detachment about you which, as you appear to dwell in high and magnificent places, can translate this feeling to others and make them feel important. You have an aristrocracy of bearing that flatters but does not overpower. You appear to be raising people to your level rather than stooping down to theirs; and despite your keen pride and arrogance, you give the impression of feeling superior without making others feel inferior. You are romantic, and in both personal and public dealings you get across the fundamental warmth and sincerity of your nature; there is nothing of the cold opportunist here, although you are an opportunist, and know how to turn everything to account in the onward march of your ambition.

The danger of this position is that your warmth and universality will find sensational, rather than constructive outlets; and this is chiefly in question with such aspects as 172, 181, 160, 161, 163, 164, 165, 200, 210, 204, 213 or 214. With these, strive for depersonalization, and objectivity of thinking. With 147, 148, 155, 156, 163, 168, 169, 173, 174 or 180, there is great driving force and luck, with probability of rise to influence. With 215, 217, 218, 226, 227, 228, 229 or 237, tremendous personal magnetism. With 237, erratic nature, alternately up and down; magnetic but unstable. With 224, large prestige, danger of sudden fall.

48

SUN IN CANCER—MOON IN PISCES

(You belong to the positive or executive group)

YOU HAVE a sailboat personality; you tack with the wind and tide, shift your ballast, alter the top rigging, and keep in cahoots with the weather conditions as you find them. This makes for progress whether on the high seas or on the sea of life. You are a diplomat and will be found not where the battle is thickest but where the entrenchments are strongest. You are a staunch upholder of the status quo and will rarely be found on the wrong side of an argument. You are so agreeable, so pleasant, so affable, that it's hard to know where you stand, or how long you are going to stand there. But your practical sense is so keen that anyone who follows your lead is likely to find himself, with you, pretty well out in front when the race is over. You are suspicious of others and do not take many into your confidence; you do not give out inside tips on the races, but play your hunches yourself, much to your advantage. You are an adept at outguessing the boss and can say "Yes" before he has a chance to turn around; thus, by anticipating his wishes, you make yourself popular and stand to advance. You are a shrewd businessman, drive a hard bargain, and understand all the profit-making methods, and, having no especial feeling for the rights of others, may be an efficiency expert of no small value. You are self-protective, defensive, and cautious, and although you think in large financial terms, are willing to get to them by small savings and judicious management; you are rarely found in want. You can be popular, in a large, broad way, with groups of people, though in personal contact you are a little suspicious and, despite a real craving for affection, hold yourself aloof for fear of being fooled or imposed on. When you overcome this, or when someone can win your confidence, you are the most loving of persons; but you always have to watch out that your suspicion doesn't arise and injure the course of true love. Learn to be somewhat less secretive, a little more open, a little less cagey, whether in personal or public dealings. Be fooled once in a while: it's good for your soul.

With 172, 181, 204, 213, 200 or 210, sensationalism increased; with

202, 212 or 149, aloof and introverted; with 163, suspicion—and success—increased. With 148, 155, 169 or 174, warmer, more open and trusting personality; with 202 or 212, likely to be imposed on. With 215, 218, 227, 228, 229 or 237, possibility of great wealth; also with 167 or 166.

49

SUN IN LEO—MOON IN ARIES

(You belong to the positive or executive group)

THIS IS a position of exceptional courage. Your life develops rapidly, for there is nothing in the world you are afraid of, and your intense emotional and physical drive carries you into new adventure, new love, new experience very early in life. In a man's horoscope this is the sign of a strong leader, both in thought and action, capable of holding down high executive positions and by courage and integrity usually "getting there." In a woman's horoscope the intensity, drive, and lack of fear is more likely to be translated into an active love-life, scornful of the conventions, or in some way willing to give all for love. In both sexes, as a matter of fact, the personal note is too strong at the beginning; personal loyalties, personal loves, strictly personal and self centered aims injure, at the outset, the scope of this configuration. You have to learn detachment, objectivity and intellectual approach, for when you have done this your worth stands a much better chance of being recognized in the world of affairs. You are capable of becoming a leader, but on the way, you'll indulge in a good deal of hero-worship, translating your ardent love-nature into an idealistic concept of right-living as you see it in one person whom you strive to emulate. You can love a person and disagree with him violently, without letting the two sides of your nature interfere with each other. You are strong for duty, justice, truth and can give your life to these ideals; you are a fighter, and will never be found on the mean, petty, or sophistical side of a debate. Your magnetism is the product of your energies, and makes you felt in whatever circle you move. You are a devoted sweetheart, a loyal friend, a sympathetic and intelligent boss, a stern but just executive.

With 147, 148, 168 or 169, authority and scope increased; you are lucky through your own efforts, and no one grudges you your success. With 163, great inner determination; with 180, cold and inflexible nature, with a set goal which you reach. With 215, 216, 217, 218, 227, 228, 229 or 226, no heights are too great for you. "Excelsior" is your motto and you do not fail to live up to it.

50
SUN IN LEO—MOON IN TAURUS

YOU ARE a strong and visionary person, seeing things in the large, with a big amount of practical idealism and hard-headedness that makes you successful in business undertakings that require foresight, courage, and executive capacity. No one ever is in doubt about where you stand, and though you are liable to errors of judgment, you are just as emphatic when you are wrong as when you are right—maybe more so. You are stubborn and lacking in innate diplomacy; you can learn to hold your tongue, but it's a lesson and not a gift. You tend to speak out your mind —"tell the truth and shame the devil" is your motto—and when what you tell is not the truth, it is from inaccuracy rather than from deceit. You are utterly honest, but you are capable of believing what suits your purposes and your momentary bias, which can be pretty stubborn. Thus you are likely to waste effort straining at gnats and tilting at windmills, where a more tactful person would compromise. Your integrity will rarely be questioned, nor will your power over people. But your good sense and judgment will often be questioned, until you learn that you can't make mountains come to you, and that you frequently make mountains out of molehills by misplaced emphasis. When you have adjusted your sense of proportion and learned the lessons of coöperation, your dynamic energies and your high sincerity will win you reward and recognition. In personal matters the same proud inflexibility stands in the way of your happiness; you're capable of quarreling with someone you really love because of a whim which you come to believe is a principle. You have a quality of huffy pride when your feelings are hurt; you can shut up like a clam and nurse your high-mindedness till you drive everyone crazy. When not in some such mood you're a gay and voluble companion, but your moods are sudden, ponderous and hard to work you out of.

With 163 or 180, tact is improved and moodiness increased; dejection gets hold of you and can be serious. With 168 or 178, aggression dangerous, and you make enemies; with 147, 148, 149, 151 or 157, considerable luck and power increased with 215, 217, 218, 227, 229 or 237. With 202 or 212, austere emotional life, somewhat hard; with 200, 210, 203, 213, 204 or 214, impulsive passional nature and trouble through it. Your intellect is subordinate to your emotional and physical forces, and your intuitions, for good and bad, will rule you rather than your reasoning power. You believe what you want to believe, and thus your mental processes follow your desires; you can rationalize yourself into thinking what you want, and if with some of the paragraphs of power and success, can make others conform to your will. With 184, 185, 186 or 187, 188, the mental powers are increased and made more logical, but they still depend largely on your intuitive and emotional biases.

51

SUN IN LEO—MOON IN GEMINI

YOU ARE a man of both action and ideas. Both rationalistic and sentimental, emotional and vigorous, you eventually get your mind and your physical energies working in unison and go far. Emotional flexibility hampers your progress at the beginning of your life. You cast about for an anchor in books, in thought, in ideology of some sort and if you don't find it, you fall back on your strong emotions. A sort of wanderlust obsesses you always—you want more worlds to conquer, either in actuality or in ideas. You love to impress yourself, and your thoughts, on people and whether you do it through the written or spoken word, or in politics or public life, you become an influence on your group. Your mind is facile, intuitive, glib rather than profound, facile rather than scientific; but in some way or other you manage to find the appeal that will win the public, and make it very persuasively. Thus you are a successful writer, journalist, editorial writer, or public speaker and through any of these mediums may work yourself into a position of influence. Your ideas, while not based in deep philosophy, have a certain plausibility about them, and your manner of expression is persuasive. You will rarely be found working hard for a living, for you believe in easy money, and seem to know how to get it; you are capable of exerting physical energy, but you'd rather not. You are romantic and not especially constant in love. This position tends to produce two marriages and a whole lot of romance outside of marriage.

With 151, very elusive personality, lots of ups and downs in life; with 147, luck powerful; 148, expansive personality, much good-fellowship and luck thereby; with 149, moody, periodically dejected. With 167, 168, 169, 173 or 174, plenty of ability and maximum return for it; with 170 or 180, iron will, for good or bad, with some of the results of each showing in the life; cyclic supremacy of will power and won't power . . . You are good company, able to smile when you don't want to, and always putting on a good front. You believe that those who have, get; and you put your best foot forward even when the other one is halfway inside the poorhouse. Some of the finest bluffs in history have been pulled off by people with this configuration, who seem to be at their best when swimming against the tide or recuperating from one of the blows of fortune which their dashing natures seem to attract. There is something of the bad child about you all your life, with an impish delight in doing or saying the dramatic, the unexpected, and the perverse. On the other hand, you're capable of doing a complete about face, and when you do, no one (not even the person you have offended worst) can resist your charm and plausibility.

52

SUN IN LEO—MOON IN CANCER

(You belong to the positive or executive group)

YOU ARE a well integrated person with an instinctive knowledge of how to make yourself live up to the best that is in you. You are intense, sensitive, and have sound common sense, so that your powers of organization and management or of artistic creation, find good, practical expression. You are devoted to your home and are hospitable and open-hearted, with a warm appreciation of the difficulties of other people. An active sense of humor keeps your feeling for the dramatic from being self-centered; you know your own worth so well that you take it for granted and do not waste time in trying to impress others with it, except in what you do. You are a realist, and whether you work through an artistic, professional, or business medium, your feet are solidly on the ground. You make your ideals work for you in the world as you find it. A keen sense of life-values gives you an extraordinary appeal to people, for you combine the intellectual approach with a touch of sentiment and heart-throbbery that is very appealing. Romance, sentiment and love are very important to you, and until you have found someone on whom to lavish the generous amount of affection you have to give, you won't be happy. Women with this aspect usually have plenty of children and love them excessively, while men have the protective instinct strongly marked and are more than ordinarily devoted to their families. You are capable of achieving wide recognition for your personal gifts and talents, for you readily catch the public imagination. You're one of them, no matter how aristocratic you may be. Soundness is the keynote of your life; everything you do bears the stamp of character, persistence, honor; and whether you become famous or whether you remain obscure, these qualities are inviolable.

With 163, 180 or 147, tremendous rise to success. With 151 or 164, nervousness and confusion interfere with progress. You need your aims clarified and your emotions controlled. With 167 or 169, great popularity; also with 146, 147 or 148. With 204 or 213, idealistic and romantic emotional nature, with much variety in the love-life. With 215, 218, 227, 229 or 237, fortunes secure and quite large; great personal magnetism and charm bring public acclaim and commensurate rewards.

53

SUN IN LEO—MOON IN LEO

(You belong to the positive or executive group)

YOU ARE deeply ambitious, concentrative, and forceful, with a drive toward success that is likely to land you where you want to be. There is a hard streak in your nature that may not be apparent on the surface, which appears jovial, sunny, and full of health, vitality, and good spirits. But a certain ruthlessness underlies your back-slappery; you'll never forgive or forget an injury or a slight to your pride or vanity. There is something magnificent about your methods of fighting, whether for yourself or for others—a scorn of your enemies that enables you to demolish them ruthlessly but without malice (unless with 163, 180, 147 or 168, when there's a tendency to downright cruelty). Even this, however, will have a detached and impersonal quality about it, for you are a broad and objective thinker, fighting ideas and not men, and even when you are unkind to men, having at heart not their plight but the cause which makes your reactions necessary. This cause assumes a sort of abstract ideality in your mind, and you depersonalize it even as you push yourself forward. You are not naturally introspective, and even with 163 (which generally makes people introspective) you are likely to act from instinct rather than from analyzed personal motive. The outer world is of more importance to you than your private inner world, and your loves, hates, ambitions, and loyalties are all tinged with an impersonal passion that gives you tremendous control over yourself and over others. In love matters you are loyal, jealous, passionate, and though warm enough in one sense, somewhat cold and detached in another. You have a good deal of pride and vanity which can be satisfied either in personal matters, such as admiration, flattery, dress, and the like, or by the broader method of satisfied ambition. The more objective you become, the harder your vanity is to satisfy, and the more it demands a broad rather than a personal satisfaction, the greater will be your happiness and success.

With 148, 155, 169 or 174, grand humanitarian outlook, the friend of all the world, of high purpose and unselfish aims. With 147, 163, 168 or 180, hardness, perhaps cruelty, and success. With 149 or 170, introversion, hardness, love turned to hate. With both 163 and 164, or 180 and 181, domineering and unconventional, sorrow through the emotions, which are powerful and likely to be uncontrolled. With 172 and 181, sensational nature needful of guidance and will power . . . Under any and all circumstances you have tremendous will power and can use it for either the advancement or the destruction of yourself and others.

54

SUN IN LEO—MOON IN VIRGO

YOU FIND ready expression for your strong opinions and emotions, chiefly through the written and spoken word. A tendency to be a man of action breaks down under a lack of true executive capacity. Some flaw in your administrative talents will drive you to seek the influence you crave through intellectual means, in which you will achieve your greatest success. You are critical, accurate in thought, somewhat too outspoken, though tact is something you can easily learn. You have a large streak of timidity under your aggressive exterior, and, if the truth could be known, you're not always so sure of yourself as you appear; in fact, your extreme aggressiveness is likely to hide some degree of inferiority complex which you try to talk yourself out of. You are ardent in love, somewhat critical and suspicious, but easily satisfied if there's some flattery and demonstrativeness thrown in. You like to be petted, though you wouldn't care to have people know it. This is a rather better position for a woman than for a man, for in women it combines ardor and constancy, making you domestic and devoted; while in a man, a sort of cool note runs through the love-nature and makes him, in spite of his romantic exterior, a little forbidding and austere—something of a Puritan at heart, though he might never be willing to admit it. Your best medium of expression in life is artistic, intellectual, or creative. You have no special feeling for the public, and if you succeed, it's rather because they like what you do or are, than because you try to give them what they want. Your independence can make enemies, for you don't ordinarily cater to anyone, and a sort of militant pride impels you frequently to do the wrong thing out of impish delight in watching the effect. Underneath this, however, you have a real desire to please; and when you have learned tact you can become very popular with a discriminating public. Your taste is good and if you will allow your natural politeness and charm to come out, you can win people to you and to respect for your attainments.

With 180, tact is increased and also purpose; with 168, 178, 147, 161, 184, 195, 187 or 188, outspokenness is your danger. With 159, 165, muddled thinking needs to be overcome, accuracy needs attention, don't tell all you know! With 186, 192, 197 or 187, fine critical mind; with 187 or 188, creative power—also with 163, and perhaps 147 or 148.

55

SUN IN LEO—MOON IN LIBRA

YOU ARE an independent, idealistic, and romantic person. Your idealism amounts to an almost visionary quality and, coupled with a keen imagination, enables you to be in the forefront of your times or your circle. You have a warm-hearted almost sentimental approach to the world which endears you to it. You are highly honorable and have a sense of your own integrity that keeps your romantic dealings on a conventional plane, although your independence frequently urges you to step aside from the beaten track. You are one of the people who, though not believing especially in the conventions, none the less live up to them for you have discovered that you cannot fly in the face of public opinion without reaping the results thereof, and the good opinion of your fellow men is very important to you. You have a sort of instinctive grasp on the public pulse, and whatever your emotional eccentricities may be, you manage to guide them in such a way as not to give offense to the powers that be. The keen edge of revolt is not developed in your nature, and somewhat to your own surprise, you find yourself leading an orderly and useful life while all your philosophy may be rebelling against the limitations and practises of the society you are supporting. Your idealism goes into action where your own wishes are concerned, but you are not interested in the welfare of groups. You and those you love are your primary concerns. You will sacrifice a good deal for love—either love of a person, love of a career, or self-love—for this is to some extent the position of Narcissus, who fell in love with his own image. Your self-respect amounts almost to idolatry and makes you a trifle vain, both of your dress, your principles, and your ambitions. Though apparently "made for love" and usually appearing romantic and ardent, you surprise people by the vast amount of common sense you bring to bear on matters of the affections. This is part of your self-respect and your rigid code of personal propriety. Nobody is likely to be so important to you as to break these down, and because your avowed ideals about love are somewhat at variance with your practises, you appear sentimental rather than ardent, theoretic rather than passionate. You are capable of envisioning great schemes, plans, and ventures, and of putting them across. You are both expressive and impressionable and, by combining the two, catch the public imagination. Your personal appearance is a great asset to your advancement in life, and women with this combination are usually of exceptional beauty.

With 200, 210, 203, 204, 213 or 214, the conventional love-nature is much altered and a hectic emotional life is indicated. With 147, 163 or 180, driving force and ambition are increased, and success attends personal efforts. If with 183, 184, 185, 186, 187 or 188, mental pursuits bring profit and advancement. With 147, 154, 148 or 155, your energies are great and you arrive easily at your goal.

56

SUN IN LEO—MOON IN SCORPIO

YOUR ANIMAL nature is strong. You have a strong vigorous body, and your temperament is shot through with good healthy animal vitality which can burst forth in temper, temperament, hate, anger, passion—or can be controlled and directed to make you a truly great person. You are probably well aware of the duality of your nature. Although you are not introspective, experience must have taught you what you are capable of when you let yourself run away and get out of control—and it also must have taught you how perfectly the world responds to your wishes when you are in full possession of yourself. Everything is colored by your personal biases; you have little capacity for objectivity or detachment. Principles mean little to you—it is human beings, worldly ambition, worldly goods, worldly loves, hates, jealousies, enthusiasms, that matter to you. "All the world's a stage" to you, and of all the players you are the most important. You are essentially dramatic, and the drama of your life will find you either the hero or the villain, for you are your own best friend—and your own worst enemy. Nobody can really help or hurt you except yourself in so far as you allow lack of self-control to give other people control over you. When at your best, you are vigilant, perceptive, intense, aspiring, with a well-defined goal toward which you strive constantly and in the seeking of which you may have to walk over other people ruthlessly. This is O. K. with you, for, as said before, abstractions don't bother you and you have little feeling for justice, and the like, for their own sake. They are all right when they suit your purposes. You are the human embodiment of the principle of the struggle for survival: you feel that if you take care of yourself everyone else will do the same for himself. You are in no sense your brother's keeper. You believe that "Down to Gehenna or up to the throne, He travels the fastest who travels alone"—and in justice to you it must be said that you're willing to live and die by this principle—willing to accept the doom that "he who lives by the sword shall die by the sword." You are a magnetic person and can make people loyal to you. You're an ardent if somewhat hard, lover, exceedingly jealous and possessive, though keeping your own freedom. You are proud, shrewd, intuitive, forceful and likely to go far, even from a pretty poor start in life.

With 147, 161, 168 or 178, the passional nature will tend to run away with you; with 200, 210, 203, 213, 204, 214, 218 or 226, sensationalism, emotional turmoil, interfere with your powers. With 224, exceptionally ambitious and ruthless; hard fall follows spectacular rise. With 216, smoother, more tactful nature, ambition well directed, and therefore more stable success. With 184, 195, 186 or 197, tendency to cruelty; also with 200 and 212. If with 202 or 212, you hurt people who are fond of you.

57

SUN IN LEO—MOON IN SAGITTARIUS

YOU ARE daring, courageous, adventurous, dashing. Your vitality and pace take the world by storm; you were undoubtedly a precocious child, and you always seem to be a couple of jumps ahead of yourself emotionally—and maybe also geographically. This position gives a passion for travel, variety, novelty, and excitement, which in a man makes a soldier of fortune and in a woman makes for romance in large and continuous doses. You have amazing energy, an expressive imaginative equipment, a magnetic effect on others, and, if you can hold in your fiery emotional nature and harness it to a constructive purpose, there is nothing you cannot do. But you tend to let your fires burn you up with their enthusiasms, and though you burn with a brilliant light, you don't focus it too well. You are likely to go through life getting by on what you are and what you appear to be—on dash, charm, and enthusiasms—rather than on what you do or know or can bring to pass. Restraint is what you chiefly need; you have a lavish gift from Fortune in your personality and the way you can charm people. But until you harness your energies to a purpose, an ambition, a goal, you are likely to zip along like a comet, which is a beautiful, but useless, wanderer in the skies. Women with this configuration make wonderful sweethearts while they're around, but they usually aren't around for long—and the same may be said of men. What you really need is to settle down, hold yourself to a job, a marriage, a purpose, a base of operation, by main strength and will power, until your energies get accustomed to the idea and learn how to work in the yoke.

With 148, 155, 149, 156, 169, 174, 175 or 176, stability is much improved, and a good deal of luck comes through flexibility and the application of the philosophic spirit to practical affairs. With 147, 161, 150, 164, 165, 168, 178, 181 or 182, super-romanticism is dangerous and the nerves have to be watched; a neurotic attitude toward love matters makes troubles. With 215, 218, 227, 229 or 237, extraordinary luck in life; with 200, 210, 167, 203, 213, 204 or 214, much sex-appeal and not so much stability in love—independence gets to be a mania. In any and all cases excess independence is your weakness and can be made into a strength only through rigid self-discipline. With 163 or 180, creative mentality results from the disciplining of the adventurous and passional nature.

58

SUN IN LEO—MOON IN CAPRICORN

THIS IS ONE of the most powerful of polarities and if with 163, 168 or 180 leads to the top. Your great energies are harnessed to a definite and well-controlled purpose. Your ardent nature is directed away from personal matters toward ambition of some very definite sort. You know what you want early in life, and you see to it that nothing, and nobody, gets in your way. You can appear passionate and ardent in love, but this is merely one expression of your generalized intensity and your desire to dominate. If, as infrequently happens, you are unsuccessful in bringing some victim to time, a little-suspected inferiority complex manifests itself—as it does under any species of frustration or bafflement. You are a spoiled child, less from being spoiled in youth than because you spoil yourself. You make demands of the world, and in seeing to it that your demands are acceded to, you achieve success. Your great strength is unswerving purpose with the energy necessary for its accomplishment, and these qualities will take you as far as your imagination can reach.

With 147, 148, 149, 168, 169, 174, 163, 180 or 175, this will be very far; you will override resistance and opposition with a kind of genial ruthlessness which people will not resent, for you have the mark of authority on you, and by and large people recognize and respect it. They expect you to excell and take delight in helping you when you need help. If with 215, 216, 217, 218, 226, 227, 228, 229 or 237, this assumes magnetic proportions, and opens all doors to you. With 150 *and* 163 purposes are muddled up more but ambition makes long if eccentric strides. With 236, alternate fixity and eccentricity of purpose. With 224, great rise and fall; you overreach yourself, your imagination runs away with you and excess pride brings your downfall — but not until you have stood at the top. This is the position of a self-made man or woman. Pride is your strength and arrogance your weakness. Sureness is your prop and over-self-confidence your enemy. You should aim at restraint of arrogance, and a respect for the rights of others.

59
SUN IN LEO—MOON IN AQUARIUS

CREATIVE IMAGINATION is your forte—what you imagine in the abstract you put into practise, either in art, letters, or mechanical creation, for this is a versatile position with a touch of the inspired. You are romantic, idealistic, and broad-minded. You are loyal in love and loyal to your ideals; and in the highest state of its development this combination will make you a leader of thought. In less highly developed natures this combination will express universality in more personal ways —in unreliability of the emotions, instability of the love-nature, and a tendency to run from one sweetheart to another from sheer restlessness and caprice. But you are fundamentally serious-minded, and even after having your fling in youth, are likely to settle down into a good husband (or wife) and surprise your friends and neighbors. You are inventive and poetic by nature, with a passion to see your dreams come true.

With 166, creative talent is marked, perhaps amounting to genius; with 215, 218, 183, 189, this is increased; with 187, 188, inspirational. With Venus in Pisces, 202, 212, hurt through too-generous affections and through having them imposed on; with 200, 210, 211, 203, 204, 213 or 214, erratic love-nature makes much trouble. With 163 or 180, strong will, much purpose and direction, usually followed to a well-defined goal, probably along creative lines. With 149, 170, 227, 148 or 169, a reformer, judge, minister. There's a great desire on your part to be in some way or another a force felt in the world of people—a sort of pervading social sense—that is likely to make you influential in whatever sphere of life you move.

60
SUN IN LEO—MOON IN PISCES

YOU KNOW when to fight and when to run away. A combination of aggression and recession, accurately timed to suit the needs of the world, brings you success. You are no coward in any sense of the word; but you understand the value of material expediency, though in moral issues you will not give an inch. You will go down with the sinking ship of Truth if necessary; but you will not be caught short in the market or play your luck past its reasonable limit. Thus you are a good business man with a large strain of humanitarianism, so that you are able to be successful without becoming hard-boiled. You take care of the people who are dependent on you, having a true feeling for noblesse oblige. You are a philanthropist. You have a keen sense of sorrow and tragedy, and under your bubbling and vigorous exterior you preserve a sort of brooding, philosophic spirit that is well aware of the sadness of life. Being a person of action, you are not content to let this remain merely dejection; you will do something about it in your own way—trying to reform the world through philosophy, donations, social work, political influence—but always animated by the broad motive. Your ambition for influence is for the good you can do rather than for personal glory; for with great self-respect, you combine a true humility of spirit and a real love for your fellow man. You are ardent in love but not constant; the expansive spirit here is likely to seek more than one person to whom to express love. But a certain idealism takes this out of the realm of philandering. You're too serious a person to be called fickle, though what you do may amount to the same thing. Whatever you do, your motives are of the highest; and if you hurt people, it is only to regret it bitterly, and perhaps in tears, later.

With 163, 164, 165, 161 in a man's chart; or 168, 178, 170, 180, 181 or 182 in a woman's chart; or 200, 210, 203, 213, 204 or 214 in either, a hectic love life is shown; if with 202 or 212, sorrow through love—hurt both to and from others. With 211, overexpansive love-nature, misplaced affections, and danger that you will be imposed on financially by those you love. With 215, 217, 218, 227, 228, 229 or 237, wealth and influence. With 215, 218 or 229, creative gifts manifest, and influence through them. You must resist a temptation to withdraw into a cell of your own building, and to allow your seriousness to degenerate into dejection and depression. Allow your energies to have active outlet, and your idealism and magnetism will carry you far.

61

SUN IN VIRGO—MOON IN ARIES

(You belong to the positive or executive group)

YOU HAVE NOT nearly the self-confidence that you impress the world with, for though you express as a dynamic and executive person, there are large gaps of timidity in you. If by any chance you work yourself into a position of authority, flaws will be found in your administration which are at variance with what you say. There are great inconsistencies in your nature, for your moral courage—which is truly great—doesn't go into action readily; after you've expressed high and noble ideas, you have trouble putting them into effect. If you can learn to start at the other end of things—act first and talk about it later—you will accomplish more and build more solid foundations. You have an excellent mental equipment of a critical and analytical rather than a creative turn; and you can sway people by sheer strength of personality. You are profoundly ambitious and insist on ruling the roost; in fact your whole emotional nature is polarized toward personal acclamation, so that in human relations you may seem a trifle cold. You are by no means the ideal sweetheart, for love as such doesn't mean much to you, and when you do marry, it's likely to be a marriage of convenience, or, at best, a marriage of true minds rather than a romantic attachment. Even if you appear to display ardor, it's of a curious kind; and there may be a streak of hardness or cruelty in you that will hurt those who love you, for you are neither aware of, nor interested in, other people's feelings. Ideas are what count to you; and the finer shades of feeling are likely to be lost on you.

This lends impersonality and detachment to your nature which gives you terrific drive, and with 168, 163, 178 or 180, will make you a power of some sort or other in your sphere, which you will ever seek to widen. With 164, 165, 182 or 171, you are apparently more romantic and erratic, but still cold beneath. With 148, 155, 169 or 179, practical business nature or professional career; a tendency to be judicial and righteous. With 149 or 170, extremely hard nature, enmities and danger of introversion through grudges, distrust of the world, and feelings of frustration. With 202 or 212, you cause much hurt to those who love you; with 216, great authority; with 224, selfish rise and eventual fall.

62

SUN IN VIRGO—MOON IN TAURUS

THIS IS ONE of the outstanding positions of luck in life; material problems rarely trouble you, though out of nervousness you may create your own worries. In some way you are taken care of; and through hereditary standing may rise to a position of considerable importance. Without squares to the Sun or Moon, however, this is not an ambitious position, and you tend to relax in luxury and ease and to lead a contented and harmonious, rather than exciting or progressive, life. You are naturally easy-going (which may be reflected in a tendency to grow fat!), and your genial nature makes friends readily, generally among rich or influential people. This is a position of hereditary prestige rather than of anything that you accomplish for yourself, for the impetus to progress, either through economic necessity or through personal drive, does not develop readily.

With 148, 161, 147, 155 or 174, you're pushed up to something, in which your integrity and common sense maintain you so long as you're not required to exert executive authority. With 215, 216, 217, 227, 228, 229 or 237 your scope and authority may be considerable. Without some of these energizing factors you're a useful, conventional, stable citizen, probably living on the fat of the land, or at least well cared for; mildly interested in intellectual and artistic matters.

With 183, 184, 185, 186, 187 or 188, the mental quickness is assisted, though there isn't likely to be much to impel creative activity; you admire artists and writers and may lionize them (especially if they are successful), but you form the appreciative and intelligent audience which art needs, rather than being a part of the arts yourself; you may be a patron of galleries, opera, the theater, or literally the patron of some deserving young artist who happens to take your fancy. In love, you are constant and loyal, rather than ardent, and have probably come through youth with a minimum of unpleasant experiences. You take a good deal for granted and are a pretty matter-of-fact person. In business, as in personal life, you are marked by soundness rather than daring; your business will run smoothly and without excitement for you stick to the conservative course, where the rocks and reefs are few. You have been sheltered and protected from the less pleasant side of the world, and it appears a pretty good place to you. You have profited under conservative business practises and achieved contentment through a harmonious, rather than an adventurous, love-life; and you are quite content to have the world continue its leisurely pace till the end of your days, which because of a sound constitution may well be long.

63

SUN IN VIRGO—MOON IN GEMINI

MIND-POWER is your strength—and your weakness. It is your strength because you are rational, capable of figuring things out analytically, and of grasping details and intricacies. It is your weakness because, through absorption with mental matters, you are likely to neglect the emotional side of your life, which nevertheless rises up to cause you trouble. Your faith is in Reason—and you are consequently confounded and baffled in the presence of emotional experience. You are sentimental rather than romantic or passionate, and either indecisive or inconstant in matters of love. Without being self-sufficient, you none the less hesitate to pin yourself down to any one person, and even when you do, your critical nature can lessen love by picking flaws. You are a good deal of an intellectual aristocrat, a little scornful of the men and women whose intellectual equipment, or training, has not been up to yours. Your adaptability is likely to bring you success in some degree, for you are a conscientious student and workman, succeeding best in personal or independent types of intellectual activity, such as the arts and the professions. You are eager for progress, an opportunist taking advantage of every opening, and not always considerate of one who gets in your way. You are impressionable but somewhat cold in response, your affinities tending to intellectual rather than romantic, for your mind always stands a censor and judges people. Thus, though you may be erratic, impulsive and independent in intellectual matters, you are not swept off your feet by your emotions. You are a little overbalanced on the mental side, and appear "good" through having few temptations to overcome —you stay on the beaten track because the by-paths don't lure you. You have to be careful that too much mental work doesn't produce nervousness—"all work and no play..."

With 150, 151, 164, 165, 171, 172, 181 or 182, this is especially dangerous, nerves being a constant problem. With 159 or 152, glib mentality; with 160, serious emotional disturbances; with 161, brilliance and some instability; with 163 or 180, depth and concentrative powers are increased; with 149 or 170, introversion; with 183, 184, 186 or 187, fine mind; with 188 or 199, day-dreamer.

Watch out for becoming a bookworm to the neglect of your physical, as well as emotional, well-being; you need exercise, rest, and relaxation to take care of your enormous mental and nervous energies.

64

SUN IN VIRGO—MOON IN CANCER

YOU ARE RESERVED, sentimental, and naturally shy, although self-confidence grows with the years. However, you don't get over a certain reticence of manner and adherence to the conventions of social usage. You have an underlying sweetness and charm which your shyness and sensitivity may conceal too effectively. You live by a code of some kind or other, usually based on the conventions of your circle but varied by you from time to time (and even from moment to moment) to suit your own purposes as they arise. You are very protective and defensive, and being agile mentally can think up reasons and excuses why what *you* do is all right, though you may condemn it sharply in another.

When you step off the beaten track in any way, you do it not from any conviction that you are doing as you should, but with an active consciousness of sin. Where your emotions are concerned and when you're in the process of defending yourself, you are capable of being illogical, and you have to be allowed to work yourself out of moods the best way you know how. Your sensitivity finds armors to protect itself with, against which both reason and affection fail. And once you have entrenched yourself in your citadel, only you can lead yourself out again. You are loving and affectionate, but a little aloof, from shyness rather than from pride, for you are really very sociable at heart and, when you let yourself go, can be the life of the party—from which hilarity you can suddenly, and for no reason, lapse into the sulks and glooms. This is probably due to physiological causes, for your vitality is not high, and your nervousness exhausts it quickly. You are very particular about matters of health and diet, and with good reason, though this can go over to finickyness and even hypochondria if you get to feeling sorry for yourself. You love attention and are capable of playing sick to get it. You are affectionate, and loyal and devoted in love. With respect to people you meet, you are alternately too suspicious and too gullible, your judgment being based on your emotions. Mentally, you are quick, clever, facile, and adaptable, with a ready intuitive grasp of details and an ability to keep several things, or jobs, going in your mind at the same time. You are temperamental with respect to work, doing it in fits and starts rather than with concentrated drive. Private nonexecutive work of a creative nature is your best medium. You are full of ideas, and expressive of them and a valuable business asset.

With 163, concentrative ability helped; with 147, much luck in material matters; with 168, 178 or 181, independence of thought marked; with 171, unusually quick and active mind; with 200, 210, 203 or 213, erratic emotional nature; with 202 or 212, self-inflicted sorrow through love.

65

SUN IN VIRGO—MOON IN LEO

YOU ARE a person of unquestioned character and absolute devotion to duty. Whatever rebellious resentments may enter your heart they never swing you from the path that you consider right and honorable. You are thus capable of being imposed upon, for if you can be made to feel that you have an obligation, you will never turn back without fulfilling it. Your inner worth frequently has difficulty in finding adequate return in the outer world. You are not good at managing people, and the executive places into which your sense of obligation or duty works you may prove too much for you. You have plenty of faith in yourself, but you have little faith in your ability to make other people see and appreciate your worth. You are likely to resign yourself to being misunderstood and frustrated. Thus you do not go out to create your own opportunities and are likely to pass up opportunities that come your way through fear that you won't be able to make good. And all the time, underneath, you have a burning sense of your own competence that you have great difficulty in bringing to the surface. You should force yourself to be independent, to take responsibility, to grasp opportunity, and to *make* the other fellow appreciate you. You rely too much on your character, your worth, your conscientiousness being rewarded, for you have a naïve faith in human nature which even years of hard blows do not completely destroy, and you have a hard time learning the ways of the world. You continue to believe that if you do right by your job you will be rewarded and are dismayed and confused when less worthy, more guileful people, go by you. In a woman's horoscope this is likely to mean that at some time or other, the family obligations will devolve on you, either through your husband's illness or through lack of success. Your worth is tested by circumstances. In a man's chart, aggressiveness is required—less faith in the reward of the just and more push. Speaking coldly and practically, you could do with less character and more guile, with some method that would make your worth known. You tend to hide your light under a bushel.

With 183, 189, 185, 191, 186 or 192, just and honorable mind; with 168, 173 or 178, more aggressiveness, and likelihood of considerable success; also with 169, 174 or 179. With 170, 180, 216 or 224, inferiority complex; with 163, inner drive is helped; artistic career likely; with 149, introversion; with 147, difficulty in expressing the really tremendous talents.

66

SUN IN VIRGO—MOON IN VIRGO

(You belong to the positive or executive group)

YOU ARE dominated and motivated by your intellectual interests. You are loyal, affectionate, sentimental rather than romantic, and can develop a great interest in domestic matters. But the lodestar of your life is the mind, its products, achievements, and possibilities. When you marry it will be for intellectual affinity as much as for anything else, for though you fall in love, you simply wouldn't fall in love with an inferior intellect. Your high sense of discrimination, amounting to an intellectual snobbery, protects you from getting involved with intellectual inferiors, for you have a very finicky taste in matters of people, dress, food and housefurnishings and can be extremely critical when your sense of good taste is offended. This sense of discrimination keeps you pretty conventional for no matter how intellectual ideas may appeal to you on the radical and daring side, an innate dislike of offending society keeps you pretty much on the straight and narrow; and when human weakness gets the better of you and you simply have to step off the beaten track you do it with such infinite care and consideration for the feelings of society, that society probably doesn't even know about it. You are something of a moralist, but your moral sense is social rather than abstract. You are a great preserver of law and order, and when you do arrive at the conclusion that things ought to be changed, you want to see them changed gradually, according to the rules of the game. You are no fire-and-sword revolutionary. Peace is important to you; no principle is worth fighting for, except in a polite and well-bred way. This position generally accompanies a good deal of breeding and family background, whence the reverence for tradition. You aren't an executive and should never by any chance try to become one. There will be major flaws in any enterprise you conduct, due largely to your conservatism and reasonableness, which sees the other fellow's viewpoint only too well and makes you less sure of your own plan of action. On the other hand you carry out orders admirably and are invaluable in important subordinate capacities that depend on the executive direction of others or in independent pursuits without executive needs—professional, or artistic. Your creations are marked by care and precision and a flawlessness that may seem cold and studied to more dashing spirits, but which is sound to the core, admirable in taste and execution.

With 146, 166, 167, 180, 168, 147, 163, 178, 181, 184, 187, 188, 215 or 218, creative gifts powerful. With 186 or 197, judicial mind, legalistic and profound; with 227 or 230, power and influence; with 155, 156, 174 or 175, influential career, easy and fluent.

67

SUN IN VIRGO—MOON IN LIBRA

YOU ARE a self-sufficient soul, intellectual, reasonable, easy to get along with, and probably easy to look at; but in some way giving the impression of detachment. You're fastidious in your tastes, in matters of dress and with respect to people, and would rather spend an evening at home with a book than go out just to be on the go. This is because you're capable of taking care of yourself and also because you're a good deal of a snob, in a quiet, unassuming way. You manage to organize your life so as to exclude those people who bore you or whom you believe to be socially or intellectually inferior. Your quietness of manner conceals a strong determination to do as you please, and your live-and-let-live policy is the corner stone of your creed. You're a moralist so far as your own life is concerned, but will rarely express criticism of others; you realize that other people probably aren't interested in your opinions, so you don't give them. You're courteous, strongly social-minded so far as the conventions are concerned, but capable of carrying on a private and perhaps secret life of your own, always within the realms of good taste and discretion. Without cynicism, you believe that what you do is your own business so long as you keep it to yourself; and without deception you go your own way simply by tactfully keeping issues from being raised. You don't like quarrels and will go to extremes of diplomacy to avoid one; in theory and practise, you're a pacifist. You are appreciative of beauty in art and letters, a great reader, and with 183, 189, 163, 187, 184 or 188, likely to have creative gifts. You're so self-sufficient that the passional-emotional life is not very important to you; consequently people with this position frequently do not marry, though not from lack of opportunity. You early get "sot in your ways," and you don't like to alter them for another. Marry young and avoid this. You reason things out so well and are so understanding, tolerant, and rational that you aren't usually hurt through your emotions and make a very satisfactory person to have around, being sympathetic of the woes of others less through experience of your own than through intuitive grasp. Your life is likely to be protected from economic worry; and if other things show creative gifts (see above) your intuitive understanding will lend a peculiarly impelling force to what you write or paint. You have a kind of universality of approach that lends scope and dignity to the most realistic, or fanciful, of themes and gives you in all walks of life a philosophic approach to problems and to your fellow men.

68

SUN IN VIRGO—MOON IN SCORPIO

YOU LOOK and behave like an intellectual but your chief driving force is found in your personal, emotional nature; and for good or ill, it colors all your thinking strongly. You are incapable of believing what is foreign to your internal emotional bias, and thus you will be found to be an ardent partisan of whatever cause appeals to you. This you may rationalize and try to give intellectual status, but as a matter of fact you select your beliefs intuitively rather than reasonably. It requires a major explosion to blast a pet idea out of you; you seem to think it is a point of personal integrity not to be convinced by argument. You are facile at thinking up reasons why your ideas are right and very persuasive in putting them across. You can outguess the other fellow and are a good debater, being more interested in winning than in truth for its own sake. You haven't yet learned that you can "win an argument" without proving anything or convincing anyone; you are the sort of person who can demonstrate logically that Charlie Ross is still alive and be sort of hurt when no one finds him. You are likely to be found among the theoretical radical thinkers, who believe in almost any kind of reform, on paper, and who can draw diagrams to show how it could work—despite the fact that it very obviously could not work. The missionary spirit is strong in you, your interest being in convincing people of what you consider the right, in the pious conviction that, if they take the pledge, they'll never tip up another glass. Your intellectual powers are strong, but you aren't a realist; you will excel as a writer of fiction, a story-teller, though you rather fancy yourself spreader of ideas. When you let your head rule your heart you can be unbeatable; when the heart is ruling the head (as it tends to do) you stand in your own light. Depersonalize your life and you can go far; live on the purely personal note and you limit your scope.

With 163 or 180, objectivity increased, ambition helped. With 147, 148, 215, 218, 229 or 237, luck in material matters. You can be a good business man, for in material matters you are more objective than in intellectual and emotional things; your practical sense comes to the front in business; your intuitions are practically accurate, and you are a valuable business asset to whomever you work for.

69

SUN IN VIRGO—MOON IN SAGITTARIUS

THERE is a wide cleavage between your intellectual and your emotional natures; you are capable of doing things you disapprove of, under the spell of adventure, romance, excitement. You are a loyal, honorable, warm-hearted, and reasonable person. But you have difficulty in getting your ideas across, and a feeling that you are misunderstood arises, perhaps because you don't understand yourself well enough to make yourself clear. You tend to think in large symbols that don't bear much relationship with your everyday life, and to idealize what are really very worldly matters. You are philosophic and somewhat introspective, but instead of looking inside yourself to find what is there, you look inside with a preconceived notion of what you ought to find or would like to find. You are sentimental rather than romantic; you fall in love with ideas, or with an ideal of love, rather than with an individual; and you tend to be baffled, frustrated, and to feel yourself cheated when the Beloved Object fails to live up to your ideal. You can daydream your life away, or you can take your ideals and your philosophies and combine them with your practical analytical nature to produce something creatively. You can be a fair business person when you have overcome a tendency to be too philosophic and idealistic, and have learned to make your vision practical in terms of the earth as you find it. Intellectually, you are interested in broad, general subjects—religion, philosophy, poetry, music, perhaps metaphysics—and you are capable of tracking a subject to its lair and making it completely yours. You have both imagination and patience, invaluable gifts for either the student or the artist. You love travel, and if you get lots of it, it will absorb your restlessness and enable you to pin yourself down to some important artistic or intellectual task. In business you will be better on the book, managerial, or fiscal side, than in buying, selling, or executive work.

With 147, 148, 168, 169, luck in life is increased; with 163, concentrative powers great; with 165, confused idealisms; with 150 and 181, erratic emotional life. With 182, sensationalist; with 173, 174, 175 or 177, strong practical bent, business instinct good; with 171 and 177, occultist, very quick mind, emotional and nerve difficulties. The nerves need strict attention, in any case, and especially if with 150, 164, 165, 171, 181, 182, 161, 163, 168, 178, 224 or 217.

70

SUN IN VIRGO—MOON IN CAPRICORN

YOU ARE a very well-integrated personality, with a fine mind, critical rather than creative; and you rise to a position of some influence and authority and to worldly security. A fundamentally serious, even morose, strain underlies your sense of humor. You are conscious of the frailties of human nature and eager to do your share to improve them intellectually... You will leave the giving of tangible charity to someone else while you're working on the human mind. Your passions tend to be of the mind rather than of the flesh; and your success comes, whether in business or professional life, through accuracy, mental soundness and devotion to duty rather than through personal magnetism. Your magnetism is late in asserting itself, and you plug through your first years by main strength and ignorance, with a fixed devotion to your purpose, incapable of being put off by unkind circumstances. Later in life your charm develops. You are quietly magnetic, restrained even when you are most eager, and have a keen sense of good taste that is a valuable social asset. You will speak your mind frankly and even brutally where an idea is in question; but you are unfailingly considerate of people's feelings. Thus, you supply in the milk of human kindness what you appear to lack in warmth, and endear people to you steadily and permanently rather than flashily and insecurely. You are constant in love and in friendship and delight in taking the unpopular side of a question, which you may well enough succeed in making the popular side, for you are extremely persuasive, with a flow of language so glib as to obscure the fundamental depth of what you have to say. You are more voluble in speech than your otherwise reserved nature would seem to warrant, but this is only part of your intellectual sureness and precision, which gives you self-confidence where ideas are involved.

With 163, 166, 168, 148 or 169, much drive and success; with 149, 170, 180, increased shyness, but great persistence and eventual recognition. With 171, 181, erratic and explosive independence; with 177, 175, 174 or 173, much success through this, though periodic unpopularity impedes progress. Nerves are an important consideration, especially with 147, 149, 150, 161, 163, 164, 165, 168, 178, 170, 180, 171, 181, 182, 187, 198 or 199.

71

SUN IN VIRGO—MOON IN AQUARIUS

YOU ARE a pretty detached sort of person, and however much your romanticism and periodic emotionalism may seem to make you otherwise, you incline to be cold and self-sufficient at heart. You view people in a rather calculating manner, and are capable of hurting those who are fond of you by the ease with which you break human ties and follow your own bent, whatever it may be. You have a good, reasonable, scientifically accurate mind, and when you have figured something out to your satisfaction, you expect everyone else to understand your logic—which you may not go to the trouble of explaining. This detachment and the apparently genial exterior that you present to the world make you a good doctor, nurse, social worker, hospital attendant, or teacher—any occupation where sympathy and understanding must be used but cannot be allowed to interfere with routine. You are able to learn readily, through application rather than intuition. You are a somewhat suspicious person, critical and judicial, though tolerant enough of your own eccentricities. If you are cold, however, you are also stable and can be a bulwark of help in time of trouble, able to absorb the woes of others without being yourself affected and thus helping them to get on their own feet when, your work being done, you go on to other matters. You are willing, rather than ardent, aggressive, or responsive, in romantic matters, and are likely to impress sweethearts with the idea that they don't really matter very much, which more likely than not is true. You can take them or you can leave them alone. Since the physical impetus to love is not powerful in you, you're capable of leading a celibate life, substituting intellect and abstract idealisms for human companionship and love.

This will be considerably altered if with 147, 149, 163, 164, 165, 168, 178, 171, 181, 182, 200, 210, 203, 213, 204 or 214, when a nervous kind of intensity will make you apparently ardent; however, this is nerves rather than passion. With 202 or 212, you cause others much hurt through coldness. You have to watch out that in both business and personal life, a certain indifference doesn't get between you and progress or contentment.

72

SUN IN VIRGO—MOON IN PISCES

INSIGHT is your great gift, an understanding mind, careful, studious, and profound. You are both intellectual and intuitive, can reason things out by cold logic, learn facts, and absorb figures, at the same time that your hunches are actively at work. You seem to know a lot of things without having to be told—to have been born wise, as it were. You are introspective, imaginative, and somewhat apprehensive; you tend to brood and worry and fall into fits of depression, for this is one of the aspects of *Weltschmerz,* and can make you feel pretty sorry for yourself in a very sentimental way. You also are capable of feeling sorry for other people, very deeply; for a wide sweep of human sympathy is yours, so that you would be an admirable social worker, nurse, doctor, settlement worker, or Salvation Army officer. There is a deeply philosophic and charitable streak in you; everything you do, whether in public or private life, is likely to be touched with this wide range of sympathy, so that you are a comfort to those around you. You believe in the Good Life, and you believe that he who would lead the good life must serve. Not innately ambitious in the ordinary sense of the word, you still have deep pride in your own worth, and in your own capacity for progress. While you are not a good executive, you feel a moral obligation to shoulder responsibility, and what you lack in aggressiveness and boldness, you more than make up in moral force and sense of duty. You are very likely to hear much of the troubles of other people as you go your way, for this is a Father-Confessor position; your friends and fellow workers will bring their troubles to you for solution.

With 148 or 155, considerable luck in life; with 169 or 174, professional career of wide influence. If Mercury has strong aspects, intellectual career, writer, speaker, philosopher—a versatile nature. Sentimentality is your besetting evil—a tendency to take your own emotions and troubles and those of the world too hard, to dramatize yourself and lose your sense of balance and proportion through overemphasizing the emotional side of your life. With 200, 210, 203 or 213, sympathy with others brings you bad companions; with 202 or 212, you're imposed on; if with 204, 209, 214, impressionability dangerous. With 149 or 170, deeply brooding spirit, must beware of fits of depression and dejection, as well as of physical trouble through nerves and worry. With 147, brilliant mind needing much self-control—danger from bad associations. With 168, aggression greater, but likely to lead into foolish actions. Go slowly!

This is one of the expressive positions and can bring you success in the literary arts after the sentimentality of youth has been overcome, for then you are able through the keenness of your insight to capture the public imagination. "Human interest" is your strong point, both in life and in letters, and can be put to good use in literary creation.

73

SUN IN LIBRA—MOON IN ARIES

YOU ARE likely to appear a good deal more daring and aggressive than you really are, for you are a fundamentally gentle soul who wants chiefly to be let alone. All you really ask of the world is that it should forget about you and let you go your own way in peace; for you are self-sufficient and believe in the "live and let live" doctrine. The difficulty is that other people have a way of demanding attention, or of asking you to alter your modes of doing, thinking, or living, and you refuse to be budged. You are apparently tractable, reasonable, and calm, but there's a bar of iron in your nature that surprises people when they first see, or feel, it. Independence is likely to lead you into weird paths, for as you go along you develop odd notions and can easily become a first-class eccentric. You seem to delight in actions and ideas that everyone else thinks are cracked, which does not in the least interfere with your serious contemplation of them. You are likely to go in for spiritualism, magnetic healing, tea-leaf reading, crystal gazing, share-the-wealth, chain letters—all with a serious absorption that is the despair of your friends. You have no hesitancy in airing the most outlandish views on all subjects. This is a romantic position, as well as that of a sensationalist, and you'll have to look out that strange companions do not lead you astray, or vice versa.

If with Mars in Libra, Venus in Scorpio, 200, 210, 202, 212, 216, 224, 147, 161, 168 or 178, emotional and sensational bents are dangerous, and there's a touch of hardness, or even cruelty, to the nature. This is a somewhat difficult position. You find coöperation with the world difficult and will succeed best in some highly practical and private occupation —craftsmanship of some sort, where you can work alone. Your independence makes it difficult for you to get married, but you really need the support and companionship of others, though you may not believe this. Coöperation is the keynote of your happiness, and if you can bring yourself to sacrifice some of your freedom and independence, life will be a much happier and more peaceful adventure for you.

74

SUN IN LIBRA—MOON IN TAURUS

YOU ARE a charming person, with plenty of independence and purpose that you know how to put across in a way that makes people like you. Your personality is your greatest asset; it's made up, among other things, of a liberal dose of sentimentality that makes a powerful appeal to the opposite sex. You need affection, sympathy, understanding; and are willing to give them generously in return. Despite your rampant sentiment and romanticism, you are constant in love, unless with 161, 164, 168, 178, 171, 181, 182, 200, 210, 203, 213 or 214, when the ideal of love does not get into active service. Here your romanticism runs away with you; like Odysseus, you seek through the world for the Ideal Companion and feel very badly about the hearts that are broken in your wanderings. But you believe in the Ideal of Love. If you are in business, this translates itself to the Rotarian Ideal of Service. You have to believe personally in what you do, with some emotional fervor, for you could not go into anything cold-bloodedly that did not appeal to your ideals. You are capable of being a high pressure salesman but you'll believe firmly that you are doing your victim a good turn. This faith in the good in things endears you to people, and it takes something pretty hard in your life, such as would be represented by 202, 212, 203, 204, 163, 164, 168, 178, 180, 181 or 182, to destroy it. Even then, though you may have been hurt through faith, you wouldn't be surprised to find it again. You can be imposed upon through this, and probably have been. Both through emotional and financial generosity, you can be fooled. This is an æsthetic position, and if you go in for creative art, your work is likely to bear the stamp of human interest and even sentimentality, which you must work to keep from getting gushy, for you love the sugary things of life and tend to think and express in very lush terms. This quality, as well as your obvious devotion to ideals, love, romance, high seriousness in human relations, will make your work popular, though it may draw down the contumely of the more hard-boiled critics. This will be true anyway—you'll be popular with the romantics and with the general public, but not so much so with the realists. And you have to be careful that sentimentality doesn't run away with you.

75

SUN IN LIBRA—MOON IN GEMINI

YOU HAVE a magnetic personality, voluble, expressive, talkative, with an ability to hold audiences. You live up to the limit of your capabilities, all your talents finding expression, and you give the impression of doing things so easily that people imagine they see great deep wells under the surface of your facility. You have a way of saying things that seems to give them significance beyond the actual ideas you convey. The illusion of universality hangs around you, and you have a kind of faith in yourself that people seem willing to accept at its face value. You are highly romantic and sentimental, and thus your appeal is very broad to the emotions, rather than to the intellect, although a certain intellectuality of manner and appearance gives the impression that you are being very profound. You always demand an audience and have an acute sense of what the public wants together with a desire, and an ability, to give it to them. In personal relationships you appear considerate and thoughtful through anticipating what your vis-à-vis wants. You are mobile, versatile, and restless, and either your travels, your studies, or your influence will cover a wide range. You are rather more likely to be varied, romantic, and appealing than profound; for you don't tend to delve deeply into things. You are quick mentally, and by running from one thing to another, appear to know a good deal. In rare cases this may lead to an exceptionally clever student, but in most cases you'll get by without too much effort. You are avid for recognition but can well be content with it on a small scale, for the inner drive of ambition is not strong. Circumstances usually conspire to reward your charming personality with a good share of adulation and the world's goods. You love the nice things of life and pretty generally manage to get some of them.

With 183, the mental powers are improved, and creative ability is possible; with 184, 185, 186, 187 or 188, more mental stability. With 161, flashy mind but liable to be inaccurate. With 163, more profound and concentrative, with liability to periods of gloom and depression. With 151, 164, erratic emotional life; with 200, 210, 203, 213, 204 or 214, trouble through over-expansive emotional dealings.

You are liable to feel sorry for yourself and dramatize yourself considerably, putting on acts of *Weltschmerz,* discouragement, woe, and gloom when even you won't know how much is real and how much is made up. This position inclines to the possibility of two marriages, and, anyway, a good deal of romance.

76

SUN IN LIBRA—MOON IN CANCER

YOU ARE exceedingly adaptable and able to take on the color of your surroundings, much to your advantage in the business and social worlds. Your adaptability, coupled with quickness of perception, endears you to people of importance and makes your rise rapid and even spectacular. Your are sensitive, intellectually as well as emotionally, and feel your way carefully, if quickly, in contacts with people. You have a habit of anticipating what another person is thinking and fitting your mood and opinion to his. Your manner is inherently flattering without being subservient or obsequious, for you have a keen sense of your own dignity and importance. Innately peaceful and tactful, you will avoid argument and strife if you possibly can, by forestalling unpleasant situations. But where your pride or your personal rights are interfered with, you will fight and are capable of a good deal of temper and temperament. You are an individualist so far as you yourself are concerned, but you have little interest in the rights of others. By minding your own business you manage not to interfere with others, but you aren't a fighter for social justice or the rights of the masses. Your aims and philosophies are pretty well centered in yourself, and though you can grasp generalities they don't interest you especially. Your flexibiliby and adaptability can amount to weakness if you allow the personal, romantic, sensational side of your nature to dominate, for then the desire to please takes destructive form, and you please people who aren't worth it and agree to ideas that are fundamentally unsound. You have to look out for this because, under the spell of romance or emotional stimulus, your "willingness" can absorb your "will."

With 151, 164, 181 or 182, these traits are accentuated, and impressionability becomes a danger because temperament and independence are marked. With 163 or 180, your purposes are stabilized, and ambition becomes a driving force that takes you far. The romantic nature is present but controlled, and an inner hardness removes the danger from your adaptability. With 200, 210, 201, 211, 203, 213, 204 or 214, emotional quirks and escapades cause excitement; with 202, 212, sorrow through sentimentality and impressionability. With 215, 216, 217, 218, 227, 228, 229 or 237, ambition is marked and leads to authority and prestige.

77

SUN IN LIBRA—MOON IN LEO

THIS IS ONE of the romantic positions whether the romanticism takes the form of poetry and art, or whether it simply makes you susceptible to romance in its less constructive form. With 163, 164, 181, 177, 200, 204, 229, 237, 215 or 217, creative art of some sort will be your best medium of expression. With 210, 203, 213, 204, 214, 171, 182 or 165, you must guard against the less desirable manifestations of romance. With some of each of these paragraphs you are a temperamental, but able, person. Some of this quality of temperament and ability will attach to you in any case. Your ideals are your guiding stars, and you will stick to them to the end, believing in them as in a religion. There is something devotional about your nature anyway, both in matters of human affection and also in a more abstract way. You have an active and conscious idealism which you always strive to live up to, and in some way or other generally succeed. You are independent, especially where your love or your ideals are concerned— or your art, if you are an artist. You believe in art for art's (and for your own) sake and are unlikely to let considerations of commercial value or of expediency interfere with either your art or your love. You are ardent, sincere, and honorable in your love, and with 200, 203, and 204, without squares to Venus, you may expect an ideal attachment to be the outcome of a rather checkered love-life.

With 210, 212, 213 or 214, the same idealism is yours, but it is less happily rewarded. With 163, 161, 164, 165 or 160 in a male horoscope, or 178, 180, 181 or 182 in a female, there is difficulty through members of the opposite sex, idealism frequently finding poor response in the people selected. This position gives you considerable ambition of a very high-minded sort, but unless there are squares to the Sun or Moon, you become relaxed and don't find or create opportunities for expression. With many triangles to the Sun and Moon, relaxation is present but it doesn't matter; you're taken care of economically and emotionally. With squares to the Sun and Moon you rise by personal effort and the creation of your own opportunities; but you have to be careful that your naturally trusting nature is not fooled by unscrupulous and unworthy people. There is a kind of naïveté about you that invites deception and you have to learn to be unforgiving and to remember your unpleasant experiences. You are such an idealist and such an optimist that the blows of the world glance off you. You remember the pleasant and forget the unpleasant — an admirable trait in personal dealings so long as you learn by experience what sort of thing to watch out for the next time.

78

SUN IN LIBRA—MOON IN VIRGO

YOUR INTELLECTUAL QUALITIES are likely to absorb a good deal of the warmth of your nature, for you are a self-sufficient person. You reason things out and are not likely to be swept off your feet by anything emotional that doesn't fit your needs. You are affectionate, love attention, and quickly learn that you can't get attention without giving something in return. You have a feeling for other people's needs that makes you appear more warm-hearted than you really are. You're analytical, critical, and observant; and you will do best in some literary or creative occupation where your mental and artistic gifts will be rewarded directly. In business you can progress through these traits, though business is foreign to your natural bent. Reasonable in argument, you are none the less capable of doing exactly what you please. You are persuasive and peace-loving and keep the peace through your reasonable method of debating things. You "get things off your chest" readily and don't go around holding grudges. You can develop tact to a high degree once you learn that everything isn't as cut and dried to everyone as it is to you. But despite this you are somewhat too positive a person to go through life without making enemies and when you've antagonized someone you have a hard time winning him back. He pursues you pretty relentlessly, and you have to give in, for you are not a fighter, and when your peaceful methods of passive resistance fail, you are bewildered.

With 168, aggression helped, but also danger of creating enemies thereby; also with 178, 147, 161; much diplomacy required. With 167, 169, 174, 176 or 177, charm increased and powerful friends are helpful; with 183, 189, 145, 146, intellectual attainments and artistic tastes marked; with 148, considerable influence and rise through these; with 163, creative powers bring success; with 149 and 227, great authority and respect.

With 200, 210, 202, 212, 203, 213, 204 or 214, marked difficulties through love affairs, but without these, you are rather self-sufficient, though 168, 178, 171, 181 or 182 will give you the appearance of being pretty romantic. With 182, 181, *and* 180, very erratic and temperamental and any one of these alone will be sufficient to bring out temperament in some marked degree, as well as 171. With 170, introversion. With 180, ambition keen, if none of the other temperamental paragraphs are included.

79

SUN IN LIBRA—MOON IN LIBRA

YOU ARE ROMANTIC with a sort of mystic faith in other people and the power of others to help you, that may meet with scant justification in the world as you find it. Sensitive, daydreaming, you are likely to be hurt by the impact of romance, and by the worldliness of other people which will seem gross and unideal to you. From this injury you are all too prone to seek flight, either in the inner recesses of your own consciousness, or in occult studies—spiritualism—anything that is otherworldly, remote, detached, ideal rather than real, spiritual rather than corporeal. You are gullible and easily led, especially when your emotional nature is appealed to, and through wearing your heart on your sleeve you are rather likely to have it punctured. There's a sort of ethereal quality about you that lends you grace and charm. You are a creature of another planet—probably Venus, the planet of love—where human relations may be as ideal as you wish them to be; but until you learn to take people as you find them here on earth, you are in for a lot of jolts. There is a certain intellectual precociousness to this position—you develop early, before your emotional nature is matured, and, in the presence of loving parents, can be the joy of the house as a child. Harshness and unkindness, sharp words, anger, are anathema to you. This is the position of Sweet Alice (Ben Bolt) who "wept with delight if you gave her a smile, and trembled with fear at your frown." In the presence of such aspect as 180 or 170, 149 or 163, you may have some success in managing others, for then your innate sympathy, kindliness, and charity receive direction and force, and you may be the kind of executive who rules by love rather than by force.

With 147, 161, 168, 178, 181, 182, 200, 202, 203, 204, 210, 212, 213, 214, 224 or 225, much hurt through the affectional nature. With 204 or 214, impressionability leads you astray. With 147, 149, 168, 170, 150 or 171, emotional introversion dangerous. Spiritualism, occultism, and all forms of abstruse studies, though appealing, only draw you further from reality and obscure, rather than solve, your problem of coping with the world and people, realistically, as they are, even at the sacrifice of some of your ideology.

80

SUN IN LIBRA—MOON IN SCORPIO

(You belong to the positive or executive group)

INDEPENDENCE of mind and action, thought and expression, are the outstanding traits of your nature. You are quick mentally, with a penetrating and absorbing curiosity, so that you are a ready student, precocious and facile. You make rapid strides in the world and are stamped with a keen ambition the following of which is an intimate need with you. You are interested in broad, sweeping matters—in ideas, philosophies, the arts and sciences—and for this reason are more likely to select a professional or artistic than a business career. Your interest is in the minds of men—what they have done and what they can do—and your respect for yourself is rooted in your respect for your own mental processes. In some way or another you will "live by your wits"—that is, by ideas rather than by hard work; and this may be in literature, science, or politics. You are, in any case, a radical, on the side of change, progress, and novelty. You are a natural born rebel, and will always be found where a battle of wits or ideas is in progress—and very likely in the minority corner. You are a keen controversialist, for you think with sharp precision and express yourself so as to leave no doubt about where you stand. You're not without your peculiar kind of tact, but you despise a pussy-footer or a kowtower and will say so to his face if the opportunity arises. You don't like to hurt people's feelings but will risk that rather than abandon the truth as you see it. You are staunch in support of merit wherever you find it and will espouse new or losing causes with all the fervor of a zealot. You are an enthusiast in loves, hates, intellectual or artistic matters, or politics. Emotionally you are ardent and intense, and although you think of yourself as being self-sufficient, you really are not at all and do best when you've settled your emotional life by having someone around you to balance your enthusiasms, although you would probably hoot at the idea that you need anyone at all. You are independent, and likely to lead your friends (sweethearts) a merry song and dance.

With 159, 161, 147, 150, 164, 165, 171 or 181 eccentricity increased, an irascible nature needful of much self-discipline, but with an inspirational quality that gets forgiveness from the world. With 163 or 180, concentrative powers helped, much success. With 149, depressed periods of great intensity. With 183 or 188, very artistic; with 184, 186 or 187, scientific, critical and brilliant mind. With 200, 210, intense emotional nature, love-life makes trouble; also with 203, 213, 214, when impressionability is dangerous. With 202 or 212, early emotionalism grows cold and produces a somewhat detached and suspicious person but very able and likely to rise to considerable power, especially if 202 is involved.

81

SUN IN LIBRA—MOON IN SAGITTARIUS

(You belong to the positive or executive group)

THIS IS an idealistic, aspiring, adventurous, and romantic position and may take the form of high-minded climbing the ladder of success, or of mere adventuresomeness and romance. With 168, 178, 181, 182, 161, 150, 164, 165, 200, 210, 203, 213 or 214, the personal, sensational side of the nature will overbalance the more idealistic and philosophic side. You will have a good time, though not without emotional ups and downs, for pleasure will mean a lot to you. With 146, 148, 163, 169, 174, 180, 185, 176 or 177, the more idealistic and aspiring side shows out; you persist in some personal career and generally arrive through your own charm and efforts. You have an ability to see things in the large and to judge the future by the present and the past, which lends an almost prophetic quality to your insight and foresight. You are too proud and independent and can make enemies through stiff-neckedness. You are gracious but don't give the impression of being warm-hearted; people tend to respect you, but whether they love you or not depends on how readily you can learn to unbend and come down to their level. You are interested in large ideas — in religion, philosophy, science — and whether you have a trained mind or not, you have a certain facility for abstract thought. This can make you completely visionary and impractical in business and personal matters if you do not deliberately pin yourself down to earth. You are physically active, fond of travel, and likely to be always on the go. A highly social sense takes you to parties and gatherings and you're never so happy as when you're getting up a big picnic. You are generous with your emotions when you are romantically inclined (which you periodically are) and can appear fickle and ardent at one and the same time. You have a rather contradictory emotional nature, your ideals failing to keep you from its expression perhaps in very independent ways. You tend to be nervous, high-strung, and impulsive.

With 147, 161, 149, 163, 150, 164, 165, 170, 171, 178, 180 or 181, nerves are a real problem to you. With 202, 212, disappointment and discontent through love. You are likely to be a little discontented anyway. Feet on the ground, and a determination to cope with the world as you find it, will bring the largest rewards to your optimism and independence.

82

SUN IN LIBRA—MOON IN CAPRICORN

YOU ARE purposeful. You know what you want, and one way or another you're likely to get it. You have tact and a gift for managing people that usually puts you out in front, whatever your scope or circle may be. With

163 and/or 180, this purpose of yours is especially well formed and your nature somewhat hardened in going after it and getting it. You are a shrewd and dangerous antagonist, subtle, sure of yourself, and capable of getting what you want by opportunistic methods. With 150 and/or 165, you are more nervous and jittery in the search of your ambition, but you will probably get there, unless also with 181 and/or 182, in which case nerves eat up your energy and your purpose.

With 168 or 178, personal problems absorb you and create destructive temperament; with 161, purpose flags after a brilliant start. But under any circumstances you are a highly reckonable person, socially competent, and able to manage your own life, your own circle, and probably a much larger circle, to your own satisfaction and their benefit. You may be a very domineering person (see paragraphs above) or you may be sweet and gracious, but whichever you may appear on the surface, those who know you understand well enough that you aren't going to be successfully opposed and that some way or other things will work out the way you want them to. You have a tremendous amount of self-respect, even ego; though unless with some of the above paragraph numbers you may be apparently reticent about it. Personal popularity you like, but you must see in your world the tangible evidence of your worth and you see to it that it is there. This is a highly variable position and may make you arrogant and bold or diplomatic and gracious; but in any case, the underlying motive is the same: you want the good opinion of your world, and you take the means which that world calls for. You're an opportunist and can build a single stone of opportunity into a whole skyscraper of success single-handed. Your driving force is great and you have a sense for the feelings and opinions of others that is an extremely valuable asset; you're highly aware of other people as they touch you, though you have no sense of impersonal social matters and aren't likely to be found in humanitarian enterprises. Life is real and earnest to you but it is also highly personal and a little selfish and self-centered. But you are so sensitive to the feelings of others and to your own need of their good opinion that you endear yourself to those around you, who both recognize your worth and love you.

83

SUN IN LIBRA—MOON IN AQUARIUS

YOU ARE a romantic of *the* romantics. Affection and love are not only physical needs but assume the proportion of a philosophy, a creed, a coat of arms. You radiate, with a sort of fragile and glamorous appeal that makes you popular with the other sex, and though there is nothing abstract or theoretic about your love-nature, you elevate your emotions with a high idealism. An overtone of good taste and breeding lends sanction to your most unconventional escapades and raises you from the purely sensational to the higher planes which your ideology demands. Apparently happy-go-lucky, there's a brooding sense of the seriousness of life underlying your flippancy. You are conscious of sorrow and tragedy and even have a way of making them up for yourself and your friends where little or no basis for them exists. You are a dramatist at heart and like nothing better than to weave patterns of blighted love, misplaced affection, lost affinities, and the like. Meantime, like as not, the pitied one is leading a contented if unexciting life with his (her) own wife (husband) utterly oblivious of the misery into which you have plunged him. Your imagination is thus capable of running away with you, and your flights of fancy may lead you to make somewhat tangled realities out of the fabric of your dreams. You are an artist at heart, and if strong intellectual indications occur you will do a lot with your romantic imagination in creative literature or in some branch of art.

With 166, 167, 183, 189, 215 or 218, this creative flair is prominent, but if there aren't any squares to the Sun or Moon, a sheltered life precludes the real experiences that would bring you into creative action. With 168 or 178, romantic difficulties are marked, bringing out talent at the same time that they don't make you happy. With 161, early promise and verge disappear early. With 147, material welfare removes the economic impetus to success, increasing romanticism by providing leisure. With 163, deep tragic sense can make a profound artist. With 149, introvert.

This is a good position for luck in life but not in itself for energy or ambition. You're protected, and things come easily to you. With 148 or 169, extraordinary luck; you marry well. This is considerably a better position for a woman than for a man, for a woman will be popular socially and protected from want and worry to a considerable extent (except what worries she makes up); while a man, though equally popular, has to fight for the drive and ambition that makes for success.

84

SUN IN LIBRA—MOON IN PISCES

YOUR RESERVE and shyness are your strengths, for in solitude and timidity you build up strength and inner poise which, when expressed in the world, lends your personality a peculiar charm that comes from your reserve. You are sociable, capable of wide popularity, yet, however charming and gracious you may be, people sense that you have depths they cannot probe and an air of mystery hangs around you that increases your interest. You're impressionable, romantic, just, and sincere. You are capable of grasping abstractions and intricacies, both mentally and emotionally and you have a trick of appearing very obvious and plausible when you may be actually very subtle and involved. You can outguess almost anyone for you are a born diplomat or detective. The crooked ways are straight to you, and, utterly honest yourself, you can scent a crook at five hundred yards and track him down. You are intuitive rather than intellectual, and you glean knowledge from observation rather than from deep study. You are a student of human nature and know your fellow men with a disturbing accuracy. You are capable, however, under the spell of romance or adventure, of being fooled in people. This is when you fail to follow your hunches for you are not likely to go far wrong when you follow your secret heart. This is a position that can bring you considerable prestige through dealings with the general public, and which will make you felt in whatever circle you move; you have an unusual personality. You can change from expansive to secretive in a minute and are capable of falling into moodiness which can be very dangerous to your peace of mind. You feel the woes of the world keenly; inequalities depress you. You are a lover of justice, and of Liberté, Egalité, Fraternité.

With 148, 155, 147, 151, 163, 169, 174, 167, 176 or 177, broad scope, and great humanitarian interests; with 215, 218, 227 or 229, wealth. With 200, 210, 211, 203, 213, 204 or 214, emotionalism makes you more personal, with trouble through love; with 202 or 212, frustrations in emotional matters depress you but broaden your interests and can lay the groundwork for a career of large scope in humanistic fields. With 183, 187, 188, 201, 203 or 204, highly idealistic mind, artistic and conscious of social needs. This is a position of the philosophic Utopian, rather than of the revolutionary, who will none the less work practically for the betterment of the people and for his own betterment.

85

SUN IN SCORPIO—MOON IN ARIES

(You belong to the positive or executive group)

YOU ARE a realist, and the center of your highly tangible world is yourself, first, last, and always. You aren't interested in generalizations or abstractions; your ambition is definite and highly personal; your loyalties are to people rather than to ideas; your loves, your hates, your resentments, are all formed in terms of individuals. You have little feeling for right, wrong, justice, philosophy, metaphysics, in the abstract; but as any one of these touches you, or someone you are interested in, you are capable of becoming strenuously interested. When you are aroused by a personal animus you are capable of voluble and forceful resentments; quarrels can occupy you to the exclusion of everything else; you love a good fight and usually don't have to live long without one. You are mentally quick, shrewd, and highly protective, with an accurate, critical mind capable of hard work and long scientific analysis. The one abstraction you find easiest to grasp is Ambition, which you promptly apply to yourself and seek out to fulfill. You are ardent and passionate in love, but not an easy person to be in love with. You are demanding, exacting, and a bit vain, and require the ultimate in devotion and consideration, which, you may by no means be willing to give in return. There's a cold streak underlying your passion, and if with 200, 210, 202, 212, 216, 224, 217, 225, 236 or 240 you may be downright cruel. With these numbers, too, you will have and cause unhappiness through love matters. You never become completely depersonalized but the more objective your viewpoint can become, the happier you will be and the happier you will make those around you. Your nature is considerably softened by 148, 155, 169 or 174; and rendered dangerously susceptible to flattery by 147, 148, 204, 214, 170 or 171—with these, also look out for bad companions—wolves in sheep's clothing—for despite your protectiveness you are not invulnerable and can be lulled into an unvigilant calm from which you are rudely awakened when it may be too late. You have a high temper which can be explosive to the danger point, and you are so wrapped up in yourself and your own purposes that you aren't a very good judge of people and can get mixed up with some pretty undesirable characters who will do you harm. By looking around you more and paying less attention to your own aims, purposes, and emotions, you develop your abilities, and stand to progress through energy, forcefulness, and a magnetic control over people.

86

SUN IN SCORPIO—MOON IN TAURUS

(You belong to the positive or executive group)

YOUR THOUGHTS, emotions, plans, and aims are all on a wide and sweeping scale; you think in the grand manner, and everything you do is touched with a bigness of purpose; little things don't interest you—small amounts of money, petty emotions, or little plans you simply don't understand. If, with your grandeur of thought and plan, you can keep your feet on the ground, you will have remarkable material success, for you have good shrewd business judgment which, hitched to the high star of your aspirations, will take you far. If you don't keep your feet on the ground, then your sweep of thought will take you into impractical realms of metaphysical speculation, mysticism, and the like. As a matter of fact, under any circumstances, you have a liberal dose of superstition. You believe in your luck, in signs, omens, and portents; you believe in your own magnetic powers with an almost devotional belief, and you are likely to have good luck charms around you, or to think some person brings good luck to you. You have a way of controlling people through your charm, a surface glamour of personality concealing the hard purposes beneath and winning people to your cause. You are an opportunist, a pragmatist—anything is right to you, if it works. You are not especially magnanimous. Your largeness of vision includes material plans and, in a sense, ideas and philosophies, but not personal dealings, in which you can be petty, vindictive, jealous, and grudge-holding. You are not a good loser, especially if loss involves what you consider loss of dignity; once you have made up your mind that something is going to happen, you take it as a personal affront if it doesn't, even if the weather is to blame. You will sulk at a rainstorm that interferes with your plans just as if the rainstorm were bent on balking you. You have excessive pride and are a jealous and imperious lover, though not especially a constant one.

With Mars in Scorpio, 147, 168, 149, 170, 163 or 180, great rise to power, and sudden fall therefrom; with 148, 149, 151 and/or 158, more stable authority of a dynamic and practical nature; possibility of great wealth and influence. With 200, 215, 218, 228, 229, great wealth; with 227, power and influence on the grand scale.

You are a judicial person, a stern and even harsh judge of your fellows, and not always inclined to temper justice with mercy; and you should remember, as you are scaling your heights and leaving the lesser ones behind, that there is a law of compensations, and that "with the same measure that ye mete withal it shall be measured to you again." In personal and business matters there comes a day of reckoning, and when the chickens come home to roost, look out for the one that you shied a shoe at.

87

SUN IN SCORPIO—MOON IN GEMINI

YOU HAVE an impressive personality, with a flair for people that makes you excessively popular; a quality of reserve lends charm to your surprisingly vocal and voluble manner of expression. You have a keen sense of humor, love a good story and tell stories exceedingly well. You give an appearance of great decision and determination, and you alone are likely to know how, inwardly, you are frequently undecisive and wavering at the very moment when you are appearing most sure of yourself. You are likely to miss opportunities through being unable to make up your mind, and to get yourself into trouble through the good-naturedness of your human relations. You are clever, quick, facile, and can learn anything; you have hobbies which may be quite intricate and take up a lot of your time; for one job, one interest, or one sweetheart is not enough to absorb you. If you are a man, this makes you very popular with women, who rather like your combination of ardor and detachment, romanticism and cynicism; however, this doesn't make you very true in love matters, which are in a class with other hobbies. What you need chiefly in all things is ability to concentrate and to integrate your purposes; for, in one way or another, life tends to be pretty easy for you. Either you are lucky and things come to you, or you are happy-go-lucky and don't care. The inner drive to success is somewhat lacking and you tend to drift through life amused by the spectacle, enjoying yourself as you go, adaptable and able to adjust yourself quickly to new circumstances. You tend to make your requirements fit your capital. Your aims and desires are not very important to you; what you want chiefly is comfort—and this comfort requires little for its satisfaction. You are a very easy person to get along with so long as you aren't interfered with; but you are capable of getting stubborn if you think someone is trying to manage you. There is a streak of perversity here, and you'll make an issue of something that you don't really care about just to show that you can't be imposed on.

With 163, 180, 147 or 168, ambition and concentrative power are helped; with 151, 164, 188, 199 or 160, unreliable and diffusive mentality, with an inclination, one way or another, to live by your wits, and by mental agility rather than by hard work. With 200, 210, 211, 203, 213 or 214, lots of romance. If with 202 or 212, much sorrow through the opposite sex.

88

SUN IN SCORPIO—MOON IN CANCER

(You belong to the positive or executive group)

YOU ARE a magnetic individual, with a tremendous amount of self-confidence, and an intuitive understanding of the world and of people. You don't go out of your way very much for people; you think well of yourself and let your friends come to you. If they don't come, that's all right, too; you are capable of self-sufficiency that can amount to smugness if you aren't careful. You are strongly opinionated, capable of defending your position by argument, although logic is not so important to you as winning your point. You have a twisting-and-turning type of mind that can be the despair of your adversaries in discussion, especially if they are so foolish as to think they can hold you down to reason. Your emotions are very powerful, your intuitions keen, and you have a great respect for your hunches. You are extremely sensitive, emotionally impressionable, and also able to impress the opposite sex. You absorb your sweethearts and demand that they toe the mark pretty strictly. Your method of reasoning in this matter is strongly tinged with emotion and especially with jealousy; the emotion of dislike or even hate can take up all your emotional force and completely drive out love, if you think your feelings have not been properly considered; and you are capable of swinging like a pendulum between extremes of emotion. You are suspicious, shrewd, especially when a personal issue is at stake, and will probe into people to get at their private lives if they give you half a chance; contrariwise, you shut up like a clam about your own private life, and things concerning yourself can't be pried out of you with a crowbar.

With 161, brilliant mind, high ambition, becoming petty as the years go on. With 168 or 178, quarrelsome and contentious nature; with 180, stable ambitions, success, a somewhat hard nature; with 215, 218, 227, 229 or 237, wealth; with 226, great personal magnetism, mystical-minded, spiritual. With 160, 200, 210 or 214, trouble through sensationalism; also with 182. With 151 and/or 164, confused mental processes, misled through fixed ideas and unwillingness to learn, stubborn, sensitive, sentimental. With 156 or 176, relaxation of energies is the danger, self-satisfaction, and smugness; lack of driving force. A good position for a doctor or a nurse.

89

SUN IN SCORPIO—MOON IN LEO

YOU HAVE a strong, positive personality; fixed opinions and emotions; great stability of purpose; and if you do not let yourself live on the strictly emotional side of your nature—which is very strong—you are capable of becoming a person of considerable influence and importance. The danger of your nature comes from emotional involvement; you are strongly impressed by romantic considerations, and you can take up all your energy dreaming and thinking about the far away and long ago, or about love in some manifestation or other. You are, with respect to love, somewhat idealistic, but with a realistic approach to matters of sex; you are no prude, though you give, and expect in return, loyalty and fidelity. You have a very complete ideology of life, not all of it too realistic; for emotional disappointments and frustrations have driven you to ideals, concepts, and abstractions of philosophy which seem visionary to more practical people. None the less, you find a lot of satisfaction in your dreams, your only danger being that they will absorb you too completely. Few people can live up to the high standards you set for them; and even when you are swept off your feet by anger, romance, hatred, jealousy, or revenge, you maintain the idea that you are really an idealist, and that your temporary lapse isn't really you at all. This is all right, if the lapses don't become habitual; but you have to hold yourself very strongly in leash, so that the Old Adam in you doesn't beat down the Regenerate Man. You can be of the earth earthy; and sensationalism can gain a tremendous hold on you if you are not careful. It is to combat this tendency, of which you are conscious (or subconscious), that you have built up your complex system of ideals.

The dangers of sensationalism are increased with 160, 147, 161, 150, 151, 165, 168, 178, 171, 181, 182, 200, 210, 203, 213, 214, 218, 226, 240, 241 or 244: with any of these your will comes to your rescue, for you have the most powerful of wills and need it. With 236, nerves are a problem; also with 170, 171, 224, 225, 226, 240 or 241. Your great magnetism, when working without the disadvantage of personal bias, can make you a leader, for you can make people do as you want, and can gain tremendous control over them when you have learned objectivity and detachment from your emotions.

90

SUN IN SCORPIO—MOON IN VIRGO

(You belong to the positive or executive group)

THERE IS never any doubt about where you stand; your mental activity, your awareness of the world around you, and your willingness to express what you think and feel, color your opinions with an amazing honesty. Even when diplomacy may dictate restraint in expression, you know well enough what you are thinking. Whoever else you may be fooling, it isn't going to be yourself. Your intellectual talents are marked, and so strongly personal is your outlook that some artistic career giving yourself personal expression is your best career medium. Your ambition is for expression, security, and personal recognition, rather than for power and authority; and whatever power you do achieve will be in influence over the minds of men, rather than in domination over their activities. Awareness of the world makes you voluble in expression of political opinions. You are a reformer, but on the intellectual rather than the social plane; you want to make men think, and you'll leave their feeding and governing to someone else. Emotionally, you are ardent and magnetic with a good deal of sex appeal. You have a curious kind of loyalty, which doesn't prevent frequent strayings from the fold; but you generally come back again. You are magnetically attractive to others and can't resist testing out your powers, which can get you into trouble, though you get out of it. You hate to have people prying into your private affairs and resist any attempt to ferret out your private life. On the other hand, you love to listen to gossip and even pass it on —not always with kindly intent. You can be very sharp-spoken when you like, capable of hating as well as loving. Your thrusts have a certain cold detachment about them that makes them the more effective, as if you scorn, rather than hate, the victim.

With 148 or 146, considerably softened nature, sentimental; with 147 or 150, excessively clever, original, and independent mind; with 149, 163, austere, ambitious. With 229 or 237, considerable influence; with 180, dispassionate determination to succeed; with 170 or 236, inertia, high temper, difficulty in expressing, deep sense of inner worth, resentful of opposition. With 183, 187, 188 or 189, creative gifts marked, an influential mind; with 183 and 192, markedly scientific, critical, and studious.

In any case, you are a highly critical person, both of other people and of abstract, artistic or literary matters. Something of a gourmet, loving food and drink and all the nice things of life, with an independence that does not run counter to the dictates of good taste and accepted usage. You have little sense of sin, but keen sense of public opinion, and generally manage to keep the good opinion of the world while you're getting away with murder.

91

SUN IN SCORPIO—MOON IN LIBRA

YOU WILL LEARN a lot of lessons through your emotional nature as you go along in life for at the beginning you are as a lamb among wolves. You have a certain naïveté and ardor combined which brings you knocks and jolts as you discover that everyone is not as direct as you are and can't be trusted to live up to your high concept of people, life, love, and human relations. As experience teaches you suspicion, your discrimination increases. You bring to your judgments a high degree of good taste and idealism that makes you a highly constructive force in whatever branch of society you may be. Your idealism becomes tinged with practicality without losing its high standards. You learn to understand people without being unduly suspicious. You develop worldliness, but it does not take the romantic glamour of idealism from your personality. You are highly sociable, with a great deal of poise and a charm of manner which makes people feel they are necessary to you—which indeed they are, though not as necessary as they may think. You are gracious, affable, and courteous at the same time that you never lose an iota of dignity. Your self-confidence amounts almost to pride, but it rarely becomes offensive. You know how to make everyone at ease and are an incomparable host or hostess. In love you are ardent, sincere, loyal, and romantic—an ideal sweetheart, tolerant of the wishes of others, and sensitive to their needs. You have feelers out constantly for other people's reactions, opinions, sensations, and can glean more from a word, a look, an expression, or a mannerism than most people can from volumes of explanation.

With 146, 148, 167 or 169, good-fellowship marked and great popularity and success; also if with 215, 217, 229 or 237. With 163 or 180, ambition marked and success comes through persistence and ability. With 147, 161, 168, 178, 164, 165, 171, 181, 182, 200, 210, 203, 204, 213 or 214, super-social—difficulties through love affairs, with tendency to go to excess in matters of the emotions. Inconstancy and unconventionality. With 184, 185, 186, 187, 188 or 183, exceptional mind, capable of high artistic, critical, or scientific development and likely to prove a wide influence through mental or creative work.

92

SUN IN SCORPIO—MOON IN SCORPIO

(You belong to the positive or executive group)

YOUR CREATIVE FORCE is terrific, and whether it expresses itself in riotous emotions, a creative-executive type of business career, or in art, depends on how you utilize the enormous energy and magnetism that are yours. In its least desirable and most negative expression this leads to sensationalists, romantics, and love-affairists. You will have a powerful sex-nature and will control your sweethearts utterly. It requires a strong degree of self-discipline for you not to dominate all those with whom you come into contact, for the coöperative spirit is not strong and the will-to-power, in personal matters, great. You are the rule-or-ruin sort, and if you run into someone you can't rule, you are likely to fight with him, separate from him, then say unkind things about him. When your devotion is fixed, you are capable of the extremes of loyalty. But it takes a strong and tactful person to hold you, and even then you require a good deal of flattery, for your vanity is great, and you like to be made to feel that you rule the roost—which, in one way or another, you pretty generally do. If you marry a person with pride in his own right (and you would despise anyone who didn't have it) this trait is likely to lead to quarrels and separations. You have a quality of subjugating people and then despising them for being weak, which makes you a tough bird to satisfy. Though desirous of personal and individual power, authority, and position, you aren't ambitious in the worldly sense. Despite your powerful executive traits, you are more likely than not to refuse to enter the arena of competition in business or politics and to devote yourself to private satisfactions. This is a strong position for creative activity if you don't waste your energies in conquering other people in romantic ways or use up your vitality in pride, anger, hatred, or contempt for the rest of the world. The missionary spirit is strong in you, and in high types you are a great preacher and reformer, having tremendous self-control and a despite for those who haven't. With 148, 155, 156, 169, 174, 175 or 173, these traits will be powerful. You control yourself and others, having an easy, satisfying, and influential life.

With 163 or 180, temperamental, gifted, erratic ups and downs, emotionally and financially. With 161 or 178, explosive temper (present in some degree anyway). With 181 or 182, unconventional and erratic nature; sensationalist. Idealism misguided leads to trouble; the will to power rebounds to your disadvantage. The Scorpio symbolism is either the Scorpion or the Eagle—crawling the depths or soaring the heights —and you are well aware of the dual power of your nature. A sort of awareness of yourself and others is your outstanding quality and you see through people with a penetrating insight and a kind of accusing understanding that makes you an associate to be reckoned with, conciliated, and perhaps feared.

93

SUN IN SCORPIO—MOON IN SAGITTARIUS

YOU ARE an unusual person, idealistic, somewhat aloof from life in your viewpoint, tending to live in a philosophic world of your own. You are an idealist, and the world tends to confuse you somewhat. You feel injustice, inequality, hardness and coldness keenly, for you are warm-hearted and affectionate and want nothing better than that men should live in peace. You are social-minded, eager to help others, and unable to understand why others are not eager to help you. You are willing to help yourself all right enough, but opportunity is lacking; a kind of visionary haze gets between you and reality, and you have difficulty getting going. You are affectionate, loyal, sincere almost to a fault, with an expansive nature that makes people love you; you are proud and conscious of your own worth. You will do best in some idealistic professional pursuit—medicine, religion, law, public life—where you can put your idealism into practise as a dedicated public servant, in social work or in the arts—music, painting, poetry. You are somewhat too idealistic for business and probably would rebel at anything that you thought smacked of shrewdness or smartness. And what you disapprove of you will not do for all the money in the world. You like nice things, luxuries, and good times, but you won't buy them at the price of your honor, and so, to your associates, you may seem too high-minded.

With 168, 178, 170, 180, 171, 181 or 182, the nature is hardened somewhat and aggression is easier for you; with 147, 161, 149, 163 or 164, idealism and independence strengthened, with more ability to put them across practically; if with 165, confusion of aims muddles up your career. Strive for education and a career in the professions or the arts, where your idealism can be put to work as it cannot be in business.

94

SUN IN SCORPIO—MOON IN CAPRICORN

INDEPENDENCE marks you for her own—you have a cavalier disregard for public opinion in respect to your private life and a judicious estimate of what the public wants in respect to your public life, so that you are a colorful figure in whatever sphere you move. Your scope and influence may become very wide, for you have the real thing in ambition and will demand recognition for your talents. You are a pioneer in thought and influence and know how to express your circle, your times, with force and with courage. You are an ardent protagonist for the right, the friend of the underdog—a sort of accusing angel, conscious of moral and social values and eager to impress your concepts on any who come within your ken. You are logical, intellectual, fair in argument, but very set in your opinions; you cannot be wheedled or coaxed from what you think is the right, but you are highly amenable to reason and can see the other fellow's side if it hasn't anything in it that you consider dishonorable. If you think it dishonorable, you see his viewpoint just as well and don't hesitate to tell him what you think of it. Despite your independence you have a just regard for the social amenities and will not do anything to offend good taste—if you can help it. But if it comes to a choice between living your private life as you want it and conciliating public opinion, then public opinion can go hang. Emotionally, you are sincere, honorable, loyal, and ardent. The sex-life is important to you.

With 200, 210, 203, 213, 204, 214, 150, 165, 168, 178, 171, 180, 181 or 182, sensationalism can take up a good deal too much of your time. With 215, 217, 218, 227, 229, 237, large amount of luck in life, influence and authority as well as wealth (true also in lesser degree if with 147, 148, 149, 154, 155, 156, 157 or 158). With 163, ambition powerfully marked, with outstanding success and recognition; if with 170 and/or 171 nerves need attention, some danger of introversion through misdirection of the emotional nature.

This is a powerful polarity and integrates the personality toward success, the extent of which is determined by the above paragraph numbers but which is likely to be felt in ambition and enterprise in any case.

95

SUN IN SCORPIO—MOON IN AQUARIUS

(You belong to the positive or executive group)

THIS IS a visionary and idealistic polarity of Sun and Moon. Pride is strongly marked in you, and you set great store by intellectual and artistic accomplishment, so that with 147, 163, or 180, your perfectionist spirit may find expression in some high form of artistic accomplishment. You are a powerful and independent thinker, a good student, bringing a philosophy and viewpoint of your own to bear on intellectual and social problems and so likely to be influential in molding the opinions of those around you. If this occurs with 215, 216, 217, 218, 227, 228, 229 or 237, your scope and influence may become very broad. There's some intolerance here of divergent opinions, which, because you do not believe in intolerance, you manage to cover up. You like flattery, and if you are a business man you are probably an executive surrounded by yes-men—whom you despise. But this is only one of the contradictions of your nature. You like adulation, but unless you know in your heart that you deserve it you have no respect for the applauders. Yet you are such a strong personality that people instinctively accept your opinions. You have to look out that you don't get in the habit of speaking *ex cathedra,* in the expectation that people will agree with you, for every once in a while someone punctures the balloon of your ego, much to your consternation. Under all your sureness you are a very sensitive person, affectionate and loving, with a great need for gentleness. You have a keen imagination, a real sense of the frustration and tragedy of life, both of your own and of others, and you are capable of being sorry for yourself and genuinely sympathetic with others, though you are reserved and don't express sympathy or any deep emotion readily. Intellectually you are voluble enough; emotionally, you tend to be inarticulate, and friends and sweethearts have to accept you at face value till they learn the depths that are there. You are likely to strike sensitive people as cold, but if they can get under the surface they are likely to be surprised.

With 202 or 212, emotional discontent and some self-pity; with 200, 210, 226, 203, 213, 204 or 214, difficulty through misplaced or misguided affections; with 170, 171 or 148, introversion, dejection dangerous to peace of mind. Your aspirations, pinned down to earth and given realistic expression, will take you far, but kept in the realm of possibility or fantasy, produce a sense of frustration and discontent.

96

SUN IN SCORPIO—MOON IN PISCES

YOU ARE an intellectual, whether in science or in the arts or merely on the appreciative side. With 151, 168, 147, 163 or 180, creative literary gifts; with 170, 216, 184, 186 or 187, scientific bent is strong. In any case you belong to that critical and appreciative public without which art and science are useless and pointless. You are sensitive, intuitive, with infinite discrimination, with respect to both works of art and people. You have an instinct for the right thing. This may make you hypercritical, especially with 147, 149, 168, 170, 171, 184, 186 or 187. You see through people, maybe better than they want you to, and there's likely to be an accusing look in your eye even when you aren't saying a word. You can make your disapproval felt, for you are a good actor by instinct and know the value of shrugs, gestures, facial expressions—and silence or the dead pan. You are romantic and imaginative, and if human companionship doesn't suit you, you are capable of retiring within yourself, from which sanctum many horses will not be sufficient to draw you. You are also capable of fits of gloom, despair, and despondency which, with 149, 163, 164, 165, 180, 181, 178, may be a real menace to your peace of mind. You can imagine and fear the worst things in the world and go through all the agonies that you would if they were real, sitting right before your own fireplace. You can have the house on fire, the children burned to ashes, and the firemen on the scene just by letting yourself go. This imagination, constructively used in creative processes, is what can make you successful in fiction and literary creation; but allowed to go into romance, daydreaming, or dramatic apprehensions of improbable woe, it simply makes you unhappy and nervous.

With 149, 163, 164, 165, 170, 171, 195, 197, 198, 199, 224, 225 or 226, nerves become a real problem, and you need to find a constructive outlet for your mental and emotional energies which otherwise run away with you. With 200, 210, 211, 203, 213, 204 or 214, romance, hectic and varied, complicates your life; with 215, 218, 227, 229 or 237, economic security with possibility of wealth.

97

SUN IN SAGITTARIUS—MOON IN ARIES

(You belong to the positive or executive group)

YOU ARE a pioneer—fearless, philosophic, dynamic, anxious and able to control others and, despite large personal ambition and vanity, capable of working for the common good—so long as you can be in the foreground. You are interested in the underdog and can see the other fellow's viewpoint at the same time that you don't sacrifice your own. You have a way of making these two viewpoints work together for mutual advantage, and thus you are a splendid organizer of large or small enterprises, with you pulling the strings and controlling the destinies of those around you. You are ardent and sincere in love, bringing your ideals to practical application in everyday affairs, so that you make a very satisfactory sweetheart. You like to have your own way but are willing to compromise up to a point, and it takes people a long time to find out that your "compromises" are usually ninety per cent your way and ten per cent someone else's. You aren't exactly diplomatic, but you have a way of saying things bluntly that doesn't really hurt people and, though they wince, they come up smiling. You're intensely honorable and will not compromise with the truth or the right as you see it. You are a practical idealist, and you know how to live in the world as it is without giving up your theories of right conduct. You aren't interested in fooling or bamboozling others, preferring straightforward dealings. And others have a hard time fooling you, for your mental powers are keen. You know your own aims down to the last detail and can carry intricate patterns of thought and action in your mind with the greatest of ease. In politics, government, law, or the ministry—any of the active professions—you are unbeatable, and, with 147 or 180, 215, 216, 224, 218, 227, 228, 229 or 149, the heights of power are not too much for you to aspire to. Your chief interest is the world around you, your career, and your personal progress and so great are your vitality and your driving force that you are pretty likely to arrive at your goal. With 224, look out for overreaching yourself. But go ahead—you are the sort of person whose integrity and force can be a public benefaction.

98

SUN IN SAGITTARIUS—MOON IN TAURUS

YOU ARE genial, courteous, idealistic, and romantic. You have a good practical understanding of the world but don't tend to get into action with it. You are philosophic and capable of abstract thinking—so much so that you are capable of letting your ideology absorb your practical purposes. You will do best in some occupation of an artistic or creative nature, where the idealism may find concrete expression and remuneration. Music is especially appealing to you. You put a high premium on education and, even if formal schooling has been brief, you will go on studying and applying yourself on your own initiative. You are aspiring rather than ambitious, and look for idealistic, rather than realistic, satisfaction from life; if you weren't well taken care of economically (which you probably are) you'd be capable of neglecting the earning of a living in some visionary pursuit. You believe the Lord will provide, and He generally does so far as you are concerned. Your faith extends to people, who are usually likely to justify it, for you have the sort of idealism that demands idealism in return. In love, you have one of the most satisfactory of natures—ardent, impulsive, loyal, and devoted. You are capable of sacrificing everything for love, but you probably won't be called on to do it.

In either a male or a female horoscope this indicates an excellent wife (or husband); and, through mutual respect and understanding for each other's aims (which may be quite different), considerable contentment and continued romance in marriage. You are constant without being puritanical—an excellent and rare virtue. You believe in the right without being a Rover Boy; you're optimistic but no Pollyanna. Worldliness and a sense of humor keeps you from smugness, while a fundamentally serious undertone keeps you from frivolity. With 147, 148, 149, 151, 168, 169 or 171, considerable luck and likelihood of artistic talents. With 171 or 181, highly independent nature without being tactless; with 182, super-romantic with danger of confusion through romance. With 215, 218, 227, 228 or 229, plenty of luck in life and much authority and prestige.

99

SUN IN SAGITTARIUS—MOON IN GEMINI

(You belong to the positive or executive group)

YOU ARE an adventurous soul and, in both romantic and geographical mobility, will range the world pretty thoroughly before you are through. You are lucky financially, and money comes in to you readily so that you're protected from want. You aren't very much concerned with security—probably because you've always had it—but in some way or other you are able to talk your way around difficult situations and pop up on the other side of them with your pockets full. You are glib, expressive, possibly eloquent with both voice and pen. This is one of the positions of those who in honorable fashion live by their wits and manage while doing so to achieve a good deal of popular prestige. It is distinctly a professional and artistic position, and if you are in a business career, get out of it and put your mind to work on what you have to offer that will bring you greater returns for less expenditure of physical energy. The idea of getting something for nothing, or for very little, is highly congenial to you. What's more, you know how to do it; you make the world pay well for what you have to give it. You have a way of dramatizing your own powers so that those in authority are eager and willing to pay well for what you have to say. You are a supersalesman of yourself, loving to hold the center of the stage. You give the impression of wisdom and great reserve strength, but how much you have that isn't in active service you know best, though you aren't likely to tell. You are highly aware of your world, though not so much of yourself, and you are likely to take yourself a shade too seriously—which may be part of the reason why others take you seriously. You have a good deal of pride which may be petty sometimes, and you are capable of saying cutting things about anyone who competes with you for the center of the stage. You are attractive to the opposite sex but not constant in love affairs; your restlessness demands variety. Despite your expressed idealism, you're pretty much of a realist and know on which side your bread is buttered. You wouldn't do a dishonorable thing, but you are able to justify a whole lot on pragmatic or practical grounds. You are an opportunist and you hate to see opportunities wasted; you are capable of pulling yourself up by your bootstraps in jig time and coming out at the top just when you were supposed to be down and out.

With Mercury in Sagittarius, 184, 188, 195, 199 or 159, talkative and gossipy; learn to keep things to yourself. With 165, 182 or 151, sensationalist, charming, magnetic. With 171, 164, rebellious, erratic, advanced thinker, and leader of thought. With 180, 212, in a female chart, much difficulty through men. With 224, high ambitions, rise and fall due to charm—and bad judgment.

This is in some way or another the position of the pioneer who is capable of influencing the minds of men to practical purpose and of advancing his own banner at the same time.

100

SUN IN SAGITTARIUS—MOON IN CANCER

THIS IS a highly intuitive, poetic, and sensitive position with an adaptability that makes it possible for you to use your abilities in almost any field that you want to. Whether you select a business, professional, or artistic career, you are likely to master and understand it. You are capable of broad abstractions of thought—and of understanding details of philosophy—and hard business sense. When you are thinking clearly you can see through anyone or anything; but you have a gullible streak in you and can be taken in by a plausible person, especially if he appeals to your emotions or your vanity. Similarly, you are capable of believing in strange doctrines, metaphysics, spiritualism and the like. This is likely to be reflected also in business, for you are an optimist and can imagine the satisfactory outcome of the most far-fetched schemes and plans. The funny thing is that by using your inventiveness and your energy you sometimes do make them work, for no task is too hard for you when you've set your mind on its accomplishment. You have to be careful, however, that through optimism and impressionability you aren't tempted to expend your energies in impossibilities. At the drop of a hat you'd go to get three golden hairs from the whiskers of a giant, if you thought you'd win the princess. Dig to the root of things before you let your enthusiasms fly—and make sure before you start a thing that you're willing to see it through, for your energies and enthusiasms have a way of falling away to nothing. You don't get discouraged, exactly, only you see something else that intrigues you. Emotionally, you're romantic and idealistic and somewhat fickle. It isn't so much that you tire of the old as that you're interested in the new. In all things—studies, business, love, ideas, philosophies—you should seek for depth rather than distance. In business, seek soundness rather than brilliance; in creation, as in the arts, quality rather than quantity; in love, concentration rather than variety. You will find the reward of your great abilities and your high ideology directly in proportion as you concentrate and refuse to scatter your energies.

With 163 or 180, concentrative abilities helped; with 151, 164, 171 or 182, erratic emotional processes need curbing; danger of nerves and nervous exhaustion and some confusion to the thinking processes. With 181, rebellious and progressive thinker; with 171, sensitive, neurasthenic dangers. With 200, 201, 203, 213, 204 or 214, emotional tangles mix you up; with 202 or 212, sentimental attitude toward love.

101

SUN IN SAGITTARIUS—MOON IN LEO

(You belong to the positive or executive group)

HONOR IS your god; all your energies, your ambitions, your strong love-nature are based and rooted in your concept of honor. Through energy, definite aims, and integrity, you are likely to go far and win wide admiration, respect, and dignity. You take life seriously, with a keen sense of the importance of making the most of it. You love justice and can temper it with mercy and through deliberate direction of your abilities get both speed and distance into your career. You are courageous both physically and morally; you are your own master and the master of your fate, and you fear no obstacle or opposition when you know your cause is right. You will defend high and low alike with justice on your side and no one could be powerful enough to offer you a bribe. You are intellectually philosophic, broad-minded, imaginative, and creative, so that any scheme you envisage, or any goal at which you imagine yourself, becomes very nearly an accomplished fact when you have the picture clearly in mind. Then all your energies work together to make a tangible reality out of what is already a reality to you in imagination. This creative, photographic imagination is your great asset, for you have the courage to imagine high and the moral, intellectual, and physical force to bring it to pass. In love you are ardent, loyal, idealistic, and constant; your ideal of love is second only to your ideal of honor. Anyone to whom you give your word has an unbreakable bond. All these qualities, naturally, make for success in life which few people could be petty enough to grudge you, since it rests on the solid foundations of work and personal integrity.

With 147, 148, 149, 154, 155, 156, 161 or 163, brilliant career; also with 167, 168, 169, 173, 175, 174 or 180. With 215, exceptional power; also with 218, 227, 228, 229 or 226. You are a person to make yourself felt in any circle, and a healthy respect for yourself sets your goal high and tends to broaden your influence and your success.

102

SUN IN SAGITTARIUS—MOON IN VIRGO

(You belong to the positive or executive group)

THIS IS A combination for intellectual power, the capacity to bring generalizations down to details and to view details in their relationship with broad concepts. Thus you are a thinker and tend in your thought to be philosophically practical. You are a realist without being hard-boiled; a romanticist without being impractical. You will do best in an intellectual or creative career, where these qualities combine to best advantage—law, religion, medicine, literature, or music. In business, while you have the capacity for it, you would feel cramped and held down. You are on the side of the underdog, willing to go to the mat for a principle which you understand so well and in such detail that you are able to make your listeners agree with you. Thus you are a good lawyer or, in social life, an influence on the thinking of your circle. There is never anything petty or small about you, and though you are a very warm-hearted person, the thing that makes your word impressive is the detachment you are able to bring to ideas. You are a diplomat and are able to win people over to your side by your manner as much as by anything you say. You have what is known as charm, and it is of the unconscious and calm variety that is most appealing.

With 148, 147, 168, 169, 173, 174, 175, 176, 177, 155, 156, 157 or 158, you have considerable luck in life; also with 215, 216, 217, 218, 227, 228 or 229; and you may acquire considerable prestige through intellectual influence. With 171, 181, 182, 150, 164, 165, nerves are dangerous; beware of confused aims. With 183, artistic, with 184, 186 or 187, critical and scientific; with 185, judicial. Look out for the somewhat judicial note anyway, for you lean to puritanism and self-righteousness, though your broad and tolerant understanding of people should forestall this unhappy result. Watch out also for remnants of an inferiority complex. Develop your capacity for details; learn to stick to things and see them through, and you may hope through intellectual pursuits to go far.

103

SUN IN SAGITTARIUS—MOON IN LIBRA

YOU ARE an exceedingly active person with broad, expansive ideas and schemes that have to be brought down to reality. With any encouragement at all you'll go off the deep end and take your soundings later, if at all. You are independent, active, courageous, and you tend to believe in your luck. You are social, convivial, and love companionship; you are romantic, with a definite need for affection, sympathy, and love, which you usually have no trouble in getting, for you are a favorite with the opposite sex. You are naturally trusting and have to learn suspicion; when once you've learned it you are a hard person to fool, for then your intuitions work overtime to warn you of fakes, frauds, four-flushers, and deadbeats. You would rather give a man your last hundred dollars than be tricked out of a dime. You are generous and can be imposed on by your friends if you aren't on the look out for them. You are highly honorable and idealistic and not especially ambitious; you like comfort and security, but you aren't interested in wealth or power, and you are so mobile that you feel secure under conditions where other people might not—home is where you hang your hat. As you grow older, however, this tends to change, especially if you marry (and you probably will), and you want a home of your own—and generally get it. In love you are a little detached, though idealistic in a sense. However, you easily feel misunderstood and get restless. Your husband (wife) is very likely to act as a good balance wheel for you, and although this makes for a steadying down, you may not like it—you feel your mobility interfered with and tend to a mild discontent, even though you expect never to do anything about it. You make the best of things, anyway, and have a philosophic attitude by which you manage not to worry or resent anything too much.

With 168, 178, 180, 171, 181, 182, 147, 161, 149, 163, 164 or 165, restlessness increased; need for watching the nerves. With 146, 147, 148, 154, 155, 156, 157, 158, 169, 167, 173, 174, 175, 176 or 177, luck is good if erratic. With 215, 216, 217, 218, 227, 228 or 229, much luck and authority; you go far and love it.

104

SUN IN SAGITTARIUS—MOON IN SCORPIO

You have a good deal of temperament and independence because of which your life develops rapidly. You step out for yourself and insist that your self-reliance be given a chance. You know what you want all your life and one way or another, contrive to get it. You have a subtle and philosophic outlook on life. Your mind works quickly and intelligently, and you have a keen sense both of your own individuality and importance and of the rights and privileges of others. You are not judicial about your friends, and though you can't help feeling approval or disapproval, you believe in a live and let live policy. Somewhat rigid and austere in matters of right and wrong, you still lack (fortunately!) the missionary spirit, and people in trouble find you a ready listener. You are sensitive and reserved and hesitate in demonstrativeness or expressions of sympathy, but the fundamental interest is there, and you make it felt in your own way. In intellectual matters you are a good student, intuitive, profound, and far-sighted, synthesizing knowledge and getting things into new and unusual combinations. You have a keen sense of the ridiculous, laugh readily, and are the best of companions, when one of your philosophic or gloomy moods is not on you. Emotionally, you combine the ardor of a romantic with the common sense of a philosopher, making romance plausible and philosophy romantic. You are somewhat nervous by nature, but strict self-discipline, poise, and restraint, hold this in check, and you translate your nervous energy into driving force and concentration of purpose, so that by will you go far. You take your obligations seriously and, despite your keen sense of humor, have a full recognition of the gravity and seriousness of living.

With 147, 161, look out for letting down tension by artificial means. With 163, concentrative powers increased; with 171, 181, 182, 168, 178, 149, 150, 163, 164 or 165, nervousness and tension increased and nerves need close watching. With 147, 148, 215, 218, 227, 228, 229 or 237, much luck and influence in life; financial security.

105

SUN IN SAGITTARIUS—MOON IN SAGITTARIUS

(You belong to the positive or executive group)

Nervous energy is your strength—and your weakness. If this position occurs with 147, 149, 150, 161, 163, 164, 165, 168, 170, 171, 178, 180,

181 or 182, nerves, in one form or another, will be a problem to you more or less continuously. In any case, even without these paragraphs, relaxation is your need. You have a philosophical mind, jumping from the particular to the general as if by second nature, and seeing things, people, problems, in large, rather than specific, terms. The devotional motif is strong in your nature, and you tend to ritualistic acceptance of some religion, code, or basic set of beliefs to which you relate the threads of your philosophy and make a working ideology for your life. Even when with 150, 164, 171 or 181, which tend to make you an advanced and perhaps radical thinker, your thought, though revolutionary, will be patterned and constructive, tending toward Utopias rather than to anarchy. The need for classification is strong in you; you put things into pigeonholes and categories and organize your information. You are very sensitive and temperamental, capable of extremes of happiness and despair, all in the space of a few seconds. Harshness and unkindness distress and bewilder you, and you can be governed only through your affections and through reason, for, despite your sensitive nature, you won't give in to unfairness, unkindness, or illogical argument. You are a good deal of a reformer, believing the world should live on your principles, your codes, your moral standards. Thus preachers, lawyers, judges are often found here and, being eloquent, logical, and persuasive are likely to achieve a good deal of influence. You love travel, and much of your nervous energy can be used up in physical motion. It is not at all unlikely that you will live and achieve your greatest success somewhere far removed from your birthplace. You are at home anywhere, settling down gypsy-like where night finds you.

With 184 or 195, talkative; with 150, 164, 171 or 181, erratic temperament; with 147, 161, 168, 178 or 225, high explosive temper; with 202 or 212, much hurt through sensitiveness; with 170, danger of introversion, psychological nooks and crannies need dusting out; with 163 or 180, power and influence through mind-strength; with 165 or 182, confusion and sensationalism; mystic tendencies should be fought down.

A great love for music accompanies this position, and music will be found very restful; also, with 215, 218 or 229, the creative bent may find expression in musical composition or performance.

106

SUN IN SAGITTARIUS—MOON IN CAPRICORN

(You belong to the positive or executive group)

YOU ARE a vigorous thinker, capable of rising to some position of importance through the strength and originality of your mind and expression. You have a considerable sense of humor, which, whether it is actively working or not, still lends charm and lift to what you say. You have an active social sense and know how to appeal to groups of people.

A large admixture of idealism in your nature, a wide scope to your vision plus the true spirit of leadership, make you a person to be reckoned with wherever you are found. Intellectually, you are both facile and profound, the readiness of your expression not making you shallow as glibness frequently does, and, except when you act on impulse, your actions will be found to be based on good sound sense. When acting on impulse you may be foolish sometimes, but always on the side of justice. You are prone to jump to conclusions, when you become indignant and act unwisely, if nobly. You have a great capacity for indignation, a righteous wrath that makes you feared by malefactors, for your moral courage is unshakable. Emotionally, you are idealistic, a trifle erratic, more able to impress others than you are impressionable yourself. You take yourself seriously, and others are likely to do the same; you demand attention, whether from an individual whom you love or from a group that you are determined to control. You think in terms of the general rather than the particular, in principals rather than in specific instances; and this broad outlook colours your love-life with a sort of impersonal detachment which, however, does not rule out physical intensity.

With 147, 163, 148 or 149, political or executive power; also with 168, 169, 167, 173, 174, 175, 176 or 177. With 150, very independent mind, rebellious and progressive; also with 165, danger of confusion and enmities. With 171, nervous disorders impede progress; with 181, a pioneer. With 182, sense of humor helped, also some confusion. This is a well-balanced position, and it takes a good deal to throw you off; with many paragraphs showing nerves, danger of overbalancing of the nature through erratic action, but in general this is a versatile and flexible position and makes for power and success through mental breadth and mobility.

107

SUN IN SAGITTARIUS—MOON IN AQUARIUS

(You belong to the positive or executive group)

YOU ARE independent, idealistic, romantic, and expressive. You don't keep much to yourself and can range from being a profound mental influence on those you meet to being a mere chatterbox. You have ideals and principles which will mean a good deal to you, and you'll fight for them, for you have great moral courage, and even when you are barking up the wrong tree, or straining at a gnat, you lose none of your zest for intellectual encounter. You have a dramatic way of putting things that adds the illusion of importance. There's a touch to your nature of what Matthew Arnold called High Seriousness, and you are capable of being a crusader for any cause that you take up, whether it be broad or petty. You tend to generalize on things and you can think up more philosophic reasons why it is right for you to be angry, or in love, or offended, than you can shake a stick at. You can also work from the general down to the particular, and your ability to put two and two together, or to split up ideas into their component parts, is the bulwark of your intellectual strength. You are romantic, highly idealistic, with a sort of feeling of personal responsibility that the world be kept as idealistic as possible, which, the world being what it is, is quite a job. There is something of the artist about you, though you are an artist in ideas rather than in color, line, or design. The abstraction of music appeals to you and with training you can become a fine performer. But ideas are your especial province. Getting them and your personality across by your force and manner of expression lends such color and drama that even your enemies admit your sincerity. You have a tendency to feel that no one is quite so high minded as you are. You are a snob in matters of ideology and love your own to the exclusion of others. This would seem intolerance if your ideology were not sound, but it usually is — according to your premises. This can make you a reformer, a missionary, a Strong Man (or woman) of the Right and you are perfectly capable of espousing some lost, or losing, or unpopular cause. This may concern itself with anything from broad social ideals to ideals of personal morality, but whatever it is, you are a zealot for it. In love, you are an idealist, and your idealism may stand in the way of what others think of as the practical side of love.

With 147, 163, 169 or 168, very powerful and influential personality; with 171, 181 or 182, more nervous, less well integrated; with 161, fine mentality, danger of ambition and verve petering out.

Strive for realism in your life and to make your idealism into practical and workable form; learn coöperation and tact: you can't always afford to express even the most high-minded of principles. Reserve in expression will smooth the path for you: you can think *what* you like.

108

SUN IN SAGITTARIUS—MOON IN PISCES

YOU ARE a philosopher. Whatever your walk in life may be, it is the broad general idea that counts with you. You lead an inner life of your own, of ideas and ideals, that may not find expression in the world of affairs, but which gives you a grip on broad realities. You aren't practical minded, thinking and living on a somewhat detached plane; and though you are lucky and therefore protected from want, you are none the less not greatly interested in the material things of the world. You are a genuine missionary with a brooding sense of the need of men for higher thinking, higher feeling, and the better things of culture, religion, and philosophy. Whether in the professions or the arts—you are little likely to be found in business—you are animated less by an art-for-art's-sake attitude than by art for man's sake. Conscious of your own worth, you none the less have true humility of spirit, which you can afford to have because you feel so closely your kinship with forces larger than man. You are a good deal of a mystic, and your insight into universal truths is remarkable. Intellectually, you are profound, broad, intuitive, able to cope with large generalizations better than with details. You must cultivate concentrative ability. Emotionally, you are impressionable and romantic and can be imposed upon by individuals who play on your general sympathetic approach for their own advantage. You are forgiving, incapable of holding a grudge, utterly free of meanness, spite, jealousy, or vengefulness; and despite your desire to better the world you live in, you have a real tolerance for its foibles. You understand all and you forgive all; you are no stern judge or avenging angel, but rather a healing doctor of the spirit, eager to serve and usually able to find ample scope for your charitable impulses.

With 148, 169, true nobility of spirit; with 147, 149, more selfish and introverted, less general, danger of depression. With 171, 181, 182, 164 or 165, erratic and somewhat sensational nature, the broadness becoming mere indiscrimination and sensationalism. With 215, 217, 227, 228, 229 or 237, tremendous scope and power, with probability of great wealth; with 226, mystic nature, capable of exerting the extremes of magnetic and spiritual influence.

109

SUN IN CAPRICORN—MOON IN ARIES

(You belong to the positive or executive group)

MIND-POWER is your great strength; you know what you want, with an intellectual determination to get there, and no one is going to say you nay. You combine tact with a kind of vigorous invulnerability—a sort of Teddy Roosevelt diplomacy is your stock in trade—the diplomacy of the Big Stick—fear God and take your own part. You are fearless, and, while you will not compromise with truth, you know how to compromise with individuals. You can't be bought, but you can find a way around a situation that will satisfy everyone—especially yourself. You are impatient, restless, nervous, but you have learned that it is expedient to control this and appear to play a waiting game, though you wait with the same intensity that a cat waits at a mouse hole, without relaxation of purpose. You are tense and high-strung. Your mind works always, and you are capable of brain feats that would exhaust a less determined person. As a matter of fact, they sometimes exhaust you, and you have to be careful of brain fag. You should learn moderation in work, in opinions, in forcefulness. You should learn that you don't have to be harsh in order to be truthful, and that it isn't necessary to hurt people's feelings in order to keep faith with honor. You have a high sense of personal integrity, and you are very chary of your good name. Emotionally, you are touchy anyway; and being not especially romantic, give the impression of coldness to the feelings of others. You have to learn to get the other fellow's point of view and to treat thin skins with gentleness. You are a fine executive, though you could stand a little more impersonality in dealing with people. When you are detached and cold you have the precision of a machine, but you can make people's blood boil or run cold with a word or a look and so upset them that they can't do a stroke of work for hours. This is a dangerous trait in an executive; look out for it.

With 147, 161, 149, 163, 170, 180, 168 or 178, very hard nature, cold and domineering, but powerful. With 150 and/or 165, erratic, temperamental; if also with 149, neurosis is the danger, through introversion of the intellectual ambitions; learn to be expressive. With 148, 155, 169, 174 or 173, power and influence; with 216, more tact and diplomacy; with 224, highly aggressive and risk of pushing the career too far, into unstable realms of ambition. With 236, jittery ambition, erratic career, temperament dangerous.

110

SUN IN CAPRICORN—MOON IN TAURUS

(You belong to the positive or executive group)

YOU HAVE a genius for people; you are capable of handling large crowds and eager to do so. Your ambition is based in a shrewd and practical worldliness—you are one of the crowd, and no matter how far above it you may soar, you always give them the comforting impression that you haven't forgotten where you came from. You have plenty of luck in life and high ability to make the most of it; but you lack somewhat in drive, and when fortuitous circumstances desert you, you are likely to relax—a sort of Achilles sulking in his tent. You are capable of sulking, being an ardent if unaggressive hater. For dislikes absorb your energies destructively and you are at your best when you are loving, not hating, and when you are loved, not opposed. Opposition baffles you, because your sense of outraged justice and dignity tells you you don't deserve it. You have charm, luck, persistence, vision, and integrity, and through these can go far.

With 163, 180, 169, 147, 148, 149 or 151, the top. With 161, brilliant start to life, not so brilliant finish. You should depend less on luck and more on your own energies. You are a genuine humanitarian, devoted not only to individuals (you are the soul of fidelity in love matters) but to large groups, and whatever your sphere in life may be there is a keen sense of service. You are interested in worldly goods, loving luxury and the good things of life. But you have a high sense of the seriousness of living and of your particular duty to make your own world a better place for you and those around you. You are a devoted wife (husband) and mother (father) with a keen sense of domestic responsibility. You are a strict disciplinarian, but you wield the rod without malice and without temper. Your disapproval is a calm and judicial rather than an emotional matter, and it has terrific force because of its sheer detachment. You can reprimand a naughty child or flay a whole group with the same glacial calm of temper and much the same effect: you make people ashamed to be anything but the best they can be. You are a pillar of society, and whether you lead a public or private life, you are a useful citizen, winning the love and admiration of those around you.

111
SUN IN CAPRICORN—MOON IN GEMINI

(You belong to the positive or executive group)

YOUR AMBITION finds its best outlet in intellectual, creative, or scientific work. The spirit of investigation is on you, and whether you're probing the mysteries of nature or of your neighbor's private life, your curiosity demands satisfaction. Glibness is likely to run away with your abilities, for you are so facile in expression that you don't have to develop your powers to the highest pitch. You can get by on a quarter of your capabilities, while less fortunate souls struggle to keep up with you with all of theirs. What you do may not bear the stamp of genius, but in some way or another it gets the attention you want. Your friends are likely to tell you that you could do better, more important work if you tried, and they are probably right. But so long as you are getting some degree of acclaim you are not likely to bother. You are not a perfectionist and may not go to the trouble to probe your own depths even throughout a long lifetime. Emotionally, you are contradictory, being fundamentally conservative and steadfast but with a sort of impish satisfaction in doing the unexpected, the unusual. Your powers of invention are enormous, and you can think up more ways to skin a cat, tell a story, or pull off a business deal, than anyone else. Your cleverness escapes the criticism of being shallow because you are a fundamentally serious person, and people are more likely to attach serious intent to what is not serious than they are to condemn you for flippancy. You run the risk of getting hypnotized by the sound of your own voice and of conceiving yourself in too heroic proportions: thus you run the risk of pomposity. You don't like to be laughed at, and while relishing a joke, prefer to have someone else the butt of it.

With 166, intellectual qualities are strengthened and deepened; with 149, 163 or 147, concentrative powers bring success; with 180, purposes are broadened and ambition increased; with 168 or 178, tactlessness needs attention; also with 159, when you'll speak your mind to your own hurt and often with too little regard for accuracy.

112

SUN IN CAPRICORN—MOON IN CANCER

(You belong to the positive or executive group)

YOU ARE sensitive and have plenty of insight into other people. You are intuitive and introspective, perhaps too introspective for your own good. If this sensitiveness is transferred to practical affairs you will rise as a manager of people, for you have a great deal of appeal to the masses, and can succeed either as an executive in business or as a writer or actor in the arts. You are domestic, very fond of your home, a good father or mother, husband or wife, willing to give and take in compromise, for you don't like quarrels and bickerings and will give a good deal to avoid them. Even if you are personally unhappy, you have a way of concealing it to keep up appearances. You are rather secretive and can carry plans around with you for a long time, working at them in your own way for weeks without taking anyone into your confidence. You have a good deal of pride and a protective shell into which you crawl when your feelings are hurt. No one is ever likely to accuse you of wearing your heart on your sleeve. There is a slight danger that this habit of concealment will turn into introversion, and with 149 or 170 this danger is emphasized. With these, and also with 147, 161, 151, 164, 163, 168, 178, 180, 171 or 182, the health is not strong and needs attention, especially from the incursions of worry and nerves. Your vitality is low and needs to be conserved. Avoid worry, touchiness, and anything which produces nervous tension, for this is destructive to you.

113

SUN IN CAPRICORN—MOON IN LEO

(You belong to the positive or executive group)

ONE OF THE combinations for public authority, a vigorous and vital personality capable of great popularity and of success in the practical world, either through business, the professions, or public life. With 168, 178, 171, 181, 182, 150, 164 or 165, a great deal of this good is interfered with because of misdirection of the passional nature. A kind of nervous enthusiasm for romance makes trouble and must be fought down if it is not to capture the entire personality. But with 148, 149, 163, 155, 167, 169, 170, 175, 180, 173, 174, 176 or 177, the ambition is well integrated toward success. The strong personality, with its ability to make friends among powerful people and subordinates alike, rises into a position of authority and influence. Your inner drive is concentrated by an insuperable will; your impatience is curbed under the yoke of expediency; you know how to be aggressive and diplomatic at the right times and in the right manner; you have that sort of aloofness and detachment that makes you seem important even before you really may be. You believe in yourself and translate your belief to others; you aren't seeking self-justification but rather self-realization, and since the good of the world and worldly authority mean much to you, you seek self-realization along those lines. You are a materialist. The abstract, the philosophic, the visionary, have no particular appeal to you. Your loyalty is to individuals rather than to ideas, and the chief individual is yourself. You are sincere but capable of veering if policy dictates. Emotionally, you are ardent but not warm-hearted. You have a kind of detached and impersonal passion, as if you could take it or leave it alone. You have, like Cassius, a lean and hungry look, for your nervous and physical energies keep you pretty well on the go. Your health is fair, but you can keep yourself going on nerve force when the vitality runs low, which it frequently does. You should learn to relax, sleep, rest, and take it easy. In relaxation, also, you will find that you develop to a greater degree the qualities of real human warmth which otherwise are insufficiently developed. You have a machine-like precision which people admire, and, if you develop a warmer attitude toward others, you will find that your progress is materially helped by the affection you will gain. Try to add to your prestige by love, rather than by fear and authority, and the two qualities, working together, will open wider vistas of success to you.

114

SUN IN CAPRICORN—MOON IN VIRGO

YOU CONCEAL a large amount of timidity under a rather impressive exterior. The result is that though you may get into positions of authority you are really better off when you are taking orders from someone else. Your best position in life is found somewhere in the middle rank—not as a complete subordinate, and not as a top executive. You have excellent principles and won't equivocate on them; you stand squarely and absolutely for the honorable course. But when you leave the realm of principle and get into action you are not nearly so forthright, for here your lack of self-assurance makes itself felt, and you waver around for decision as to action even when the principle involved is perfectly plain to you. You will do best in the professions, corporation law, the arts—anything where you can progress by sticking to the rules of the game. In business, where decisions must be made boldly, you are likely to have troubles; opportunities pass you by while you're trying to make up your mind, and less worthy, more flashy and decisive people, go by you on the road to fame and fortune. You have ambition enough and a certain amount of material luck, but when your fate rests in your own hands you juggle it as if it were a hot potato. Emotionally, you are something of a sensationalist—in fact, a good deal of a sensationalist. You are high-strung and highly organized and demand satisfaction of your desires. You are extremely popular with the opposite sex and never should lack for sweethearts except when indecision rears its ugly head. The emotional life is very important to you, despite the highly intellectual bent of your fundamental nature. You will marry for a combination of these. You are never likely to be swept off your feet by romance, however great, if it should present itself in the form of a person of low intellect. You are a good deal of an intellectual (and for that matter, social) snob and instinctively seek the right people and live in the right part of town. You are conventional, no matter how erratic you may appear.

With 200, 210, 202 or 212, serious emotional quirks need straightening out; with 216 or 224, wavering or erroneous judgment causes serious trouble at some time; with 170 or 180, periodic fits of depression are dangerous, health needs attention. With 227 or 230, powers of decision are strengthened, and authority follows, possibly very great if also with 155. With 233, low aims, lack of ambition and energy. You should strive for self-sufficiency, self-reliance, and aggressiveness along constructive lines and resist all through your life the temptation to lean and depend on someone else.

115

SUN IN CAPRICORN—MOON IN LIBRA

(You belong to the positive or executive group)

YOU HAVE a kind of inspirational faith in your own infallibility which can make you merely an eccentric, a dogmatist, a rigid and inflexible personality, or can carry you to the heights if you combine your self-assurance with the will to action. You are something of a fighter and must overcome a tendency to touchiness and quarrelsomeness. You have a visionary and imaginative viewpoint on many things, and unless you have terrific drive, people will merely think you strange. With 147, 161, 148, 149, 150, 163, 168, 169, 170, 180, 215, 218, 226, 227, 228, 229, 236 or 237, you have a magnificent chance to rise to great heights through continuous and almost monomaniac plugging at your individual ideal or goal; under these circumstances you have a magnetic power over people, which will be felt also but in lesser degree with 166 and 167. Without any of these bolstering influences, look out for mere eccentricity, oddness, peculiarity, for you have very unusual viewpoints, and impatience makes it hard for you to sell yourself or your notions to your public. You are not exactly romantic. There is a sort of detachment about you that belies your need for people. You are extremely social and like to have people around you but, at the same time, you do not warm up to them very quickly; you are suspicious, proud, and a little aloof. With 200, 210, 203, 213, 204 or 214, this may be changed into super-sociability and much trouble through erratic and impulsive emotions. Your emotional and intellectual concepts get mixed up with each other. You believe for a fact what you feel emotionally, and yet become hopelessly involved through gullibility when your suspicions aren't working. When they are working, you tend to alienate people. This is a rather difficult position and your chief lesson is to give up some of your ideas and some of your independence in compromise with the world as it is. Your success will come through ability to compromise, both with people and with ideas; and in proportion as you learn coöperation you will achieve success.

116

SUN IN CAPRICORN—MOON IN SCORPIO

(You belong to the positive or executive group)

YOU HAVE tremendous inner drive and "temperament." You have been highly independent in your day, with a keen sense of your own importance as an individual. This you never lose; a certain rigid inner pride keeps your self-respect always at a high level. As you grow older, however, a natural social sense asserts itself. You learn the need for coöperating with people, and you learn that, though you have rights, others have rights also. Naturally of a judicial and rather stern nature, you have your own private opinions of what people do, a keen sense of moral values, and a devotion to the orthodox in conduct. However, sensitiveness and reserve keep you from expressing everything you feel, though you can make your disapproval felt without a word. You are a sort of accusing angel with a powerful feeling that your judgment is one with the judgment of God and the universe. It is difficult to persuade you that you are wrong, for although apparently reasonable, you have an inflexible core within and a trick of appearing not to understand the other fellow's viewpoint when you understand it perfectly but think it better tactics not to admit it. You are unswervingly honorable, loyal, and devoted, with a keen sense of the sobriety of life, and of your duty as a part of it. You are able to understand and feel the problems of other people without their telling you—and sometimes understand where the other fellow would rather you didn't. You trust your first impressions of people and, whether you're right or wrong, you rarely change, especially if the first impression has been bad. Though apparently tolerant, you are not really tolerant, a stern quality of judgment underlying your sympathy. You will help people of whom you disapprove, but you don't bargain to take them to your heart. You are capable of infinite detachment; your emotions do not interfere with your reasoning powers, except when you are deeply touched through your affections, at which time you can go to pieces pretty thoroughly and be unreasonable. But generally, by strict self-discipline and a sort of permanent vigilance, you are reasonable, detached, and calm.

With 147, 161 or 163, brilliant mind, periods of dejection and depression need attention. With 148, 169, 180, 215, 217, 218, 227, 228, 229 or 237, great authority and power; with 149, 170, 171, 181, 182, 150, 164 or 165, nerves need attention. With 200, 210, 225, 226 or 223, difficulty through romantic matters; with 216, much tact, danger of too little aggression; with 224, over-bold, misdirected courage leads to rise and fall.

117

SUN IN CAPRICORN—MOON IN SAGITTARIUS

(You belong to the positive or executive group)

WIT, FLUENCY and ambition combine to take you a long way. You are a voluble and expressive person with a keen sense of values and discrimination and an ability to make your opinions felt. Thus, in the world of ideas you are likely to be a power, whether that world is narrow and limited or broad and inclusive. You are a great traveler, restless, needful of being on the go all the time, and, either in geographic mobility or intellectual variety, pretty sure never to be at rest. A sort of nervous enthusiasm pervades all that you do—an enthusiasm that works on nerve force rather than physical vitality. Your imagination outruns your body, and your mind works overtime, even when you may be physically exhausted. You have to learn to relax, for if you follow your natural bent, you will come a cropper of nerves. You are a severe critic but also an enthusiastic one—a person of strong likes and dislikes—and with reasons for all of them. Both your loves and your friends are dictated by intellectual rather than romantic considerations, though when you are satisfied about the intellectual content of your companion, you are capable of great sentimentality. The same may be said for ideas: you look first for the mind and, after that, you can let yourself go. You are a kind of snob of the intellect. When you know that you are in the company of the elect you can be as sentimental, as romantic, as emotional as all get-out. But in the presence of intellectual inferiority you freeze up and achieve an austerity that surprises even yourself. You are a broad, inclusive person in more ways than one, and your intellectual discrimination does not really interfere with your humanitarian qualities.

If with 166, 180, 186 or 197, depth increased; with 145 or 159, garrulity, talkativeness, indiscrimination of what you say and believe. With 147, 149, 148, 155, 156, 169, 174, 175, 176, 177, 173 or 167, influence, authority. With 150, 164, 165, 171, 181 or 182, nerves need attention. With 181, 182 and 180, highly nervous inclinations with danger to health from eccentricities of the emotions.

118

SUN IN CAPRICORN—MOON IN CAPRICORN

(You belong to the positive or executive group)

EARLY PHYSICAL HANDICAPS—infantile or youthful bad health—polarize your nature toward success which in middle and later life can become very great. Ambition is powerful, and self-control almost a fetish. Worldliness comes naturally to you, and a passion to impress yourself on the world through an ideal, an idea, or a moral formula gives impetus to your career. Inherently selfish and self-centered, you know how to translate this to the people of your world so as to gain power over them—and power is your goal rather than material wealth. There is a cold, hard, invulnerable streak in you that resists close personal associations at the same time that it knows how to appeal to the imagination of the people en masse. You aren't especially interested in art for its own sake but may use it as a medium for the expressing of ideas. Further, you aren't even much interested in ideas for their own sake, except to gain authority and power for yourself. You are a realist, first, last, and always. The ideal to you is only a means to an end. You are a stern judge, an exacting boss, and a stiff executive, for your devotion to justice and duty is strong, and though you might strain a point for your own purposes, you aren't likely to strain one for anyone else. Your force arises from your self-control, and you will accumulate power directly in proportion as you accumulate self-discipline. In the end, your downfall, if it comes, will come because you forget this basic principle and push your luck or power too far. You have only to be careful that when you arrive at the summit you don't, in your elation and self-satisfaction, fall over the edge. You aren't amenable to an appeal to the affections; you rule by force and must be ruled the same way. Reason only will appeal to you and only that reason which fits in with your purposes. You will listen to and understand reason—and then do as you please. Your blindness to the other fellow's viewpoint is merely a trick to confuse him—you really see it perfectly.

With 163 or 180, extremes of authority—and danger of fall therefrom; with 171 or 182, or both, early ill health needs constant care. With 171, erotic impulses strong making difficulties; with 224, bad judgment causes much trouble, indecision and wavering lead to dangerous actions that succeed for a while and then collapse. With 202 or 212, hardened emotional nature through experience. With both 171 and 180, or 182 and 180, or 161 or 178, or 149 or 170, health an especially necessary consideration.

119

SUN IN CAPRICORN—MOON IN AQUARIUS

(You belong to the positive or executive group)

YOU HAVE a hard determination within you that makes itself felt by others in the world of business or professional affairs and carries you far. A good healthy respect for yourself and your own talents demands the respect of others. If this is polarized by 147, 180, 170 or 148, you are eager for fame and likely to get it in some degree or other. Even if without these, you have a great deal of drive and push which carry you up. You are conventional, believing in the status quo; eager to go with the right people and to live in the right part of town, and even your good business judgment may not keep you from living right up to the hilt of your income. But this is not likely ever to cause you any trouble. Your credit is good, and you are apt at turning to, in one way or another, when the checking account gets low. Intellectually, you are practical; knowledge for its own sake has no meaning to you and you will be a good student just so long as you are learning something of which you can see the practical advantage. You are an opportunistic student all your life and will excel in professional or vocational school rather than in a general cultural course. Similarly, in other walks of life, anything which is grist to your mill you will be interested in—people, clubs, meetings, and the like, for whether your ambitions are business or social, they are always in the forefront of your mind. Emotionally, you can be intense, but your intensity is not likely to be directed toward someone lower in the social or financial scale. Your calm and intelligence make you an admirable, companionable, and easy-going spouse provided your independence is not interfered with. What you lack in ardor you make up in stability. You won't go out of your way for people you find dull or profitless, and your diplomacy is likely to break down in the presence of stupidity. Your pride is great and is likely to be based in your capabilities, your attainments, and your purchases rather than social prestige, for although you insist on having the right people around you, you insist, to yourself, that your worth must be proved. With 146, 148, 167 or 209 the nature is softened considerably, and a really humanitarian spirit may be felt. With 215, 218, 227 or 229, great luck in life and possibility of great wealth through your own efforts.

120

SUN IN CAPRICORN—MOON IN PISCES

(You belong to the positive or executive group)

YOU ARE highly aware of your world, especially of the seriousness and sorrows of people. You have an insight into their hearts and lives which seems intuitive. You are a moralist and a humanitarian; you think in terms of the whole mass of society with a real personal feeling for the underprivileged. Through the development of this quality and your own insight and sympathetic understanding you can go far and achieve considerable respect and love. You are not interested in power, but rather in the obscure things you can do to help. You have the real spirit of charity and detachment, preferring to give in secret. Your kindnesses will never be shouted from the housetops—not, at least, by you. Your satisfactions in life are personal, spiritual, internal; for you have a keen sense of soul values, and the real worth, the real person, the real idea, appeals to you rather than the superficial acclaim or glitter that takes the shallower mind. This is likely to make you a little lonely, but it also can bring you outstanding success and personal satisfaction in any of the social sciences, medicine, nursing, institutional work, detective work, or teaching. You are a deep, careful, and understanding student and can go far through intellectual endeavor.

With 148, 155, 169, 174, 167, 176 or 177, magnificent humanitarian, with brilliant opportunities for doing good. With 147, 163, 180 or 168, drive and persistence helped, ambition fixed and likely to be achieved. With 166, 186, 197, 187 or 198, critical and shrewd mind—an admirable position for a detective.

You have a true love for justice and equity in human relations and the ability to detach yourself from personal considerations. Your sensitiveness, instead of making for self-pity and a sense of your own woes, transfers itself to sympathy with and understanding for others. You assume responsibilities so readily that you are likely to be imposed upon, but you consider it no more than right that you should take them. You have a true feeling for noblesse oblige and will be found wherever there is something you can do for someone less fortunate than yourself. Only look out that this bent doesn't lead you to marry someone to reform him (her). That never works.

121

SUN IN AQUARIUS—MOON IN ARIES

YOU HAVE a quick, aggressive mind, a keen sense of your own intellectual powers, and a sort of judicial attitude toward the rest of the world. This is one of the positions of a genuine superiority complex, and you have to look out that smugness and self-satisfaction do not make you unpopular. You have a detached intellectual interest in all manner of things, a broad, deep, and honest mind; but you need bolstering up on the emotional side. You tend to be cold, aloof, detached—at the same time that you are very eager to have people listen to you. You are sound; what you know is accurate, well thought out, and well put. But your great abilities will go unrewarded until you learn that you can't be a walking mind. You have a real need for people and for social activity; you probably come of a good family with a good heritage both of blood and brain, and doors are opened to you automatically that are closed to many. If you improve on your social opportunities by learning to be less arrogant, to appear less sure of yourself, to look once in a while as if you needed sympathy, you will find people warming up to you much more. Naturally these qualities get in the way of your expression of love, for though you are needful of affection, a certain awareness, rising from your mind processes, makes you appear less warm-hearted than you really are, and your utter independence is not good for awakening the Gentler Passions.

With 147, 161, 149, 163, 170 or 180, very hard and ambitious nature, which usually gets there; with 146, 148, 162, 155, 158, 169, 174 or 167, warmer and more genial, less calculating; with 181 or 164, erratic, independent, and rebellious mentality; with 165 or 182, muddled thinking, equally aggressive, but less sound. With 183, 188 or 187, artistic mind; with 184, 186 or 187, sharp, critical, analytical; with 185, judicial. With 227, 236, 237, 216, great influence; with 236 and 181, jittery ambitions, high temperament, an aloof and cold nature, though emotionally intense.

122

SUN IN AQUARIUS—MOON IN TAURUS

(You belong to the positive or executive group)

YOU HAVE a nice blend of the emotional and intellectual natures—an efficient mind, purposeful, reasonable, and logical. You have all the qualities necessary to be a good executive except the desire to be one, but, unless with 147, 161, 163, 180, 168 or 178, you aren't interested in gaining control over other people. You are impelled to personal development rather than to those pursuits that lead to public acclaim. You are devoid of the domineering or missionary spirit, willing to "live and let live." This gives you a certain detachment that may be interpreted as snobbishness. You estimate people, not according to their wealth and position, but according to whether or not they interest you. If they don't interest you, you simply don't bother with them. You are romantic, but with romanticism you combine a deep sense of loyalty and dependability. Loyalty holds you in check where conventions would not, for with respect to the conventions you are theoretically scornful, though in actual practise you rarely do anything to violate them, unless with 181, 178, 164, 200, 210, 203, 213, 204 or 214 when your transgressions will leave you with a consciousness of error or sin! You are a lover of peace and harmony and will use all your tact and graciousness to avoid a quarrel. You are able in your private life to achieve peace with honor—that is, in your quiet way, you pretty generally get what you want and make the other fellow like it. In early youth this amounts to stubbornness, but with maturity it develops into fixity of purpose. You are willing to wait for results, and you know the futility of forcing issues. Socially, you are gracious and sympathetic, but you don't go out of your way for people. Your friends seek you. You are interested in the arts, but unless with 147, 161, 163, 180, 178, 181, 200, 215 or 218, not creative. You are likely to be associated with artistic people, however, and to be in some way connected with art professionally, perhaps on the executive or directing side of institutions and the like, where your executive ability finds a congenial outlet.

123

SUN IN AQUARIUS—MOON IN GEMINI

YOU ARE a romantic, and unless you translate this quality into an artistic career or overcome it entirely, your emotions will run away with you. Your idealism is strongly mixed with critical tendencies, and discontent arises through disappointment when people do not live up to the impossibly high romantic standards you set for them. You incline to jump into romances readily, with high motives and high enthusiasms, and when enthusiasm wanes, or the high motives are in any way doubted, you jump out again. You are a great self-dramatist; nothing that happens to you loses any fat when you tell about it. Your sweetheart is always the most wonderful in the world—and after he (she) has gone away, you still cling to the ideal, trying to justify yourself both in loving her (him) and in leaving (her) him. You believe in the sadness that goes with true love—in fact, you seem more convinced that it's bound to be sad than that it's bound to be happy, with the result that you frequently see to it single-handed that it is sad. Intellectually, you are quick, apt, intuitive, inclining to skim the surface of many and varied things. In business or occupation this is a decided handicap. You tire rapidly, and if you don't get all the breaks, drift from job to job, as you do from sweetheart to sweetheart. This is a somewhat better position for a woman than for a man, for the romantic note is not so destructive in practical ways, in a woman. But in a man it makes for considerable instability, a lack of decisiveness, and a sort of helplessness before the world that seems unjust in the face of idealism. Learn to pin yourself down to reality, to cope with the world as it is—especially, learn to stick. If with 163, 170 or 180, early hectic life settles down to real purpose and drive though the necessity for decisiveness is always present; with 200, 210, 203, 204, 213 or 214, turbulent emotions; with 202 or 212, much hurt through the fickleness of others, which fickleness you learn to use yourself, protectively.

Overcome a tendency to drift, both in emotional, intellectual, and business matters; put your personality constructively to work in the world — it is a social asset and can be made into a business asset as well when you decide what you are after.

124

SUN IN AQUARIUS—MOON IN CANCER

(You belong to the positive or executive group)

YOU ARE an ultra-social person, needful of companionship and very sensitive, both in your own feelings and perceptions and with regard to the feelings of others. You have an almost uncanny faculty for responding to other people, with the result that you are extremely popular. You probably have unusual hereditary endowments and position, but this doesn't prevent you from endearing yourself to those in all walks of life. For there's a touch of the true democrat here that all the sheltering in the world cannot down. Servants love you and you do much to deserve their love. In worldly matters this quality has a good commercial value; you are able to be yourself without equivocation and at the same time to make people like you and pay you well. Thus, whether you are in business, politics, or the arts, you appeal to a wide circle. You are tactful in speech and writing and able to calculate nicely the effect of what you say. Your impulses and intuitions bear the stamp of practical good sense, although your ideas are likely to be visionary. You feel with far greater accuracy than you think; your creations have emotional rather than intellectual appeal. This doesn't mean that you haven't a good mind, for your mind is quick, facile, penetrating, with a touch of the inspirational; but it does mean that your emotions are capable of running away with your intellect and of leading you into paths that are not rationally defensible. You are a romantic, and no matter in what walk of life or occupation you may be found, a personal adventurous feeling underlies all that you say or do or think.

With 147, 163, 168, 180, 148, 150, 169, 186 or 202, you rise to considerable influence; with 212, serious emotional disappointment; with 200, 210, 203, 213, 204 or 214, misdirection of the emotional nature needs attention; with 188 or 199, purely visionary and impractical schemes need practicalizing; if with 229, 237, 215, 216, 217 or 218, a powerful personality bound to be recognized and appreciated.

125

SUN IN AQUARIUS—MOON IN LEO

YOUR INTELLECT and your emotions have a constant struggle for the center of the stage, for, although you are a strongly mental type, your imagination is so active that it can interfere with your logical processes. In the realm of pure thought you tend to wander from the scientific to the speculative; while in dealing with people your ardent and expansive nature is capable of being fooled by anyone who, in some way or other, makes an appeal to your need for affection or who seems to need affection himself. Since you are warm-hearted, idealistic, and romantic, you throw a sort of glamour around people, taking them to your heart and finding excuses for doing so even after they have proved themselves unworthy. You are proud, independent, and self-reliant, and you don't like to have your original good opinion of people upset. Thus you are capable of making the best of a bad bargain in friendship or in love for a long time. But if your pride is ever hurt by the person directly, you can break and run—and never come back. You have strong artistic leanings and a powerful creative flair which, with 147, or 180, or 163 without 170, may result in productive activity along creative lines. You are persistent, once you have pinned yourself down to reality.

With 187, 198 or 182, much interest in occult matters. With 184 or 195 scientific ability—the speculative bent proves things imagined by experimentation and may do pioneering in science or philosophy. With 151 or 182, mystic leanings dangerous; a highly impressionable nature, leaning to the sensational. With 181 or 164, explosive and romantic temperament, erratic and idealistic, but somewhat unstable. With 200, 210, 211, 203, 204, 213 or 214, the romantic nature needs careful watching; with 202 or 212, much difficulty through this. With 186, powerful mind, good business ability, thorough and efficient.

You must pin yourself strictly down to the realities of your life for your highest development and greatest happiness.

126

SUN IN AQUARIUS—MOON IN VIRGO

(You belong to the positive or executive group)

MIND POWER and ability to detach yourself from personal considerations are your chief assets. You can reason things out with a fine, hard, critical analysis and, through being able to keep your emotions out of situations you achieve an unusually sane judgment. If you have had a good education you go far in an intellectual, creative, or professional career. You are expressive and can be eloquent in either writing or speech. You can reason from a minimum of evidence and through intellectual subtlety can make the worse appear the better cause. You are a hard opponent in argument or debate, and even in personal matters you bring your reason and your argumentativeness to bear. You believe in the power of the spoken and written word, and this is likely to make oddities in your emotional life. You can think up reasons and excuses for your affections and emotions and expect other people to do the same. You aren't an especially good loser, either in intellectual or emotional matters, and you have a way of seeming hurt if people don't agree with you or if your persuasiveness fails. Your emotions are so bound up with your thinking processes that you think those who love you ought to agree with you and those who agree with you must love you. Since the rest of the world doesn't understand this attitude, you are likely to feel pretty lonely. A good deal of self-pity accompanies this position. You take yourself pretty seriously and feel aggrieved when others do not do the same. A peculiarly detached approach to matters of affection and love brings you disappointments, for you are much in need of companionship, which you do not make apparent in the most direct manner possible. You are sensitive and very conscious of rebuffs, perhaps imagining them when they do not actually exist. You are proud and therefore appear self-sufficient, which you are not really at all. With 160, 200, 210, 213 or 214, much hurt through the emotions. With 147, 148, 149 or 150, great mind power and success and rise through it, though danger of fall thereafter. With 170, austere nature; with 180 or 181, erratic and temperamental; with 168 or 178, high temper and danger of the passional nature running away with you; anger and strife dangerous.

127

SUN IN AQUARIUS—MOON IN LIBRA

YOU ARE highly social-minded, romantic in the extreme, and will have your share of the ups and downs of love. You are constantly being disappointed by the duplicity, the infidelity, the faithlessness, and the fickleness in those you love. You are able to give your affections to the most outlandish people and to be surprised when you aren't able to hold them. On the other hand, they may have a hard time holding you, for you are an elusive creature, liking what you like when you like it and tending to tire of it rather quickly. You hold the illusion that you are fidelity itself, but, at the drop of a hat, you can find a reason why you shouldn't be faithful. You are well able to understand the sentimentality of "I have been true to you, Cynara, in my fashion." Your fashion may indeed be a strange one. But you are a person of considerable charm, magnetism, personality, and fundamental sincerity, and when you get your emotional life settled—marriage is a real necessity to you!—you are a most charming, constructive person. You understand people and, knowing well the foibles of humanity, you are tolerant and sympathetic; an ideal confidant. You will succeed best in some artistic or professional career where your idealism and expressiveness has full sway; or in business, for you are a good salesman, persuasive and forceful without being objectionable. You know how to sell your product along with yourself, and vice versa. You lack persistence, and if you can't put things over in one fell swoop, you are likely to lose interest—unless with 149, 163, 170 or 180, when you can hang on like grim death.

With 200, 210, 203, 214, 213 or 204, turbulent and varied love-life. With 202 or 212, disappointments in love to and from others. With 183 or 189, artistic ability; also with 203, 204, 187 or 188. The development of the aesthetic side of your nature, either on the critical, appreciative, or creative side, will do much to stabilize your purposes and give you a goal that is compatible with your highly idealistic bent.

128

SUN IN AQUARIUS—MOON IN SCORPIO

(You belong to the positive or executive group)

YOUR GOOD OPINION of yourself is the lodestar of your life. Nobody is likely to be so important to you as yourself and your ambition, and this, if it occurs with 147, 161, 149, 163, 168, 170 or 180, may amount to an egomania and a driving force that commands recognition, though it frequently collapses through resting on insecure foundations. You have a highly personalized approach to life, and, even when you are most intellectual, most detached, most abstracted in your thinking and reasoning, there is a strong personal underlying motif and a deep consciousness that You are important. You are a tremendous personality in your circle and can become an influence for good or evil on all you reach. You are magnetic, commanding, intellectually brilliant and intense, and you translate to your listeners a sense of your own importance that is hypnotic. Once your spell is working, your followers feel that you can do no wrong. But so personal is this charm and so bound up with your own vitality that if you relax it collapses; you don't train lieutenants to carry on your work or impel people to cheer for you when you aren't there. They are sold on you, personally, rather than on what you do or fail to do, and when you need defenders or apologists, few will be forthcoming. You accept the responsibility of your life and build it yourself, and with your efforts it ceases. If you can learn to detach yourself and your thinking and emotional processes from the all-absorbing you, then you can achieve a more objective grip on things which will rest on more secure foundations. But you tend to build everything on your own vitality, demanding, rather than wooing, recognition and love. The result is that when you are no longer able to demand you find you have built no strong foundations on which these things can continue to rest. You are not a superficial person, being deep and intense; but you may appear superficial through your self-absorption. Also, unless the driving forces listed above are present, there is a sort of inertia and, especially with 161 or 180, some essential flaw in the personality, the philosophy, or the approach will tear down your structure as soon as it is built. With these and with 224, look carefully at the premises on which your life rests. Dig deeply into your consciousness to see on what essential fallacies you are working, and in any case, try to find the method by which your tremendous powers can be released, impersonally, to gain you an emotional and intellectual, rather than a purely personal, hold on your public.

129

SUN IN AQUARIUS—MOON IN SAGITTARIUS

(You belong to the positive or executive group)

INDEPENDENCE of mind and action, thought and expression, are the keynotes of your nature. You are an intellectual and, as your life has gone on, you have become able to focus your emotional and passional nature in intellectual concepts, and to approach the philosophic ideal of objectivity. This was not all the case in the beginning of your life, when emotions ran very high and strong and threatened to gallop away with the whole personality. You have qualities of uncompromising intellectual honesty, strong opinions, and a broad viewpoint on world affairs. Your tendency to wide interests can make you a visionary and impractical dilettante, if it is not with 147, 161, 149, 163, 168, 178, 170, 180, 183, 186, 192 or 197. But, if with any of these, you have depth, vision, and scope of intellect and will always be found fighting on the side of the fundamental truth. Independence, courage, and efficiency give you a fine foundation for success. You are an executive by nature and will not stay long in a subordinate position, rising by industry, honesty, intelligence, and a strict regard for duty. You may be a little outspoken (especially if Mercury is in Sagittarius with the Moon), and a high-spirited and righteous independence must be curbed and brought in line with the world as it is. You are never likely to learn to compromise with truth and honor, but you should learn to compromise with people. There is a tendency to arts and letters here, a love for the beautiful in all things, with a touch of the Keatsian thesis that "Beauty is truth, truth beauty" and a feeling that "Euclid alone has looked on beauty bare." Line, design, logic, and reason are your concepts of beauty, rather than the more sensual beauty of the ultra-romantic.

Emotionally, this is a romantic position, inclining to produce several intense and idealistic love affairs and showing the likelihood of more than one marriage. There's great personal magnetism, which lasts till late in life—you seem to have drunk from the fountain of youth, for the continuous freshness of your outlook keeps you young for a surprisingly long time. Thus, through traits of personality and character and through help from influential friends, you are likely to have what is known as luck in life.

130

SUN IN AQUARIUS—MOON IN CAPRICORN

(You belong to the positive or executive group)

YOU ARE a hundred per cent American, a supporter of the status quo, an upholder of law and order, a rugged individualist. The fact of outstanding interest about this combination is that it has produced more eminent Americans than any other solar-lunar combination. It has an affinity with the horoscope of the United States and will carry you far in public life—politics preferably, but any activity that deals with the general (American) public. You are automatically able to catch the imagination of those around you, for you combine a warm humanism with strict and logical adherence to the facts—a combination peculiarly calculated to win support from the people. Thus, whether you are a president (Lincoln)—inventor (Edison)—a pioneer (Lindbergh)—an actor (John Barrymore)—a critic (George Jean Nathan)—an actress (Katherine Cornell)—a poet (William Ellery Leonard)—a novelist (Dorothy Canfield Fisher)—or a poet (William Rose Benet), in some way or another, your work bears the mark of distinction and your achievement carries home to the public.

Note: All the above have this solar-lunar combination except Lindbergh, who may have the Moon in Sagittarius or Capricorn, depending on the accuracy of his birth data, which so far has been unverifiable. We suspect he has the Moon in Capricorn, for he surely belongs in this galaxy of stars who have captured the American imagination.

The qualities which seal you with the seal of success are qualities of imagination, foresight, fearlessness, self-confidence, and fundamental honesty of purpose, which you never lose sight of for a moment. Your ambition is important to you, but your honor more so, and if you had to sacrifice one or the other it would be your ambition. It is this very integrity that endears you to those around you, so that while warmer-hearted, more expressive, more voluble people are all well enough, you, with your austerity, your pride, your strict sense of right and wrong, none the less can win their affection and love. No one begrudges you your success; it is felt to be deserved because you have created it for yourself and have not compromised with truth or with your convictions on the way. You can succeed in public life—though if rugged individualism breaks down this won't be true any longer. There is nothing of the radical about you. You are humanitarian, but you don't believe in the people even though you love them; you think they have to be taken care of and therefore your political chances get less as various phases of socialism come in. But in any world you are an admirable, admired, and respected person, capable of assuming authority and carrying it well; of envisioning and putting through large enterprises, and of remaining untouched and unspoiled even at the height of success and acclaim.

131

SUN IN AQUARIUS—MOON IN AQUARIUS

(You belong to the positive or executive group)

THE SCIENTIFIC BENT is strong in you. You are an analyst, an organizer as well as a finder of information and knowledge, and you see your knowledge in broad, social, and philosophic sweeps. Your bent is critical rather than creative or executive, though in your executive power over the minds of men you are not easily excelled. In your personal life you are romantic, though a tendency to relate your personal feelings to large principles and generalizations makes you more like a book of poetry than a realistic lover. If Venus is in Aquarius, you may be extremely idealistic and romantic in love matters, and if Venus is in Pisces you may be soft-hearted enough to be imposed on. If Venus is in Capricorn, you are hard-headed enough to take care of yourself and will no doubt make a judicious compromise between love and money when you marry, believing with the Quakers, "Thee shouldst marry for love, but it is just as easy to love where there is money." You aren't likely to marry beneath you for, despite a wide interest in people, your discrimination is strong and your innate fineness and good taste will lead you to a choice of a mate from your own social station, if not above it. You are a great reader and student, self-sufficient at times, while at others you crave society — any company being preferable to none. And you are likely to collect odd assortments of people around you, all sorts of waifs and strays who fascinate you despite your underlying snobbery.

With 147, 150, 161, 164, 168, 178, 171, 181, 200, 210, 202, 212, 203, 213, 204 or 214, this may lead to your running with your inferiors more than is good for you; with 180, you love to dominate and will seek those whom you can dominate and run away from those you can't. You are jealous and irascible and will rule or quit. Often as not you quit. With 180, ambition leads you sternly upwards—look out for organic physical difficulties through overwork and nerve tension. Nerves will always beset you more or less, and a tendency to live on nervous energy must be suppressed; learn to relax.

132

SUN IN AQUARIUS—MOON IN PISCES

YOU ARE intuitive, something of a mystic, leaning on your hunches and your inspirations and capable of going far, either toward truth or toward fallacies through the following of your swift mental processes. You have a feeling for poetry that makes it appear a science, and for science that makes of it a sort of poetry, and a combination of the real and the abstract, the imaginative and the demonstrable, the mystic and the earthly, gives you a broad hold on all branches of human knowledge and thought. You need a good education, strict discipline in logic, and the development of a respect for accuracy and fact. Without this intellectual training you can become a first-class visionary, spiritualist, medium, or clairvoyant, believing in ghosts, fairies, and hobgoblins. In any case you will be fascinated throughout life by the unseen, the mysterious, and the strange, which may give you strange bogies and phobias and cause you to be gullible on some points at the same time that you are completely rational on others. You lead a private life of your own, into which few other people ever penetrate. You may have delusions either of grandeur or persecution, genius, a belief in witches and warlocks, a propensity to believe in alchemy, or that the world is flat, or that there will befall woe if a black cat crosses your path. There is an odd admixture of the irrational with all the otherwise completely sane things that you do and believe but so great is your grip on reality that these oddities rarely amount to anything and really lend color and mystery to your personality. In your emotional life you are idealistic, loyal, sensitive, and easily imposed upon and will be hurt rather than angry at being fooled.

With 202 or 212, you are hurt through your sensitiveness; with 200, 210, 203, 204 or 214, sensationalism, curious ideas of love, make trouble; with 165, 182, 188 or 199, muddled thinking; with 149, danger of introversion; with 163 or 180, great concentrative and driving force; with 184, 185, 186 or 187, critical and careful mind; with 187, inspirational along scientific or poetic lines, or both — a very versatile person.

133
SUN IN PISCES—MOON IN ARIES

YOU HAVE a judicial type of mind, aware, alert, and intuitive, relating knowledge, life, principles and ideals strictly to yourself, and then allowing your concepts to take in general principles. You are naturally reserved, although a vitality of manner makes you appear less so than you really are. Behind the expansiveness of approach you have a private life of your own that remains untouched, and you are forming judgments of people and events all the time. You are rather more self-sufficient than you appear; you like to reach forth from your private world and influence other people at the same time that you remain detached and a little proud and aloof. Your self-respect is tremendous and, working hand in hand with your independence of spirit, carries you along in the world. There is something solid and substantial about you that other people trust. You are affectionate and somewhat ardent in love, though you are touchy and easily offended. You are a trifle quarrelsome and have something of a chip on your shoulder—in your manner, at least. You are temperamental in the real sense, and temperament, anger, bafflement, and frustration make you nervous and rebound on you so that you are likely to be more hurt than your opponent. You need peace and calm and shouldn't let the more aggressive side of your nature disturb the repose that is so needful to the other side. You have about you an air of authority which is confusing to less positive people who are always relieved to find out that you aren't as unyielding as you appear. You are very sympathetic and understanding, and your bravado is in the nature of a protective shell around a very sensitive core.

With 147, 161, 168 or 178, quarrelsomeness dangerously increased, and health suffers through anger; with 181, highly temperamental and somewhat unconventional nature; with 182, sensational, dreamy, mystical, and danger through erratic impressionability. With 163 or 180, moody, trouble through love matters; with 200, 210, 201, 211, 203, 213, 204 or 214, super-social, and difficulty through emotional jumpiness. This is a business and professional rather than an artistic position. Your aggressive nature deals with other people better than with abstractions or ideals, and your magnetism helps you to success in material matters through your ability to organize and manage.

134

SUN IN PISCES—MOON IN TAURUS

YOU ARE an extremely sociable person with much social tact. You are sensitive almost to a fault, but you make up for this with an equally acute sense of the other person's feelings and wishes, which you'll go out of your way to avoid hurting. You are thus very easy to get along with, tractable and agreeable—except when you are opposed, when you can be very stubborn. You will not be imposed upon and have an equal dislike for imposing upon others. You tend to be somewhat formal in social matters and like to have the give-and-take evened off so that no one is in anyone else's debt. You are artistic either in a creative or appreciative way, and, although you have innate sense for business, will generally be found in the artistic or professional careers. Medicine, the ministry, writing, singing, music of some sort—these interest you more than competitive matters. The struggle for existence is likely to be easy for you, for this is a lucky position and, through inherited security, or the ready flow of money to you, economic matters are generally taken care of. You are especially sensitive to music and probably play or sing well; in any case, you will be found among the patrons of the opera or concerts. You will rarely be found doing anything gauche or ill-mannered or saying the wrong thing. You are especially flattering in speech, apparently having kissed the Blarney Stone, and you like flattery. You have a lot of self-respect and like to feel that other people appreciate you. This is because, despite all your apparent poise and social graces, you are really a rather uncertain person, not sure of yourself, and therefore liking to hear nice things about yourself, to which you react with true gratitude. You are a loyal friend and will have loyal friends around you. In love, you are devoted, though your highly sensitive nature may make trouble in matters of the emotions. You can be ruled by love but not by anger or in fact by any kind of discipline, for you kick over the traces and run away if you think anyone is trying to lord it over you.

With 147, 148, 155, 156, 157 or 158, powerful careerist, with a good deal of energy and luck; with 163, 181, 182 or 180, difficulty in marriage or love; with 200, 210, 202, 212, 203, 213, 204 or 214, erratic and somewhat hectic emotional life; with 215, 218, 229 or 237, tremendous luck and probability of wealth; with 151, music prominent; 163, 147, 146, 215, 218 or 229, heighten the artistic nature and produce success and recognition through the arts.

135

SUN IN PISCES—MOON IN GEMINI

ALTERNATE FLEXIBILITY and stubbornness, both badly timed, cause you trouble. You will yield when you should be firm and stand your ground when the part of good sense is to give way. This is a result of a fundamental lack of self-confidence, which your extremely voluble and expressive nature belies. You can talk readily and convincingly, and until your associates learn that you talk chiefly to convince yourself they will think you a highly opinionated person. What you must learn is *not* to talk until your mind is made up, for frequently what issues from your mouth is a great surprise to your ears, and you have to get used to your own ideas even as you are trying to sell them to someone else. This is true in both intellectual and emotional matters—it isn't exactly that you jump to conclusions, but that you simply jump and take a gamble on what conclusion you will land in. There is a good deal of timidity here, and you are thrown off your balance and confused by hard, determined, unkind, or very opinionated people. In the presence of weaker intellects you are reasonable and delight in your tolerance; but in the presence of someone whom you feel to be stronger than yourself you assert yourself with arguments and, since your reasoning is not always right, you lose out. Thus you are beloved of people who work under you but not by your bosses and, until you learn not to be so stubborn when opposed, your path of progress will be made difficult by your handling of opposition. This is a rather better position for a woman than for a man, for in a woman it is intellectual mobility rather than indecision. But in either sex the chief danger in life is from lack of ability to make up the mind constructively.

With 223, 224, 216, 195, 196, 197, 198, 199, 233, 234, 235, 240, 241 or 244, this indecision is emphasized dangerously. With 147 or 161, aggression is misdirected and makes enemies; with 180, determination increased—and inferiority complex takes constructive action. With 151, 164, 181 or 182, nerves very much of a problem; with 159, muddled thinking, mind needs training.

This position inclines, in either sex, to more than one marriage and popularity with the other sex; also to considerable variety in the emotional life and some depression and dejection through it.

136

SUN IN PISCES—MOON IN CANCER

(You belong to the positive or executive group)

YOU ARE a dramatist, and the play you are most interested in is the drama of You. You are sensitive, alert to the opinion and feelings of the world around you and, through a sort of sixth sense, able to give the public what it wants almost before it knows it wants it. You are courteous, kind, considerate, and genuinely charitable, willing to give to the poor and needy even if you have to make sacrifices yourself to do it. You are really a very shy person, and your personality and forcefulness is the product of rigid self-discipline, for you have overcome timidity and stage fright and *made* yourself go forward into the public eye. You have converted timidity into sensitiveness and fear into an understanding of other people—and after you understand them you don't have to be afraid of them: you know how to handle them. You can be successful as an actor, doctor, nurse, minister, diplomat, or detective—any place where a knowledge of the mental and emotional workings of others is an asset. You have a certain flair for business, but this will probably show forth in your management of your own property rather than in a business career, for you seek a purely personal type of expression and will do best if you land in the arts or the professions. Emotionally, you are so acutely sensitive to impressions that you have a very romantic life, not without its ups and downs and inconstancies. You take offense readily and can drive people crazy with the intensity of your hurt and bewilderment over apparently trifling things. You are moody and temperamental, after the manner of an April day. This is a good position for material well-being. With 147, 148, 151, 168, 169 or 172, exceptionally so.

With 215, 218, 227, 229, great authority and possessions. With 164, 151, 181 or 182, sensationalism needs combating; with 200, 210, 203, 213 or 214, highly romantic career, many loves. The same paragraphs which increase the fortunes (see above) tend to increase the creative gifts and to bring recognition and financial return through the arts or the professions. You are so versatile that you are likely to follow two careers (not to mention two sweethearts) at the same time, and do well with each. One way or another, you tend to lead a "double life" and obey the Biblical injunction of not letting the left hand know what the right doeth. O. K. so long as you don't get snarled up.

137

SUN IN PISCES—MOON IN LEO

YOU ARE a somewhat contradictory person, alternately aggressive and reticent, and at all times overcoming a fundamental timidity which your rather expansive personality belies if one doesn't look below the surface. You have private fears, forebodings, and worries that do not find expression in your apparently fearless and competent manner. There are deep wells of your consciousness that few people are aware of and of which you yourself are not completely aware. You are sociable, many times, when you would rather be alone—and contrariwise, you are frequently discontented when you are alone and long for companionship. You can, in a very genuine sense, be "alone in a crowd"—not for lack of personality or popularity, but because you tend to withdraw into yourself. You have great abilities, mental and artistic, which do not find ready expression. You give the impression that there are many things you could do if you wanted to. You fail to because of a fundamental lack of willingness to engage in competition. Your apparent sureness is a manner rather than an actuality; you have a great admiration for accomplishment in others but probably won't try to equal or surpass what has already been done. When you are not in a mood or a dejected state, you are excellent company, with a lively sense of humor, kind and considerate of others, generous and charitable, broad-minded in your outlook. If you ever become cross, snappy, or ill-tempered, it is because in some way you have been reminded of your lack of sureness—because you are putting up a defense against some real or imagined enemy of your emotional security. Emotionally, you are romantic, imaginative, impressionable, sensitive, and loyal—loyalty is a fetish with you, and your affections once given are never withdrawn. You are very needful of affection, sympathy, love, and understanding and will be the devoted servant of anyone who gives them to you.

This position is indicative of considerable luck in life, and if with 215, 218, 229 or 237, may accompany wealth, or at least security—though part of your nervousness is based in a fear of the loss of security. Your hardest lesson is the cultivation of inner poise to match the outward manifestations of courage and conviction. And your effort should be to see the world as it is rather than as your apprehensive spirit tends to imagine it. Realism is your safest and surest guide and you should avoid tendencies to metaphysics, spiritualism, and psychic research, which can gain a dangerously strong hold on you.

138

SUN IN PISCES—MOON IN VIRGO

YOU ARE able to put your intuitions over and to bring them to bear logically on your life. You are a good judge of people, with an absolute determination of the correctness of your judgments. Once you are determined about the inner worth of an individual, nothing he can do, however erratic or unreasonable or reprehensible, will shake your faith in him; you understand him from the inside out, and you are willing to let him work out his own problems in his own way. You believe that "to understand all is to forgive all," and though you are a harsh judge when you estimate a person to be fundamentally unsound, you are equally lenient when you know that the core of his being is sound. Your tolerance is specific rather than universal, intellectual rather than emotional, for you apply to your intuitions a high degree of logic and common sense by which you can make them plausible, both to yourself and others. This integration of facts felt and facts known gives you a quiet self-assurance which rises from the working together of your mental and emotional natures; these are not generally found at variance with each other. You don't find yourself doing by impulse things of which you disapprove; and though you may do things of which others disapprove, you have a good reason of your own why you are all right. Your conscience is a real force, but as you are tolerant of others you are also tolerant of yourself, and though you won't often stray from the beaten track, when you do, you do it calmly and without excitement—with a quiet conviction that you are acting according to some code or other, which you may have made up for the occasion, but which is very real and definite to you. But, by and large, you will lead a conventional, orderly, and understanding life. You have a keen sense of humor, laughing readily, which may not give an accurate impression of your fundamentally serious nature. You are amused by life at the same time that you are acutely conscious of its underlying tragic implications. But this consciousness does not interfere with your enjoyment. You have a private litany of faith, a sort of exclusive metaphysics of your own, by which you weave together apparent contradictions into the integrated philosophy by which you live and estimate life. This position is mildly good for business activity of the non-executive variety, and also for such creative work as calls for accuracy, thought, and application, rather than inspirational creativeness. Makes good humorists and jokesmiths.

139

SUN IN PISCES—MOON IN LIBRA

YOUR ÆSTHETIC QUALITIES are strongly marked; you strive for self-expression through the arts or through religion or philosophy. Whatever you go in for, you have a sort of consecrated and devotional attitude toward it. You are strongly sensuous, and you give whatever you touch a romantic and idealistic glamour. Appeal to the emotions rather than to the intellect is your aim or should be your aim. Intellectually, you are capable of taking a fine education, but you are fundamentally not an intellectual but an intuitive type. You can drown your gifts in a sea of facts, and verbiage if you go in for too technical matters. Your control can be over the hearts, rather than over the minds, of men and when your intellect is working under the spell of inspiration you can produce marvels that strike to the roots of humanity with a strange eerie quality. You should not go in for spiritualism, mediumship, or mysticism of any sort, for this can gain a great hold on you; but you should develop an automatic quality to what you say, do, write, or speak, for your best self comes out when you are completely off guard. You have a deep and active subconscious, and to bring about the fluent expression of it, unhindered by the world and even by intellectual considerations, should be your aim. You are capable of falling into bad emotional muddles through a sort of irritating consciousness that you aren't working as a unit and of trying to rationalize yourself out of them. As a matter of fact, rationalization is one of your worst enemies. You can believe anything which it suits your emotional purposes to believe and, under stress of disappointment, frustration, or slow progress, can further impede your getting ahead by thinking too much, analyzing too much, and acting too little on impulse. You are one of the few people in the world who is best when undisciplined, for although a certain amount of education and self-control is necessary, you tend to press yourself into a mold more completely than is necessary, and to set up complexes due to the repression. Contrary to psychoanalytical dogma, in your case this is not sexual repression but emotional and intellectual repression. You need to let go, internally, so that the expression which is so important to you may flow of its own volition. When you do this you will be amazed at the increased happiness, fluency, and success of your life. With 183 or 189, highly idealistic and artistic mind, creative ability high. With 202 or 212, emotional disappointment mixes you up; with 200, 210, 203, 204, 213 or 214, hectic emotional life, emotional perversity and eccentricity. With 147, brilliant creative mind; with 161, equally brilliant, but purpose flags.

140

SUN IN PISCES—MOON IN SCORPIO

YOU ARE a keen person, perceptive, intuitive, with a razor-like swiftness of thought and an ability to put things together in strange and unusual combinations. Your sense of humor is extraordinary, and you can see the whimsical, the humorous, the ridiculous, or the pathetic in your fellow creatures—and in yourself. Fundamentally a serious person, you have a kind of perverse habit of philosophic laughter. Even when you appear to be clowning, there is a serious undercurrent to your ludicrousness. You brood a good deal and are capable of falling into profound periods of dejection and depression. You lead a private life of your own that is not always a happy one, for when you aren't thinking of the woes of the world you are thinking of your own private troubles. You have a lively imagination and if you aren't careful can believe in things that aren't true. You are especially liable to superstition and very likely believe in dreams and fancy yourself something of a Joseph in matters of dream interpretation. You have a somewhat morbid interest in death, the fate of the dead, and your own fate. You believe in the survival of personality and may think you have reason to believe it proved. You are a fair business man, if you let yourself go in for business. But your best bent is professional, artistic, or musical, for you need self-expression of a personal sort. In romantic matters, you are impressionable and impressive, having a profound effect on members of the opposite sex and meriting their love by giving love in return. This isn't a position that makes for fidelity, but rather for variety, in the love-life.

With 200, 210, 211, 203, 213, 204 or 214, much variety; with 202 or 212, hurt through, and to, others; with 147, 161, 168, 178, 165 or 182, tension, which you let down with artificial means—look out for drugs and soporifics. With 163, great intensity and drive; with 150, 164, 165, 181 or 182, nerves are a problem; with 148, 155, 169 or 174, lots of luck; with 215, 218, 227, 228, 229, 237 or 226, great magnetism, luck, and probably wealth and influence.

141

SUN IN PISCES—MOON IN SAGITTARIUS

(You belong to the positive or executive group)

YOU ARE a progressive thinker, in the forefront of the thought of your times and possibly ahead of it. Through vision, foresight, and expressiveness you can be a large influence on those around you; you think in large, broad terms, in either scientific or social matters. You think so naturally in abstractions and generalities that, without strict intellectual training, you may be a completely impractical visionary, unable to cope with the world, unable to see the trees because of the forest, and thus making progress difficult. With education—whether formal or self-gained—your extraordinary breadth of viewpoint and your deep wisdom of insight bring you to the fore rank of thinkers; and either in science, sociology, or literature you rise to respect and authority. You are a highly expansive person and may try to spread your energies too thinly, over too wide a field of knowledge or endeavor; you should pin yourself down to a specialty and master it. A certain spiritual quality attaches to everything you do; you seem at one moment of the earth earthy; and at another like a prophet from another plane. You have tremendous confidence in yourself and your mission, whether you feel that it is world-shaking or confined to a narrow circle of intimates. You create your own opportunities, and doors open up to you; though, on the face of things, you are not really aggressive. Your imagination works in staggering symbols, huge canvases, in great sweeping thoughts and magnificant expressions of them. There is something heroic about your intellectual and imaginative processes that dwarfs competitors, who may none the less reap more material rewards than you do. Definitely, you are not a materialist, and if the world gives you a living you are content to go on with your work. You are an idealist through and through and have some of the naïveté that attaches to idealism, in spite of your intuitive wisdom.

With 148, 155, 169, 174, 173, 175, 176, 177, 152, 153, 154, 156, 157 or 158, wide influence and protection from material want; with 163, 180, concentrative powers marked, worldliness less marked; with 150, 164, 165, 181 or 182, nervousness a great problem.

You should learn concentration and through development of your intellectual and imaginative powers seek to express the ideas, thoughts, and concepts that are so natural to you. Stay away from metaphysics, which tempts you, and stick to the provable and demonstrable facts of either science or the professions or arts.

142

SUN IN PISCES—MOON IN CAPRICORN

(You belong to the positive or executive group)

YOU ARE worldly wise, and you combine with your sensitiveness and perceptivity a large amount of concentrated driving power which impels you to worldly success. You are conscious of large values, philosophic and abstract concepts, but they are significant to you chiefly in terms of what use the world can make of them and what use you can make of them in your own progress. Through being able to combine the ideal and the practical, the abstract and the concrete, you capture the imagination of men. You are deeply ambitious, eager that your worth should find recognition in the world; and through adaptability and a sense of other people's emotions and motives you are likely to go far in the business or political world. You are daring, though not exactly courageous; you are willing to take a chance, even when you are timid about the outcome; and you are able to cover over your inner jitteriness with a great show of bravado. You have a strong personality, considerable reserve, and a good deal of secretiveness; before you take people into your confidence you work things out in your own mind till the plans are complete. You are in this way an executive, a planner, and a doer, able both to do yourself and to get others to do for you. You are strong for duty and the fulfilling of obligations, and your word is as good as your bond; similarly you expect every man to do his duty and won't brook loafing on the job in those who work for you. Emotionally you are a most satisfactory person, both sensitive and reserved and not generally demanding much from those you love except fair treatment and a judicious amount of affection. You are only moderately jealous, but can appear more so if you want to make a point. You are something of an actor, anyway, and you have an accurate sense of the audience you are dealing with.

With 163, tremendous ambition, which meets with success; with 148, 155, 169 or 174, good-fellowship marked, and also much material success; with 215, 216, 218, 227, 228, 229 or 237, rise to great influence and power, with probability of wealth.

Material things are important to you, though with this materialism you combine a philosophic approach to things that makes you a balanced and interesting, as well as a successful, person.

143

SUN IN PISCES—MOON IN AQUARIUS

(You belong to the positive or executive group)

YOU ARE a humanitarian, believing in people in the large, and likely to be at home in adventures of reform, social service, public duty, religion, and the like. If you go into public life it is as the devoted public servant rather than as the careerist. The missionary spirit is strong in you; you believe in the homely virtues, in moderation, in truth, in honor, and they form a sort of creed with you which you try to impress on others. You are not a very tolerant person and condemn roundly those who are of frailer mold than yourself, at the same time that you are eager to help them achieve strength. You are orthodox in your religious beliefs—in fact, somewhat pious; and if you aren't careful you'll find yourself developing a holier-than-thou attitude. Try to believe that other people know what they are about even if their methods and beliefs are different from yours—even the heathen Chinee. You are emotionally ardent and sincere, with a real sympathy and understanding for people you love, and you endear yourself to those around you through courtesy, affability, and a sense of humor which does not, however, interfere with your fundamentally serious attitude toward life. You are temperamental, capable of enjoying yourself in company—and going home to brood and gloom about the state of the nation or the fact that there is a war on in Ethiopia. If you get something like this on your mind with sufficient intensity, you are perfectly capable of trying to do something about it single-handed; or at least you will sit down and write a letter to the editor about it, signed "Pro Bono Publico" or "Pax Vobiscum." You have great faith in the power of the spoken or written word to make converts to a cause and are a powerful and persuasive speaker or writer. You are likely to keep after someone in your circle till you have made him a convert to your cause, which may be Prohibition, the Church, the League for Peace, or any one of the humanitarian movements that are so important to you. In private life you are an upright citizen, a pillar of the Church, and of government, law, and order; and because of these qualities you are respected, loved, and trusted.

144

SUN IN PISCES—MOON IN PISCES

(You belong to the positive or executive group)

YOU ARE an unusual person, interested in unusual and out-of-the-way studies, people, ideas—and a good deal interested in yourself. You are highly introspective, with the result that the outer world seems an odd, if not completely insane, place to you and most people either crazy, stupid, or full of weird notions. Did it ever occur to you that maybe *you're* the one with the weird notions, and that you are like the soldier who wrote home that the whole company was out of step except himself? A tendency to withdraw into yourself to nurse some private idea that you can't get across or won't bother to get across makes you strangely inaccessible, and though you appear tractable, reasonable, interested in other people and other ideas, you are in reality all wound up inside, building more stately mansions for your soul—like the chambered Nautilus—while you are letting the world go hang. You need to keep a firm grip on reality, and the more conventionally you live and think, and the more you try to understand and conform with other people's ideas and methods, the happier you will be. The danger of your private life—your internal existence—is that you will gradually become so isolated in your viewpoint, thinking, and living as to be very lonely. You are so sensitive that you are afraid of being hurt by contact with the world; you are not courageous and prefer withdrawal to encounter. Although in exceptional cases your tact and sensitiveness may lead you to positions of authority, your execution is likely to be weak, though you are painstaking and accurate in details and very strong for duty and fulfilling obligations. Mentally you are quick, perceptive, intuitive, with an almost mystic belief in your hunches; and when not emotionally involved, your hunches are likely to be all right. Emotion throws you off, and if with 200, 210, 202, 212, 203, 213, 204, 214, 216, 224, 147, 161, 168, 178, 164, 165, 181 or 182, much trouble through emotional matters, with danger of complexes and unconventional ideas.

With 163 or 180, objectivity is helped; you are able to exteriorize powerfully and to good practical purpose. Watch health. With 148, 155, 169, 174, luck in material matters; with 215, 218 or 229, wealth; with 149 or 170, introversion must be guarded against; with 186 or 197, mentally depressed periods; with 161, erratic mentality; if Mercury is in Pisces, garrulous, or if with 184, 195, 188 or 199.

Insight is your great strength, and you have an uncanny way of seeing the core and substance of things; use this creatively and constructively, rather than critically or introvertedly, and your understanding will make you valuable in the world of practical affairs. Avoid spiritualism, occultism, and the like.

REGULAR PARAGRAPHS

THE FOLLOWING REGULAR PARAGRAPHS REFER TO PLANETARY ASPECTS. THE BASIC PARAGRAPHS INTERPRETING THE SUN AND MOON BEGIN ON PAGE 25.

145
MOON CONJUNCTION[1] MERCURY ☽ ☌ ☿

WIT, CLEVERNESS, intellectual aptness are your especial gifts—and the danger of this aspect is that you will coast through life on your wits, skimming the surface of things, getting information without much effort and also without much depth. Unless with 149, 163, 148, 166, 178, 180 or 181, you won't try to get far under the outer skin of intellectual matters. You are charming company, never without something to say that's witty and entertaining. You have a certain creative flair which, without one or more of the paragraphs listed above, will bring you success in intellectual endeavors that don't require true creative ability. Successful advertising people, reporters, radio speakers, and the like, who depend on pleasant voices, glibness of expression, quickness of phrasing and expression, come under this clever and facile influence. On the other hand, if this is supported by one of the numbers listed above, the profundity is increased and you then become a careful as well as an apt student, intellectually eager for knowledge, and capable of sticking to your guns until your curiosity is satisfied. If to this is added 147, 184, 188, 215, 218 or 226, created ability will be marked along either literary, dramatic, musical, or artistic lines. With 161, preciosity—and sharp tongue; with 164, erratic mentality; with 151, confused, inspirational, and mystic; with 196, careless mind, somewhat tricky; with 195 and 197, yarn spinners. With 183 or 189, much appreciation of the arts and of belles lettres, but unless with one of the creative aspects listed in this paragraph, the yearning to create is not likely to be satisfied.

This is a good business position, making salesmen and contact men, and if with 161, 163, 178, 179 or 180 you are likely to go far and turn your mental agility to good practical account in the coin of the realm.

146
MOON CONJUNCTION[1] VENUS ☽ ☌ ♀

GRACE AND CHARM if a woman, and personality or its equivalent if a man, make human relations and therefore life easy for you. You are likely to be one of the spoiled darlings of society, capable of winning people over simply by appearing on the scene. Considerable beauty generally accompanies this position, and even if your features don't look regular to you, there'll always be lots of people who see something there that they find easy to look at. You are a trifle vain and will spend money for adornment even if you have to go without something else that you may need more. But this is unlikely to happen, for there is a good deal of material luck with this position, and someone or something will probably pop up at the last minute to save you from financial

[1] In the same space with.

distress. This aspect in itself doesn't make you very aggressive in either profession or personal life, but with other aggressive indications will insure the success of your ventures. A woman with this aspect may be a social leader of some importance or in some way the center of her circle; while a man is sure to have a charming, popular, and helpful wife. With 161, 164 or 150, she may be too popular for his comfort, though generally loyal and devoted even when flirtatious. If you have this in your chart, you will find that your business and professional career is materially helped by social contacts, and that society is important to you. You thrive on people, parties, and amusements; while anything connected with these (singing, acting, producing, drama, music, writing for the public) will provide your best medium of expression and your surest way to success.

If this occurs in Libra, or Taurus, the best qualities are brought out for business purposes; if in Cancer, you are very domestic and profit through your home or your heredity—this makes for wonderful wives, mothers, and hostesses among women, and good fathers and husbands among men, who find their career magically developing after they've established their homes.

If this conjunction takes place in Scorpio, magnetism is increased—an angle of power; if it takes place in Aries, intellectual vigor wins the public;

in Capricorn, public influence;

in Aquarius, romantic, aristocratic, success either in arts, science, or business—a remarkably versatile and charming nature;

in Leo, dramatic; in Virgo, critical and scientific success;

in Gemini, for a man, vigorous, and maybe fickle, love-nature, but eventual success through intellectual control; in Pisces, danger of being imposed on through the affections; in Sagittarius, large and generous mind, philosophic and idealistic, and success through professional pursuits such as law, politics, or the ministry.

147

MOON CONJUNCTION[1] MARS ☽ ☌ ♂

WITH ANY KIND of break at all, this aspect will give you authority, power, and a commensurate financial return. Its material benefits work best in the horoscope of a man. In women it gives great charm, magnetism, and artistic ability, but doesn't produce the public acclaim that it does in a man's chart. In either case it gives great independence of spirit, frequently the result of early restriction. These early restrictions arose either in the parental home, or as the result of some early illness which has left you with a psychological demand for success. This demand is compensation for a physical weakness of some kind, or for an inferiority complex. You have a quick, facile, and expressive mind, knowing how to deal with both individuals and large bodies of people. You are a fighter

[1] In the same space with.

and a foeman worthy of anyone's steel.

In a woman's horoscope the quarrelsome tendencies are less marked after the girl has left her parents' home—previous to this, it makes friction between the girl and her mother; later, it develops in artistic or musical ability, and with 200, 215 or 218, may produce a truly great creative artist. Sexual tendencies are strongly marked and need guiding and controlling, while with 224 there is danger of neurosis through suppression and strange, conflicting ideas of love.

In a man's horoscope, with 180, political and business power is assured; this combination of 147 and 180 has produced a long line of Presidents of the United States and other officials in public and private authority. Here tact, self-assurance, and determination are added to the mental agility and energy; and a fixed ambition generally meets with outstanding recognition and success.

With 219, 220, 215, 200 or 205, likelihood of inherited wealth, or position from which to make wealth. With 160, erratic love-nature extravagance, and risk of unhappiness through these; also with 212, 213, 214, 202, 203 or 204. With 226, religious and mystic turn, usually leading to some position of authority in church or occult matters.

148

MOON CONJUNCTION[1] JUPITER ☽ ☌ ♃

CHARACTER is your god. You believe in your own personal worth from a moral and character viewpoint. Your abilities may be high or low, depending on other things, but you are utterly dependable and can be counted on to do the right thing and think the right thoughts. This doesn't make you puritanical or cold, because you have a naturally cheerful and optimistic nature, very sympathetic with other people and their troubles. You have a genuine feeling for your fellow man, his problems and difficulties. This is the aspect of the missionary who may be interested in people's souls, but chiefly wants to take care of their physical comforts on earth. Here are found social workers, doctors, nurses, and executives in these fields, to whom their occupation is more than a means of livelihood—it's a conviction and a passion. You have a certain nobility of approach and of motive—you couldn't be mean or petty if you tried, and thus your popularity and luck are well deserved, and nobody grudges them to you. You can be a stern judge, but you will always temper justice with mercy. You will condemn people, perhaps, morally, but be reluctant to punish them, and you are never vindictive.

With 227 you are virtually assured of a long and honorable career, or great personal influence and public recognition.

If this conjunction of the Moon and Jupiter occurs in Cancer, Scorpio, Pisces, Sagittarius, Aries, or Leo, you're well fixed financially, increasingly so if with 215, 219, 230 or 229.

[1] In the same space with.

In Pisces, very charitable in tangible fashion.

In Gemini or Virgo, clear, judicial, and critical mind, a little puritanical and austere, but generous. In Scorpio, the Accusing Angel.

In Libra or Aquarius, romantic, liberal with affection, a lover of humanity both in particular and the abstract.

In Capricorn, great power over people, increased if with 227 or 230.

In Taurus, materialistic, delighting in giving largesse; success in business and handling funds or real estate . . . It takes extraordinary combinations to injure the moral good of this aspect, and only such aspects as 200 with 224 or 212 with 236 or 225 can destroy the goodness of this conjunction, and pervert its uses to mere love of power for its own sake. Without these interfering factors, the humanitarian motive is uppermost and makes you an extraordinarily fine person.

149

MOON CONJUNCTION[1] SATURN ☽ ☌ ♄

YOU ARE sober, serious-minded, a bit somber and inclined to dejection of spirits, moody and temperamental. You have a deep, somewhat ponderous mind, careful and painstaking rather than brilliant. You are a good thorough student and prone to philosophize about knowledge. You take very little for granted, being both curious and suspicious; and you are continuously asking the Why? Whence? Whither? and How? questions that are the litany both of the scientific investigator and of the metaphysical speculator. You are a digger, a prober both into abstract facts and knowledge—and into people, delighting in getting at the personal history of your friends and relatives and sometimes giving them quite a problem if they have things they don't want to tell you. Emotionally, you are sensitive, jealous, quick to take offense, and adept at demanding an explanation as balm to aggrieved feelings. For all this, however, you are not especially considerate of the feelings of others; and either with or without meaning to, you can injure people with bluntness. You tend somewhat to introversion, and you nurse your private theories, ailments, troubles, woes, and ideas with a disregard for the outer world that can be very annoying. This is one of the positions of egocentricity. You are the hub of your universe, and it seems only right and proper to you that everything should revolve around you—an opinion which may not be shared by everyone. In some way or other you contrive to hold the center of the stage, if not actively by leading the conversation, then passively by sulking in a corner till someone asks you what's the matter.

This is one of the positions that gives the appearance of genius or ability of a high order; yet so personal and intimate is your viewpoint that you may never get outside yourself enough to express in an artistic or scientific way. You took on responsibilities early in life, and were precocious. But experience has in some way driven you into yourself,

[1] In the same space with.

and in order to release the energies of your really excellent mind you have to learn to depersonalize your outlook. Take yourself *less* seriously, and the world around you *more* seriously. Give your own pet ideas less emphasis and the viewpoint of other people more.

In a man's horoscope this gives a fine wife, more mature and worldly-wise in viewpoint if not in years. She is a great help and, through her very excellence, likely to exaggerate the latent inferiority feeling in the man. With 247, this is emphasized; if with 164 or 165, an erratic emotional nature, stormy temperament; if with 153, exceptional wife.

If with 224, this paragraph give egocentricity and quarrelsomeness of a dangerous order, and risk of loss of position and fortune through the headstrong following of your own hunches. If with many triangles and conjunctions it shows a sheltered life with private, and possibly meaningless, woes. In a woman's chart this inclines to poor health—and does she love it!

150
MOON CONJUNCTION[1] URANUS ☽ ☌ ♅

YOU ARE one of the outstanding people of your circle. You are a character, with markedly individualistic traits, original, fearless in thought and expression, a trifle eccentric, uncompromisingly independent. Given a choice of two modes of conduct, a usual and an unusual, you will unhesitatingly select the unusual, the unconventional, the aggressive. You lean to the bizarre, the revolutionary, the daring, so that in a constructive, creative, or executive horoscope, you become an important person, respected for your intelligence and authority, and somewhat feared because no one ever knows what you are likely to do next. If with 183, 184, 185, 186, 187, 188, 180, 215, 216, 217, 218, 227, 228 or 237, extraordinary prestige through the original exercise of mentality is shown; if with 180, business or political leadership is possible; with 217, 221, military career likely. So idealistic and expansive is your mental outlook that money is of secondary importance to you, though you know how to spend it—or rather, how not to hang on to it. You are emotionally erratic, sure to have a large fund of experience, and some difficulty in marriage through the outbursting of your temperament.

In a man's horoscope you are sure to have at least one wife who will bring out the worst of this configuration. You run to odd, strange, unconventional associates, and will probably at some time link yourself with the oddest and most intractable person you can find. This position gives you tense nerves, and a continuous strain seems to be on you so that, unless controlled and guided, your health suffers from nervous ailments that can amount to neurosis. With 245, 145, 146, 147 or 149, this danger is emphasized; with 151, curious psychic and psychological conditions confuse you and require a maximum of control and realism on your part. Your intellectual potentialities are tremendous and depend for

[1] In the same space with.

their development on your control of the eccentric, erratic, emotional, and nervous elements in your nature which are so destructive to integrated progress. With 243, interest in occult matters marked and profitable—even without this, there is some interest in obscure and out-of-the-way subjects, occult rather than metaphysical.

151

MOON CONJUNCTION[1] NEPTUNE ☽ ☌ ♆

YOU HAVE great insight into studies, facts, and people. Your intuitions and hunches are keen and very realistic to you. There is a danger of your becoming confused and muddled in your mental processes, either through absorption in imagination, lack of facts, or physchological biases arising from heredity and early experience. You believe so strongly in yourself, your intuitions, and your opinions, that you are likely to fly in the face of good sound horse sense. Your imagination runs away with you and you think that because you believe it and will it, it must be so. This is one of the insidious aspects of introversion, and you are capable of withdrawing into yourself or into a dream world with your pet theories, to the injury of your progress in the world outside. In a creative artist, this position lends inspiration of a high order. In executives and business people, it lends intuitions and magnetism, which aid progress. But in negative horoscopes it must be guarded against, for its danger is subtle and undermining. In Taurus, the best of this shows forth; in Gemini and Cancer, mental confusion is likely; in Leo, sensationalism is dangerous. If with 159, broken education, lack of facts, impedes progress, which, however, develops pretty well anyway through mental facility; but an inferiority feeling with respect to mental achievements gnaws at you and should be ridden down. If with 160, emotional conflict, probably stemming from the relationship with the mother, makes psychological difficulty—you are touchy about your popularity, and your contacts with people suffer thereby. If with 163 or 164, mysticism is confusing, your mind wanders, and is erratic, pliable, and non-concentrative, needing to be pinned down. Sensationalism is dangerous to you. If with 229, 232, 243, 237, 215, 154, 155, 156 or 246, the material side of this shows out and wealth may accrue. If with 237 or 243, interest in the occult, metaphysical, and spiritual is marked; if with 226, you become a spiritual leader of great magnetism but must always guard against your own hypnosis. The need for this position is exactness (the power to pin things down to facts) and reserve (the holding in of information, emotions, and plans, for you tend to tell everything, and thus to weaken your concentrative powers which should help you in achievement).

[1] In the same space with.

152
MOON TRINE MERCURY ☽ △ ☿

THIS IS a good aspect for sound common sense, strengthening the sanity of the mind and giving you the power to absorb knowledge readily and quickly. You are inquisitive, eager, intelligent, an apt student, and a good conversationalist, witty and apt in expression, logical and reasonable. You have some adaptability for business, especially salesmanship. You can succeed in one of the "vocal" occupations, such as speaking or radio announcing. You have manual aptitude and can do things with your hands, although you'd rather use your mind. Through cleverness you can generally succeed in life without too much hard work for you're a good talker and can sell yourself as well as your product, which eases the road for you.

153
MOON TRINE VENUS ☽ △ ♀

YOU ARE gracious and no doubt easy to look at. If you are a woman you are probably a social leader; if a man, a favorite with the social leaders. You probably were born to a good social status—or if not, you are a lucky child who rises far above your original social level. It is one of the positions for material luck and always keeps you from the worst degrees of want. You can make a little go a long way if you have to, but if you don't have to, your patrician taste can prove expensive in matters of dress, house furnishings, and personal adornments. You wouldn't live in a shabby place, and even when times are hard, would have a home of grace, charm, and (somehow) of luxury. It is one of the indexes of a happy marriage, and even if other indications are unfavorable, this will in some degree give happiness in the married state. In a male horoscope, gives a beautiful and talented wife; in a female horoscope, gives these qualities to the native herself.

154
MOON TRINE MARS ☽ △ ♂

YOU HAVE a vigorous mind—sharp, quick, satiric—and a clipped manner of speech. You have an aggressive spirit which may or may not be manifest in your actions, but which causes your plans to soar and your ideas to expand. You have good control over your passions, which are strong; and use your anger to good purpose. You are a dangerous enemy because your fires are leashed and directed to go to the mark. With 184, a very brilliant mind; with 195, equally brilliant, but not so well organized, and pretty cutting in your speech. In a man's horoscope this gives an aggressive wife, possibly a shrew, who none the less is good for him, stimulating him to action at the same time that she makes him mad.

155

MOON TRINE JUPITER ☽ △ ♃

YOU ARE idealistic, humanitarian, and expansive in your outlook, animated by genuine charity, and probably in a position to make it practical. You are cheerful, optimistic, good-humored, and tactful. Courtesy is innate in you—one of nature's gentlefolk. You have excellent family connections especially on your mother's side, and probably some financial help from them in gifts or legacies. Necessity has never taught you to be careful of money, which you more or less take for granted. If put to it, your earning powers are good, for friends put you in the way of earning. Character is your strong point: you have a keen sense of right and wrong. Your ideas run along conventional lines; you belong to the conservative, right-wing, pillar-of-society group, believing in noblesse oblige rather than in socialism. You are devotional and probably religious in an orthodox sense, but the pillar of your religion is the god in you—that is, character—rather than metaphysics and dogma.

156

MOON TRINE SATURN ☽ △ ♄

IN CONVENTIONALITY, sobriety, character, this is very similar to the trine of the Moon to Jupiter (above) except that it does not give you the humanitarian and charitable qualities of that expansive and good-natured planet. You incline to be serious, sober, a trifle proud and reserved, and maybe a little forbidding. Life is real and life is earnest to you, and you take yourself rather seriously. You inherit your mental traits directly from your mother, resembling her and her side of the family in your internal make-up if not in your appearance. Duty is important to you; you will never shirk a job and are capable of considerable self-sacrifice if you think your duty requires it. You are able to achieve this without self-pity, taking certain obligations for granted as your lot in life and approaching them with sobriety and philosophy. Concentrative powers are not strongly marked, and you have some tendency merely to accept what comes in the way of duty, without going out and creating opportunities for yourself. You lack aggression and that internal tension that pushes men and women to the heights. Relaxation and contentment are your two worst enemies, for although they keep you from the blows of the world and allow you to maintain inner poise and calm, they also keep you from getting too far ahead. If you aren't contented you are likely to go on being discontented for a long time without doing anything about it. Control the restlessness of your body and put some restlessness into your mind, your spirit. What you need to do is work up steam in the boiler so that the engine can get places.

157

MOON TRINE URANUS ☽ △ ♅

THERE ARE dash and vitality here, preceding from an alert, quick mind, eager for knowledge, absorptive, and magnetic. You are able to see all sides of any question, from the other fellow's viewpoint as well as from your own; this makes you tolerant and intelligent, a good listener, a fair opponent in a detached intellectual encounter. You are capable of a good deal of mental objectivity; large ideas appeal to you, and you can think abstractly. Artistic and intellectual matters interest you, as well as social and political ideas and theories; but on these matters there is so much tolerance that you have difficulty making a firm stand for your opinions, and unless some other aspect shows decisiveness, this may be a debating-society position, under which things are talked out and mulled over and few decisions arrived at. Learn to see all sides, and then choose one and stick to it, and remember that too much tolerance and understanding of the other fellow's opinions amounts to having none of your own. You have advanced ideas, in theory, and may talk like a radical straight from Moscow; but you are little likely to put these into practise in your own life. This is one of the positions of the Parlor Pink, who talks a good revolution but doesn't get around to doing very much about it.

158

MOON TRINE NEPTUNE ☽ △ ♆

CHARM AND GRACE of manner and speech mark you—a certain fluency to your movements and manner of expression attract attention. You are rather a striking personality, in a quiet and unassuming way. You have a keen sense of other people's feelings and wishes. You put two and two together instinctively and thus are able to draw conclusions that are lost on less intuitive souls. Beauty in all forms has a strange effect upon you, and conversely discord, strife, and loud noises throw you off. You will give your all for peace and quiet, and for this reason frequently go off by yourself for periods of repose and relaxation, far from the madding crowd. If there are any artistic or creative indications in the horoscope, this will assist them greatly, although by itself it gives the appreciative, receptive artistic qualities. You are a lover of music and really require it, finding comfort and relaxation in the rhythm, tone, and color of what you hear. Your sense perceptions are all acute, and sights, sounds, odors, colors, and the feel of things give you a curious sensuous satsifaction. You should cultivate objectivity, and detachment from your private æsthetic world, which pleasant though it is can interfere with realistic problems.

159
MOON SQUARE MERCURY ☽ □ ☿

YOU ARE talkative, expressive, witty—if with 151 or 188, extraordinarily witty. If with 184 or 195, sarcastic, with a sharp tongue. You may not have a trained mind, but this doesn't keep you from occupying yourself with mental pursuits, either as a hobby or as a mode of gaining a livelihood. What you lack in persistence you make up in glibness and facility. Only in extraordinary instances will this accompany the artistically creative ability of the poet or dramatist; but it will lead you into some writing or speaking occupation—secretarial, advertising, public speaking such as radio, salesmanship, etc.—anything where wit, cleverness, and knowing all the answers is an asset. You have a tendency to talk too much, and if with 151, 165, 184, 195, 188 or 199, this may amount to a mania for telling everything you know, even those things that you ought to keep to yourself. You have to cultivate reserve in speech; for keeping things to yourself will help them to develop. You waste your mental powers by expressing everything. You are not logical and have to make a conscious and serious effort to keep to the main track of the discussion. Mental training is what you need—strict schooling, which likely as not you ran away from when you were very young. You are likely to skim over the surface of things mental and get by on your wits rather than by intense application. But with your cleverness, wit, and adaptability you will get by!

160
MOON SQUARE VENUS ☽ □ ♀

THIS ASPECT doesn't make you very sociable and is likely to impair popularity by making you scornful of the things that have to be done to achieve it. Your attitude is that you just won't be bothered—if they want you, let them come for you. You have to learn to go out of your way more for people. The truth of the matter is that you are sensitive, have a sort of inferiority complex about your popularity, and dread the idea of pushing yourself forward, with the result that periodically, through sheer discouragement, you push yourself in the wrong way and at the wrong time. Look around you at the people who are well liked and try to take a leaf from their book. If with 200, 204, 210 or 214, very much impressed by sex matters, which are dangerous and need controlling. If with 202 or 212, much sorrow through social and romantic matters. This is a difficult aspect for material matters, for you spend money foolishly, and have to cultivate good business sense. You are a real spendthrift at heart; getting rid of money amounts to a genius with you. You are emotionally temperamental and can weep buckets when you are hurt, or when you realize you've hurt someone else; for you are gentle, and wouldn't wilfully hurt anyone. But for all that, you do.

161
MOON SQUARE MARS ☽ □ ♂

YOU STARTED OUT in life like a house afire—all energy and intelligence and even brilliance, for this is the aspect of the child who is thought to be a genius in his early and formative years. Your mind was quick, apt, facile, expressive, and able to absorb and give back knowledge readily, so that you were the delight of your parents and teachers, giving promise of great achievement in later life. In many ways you were extraordinarily precocious throughout youth; and at any time in life you possess an exceptional mentality and great possibilities. Your mind is analytic and scientific rather than artistic and creative; and although the creative *urge* is powerful, the creative *force* is not usually present with this configuration. Anything that requires knowledge, factual application, technical ease, or critical insight, is your forte, and in these fields you can go far. As a scientist, mathematician, critic, or technician, your mind is invaluable, and the independence and originality of your thought processes enable you to forge to the front. There is with this aspect some danger that after the first glow and flush of youth is past, the great urge to better and improve yourself will in some subtle and inexplicable way be dissipated and lost. Unless with some such aspect as 180, or 186, or 192 or 197, a sort of mental inertia may settle over you in which accomplishment becomes difficult. It requires a tremendous amount of will power to bring the promise of this aspect to fruition. There is a tendency to relax internally, with an intimate knowledge of your own worth as your pillow, and forget that no worth is worth anything if it is not made apparent in the world as it is. This is a position also of great nervous tension, of the sort which is classically supposed to accompany genius. You may be tempted to seek escape from this tension in a variety of artificial anodynes—either in simple daydreaming and imagining what you might be or what you have been or what you are going to be; or in the more concrete escapes, which are also the more dangerous escapes. Liquor or alcohol in any form is poison to you, either to your digestive tract, or to your psychic, mental, and nervous state. Similarly, you should avoid the use of any drug or soporific stronger, let us say, than aspirin, and seek to find the solution to your tensions in more constructive mediums. You should practise relaxation deliberately. Get plenty of sleep, and in every way try to cut down the stress of your existence, both internal and external. You have tremendous possibilities—perhaps even genius—and you owe it to yourself and the world to make the most of them.

With 184, 186, 187 or 188, extraordinary mind, capable of any heights of achievement; with both 183 and 184, remarkable combination of scientific and artistic gifts; with Sun in Gemini, Libra, or Aquarius, genius (if with 215, financial genius; 216, political).

162

MOON SQUARE JUPITER ☽ □ ♃

YOU ARE optimistic with respect to financial matters. You have a feeling that the purse will always be full, and the extravagance resulting therefrom may become dangerous to your security, especially if with 147, 161, 151, 165 or 178, 179. If other aspects show material success and well-being you have a cavalier attitude toward expenses and love to spend. This is a Falstaffian position—there's a hankering for rich and fancy food, a tendency to eat too much of it, and an accompanying danger of fleshiness, diabetes, gout, blood disorders. This is one of the aspects of indulgence. You are sunny and open-hearted, tolerant of other people and of yourself as well; a kind of happy-go-lucky individual, taking people as you find them, and consequently popular. If with 149, 163, 170, 180, 186 or 197, this expansiveness may be curbed somewhat, but you are genial at heart. You usually have some share of the world's goods, though this doesn't in itself make for security—money comes in and goes out without causing you much worry or trouble, but unless with 149, 163, 170, 180, 186, 197, 207, 230 or 216, it does not get saved very consistently.

163

MOON SQUARE SATURN ☽ □ ♄

THIS IS PERHAPS the most powerful single aspect you can have in a horoscope. It gives both ambition and the ability to concentrate on it. You are serious-minded, at times changing to moody, depressed, and dejected; but as you grow older an early tendency to fall into the doldrums gradually disappears as your mind becomes organized into a smooth-running unit driving always toward a well-defined goal. Whatever your physical energy may or may not be, your mental and psychic energy is high and well directed. You do not waste yourself in profitless ventures or very much in nerves, anger, or displays of temperament; these belonged to your early years, and you learned as you grew older the futility and waste which such displays involve. Your greatest asset is your ability to learn by experience, for though you have made many, and probably great, mistakes, your self-knowledge is your salvation. At the bottom of the pit of depression or despair or error, you are able to look yourself squarely in the face and start building your way back to where you want to be. You have an inner drive and a sense of your own worth amounting almost to a neurosis, which you are able to express on the constructive side. Psychologically this marks you as somehow extraordinarily influenced by one or both parents. Thus, in whatever field you choose to operate—business, the professions, or the arts—you have the jump on competitors who are not assisted by the mental energy and the psychological drive of this aspect. Although determined and apparently ardent in emotional matters, you are capable of being pretty cold when it suits your purposes. Nothing personal is allowed to interfere with the main stream of your intentions once youth is past and your purposes are set. Prior to this, in youth, this aspect gives a hectic emotional life, and you may be the despair of yourself and your friends and relatives. Through excessive independence you hurt your parents; through erratic action, your sweethearts. But as you mature, these temperamental qualities fall away. What has happened goes deeply into your consciousness; and your fund of experience, falling under the scrutiny of an analytical mentality, contributes to that knowledge of the world, of people, and of yourself which becomes the cornerstone of your success. If your horoscope has a negative (non-executive) combination of the Sun and Moon and shows none of the other major aspects (marked*), then this aspect may lead merely to depression of spirits, dejection, and a sense of frustration. But the power of it is so great that with any encouragement from any other aspect, it will produce success along some line or other. Its genius varies according to other indications as follows:

If with 169, 174, 179 or 192, business; 168 or 173, military, government, political; 180, business or government; 215, financial (if also with 218, highly creative); 183, 189 or 188, creative, dramatic, poetic.

If with 148, 155, 185 or 186, legal, judicial; 184 or 186, scientific, analytic; 187, creative-critical; scientific or artistic; versatile.

This is a more powerful position in a male than in a female horoscope, though in either case its significance is marked. The psychological bias is toward the mother and thus operates more constructively in men than in women. In men this aspect tends to some unhappiness in marriage, less the fault of the wife (who usually proves an admirable balance wheel) than of the psychological complexity of the man. Maturity brings more happiness, as this aspect steadies down. In women, in addition to producing the admirable mental qualities indicated, it may also tend to poor health, self-pity, and, in extreme cases hypochondria.

164

MOON SQUARE URANUS ☽ □ ♅

YOU HAVE had a high temper in your day, and if you've controlled it the credit goes to your good sense. You are rebellious, headstrong, abrupt in speech, quick on the draw—a sort of hair-trigger personality, full of fire and dash that need the control of a vigorous intellect. With 163 or 180, self-knowledge and self-discipline enable you to get yourself in hand after first youth is past; but with 149 and 165, a sort of perpetual confusion hangs over you, and you have a hard time getting the straight of your own nature. This is one of the marks of the advanced thinker, the Bohemian who is a law unto himself and must make a conscious effort to get in line with society. You are on the side of the underdog, the downtrodden, the underprivileged and believe in some form of social control where inequalities may be ironed out. A great individualist, you none the less believe that society has duties to is members, that their individuality may be able to thrive the better. You are ardent in your loves, idealistic and impulsive and capable of deep loyalties through which, however, you can see the faults of the beloved—and say so in no uncertain terms. Tact is something you have to learn, for your uncompromising truthfulness and honesty make tact seem wasted time to you. You are sensitive of the feelings of others, and once your high-spiritedness is reined you are the most sympathetic and understanding of friends.

165

MOON SQUARE NEPTUNE ☽ □ ♆

THIS IMPAIRS the creative gifts, and your manner of thought and expression, intruding an unrealistic note into your notions and confusing practical issue with hazy and misty generalizations. In business, thought, romance, you have to keep your feet on the ground, for you love the clouds. You are capable of daydreaming by the hour and of concocting brave plans that would be marvelous—if you or anyone else could make them happen. This adds a sort of naïve charm to your nature. You can believe in fairies, Santa Claus and ghosts, just as others can believe in Herbert Hoover, and your perpetual love for the mystic will intrigue those who love the innocent, the childish, the unspoiled. But all this doesn't help you much in the world of affairs, and an impractical approach to many things will stand in the way of your progress until such a time as you get your feet on the ground and hitch your wagon to a fence post.

166

SUN CONJUNCTION[1] MERCURY ☉ ☌ ☿

YOU HAVE a *sound* mentality. Along whatever lines you work you are fundamentally sane. Even with such erratic aspects as 161, 178, 181, 182, 224, 217, 225, 236, 240 or 244, which make for nervousness, you have a hitching post of normalcy in this stable conjunction. Men and women with this aspect have an assurance against serious or permanent mental difficulties which will carry them through a whole lot of stress and bring them out the right side.

You have fixed opinions though unless in Taurus, Leo, Scorpio, you are not stubborn. In these signs stubbornness is marked, and you are a tough customer to make change your mind once you have it made up.

[1] In the same space with.

In Gemini, Sagittarius, Virgo, you may appear wavering and flexible, but under this surface agreement, you are as likely as not to keep your own private theories very close to your heart.

In Aries, you are argumentative and contentious—and hard to deal with in an argument. You don't get the other fellow's viewpoint too well, and you aren't interested in talking his language.

In Cancer or Libra, tactful and considerate of the opinions of others.

In Capricorn, eager to get your own ideas across, but not too sure of yourself, though a fine, accurate mind in scientific matters.

In Aquarius, tolerant, versatile, sound.

In Pisces, self-abnegating until opposed, and then capable of bull-like stubbornness—the apotheosis of won't power. You are studious and sound in your intellectual work, but this position does not in itself make for creative ability. This will make for perseverance—the ability to add the ninety-nine percent of perspiration to genius's one percent of inspiration.

167

SUN CONJUNCTION[1] VENUS ☉ ☌ ♀

YOU ARE popular, a favorite with the other sex, with a robust magnetism and fire to your personality that comes from high good spirits, and a sort of all-pervading optimism and good-fellowship. In a woman's horoscope this will give you more than your share of admirers, and they will have good financial and social backgrounds; girls with this position generally marry above their station without sacrificing love. Women under this aspect frequently trip to the altar with the boss or his son. In a man's horoscope you are a favorite with women, lucky in love and in other things too; loyal, devoted, and ardent, the prototype of the Great Lover. Idealism lends a curious glamour to your appearance, for you are easy to look at, and your idealism sticks out all over you, throwing a kind of magnetic aura around you. It's sex appeal but also something more idealistic than that—the appeal of a Janet Gaynor rather than of a Mae West. You love nice things and have an exquisite, as well as a lavish, taste. In both emotional and material matters this is a highly intensifying influence and will heighten and tend to improve any other paragraphs referring either to the Sun or to Venus.

168

SUN CONJUNCTION[1] MARS ☉ ☌ ♂

LITTLE BOYS and girls with this aspect are generally known as "fresh kids" and more likely than not they never get over it. You are marked by a certain audacity—you speak out your mind at the drop of a hat—and not very tactfully either. You don't know the meaning of the word fear, either in a physical or a mental sense. You will attack a roaring

[1] In the same space with.

lion bare-handed, or endeavor to debate a legal point with a Supreme Court justice—all with the same aggressive assurance in your own ability. This is admirable, but it isn't always good sense. You come in for a good many trimmings both verbal and otherwise, through an unwise selection of opponents, and throughout life you have to be careful of trying to push over stone walls with your head. You're the kid who wouldn't holler Uncle no matter how your arm was being twisted. With the Moon in Scorpio or Aries, or with 147, 161, 184, 195, 181 or 179, these traits are emphasized dangerously so that quarrels and enmities beset you. With the Moon in Taurus, Virgo, or Capricorn, or with 163, 186, 197, 175 or 174, the dangers of your aggressiveness are much moderated, and self-confidence and courage bring success through your own efforts. With 224, 225, 223, quarrels are destructive; boldness elates you and then casts you down materially as well as spiritually and mentally. In any case, you will have to curb aggressiveness which can range from mere cockiness to downright egomania. You have abundant energies both mental and physical. It is too bad if your abilities are lost through antagonism, or your powers dissipated in temper. Self-control should be your constant aim in both personal and business matters and you should remember when you are tempted to do or say something bold that "fools rush in where angels fear to tread." Your vigorous personality and quick mind will carry you far when you have learned to overcome the quirks of your own nature. In a woman's horoscope this generally brings trouble through men. If you marry a girl with this aspect prepare to let her rule the roost.

169

SUN CONJUNCTION[1] JUPITER ☉ ☌ ♃

YOU HAVE high vitality, courage, and magnanimity. A certain amount of material luck, even in adversity, will always hover around you to preserve you from the worst blows that the material world might otherwise deal you. You are lavish with money, generous and charitable, and you derive a certain satisfaction from giving largesse. Money, influence, and honors sit on you naturally. You take them for granted, for you have natural pride, self-confidence and self-assurance. There's a kind of glow to your personality which even though you may be somewhat reserved makes itself felt on those around you. With 168, 178, 172 or 181 this is translated into artistic, creative energy. Also with 147, 161 or 163. With 162 the creative urge is present but not the capacity, unless with some of the other afore-mentioned paragraphs. Creative ability is also helped by 183, 187, 188, 217 or 218. If with 227 or 223, executive, business or government, success. Also with 173, 175, 176 or 177. This is one of the positions of luck in life, and indicates an excellent heredity from which the best qualities of the father's line show forth in you and

[1] In the same space with.

may easily reach the peak of their expression in your life and achievements. It frequently accompanies a legacy from the father, or, if there is no legacy, he gave freely to you at some time in your life. Thus this may indicate a spoiled child, except that your sound good sense and self-reliance come to your aid and you take constructive advantage of your benefits.

170

SUN CONJUNCTION[1] SATURN ☉ ☌ ♄

YOUR INTENSE NATURE generally finds plenty to overcome in this world, for your nervous vigor is not accompanied by a commensurate physical vitality. You tire easily, and should not let your nervousness drive you faster than you can comfortably go. Responsibilities devolve on you early in life and they discourage you somewhat, causing you to withdraw into yourself. You dislike competition and want chiefly for the world to leave you alone. Your help is demanded, probably by a parent or by early domestic duties, and if you rebel against this and seek a career of your own you find obstacles to overcome. You are independent without being aggressive, and in the search for independence you are likely to fall into an easy rut from which you have difficulty in rising. You are a little self-centered for executive work and not coöperative enough for subordinate work. This is a lone-wolf position, and you may find yourself pretty lonely. In a woman's horoscope this indicates difficulty through men because of an early-formed psychological bias toward the father or an older relative.

In a man's horoscope something of the same condition exists—a sort of father- or mother-worship contributing to an inferiority complex. You need the real, rather than the pseudo, self-confidence, for most of your independence is bravado and is not backed by self-reliance. You should develop this through increasing your contact with the world around you, by avoiding the secretive life you seek defensively, and by developing a willingness to compete in the world of affairs. Ignore your own emotions and sensitiveness which in the end will harden you if you don't watch them. Your intellectual powers and powers of concentration are good. With 173, 174, 176, 177, 153, 154, 155, 156, 157 or 158, you may develop them to good business activity and achieve considerable power, prestige, and authority for you are a magnetic person and have only to let your magnetism work outward instead of inward to get pretty much what you want out of the world.

171

SUN CONJUNCTION[1] URANUS ☉ ☌ ♅

A CONTINUOUS nervous tension pervades you which you have to fight down and bring in line with the needs of your life. You have a quick

[1] In the same space with.

sharp mind, highly intellectual if trained, but inclining to the sensational if left untrained, and in any case erratic, high-strung, and worrisome. Abstractions appeal to you more than realities; the intellectual more than the material. The result is that you are baffled, confused, and made nervous when the realistic world demands attention. You should practise relaxation and resist an impulse to get along without sleep, which you need if you are going to keep your nerves in shape. Your mind has a way of working overtime even when you are asleep—with the result that this position often accompanies attacks of insomnia, especially if with 161. If with 173, 174, 175 or 177, the nervous energy is given constructive bent, and through aptness, perceptivity, and perseverance you will go far along intellectual or creative lines. You are not cut out for business, though your versatility will permit you to do anything. You have a kind of pride in emulating Goethe's Universal Man, to whom no field was closed and who could master any branch of knowledge or endeavor. Health is an important consideration in your life, and you should take especial care that you aren't made ill by nervousness, worry, or by one of the so-called neurotic ailments. If with 182 and/or 180, this is especially pertinent. With 217 or 225 temperament and anger dangerous to stability of health; also likelihood of accidents, falls, etc. Your emotional nature, after having been pretty turbulent, settles down to a sort of cold, dispassionate, and analytical acceptance of human relations as you have found or created them—unless with 180, 178, 200, or 210, when a sort of perpetual rebellion will keep your emotional life in turmoil till you master it. Impersonality and objectivity will show you the way to success and contentment—and you are well equipped to know the significance of the ideal state in which (to quote Walter Lippmann) "The intellect has become a passion, and the passions are cold." With 236, danger of inertia due to frustration or subconscious remnants that need cleaning out. With 243, interest in the occult, from which you could make a successful career or a stimulating hobby.

172

SUN CONJUNCTION[1] NEPTUNE ☉ ☌ ♆

YOU HAVE a strong mystic, inspirational bent which can take either a constructive or destructive form. If in the powerful sign Taurus, you have great creative powers, especially if with 14, 151, 188, 204, 218, 229 or 237; and if in addition to one of these you have 176, success is pretty well assured . . . In any other sign the tendency is to mental confusion, impressionability, mysticism, scattered mental and emotional energies are likely to swamp you. You have to fight to keep your feet on the ground. Romanticism will rule your life dangerously, and you will fall in with difficult and unreliable people whose unstable notions you will take too seriously for your own good. Drugs, alcohol, soporifics fascinate you, and

[1] In the same space with.

even if you don't indulge actually, you're prone to "drug" your mind from reality with daydreams, abstract visions, and imaginings which you can't put into practise. With 181 and/or 180, sensationalism in one form or another besets you, and at some time in your life you are likely to come a cropper through letting your good judgment go to sleep and following some destructive path of least resistance. You have to fight constantly for awareness, perception of the world as it realistically is, and submergence of the impractical and visionary ideas and dreams that throng your consciousness. Unconventionality takes on a peculiarly insidious form under these conditions and presents itself in glowing colors. With 200, 210, 212 or 202, love dangerous; disappointments and breaks likely and should be guarded against. With 218, you are too magnetic for your own good but lucky materially. With 229, wealth; with 173, 175 or 174, luck through your own efforts and material progress. With Moon in Scorpio, Cancer, Pisces, highly impressionable—look out for the recoil of your emotions. If with 243, magnetic control over others once you have controlled yourself.

173

SUN TRINE MARS ☉△♂

YOU HAVE abundant physical vitality and little hesitancy in using it. You are always on the move. Your aims and purposes, being direct and clear and animated by a good physical equipment, carry you to success. You are forceful, hard-hitting, aggressive, knowing where you stand and where you are going. You wear out less energetic souls by the speed and continuousness of your activities, for you are seemingly tireless and can stand shoulder to shoulder with the strongest when it comes to matters of endurance. Since a good deal of the success of this world in material matters depends on physical vitality, you have an edge on competitors. You are an excellent leader not so much of thought as of action (unless Mercury is powerful) and frequently choose the army or navy as your field of activity, where you speedily rise to authority; or business, where you won't long stay in a subordinate position. You overwhelm people, and they naturally give way to you. If this occurs with strong intellectual and creative bents (163, 183, 186, 197, 187 or 188) you are a leader of thought and a powerful personality.

174

SUN TRINE JUPITER ☉△♃

THE QUALITIES of luck, energy, magnanimity, and good spirits here are very similar to those shown under 169. The creative urge, however, depends on other things and requires some such aspects as 163, 181, 147 or 180 to be brought out. You have lots of vitality and optimism, together with a broad, tolerant, philosophic viewpoint—a sort of hail-fellow-well-met person making friends readily and generally keeping them. This is an excellent position for business. With any such combination as 215, 227, 228, 229, or 163, 147, 180, 230, it will give you a successful career of considerable scope and influence. In a professional or artistic career this insures financial return. No poet with this aspect ever starved in a garret, or anywhere else, for that matter. You spend freely and convivially, and your abundant vitality makes it possible for you to keep going for a long time.

175

SUN TRINE SATURN ☉ △ ♄

YOU ARE LUCKY, coming of good stock and being born into a favorable environment. Elders have done a good deal for you, and no matter how poor your parents may have been or how rich, they have seen to it that responsibility was removed from you as much as possible and that the hardships of life did not touch you (unless with 163, in which case you assumed a good deal of responsibility early and carried it well). You have a good sound body and mind. You are serious without being dejected or depressed, and are capable of concentrated effort. If this exists without 163, 147, 178 or 181, then there is a tendency to relaxation and absence of direction and purpose—luck helps you out, but you don't seize or create opportunities. With one of these above-mentioned energizing aspects a large element of luck. Doors open to you, opportunities come, or you create them. Without these energizing aspects, look out. The tendency of this aspect is to smugness and self-satisfaction, pride and relaxation of ambition and energies, so that, despite a sound mind in a sound body, you don't seem to get very far. If with 215, 218 or 220, lots of luck with very little effort; maximum return for minimum work; material security. If with 227, high authority and influence—a judicial nature. This aspect is frequently found in horoscopes that show legacy or some circumstance that removes financial worry—and thus also removes the economic impetus to ambition.

176

SUN TRINE URANUS ☉ △ ♅

ONE OF THE indexes of long life, a strong physical heredity, and vitality. In addition to these physical qualities, you have a progressive mental outlook, strongly tinged with originality, and any plans that you organize will be pushed through with a certain dash and comprehension of total results that knits the parts together strongly. Organization, either of undertakings or of knowledge, is your strong point. You see things in the large rather than the particular. If with 161, 163, 180, 215,

216, 224 or 218, this position makes you a leader of thought and action. Your originality is not tinged with the bizarre, but has a wholesome practical quality about it. You are a very expansive person, looking at things in the large. If this occurs in a nativity where the Sun-Moon polarization is in executive combination, or with any of the above paragraphs, you'll indulge in large independent ventures which will succeed or fail according to the other indications of the horoscope. If with 220, you build strongly and forever; if with 224, less permanently, but always on the grand scale, and in the grand manner, for a certain magnanimity of approach and magnificence of outlook characterizes you.

177

SUN TRINE NEPTUNE ☉ △ ♆

YOUR EMOTIONAL and intellectual sides are nicely blended and give you a good deal of quiet charm and magnetism. Your intuitions are strong, and your critical faculties are aided by innate good taste. You are likely to have the wish to create artistically, but this aspect alone will not bring the power, though if other aspects to the Sun, Moon, Venus, and Mercury show creative powers, this will materially aid their expression and help to bring recognition. You have in any case a genuine appreciation for beauty, poetry, and music and will be found among the patrons of art galleries, operas, concerts, and the theater. This aspect also supports the health and aids the general material welfare.

178

SUN SQUARE MARS ☉□ ♂

ENERGY IS the keynote of your nature. You have a sort of quivering intensity which, if directed and controlled by 167, 168 or 163, makes you an efficient and forceful person driving toward some well-defined goal. Without these, your energies are just as strong but your goal is less well defined, and you tend to spend your energies in nerves and in emotional and sensational matters. Your passional nature in any case is strong—love, anger, hate, fear: all the personal passions can take strong hold of you and, unless with a powerful will, can take hold pretty destructively. You can fly into rages, become absorbed in love, or give yourself up to hating with a whole-heartedness that is in many ways admirable but which, at the same time, absorbs too much of you. Your approach to things, facts, and people is strictly personal—you have little capacity for detachment and objectivity, and your outlook depends entirely on the state of your emotions, on the way people treat you, and on the status of your private life at the time. Thus you are capable of being a little petty when your feelings are hurt or you are aggrieved or injured; you don't take a broad view of these things, and you are capable of being vindictive and revengeful, of holding grudges and "getting even." Mars is the great get-evener, and one way or another you'll settle your score with anyone who has offended you. If with 167, 169, 183, 185, 201 or 174, the mind is depersonalized somewhat, but in any case the fundamental traits remain to some degree. In a man's horoscope this makes a fighter going through life with a chip on his shoulder and a pretty dangerous fellow to attack. He'll fight like a cornered bull and very often win. In a woman's horoscope the quarrelsomeness is not so great, though under the surface calm there's a boiling sea, and it indicates likelihood of emotional psychic involvement through the father and some ill health too, or difficulty with, the husband. A woman with this aspect very often rules her home—and not always by subtlety either. She has a way of making men toe the mark which they generally seem to like.

179

SUN SQUARE JUPITER ☉□♃

YOU ARE full of vitality, good spirits, and fun. You are likely to waste your energies and your money in having a good time, for this is a happy-go-lucky position and adds a lift and verve even to a pretty sober nature. It generally accompanies comfortable worldly status and keeps bringing in the shekels, even if you manage to get rid of them pretty quickly. You have a great deal of pride. Social prestige is important to you and you feed your vanity on it. You are still genial and humane and will gladly help people in distress, for a goodly amount of charity accompanies this aspect. You love food and drink and tend to overindulge. You are lavish with your expenditures not only of money, but of affection, passion, friendship; an all-pervasive expansiveness runs through your life. This is a sort of Falstaffian position. You're markedly convivial, the best of companions, but through flaunting the precepts of moderation, you can cause yourself a good deal of unhappiness, ruin your digestion, and get fat. If with 168, 200 or 210, excesses are very dangerous and in addition to crippling your fortunes, will have an effect on your health through blood disorders, gout, diabetes, or one of the ailments that goes with excess.

180

SUN SQUARE SATURN ☉□♄

YOU HAVE ambition strongly marked, a sense of your own dignity and worth, and a determination to make the world recognize you. You have a tremendous inner drive, together with a well-formed purpose. In a man's horoscope especially, this will meet with a high degree of success in the material world. You do best when working independently, away from the place of your birth and the home of your parents. So long as you stick closely to home and mother, or the hereditary pattern, responsibilities will weigh you down, and obligations will be foisted on you which impede your material progress though they strengthen your ultimate purpose. But as soon as you are on your own, among strangers, your rise begins, and it usually goes on steadily till you stand at some point of importance. You create your own opportunities. You take advantage of every twist and turn of circumstance. A sort of shrewd hardness develops with the years, and the way of the world is an open book to you. You are steady, calm, persistent, wary, suspicious, and skeptical. You know which side your bread is buttered on, and how to get the butter. You are capable of living a very austere life if it suits your purposes. No personal matter is likely to interfere with your ambition, and you gain a reputation for being machine-like in your precision and purposes. This is a somewhat Machiavellian position, and with 163, 147 or 168 can lead to the top of the heap. The danger is always that pride and an inability to flex with later circumstances will cause your downfall. You stick to the ship till it sinks, less from principle than from pride, and go down with flying colors, arrogant and defiant to the end, and still conscious of your own worth and right. In a woman's horoscope these same qualities appear to some extent with less aggression and more tact, and they do not make for the same progress in a woman's chart, nor for the same high achievement. Restrictions and responsibilities are likely to hem you in, for you are strong for duty and obligations and stick with an admirable adhesiveness to any task which life sets you. Also, in a woman's chart, this means early trouble through men, frequently starting with the father, who may be poor and unsuccessful, and continuing with difficulty in one form or another through sweethearts and husband. If with 224, this difficulty is increased greatly, but this aspect gives you fortitude, philosophy, and the ability to see through the difficult experiences which life may offer.

181

SUN SQUARE URANUS ☉□♅

YOU'VE SOWN your wild oats—and how! Your intellectual development was a good deal in advance of your emotional development, and as a result you had ideas, notions, theories, of independence and of human relations which you put into practise, considerably to the despair of your elders. You're a liberal in every way, with advanced social, political, and personal ideas. Individualism is very important to you, and your own ego comes first. As you grow older this outlook broadens from the purely personal to the more general; you turn from egocentric to humanitarian, interested in large ideas, large groups of people, social problems in the large. Especially with 163, 183, 185, 186, 188, 189, 167 or 174, the mental outlook is very inclusive, developing out of a strictly selfish rut into a genuine feeling for humanity. This is one of the aspects of idealism but on its way to that state it goes through many ramifications. You have been dejected and depressed and discouraged; probably you've had your share of unconventional and erratic love affairs. You always tend to be something of a romantic; no matter how much you control, or how much you learn to translate the personal into the impersonal, an adventurous spirit keeps gnawing at you. This is the aspect of Ulysses, forever wandering the seas—even when he's sitting by his hearth with Penelope. This adventurous urge, leashed and controlled and directed by a sound mind such as is indicated by the above paragraph numbers, will produce works of art, for the creative urge is powerful, with a touch of inspirationalism. Translate your adventuresomeness to intellectual, rather than geographical or personal variety, and the world is at your feet.

With 172 or 182, emotionalism will dominate you. You are a sensationalist and need to depersonalize yourself consciously. With 170, danger of introversion and nervous disorders. With 236, violently temperamental nature capable of being leashed by an equally great will power into big constructive action. With 243, mystic nature. Occultism is interesting to you but unless with a powerful mentality, dangerous. With Moon in Scorpio, Venus in Taurus, 147, 161, 200 or 210, sex-nature needs control. With 163, temperament through love matters.

In any case, you have a periodically explosive temper and must learn the lessons of coöperation both with the world in general and with individuals. You tend to think that you are right and all the rest of the world is crazy, which may be true but doesn't make much of a hit with the world.

182

SUN SQUARE NEPTUNE ☉□♆

THIS IS a treacherous aspect, subtly weakening the will power and making you susceptible to influences that arise not always from worthy sources. You are a sensationalist and will go out of your way for the bizarre, the unusual, or the mysterious in experience. You have to look out for this tendency, which leads you to seek strange and unreliable associates. A certain nebulous and impractical idealism attaches to your emotional and thought processes. You are likely to think in beautiful and vague circles and to give yourself up to dreams and emotions of a hypnotic and dangerous quality. Reason should be your constant aim, and you should avoid thinking or acting along inspirational, intuitive, or sensational lines.

183

MERCURY CONJUNCTION[1] VENUS ☿ ☌ ♀

THIS ASPECT gives perhaps the most idealistic mental outlook possible. It shows strong leanings to the artistic and beautiful things of life which may become creative activity if with 163, 180, 161, 188, 194, 215, 218, 184, 168, 178, 181, 171 or 172. If with none of these, though creative powers aren't there, there is a good deal of appreciation of fine things, and innate discrimination. The champagne taste that so often has to get along on the beer pocketbook. You will have friends among clever and intellectual people. You will no doubt marry someone from this group, for your affections are much bound up in your opinion of the loved one's mentality. You have a good deal of charm of manner, wit, and gayety to your speech, and probably have a very pleasant speaking (and perhaps also singing) voice. You don't shout even when you're angry, and you have a persuasive manner that wins people over. This is therefore good for a salesmanship or in the professions, where personal contacts are of paramount importance. With 202, the intellectual life replaces the romantic; also, to a lesser extent, with 197 and 192; with any of these three, your mind is deep, studious, serious, and critical, and well fitted for an academic or professional career. With 185, business—with 215 also, great success and wealth through business endeavors. With 218, creative genius; also likely with 215; with both, unlimited artistic ability; with 190 and 192, painting, sculpture, architecture.

184

MERCURY CONJUNCTION[1] MARS ☿ ☌ ♂

YOU HAVE a quick, brilliant mind, a sharp penetrating insight and grasp of mathematical and scientific intricacies. You also have an abrupt manner of speech, not marked by diplomacy. Facts interest you, not speculations; you speak your mind and can make trouble for yourself by this quality. You are contentious, loving a good argument. Ease of perception and quickness of grasp open the doors of knowledge to you readily, but unless with 163, 180, 183, 189, 185, 191, 186, 192, 193 or 194, your learning may be merely superficial. If with any of these, your mind develops fluently and with much promise, and unless with 161, 198 or 199, you will go far. With these latter, confusion and erratic actions disintegrate the early promise. With 161, read that paragraph carefully, for your entire life problem is found therein. With 197, 198, 199 or 236, serious errors of judgment will crack in a minute the foundations of your progress, and you have to guard every move you make and every decision you arrive at, with the most careful of judgment. With 216, unusual mind, facile, quick, tactful, and absorptive; aggressive

[1] In the same space with.

without being offensive, knowing social tact instinctively. With 168, heavy-handed and tactless, needful of the check-rein on the speech and actions, but a good clear mind capable of depth and distance when the temperamental qualities are mastered.

185

MERCURY CONJUNCTION[1] JUPITER ☿ ☌ ♃

YOU HAVE a fine, ultra-honorable, mind, with a high degree of stick-to-it-ive-ness which, if in Taurus, Leo, Scorpio, or Aquarius, amounts to great stubbornness, and in any sign makes you a hard person to sway from an opinion. If the opinion involves right and wrong, you can't be swayed from the right. You are the man whom "no one dared offer a bribe." You are judicial, a little puritanical, and likely to be found in the law, the ministry, or politics, where your integrity and high standards carry you far. You are a good business man, optimistic but sound, capable of executive leadership; a super-salesman, persuasive and forceful. You love a good story, especially if with 188 or 194, and when not in your solemn mood can appreciate a joke on anyone, including yourself, despite the fact that you take yourself and the world pretty seriously. With this aspect in your horoscope, other aspects to Mercury assume additional importance. If there are no other aspects to Mercury, then your mental processes are simple and direct, without complexity or involvement, proceeding from cause to effect with admirable precision and not likely very often to be wrong.

186

MERCURY CONJUNCTION[1] SATURN ☿ ☌ ♄

YOU HAVE a deep, precise, and above all serious mental outlook, ranging from the profound to the melancholy but never frivolous or light. Knowledge is sacred to you. The Law is the Law. You stick by the Code as you understand it. With 185, 191, 183 or 189, very lofty mind, capable of the heights of idealism, and the profundities of philosophy. With 193, 194, 198, 199, mystic bent, intuitive, inspirational, and with flashes of deep wisdom, perhaps in science, religion, or philosophy. With 195, 196, 198, 199, the sobriety of this aspect is not injured; you are still profound and deep-running enough but the depth may turn to trickery in mental processes and the moral sense be somewhat upset. If with 240 and/or 241, danger of melancholia. Also with 163, 145 or 149. You are an impressive speaker and logician, whether you're fighting on the side of the angels or against them. A certain power and authority, amounting almost to pompousness, attaches to your manner of speech. You don't merely say things, you state them; and this has its effect on your listeners, who will have to have strong wills not to fall in line with your

[1] In the same space with.

subtle reasoning. You can outguess most people, and, being suspicious, are rarely fooled. You have it in you to bamboozle the world. Nobody is ever going to sell you any gold bricks or phony oil stock.

187

MERCURY CONJUNCTION[1] URANUS ☿ ☌ ♅

A SHARP, brilliant, critical mind, with strong mechanical leanings. You are likely to work your way to a position of respect and authority in criticism, the arts, mechanics, or electricity. Your manner of speech is quick and incisive—sometimes jerky; but the words come out with a clipped force and a curiously inexplicable charm. You don't pull your punches; your judgments bear the mark of a certain detachment that removes the personal sting. You are capable of a high order of objectivity in your mental processes and, in the middle of emotional turmoil, can think things through swiftly and with the utmost logic (unless with 150 or 164, when your emotions muddle you up considerably). You love conversation, reading, the drama. You are an individualist and strive to satisfy your individuality realistically. You are opinionated, but considerate of the opinions of others even when you don't agree with them. If with 197 or 199, mental confusion; if with 195, explosive high temper and very cutting speech; if with 183 or 189, artistic; if with 161, brilliance; if with 163 or 180, power through your own efforts.

188

MERCURY CONJUNCTION[1] NEPTUNE ☿ ☌ ♆

YOU HAVE a sensitive mind, plastic and impressionable, sensational and romantic. Smells and tastes mean a great deal to you, and you respond to color, music, and odor as a photographic plate responds to light. You try to find the expression for what you feel, for a desire to articulate beauty is inherent in you. This causes you to write poetry or music, at which you may be very successful if either 183, 189, 190, 192, 193, and 163 or 180 is present. A tendency to fall into sensationalism is dangerous, markedly so if with 184, 195, 197, 198, 200, 210, 203, 204, 213, 214, 150, 151, 164, 165, 168, 178, 171, 172 or 181; and even with these, the mind runs to sensuous thoughts and must be strictly controlled and guarded. These may range from the spiritual and idealistic to the gross and bestial, and a touch of earth is generally mixed with even the highest amount of idealism. This is an aspect of Pan the Earth God, who despite the goat hooves piped the most ethereal of songs and won the hearts of the maidens. This sensationalism, controlled and guided, produces art, poetry, charm; but allowed to run rampant, can absorb and hypnotize the whole personality destructively. You should avoid mysticism, spiritualism, and anything that is not logically provable. Once you pin

[1] In the same space with.

yourself down to logic and reasonableness and avoid sensationalism, your mind is capable of extraordinary feats.

189

MERCURY TRINE VENUS ☿ △ ♀

THIS GIVES much the same qualities as 183 (Mercury in the same space with Venus) with slightly less emphasis. The same idealism is manifest, and also the same leaning of the arts, either on the creative or the appreciative side. Read 183. The combinations which give artistic gifts with this aspect (189) are as follows: 163, 180, 188, 204, 146, 215, 218, 168, 178 or 181; and possibly 172. If also with 178, 179, 180 or 181.

190

MERCURY TRINE MARS ☿ △ ♂

YOU HAVE a facile quick mind, capable of grasping scientific facts and interested in them. But there's a good deal of a tendency to wasting your mental energies through lack of purpose, direction, and concentrative faculties. If other things show concentration, then this adds to the facility; if not, you'll have to fight against a tendency to skim the surface. If with 215 or 218 and 192, this shows facility at sculpture or one of the manual arts or sciences (surgery, etc.), for your fingers and hands are strong and capable, and if trained and guided by a strong purpose, become directly responsible for your success. A temptation to live by your wits is always present. If you hold yourself to a purpose your road to success is eased by quickness, perception, and ready grasp of details.

191

MERCURY TRINE JUPITER ☿ △ ♃

YOU HAVE HAD a fine education, and a trained mind makes life easy. You are just, honorable, and somewhat proud of your mental achievements. You are anxious to impress people with your knowledge and very sure of yourself. This doesn't necessarily make you accurate and a tendency to elaborate tinges your giving out of information, though not in a way to make you untruthful, You philosophize a good deal, thinking in general rather than specific terms, and may be hard to pin down to details. You are judicial—this may accompany downright Puritanism and in any case contributes to the puritanical side of your nature. You incline to the professions, your mental bent being somewhat more philosophic and academic than the bent that normally leads to business. If by any chance you get into business, your ability to see things in the large will contribute to your advancement, and your integrity will be appreciated and rewarded. Keep your feet on the ground, for an inclination to go into generalities can destroy your business sense.

192

MERCURY TRINE SATURN ☿ △ ♄

THIS ADDS to the intuitive faculties which in turn add to the reasoning power. You have a nicely balanced mind, capable of great concentrative action, probably on the critical or executive side unless other creative forces are shown in the horoscope. You are likely to have a wide variety of interests for you are accurate and profound, a student and philosopher, interested in ideas as well as in the practical workaday routine, for which you have a great capacity. You have good insight and a good business head, not easily deceived. You're utterly honest and trustworthy, a stickler for duty and the sanctity of obligations. This aspect will do a good deal to balance an entire horoscope by giving you the power to control things through logical analysis.

193

MERCURY TRINE URANUS ☿ △ ♅

READ 176. The mental outlook, scope, and breadth are like this paragraph, though 193 does not give the physical vitality that is given by 176. You are quick, inventive, and broad-minded and have advanced views and ideas which you are able to make practically workable and of which you are able to convince the world. You are very likely to be a leader of thought and opinion in whatever sphere of activity you move.

194

MERCURY TRINE NEPTUNE ☿ △ ♆

THIS AIDS intuition and reasoning powers; and with other indications of creative and concentrative gifts lends an inspirational quality to the work. If no creative power is shown this aspect is unimportant, giving balance to the mind, glibness and facility to the speech, and lending charm to the voice. You have a kind of detached and abstract viewpoint on knowledge, loving it for its own sake. You are thus anxious to satisfy your intellectual curiosity even with odds and ends of information that you may never use. It helps the memory and makes you a good storyteller, for you don't forget much, and something is always reminding you.

195

MERCURY SQUARE MARS ☿ □ ♂

You have a keen, scientifically sharp mind and a tongue of rapier-like speed—and edge. You can, and do, say cutting things. You don't mince words. Despite your excellent mental equipment, you may not develop intellectual gifts, for you are prone to jump to conclusions and unless with 186, 180, 163 do not tend to get far below the surface of anything that requires hard work. Where intuitive grasp and shrewdness are called for you get to the heart of things in a second. Your judgment is not sound. In business you are someone to be watched and need a strong and cautious person around you to keep you from flying up meaningless alleys. You are always jumping into holes feet first and finding out later how deep they are.

With 188 or 199, a tricky mind; with 186 or 197, depth is aided, subtlety increased—which subtlety may some day prove a boomerang. With 197, 198 or 199, the mind has more balance and poise, but periodic indiscretions cause trouble; with 183, a rather hard and calculating emotional nature, intense but wary.

A sharp suspiciousness attaches to this position. You know your own mental processes, and suspect them in others. You'd make a good detective, sensing all the tricks of evasion that might be used against you.

196

MERCURY SQUARE JUPITER ☿ □ ♃

You love to spin yarns—harmless yarns, to be sure, but highly exaggerated and colored; nothing ever loses any fat in the telling when you tell it. Though you worship educated and intellectual people, your own mind is not highly trained. You are capable of error in judgment through misconception of the facts, misinterpretation of the facts, exaggerated notions, or just plain ignorance. You are likely to barge ahead in a plan or an idea without any least notion of the underlying necessities of the situation. You aren't easy to persuade that you are wrong, for even when faced with evidence, you have a way of sticking to your guns though your ammunition is gone. If with 145, 159, 187, 195 or 199, fuzzy thinking can get you into a lot of trouble. There is likely to be a flaw in your judgment, especially your business judgment, that can be costly. You need mental training, facts and figures, a respect for authority, and a willingness to learn from books and from individuals, as well as in the expensive school of experience.

197

MERCURY SQUARE SATURN ☿ □ ♄

YOU ARE liable to fits of depression, for your deep and subtle mind feels the woes of the world, and your own woes, very keenly. You are sensitive in a peculiarly brooding sort of way, not striking back when hurt, but nursing your grief and feeling sorry for yourself. You have a profound mind. Shallowness, stupidity, and deceit throw you off balance—though you yourself are capable of subtleties that others may think deceit. But knowing your purposes you can justify yourself with a sort of pragmatic philosophy—the ends justify the means. You are selfish, and capable of what is known in the divorce as "mental cruelty" especially if with 184 or 195. You are a prober and a pryer and can get inside people even when they try to keep you out—this is a detective-like position. You are a subtle opponent in argument, having facts and figures at your command, and there's nothing flimsy about the logical structure you build. You thus make a good lawyer and a just, if stern, judge. If with 198, 199 or 195, a tricky mind; if with 234, exactitude is injured, subtlety increased. If with 188, evasive; if with 187, scientifically exact, somewhat inspired, and inventive.

198

MERCURY SQUARE URANUS ☿ □ ♅

QUICKNESS and mental facility are your gifts, with a periodic insight of great swiftness and accuracy but no great stability. Your mental control is not good, and your energies are wasted in temperament. You are independent in thought and action and your own mentor of opinion, frequently differing violently from established authority—and more likely than not to get into trouble through tactlessness. You like to talk back to policemen. The revolutionary spirit is strong in you with a "whatever it is, I'm against it" attitude. You like a battle of wits and will take the other side of the argument just for the fun of it or to help out the underdog. Your great independence and vigor of mind can make you a leader of thought when you have learned to get the chip off your shoulder. With 244, confused mental processes; with 240, you learn tact slowly, but steadily, and your influence rises. With 185, judicial nature, just and independent; with 196, unreliable mental processes, erratic and inexact.

199

MERCURY SQUARE NEPTUNE ☿ □ ♆

YOU ARE a daydreamer. You think abstract and impractical thoughts which you weave into a web of reality but can't put into practise. You love beauty, music, and art and should try to master the creative technique of one of these to put your inspirational faculties to work. You have difficulty concentrating. You are easily distracted, not so much by things or people around you as by the wandering tendencies of your own mind. Even when you are shut up alone in a quiet room, little is likely to be accomplished. If with 196, concentration is helped periodically, but the old wanderlust of the intellect needs attention in the interims; if with 196, expansive and active mind, needful of being pinned down to details of accomplishment.

200

VENUS CONJUNCTION[1] MARS ♀ ☌ ♂

YOU ARE extremely attractive to the opposite sex. This is the position par excellence of those who have what is known as IT. Others have it, to be sure, but you have it in a peculiarly magnetic form, and there is nothing that can take it away from you. You are also somewhat lucky in financial matters, even though you love to spend money perhaps not always in practical ways. You seem protected from want despite the fact that money has a way of running through your fingers. While impressionable in love matters you have a certain hard streak in you that may be the despair of sweethearts and admirers. You are conscious of your powers and do not hesitate to use them. You crave admiration, excitement, adulation—and above all you need the devotion of one person—that is, of one at a time; for you are not constant in the strict sense of that word. You may regard yourself as a model of devotion and loyalty, but this isn't going to keep you from flirtations when the mood is upon you. This is an excellent aspect for dealing with large bodies of people and for artistic work of any sort. There is a sort of fire to your manner of expression that catches the public imagination. Your magnetism is capable of spreading far and wide under other favorable conditions. On the other hand, your emotions are likely to get you into trouble and to cause you a good deal of sorrow. With 212 this is especially true. Some early disappointment in the matter of love has been sitting on you for a long time like a heavy weight, and not allowing you to enjoy the admiration you get. You have to be careful that a somewhat adolescent attitude toward romance doesn't follow you into maturity. You are one of these people who is perennially youthful—just be sure you aren't perpetually childish! With 203 or 217, unconventional nature, strange and unusual ideas about love. With 204 or 218, like the above in addition to being very impressionable, with an almost mystic and reverential attitude toward love. In any case, your love-life probably started very early—almost shockingly early—and is likely to continue late—"Age does not wither, nor custom stale, its infinite variety!"

[1] In the same space with.

201
VENUS CONJUNCTION[1] JUPITER ♀ ☌ ♃

YOU ARE gentle and idealistic and likely to have your feelings imposed upon. With 202 or 212, cyclic emotional life, many ups and downs, smiles and tears in the space of a minute. With 200 or 210, idealism and sensationalism curiously mixed, a varied love career—also with 203, 213, 204 or 214. Idealism will be the keynote of your nature at the start of your life, but the world will doubtless take a great deal of this out of you especially if with the above numbers, though it can never destroy it entirely. A naïve faith in goodness prevails to the end. You are religious according to some faith or fashion, probably orthodox, believing in the reward of the righteous. Some wealth is shown by this position, and with 200, 215 or 218, this is increased. With 207, 208, 209 or 205, much contentment and security, a sheltered life, peaceful and calm.

202
VENUS CONJUNCTION[1] SATURN ♀ ☌ ♄

YOU HAVE an extremely complex emotional nature subject to dejection, depression of spirits, and discontent arising from emotional causes. This usually goes back to your childhood, and the cold or unsympathetic treatment of you by one or both parents which has tended to warp your emotional nature. You are sensitive and have been hurt much too easily, so that you have withdrawn into yourself and give the appearance of being detached and a little hard—which of course you are not (unless with 200, 210 or 224). You have a somewhat sacrificial attitude toward love matters, believing that pain and suffering are the lot of those who love; and a liberal dose of self-pity generally accompanies this position. Your emotional troubles arise not only from the unkindness of others, but also from your somewhat suspicious attitude toward those who love you, which irritates and angers them and in the end may cause them to act toward you in just the manner you don't wish—a sort of "that which I have feared hath come upon me" condition. It is true that you have been imposed on in the past, but you must not judge all men or women by the few people who have disappointed you, and you should cultivate trust in those you love. You are extremely loyal—in fact, loyalty is a god to you. You will stick to someone long after he (she) has ceased to love you or you to love him (her). Divorce is rare with this position, not because you are happy but because you are conventional and have a grim determination to bear all in silence rather than go through the "ignominy" of the courts. There is a tendency to marry beneath your station, either socially or intellectually, or to marry someone for purposes of reform—which isn't likely to work at all. This position, especially if

[1] In the same space with.

with 227, 215, 219, 216, 224 or 220, frequently accompanies hereditary wealth, which may be lost. It is a somewhat good business position and in an executive type of horoscope makes for hard-headedness. Care in the handling of money can be altered considerably with 200, 210, 201 or 211; then there is a penny-wise and pound-foolish attitude, scrimping with one hand and wasting with the other. This position usually makes it *necessary* for you to be careful of money at some time or other, and the more careful you are early in life, the less likely you are to have to be careful later. It behooves you to deal with extreme caution in all business matters, which have a way of turning on you suddenly and creating unexpected situations that have to be coped with, with great discernment.

203

VENUS CONJUNCTION[1] URANUS ♀ ☌ ♅

THIS GIVES an emotional nature alternately repressed and explosive, apparently somewhat conventional and cold but actually very independent and erratic in the love-life. A highly nervous quality accompanies all of your emotional dealings. You are an idealist in the realms of love, full of theories about sex and human relations in general, which complicate relationships that to other people are much more simple. You think much on emotional matters and are capable of hasty and jumpy action with respect to them; the motivating force behind your impulses is rational rather than physical—you can be swept off your feet by an idea, an ideal, a theory, more quickly than by the physical beauty of an individual. This ideology of yours is likely to take quite unusual forms, and to lead to strange relationships among strange and out-of-the-way people, because of whom you gain the reputation for being an eccentric. With 201, 206 or 209, highly idealistic and trusting; with 183, the intellectual life absorbs the emotional, giving artistic talent; with 200, 202, 210 or 214, much trouble through emotional matters, and some isolation from ordinary social contacts in search of the sensational and bizarre. An idealistic, generalized, and humanistic quality colors all your emotions, and elevates them from the purely personal plane to a kind of abstracted passion.

204

VENUS CONJUNCTION[1] NEPTUNE ♀ ☌ ♆

YOU ARE artistic, ultra-romantic, and impressionable. You fascinate others with a kind of other-worldly charm. There is something ethereal about you that isn't completely explained by your appearance, which doubtless is handsome or beautiful, depending on your sex. To men this gives a grace and charm of appearance and manner that is especially acceptable to women. To women it gives a sort of fragile and transparent

[1] In the same space with.

beauty that is magnetically captivating. You have to look out that your own charms don't run away with you, for there's a touch of sensationalism here, and an "all-for-love-and-the-world-well-lost" attitude that makes your emotions dangerous. You play hunches with respect to people, staking everything on your first impressions which can be woefully wrong. You are attracted by the unusual rather than by the sound in human beings, and can get mixed up with odd creatures if you let yourself go. You react rapidly to sense impressions and also to alcohol and drugs, which awaken the least desirable side of your emotional nature, for under your idealism there's a thick strata of earth. This assists material well-being, especially if with 229 or 218. With 213, erratic and irresponsible love-nature, periodically going off at a tangent. With 202 or 212, alternate heights and depths of emotional variety, subject to elation and depression from the feelings. With 200 or 210, sensuous. With 211, overexpansive and generous with the affections. This position aids creative power, and with other indications of concentrative and artistic ability lends appeal and assists recognition.

205

VENUS TRINE MARS ♀ △ ♂

STRONG and magnetic personality with a large amount of sex appeal of the more desirable sort, intense without being erratic; and emotionally reliable. You are likely to marry well so far as money is concerned, and also to have good earning powers of your own if you should need them. You spend freely especially in the pursuit of pleasure or the purchase of finery. You profit materially through your parents and probably will have some legacy from them or from someone else. Money is important to you. You are a materialist, and your ideals have a touch of earth in them. You are ardent rather than romantic though if other positions show romanticism this will lend vitality and realism to what might otherwise be a nebulous ideology. You will never want for sweethearts, and you'll be popular always, a social leader gathering people around you—and loving it!

206

VENUS TRINE JUPITER ♀ △ ♃

YOU HAVE a gentle nature, sensitive and anxious not to hurt people or to be hurt by them. There is danger of your being imposed on, either personally or financially, through your emotions and sympathies. Without squares □ or harmful conjunctions to Venus, you have a placid and harmonious emotional life and a degree of financial security. You have a somewhat matter-of-fact attitude toward love and will no doubt make a "good" marriage; you wouldn't be likely to marry beneath your station.

This is not an "all-for-love-and-the-world-well-lost" configuration, but one that achieves satisfaction in love without going far afield from the hereditary and socially set pattern. You love the nice things of life and one way or another will manage to have them around you. This aspect doesn't create much for good or evil in itself, but supports other tendencies. If there are not other aspects to Venus the indications here will be significant, but almost any other aspect except 183 will fundamentally absorb this one and submerge its influence.

207

VENUS TRINE SATURN ♀ △ ♄

THIS STEADIES the emotional nature and if there is no aspect between Venus and Mars, Venus and Neptune, Venus and Uranus, or Venus and the Sun, makes you cold, aloof, and rather self-sufficient. You have extraordinary business judgment and through conservative and sound tactics usually build yourself a fortune, if you don't have one left to you —for this is one of the positions of hereditary security and, with other indications, wealth. If Venus is not with Mars, Uranus, or Neptune, you are ultra-conventional. You are so self-controlled yourself that you don't understand why other people have to be otherwise. You are peace-loving and wish nothing better than to live in harmony with your fellow men, although you aren't especially tolerant of them. You haven't had the emotional variety to your life to make you understanding of human weakness. If Venus is with Mars, Neptune, or Uranus, this condition may be changed. There will be emotional variety, and this aspect (207) will enable you to steady down your life and recuperate from the ups and downs. A philosophic calm will underlie your greatest turmoil and give you the foundation on which to rebuild either your emotional stability or your material fortunes. This is one of the best of the *passive* aids to good fortune, standing by to give you self-confidence and sound good sense.

208

VENUS TRINE URANUS ♀ △ ♅

YOU ARE magnetic and charming, attractive to the opposite sex, and mildly unconventional in regard to sex matters. You have a broad emotional viewpoint tending to the generally humane rather than to the strictly personal. Eccentric friends are helpful; you gather strange birds around you. You love to help the underdog. An active social nature brings you in contact with strong people and assists your advancement. This adds to the luck in life and suggests a marriage that is happy romantically and financially helpful at the same time. It is a mild aspect in itself and produces little but strengthens the good and mitigates the evil, as shown by the rest of the chart.

209
VENUS TRINE NEPTUNE ♀ △ ♆

YOU ARE romantic, charming, alluring—and impressionable. You are idealistic, always looking for perfection in your sweethearts and in the world and blissfully certain that even though it may elude you, it's there and will be found eventually. You are more trusting than erring mankind deserves. You can be fooled by one person and, in the twinkling of an eye, trust someone else who may be even less trustworthy. You are attracted to out-of-the-way people—waifs and strays, down-and-outers, and can get yourself into a lot of trouble by believing in crooks, frauds, sensationalists, adventurers, and out-right seducers. Unless you lead a pretty sheltered life you will be taken in and shaken down at some time or other. With 200, 210, 218 or 226, much deception and treachery with respect to love matters. With 202 or 212, disappointment makes you reserved but doesn't destroy your faith in the ultimate goodness of everyone. This is one of the supporting factors for material luck in life, and, with 200, 215, 218, 201 or 229, may accompany great wealth.

210
VENUS SQUARE MARS ♀ □ ♂

THIS STRENGTHENS your emotions and passions and will bring you some turbulent experience through love and sex at some time during your life. It adds a note of inharmony and strangeness to the love-life, making you extremely self-willed and independent. With 202 or 212, danger of psychopathic independence in sex matters, due to some distressing experience. With 201, 211, overexpansive sex-nature—"super-social." With 203, 204, 213, 214, highly unconventional and stormy sex-life. You are temperamental, and if the intellectual qualities are not markedly strong, or with 151, 165, 173, 182, 188, 199, 160 or 181, this aspect will lead you to serious involvements through the misdirection of the passional and sensational nature. If the mental qualities are strong, this increases romanticism and intrudes a sensual note into the nature. It also inclines to financial extravagance in the matters of pleasure, dress, personal and domestic finery. There is a good deal of spice to your personality. You are magnetic, love company and a good time, and there is very little prudery about you. You'll swap yarns with the best of 'em, and maybe not always Sunday-school stories either.

211

VENUS SQUARE JUPITER ♀ □ ♃

YOU HAVE an expansive emotional nature; what you lack in intensity you make up in variety. You are extravagant, with both your affections and your finances. You aren't a good manager of funds and spend freely for love or for pleasure. If you are a man gold-diggers find you easy prey; and if you are a woman your vanity proves expensive. With 200 or 210, these traits are emphasized dangerously. Love affairs and financial indiscretion keep you in turmoil and excitement.

With 204 or 214, very impressionable, naïve, and affectionate nature, likely to be imposed on. With 202 or 212, sorrow through unreliable emotions, either your own or someone else's. With 203 or 213, erratic, irresponsible, and unconventional friends and sweethearts and a lot of stress and storm due to your emotional independence. This is a somewhat idealistic position, heightening the love-nature and giving you a curious sort of ideology with respect to love.

212

VENUS SQUARE SATURN ♀ □ ♄

THIS IS very similar to 202 (Venus in the same space with Saturn) which you should read. The emotional qualities of these two aspects are practically identical. With respect to financial and economic conditions this does not indicate inheritance, in fact takes it away. Even if you were born into a family of wealth, it is likely to disappear before it gets to you or to be less than you had thought it would be. You receive little help from your parents and should not live around them any longer than you can help. You do best when you are on your own. Work for and live among strangers. You are careful of money but never seem to have enough. You should make a budget and stick to it. You have good business sense of a temperamental sort. You don't plan things out too well, but your instincts are pretty good because conservative. On the other hand, you are capable of scrimping for a long time and then spending your savings foolishly. You're the fellow Benjamin Franklin was aiming at when he wrote, "Never buy what you do not need because it is cheap." You have a fear and dread of poverty which may not be at all justified, but which you should guard against by always keeping something laid up for a rainy day. Property rights are sacred to you, and you love to own things, especially land and your own house. You will make no end of sacrifices to have a place of your own. Read 202 for an analysis of your emotional qualities.

213
VENUS SQUARE URANUS ♀ □ ♅

THIS IS like 203 (Venus in the same space with Uranus) in the quality of the emotional life. Read that paragraph. In addition to the characteristics given there, this will bring an additional somberness and sobriety to your outlook on human relations and will cause you at some time some considerable disappointment through misplaced or frustrated affections. You tend strongly to the unconventional in love matters, making a fetish of independence in your love-life. A certain austerity attaches to you, and you can be unyielding when it does not suit your purpose to yield, at which time your detachment and objectivity can amount to cruelty. But at other times look out for impulse and temperament, for this is an erratic and unreliable position and makes you liable to periodic destructive impulses.

214
VENUS SQUARE NEPTUNE ♀ □ ♆

SOMEWHAT SIMILAR in force to the above paragraph (213) with a touch more of abstract idealism and less hardness to the love-nature. You are sensational rather than intellectual in your emotions and find it difficult to say no to an appeal to your feelings, especially with 200, 210, 201 or 211. With 244, 202 or 212, you say no at the wrong time, the judgment in love matters being bad and making you capricious—alternately yielding, affectionate, loving, and then suddenly, for no reason, uncompromising and independent. Unreliable and treacherous friends make trouble for you. Read 204, which is similar in effect to this aspect.

215
MARS CONJUNCTION[1] JUPITER ♂ ☌ ♃

YOU HAVE energy, dash, fire, enthusiasm, and magnetism. The creative urge is powerful in you. You have the sort of personality that less fortunate mortals pray for, and even if you don't do anything but sit on the side lines of life you give the impression that you could play the game with the best of them if you wanted to. If there aren't any squares □ in your horoscope you may sit on the side lines always, protected from economic worry and simply enjoying yourself; for this is an aspect of the *joie de vivre*. But if you are energized by a strong polarity of Sun and Moon, or by squares to the Sun or Moon; or by any such aspect as 218, 178, 163, 181, 180, 166, 167, 186 or 187, you will have mentality and ability of an extraordinary order. In any case, this is a condition of luck in life. If you aren't making money through

[1] In the same space with.

your own efforts then it's being left to you, or in some way put into your hands—through which it speedily flows out again.

With 224, gambling tendencies are strong—and dangerous. With 200 or 210, dangerous magnetism for the opposite sex makes trouble. If also with 212, rocks and reefs on the course of true love—romanticism meets scant encouragement. With 163 or 218, artistic and creative force strong; with 169, 180, business or government career best; with 161, early brilliance likely to peter out.

216

MARS CONJUNCTION[1] SATURN ♂ ☌ ♄

YOU WILL have to watch out for a tendency to be too accommodating and obliging. Your good-nature will either get you into trouble or cause you to be imposed on. You are so aware of social matters that you know how to please people and you are inclined to be, if possible, too self-sacrificing and self-effacing. This, in a selfish world, is a charming quality, but if carried too far it can nullify your individuality and your abilities. You are sure of yourself. You don't efface yourself through timidity but rather through being so sure that you don't feel the need to argue about it. If you can learn to translate this assurance into action and expression your calm and balanced nature will carry you far. If there are squares □ to your Sun and Moon, you'll learn to do this without any trouble. But if there are only trines △ and conjunctions (in the same space) ☌ to your Sun and Moon, you are likely to lead a placid, popular, and easy life without any need for developing your talents. Be a little more aggressive—too much tolerance amounts to mere weakness. An artistic or professional career is your best medium. Medicine, the law, and especially the ministry may appeal to you, from the idealistic, sacrificial, and service viewpoint, for this is the aspect of the soul dedicated to an ideal. Your mental qualities are excellent, inclining on the creative side to be imitative in the beginning and then strikingly original.

With 184 and 186, danger of overtaxing the mind and the eyes through too constant application to study and books; with 202, hectic and distressing love-life early; with 178, quarrels and disputes destructive and exhausting; with 149, genius; with 163, 181 or 179, plenty of energy and ability; with 166, 167 or 169, luck in financial matters and business deals; with 172, confusion of purposes, impressionability, and danger from mystic leanings.

A private and personal career may carry you to a position of influence, authority, and even fame, far beyond the ordinary confines of your occupation.

[1]In the same space with.

217
MARS CONJUNCTION[1] URANUS ♂ ☌ ♅

YOU HAVE a strong personality and are a little cold and impersonal. You are mental rather than emotional in your bias toward life; capable, and quick in your perceptions. You are best when working in impersonal matters for your emotions are inaccurate and unreliable and (as the palmists say) you should let the head rule the heart. This makes good leaders, teachers, and government officials. Personal considerations don't interfere with what you have to do. You can be hard and even cruel if it suits your purposes. While you can be kind in theory and to groups, you are capable of being unkind in personal dealings and of hurting those who love you. A sort of rigidity pervades your emotions, and you have difficulty in unbending. There is something a little forbidding about you. You have periodically high temper, especially with 161, 178, 195 or 240. With 244, confused, indirect, and a little disorganized mentally—emotions and sensations interfere with logic and set up conflicts. With 147 or 168, health a problem; also to some extent with 161 and 178.

218
MARS CONJUNCTION[1] NEPTUNE ♂ ☌ ♆

THE MOST POWERFUL magnetic aspect in the horoscope. You have poise, charm, ability, power over people—and a determination to get ahead in the world that rarely fails to succeed. Your aims are definite, and your physical, mental, and intuitive powers work in unison to help you. You have a superstitious belief in many things including your own powers, and something of the magician hovers about you. Doors open at your word, men obey you, and the good things of the world come to you. You live up to the hilt of your possibilities and appear to have a guardian angel at your side, holding you to your task and encouraging you. You are selfish and self-centered, but you think these are virtues. You are capable of being pretty ruthless in the pursuit of what you are after. With 180, 163, 168, 178, 148, 149, 150, 151, 167, 169, 154, 155, 156, 157, 173, 174, 175 or 176, you will go very far. Without these, luck is still on your side but you don't make or find opportunities quite so readily. With 200, 210, 224, 225 or 241, sensationalism and indulgence will sap the powers; with 160, much difficulty through sex matters; with 224, great rise and fall. In itself this is a powerful position to have and, with any degree of will at all, it will give you something of the power over the world that the Magic Lamp gave to Aladdin.

[1] In the same space with.

219

MARS TRINE JUPITER ♂ △ ♃

ONE OF THE INDICES of wealth, either inherited or made by your own efforts or both. Frequently accompanies a rich marriage, especially if with 147 or 148 in a male chart, or 168, 169 or 174 in a female chart. Large ventures provide income and security. This is no scrimping-and-accumulating aspect for materially you do things in the grand manner. You are something of a gambler, and willing to risk it all in a game of pitch and toss. You're pretty lucky, which may account for your willingness to try. Business hunches are sound. Your financial structure is solid, and you're able continuously to add to the superstructure. Congratulations!

220

MARS TRINE SATURN ♂ △ ♄

YOU ARE a builder, willing to start at the bottom of a career and work your way deliberately to the top. There's nothing flimsy about the structure you build. This may make you an actual architect, or it may make you figuratively an architect of your own fate, laying your plans far in advance, and working soundly for their accomplishment. You have an excellent balance of boldness and reticence, aggressiveness and tact. You know when to fight and when to run away, when to push your affairs and when to let them bide their time. Your great asset is a sense of balance and proportion. Your judgment is excellent, and you always know where you are going and how each brick, however small, is going to fit into the eventual product. If this exists with any of the concentrative aspects (163, 180, 147, 168 or 178), driving force is terrific and always well aimed. If with 215, 217, 218, 227 or 230, material "luck" rises from carefully laid plans and great power and wealth may easily accrue. This is one of the best of all aspects (except those to the Sun and Moon) for self-reliance, progress, and sound success, the extent and nature of which will depend on other indications. But as insurance that your energies will find constructive and progressive outlet, you wouldn't want anything better than this.

221

MARS TRINE URANUS ♂ △ ♅

YOU ARE inventive and mechanically inclined and if with 184, 195, 187 or 198, likely to be a mechanical genius. Electricity, railroads, steel, iron, metals, and mechanics of all sorts are the natural media in which you work, and your highly original turn of mind will find new uses and combinations in connection with all these things. On the purely intellectual side, you are critical and analytical—cold, detached, and impersonal rather than emotional. You love speed and will drive a car, run an aëroplane or a speed boat at breakneck pace. You are a gambler with safety as well as with finances and ideas and will stake your all on a scheme or a plan the success of which you are convinced.

222

MARS TRINE NEPTUNE ♂ △ ♆

YOU HAVE marked personal magnetism. Opportunities open up to you readily. You have a somewhat mystical, spiritual, or religious nature—a degree of superstition, and a belief in your internal powers. This frequently accompanies belief in Christian Science, Unity, or cults that deal in mind power. It isn't a very important aspect in itself but it lends color to your personality and sharpens your æsthetic and artistic senses. You control people by charming them. A mildly hypnotic power of which you may not be conscious assists all human relationships. You rely a good deal on hunches, especially about people. If this aspect is accompanied by strong and reasonable mental tendencies you may not even be conscious of its action, but rest assured it is responsible for the quickness of your insight, reasoning powers, and general mental astuteness. It eases the course of emotional matters somewhat; it is a passive rather than an active ally to accomplishment in all fields.

223

MARS SQUARE JUPITER ♂ □ ♃

YOU ARE a gambler and you gamble in large sums—no penny ante for you. But gambles are dangerous, and in the end you'll win less than you lose. In both financial and other matters you don't know when you've had enough. Enthusiasm and high vitality carry you optimistically onward till your luck vanishes and you're back behind the starting line again. This makes you a partner to be looked out for in business matters for you'll ride a willing horse to death.... You have to learn moderation in all things. Control and direction of your energies and enthusiasms is what you chiefly need, for your capabilities and vision are great and if harnessed by some such concentrative and directing aspect as 180, 163 or 169 will carry you far. In a woman's horoscope this shows difficulty through men. Employers don't benefit you despite your capabilities, and men are likely as not to cause you losses or difficulties. If you are not extravagant yourself, then your men-folks are. Emotionally, this is a somewhat hectic position inclining to an extravagance and daring of emotions similar to the financial and business extravagance and daring.

224
MARS SQUARE SATURN ♂ □ ♄

THIS IS an aspect of bad judgment and of that peculiarly insidious form of bad judgment which for years may appear to be "getting away with it" until the accumulated flaws in your life topple over the structure of your existence. If you have this aspect in your chart you will do well to sit down right now and make a thorough analysis of your life, your position, and your security, to see whether you are not operating on a major fallacy—a fallacy concerning either your own capabilities or the nature of the world in which you are working. Somewhere along the line you are making a fundamental mistake in estimating your own capacity, or the extent of your security.

If the Sun-Moon reading and/or other readings show marked executive leanings, this aspect will increase the executive talent, make you arrogant, dynamic, forceful, magnetic, able to control other people—often to their own hurt but with the best of intentions on your part. You will push your affairs too hard, too far, and too fast; get yourself financially out on a limb—and find too late that the limb is cracking. This is the aspect of the plunger who burns his bridges behind him, arrogantly certain of his own luck and his own infallibility until he discovers too late that his structure is a house of cards. In youth you will have had responsibility, or started your career early, having been precocious in either mental or material matters. You have built up an inordinate amount of faith in your own ability. The danger is that you will push your luck past the safety zone—that either in business or speculation or professional activity, you will trust to your own infallibility once too often and come a cropper. This is the aspect of fortunes made and lost—of shirt-sleeves to shirt-sleeves in three generations—or in one; of arrogant overlords either of men or of money whose stars rise and set all in the course of a single lifetime. If you have this aspect the good may be reaped and the evil avoided, if you will pause at the height of your success—and deliberately refuse to go any further. But the hypnotic influence of this aspect makes such withdrawal difficult though not impossible. You must be satisfied with moderation and content to draw down your winnings without waiting for the last roll of the dice.

If the Sun-Moon reading and/or other readings show nonexecutive leanings, this aspect will give you some sort of an inferiority complex to bring you under the dominance of older people. In general it will retard your development, making you indecisive and too willing to take advice and guidance. You are likely to be imposed upon—with periodic and depressing bursts of rebellious temperament which serve to wear you out without accomplishing anything else. You struggle for a decision, letting things mill around in your mind for a long time indeterminately without really concentrating on the facts and figures; and finally, out of sheer impatience you jump to a conclusion which may not have any relationship with the facts or with your mullings. The dominance of others, early responsibilities, and a sort of nervous rebellion toward them cause you difficulty in orienting yourself to the world. None of these things, of course, is fated, and the difficulty may be overcome by the assumption of independence in youth; by a philosophic attitude toward obligations which cannot be avoided, and an accompanying determination not to be imposed upon, or by a strict course of self-analysis, to get at the roots of your indecision—if necessary, to change your environment and your occupation in order to rout out those factors which are psychologically distressing.

In either of the above cases finances will bear watching especially with respect to sudden losses due to bad judgment in business matters, and the emotional nature must be carefully guarded against the incursion of factors that make for psychic biases in human relations. In a woman's horoscope this usually means disagreement between husband and father, or husband and brother, or husband and sons—or all of them. Such a girl frequently has to defy her father to get married at all, or throw off some obligation or tie which someone is trying to foist on her. In a man's horoscope it has no especial effect on his wife or his marriage unless with 147, 149, 161 or 163, in which case her health is likely not to be of the best. Whatever other factors do or do not exist, however, the Nemesis of erroneous judgment very temptingly presented, must be watched, and you must make every effort to analyze strictly what you do from a purely rational, logical, and unemotional viewpoint.

With 200, 210, 202 or 212, difficulty through love matters and danger of deep-rooted emotional biases with respect to love. With 227, 215, 223, 147 or 149, fortunes made and lost, either by the native, or by someone who would have left it to him. With 184, sharp and shrewd mind—look out for this fellow in a trade or a business deal! He's good. But he should also look out for himself—maybe someday he'll be too good! With 168 or 170, violent temper.

225

MARS SQUARE URANUS ♂ □ ♅

TEMPER! This is the aspect par excellence of an explosive and apparently uncontrollable temper which has to be curbed lest it run away with the whole personality. It is especially destructive if with 224 or 226, when rages take command of your entire being. Anger will lead to serious emotional and psychic disturbances if you don't learn to curb it. This also tends to break down the structure of your plans, to present sudden and insurmountable obstacles, and to put a strata of quicksand under what you try to build. You must examine the foundations of your plans, your emotions, your human relationships very carefully to make sure that fundamental flaws in theory or practise are not jeopardizing them. You have an independent mind—too independent. Rash and tactless speech cause you much trouble. This position also carries with it a likelihood of accidents — stay out of aëroplanes, speed-boats, racing cars, and roller coasters. You love speed and are something of a daredevil—don't let it run away with you!

226

MARS SQUARE NEPTUNE ♂ □ ♆

THIS ASPECT accompanies spiritual thought and spiritual leadership and is found in the executives of the Church and of spiritual and occult organizations as well as occasionally among great military leaders who have an unusually magnetic personal hold over their men. It gives you a spiritual insight into the affairs of earth, and a practical viewpoint about ideas of heaven. You are conscious of the two worlds which are not separate entities to you but related and integrated parts of the same whole. Thus, in strong executive horoscopes, this spirituo-practical approach gives your personality the ring of authenticity and divine right. You speak "not as the Scribes and Pharisees, but as one having authority," and you somewhat overawe those who come in contact with you. Whatever possibilities your horoscope shows, this will lend subtle but powerful force to it and give you a grip on the minds and hearts of men that is invaluable.

227

JUPITER CONJUNCTION[1] SATURN ♃ ☌ ♄

THIS ASPECT occurs about every nineteen years, lasts for a considerable period, and thus affects large numbers of people born during these times. In general, it indicates a period of law and order, and people born under it are pillars of society, quietly and nobly ambitious to succeed, but willing to do so only in orthodox and utterly honorable fashion. If you have this aspect you are conventional, orderly, proud, aspiring, with a quiet dignity about you that impresses your friends. In whatever sphere you may be you are supported and made prosperous and secure to some extent. With 148, 155, 169 or 174, you will rise to considerable honor, or even fame, though you will have a long apprenticeship to serve before your value and worth are recognized. You are eager for recognition but hate notoriety, so your recognition when it comes will rest on secure foundations.

With 224, swifter rise, more aggressive nature, and less certain tenure of public approval. With 220, 231, 232, probability of wealth. With 1, 14, 40, 66, 92 or 118, unlimited prestige and authority . . .

[1] In the same space with.

This position is somewhat late in bringing its benefits, generally not being felt until after the thirtieth year, except in setting the mold of your personality and your ambitions; but after this it works steadily on your side. Positions of influence are most likely—government, army, ministry, the law. You may be an author, leaving your imprint on literature for generations.

228

JUPITER CONJUNCTION[1] URANUS ♃ ☌ ♅

YOU HAVE a certain amount of material luck, and do well in large enterprises—government, railroading, large corporations—for this is an aspect of Big Business. You are an organizer, a planner, and a doer. The fact that your most practical plans have a touch of high idealism lends force to your authority. You are philosophical, capable of objectivity and detachment. You think in great sweeps and express yourself in the grand manner. As an orator you have the power to sway audiences both with the scope of your thought and with your manner of expression. This aspect, though it does little of itself, lends force to an aggressive horoscope, heightens the possibility of recognition, and gives you luck and prestige as well as the possibility of sudden and unexpected gains.

229

JUPITER CONJUNCTION[1] NEPTUNE ♃ ☌ ♆

A MATERIAL ASPECT which will make wealth if the rest of the horoscope shows security and material fortune. Money through inheritance, luck, oil wells, liquids of all kinds; or, without these, general good luck. You are idealistic and expansive in your ideas, spiritual, high minded, and both impressive and impressionable. If other indications show happy marriage this will make it ideal, from a material as well as an emotional angle. It also does something to mitigate the indications of an unhappy marriage. It is primarily an aspect of fortune and may bring you gains from unusual sources.

230

JUPITER TRINE SATURN ♃ △ ♄

YOU HAVE in this aspect the best possible insurance against want and poverty for no matter how bad things may be, you always seem to get what you need. When everyone else is broke you can fish a dollar out of some place. In a similar way, when you're broke, someone or something will come to your rescue. Even in an otherwise weak horoscope this aspect is so strong that it takes the edge from the worst cuts of life, holding up your head and your fortunes, and giving you, in varying

[1] In the same space with.

degrees, dignity and security which by careful and conservative expenditures you can make into wealth. You are an excellent manager of funds and can stretch a dollar to the limit without being penurious or petty. You simply know how to get your money's worth, and, being utterly fair and honorable, are just as willing to give fair value when you're on the selling end. You won't fleece others, and you won't be fleeced yourself. You can deal with large numbers of people and, having an eminent sense of justice in abstract as well as practical matters, you make a fine judge, minister, social worker, or executive. Whether you are prominent and powerful or quiet and reserved, your character wins you respect and a certain prestige and authority in whatever sphere you move. This is an aspect of maturity and may not be felt before the thirtieth year in any except the security sense. Under it you will develop steadily and forcefully as you grow older and in middle and later life feel the stability that you derive from these two most powerful of the planets.

231

JUPITER TRINE URANUS ♃ △ ♅

THIS IS MERELY a contributing aspect and has little force of its own. It adds stability to the character and in some degree to the fortunes, giving an element of luck to the economic status and broadening the outlook. If creative power is shown, this will give it great breadth, scope, and social humanitarian appeal. If a business career is indicated, this builds the fortunes and makes beloved executives and managers. If public life, this tinges the purpose with a broad social outlook that may reach the constructively radical.

232

JUPITER TRINE NEPTUNE ♃ △ ♆

THIS ADDS to the spiritual insight, increasing any latent intuitive faculties and enabling you to give practical application to your hunches. Aids creative artists by adding charm and facility to their expression and by making it salable. Helps business men by enabling them to follow their hunches to good advantage. Aids all those who deal with people (professional men, politicians) by adding a peculiar magnetism to the personality and making them appear jovial, humanitarian, and charitable.

233

JUPITER SQUARE SATURN ♃ □ ♄

YOU HOLD yourself back by being unable to imagine yourself in a higher place than you are. Your ambition is limited, and a certain humility hangs over you that keeps you from recognition. It isn't so much that your luck is bad or your abilities low, for you are a careful and conscientious workman—what really hurts is the narrow range of your imagination. Where other people see themselves forging ahead, you think you're lucky if you can keep the wolf from the door. You have to set your goal in the stars if you're going to so much as get your head above water, the competitive world being what is is. Read the poetry of Robert Browning, get inspired, and realize the "Not failure, but low aim, is sin."

234

JUPITER SQUARE URANUS ♃ □ ♅

YOU ARE EXPANSIVE in your imagination and plans, thinking up huge business structures and schemes which may or may not have practical merit to them. As often as not they are visionary, radically advanced, and out of step with business as it really is. Your organization of material, men, or business is likely to be brilliant but unsound. You are a visionary and must continuously hold yourself down to reality. If other indications in the horoscope show a strong practical bent, this will add zest and flair to it, but if there are romantic, adventurous, or flighty tendencies, you will be going off on unfeasible tangents that are costly in money as well as energy. Sudden losses due to this unsoundness are likely to fall on you and, in both schemes and financial matters, you should stay away from the long-shot gambles that are so tempting to you.

235

JUPITER SQUARE NEPTUNE ♃ □ ♆

YOU ARE a good deal of a visionary, idealistic in matters of philosophy and religion, with a kind of nebulous and unsound approach to abstract matters. You are capable of believing in things that never were on land or sea. A strata of mysticism underlies your thinking, a mist of unreality gets between your eyes and the outer world. Concrete evidence should be your constant aim, and you should forget the Pauline definition of faith as "the evidence of things unseen," for you are all too prone to believe and must cultivate skepticism. In material and personal matters this makes you pretty gullible, and, unless other indications show a marked degree of suspicion and shrewdness, this will get you into trouble and cause losses. Even with the most practical of indications you will have periodic fits of playing hunches or inspirations that will be costly. Stay away from seances, spiritualism, abstract philosophy, and religion, and pin your thinking, your emotions, and your business strictly down to earth.

236

SATURN CONJUNCTION[1] URANUS ♄ ☌ ♅

THIS STRENGTHENS a strong horoscope with a steely magnetism and weakens a poor one with confusion. It gives you a periodically explosive, violent temper. With 163, 180, 212 or 224, much trouble through your erratic emotional nature. You have a queer interest in out-of-the-way things, people, and studies and lead a private life of your own that you don't like other people to know about. You are secretive, suspicious, reserved, and rather proud; with 195, very strangely working mind, involved and indirect mental processes, difficulty of expression, independent and irascible, despite (or because of?) a subtle inferiority complex. You are a subtle person anyway, keeping your purposes well to yourself, with a sort of quivering ambition that you have difficulty integrating into action. You get muddled between the practical and the ideal, the visionary and the real, the theoretic and the actual.

237

SATURN CONJUNCTION[1] NEPTUNE ♄ ☌ ♆

THIS ADDS luck, magnetism, material good fortune, which you are able to control through control of yourself. It is a somewhat imperious position, under favorable circumstances giving you unusual charm of manner and a sort of hypnotic power over people. This will be true of greater or less degree, depending on the strength of the rest of the horoscope. In powerful, aggressive nativities it can lead to the heights of acclaim. In weaker ones, it bolsters up the weaknesses and gives you a charm that keeps off the worst of the evils. With 243 you belong to a sort of freemasonry of the elect. With 216, automatic rise; with 224, rise and fall; sensationalist. With 240, confusion, eccentricity, poor structure to the career, lack of organization. With 233, low order of ambition keeps dream from being realized—material humility accompanies spiritual exaltation.

238

SATURN TRINE URANUS ♄ △ ♅

YOU ARE supported by apparently inexplicable forces, able to put across plans that others fail in, and if there are conjunctions to either Saturn or Uranus in your horoscope, you will build your plans swiftly. With 163 or 180 your faculties of concentration and purposefulness meet with almost magical success. If you are an artist, engineer, architect, railroad man, military or naval leader, or politician, there is a touch of the unusual about you or your work. If with conjunctions or oppositions to either planet, or if with 156 or 175, you are a striking personality, able to "get

[1] In the same space with.

away with" very odd ideas which unaccountably work out. There's a touch of inspirationalism about you, a quick constructive perceptivity, that wins supporters and seems magnetically to attract success.

239

SATURN TRINE NEPTUNE ♄ △ ♆

THE EFFECT of this is very similar to that of 238 in that it bolsters and supports powerfully whatever other tendencies are shown in the horoscope. This aspect is more helpful on the purely creative and artistic side, and if you are engaged in such work your practical idealism shows forth in it to give worldly significance to a touch of other-worldliness. The concrete yet fantastic art of Arthur Rackham is symbolic of the sort of expression that this aspect makes possible—earth magic, which, whether you are an artist or not, lends an elusive but perpetual support to all your material activities.

240

SATURN SQUARE URANUS ♄ □ ♅

YOU ARE a pioneer and in some way an eccentric, independent in thought and action. Your independence doesn't work very strongly for your success, and you have to learn cooperation, tact, and diplomacy. In a horoscope that shows inventiveness, originality, and executive force, this increases those traits adding a note of quarrelsomeness, but none the less making you a strong and influential character. You are forceful in an electric sort of way and impress people even when they don't like your manner or your methods. In a non-executive horoscope the benefits of this position will not be felt. You have a peculiarly destructive temper—destructive to yourself chiefly—and must guard against the temperament that underlies your disposition.

241

SATURN SQUARE NEPTUNE ♄ □ ♆

AMBITION has a way of going to sleep on you. A sense of your own power works subtly inward giving you a peculiar brand of good opinion of yourself, which likely as not you don't get around to doing anything about. A sort of mystic faith in your own worth pervades your thinking—you know you could do it if you wanted to, but you have to fight to want to. This will prop self-confidence if other things show aggression, but it will forestall accomplishment if you do not integrate your purposes and translate them by will power and a set goal, into action.

242

URANUS CONJUNCTION[1] NEPTUNE ♅ ☌ ♆

THIS HAS NOT occurred since 1819, and will not occur again till 1993. Skip it!

243

URANUS TRINE NEPTUNE ♅ △ ♆

THIS ASPECT occurred from September, 1878, to October, 1884, in the earth signs Virgo and Taurus and has not been repeated since.* Everyone born in those years has some of the force of this aspect, which amounted to a world condition and required rather special factors in the individual horoscopes to make it show forth. In general, it is a supporting aspect of material benefit, helping to improve a good horoscope and lending some support even to a bad one. It inclines to a practical interest in the occult. It sharpens the perceptions and with 187 or 188, gives an extraordinarily broad and capable mind. With 164, 165, 181 or 182, danger of mental confusion through occult studies; with 164 or 191, inventive and unconventional nature; with 165 or 182, dreamy, mystic, sensational. With 203 or 204, magnetic and charming to an extraordinary degree, danger of difficulty through the people you attract. If with 217, inventive genius; with 218, wealth. With 237 or 229, and 180 or 147, extraordinary power and charm. President Roosevelt is significant of the race of giants which this aspect is capable of producing.

244

URANUS SQUARE NEPTUNE ♅ □ ♆

THIS POSITION, because of the slow motion of the two planets involved, lasts for many years at a time and consequently influences many people. It is the aspect of the so-called "Younger Generation" that ran rampant right after the World War overturning law, order, and especially personal morality, and creating a new social order on the ashes of an old one. It is the aspect of Rebellion, and its relationship to your planets has been dealt with in the "with" passages of your horoscope. It makes pioneers in thought and action, individualists who think things through for themselves with a peculiarly ritualistic sense of their own special importance in the scheme of things and a broad social outlook at the same time. It is an aspect of idealism which has a strong touch of earth in it and a practical note underlies even your most visionary opinion. In itself, unless activated by other aspects, this will not be felt in your life but in an executive and aggressive horoscope this lends flavor to the personality, courage and independence, and warns you against the faults of these virtues, which are rashness, indiscretion, and tactlessness.

[1] In the same space with.

* It had not happened again when this book was written, but did happen later when Uranus in Taurus was Trine to Neptune in Virgo.

245

MOON CONJUNCTION[1] SUN ☽ ☌ ☉

THIS LENDS concentrative force to the nature. In a woman's horoscope this is a bad position for health, and indeed in any horoscope the health needs watching. The vitality is not of the best except in Taurus, Leo, and Scorpio. Even here, though vitality is all right, organic difficulties are likely to crop up. This position warns you against pushing your mental energies past the limits of your physical capacity.

246

MOON TRINE SUN ☽ △ ☉

THIS ADDS an element of luck to the life and will tend to strengthen any good, or minimize any evil, that may be indicated by the rest of the chart. It inclines to a strong, sound body and an ability to take the ups and downs of the world in your stride. While it will not negate in any large degree the difficulties of the powerful (*) aspects, it will cushion the blow, give you internal resilience and external poise, as well as an elastic power to bounce back to normal from any personal or economic difficulty.

247

MOON SQUARE SUN ☽ □ ☉

THE SQUARE aspect between the Sun and Moon energizes the mentality giving drive, force, and quickness to the mind, and tends to objectify the desires (unless Sun is in Aries and Moon in Libra, Sun in Pisces and Moon in Virgo). It adds quickness and perceptive power to whatever other intellectual gifts are indicated, and warns of letting the mind run ahead of the body and exhaust it. Frequently this indicates some difficulty between the parents around the time of your birth—personal or financial tension in the family or in the family environment. An environmental or hereditary bias is set up giving one of those psychological quirks which makes for success. Rapid mental development follows, and success through ability to objectify and depersonalize your life by mental processes.

248

SUN TRINE VENUS

IGNORE this.

[1] In the same space with.

* It can't happen here! If you are on the Earth or any outer planet it is impossible for the Sun and Venus to be trine or 120 degrees apart. It could happen if you lived on Mercury.

249

GENERAL CONSIDERATION OF SORT OF ASPECTS TO THE SUN

IF THERE ARE *only triangles* to the Sun in your horoscope, then, though your luck and energy may be good, you need to work up drive, direction, and purpose. If there are *triangles* and *conjunctions* and no squares, energy, luck, and direction work well together, and accomplishment is easy and fluent. If the only conjunction is to Mercury, it is almost as if there were no conjunction at all, but with Jupiter, Venus, or Mars, progress is rapid and satisfying. If to the Moon only, good concentrative facilities periodically burst forth with long-lasting results. If there are *squares* only, great energy, persistence, and overcoming of obstacles, but little luck. If both *squares* and *conjunctions*, the top!

In a general way, trines make ease, contentment, happiness, luck; while squares give energy, drive, success, ambition. Conjunctions bring both energy and luck, and are translatable in terms of whether the Sun receives squares or trines, along with the conjunction. Similarly, squares and trines to the Sun together bring success through work and perseverance, and luck develops in proportion to the work done and the effort expended.

250

GENERAL CONSIDERATIONS OF THE KIND OF ASPECTS TO THE MOON

IF THERE ARE only *triangles* to the Moon, then your personality is charming, magnetic; you are clear-thinking, but you lack inner concentration drive and force. If there are *triangles* and *conjunctions,* then you have fine concentrative force, plus good expressive qualities—this condition is one of the symptoms of success. If the conjunction is with Saturn, introversion likely, but otherwise, excellent powers of reason, creation, and expression are exhibited when the Moon has both conjunctions and trines. If there are *squares* only, temperament in youth gives way to concentrative force later, especially if paragraph 163 is circled. Ambition forces you to work and you learn to integrate your internal forces successfully. If conjunctions (except to Mercury and Neptune) are accompanied by squares (except to Mercury, Neptune, or Venus) you overcome psychological handicaps for an intellectual triumph over yourself; this gives the mind-that-found-itself-type of person, though not necessarily in extreme form.

No aspects to the Moon gives deficiency of purpose and internal stamina, just as no aspects to the Sun gives lack of direction and ambition in the material world.

HOW TO CAST YOUR OWN HOROSCOPE

1. Tear a Horoscope Blank from the back of the book.
2. Look up your birth date in the correct table and write the numbers you find in the exact order that you find them, under the corresponding abbreviations in the box provided on the Horoscope Blank.
3. Write each abbreviation in its corresponding numbered space on the circle on the Horoscope Blank.
4. Note the Zodiac names in which the Sun and Moon appear. Look these up in Table I and record this with the paragraph number in the space provided on the Horoscope Blank.
5. Note what planets appear in the same space with one another or the Sun or Moon and refer to the bottom of the sheet for the correct paragraph number and underline for future reference.
6. Place the wheel (cut from last printed page in the back of the book) on the chart, pointing the arrow to the space where the Moon appears. Note where the triangles and squares come and look them up at the bottom of the sheet under "Moon △ this" and "Moon □ that." Underline these paragraph numbers for future reference.
7. Place the arrow at the Sun and note where the triangles and squares appear, proceeding as before.
8. Continue this through the seven planets, placing the arrow to each planet in turn and noting where the triangles and squares appear. Always refer to the bottom of the sheet for the correct paragraph numbers.
9. Collect all these paragraph numbers and look them up in the book—reading the basic number (the paragraph number on the Horoscope Blank) first, then the numbers with the asterisk, and lastly the underlined numbers.

Rule.

1. If you were born *early in the day,* read the basic paragraph *preceding* the one you obtained from table of Solar-Lunar polarity.
2. If you were *born late in the day,* read the basic paragraph *following* the one you found in the Solar-Lunar table.
3. *If you do not know the hour* of your birth, and the basic paragraph does not fit you, it is probable that the Moon had moved on another sign, or was not yet advanced to that sign, at the hour of your birth. In that case, you will find that either the paragraph following or the one preceding will fit your case.

VERY IMPORTANT: Regardless of the above consideration, *do not move the Moon* in your horoscope from the place it is given on your birth date; the aspects there indicated are yours and must not be tampered with!

	JAN	FEB	MAR	APR	MAY	JUNE	JULY	AUG	SEPT	OCT	NOV	DEC
1	30 6 30 27 22 30 16 21 7	33 10 31 31 24 30 16 21 7	35 11 32 35 25 31 16 21 7	1 15 1 3 25 31 15 21 7	5 18 6 6 25 31 15 21 7	7 24 7 10 25 31 15 21 7	10 27 9 13 25 31 16 21 7	13 33 15 18 25 31 16 21 7	16 2 19 21 25 31 16 21 7	19 6 19 24 28 31 16 21 7	22 10 21 26 30 31 17 21 7	26 13 26 26 32 31 17 21 7
2	30 7 30 28 22 30 16 21 7	33 11 31 31 24 30 16 21 7	35 12 32 35 25 31 16 21 7	1 16 1 3 25 31 15 21 7	5 20 7 7 25 31 15 21 7	7 25 7 10 25 31 15 21 7	11 28 9 13 25 31 16 21 7	13 24 15 18 25 31 16 21 7	16 3 19 21 27 31 16 21 7	19 7 19 24 28 31 16 21 7	22 11 22 26 30 31 17 21 7	26 14 26 26 32 31 17 21 7
3	30 8 30 28 22 30 16 21 7	33 12 31 32 24 30 16 21 7	35 13 32 35 25 30 16 21 7	1 18 1 3 25 31 15 21 7	5 21 7 7 25 31 15 21 7	7 26 7 10 25 31 15 21 7	11 30 9 13 25 31 16 21 7	13 36 15 18 25 31 16 21 7	16 4 19 21 27 31 16 21 7	19 8 19 24 28 31 16 21 7	23 12 22 26 30 31 17 21 7	26 16 26 26 32 31 17 21 7
4	30 9 30 28 22 30 16 21 7	33 13 31 32 24 30 16 21 7	35 15 32 35 25 31 16 21 7	1 19 1 3 25 31 15 21 7	5 22 7 7 25 31 15 21 7	7 28 7 11 25 31 15 21 7	11 31 9 13 25 31 16 21 7	13 1 15 18 25 31 16 21 7	16 6 19 21 27 31 16 21 7	19 9 19 24 28 31 16 21 7	23 14 22 26 30 31 17 21 7	26 17 26 26 32 31 17 21 7
5	30 10 31 28 22 30 16 21 7	33 15 31 32 24 30 16 21 7	35 16 32 35 25 31 16 21 7	1 21 1 3 25 31 15 21 7	5 24 7 7 25 31 15 21 7	7 29 7 11 25 31 15 21 7	11 33 9 13 25 31 16 21 7	13 2 15 18 25 31 16 21 7	16 7 19 21 27 31 16 21 7	20 10 19 24 28 31 16 21 7	23 15 22 26 30 31 17 21 7	26 18 26 26 33 31 17 21 7
6	30 12 31 28 22 30 16 21 7	33 16 31 32 24 30 16 21 7	35 17 33 35 25 31 16 21 7	1 22 1 3 25 31 15 21 7	5 25 7 7 25 31 15 21 7	8 31 7 11 25 32 16 21 7	11 34 10 15 25 31 16 21 7	13 4 15 18 25 31 16 21 7	16 9 20 21 27 31 16 21 7	20 12 19 24 28 31 16 21 7	23 16 22 26 31 31 17 21 7	26 19 26 26 33 31 17 21 7
7	30 13 31 28 22 30 16 21 7	33 17 31 32 24 30 16 21 7	36 18 33 36 25 31 16 21 7	1 23 1 3 25 31 15 21 7	5 27 7 7 25 31 15 21 7	8 32 7 11 25 32 16 21 7	11 36 10 15 25 31 16 21 7	13 5 16 18 25 31 16 21 7	16 10 20 22 27 31 16 21 7	20 13 19 24 28 31 16 21 7	23 17 22 26 31 31 17 21 7	26 21 27 26 33 31 17 21 7
8	30 14 31 28 22 30 16 21 7	33 19 31 33 24 30 16 21 7	36 19 33 36 25 31 16 21 7	3 24 3 4 25 31 15 21 7	5 28 7 7 25 31 15 21 7	8 34 7 11 25 32 16 21 7	12 1 10 15 25 31 16 21 7	15 6 16 18 25 31 16 21 7	16 11 20 22 27 31 16 21 7	20 14 19 25 26 31 16 21 7	23 18 23 26 31 31 17 21 7	26 22 27 26 33 31 17 21 7
9	30 15 31 28 22 30 16 21 7	33 20 31 33 24 30 16 21 7	36 21 33 36 25 31 16 21 7	3 25 3 4 25 31 15 21 7	6 30 7 7 25 31 15 21 7	8 35 7 12 25 32 16 21 7	12 3 10 15 25 31 16 21 7	15 7 16 18 25 31 16 21 7	16 12 20 22 27 31 16 21 7	20 15 19 25 28 31 16 21 7	23 20 23 26 31 31 17 21 7	26 23 27 26 33 31 17 21 7
10	30 16 31 28 22 30 16 21 7	33 21 31 33 24 30 16 21 7	36 22 33 36 25 31 16 21 7	3 27 3 4 25 31 15 21 7	6 31 7 7 25 31 15 21 7	8 36 7 12 25 32 16 21 7	12 4 10 15 25 31 16 21 7	15 9 16 18 25 31 16 21 7	18 13 20 22 27 31 16 21 7	20 16 19 25 28 31 16 21 7	23 21 23 26 31 31 17 21 7	26 24 28 25 33 32 17 21 7
11	30 18 31 30 22 30 16 21 7	33 22 31 33 24 30 16 21 7	36 24 34 36 25 31 16 21 7	3 28 3 4 25 31 15 21 7	6 33 7 7 25 31 15 21 7	9 2 7 12 25 32 16 21 7	12 5 10 15 25 31 16 21 7	15 10 16 19 25 31 16 21 7	18 14 20 22 27 31 16 21 7	21 18 19 25 28 31 16 21 7	23 22 23 26 31 31 17 21 7	26 26 28 25 33 32 17 21 7
12	30 19 31 30 22 30 16 21 7	33 24 31 33 24 30 16 21 7	36 25 24 36 25 31 16 21 7	3 30 3 4 25 31 15 21 7	6 34 7 7 25 31 15 21 7	9 3 7 12 25 32 16 21 7	12 7 10 16 25 31 16 21 7	15 11 16 19 25 31 16 21 7	18 16 20 22 27 31 16 21 7	21 19 19 25 28 31 16 21 7	24 23 23 26 31 31 17 21 7	26 27 28 25 33 32 17 21 7
13	30 20 31 30 22 30 16 21 7	33 25 32 33 24 30 15 21 6	36 26 34 36 25 31 16 21 7	3 31 3 4 25 31 15 21 7	6 36 7 7 25 31 15 21 7	9 4 7 12 25 32 16 21 7	12 8 11 16 25 31 16 21 7	15 12 16 19 25 31 16 21 7	18 16 20 22 27 31 16 21 7	21 20 19 25 28 31 16 21 7	24 25 23 26 31 31 17 21 7	26 28 28 25 33 32 17 21 7
14	30 21 31 30 22 30 16 21 7	33 26 30 33 24 30 15 21 6	36 27 34 36 25 31 16 21 7	3 33 4 4 25 31 15 21 7	6 1 7 7 25 31 15 21 7	9 6 7 12 25 32 16 21 7	12 9 11 16 25 31 16 21 7	15 13 16 19 25 31 16 21 7	18 18 20 22 27 31 16 21 7	21 21 19 25 28 31 16 21 7	24 26 24 26 31 31 17 21 7	26 30 28 25 33 32 17 21 7
15	30 23 21 30 22 30 16 21 7	33 28 30 33 24 30 15 21 6	36 29 34 1 25 31 16 21 7	3 34 4 4 25 31 15 21 7	6 2 7 7 25 31 15 21 7	9 7 7 12 25 32 16 21 7	12 10 12 16 25 31 16 21 7	15 15 16 19 25 31 16 21 7	18 19 20 22 27 31 16 21 7	21 22 19 25 28 31 16 21 7	24 28 24 26 31 31 17 21 7	26 31 28 25 33 32 17 21 7
16	30 24 31 30 22 30 16 21 7	33 30 30 33 24 30 15 21 6	36 30 34 1 25 31 15 21 7	3 36 4 4 25 31 15 21 7	6 3 7 7 25 31 15 21 7	9 8 7 12 25 32 16 21 7	12 12 12 16 25 31 16 21 7	15 16 17 19 25 31 16 21 7	18 21 20 22 27 31 16 21 7	21 24 19 25 28 31 16 21 7	24 29 24 26 31 31 17 21 7	26 33 29 25 33 32 17 21 7
17	30 25 31 30 22 30 16 21 7	33 31 30 33 24 30 15 21 6	36 31 34 1 25 31 15 21 7	3 1 4 4 25 31 15 21 7	6 5 7 9 25 31 15 21 7	9 9 7 12 24 31 15 21 7	12 13 12 16 25 31 16 21 7	15 17 17 19 25 31 16 21 7	18 22 20 22 27 31 16 21 7	21 25 19 25 28 31 16 21 7	24 30 24 26 31 31 17 21 7	26 35 29 25 34 32 17 21 7
18	30 27 31 30 22 30 16 21 7	33 33 30 33 24 30 15 21 6	36 33 34 1 25 31 15 21 7	3 3 4 4 25 31 15 21 7	6 6 7 9 25 31 15 21 7	9 10 7 12 24 31 15 21 7	12 14 12 16 25 31 16 21 7	15 18 17 19 25 31 16 21 7	18 23 20 22 27 31 16 21 7	21 27 19 25 28 31 16 21 7	24 31 24 26 31 31 17 21 7	26 36 29 25 34 32 17 22 7
19	30 28 31 31 22 30 16 21 7	34 34 30 34 25 30 16 22 7	36 34 34 1 25 31 15 21 7	3 4 4 4 25 31 15 21 7	6 7 7 9 25 31 15 21 7	9 12 1 12 24 31 15 21 7	12 15 12 16 25 31 16 21 7	15 19 17 19 25 31 16 21 7	18 24 20 22 27 31 16 21 7	21 28 19 25 28 31 16 21 7	24 33 24 26 31 31 17 21 7	27 1 29 25 34 32 17 22 7
20	31 30 31 30 22 30 16 21 7	34 35 30 34 25 30 16 22 7	36 36 34 1 25 31 15 21 7	4 5 5 5 25 31 15 21 7	6 9 7 9 25 31 15 21 7	9 13 7 12 24 31 15 21 7	12 16 12 16 25 31 16 21 7	15 21 18 19 25 31 16 21 7	18 25 20 22 27 31 16 21 7	21 30 19 25 28 31 16 21 7	24 35 24 26 31 31 17 21 7	27 2 29 25 34 32 17 22 7
21	31 32 32 30 23 30 16 21 7	34 1 31 34 25 30 16 22 7	1 1 34 1 25 31 15 21 7	4 6 5 5 25 31 15 21 7	7 10 7 9 25 31 15 21 7	10 14 7 12 24 31 15 21 7	12 17 12 16 25 31 16 21 7	15 22 18 19 25 31 16 21 7	18 27 20 23 27 31 16 21 7	21 31 20 26 29 31 17 21 7	24 36 24 26 31 31 17 21 7	27 4 29 25 34 32 17 22 7
22	31 33 32 30 23 30 16 21 7	34 2 31 34 25 30 16 22 7	1 3 34 1 25 31 15 21 7	4 7 5 5 25 31 15 21 7	7 11 7 9 25 31 15 21 7	10 15 7 12 24 31 15 21 7	12 19 12 16 25 31 16 21 7	15 23 18 19 25 31 16 21 7	18 28 20 23 27 31 16 21 7	21 32 20 26 29 31 17 21 7	25 1 25 26 31 31 17 21 7	28 5 29 25 34 32 17 22 7
23	31 34 32 30 23 30 16 21 7	34 3 31 34 25 30 16 22 7	1 4 35 1 25 31 15 21 7	4 9 5 5 25 31 15 21 7	7 12 7 9 25 31 15 21 7	10 16 7 12 24 31 15 21 7	13 20 13 16 25 31 16 21 7	17 26 18 20 26 31 17 21 7	19 30 20 23 28 31 16 21 7	22 34 20 26 29 31 17 21 7	25 3 25 26 31 31 17 21 7	28 7 29 25 34 32 17 22 7
24	32 36 32 30 23 30 16 21 7	34 5 31 34 25 30 16 22 7	1 6 35 1 25 31 15 21 7	4 10 6 6 25 31 15 21 7	7 13 7 9 25 31 15 21 7	10 18 7 12 24 31 15 21 7	13 21 13 16 25 31 16 21 7	17 26 18 20 26 31 17 21 7	19 31 20 23 28 31 16 21 7	22 35 20 26 29 31 17 21 7	25 4 25 26 31 31 17 21 7	28 8 29 25 34 32 17 22 7
25	32 1 32 30 23 30 16 21 7	34 6 31 34 24 30 15 21 6	1 7 36 1 25 31 15 21 7	4 11 6 6 25 31 15 21 7	7 15 7 9 25 31 15 21 7	10 19 7 13 24 31 15 21 7	13 22 13 17 25 31 16 21 7	17 27 18 20 26 31 17 21 7	19 33 20 23 28 31 16 21 7	22 1 20 26 29 31 17 21 7	25 5 25 26 31 31 17 21 7	28 9 29 25 34 32 17 22 7
26	32 3 32 31 23 30 16 21 7	34 7 31 34 24 30 15 21 7	1 8 36 1 25 31 15 21 7	4 12 6 6 25 31 15 21 7	7 16 7 9 25 31 15 21 7	10 20 7 13 24 31 15 21 7	13 24 13 17 25 31 16 21 7	17 29 18 20 26 31 17 21 7	19 34 19 23 28 31 16 21 7	22 2 20 26 30 31 17 21 7	25 7 26 26 31 31 17 21 7	28 10 31 25 34 32 17 22 7
27	32 4 32 31 23 30 16 21 7	34 8 31 34 24 30 15 21 6	1 9 36 2 25 31 15 21 7	4 13 6 6 25 31 15 21 7	7 17 7 10 25 31 15 21 7	10 21 7 13 24 31 15 21 7	13 25 13 17 25 31 16 21 7	16 30 19 20 26 31 16 21 7	19 36 19 24 28 31 16 21 7	22 3 21 26 30 31 17 21 7	25 9 26 26 31 31 17 21 7	28 11 31 25 34 32 17 22 7
28	32 5 32 31 23 30 16 21 7	34 10 31 34 24 30 15 21 6	1 10 36 2 25 31 15 21 7	4 15 6 6 25 31 15 21 7	7 18 7 10 25 31 15 21 7	10 22 7 13 24 31 15 21 7	13 26 13 17 25 31 16 21 7	16 31 19 21 25 31 16 21 7	19 1 19 24 28 31 16 21 7	22 5 21 26 30 31 17 21 7	25 10 26 26 31 31 17 21 7	28 13 31 25 34 32 17 22 7
29	32 7 32 31 23 30 16 21 7		1 12 36 3 25 31 15 21 7	4 16 6 6 25 31 15 21 7	7 19 7 10 25 31 15 21 7	10 24 7 13 24 31 15 21 7	13 28 13 17 25 31 16 21 7	16 33 19 21 25 31 16 21 7	19 2 19 24 28 31 16 21 7	22 6 21 26 30 31 17 21 7	26 11 26 26 31 31 17 21 7	28 14 31 25 34 32 17 22 7
30	32 8 32 31 23 30 16 21 7	**1890**	1 13 36 3 25 31 15 21 7	4 17 6 6 25 31 15 21 7	7 21 7 10 25 31 15 21 7	10 25 7 13 24 31 15 21 7	13 29 14 17 25 31 17 21 7	16 34 19 21 25 31 16 21 7	19 4 19 24 28 31 16 21 7	22 7 21 26 30 31 17 21 7	26 12 26 26 31 31 17 21 7	28 15 31 25 34 32 17 22 7
31	32 9 32 32 23 30 16 21 7		1 14 1 3 25 31 15 21 7		7 22 7 10 25 31 15 21 7		13 31 14 17 25 31 17 31 7	16 36 19 21 25 31 16 21 7		22 9 21 26 30 31 17 21 7		28 16 31 25 34 32 17 22 7

	JAN	FEB	MAR	APR	MAY	JUNE	JULY	AUG	SEPT	OCT	NOV	DEC
1	29 17 31 25 35 32 17 22 7	33 22 29 27 1 33 17 22 7	35 23 33 30 3 33 17 22 7	2 28 3 34 5 34 17 21 7	4 31 6 1 7 34 16 21 7	8 1 5 5 9 35 17 21 7	11 5 10 8 11 35 17 21 7	13 10 16 12 13 35 17 21 7	16 15 18 16 15 35 17 21 7	19 18 18 19 18 34 18 22 7	22 22 23 24 19 34 18 22 7	25 25 27 27 21 34 18 22 7
2	29 19 31 25 35 32 17 22 7	33 23 29 27 1 33 17 22 7	35 24 33 30 3 33 17 22 7	2 29 3 34 5 34 17 21 7	4 33 6 1 7 34 16 21 7	8 2 5 5 9 35 17 21 7	11 6 10 8 11 35 17 21 7	13 11 16 12 13 35 17 21 7	16 16 18 16 15 35 17 21 7	19 19 18 19 18 34 18 22 7	22 24 23 24 19 34 18 22 7	25 27 27 27 21 34 18 22 7
3	29 20 31 25 35 32 17 22 7	33 25 29 27 1 33 17 22 7	35 26 33 30 3 33 17 22 7	2 31 3 34 5 34 17 21 7	4 34 6 1 7 34 16 21 7	8 4 5 5 9 35 17 21 7	11 8 10 8 11 35 17 21 7	13 12 16 12 13 35 17 21 7	17 17 18 16 15 35 17 21 7	19 20 18 19 18 34 18 22 7	22 25 23 24 19 34 18 22 7	25 28 27 27 21 34 18 22 7
4	29 21 31 25 35 32 17 22 7	33 26 29 27 1 33 17 22 7	35 26 33 30 3 33 17 22 7	2 32 3 34 5 34 17 21 7	4 36 6 1 7 34 16 21 7	8 5 5 5 9 35 17 21 7	11 9 10 8 11 35 17 21 7	13 13 16 12 13 35 17 21 7	17 18 18 16 15 35 17 21 7	19 21 18 19 18 34 18 22 7	22 26 23 24 19 34 18 22 7	25 30 28 28 22 34 18 22 7
5	29 22 31 25 35 32 17 22 7	33 27 29 27 1 33 17 22 7	35 28 33 30 3 33 17 22 7	2 33 3 34 5 34 17 21 7	4 1 6 1 7 34 16 21 7	8 7 5 5 10 35 17 21 7	11 10 11 8 11 35 17 21 7	13 15 17 13 13 35 17 21 7	17 19 17 17 16 35 17 21 7	19 22 18 19 18 34 18 22 7	22 27 23 24 19 34 18 22 7	25 31 28 28 22 34 18 22 7
6	29 24 31 25 35 32 17 22 7	33 28 29 28 1 33 16 22 7	35 29 33 31 3 33 17 22 7	2 34 3 34 5 34 17 21 7	4 3 6 1 7 34 16 21 7	8 8 5 5 10 35 17 21 7	11 11 11 9 11 35 17 21 7	13 16 17 13 13 35 17 21 7	17 20 17 17 16 35 17 21 7	20 24 18 20 18 34 18 22 7	22 28 23 24 19 34 18 22 7	25 32 28 28 22 34 18 22 7
7	29 25 31 25 35 32 17 22 7	33 29 29 28 1 33 16 22 7	35 31 33 31 3 33 17 22 7	2 36 3 34 6 34 16 21 7	4 4 6 1 7 34 16 21 7	8 9 5 5 10 35 17 21 7	11 13 11 9 11 35 17 21 7	13 17 17 13 13 35 17 21 7	17 22 17 17 16 35 17 21 7	20 25 18 20 18 34 18 22 7	22 30 24 24 20 34 18 22 7	25 34 28 28 22 34 18 22 7
8	29 26 31 26 35 32 17 22 7	33 32 29 28 1 33 16 22 7	35 32 34 31 4 34 17 22 7	2 2 4 34 6 34 16 21 7	4 6 6 1 7 34 16 21 7	8 10 5 5 10 35 17 21 7	11 14 11 9 11 35 17 21 7	13 18 17 13 13 35 17 21 7	17 23 17 17 16 35 17 21 7	20 26 19 20 18 34 18 22 7	23 31 24 24 20 34 18 22 7	25 35 28 28 22 34 18 22 7
9	29 28 31 26 35 32 17 22 7	33 33 29 29 2 33 16 22 7	35 34 34 31 4 34 17 22 7	3 3 4 34 6 34 16 21 7	5 7 6 2 8 34 16 21 7	8 12 5 5 10 35 17 21 7	11 15 11 9 12 35 17 21 7	13 19 17 13 13 35 17 21 7	17 24 17 17 16 35 17 21 7	21 27 19 21 18 34 18 22 7	23 33 24 25 20 34 18 22 7	25 36 28 28 22 34 18 22 7
10	29 29 31 26 35 32 17 22 7	33 35 31 29 2 33 16 22 7	35 35 35 31 4 34 17 22 7	3 4 4 34 6 34 16 21 7	5 8 5 2 8 34 16 21 7	8 13 5 5 10 35 17 21 7	11 17 12 9 12 35 17 21 7	13 21 17 13 13 35 17 21 7	17 25 17 17 16 34 17 21 7	21 29 19 21 18 34 18 22 7	23 34 24 25 20 34 18 22 7	26 1 28 28 22 34 18 22 7
11	29 31 31 26 35 32 17 22 7	33 36 31 29 2 33 16 22 7	35 1 35 31 4 34 17 22 7	3 6 4 34 6 34 16 21 7	5 10 5 2 8 34 16 21 7	8 14 6 6 10 35 17 21 7	11 17 12 10 12 35 17 21 7	13 22 17 13 13 35 17 21 7	17 26 17 17 16 34 17 21 7	21 30 19 21 18 34 18 22 7	23 35 24 25 20 34 18 22 7	26 3 28 28 22 34 18 22 7
12	29 32 30 26 35 32 17 22 7	33 2 31 29 2 33 16 22 7	35 2 35 31 4 34 17 22 7	3 7 4 34 6 34 16 21 7	5 11 5 2 8 34 16 21 7	8 16 6 6 10 35 17 21 7	11 19 12 10 12 35 17 21 7	13 23 17 13 13 35 17 21 7	17 28 17 17 16 34 17 21 7	21 31 19 22 18 34 18 22 7	23 1 24 25 20 34 18 22 7	27 5 28 28 22 34 18 22 7
13	29 34 29 26 35 32 17 22 7	33 3 31 29 2 33 16 22 7	35 4 35 31 4 34 17 22 7	3 9 4 34 6 34 16 21 7	6 12 5 2 8 34 16 21 7	8 17 6 6 10 35 16 21 7	12 20 12 10 12 35 17 21 7	14 24 17 14 14 35 17 21 7	17 29 17 17 16 34 17 21 7	21 33 19 22 18 34 18 22 7	23 2 25 25 20 34 18 22 7	27 6 28 28 22 34 18 22 7
14	29 35 29 26 35 32 17 22 7	33 4 31 29 2 33 16 22 7	36 5 35 31 4 34 17 22 7	3 10 4 34 6 34 16 21 7	6 13 5 2 8 34 16 21 7	8 18 6 6 10 35 16 21 7	12 21 13 10 12 35 17 21 7	14 26 17 14 14 35 17 21 7	17 31 17 17 16 34 17 21 7	21 34 19 22 18 24 18 22 7	24 4 25 25 20 24 18 22 7	27 7 28 28 22 34 18 22 7
15	29 1 29 26 35 32 17 22 7	36 6 31 29 2 33 16 22 7	36 7 35 31 4 34 17 22 7	3 12 4 34 6 34 16 21 7	6 15 5 2 8 34 16 21 7	8 19 6 6 11 35 16 21 7	12 22 13 10 12 35 17 21 7	14 27 17 14 14 35 17 21 7	17 32 17 17 16 34 17 21 7	21 36 19 22 18 34 18 22 7	24 5 25 25 20 34 18 22 7	27 9 28 28 22 34 18 22 7
16	30 2 29 26 35 32 17 22 7	33 7 31 29 2 33 16 22 7	36 8 35 31 4 34 17 22 7	3 13 4 34 6 34 16 21 7	6 16 5 2 8 34 16 21 7	9 20 6 6 11 35 16 21 7	12 23 13 10 12 35 17 21 7	14 28 17 14 14 35 17 21 7	17 33 17 17 16 34 17 21 7	21 1 20 21 18 34 18 22 7	24 7 25 25 20 34 18 22 7	27 10 28 28 22 34 18 22 7
17	30 4 29 26 35 32 17 22 7	33 8 21 29 2 33 16 22 7	36 9 36 31 4 34 17 22 7	3 14 4 34 6 34 16 21 7	6 17 5 2 8 34 16 21 7	9 21 7 7 11 35 16 21 7	12 25 13 10 12 35 17 21 7	14 30 17 14 14 35 17 21 7	17 35 17 17 16 34 17 21 7	21 3 20 21 16 34 18 21 7	24 8 25 25 20 34 18 22 7	27 12 28 29 22 34 18 22 7
18	30 5 29 26 35 32 17 22 7	33 10 31 29 2 33 16 22 7	36 11 36 31 4 34 17 22 7	3 15 5 35 6 34 16 21 7	6 18 5 2 8 34 16 21 7	9 23 7 7 11 35 16 21 7	12 26 13 10 12 35 17 21 7	14 31 17 14 14 35 17 21 7	17 1 17 17 16 34 17 21 7	21 4 20 21 18 34 18 21 7	24 9 25 25 20 34 18 22 7	27 13 28 29 22 34 18 22 7
19	30 6 29 26 35 32 17 22 7	34 11 31 29 2 33 16 22 7	36 12 26 31 4 34 17 22 7	3 16 5 35 6 34 16 21 7	6 19 5 2 8 34 16 21 7	9 24 7 7 11 35 16 21 7	12 27 13 11 12 35 17 21 7	14 32 17 14 14 35 17 21 7	17 2 17 17 16 34 17 21 7	21 6 20 21 18 34 18 21 7	24 11 25 25 20 34 18 22 7	27 14 28 29 22 34 18 22 7
20	31 7 29 26 35 32 17 22 7	34 12 31 29 2 33 16 22 7	36 13 36 32 5 34 17 22 7	4 18 5 36 7 34 16 21 7	6 21 5 2 8 34 16 21 7	9 25 7 7 11 35 16 21 7	12 29 13 11 13 35 17 21 7	14 34 17 14 14 35 17 21 7	17 4 17 17 16 34 17 21 7	21 7 21 21 18 34 18 21 7	24 12 25 25 20 34 18 22 7	27 15 28 29 22 34 18 22 7
21	31 8 29 26 36 32 17 22 7	34 13 32 29 2 33 16 22 7	1 14 1 32 5 34 17 22 7	4 19 5 36 7 34 16 21 7	7 22 5 3 9 34 16 21 7	9 27 8 8 11 35 17 21 8	12 30 13 11 13 35 17 21 7	15 36 18 15 15 35 17 21 7	17 5 17 18 16 34 17 21 7	21 9 21 21 18 34 18 21 7	24 13 26 26 20 34 18 22 7	27 17 28 29 22 34 18 22 7
22	31 10 29 26 36 32 17 22 7	34 15 32 29 2 33 16 22 7	1 16 1 32 5 34 17 22 7	4 20 6 36 7 34 16 21 7	7 23 5 3 9 34 16 21 7	10 28 8 8 11 35 17 21 8	12 32 14 11 13 35 17 21 7	15 1 18 15 15 35 17 21 7	17 6 17 19 16 34 17 21 7	21 10 21 21 19 34 18 21 7	24 15 26 26 21 34 18 22 7	28 18 28 31 22 34 19 22 7
23	31 11 29 26 36 32 17 22 7	34 16 32 29 2 33 16 22 7	1 17 1 32 5 34 17 22 7	4 21 6 36 7 34 16 21 7	7 24 5 4 9 34 16 21 7	10 30 8 8 11 35 17 21 8	13 33 14 11 13 35 17 21 7	16 3 18 15 15 35 17 21 7	19 7 17 19 16 34 17 21 7	21 12 21 21 19 34 18 21 7	24 16 26 26 21 34 18 22 7	28 19 28 31 22 34 19 22 7
24	31 12 29 26 36 32 17 22 7	34 17 32 29 2 33 16 22 7	1 18 1 32 5 34 17 22 7	4 22 6 36 7 34 16 21 7	7 26 5 4 9 34 16 21 7	10 31 8 8 11 35 17 21 8	13 35 14 11 13 35 17 21 7	16 4 18 15 15 35 17 21 7	19 8 16 19 16 34 16 22 7	22 13 21 22 19 34 18 22 7	25 17 26 26 21 34 18 22 7	28 20 28 31 22 34 19 22 7
25	31 14 29 26 36 33 17 22 7	34 18 32 29 2 33 16 22 7	1 19 1 33 5 34 17 22 7	4 24 6 36 7 34 16 21 7	7 27 5 4 9 34 16 21 7	10 32 8 8 11 35 17 21 8	13 36 15 11 13 35 17 21 7	16 5 18 15 15 35 17 21 7	19 10 16 19 16 34 16 22 7	22 14 22 23 19 34 18 22 7	25 18 27 27 21 34 18 22 7	28 21 28 31 22 34 19 22 7
26	31 15 29 26 1 33 17 22 7	35 19 33 29 2 33 16 22 7	1 20 1 33 5 34 17 22 7	4 25 6 36 7 34 16 21 7	7 28 5 4 9 34 16 21 7	10 34 8 8 11 35 17 21 8	13 2 15 11 13 35 17 21 7	16 7 18 15 15 35 17 21 7	19 12 16 19 16 34 16 22 7	22 15 22 23 19 34 18 22 7	25 19 27 27 21 34 18 22 7	28 22 28 31 22 34 19 22 7
27	31 16 29 26 1 33 16 22 7	35 21 33 29 2 33 16 22 7	2 21 2 33 5 34 17 22 7	4 26 6 1 7 34 16 21 7	7 30 5 5 9 34 16 21 7	10 35 8 8 11 35 17 21 8	13 3 15 11 13 35 17 21 7	16 8 18 15 15 35 17 21 7	19 13 16 19 16 34 16 22 7	22 16 22 23 19 34 18 22 7	25 21 27 27 21 34 18 22 7	28 24 28 31 22 34 19 22 7
28	31 17 29 26 1 33 16 22 7	35 22 33 29 2 33 16 22 7	2 23 2 33 5 34 17 22 7	4 27 6 1 7 34 16 21 7	7 31 5 5 9 34 16 21 7	10 1 9 8 11 35 17 21 8	13 5 15 11 13 35 17 21 7	16 9 18 15 15 35 17 21 7	19 14 16 19 16 34 16 22 7	22 18 22 23 19 34 18 22 7	25 22 27 27 21 34 18 22 7	28 25 28 31 22 34 19 22 7
29	32 18 29 26 1 33 16 22 7	**1891**	2 24 2 33 5 34 17 22 7	4 29 6 1 7 34 16 21 7	7 33 5 5 9 34 16 21 7	10 2 9 8 11 35 16 21 8	13 6 15 12 13 35 17 21 7	16 11 18 15 15 35 17 21 7	19 15 16 19 16 34 16 22 7	22 19 22 23 19 34 18 22 7	25 23 27 27 21 34 18 22 7	28 27 28 31 22 34 19 22 7
30	32 20 29 26 1 33 16 22 7		2 25 2 33 5 34 17 22 7	4 30 6 1 7 34 16 21 7	7 35 5 5 9 34 16 21 7	10 3 9 8 11 35 16 21 8	13 7 15 12 13 35 17 21 7	16 12 18 15 15 35 17 21 7	19 16 16 19 16 34 16 22 7	22 20 22 23 19 34 18 22 7	25 24 27 27 21 34 18 22 7	28 28 28 31 22 34 19 22 7
31	32 21 29 26 1 33 16 22 7		2 26 2 33 5 34 17 22 7		7 26 5 5 9 34 16 21 7		13 8 16 12 13 35 17 21 7	16 13 18 15 15 35 17 21 7		22 21 22 23 19 34 18 22 7		28 29 28 31 22 34 19 22 7

	JAN	FEB	MAR	APR	MAY	JUNE	JULY	AUG	SEPT	OCT	NOV	DEC
1	29 30 28 31 23 35 19 22 7	31 36 30 36 25 36 18 22 7	34 2 34 3 27 36 18 22 7	2 7 4 6 29 1 18 22 7	4 11 3 9 30 1 18 22 7	9 16 6 12 33 3 18 22 7	11 19 12 12 33 3 18 22 8	14 23 16 10 32 3 18 22 7	16 28 15 12 31 3 19 22 7	19 31 19 15 31 3 19 22 7	22 36 24 18 33 3 19 22 7	25 4 27 22 34 2 19 22 7
2	29 31 28 31 23 35 19 22 7	31 1 30 36 25 36 18 22 7	35 3 34 3 27 36 18 22 7	2 9 4 6 29 1 18 22 7	4 12 3 9 30 1 18 22 7	9 17 6 12 33 3 18 22 7	11 20 12 12 33 3 18 22 8	14 24 16 10 32 3 18 22 7	16 29 15 12 31 3 19 22 7	19 33 19 15 31 3 19 22 7	22 1 24 18 33 3 19 22 7	25 6 27 22 34 2 19 22 7
3	29 33 28 31 23 35 19 22 7	31 2 30 36 25 36 18 22 7	34 5 34 3 27 36 18 22 7	2 10 4 6 29 1 18 22 7	5 13 3 9 30 1 18 22 7	9 18 6 12 33 3 18 22 7	11 21 12 12 33 3 18 22 8	14 26 16 10 32 3 18 22 7	16 30 15 12 31 3 19 22 7	19 34 19 15 31 3 19 22 7	22 3 24 19 33 3 19 22 7	25 7 27 22 34 2 19 22 7
4	29 35 28 31 23 35 19 22 7	31 4 30 26 25 36 18 22 7	34 6 34 3 27 36 18 22 7	2 11 4 6 29 1 18 22 7	5 15 3 9 30 1 18 22 7	9 19 6 12 33 3 18 22 7	11 22 12 12 33 3 18 22 8	14 27 16 10 32 3 18 22 7	16 32 15 12 31 3 19 22 7	19 35 19 15 31 3 19 22 7	22 4 24 19 33 2 19 22 7	25 9 27 22 34 2 19 22 7
5	29 36 28 32 23 35 19 22 7	32 6 30 36 25 36 18 22 7	35 8 35 3 27 36 18 22 7	2 13 4 7 29 1 18 22 7	5 16 3 10 30 1 18 22 7	9 21 7 12 33 3 18 22 7	11 24 13 12 33 3 18 22 8	14 28 16 10 32 3 18 22 7	16 33 15 12 31 3 19 22 7	19 1 19 15 31 3 19 22 7	22 6 24 19 33 2 19 22 7	25 10 27 22 34 2 19 22 7
6	29 1 28 32 23 35 19 22 7	32 7 30 36 25 36 18 22 7	35 9 35 3 27 36 18 22 7	2 14 4 7 29 1 18 22 7	5 17 3 10 30 1 18 22 7	9 22 7 12 33 3 18 22 7	11 25 13 12 33 3 18 22 8	14 30 16 10 32 3 18 22 7	16 34 15 12 31 3 19 22 7	19 3 19 15 31 3 19 22 7	22 7 25 19 33 2 19 22 7	25 12 27 22 34 2 19 22 7
7	29 3 28 32 23 35 19 22 7	32 8 30 36 25 36 18 22 7	35 10 35 3 27 36 18 22 7	2 15 4 7 29 1 18 22 7	5 18 3 10 31 1 18 22 7	9 23 7 12 33 3 18 22 7	12 26 13 12 33 3 18 22 8	14 31 16 10 32 3 18 22 7	16 36 15 12 31 3 19 22 7	20 4 20 15 32 3 19 22 7	22 9 25 19 33 2 19 22 7	25 13 27 22 34 2 19 22 7
8	29 4 28 32 23 35 19 22 7	32 9 31 26 25 36 18 22 7	36 12 36 3 27 36 18 22 7	2 16 4 7 29 1 18 22 7	5 20 3 10 31 1 18 22 7	9 24 7 12 33 3 18 22 7	12 27 13 12 33 3 18 22 8	14 33 16 10 32 3 18 22 7	16 1 15 13 31 3 19 22 7	20 5 20 16 32 2 19 22 8	23 10 25 19 33 2 19 22 7	25 14 27 22 34 2 19 22 7
9	29 5 28 32 23 35 19 22 7	32 11 31 36 25 36 18 22 7	36 13 36 3 27 26 18 22 7	2 18 4 7 29 1 18 22 7	5 21 3 10 31 1 18 22 7	9 25 7 12 33 3 18 22 7	12 29 13 12 33 3 18 22 8	15 34 16 10 31 3 18 22 7	16 3 15 13 31 3 19 22 7	20 7 20 16 32 2 19 22 8	23 12 25 19 34 2 19 22 7	25 16 27 22 34 2 19 22 7
10	29 7 28 32 23 35 19 22 7	33 12 31 36 25 36 18 22 7	36 14 36 4 27 36 18 22 7	2 19 4 7 30 1 18 22 7	5 22 3 10 31 1 18 22 7	9 27 7 12 33 3 18 22 7	12 30 13 12 33 3 18 22 8	15 35 16 10 31 3 18 22 7	16 4 16 13 31 3 19 22 7	20 8 20 16 32 2 19 22 8	23 13 25 19 34 2 19 22 7	25 17 26 22 34 2 19 22 7
11	29 8 28 32 23 35 19 22 7	33 13 31 36 25 36 18 22 7	36 15 36 4 27 36 18 22 7	2 20 4 7 30 1 18 22 7	6 23 4 10 31 1 18 22 7	9 28 7 12 33 3 18 22 7	12 31 13 12 33 3 18 22 8	15 1 16 10 31 3 18 22 7	18 6 16 13 31 3 19 22 7	20 10 21 16 32 2 19 22 8	23 15 25 19 34 2 19 22 7	25 18 26 22 34 2 19 22 7
12	29 10 28 32 23 35 19 22 7	33 14 31 36 25 36 18 22 7	36 16 36 4 27 36 18 22 7	2 21 4 7 30 1 18 22 7	6 24 4 10 31 1 18 22 7	9 29 9 12 33 3 18 22 7	12 33 15 12 33 3 18 22 8	15 2 16 11 31 3 18 22 7	18 7 16 13 31 3 19 22 7	20 11 21 17 32 2 19 22 8	23 16 25 19 34 2 19 22 7	25 19 26 22 34 2 19 22 7
13	29 11 28 32 23 35 19 22 7	33 16 31 36 25 36 18 22 7	36 18 36 4 27 36 18 22 7	2 22 4 7 30 1 18 22 7	6 26 4 10 31 1 18 22 7	9 30 9 12 33 3 18 22 7	12 34 15 11 33 3 18 22 8	15 3 16 11 31 3 18 22 7	18 9 16 13 31 3 19 22 7	20 12 21 17 32 2 19 22 8	24 17 25 19 34 2 19 22 7	26 21 26 23 35 2 19 22 7
14	29 12 28 32 23 35 19 22 7	33 17 31 36 25 36 18 22 7	36 19 36 4 27 36 18 22 7	2 24 4 7 30 1 18 22 7	6 27 4 10 31 1 18 22 7	9 32 9 12 33 3 18 22 7	12 36 15 11 33 3 18 22 8	15 5 16 11 31 3 18 22 7	18 10 16 13 31 3 19 22 7	20 14 21 17 32 2 19 22 8	24 18 25 19 34 1 19 22 7	27 22 26 24 36 2 19 22 7
15	29 13 28 32 23 35 19 22 7	33 18 31 36 25 36 18 22 7	36 20 36 4 27 36 18 22 7	2 25 4 7 30 1 18 22 7	6 28 4 10 31 1 18 22 7	9 33 9 12 33 3 18 22 7	12 1 15 11 33 3 18 22 8	15 6 16 11 31 3 18 22 7	18 12 16 13 31 3 19 22.7	20 15 21 17 32 2 19 22 8	24 19 25 19 34 1 19 22 7	27 23 26 24 36 2 19 22 7
16	29 14 28 32 23 35 19 22 7	33 19 33 36 27 36 18 22 7	36 21 36 4 27 36 18 22 7	2 26 4 7 30 1 18 22 7	6 30 4 10 31 1 18 22 7	9 34 9 12 33 3 18 22 7	12 3 15 11 33 3 18 22 8	15 7 16 11 31 3 18 22 7	18 13 16 13 31 3 19 22 7	20 16 21 17 32 2 19 22 8	24 21 25 19 34 1 19 22 7	27 24 26 24 36 2 19 22 7
17	29 16 28 32 23 35 19 22 7	33 21 33 36 27 36 18 22 7	36 22 36 4 27 36 18 22 7	2 27 4 7 30 1 18 22 7	6 31 4 11 31 2 17 22 7	9 36 9 12 33 3 18 22 7	12 4 15 11 33 3 18 22 8	15 9 16 11 31 3 18 22 7	18 14 16 13 31 3 19 22 7	20 17 22 17 32 2 19 22 8	24 22 25 19 34 1 19 22 7	27 25 26 24 36 2 19 22 7
18	30 18 27 33 24 35 19 22 7	33 22 33 1 27 36 18 22 7	36 24 36 4 27 36 18 22 7	2 28 4 8 30 1 18 22 7	6 32 4 11 31 2 17 22 7	9 1 9 12 33 3 18 22 7	12 5 15 11 33 3 18 22 8	15 10 16 11 31 3 18 22 7	18 15 16 13 31 3 19 22 7	20 19 22 17 32 2 19 22 8	24 23 25 19 34 1 19 22 7	27 27 26 24 36 2 19 22 7
19	30 19 27 33 24 35 19 22 7	34 23 33 1 27 36 18 22 7	36 25 36 4 27 36 18 22 7	2 30 4 8 30 1 18 22 7	6 33 4 11 31 2 17 22 7	9 3 9 12 33 3 18 22 7	12 6 15 11 33 3 18 22 8	15 12 16 11 31 3 18 22 7	18 16 16 13 31 3 19 22 7	20 20 22 17 32 2 19 22 8	24 24 26 20 34 2 19 22 7	27 28 26 24 36 2 19 22 7
20	30 20 27 33 24 35 19 22 7	34 24 33 1 27 36 18 22 7	1 26 2 4 28 1 18 22 7	4 31 4 9 30 1 18 22 7	6 35 4 11 31 2 17 22 7	9 4 9 12 33 3 18 22 7	12 8 15 11 33 3 18 22 8	15 13 16 11 31 3 18 22 7	18 18 16 13 31 3 19 22 7	20 21 22 17 32 2 19 22 8	24 25 26 20 34 2 19 22 7	27 29 26 24 36 2 19 22 7
21	31 21 28 34 25 35 19 22 7	34 25 33 1 27 36 18 22 7	1 28 2 4 28 1 18 22 7	4 32 4 9 30 1 18 22 7	7 36 4 11 31 2 17 22 7	10 6 10 12 33 3 18 22 7	12 9 15 11 33 3 18 22 8	15 15 16 11 31 3 18 22 7	18 19 17 14 31 3 19 22 7	20 22 22 17 33 3 19 22 7	24 26 26 20 34 2 19 22 7	28 30 26 24 36 2 19 22 7
22	31 22 28 34 25 35 19 22 7	34 27 33 3 27 36 18 22 7	1 29 2 5 28 1 18 22 7	4 34 4 9 30 1 18 22 7	7 1 4 11 31 2 17 22 7	10 7 10 12 33 3 18 22 7	13 11 15 11 33 3 18 22 8	15 16 16 11 31 3 18 22 7	18 20 17 14 31 3 19 22 7	20 24 22 17 33 3 19 22 7	25 28 26 20 34 2 19 22 7	28 31 26 24 36 2 19 22 7
23	31 23 29 34 25 35 19 22 7	34 28 33 3 27 36 18 22 7	1 30 2 5 28 1 18 22 7	4 36 4 9 30 1 18 22 7	7 3 4 11 31 2 17 22 7	10 9 10 12 33 3 18 22 7	13 12 15 10 33 3 18 22 8	16 17 16 11 31 3 18 22 7	19 21 17 14 31 3 19 22 7	22 25 22 17 33 3 19 22 7	25 29 26 20 34 2 19 22 7	28 33 26 25 1 2 19 22 7
24	31 25 29 34 25 35 19 22 7	34 30 33 3 27 36 18 22 7	1 31 2 5 28 1 18 22 7	4 1 4 9 30 1 18 22 7	7 4 4 11 31 2 17 22 7	10 10 10 12 33 3 18 22 7	13 13 15 10 32 3 18 22 8	16 18 16 11 31 3 18 22 7	19 22 17 14 31 3 19 22 7	22 26 22 17 33 3 19 22 7	25 30 26 21 34 2 19 22 7	28 34 26 25 1 2 19 22 7
25	31 26 29 34 25 35 19 22 7	34 31 33 3 27 36 18 22 7	1 33 3 5 28 1 18 22 7	4 3 3 9 30 1 18 22 7	7 6 4 11 31 2 17 22 7	10 12 11 12 33 3 18 22 7	14 15 15 10 32 3 18 22 8	16 19 16 11 31 3 18 22 7	19 24 19 14 31 3 19 22 7	22 27 24 18 33 3 19 22 7	25 31 27 21 34 2 19 22 7	28 35 26 25 1 2 19 22 7
26	31 27 29 34 25 35 19 22 7	34 32 34 3 27 36 18 22 7	1 34 3 6 28 1 18 22 7	4 4 3 9 30 1 18 22 7	7 7 4 11 31 2 17 22 7	10 13 11 12 33 3 18 22 7	14 17 16 10 32 3 18 22 8	16 21 16 12 31 3 18 22 7	19 25 19 14 31 3 19 22 7	22 28 24 18 33 3 19 22 7	25 33 27 21 34 2 19 22 7	28 1 26 25 1 2 19 22 7
27	31 28 29 34 25 35 19 22 7	34 34 34 3 27 36 18 22 7	1 36 3 6 28 1 18 22 7	4 5 3 9 30 1 18 22 7	7 8 4 11 31 2 17 22 7	10 15 11 12 33 3 18 22 7	14 18 16 10 32 3 18 22 8	16 22 16 12 31 3 18 22 7	19 26 19 14 31 3 19 22 7	22 30 24 18 33 3 19 22 7	25 34 27 21 34 2 19 22 7	28 2 26 25 1 2 19 22 7
28	31 29 29 35 25 35 19 22 7	34 35 34 3 27 36 18 22 7	1 1 3 6 28 1 18 22 7	4 7 3 9 30 1 18 22 7	7 10 4 11 31 2 17 22 7	10 15 12 12 33 3 18 22 7	14 19 16 10 32 3 18 22 8	16 23 16 12 31 3 18 22 7	19 27 19 14 31 3 19 22 7	22 31 24 18 33 3 19 22 7	25 36 27 22 34 2 19 22 7	28 3 26 25 1 2 19 22 7
29	31 31 29 35 25 35 19 22 7	34 36 34 3 27 36 18 22 7	1 3 3 6 28 1 18 22 7	4 8 3 9 30 1 18 22 7	7 12 4 11 31 2 17 22 7	10 16 12 12 33 3 18 22 7	14 20 16 10 32 3 18 22 8	16 24 16 12 31 3 19 22 7	19 28 19 14 31 3 19 22 7	22 32 24 18 33 3 19 22 7	25 1 27 22 34 2 19 22 7	28 4 26 25 1 2 19 22 7
30	31 33 29 35 25 35 19 22 7	**1892**	1 4 3 6 28 1 18 22 7	4 9 3 9 30 1 18 22 7	7 13 4 11 31 2 17 22 7	10 18 12 12 33 3 18 22 7	14 21 16 10 32 3 18 22 8	16 25 16 12 31 3 19 22 7	19 30 19 14 31 3 19 22 7	22 33 24 18 33 3 19 22 7	25 2 27 22 34 2 19 22 7	28 6 26 25 1 2 19 22 7
31	31 34 29 35 25 35 19 22 7		1 6 4 6 28 1 18 22 7		7 14 4 11 31 2 17 22 7		14 22 16 10 32 3 18 22 8	16 26 16 12 31 3 19 22 7		22 34 24 18 33 3 19 22 7		28 8 26 25 1 2 19 22 7

	JAN	FEB	MAR	APR	MAY	JUNE	JULY	AUG	SEPT	OCT	NOV	DEC
1	29 9 26 26 2 2 20 22 8	32 15 31 30 3 3 20 22 7	34 15 36 33 4 3 19 22 7	1 30 1 1 7 4 19 22 7	4 23 1 4 9 4 19 22 7	7 28 7 9 11 5 19 22 7	10 31 13 12 13 6 19 22 7	13 36 15 16 15 6 19 22 7	17 5 15 20 17 7 20 22 8	20 9 20 23 19 7 20 22 8	22 14 25 26 20 6 20 22 7	26 18 24 30 23 6 21 23 8
2	29 11 26 26 2 2 20 22 8	31 16 31 30 3 3 20 22 7	34 17 36 33 4 3 19 22 7	1 21 1 1 7 4 19 22 7	4 25 1 4 9 4 19 22 7	7 29 7 9 11 5 19 22 7	10 32 13 12 13 6 19 22 7	13 1 15 16 15 6 19 22 7	17 7 15 20 17 7 20 22 8	20 11 20 23 19 7 20 22 8	22 16 25 26 20 6 20 22 8	26 19 24 30 23 6 21 23 8
3	29 12 26 26 2 2 20 22 8	31 17 31 30 3 3 19 22 7	34 18 36 33 4 3 19 22 7	1 22 1 1 7 4 19 22 7	4 26 2 4 9 4 19 22 7	7 30 7 9 11 5 19 22 7	10 34 13 12 13 6 19 22 7	13 3 15 16 15 6 19 22 7	17 8 15 20 17 7 20 22 8	20 12 20 23 19 7 20 22 8	22 17 25 26 20 6 20 22 8	26 21 24 30 23 6 21 23 8
4	29 14 26 26 2 2 20 22 8	31 18 31 30 3 3 19 22 7	34 19 26 33 4 3 19 22 7	1 24 1 1 7 4 19 22 7	4 27 2 4 9 4 19 22 7	7 31 7 9 11 5 19 22 7	10 35 13 12 13 6 19 22 7	13 4 15 16 15 6 19 22 7	17 9 15 20 17 7 20 22 8	20 13 20 24 19 7 20 22 8	22 18 25 26 20 6 20 22 8	26 22 24 30 23 6 21 23 8
5	29 15 26 26 2 2 20 22 8	31 19 31 30 3 3 19 22 7	34 20 36 34 4 3 19 22 7	1 25 1 1 7 4 19 22 7	4 28 2 4 9 4 19 22 7	7 32 7 9 11 5 19 22 7	10 36 13 13 13 6 19 22 7	13 5 15 16 15 6 19 22 7	17 11 15 20 17 7 20 22 8	20 15 20 24 19 7 20 22 8	22 19 25 26 20 6 20 22 8	26 23 24 31 23 6 20 23 8
6	29 16 26 26 2 2 20 22 8	33 21 31 30 3 3 19 22 7	34 22 1 34 4 3 19 22 7	1 26 1 1 7 4 19 22 7	4 29 3 4 9 4 19 22 7	7 34 8 9 11 5 19 22 7	10 1 13 13 13 6 19 22 7	13 7 15 16 15 6 19 22 7	17 12 16 20 17 7 20 22 7	20 16 21 24 19 7 20 22 8	22 20 26 28 20 6 20 22 8	26 24 24 31 23 6 21 23 8
7	29 18 26 26 2 2 20 22 8	33 22 31 30 3 3 19 22 7	34 23 1 34 4 3 19 22 7	1 27 1 1 7 4 19 22 7	4 30 3 5 9 4 19 22 7	7 35 8 9 11 5 19 22 7	11 3 13 13 13 6 19 22 7	13 8 15 16 15 6 19 22 7	17 13 16 30 17 7 20 22 8	20 17 21 24 19 7 20 22 8	22 22 26 28 20 6 20 22 8	26 26 24 31 23 6 21 23 8
8	29 19 26 26 2 2 20 22 8	33 23 31 30 3 3 20 22 7	35 24 1 34 4 3 19 22 7	2 28 1 1 7 4 19 22 7	5 31 3 5 9 4 19 22 7	7 1 9 9 11 5 19 22 7	11 4 13 13 13 6 19 22 7	13 10 15 16 15 6 19 22 7	17 15 16 20 17 7 20 22 8	20 19 21 24 19 7 20 22 8	22 22 26 28 20 6 20 22 8	26 27 24 31 28 6 21 23 8
9	29 20 26 26 2 2 20 22 8	33 24 32 31 3 3 20 22 7	35 25 1 34 4 3 19 22 7	2 30 1 1 7 4 19 22 7	5 33 3 6 9 4 19 22 7	8 2 9 9 11 5 19 22 7	11 6 13 13 13 6 19 22 7	13 11 13 16 15 6 19 22 7	17 16 16 20 17 7 20 22 8	20 19 21 24 19 7 20 22 8	22 24 26 28 20 6 20 22 8	27 28 24 31 23 6 21 23 8
10	29 21 26 26 2 2 20 22 8	33 25 32 31 3 3 20 22 7	35 26 1 34 4 3 19 22 7	3 31 1 1 7 4 19 22 7	5 34 3 6 9 4 19 22 7	8 3 9 10 11 5 19 22 7	11 7 13 13 13 6 19 22 7	15 12 13 16 15 6 19 22 7	17 17 16 21 17 7 20 22 8	20 21 22 24 19 7 20 22 8	22 26 26 28 20 6 20 22 8	27 29 24 32 23 5 21 23 8
11	29 22 28 26 2 2 20 22 8	33 27 33 31 4 3 20 22 7	36 27 1 34 4 3 19 22 7	3 32 1 1 7 4 19 22 7	6 36 3 6 9 4 19 22 7	9 4 9 10 11 5 19 22 7	11 9 14 13 13 6 19 22 7	15 13 13 16 15 6 19 22 7	17 19 17 21 17 7 20 22 8	20 22 22 24 19 7 20 22 8	22 27 26 28 21 6 21 22 8	27 30 24 32 23 5 21 23 8
12	29 24 28 26 2 2 20 22 8	33 28 33 31 4 3 19 22 7	36 28 1 34 6 3 19 22 7	3 34 1 1 7 4 19 22 7	6 1 3 6 9 4 19 22 7	9 6 10 10 11 5 19 22 7	12 10 14 13 13 6 19 22 7	15 15 13 16 15 6 19 22 7	17 20 17 21 17 7 20 22 8	20 24 22 25 19 7 20 22 8	22 28 26 28 21 6 21 22 8	27 32 24 32 23 5 21 23 8
13	29 25 28 26 2 2 20 22 8	33 28 33 31 4 3 19 22 7	36 30 1 34 6 3 19 22 7	3 35 1 3 7 4 19 22 7	6 3 3 6 9 4 19 22 7	9 7 10 10 11 5 19 22 7	12 12 15 13 13 6 19 22 7	15 16 13 16 15 6 19 22 7	17 22 17 21 17 7 20 22 8	20 25 22 25 20 7 20 22 8	24 29 26 28 21 6 21 22 8	27 33 25 32 23 5 21 23 8
14	29 26 28 27 2 2 20 22 8	33 31 33 31 4 3 19 22 7	36 31 1 34 6 3 19 22 7	3 36 1 3 7 4 19 22 7	6 4 4 6 10 4 19 22 7	9 9 10 10 11 5 19 22 7	12 13 15 13 13 6 19 22 7	15 18 13 18 15 6 19 22 7	17 22 17 21 17 7 20 22 8	20 26 22 25 20 7 20 22 8	24 30 26 28 21 6 21 22 8	37 34 25 32 23 5 21 23 8
15	30 27 29 27 2 2 20 22 8	33 32 33 31 4 3 19 22 7	36 33 1 34 6 3 19 22 7	3 1 1 3 7 4 19 22 7	6 6 4 6 10 4 19 22 7	9 10 10 10 12 6 19 22 7	12 15 15 13 13 6 19 22 7	15 19 13 18 15 6 19 22 7	17 24 17 21 17 7 20 22 8	20 27 22 25 20 7 20 22 8	24 31 26 28 21 6 21 22 8	27 35 25 32 23 5 21 23 8
16	30 28 29 28 2 2 20 22 8	33 33 33 31 4 3 19 22 7	36 34 1 34 6 3 19 22 7	3 3 1 3 7 4 19 22 7	6 7 4 6 10 4 19 22 7	9 12 10 10 12 6 19 22 7	12 16 15 13 13 6 19 22 7	15 21 14 19 16 7 20 22 8	17 25 17 21 17 7 20 22 8	20 28 22 26 20 7 20 22 8	24 33 26 28 21 6 21 22 8	27 36 25 32 23 5 21 23 8
17	30 29 29 28 2 2 20 22 8	33 34 33 31 4 3 19 22 7	36 35 1 34 6 3 19 22 7	3 4 1 3 7 4 19 22 7	6 8 4 7 10 4 19 22 7	9 14 10 10 12 6 19 22 7	12 17 15 13 13 6 19 22 7	15 22 14 19 16 7 20 22 8	17 26 17 22 17 7 20 22 8	20 29 22 26 20 7 20 22 8	24 34 26 28 22 6 21 22 8	27 2 25 32 23 5 21 23 8
18	30 31 29 28 2 2 20 22 8	34 36 34 31 4 3 19 22 7	36 1 34 34 6 3 19 22 7	3 6 1 3 7 4 19 22 7	6 10 4 7 10 4 19 22 7	9 15 10 10 12 6 19 22 7	12 19 15 13 13 6 19 22 7	15 23 14 19 16 7 20 22 8	17 28 17 22 17 7 20 22 8	20 31 22 26 20 7 20 22 8	24 36 26 30 22 6 21 22 8	27 3 26 32 23 5 21 23 8
19	30 32 29 28 2 2 20 22 8	34 1 34 31 4 3 19 22 7	36 3 1 34 6 3 19 22 7	3 7 1 3 7 4 19 22 7	6 11 4 7 10 4 19 22 7	9 16 10 10 12 6 19 22 7	12 20 15 13 13 6 19 22 7	15 24 14 19 16 7 20 22 8	17 29 17 22 17 7 20 22 8	21 32 22 26 20 7 20 22 8	24 1 26 30 22 6 21 22 8	27 4 26 32 23 5 21 23 8
20	31 34 29 28 2 2 20 22 7	34 3 34 31 4 3 19 22 7	1 4 1 36 6 3 19 22 7	4 9 1 3 7 4 19 22 7	6 13 4 7 10 4 19 22 7	9 18 10 10 12 6 19 22 7	12 21 15 15 15 6 19 22 7	15 25 14 19 16 7 20 22 8	17 30 17 22 17 7 20 22 8	21 33 22 26 20 5 20 22 8	24 2 26 30 22 6 21 22 8	27 6 26 32 23 5 21 23 8
21	31 35 29 29 2 2 20 22 7	34 4 34 31 4 3 19 22 7	1 6 1 36 6 3 19 22 7	4 10 1 3 7 4 19 22 7	7 14 4 7 10 4 19 22 7	10 19 12 12 12 6 19 22 7	12 22 15 15 15 6 19 22 7	15 27 14 19 16 7 20 22 8	17 31 17 22 17 7 20 22 8	21 34 22 26 20 6 20 22 8	24 3 26 30 22 6 21 22 8	27 8 26 32 23 5 21 23 8
22	31 36 29 29 2 2 20 22 7	34 5 34 31 4 3 19 22 7	1 7 1 36 6 3 19 22 7	4 12 1 3 7 4 19 22 7	7 16 5 7 10 4 19 22 7	10 20 12 12 12 6 19 22 7	12 24 15 15 15 6 19 22 7	15 28 14 19 16 7 20 22 8	17 32 19 22 17 7 20 22 8	21 36 22 26 20 6 20 22 8	26 4 26 30 22 6 21 22 8	28 9 26 33 24 6 21 23 8
23	31 2 29 29 2 2 20 22 7	34 7 34 31 4 3 19 22 7	1 8 1 36 6 3 19 22 7	4 13 1 4 7 4 19 22 7	7 17 5 7 10 4 19 22 7	10 22 12 12 12 6 19 22 7	13 25 15 15 15 6 19 22 7	16 29 14 19 16 7 20 22 8	17 34 19 22 7 7 20 22 8	22 1 24 26 20 6 20 22 8	26 6 26 30 22 6 21 22 8	28 11 26 33 24 6 21 23 8
24	32 3 29 29 2 2 20 22 8	34 9 34 33 4 3 19 22 7	1 9 1 36 6 3 19 22 7	4 15 1 4 8 4 19 22 7	7 18 5 7 10 4 19 22 7	10 24 12 12 12 6 19 22 7	13 26 15 15 15 6 19 22 7	16 30 13 19 16 7 19 22 7	19 35 19 22 19 7 20 22 8	22 2 24 26 20 6 20 22 8	26 7 26 30 22 6 21 22 8	28 12 26 33 24 6 21 23 8
25	32 4 29 29 2 2 20 22 8	34 10 34 33 4 3 19 22 7	1 10 1 36 6 4 19 22 7	4 16 1 4 8 4 19 22 7	7 19 5 7 10 4 19 22 7	10 24 12 12 12 6 19 22 7	13 27 15 15 15 6 19 22 7	16 31 13 19 16 7 19 22 7	19 36 19 22 19 7 20 22 8	22 4 24 26 20 6 20 22 8	26 9 26 30 22 6 21 22 8	28 13 26 33 24 6 21 23 8
26	32 6 29 29 2 2 20 22 8	34 12 34 33 4 3 19 22 7	1 12 1 36 6 4 19 22 7	4 17 1 4 8 4 19 22 7	7 21 6 7 10 4 19 22 7	10 25 12 12 12 6 19 22 7	13 28 15 15 15 6 19 22 7	16 33 13 19 16 7 19 22 7	19 2 19 22 19 7 20 22 8	22 6 24 26 20 6 20 22 8	26 11 26 30 22 6 21 22 8	28 15 26 33 24 6 21 23 8
27	32 7 29 29 2 2 20 22 8	34 13 35 33 4 3 19 22 7	1 14 1 36 6 4 19 22 7	4 18 1 4 8 4 19 22 7	7 22 6 7 10 4 19 22 7	10 26 12 12 12 6 19 22 7	13 30 15 15 15 6 19 22 7	16 34 13 19 16 7 19 22 7	19 3 19 22 19 7 20 22 8	22 7 24 26 20 6 20 22 8	26 12 26 30 22 6 21 22 8	29 16 26 33 24 6 21 23 8
28	32 9 29 29 2 2 20 22 8	34 15 35 33 4 3 19 22 7	1 15 1 36 6 4 19 22 7	4 19 1 4 8 4 19 22 7	7 23 6 7 10 4 19 22 7	10 27 12 12 12 6 19 22 7	13 31 15 15 15 6 19 22 7	16 36 13 19 16 7 19 22 7	19 4 19 22 19 7 20 22 8	22 8 24 26 20 6 20 22 8	26 13 26 30 22 6 21 22 8	29 18 26 33 24 6 21 23 8
29	32 10 29 29 2 2 20 22 8	1893	1 16 1 1 7 4 19 22 7	4 21 1 4 9 4 19 22 7	7 24 7 7 10 4 19 22 7	10 28 13 12 12 6 19 22 7	13 32 15 16 15 6 19 22 7	16 1 13 19 16 7 19 22 7	19 6 19 22 19 7 20 22 8	22 10 24 26 20 6 20 22 8	26 15 26 30 22 6 21 22 8	29 19 26 33 24 6 21 23 8
30	32 11 30 29 2 2 20 22 8		1 18 1 1 7 4 19 22 7	4 22 1 4 9 4 19 22 7	7 25 7 7 10 4 19 22 7		13 33 15 16 15 6 19 22 7	16 2 13 19 16 7 19 22 7	19 7 19 22 19 7 20 22 8	22 11 24 26 20 6 20 22 8	26 16 24 30 22 6 21 22 8	29 20 27 33 24 6 21 23 8
31	32 13 31 29 2 2 20 22 8		1 19 1 1 7 4 19 22 7		7 27 7 7 10 4 19 22 7		13 34 15 16 15 6 19 22 7	16 4 13 19 16 7 19 22 7		22 13 25 26 20 6 20 22 8		29 21 27 33 24 6 21 23 8

	JAN	FEB	MAR	APR	MAY	JUNE	JULY	AUG	SEPT	OCT	NOV	DEC
1	30 24 27 33 25 6 21 24 7	33 27 33 34 27 6 21 24 7	35 28 36 33 29 6 21 23 8	2 32 35 33 31 7 21 23 8	5 35 2 36 32 7 20 23 8	8 4 9 3 35 8 20 23 8	10 8 13 7 1 8 20 22 8	14 14 12 10 3 9 21 23 8	16 19 16 15 4 10 21 22 8	19 23 21 18 4 10 21 23 8	23 27 24 21 3 10 21 23 8	26 30 23 26 2 10 22 23 8
2	30 24 27 33 25 6 21 24 7	33 28 33 34 27 6 21 24 7	35 29 36 33 29 6 21 23 8	2 33 35 33 31 7 21 23 8	5 1 2 36 32 7 20 23 8	8 6 9 3 35 8 20 23 8	10 10 13 7 1 8 20 22 8	14 15 12 10 3 9 21 23 8	17 21 17 15 4 10 21 22 8	19 24 21 18 4 10 21 23 8	23 28 24 21 3 10 21 23 8	26 31 23 26 2 10 22 23 8
3	30 25 27 33 25 6 21 24 7	33 30 33 34 27 6 21 24 7	35 30 36 33 29 6 21 23 8	3 35 35 34 31 7 21 23 8	5 2 2 36 32 7 20 23 8	8 7 9 4 35 8 20 23 8	11 11 13 7 1 8 20 22 8	14 16 12 12 3 9 21 23 8	17 22 17 15 4 10 21 22 8	19 25 22 18 4 10 21 23 8	23 29 24 21 3 10 21 23 8	26 33 23 26 2 10 22 23 8
4	30 27 27 33 25 6 21 24 7	33 31 33 34 27 6 21 24 7	35 31 36 33 29 6 21 23 8	3 36 35 34 31 7 21 23 8	5 4 2 36 32 7 20 23 8	8 9 10 4 35 8 20 23 8	11 13 13 7 1 8 20 22 8	14 18 12 12 3 9 21 23 8	17 22 17 15 4 10 21 22 8	19 26 22 18 4 10 21 23 8	23 31 24 22 3 10 21 23 8	26 34 23 26 2 10 22 23 8
5	30 28 28 33 25 6 21 24 7	33 32 33 34 27 6 21 24 7	35 33 36 33 29 6 21 23 8	3 1 35 34 31 7 21 23 8	5 5 2 36 32 7 20 23 8	8 10 10 4 35 8 20 23 8	11 14 13 7 1 8 20 22 8	14 19 12 12 3 9 21 23 8	17 24 17 15 4 10 21 22 8	19 27 22 18 4 10 21 23 8	23 32 24 22 3 10 21 23 8	26 35 23 26 2 10 22 23 8
6	30 29 28 33 25 6 21 24 7	33 33 33 34 27 6 21 24 7	35 34 36 33 29 6 21 23 8	3 3 36 34 31 7 21 23 7	5 6 4 1 32 7 20 23 8	8 11 10 4 35 8 20 23 8	11 16 13 8 1 8 20 22 8	14 21 12 12 3 9 21 23 8	17 25 17 15 4 10 21 22 8	20 29 22 18 4 10 21 23 8	23 33 24 22 3 10 21 23 8	26 36 23 26 2 10 22 23 8
7	30 30 28 33 25 6 21 24 7	33 34 33 34 27 6 21 24 7	35 35 36 33 29 6 21 23 8	3 4 36 34 31 7 21 23 7	5 7 4 1 33 7 20 23 8	8 13 10 4 35 8 20 23 8	11 17 13 8 1 8 20 22 8	14 22 12 12 3 9 21 23 8	17 27 17 15 4 10 21 22 8	20 30 22 19 4 10 21 23 8	23 34 23 23 2 10 21 23 8	26 1 24 26 2 10 22 23 8
8	30 31 28 33 25 6 21 24 7	33 36 33 34 27 6 21 24 7	35 36 36 33 29 6 21 23 8	3 6 36 34 31 7 21 23 7	5 8 5 1 33 7 20 23 8	8 15 11 5 35 8 20 23 8	11 18 13 8 1 8 20 22 8	14 23 12 12 3 9 21 23 8	17 28 17 15 4 10 21 22 8	20 31 22 19 4 10 21 23 8	23 36 23 23 2 10 22 23 8	26 2 24 26 2 10 22 23 8
9	30 32 30 34 25 6 21 24 7	33 1 34 34 27 6 21 24 7	35 2 36 33 29 6 21 23 8	3 7 36 34 31 7 21 23 7	5 11 5 1 34 7 20 23 8	8 16 11 5 35 8 20 23 8	11 20 13 8 2 8 20 22 8	14 25 12 12 3 9 21 23 8	17 29 17 15 4 10 21 22 8	21 32 22 19 3 10 21 23 8	23 1 33 23 2 10 22 23 8	26 4 25 26 2 10 22 23 8
10	30 33 30 34 25 6 21 24 7	33 2 34 34 27 6 21 24 7	36 3 36 33 30 6 21 23 8	3 9 36 34 31 7 21 23 7	5 12 5 1 34 7 20 23 8	8 18 11 5 35 8 20 22 8	11 21 13 8 2 8 20 22 8	15 26 12 12 3 9 21 23 8	17 30 17 15 4 10 21 22 8	21 33 22 19 3 10 21 23 8	23 2 23 23 2 10 22 23 8	26 5 25 26 2 10 22 23 8
11	30 34 30 34 25 6 21 24 7	33 3 34 34 27 6 21 24 7	36 4 36 33 30 6 21 23 8	3 10 36 35 32 7 21 23 8	5 14 5 1 34 7 20 23 8	8 19 11 4 35 8 20 22 8	11 22 13 8 2 8 20 22 8	15 27 13 12 3 9 21 23 8	17 31 18 15 4 10 21 22 8	21 34 23 19 3 10 21 23 8	23 3 23 23 2 10 22 23 8	26 7 25 26 2 10 22 23 8
12	30 36 30 34 25 6 21 24 7	33 5 34 34 27 6 21 24 7	36 6 36 33 30 6 21 23 8	3 12 36 35 32 7 21 23 8	5 15 5 1 34 7 20 23 8	8 20 11 4 35 8 20 22 8	11 24 13 8 2 8 20 22 8	15 28 13 12 3 9 21 23 8	17 33 18 15 4 10 21 22 8	21 36 23 19 3 10 21 23 8	23 4 23 23 2 10 22 23 8	26 8 25 26 2 10 22 23 8
13	30 1 30 34 25 6 21 24 7	33 6 34 33 27 6 21 24 7	36 7 36 33 30 6 21 23 8	3 13 36 35 32 7 21 23 8	6 16 5 1 34 7 20 23 7	8 21 11 4 35 8 20 22 8	11 25 13 8 2 8 20 22 8	15 29 13 12 3 9 21 23 8	17 34 18 16 4 10 21 22 8	21 1 23 19 3 10 21 23 8	23 6 23 23 2 10 22 23 8	27 10 26 27 3 10 22 23 8
14	30 3 30 34 25 6 21 24 7	33 7 34 33 28 6 21 24 7	36 9 36 33 30 6 21 23 8	3 14 36 35 32 7 21 23 8	6 18 5 1 34 7 20 23 7	8 23 11 4 35 8 20 22 8	11 26 13 8 2 8 20 22 8	15 30 14 12 3 9 21 23 8	17 35 19 16 4 10 21 22 8	21 3 23 19 3 10 21 23 8	23 8 23 23 2 10 22 23 8	27 12 26 27 3 10 22 23 8
15	30 4 30 34 25 6 21 24 7	33 9 34 33 28 6 21 24 7	36 10 36 33 30 6 21 23 8	3 15 1 35 32 7 21 23 8	6 19 5 1 34 7 20 23 7	8 24 11 4 35 8 20 22 8	11 27 13 8 2 8 20 22 8	15 32 14 12 3 9 21 23 8	17 36 19 16 4 10 21 22 8	21 4 23 19 3 10 21 23 8	23 9 23 23 2 10 22 23 8	27 13 26 27 3 10 22 23 8
16	30 6 30 34 25 6 21 24 7	33 10 36 33 28 6 21 24 7	36 12 36 33 30 6 21 23 8	3 17 1 35 32 7 21 23 8	6 21 5 1 34 7 20 23 7	8 25 11 4 36 8 20 22 8	12 28 12 9 3 9 21 23 9	15 33 14 12 3 9 21 23 8	17 1 19 16 4 10 21 22 8	21 5 23 20 3 10 21 23 8	23 10 23 23 2 10 22 23 8	27 14 26 27 3 9 22 23 8
17	30 7 30 34 25 6 21 24 7	33 12 36 33 28 6 21 24 7	36 13 36 33 30 6 21 23 8	3 18 1 35 32 7 21 23 8	6 22 5 2 35 8 20 23 8	8 26 11 4 36 8 20 22 8	12 30 12 9 3 9 21 23 9	15 34 14 12 3 9 21 23 8	17 3 19 16 4 10 21 22 8	21 6 23 20 3 10 21 23 8	23 12 23 23 2 10 22 23 8	27 16 26 27 3 9 22 23 8
18	30 8 30 34 25 6 21 24 7	33 13 36 33 28 6 21 24 7	36 15 36 33 30 6 21 23 8	3 20 1 35 32 7 21 23 8	6 23 6 2 35 8 20 23 8	9 28 11 4 36 8 20 22 8	12 31 12 9 3 9 21 23 9	15 35 14 13 4 10 21 23 8	18 4 19 16 4 10 21 22 8	21 8 23 20 3 10 21 23 8	24 13 23 23 2 10 22 23 8	27 17 26 27 3 9 22 23 8
19	30 10 30 34 25 6 21 24 7	34 15 36 33 28 6 21 24 7	36 16 36 33 30 6 21 23 8	2 21 1 35 32 7 20 23 7	6 24 6 2 35 8 20 23 8	9 29 11 4 36 8 20 22 8	12 32 12 9 3 9 21 23 8	15 1 14 13 4 10 21 23 8	18 5 19 16 4 10 21 22 7	21 9 23 20 3 10 21 23 8	24 14 23 23 2 10 22 23 8	27 18 26 27 3 9 22 23 8
20	31 11 30 34 25 6 21 24 7	34 16 36 33 28 6 21 24 7	36 17 36 33 30 6 21 23 8	4 22 1 35 32 7 20 23 7	6 26 6 2 35 8 20 23 8	10 30 11 4 1 8 20 22 8	12 33 12 9 3 9 21 23 8	15 2 14 13 4 10 21 23 8	18 7 19 16 4 10 21 22 7	21 11 23 20 3 10 21 23 8	24 16 23 23 2 10 22 23 8	27 20 26 27 3 9 22 23 8
21	31 12 30 34 25 6 21 24 7	34 18 36 33 29 6 21 23 7	1 19 35 33 30 6 21 23 8	4 23 1 35 32 7 20 23 7	7 27 7 2 35 8 20 23 8	10 31 11 6 1 8 20 22 8	12 34 12 9 3 9 21 23 8	15 3 14 13 4 10 21 23 8	18 9 20 16 4 10 21 22 7	21 12 23 20 3 10 21 23 8	24 17 23 24 2 10 22 23 8	27 21 26 27 3 9 23 23 8
22	31 14 30 34 25 6 21 24 7	34 19 36 33 29 6 21 23 7	1 20 35 33 30 6 21 23 8	4 25 1 35 32 7 20 23 7	7 28 7 2 35 8 20 23 8	10 32 11 6 1 8 20 22 8	12 36 12 9 3 9 21 23 8	15 4 14 13 4 10 21 23 8	18 10 20 16 4 10 21 22 7	21 13 23 20 3 10 21 23 8	25 19 23 24 2 10 22 23 8	28 22 26 28 4 10 22 23 8
23	31 15 30 34 25 6 21 24 7	34 21 36 33 29 6 21 23 7	1 21 35 33 30 6 21 23 8	4 26 1 35 32 7 20 23 7	7 29 8 2 35 8 20 23 8	10 33 12 6 1 8 20 22 8	13 1 12 9 3 9 21 23 8	16 6 14 13 4 10 21 23 8	19 10 21 16 4 10 21 22 7	22 15 23 21 3 10 21 23 8	25 20 23 24 2 10 22 23 8	28 24 26 28 4 10 22 23 8
24	31 17 31 34 25 6 21 24 7	34 22 36 33 29 6 21 23 7	1 22 35 33 30 6 21 23 7	5 27 1 35 32 7 20 23 7	7 30 8 2 35 8 20 23 8	10 35 12 6 1 8 20 22 8	13 3 12 9 3 9 21 23 8	16 7 15 13 4 10 21 22 8	19 12 21 16 4 10 21 22 7	22 16 24 21 3 10 21 23 8	25 21 23 25 2 10 22 23 8	28 25 27 28 4 10 22 23 8
25	31 18 31 34 25 6 21 24 7	34 24 36 33 29 6 21 23 7	1 24 35 33 30 6 21 23 7	5 28 1 35 32 7 20 23 7	8 32 8 2 35 8 20 23 8	10 36 12 6 1 8 20 22 8	13 3 12 9 3 9 21 23 8	16 8 15 13 4 10 21 22 8	19 13 21 16 4 10 21 22 7	22 18 24 21 3 10 21 23 8	25 22 23 25 2 10 22 23 8	28 26 27 29 4 10 22 23 8
26	31 20 31 34 25 6 21 24 7	34 24 36 33 29 6 21 23 7	1 25 35 33 30 6 21 23 7	5 30 2 36 32 7 20 23 7	8 33 8 2 35 8 20 23 8	10 1 12 6 1 8 20 22 8	13 5 12 9 3 9 21 23 8	16 10 15 13 4 10 21 22 8	19 15 21 17 4 10 21 23 8	22 19 24 21 3 10 21 23 8	25 24 23 25 2 10 22 23 8	28 27 28 29 4 10 22 23 8
27	31 21 31 34 27 6 21 24 7	34 25 36 33 29 6 21 23 7	1 26 35 33 30 6 21 23 7	5 31 3 36 33 7 21 23 8	8 34 8 2 35 8 20 23 8	10 2 13 6 1 8 20 22 8	14 6 12 9 3 9 21 23 8	16 11 15 13 4 10 21 22 8	19 17 21 17 4 10 21 23 8	22 21 24 21 3 10 21 23 8	25 25 23 25 2 10 22 23 8	28 28 28 29 4 10 22 23 8
28	33 22 33 34 27 6 21 24 7	34 27 36 33 29 6 21 23 7	1 27 35 33 30 6 21 23 7	5 32 3 36 33 7 21 23 8	8 35 8 2 35 8 20 23 8	10 4 13 6 1 8 20 22 8	14 7 12 9 3 9 21 23 8	16 13 15 13 4 10 21 22 8	19 18 21 17 4 10 21 23 8	23 22 24 21 3 10 21 23 8	26 26 23 26 2 10 22 23 8	28 30 28 29 4 10 22 23 8
29	33 24 33 34 27 6 21 24 7		1 29 35 33 30 6 21 23 7	5 33 3 36 33 7 21 23 8	8 36 8 2 35 8 20 23 8	10 5 13 6 1 8 20 22 8	14 9 12 9 3 9 21 23 8	16 4 16 14 4 10 21 23 8	19 19 21 17 4 10 21 23 8	23 23 24 21 3 10 21 23 8	26 28 23 26 2 10 22 23 8	28 31 28 29 4 10 22 23 8
30	33 25 33 34 27 6 21 24 7	**1894**	1 30 35 33 30 6 21 23 7	5 34 3 36 33 7 21 23 8	8 2 8 2 35 8 20 23 8	10 7 13 7 1 8 20 23 8	14 10 12 9 3 9 21 23 8	17 16 16 14 4 10 21 23 8	19 21 21 17 4 10 21 23 8	23 24 24 21 3 10 21 23 8	26 29 23 26 2 10 22 23 8	29 32 28 29 4 10 22 23 8
31	33 26 33 34 27 6 21 24 7		1 31 35 33 30 6 21 23 7		8 3 8 2 35 8 20 23 8		14 12 12 9 3 9 21 23 8	17 17 16 14 4 10 21 23 8		23 25 24 21 3 10 21 23 8		29 33 28 29 4 10 22 23 8

	JAN	FEB	MAR	APR	MAY	JUNE	JULY	AUG	SEPT	OCT	NOV	DEC
1	29 34 28 29 4 10 22 23 8	31 3 33 33 4 9 22 23 8	35 4 33 36 6 9 22 23 8	2 9 35 5 8 9 22 23 8	4 13 4 8 10 10 22 23 8	8 18 10 12 12 10 22 23 8	10 22 10 16 14 11 22 23 8	13 27 11 17 16 11 22 23 8	16 31 17 19 17 13 22 23 8	20 35 22 17 20 13 22 23 8	22 3 21 17 22 13 22 23 8	25 7 24 21 24 13 22 24 8
2	29 36 28 29 4 10 22 23 8	31 4 33 33 4 9 22 23 8	35 5 33 1 7 9 22 23 8	2 11 35 5 8 9 22 23 8	4 14 4 8 10 10 22 23 8	8 19 10 12 12 10 22 23 8	10 23 10 16 14 11 22 23 8	13 28 11 17 16 11 22 23 8	16 33 17 19 17 13 22 23 8	20 36 22 17 20 13 22 23 8	22 4 21 17 22 13 22 23 8	25 8 25 21 24 13 22 24 8
3	29 1 28 29 4 10 22 23 8	31 6 33 33 4 9 22 23 8	35 7 33 1 7 9 22 23 8	2 12 35 5 8 9 22 23 8	4 16 4 8 10 10 22 23 8	8 21 10 12 12 10 22 23 8	10 25 10 16 14 11 22 23 8	13 29 13 17 16 11 22 23 8	16 34 17 19 17 13 22 23 8	20 1 22 17 20 13 22 23 8	22 5 21 18 22 13 22 23 8	25 9 25 21 24 13 22 24 8
4	29 2 28 29 4 10 22 23 8	31 7 34 34 4 9 22 23 8	35 8 33 1 7 9 22 23 8	2 13 35 5 8 9 22 23 8	5 17 5 8 10 10 22 23 8	8 22 10 12 12 10 22 23 8	10 26 10 16 14 11 22 23 8	14 31 13 17 16 11 22 23 8	16 35 17 19 17 13 22 23 8	20 2 22 17 20 13 22 23 8	22 7 21 18 22 13 22 23 8	26 10 25 21 24 13 22 24 8
5	29 4 29 29 4 10 22 23 8	21 8 34 34 4 9 22 23 8	35 9 33 1 7 9 22 23 8	2 15 35 5 8 9 22 23 8	5 18 5 8 10 10 22 23 8	8 23 10 13 13 10 22 23 8	11 27 10 16 14 11 22 23 8	14 32 13 17 16 11 22 23 8	17 36 17 19 17 13 22 23 8	20 4 22 17 20 13 22 23 8	22 8 21 18 22 13 22 23 8	26 12 25 21 24 13 22 24 8
6	29 5 29 29 4 10 22 23 8	32 10 34 34 5 9 22 23 8	35 11 33 1 7 9 22 23 8	2 16 35 5 8 9 22 23 8	5 20 5 8 10 10 22 23 8	8 25 10 13 13 10 22 23 8	11 28 10 16 14 11 22 23 8	14 33 13 18 16 11 22 23 8	17 1 17 19 17 13 22 23 8	20 5 22 17 20 13 22 23 8	22 10 21 18 22 13 22 23 8	26 13 25 21 24 13 22 24 8
7	29 6 29 30 4 10 22 23 8	32 11 34 34 5 9 22 23 8	35 12 33 1 7 9 22 23 8	2 18 35 5 8 9 22 23 8	5 21 5 9 10 10 22 23 8	8 26 10 13 13 10 22 23 8	11 30 10 16 14 11 22 23 8	14 34 13 18 16 11 22 23 8	17 3 19 19 19 13 22 23 8	20 6 22 17 20 13 22 23 8	22 11 21 19 22 13 22 23 8	26 15 25 21 24 13 22 24 8
8	29 8 29 30 4 10 22 23 8	32 13 34 34 5 9 22 23 7	35 13 33 1 7 9 22 23 8	2 19 35 5 8 9 22 23 8	5 22 5 9 10 10 22 23 8	8 28 10 13 13 10 22 23 8	11 31 10 16 14 11 22 23 8	14 35 13 18 16 11 22 23 8	17 4 19 19 19 13 22 23 8	20 7 22 17 20 13 22 23 8	22 12 21 19 22 13 22 23 8	26 16 25 21 24 13 22 24 8
9	29 9 29 30 4 10 22 23 8	32 14 34 34 5 9 22 23 7	35 15 33 1 7 9 22 23 8	2 21 35 5 9 9 22 23 8	5 23 5 9 10 10 22 23 8	8 28 11 13 13 11 22 23 8	11 32 10 16 14 11 22 23 8	14 1 13 18 16 11 22 23 8	17 5 19 19 19 13 22 23 8	20 8 22 17 20 13 22 23 8	22 13 21 19 22 13 22 23 8	26 18 25 22 24 13 22 24 8
10	29 10 29 30 4 10 22 23 8	32 16 34 34 5 9 22 23 7	35 17 33 1 7 9 22 23 7	2 22 36 5 9 9 22 23 8	5 25 6 9 10 10 22 23 8	8 30 11 13 13 11 22 23 8	11 33 10 16 14 11 22 23 8	14 2 13 18 16 11 22 23 8	17 6 19 19 19 13 22 23 8	20 10 22 17 20 13 22 23 8	22 14 21 19 22 13 22 23 8	26 19 25 22 24 13 22 24 8
11	29 12 29 31 4 10 22 23 8	32 17 34 34 5 9 22 23 7	35 18 33 1 7 9 22 23 7	3 23 36 5 10 10 22 23 8	5 27 6 9 10 10 22 23 8	8 31 11 13 13 11 22 23 8	11 34 10 16 14 11 22 23 8	14 3 14 18 16 11 22 23 8	17 8 19 19 19 13 22 23 8	20 11 22 17 20 13 22 23 8	22 16 21 19 22 13 22 23 8	26 21 25 22 24 13 22 24 8
12	29 13 29 31 4 10 22 23 8	32 19 34 34 5 9 22 23 7	35 19 33 1 7 9 22 23 7	3 25 1 5 10 10 22 23 8	5 28 7 9 10 10 22 23 8	8 32 11 13 13 11 22 23 8	11 35 10 16 14 11 22 23 8	14 4 14 18 17 11 22 23 8	17 9 19 19 19 13 22 23 8	20 13 22 17 20 13 22 23 8	22 17 22 19 22 13 22 23 8	26 22 26 22 25 13 22 24 8
13	29 15 29 31 4 10 22 23 8	32 20 34 34 5 9 22 23 7	35 21 33 2 7 9 22 23 7	3 26 1 5 10 10 22 23 8	5 29 7 10 10 10 22 23 8	8 34 11 13 13 11 22 23 8	11 1 10 16 14 11 22 23 8	14 5 14 18 17 11 22 23 8	17 10 20 19 19 13 22 23 8	20 14 22 17 20 13 22 23 8	22 19 22 19 22 13 22 23 8	26 24 26 22 25 13 22 24 8
14	29 17 29 31 4 10 22 23 8	33 22 34 34 6 9 22 23 7	35 22 33 2 7 9 22 23 7	3 27 1 5 10 10 22 23 8	5 31 7 10 10 10 22 23 8	8 35 11 13 13 11 22 23 8	11 2 10 16 14 11 22 23 8	14 7 14 19 17 11 22 23 8	17 11 20 19 19 13 22 23 8	20 15 22 17 20 13 22 23 8	22 21 22 19 22 13 22 23 8	26 25 26 22 25 13 22 24 8
15	29 18 30 31 4 9 22 23 7	33 23 34 34 6 9 22 23 7	35 23 33 2 7 9 22 23 7	3 28 2 5 10 10 22 23 8	5 32 8 10 10 10 22 23 8	8 36 11 13 13 11 22 23 8	1 3 10 17 14 11 22 23 8	14 8 14 19 17 11 22 23 8	17 13 20 19 19 13 22 23 8	20 17 22 17 20 13 22 23 8	23 23 23 20 23 14 23 23 8	26 26 26 22 25 13 22 24 8
16	29 19 31 31 4 9 22 23 7	33 24 35 35 6 9 22 23 8	36 25 33 3 7 9 22 23 7	3 30 2 6 10 10 22 23 8	5 33 8 10 11 10 22 23 8	9 1 11 13 13 11 22 23 8	11 4 10 17 14 11 22 23 8	14 9 14 19 17 12 22 23 8	17 14 20 19 19 13 22 23 8	20 18 22 17 20 13 22 23 8	23 23 23 20 23 14 23 23 8	26 27 26 22 25 13 22 24 8
17	29 21 31 31 4 9 22 23 7	33 25 35 35 6 9 22 23 8	36 26 34 3 7 9 22 23 7	3 31 2 6 10 10 22 23 8	5 34 8 10 11 10 22 23 8	9 2 11 13 13 11 22 23 8	11 6 10 17 14 11 22 23 8	14 11 14 19 17 12 22 23 8	17 16 20 19 19 13 22 23 8	20 20 22 17 20 13 22 23 8	23 25 23 20 23 14 23 23 8	27 29 26 22 25 13 22 24 8
18	30 22 31 31 4 9 22 23 7	33 27 35 35 6 9 22 23 8	36 28 34 3 7 9 22 23 7	3 32 2 7 10 10 22 23 8	6 35 8 10 11 10 22 23 8	9 4 11 14 13 11 22 23 8	11 7 10 17 14 11 22 23 8	14 12 14 19 17 12 22 23 8	17 18 20 19 19 13 22 23 8	20 22 22 17 20 13 22 23 8	23 26 23 20 23 14 23 23 8	27 30 26 22 25 13 22 24 8
19	30 23 31 31 4 9 22 23 7	34 28 35 35 6 9 22 23 8	36 29 34 3 8 9 22 23 8	3 33 2 7 10 10 22 23 8	6 1 8 10 11 10 22 23 8	9 5 11 14 13 11 22 23 8	11 8 10 17 14 11 22 23 8	15 13 16 19 17 12 22 23 8	17 19 20 19 19 13 22 23 8	20 23 22 17 20 13 22 23 8	23 28 23 20 23 14 23 23*8	27 31 26 22 25 13 22 24 8
20	31 25 31 31 4 9 22 23 7	34 29 34 35 6 9 22 23 8	36 30 34 3 8 9 22 23 8	4 34 2 7 10 10 22 23 8	6 2 8 10 11 10 22 23 8	9 6 11 14 13 11 22 23 8	11 10 10 17 15 11 22 23 8	15 14 16 19 17 12 22 23 8	17 20 20 17 19 13 22 23 8	20 24 22 17 20 13 22 23 8	23 29 23 20 23 14 23 23 8	27 33 27 22 25 13 22 24 8
21	31 26 31 31 4 9 22 23 7	34 30 34 35 6 9 22 23 8	1 31 34 3 8 9 22 23 8	4 36 2 7 10 10 22 23 8	7 3 8 10 11 10 22 23 8	9 8 11 14 13 11 22 23 8	11 11 10 17 15 11 22 23 8	15 17 16 19 17 12 22 23 8	18 22 20 17 19 13 22 23 8	20 26 22 17 20 13 22 23 8	23 30 23 20 23 14 23 23 8	27 34 27 22 25 13 22 24 8
22	31 27 31 31 4 9 22 23 7	34 31 34 36 6 9 22 24 8	1 32 34 3 8 9 22 23 8	4 1 2 8 10 10 22 23 8	7 4 8 11 11 10 22 23 8	10 9 11 14 13 11 22 23 8	11 13 10 17 15 11 22 23 8	15 18 16 19 17 12 22 23 8	18 23 20 17 19 13 22 23 8	20 27 22 17 20 13 22 23 8	23 32 23 20 23 14 23 23 8	28 35 27 22 25 13 22 24 8
23	31 28 31 31 4 9 22 23 7	34 33 34 36 6 9 22 24 8	1 34 34 3 8 9 22 23 8	4 2 2 8 10 10 22 23 8	7 5 8 11 11 10 22 23 8	10 11 11 14 13 11 22 23 8	13 15 11 17 15 11 22 23 8	16 19 16 19 16 12 22 23 8	19 25 20 17 19 13 22 23 8	20 28 22 17 20 13 22 23 8	24 32 23 20 23 14 23 23 8	28 36 28 23 25 13 23 23 8
24	31 30 31 31 4 9 22 23 7	34 34 34 36 6 9 22 24 8	1 35 34 4 8 9 22 23 8	4 3 3 8 10 10 22 23 8	7 7 8 11 11 10 22 23 8	10 12 11 14 13 11 22 23 8	13 16 11 17 15 11 22 23 8	16 21 16 19 17 12 22 23 8	19 26 20 17 19 13 22 23 8	22 30 22 17 21 13 22 23 8	24 34 23 20 23 14 23 23 8	28 1 28 23 26 14 23 23 8
25	31 31 31 35 4 9 22 23 7	34 35 34 36 6 9 22 24 8	1 36 34 4 8 9 22 23 8	4 5 3 8 10 10 22 23 8	7 9 9 11 11 10 22 23 8	10 13 11 14 14 11 22 23 8	13 17 11 17 15 11 22 23 8	16 22 17 19 17 12 22 23 8	19 28 22 17 19 13 22 23 8	22 31 22 17 21 13 22 23 8	24 35 23 20 23 14 23 23 8	28 2 28 23 26 14 23 23 8
26	31 31 31 31 4 9 22 23 7	34 36 34 36 6 9 22 24 8	1 1 34 4 8 9 22 23 8	4 6 3 8 10 10 22 23 8	8 10 9 11 11 10 22 23 8	10 14 11 14 14 11 22 23 8	13 19 11 17 15 11 22 23 8	16 23 17 19 17 12 22 23 8	19 29 22 17 19 13 22 23 8	22 32 21 17 21 13 22 23 8	24 36 23 20 23 14 23 23 8	29 4 29 23 26 14 23 23 8
27	31 33 32 32 4 9 22 23 7	34 1 34 36 6 9 22 24 8	1 3 34 4 8 9 22 23 8	4 7 3 8 10 10 22 23 8	8 11 9 11 11 10 22 23 8	10 16 11 14 14 11 22 23 8	13 21 11 17 15 11 22 23 8	16 25 17 19 17 12 22 23 8	19 30 22 17 19 13 22 23 8	22 33 21 17 21 13 22 23 8	24 1 23 20 23 14 23 23 8	29 5 29 23 26 14 23 23 8
28	31 34 33 33 4 9 22 23 7	34 3 34 36 6 9 22 24 8	2 4 34 4 8 9 22 23 8	4 8 4 8 10 10 22 23 8	8 13 9 11 11 10 22 23 8	11 17 11 14 14 11 22 23 8	13 22 11 17 15 11 22 23 8	16 26 17 19 17 12 22 23 8	19 31 22 17 19 13 22 23 8	22 34 21 17 21 13 22 23 8	24 2 23 20 23 14 23 23 8	29 6 29 23 26 14 23 23 8
29	31 35 33 33 4 9 22 23 7	**1895**	2 5 35 4 8 9 22 23 8	4 10 4 8 10 10 22 23 8	8 14 10 11 11 10 22 23 8	11 19 11 14 14 11 22 23 8	13 23 11 17 16 11 22 23 8	16 28 17 19 17 12 22 23 8	19 32 22 17 19 13 22 23 8	22 35 21 17 21 13 22 23 8	24 4 23 20 23 14 23 23 8	29 8 29 23 26 14 23 23 8
30	31 1 33 33 4 9 22 23 7		2 6 35 4 8 9 22 23 8	4 11 4 8 10 10 22 23 8	8 15 10 11 11 10 22 23 8	11 20 11 14 14 11 22 23 8	13 25 11 17 16 11 22 23 8	16 29 17 19 17 12 22 23 8	19 34 22 17 19 13 22 23 8	22 1 22 17 22 13 22 23 8	24 5 23 20 23 14 23 23 8	29 9 29 23 26 14 23 23 8
31	31 2 33 33 4 9 22 23 7		2 8 35 4 8 9 22 23 8		8 17 10 11 11 10 22 23 8		13 26 11 17 16 11 22 23 8	16 30 17 19 17 12 22 23 8		22 2 22 17 22 13 22 23 8		29 10 29 23 26 14 23 23 8

	JAN	FEB	MAR	APR	MAY	JUNE	JULY	AUG	SEPT	OCT	NOV	DEC
1	29 11 29 23 26 13 23 23 8	32 17 32 28 28 13 23 23 8	35 19 33 33 30 12 24 24 8	2 25 36 36 33 12 24 24 8	5 28 7 3 35 13 23 23 8	7 33 8 7 1 13 23 24 8	11 36 8 11 3 14 23 24 8	14 4 14 14 5 14 23 23 8	16 8 19 17 7 15 24 24 8	19 12 21 22 9 16 24 24 9	22 18 21 25 9 16 24 24 9	25 21 25 30 9 16 24 24 9
2	29 13 29 23 26 13 23 23 8	32 18 32 28 28 13 23 23 8	35 21 33 33 30 12 24 24 8	2 26 36 36 33 12 24 24 8	5 29 7 3 35 13 23 23 8	7 34 8 7 1 13 23 24 8	11 1 8 11 4 14 23 24 8	14 5 14 14 5 14 23 23 8	16 10 19 17 7 15 24 24 8	19 13 21 22 9 16 24 24 9	22 19 21 25 9 16 24 24 9	27 22 27 30 9 16 24 24 9
3	29 14 29 23 26 13 23 23 8	32 19 32 28 28 13 23 23 8	35 22 33 33 30 12 24 24 8	2 27 36 36 33 12 24 24 8	5 31 7 3 35 13 23 23 8	7 35 8 7 1 13 23 24 8	11 2 8 11 4 14 23 24 8	14 7 14 14 5 14 23 23 8	17 12 20 17 8 15 24 24 8	19 15 21 22 9 15 24 24 9	22 21 21 25 9 15 24 24 9	27 24 27 30 9 16 24 24 9
4	29 16 29 25 26 13 23 23 8	32 21 32 28 28 13 23 23 8	35 24 33 33 30 12 24 24 8	2 28 1 36 33 12 24 24 8	5 32 7 4 35 13 23 23 8	8 36 8 7 1 13 23 24 8	11 3 8 11 4 14 23 24 8	14 8 14 14 5 14 23 23 8	17 13 20 18 8 15 24 24 8	19 16 21 22 9 15 24 24 9	24 22 21 27 9 16 24 24 9	27 25 27 30 9 16 24 24 9
5	29 17 29 25 26 13 23 23 8	32 22 32 28 28 13 23 23 8	35 25 33 33 30 12 24 24 8	2 30 1 36 33 12 24 24 8	5 33 7 4 35 13 23 23 8	8 1 8 7 1 13 23 24 8	11 5 8 11 4 14 23 24 8	14 9 14 14 5 14 23 23 8	17 15 20 18 8 15 24 24 8	21 18 21 22 9 15 24 24 9	24 24 22 27 9 16 24 24 9	27 27 27 30 9 16 24 24 9
6	29 29 29 25 26 13 23 23 8	32 23 32 29 29 13 23 23 8	35 26 33 33 30 12 24 24 8	2 31 1 36 33 12 24 24 8	5 34 7 4 35 13 23 23 8	8 3 8 8 2 13 23 24 8	11 6 8 11 5 14 23 24 8	14 10 14 14 5 14 23 23 8	17 16 20 19 8 15 24 24 8	21 19 21 22 9 15 24 24 9	24 25 22 27 9 16 24 24 9	27 28 27 30 9 16 24 24 9
7	29 20 29 25 26 13 23 23 8	32 25 32 29 29 13 23 23 8	36 28 33 33 30 12 24 24 8	2 33 2 36 33 12 24 24 8	5 35 7 4 35 13 23 23 8	8 4 8 8 2 13 23 24 8	11 7 8 11 5 14 23 24 8	14 11 14 14 5 14 23 23 8	17 17 20 19 8 15 24 24 8	21 21 21 22 9 15 24 24 9	24 27 22 27 9 16 24 24 9	27 30 27 30 9 16 24 24 9
8	29 21 29 25 26 13 23 23 8	32 27 32 29 29 13 23 23 8	36 29 33 33 31 13 24 24 8	2 33 2 36 33 12 24 24 8	5 1 7 4 35 13 23 23 8	8 5 8 8 2 13 23 24 8	11 8 8 11 5 14 23 24 6	14 13 14 14 5 14 23 23 8	17 19 20 19 8 15 24 24 8	21 22 21 22 9 15 24 24 9	24 28 22 27 9 16 24 24 9	27 31 27 30 9 16 24 24 9
9	29 23 31 25 26 13 23 23 8	32 28 32 29 29 13 23 23 8	36 30 33 33 31 13 24 24 8	2 35 2 36 33 12 24 24 8	5 2 7 4 35 13 23 23 8	8 6 8 8 2 13 23 24 8	11 10 8 11 5 14 23 24 8	14 14 14 14 5 14 23 23 8	17 20 20 19 8 15 24 24 8	21 24 21 24 9 15 24 24 9	24 30 22 27 9 16 24 24 9	27 33 27 30 9 16 24 24 9
10	29 23 31 25 26 13 23 23 8	32 29 32 29 29 13 23 23 8	36 31 33 33 31 13 24 24 8	2 36 2 36 33 12 24 24 8	5 3 8 4 35 13 23 23 8	6 8 8 8 2 13 23 24 8	11 11 9 11 5 14 23 24 8	14 16 14 14 5 14 23 23 8	17 22 20 19 8 15 24 24 8	21 25 21 24 9 15 24 24 9	24 30 22 27 9 16 24 24 9	27 34 27 30 9 16 24 24 9
11	29 25 31 25 26 13 23 23 8	32 31 32 29 29 13 23 23 8	36 33 33 33 31 13 24 24 8	2 1 2 36 33 12 24 24 8	5 4 8 4 35 13 23 23 8	8 9 8 8 2 13 23 24 8	11 13 9 11 5 14 23 24 8	14 17 14 14 5 14 23 23 8	17 24 20 20 8 15 24 24 8	21 27 21 24 9 15 24 24 9	24 32 22 27 9 16 24 24 9	27 35 27 30 9 16 24 24 9
12	29 27 31 25 26 13 23 23 8	32 32 32 29 29 13 23 23 8	36 34 33 33 31 13 24 24 8	2 2 2 36 34 12 24 24 8	5 5 8 4 35 13 23 23 8	8 11 8 8 2 13 23 24 8	12 14 10 12 5 14 23 24 8	14 19 14 14 5 14 23 23 8	17 24 20 20 8 15 24 24 8	21 28 21 24 9 15 24 24 9	24 33 22 27 9 16 24 24 9	27 36 27 30 9 16 24 24 9
13	29 28 31 25 26 13 23 23 8	32 32 32 29 29 13 23 23 8	36 35 33 33 31 13 24 24 8	3 3 2 1 34 12 24 24 8	5 7 8 5 35 13 23 23 8	8 12 8 8 2 13 23 24 8	12 15 10 12 5 14 23 24 8	14 20 16 16 7 14 23 23 8	17 26 20 20 8 15 24 24 8	21 30 20 24 9 15 24 24 9	24 34 22 27 9 16 24 24 9	27 1 28 31 9 16 24 24 9
14	29 29 31 25 26 13 23 23 8	32 34 32 29 29 13 23 23 8	36 36 33 33 32 13 24 24 8	3 4 2 1 34 12 24 24 8	5 8 8 5 35 13 23 23 8	8 13 8 8 2 13 23 24 8	12 17 10 12 5 14 23 24 8	14 22 16 16 7 14 23 23 8	17 27 20 20 8 15 24 24 8	21 31 20 24 9 15 24 24 9	24 36 24 27 9 16 24 24 9	26 3 28 31 8 17 24 24 8
15	29 31 31 25 26 13 23 23 8	32 35 32 29 29 13 23 23 8	36 1 33 33 32 13 24 24 8	3 6 2 1 34 12 24 24 8	6 9 8 5 36 13 23 24 8	8 14 8 8 2 13 22 24 8	12 18 11 12 5 14 23 24 8	14 23 16 16 7 14 23 23 8	17 28 20 20 8 15 24 24 8	21 33 20 24 9 15 24 24 9	24 1 24 27 9 16 24 24 9	26 4 28 31 8 17 24 24 8
16	29 32 32 26 27 18 23 23 8	32 36 32 29 29 13 23 23 8	36 3 34 33 32 13 24 24 8	3 7 3 1 34 12 24 24 8	6 10 8 5 36 13 23 24 8	8 16 8 8 2 13 22 24 8	12 19 11 12 5 14 23 24 8	14 25 16 16 7 14 23 23 8	17 30 20 20 8 15 24 24 8	21 33 19 24 9 15 24 24 9	24 2 24 27 9 16 24 24 9	26 5 28 31 8 17 24 24 8
17	29 33 32 26 27 13 23 23 8	32 1 32 29 29 13 23 23 8	36 4 34 33 33 12 24 24 8	3 8 3 1 34 12 24 24 8	6 11 8 5 36 13 23 24 8	8 17 8 8 2 13 22 24 8	12 21 11 12 5 14 23 24 8	14 26 16 16 7 14 23 23 8	17 31 20 20 8 15 24 24 8	21 34 19 24 9 15 24 24 9	24 3 24 27 9 16 24 24 9	26 6 28 31 8 17 24 24 8
18	29 34 32 26 27 13 23 23 8	32 3 32 29 29 13 23 23 8	36 5 34 33 33 12 24 24 8	3 10 3 2 34 13 24 24 8	6 13 8 5 36 13 23 24 8	8 18 8 8 2 13 22 24 8	12 23 11 12 5 14 23 24 8	14 28 17 16 7 14 23 23 8	17 33 20 20 8 15 24 24 8	21 36 19 24 9 15 24 24 9	24 4 24 28 9 16 24 24 9	26 7 28 31 8 17 24 24 8
19	29 35 32 26 27 13 23 23 8	34 4 32 29 29 13 23 23 8	36 6 34 34 33 12 24 24 8	3 11 4 2 34 13 24 24 8	6 14 8 5 36 13 23 24 8	9 20 8 8 2 13 22 24 8	12 23 11 12 5 14 23 23 8	14 29 17 16 7 14 23 23 8	18 34 20 20 8 15 24 24 8	21 1 19 24 9 15 24 24 9	24 6 24 28 9 16 24 24 9	27 8 28 32 8 17 24 24 8
20	29 1 32 26 27 13 23 23 8	34 5 32 29 29 13 23 23 8	1 7 34 34 33 12 24 24 8	4 12 4 2 34 13 24 24 8	6 16 8 5 36 13 23 24 8	9 21 8 8 2 13 22 24 8	12 25 11 25 5 14 23 23 8	14 30 17 16 7 14 23 23 8	18 35 20 20 8 15 24 24 8	21 2 20 24 9 15 24 24 9	24 7 24 28 9 16 24 24 9	27 10 28 32 8 17 24 24 8
21	31 2 32 26 27 13 23 23 8	34 5 32 29 29 13 23 23 8	1 9 35 34 33 12 24 24 8	4 14 5 2 35 13 23 24 8	7 17 8 5 36 13 23 24 8	10 22 8 8 2 13 22 24 8	12 26 11 12 5 14 23 23 8	14 32 17 16 7 14 23 23 8	18 36 20 20 8 15 24 24 8	21 3 20 24 9 15 24 24 9	24 8 24 28 9 16 24 24 9	28 12 28 32 8 17 24 24 8
22	31 3 32 26 27 13 23 23 8	34 7 32 29 29 13 23 23 8	1 10 35 34 33 12 24 24 8	4 15 5 2 35 13 23 24 8	7 19 8 6 1 13 24 24 8	10 24 8 8 2 13 22 24 8	13 28 11 13 5 14 23 23 8	16 32 17 17 7 14 23 23 8	18 1 20 20 8 15 24 24 8	21 4 20 24 9 15 24 24 9	25 9 24 28 9 16 24 24 9	28 12 28 32 8 17 24 24 8
23	31 4 32 26 28 13 23 23 8	34 9 32 29 29 11 23 23 8	1 12 35 34 33 12 24 24 8	4 16 5 2 35 13 23 24 8	7 20 8 6 1 13 24 24 8	10 26 8 8 2 13 22 24 8	14 29 11 14 5 14 23 23 8	16 34 17 17 7 14 23 23 8	19 3 21 21 9 15 24 24 9	22 6 21 24 9 15 24 24 9	25 10 24 28 9 16 24 24 9	28 14 28 32 8 17 24 24 8
24	31 5 32 26 28 13 23 23 8	34 10 32 21 29 11 23 23 8	1 13 35 34 33 12 24 24 8	4 18 5 2 35 13 23 24 8	7 22 8 6 1 13 24 24 8	10 26 8 8 2 13 22 24 8	13 41 11 14 5 14 23 23 8	16 35 17 17 7 14 23 23 8	19 4 21 21 9 15 24 24 9	22 7 21 24 9 15 24 24 9	25 12 24 28 9 16 24 24 9	28 15 30 32 8 17 24 24 8
25	31 7 32 26 28 13 23 23 8	35 11 32 31 29 11 23 23 8	1 15 35 35 33 12 24 24 8	4 19 5 2 35 13 23 24 8	7 24 8 6 1 13 24 24 8	10 28 8 10 2 13 22 24 8	14 32 11 14 5 14 23 23 8	16 36 17 17 7 14 23 23 8	19 6 21 21 9 15 24 24 9	22 8 21 25 9 15 24 24 9	25 13 25 28 9 16 24 24 9	28 16 30 32 8 17 24 24 8
26	31 8 32 28 28 13 23 23 8	35 13 32 31 29 11 23 23 8	1 15 35 35 33 12 24 24 8	4 21 5 2 35 13 23 24 8	7 25 8 6 1 13 24 24 8	10 30 8 10 3 13 22 24 8	14 33 12 14 5 14 23 23 8	16 1 17 17 7 14 23 23 8	19 6 21 21 9 15 24 24 9	22 9 21 25 9 15 24 24 9	25 15 25 28 9 16 24 24 9	28 17 20 32 8 17 24 24 8
27	31 10 32 28 28 13 23 23 8	35 14 32 31 29 11 23 23 8	2 18 36 35 33 12 24 24 8	5 23 6 2 35 13 23 24 8	7 26 8 6 1 13 23 24 8	10 31 8 10 3 13 22 24 8	14 34 13 14 5 14 23 23 8	16 2 17 17 7 14 23 23 8	19 7 21 21 9 15 24 24 9	22 10 21 25 9 15 24 24 9	25 15 25 28 9 16 24 24 9	28 19 30 33 8 17 24 24 8
28	31 11 32 28 28 13 23 23 8	35 16 32 31 29 11 23 23 8	2 19 36 35 33 12 24 24 8	5 24 6 2 35 13 23 24 8	7 27 8 6 1 13 23 24 8	10 33 8 10 3 13 22 24 8	14 35 13 14 5 14 23 23 8	16 4 17 17 7 14 23 23 8	19 9 21 21 9 15 24 24 9	22 12 21 25 9 15 24 24 9	25 16 25 28 9 16 24 24 9	28 21 30 33 8 17 24 24 8
29	31 12 32 28 28 13 23 23 8	35 17 32 31 29 11 23 23 8	2 20 36 35 33 12 24 24 8	5 25 6 2 35 13 23 24 8	7 29 8 6 1 13 23 24 8	10 34 8 10 3 13 22 24 8	14 1 13 14 5 14 23 23 8	16 5 17 17 7 14 23 23 8	19 10 21 21 9 15 24 24 9	22 13 21 25 9 15 24 24 9	25 18 25 28 9 16 24 24 9	28 22 30 33 8 17 24 24 8
30	31 14 32 28 28 13 23 23 8	**1896**	2 21 36 35 33 12 24 24 8	5 27 6 2 35 13 23 24 8	8 30 8 6 1 13 23 24 8	10 35 8 10 3 13 22 24 8	14 2 14 14 5 14 23 23 8	16 6 19 17 7 14 23 23 8	19 12 21 22 9 15 24 24 9	22 15 21 25 9 15 24 24 9	25 19 25 28 9 16 24 24 9	28 24 30 33 8 17 24 24 8
31	32 15 32 28 28 13 23 23 8		2 24 36 35 33 12 24 24 8		8 31 8 6 1 13 23 24 8		14 3 14 14 5 14 23 23 8	16 7 19 17 7 14 23 23 8		22 16 21 25 9 15 24 24 9		28 25 30 33 8 17 24 24 8

	JAN	FEB	MAR	APR	MAY	JUNE	JULY	AUG	SEPT	OCT	NOV	DEC
1	29 26 30 33 8 17 24 24 8	32 32 30 36 8 17 24 24 8	35 33 32 2 8 16 24 24 8	2 1 2 5 10 16 24 24 8	4 4 7 4 12 16 24 24 8	8 8 6 5 14 16 24 24 8	10 12 9 6 15 16 24 24 9	13 17 15 8 17 17 24 24 8	16 22 19 13 19 18 24 24 9	19 27 18 16 21 18 24 24 9	22 31 22 21 23 18 24 24 9	25 35 27 24 25 19 25 25 9
2	29 28 30 33 8 17 24 24 8	32 33 30 36 8 17 24 24 8	35 34 32 2 8 16 24 24 8	2 2 2 5 10 16 24 24 8	4 6 7 9 12 16 24 24 8	8 10 6 5 14 16 24 24 8	10 13 9 6 15 16 24 24 9	13 18 15 8 17 17 24 24 8	16 24 19 13 19 18 24 24 9	19 28 18 16 21 18 24 24 9	22 33 22 21 23 18 24 24 9	25 36 27 24 25 19 25 25 9
3	29 30 30 33 8 17 24 24 8	32 24 30 36 8 17 24 24 8	35 35 32 2 8 16 24 24 8	2 3 2 5 10 16 24 24 8	5 7 7 4 12 16 24 24 8	8 11 6 5 14 16 24 24 8	10 15 9 6 15 16 24 24 9	13 20 15 8 17 17 24 24 8	18 25 19 13 19 18 24 24 9	20 29 18 16 21 18 24 24 9	23 35 23 21 23 18 24 24 9	25 1 27 25 25 19 25 25 9
4	29 31 30 33 8 17 24 24 8	32 35 30 36 8 17 24 24 8	35 36 33 2 8 16 24 24 8	2 5 2 5 10 16 24 24 8	5 8 7 4 12 16 24 24 8	8 12 6 5 14 16 24 24 8	10 16 9 6 15 16 24 24 9	13 21 16 8 17 17 24 24 8	18 27 19 13 19 18 24 24 9	20 30 18 16 21 18 24 24 9	23 36 23 21 23 18 24 24 9	25 3 27 25 25 19 25 25 9
5	29 32 30 33 8 17 24 24 8	32 36 30 36 8 17 24 24 8	35 1 33 4 8 16 24 24 8	2 6 2 5 10 16 24 24 8	5 9 7 4 12 16 24 24 8	8 14 6 5 14 16 24 24 8	10 17 10 6 15 16 24 24 9	13 22 16 9 18 18 24 24 9	18 28 19 13 19 18 24 24 9	20 32 18 17 21 18 24 24 9	23 1 23 21 23 18 24 24 9	25 4 27 25 25 19 25 25 9
6	29 33 32 33 8 17 24 24 8	32 2 30 36 8 17 24 24 8	35 2 33 4 8 16 24 24 8	2 7 2 5 10 16 24 24 8	5 10 7 4 12 16 24 24 8	8 15 6 5 14 16 24 24 8	10 19 10 6 15 16 24 24 9	14 24 16 10 18 18 24 24 9	18 30 19 13 19 18 24 24 9	21 33 18 17 21 18 24 24 9	23 2 23 21 23 18 24 24 9	25 5 27 25 25 19 25 25 9
7	29 35 32 33 8 17 24 24 8	32 3 30 1 8 17 24 24 8	35 4 33 4 8 16 24 24 8	2 8 2 5 10 16 24 24 8	5 12 7 4 12 16 24 24 8	8 16 6 5 14 16 24 24 8	11 20 10 6 15 16 24 24 9	15 26 16 10 18 18 24 24 9	18 31 19 13 19 18 24 24 9	21 35 18 17 21 18 24 24 9	23 3 23 21 23 18 24 24 9	27 6 28 25 27 19 25 25 9
8	29 36 32 33 8 17 24 24 8	32 4 30 1 8 17 24 24 8	35 5 33 4 8 16 24 24 8	2 9 2 5 10 16 24 24 8	6 13 7 4 12 16 24 24 8	8 18 6 5 14 16 24 24 8	11 21 10 6 15 16 24 24 9	15 27 16 10 18 18 24 24 9	18 33 19 13 19 18 24 24 9	21 36 18 17 21 18 24 24 9	24 4 24 21 24 18 24 24 9	27 7 28 25 27 19 25 25 9
9	30 1 32 35 8 17 24 24 8	32 6 30 2 8 17 24 24 8	35 6 33 4 8 16 24 24 8	2 11 3 5 11 16 24 24 8	6 14 7 4 12 16 24 24 8	8 19 6 5 14 16 24 24 8	11 23 10 6 15 16 24 24 8	15 28 16 10 18 18 24 24 9	18 33 19 13 19 18 24 24 9	21 1 18 17 21 18 24 24 9	24 6 24 21 24 18 24 24 9	27 9 28 25 27 19 25 25 9
10	30 2 32 35 8 17 24 24 8	32 7 30 2 8 16 24 24 8	35 7 34 4 8 16 24 24 8	2 12 4 5 11 16 24 24 8	6 15 7 4 12 16 24 24 8	8 20 6 5 14 16 24 24 8	11 24 10 6 15 16 24 24 8	15 30 16 10 18 18 24 24 9	18 35 20 14 20 18 24 24 9	21 2 18 17 22 18 24 24 9	24 7 24 21 24 18 24 24 9	27 10 28 25 27 19 25 25 9
11	30 3 32 35 8 17 24 24 8	33 8 30 2 8 16 24 24 8	35 8 34 4 8 16 24 24 8	2 13 4 5 11 16 24 24 8	6 16 7 4 12 16 24 24 8	8 22 6 5 14 16 24 24 8	12 26 10 7 16 16 24 24 9	15 31 18 10 18 18 24 24 9	18 36 20 14 20 18 24 24 9	21 3 18 18 22 18 24 24 9	24 8 24 21 24 18 24 24 9	27 11 28 25 27 19 25 25 9
12	30 4 32 35 8 17 24 24 8	33 9 30 2 8 16 24 24 8	35 10 34 4 8 16 24 24 8	2 15 4 5 11 16 24 24 8	6 18 6 3 12 15 24 24 8	8 24 6 5 14 16 24 24 8	12 27 10 7 16 16 24 24 9	15 33 18 10 18 18 24 24 9	18 1 20 14 20 18 24 24 9	21 4 19 18 22 18 24 24 9	24 9 24 21 24 18 24 24 9	27 12 28 25 27 19 25 25 9
13	30 6 32 35 8 17 24 24 8	33 10 30 2 8 16 24 24 8	35 11 34 4 8 16 24 24 8	2 16 4 5 11 16 24 24 8	6 19 6 3 12 15 24 24 8	8 25 6 5 14 16 24 24 8	12 29 12 7 16 16 24 24 9	15 34 18 10 18 18 24 24 9	18 3 20 14 20 18 24 24 9	21 6 19 18 22 18 24 24 9	24 10 24 21 24 18 24 24 9	27 13 28 25 27 19 25 25 9
14	30 7 32 35 8 17 24 24 8	33 12 30 2 8 16 24 24 8	35 12 34 4 8 16 24 24 8	2 17 4 5 11 16 24 24 8	6 21 6 3 12 15 24 24 8	8 26 6 5 14 16 24 24 8	12 30 12 7 16 16 24 24 9	15 36 18 10 18 18 24 24 9	18 4 20 14 20 18 24 24 9	21 7 19 18 22 18 24 24 9	24 12 24 22 24 18 24 24 9	27 15 28 25 27 19 25 25 9
15	30 8 32 35 8 17 24 24 8	33 13 30 2 8 16 24 24 8	35 14 34 4 8 16 24 24 8	2 19 5 5 11 16 24 24 8	6 22 6 3 12 15 24 24 8	8 28 7 5 14 16 24 24 8	12 32 12 7 16 16 24 24 9	15 1 18 11 18 18 24 24 9	18 5 20 14 20 18 24 24 9	21 8 19 18 22 18 24 24 9	24 13 24 22 24 18 24 24 9	27 16 28 25 27 19 25 25 9
16	30 10 32 35 8 17 24 24 8	33 15 30 2 8 16 24 24 8	36 15 35 4 9 16 24 24 8	2 20 5 5 11 16 24 24 8	6 24 6 3 12 15 24 24 8	8 30 7 5 14 16 24 24 8	12 33 12 7 16 16 24 24 9	15 2 18 11 18 18 24 24 9	18 6 20 14 20 18 24 24 9	21 9 19 18 22 18 24 24 9	24 14 24 22 24 18 24 24 9	27 18 28 25 27 19 25 25 9
17	30 11 32 35 8 17 24 24 8	33 16 30 2 8 16 24 24 8	36 16 35 4 9 16 24 24 8	3 22 5 5 11 16 24 24 8	6 26 6 3 12 15 24 24 8	8 31 7 5 14 16 24 24 8	12 34 12 7 16 16 24 24 9	15 3 18 11 18 18 24 24 9	18 7 19 15 21 18 24 24 9	21 11 20 18 22 18 24 24 9	24 15 24 22 24 18 24 24 9	27 19 28 25 27 19 25 25 9
18	30 12 32 35 8 17 24 24 8	34 17 30 2 8 16 25 25 8	36 18 35 4 9 16 24 24 8	3 24 5 5 11 16 24 24 8	6 27 6 3 12 15 24 24 8	8 33 7 5 14 16 24 24 8	12 36 12 7 16 16 24 24 9	15 4 18 11 18 18 24 24 9	18 9 19 15 21 18 24 24 9	21 12 20 18 22 18 24 24 9	24 16 24 22 24 18 24 24 9	27 20 28 25 27 19 25 25 9
19	30 13 32 35 8 17 24 24 8	34 19 30 2 8 16 25 25 8	36 19 35 5 9 16 24 24 8	4 25 5 5 11 16 24 24 8	6 28 6 3 12 15 24 24 8	9 34 7 5 14 16 24 24 8	12 1 12 7 16 16 24 24 9	15 6 18 12 18 18 24 24 9	18 10 19 15 21 18 24 24 9	21 13 21 18 22 18 24 24 9	24 18 24 22 24 18 24 24 9	27 21 28 25 27 19 25 25 9
20	32 15 32 35 8 17 24 24 8	34 20 31 2 8 16 25 25 8	1 20 35 5 10 16 24 24 8	4 26 5 5 11 16 24 24 8	6 30 6 3 12 15 24 24 8	9 35 7 5 14 16 24 24 8	12 3 12 7 16 16 24 24 9	15 7 18 12 18 18 24 24 9	18 11 19 15 21 18 24 24 9	21 15 21 18 22 18 24 24 9	24 19 24 22 24 18 24 24 9	27 22 29 27 27 19 25 25 9
21	32 17 32 35 8 17 24 24 8	34 21 31 2 8 16 25 25 8	1 22 35 5 10 16 24 24 8	4 28 6 5 11 16 24 24 8	7 31 6 3 12 16 24 24 8	10 36 7 6 15 16 24 24 9	12 3 13 7 16 16 24 24 9	15 8 18 12 18 18 24 24 9	18 12 18 15 21 18 24 24 9	21 15 21 19 22 18 24 24 9	24 21 24 22 24 18 24 24 9	27 25 29 27 27 19 25 25 9
22	32 17 32 35 8 17 24 24 8	34 22 31 2 8 16 25 25 8	1 24 35 5 10 16 24 24 8	4 29 6 5 11 16 24 24 8	7 33 6 3 12 16 24 24 8	10 1 7 6 15 16 24 24 9	12 5 14 8 16 16 24 24 8	15 9 18 12 18 18 24 24 9	18 14 18 15 21 18 24 24 9	21 16 21 19 22 18 24 24 9	25 22 25 23 25 19 25 25 9	28 25 30 27 27 19 25 25 9
23	32 19 30 35 8 17 24 24 8	33 24 31 2 8 16 24 24 8	1 25 35 5 10 16 24 24 8	4 30 6 5 11 16 24 24 8	7 34 7 4 13 15 25 25 8	10 3 9 6 15 16 24 24 9	13 6 14 8 16 16 24 24 8	16 10 18 12 18 18 24 24 9	19 15 18 15 21 18 24 24 9	22 18 21 19 22 18 24 24 9	25 24 26 23 25 19 25 25 9	28 27 30 27 27 19 25 25 9
24	32 20 30 35 8 17 24 24 8	34 26 32 2 8 16 25 25 8	1 27 35 5 10 16 24 24 8	4 32 6 5 11 16 24 24 8	7 35 7 4 13 15 25 25 8	10 4 9 6 15 16 24 24 9	13 7 14 8 16 16 24 24 8	16 12 18 12 18 18 24 24 9	19 16 18 15 21 18 24 24 9	22 19 21 19 22 18 24 24 9	25 25 26 23 25 19 25 25 9	28 28 30 27 27 19 25 25 9
25	32 22 30 36 8 17 24 24 8	34 27 32 2 8 16 24 24 8	1 28 36 5 10 16 24 24 8	4 33 6 5 11 16 24 24 8	7 36 6 3 13 16 24 24 8	10 5 9 6 15 16 24 24 9	13 8 14 8 16 16 24 24 8	16 13 18 12 18 18 24 24 9	19 18 18 15 21 18 24 24 9	22 21 21 19 22 18 24 24 9	25 27 27 23 25 19 25 25 9	28 30 30 27 27 19 25 25 9
26	32 24 30 36 8 17 24 24 8	34 28 32 2 8 16 24 24 8	1 29 36 5 10 16 24 24 8	4 34 6 4 11 16 24 24 8	7 1 6 4 13 16 24 24 8	10 6 9 6 15 16 24 24 9	13 9 14 8 16 16 24 24 8	16 14 19 12 19 18 24 24 9	19 19 18 16 21 18 24 24 9	22 22 21 19 22 18 24 24 9	25 28 27 23 25 19 25 25 9	28 31 30 27 27 19 25 25 9
27	32 25 30 36 8 17 24 24 8	34 30 32 2 8 16 24 24 8	1 31 1 5 10 16 24 24 8	4 36 6 4 11 16 24 24 8	7 2 6 4 13 16 24 24 8	10 7 9 6 15 16 24 24 9	13 10 15 9 16 16 24 24 8	16 15 19 12 19 18 24 24 9	19 21 18 16 21 18 24 24 9	22 24 21 19 22 18 24 24 9	25 29 27 23 25 19 25 25 9	28 33 30 27 27 19 25 25 9
28	32 26 30 36 8 17 24 24 8	35 31 32 2 8 16 24 24 8	1 32 1 5 10 16 24 24 8	4 2 6 4 12 16 24 24 8	7 5 6 4 13 16 24 24 8	10 10 9 6 15 16 24 24 9	13 12 15 9 17 16 24 24 8	16 16 19 12 19 18 24 24 9	19 22 18 16 21 18 24 24 9	22 25 21 19 22 18 24 24 9	25 31 27 23 25 19 25 25 9	28 34 30 27 27 19 25 25 9
29	32 27 30 36 8 17 24 24 8	1897	1 33 1 5 10 16 24 24 8	4 3 7 4 12 16 24 24 8	7 6 6 4 13 16 24 24 8	10 12 9 6 15 16 24 24 9	13 13 15 9 17 17 24 24 8	16 18 19 12 19 18 24 24 9	19 24 18 16 21 18 24 24 9	22 27 22 20 22 18 24 24 9	25 33 27 23 25 19 25 25 9	28 36 30 27 27 19 25 25 9
30	32 29 30 36 8 17 24 24 8		1 34 1 5 10 16 24 24 8	4 3 7 4 12 16 24 24 8	7 6 6 4 13 16 24 24 8	10 12 9 6 15 16 24 24 9	13 15 15 9 17 17 24 24 8	16 19 19 12 19 18 24 24 9	19 25 18 16 21 18 24 24 9	22 29 22 20 22 18 24 24 9	25 34 27 23 25 19 25 25 9	28 1 30 27 27 19 25 25 9
31	32 30 30 36 8 17 24 24 8		1 36 1 5 10 16 24 24 8		7 8 6 4 13 16 24 24 8		13 16 15 9 17 17 24 24 8	16 21 19 12 19 18 24 24 9		22 30 22 20 22 18 24 24 9		28 3 30 27 27 19 25 25 9

	JAN	FEB	MAR	APR	MAY	JUNE	JULY	AUG	SEPT	OCT	NOV	DEC
1	28 4 30 27 27 19 25 25 9	31 9 30 31 30 19 25 25 9	35 9 33 35 32 20 26 25 8	2 13 3 3 35 19 26 25 8	5 17 5 7 1 19 26 25 9	7 22 5 10 3 19 25 25 9	11 25 11 14 5 19 25 25 9	13 31 16 18 7 19 25 25 9	17 36 17 21 9 19 25 24 9	19 3 18 24 12 21 25 24 9	22 8 24 26 13 21 26 25 9	26 11 28 26 14 22 26 25 9
2	28 5 30 28 28 19 25 25 9	31 9 30 31 30 19 25 25 9	35 10 34 35 32 20 26 25 8	2 14 3 3 35 19 26 25 8	5 18 5 7 1 19 26 25 9	8 23 5 10 3 19 26 25 9	11 27 11 14 5 19 25 25 9	13 32 16 18 7 19 25 24 9	17 1 17 21 9 19 25 24 9	19 5 18 24 12 21 25 24 9	23 9 24 26 13 21 26 25 9	26 12 28 26 14 22 26 25 9
3	28 6 30 28 28 19 25 25 9	31 10 30 31 30 19 25 25 9	35 11 34 35 32 20 26 25 8	2 16 3 3 35 19 26 25 8	5 19 5 7 1 19 26 25 9	8 24 5 11 3 19 26 25 9	11 28 11 14 5 19 25 25 9	13 33 16 18 7 19 25 24 9	17 3 17 21 9 19 25 24 9	19 6 18 24 12 21 25 24 9	23 10 24 26 13 21 26 25 9	26 14 28 26 14 22 26 25 9
4	28 7 29 28 28 19 25 25 9	31 12 30 31 30 19 25 25 9	35 12 34 35 32 20 26 25 8	2 17 3 3 35 19 26 25 8	5 21 5 7 1 19 26 25 9	8 26 6 11 3 19 26 25 9	11 30 11 14 5 19 25 25 9	13 34 16 18 7 19 25 24 9	17 4 17 21 9 19 25 24 9	19 7 18 24 12 21 25 24 9	23 12 24 26 13 21 26 25 9	26 15 28 26 14 22 26 25 9
5	28 8 29 28 28 19 25 25 9	31 13 30 31 30 19 25 25 9	35 14 34 35 32 20 26 25 8	2 18 3 3 35 19 26 25 8	5 23 5 7 1 19 25 25 9	8 27 6 11 3 19 26 25 9	11 31 12 15 6 19 25 24 9	13 36 16 18 7 19 25 24 9	17 5 17 21 9 19 25 24 9	21 9 19 24 12 21 25 24 9	23 13 24 26 13 21 26 25 9	26 16 28 26 14 22 26 25 9
6	28 9 28 28 28 19 25 25 9	31 14 30 31 30 19 25 25 9	35 15 35 36 32 20 26 25 8	2 19 3 3 35 19 26 25 8	5 24 5 7 1 19 25 25 9	8 28 6 11 3 19 26 25 9	11 33 12 15 6 19 25 24 9	13 1 16 18 7 19 25 24 9	17 6 17 21 9 19 25 24 9	21 10 19 24 12 21 25 24 9	23 14 24 26 13 21 26 25 9	26 17 28 26 14 22 26 25 9
7	28 10 28 28 28 19 25 25 9	33 15 30 33 30 19 25 25 9	35 16 35 36 32 20 26 25 8	2 20 4 4 35 19 26 25 8	5 25 5 7 1 19 25 25 9	8 30 6 11 3 19 26 25 9	11 34 12 15 6 19 25 24 9	13 3 16 18 7 19 25 24 9	17 7 17 22 10 19 25 24 9	21 11 19 24 12 21 25 24 9	23 15 24 26 13 21 26 25 9	26 18 28 26 14 22 26 25 9
8	29 12 28 28 28 19 25 25 9	33 17 30 33 30 19 25 25 9	35 17 35 36 32 20 26 25 8	2 23 5 4 35 19 26 25 8	5 27 4 7 1 19 25 25 9	9 32 6 11 4 19 25 25 9	11 36 12 15 6 19 25 24 9	13 4 16 18 7 19 25 24 9	17 9 16 22 10 19 25 24 9	21 12 19 25 12 21 25 25 9	23 17 24 26 13 21 26 25 9	26 20 28 26 14 22 26 25 8
9	29 13 28 28 28 19 25 25 9	33 18 30 33 30 19 25 25 9	35 20 35 36 32 20 26 25 8	2 24 5 4 35 19 26 25 8	5 28 4 7 1 19 25 25 9	9 33 6 11 4 19 25 25 9	11 1 12 15 6 19 25 24 9	13 6 16 18 7 19 25 24 9	17 10 16 22 10 19 25 24 9	21 13 19 25 12 21 25 25 9	23 18 24 26 13 21 26 25 9	26 21 28 25 13 22 26 25 8
10	30 14 28 28 28 19 25 25 9	33 19 30 33 30 19 25 25 9	35 20 35 36 32 20 26 25 8	2 25 5 4 35 19 25 25 8	5 30 4 7 1 19 25 25 9	9 35 6 11 4 19 25 25 9	11 2 12 15 6 19 25 24 9	13 7 16 18 7 19 25 24 9	18 11 16 22 10 19 25 24 9	21 15 19 25 12 21 25 25 9	23 19 25 26 13 21 25 25 9	26 22 28 25 13 22 26 25 8
11	30 16 28 28 28 19 25 25 9	33 21 31 33 31 19 25 25 9	35 22 35 36 32 20 26 25 8	2 27 5 4 35 19 26 25 8	6 31 4 7 1 19 25 25 9	9 36 7 11 4 19 25 25 9	12 3 13 15 6 19 25 24 9	13 8 16 19 7 19 25 24 9	18 12 17 23 11 20 25 25 9	21 16 21 25 12 21 25 25 9	24 21 25 25 13 21 25 25 9	26 24 28 25 13 22 26 25 8
12	30 17 28 28 28 19 25 25 9	33 22 31 33 31 19 25 25 9	36 23 35 36 32 20 26 25 8	2 28 5 4 35 19 26 25 8	6 32 4 7 1 19 25 25 9	9 1 7 12 4 19 25 25 9	12 5 13 15 6 19 25 24 9	15 9 18 19 9 19 25 24 9	18 13 17 23 11 20 25 25 9	21 17 21 25 12 21 25 25 9	24 22 25 25 13 21 25 25 9	26 25 28 25 13 22 26 25 8
13	30 18 28 28 28 19 25 25 9	33 24 31 33 31 19 25 25 9	36 24 35 36 32 20 26 25 8	3 29 5 4 35 19 26 25 8	6 34 4 8 2 18 26 25 9	9 3 7 12 4 19 25 25 9	12 6 13 15 6 19 25 24 9	15 10 18 19 9 19 25 24 9	18 15 17 23 11 20 25 25 9	21 18 21 25 12 21 25 25 9	24 23 25 25 13 21 25 25 9	26 26 28 25 13 22 26 25 8
14	30 19 28 28 28 19 25 25 9	33 25 31 33 31 19 25 25 9	36 26 35 1 32 20 26 25 8	3 31 5 4 35 19 26 25 8	6 35 4 8 2 18 26 25 9	9 4 7 12 4 19 25 25 9	12 7 13 15 6 19 24 24 8	15 12 18 19 9 19 25 24 9	18 16 17 23 11 20 25 25 9	21 19 21 25 12 21 25 25 9	24 24 25 25 13 21 25 25 9	26 28 28 25 13 22 26 25 8
15	30 21 28 28 28 19 25 25 9	33 26 32 33 32 20 26 25 8	36 27 35 1 33 19 26 25 8	3 32 5 5 35 19 26 25 8	6 36 4 8 2 18 26 25 9	9 5 7 12 4 19 25 25 9	12 8 13 15 6 19 24 24 8	15 13 18 19 9 19 25 24 9	18 18 17 23 11 20 25 25 9	21 21 21 25 12 21 25 25 9	24 25 25 25 13 21 25 25 9	26 29 28 25 13 22 26 25 8
16	30 22 28 28 28 19 25 25 9	33 28 32 33 32 20 26 25 8	36 29 36 1 33 19 26 25 8	3 34 5 5 35 19 26 25 8	6 2 4 8 2 18 26 25 9	9 6 7 12 4 19 25 25 9	12 9 13 15 6 19 24 24 8	15 14 18 19 9 19 25 24 9	18 19 17 23 11 20 25 25 9	21 22 21 25 12 21 25 25 9	24 27 25 25 13 21 25 25 9	26 31 28 25 13 22 26 25 8
17	30 24 28 28 28 19 25 25 9	33 29 32 33 32 20 26 25 8	36 30 36 1 33 19 26 25 8	3 35 5 5 35 19 26 25 8	6 3 4 9 2 18 26 25 9	9 7 7 12 4 19 25 25 9	12 10 14 15 6 19 24 24 8	15 15 18 19 9 19 25 24 9	19 20 17 23 11 20 25 24 9	21 24 21 25 12 21 25 25 9	24 29 25 25 13 21 25 25 9	27 32 28 25 13 22 26 25 9
18	30 25 28 28 28 19 25 25 9	34 31 32 34 32 20 26 25 8	36 31 1 1 33 19 26 25 8	3 1 6 6 36 19 26 25 9	6 4 4 9 2 18 26 25 9	9 9 7 12 4 19 25 25 9	12 12 14 15 6 19 24 24 8	15 16 18 19 9 19 25 24 9	18 21 17 23 11 20 25 24 9	21 25 21 25 12 21 25 25 9	24 30 25 25 13 21 25 25 9	27 34 28 25 13 22 26 25 9
19	30 27 28 30 28 19 25 25 9	34 32 32 34 32 20 26 25 8	36 33 1 1 33 19 26 25 8	3 2 6 6 36 19 26 25 9	6 5 4 9 2 18 26 25 9	9 10 7 12 4 19 25 25 9	12 13 14 15 6 19 24 24 8	15 18 18 19 9 19 25 24 9	18 22 17 23 11 20 25 24 9	21 27 21 25 12 21 25 25 9	24 31 25 25 13 21 25 25 9	27 35 28 25 13 22 26 25 9
20	31 28 28 30 28 19 25 25 9	34 33 32 34 32 20 26 25 8	36 34 1 1 33 19 25 25 8	4 3 6 6 36 19 26 25 9	6 7 4 9 2 18 26 25 9	9 11 9 13 5 19 25 25 9	12 14 14 15 6 19 24 24 8	15 19 18 19 9 19 25 24 9	18 24 17 23 11 20 25 24 9	21 28 21 25 12 21 25 25 9	24 33 25 25 13 21 25 25 9	27 1 28 25 13 22 26 25 9
21	31 30 28 30 28 19 25 25 9	34 35 32 34 32 20 26 25 8	1 36 1 1 34 19 26 25 8	4 4 6 6 36 19 26 25 9	7 8 4 10 2 19 26 25 9	10 12 9 12 5 19 25 25 9	12 15 14 15 6 19 24 24 8	15 20 18 19 9 19 25 24 9	18 25 17 23 11 20 25 24 9	21 30 21 26 12 21 25 25 9	24 34 25 25 13 21 25 25 9	27 3 28 25 13 22 26 25 9
22	31 31 28 30 28 19 25 25 9	34 36 32 34 32 20 26 25 8	1 1 1 1 34 19 26 25 8	4 6 6 6 36 19 26 25 9	7 9 4 10 2 19 25 25 9	10 14 9 13 5 19 25 25 9	12 17 14 15 6 19 24 24 8	15 22 18 19 9 19 25 24 9	18 27 17 23 11 20 25 24 9	21 31 21 26 12 21 26 25 9	25 36 27 25 13 21 25 25 9	28 4 27 25 13 22 26 25 9
23	31 33 28 30 28 19 25 25 9	35 2 32 35 32 20 26 25 8	1 2 1 1 34 19 26 25 8	4 7 6 6 36 19 26 25 9	7 10 4 10 3 19 25 25 9	10 15 9 13 5 19 25 25 9	13 18 15 16 7 19 25 24 9	16 23 18 19 9 19 25 24 9	19 28 17 23 11 20 25 25 9	22 32 22 26 12 21 26 25 9	25 1 27 25 13 21 25 25 9	28 4 27 25 13 22 26 25 9
24	31 34 28 30 28 19 25 25 9	35 3 32 35 32 20 26 25 8	1 4 1 1 34 19 25 25 8	5 8 5 6 36 19 26 25 9	7 11 4 10 3 19 25 25 9	10 16 9 13 5 19 25 25 9	13 19 15 16 7 19 25 24 9	16 24 18 19 9 19 25 24 9	19 29 17 23 11 20 25 25 9	22 34 22 26 12 21 26 25 9	25 3 27 25 13 21 25 25 9	28 6 27 25 13 22 26 25 9
25	31 36 28 31 28 19 25 25 9	35 4 33 35 32 20 26 25 8	1 5 1 1 34 19 25 25 8	5 9 5 6 36 19 26 25 9	7 12 5 10 3 19 25 25 9	10 17 9 13 5 19 25 25 9	13 21 15 16 7 19 25 24 9	16 25 18 21 9 19 25 24 9	19 31 17 23 11 20 25 25 9	22 35 22 26 12 21 26 25 9	25 4 27 25 13 21 25 25 9	28 7 27 25 13 22 26 25 9
26	31 1 28 31 28 19 25 25 9	35 5 33 35 32 20 26 25 8	1 6 2 2 34 19 25 25 8	5 10 5 6 36 19 26 25 9	7 14 5 10 3 19 25 25 9	10 18 10 13 5 19 25 25 9	13 22 15 17 7 19 25 24 9	16 27 18 21 9 19 25 24 9	19 33 17 23 11 21 25 25 9	22 36 22 26 12 21 26 25 9	25 5 27 25 13 21 25 25 9	28 9 27 25 13 22 26 25 9
27	31 2 28 31 28 19 25 25 9	35 7 33 35 32 20 26 25 8	1 7 2 2 34 19 25 25 8	5 12 5 6 36 19 26 25 9	7 15 5 10 3 19 25 25 9	10 19 10 13 5 19 25 25 9	13 24 15 17 7 19 25 24 9	16 28 18 21 9 19 25 24 9	19 34 18 24 12 21 25 25 9	22 1 22 26 12 21 26 25 9	25 6 27 25 13 21 25 25 9	28 10 27 25 13 22 26 25 9
28	31 3 28 31 28 19 25 25 9	35 8 33 35 32 20 26 25 8	1 8 2 2 34 19 25 25 8	5 13 5 6 36 19 26 25 9	7 16 5 10 3 19 25 25 9	10 21 10 13 5 19 25 25 9	13 25 16 18 7 19 25 25 9	16 30 18 21 9 19 25 24 9	19 36 18 24 12 21 25 25 9	22 3 22 26 12 21 26 25 9	25 7 27 25 13 21 25 25 9	28 11 27 25 13 22 26 25 9
29	31 4 28 31 28 19 25 25 9		1 10 2 2 34 19 25 25 8	5 14 5 7 1 19 26 25 9	7 17 5 10 3 19 25 25 9	10 22 10 13 5 19 25 25 9	13 26 16 18 7 19 25 25 9	16 31 18 21 9 19 25 24 9	19 1 18 24 12 21 25 25 9	22 4 22 26 12 21 26 25 9	25 9 27 25 13 21 25 25 9	28 12 27 25 13 22 26 25 9
30	31 6 28 31 28 19 25 25 9	**1898**	1 11 2 2 34 19 25 25 8	5 15 5 6 36 19 26 25 9	7 19 5 10 3 19 25 25 9	10 23 10 13 5 19 25 25 9	13 28 16 18 7 19 25 25 9	13 33 18 21 9 19 25 24 9	19 2 18 24 12 21 25 25 9	22 6 22 26 12 21 26 25 9	25 10 27 25 13 21 25 25 9	28 13 27 25 13 22 26 25 9
31	31 7 28 31 28 19 25 25 9		1 12 2 2 34 19 25 25 8		7 21 5 10 3 19 25 25 9		13 29 16 18 7 19 25 25 9	16 34 18 21 9 19 25 24 9		22 7 22 26 12 21 26 25 9		28 14 27 25 13 22 26 25 9

	JAN	FEB	MAR	APR	MAY	JUNE	JULY	AUG	SEPT	OCT	NOV	DEC
1	28 16 26 25 13 22 26 25 8	32 20 30 26 12 23 26 25 8	34 21 34 30 12 22 27 25 9	1 27 3 34 12 22 27 25 9	4 30 3 1 13 22 27 25 9	7 36 6 5 15 22 27 25 9	10 3 13 8 16 22 26 25 9	13 8 16 12 18 22 26 25 9	16 13 14 16 20 22 26 25 9	20 16 20 20 23 23 26 25 9	22 21 23 23 23 23 27 25 9	25 24 27 27 27 24 27 25 9
2	28 17 26 25 13 22 26 25 8	32 21 30 26 12 23 26 25 8	34 22 36 20 12 22 27 25 9	1 28 3 34 12 22 27 25 9	4 31 3 1 13 22 27 25 9	7 1 6 6 15 22 27 25 9	10 4 13 8 16 22 26 25 8	13 9 16 12 18 22 26 25 9	16 14 14 16 20 22 26 25 9	20 17 20 20 23 23 26 25 9	22 22 23 23 23 23 27 25 9	25 25 27 27 27 24 27 25 9
3	28 18 26 25 13 22 26 25 8	32 22 30 26 12 23 26 25 8	34 24 36 30 12 22 27 25 9	1 29 3 34 12 22 27 25 9	4 33 3 1 13 22 27 25 9	9 2 6 6 15 22 27 25 9	10 6 13 8 16 22 26 25 8	14 10 16 12 18 22 26 25 9	16 15 15 16 20 22 26 25 9	20 18 20 20 23 23 26 25 9	23 23 25 23 25 23 27 25 9	25 27 27 28 27 24 27 25 9
4	28 19 26 25 13 22 26 25 8	32 24 31 26 12 23 26 25 8	34 25 36 30 12 22 27 25 9	1 30 3 34 12 22 27 25 9	4 34 3 1 13 22 27 25 9	9 3 7 6 15 22 27 25 9	11 7 13 8 16 22 26 25 8	14 12 16 13 18 22 26 25 9	17 16 15 17 20 22 26 25 9	20 19 20 20 23 23 26 25 9	23 23 25 23 25 23 27 25 9	25 28 27 28 27 24 27 25 9
5	28 20 26 25 13 22 26 25 8	32 25 31 26 13 23 26 25 8	34 27 36 30 12 22 27 25 9	3 31 3 34 12 22 27 25 9	4 36 3 1 13 22 27 25 9	9 5 7 6 15 22 27 25 9	11 8 13 8 17 22 27 25 8	14 13 16 13 18 22 26 25 9	17 17 15 17 20 22 26 25 9	20 20 20 20 23 23 26 25 9	23 25 25 23 25 23 27 25 9	25 30 25 28 27 24 27 25 9
6	29 22 26 25 13 22 26 25 8	32 26 31 28 12 23 26 25 8	36 28 36 31 12 22 27 25 9	3 33 3 34 12 22 27 25 9	4 1 3 1 13 22 27 25 9	9 6 7 6 15 22 27 25 9	11 10 13 8 17 22 27 25 8	14 14 16 13 19 22 26 25 9	17 18 15 17 20 22 26 25 9	20 22 20 20 23 23 26 25 9	23 27 25 23 25 23 27 25 9	25 31 25 28 27 24 27 25 9
7	29 23 26 25 13 22 26 25 8	33 28 31 28 12 22 27 25 9	36 30 36 31 12 22 27 25 9	3 34 3 34 12 22 27 25 9	4 3 3 1 13 22 27 25 9	9 7 7 6 15 22 27 25 9	11 11 13 8 16 22 27 25 8	14 15 16 13 19 22 26 25 9	17 19 15 17 20 22 26 25 9	20 23 20 20 23 23 26 25 9	23 28 25 24 25 23 27 25 9	27 32 25 28 27 24 27 25 9
8	29 25 26 25 13 22 26 25 8	33 30 31 28 12 22 27 25 9	36 31 36 31 12 22 27 25 9	3 36 3 34 12 22 27 25 9	5 4 3 1 13 22 27 25 9	9 9 7 6 15 22 27 25 9	11 12 13 9 17 22 26 25 9	14 16 16 13 19 22 26 25 9	17 20 15 17 20 22 26 25 9	21 24 21 21 23 23 27 25 9	23 29 25 24 25 23 27 25, 9	27 33 25 28 27 24 27 25 9
9	29 26 26 25 13 22 26 25 8	33 31 31 28 12 22 27 25 9	36 33 36 31 12 22 27 25 9	3 1 3 34 12 22 27 25 9	5 5 3 1 13 22 27 25 9	9 10 9 6 15 22 27 25 9	11 13 14 9 17 22 26 25 9	14 18 16 13 19 22 26 25 9	17 22 15 17 20 22 26 25 9	21 25 21 21 23 23 27 25 9	23 31 25 25 25 23 27 25 9	27 34 25 28 27 24 27 25 9
10	30 28 26 25 13 22 26 25 8	33 33 31 28 12 22 27 25 9	36 34 36 31 12 22 27 25 9	3 3 3 34 12 22 27 25 9	5 7 3 1 13 22 27 25 9	9 11 9 6 15 22 27 25 9	11 14 14 9 17 22 26 25 9	14 19 16 13 19 22 26 25 9	17 23 16 17 20 22 26 25 9	21 27 21 21 23 23 27 25 9	23 33 25 25 25 23 27 25 9	27 36 25 28 27 24 27 25 9
11	30 29 26 25 13 22 26 25 8	33 34 31 28 12 22 27 25 9	36 36 1 31 12 22 27 25 9	3 4 3 34 12 22 27 25 9	6 8 3 3 13 22 27 25 9	9 12 9 6 15 22 27 25 9	11 16 14 10 17 22 26 25 9	14 20 16 13 19 22 26 25 9	17 25 16 17 20 22 26 25 9	21 28 21 21 23 23 27 25 9	23 34 25 25 25 23 27 25 9	27 2 25 29 27 24 27 25 9
12	30 31 26 25 13 22 26 25 8	33 36 32 28 12 22 27 25 9	36 1 1 31 12 22 27 25 9	3 6 3 34 12 22 27 25 9	6 9 3 3 13 22 27 25 9	9 13 9 6 15 22 27 25 9	11 17 14 10 17 22 26 25 9	14 21 16 14 19 22 26 25 9	17 26 16 17 21 22 26 25 9	21 29 21 21 23 23 27 25 9	23 35 25 25 25 23 27 25 9	27 3 25 29 27 24 27 25 9
13	30 32 26 25 13 22 26 25 8	33 1 33 28 12 22 27 25 9	36 3 1 31 12 22 27 25 9	3 7 3 34 12 22 27 25 9	6 10 3 3 13 22 27 25 9	9 15 9 6 15 21 27 25 9	11 18 14 10 17 22 26 25 9	14 22 16 14 19 22 26 25 9	17 27 16 17 21 22 26 25 9	21 31 21 21 23 23 27 25 9	23 36 25 25 25 23 27 25 9	27 4 25 29 27 24 27 25 9
14	30 34 28 26 12 22 26 25 8	33 3 33 28 12 22 27 25 9	36 4 1 31 12 22 27 25 9	3 9 3 36 12 22 27 25 9	6 12 3 3 13 22 27 25 9	9 16 9 6 15 21 27 25 9	11 19 14 10 17 22 26 25 9	14 24 16 14 19 22 26 25 9	17 29 16 17 21 22 26 25 9	21 32 21 21 23 23 27 25 9	23 2 27 25 25 23 27 25 9	27 6 25 29 28 24 27 25 9
15	30 35 28 26 12 22 26 25 8	33 4 33 28 12 22 27 25 9	36 5 1 31 12 22 27 25 9	3 9 3 36 13 22 27 25 9	6 13 3 3 15 22 27 25 9	9 18 9 6 15 21 27 25 9	11 21 14 10 17 22 26 25 9	14 25 16 14 19 22 26 25 9	17 30 16 17 21 22 26 25 9	21 34 21 21 23 23 27 25 9	23 3 27 25 25 23 27 25 9	27 7 25 29 28 24 27 25 9
16	30 36 28 26 12 22 26 25 8	33 6 33 28 12 22 27 25 9	36 6 1 31 12 22 27 25 9	3 10 3 36 13 22 27 25 9	6 14 4 3 15 22 27 25 9	9 18 9 7 16 21 27 25 9	12 22 15 10 18 22 27 25 9	15 26 15 14 19 22 26 25 9	17 31 16 17 21 22 26 25 9	21 36 22 22 23 23 27 25 9	23 5 27 27 27 23 27 25 9	27 9 25 29 28 24 27 25 9
17	30 2 28 26 12 22 26 25 8	33 7 33 29 11 23 27 25 9	36 7 3 33 12 22 27 25 9	3 12 3 36 13 22 27 25 9	6 15 4 3 15 22 27 25 9	9 19 9 7 16 21 27 25 9	12 23 15 10 18 22 27 25 9	15 28 15 14 19 22 26 25 9	17 33 17 17 21 22 26 25 9	21 1 22 22 23 23 27 25 9	23 6 27 27 27 23 27 25 9	27 10 25 29 28 24 27 25 9
18	30 3 28 26 12 22 26 25 8	33 8 33 29 11 23 27 25 9	36 9 3 33 12 22 27 25 9	3 13 3 36 13 22 27 25 9	6 16 4 3 15 22 27 25 9	9 21 10 7 16 21 27 25 9	12 24 15 10 18 22 27 25 9	15 29 15 14 19 22 26 25 9	17 35 17 17 21 22 26 25 9	21 3 22 22 23 23 27 25 9	23 7 27 27 27 23 27 25 9	27 11 25 30 28 24 27 25 9
19	30 4 28 26 12 22 26 25 8	34 9 33 29 11 23 27 25 9	36 10 3 33 12 22 27 25 9	3 15 3 36 13 22 27 25 9	6 18 4 3 15 22 27 25 9	9 22 10 7 16 21 27 25 9	12 25 15 11 18 22 27 25 9	15 31 15 14 19 22 26 25 9	17 36 17 17 21 22 26 25 9	21 4 22 22 23 23 27 25 9	23 9 27 27 27 23 27 25 9	27 12 25 30 28 24 27 25 9
20	31 6 28 26 13 22 26 25 8	34 10 33 29 11 22 27 25 9	36 12 3 33 12 22 27 25 9	4 16 3 36 13 22 27 25 9	6 19 4 3 15 22 27 25 9	9 23 10 7 16 21 27 25 9	12 27 15 11 18 22 27 25 9	15 32 15 14 19 22 26 25 9	18 2 17 18 21 22 26 25 9	21 5 22 22 23 23 27 25 9	23 10 27 27 27 23 27 25 9	27 13 25 30 28 24 27 25 9
21	31 7 28 26 13 22 26 25 8	34 11 33 29 11 22 27 25 9	1 12 3 33 12 22 27 25 9	4 17 3 36 13 22 27 25 9	7 20 4 3 15 22 27 25 9	9 25 10 7 16 21 27 25 9	12 28 15 11 18 22 27 25 9	15 34 15 14 20 22 26 25 9	18 3 17 18 21 22 26 25 9	21 7 23 23 23 23 27 25 9	23 11 27 27 27 23 27 25 9	27 15 25 30 28 24 27 25 9
22	31 9 28 26 13 22 27 25 9	34 13 33 29 11 22 27 25 9	1 13 3 33 12 22 27 25 9	4 18 3 36 13 22 27 25 9	7 21 4 4 15 22 27 25 9	10 27 11 7 16 22 27 25 9	12 30 15 11 18 22 27 25 9	15 35 15 15 20 22 26 25 9	18 4 17 18 22 22 26 25 9	21 8 23 23 23 23 27 25 9	25 13 27 27 27 23 27 25 9	28 16 25 30 28 24 28 25 9
23	31 9 28 27 13 22 27 25 9	34 14 34 29 11 22 27 25 9	1 15 3 33 12 22 27 25 9	4 19 3 36 13 22 27 25 9	7 22 4 4 15 22 27 25 9	10 28 11 7 16 22 27 25 9	13 31 15 11 18 22 27 25 9	16 1 14 15 20 22 26 25 9	19 5 17 19 22 22 26 25 9	21 9 23 23 23 23 27 25 9	25 14 27 27 27 23 27 25 9	28 17 25 30 28 24 28 25 9
24	31 10 28 27 12 22 27 25 9	34 15 34 29 11 22 27 25 9	1 16 3 33 12 22 27 25 9	4 21 3 36 13 22 27 25 9	7 24 6 4 15 22 27 25 9	10 29 11 7 16 22 27 25 9	13 33 15 11 18 22 27 25 9	16 2 14 15 20 22 26 25 9	19 7 17 19 22 22 26 25 9	22 10 23 23 23 23 27 25 9	25 15 27 27 27 23 27 25 9	28 18 25 30 28 24 28 25 9
25	31 12 28 27 12 22 27 25 9	34 16 34 29 11 22 27 25 9	1 17 3 33 12 22 27 25 9	4 22 3 36 13 22 27 25 9	7 25 6 4 15 22 27 25 9	10 31 11 9 16 22 27 25 9	13 34 16 11 18 22 27 25 9	16 4 14 15 20 22 26 25 9	19 8 18 19 22 22 26 25 9	22 11 23 23 23 23 27 25 9	25 16 27 27 27 23 27 25 9	28 19 25 30 28 24 28 25 9
26	31 13 28 27 12 22 27 25 9	34 18 34 29 11 22 27 25 9	1 18 3 33 12 22 27 25 9	4 23 3 36 13 22 27 25 9	7 27 6 4 15 22 27 25 9	10 33 11 9 16 22 27 25 9	13 36 16 11 18 22 27 25 9	16 5 14 15 20 22 26 25 9	19 10 18 19 22 22 26 25 9	22 13 23 23 23 23 27 25 9	25 18 27 27 27 23 27 25 9	28 21 25 30 28 24 27 25 9
27	31 15 30 27 12 22 27 25 9	34 19 34 29 11 22 27 25 9	1 19 3 33 12 22 27 25 9	4 24 3 1 13 22 27 25 9	7 28 6 4 15 22 27 25 9	10 34 11 9 16 22 27 25 9	13 1 16 12 18 22 27 25 9	16 7 14 15 20 22 26 25 9	19 11 19 19 22 22 26 25 9	22 14 23 23 23 23 27 25 9	25 19 27 27 27 23 27 25 9	28 22 25 31 29 25 27 25 9
28	31 15 30 27 12 22 27 25 9	34 20 34 29 11 22 27 25 9	1 21 3 33 12 22 27 25 9	4 25 3 1 13 22 27 25 9	7 30 6 4 15 22 27 25 9	10 36 12 9 16 22 27 25 9	13 3 16 12 18 22 27 25 9	16 8 14 15 20 22 26 25 9	19 12 19 19 22 22 26 25 9	22 15 23 23 23 23 27 25 9	25 20 27 27 27 23 27 25 9	28 23 25 31 28 25 27 25 9
29	31 16 30 27 12 22 27 25 9		1 22 3 33 12 22 27 25 9	4 27 3 1 13 22 27 25 9	7 31 6 4 15 22 27 25 9	10 1 12 9 16 22 27 25 9	13 4 16 12 18 22 27 25 9	16 9 14 16 20 22 26 25 9	19 13 19 19 22 22 26 25 9	22 16 23 23 23 23 27 25 9	25 21 27 27 27 23 27 25 9	28 24 25 31 28 25 27 25 9
30	31 18 30 27 12 22 27 25 9	**1899**	1 24 3 33 12 22 27 25 9	4 28 3 1 13 22 27 25 9	7 33 6 5 15 22 27 25 9	10 2 12 9 16 22 27 25 9	13 6 16 12 18 22 27 25 9	16 10 14 16 20 22 26 25 9	19 14 19 19 22 22 26 25 9	22 18 23 23 23 23 27 25 9	25 22 27 27 27 23 27 25 9	28 25 27 31 28 25 27 25 9
31	31 19 30 27 12 22 27 25 9		1 25 3 33 12 22 27 25 9		7 34 6 5 15 22 27 25 9		13 7 16 12 18 22 27 25 9	16 12 14 16 20 22 26 25 9		22 19 23 23 23 23 27 25 9		28 27 27 31 28 25 27 25 9

	JAN	FEB	MAR	APR	MAY	JUNE	JULY	AUG	SEPT	OCT	NOV	DEC
1	29 29 27 31 29 25 27 25 9	31 34 31 34 31 25 27 25 9	34 34 36 3 34 25 28 25 9	2 4 36 6 36 26 29 26 9	4 7 3 9 3 25 28 25 9	7 13 7 12 4 25 28 25 9	11 16 13 11 7 25 28 25 9	13 20 13 10 9 25 27 25 9	16 25 15 12 10 25 27 25 9	19 28 21 15 13 25 27 25 9	22 33 25 19 15 26 28 26 9	26 1 24 22 16 26 28 26 9
2	29 30 27 31 29 25 27 25 9	31 36 31 34 31 25 27 25 9	34 36 36 3 34 25 27 25 9	2 6 36 6 36 26 29 26 9	4 9 3 9 3 25 28 25 9	7 14 7 12 4 25 28 25 9	11 17 13 11 7 25 28 25 9	13 21 13 10 9 25 27 25 9	16 26 15 12 10 25 27 25 9	19 29 21 15 13 25 27 25 9	22 34 25 19 15 26 28 26 9	26 2 24 22 16 26 28 26 9
3	29 31 27 31 29 25 27 25 9	31 1 31 36 31 25 28 25 9	34 1 1 3 34 25 27 25 9	2 7 36 6 36 26 29 26 9	4 10 3 9 3 25 28 25 9	7 15 7 12 4 25 28 25 9	11 18 13 11 7 25 28 25 9	13 22 13 10 9 25 27 25 9	16 26 16 12 10 25 27 25 9	19 31 21 15 13 25 27 25 9	23 36 25 19 15 26 28 26 9	26 4 24 22 16 26 28 26 9
4	29 33 27 31 29 25 27 25 9	31 2 31 36 31 25 27 25 9	34 3 1 3 34 25 27 25 9	2 8 36 6 36 26 28 26 9	4 12 3 9 3 25 28 25 9	7 16 9 12 6 25 28 25 9	11 19 13 11 7 25 28 25 9	13 24 13 10 9 25 27 25 9	16 28 16 12 10 25 27 25 9	19 32 21 15 13 25 27 25 9	23 1 25 19 15 26 28 26 9	26 6 24 22 16 26 28 26 9
5	29 34 27 31 29 25 27 25 9	31 4 31 36 31 25 27 25 9	34 4 1 3 34 25 27 25 9	2 10 36 6 1 26 28 26 9	5 13 3 9 3 25 28 25 9	8 18 9 12 6 25 28 25 9	11 21 13 11 7 25 28 25 9	13 25 13 10 9 25 27 25 9	16 30 16 12 10 25 27 25 9	19 33 21 15 13 25 27 25 9	23 3 25 19 15 26 28 26 9	26 7 24 22 16 26 28 26 9
6	29 36 27 31 29 25 27 25 9	31 5 31 36 31 25 27 25 9	36 6 1 3 34 25 27 25 9	2 11 36 7 1 26 28 26 9	5 14 3 10 3 25 28 25 9	8 19 9 12 6 25 28 25 9	11 22 13 11 7 25 28 25 9	13 27 13 10 9 25 27 25 9	16 31 16 12 10 25 27 25 9	19 35 21 15 13 25 27 25 9	24 4 25 19 15 26 28 26 9	26 8 24 22 16 26 28 26 9
7	29 1 27 31 29 25 27 25 9	31 6 31 36 31 25 27 25 9	36 7 1 3 34 25 27 25 9	2 12 36 7 1 26 28 26 9	5 15 3 10 3 25 28 25 9	9 20 9 12 6 25 28 25 9	11 23 13 11 7 25 28 25 9	14 27 13 10 9 25 27 25 9	16 33 16 12 10 25 27 25 9	19 36 21 15 13 25 27 25 9	24 6 25 19 15 26 28 26 9	26 9 24 22 16 26 28 26 9
8	29 2 27 32 29 25 26 25 8	31 7 31 36 31 25 27 25 9	36 9 1 3 34 25 27 25 9	2 13 36 7 1 26 28 26 9	5 16 3 10 3 25 28 25 9	9 21 10 12 6 25 28 25 9	11 24 13 11 7 25 28 25 9	14 29 13 10 9 25 27 25 9	16 34 16 12 10 25 27 25 9	19 2 21 15 13 25 27 25 9	24 8 25 19 15 26 28 26 9	26 10 24 22 16 26 28 26 9
9	29 4 27 32 29 25 27 25 9	31 9 31 36 31 25 27 25 9	36 10 1 3 34 25 27 25 9	2 14 36 8 1 26 28 26 9	5 18 3 10 3 25 28 25 9	9 22 10 12 6 25 28 25 9	11 25 13 11 7 25 28 25 9	14 30 13 10 9 25 27 25 9	16 36 16 13 10 25 27 25 9	19 3 22 16 13 25 27 25 9	24 9 25 19 15 25 28 25 9	26 12 24 22 16 26 28 26 9
10	30 6 27 33 30 25 27 25 9	31 10 31 36 31 25 27 25 9	36 11 1 3 34 25 27 25 9	3 16 36 8 1 26 28 26 9	5 19 3 10 3 25 28 25 9	9 24 10 12 6 25 28 25 9	11 27 13 11 7 25 28 25 9	14 31 13 10 9 25 27 25 9	17 1 16 13 11 25 27 25 9	19 4 22 16 13 25 27 25 9	24 10 25 19 15 25 28 25 9	26 13 24 22 16 26 28 26 9
11	30 7 28 33 30 25 27 25 9	31 12 31 1 31 25 28 25 9	36 12 1 4 34 25 27 25 9	3 17 36 8 1 26 28 26 9	6 20 4 10 3 25 28 25 9	9 25 10 12 6 25 28 25 9	11 28 13 11 7 25 28 25 9	14 33 13 11 9 25 27 25 9	17 2 16 13 11 25 27 25 9	20 6 22 16 13 25 27 25 9	24 12 25 19 15 25 28 25 9	26 15 24 23 16 26 28 26 9
12	30 8 28 33 30 25 27 25 9	33 13 33 1 33 25 28 25 9	36 13 1 4 34 25 28 25 9	3 18 36 8 1 26 28 26 9	6 21 4 10 3 25 28 25 9	9 25 10 12 6 25 28 25 9	11 29 13 11 7 25 28 25 9	14 35 13 11 9 25 27 25 9	18 4 17 13 12 25 27 25 9	20 7 22 16 13 25 27 25 9	24 13 25 19 15 25 27 25 9	26 16 24 23 16 26 28 26 9
13	30 9 28 33 30 25 28 25 9	33 14 33 1 33 25 28 25 9	36 15 1 4 34 25 28 25 9	3 19 36 7 1 25 28 25 9	6 22 4 10 3 25 28 25 9	9 27 10 12 6 25 28 25 9	11 31 13 11 7 25 28 25 9	15 36 13 11 9 25 27 25 9	18 6 18 13 12 25 27 25 9	20 9 22 16 13 25 27 25 9	24 14 25 19 15 25 27 25 9	26 17 25 23 16 26 28 26 9
14	30 10 28 33 30 25 27 25 9	33 15 34 1 33 25 28 25 9	36 16 1 4 34 25 28 25 9	3 21 36 7 1 25 28 25 9	6 24 4 10 3 25 28 25 9	9 28 10 12 6 25 28 25 9	11 33 13 11 7 24 28 25 9	15 2 13 11 9 25 27 25 9	18 7 18 13 12 25 27 25 9	20 10 22 16 13 25 27 25 9	24 15 25 20 15 26 27 26 9	26 18 25 23 16 26 28 26 9
15	30 12 28 33 30 25 27 25 9	33 16 34 1 33 25 28 25 9	36 17 2 5 35 26 28 26 9	3 22 36 7 1 25 28 25 9	6 25 4 10 3 25 28 25 9	9 30 10 12 6 25 28 25 9	12 34 13 11 7 24 28 25 9	15 3 13 11 9 25 27 25 9	18 9 18 13 12 25 27 25 9	21 12 22 16 13 25 27 25 9	24 17 24 20 15 26 27 26 9	27 20 26 24 17 27 29 26 9
16	30 13 29 33 30 25 27 25 9	33 18 34 1 33 25 28 25 9	36 18 2 5 35 26 28 26 9	3 23 36 7 1 25 28 25 9	6 27 4 10 3 25 28 25 9	9 31 11 12 6 25 28 25 9	12 36 13 11 7 24 28 25 9	15 5 13 11 9 25 27 25 9	18 10 18 13 12 25 27 25 9	21 13 22 16 13 25 27 25 9	24 18 24 20 15 26 27 26 9	27 21 26 24 17 27 29 26 9
17	30 15 29 33 30 25 27 25 9	33 19 34 1 33 25 28 25 9	36 20 2 5 35 26 28 26 9	3 24 1 7 1 25 28 25 9	6 28 4 10 4 25 28 25 9	9 33 12 12 6 25 28 25 9	12 1 13 11 7 24 28 25 9	15 6 13 11 9 25 27 25 9	18 11 18 13 12 25 27 25 9	21 14 22 16 13 25 27 25 9	24 19 24 20 15 26 28 26 10	27 22 26 24 17 27 29 26 9
18	30 15 29 33 30 25 27 25 9	33 20 34 1 33 25 28 25 9	36 21 2 5 35 26 28 26 9	3 25 1 7 1 25 28 25 9	6 29 4 10 4 25 28 25 9	9 34 12 12 6 25 28 25 9	12 2 13 11 7 24 28 25 9	15 7 13 11 9 25 27 25 9	18 12 18 13 12 25 27 25 9	21 16 22 16 13 25 27 25 9	24 20 24 20 15 26 27 26 9	27 24 26 24 17 27 29 26 9
19	30 16 29 33 30 25 27 25 9	34 21 34 1 33 25 28 25 9	36 22 2 5 35 26 28 26 9	3 27 1 7 1 25 28 25 9	6 30 4 10 4 25 28 25 9	9 36 12 12 6 25 28 25 9	12 4 13 10 7 24 27 25 9	15 9 13 11 9 25 27 25 9	18 13 19 13 12 25 27 25 9	21 16 22 16 13 25 27 25 9	24 21 24 20 15 26 27 26 9	27 24 26 24 17 27 29 26 9
20	31 18 29 34 31 25 27 25 9	34 22 34 1 33 25 28 25 9	36 23 2 5 35 26 28 26 9	3 28 1 7 1 25 28 25 9	6 31 4 10 4 25 28 25 9	9 1 12 12 6 25 28 25 9	12 5 13 10 7 24 27 25 9	15 10 13 11 10 25 27 25 9	18 15 19 13 12 25 27 25 9	21 18 23 17 14 26 27 26 9	24 22 24 20 15 26 27 26 9	27 26 26 24 17 27 29 26 9
21	31 19 29 34 31 25 27 25 9	34 24 34 1 33 25 27 25 9	1 24 2 5 35 26 28 26 9	4 29 1 7 1 25 28 25 9	6 33 5 11 4 25 28 25 9	9 3 12 12 6 25 28 25 9	12 6 13 10 7 24 27 25 9	15 11 13 11 10 25 27 25 9	18 16 19 13 12 25 27 25 9	21 19 23 17 14 26 27 26 9	24 24 24 20 15 26 27 26 9	27 27 26 24 17 27 29 26 9
22	31 20 30 34 31 25 27 25 9	34 25 34 1 33 25 27 25 9	1 26 2 5 35 26 28 26 9	4 31 1 7 1 25 28 25 9	7 34 6 12 4 25 28 25 9	10 4 12 12 6 25 28 25 9	12 7 13 10 7 25 27 25 9	15 12 13 11 10 25 27 25 9	18 17 19 13 12 25 27 25 9	21 20 23 17 14 26 27 26 9	24 25 24 20 15 26 27 26 9	29 29 26 24 17 27 29 26 9
23	31 21 30 34 31 25 27 25 9	34 26 34 1 33 25 27 25 9	1 27 2 5 35 26 28 26 9	4 32 1 9 1 25 28 25 9	7 36 6 12 4 25 28 25 9	10 6 12 12 6 25 28 25 9	13 9 13 10 9 25 27 25 9	15 13 14 11 10 25 27 25 9	18 18 19 13 12 25 27 25 9	21 21 23 17 14 26 27 26 9	25 26 24 21 16 26 28 26 9	29 30 26 25 17 27 29 26 9
24	31 22 30 34 31 25 27 25 9	34 27 34 1 33 25 27 25 9	1 28 2 5 35 26 28 26 9	4 33 1 9 1 25 28 25 9	7 1 6 12 4 25 28 25 9	10 7 12 12 6 25 28 25 9	13 10 13 10 9 25 27 25 9	16 15 14 11 10 25 27 25 9	19 19 19 14 13 25 27 25 9	22 23 23 17 14 26 28 26 10	25 27 24 21 16 26 28 26 9	29 31 26 25 17 27 29 26 9
25	31 24 30 34 31 25 27 25 9	34 29 36 1 33 25 27 25 9	1 30 1 5 35 26 28 26 9	4 34 1 9 1 25 28 25 9	7 3 6 12 4 25 28 25 9	10 8 12 12 6 25 28 25 9	13 11 13 10 9 25 27 25 9	16 16 14 11 10 25 27 25 9	19 20 19 14 13 25 27 25 9	22 24 23 17 14 26 28 26 10	25 28 24 21 16 26 28 26 9	29 33 27 26 17 27 29 26 9
26	31 25 30 34 31 25 27 25 9	34 30 36 1 33 25 27 25 9	2 32 1 5 35 26 29 26 9	4 36 3 9 3 25 28 25 9	7 4 7 12 4 25 28 25 9	10 9 12 12 6 25 28 25 9	13 13 13 10 9 25 27 25 9	16 18 14 11 10 25 27 25 9	19 22 19 14 13 25 27 25 9	22 26 24 18 14 26 28 26 10	25 30 24 21 16 26 28 26 9	29 35 27 26 17 27 29 26 9
27	31 27 30 34 31 25 27 25 9	34 31 36 1 33 25 27 25 9	2 33 1 6 36 26 29 26 9	4 3 3 9 3 25 28 25 9	7 6 7 12 4 25 28 25 9	10 10 13 12 7 25 28 25 9	13 15 13 10 9 25 27 25 9	16 19 14 11 10 25 27 25 9	19 23 19 14 13 25 27 25 9	22 27 24 18 14 26 28 26 10	25 31 24 22 16 26 28 26 9	29 35 27 26 17 27 29 26 9
28	31 28 30 34 31 25 27 25 9	34 33 36 1 33 25 27 25 9	2 35 1 6 36 26 29 26 9	4 3 3 9 3 25 28 25 9	7 7 7 12 4 25 28 25 9	10 12 13 12 7 25 28 25 9	13 15 13 10 9 25 27 25 9	16 20 15 12 10 25 27 25 9	19 24 20 14 13 25 27 25 9	22 28 24 18 14 26 28 26 10	25 33 24 22 16 26 28 25 9	29 36 27 26 17 27 29 26 9
29	31 29 21 34 31 25 27 25 9	1900	2 36 36 6 36 26 29 26 9	4 5 3 9 3 25 28 25 9	7 9 7 12 4 25 28 25 9	10 13 13 12 7 25 28 25 9	13 16 13 10 9 25 27 25 9	16 21 15 12 10 25 27 25 9	19 25 20 15 13 25 27 25 9	22 29 24 18 14 26 28 26 10	25 34 24 22 16 26 28 25 9	29 2 27 26 17 27 29 26 9
30	31 31 31 34 31 25 27 25 9		2 2 36 6 36 26 29 26 9	4 6 3 9 3 25 28 25 9	7 10 7 12 4 25 28 25 9	10 14 13 12 7 25 28 25 9	13 18 13 10 9 25 27 25 9	16 22 15 12 10 25 27 25 9	19 27 20 15 13 25 27 25 9	22 30 24 18 14 26 28 26 10	25 36 24 22 16 26 28 25 9	29 3 27 26 17 27 29 26 9
31	31 33 31 34 31 25 27 25 9		2 3 36 6 36 26 29 26 9		7 12 7 12 4 25 28 25 9		13 19 13 10 9 25 27 25 9	16 24 15 12 10 25 27 25 9		22 31 24 18 14 26 28 26 10		29 5 27 26 17 27 29 26 9

	JAN	FEB	MAR	APR	MAY	JUNE
1	29 6 27 26 17 27 29 26 9	32 11 33 30 17 29 29 26 9	35 12 36 33 15 29 29 26 9	2 17 35 1 15 29 29 26 9	5 20 3 5 15 29 29 26 9	8 25 11 9 17 29 29 26 9
2	29 8 27 26 17 27 29 26 9	32 13 33 30 17 29 29 26 9	35 13 36 33 15 29 29 26 9	2 18 35 1 15 29 29 26 9	5 21 3 5 15 29 29 26 9	8 26 11 9 17 29 29 26 9
3	29 9 29 26 17 27 29 26 9	32 14 33 30 17 29 29 26 9	35 15 36 33 15 29 29 26 9	2 19 35 2 15 29 29 26 9	5 22 3 5 15 29 29 26 9	8 27 11 9 17 29 29 26 9
4	29 11 29 26 17 27 29 26 9	32 15 33 30 17 29 29 26 9	35 16 36 33 15 29 29 26 9	2 20 35 2 15 29 29 26 9	5 24 4 5 15 29 29 26 9	8 28 11 9 17 29 29 26 9
5	29 12 29 26 17 27 29 26 9	32 17 33 30 17 29 29 26 9	35 17 35 33 15 29 29 26 9	2 22 35 2 15 29 29 26 9	5 25 4 5 15 29 29 26 9	8 29 11 9 17 29 29 26 9
6	29 13 29 26 17 27 29 26 9	32 18 33 30 17 29 29 26 9	35 18 35 33 15 29 29 26 9	2 23 35 2 15 29 29 26 9	5 26 5 5 15 29 29 26 9	8 31 11 9 17 29 29 26 9
7	29 15 29 26 17 27 29 26 9	32 19 34 30 16 28 28 26 9	35 20 35 33 15 29 29 26 9	2 24 35 2 14 29 29 26 9	5 27 5 5 15 29 29 26 9	8 32 11 9 17 29 29 26 9
8	29 16 29 26 17 27 29 26 9	33 20 34 30 16 28 28 26 9	35 21 35 33 15 29 29 26 9	2 25 35 2 14 29 29 26 9	5 29 5 5 15 29 29 26 9	8 33 11 9 17 29 29 26 9
9	29 17 29 26 17 27 29 26 9	33 21 34 31 16 28 28 26 9	35 22 35 33 15 29 29 26 9	2 27 35 2 14 29 29 26 9	5 30 5 5 15 29 29 26 9	8 35 11 9 17 29 29 26 9
10	29 18 29 27 17 27 29 26 9	33 22 34 31 16 28 28 26 9	35 23 35 35 15 29 29 26 9	2 28 36 2 14 29 29 26 9	5 31 5 5 15 29 29 26 9	8 36 11 9 17 29 29 26 9
11	29 20 29 27 17 27 29 26 9	33 24 34 31 16 28 28 26 9	35 24 35 35 15 29 29 26 9	2 29 36 2 14 29 29 26 9	5 33 5 5 16 29 29 26 9	8 2 11 10 17 29 29 26 9
12	29 21 29 27 17 27 29 26 9	33 25 34 31 16 28 28 26 9	36 26 35 35 15 29 29 26 9	2 30 36 2 14 29 29 26 9	5 34 5 5 16 29 29 26 9	8 3 11 10 17 29 29 26 9
13	29 22 29 27 17 27 29 26 9	33 26 34 31 16 28 28 26 9	36 27 35 35 15 29 29 26 9	2 31 36 2 14 29 29 26 9	5 35 5 5 16 29 29 26 9	8 5 11 10 17 29 29 26 9
14	30 23 30 27 17 27 29 26 9	33 27 34 31 16 28 28 26 9	36 29 35 35 15 29 29 26 9	2 32 36 2 14 29 29 26 9	5 1 5 5 16 29 29 26 9	8 6 11 11 17 29 29 26 9
15	30 24 30 27 17 27 29 26 9	33 28 34 31 16 28 28 26 9	36 29 35 35 15 29 29 26 9	2 35 36 2 14 29 29 26 9	5 2 5 5 16 29 29 26 9	9 8 11 11 17 29 29 26 9
16	30 25 30 27 17 27 29 26 9	33 30 34 31 16 28 28 26 9	36 31 35 35 15 29 29 26 9	2 36 1 2 14 29 29 26 9	5 4 7 7 16 29 29 26 9	9 9 11 11 17 29 29 26 9
17	30 26 30 27 17 27 29 26 9	33 31 35 31 16 28 28 26 9	36 33 35 35 15 29 29 26 9	3 1 1 3 15 29 29 26 9	6 5 7 7 16 29 29 26 9	9 11 11 11 17 29 29 26 9
18	30 29 30 29 17 29 29 26 9	33 33 36 32 16 28 28 26 9	36 33 35 35 15 29 29 26 9	3 2 1 3 15 29 29 26 9	6 7 7 7 16 29 29 26 9	9 12 11 11 17 29 29 26 9
19	30 29 30 29 17 29 29 26 9	34 34 36 32 16 28 28 27 9	36 35 35 36 15 29 29 26 9	3 5 1 3 15 29 29 26 9	6 8 7 7 16 29 29 26 9	9 13 11 11 17 29 29 26 9
20	30 30 30 29 17 29 29 26 9	34 36 36 32 16 28 28 27 9	36 36 35 36 15 29 29 26 9	3 6 1 3 15 29 29 26 9	6 10 7 7 16 29 29 26 9	9 14 11 11 17 29 29 26 9
21	31 32 31 29 17 29 29 26 9	34 1 36 32 16 28 28 27 9	1 2 35 36 15 29 29 26 9	4 7 2 3 15 29 29 26 9	6 11 7 7 16 29 29 26 9	9 16 11 11 17 29 29 26 9
22	31 33 31 29 17 29 29 26 9	34 3 36 32 16 28 28 27 9	1 3 35 36 15 29 29 26 9	4 9 2 3 15 29 29 26 9	8 12 8 8 17 29 29 26 9	10 17 11 11 17 28 29 26 9
23	31 35 31 29 17 29 29 26 9	34 4 36 33 16 28 28 27 9	1 5 35 36 15 29 29 26 9	4 10 2 4 15 29 29 26 9	8 13 8 8 17 29 29 26 9	10 18 11 11 17 28 29 26 9
24	32 36 32 29 17 29 29 26 9	34 6 36 33 16 28 28 27 9	1 6 35 36 15 29 29 26 9	4 11 2 4 15 29 29 26 9	8 15 8 8 17 29 29 26 9	10 19 11 11 17 28 29 26 9
25	32 3 32 29 17 29 29 26 9	34 7 36 33 16 28 28 27 9	1 8 35 36 15 29 29 26 9	4 13 2 4 15 29 29 26 9	8 17 8 8 17 29 29 26 9	10 20 11 11 17 28 29 26 9
26	32 3 32 29 17 29 29 26 9	34 8 36 33 16 28 28 27 9	1 9 35 36 15 29 29 26 9	5 15 2 5 15 29 29 26 9	8 17 8 8 17 29 29 26 9	10 22 11 11 17 28 29 26 9
27	32 5 32 29 17 29 29 26 9	34 10 36 33 16 28 28 27 9	1 11 35 36 15 29 29 26 9	5 15 2 5 15 29 29 26 9	8 19 8 8 17 29 29 26 9	10 23 11 11 17 28 29 26 9
28	32 6 32 29 17 29 29 26 9	34 10 36 33 16 28 28 27 9	1 12 35 36 15 29 29 26 9	5 17 2 5 15 29 29 26 9	8 20 8 8 17 29 29 26 9	11 24 12 12 18 29 29 26 9
29	32 7 32 29 17 29 29 26 9		2 13 35 36 15 29 29 26 9	5 18 2 5 15 29 29 26 9	8 21 9 8 17 29 29 26 9	11 26 12 12 18 29 29 26 9
30	32 8 32 29 17 29 29 26 9	**1901**	2 15 35 1 15 29 29 26 9	5 19 2 5 15 29 29 26 9	8 23 9 8 17 29 29 26 9	11 27 12 12 18 29 29 26 9
31	32 11 32 29 17 29 29 26 9		2 16 35 1 15 29 29 26 9		8 23 9 8 17 29 29 26 9	

	JULY	AUG	SEPT	OCT	NOV	DEC
1	11 29 12 12 18 29 29 26 9	14 33 11 17 20 29 29 26 9	16 2 17 19 22 28 28 25 10	19 6 22 24 24 28 28 25 10	23 11 23 21 26 29 29 26 10	26 15 24 30 29 29 29 26 10
2	11 29 12 12 18 29 29 26 9	14 33 12 17 20 29 29 26 10	16 4 17 19 22 28 28 25 10	19 7 22 24 24 28 28 25 10	23 13 23 27 26 29 29 26 10	26 16 24 30 29 29 29 26 10
3	11 31 12 12 18 29 29 26 9	14 36 12 17 20 29 29 26 10	16 5 17 19 22 28 28 25 10	19 9 22 24 24 28 28 25 10	23 14 23 27 26 29 29 26 10	26 17 24 30 29 29 29 26 10
4	11 32 12 12 18 29 29 26 9	14 1 12 17 20 29 29 26 10	16 6 17 19 22 28 28 25 10	19 10 22 24 24 28 28 25 10	23 15 23 27 26 29 29 26 10	26 19 24 30 29 29 29 26 10
5	11 33 12 13 18 29 29 26 9	14 2 12 17 20 29 29 26 10	16 7 17 20 22 28 28 25 10	19 12 22 24 24 28 28 25 10	23 17 23 27 26 29 29 26 10	26 20 24 30 29 29 29 26 10
6	11 34 12 13 18 29 29 26 9	14 4 12 17 20 28 29 26 10	16 9 17 20 22 28 28 25 10	19 13 22 24 24 28 28 25 10	23 18 23 27 26 29 29 26 10	26 21 25 31 29 29 29 26 10
7	11 36 12 13 18 29 29 26 9	14 5 12 17 20 28 29 26 10	16 10 18 20 22 28 28 25 10	19 15 22 24 24 28 28 25 10	23 19 23 27 26 29 29 26 10	26 22 25 31 29 29 29 26 10
8	11 2 12 13 18 29 29 26 9	14 7 12 17 20 28 29 26 10	16 12 18 20 22 28 28 25 10	19 15 22 24 24 28 28 25 10	23 20 23 29 26 29 29 26 10	26 23 25 31 29 29 29 26 10
9	11 3 12 14 18 29 29 26 9	14 8 12 17 20 28 29 26 10	16 13 18 20 22 28 28 25 10	19 16 22 24 24 28 28 25 10	23 21 23 29 26 29 29 26 10	26 25 25 31 29 29 29 26 10
10	11 5 12 14 18 29 29 26 9	14 10 13 17 20 28 29 26 10	16 15 18 20 22 28 28 26 10	19 18 22 24 24 28 28 25 10	23 22 23 29 26 29 29 26 10	26 26 25 31 29 29 29 26 10
11	11 6 11 14 18 29 29 26 9	14 11 13 17 20 28 29 26 10	17 16 19 21 22 28 28 26 10	19 19 22 24 24 28 28 25 10	23 23 23 29 26 29 29 26 10	26 27 25 31 29 29 29 26 10
12	11 7 11 14 18 29 29 26 9	14 12 13 17 20 28 29 26 10	17 17 19 21 22 28 28 26 10	19 21 22 24 24 28 28 25 10	24 25 23 29 26 29 29 26 10	26 28 26 32 29 29 29 26 10
13	11 8 11 14 18 29 29 26 9	14 14 14 17 20 28 29 26 10	17 18 19 21 22 28 28 26 10	19 22 22 24 24 28 28 25 10	24 26 23 29 26 29 29 26 10	26 29 26 32 29 29 29 26 10
14	11 10 11 14 19 28 29 26 9	14 15 14 17 20 28 29 26 10	17 19 19 21 22 28 28 26 10	21 23 22 24 24 28 28 26 10	24 27 23 29 26 29 29 26 10	26 31 26 32 29 29 29 26 10
15	11 11 11 14 19 28 29 26 9	14 16 14 17 20 28 29 26 10	17 21 19 21 22 28 28 26 10	21 24 22 25 25 28 28 26 10	24 29 23 29 26 29 29 26 10	26 32 26 32 29 29 29 26 10
16	12 13 11 14 19 28 29 26 9	15 17 14 17 21 28 29 26 10	17 22 20 22 23 28 29 26 10	21 25 22 25 25 28 28 26 10	24 30 23 29 26 29 29 26 10	26 33 26 32 29 29 29 26 10
17	12 14 11 14 19 28 29 26 9	15 19 14 18 21 28 29 26 10	18 23 20 22 23 28 29 26 10	21 26 22 25 25 28 28 25 10	24 31 23 29 28 29 29 26 10	26 35 26 32 29 29 29 26 10
18	12 15 11 14 19 28 29 26 9	15 20 14 18 21 28 29 26 10	18 24 20 22 23 28 29 26 10	21 28 22 25 25 28 28 25 10	24 32 23 29 28 29 29 26 10	26 36 26 32 29 29 29 26 9
19	12 17 11 14 19 28 29 26 9	15 21 15 18 21 28 29 26 10	18 26 20 22 23 28 29 26 10	21 28 23 25 25 28 28 25 10	24 33 23 29 28 29 29 26 10	27 1 26 32 29 29 29 26 9
20	12 18 11 14 19 28 29 26 9	15 22 15 18 21 28 29 26 10	18 27 20 22 23 28 29 26 10	21 30 23 25 25 28 28 25 10	24 35 23 29 28 29 29 26 10	27 2 26 32 29 29 29 26 9
21	12 19 11 14 19 28 29 26 9	15 24 15 18 21 28 29 26 10	18 29 20 23 23 29 29 26 10	21 31 23 25 25 28 28 25 10	24 36 23 29 28 29 29 26 10	27 4 26 32 29 29 29 26 9
22	12 20 11 15 20 29 29 26 10	15 25 15 18 21 28 29 26 10	18 30 20 23 23 28 29 26 10	21 33 23 26 26 28 28 26 10	24 2 23 29 28 29 29 26 10	27 5 26 32 29 29 29 26 9
23	12 22 11 15 20 29 29 26 10	15 26 15 18 21 28 29 26 10	18 30 20 23 23 28 29 26 10	21 34 23 26 26 28 28 26 10	35 3 23 29 28 29 29 26 10	28 7 26 32 29 29 29 26 9
24	14 23 11 15 20 29 29 26 10	16 27 16 19 22 28 29 26 10	19 32 20 23 23 28 29 26 10	22 36 23 26 26 28 28 26 10	25 5 23 29 28 29 29 26 10	28 8 28 32 29 29 29 26 10
25	14 24 11 15 20 29 29 26 10	16 29 16 19 22 28 29 26 10	19 33 21 23 23 28 28 26 10	22 1 23 26 26 28 28 26 10	25 6 23 29 28 29 29 26 10	28 10 28 32 29 29 29 26 10
26	14 25 11 15 20 29 29 26 10	16 30 16 19 22 28 29 26 10	19 35 21 23 23 28 28 26 10	22 2 23 26 26 28 28 26 10	25 8 23 29 28 29 29 26 10	28 11 28 32 29 29 29 26 9
27	14 26 11 16 20 29 29 26 10	16 31 16 19 22 28 29 26 10	19 36 21 23 23 28 28 26 10	22 4 23 26 26 28 28 26 10	25 9 23 29 28 29 29 26 10	28 13 28 32 29 29 29 26 9
28	14 28 11 16 20 29 29 26 10	16 32 16 20 22 28 29 26 10	19 1 21 23 23 28 28 26 10	22 5 23 26 26 28 28 26 10	25 11 23 29 28 29 29 26 10	23 14 28 32 29 29 29 26 9
29	14 29 11 16 20 29 29 26 10	16 34 16 20 22 28 29 26 10	19 3 21 23 23 28 28 26 10	22 8 23 26 26 28 28 26 10	25 12 23 29 28 29 29 26 10	28 16 28 32 29 29 29 26 9
30	14 30 11 16 20 29 29 26 10	16 35 16 20 22 28 29 26 10	19 4 21 23 23 28 28 26 10	22 8 23 26 26 28 28 26 10	26 13 23 29 28 29 29 26 10	28 17 28 32 29 29 29 26 9
31	14 31 11 16 20 29 29 26 10	16 1 16 20 22 28 29 26 10		22 10 23 26 26 28 28 26 10		28 18 28 32 29 29 29 26 9

	JAN	FEB	MAR	APR	MAY	JUNE	JULY	AUG	SEPT	OCT	NOV	DEC
1	30 19 28 33 30 30 30 27 9	32 24 33 33 33 30 30 26 9	34 25 32 32 35 31 30 26 9	2 29 36 33 2 32 30 27 9	5 32 5 36 5 32 30 26 9	8 1 10 4 6 32 30 26 10	10 5 10 7 8 32 30 26 10	14 10 12 10 10 32 30 26 10	16 16 18 14 12 31 30 26 10	19 19 22 18 14 31 30 26 10	22 24 21 22 16 31 30 27 10	26 27 26 26 18 32 30 27 10
2	30 21 30 33 31 30 30 27 9	32 25 33 33 33 30 30 26 9	34 26 32 32 35 31 30 26 9	2 30 36 33 2 32 30 27 9	5 33 5 36 5 32 30 26 9	8 3 9 3 6 32 30 26 9	10 6 10 7 8 32 30 26 10	14 12 12 10 10 32 30 26 10	16 17 18 14 12 31 30 26 10	19 21 22 18 14 31 30 26 10	22 25 21 22 16 31 30 27 10	26 28 26 26 18 32 30 27 10
3	30 22 30 33 31 30 30 27 9	32 26 33 33 33 30 30 26 9	34 26 32 32 35 31 30 26 9	2 31 36 33 2 32 30 27 9	5 35 6 36 5 32 30 26 9	8 4 10 4 6 32 30 26 10	10 8 10 7 8 32 30 26 10	14 13 13 10 10 32 30 26 10	17 18 18 14 12 31 30 26 10	19 22 22 18 14 31 30 26 10	22 27 21 22 16 31 30 27 10	26 30 26 26 18 32 30 27 10
4	30 24 30 33 31 30 30 27 9	32 27 33 33 33 30 30 26 9	35 28 32 32 35 31 30 26 9	2 33 36 33 2 32 30 27 9	5 36 6 36 5 32 30 26 9	8 6 10 4 6 32 30 26 10	11 9 10 7 8 32 30 26 10	14 14 14 10 10 32 30 26 10	17 19 19 14 13 31 30 26 10	19 23 22 18 14 31 30 26 9	22 27 21 22 16 31 30 27 10	26 31 26 26 18 32 30 27 10
5	30 24 30 33 31 30 30 27 9	32 28 33 33 33 30 30 26 9	35 30 32 32 35 31 30 26 9	2 34 36 34 2 32 30 26 9	5 2 6 36 5 32 30 26 9	8 7 10 4 6 32 30 26 10	11 11 10 7 8 32 30 26 10	14 16 14 10 10 32 30 26 10	17 21 19 14 13 31 30 26 10	19 24 22 18 14 31 30 26 9	22 28 21 22 16 31 30 27 10	26 32 26 26 18 32 30 27 10
6	30 25 30 33 31 30 30 27 9	32 30 33 33 33 30 30 26 9	35 31 32 32 35 31 30 26 9	2 36 36 34 2 32 30 26 9	5 3 6 36 5 32 30 26 9	8 8 10 4 6 32 30 26 10	11 12 10 7 8 32 30 26 10	14 17 14 10 10 32 30 26 10	17 22 19 14 13 31 30 26 10	19 25 22 18 14 31 30 26 9	22 30 21 22 16 31 30 27 10	26 33 26 26 18 32 30 27 10
7	30 27 30 33 31 30 30 26 9	32 31 33 33 33 31 30 27 9	35 32 32 32 35 31 30 26 9	2 1 36 34 2 32 30 26 9	5 5 7 1 5 32 30 26 9	8 10 10 4 6 32 30 26 10	11 14 10 7 8 32 30 26 10	14 19 14 10 10 32 30 26 10	17 23 19 14 13 31 30 26 10	19 26 22 19 14 31 29 26 10	22 31 21 22 16 31 30 27 10	27 34 27 27 18 32 30 27 10
8	30 28 30 33 31 30 30 26 9	32 33 33 33 33 31 30 27 9	35 33 32 32 35 31 30 26 9	2 3 36 34 2 32 30 26 9	5 6 7 1 5 32 30 26 9	8 12 10 4 6 32 30 26 10	11 15 10 7 8 32 30 26 10	14 20 14 12 12 32 30 26 10	17 25 19 14 13 31 30 26 10	20 27 22 19 14 31 29 26 10	22 32 21 22 16 31 30 27 10	27 36 27 27 18 32 30 27 10
9	30 30 30 33 31 30 30 26 9	32 34 33 33 33 31 30 27 9	36 35 33 33 36 31 30 27 9	2 4 1 34 2 32 30 26 9	5 7 7 1 5 32 30 26 9	8 13 10 4 6 32 30 26 10	12 17 10 8 8 32 30 26 10	14 21 14 12 12 32 30 26 10	17 26 19 14 13 31 30 26 10	20 29 22 19 14 31 29 26 10	24 33 21 22 16 31 30 26 10	27 1 27 27 18 32 30 27 10
10	30 30 30 33 31 30 30 26 9	32 36 33 33 33 30 30 27 9	36 36 33 33 36 31 30 27 9	2 6 1 34 2 32 30 26 9	5 9 7 1 5 32 30 26 9	8 14 10 4 6 32 30 26 10	12 18 10 8 8 32 30 26 10	14 22 14 12 12 32 30 26 10	17 27 19 14 13 31 30 26 10	20 29 22 19 14 31 29 26 10	24 34 21 22 16 31 30 26 10	27 2 27 27 18 32 30 27 10
11	30 31 30 33 31 30 30 26 9	33 36 33 33 33 30 30 27 9	36 1 33 33 36 31 30 27 9	2 7 1 34 2 32 30 26 9	6 10 7 1 5 32 30 26 9	8 16 10 4 7 32 30 26 10	12 19 10 8 8 32 30 26 10	14 24 14 12 12 32 30 26 10	17 28 19 16 13 31 30 26 10	20 31 22 19 14 31 29 26 10	24 36 22 23 17 31 30 26 10	27 3 27 27 18 32 30 27 10
12	30 33 30 33 31 30 30 26 9	32 2 33 33 33 30 30 27 9	36 3 33 33 36 31 30 27 9	2 8 1 34 2 32 30 26 9	6 12 7 1 5 32 30 26 9	8 17 10 4 6 32 30 26 10	12 21 9 8 8 32 30 26 10	14 25 14 12 12 32 30 26 10	17 30 19 16 13 31 30 26 10	20 32 22 19 14 31 29 26 10	24 1 22 23 17 31 30 26 10	27 5 27 27 18 32 30 27 10
13	30 34 30 33 31 30 30 26 9	33 3 34 33 34 30 30 27 9	36 4 33 33 36 31 30 27 9	2 9 2 34 2 32 30 26 9	6 14 7 1 5 32 30 26 9	8 18 10 4 7 32 30 26 10	12 22 10 8 8 32 30 26 10	14 26 14 12 12 32 30 26 10	17 31 19 16 13 31 30 26 10	20 34 22 19 14 31 29 26 10	24 3 22 23 17 31 30 26 10	27 6 27 27 18 32 30 27 10
14	30 36 31 33 31 30 30 26 9	33 4 34 33 34 30 30 27 9	36 6 33 33 36 31 30 27 9	2 11 2 34 2 32 30 26 9	6 15 7 1 5 32 30 26 9	8 20 10 4 7 32 30 26 10	12 23 10 8 8 32 30 26 10	14 27 14 12 12 32 30 27 10	17 32 19 16 13 31 30 26 10	20 35 22 19 14 31 29 26 10	24 4 22 23 17 31 30 26 10	27 8 27 27 18 32 30 27 10
15	30 1 31 33 32 30 30 26 9	33 6 34 33 34 30 30 27 9	36 7 33 33 36 31 30 27 9	2 12 2 34 2 32 30 26 9	6 16 8 2 5 32 30 26 9	8 21 10 4 7 32 30 26 10	12 24 10 8 8 32 30 26 10	15 28 15 12 12 32 30 27 10	17 33 19 16 13 31 30 26 10	20 36 22 19 14 31 29 26 10	24 6 22 24 18 31 30 27 10	27 9 27 27 18 32 30 27 10
16	30 3 31 33 32 30 30 26 9	33 7 34 33 34 30 30 27 9	36 9 33 33 36 31 30 27 9	2 14 2 34 2 32 30 26 9	6 17 8 2 5 32 30 26 9	8 22 10 5 7 32 30 26 10	12 25 9 8 9 32 30 26 9	15 30 15 12 12 32 30 27 10	18 34 21 16 13 31 30 27 10	21 1 21 19 13 31 30 25 10	24 7 22 24 18 31 30 27 10	27 10 27 27 18 32 30 27 10
17	30 4 31 33 32 30 30 26 9	33 9 34 33 34 30 30 27 9	36 10 33 33 36 31 30 27 9	3 15 3 35 3 32 30 27 9	6 19 8 2 5 32 30 26 9	8 23 10 5 7 32 30 26 10	12 26 9 8 9 32 30 26 9	15 31 15 12 12 32 30 27 10	18 36 21 16 13 31 30 27 10	21 3 21 19 13 31 30 25 10	24 9 22 24 18 31 30 27 10	27 12 27 27 18 32 30 27 10
18	30 4 31 33 32 30 30 26 9	33 10 33 33 34 30 30 27 9	36 12 33 33 36 31 30 27 9	3 16 3 35 3 32 30 27 9	6 20 8 2 5 32 30 26 9	9 24 9 5 7 32 30 26 9	12 28 10 8 10 32 30 36 10	15 32 16 12 12 32 30 27 10	18 1 21 16 13 31 30 27 10	21 5 21 19 13 31 30 27 10	24 10 22 24 18 31 30 27 10	27 14 27 27 18 32 30 27 10
19	30 6 31 33 32 30 30 26 9	33 12 33 33 34 30 30 27 9	36 13 34 33 36 31 30 27 9	3 18 3 35 3 32 30 27 9	6 21 8 2 5 32 30 26 9	9 26 9 5 8 32 30 26 9	12 29 9 8 9 32 30 36 9	15 33 16 12 12 32 30 27 10	18 3 21 16 13 31 30 27 10	21 4 21 19 13 31 30 27 10	24 12 24 24 18 31 30 27 10	27 15 27 27 18 32 30 27 10
20	30 8 32 33 32 30 30 26 9	34 13 33 33 34 30 30 27 9	36 14 34 33 36 31 30 27 9	3 19 3 35 3 32 30 27 9	6 22 8 2 5 32 30 26 9	9 27 9 5 8 32 30 26 9	12 30 10 10 10 32 30 26 10	15 34 16 13 12 32 30 27 10	18 4 21 16 13 31 30 27 10	21 7 21 19 13 31 30 27 10	24 13 24 24 18 31 30 27 10	27 17 27 27 18 32 30 27 10
21	31 9 32 33 32 30 30 26 9	34 15 33 33 34 30 30 27 9	1 15 34 33 1 31 30 27 9	4 20 4 36 4 32 31 27 9	6 23 8 2 5 32 30 26 9	9 28 9 5 8 32 30 26 9	12 31 10 10 10 32 30 26 10	15 36 16 14 12 32 30 26 10	18 5 21 16 13 31 30 27 10	21 9 21 20 15 31 30 26 10	24 15 24 24 18 31 30 27 10	27 18 27 27 18 32 30 27 10
22	31 12 32 33 32 30 30 26 9	34 16 33 33 34 30 30 27 9	1 17 34 33 1 31 30 27 9	4 22 4 36 4 32 31 27 9	7 25 8 2 5 32 30 26 10	10 29 10 5 8 32 30 26 10	12 33 11 10 10 32 30 26 10	15 2 17 14 12 32 30 26 10	18 7 21 17 14 32 30 26 10	21 10 21 20 15 31 30 26 10	24 16 24 24 18 31 30 27 10	27 19 27 27 18 32 30 27 10
23	31 12 32 33 32 30 30 26 9	34 18 32 32 35 31 30 26 9	1 18 34 33 1 31 30 27 9	4 23 4 36 4 32 31 27 9	7 26 8 2 5 32 30 26 9	10 30 10 5 8 32 30 26 10	12 34 11 10 10 32 30 26 10	15 3 17 14 12 32 30 26 10	18 8 21 17 14 32 30 26 10	21 12 21 20 15 31 30 26 10	25 18 24 25 18 31 30 27 10	28 21 28 28 19 32 30 26 10
24	31 13 32 33 32 30 30 26 9	34 19 32 32 35 31 30 26 9	1 19 34 33 1 31 30 27 9	4 24 4 36 4 32 31 27 9	7 27 8 2 5 32 30 26 9	10 32 10 6 8 32 30 26 10	13 35 11 10 10 32 30 26 10	15 5 17 14 12 32 30 26 10	20 10 21 17 14 32 30 26 10	22 13 21 20 16 31 30 26 10	25 18 24 25 18 31 30 27 10	28 22 28 28 19 32 30 26 10
25	31 14 32 33 32 30 30 26 9	34 20 32 32 35 31 30 26 9	1 21 34 33 1 31 30 27 9	4 25 4 36 4 32 31 27 9	7 28 9 3 6 33 30 27 9	10 33 10 6 8 32 30 26 10	13 36 12 10 10 32 30 26 10	16 6 17 14 12 32 30 26 10	20 11 21 17 14 32 30 26 10	22 15 21 20 16 31 30 26 10	25 19 24 25 18 31 30 27 10	28 23 28 28 19 32 30 26 10
26	31 16 33 33 33 30 30 27 9	34 21 32 32 35 31 30 26 9	1 22 34 33 1 31 30 27 9	4 26 4 36 4 32 31 27 9	7 30 9 3 6 33 30 27 9	10 34 10 6 8 32 30 26 10	13 1 12 10 10 32 30 26 10	16 7 17 14 12 32 30 26 10	20 12 21 17 14 32 30 26 10	22 16 21 20 16 31 30 26 10	25 21 24 25 18 31 30 27 10	28 24 28 28 19 32 30 26 10
27	31 18 33 33 33 30 30 27 9	34 22 32 32 35 31 30 26 9	1 23 34 33 1 31 30 27 9	4 27 4 36 4 32 31 27 9	7 31 9 3 6 33 30 27 9	10 35 10 6 8 32 30 26 10	13 3 12 10 10 32 30 26 10	16 8 17 14 12 32 30 26 10	20 14 21 17 14 32 30 26 10	22 17 21 20 16 31 30 26 10	25 22 24 25 18 31 30 27 10	28 25 28 28 19 32 30 26 10
28	31 19 33 33 33 30 30 27 9	34 24 32 32 35 31 30 26 9	1 24 34 33 1 31 30 27 9	4 29 4 36 4 32 31 27 9	7 33 9 3 6 33 30 27 9	10 1 10 6 8 32 30 26 10	14 5 12 10 10 32 30 27 10	16 10 17 14 12 32 30 27 10	20 15 22 17 14 32 30 26 10	22 19 21 20 16 31 30 26 10	25 24 24 25 18 31 30 27 10	28 27 29 29 19 32 30 26 10
29	31 21 33 33 33 30 30 27 9		1 25 34 33 1 31 30 27 9	4 30 4 36 3 32 30 27 9	7 33 9 3 6 33 30 27 9	10 2 10 6 8 32 30 26 10	14 6 12 10 10 32 30 27 10	16 12 18 14 12 32 30 27 10	20 17 22 17 14 32 30 26 10	22 20 21 20 16 31 30 26 10	25 25 24 25 18 31 30 27 10	28 28 29 29 19 32 30 26 10
30	31 21 33 33 33 30 30 27 9	**1902**	1 27 36 33 1 31 30 27 9	4 31 5 36 5 32 30 27 9	7 34 9 3 6 33 30 27 9	10 3 10 6 8 32 30 26 10	14 7 12 10 10 32 30 27 10	16 13 18 14 12 32 30 27 10	20 18 22 17 14 32 30 26 10	22 21 21 22 16 31 30 26 10	25 25 25 25 18 31 30 27 10	28 30 30 30 19 32 30 26 10
31	31 22 33 33 33 30 30 27 9		1 28 36 33 1 31 30 27 9		7 36 9 3 6 33 30 27 9		14 9 12 10 10 32 30 27 10	16 14 18 14 12 32 30 27 10		22 22 21 22 16 31 30 26 10		28 30 30 30 19 32 30 26 10

	JAN	FEB	MAR	APR	MAY	JUNE	JULY	AUG	SEPT	OCT	NOV	DEC
1	28 31 30 30 19 33 30 27 10	32 36 32 33 20 33 31 27 9	34 1 31 1 19 34 31 27 10	1 6 1 4 19 34 31 27 10	5 10 6 8 18 35 32 27 10	7 15 7 12 19 36 31 27 10	10 19 9 15 19 36 31 27 10	13 23 15 18 21 36 31 27 10	16 28 19 19 23 35 31 26 10	19 31 19 17 25 35 31 27 10	22 36 21 18 27 34 31 27 10	26 2 26 20 29 35 31 27 10
2	28 33 30 30 19 33 30 27 10	32 1 32 33 20 33 31 27 9	34 3 31 1 19 34 31 27 10	1 7 1 4 19 34 31 27 10	5 11 6 8 18 35 32 27 9	7 16 7 12 19 36 31 27 10	10 21 9 15 19 36 31 27 10	13 25 15 18 21 36 31 27 10	16 30 19 19 23 35 31 26 10	19 33 19 17 25 35 31 27 10	22 1 21 18 27 34 31 27 10	26 4 26 20 29 35 31 26 10
3	28 34 30 30 19 33 30 27 10	32 2 32 33 20 33 31 27 9	34 4 31 1 19 34 31 27 10	1 9 1 4 19 34 31 27 10	5 13 7 8 18 35 32 27 9	7 18 7 12 19 36 31 27 10	10 22 9 15 19 36 31 27 10	13 26 15 18 21 36 31 27 10	16 31 19 19 23 35 31 26 10	19 34 19 17 25 35 31 27 10	22 3 22 18 28 34 31 27 10	26 6 26 20 29 35 31 26 10
4	28 35 30 30 19 33 30 27 10	32 4 32 33 20 33 31 27 9	35 5 31 1 19 34 31 27 10	1 10 1 4 19 34 31 27 10	5 15 7 9 18 35 32 27 9	7 19 7 12 19 26 31 27 10	10 23 9 15 19 36 31 27 10	13 27 15 18 22 36 31 27 10	16 32 19 19 23 35 31 26 10	19 35 19 17 26 35 31 27 10	22 4 22 18 28 34 31 27 10	26 7 26 20 29 35 31 26 10
5	28 36 30 30 19 33 30 27 10	32 5 31 33 20 33 31 27 9	35 6 33 1 19 34 31 27 10	1 10 1 4 19 34 31 27 10	5 16 7 9 19 35 32 27 9	7 21 7 12 19 36 31 27 10	10 24 9 15 19 36 31 27 10	13 29 15 18 22 36 31 27 10	17 33 19 19 23 35 31 26 10	19 36 19 17 26 35 31 27 10	22 5 22 18 28 34 31 27 10	26 9 26 21 30 35 31 26 10
6	28 2 30 30 19 33 30 27 10	32 7 31 33 20 33 31 27 9	35 7 33 1 19 34 31 27 10	2 18 1 4 19 34 31 27 10	5 17 7 9 19 35 32 27 9	7 22 7 13 19 36 31 27 10	10 25 9 15 19 36 31 27 10	13 30 15 18 22 36 31 27 10	17 34 19 19 23 35 31 26 10	19 1 19 17 26 35 31 27 10	22 6 22 18 28 34 31 27 10	26 10 26 21 30 35 31 26 10
7	28 3 30 30 19 33 30 27 10	32 8 31 33 20 33 31 27 9	35 9 33 1 19 34 31 27 10	2 14 1 5 19 35 31 27 10	5 18 7 9 18 35 32 27 9	7 23 7 13 19 36 31 27 10	10 27 9 15 19 36 31 27 10	13 31 15 18 22 36 31 27 10	17 35 19 17 23 35 31 26 10	19 3 19 17 26 35 31 27 10	23 8 22 18 28 35 31 27 10	26 12 26 21 30 35 31 26 10
8	29 4 30 30 19 33 30 27 10	33 9 31 34 21 33 31 27 9	36 10 33 1 19 34 31 27 10	3 16 1 5 19 35 31 27 10	5 19 7 9 18 35 32 27 9	7 24 7 13 19 36 31 27 10	10 28 9 16 19 34 31 27 10	14 32 15 18 22 36 31 27 10	17 1 19 17 23 35 31 26 10	20 5 19 17 26 35 31 27 10	23 9 22 18 28 35 31 27 10	26 13 26 21 30 35 31 26 10
9	29 6 30 30 19 33 30 27 10	33 11 31 34 21 33 31 27 9	36 12 33 1 19 34 31 27 10	3 18 1 5 19 35 31 27 10	5 21 7 9 18 35 32 27 9	9 25 7 13 19 36 31 27 10	10 28 9 16 19 36 31 27 10	14 33 15 18 22 36 31 27 10	17 2 20 17 23 35 31 26 10	20 6 19 17 26 35 31 27 10	23 11 22 19 28 35 31 27 10	26 15 26 21 30 35 31 26 10
10	30 7 30 30 19 33 30 27 10	33 13 31 34 21 33 31 27 9	36 13 33 1 19 34 31 27 10	8 19 1 5 19 35 31 27 10	5 22 7 9 18 35 32 27 9	9 27 7 13 19 36 31 27 10	10 30 9 16 19 36 31 27 10	15 35 16 18 22 36 31 27 10	17 3 20 17 23 35 31 26 10	20 7 19 17 26 35 31 27 10	23 12 22 19 28 34 31 27 10	26 16 26 22 31 35 31 26 10
11	30 9 30 30 19 33 30 27 10	33 14 31 34 21 33 31 27 9	36 15 33 1 19 34 31 27 10	3 20 3 6 19 35 31 27 10	6 24 8 9 18 36 31 27 9	9 28 7 13 19 36 31 27 10	10 31 10 16 19 36 31 27 10	15 36 16 18 22 36 31 27 10	17 4 20 17 23 35 31 26 10	20 8 19 17 26 35 31 27 10	23 13 22 19 28 34 31 27 10	26 17 26 22 31 35 31 26 10
12	30 10 30 30 19 33 30 27 10	33 15 31 35 21 33 31 27 9	36 16 33 1 19 34 31 27 10	3 21 3 6 19 35 31 27 10	6 25 8 9 18 36 31 27 9	9 29 7 13 19 36 31 27 10	10 33 10 16 19 36 31 27 10	15 1 16 18 22 36 31 27 10	17 5 20 17 23 35 31 26 10	20 10 19 17 26 35 31 27 10	28 15 22 19 28 34 31 27 10	26 19 28 22 31 35 31 27 10
13	30 12 30 30 19 33 30 27 10	33 17 31 35 21 33 31 27 9	36 18 33 1 19 34 31 27 10	3 22 3 6 19 35 31 27 10	6 26 8 9 18 36 31 27 9	9 30 7 13 19 36 31 27 10	10 34 10 16 19 36 31 27 10	15 2 16 18 22 36 31 27 10	17 7 20 17 23 35 31 26 10	20 11 19 17 26 35 21 26 10	23 16 22 19 28 34 31 27 10	27 21 28 22 31 35 31 27 10
14	30 13 30 30 19 33 30 27 10	33 18 31 35 21 33 31 27 9	36 19 33 1 19 34 31 27 10	3 24 3 6 19 35 31 27 10	6 27 8 9 18 36 31 27 9	9 31 7 13 19 36 31 27 10	12 35 10 16 21 36 31 27 10	15 4 16 18 22 36 31 27 10	17 8 20 17 23 35 31 26 10	20 12 19 17 26 35 21 26 10	23 18 22 19 28 34 31 27 10	27 22 28 22 31 35 31 27 10
15	30 15 31 31 19 33 30 27 10	33 21 31 35 21 33 31 27 9	36 19 34 1 19 34 31 27 9	3 25 3 6 19 35 31 27 10	6 28 8 9 18 36 31 27 9	9 33 7 13 19 36 31 27 10	12 36 10 16 21 36 31 27 10	15 5 16 18 22 36 31 27 10	17 10 20 17 23 35 31 26 10	20 14 19 17 26 35 21 26 10	24 19 24 19 28 34 31 27 10	27 23 28 22 31 35 31 27 10
16	30 16 32 32 20 33 30 27 10	33 21 31 36 21 33 31 27 9	36 22 34 1 19 34 31 27 9	3 27 3 6 19 35 31 27 10	6 30 8 9 18 36 31 27 9	9 34 7 13 19 36 31 27 10	12 1 10 16 21 36 31 27 10	15 6 16 18 22 36 31 27 10	17 11 20 17 23 35 31 26 10	20 15 19 17 26 35 21 26 10	24 21 24 19 28 34 31 27 10	27 24 28 22 31 34 31 27 10
17	30 18 32 32 20 33 30 27 10	33 22 31 36 21 33 31 27 9	36 23 34 3 19 34 31 27 9	3 28 4 6 19 35 31 27 10	6 31 8 9 18 36 31 27 9	9 36 7 13 19 36 31 27 10	12 3 12 16 21 36 31 27 10	15 7 16 18 22 36 31 27 10	17 33 20 17 23 35 31 26 10	20 17 19 17 26 35 21 26 10	24 22 24 19 28 34 31 27 10	27 25 28 22 31 34 31 27 10
18	30 19 32 32 20 33 30 27 10	33 24 31 36 21 33 31 27 9	36 24 34 3 19 34 31 27 9	3 29 4 7 19 35 31 27 10	6 32 8 9 18 35 31 27 9	9 36 7 13 19 36 31 27 10	12 4 12 16 21 36 31 27 10	15 9 16 19 22 36 31 27 10	17 14 20 17 25 35 31 26 10	20 18 19 17 26 35 21 26 10	24 24 24 19 28 34 31 27 10	27 27 28 22 31 34 31 27 10
19	30 20 32 32 20 33 30 27 10	33 25 31 36 21 33 31 27 9	36 26 34 3 19 34 31 27 9	3 30 4 7 19 35 31 27 10	6 33 8 10 18 35 31 27 9	9 1 7 13 19 36 31 27 10	12 6 12 16 21 36 31 27 10	15 10 16 19 22 36 31 27 10	17 16 20 17 25 35 31 26 10	20 19 19 17 26 35 21 26 16	24 25 24 19 28 34 31 27 10	27 28 28 22 31 34 31 27 10
20	30 21 32 32 20 33 30 27 10	34 26 31 36 20 34 31 27 10	36 27 34 3 19 34 31 27 9	3 31 4 7 18 34 31 27 9	6 34 8 10 18 35 31 27 9	9 3 7 13 19 36 31 27 10	12 7 12 16 21 36 31 27 10	15 12 18 19 22 36 31 27 10	17 17 20 17 25 35 31 26 10	20 21 19 17 26 35 21 26 10	24 26 24 19 28 34 31 27 10	27 28 28 22 31 34 31 27 10
21	31 23 32 32 20 32 31 27 10	34 27 31 36 20 34 31 27 10	36 28 34 3 19 34 31 27 9	4 33 4 7 18 34 31 27 9	6 35 8 10 18 35 31 27 9	9 4 7 13 19 36 31 27 10	12 8 12 17 21 36 31 27 10	15 13 18 19 22 36 31 27 10	17 19 20 17 25 35 31 26 10	20 22 19 17 26 35 21 26 10	24 27 24 20 29 35 31 27 10	27 30 28 22 31 34 31 27 11
22	31 24 32 32 20 32 31 27 10	34 28 31 36 20 34 31 27 10	1 29 34 3 19 34 31 27 10	4 34 4 7 18 34 31 27 9	7 1 8 10 18 35 31 27 9	9 6 7 13 19 36 31 27 10	12 9 12 17 21 36 31 27 10	15 15 18 19 22 36 31 27 10	17 20 20 17 25 35 31 26 10	20 24 19 17 26 35 21 26 10	24 28 24 20 29 35 31 27 10	27 31 28 22 31 34 31 27 11
23	31 25 32 32 20 32 31 27 10	34 30 31 36 19 34 31 27 10	1 30 34 3 19 34 31 27 10	4 34 4 7 18 34 31 27 9	7 2 8 10 18 35 31 27 9	10 7 7 13 19 36 31 27 10	12 11 12 18 21 36 31 27 10	15 16 18 19 22 36 31 27 10	17 22 20 17 25 35 31 26 10	20 25 19 17 26 35 21 26 10	25 29 25 20 29 35 31 27 10	27 33 28 22 31 34 31 27 11
24	31 26 32 32 20 32 31 27 10	34 31 31 36 19 34 31 27 10	1 31 34 4 19 34 31 27 10	4 36 4 7 18 34 31 27 9	7 4 8 11 18 35 31 27 9	10 9 7 13 19 36 31 27 10	13 13 13 18 21 36 31 27 10	16 18 18 19 22 36 31 27 10	19 23 20 17 25 35 31 26 10	20 26 20 18 26 35 21 26 10	25 31 25 20 29 35 31 27 10	29 35 28 22 31 34 31 27 11
25	31 28 32 32 20 32 31 27 10	34 32 31 36 19 34 31 27 10	1 33 34 4 19 34 31 27 10	4 1 4 7 18 34 31 27 9	7 5 8 11 18 35 31 27 9	10 10 7 13 19 36 31 27 10	13 15 12 18 21 36 31 27 10	16 19 18 19 22 36 31 27 10	19 24 20 17 25 35 31 26 10	22 28 21 18 27 35 21 27 10	25 32 25 20 29 35 31 27 10	29 34 28 22 31 34 31 27 11
26	31 29 32 32 20 32 31 27 10	34 33 31 36 19 34 31 27 10	1 34 36 4 19 34 31 27 10	4 3 6 7 18 34 31 27 9	7 6 8 11 18 35 31 27 9	10 12 7 15 19 36 31 27 10	13 16 13 18 21 36 31 27 10	16 21 18 19 22 36 31 27 10	19 25 20 17 25 35 31 26 10	22 29 21 18 27 35 21 27 10	25 33 25 20 29 35 21 26 10	29 34 28 22 31 34 31 27 11
27	31 30 32 32 20 32 31 27 10	34 34 31 36 19 34 31 27 10	1 34 36 4 19 34 31 27 10	4 4 6 7 18 34 31 27 9	7 8 8 11 18 35 31 27 9	10 13 7 15 19 36 31 27 10	13 18 13 18 21 36 31 27 10	16 22 18 19 22 36 31 27 10	19 26 20 17 25 35 31 26 10	22 30 21 18 27 35 21 27 10	25 34 25 20 29 35 31 26 10	29 2 28 22 31 34 31 27 11
28	31 31 32 32 20 32 31 27 10	34 36 31 36 19 34 31 27 10	1 1 36 4 19 34 31 27 10	4 6 6 7 18 34 21 27 9	7 9 7 11 18 35 31 27 9	10 15 7 15 19 36 31 27 10	13 19 13 18 21 36 31 27 10	16 24 19 19 23 35 31 26 10	19 28 20 17 25 35 31 26 10	22 31 21 18 27 35 21 27 10	25 35 25 20 29 35 31 26 10	29 1 28 22 31 34 31 27 11
29	31 32 32 32 20 32 31 27 10		1 1 36 4 19 34 31 27 10	4 7 6 7 18 34 31 27 9	7 11 7 11 18 35 31 27 9	10 16 7 15 19 36 31 27 10	13 20 13 18 21 36 31 27 10	16 25 19 19 23 35 31 26 10	19 29 20 17 25 35 31 26 10	22 32 21 18 27 35 21 27 10	25 1 25 20 29 35 31 26 10	29 5 28 22 31 34 31 27 11
30	32 34 32 32 20 32 31 27 10	**1903**	1 3 36 4 19 34 31 27 10	4 9 6 7 18 34 31 27 9	7 12 7 11 18 35 31 27 9	10 18 7 15 19 36 31 27 10	13 21 13 18 21 36 31 27 10	16 26 19 19 23 35 31 26 10	19 30 20 17 25 35 31 26 10	22 34 21 18 27 35 21 27 10	25 2 25 20 29 35 31 26 10	29 4 28 22 31 34 31 27 11
31	32 35 32 32 20 32 31 27 10		1 4 36 4 19 34 31 27 10		7 14 7 11 18 35 31 27 9		13 22 13 18 21 36 31 27 10	16 27 19 19 23 35 31 26 10		22 35 21 18 27 35 21 27 10		29 7 28 22 31 34 31 27 11

	JAN	FEB	MAR	APR	MAY	JUNE	JULY	AUG	SEPT	OCT	NOV	DEC
1	28 9 30 24 31 36 31 27 10	32 14 30 28 34 36 32 27 10	34 16 32 32 1 1 32 28 10	1 21 2 35 3 1 32 27 10	5 25 5 2 5 2 32 27 10	7 29 5 7 7 2 32 27 10	10 33 10 10 10 3 33 27 10	14 1 15 14 12 3 32 27 9	16 5 19 18 14 3 32 27 10	19 9 18 22 16 3 32 27 10	23 14 23 26 18 3 32 27 11	25 18 27 29 19 3 31 27 10
2	28 10 30 24 31 36 31 27 10	32 15 30 28 34 36 32 27 10	34 18 32 32 1 1 32 28 10	1 22 2 35 3 1 32 27 10	5 26 5 2 5 2 32 27 10	7 31 5 7 7 2 32 27 10	10 34 10 10 10 3 33 27 10	14 2 15 14 12 3 32 27 9	16 7 19 18 14 3 32 27 10	19 10 18 22 16 3 32 27 10	23 16 23 26 18 3 32 27 11	25 19 27 29 19 2 31 27 10
3	28 12 30 24 31 36 31 27 10	32 16 30 28 34 36 32 27 10	34 19 32 32 1 1 32 28 10	1 23 3 35 3 1 32 27 10	5 27 5 2 5 2 32 27 10	7 32 5 7 7 2 32 27 10	10 35 10 10 10 3 33 27 10	14 3 15 14 12 3 32 27 9	16 8 19 18 14 3 32 27 10	19 12 18 22 16 3 32 27 10	23 17 23 26 18 3 32 27 11	25 21 27 29 19 2 31 27 10
4	30 13 31 25 33 36 31 27 10	32 18 30 28 34 36 32 27 10	35 20 34 32 1 1 32 28 10	2 25 3 35 3 1 32 27 10	5 29 5 2 5 2 32 27 10	8 32 5 8 8 2 32 27 10	10 36 10 10 10 3 33 27 10	14 5 15 14 12 3 32 27 9	16 9 18 18 14 3 32 27 10	20 13 18 22 16 3 32 27 11	23 18 23 26 18 3 32 27 11	25 22 27 29 19 2 31 27 10
5	30 15 31 25 33 36 31 27 10	32 19 29 29 35 35 32 27 10	35 22 34 32 1 1 32 28 10	2 26 3 36 3 1 32 26 10	5 30 5 3 5 2 32 27 10	8 34 5 8 8 2 32 27 10	10 1 10 10 10 3 33 27 10	14 6 16 14 12 3 32 27 10	16 11 18 18 14 3 32 27 10	20 14 18 23 17 3 32 27 11	23 20 23 26 18 3 32 27 11	25 23 28 29 19 2 31 27 10
6	30 16 31 25 33 36 31 27 10	32 20 29 29 35 35 32 27 10	35 23 34 32 1 1 32 28 10	2 28 3 36 3 1 32 26 10	5 31 5 3 5 2 32 27 10	8 35 5 8 8 2 32 27 10	10 3 10 10 10 3 33 27 10	14 7 16 14 12 3 32 27 10	16 12 18 18 14 3 32 27 10	20 16 18 23 17 3 32 27 11	23 21 23 27 18 3 32 27 10	25 25 28 29 19 2 31 27 10
7	30 18 31 25 33 36 31 27 10	32 22 29 29 35 35 32 27 10	35 25 34 32 1 1 32 28 10	2 29 3 36 4 1 32 26 10	5 32 5 3 5 2 32 27 9	8 1 5 8 8 2 32 27 10	10 4 10 10 10 3 33 27 10	14 9 16 14 12 3 32 27 10	16 14 18 18 14 3 32 27 10	20 18 18 23 17 3 32 27 11	23 23 23 27 18 3 32 27 10	25 27 28 29 19 2 31 27 10
8	30 19 31 25 33 36 31 27 10	32 23 29 29 35 35 32 27 10	35 26 34 32 1 1 31 28 10	2 30 4 36 4 1 32 26 10	5 34 5 3 5 2 32 27 9	8 2 5 8 8 2 32 27 10	10 6 10 10 10 3 33 27 10	14 10 16 14 12 3 32 27 10	16 15 18 18 14 3 32 27 10	20 19 19 23 17 3 32 27 11	23 24 23 27 18 3 32 27 10	25 28 28 29 19 2 31 27 10
9	30 20 31 25 33 36 31 27 10	32 25 29 29 35 35 32 27 10	35 27 34 32 1 1 31 28 10	2 31 4 36 4 1 32 26 10	5 35 5 3 5 2 32 27 9	8 2 5 8 8 2 32 27 10	11 6 11 11 10 3 33 27 10	14 12 16 14 12 3 32 27 10	18 17 18 18 14 3 32 27 10	20 21 20 23 17 3 32 27 11	23 26 23 27 18 3 32 27 10	26 29 29 29 20 2 32 27 11
10	30 21 31 25 33 36 31 27 10	32 26 29 29 35 35 32 27 10	26 28 34 32 1 1 31 27 10	2 32 4 36 4 1 32 26 10	5 36 5 3 5 2 32 27 9	8 4 5 8 8 2 32 27 10	12 8 12 12 10 3 33 27 10	14 13 16 14 12 3 32 27 10	18 18 18 19 14 3 32 27 10	20 22 20 23 17 3 32 27 11	23 27 23 27 18 3 32 27 10	26 31 29 29 20 2 32 27 11
11	30 22 31 25 33 36 31 27 10	32 27 29 29 35 35 32 27 10	36 30 34 32 1 1 31 27 10	2 34 4 36 4 1 32 26 10	5 1 5 3 5 2 32 27 9	9 6 6 9 9 3 33 27 10	12 9 12 12 10 3 33 27 10	15 15 16 15 12 3 33 27 10	18 19 18 19 14 3 32 27 10	21 23 20 23 17 3 32 27 11	23 28 23 27 18 3 32 27 10	27 32 29 29 20 2 32 27 11
12	30 24 31 25 33 36 31 27 10	32 28 29 29 35 35 32 27 10	36 33 34 32 1 1 31 27 10	2 36 5 36 5 1 32 26 10	5 2 5 4 5 2 32 27 10	9 7 6 9 9 3 33 27 10	10 10 12 12 10 3 33 27 10	15 16 16 15 12 3 33 27 10	18 21 18 19 15 3 33 27 10	21 25 20 23 17 3 32 27 11	23 30 23 27 18 3 32 27 10	27 33 29 29 20 2 32 27 11
13	30 25 31 25 33 36 31 27 10	32 30 30 30 36 36 32 27 10	36 31 35 31 1 1 31 27 10	2 35 5 1 5 1 32 26 10	5 3 5 4 5 2 32 27 10	9 9 6 9 9 3 33 27 10	12 12 12 12 10 3 33 27 10	15 18 16 15 12 3 33 27 10	18 24 18 19 15 3 33 27 10	21 27 20 23 17 3 32 27 11	23 31 23 27 18 3 32 27 10	27 34 29 31 20 2 32 27 11
14	30 27 30 25 33 36 31 27 10	33 31 30 30 36 36 32 27 10	36 32 35 32 1 1 31 27 10	2 1 5 1 5 1 32 26 10	5 4 5 4 5 2 32 27 10	9 10 7 9 9 3 33 27 10	12 13 12 12 10 3 33 27 10	15 19 16 15 12 3 33 27 10	18 24 18 21 15 3 33 27 10	21 28 20 23 17 3 32 27 11	23 32 23 27 18 3 32 27 10	27 35 29 31 20 2 32 27 11
15	30 28 30 25 33 36 31 27 10	33 32 31 30 36 36 32 27 10	36 34 35 32 2 1 32 27 10	2 2 5 1 5 1 32 26 10	5 5 5 4 5 2 32 27 10	9 11 7 9 9 3 33 27 10	12 15 12 12 10 3 33 27 10	15 21 18 16 13 4 33 27 10	18 25 18 21 15 3 33 27 10	21 29 20 23 16 3 32 27 10	23 33 25 27 18 3 32 27 10	27 36 29 31 20 2 32 27 11
16	30 29 30 27 33 36 31 27 10	33 33 31 30 36 36 32 27 10	36 36 35 33 2 1 32 27 10	2 5 5 1 5 1 32 26 10	5 7 5 5 5 2 32 27 10	9 13 7 9 9 3 33 27 10	12 16 12 12 10 3 33 27 10	15 22 18 16 13 4 33 27 10	18 27 18 21 15 3 33 27 10	21 30 20 23 16 3 32 27 10	23 34 25 27 18 3 32 27 10	27 2 29 31 20 2 32 27 11
17	30 30 30 27 33 36 31 27 10	33 34 31 30 36 36 32 27 10	36 1 35 33 2 1 32 27 10	2 5 5 1 5 1 32 26 10	5 9 5 5 5 2 32 27 10	9 15 7 9 9 3 33 27 10	12 18 12 12 10 3 33 27 10	15 24 18 16 13 4 33 27 10	18 28 18 21 15 3 33 27 10	21 31 20 23 16 3 32 27 10	23 36 25 27 18 3 32 27 10	27 3 29 31 20 2 32 27 11
18	30 31 30 27 33 36 31 27 10	33 36 31 30 36 36 32 27 10	36 2 35 33 2 1 32 27 10	2 6 5 1 5 1 32 26 10	5 10 5 5 5 2 32 27 10	9 15 7 9 9 3 33 27 10	12 19 13 12 10 3 33 27 10	15 25 18 16 13 4 33 27 10	18 30 18 21 15 3 33 27 10	21 32 20 23 16 3 32 27 10	24 1 25 27 18 3 32 27 10	27 4 29 31 20 2 32 27 11
19	30 33 30 27 33 36 31 27 10	33 1 32 30 36 36 32 27 10	36 3 36 33 2 1 32 27 10	3 8 5 1 5 1 32 27 10	5 11 5 5 5 2 32 27 10	9 17 7 9 9 3 33 27 10	12 21 13 12 10 3 33 27 10	15 26 18 16 13 4 33 27 10	18 31 18 21 15 3 33 27 10	21 34 20 23 16 3 32 27 10	24 2 26 27 18 3 32 27 10	27 5 29 31 20 2 32 27 11
20	20 34 30 27 34 36 31 27 10	34 2 32 30 36 36 32 27 10	36 4 36 34 2 1 32 27 10	3 9 5 2 5 2 32 27 10	5 13 5 5 5 2 32 27 10	9 18 7 9 9 3 33 27 10	12 22 13 12 10 3 32 27 10	15 27 18 16 13 4 32 27 10	18 33 18 21 15 3 33 27 10	21 35 20 24 16 3 32 27 10	24 3 26 27 18 3 32 27 10	27 7 29 32 20 2 32 27 10
21	31 35 30 27 34 36 31 27 10	34 3 32 30 36 36 32 27 10	1 5 36 34 2 1 32 27 10	4 10 5 2 5 2 32 27 10	5 14 5 5 5 2 32 27 10	9 19 7 9 9 3 33 27 10	12 24 14 12 10 3 32 27 10	15 28 18 16 13 4 32 27 10	18 33 18 21 15 3 33 27 10	21 36 21 24 16 3 32 27 10	24 4 26 27 18 3 32 27 10	27 8 29 32 20 2 32 27 10
22	31 36 30 27 34 36 31 27 10	34 5 32 30 36 36 32 27 10	1 7 36 34 2 1 32 27 10	4 12 5 2 5 2 32 27 10	7 16 5 5 7 2 32 27 10	10 21 7 9 9 3 33 27 10	12 25 14 12 10 3 32 27 10	15 29 18 16 13 4 32 27 10	18 34 18 21 15 3 33 27 10	21 1 21 24 16 3 32 27 10	24 5 26 27 18 3 32 27 10	28 10 29 32 20 2 32 28 10
23	31 1 30 27 34 36 31 27 10	34 6 32 30 36 36 32 27 9	1 8 36 34 2 1 32 27 10	4 13 5 2 5 2 32 27 10	7 17 5 5 7 2 32 27 10	10 22 9 9 9 3 33 27 10	13 26 14 13 10 3 32 27 10	15 31 18 16 13 4 32 27 10	19 36 18 21 15 3 32 27 10	21 3 21 24 16 3 32 27 10	25 7 26 28 19 3 32 27 10	28 10 29 32 20 2 32 28 10
24	31 3 30 27 34 36 31 27 10	34 7 32 30 36 36 32 27 9	1 10 1 34 3 1 33 27 10	4 14 5 2 5 2 32 27 10	7 19 5 5 7 2 32 27 10	10 24 9 9 9 3 33 27 10	13 27 14 13 10 3 32 27 10	16 32 18 16 13 4 32 27 10	19 36 18 21 15 3 32 27 10	22 4 21 24 17 3 32 27 10	25 9 26 28 19 3 32 27 10	28 12 29 32 20 2 32 28 10
25	31 4 30 27 34 36 31 27 10	34 9 32 30 36 36 32 27 9	1 11 1 34 3 1 33 27 10	4 16 5 2 5 2 32 27 10	7 20 5 5 7 2 32 27 10	10 25 9 9 9 3 33 27 10	13 29 14 13 11 3 32 27 10	16 33 18 16 13 4 32 27 10	19 2 18 21 15 3 32 27 10	22 5 21 24 17 3 32 27 10	25 10 26 28 19 3 32 27 10	28 13 29 32 20 2 32 28 10
26	31 5 30 27 34 36 31 27 10	34 10 32 30 36 36 32 27 9	1 12 1 34 3 1 33 27 10	4 18 5 2 5 2 32 27 10	7 21 5 5 7 2 32 27 10	10 27 9 10 9 3 33 27 10	13 30 14 13 11 3 32 27 10	16 34 18 18 13 4 32 27 10	19 3 18 21 15 3 32 27 10	22 6 21 25 17 3 32 27 10	25 11 26 28 19 3 32 27 10	28 14 29 32 20 2 32 28 10
27	31 6 30 27 34 36 31 27 10	34 12 32 30 36 36 32 27 9	1 14 1 34 3 1 33 27 10	5 19 5 2 5 2 32 27 10	7 23 5 5 7 2 32 27 10	10 28 9 10 9 3 33 27 10	14 31 14 14 11 3 32 27 10	16 36 18 17 14 4 32 27 10	19 4 18 21 15 3 32 27 10	22 7 22 25 17 3 32 27 10	25 12 27 28 19 3 32 27 10	28 16 29 32 20 2 32 28 10
28	31 7 30 27 34 36 31 27 10	34 13 32 30 36 36 32 27 9	1 15 1 35 3 1 33 27 10	5 20 5 2 5 2 32 27 10	7 23 5 5 7 2 32 27 10	10 29 9 10 9 3 33 27 10	14 32 14 14 11 3 32 27 10	16 1 19 18 14 4 32 27 10	19 5 18 21 15 3 32 27 10	22 9 22 25 17 3 32 27 10	25 14 27 28 19 3 32 27 10	28 18 29 32 20 2 32 28 10
29	31 9 30 27 34 36 31 27 10	34 14 32 30 36 36 32 27 9	1 16 1 35 3 1 33 27 10	5 22 5 2 5 2 32 27 10	7 25 5 5 7 2 32 27 10	10 30 9 10 9 3 33 27 10	14 34 14 14 11 3 32 27 10	16 2 19 18 14 4 32 27 10	19 6 18 21 15 3 32 27 10	22 10 22 25 17 3 32 27 10	25 15 27 28 19 3 32 27 10	28 19 29 32 20 2 32 28 10
30	31 10 30 28 34 36 31 27 10	**1904**	1 18 1 35 3 1 33 27 10	5 23 5 2 5 2 32 27 10	7 27 5 5 7 2 32 27 10	10 31 9 10 9 3 33 27 10	14 35 14 14 11 3 32 27 10	16 3 19 18 14 4 32 27 10	19 7 18 21 15 3 32 27 10	23 12 22 25 18 3 32 27 11	25 16 27 28 19 3 32 27 10	28 20 29 32 20 2 32 28 10
31	31 12 30 28 34 36 31 27 10		1 19 1 35 3 1 33 27 10		7 28 5 5 7 2 32 27 10		14 36 15 14 12 3 32 27 10	16 4 19 18 14 4 32 27 10		23 13 22 25 18 3 32 27 11		28 22 29 32 20 2 32 28 10

	JAN	FEB	MAR	APR	MAY	JUNE	JULY	AUG	SEPT	OCT	NOV	DEC
1	28 24 28 33 21 3 33 28 10	31 28 30 1 22 3 33 28 10	34 29 34 3 24 3 33 28 10	1 34 3 4 24 4 33 28 10	5 1 3 3 23 5 33 27 9	7 5 6 4 22 5 34 28 10	10 9 12 6 22 6 34 28 10	13 14 16 9 23 7 34 27 10	16 19 16 13 25 7 34 28 10	19 22 18 16 27 7 33 27 10	22 28 23 20 29 7 33 28 10	25 31 27 24 31 7 33 28 10
2	28 25 28 33 21 3 33 28 10	31 30 30 1 22 3 33 28 10	34 31 34 3 24 3 33 28 10	1 35 4 4 24 4 33 28 10	5 3 3 3 23 5 33 27 9	7 7 6 4 22 6 34 28 10	10 10 12 6 22 6 34 28 10	13 15 16 9 24 7 34 27 10	16 21 16 13 25 7 34 28 11	19 25 18 16 27 7 33 27 10	22 29 23 20 29 7 33 28 10	25 33 28 24 31 7 33 28 10
3	28 26 28 33 21 3 33 28 10	31 31 30 1 22 3 33 28 10	34 32 34 3 24 3 33 28 10	1 36 4 4 24 4 33 28 10	5 4 4 4 23 5 34 27 9	8 8 6 4 22 6 34 28 10	11 12 12 6 23 6 33 28 10	14 16 16 9 24 7 34 27 10	16 22 16 13 25 7 34 28 11	19 26 18 16 27 7 33 27 10	22 31 23 20 29 7 33 28 10	25 34 28 24 31 7 33 28 10
4	28 28 28 33 21 3 33 28 10	31 32 30 1 22 3 33 28 10	36 33 36 3 24 3 33 28 10	1 1 4 4 24 4 33 28 10	5 5 3 3 23 5 33 28 10	8 9 6 4 22 6 34 28 10	11 13 12 6 23 6 33 28 10	14 18 16 9 24 7 34 27 10	16 24 16 13 25 7 34 28 11	19 27 19 16 27 7 33 27 10	23 32 23 20 29 7 33 28 10	25 36 28 24 31 7 33 28 10
5	30 29 28 33 21 3 33 28 10	33 33 30 1 24 3 33 28 10	36 34 36 3 24 3 33 28 10	2 3 4 4 24 4 33 28 10	5 6 3 3 23 5 33 28 10	8 10 6 4 22 6 34 28 10	11 14 12 6 23 6 33 28 10	14 20 16 9 24 7 34 27 10	16 25 16 13 25 7 34 28 11	19 28 19 16 27 7 33 27 10	23 33 24 21 30 7 33 28 10	26 1 28 24 32 6 33 28 10
6	30 30 28 33 21 3 33 28 10	33 34 30 1 24 3 33 28 10	36 36 36 4 24 4 33 28 10	2 4 4 4 24 4 33 28 10	5 7 3 3 23 5 33 28 10	8 12 6 4 22 6 33 28 10	11 16 12 6 23 6 34 28 10	14 21 16 10 24 7 34 28 10	16 27 16 13 25 7 34 28 11	19 30 19 16 27 7 33 27 10	23 34 24 21 30 7 33 28 10	26 2 28 24 32 6 33 28 10
7	30 31 28 33 21 3 33 28 10	33 36 30 1 24 3 33 28 10	36 1 36 4 24 4 33 28 10	2 5 4 4 24 4 33 28 10	5 9 3 3 23 5 33 28 10	8 13 6 4 22 6 33 28 10	11 17 12 6 23 6 33 28 10	14 22 16 10 24 7 33 28 10	16 28 16 13 25 7 34 28 11	19 31 19 16 27 7 33 27 10	24 36 24 21 30 7 33 28 10	26 3 28 24 32 6 33 28 10
8	30 33 28 34 21 3 33 28 10	33 1 30 1 24 3 33 28 10	36 2 36 4 24 4 33 28 10	2 6 4 4 24 4 33 28 10	5 10 3 3 23 5 33 28 10	8 15 6 4 22 6 33 28 10	11 19 13 7 23 6 34 28 10	14 24 16 10 24 7 33 28 10	16 29 16 13 25 7 34 28 11	19 33 19 16 27 7 33 27 10	24 1 25 21 30 7 33 28 10	26 5 28 24 32 6 33 28 10
9	30 34 28 34 21 3 33 28 10	33 2 31 1 24 3 33 28 10	36 3 36 4 24 4 33 28 10	2 7 4 4 24 4 33 28 10	5 11 3 3 23 5 33 28 10	8 16 7 4 22 6 34 28 10	11 20 13 7 23 6 34 28 10	14 25 16 10 24 7 33 28 10	16 30 16 13 25 7 34 28 11	19 34 19 16 27 7 33 27 10	24 2 25 21 30 7 33 28 10	26 6 28 24 32 6 33 28 10
10	30 35 28 34 21 3 33 28 10	33 3 31 1 24 3 33 28 10	36 4 36 4 24 4 33 28 10	2 9 4 4 24 4 33 28 10	5 12 3 3 23 5 33 28 10	8 18 7 4 22 6 34 28 10	11 21 13 7 23 6 34 28 10	14 27 16 10 24 7 33 28 10	16 32 16 13 25 7 34 28 11	19 35 19 16 27 7 33 27 10	24 3 25 21 30 7 33 28 10	26 7 27 24 32 6 33 28 10
11	30 36 28 34 21 3 33 28 10	33 6 31 1 24 3 33 28 10	36 6 36 4 24 4 33 28 10	3 10 4 4 24 4 33 28 10	5 14 3 3 23 5 33 28 10	8 19 7 4 22 6 34 28 10	11 23 13 7 23 6 34 28 10	14 28 16 10 24 7 33 28 10	16 33 16 13 25 7 33 28 11	20 36 20 16 29 7 33 28 11	24 5 25 21 30 7 33 28 10	26 8 27 24 32 6 33 28 10
12	30 1 28 34 21 3 33 28 10	33 6 31 1 24 3 33 28 10	36 7 36 4 24 4 33 28 10	3 12 4 4 24 4 33 28 10	5 15 3 3 23 5 33 28 10	9 20 7 4 22 6 34 28 10	11 24 13 17 23 6 34 28 10	14 30 16 10 24 7 33 28 10	16 34 16 13 25 7 34 28 11	20 2 20 16 29 7 33 28 11	24 6 25 21 30 7 33 28 10	27 9 27 25 33 6 33 28 10
13	30 3 28 34 21 3 33 28 10	33 7 31 1 24 3 33 28 10	36 8 36 4 24 4 33 28 10	3 13 4 4 24 4 33 28 10	5 16 3 3 23 5 33 28 10	9 22 7 4 22 6 34 28 10	11 26 13 7 23 6 34 28 10	15 31 16 10 24 6 33 28 10	16 35 16 13 25 7 34 28 11	21 3 21 17 29 7 33 28 11	24 7 25 21 30 7 33 28 10	27 10 27 25 33 6 33 28 10
14	30 4 28 34 22 3 33 28 10	33 8 31 1 24 3 33 28 10	36 9 36 4 24 4 33 28 10	3 14 4 4 24 4 33 28 10	5 18 3 3 23 5 33 28 10	9 24 7 4 22 6 34 28 10	11 27 13 7 23 6 34 28 10	15 32 16 10 24 6 33 28 10	16 1 16 13 25 7 34 28 11	21 4 21 18 29 7 33 28 11	24 8 26 21 30 6 33 28 10	27 12 27 25 33 6 33 28 10
15	30 5 28 34 22 3 33 28 10	33 10 31 1 24 3 33 28 10	36 10 36 4 24 4 33 28 10	3 15 4 4 24 4 33 28 10	5 19 3 3 23 5 33 28 10	9 25 8 4 22 6 34 28 10	11 28 13 7 23 6 34 28 10	15 33 16 10 24 7 33 27 10	16 2 16 13 25 7 34 28 11	21 5 21 19 29 7 33 28 11	24 10 26 21 30 6 33 28 10	27 13 27 25 33 6 33 28 10
16	30 6 28 35 22 3 33 28 10	33 11 33 3 24 3 33 28 10	36 12 1 4 24 4 33 28 10	3 16 4 4 24 4 33 28 10	6 21 4 4 24 6 33 28 10	9 26 8 4 22 6 34 28 10	12 30 13 7 23 6 34 28 10	15 34 16 10 24 7 33 27 10	16 3 16 13 25 7 34 28 11	21 6 21 19 29 7 33 28 11	24 10 26 21 30 6 33 28 10	27 15 27 25 33 6 33 28 10
17	30 7 28 35 22 3 33 28 10	33 12 33 3 24 3 33 28 10	36 13 1 4 24 4 33 28 10	3 18 4 4 24 4 33 28 10	6 22 4 4 24 6 33 28 10	9 28 8 4 22 6 34 28 10	12 31 13 7 23 6 34 28 10	15 36 16 10 24 7 33 27 10	18 4 16 15 27 7 34 28 11	21 7 21 19 29 7 33 28 11	24 12 26 21 30 6 33 28 10	27 15 27 26 33 6 33 28 10
18	30 9 28 35 22 3 33 28 10	33 14 33 3 24 3 33 28 10	36 15 1 4 24 4 33 28 10	3 19 4 4 24 4 33 28 10	6 24 4 4 23 5 33 28 10	9 29 8 4 22 6 34 28 10	12 32 14 7 23 6 34 28 10	15 1 16 10 24 7 33 27 10	18 5 16 15 27 7 33 28 11	21 9 21 19 29 7 33 28 11	24 13 26 21 30 6 33 28 10	27 17 27 26 33 6 33 28 10
19	30 10 28 35 22 3 33 28 10	34 15 33 3 24 3 33 28 10	36 16 1 4 24 4 33 28 10	3 21 4 4 24 4 33 28 10	6 25 4 4 23 5 33 28 10	9 30 9 4 22 6 34 28 10	12 34 14 7 23 6 34 28 10	15 2 16 10 24 7 33 27 10	18 6 16 15 27 7 33 28 11	21 10 22 19 29 7 33 28 11	24 15 27 21 30 6 33 28 10	27 18 26 26 33 6 33 28 10
20	30 12 28 35 22 3 33 28 10	34 17 33 3 24 3 33 28 10	36 18 1 4 24 4 33 28 10	3 22 4 4 24 4 33 28 10	6 27 4 4 23 5 33 28 10	9 31 9 4 22 6 34 28 10	12 35 14 8 23 6 34 28 10	15 3 16 10 24 7 33 27 10	18 7 18 15 27 7 33 28 11	21 11 22 19 29 7 33 28 11	24 16 27 21 30 6 33 28 10	27 20 26 26 33 6 33 28 10
21	31 13 28 35 22 3 33 28 10	34 18 33 3 24 3 33 28 10	1 19 1 4 24 4 33 28 10	4 24 4 4 24 4 33 28 10	6 28 5 4 23 5 33 28 10	9 33 9 4 22 6 34 28 10	12 36 15 8 23 7 34 28 10	15 5 16 11 24 7 33 28 10	18 9 18 15 27 7 33 28 11	21 12 22 19 29 7 33 28 11	24 18 27 21 30 6 33 28 10	27 21 26 26 33 6 33 28 10
22	31 15 28 35 22 3 33 28 10	34 19 33 3 24 3 33 28 10	1 21 1 4 24 4 33 28 10	4 26 4 4 24 4 34 28 10	7 30 5 4 23 5 34 28 10	10 34 10 4 22 6 34 28 10	12 1 15 8 23 7 34 28 10	15 6 16 11 24 7 33 28 10	18 10 18 15 27 7 33 28 11	21 13 23 19 29 7 33 28 11	24 19 27 21 30 6 33 28 10	27 22 26 26 33 6 33 28 10
23	31 16 28 35 22 3 33 28 10	34 21 33 3 24 3 33 28 10	1 22 2 4 24 4 33 28 10	4 27 4 4 24 4 34 28 10	7 31 5 4 23 5 34 28 10	10 35 10 4 22 6 34 28 10	12 3 15 8 23 7 34 28 10	15 7 16 11 24 7 33 28 10	18 11 18 15 27 7 33 28 11	21 15 23 19 29 7 33 28 11	25 21 27 22 31 7 33 28 10	28 25 26 26 34 6 34 28 10
24	31 18 28 35 22 3 33 28 10	34 24 33 3 24 3 33 28 10	1 24 2 4 24 4 33 28 10	4 29 4 4 24 4 34 28 10	7 32 5 4 23 5 34 28 10	10 1 10 4 22 6 34 28 10	13 4 15 8 23 7 34 28 10	16 8 16 11 25 7 34 28 10	19 13 18 15 27 7 33 28 11	22 16 23 19 29 7 33 28 11	25 22 27 22 31 7 33 28 10	28 26 26 26 34 6 34 28 10
25	31 19 28 35 22 3 33 28 10	24 24 33 3 24 3 33 28 10	1 25 2 4 24 4 33 28 10	4 30 4 4 24 4 34 28 10	7 33 5 4 23 5 34 28 10	10 2 10 6 22 6 34 28 10	13 5 16 8 23 7 34 28 10	16 9 16 12 25 7 34 28 10	19 15 18 15 27 7 33 28 11	22 18 23 20 29 7 33 28 11	25 24 27 22 31 7 33 28 10	28 27 26 26 34 6 34 28 10
26	31 21 28 36 22 3 33 28 10	34 25 33 3 24 3 33 28 10	1 27 3 4 24 4 33 28 10	4 31 4 4 24 4 34 28 10	7 34 5 4 23 5 34 28 10	10 3 10 6 22 6 34 28 10	13 6 16 8 23 7 34 28 10	16 10 16 12 25 7 34 28 10	19 16 18 15 27 7 33 27 11	22 20 23 20 29 7 33 28 11	25 25 27 22 31 7 33 28 10	28 28 26 28 34 6 34 28 10
27	31 22 28 36 22 3 33 28 10	34 27 33 3 24 3 33 28 10	1 28 3 4 24 4 33 28 10	4 33 4 4 24 4 34 28 10	7 36 5 4 23 5 34 28 10	10 4 10 6 22 6 34 28 10	13 7 16 8 23 7 34 28 10	16 12 16 12 25 7 34 28 10	19 17 18 15 27 7 33 27 11	22 21 23 20 29 7 33 28 11	25 27 27 22 31 7 33 28 10	28 30 26 28 34 6 34 28 10
28	31 23 29 36 22 3 33 28 10	34 28 34 3 24 3 33 28 10	1 29 3 4 24 4 33 28 10	4 34 4 4 24 4 34 28 10	7 1 5 4 23 5 34 28 10	10 6 10 6 22 6 34 28 10	13 9 16 9 23 7 34 28 10	16 13 16 12 25 7 34 28 10	19 18 18 15 27 7 33 27 11	22 22 23 20 29 7 33 28 11	25 28 27 22 31 7 33 28 10	28 31 26 28 34 6 34 28 10
29	31 24 29 36 22 3 33 28 10		1 30 3 4 24 4 33 28 10	5 35 3 4 23 5 33 28 10	7 2 5 4 23 5 34 28 10	10 6 11 6 22 6 34 28 10	13 10 16 9 23 7 34 28 10	16 15 16 12 25 7 34 28 10	19 20 18 15 27 7 33 27 11	22 23 23 20 29 7 33 28 11	25 29 27 23 31 7 33 28 10	28 32 26 28 34 6 34 28 10
30	31 25 29 36 22 3 33 28 10	1905	1 31 3 4 24 4 33 28 10	5 36 3 4 23 5 33 28 10	7 3 5 4 23 5 34 28 10	10 7 11 6 22 6 34 28 10	13 11 16 9 23 7 34 28 10	16 16 16 12 25 7 34 28 10	19 21 18 15 27 7 33 27 11	22 25 23 20 29 7 33 28 11	25 30 27 23 31 7 33 28 10	28 34 26 28 34 6 34 28 10
31	31 26 29 36 22 3 33 28 10		1 33 3 4 24 4 33 28 10		7 5 5 4 23 5 34 28 10		13 12 16 9 23 7 34 28 10	16 18 16 12 25 7 34 28 10		22 27 23 20 29 7 33 28 11		28 35 26 28 34 6 34 28 10

	JAN	FEB	MAR	APR	MAY	JUNE	JULY	AUG	SEPT	OCT	NOV	DEC
1	28 36 26 28 34 6 34 28 10	31 5 30 31 36 6 34 28 10	34 6 34 34 2 6 34 28 10	1 10 3 3 4 7 34 28 10	4 13 1 7 7 7 34 28 10	8 18 7 11 8 8 35 28 10	11 22 13 14 11 9 35 29 11	13 27 15 17 13 10 35 28 11	16 33 15 21 15 10 34 28 10	19 36 19 24 16 10 34 28 10	23 5 25 26 19 11 35 28 11	25 9 25 25 20 10 34 28 10
2	28 1 26 28 34 6 34 28 10	31 6 31 31 36 6 34 28 10	34 7 34 34 2 6 34 28 10	1 11 3 3 4 7 34 28 10	4 15 1 7 7 7 34 28 10	8 19 7 11 8 8 35 28 10	11 23 13 14 11 9 35 29 11	13 29 15 17 13 10 35 28 11	16 34 15 21 15 10 34 28 10	19 1 19 24 16 10 34 28 10	23 6 25 26 19 11 35 28 11	25 9 25 25 20 10 34 28 10
3	28 3 26 28 34 6 34 28 10	32 7 32 32 36 6 34 28 10	34 8 36 36 2 6 34 28 10	1 12 3 3 4 7 34 28 10	4 16 1 7 7 7 34 28 10	8 20 7 11 8 8 35 28 10	11 25 13 14 11 9 35 29 11	13 30 15 17 13 10 35 28 11	16 34 15 21 15 10 34 28 10	19 3 19 24 16 10 34 28 10	23 7 25 26 19 11 35 28 11	25 10 25 25 20 10 34 28 10
4	28 4 27 28 34 6 34 28 10	32 8 32 32 36 6 34 28 10	34 9 36 36 3 6 34 28 10	1 14 1 3 4 7 34 28 10	4 18 1 7 7 7 34 28 10	8 22 7 11 8 8 35 28 10	11 26 13 14 11 9 35 29 11	13 31 14 17 13 10 35 28 11	16 1 15 21 15 10 34 28 10	19 4 19 24 16 10 34 28 10	23 8 25 26 19 11 35 28 11	25 12 25 25 20 10 34 28 10
5	29 5 27 28 34 6 34 28 10	32 10 32 32 1 6 34 28 10	34 10 36 36 3 6 34 28 10	1 15 1 3 4 7 34 28 10	4 19 1 7 7 7 34 28 10	8 24 8 11 8 8 35 28 10	11 28 14 15 11 9 35 29 11	13 33 14 18 13 10 35 28 11	16 2 15 21 15 10 34 28 10	19 5 19 24 16 10 34 28 10	23 10 25 26 19 11 35 28 11	25 13 25 25 20 10 34 28 10
6	29 6 27 28 34 6 34 28 10	32 10 32 32 1 6 34 28 10	36 12 36 36 3 6 34 28 10	1 16 1 3 4 7 34 28 10	4 20 2 7 7 7 34 28 10	8 25 8 11 8 8 35 28 10	11 29 14 15 11 9 35 28 11	13 35 14 18 13 10 35 28 11	16 3 15 21 15 10 34 28 10	19 6 21 24 16 10 34 28 10	23 11 25 26 19 11 35 28 11	25 14 25 25 20 10 34 28 10
7	29 7 27 28 34 6 34 28 10	32 12 32 32 1 6 34 28 10	36 13 36 36 3 6 34 28 10	2 18 1 3 4 7 34 28 10	4 22 2 7 7 7 34 28 10	8 26 8 11 8 8 35 28 10	11 31 14 15 11 9 35 28 11	13 36 13 18 13 10 35 28 11	16 4 15 21 15 10 34 28 10	19 7 21 24 16 10 34 28 10	22 12 25 25 19 10 34 28 10	25 15 25 25 20 10 34 28 10
8	29 9 27 28 34 6 33 28 10	32 13 32 32 1 6 34 28 10	36 15 1 36 3 6 34 28 10	2 19 1 4 5 7 34 28 10	4 23 2 7 7 7 34 28 10	8 28 8 11 8 8 35 28 10	11 33 14 15 11 9 35 28 11	13 1 13 18 13 10 35 28 11	17 6 16 22 15 10 34 28 10	19 9 21 24 16 10 34 28 10	22 13 25 25 19 10 34 28 10	25 16 25 25 20 10 34 28 10
9	29 10 27 28 34 6 33 28 10	33 15 33 33 1 6 34 28 10	36 16 1 36 3 6 34 28 10	2 21 1 4 5 7 34 28 10	4 25 3 7 7 7 34 28 10	8 29 8 11 8 8 35 28 10	11 34 14 15 11 9 35 28 11	13 2 13 18 13 10 35 28 11	17 7 16 22 15 10 35 28 11	19 10 21 25 17 10 34 28 10	22 14 25 25 19 10 34 28 10	26 18 25 25 20 10 34 28 10
10	29 12 27 28 34 6 33 28 10	33 16 33 33 1 6 34 28 10	36 17 1 36 3 7 34 28 10	2 22 1 4 5 7 34 28 10	4 26 3 7 7 7 34 28 10	8 31 8 11 9 8 35 28 10	11 35 14 15 11 9 35 28 11	13 4 13 18 13 10 35 28 10	17 8 17 22 15 10 35 28 11	19 11 21 25 17 10 34 28 10	22 15 25 25 19 10 34 28 10	26 19 25 25 20 10 34 28 10
11	30 13 27 28 34 6 33 28 10	33 18 33 33 1 6 34 28 10	36 19 1 1 3 7 34 28 10	2 24 1 4 5 7 34 28 10	6 28 3 7 7 7 34 28 10	8 32 8 11 9 8 35 28 10	11 36 14 15 11 9 35 28 10	13 4 13 19 13 10 35 28 10	17 9 17 22 15 10 35 28 11	19 12 21 25 17 10 34 28 10	22 16 25 25 19 10 34 28 10	26 20 25 25 20 10 34 28 10
12	30 14 27 28 34 6 33 28 10	33 19 33 33 1 6 34 28 10	36 20 1 1 3 7 34 28 10	3 25 1 4 5 7 34 28 10	6 29 3 7 7 7 34 28 10	8 34 8 11 10 8 35 28 10	11 2 14 15 11 9 35 28 10	14 6 14 19 14 10 35 28 10	17 10 17 22 15 10 35 28 11	19 13 22 25 17 10 34 28 10	22 18 25 25 19 10 34 28 10	26 22 25 25 20 10 34 28 10
13	30 15 28 29 35 6 34 28 10	33 21 33 33 1 6 34 28 10	36 21 1 1 3 7 34 28 10	3 27 1 4 5 7 34 28 10	6 31 3 8 8 8 35 29 11	8 35 10 11 10 8 35 28 10	11 3 14 15 11 9 35 28 10	14 7 14 19 14 10 35 28 10	17 11 17 22 16 10 35 28 11	19 15 22 25 17 10 34 28 10	22 19 25 25 19 10 34 28 10	26 24 25 25 20 10 34 28 10
14	30 17 28 29 35 6 34 28 10	33 22 33 33 1 6 34 28 10	36 23 1 1 3 7 34 28 10	3 28 1 4 5 7 34 28 10	6 32 3 8 8 8 35 29 11	8 1 10 11 10 8 35 28 10	11 4 15 15 11 9 35 28 10	14 8 14 19 14 10 35 28 10	17 13 17 22 16 10 35 28 11	19 16 22 25 17 10 34 28 10	24 21 25 25 19 10 34 28 10	27 25 25 25 21 10 34 28 10
15	30 18 28 29 35 6 34 28 10	33 24 33 33 1 6 34 28 10	36 25 1 1 3 7 34 28 10	3 30 1 4 6 7 34 28 10	6 33 5 8 8 8 35 29 11	8 2 10 11 10 8 35 28 10	11 5 15 15 11 9 35 28 10	14 9 14 19 14 10 35 28 10	17 14 16 22 16 10 34 28 10	21 17 22 25 17 10 34 28 10	24 22 25 25 19 10 34 28 10	27 27 25 25 21 10 34 28 10
16	30 19 28 29 35 6 34 28 10	33 25 33 33 1 6 34 28 10	36 26 1 1 3 7 34 28 10	3 31 1 4 6 7 34 28 10	6 35 5 8 8 8 35 29 11	9 3 10 12 10 9 35 28 10	11 6 15 16 11 9 35 28 10	14 10 14 19 14 10 35 28 10	17 15 16 22 16 10 34 28 10	21 19 22 25 17 10 34 28 10	24 24 25 25 19 10 34 28 10	27 28 25 25 21 10 34 28 10
17	30 21 28 29 25 6 34 28 10	33 26 33 33 1 6 34 28 10	36 27 1 1 4 7 34 28 10	3 32 1 4 6 7 34 28 10	6 36 5 8 8 8 35 29 11	9 4 10 12 10 9 35 28 10	11 8 15 16 11 9 35 28 10	14 12 14 20 14 10 35 28 11	17 16 16 22 16 10 34 28 10	21 21 22 25 18 10 34 28 10	24 25 25 25 19 10 34 28 10	27 30 25 25 22 10 34 28 10
18	30 22 28 29 35 6 34 28 10	33 28 33 33 1 6 34 28 10	36 28 2 1 4 7 34 28 10	3 34 1 4 6 7 34 28 10	6 2 5 8 8 8 35 29 11	9 5 10 12 10 9 35 28 10	12 9 15 16 12 9 35 28 10	15 13 14 20 14 10 35 28 11	17 18 16 22 16 10 34 28 10	21 22 22 25 18 10 34 28 10	24 27 25 25 19 10 34 28 10	27 31 25 24 22 10 34 28 10
19	30 24 28 30 36 6 34 28 10	34 29 34 34 1 6 34 28 10	36 30 2 1 4 7 34 28 10	3 34 1 4 6 7 34 28 10	6 2 5 8 8 8 35 29 11	9 7 10 12 10 9 35 28 10	12 10 15 16 12 9 35 28 10	15 14 14 20 14 10 35 28 11	18 19 18 22 16 10 34 28 10	21 24 22 25 18 10 34 28 10	24 28 25 25 19 10 34 28 10	27 33 25 24 22 10 34 28 10
20	30 25 28 30 36 6 34 28 10	34 30 34 34 1 6 34 28 10	36 31 2 1 4 7 34 28 10	3 36 1 4 6 7 34 28 10	6 3 5 8 8 8 35 29 11	9 8 10 12 10 9 35 28 10	12 11 15 16 12 9 35 28 10	15 16 14 20 14 10 35 28 11	18 21 18 22 16 10 34 28 10	21 25 22 25 18 10 34 28 10	24 30 25 25 19 10 34 28 10	27 34 25 24 22 10 34 28 10
21	31 27 28 30 36 6 34 28 10	34 31 34 34 1 6 34 28 10	1 33 2 1 4 7 34 28 10	4 1 1 6 6 7 34 28 10	6 5 5 8 8 8 35 29 11	9 9 10 13 10 9 35 28 10	12 12 15 17 12 9 35 28 10	15 17 14 20 14 10 35 28 11	18 22 18 22 16 10 34 28 10	21 27 22 25 18 10 34 28 10	24 32 25 25 19 10 34 28 10	27 35 25 24 22 10 34 28 10
22	31 29 29 30 36 6 34 28 10	34 33 34 34 1 6 34 28 10	1 34 2 1 4 7 34 28 10	4 3 1 6 6 7 34 28 10	7 6 5 8 8 8 35 29 11	10 10 10 13 10 8 35 28 10	12 13 15 17 12 9 35 28 10	15 19 14 20 14 10 35 28 11	18 24 18 22 16 10 34 28 10	21 28 22 25 18 10 34 28 10	24 33 25 25 19 10 34 28 10	27 36 25 24 22 10 34 28 10
23	31 30 29 30 36 6 34 28 10	34 34 34 34 1 6 34 28 10	1 35 2 1 4 7 34 28 10	4 4 1 6 6 7 34 28 10	7 7 5 9 8 8 35 29 11	10 11 11 13 10 8 35 28 10	12 15 15 17 12 9 35 28 10	15 20 14 20 14 10 35 28 11	18 25 18 22 16 10 34 28 10	21 30 22 25 18 10 34 28 10	25 34 25 25 19 10 34 28 10	28 1 25 24 22 10 34 28 10
24	31 31 29 30 36 6 34 28 10	34 36 34 34 1 6 34 28 10	1 36 2 1 4 7 34 28 10	4 5 1 6 6 7 34 28 10	7 8 5 9 8 8 35 29 11	10 13 11 13 11 8 35 29 11	13 16 15 17 13 9 35 28 10	16 21 14 20 14 10 35 28 11	19 27 19 22 16 10 34 28 10	22 31 22 25 18 10 34 28 10	25 36 25 25 19 10 34 28 10	28 3 25 24 22 10 34 28 10
25	31 32 30 31 36 6 34 28 10	34 1 34 34 1 6 34 28 10	1 1 2 1 4 7 34 28 10	4 6 1 6 6 7 34 28 10	7 9 6 9 8 8 35 29 11	10 14 12 13 11 8 35 29 11	13 17 15 17 13 9 35 28 10	16 23 14 20 14 10 35 28 11	19 28 19 22 16 10 34 28 10	22 32 24 25 18 10 34 28 10	25 1 25 25 19 10 34 28 10	28 4 25 25 22 10 34 28 10
26	31 33 30 31 36 6 34 28 10	34 2 34 34 2 6 34 28 10	1 3 2 1 4 7 34 28 10	4 7 1 6 6 7 34 28 10	7 11 6 9 8 8 35 29 11	10 15 12 13 11 8 35 29 11	13 19 15 17 13 9 35 28 10	16 24 14 20 14 10 35 28 11	19 30 19 23 16 10 34 28 10	22 33 24 25 18 10 34 28 10	25 1 25 25 19 10 34 28 10	28 5 25 25 22 10 34 28 10
27	31 34 30 31 36 6 34 28 10	34 3 34 34 2 6 34 28 10	1 4 2 2 4 7 34 28 10	4 8 1 6 6 7 34 28 10	7 12 6 11 8 8 35 29 11	10 16 12 13 11 8 35 29 11	13 21 15 17 13 9 35 28 10	16 26 14 20 14 10 34 28 10	19 31 19 23 16 10 34 28 10	22 34 24 25 18 10 34 28 10	26 3 26 26 19 10 34 28 10	28 7 25 25 22 10 34 28 10
28	31 36 30 31 36 6 34 28 10	34 4 34 34 2 6 34 28 10	1 5 2 2 4 7 34 28 10	4 10 1 6 6 7 34 28 10	7 13 6 11 8 8 35 29 11	10 17 12 13 11 8 35 29 11	13 22 15 17 13 9 35 28 10	16 27 14 20 14 10 34 28 10	19 32 19 24 16 10 34 28 10	22 36 24 25 18 10 34 28 10	26 4 26 26 19 10 35 28 10	28 7 25 25 22 10 34 28 10
29	31 1 30 31 36 6 34 28 10		1 6 2 2 4 7 34 28 10	5 11 2 7 7 7 35 29 11	8 14 6 11 8 8 35 29 11	10 19 12 14 11 8 35 29 11	13 23 15 17 13 9 35 28 10	16 28 14 20 14 10 34 28 10	19 33 19 24 16 10 34 28 10	22 1 24 25 18 10 34 28 10	26 6 26 26 19 10 35 28 10	28 9 25 25 22 10 34 28 10
30	31 3 30 31 36 6 34 28 10	**1906**	1 7 2 2 4 7 34 28 10	5 12 2 7 7 7 35 29 11	8 15 6 11 8 8 35 29 11	10 20 12 14 11 8 35 29 11	13 24 15 17 13 9 35 28 10	16 30 14 20 14 10 34 28 10	19 34 19 24 16 10 34 28 10	22 3 24 25 18 10 34 28 10	26 8 26 26 19 10 35 28 10	28 10 26 25 22 10 34 28 10
31	31 4 30 31 36 6 34 28 10		1 9 2 2 4 7 34 28 10		8 17 6 11 8 8 35 29 11		13 26 15 17 13 9 35 28 10	16 31 14 20 14 10 34 28 10		22 4 24 25 18 10 34 28 10		28 11 26 25 22 10 34 28 10

	JAN	FEB	MAR	APR	MAY	JUNE	JULY	AUG	SEPT	OCT	NOV	DEC
1	28 13 27 25 22 10 34 28 10	32 16 32 27 24 10 35 29 11	35 17 36 30 26 10 35 28 10	1 24 36 33 27 10 36 28 10	5 27 2 2 29 11 36 29 11	7 32 8 5 29 11 36 29 11	11 36 13 9 29 12 36 29 11	13 5 12 12 29 12 36 29 11	17 9 17 17 29 13 36 29 11	19 12 21 19 30 13 36 28 10	23 17 24 24 32 14 36 28 11	26 20 24 27 34 14 36 29 11
2	28 14 27 25 22 10 34 28 10	32 18 32 27 24 10 35 29 11	35 19 36 30 26 10 35 28 10	1 25 36 34 28 10 36 28 10	5 29 2 2 29 11 36 29 11	7 34 9 5 29 11 36 29 11	11 2 13 9 29 12 36 29 11	13 6 12 12 29 12 36 29 11	17 11 17 17 29 13 36 29 11	19 13 21 19 30 13 36 29 11	23 18 24 24 32 14 36 28 11	26 22 24 27 34 14 36 29 11
3	28 15 27 25 22 10 34 28 10	32 20 32 27 24 10 35 29 11	35 20 36 30 26 10 35 28 10	1 26 36 34 28 10 36 28 10	5 30 2 2 29 11 36 29 11	7 35 9 5 29 11 36 29 11	11 3 13 9 29 12 36 29 11	13 7 12 12 29 12 36 29 11	17 12 17 17 29 13 36 29 11	19 15 21 19 30 13 36 28 10	23 19 24 24 32 14 36 28 11	26 23 24 28 34 14 36 29 11
4	28 16 27 25 22 10 34 28 10	32 21 32 27 25 10 35 29 11	35 22 1 31 26 10 35 28 10	1 28 36 34 28 10 36 28 10	5 31 3 2 29 11 36 29 11	7 36 9 5 29 11 36 29 11	11 4 13 9 29 11 36 29 11	13 9 12 12 29 12 36 29 11	17 13 17 17 29 13 36 29 11	19 16 21 19 30 13 36 28 10	23 21 24 24 32 14 36 28 11	26 25 24 28 34 14 36 29 11
5	28 17 27 25 22 10 34 28 10	32 23 32 27 25 10 35 29 11	35 24 1 31 26 10 35 28 10	1 28 36 34 28 10 36 28 10	5 33 3 2 29 11 36 29 11	7 2 9 5 29 11 36 29 11	11 5 13 9 29 11 36 29 11	13 10 12 12 29 12 36 29 11	17 14 17 17 29 13 36 29 11	19 18 22 21 30 13 36 28 10	23 23 24 24 32 14 36 28 11	26 26 24 29 34 15 36 29 11
6	28 19 27 25 22 10 34 28 10	32 23 32 27 25 10 35 29 11	35 25 1 31 26 10 35 28 10	1 30 36 34 28 10 36 28 10	5 34 3 2 29 11 36 29 11	7 3 9 5 29 11 36 29 11	11 6 13 9 29 11 36 29 11	14 11 12 12 29 12 36 29 11	17 15 17 17 29 13 36 29 11	19 19 22 21 30 13 36 28 10	23 24 24 24 32 14 36 28 11	27 27 24 29 34 15 36 29 11
7	28 20 28 25 22 10 34 28 10	32 25 32 28 25 10 35 29 11	35 26 1 31 26 10 35 28 10	1 32 36 34 28 10 36 28 10	5 36 3 2 29 11 36 29 11	7 4 10 5 29 11 26 29 11	11 8 13 9 29 11 36 29 11	14 12 12 12 29 12 36 29 11	17 16 17 17 29 13 36 29 11	19 20 22 21 30 13 36 28 10	23 25 24 24 32 14 36 28 11	27 29 24 29 35 15 36 29 11
8	28 21 28 25 22 10 34 28 10	32 27 32 28 25 10 35 29 11	35 28 1 31 26 10 35 28 10	1 33 36 34 28 10 36 28 10	5 1 3 2 29 11 36 29 11	7 5 10 5 29 11 36 29 11	11 9 13 9 29 11 36 29 11	14 13 12 12 29 12 36 29 11	17 18 17 17 29 13 26 29 11	19 21 22 21 30 13 36 28 10	23 27 24 24 32 14 36 28 11	27 30 24 29 35 15 36 29 11
9	28 22 28 25 22 10 34 28 10	32 29 32 28 25 10 35 29 11	35 29 1 31 26 10 35 28 10	1 34 36 34 28 10 36 28 10	5 2 4 2 29 11 36 29 11	9 7 11 6 29 11 36 29 11	11 10 13 9 29 11 36 29 11	14 14 12 13 29 12 36 29 11	18 19 18 18 30 13 36 28 12	19 22 22 21 30 13 36 28 10	23 28 24 25 32 14 36 28 11	27 33 24 29 35 15 36 29 11
10	29 24 28 25 22 10 34 28 10	33 30 33 28 25 10 35 29 11	35 31 1 31 26 10 35 28 10	1 36 36 34 28 10 36 28 10	5 3 5 2 29 11 36 29 11	9 8 11 6 29 11 36 29 11	11 11 13 9 29 11 36 29 11	14 16 12 14 29 12 36 29 11	18 21 18 18 30 13 36 28 12	19 24 22 21 30 13 36 28 12	23 29 24 25 32 14 36 28 11	27 32 24 29 35 15 36 29 11
11	29 25 28 25 22 10 34 28 10	33 31 33 29 25 10 35 29 11	35 32 1 31 26 10 35 28 10	2 1 36 34 28 10 36 28 10	5 5 5 2 29 11 36 29 11	9 9 11 6 29 11 36 29 11	11 12 13 9 29 11 36 29 11	14 17 12 14 29 12 36 29 11	18 22 18 18 30 13 36 28 12	21 25 22 21 30 13 36 28 12	23 31 23 25 32 14 35 28 11	27 35 25 29 35 15 36 29 11
12	29 27 28 25 22 10 34 28 10	33 33 34 29 25 10 35 29 11	35 34 36 31 26 10 35 28 10	2 2 36 34 28 10 36 28 10	5 6 5 2 29 11 36 29 11	9 10 11 6 29 11 36 29 11	11 13 13 9 29 11 36 29 11	14 18 12 14 29 12 36 29 11	18 23 18 18 30 13 36 28 12	21 27 22 21 30 13 36 28 12	23 32 23 26 32 14 35 28 11	27 36 26 29 35 15 36 29 11
13	30 28 28 25 22 10 34 28 10	33 34 34 29 25 10 35 29 11	36 36 36 31 27 10 36 28 10	2 4 36 36 28 10 36 28 10	5 7 5 2 29 11 36 29 11	9 11 11 6 29 11 36 29 11	11 15 13 9 29 11 36 29 11	14 19 12 14 29 12 36 29 11	18 24 18 18 30 13 36 28 12	21 28 22 21 30 13 36 28 12	23 34 23 26 32 14 35 28 11	27 2 26 29 35 15 36 29 11
14	30 30 28 25 22 10 34 28 10	33 35 34 29 25 10 35 29 11	36 36 36 31 27 10 36 28 10	2 5 36 36 28 10 36 28 10	6 8 5 2 29 11 36 29 11	9 13 11 6 29 11 36 29 11	12 16 13 11 29 12 36 29 11	14 21 12 14 29 12 36 29 11	18 25 18 18 30 13 36 28 12	21 30 23 22 31 13 36 28 12	23 36 23 26 32 14 35 28 11	27 3 26 29 35 15 36 29 11
15	30 31 28 25 22 10 34 28 10	33 1 34 29 25 10 35 29 11	36 1 36 31 27 10 36 28 10	2 6 36 36 28 10 36 28 10	6 10 5 2 29 11 36 29 11	9 14 11 6 29 11 36 29 11	12 17 13 11 29 12 36 29 11	14 22 12 14 29 12 36 29 11	18 27 18 18 30 13 36 28 12	21 31 23 22 31 13 36 28 12	23 36 23 26 32 14 35 28 11	27 5 26 29 35 15 36 29 11
16	30 33 28 25 22 10 34 28 10	33 2 35 29 26 10 35 29 11	36 3 36 32 27 10 36 28 10	2 7 36 36 28 10 36 28 10	6 11 5 2 29 11 36 29 11	9 15 11 6 29 11 36 29 11	12 18 13 11 29 12 36 29 11	15 24 12 15 29 12 36 29 11	18 28 19 18 30 13 36 28 12	21 32 23 22 31 13 36 28 12	23 2 23 26 32 14 35 28 11	26 6 26 29 35 14 35 29 11
17	30 34 28 25 22 10 34 28 10	33 3 35 29 26 10 35 29 11	36 4 36 32 27 10 36 28 10	2 9 36 36 28 10 36 28 10	6 12 6 2 29 11 36 29 11	9 16 11 7 29 11 36 29 11	12 20 13 11 29 12 36 29 11	15 25 12 15 29 12 36 29 11	18 30 19 18 30 13 36 28 12	21 34 24 22 31 13 26 28 12	23 3 23 26 32 14 35 28 11	26 8 26 29 35 14 35 29 11
18	30 36 28 25 22 10 34 28 10	33 5 35 29 26 10 35 29 11	36 5 36 33 27 10 36 28 10	3 10 1 36 28 10 36 28 10	6 13 6 3 29 11 36 29 11	9 17 11 7 29 11 36 29 11	12 21 13 11 29 12 36 29 11	15 26 12 15 29 12 36 29 11	18 31 19 18 30 13 36 28 12	21 36 24 22 31 13 36 28 12	23 4 23 26 32 14 35 28 11	26 8 26 29 35 14 35 29 11
19	30 1 28 25 22 10 34 28 10	33 6 35 29 26 10 35 29 11	36 7 36 33 27 10 36 28 10	3 10 1 36 28 10 36 28 10	6 14 6 3 29 11 36 29 11	9 19 11 7 29 11 36 29 11	12 23 13 11 29 12 36 29 11	15 27 13 15 29 12 36 29 11	18 33 19 18 30 13 36 28 12	21 1 24 22 31 13 36 28 12	24 6 23 26 33 14 35 28 11	26 9 26 29 35 14 35 29 11
20	30 3 29 25 23 10 34 28 10	34 7 35 29 26 10 35 29 11	36 8 36 33 27 10 36 28 10	3 12 1 36 28 10 36 28 10	6 15 6 3 29 11 36 29 11	9 20 11 7 29 11 36 29 11	12 24 13 11 29 13 36 29 11	15 29 13 15 29 12 36 29 11	18 34 19 18 30 13 36 28 12	21 3 24 22 31 13 36 28 10	24 7 23 26 33 14 35 28 11	26 11 26 29 35 14 35 29 11
21	31 4 29 25 23 10 34 28 10	34 8 35 29 26 10 35 29 11	36 9 36 33 27 10 36 28 10	4 13 1 36 28 10 36 28 10	6 17 6 3 29 11 36 29 11	9 22 11 7 29 11 36 29 11	12 25 13 11 29 12 36 29 11	15 31 13 15 29 12 36 29 11	18 36 19 18 30 13 36 28 12	21 4 24 22 31 13 36 28 10	24 9 23 26 33 14 35 28 11	26 11 26 30 35 14 35 29 11
22	31 5 29 25 23 10 34 28 10	34 9 35 29 26 10 35 29 11	1 10 36 33 27 10 36 28 10	4 15 1 36 28 10 36 28 10	7 18 7 3 29 11 36 29 11	9 23 11 7 29 11 36 29 11	12 27 13 11 29 12 36 29 11	15 32 15 15 29 12 36 29 11	18 1 19 18 30 13 36 28 12	21 4 24 22 31 13 36 28 10	24 9 23 26 33 14 35 28 11	26 13 26 30 35 14 35 29 11
23	31 6 31 25 23 10 34 28 10	34 11 35 29 26 10 35 29 11	1 12 36 33 27 10 36 28 10	4 16 1 36 28 10 36 28 10	7 20 7 4 29 11 36 29 11	9 24 11 7 29 11 36 29 11	12 29 13 11 29 12 36 29 11	15 34 15 15 29 12 36 29 11	18 3 21 18 30 13 36 28 12	21 6 24 22 31 13 36 28 10	25 11 23 26 34 14 35 28 11	28 14 26 30 35 14 35 29 11
24	31 7 31 25 23 10 34 28 10	34 12 35 29 26 10 35 29 11	1 13 36 33 27 10 36 28 10	1 18 1 36 28 10 36 28 10	7 20 7 4 29 11 36 29 11	10 26 13 7 29 11 1 29 11	13 30 13 11 29 13 1 29 11	16 35 16 16 29 12 36 29 11	19 4 21 19 30 13 36 28 12	21 7 24 22 31 13 36 28 10	25 12 23 26 34 14 35 28 11	28 15 26 30 35 14 35 29 11
25	31 9 31 25 23 10 34 28 10	34 13 35 29 26 10 35 29 11	1 14 36 33 27 10 36 28 10	4 18 1 36 28 10 36 28 10	7 22 7 4 29 11 36 29 11	10 27 13 8 29 11 1 29 11	13 31 13 11 29 13 1 29 11	16 36 16 16 29 12 36 29 11	19 6 21 19 30 13 36 28 12	22 9 24 22 31 13 36 28 10	25 13 23 26 34 13 35 28 11	28 16 26 30 35 14 35 29 11
26	31 10 31 25 24 10 34 28 10	34 14 35 29 26 10 35 29 11	1 15 36 33 27 10 36 28 10	4 19 1 36 28 10 36 28 10	7 24 7 5 29 11 36 29 11	10 29 13 8 29 11 1 29 11	13 33 13 11 29 13 1 29 11	16 2 16 16 29 12 36 29 11	19 7 21 19 30 13 36 28 12	22 10 24 22 31 13 36 28 10	25 14 23 26 34 13 35 28 11	28 17 26 30 35 14 35 29 11
27	31 11 31 25 24 10 34 28 10	35 16 36 30 26 10 35 29 11	1 16 36 33 27 10 36 28 10	4 21 1 36 28 10 36 28 10	7 25 7 5 29 11 36 29 11	10 30 13 8 29 11 1 29 11	13 35 12 12 29 12 36 29 11	16 3 16 16 29 12 36 29 11	19 8 21 19 30 13 36 28 12	22 10 24 22 31 13 36 28 10	25 15 23 26 34 13 35 28 11	29 19 26 31 35 14 35 29 11
28	31 12 31 26 24 10 34 28 10	35 17 36 30 26 10 35 29 11	1 18 36 33 27 10 36 28 10	4 22 1 1 28 10 36 28 10	7 27 7 5 29 11 36 29 11	11 32 13 8 29 11 36 29 11	13 36 12 12 29 13 36 29 11	16 4 16 16 29 12 36 29 11	19 9 21 19 30 13 36 28 12	22 12 24 22 31 13 36 28 10	25 16 23 26 34 13 35 28 11	29 20 26 31 35 14 35 29 11
29	31 13 31 27 24 10 34 28 10		1 19 36 33 27 10 36 28 10	4 24 1 1 28 10 36 28 10	7 28 7 5 29 11 36 29 11	11 33 13 8 29 11 36 29 11	13 2 12 12 29 12 36 29 11	17 6 17 17 29 12 36 29 11	19 10 21 19 30 13 36 28 12	22 13 24 22 31 13 36 28 10	25 18 23 26 34 13 35 28 11	29 21 27 31 36 14 36 29 11
30	31 15 31 27 24 10 34 28 10	**1907**	1 21 36 33 27 10 36 28 10	4 25 1 1 28 10 36 28 10	7 29 7 5 29 11 36 29 11	11 35 13 8 29 11 36 29 11	13 2 12 12 29 12 36 29 11	17 7 17 17 29 12 36 29 11	19 12 21 19 30 13 36 28 12	22 15 24 22 31 13 36 28 10	25 19 23 26 34 13 35 28 11	29 22 27 31 36 14 36 29 11
31	31 16 31 27 24 10 34 28 10		1 22 36 33 27 10 36 28 10		7 31 7 5 29 11 36 29 11		13 4 12 12 29 12 36 29 11	17 8 17 17 29 12 36 29 11		22 16 24 23 31 13 36 28 10		29 24 28 31 36 14 36 29 11

	JAN	FEB	MAR	APR	MAY	JUNE	JULY	AUG	SEPT	OCT	NOV	DEC
1	29 25 28 32 36 14 36 29 11	32 31 33 35 2 14 36 29 11	34 33 34 1 4 13 36 28 10	2 2 35 6 6 13 1 29 11	4 6 4 9 8 13 1 29 11	8 11 11 11 11 14 2 29 11	11 14 11 11 11 14 2 29 11	15 17 11 12 15 15 3 29 11	17 23 17 11 17 15 2 29 11	19 27 22 15 18 16 1 29 11	23 31 22 19 20 17 1 29 11	25 35 25 22 22 17 1 29 11
2	29 27 29 32 36 14 36 29 11	32 32 33 36 2 14 36 29 11	34 34 34 1 4 13 36 28 10	2 4 35 6 6 13 1 29 11	4 7 4 9 8 13 1 29 11	8 11 11 11 11 14 2 29 11	11 15 11 11 12 14 2 29 11	15 21 11 12 15 15 3 29 11	17 24 17 11 17 15 2 29 11	19 28 22 15 18 16 1 29 11	23 32 21 19 20 17 1 29 11	25 1 25 22 22 17 1 29 11
3	29 29 29 32 36 14 36 29 11	32 33 33 36 2 14 36 29 11	34 36 34 1 4 13 36 28 10	2 5 35 6 6 13 1 29 11	4 9 4 9 8 13 1 29 11	8 13 11 11 11 14 2 29 11	11 16 11 11 12 14 2 29 11	15 21 11 12 15 15 3 29 11	17 26 17 11 17 15 2 29 11	20 29 22 15 18 16 2 29 11	23 35 21 19 20 17 1 29 11	25 2 25 23 23 17 1 29 11
4	29 30 29 32 36 14 36 29 11	32 35 33 36 2 13 36 29 11	34 1 34 1 4 13 36 28 10	2 6 35 6 6 13 1 29 11	4 10 4 10 8 13 1 29 11	8 14 11 11 11 14 2 29 11	11 17 11 11 12 14 2 29 11	15 22 11 12 15 15 3 29 11	17 27 18 12 17 15 2 29 11	20 30 22 15 18 16 2 29 11	23 36 21 19 20 17 1 29 11	25 4 25 23 23 17 1 29 11
5	29 32 29 32 36 14 36 29 11	32 36 34 36 2 13 36 29 11	34 2 34 3 4 13 36 28 10	2 7 35 6 6 13 1 29 11	4 11 4 10 8 13 1 29 11	8 15 11 11 11 14 2 29 11	11 18 11 11 12 14 2 29 11	15 24 11 12 15 15 3 29 11	17 28 18 12 17 15 2 29 11	20 32 22 15 18 16 2 29 11	23 1 21 19 20 17 1 29 11	25 5 25 23 23 17 1 29 11
6	29 33 29 32 36 14 36 29 11	32 2 34 36 2 13 36 29 11	34 4 34 3 4 13 36 28 10	2 9 35 6 6 13 1 29 11	5 12 5 10 8 13 1 29 11	8 17 11 11 11 14 2 29 11	11 20 11 11 12 14 2 29 11	15 23 11 12 15 15 3 29 11	17 29 17 11 17 15 2 29 11	20 33 22 15 18 16 2 29 11	23 2 21 19 20 17 1 29 11	25 6 25 23 23 17 1 29 11
7	29 35 29 32 36 14 36 29 11	32 3 34 36 2 13 36 29 11	34 6 34 3 4 13 36 28 10	2 10 35 7 7 13 1 29 11	5 13 5 10 9 13 1 29 11	8 17 11 11 11 14 2 29 11	11 21 11 11 12 14 2 29 11	15 27 13 12 15 15 3 30 12	17 31 18 12 17 15 2 29 11	20 34 22 15 18 16 2 29 11	23 4 21 19 20 17 1 29 11	25 8 25 23 23 17 1 29 11
8	29 36 29 32 36 14 36 29 11	32 5 35 36 2 13 36 29 11	34 7 34 3 4 13 36 28 10	2 11 36 7 7 13 1 29 11	5 14 5 10 9 13 1 29 11	8 19 11 11 11 14 2 29 11	11 22 11 11 13 14 2 29 11	15 27 13 12 15 15 3 30 12	17 33 18 12 17 15 2 29 11	20 36 22 16 18 16 2 29 11	23 5 21 19 20 17 1 29 11	25 9 25 23 23 17 1 29 11
9	29 2 29 32 36 14 36 29 11	32 6 35 36 2 13 36 29 11	34 8 34 3 4 13 36 28 10	2 13 36 7 7 13 1 29 11	5 16 5 10 9 13 1 29 11	9 20 11 11 11 14 2 29 11	11 23 11 11 13 14 2 29 11	15 30 13 12 15 15 3 30 12	17 34 19 13 17 15 1 29 11	20 2 22 16 18 16 2 29 11	23 7 21 19 20 17 1 29 11	25 10 25 23 23 17 1 29 11
10	29 2 29 32 36 14 36 29 11	32 7 35 36 2 13 36 29 11	35 9 34 4 4 13 36 28 10	2 14 1 7 7 13 1 29 11	5 17 5 11 9 14 2 29 11	9 21 11 11 11 14 2 29 11	11 25 11 11 13 14 2 29 11	15 29 13 12 15 15 3 30 12	17 35 19 13 17 15 1 29 11	20 3 22 16 19 16 1 29 11	23 8 21 19 20 17 1 29 11	25 11 26 23 23 17 1 29 11
11	29 4 29 32 1 14 36 29 11	32 9 35 36 2 13 36 29 11	36 11 34 4 4 13 36 28 10	2 15 1 7 7 13 1 29 11	5 18 5 11 9 14 2 29 11	9 23 11 11 11 14 2 29 11	11 26 11 11 14 14 2 29 11	15 32 14 11 15 15 2 29 11	17 1 19 13 17 15 1 29 11	20 4 22 16 19 16 1 29 11	23 10 21 19 20 17 1 29 11	25 13 26 23 23 17 1 29 11
12	29 5 29 33 1 14 36 29 11	33 10 35 36 3 13 36 29 11	36 12 34 4 4 13 36 28 10	2 16 1 7 7 13 1 29 11	5 19 5 11 9 14 2 29 11	9 24 11 11 11 14 2 29 11	11 28 11 11 14 14 2 29 11	15 33 14 11 15 15 2 29 11	17 2 19 13 17 16 1 29 11	20 6 22 16 19 16 1 29 11	24 11 22 19 20 17 1 29 12	25 14 26 23 23 17 1 29 11
13	30 6 30 33 1 14 36 29 11	33 11 35 36 3 13 36 29 11	36 13 34 4 4 13 36 28 10	2 17 1 7 7 13 1 29 11	5 21 5 11 9 14 2 29 11	9 25 11 11 11 14 2 29 11	11 29 11 11 14 14 2 29 11	15 35 14 11 15 15 2 29 11	17 4 19 13 17 16 1 29 11	20 7 22 16 19 16 1 29 11	24 12 22 19 20 17 1 29 12	25 15 26 23 23 17 1 29 11
14	30 7 30 33 1 13 36 29 11	33 12 35 1 3 13 36 29 11	36 14 34 4 4 13 36 28 10	3 19 1 7 7 13 1 29 11	5 22 8 11 9 14 2 29 11	9 27 11 11 11 14 2 29 11	11 31 11 11 14 14 2 29 11	15 36 14 11 15 15 2 29 11	17 5 19 13 17 16 1 29 11	20 9 22 16 19 16 1 29 11	24 13 23 20 20 17 1 29 12	25 16 26 23 23 17 1 29 11
15	30 9 30 33 1 13 36 29 11	33 13 35 1 3 13 36 29 11	36 15 34 4 4 13 36 28 10	3 20 1 7 7 13 1 29 11	5 23 8 11 9 14 2 29 11	9 29 11 11 11 14 2 29 11	11 32 11 11 14 14 2 29 11	15 2 15 11 15 15 2 29 11	17 7 19 13 17 16 1 29 11	20 10 22 16 19 16 1 29 11	24 14 23 20 20 17 1 29 12	25 17 26 23 23 17 1 29 11
16	30 10 30 33 1 13 36 29 11	33 14 35 1 3 13 36 29 11	36 16 34 4 4 13 36 28 10	3 21 1 7 7 13 1 29 11	6 25 8 11 9 14 2 29 11	9 29 11 11 11 14 2 29 11	11 34 11 11 14 14 2 29 11	15 3 15 11 15 15 2 29 11	17 8 19 13 17 16 1 29 11	20 11 23 17 19 17 1 29 11	24 16 23 20 20 17 1 29 12	27 19 26 23 23 17 1 29 11
17	30 11 30 33 1 13 36 29 11	33 15 35 1 3 13 36 29 11	36 18 34 4 4 13 36 28 10	3 22 1 7 7 13 1 29 11	6 26 8 11 9 14 2 29 11	9 32 11 11 11 14 2 29 11	12 35 11 11 14 14 2 29 11	15 5 15 11 15 15 2 29 11	17 9 19 13 17 16 1 29 11	20 12 23 17 19 17 1 29 11	24 17 23 20 20 17 1 29 12	27 20 26 23 23 17 1 29 11
18	30 12 30 33 1 13 36 29 11	33 17 35 1 3 13 36 29 11	36 19 34 4 4 13 36 28 10	3 24 1 7 7 13 1 29 11	6 27 8 11 9 14 2 29 11	9 33 11 11 11 14 2 29 11	12 1 11 11 14 14 2 29 11	15 6 15 11 15 15 2 29 11	17 10 20 13 17 16 1 29 11	20 13 23 17 19 17 1 29 11	24 18 23 20 20 17 1 29 12	27 21 26 23 23 17 36 29 11
19	30 14 30 33 2 14 36 29 11	33 18 35 1 3 13 36 29 11	36 20 35 4 4 13 36 28 10	3 25 1 7 7 13 1 29 11	6 29 8 11 9 14 2 29 11	9 34 11 11 11 14 2 29 11	12 2 11 11 14 14 2 29 11	15 8 15 11 15 15 2 29 11	17 11 20 13 17 16 1 29 11	20 15 23 17 19 17 1 29 11	24 19 23 21 21 17 1 29 11	27 23 27 24 23 17 36 29 11
20	30 15 30 33 2 14 36 29 11	34 19 35 2 4 13 36 29 11	36 21 34 5 5 13 36 29 11	3 27 1 7 7 13 1 29 11	6 30 8 11 9 14 2 29 11	9 35 11 11 11 14 2 29 11	12 3 11 11 14 14 2 29 11	15 9 15 11 15 15 2 29 11	18 13 20 13 17 16 1 29 11	21 16 23 17 19 17 1 29 11	24 20 23 21 21 17 1 29 11	27 23 27 24 23 17 36 29 11
21	32 16 32 34 2 14 36 29 11	34 21 35 2 4 13 36 29 11	1 23 34 5 5 13 1 29 11	4 28 2 7 7 13 1 29 11	8 31 8 11 9 14 2 29 11	9 1 11 11 11 13 1 29 11	12 5 11 11 14 14 2 29 11	15 10 15 11 15 15 2 29 11	18 14 20 13 17 16 1 29 11	21 17 23 17 19 17 1 29 11	24 21 23 21 21 17 1 29 11	27 25 27 24 23 17 36 29 11
22	32 17 32 34 2 14 36 29 11	34 22 35 2 4 13 36 29 11	1 24 34 5 5 13 1 29 11	4 29 2 7 7 13 1 29 11	8 33 9 11 9 14 2 29 11	10 2 11 11 11 13 1 29 11	12 6 11 11 14 14 2 29 11	15 11 15 11 15 15 2 29 11	18 15 20 13 17 16 1 29 11	21 18 23 17 19 17 1 29 11	24 23 23 21 21 17 1 29 11	28 26 28 25 23 17 1 29 11
23	32 18 32 34 2 14 36 29 11	34 23 35 2 4 13 36 29 11	1 25 35 5 5 13 1 29 11	4 31 2 7 7 13 1 29 11	8 34 9 11 11 14 2 29 11	10 4 11 11 11 13 1 29 11	14 7 11 11 14 14 2 29 11	15 12 15 11 15 15 2 29 11	19 16 20 13 17 16 1 29 11	21 19 20 13 17 17 1 29 11	25 24 23 21 21 17 1 29 11	28 28 28 25 23 17 1 29 11
24	32 20 32 34 2 14 36 29 11	34 24 35 2 4 13 36 29 11	1 27 35 5 5 13 1 29 11	4 32 2 7 7 13 1 29 11	8 36 9 11 11 14 2 29 11	10 5 11 11 11 13 1 29 11	14 8 11 11 14 14 2 29 11	16 13 16 11 16 16 2 29 11	19 17 20 13 17 16 1 29 11	22 21 22 17 20 16 2 29 11	25 25 23 21 21 17 1 29 11	28 29 28 25 23 17 1 29 11
25	32 21 32 35 2 14 36 29 11	34 26 34 1 4 13 36 28 10	1 28 35 5 5 13 1 29 11	4 33 2 7 7 13 1 29 11	8 1 9 11 11 14 2 29 11	10 6 11 11 11 13 1 29 11	14 10 11 11 14 14 2 29 11	16 15 16 11 16 16 2 29 11	19 19 20 13 17 16 1 29 11	22 22 22 17 20 16 2 29 11	25 27 23 21 21 17 1 29 11	28 31 28 25 23 17 1 29 11
26	32 23 32 35 2 14 36 29 11	34 27 34 1 4 13 36 28 10	1 29 35 5 5 13 1 29 11	4 34 2 7 7 13 1 29 11	8 2 9 11 11 14 2 29 11	10 7 11 11 11 13 1 29 11	14 11 11 11 14 14 2 29 11	16 16 16 11 16 16 2 29 11	19 20 21 14 17 16 1 29 11	22 23 22 17 20 16 2 29 11	26 28 23 22 22 17 1 29 11	28 32 28 25 23 17 1 29 11
27	32 24 32 35 2 14 36 29 11	34 28 34 1 4 13 36 28 10	1 31 35 5 5 13 1 29 11	4 36 1 7 7 13 1 29 11	8 4 10 11 10 13 1 29 11	10 9 11 11 11 13 1 29 11	14 12 11 11 14 14 2 29 11	16 17 16 11 16 16 2 29 11	19 21 21 14 17 16 1 29 11	22 25 22 17 20 16 2 29 11	26 29 23 22 22 17 1 29 11	28 34 28 25 23 17 1 29 11
28	32 25 32 35 2 14 36 29 11	34 30 34 1 4 13 36 28 10	1 32 35 5 5 13 1 29 11	4 1 3 9 8 13 1 29 11	7 5 10 11 10 13 1 29 11	10 10 11 11 11 13 1 29 11	14 14 11 11 14 14 2 29 11	16 17 16 11 16 16 2 29 11	19 22 21 14 17 16 1 29 11	22 26 22 17 20 16 2 29 11	26 31 23 22 22 17 1 29 11	28 35 28 25 23 17 1 29 11
29	32 26 33 35 2 14 36 29 11	34 31 34 1 4 13 36 28 10	1 34 35 6 6 13 1 29 11	5 3 3 9 8 13 1 29 11	7 7 10 11 10 13 1 29 11	10 11 11 11 11 13 1 29 11	14 14 11 11 14 14 2 29 11	16 20 16 11 16 16 2 29 11	19 23 22 15 17 16 1 29 11	22 27 22 17 20 16 2 29 11	26 32 24 22 22 17 1 29 11	28 36 29 25 23 17 1 29 11
30	32 27 33 35 2 14 36 29 11	**1908**	2 35 35 6 6 13 1 29 11	5 4 3 9 8 13 1 29 11	7 8 10 11 10 13 1 29 11	10 12 11 11 11 13 1 29 11	14 16 11 11 14 14 2 29 11	16 20 16 11 16 16 2 29 11	19 25 22 15 17 16 1 29 11	22 29 22 17 20 16 2 29 11	26 34 24 22 22 17 1 29 11	28 1 29 25 23 17 1 28 10
31	32 29 33 35 2 14 36 29 11		2 1 35 6 6 13 1 29 11		7 9 10 11 10 13 1 29 11		14 17 11 11 14 14 2 29 11	16 21 16 11 16 16 2 29 11		22 30 22 17 20 16 2 29 11		28 3 29 25 23 17 1 29 11

	JAN	FEB	MAR	APR	MAY	JUNE	JULY	AUG	SEPT	OCT	NOV	DEC
1	29 5 29 26 24 17 1 29 11	31 9 33 29 25 16 1 29 11	34 10 32 33 28 16 1 29 11	2 15 36 2 29 16 2 29 11	5 18 5 5 32 16 2 29 11	7 22 9 9 34 16 3 30 12	11 26 9 12 36 17 3 30 11	13 31 13 16 1 18 3 30 12	16 36 19 19 1 18 3 30 12	19 4 20 23 36 18 2 29 11	22 9 20 26 35 19 2 29 11	25 13 25 30 1 19 2 29 11
2	29 6 29 26 24 17 1 29 11	31 11 33 29 25 16 1 29 11	34 11 32 33 28 16 1 29 11	2 16 36 2 29 16 2 29 11	5 19 5 5 32 16 2 29 11	7 24 9 9 34 16 3 30 12	11 27 9 12 36 17 3 30 11	13 33 13 16 1 18 3 30 12	16 1 19 19 1 18 3 30 12	19 5 20 23 36 18 2 29 11	22 10 20 26 35 19 2 29 11	25 14 25 30 1 19 2 29 11
3	29 7 29 26 24 17 1 29 11	32 12 33 29 26 17 1 29 11	34 13 32 33 28 16 1 29 11	2 17 36 2 29 16 2 29 11	5 20 5 5 32 16 2 29 11	7 25 9 9 34 16 3 30 12	11 29 9 12 36 17 3 30 11	13 34 13 18 1 18 3 30 12	16 3 19 19 1 18 3 30 12	19 7 20 24 36 18 2 29 11	23 11 20 27 36 19 2 29 11	25 15 25 30 1 19 2 29 11
4	29 8 29 26 24 17 1 29 11	32 13 33 29 26 17 1 29 11	34 14 32 33 28 16 1 29 11	2 19 36 2 29 16 2 29 11	5 22 6 5 32 16 2 29 11	7 27 9 9 34 16 3 30 12	11 30 9 13 36 17 3 30 11	13 36 13 18 1 18 3 30 12	18 5 19 21 1 18 3 30 12	20 9 20 24 36 18 2 29 11	23 13 20 27 36 19 2 29 11	26 16 26 30 2 20 2 29 11
5	29 10 29 26 24 17 1 29 11	32 15 33 29 26 17 1 29 11	34 15 32 34 28 16 1 29 11	2 20 36 2 29 16 2 29 11	5 23 6 5 32 16 2 29 11	7 28 9 9 34 16 3 30 12	11 31 9 13 36 17 3 30 11	13 1 13 18 1 18 3 30 12	18 6 19 21 1 18 3 30 12	20 10 20 24 36 18 2 29 11	23 14 20 27 36 19 2 29 11	26 17 26 30 2 20 2 29 11
6	29 11 29 26 25 17 1 29 11	32 16 33 29 26 17 1 29 11	34 16 32 34 28 16 1 29 11	2 21 1 2 29 16 2 29 11	5 24 7 5 32 16 2 29 11	9 30 9 9 34 16 3 30 12	11 33 9 13 36 17 3 30 11	13 3 13 18 1 18 3 30 12	18 7 19 21 1 18 3 30 12	20 11 20 24 36 18 2 29 11	23 16 21 27 36 19 2 29 11	26 19 26 32 2 20 2 29 11
7	29 12 29 26 25 17 1 29 11	32 17 32 30 26 17 1 29 11	34 17 32 34 28 16 1 29 11	2 22 1 2 29 16 2 29 11	5 25 7 5 32 16 2 29 11	9 31 9 9 34 16 3 30 12	11 35 9 13 36 17 3 30 11	13 4 13 18 1 18 3 30 12	18 9 19 21 1 18 3 30 12	20 12 20 24 36 18 2 29 11	23 17 21 27 36 19 2 29 11	26 20 26 32 2 20 2 29 11
8	29 13 31 26 25 17 1 29 11	32 18 32 30 26 17 1 29 11	34 19 32 34 28 16 1 29 11	2 23 2 2 29 16 2 29 11	5 27 7 5 32 16 2 29 11	9 32 9 9 34 16 3 30 12	11 36 9 13 36 17 3 30 11	15 6 15 18 1 18 3 30 12	18 10 21 21 1 18 3 30 12	20 14 20 24 36 18 2 29 11	23 18 22 28 36 19 2 29 11	26 21 26 32 2 20 2 29 11
9	29 15 31 26 25 17 1 29 11	32 19 32 31 26 17 1 29 11	35 20 32 34 28 16 1 29 11	2 25 2 2 29 16 2 29 11	5 28 7 5 32 16 2 29 11	9 33 9 9 34 16 3 30 12	11 1 9 13 36 17 3 30 11	15 7 15 18 1 18 3 30 12	18 12 21 21 1 18 3 30 12	20 15 20 24 36 18 2 29 11	23 19 22 28 36 19 2 29 11	26 22 26 32 2 20 2 29 11
10	29 16 31 26 25 17 1 29 11	32 20 32 31 26 17 1 29 11	35 21 33 34 28 16 1 29 11	2 26 2 2 31 16 2 29 11	5 29 7 5 32 16 2 29 11	9 34 9 10 34 16 3 30 12	12 3 9 13 36 17 3 30 11	15 8 15 18 1 18 3 30 12	18 13 21 21 1 18 3 30 12	20 16 20 24 36 18 2 29 11	23 20 22 28 36 19 2 29 11	26 23 26 32 2 20 2 29 11
11	29 17 31 27 25 17 1 29 11	33 22 33 31 27 16 1 29 11	35 22 33 34 28 16 1 29 11	2 27 2 2 31 16 2 29 11	5 31 7 5 32 16 2 29 11	9 36 9 11 35 17 3 30 11	11 4 9 13 36 17 3 30 11	15 9 15 18 1 18 3 30 12	18 14 21 21 1 18 3 30 12	20 17 20 24 36 18 2 29 11	23 22 22 28 35 19 2 29 11	26 25 26 32 2 20 2 29 11
12	29 18 31 27 25 17 1 29 11	33 23 33 31 27 16 1 29 11	35 23 33 34 28 16 1 29 11	2 29 2 2 31 16 2 29 11	5 32 7 5 32 16 2 29 11	9 1 9 11 35 17 3 30 11	12 6 9 13 36 17 3 30 11	15 10 15 18 1 18 3 30 12	18 15 21 21 1 18 3 30 12	20 18 20 24 36 18 2 29 11	23 23 22 28 35 19 2 29 11	26 26 26 32 2 20 2 29 11
13	29 19 31 28 25 17 1 29 11	33 24 33 31 27 16 1 29 11	35 25 33 34 28 16 1 29 11	2 29 2 2 31 16 2 29 11	5 34 7 5 32 16 2 29 11	9 3 9 11 35 17 3 30 11	12 7 10 13 36 17 3 30 11	15 12 15 18 1 18 3 30 12	18 16 21 21 1 18 3 30 12	20 20 20 24 36 18 2 29 11	23 24 22 28 35 19 2 29 11	26 28 27 32 2 20 2 29 11
14	29 20 31 28 25 17 1 29 11	33 25 33 31 27 16 1 29 11	35 26 33 34 28 16 1 29 11	2 31 2 2 31 16 2 29 11	5 35 8 5 32 16 2 29 11	9 5 9 11 35 17 3 30 11	12 8 10 13 36 17 3 30 11	15 13 16 18 1 18 3 30 12	18 18 21 21 1 18 3 30 12	20 20 20 24 36 18 2 29 11	23 25 22 28 35 19 2 29 11	26 29 27 32 2 20 2 29 11
15	30 22 31 28 25 17 1 29 11	33 27 33 31 27 16 1 29 11	35 27 33 34 28 16 1 29 11	3 33 3 3 31 16 2 30 11	5 36 8 5 32 16 2 29 11	9 6 9 11 35 17 3 30 11	12 10 10 15 36 17 3 30 12	15 15 16 18 1 18 3 30 12	18 19 21 21 1 18 3 30 12	20 22 20 24 36 18 2 29 11	23 26 22 28 35 19 2 29 11	26 30 27 32 2 20 2 29 11
16	30 23 31 28 25 17 1 29 11	33 28 31 31 27 16 1 29 11	35 29 33 34 29 16 1 29 11	3 34 3 3 31 16 2 30 11	5 2 8 5 32 16 2 29 11	9 7 9 11 35 17 3 30 11	12 11 10 15 36 17 3 30 12	15 16 16 18 1 18 3 30 12	18 20 21 21 1 18 3 30 12	20 23 20 24 36 18 2 29 11	23 28 23 29 35 19 2 29 11	26 31 28 32 2 20 2 29 11
17	30 25 31 28 25 17 1 29 11	33 29 31 31 27 16 1 29 11	35 30 34 35 29 16 2 29 11	3 35 3 3 31 16 2 30 11	5 3 8 7 32 16 2 29 11	9 9 9 11 35 17 3 30 11	12 12 10 15 36 17 3 30 12	15 17 16 18 1 18 3 30 12	18 21 21 22 1 18 3 30 12	20 24 20 24 36 18 2 29 11	23 29 23 29 35 19 2 29 11	26 32 28 32 2 20 2 29 11
18	30 26 31 28 25 17 1 29 11	33 32 31 31 27 16 1 29 11	35 32 34 35 29 16 2 29 11	3 1 3 3 31 16 2 30 11	5 5 8 7 32 16 2 29 11	9 10 9 11 35 17 3 30 11	12 14 11 15 36 17 3 30 12	15 18 18 18 1 18 3 30 12	18 22 21 22 36 18 2 29 11	20 26 20 24 36 18 2 29 11	23 30 23 29 35 19 2 29 11	26 34 29 32 2 20 2 29 11
19	30 27 32 28 25 16 1 29 11	34 31 31 31 27 16 1 29 11	35 33 34 35 29 16 2 29 11	3 3 3 3 31 16 2 30 11	5 6 8 7 32 16 2 29 11	9 11 9 11 35 17 3 30 11	12 15 11 15 36 17 3 30 12	15 19 18 18 1 18 3 30 12	18 24 21 22 36 18 2 29 11	20 27 20 24 36 18 2 29 11	23 32 23 29 35 19 2 29 11	26 35 29 32 2 20 2 29 11
20	30 28 32 28 25 16 1 29 11	34 34 31 31 27 16 1 29 11	35 35 34 35 29 16 2 29 11	3 4 3 3 31 16 2 30 11	5 7 8 7 32 16 2 29 11	9 13 9 11 35 17 3 30 11	12 16 11 15 36 17 3 30 11	15 21 18 18 1 18 3 30 12	18 25 21 22 36 18 2 29 11	20 28 20 26 36 18 2 29 11	24 33 23 29 36 19 2 29 11	27 1 29 32 2 20 2 29 11
21	31 29 32 28 25 16 1 29 11	34 35 32 32 27 16 1 29 11	1 36 34 35 29 16 2 29 11	4 6 4 4 31 16 1 29 11	5 8 8 7 32 16 2 29 11	9 14 9 11 35 17 3 30 11	12 17 11 15 36 17 3 30 11	15 21 18 19 1 18 3 30 12	18 26 21 22 36 18 2 29 11	20 29 20 26 36 18 2 29 11	24 34 23 29 36 19 2 29 11	27 2 29 32 2 20 2 29 11
22	31 31 32 28 35 16 1 29 11	34 1 32 32 28 16 1 29 11	1 2 34 35 29 16 2 29 11	4 7 4 4 31 16 1 29 11	7 10 8 7 34 16 2 29 11	10 15 9 11 35 17 3 30 11	12 18 11 15 36 17 3 30 11	15 23 18 19 1 18 3 30 12	18 27 21 22 36 18 2 29 11	20 31 20 26 36 18 2 29 11	24 35 23 29 36 19 2 29 11	28 4 29 32 2 20 2 29 11
23	31 33 32 28 25 16 1 29 11	34 2 32 32 28 16 1 29 11	1 3 34 35 29 16 2 29 11	4 9 4 4 31 16 1 29 11	7 11 8 7 34 16 2 29 11	10 16 9 12 36 16 3 30 12	12 20 11 15 36 17 3 30 11	15 24 18 19 1 18 3 30 12	18 28 21 22 36 18 2 29 11	21 32 20 26 36 18 2 29 11	25 1 23 29 1 19 2 29 11	28 5 29 32 2 20 2 29 11
24	31 34 33 28 25 16 1 29 11	34 4 33 33 28 16 1 29 11	1 5 34 35 29 16 2 29 11	4 10 4 4 31 16 1 29 11	7 13 8 7 34 16 2 29 11	10 18 9 12 36 16 3 30 12	13 21 11 15 1 17 3 30 11	16 25 18 19 1 18 3 30 12	19 29 21 22 1 19 2 29 11	22 34 20 26 36 18 2 29 11	25 2 25 29 1 19 2 29 11	28 7 29 32 2 20 2 29 11
25	31 35 33 28 25 16 1 29 11	34 6 33 33 28 16 1 29 11	1 6 34 35 29 16 2 29 11	4 11 4 4 31 16 1 29 11	7 14 8 7 34 16 2 29 11	10 19 9 12 36 16 3 30 12	13 22 11 15 1 17 3 30 11	16 27 18 19 1 18 3 30 12	19 31 21 23 1 19 2 29 11	22 35 20 26 36 18 2 29 11	25 4 25 29 1 19 2 29 11	28 8 29 32 2 20 2 29 11
26	31 1 33 28 25 16 1 29 11	34 7 33 33 28 16 1 29 11	1 7 34 35 29 16 2 29 11	4 12 4 4 31 16 1 29 11	7 16 8 7 34 16 2 29 11	10 20 9 12 36 16 3 30 11	13 23 12 15 1 17 3 30 11	16 28 18 19 1 18 3 30 12	19 32 21 23 1 19 2 29 11	22 36 20 26 36 18 2 29 11	25 5 25 29 1 19 2 29 11	28 10 29 32 2 20 2 29 11
27	31 2 33 29 25 16 1 29 11	34 8 32 32 28 16 1 29 11	1 9 35 35 29 16 2 29 11	4 13 4 4 31 16 1 29 11	7 17 8 7 34 16 2 29 11	10 21 9 12 36 16 3 30 12	13 24 12 15 1 17 3 30 11	16 30 18 19 1 18 3 30 12	19 34 21 23 1 19 2 29 11	22 2 20 26 36 18 2 29 11	25 7 25 29 1 19 2 29 11	28 11 29 32 2 20 2 29 11
28	31 4 33 29 25 16 1 29 11	34 9 33 33 28 16 1 29 11	1 10 35 35 29 16 2 29 11	4 15 4 4 31 16 1 29 11	7 18 8 7 34 16 2 29 11	10 22 9 12 36 16 3 30 12	13 25 12 15 1 17 3 30 11	16 30 18 19 1 18 3 30 12	19 36 21 23 36 18 2 29 11	22 3 20 26 35 18 2 29 11	25 8 25 29 1 19 2 29 11	29 12 29 32 2 20 2 29 11
29	31 5 33 29 25 16 1 29 11		1 11 35 1 29 16 1 29 11	4 16 4 4 31 16 1 29 11	7 19 8 8 34 16 2 29 11	10 24 9 12 36 16 3 30 12	13 27 12 16 1 17 3 30 11	16 32 18 19 1 18 3 30 12	19 1 21 23 36 18 2 29 11	22 5 20 26 35 18 2 29 11	25 10 25 29 1 19 2 29 11	29 13 29 32 2 20 2 29 11
30	31 7 33 29 25 16 1 29 11	**1909**	1 13 35 1 29 16 1 29 11	4 18 4 4 31 16 1 29 11	7 20 8 8 34 16 2 29 11	10 25 9 12 36 16 3 30 12	13 28 13 16 1 17 3 30 11	16 33 18 19 1 18 3 30 12	19 2 21 23 36 18 2 29 11	22 6 20 26 35 18 2 29 11	25 11 25 29 1 19 2 29 11	29 14 29 32 2 20 2 29 11
31	31 7 33 29 25 16 1 29 11		1 14 35 2 29 16 1 29 11		7 20 8 8 34 16 2 29 11		13 30 13 16 1 17 3 30 11	16 35 18 19 1 18 3 30 12		22 8 20 26 35 18 2 29 11		29 16 29 32 2 20 2 29 11

	JAN	FEB	MAR	APR	MAY	JUNE	JULY	AUG	SEPT	OCT	NOV	DEC
1	29 17 30 32 2 20 2 29 11	32 22 29 33 5 20 2 29 11	35 22 32 32 5 20 2 29 11	1 27 1 33 7 19 3 30 10	5 30 7 36 9 19 3 30 11	7 36 7 4 12 19 4 30 12	10 3 9 7 13 19 4 30 12	13 9 15 10 15 19 4 30 12	17 14 19 14 17 20 5 29 11	19 18 18 18 19 20 4 29 11	22 22 22 22 21 21 4 30 12	25 25 26 25 24 22 4 30 12
2	29 19 30 32 2 20 2 29 11	32 23 29 33 5 20 2 29 11	35 23 32 32 5 20 2 29 11	1 28 1 33 7 19 3 30 10	5 31 7 1 10 19 3 30 11	7 1 6 4 12 19 4 30 12	10 4 9 7 13 19 4 30 12	13 10 15 10 15 19 4 30 12	17 15 19 14 17 20 4 29 11	19 19 18 18 19 20 4 29 11	22 23 22 22 21 21 4 30 12	26 27 27 26 24 22 4 30 12
3	29 20 30 32 2 20 2 29 11	32 24 29 33 5 20 2 29 11	35 25 32 32 5 20 2 29 11	1 30 1 33 7 19 3 30 10	5 33 7 1 10 19 3 30 11	7 3 6 4 12 19 4 30 12	10 6 9 7 13 19 4 30 12	13 12 15 10 15 19 4 30 12	17 16 20 14 17 20 4 29 11	19 20 18 18 19 20 4 29 11	22 24 22 22 21 21 4 30 12	26 28 27 26 24 22 4 30 12
4	29 21 31 32 2 20 2 29 11	32 25 29 33 5 20 2 29 11	35 26 32 32 5 20 2 29 11	1 31 1 33 7 19 3 30 10	5 34 7 1 10 19 3 30 11	7 4 6 4 12 19 4 30 12	10 7 9 7 13 19 4 30 12	13 13 15 10 15 19 4 30 12	17 17 20 14 17 20 4 29 11	19 21 18 18 19 20 4 29 11	22 25 22 22 21 21 4 30 12	26 29 27 26 24 22 4 30 12
5	29 22 31 32 2 20 2 29 11	32 26 29 33 5 20 2 29 11	35 27 32 32 5 20 2 29 11	1 33 1 34 7 19 3 30 10	5 36 7 1 10 19 3 30 11	7 6 6 4 12 19 4 30 12	10 9 9 7 13 19 4 30 12	13 15 15 10 15 19 4 30 12	17 19 20 14 17 20 4 29 11	19 22 18 18 20 20 4 29 11	23 27 22 22 22 22 4 30 12	26 30 27 26 24 22 4 30 12
6	29 23 31 32 2 20 2 29 11	32 28 29 33 4 20 2 29 11	36 29 33 32 6 20 3 30 11	1 34 1 34 7 19 3 30 10	5 1 7 1 10 19 3 30 10	8 7 6 4 12 19 4 30 12	12 10 9 7 13 19 4 30 12	13 16 16 11 16 20 4 29 11	17 20 20 14 17 20 4 29 11	20 24 18 18 20 20 4 29 11	23 28 22 22 22 22 4 30 12	26 31 27 26 24 22 4 30 12
7	29 25 32 32 2 20 2 29 11	32 29 29 33 4 20 2 29 11	36 30 33 32 6 20 3 30 11	3 36 3 34 9 19 3 30 12	5 3 7 1 10 19 3 30 10	8 8 6 4 12 19 4 30 12	12 12 10 7 13 19 4 30 12	13 17 16 11 16 20 4 29 11	17 20 20 14 17 20 4 29 11	20 25 18 19 20 20 4 29 11	23 29 22 22 22 22 4 30 12	26 32 27 26 24 22 4 30 12
8	29 26 32 32 2 20 2 29 11	32 30 29 32 4 20 2 29 11	36 31 33 32 6 20 3 30 11	3 1 3 34 9 19 3 30 12	6 4 7 1 10 19 3 30 10	8 10 6 4 12 19 4 30 12	12 13 10 7 13 19 4 30 12	13 18 16 11 16 20 4 29 11	17 22 20 14 17 20 4 29 11	20 26 18 19 20 20 4 29 11	23 30 22 22 22 22 4 30 12	26 34 27 26 24 22 4 30 12
9	29 27 32 32 2 20 2 29 11	32 31 29 32 4 20 2 29 11	36 33 33 32 6 20 3 30 11	3 1 3 34 9 19 3 30 12	6 6 7 1 10 19 3 30 10	8 11 6 4 12 19 4 30 12	12 15 10 7 13 19 4 30 12	14 20 16 11 16 20 4 29 11	17 23 20 14 17 20 4 29 11	20 27 18 19 20 20 4 29 11	23 31 23 23 22 22 4 30 12	26 35 28 26 24 22 4 30 12
10	29 28 32 32 2 20 2 29 11	32 32 29 32 4 20 2 29 11	36 34 33 32 6 20 3 30 11	3 3 3 34 9 19 3 30 12	6 7 7 1 10 19 3 30 10	8 12 6 4 12 19 4 30 12	12 16 10 7 13 19 4 30 12	14 21 16 11 16 20 4 29 11	17 25 20 15 17 20 4 29 11	20 28 18 19 20 20 4 29 11	23 32 23 23 22 22 4 30 12	26 36 28 26 24 22 4 30 12
11	29 29 32 32 2 20 2 29 11	32 34 29 32 4 20 2 29 11	36 36 33 32 6 20 3 30 11	3 5 3 34 9 19 3 30 12	6 9 7 1 10 19 3 30 10	9 14 6 4 12 19 4 30 12	12 18 10 7 13 19 4 30 12	14 22 16 11 16 20 4 29 11	17 26 20 15 17 20 4 29 11	20 30 18 20 20 20 4 29 11	23 34 23 23 22 22 4 30 12	26 2 28 26 24 22 4 30 12
12	29 31 32 32 2 20 2 29 11	32 35 29 32 4 20 2 29 11	36 1 33 32 6 20 3 30 11	3 6 3 34 9 19 3 30 12	6 10 7 1 10 19 3 30 10	9 15 7 4 12 19 4 30 12	12 19 10 7 13 19 4 30 12	14 23 16 12 16 19 4 30 12	17 27 20 15 17 20 4 29 11	20 31 20 20 20 20 4 29 11	23 36 23 23 22 22 4 30 12	26 3 28 26 24 22 4 30 12
13	29 32 32 32 2 20 2 29 11	32 2 29 32 4 20 2 29 11	36 3 33 32 6 20 3 30 11	3 9 4 34 9 19 3 30 12	6 12 7 1 10 19 3 30 10	9 16 7 4 12 19 4 30 12	12 19 10 8 14 19 4 30 12	14 24 16 12 16 19 4 30 12	17 28 20 16 17 20 4 29 11	20 32 20 20 20 20 4 29 11	23 1 23 23 22 22 4 29 11	27 4 28 27 24 22 4 30 12
14	29 34 32 32 2 20 2 29 11	32 2 29 32 5 20 2 29 11	36 4 33 32 6 20 3 30 11	3 9 4 34 9 19 3 30 12	6 13 7 1 10 19 3 30 10	9 18 7 4 12 19 4 30 12	12 21 12 8 14 19 4 30 12	14 25 16 12 16 19 4 30 12	17 29 20 16 17 20 4 29 11	21 33 21 21 21 21 4 30 12	23 3 23 23 22 22 4 30 12	27 6 28 27 24 22 4 30 12
15	29 35 32 32 2 20 2 29 11	32 5 29 32 5 20 2 29 11	35 6 34 32 7 20 2 29 11	3 10 4 34 9 19 3 30 12	6 15 7 1 10 19 3 30 10	9 19 7 4 12 19 4 30 12	12 22 12 8 14 19 4 30 12	15 27 18 12 16 19 4 30 12	17 31 20 16 17 20 4 29 11	21 34 21 21 21 21 4 30 12	24 4 24 24 22 22 4 30 12	27 7 28 27 24 22 4 30 12
16	29 1 32 32 2 20 2 29 11	32 5 31 32 5 20 2 29 11	35 7 34 32 7 20 2 29 11	3 12 4 34 9 19 3 30 12	6 16 7 1 10 19 3 30 10	9 21 7 6 13 19 4 30 12	12 23 12 8 14 19 4 30 12	15 28 18 12 16 19 4 30 12	17 32 20 16 17 20 4 29 11	21 36 21 21 21 21 4 30 12	24 6 24 24 22 20 4 30 12	27 9 28 27 24 22 3 30 12
17	29 2 32 32 2 20 2 29 11	32 7 31 32 5 20 2 29 11	35 8 34 32 7 20 2 29 11	3 13 5 35 9 19 3 30 11	6 17 7 1 10 19 3 30 10	9 21 7 6 12 19 4 30 12	12 25 12 8 14 19 4 30 12	15 29 18 12 16 19 4 30 12	17 34 20 16 17 20 4 29 11	21 1 21 21 21 21 4 30 12	24 7 24 24 22 22 4 30 12	27 10 30 27 24 22 3 30 12
18	30 3 32 33 3 20 2 29 11	33 8 31 32 5 20 2 29 11	35 10 34 32 7 20 2 29 11	3 15 5 35 9 19 3 30 11	6 18 7 1 10 19 3 30 10	9 23 7 6 13 19 4 30 12	12 25 12 8 14 19 4 30 12	15 30 18 12 16 19 4 30 12	17 35 19 16 17 20 4 29 11	21 3 21 21 21 21 4 30 12	24 9 24 24 22 22 4 30 12	27 12 30 27 24 22 3 30 12
19	30 5 32 33 3 20 2 29 11	33 10 31 32 5 20 2 29 11	35 11 35 32 7 20 2 29 11	3 16 6 36 9 19 3 30 11	6 19 7 1 10 19 3 30 10	9 24 7 6 13 19 4 30 12	12 26 12 8 14 19 4 30 12	15 32 18 13 16 20 4 29 11	17 1 19 16 17 20 4 29 11	21 4 21 21 21 21 4 30 12	24 10 24 24 22 22 4 30 12	27 13 30 28 24 22 3 30 12
20	30 6 32 33 3 20 2 29 11	34 11 31 32 5 20 2 29 11	35 12 35 32 7 20 2 29 11	3 18 6 36 9 19 3 30 11	6 21 7 2 11 19 3 30 10	9 25 7 6 13 19 4 30 12	12 28 12 9 15 19 4 30 12	15 33 17 13 16 20 4 29 11	17 2 19 16 17 20 4 29 11	21 6 21 21 21 21 3 30 12	24 12 24 24 22 22 4 30 12	27 15 30 28 24 22 3 30 12
21	31 8 32 34 4 20 2 29 11	34 13 32 32 5 20 2 29 11	35 13 35 32 7 20 2 29 11	4 18 6 36 9 19 3 30 11	6 22 7 2 11 19 4 30 10	9 26 7 6 13 19 4 30 12	12 30 12 9 15 19 4 30 12	15 34 17 13 16 20 4 29 11	17 4 19 16 17 20 4 29 11	21 7 21 21 21 21 3 30 12	24 13 24 24 22 22 4 30 12	27 16 30 28 25 22 3 30 12
22	31 9 31 34 4 20 2 29 11	34 14 32 32 5 20 2 29 11	1 14 35 32 7 20 2 29 11	4 19 6 36 9 19 3 30 11	7 23 7 2 11 19 3 30 11	10 27 7 6 13 19 4 30 12	12 31 13 9 15 19 4 30 12	15 35 17 13 16 20 4 29 11	18 5 19 16 18 20 4 29 11	21 9 21 21 21 21 3 30 12	24 14 24 24 22 22 4 30 12	27 18 30 28 25 22 3 30 12
23	31 10 31 34 4 20 2 29 11	34 15 32 32 5 20 2 29 11	1 16 35 32 7 20 2 29 11	4 21 6 36 9 19 3 30 11	7 24 7 2 11 19 3 30 11	10 28 7 6 13 19 4 30 12	12 32 13 9 15 19 4 30 12	15 1 17 13 16 20 4 29 11	18 6 19 16 18 20 4 29 11	21 10 21 21 21 21 3 30 12	25 15 25 25 22 22 4 30 12	28 19 30 28 25 22 3 30 12
24	31 11 31 34 4 20 2 29 11	34 16 32 32 5 20 2 29 11	1 17 35 32 7 20 2 29 11	4 22 6 36 9 19 3 30 11	7 25 7 2 11 19 3 30 11	10 30 7 6 13 19 4 30 12	12 33 13 9 15 19 4 30 12	16 2 17 13 16 20 4 29 11	19 8 19 17 19 20 4 29 11	22 12 21 21 21 21 4 30 12	25 16 25 25 23 22 4 30 12	28 20 30 28 25 22 3 30 12
25	31 13 31 34 4 20 2 29 11	34 17 32 32 5 20 2 29 11	1 19 35 32 7 20 2 29 11	4 23 6 36 9 19 3 30 11	7 26 7 2 11 19 3 30 11	10 31 7 6 13 19 4 30 12	13 35 13 10 15 19 4 30 12	16 4 17 13 16 20 4 29 11	19 9 19 17 19 20 4 29 11	22 13 21 21 21 21 4 30 12	25 18 25 25 23 22 4 30 12	28 21 30 28 25 22 3 30 12
26	32 14 32 34 5 20 2 29 11	34 19 32 32 5 20 2 29 11	1 20 36 33 7 19 3 30 11	4 24 6 36 9 19 3 30 11	7 27 7 2 11 19 3 30 11	10 33 7 6 13 19 4 30 12	13 36 13 10 15 19 4 30 12	16 5 17 13 16 20 4 29 11	19 10 19 17 19 20 4 29 11	22 15 21 21 21 21 4 30 12	25 19 25 25 24 22 4 30 12	28 22 30 28 25 22 3 30 12
27	32 16 32 34 5 20 2 29 11	34 20 32 32 5 20 2 29 11	1 21 36 33 7 19 3 30 11	4 25 6 36 9 19 3 30 11	7 29 7 2 11 19 3 30 11	10 34 7 6 13 19 4 30 12	13 1 13 10 15 19 4 30 12	16 7 19 13 16 20 4 29 11	19 11 19 17 19 20 4 29 11	22 16 21 21 21 21 4 30 12	25 20 25 25 24 22 4 30 12	28 24 30 28 25 22 3 30 12
28	32 17 32 34 5 20 2 29 11	34 21 32 32 5 20 2 29 11	1 22 36 33 7 19 3 30 11	4 27 6 36 9 19 3 30 11	7 30 7 3 12 19 4 30 12	10 35 8 6 13 19 4 30 12	13 3 13 10 15 19 4 30 12	16 8 19 13 16 20 4 29 11	19 13 19 17 19 20 4 29 11	22 17 21 21 21 21 4 30 12	25 22 25 25 24 22 4 30 12	28 25 30 28 25 22 3 30 12
29	32 18 32 33 5 20 2 29 11		1 23 1 33 7 19 3 30 11	4 28 6 36 9 19 3 30 11	7 31 7 3 12 19 4 30 12	10 36 8 6 13 19 4 30 12	13 4 15 10 15 19 4 30 12	16 10 19 13 17 20 4 29 11	19 15 17 17 19 20 4 29 11	22 18 21 21 21 21 4 30 12	25 23 25 25 24 22 4 30 12	28 26 30 28 25 22 3 30 12
30	32 19 32 33 5 20 2 29 11	1910	1 25 1 33 7 19 3 30 11	4 29 6 36 9 19 3 30 11	7 33 7 3 12 19 4 30 12	10 1 8 7 13 19 4 30 12	13 6 15 10 15 19 4 30 12	16 11 19 13 17 20 4 29 11	19 16 17 17 19 20 4 29 11	22 19 21 21 21 21 4 30 12	25 24 25 25 24 22 4 30 12	28 27 30 30 25 22 3 30 12
31	32 20 30 33 5 20 2 29 11		1 26 1 33 7 19 3 30 11		7 34 7 3 12 19 4 30 12		13 7 15 10 15 19 4 30 12	16 12 19 13 17 20 4 29 11		22 21 22 22 21 21 4 30 12		28 28 30 30 25 22 3 30 12

	JAN	FEB	MAR	APR	MAY	JUNE	JULY	AUG	SEPT	OCT	NOV	DEC
1	28 30 30 30 25 22 3 30 12	32 35 29 34 28 23 4 30 11	34 34 34 1 30 22 4 30 12	1 4 3 4 31 22 4 30 10	4 8 4 8 34 22 4 30 12	7 14 5 12 36 22 5 30 12	10 18 10 15 3 22 6 30 12	14 23 17 17 5 23 5 30 12	16 27 18 18 6 22 6 30 12	20 30 18 17 8 23 5 30 12	24 34 24 18 7 24 6 30 12	25 1 27 21 6 24 5 30 12
2	28 31 30 30 25 22 3 30 12	32 36 29 34 28 23 4 30 11	34 1 34 1 30 22 4 30 12	1 6 3 4 31 22 4 30 10	4 10 4 8 34 22 4 30 12	8 15 5 12 36 22 5 30 12	10 19 10 15 3 22 6 30 12	14 23 17 17 5 23 5 30 12	16 27 18 18 6 22 6 30 12	20 31 18 17 8 23 5 30 12	24 36 24 18 7 24 6 30 12	25 3 27 21 6 24 5 30 12
3	28 32 30 30 25 22 3 30 12	32 1 29 34 28 23 4 30 11	34 2 34 1 30 22 4 30 12	1 7 3 4 31 22 4 30 10	4 11 4 8 34 22 4 30 12	8 16 5 12 1 22 5 30 12	10 20 10 15 3 22 6 30 12	14 24 17 17 5 23 5 30 12	16 28 18 18 6 22 6 30 12	20 32 18 17 8 23 5 30 12	24 1 24 18 7 24 6 30 12	25 5 28 21 6 24 5 30 12
4	29 33 30 30 25 23 3 30 11	32 3 29 34 28 23 4 30 11	35 3 34 1 29 23 4 29 11	1 9 3 4 31 22 4 30 10	4 12 4 8 34 22 4 30 12	8 18 5 12 1 22 5 30 12	12 21 12 15 3 22 6 30 12	14 25 17 17 5 23 5 30 12	16 30 18 18 6 22 6 30 10	20 33 18 17 8 23 5 30 12	24 2 24 18 7 24 6 30 12	25 6 28 21 6 24 5 30 12
5	29 34 30 30 25 23 3 30 11	32 4 30 34 28 23 4 30 11	35 4 34 1 29 23 4 29 11	1 10 4 5 32 23 4 30 11	4 14 4 8 34 22 4 30 12	8 19 5 12 1 22 5 30 12	12 22 12 15 3 22 6 30 12	14 26 17 17 5 23 5 30 12	16 31 18 18 7 22 6 30 12	20 35 18 17 8 23 5 30 12	24 3 24 18 7 24 6 30 12	26 7 28 21 6 24 5 30 12
6	29 36 30 30 26 23 3 30 11	31 5 30 34 28 22 4 30 11	35 5 34 1 29 23 4 29 11	2 12 4 5 32 23 4 30 11	4 15 4 9 34 22 4 30 12	8 21 5 12 1 22 5 30 12	12 24 12 15 3 22 6 30 12	14 28 17 17 5 23 5 30 12	18 33 18 18 7 22 6 30 12	20 36 18 17 8 23 5 30 12	24 6 24 18 7 24 6 30 12	26 9 28 21 6 24 5 30 12
7	30 1 30 30 26 23 3 30 12	31 7 30 34 28 22 4 30 11	35 7 34 1 29 23 4 29 11	2 13 4 5 32 23 4 30 11	4 16 4 9 34 22 4 30 12	8 21 5 12 1 22 5 30 12	12 25 12 15 3 22 6 30 12	14 29 17 17 5 23 5 30 12	18 34 18 18 7 22 6 30 12	20 1 20 17 8 23 5 30 12	24 6 24 18 7 24 6 30 12	26 10 29 21 6 24 5 30 12
8	30 3 30 30 26 23 3 30 12	31 8 30 34 28 22 4 30 11	35 9 34 2 29 23 4 29 11	2 13 4 5 32 23 4 30 11	4 18 4 9 34 22 4 30 12	8 22 6 12 1 22 5 30 12	12 26 12 16 3 22 6 30 12	14 30 17 17 5 23 5 30 12	18 36 18 18 7 22 6 30 12	20 3 20 17 8 23 5 30 12	24 7 24 18 7 24 6 30 12	26 12 29 22 6 24 5 30 12
9	30 4 30 30 26 23 3 30 12	31 10 30 34 28 22 4 30 11	35 10 35 2 29 23 4 29 11	2 16 4 5 32 23 4 30 11	4 19 4 9 34 22 4 30 12	8 23 6 13 1 22 5 30 12	12 27 12 16 3 22 6 30 12	14 31 17 17 5 23 5 30 12	18 36 18 18 7 22 6 30 12	20 4 20 17 8 23 5 30 12	24 9 24 19 7 24 6 30 12	26 13 29 22 6 24 5 30 12
10	30 6 30 30 26 23 3 30 12	31 11 30 34 28 22 4 30 11	35 11 35 2 29 23 4 29 11	2 17 4 5 32 23 4 30 11	4 21 4 9 34 22 4 30 12	8 25 6 13 1 22 5 30 12	12 28 12 16 3 22 6 30 12	15 33 18 18 6 22 6 30 12	18 1 18 18 7 22 6 30 12	20 5 20 17 8 23 5 30 12	24 10 24 19 7 24 6 30 12	26 14 29 22 6 24 5 30 12
11	30 7 30 30 26 23 3 30 12	31 12 31 34 28 22 4 30 11	35 13 35 2 29 23 4 29 11	3 18 4 6 33 23 4 30 12	4 22 4 9 34 22 4 30 12	8 26 6 13 1 22 5 30 12	12 30 12 16 3 22 6 30 12	15 34 18 18 6 22 6 30 12	18 3 18 18 7 22 6 30 12	20 7 20 17 8 23 5 30 12	24 12 24 19 7 24 6 30 12	26 16 29 22 6 24 5 30 12
12	30 9 30 30 26 23 3 30 12	31 13 31 34 28 22 4 30 11	35 14 35 2 31 23 4 29 11	3 19 4 6 33 23 4 30 12	6 22 4 9 34 22 4 30 12	9 27 6 13 1 22 5 30 12	12 31 12 15 3 21 6 30 12	15 36 18 18 6 22 6 30 12	18 4 18 18 7 22 6 30 12	20 8 20 17 8 23 5 30 12	24 13 25 19 7 24 6 30 12	26 18 29 22 6 24 5 30 12
13	30 10 30 30 26 23 3 30 12	31 15 31 34 28 22 4 30 11	35 16 35 2 31 23 4 29 11	3 21 4 6 33 23 4 30 12	6 24 4 10 34 22 4 30 12	9 29 8 14 2 23 5 30 12	12 32 12 15 3 21 6 30 12	15 1 18 18 6 22 6 30 12	18 6 17 18 7 23 6 30 12	21 10 20 17 8 23 5 30 12	24 15 25 19 7 24 6 30 12	27 19 29 22 6 24 5 30 12
14	30 12 29 30 26 23 3 30 12	33 16 31 34 28 22 4 30 11	35 17 35 2 31 23 4 29 11	3 22 4 6 33 23 4 30 12	6 25 4 10 34 22 4 30 12	9 30 8 14 2 23 5 30 12	12 33 12 15 3 21 6 30 12	15 2 18 18 6 22 6 30 12	18 7 17 18 7 23 6 30 12	21 11 20 17 8 23 5 30 12	24 16 25 19 7 24 6 30 12	27 20 29 23 6 24 5 30 12
15	30 13 29 30 26 23 3 30 12	33 18 31 34 28 22 4 30 11	35 19 35 2 31 23 4 29 11	3 23 4 6 33 23 4 30 12	6 25 4 10 34 22 4 30 12	9 31 8 14 2 23 5 30 12	12 34 12 15 3 21 6 30 12	15 3 18 18 6 22 6 30 12	18 9 17 18 7 23 6 30 12	21 12 20 17 8 23 5 30 12	24 18 25 19 7 24 6 30 12	27 21 29 23 6 24 5 30 12
16	30 15 29 32 26 23 3 30 12	33 19 31 35 29 23 4 30 11	36 20 36 3 31 23 4 30 11	3 24 4 6 33 23 4 30 12	6 28 4 10 35 22 4 30 11	9 32 8 14 2 23 5 30 12	12 35 13 16 4 22 5 30 12	15 4 18 18 6 22 6 30 12	18 10 17 18 7 23 6 30 12	21 14 20 17 8 23 5 30 12	24 19 25 19 7 24 6 30 12	27 23 29 23 6 24 5 30 12
17	30 16 29 32 26 23 3 30 12	33 21 31 35 29 23 4 30 11	36 21 36 3 31 23 4 30 11	3 25 4 6 33 23 4 30 12	6 29 4 10 35 22 4 30 11	9 33 8 14 2 23 5 30 12	12 1 13 16 4 22 5 30 12	15 6 18 18 6 22 6 30 12	18 12 17 18 7 23 6 30 12	21 15 21 17 8 23 5 30 12	24 21 25 19 7 24 6 30 12	27 24 29 23 6 24 5 30 12
18	30 17 29 32 26 23 3 30 12	33 22 31 35 29 23 4 30 11	36 22 36 3 31 23 4 30 11	3 27 4 6 33 23 4 30 12	6 30 4 10 35 22 4 30 11	9 35 8 14 2 23 5 30 12	12 3 13 16 4 22 5 30 12	15 7 18 18 6 22 6 30 12	18 14 17 18 7 23 6 30 12	21 17 21 17 8 23 5 30 12	24 22 25 19 7 24 6 30 12	27 25 29 23 6 24 5 30 12
19	30 18 29 32 27 23 3 30 12	33 23 31 35 29 23 4 30 11	36 24 36 3 31 23 4 30 11	3 28 4 6 33 23 4 30 12	6 31 4 10 35 22 4 30 11	9 36 8 14 2 23 5 30 12	12 4 13 17 4 22 5 30 12	15 9 18 18 6 22 6 30 12	18 15 17 18 7 23 6 30 12	21 18 21 17 8 23 5 30 12	24 33 25 19 7 24 5 30 12	27 26 29 23 6 24 5 30 12
20	30 19 29 32 27 23 3 30 12	34 24 32 35 29 23 4 30 11	36 25 36 3 31 23 4 30 11	3 29 5 6 33 23 4 30 12	6 32 4 10 35 22 4 30 11	9 1 8 14 2 23 5 30 12	12 5 13 17 4 22 5 30 12	15 10 18 18 6 22 6 30 12	18 16 17 18 7 23 6 30 12	21 20 21 17 8 23 5 30 12	24 24 26 20 6 24 5 30 12	27 27 29 23 6 24 5 30 12
21	31 21 29 32 28 23 4 31 11	34 25 32 35 29 23 4 30 11	36 26 36 3 31 23 4 30 11	4 30 5 7 34 23 4 30 12	6 34 4 10 35 22 4 30 11	9 3 8 14 2 23 5 30 12	12 6 15 18 4 22 6 30 12	15 12 18 18 6 22 6 30 12	18 17 17 18 7 23 6 30 12	21 21 21 17 8 23 5 30 12	24 25 26 20 6 24 5 30 12	27 29 29 23 6 24 5 30 12
22	31 22 29 32 28 23 4 31 11	34 27 32 35 29 23 4 30 11	1 27 1 3 31 22 4 30 10	4 31 5 7 34 22 4 30 12	7 35 4 10 35 22 4 30 11	10 4 9 15 3 22 6 30 12	12 9 15 18 4 22 6 30 12	15 13 18 18 6 22 6 30 12	18 18 17 18 7 23 6 30 12	21 22 21 17 8 23 5 30 12	24 27 26 20 6 24 5 30 12	27 30 29 23 6 24 5 30 12
23	31 23 29 32 28 23 4 31 11	34 28 32 35 29 23 4 30 11	1 28 1 3 31 22 4 30 10	4 33 4 7 34 22 4 30 12	7 36 4 10 36 22 4 30 12	10 6 9 15 3 22 6 30 12	12 8 15 18 4 22 6 30 12	15 15 18 18 6 22 6 30 12	18 19 17 18 7 23 6 30 12	21 23 21 17 8 23 5 30 12	25 28 26 20 7 25 5 30 12	28 31 29 23 6 24 5 30 12
24	31 25 29 32 28 23 4 31 11	34 30 33 36 30 22 4 30 12	1 30 1 4 31 22 4 30 10	4 34 4 7 34 22 4 30 12	7 2 4 10 36 22 4 30 12	10 7 9 15 3 22 6 30 12	13 11 15 18 4 22 6 30 12	16 16 18 18 6 22 6 30 12	20 21 17 17 8 23 5 30 12	22 24 22 17 8 23 5 30 12	25 29 26 20 7 25 5 30 12	28 32 28 24 6 25 6 30 12
25	31 26 29 32 28 23 4 31 11	34 30 33 36 30 22 4 30 12	1 31 1 4 31 22 4 30 10	4 36 4 7 34 22 4 30 12	7 3 4 10 36 22 4 30 12	10 9 9 15 3 22 6 30 12	13 12 15 18 4 22 6 30 12	16 18 18 18 6 22 6 30 12	20 22 17 17 8 23 5 30 12	22 26 22 17 8 23 5 30 12	25 30 27 21 7 25 5 30 12	28 33 28 24 6 25 6 30 12
26	31 27 29 32 27 23 3 30 11	34 31 33 36 30 22 4 30 12	1 31 1 4 31 22 4 30 10	4 1 4 7 34 22 4 30 12	7 4 4 10 36 22 4 30 12	10 10 9 15 3 22 6 30 12	13 14 15 18 4 22 6 30 12	16 19 18 18 6 22 6 30 12	20 23 17 17 8 23 5 30 12	22 27 22 18 8 24 6 30 12	25 31 27 21 7 25 5 30 12	28 34 28 24 6 25 6 30 12
27	31 28 29 32 28 23 4 30 11	34 33 33 36 30 22 4 30 12	1 33 2 4 31 22 4 30 10	4 3 4 7 34 22 4 30 12	7 6 4 12 36 22 4 30 12	10 12 9 15 3 22 6 30 12	13 15 15 18 4 22 6 30 12	16 21 18 18 6 22 6 30 12	20 25 17 17 8 23 5 30 12	22 28 22 18 8 24 6 30 12	25 32 27 21 7 25 5 30 12	29 36 29 24 6 25 6 30 12
28	31 29 29 34 28 23 4 30 11	34 34 33 1 30 22 4 30 12	1 35 2 4 31 22 4 30 10	4 4 4 7 34 22 4 30 12	7 7 4 12 36 22 4 30 12	10 13 9 15 3 22 6 30 12	13 16 15 18 4 22 6 30 12	16 21 18 18 6 22 6 30 12	20 26 17 17 8 23 5 30 12	22 29 22 18 8 24 6 30 12	25 34 27 21 7 25 5 30 12	29 1 27 24 6 25 6 30 12
29	32 30 29 34 28 23 4 30 11	1911	1 36 2 4 31 22 4 30 10	4 6 4 7 34 22 4 30 12	7 9 4 12 36 22 4 30 12	10 15 10 15 3 22 6 30 12	13 18 15 18 4 22 6 30 12	16 22 18 18 6 22 [illegible] 30 12	20 27 17 17 8 23 5 30 12	22 30 22 18 8 24 6 30 12	25 35 27 21 7 25 5 30 12	29 3 27 24 6 25 5 30 12
30	32 31 29 34 28 23 4 30 11		1 1 2 4 31 22 4 30 10	4 7 4 8 34 22 4 30 12	7 10 4 12 36 22 4 30 12	10 16 10 15 3 22 6 30 12	13 19 15 18 4 22 6 30 12	16 24 18 18 6 22 6 30 12	20 28 17 17 8 23 5 30 12	24 32 24 18 8 24 6 30 12	25 36 27 21 6 24 5 30 12	29 3 27 24 6 25 5 30 12
31	32 33 29 34 28 23 4 30 11		1 3 2 4 31 22 4 30 10		7 12 4 12 36 22 4 30 12		14 21 16 17 5 23 5 29 11	16 25 18 18 6 22 6 30 12		24 33 24 18 8 24 6 30 12		29 5 27 24 6 25 5 30 12

	JAN	FEB	MAR	APR	MAY	JUNE	JULY	AUG	SEPT	OCT	NOV	DEC
1	29 6 27 24 6 25 5 30 12	32 11 31 28 7 26 5 31 12	35 14 35 32 8 26 5 31 12	2 19 2 25 9 26 5 31 11	5 23 2 2 11 26 5 31 11	7 27 6 7 13 25 6 31 12	10 31 12 10 15 25 6 31 12	13 34 16 14 16 25 7 31 12	16 4 15 19 19 25 7 31 12	19 7 19 22 21 25 7 31 12	22 13 24 25 22 25 7 30 12	25 16 27 30 25 27 7 31 12
2	29 7 27 24 6 25 5 30 12	32 13 31 29 7 26 5 31 12	35 16 35 32 8 26 5 31 12	2 20 2 35 9 26 5 31 11	5 23 2 2 11 26 5 31 11	7 28 6 7 13 25 6 31 12	10 32 12 10 15 25 6 31 12	13 36 16 14 16 25 7 31 12	16 5 15 19 19 25 7 31 12	19 9 19 22 21 25 7 31 12	22 14 24 25 22 25 7 30 12	25 18 27 30 25 27 7 31 12
3	29 9 27 24 6 25 5 30 12	32 14 31 29 7 26 5 31 12	35 17 35 32 8 26 5 31 12	3 22 3 1 10 27 6 31 12	5 26 2 2 11 26 5 31 11	7 30 6 7 13 25 6 31 12	10 33 12 10 15 25 6 31 12	13 1 16 14 16 25 7 31 12	16 6 15 19 19 25 7 31 12	19 10 19 22 21 25 7 31 12	22 16 24 25 22 25 7 30 12	25 19 27 30 25 27 7 31 12
4	29 11 27 24 6 25 5 30 12	32 17 31 29 7 26 5 31 12	35 19 35 32 8 26 5 31 12	3 24 3 1 10 27 6 31 12	5 27 2 2 11 26 5 31 11	7 31 6 7 13 25 6 31 12	10 34 13 10 15 25 6 31 12	13 3 16 14 16 25 7 31 12	16 7 15 19 19 25 7 31 12	19 12 *19 22 21 25 7 31 12	22 17 25 26 22 26 7 30 12	25 21 27 30 25 27 7 31 12
5	29 12 27 25 6 25 5 30 12	32 18 31 29 7 26 5 31 12	35 20 35 32 8 26 5 31 12	3 25 3 1 10 27 6 31 12	5 28 2 2 11 26 5 31 11	7 32 7 7 13 25 6 31 12	10 36 13 10 15 25 6 31 12	13 4 16 15 16 25 7 31 12	16 9 15 19 19 25 7 31 12	19 13 19 22 21 25 7 31 12	22 18 25 26 22 26 7 30 12	27 22 27 30 25 27 7 31 12
6	29 14 27 25 6 25 5 30 12	32 19 31 29 7 26 5 31 12	35 21 35 32 8 26 5 31 12	3 26 3 1 10 27 6 31 12	5 29 2 2 11 26 5 31 11	7 33 7 7 13 25 6 31 12	10 1 13 10 15 25 6 31 12	13 6 16 15 16 25 7 31 12	16 10 15 19 19 25 7 31 12	19 15 19 22 21 25 7 31 12	22 20 25 26 22 26 7 30 12	27 23 27 31 25 27 7 31 12
7	29 14 27 25 5 25 5 30 11	32 21 31 29 7 25 5 31 11	35 22 35 32 8 26 5 31 12	3 27 3 1 10 27 6 31 12	5 30 2 4 11 26 5 31 11	7 34 7 7 13 25 6 31 12	10 2 13 10 15 25 6 31 12	13 7 16 15 16 25 7 31 12	16 12 16 19 19 25 7 30 12	20 16 20 23 21 26 7 30 12	22 21 25 26 22 26 7 30 12	27 25 27 31 25 27 7 31 12
8	29 17 27 25 5 25 5 30 11	32 22 31 29 7 25 5 31 11	35 24 35 32 8 26 5 31 12	3 28 3 1 10 27 6 31 12	5 31 2 4 11 26 5 31 11	7 36 7 7 13 25 6 31 12	12 3 13 12 15 25 6 31 12	14 8 16 16 17 25 7 31 12	18 13 16 19 19 25 7 30 12	20 18 20 23 21 26 7 30 12	22 22 25 26 22 26 7 30 12	27 26 27 31 25 27 7 31 12
9	29 18 27 25 5 25 5 30 11	32 23 31 29 7 25 5 31 11	35 25 36 32 8 26 5 31 12	3 29 3 1 10 27 6 31 12	5 33 2 4 11 26 5 31 11	7 1 7 7 13 25 6 31 12	12 4 13 12 15 25 6 31 12	14 10 16 16 17 25 7 31 12	18 15 16 19 19 25 7 31 12	20 19 20 23 21 26 7 30 12	23 24 25 26 23 26 7 30 12	27 27 27 31 25 27 7 31 12
10	29 19 27 25 5 25 5 30 11	32 24 31 29 7 25 5 31 11	35 26 36 32 8 26 5 31 12	3 31 3 1 10 27 6 31 12	5 34 2 4 11 26 5 31 11	7 3 7 7 13 25 6 31 12	12 6 13 12 15 25 6 31 12	14 12 16 16 18 25 7 31 12	18 16 16 19 19 25 7 31 12	20 21 20 23 21 26 7 30 12	23 25 25 26 23 26 7 30 11	27 28 27 31 25 27 7 31 12
11	29 21 27 25 5 25 5 30 11	32 25 31 29 7 25 5 31 11	35 27 36 32 8 26 5 31 12	3 32 3 1 10 27 6 31 12	5 35 2 4 11 26 5 31 11	8 4 8 8 13 25 6 31 12	12 7 13 12 15 25 6 31 12	14 13 16 16 18 25 7 31 12	18 18 16 19 19 25 7 31 12	21 21 21 23 21 26 7 30 12	23 26 25 26 23 26 7 30 11	27 30 27 31 25 27 7 31 12
12	29 22 27 25 5 25 5 30 11	32 27 31 29 7 25 5 31 11	35 28 1 32 8 26 5 31 12	3 33 3 1 10 27 6 31 12	6 36 3 4 12 26 6 31 12	8 5 8 8 13 25 6 31 12	12 9 14 12 15 25 6 31 12	14 14 16 16 18 25 7 31 12	18 19 16 19 19 25 7 31 12	21 23 21 23 21 26 7 30 12	23 28 25 26 23 26 7 30 11	27 31 27 31 25 27 7 31 12
13	30 23 27 25 6 25 5 30 12	32 28 31 29 7 25 5 31 11	35 30 1 32 8 26 5 31 12	3 34 3 1 10 27 6 31 12	6 1 3 4 12 26 6 31 12	8 6 8 8 13 25 6 31 12	12 10 14 12 15 25 6 31 12	14 16 16 16 18 25 7 31 12	18 21 16 19 19 25 7 30 12	21 24 21 23 21 26 7 30 12	23 29 26 26 23 26 7 30 11	27 32 26 31 25 27 7 31 12
14	30 24 27 25 6 25 5 30 12	33 29 31 29 7 25 4 31 11	35 31 1 32 8 26 5 31 12	3 36 3 1 10 27 6 31 12	6 3 3 4 12 26 6 31 12	8 8 8 8 13 25 6 31 12	12 12 14 12 15 25 6 31 12	14 17 16 16 18 25 7 31 12	18 22 16 19 19 25 7 30 12	21 25 21 24 21 26 7 30 12	23 30 26 26 23 26 7 30 11	27 33 25 31 25 27 7 31 12
15	30 25 28 25 6 25 5 30 12	33 30 31 29 7 25 4 31 11	35 32 1 32 8 26 5 31 12	3 1 3 1 10 26 6 31 12	6 4 3 4 12 26 6 31 12	8 9 8 8 13 25 6 31 12	12 13 14 12 15 25 6 30 12	15 19 16 16 18 25 7 31 12	18 24 16 19 19 25 7 30 12	21 27 21 24 21 26 7 30 12	24 31 26 26 24 26 7 30 12	27 34 25 31 25 27 7 31 12
16	30 27 28 25 6 25 5 30 12	33 31 31 29 7 25 4 31 11	36 33 2 32 9 26 5 31 12	3 2 3 1 10 26 6 31 12	6 6 4 5 12 26 6 31 12	8 11 8 8 13 25 6 31 12	12 15 14 12 15 25 6 30 12	15 20 16 16 18 25 7 31 12	18 25 16 19 19 25 7 30 12	21 28 21 24 21 26 7 30 12	24 33 26 26 24 26 7 30 12	27 36 25 31 25 27 7 31 12
17	30 28 28 25 6 25 5 30 12	33 32 31 29 7 25 4 31 11	36 35 2 33 9 26 5 31 12	3 3 3 1 10 26 6 31 12	6 7 4 6 12 26 6 31 12	8 12 8 8 13 25 6 31 12	12 16 14 12 15 24 6 30 12	15 21 16 16 18 25 7 31 12	18 26 16 19 19 25 7 30 12	21 30 21 24 21 26 7 30 12	24 34 26 27 24 26 7 30 12	27 1 25 31 25 27 7 31 12
18	30 29 28 25 6 25 5 30 12	33 34 31 29 7 25 4 31 11	36 36 2 33 9 26 5 31 12	3 5 3 1 10 26 6 31 12	6 8 4 6 12 26 6 31 12	9 13 9 9 13 26 6 31 12	12 18 14 12 15 24 6 30 12	15 23 16 16 18 25 7 31 12	18 27 16 19 19 25 7 30 12	21 30 21 24 21 26 7 30 12	24 35 26 28 24 26 7 30 12	27 2 25 31 25 27 7 31 12
19	30 30 29 26 6 25 5 30 12	33 35 32 29 7 25 5 31 11	36 1 2 34 9 26 5 31 12	3 6 3 1 10 26 6 31 12	6 10 4 6 12 26 6 31 12	9 15 9 9 14 26 6 31 12	12 19 14 12 15 24 6 30 12	15 24 15 15 18 24 6 30 12	18 28 16 19 19 25 7 30 12	21 32 21 24 21 26 7 30 12	24 36 26 28 24 26 7 30 12	27 3 25 31 26 27 6 31 12
20	30 32 29 26 6 25 5 30 12	34 36 32 31 7 25 5 31 11	36 3 2 34 9 26 5 31 12	4 7 3 1 10 26 6 31 12	7 12 4 6 12 26 6 31 12	9 17 9 9 14 26 6 31 12	12 21 14 12 15 24 6 30 12	15 25 15 15 18 24 6 30 12	18 30 16 19 19 25 7 30 12	21 33 21 24 21 26 7 30 12	24 1 26 28 24 26 7 30 12	27 4 25 31 26 27 6 31 12
21	31 33 29 26 7 25 5 31 12	34 1 32 31 7 25 5 31 11	1 4 2 34 9 26 5 31 12	4 9 3 1 10 26 6 31 12	7 13 4 6 12 26 6 31 12	9 18 9 9 14 26 6 31 12	12 22 15 12 15 24 6 30 12	15 27 15 15 18 24 6 30 12	18 31 18 19 19 25 7 30 12	21 34 22 24 21 26 7 30 12	24 2 26 28 24 26 7 30 12	27 6 25 31 26 27 6 31 12
22	31 34 29 27 7 25 5 31 12	34 3 33 31 7 25 5 31 11	1 5 2 34 9 26 5 31 12	4 10 1 1 10 26 6 31 12	7 15 4 6 12 26 6 31 12	10 19 10 10 14 26 6 31 12	12 23 15 12 15 24 6 30 12	15 28 15 15 18 24 6 30 12	18 32 18 19 19 25 7 30 12	21 36 22 24 21 26 7 30 12	24 4 26 28 24 26 7 30 12	28 8 25 31 26 28 7 31 12
23	31 35 29 27 7 25 5 31 12	34 4 33 31 7 25 5 31 11	1 7 2 34 9 26 5 31 12	4 12 1 1 10 26 6 31 12	8 16 4 6 12 25 6 31 12	10 21 10 10 14 26 6 31 12	13 25 16 13 16 25 7 31 12	15 29 15 17 18 24 6 30 12	19 33 18 19 19 25 7 30 12	21 1 22 25 21 26 7 30 12	25 5 26 28 25 26 7 31 12	28 9 26 32 26 28 7 31 12
24	31 1 29 27 7 25 5 31 12	34 5 33 31 7 25 5 31 11	1 8 3 35 9 26 5 31 12	4 13 1 1 10 26 6 31 12	8 17 4 6 12 25 6 31 12	10 22 10 10 14 26 6 31 12	13 26 16 13 16 25 7 31 12	16 30 15 17 18 25 7 31 12	19 34 18 21 20 26 7 31 12	22 2 23 25 22 26 7 31 12	25 7 26 28 25 26 7 31 12	28 10 26 32 26 28 7 31 12
25	32 2 29 27 6 26 5 30 12	34 7 34 31 7 25 5 31 11	1 9 3 35 9 26 5 31 12	4 15 1 1 10 26 6 31 12	8 19 4 6 12 25 6 31 12	10 24 11 10 14 26 6 31 12	13 27 16 13 16 25 7 31 12	16 31 15 18 18 25 7 31 12	19 36 18 21 20 26 7 21 12	22 3 23 25 22 26 7 31 12	25 8 26 28 25 26 7 31 12	28 12 26 32 26 28 7 31 12
26	32 3 29 27 6 26 5 30 12	34 8 34 31 7 25 5 31 11	2 11 3 35 9 26 5 31 12	4 16 2 2 11 26 5 31 11	8 20 5 6 12 25 6 31 12	10 25 11 10 14 25 6 31 12	13 28 16 13 16 25 7 31 12	16 33 15 18 18 25 7 31 12	19 1 18 21 20 26 7 31 12	22 4 24 25 22 26 7 31 12	25 9 26 29 25 26 7 31 12	28 13 26 32 26 28 7 31 12
27	32 5 29 27 6 26 5 30 12	34 10 34 31 7 25 5 31 11	2 12 3 35 9 26 5 31 12	4 18 2 2 11 26 5 31 11	8 21 5 6 12 25 6 31 12	10 26 12 10 14 25 6 31 12	13 29 16 13 16 25 7 31 12	16 34 15 18 18 25 7 31 12	19 2 18 21 20 26 7 31 12	22 6 24 25 22 26 7 31 12	25 11 26 29 25 26 7 31 12	28 15 27 33 27 27 7 31 12
28	32 6 29 27 6 26 5 30 12	34 11 34 31 7 25 5 31 11	2 13 3 35 9 26 5 31 12	4 19 2 2 11 26 5 31 11	8 22 6 6 13 25 6 31 12	10 27 12 10 14 25 6 31 12	13 30 16 13 16 25 7 31 12	16 36 15 18 18 25 7 31 12	19 4 19 21 20 25 7 31 12	22 7 24 25 22 26 7 31 12	25 12 26 29 25 26 7 30 12	28 16 27 33 27 27 7 31 12
29	32 7 29 27 6 26 5 30 12	34 12 34 31 7 25 5 31 11	2 15 3 35 9 26 5 31 12	4 20 2 2 11 26 5 31 11	8 24 6 6 13 25 6 31 12	10 28 12 10 14 25 6 31 12	13 31 16 13 16 25 7 31 12	16 36 15 18 18 25 7 31 12	19 5 19 21 20 25 7 31 12	22 8 24 25 22 26 7 31 12	25 32 26 29 25 26 7 31 12	28 18 27 33 27 27 7 31 12
30	32 9 29 28 6 26 5 30 12	1912	2 16 3 35 9 26 5 31 12	4 21 2 2 11 26 5 31 11	8 25 6 6 13 25 6 31 12	10 30 12 10 14 25 6 31 12	13 33 16 13 16 25 7 31 12	16 1 15 18 18 25 7 31 12	19 6 19 22 21 25 7 31 12	22 10 24 25 22 26 7 31 12	25 32 26 29 25 26 7 31 12	28 19 27 33 27 27 7 31 12
31	32 10 29 28 7 26 5 31 12		2 18 3 35 9 26 5 31 12		8 26 6 6 13 25 6 31 12		13 34 16 13 16 25 7 31 12	16 3 15 18 18 25 7 31 12		22 12 24 25 22 26 7 31 12		28 21 27 33 27 27 7 31 12

	JAN	FEB	MAR	APR	MAY	JUNE	JULY	AUG	SEPT	OCT	NOV	DEC
1	28 22 27 33 27 27 6 31 12	32 27 31 36 30 28 6 31 12	34 28 36 3 31 28 6 31 12	1 32 1 4 34 28 7 31 12	4 35 2 4 35 29 7 31 11	7 4 7 4 2 29 7 31 11	10 7 13 6 4 28 7 31 12	13 12 14 9 7 28 8 31 12	16 17 15 13 8 28 8 31 12	19 21 20 16 10 28 8 31 12	22 26 25 20 11 29 8 31 11	25 30 23 23 11 29 8 31 11
2	28 23 27 33 27 27 6 31 12	32 28 31 36 30 28 6 31 12	34 28 36 3 31 28 6 31 12	1 33 1 4 34 28 7 31 12	4 36 2 3 35 29 7 31 11	7 5 7 4 2 29 7 31 11	10 9 13 6 4 28 7 31 12	13 13 14 9 7 28 8 31 12	16 19 15 13 8 28 8 31 12	19 23 20 16 10 28 8 31 12	22 28 25 20 11 29 8 31 11	25 31 23 23 11 29 8 31 11
3	28 24 27 33 27 27 6 31 12	32 29 31 1 30 28 6 31 12	34 30 36 3 31 28 6 31 12	1 34 1 4 34 28 6 31 12	4 2 2 3 35 29 7 31 11	7 6 7 4 2 29 7 31 11	10 10 13 6 4 28 7 31 12	13 15 14 9 7 28 8 31 12	16 21 15 13 8 28 8 31 12	19 24 20 16 10 28 8 31 12	22 29 25 20 11 29 8 31 11	26 32 23 23 11 29 8 31 11
4	28 26 27 33 27 27 6 31 12	32 30 31 1 30 28 6 31 12	34 31 36 3 31 28 6 31 12	1 36 1 4 34 28 6 31 12	5 3 2 3 36 29 7 31 12	7 7 7 4 2 29 7 31 11	10 12 13 6 4 28 7 31 12	13 17 14 9 7 28 8 31 12	17 22 16 13 8 28 8 31 12	19 25 20 16 10 28 8 31 12	22 30 25 20 11 29 8 31 11	26 34 23 23 11 29 8 31 11
5	28 27 27 33 27 27 6 31 12	32 31 31 1 30 28 6 31 12	35 32 1 3 31 29 6 31 11	1 1 1 4 34 28 6 31 12	5 4 2 3 36 29 7 31 12	7 9 7 4 2 29 7 31 11	10 13 13 6 4 28 7 31 12	13 18 14 9 7 28 8 31 12	17 24 16 13 8 28 8 31 12	20 26 21 17 11 29 8 31 12	23 31 25 20 11 29 8 31 11	26 35 23 23 11 29 8 31 11
6	28 28 27 33 27 27 6 31 12	32 33 31 1 30 28 6 31 12	35 33 1 4 31 29 6 31 11	1 2 1 4 34 28 6 31 12	5 6 3 3 36 29 7 31 12	7 10 7 4 2 29 7 31 11	10 13 13 6 4 28 7 31 12	13 19 14 10 7 28 8 31 12	17 25 16 13 8 28 8 31 12	20 28 21 17 11 29 8 31 12	23 32 25 20 11 29 8 31 11	26 36 23 23 11 29 8 31 11
7	29 29 28 34 28 28 6 31 12	33 34 33 1 30 28 6 31 12	35 35 1 4 31 29 6 31 11	2 3 1 4 34 29 7 31 11	5 7 3 3 36 29 7 31 12	8 12 8 4 2 29 7 31 11	10 16 13 6 4 28 7 31 12	13 20 14 10 7 28 8 31 12	17 26 16 13 8 28 8 31 12	20 29 21 17 11 29 8 31 12	23 34 25 20 11 29 8 31 11	26 1 23 23 11 29 8 31 11
8	30 31 28 34 28 28 6 31 12	33 35 33 1 30 28 6 31 12	35 36 1 4 31 29 6 31 11	2 4 1 4 34 29 7 31 11	5 8 3 3 1 29 7 31 12	8 13 8 4 2 29 7 31 11	10 16 13 7 4 28 7 31 12	13 22 13 10 7 28 7 31 12	17 27 16 13 8 28 8 31 12	20 31 21 17 11 29 8 31 12	23 35 25 20 11 29 8 31 11	26 2 23 25 11 29 8 31 11
9	30 32 28 34 28 28 6 31 12	33 36 33 1 30 28 6 31 12	35 1 1 4 31 29 6 31 11	2 6 1 4 34 29 7 31 11	5 9 3 3 1 29 7 31 11	8 14 9 4 2 29 7 31 11	10 18 13 7 4 28 7 31 12	13 24 13 10 7 28 7 31 12	17 28 16 13 8 28 8 31 12	20 32 22 17 11 29 8 31 12	23 36 25 20 11 29 8 31 11	26 4 23 25 11 29 8 31 11
10	30 33 28 34 28 28 6 31 12	33 1 33 1 30 28 6 31 12	35 2 1 4 31 29 6 31 11	2 7 1 4 34 29 7 31 11	5 10 3 3 1 29 7 31 11	8 16 9 4 3 29 7 31 12	11 19 13 7 5 29 7 31 12	13 25 13 10 7 28 7 31 12	17 30 16 13 9 28 8 31 12	20 33 22 17 11 29 8 31 12	23 1 25 20 11 29 8 31 11	26 5 24 25 12 30 8 31 12
11	30 34 28 34 28 28 6 31 12	33 3 33 1 30 28 6 31 12	35 3 1 4 31 29 6 31 11	2 8 1 4 34 29 7 31 11	5 12 3 3 1 29 7 31 11	8 18 10 4 3 29 7 31 12	11 21 14 7 5 29 8 31 12	13 25 13 10 7 28 7 31 12	17 31 16 14 9 28 8 31 12	20 34 22 17 11 29 8 31 12	23 2 25 20 11 29 8 31 11	26 6 24 25 12 30 8 31 12
12	30 35 28 34 28 28 6 31 12	33 4 33 1 30 28 6 31 12	35 5 1 4 32 29 6 31 11	2 10 1 4 34 29 7 31 11	5 13 4 3 1 29 7 31 11	9 19 10 4 3 29 7 31 12	11 23 14 7 5 29 8 31 12	13 28 13 10 7 28 7 31 12	17 32 16 14 9 28 8 31 12	20 35 23 17 11 29 8 31 12	23 4 25 20 11 29 8 31 11	26 7 24 26 12 30 8 31 12
13	30 36 28 34 28 28 6 31 12	33 5 33 1 30 28 6 31 12	35 6 1 4 32 29 6 31 11	2 11 1 4 34 29 7 31 11	5 15 4 3 1 29 7 31 11	9 20 10 4 3 29 7 31 12	11 24 14 8 5 29 8 31 12	13 29 13 10 7 28 7 31 12	17 33 17 14 9 28 8 31 12	20 1 23 17 11 29 8 31 12	23 5 25 20 11 29 8 31 11	26 8 25 26 12 30 8 31 12
14	30 2 28 34 28 28 6 31 12	33 6 33 1 30 28 6 31 12	36 7 1 4 32 28 6 31 12	2 12 1 4 34 29 7 31 11	5 16 4 3 1 29 6 31 11	9 21 10 4 3 29 7 31 12	11 25 14 8 5 29 8 31 12	13 30 13 10 7 28 7 31 12	17 34 17 14 9 28 8 31 12	20 2 23 17 11 29 8 31 12	23 5 25 22 11 29 8 31 11	26 10 25 26 12 30 8 31 12
15	30 3 28 34 28 28 6 31 12	33 8 33 1 30 28 6 30 12	36 8 1 4 32 28 6 31 12	2 13 1 4 35 29 7 31 11	5 18 4 3 1 29 6 31 11	9 23 10 4 3 29 7 31 12	11 26 14 8 5 29 8 31 12	13 31 13 10 7 28 7 31 12	17 35 18 14 9 28 8 31 12	20 3 23 17 11 29 8 31 12	23 8 25 22 11 29 8 31 11	26 12 25 26 12 30 8 31 12
16	30 4 28 34 28 28 6 31 12	33 9 33 1 30 28 6 30 12	36 10 1 4 32 28 6 31 12	2 15 1 4 35 29 7 31 11	5 19 4 3 1 29 6 31 11	9 24 10 4 3 29 7 31 12	12 28 14 8 6 29 8 31 12	13 32 13 10 7 28 7 31 12	17 1 18 14 10 28 8 31 12	20 4 23 17 11 29 8 31 12	23 9 25 22 11 29 8 31 11	27 13 25 26 12 30 8 31 12
17	30 6 28 34 28 28 6 31 12	33 10 33 1 30 28 6 30 12	36 12 1 4 33 28 6 31 12	2 16 1 4 35 29 7 31 11	5 21 4 3 1 29 6 31 11	9 25 11 5 4 29 7 31 12	12 29 14 8 6 29 8 31 12	13 34 13 10 7 28 7 31 12	17 2 18 14 10 28 8 31 12	20 5 23 18 11 29 8 31 12	23 10 25 22 11 29 8 31 11	27 14 25 26 12 30 8 31 12
18	30 7 28 34 28 28 6 31 12	33 12 33 1 30 28 6 30 12	36 13 1 4 33 28 6 31 12	3 18 1 4 35 29 7 31 12	5 22 4 3 1 29 6 31 11	9 27 11 5 4 29 7 31 12	12 30 14 8 6 29 8 31 12	13 34 13 10 7 28 7 31 12	17 3 18 14 10 28 8 31 12	20 7 23 18 11 29 8 31 12	23 11 25 22 11 29 8 31 11	27 15 25 26 12 30 8 31 12
19	30 8 28 34 28 28 6 31 12	34 13 34 3 31 28 6 31 12	36 15 1 4 33 28 6 31 12	3 19 1 4 35 29 7 31 12	6 24 4 3 1 29 7 31 12	9 29 11 5 4 29 7 31 12	12 31 14 8 6 29 8 31 12	15 36 13 10 7 28 7 31 12	17 4 18 14 10 28 8 31 12	20 8 23 18 11 29 8 31 12	23 13 25 22 11 29 8 31 11	27 16 25 26 12 30 8 31 12
20	30 10 30 36 28 28 6 31 12	34 15 34 3 31 28 6 31 12	36 16 1 4 33 28 6 31 12	3 21 1 4 35 29 7 31 11	6 25 5 3 1 29 7 31 12	9 30 11 5 4 29 7 31 12	12 33 14 8 6 29 8 31 12	15 1 14 12 8 28 8 31 12	17 6 19 14 10 28 8 31 12	20 9 23 19 11 29 8 31 12	23 14 25 22 11 29 8 31 11	27 17 25 26 12 30 8 31 12
21	31 12 30 36 28 28 6 31 12	34 16 34 3 31 28 6 31 12	1 18 2 5 34 29 7 32 12	4 22 1 4 35 29 7 31 11	6 26 5 3 1 29 7 31 12	9 31 11 5 4 29 7 31 12	12 34 14 8 6 29 8 31 12	15 2 14 12 8 28 8 31 12	17 7 19 14 10 28 8 31 12	21 10 23 19 11 29 8 31 12	23 16 25 22 11 29 8 31 11	27 19 26 26 12 30 8 31 12
22	31 13 30 36 28 28 6 31 12	34 18 34 3 31 28 6 31 12	1 19 2 5 34 29 7 32 12	4 24 1 4 35 29 7 31 11	7 27 5 3 1 29 7 31 12	10 32 11 5 4 29 7 31 12	12 35 14 8 6 29 8 31 12	15 4 14 12 8 28 8 31 12	18 8 19 14 10 28 8 31 12	21 12 24 19 11 29 8 31 12	23 17 25 23 11 29 8 31 11	28 20 26 26 12 30 8 31 12
23	31 14 30 36 28 28 6 31 12	34 19 34 3 31 28 6 31 12	1 21 2 5 34 29 7 32 12	4 25 1 4 35 29 7 31 11	7 29 5 3 1 29 7 31 12	10 33 11 5 4 29 7 31 12	12 36 14 8 6 29 8 31 12	15 5 14 12 8 28 8 31 12	18 10 19 14 10 28 8 31 12	21 13 24 19 11 29 8 31 12	25 19 25 23 11 29 8 31 11	28 22 26 26 12 30 8 31 12
24	31 16 30 36 28 28 6 31 12	34 21 34 3 31 28 6 31 12	1 22 2 5 34 29 7 32 12	4 27 1 4 35 29 7 31 11	7 30 5 3 1 29 7 31 12	10 34 11 5 4 29 7 31 12	13 1 14 8 6 29 8 31 12	16 6 14 12 8 28 8 31 12	19 11 19 15 10 28 8 31 12	22 15 24 19 11 29 8 31 12	25 20 25 23 11 29 8 31 11	28 24 26 26 12 30 8 31 12
25	31 17 30 36 28 28 6 31 12	34 22 36 3 31 28 6 31 12	1 23 2 5 34 29 7 32 12	4 28 1 4 35 29 7 31 11	7 31 6 3 1 29 7 31 12	10 36 12 5 4 28 7 31 12	13 3 14 8 6 29 8 31 12	16 7 14 12 8 28 8 31 12	19 12 19 15 10 28 8 31 12	22 16 24 19 11 29 8 31 12	25 20 23 23 11 29 8 31 11	28 25 26 26 12 30 8 31 12
26	31 19 30 36 28 28 6 31 12	34 24 36 3 31 28 6 31 12	1 25 2 5 34 29 7 32 12	4 29 1 4 35 29 7 31 11	7 33 6 3 2 29 7 31 12	10 1 12 5 4 28 7 31 12	13 4 14 8 6 29 8 31 12	16 8 14 12 8 28 8 31 12	19 13 19 15 10 28 8 31 12	22 17 24 19 11 29 8 31 12	25 23 23 23 11 29 8 31 11	28 26 26 26 12 30 8 31 12
27	31 20 30 36 28 28 6 31 12	34 25 36 3 31 28 6 31 12	1 26 1 4 33 28 6 31 12	4 31 1 4 35 29 7 31 11	7 34 6 3 2 29 7 31 11	10 2 12 5 4 28 7 31 12	13 5 14 8 6 29 8 31 12	16 10 14 12 8 28 8 31 12	19 15 20 16 10 28 8 31 12	22 19 25 19 11 29 8 31 11	25 23 23 23 11 29 8 31 11	28 28 26 27 12 30 8 31 12
28	31 21 30 36 28 28 6 31 12	34 27 36 3 31 28 6 31 12	1 27 1 4 33 28 6 31 12	4 32 1 4 35 29 7 31 11	7 35 7 3 2 29 7 31 11	10 3 13 5 4 28 7 31 12	13 6 14 8 6 29 8 31 12	16 12 14 12 8 28 8 31 12	19 17 20 16 10 28 8 31 12	22 20 25 19 11 29 8 31 11	25 26 23 23 11 29 8 31 11	28 30 26 27 12 30 8 31 12
29	31 23 30 36 28 28 6 31 12	**1913**	1 28 1 4 33 28 6 31 12	4 33 1 4 35 29 7 31 11	7 36 7 3 2 29 7 31 11	10 4 13 5 4 28 7 31 12	13 8 14 8 7 29 8 31 12	16 13 14 12 8 28 8 31 12	19 18 20 16 10 28 8 31 12	22 22 25 20 11 29 8 31 11	25 27 23 23 11 29 8 31 11	28 31 27 27 12 30 8 31 12
30	31 24 31 36 28 28 6 31 12		1 30 1 4 33 28 6 31 12	4 34 1 4 35 29 7 31 11	7 1 7 3 2 29 7 31 11	10 6 13 6 4 28 7 31 12	13 9 14 8 7 29 8 31 12	16 14 14 12 8 28 8 31 12	19 20 20 16 10 28 8 31 12	22 23 25 20 11 29 8 31 11	25 28 23 23 11 29 8 31 11	28 32 27 27 12 30 8 31 12
31	31 25 31 36 28 28 6 31 12		1 31 1 4 33 28 6 31 12		7 2 7 4 2 29 7 31 11		13 10 14 8 7 29 8 31 12	16 15 14 12 8 28 8 31 12		22 25 25 20 11 29 8 31 11		28 33 27 27 12 30 8 31 12

	JAN	FEB	MAR	APR	MAY	JUNE	JULY	AUG	SEPT	OCT	NOV	DEC
1	29 34 27 28 11 30 7 31 12	31 3 31 31 10 31 7 31 12	34 4 36 34 10 31 7 31 12	2 8 35 2 11 32 8 32 12	5 12 3 6 12 33 9 32 12	9 16 9 10 15 33 9 33 12	10 21 12 14 16 32 8 32 12	14 26 12 18 18 32 9 32 12	16 31 16 21 20 32 10 32 12	19 34 22 24 22 31 10 31 13	22 3 22 25 24 31 10 31 13	26 6 24 25 26 32 9 31 12
2	29 36 27 28 11 30 7 31 12	31 4 31 31 10 31 7 31 12	34 4 36 34 10 31 7 31 12	2 9 35 2 11 32 8 32 12	5 13 3 7 13 33 9 32 12	9 18 9 10 15 33 9 33 12	10 22 12 14 16 32 8 32 12	14 27 12 18 18 32 9 32 12	17 32 17 21 20 32 10 32 12	19 36 22 24 22 31 10 31 13	22 4 22 25 24 31 10 31 13	26 7 24 25 26 32 9 31 12
3	29 1 27 28 11 30 7 31 12	31 5 31 31 10 31 7 31 12	34 6 36 34 10 31 7 31 12	2 11 35 2 11 32 8 32 12	5 14 3 7 13 33 9 32 12	9 19 11 10 15 33 9 33 12	10 24 12 14 16 32 8 32 12	14 28 12 18 18 32 9 32 12	17 33 17 21 20 32 10 32 12	19 1 22 24 22 31 10 31 13	22 5 22 25 24 31 10 31 13	26 8 24 25 26 32 9 31 12
4	29 2 28 28 11 30 7 31 12	31 6 32 31 10 31 7 31 12	34 7 36 34 10 31 7 31 12	2 12 35 2 11 32 8 32 12	5 15 3 7 13 33 9 32 12	9 21 11 11 15 33 9 33 12	10 25 12 14 16 32 8 32 12	14 30 12 18 18 32 9 32 12	17 35 17 21 20 32 10 32 12	19 2 22 24 22 31 10 31 13	23 6 23 26 24 32 10 32 13	26 10 24 25 26 32 9 31 12
5	29 3 29 29 11 30 7 31 12	31 7 33 31 10 31 7 31 12	34 9 36 34 10 31 7 31 12	2 13 35 2 11 32 8 32 12	5 18 4 7 13 33 9 32 12	9 22 11 11 15 33 9 33 12	10 27 12 14 16 32 8 32 12	14 31 12 18 18 32 9 32 12	17 36 17 21 20 32 10 32 12	19 3 22 24 22 31 10 31 13	23 8 23 26 24 32 10 32 13	26 11 24 24 26 32 9 31 12
6	29 4 29 29 11 30 7 31 12	31 9 33 31 10 31 7 31 12	34 10 36 36 10 31 7 31 12	3 14 36 4 12 32 8 32 12	5 17 5 7 13 33 9 32 12	9 24 11 11 15 33 9 33 12	10 28 12 14 16 32 8 32 12	14 32 12 18 18 32 9 32 12	17 1 17 21 20 32 10 32 12	19 4 22 24 22 31 10 31 13	23 9 23 26 24 32 10 32 13	26 12 24 24 26 32 9 31 12
7	29 6 29 29 11 30 7 31 12	31 10 33 31 10 31 7 31 12	34 10 36 36 10 31 7 31 12	3 16 36 4 12 32 8 32 12	5 20 5 7 13 33 9 32 12	9 25 11 11 15 33 9 33 12	10 29 12 15 16 33 9 31 12	14 34 12 18 18 32 9 32 12	18 2 18 22 20 32 10 31 12	19 6 22 25 22 31 10 31 13	23 10 23 26 24 32 10 32 13	26 13 24 24 26 32 9 31 12
8	29 7 29 29 11 30 7 31 12	31 12 33 31 10 31 7 31 12	34 12 36 36 10 31 7 31 12	3 17 36 5 12 32 8 32 12	5 21 5 7 13 33 9 32 12	9 27 11 11 15 33 9 32 12	10 30 12 15 16 33 9 31 12	14 35 12 18 18 32 9 32 12	18 3 18 22 20 32 10 31 12	19 7 22 25 22 31 10 31 13	23 11 23 26 24 32 10 32 13	26 14 25 24 26 32 9 31 12
9	29 8 29 29 11 30 7 31 12	31 13 34 31 10 31 7 31 12	35 14 35 36 10 32 8 32 12	3 19 36 5 12 32 8 32 12	5 23 5 7 13 33 9 32 12	9 28 12 12 15 33 9 33 12	10 31 12 15 16 33 9 31 12	14 36 12 18 18 32 9 32 12	18 5 18 22 20 32 10 31 12	19 8 22 25 22 31 10 31 13	23 13 23 26 24 32 10 32 13	27 16 25 24 27 33 9 31 12
10	29 9 29 29 11 30 7 31 12	31 15 34 31 10 31 7 31 12	35 15 35 36 10 32 8 32 12	3 21 36 5 12 32 8 32 12	6 24 5 9 14 33 9 32 12	9 30 12 12 15 33 9 31 12	10 33 12 15 16 33 9 31 12	14 1 12 18 18 32 9 32 12	18 6 18 22 20 32 10 31 12	19 9 22 25 22 31 10 31 13	23 14 22 26 24 32 10 31 13	27 18 25 24 27 33 9 31 12
11	29 11 29 29 11 30 7 31 12	33 16 34 33 10 31 7 31 12	35 17 35 36 11 32 8 32 12	3 22 36 5 12 32 8 32 12	6 27 5 9 14 33 9 32 12	9 31 12 12 15 33 9 31 12	12 34 12 15 16 33 9 31 12	14 3 13 18 18 32 9 31 12	18 7 18 23 20 32 10 32 12	19 10 22 25 22 31 10 31 13	23 15 22 26 25 32 10 31 13	27 19 25 24 27 33 9 31 12
12	29 12 29 29 11 30 7 31 12	33 18 34 33 10 31 7 31 12	35 18 35 36 11 32 8 32 12	3 23 36 5 12 32 8 32 12	6 27 5 9 14 33 9 32 12	9 33 12 12 15 33 9 31 12	12 36 12 15 16 33 9 31 12	14 4 13 18 18 32 9 31 12	18 8 18 23 20 32 10 32 12	19 12 22 25 22 31 10 31 13	23 16 22 26 25 32 10 31 13	27 21 25 24 27 33 9 31 12
13	30 13 29 29 11 30 7 31 12	33 19 34 33 10 31 7 31 12	36 20 35 36 11 32 8 32 12	3 25 36 5 12 32 8 32 12	6 29 6 9 14 33 9 32 12	9 33 12 12 15 33 9 31 12	12 1 12 15 16 33 9 31 12	14 5 13 18 18 32 9 31 12	18 10 19 22 20 32 10 31 12	19 13 22 25 22 31 10 31 13	23 17 22 26 25 32 10 31 13	27 22 25 24 27 33 9 31 12
14	30 15 29 29 11 30 7 31 12	33 21 34 33 10 31 7 31 12	36 21 35 1 11 32 8 32 12	3 26 36 5 12 32 8 32 12	6 30 6 9 14 33 9 32 12	9 35 12 12 15 33 9 31 12	12 2 12 15 16 33 9 31 12	14 6 13 18 18 32 9 31 12	18 11 19 22 20 32 10 31 11	19 14 22 25 22 31 10 31 13	23 19 22 26 25 32 10 31 13	27 24 25 24 27 33 9 31 12
15	30 16 29 29 11 30 7 31 12	33 22 34 33 10 31 7 31 12	36 23 35 1 11 32 8 32 12	3 28 36 5 12 32 8 32 12	6 32 6 9 14 33 9 32 12	9 36 12 12 15 33 9 31 12	12 3 12 15 16 33 9 31 12	14 7 13 18 18 32 9 31 12	18 12 20 23 20 32 10 32 11	19 16 22 25 22 31 10 31 13	23 20 22 25 25 32 10 31 13	27 25 25 24 27 33 9 31 12
16	30 18 30 30 11 30 7 31 12	33 24 34 33 10 31 7 31 12	36 24 35 2 11 32 8 32 12	3 29 36 5 12 32 8 32 12	6 33 6 9 14 33 9 32 12	9 1 12 12 15 33 9 31 12	12 4 12 16 17 33 9 31 12	15 9 13 18 18 32 9 31 12	18 14 20 23 20 32 10 32 11	21 17 22 25 22 31 9 31 13	23 22 22 25 25 32 10 31 13	27 27 25 24 27 33 9 31 12
17	30 19 30 30 11 30 7 31 12	33 25 34 33 10 31 7 31 12	36 26 35 2 11 32 8 32 12	3 30 1 5 12 32 8 32 12	6 34 6 9 14 33 9 32 12	9 2 12 12 15 33 9 31 12	12 6 12 16 17 33 9 31 12	15 10 13 18 18 32 9 31 12	18 15 20 23 20 32 9 32 11	21 18 22 25 22 31 9 31 13	24 24 22 25 25 32 10 31 12	27 28 25 24 27 33 9 31 12
18	30 21 30 30 10 30 7 31 12	33 25 34 33 10 31 7 31 12	36 27 35 2 11 32 8 32 12	3 32 1 5 12 32 8 32 12	6 35 6 9 14 33 9 32 12	9 3 12 12 15 33 9 31 12	12 7 12 16 17 33 9 31 12	15 11 13 18 18 32 9 31 12	18 16 20 23 21 32 10 32 12	21 19 22 25 22 31 9 31 13	24 25 22 25 25 32 10 31 12	27 29 27 24 27 33 9 31 12
19	30 22 30 30 10 30 7 31 12	34 27 34 34 10 31 7 31 12	36 29 35 2 11 32 8 32 12	3 33 1 5 12 32 8 32 12	6 36 7 9 14 33 9 32 12	9 5 12 12 15 33 9 31 12	12 8 12 17 17 33 9 31 12	15 13 14 19 19 32 9 31 12	18 18 20 23 21 32 10 32 12	21 21 22 25 22 31 9 31 13	24 27 22 25 25 32 10 31 12	27 30 27 24 27 33 9 31 12
20	30 24 30 30 10 30 7 31 12	34 28 36 34 10 31 7 31 12	36 30 35 2 11 32 8 32 12	3 34 2 5 12 32 8 32 12	5 2 8 9 14 33 9 32 12	9 6 12 13 15 33 9 31 12	12 9 12 17 17 33 9 31 12	15 14 14 19 19 32 9 31 12	18 19 20 23 21 32 10 32 12	21 22 22 25 22 31 9 31 13	24 28 22 25 25 32 10 31 12	27 31 27 24 27 33 9 31 12
21	31 25 31 31 10 31 7 31 12	34 30 36 34 10 31 7 31 12	1 31 35 2 11 32 8 32 12	4 35 2 5 12 32 8 32 12	6 3 8 9 14 33 9 32 12	9 7 12 13 15 33 9 31 12	12 10 12 17 17 33 9 31 12	15 15 14 19 19 32 9 31 12	18 21 20 23 21 32 10 32 12	21 24 22 25 22 31 9 31 13	24 30 22 25 25 32 10 31 12	27 33 27 24 27 33 9 31 12
22	31 26 31 31 10 31 7 31 12	34 31 36 34 10 31 7 31 12	1 32 35 2 11 32 8 32 12	4 36 2 5 12 32 8 32 12	7 4 8 9 14 33 9 32 12	10 9 12 13 15 33 9 31 12	12 12 12 17 17 33 9 31 12	15 17 14 19 19 32 9 31 12	18 22 20 23 21 32 10 32 12	21 25 22 25 22 31 9 31 13	24 31 22 25 25 32 10 31 12	27 34 27 24 27 33 9 31 12
23	31 28 31 31 10 31 7 31 12	34 33 36 34 10 31 7 31 12	1 33 35 2 11 32 8 32 12	4 2 2 5 12 32 8 32 12	7 5 8 9 14 33 9 32 12	10 10 12 13 15 33 9 31 12	12 13 12 17 17 33 9 31 12	15 18 14 19 19 32 9 31 12	18 23 20 23 21 32 10 32 12	21 27 22 25 22 31 9 31 13	26 32 23 26 26 32 10 32 13	28 36 28 24 28 32 10 31 12
24	31 29 31 31 10 31 7 31 12	34 34 36 34 10 31 7 31 12	2 35 35 2 11 32 8 32 12	5 3 2 6 12 32 8 32 12	7 6 8 9 14 33 9 32 12	10 11 12 13 15 33 9 31 12	13 15 12 17 17 33 9 31 12	16 20 16 20 20 32 10 32 12	19 25 20 23 22 32 10 32 13	22 28 23 25 23 32 10 31 13	26 34 23 26 26 32 10 32 13	28 1 28 24 28 32 10 31 12
25	31 30 31 31 10 31 7 31 12	34 34 36 34 10 31 7 31 12	2 36 35 2 11 32 8 32 12	5 4 2 6 12 32 8 32 12	8 8 9 9 14 33 9 32 12	10 12 12 13 15 33 9 31 12	13 16 12 18 18 33 9 31 12	16 21 16 20 20 32 10 32 12	19 26 20 23 22 32 10 32 13	22 30 23 25 23 32 10 31 13	26 35 23 26 26 32 10 32 13	28 2 28 24 28 32 10 31 12
26	31 31 31 31 10 31 7 31 12	34 36 36 34 10 31 7 31 12	2 1 35 2 11 32 8 32 12	5 5 2 6 12 32 8 32 12	8 9 9 10 14 33 9 32 12	10 13 12 13 16 33 9 31 12	13 18 12 18 18 33 9 31 12	16 23 15 20 20 32 10 32 12	19 28 20 23 22 32 10 32 13	22 31 23 25 23 32 10 31 13	26 36 23 26 26 32 10 32 13	28 3 28 24 28 32 10 31 12
27	31 32 31 31 10 31 7 31 12	34 1 36 34 10 31 7 31 12	2 2 35 2 11 32 8 32 12	5 6 2 6 12 32 8 32 12	8 10 9 10 14 33 9 32 12	10 15 12 13 16 33 9 31 12	13 19 12 18 18 33 9 31 12	16 24 16 20 20 32 10 32 12	19 29 22 23 22 32 10 32 13	22 32 23 25 23 32 10 31 13	26 1 23 26 26 32 10 32 13	28 4 28 24 28 32 10 31 12
28	31 34 31 31 10 31 7 31 12	34 3 36 34 10 31 7 31 12	2 3 35 2 11 32 8 32 12	5 8 2 6 12 32 8 32 12	8 11 9 10 14 33 9 32 12	10 16 12 13 16 33 9 31 12	13 21 12 18 18 33 9 31 12	16 25 16 20 20 32 10 32 12	19 31 22 24 22 32 10 32 13	22 34 23 25 23 32 10 31 13	26 3 23 26 26 32 10 32 13	28 5 28 24 28 32 10 31 12
29	31 35 31 31 10 31 7 31 12		2 5 35 2 11 32 8 32 12	5 9 2 6 12 32 8 32 12	8 12 9 10 14 32 9 32 12	10 18 12 13 16 33 9 31 12	13 21 12 18 18 33 9 31 12	16 27 16 20 20 32 10 32 12	19 32 22 24 22 32 10 32 13	22 35 23 25 23 32 10 31 13	26 4 23 26 26 32 10 32 13	28 7 28 24 28 32 10 31 12
30	31 36 31 31 10 31 7 31 12	**1914**	2 6 35 2 11 32 8 32 12	5 10 2 6 12 32 8 32 12	8 14 9 10 14 33 9 32 12	10 19 12 13 16 33 9 31 12	13 22 12 18 18 33 9 31 12	16 28 16 20 20 32 10 32 12	19 33 22 24 22 32 10 32 13	22 1 23 25 23 32 10 31 13	26 5 23 26 26 32 10 32 13	28 8 28 24 28 33 10 31 12
31	31 1 31 31 10 31 7 31 12		2 7 35 2 11 32 8 32 12		8 15 9 10 14 33 9 32 12		13 24 12 18 18 33 9 31 12	16 29 16 20 20 32 10 32 12		22 2 23 25 23 32 10 31 13		28 10 28 24 28 33 10 31 12

	JAN	FEB	MAR	APR	MAY	JUNE	JULY	AUG	SEPT	OCT	NOV	DEC
1	28 10 28 25 28 33 9 31 12	32 15 33 27 32 33 9 32 12	34 16 33 30 33 34 9 32 12	2 21 35 33 35 35 8 32 12	5 26 5 2 2 35 9 32 12	8 31 10 5 5 36 10 32 12	10 34 10 9 6 32 10 32 12	14 3 12 12 8 36 11 32 13	17 7 18 17 11 32 11 32 13	20 11 22 20 12 36 11 32 13	23 15 20 23 14 35 11 32 13	25 18 25 27 15 35 11 32 13
2	28 12 28 25 28 33 9 31 12	32 17 33 27 32 33 9 32 12	34 18 33 30 33 34 9 32 12	2 23 35 34 35 35 8 32 12	5 27 5 2 2 35 9 32 12	8 32 10 5 5 36 10 32 12	10 36 10 9 6 36 10 32 12	14 4 12 12 8 36 11 32 13	17 8 18 17 11 36 11 32 13	20 12 22 20 12 36 11 32 13	23 16 20 23 14 35 11 32 13	25 20 25 27 15 35 11 32 13
3	28 13 28 25 28 33 9 31 12	32 18 33 27 32 33 9 32 12	34 19 33 30 33 34 9 32 12	2 24 35 34 35 35 8 32 12	5 28 5 2 2 35 9 32 12	8 33 10 5 5 36 10 32 12	10 1 10 9 6 36 10 32 12	14 5 12 12 9 36 11 32 13	17 10 18 17 11 36 11 32 13	20 13 22 20 12 36 11 32 13	23 17 20 23 14 35 11 32 13	25 21 25 28 15 35 11 32 13
4	28 15 28 25 28 33 9 31 12	32 19 33 27 32 33 9 32 12	34 21 33 30 33 34 9 32 12	2 26 35 34 35 35 8 32 12	5 30 5 2 2 35 9 32 12	8 34 10 5 5 36 10 32 12	10 2 10 9 6 36 10 32 12	14 6 13 13 9 36 11 32 13	17 11 18 17 11 36 11 32 13	20 14 22 20 12 36 11 32 13	23 19 20 23 14 35 11 32 13	25 22 25 28 15 35 11 32 13
5	29 16 29 25 29 33 9 31 12	32 21 33 27 32 33 9 32 12	34 22 33 30 33 34 9 32 12	2 26 35 34 35 35 8 32 12	5 31 5 2 2 35 9 32 12	8 36 10 5 5 36 10 32 12	10 3 10 9 6 36 10 32 12	14 8 13 13 9 36 11 32 13	17 12 19 17 11 36 11 32 13	20 15 22 20 13 35 11 32 13	23 20 20 23 14 35 11 32 13	25 23 25 28 15 35 11 32 13
6	29 17 29 25 29 33 9 31 12	32 22 33 27 32 33 9 32 12	34 24 33 30 33 34 9 32 12	2 28 35 34 35 35 8 32 12	5 32 5 2 2 35 9 32 12	8 1 10 5 5 36 10 32 12	10 4 10 9 6 36 10 32 12	14 9 14 14 9 36 11 32 13	17 13 19 17 11 36 11 32 13	20 17 22 20 13 35 11 32 13	23 22 20 23 14 35 11 32 13	25 25 25 28 15 35 11 32 13
7	29 18 29 25 29 33 9 31 12	32 24 34 28 32 34 9 32 12	34 25 33 31 33 34 9 32 12	2 30 35 34 35 35 8 32 12	5 34 5 2 2 35 9 32 12	8 2 10 5 5 36 10 32 12	10 6 10 9 6 36 10 32 12	14 10 14 14 9 36 11 32 13	17 14 19 17 11 36 11 32 13	20 18 22 20 13 35 11 32 13	23 23 20 24 14 35 11 32 13	26 26 26 28 15 35 11 32 13
8	29 20 29 25 29 33 9 31 12	32 25 34 28 32 34 9 32 12	36 27 33 31 33 34 9 32 12	2 32 35 34 35 35 8 32 12	5 35 6 2 2 35 9 32 12	8 3 10 5 5 36 10 32 12	10 7 10 9 6 36 10 32 12	14 11 14 14 9 36 11 32 13	17 16 20 17 11 36 11 32 13	20 20 22 20 13 35 11 32 13	23 25 20 24 14 35 11 32 13	26 29 26 29 15 35 11 32 13
9	29 21 29 25 29 33 9 31 12	32 27 34 28 32 34 9 32 12	36 28 33 31 33 34 9 32 12	2 33 35 34 35 35 8 32 12	5 36 6 2 2 35 9 32 12	8 5 10 6 5 36 10 32 12	10 8 10 9 7 36 10 32 12	14 13 14 14 9 36 11 32 13	17 17 20 17 11 36 11 32 13	20 21 22 20 13 35 11 32 13	23 26 22 25 14 35 11 32 13	26 30 26 29 15 35 11 32 13
10	29 22 29 25 29 33 9 31 12	32 28 34 28 32 34 9 32 12	36 29 33 32 34 34 9 32 12	3 34 36 35 36 35 9 32 12	5 1 6 2 2 35 9 32 12	8 6 10 6 5 36 10 32 12	11 9 10 9 7 36 10 32 12	14 14 14 14 9 36 11 32 13	17 19 20 17 11 36 11 32 13	20 22 22 20 13 35 11 32 13	23 28 22 25 14 35 11 32 13	27 32 27 29 15 36 11 32 13
11	30 24 30 25 30 33 9 31 12	33 30 34 28 32 34 9 32 12	36 30 33 32 34 34 9 32 12	3 35 36 35 36 35 9 32 12	5 3 6 3 3 35 9 32 12	8 7 10 6 5 36 10 32 12	11 10 10 10 7 32 10 32 12	14 15 14 14 9 36 11 32 13	17 20 20 17 11 36 11 32 13	20 24 22 20 13 35 11 32 13	23 29 22 25 14 35 11 32 13	27 33 27 29 15 36 11 32 13
12	30 25 30 25 30 33 9 31 12	33 31 34 28 32 34 9 32 12	36 32 33 32 34 34 9 32 12	3 36 36 35 36 35 9 32 12	5 4 6 3 3 35 9 32 12	9 8 10 6 5 36 10 32 12	12 12 10 10 7 36 10 32 12	14 16 14 14 9 36 11 32 13	17 22 20 17 11 35 11 32 13	20 25 22 20 13 35 11 32 13	23 31 22 25 14 35 11 32 13	27 35 27 29 15 36 11 32 13
13	30 27 30 25 30 33 9 31 12	33 32 34 28 32 34 9 32 12	36 33 33 32 34 34 9 32 12	3 2 36 35 36 35 9 32 12	5 5 6 3 3 35 9 32 12	9 10 10 6 5 36 10 32 12	12 13 10 10 8 36 10 32 12	14 18 14 14 9 36 11 32 13	17 23 20 17 11 35 11 32 13	20 27 22 22 13 35 11 31 13	23 32 22 25 14 35 11 32 13	27 36 27 29 15 36 11 32 13
14	30 28 30 25 30 33 9 31 12	33 34 34 28 32 34 9 32 12	36 34 33 32 34 34 9 32 12	3 3 2 35 36 35 9 32 12	5 6 8 3 3 35 9 32 12	9 11 10 6 5 36 10 32 12	12 14 10 10 8 36 10 32 12	14 19 14 14 9 36 11 32 13	17 24 20 17 11 35 11 32 13	20 28 22 22 13 35 11 31 13	23 33 22 26 14 35 11 32 13	27 1 27 29 15 36 11 32 13
15	30 30 31 25 30 33 9 31 12	33 35 33 28 32 33 9 32 12	36 36 33 32 34 34 9 32 12	3 4 2 35 36 35 9 32 12	5 8 8 3 3 35 9 32 12	9 12 10 6 5 36 10 32 12	12 15 10 10 8 36 10 32 12	14 21 14 14 9 36 11 32 13	17 26 20 17 11 35 11 32 13	20 29 22 22 13 35 11 31 13	23 35 22 26 14 35 11 32 13	27 2 27 29 15 36 11 32 13
16	30 31 31 25 30 33 9 31 12	33 36 33 29 32 33 9 32 12	36 1 33 32 34 34 9 32 12	3 6 2 35 36 35 9 32 12	6 9 8 3 3 36 9 32 12	9 13 10 7 5 36 10 32 12	12 16 10 10 8 36 10 32 12	14 22 14 14 9 36 11 32 13	17 29 20 17 11 35 11 32 13	20 31 22 22 13 35 11 31 13	23 35 22 26 14 35 11 32 13	27 4 27 29 15 36 11 32 13
17	30 33 31 25 30 33 9 31 12	33 1 33 29 32 33 9 32 12	36 2 33 32 34 34 9 32 12	3 7 2 36 36 35 9 32 12	6 10 8 3 3 36 9 32 12	9 15 10 7 5 36 10 32 12	12 18 10 10 8 36 10 32 12	15 23 15 14 9 36 11 32 13	17 29 20 17 11 35 11 32 13	20 32 22 22 13 35 11 31 13	23 1 22 26 14 35 11 32 13	27 5 27 29 15 36 11 32 13
18	30 34 31 25 30 33 9 31 12	33 2 33 29 32 33 9 32 12	36 3 33 32 34 34 9 32 12	3 8 2 36 36 35 9 32 12	6 11 8 3 3 36 9 32 12	9 16 10 7 5 36 10 32 12	12 19 10 10 8 36 10 32 12	15 25 15 14 9 36 11 32 13	17 30 20 17 11 35 11 32 13	20 34 22 22 13 35 11 31 13	23 2 23 26 14 35 11 32 13	27 6 27 29 15 36 11 32 13
19	30 35 31 25 30 33 9 31 12	33 4 33 29 32 33 9 32 12	36 4 35 32 35 35 9 32 12	3 9 2 36 36 35 9 32 12	6 12 8 3 3 36 9 32 12	9 17 10 7 5 36 10 32 12	12 20 10 10 8 36 10 32 12	15 26 15 14 9 36 11 32 13	17 31 20 17 11 35 11 32 13	20 35 22 22 13 35 11 31 13	23 4 23 26 14 35 11 32 13	27 7 27 29 15 36 11 32 13
20	30 36 31 25 30 33 9 31 12	34 5 34 29 32 34 8 32 12	36 6 35 32 35 35 9 32 12	3 10 2 36 36 35 9 32 12	6 14 8 3 3 36 9 32 12	9 18 10 7 6 36 10 33 12	12 22 10 10 8 36 10 32 12	15 27 15 15 9 36 11 32 13	17 32 20 17 11 35 11 32 13	21 36 22 22 13 35 11 31 13	23 5 23 26 14 35 11 32 13	27 8 27 29 15 36 11 32 13
21	31 2 31 25 30 33 9 31 12	34 6 34 29 32 34 8 32 12	36 7 35 32 35 35 9 32 12	4 11 2 36 36 35 9 32 12	6 15 8 3 3 36 9 32 12	9 19 10 9 6 36 10 33 12	12 24 10 10 8 36 10 32 12	15 29 15 15 9 36 11 32 13	17 34 20 17 11 35 11 32 13	21 2 22 22 13 35 11 31 13	23 6 23 26 14 35 11 32 13	27 9 27 29 15 36 11 32 13
22	31 3 31 25 30 33 9 31 12	34 7 34 29 32 34 8 32 12	1 8 35 32 35 35 9 32 12	4 12 2 36 36 35 9 32 12	7 16 8 3 3 36 9 32 12	9 21 10 9 6 36 10 33 12	12 25 10 10 8 36 10 32 12	15 31 15 15 9 36 11 32 13	17 35 20 19 11 35 11 32 13	21 3 22 22 13 35 11 31 13	23 7 23 26 14 35 11 32 13	27 11 27 29 15 36 11 32 13
23	31 4 31 25 30 33 9 31 12	34 8 34 29 32 34 8 32 12	1 9 35 32 35 35 9 32 12	4 14 2 36 1 35 9 32 12	7 18 8 3 3 36 9 32 12	10 22 10 9 6 36 10 33 12	12 27 10 10 8 36 10 32 12	15 32 15 15 9 36 11 32 13	17 1 20 19 11 35 11 32 13	21 4 22 22 13 35 11 31 13	25 8 23 26 14 35 11 32 13	28 12 28 31 15 35 11 32 13
24	31 6 31 25 30 33 9 31 12	34 10 34 29 32 34 8 32 12	1 11 35 32 35 35 9 32 12	4 15 3 36 1 35 9 32 12	7 19 9 3 3 36 9 32 12	10 24 10 9 6 36 10 33 12	13 28 10 10 8 36 10 32 13	17 33 17 15 11 36 11 32 13	19 2 22 19 11 35 11 32 13	21 5 20 22 13 35 11 31 13	25 10 23 26 14 35 11 32 13	28 13 28 31 15 35 11 32 13
25	31 7 33 27 30 33 9 31 12	34 11 32 30 32 34 8 32 12	1 12 35 32 35 35 9 32 12	4 16 3 36 1 35 9 32 12	7 20 9 3 3 36 9 32 12	10 27 10 9 6 36 10 33 12	13 30 10 10 8 36 10 32 13	17 35 17 15 11 36 11 32 13	19 3 22 19 11 35 11 32 13	22 6 20 22 13 35 11 31 13	25 11 24 27 15 35 11 32 13	28 14 28 31 15 35 11 32 13
26	31 8 33 27 30 33 9 31 12	34 12 32 30 32 34 8 32 12	1 13 35 32 35 35 9 32 12	4 18 3 36 2 35 9 32 12	7 21 9 5 5 36 9 32 12	10 27 10 9 6 36 10 33 12	13 31 12 12 8 36 10 32 13	17 36 17 15 11 36 11 32 13	19 4 22 19 11 35 11 32 13	22 8 30 22 13 35 11 31 13	25 12 24 27 15 35 11 32 13	29 15 29 31 15 35 11 32 13
27	31 9 33 27 30 33 9 31 12	34 13 32 30 32 34 8 32 12	2 15 35 33 35 35 9 32 12	5 20 5 36 2 35 9 32 12	7 23 9 5 5 36 9 32 12	10 28 10 9 6 36 10 33 12	13 32 12 12 8 36 10 32 13	17 1 17 15 11 36 11 32 13	19 5 22 19 11 35 11 32 13	22 9 20 22 13 35 11 31 13	25 13 24 27 15 35 11 32 13	29 17 29 31 15 35 11 32 13
28	31 10 33 27 30 33 9 31 12	34 14 32 30 32 34 8 32 12	2 16 35 33 35 35 9 32 12	5 21 5 36 2 35 9 32 12	8 25 9 5 5 36 9 32 12	10 30 10 9 6 36 10 32 12	13 34 12 12 8 36 10 32 13	17 2 18 15 11 36 11 32 13	20 7 22 20 11 35 11 32 13	22 10 20 22 13 35 11 31 13	25 14 24 27 15 35 11 32 13	29 18 29 31 15 35 11 32 13
29	31 12 33 27 30 33 9 31 12		2 17 35 33 35 35 9 32 12	5 22 5 36 2 35 9 32 12	8 26 9 5 5 36 9 32 12	10 32 10 8 6 36 10 32 12	14 35 12 12 8 36 10 32 13	17 4 18 17 11 36 11 32 13	20 8 22 20 12 36 11 31 13	22 11 20 22 13 35 11 31 13	25 16 24 27 15 35 11 32 13	29 20 29 31 15 35 11 32 13
30	31 13 33 27 30 33 9 31 12	1915	2 18 35 33 35 35 9 32 12	5 24 5 36 2 35 9 32 12	8 28 9 5 5 36 10 32 12	10 33 10 8 6 36 10 32 12	14 36 12 12 8 36 10 32 13	17 5 18 17 11 36 11 32 13	20 9 22 20 12 36 11 32 13	22 13 20 22 13 35 11 31 13	25 17 24 27 15 35 11 32 13	29 21 29 32 15 35 11 32 13
31	31 14 33 27 30 33 9 31 12		2 20 35 33 35 35 9 32 12		8 29 9 5 5 36 10 32 12		14 1 12 12 8 36 10 32 13	17 6 18 17 11 36 11 32 13		22 13 20 22 13 35 11 31 13		29 23 29 32 15 35 11 32 13

	JAN	FEB	MAR	APR	MAY	JUNE	JULY	AUG	SEPT	OCT	NOV	DEC
1	29 24 29 32 15 36 11 32 14	32 29 32 35 14 36 11 32 13	34 31 31 2 13 1 10 31 12	2 36 36 6 14 2 11 32 12	5 4 6 9 14 2 11 32 12	8 8 8 11 16 3 11 32 12	11 11 8 11 17 4 11 32 13	14 16 14 10 19 4 12 32 13	16 21 19 12 21 4 12 32 13	19 25 20 15 23 4 12 32 13	22 30 21 18 25 3 13 32 13	25 34 26 22 28 4 13 32 13
2	29 25 29 32 15 36 11 32 14	32 30 32 35 14 36 11 32 13	34 31 31 2 13 1 10 31 12	2 2 1 6 14 2 11 32 12	5 5 6 9 14 2 11 32 12	8 10 8 11 16 3 11 32 12	11 13 8 11 17 4 11 32 13	14 18 14 10 19 4 12 32 13	16 22 19 12 21 4 12 32 13	19 26 20 15 23 4 12 32 13	22 31 21 18 25 3 13 32 13	25 35 26 22 28 4 13 32 13
3	29 27 29 32 15 36 11 32 14	32 32 32 35 14 36 11 32 13	34 34 31 3 13 1 10 31 12	2 3 1 6 14 2 11 32 12	5 6 7 9 14 2 11 32 12	8 11 8 11 16 3 11 32 12	11 14 8 11 17 4 11 32 13	14 19 14 10 19 4 12 32 13	16 23 19 12 21 4 12 32 13	19 27 20 15 23 4 12 32 13	23 32 21 19 25 3 13 32 13	26 1 26 22 28 4 13 32 13
4	29 28 30 32 15 36 11 32 13	32 32 32 35 14 36 11 32 13	34 36 31 3 13 1 10 31 12	2 4 1 6 14 2 11 32 12	5 7 7 9 14 2 11 32 12	8 12 8 11 16 3 11 32 12	11 15 8 11 17 4 11 32 13	14 20 14 10 19 4 12 32 13	16 25 19 12 21 4 12 32 13	20 29 20 16 23 4 12 32 13	23 34 21 19 25 3 13 32 13	26 2 26 22 28 4 13 31 13
5	29 29 30 32 15 36 11 32 13	32 35 32 36 14 36 11 32 13	34 1 31 3 13 1 10 31 12	2 5 2 6 14 2 11 32 12	5 8 7 9 14 2 11 32 12	8 13 8 11 16 3 11 32 12	11 16 8 11 17 4 11 32 13	14 21 14 10 19 4 12 32 13	16 26 20 12 21 4 12 32 13	20 30 20 16 23 4 12 32 13	23 35 22 19 25 3 13 32 13	26 3 26 22 28 4 13 31 13
6	29 31 30 32 15 36 11 32 13	32 36 32 36 14 36 11 32 13	34 2 31 3 13 1 10 31 12	2 7 2 7 14 2 11 32 13	5 10 7 10 14 2 11 32 12	8 14 8 11 16 3 11 32 12	11 17 8 10 17 4 11 32 13	14 23 14 10 19 4 12 32 13	16 28 20 12 21 4 12 32 13	20 32 30 16 23 4 12 32 13	23 1 22 19 25 4 13 32 13	26 4 26 22 28 4 13 31 13
7	29 33 30 33 15 36 11 33 13	32 2 32 36 14 36 11 32 13	34 3 31 3 13 1 10 31 12	2 8 2 7 14 2 11 32 12	5 11 7 10 14 2 11 32 12	8 16 8 11 16 3 11 32 12	11 19 8 10 17 4 11 32 13	14 24 14 10 19 4 12 32 13	16 29 20 12 21 4 12 32 13	20 33 20 16 23 4 12 32 13	23 2 22 19 25 4 13 32 13	26 5 26 22 28 4 13 31 13
8	29 34 21 32 15 36 11 32 13	32 3 32 36 14 36 11 32 13	34 4 31 3 13 1 10 31 12	2 9 2 7 14 2 11 32 12	5 12 7 10 14 2 11 32 12	8 17 8 11 16 3 11 32 12	11 20 8 10 17 4 11 32 13	14 25 14 10 19 4 12 32 13	17 30 20 12 21 4 12 32 13	20 34 20 16 23 4 12 32 13	23 4 22 19 25 4 13 32 13	25 7 27 22 28 3 12 31 13
9	29 35 31 32 15 36 11 32 13	32 4 32 36 14 36 11 32 13	34 6 31 3 13 1 10 31 12	2 11 2 8 14 2 11 32 12	5 13 7 10 14 2 10 32 12	8 18 8 11 16 3 11 32 12	11 22 8 10 17 4 11 32 13	14 26 15 10 19 4 12 32 13	17 32 20 13 22 4 12 32 13	20 36 20 16 23 4 12 32 13	23 5 22 19 25 4 13 32 13	25 8 27 22 28 3 12 31 13
10	29 36 31 32 15 36 11 32 13	32 5 32 36 14 36 11 32 13	35 7 33 4 13 1 10 31 12	2 12 2 8 14 2 10 32 12	5 14 7 10 14 2 10 32 12	8 19 8 11 16 3 11 32 13	11 23 8 10 17 4 11 32 13	14 28 16 10 19 4 12 32 13	17 33 20 13 22 4 12 32 13	20 1 19 16 23 4 12 32 13	23 6 23 20 26 4 13 32 13	25 9 27 22 28 3 12 31 13
11	29 2 32 32 15 36 11 32 13	32•6 32 36 14 36 11 32 13	35 7 33 4 13 1 10 31 12	2 13 2 8 14 2 10 32 12	6 16 9 11 15 3 11 33 12	8 20 8 11 16 2 11 32 12	11 24 10 10 17 4 11 32 13	14 30 16 10 19 4 12 32 13	18 35 20 13 22 4 12 32 13	20 3 19 16 23 4 12 32 13	23 7 23 20 26 4 13 32 13	26 11 27 23 28 3 12 32 13
12	29 3 32 33 15 36 11 32 13	32 8 32 1 14 1 11 32 13	36 9 33 4 13 1 10 31 12	2 14 2 8 14 2 10 32 12	6 17 9 11 15 3 11 33 12	9 22 8 11 17 3 11 32 12	11 26 10 10 17 4 11 32 13	14 31 16 10 19 4 12 32 13	18 36 20 13 22 4 12 32 13	20 4 19 16 23 4 12 32 13	23 8 23 20 26 4 13 32 13	26 12 28 23 28 3 12 32 13
13	30 4 32 33 15 36 11 32 13	32 9 32 1 14 1 11 32 13	36 10 33 4 13 1 10 31 12	2 15 2 8 14 2 10 32 12	6 18 9 11 15 3 11 33 12	9 23 8 11 17 3 11 32 12	11 26 10 10 17 4 11 32 13	14 32 16 11 20 4 12 32 13	18 2 20 13 22 4 12 32 13	20 5 19 16 23 4 12 32 13	23 10 23 20 26 4 13 32 13	26 13 28 23 28 3 12 32 13
14	30 6 32 33 15 36 11 33 13	32 10 31 1 14 1 11 32 13	36 12 33 4 13 1 10 31 12	2 16 2 8 14 2 10 32 12	6 20 9 11 15 3 11 33 12	9 25 8 11 17 3 11 32 12	11 29 10 10 17 4 11 32 13	14 34 16 11 20 4 12 32 13	18 3 20 13 22 4 12 32 13	21 7 19 16 23 4 12 32 13	23 11 23 20 26 4 13 32 13	26 14 28 23 28 3 12 32 13
15	30 7 32 33 15 36 11 32 13	32 10 31 1 14 1 10 32 13	36 13 34 4 13 1 10 31 12	3 18 3 8 14 2 10 32 12	6 21 9 11 15 3 11 33 12	9 27 8 11 17 3 11 32 12	11 30 10 10 17 4 11 32 13	14 35 16 11 20 4 12 32 13	18 4 20 13 22 4 12 32 13	21 8 19 16 24 4 12 32 13	23 12 23 20 26 4 13 32 13	27 15 28 23 28 3 11 32 13
16	30 8 32 33 15 36 11 32 13	32 13 31 1 14 1 10 32 13	36 13 34 4 13 1 10 31 12	3 19 3 8 14 2 10 32 12	6 23 9 11 15 3 11 33 12	9 28 8 11 17 3 11 32 12	11 32 10 10 17 4 11 32 13	14 1 16 11 20 4 12 32 13	18 6 20 13 22 4 12 32 13	21 9 19 16 24 3 12 32 13	23 13 23 20 26 2 13 32 13	27 17 28 23 28 3 11 32 13
17	30 9 32 33 15 36 11 32 13	32 14 31 1 14 1 10 32 13	36 16 34 4 13 1 10 31 12	3 20 3 8 14 2 10 32 12	6 24 9 11 15 3 11 33 12	9 29 8 11 17 3 11 32 12	11 33 11 10 17 4 11 32 13	14 3 18 12 21 4 12 32 13	18 7 20 13 22 4 12 32 13	21 10 19 17 24 3 12 32 13	23 14 23 20 26 2 12 32 12	27 18 28 23 28 3 11 32 13
18	30 11 32 33 15 36 11 32 13	33 15 31 1 14 1 10 32 13	36 17 34 4 13 1 10 31 12	3 22 4 8 14 2 10 32 12	6 25 9 11 15 3 11 33 12	9 31 8 11 17 3 11 32 12	11 35 11 10 17 4 11 32 13	14 4 18 12 21 4 12 32 13	18 8 20 13 22 4 12 32 13	21 12 19 17 24 3 12 32 13	24 16 23 20 26 2 12 32 12	27 19 28 23 28 3 11 32 13
19	30 12 32 33 15 36 11 32 13	33 16 31 1 13 1 10 31 12	36 18 34 4 13 1 10 31 12	3 23 4 8 14 2 10 32 12	6 27 9 11 15 3 11 33 12	9 32 8 11 17 3 11 32 12	11 36 11 10 17 4 11 32 13	14 5 18 12 21 4 12 32 13	18 10 20 13 22 4 12 31 13	21 13 19 17 24 3 12 32 13	24 17 23 20 26 2 12 32 12	27 21 28 24 28 3 12 33 13
20	30 13 32 33 15 36 11 32 13	34 18 31 1 13 1 10 31 12	36 19 34 4 13 1 10 31 12	4 25 4 8 14 2 10 32 12	6 28 9 11 15 3 11 33 12	9 34 8 11 17 3 11 32 12	11 1 11 10 17 4 11 32 13	15 6 18 12 21 4 12 32 13	18 11 20 13 22 4 12 31 13	21 14 20 17 24 3 12 32 13	24 18 23 20 26 2 12 32 12	27 22 28 24 28 3 12 32 13
21	31 14 32 33 15 36 11 32 13	34 19 31 1 13 1 10 31 12	1 21 34 4 13 1 10 31 12	4 26 5 8 14 2 10 32 12	7 30 9 11 15 3 11 33 12	9 35 8 11 17 3 11 32 12	11 2 11 10 17 4 11 32 13	15 7 18 12 21 4 12 32 13	18 12 20 13 22 4 12 31 13	21 15 20 17 24 3 12 32 13	24 19 24 21 27 3 12 32 12	27 23 29 24 29 3 12 32 13
22	31 15 32 33 15 36 11 32 13	34 19 31 1 13 1 10 31 12	1 22 34 4 13 1 10 31 12	4 28 5 8 14 2 10 32 12	7 31 9 11 '15 3 11 33 12	10 1 8 11 17 4 11 32 13	11 4 11 10 17 4 11 32 13	15 8 18 12 21 4 12 32 13	18 13 20 13 22 4 12 31 13	21 16 20 17 24 3 12 32 13	24 21 24 21 27 3 12 32 12	28 24 29 25 29 3 12 32 13
23	31 16 33 35 15 36 11 32 13	34 21 31 1 13 1 10 31 12	1 24 34 4 13 1 10 31 12	4 29 5 8 14 2 10 32 12	7 33 9 11 15 3 11 33 12	10 2 8 11 17 4 11 32 13	13 5 11 10 19 4 11 32 13	15 10 18 12 21 4 12 32 13	19 14 20 13 22 4 12 31 13	21 18 20 17 24 3 12 32 13	25 22 25 22 28 4 13 32 13	28 26 29 25 29 3 12 32 13
24	31 18 33 35 15 36 11 32 13	34 22 31 1 13 1 10 31 12	1 25 34 4 13 1 10 31 12	4 30 5 8 14 2 10 32 12	7 34 9 11 15 3 11 33 12	10 3 8 11 17 4 11 32 13	13 7 11 10 19 4 11 32 13	16 11 18 12 21 4 12 32 13	19 15 20 13 22 4 12 31 13	22 19 20 17 25 4 13 32 13	25 24 25 22 28 4 13 32 13	28 27 29 25 29 3 12 32 13
25	31 19 33 35 15 36 1.1 32 13	34 24 31 1 13 1 10 31 12	1 25 34 4 13 1 10 31 12	4 32 5 8 14 2 10 32 12	7 36 9 11 15 3 11 33 12	10 4 8 11 17 4 11 32 13	13 8 11 10 19 4 11 32 13	16 12 18 12 21 4 12 32 13	19 17 20 13 22 4 12 31 13	22 20 20 18 25 4 13 32 13	25 25 25 22 28 4 13 32 13	28 29 29 25 29 3 12 32 13
26	31 20 33 35 15 36 11 32 13	34 25 32 1 13 1 10 31 12	1 28 34 4 13 1 10 32 12	4 33 5 8 14 2 10 32 12	7 1 9 11 15 3 11 33 12	10 5 8 11 17 4 11 32 13	13 9 13 10 19 4 11 32 13	16 13 18 12 21 4 12 32 13	19 18 20 13 22 4 12 31 13	22 22 20 18 25 4 13 32 13	25 27 25 22 28 4 13 32 13	28 30 30 25 30 3 12 32 13
27	32 22 33 35 15 36 11 32 13	34 27 32 1 13 1 10 31 12	1 30 35 5 13 1 10 32 12	4 34 5 8 14 2 10 32 12	7 3 9 11 15 3 11 33 12	10 7 8 11 17 4 11 32 13	13 10 13 10 19 4 11 32 13	16 14 18 12 21 4 12 32 13	19 19 20 13 22 4 12 31 13	22 23 20 18 25 4 13 32 13	25 28 25 22 28 4 13 32 13	28 32 30 25 30 3 12 32 13
28	32 23 33 35 15 36 11 32 13	34 28 32 1 13 1 10 31 12	1 31 35 5 13 1 10 32 12	4 36 5 8 14 2 10 32 12	7 4 9 11 15 3 11 33 12	10 8 8 11 17 4 11 32 13	13 11 13 10 19 4 11 32 13	16 16 18 12 21 4 12 32 13	19 21 20 14 23 4 12 32 13	22 24 20 18 25 4 13 32 13	26 30 25 22 28 4 13 32 13	28 33 30 25 30 3 12 32 13
29	32 24 33 35 15 36 11 32 13	34 29 32 2 13 1 10 31 12	1 32 35 5 13 1 10 32 12	5 2 5 8 14 2 11 32 12	7 5 9 11 16 3 11 33 12	10 9 8 11 17 4 11 32 13	13 13 13 10 19 4 11 32 13	16 17 19 12 21 4 12 32 13	19 22 20 14 23 4 12 32 13	22 25 20 18 25 4 13 32 13	25 31 25 22 28 4 13 32 13	28 35 30 26 30 3 12 32 13
30	32 26 33 35 15 36 11 32 13	1916	1 34 35 5 13 1 10 32 12	5 2 5 8 14 2 11 32 12	7 6 9 11 16 3 11 33 12	10 10 8 11 17 4 11 32 13	13 14 13 10 19 4 11 32 13	16 18 19 12 21 4 12 32 13	19 23 20 14 23 4 12 32 13	22 27 20 18 25 4 13 32 13	25 32 25 22 28 4 13 32 13	28 36 30 26 30 3 12 32 13
31	32 27 33 35 15 36 11 32 13		1 35 35 5 13 1 10 32 12		7 7 9 11 16 3 11 33 12		13 15 13 10 19 4 11 32 13	16 19 19 12 21 4 12 32 13		22 28 20 18 25 4 13 32 13		28 2 30 26 30 3 12 32 13

	JAN	FEB	MAR	APR	MAY	JUNE	JULY	AUG	SEPT	OCT	NOV	DEC
1	30 3 30 26 30 3 12 32 12	33 9 30 30 33 3 12 33 13	34 9 33 33 34 4 12 33 13	1 13 1 1 1 4 12 33 13	6 16 6 6 3 6 12 33 13	7 21 6 9 6 6 12 33 13	10 24 9 12 8 6 12 33 12	13 29 15 16 10 7 13 33 13	16 34 19 19 12 7 13 33 13	20 2 18 23 14 8 14 32 14	23 7 22 27 15 7 14 32 13	25 11 27 30 16 7 14 32 13
2	29 4 30 26 30 3 12 32 12	33 9 30 30 33 3 12 33 13	34 10 33 33 34 4 12 33 13	1 15 3 1 1 4 12 33 13	6 18 6 6 3 6 12 33 13	7 22 6 9 6 6 12 33 13	10 26 9 13 8 7 13 33 13	13 31 15 16 10 7 13 33 13	16 36 19 19 12 7 13 33 13	20 4 18 23 14 8 14 32 14	23 8 23 28 16 7 14 32 13	25 12 27 30 16 7 14 32 13
3	29 6 30 26 30 3 12 32 12	33 10 30 30 33 3 12 33 13	34 11 33 33 34 4 12 33 13	1 15 3 1 1 4 12 33 13	6 19 6 6 3 6 12 33 13	8 24 6 9 6 6 12 33 13	10 27 10 13 8 7 13 33 13	13 33 16 16 10 7 13 33 13	16 1 19 21 12 7 13 33 13	20 5 18 23 14 8 14 32 14	23 10 23 28 16 7 14 32 13	26 13 27 30 17 7 14 32 13
4	29 7 30 26 30 3 12 32 12	33 11 30 30 33 3 12 33 13	34 12 33 33 34 4 12 33 13	3 16 3 1 1 4 12 33 13	6 20 6 6 3 6 12 33 13	8 25 6 9 6 6 12 33 13	10 28 10 13 8 7 13 33 13	13 34 16 16 10 7 13 33 13	16 3 19 21 12 7 13 33 13	20 7 18 23 14 8 14 32 14	23 11 23 28 16 7 14 32 13	26 14 27 30 17 7 14 32 13
5	29 8 30 26 30 3 12 32 13	33 12 30 30 33 3 12 33 13	35 13 33 34 35 4 12 33 13	3 18 3 1 1 4 12 33 13	6 21 6 6 4 6 12 33 13	8 26 6 9 6 6 12 33 13	10 30 10 13 9 7 13 33 13	13 35 16 16 10 7 13 33 13	16 4 19 21 12 7 13 33 13	20 8 18 23 14 8 14 32 14	23 13 23 28 16 7 14 32 13	26 16 27 30 17 7 14 32 13
6	29 9 30 26 30 3 12 32 12	33 13 30 30 33 3 12 33 13	35 15 33 34 35 4 12 33 13	3 19 3 1 1 4 12 33 13	6 22 6 6 4 6 12 33 13	9 27 6 9 6 6 12 33 13	11 31 11 13 9 7 13 33 13	13 1 16 16 10 7 13 33 13	16 6 19 21 12 7 13 33 13	20 9 18 23 14 8 14 32 14	23 14 23 28 16 7 14 32 13	26 17 28 31 17 7 14 32 13
7	29 10 30 27 30 3 12 32 12	33 15 30 30 33 3 12 33 13	36 16 33 34 36 4 12 33 13	3 21 3 1 1 4 12 33 13	6 24 6 6 4 6 12 33 13	9 29 6 9 6 6 12 33 13	11 33 11 13 9 7 13 33 13	15 2 16 16 10 7 13 33 13	16 7 19 21 12 7 13 33 13	20 10 18 23 14 8 14 32 14	23 14 23 28 16 7 14 32 13	26 18 28 31 17 7 14 32 13
8	30 12 30 27 30 3 12 32 12	33 16 30 31 33 3 12 33 13	36 17 33 34 36 4 12 33 13	3 21 3 1 1 4 12 33 13	6 25 6 6 4 6 12 33 13	9 30 6 9 6 6 12 33 13	11 34 11 13 9 7 13 33 13	15 4 16 16 10 7 13 33 13	16 9 19 21 12 7 13 33 13	20 12 18 23 14 8 14 32 14	23 16 23 28 16 7 14 32 13	26 19 28 31 17 7 14 32 13
9	30 13 30 27 30 3 12 32 13	33 17 30 31 33 3 12 33 13	36 18 34 34 36 4 12 33 13	3 22 4 1 1 4 12 33 13	6 27 6 6 4 6 12 33 13	9 31 6 9 6 6 12 33 13	11 36 11 13 9 7 13 33 13	15 5 16 16 10 7 13 33 13	16 10 19 21 12 7 13 33 13	20 13 18 23 14 8 14 32 14	23 17 23 28 16 7 14 32 13	26 20 28 31 17 7 14 32 13
10	30 14 30 27 30 3 12 32 12	33 18 30 31 33 3 12 33 13	36 19 34 34 36 4 12 33 13	3 24 4 3 3 5 12 33 13	6 28 6 6 4 6 12 33 13	9 33 6 10 6 6 12 33 13	11 1 11 13 9 7 13 33 13	15 6 16 16 10 7 13 33 13	16 11 19 21 12 7 13 33 13	20 14 19 23 14 8 14 32 14	23 18 23 28 16 7 14 32 13	26 22 28 31 17 7 14 32 13
11	30 15 30 27 30 3 12 32 12	33 19 30 31 33 3 12 33 13	36 21 34 34 36 4 12 33 13	3 25 5 3 3 5 12 33 13	6 30 6 6 4 6 12 33 13	9 34 6 10 6 6 12 33 13	11 3 11 13 9 7 13 33 13	15 7 17 17 11 7 13 33 13	16 12 19 21 12 7 13 33 13	20 14 19 24 14 8 14 32 14	23 20 23 28 16 7 14 32 13	26 23 28 31 17 7 13 32 13
12	30 16 30 27 30 3 12 32 12	33 21 30 31 33 3 12 33 13	36 22 36 36 36 4 12 33 13	3 27 5 3 3 5 12 33 13	6 31 6 6 4 6 12 33 13	9 36 6 10 6 6 12 33 13	11 4 11 13 9 7 13 33 13	15 9 17 17 11 7 13 33 13	16 13 19 22 13 7 13 33 13	20 16 19 25 14 7 14 32 13	23 20 23 28 16 7 14 32 13	26 24 28 31 17 7 13 32 13
13	30 18 30 27 30 3 12 32 13	33 22 30 31 33 3 12 33 13	36 24 36 36 36 4 12 33 13	3 28 5 3 3 5 12 33 13	6 33 6 6 4 6 12 33 13	9 1 6 10 6 6 12 33 13	11 6 11 13 9 7 13 33 13	15 10 17 17 11 7 13 33 13	18 15 19 22 13 7 13 33 13	20 18 19 25 14 7 14 32 13	23 22 23 28 16 7 14 32 13	26 25 29 31 17 7 13 32 13
14	30 19 30 27 30 3 12 32 12	33 24 30 31 33 3 12 33 13	36 23 36 36 36 4 12 33 13	3 30 5 3 3 5 12 33 13	6 33 6 6 4 6 12 33 13	9 3 6 10 6 6 12 33 13	12 6 12 13 9 7 13 33 13	15 11 17 17 11 7 13 33 13	18 16 19 22 13 7 13 33 13	20 19 19 25 14 7 14 32 13	23 23 23 28 16 7 14 32 13	26 26 29 31 17 7 13 32 13
15	30 20 30 27 30 3 12 32 12	33 25 31 31 33 3 12 33 13	36 25 36 36 36 4 12 33 13	3 32 5 3 3 5 12 33 13	6 35 6 6 4 6 12 33 13	9 4 7 10 7 6 12 33 13	12 7 12 15 9 7 13 33 13	15 12 17 17 11 7 13 33 13	18 16 18 22 13 7 13 33 13	20 20 19 25 14 7 14 32 13	23 25 23 28 16 7 14 32 13	26 28 29 31 17 7 13 32 13
16	30 21 30 27 31 3 12 32 13	33 27 31 31 33 3 12 33 13	36 27 36 36 36 4 12 33 13	3 33 5 3 3 5 12 33 13	6 36 6 7 4 6 12 33 13	9 6 7 10 7 6 12 33 13	12 9 12 15 9 7 13 33 13	15 13 18 18 11 7 13 33 13	18 18 18 22 13 7 13 33 13	20 21 19 25 14 7 14 32 13	23 26 25 28 16 7 14 32 13	26 29 29 31 17 7 13 32 13
17	30 22 30 27 31 3 12 32 13	33 28 31 33 33 3 12 33 13	36 28 36 36 36 4 12 33 13	3 35 5 3 3 5 12 33 13	6 2 6 7 4 6 12 33 13	9 7 7 10 7 6 12 33 13	12 10 12 15 9 7 13 33 13	15 15 18 18 11 7 13 33 13	18 19 18 22 13 7 13 33 13	20 23 19 25 14 7 14 32 13	23 27 25 28 16 7 14 32 13	26 31 29 32 17 7 14 32 13
18	30 23 30 28 31 3 12 32 13	33 29 31 33 33 3 12 33 12	36 30 36 36 36 4 12 33 13	3 36 5 3 3 5 12 33 13	6 3 6 7 4 6 12 33 13	9 8 7 11 7 6 12 33 13	12 12 13 15 9 7 13 33 13	15 16 18 18 11 7 13 33 13	18 21 18 22 13 7 13 33 13	20 23 19 25 14 7 14 32 13	23 28 25 28 16 7 14 32 13	27 32 30 32 18 7 14 32 13
19	30 25 30 28 31 3 12 32 13	34 30 31 33 34 4 12 33 13	36 31 36 36 36 4 12 33 13	3 1 6 3 3 6 12 33 13	6 4 6 7 4 6 12 33 13	9 9 7 11 7 6 12 33 13	12 13 13 15 9 7 13 33 13	15 17 18 18 11 7 13 33 13	18 22 18 22 13 7 13 33 13	20 25 19 25 14 7 14 32 13	23 30 25 28 16 7 14 32 13	27 34 30 32 18 7 14 32 13
20	30 27 30 28 31 3 12 32 13	34 33 31 33 34 4 12 33 13	36 33 36 36 36 4 12 33 13	3 3 6 3 3 6 12 33 13	6 6 6 7 6 6 12 33 13	9 11 7 11 7 6 12 33 13	12 14 13 15 9 7 13 33 13	15 18 18 18 11 7 13 33 13	18 23 18 22 13 7 13 33 13	20 26 19 25 14 7 14 32 13	23 31 25 28 16 7 14 32 13	27 36 30 32 18 7 14 32 13
21	31 28 30 28 32 3 12 32 13	34 34 31 33 34 4 12 33 13	36 34 36 36 36 4 12 33 13	4 3 6 4 3 6 12 33 13	6 7 6 7 6 6 12 33 13	9 12 7 11 7 6 12 33 13	12 15 13 15 9 7 13 33 13	15 19 18 18 11 7 13 33 13	18 24 18 22 13 7 13 33 13	21 28 20 26 15 8 14 33 14	23 32 25 28 16 7 14 32 13	27 1 30 32 18 7 14 32 13
22	31 30 30 28 32 3 12 32 13	34 35 31 33 34 4 12 33 13	1 36 1 1 1 4 12 33 13	4 6 6 4 3 6 12 33 13	7 9 6 7 6 6 12 33 13	10 13 7 11 7 6 12 33 13	12 16 13 15 9 7 13 33 13	15 20 18 19 11 7 13 33 13	18 25 18 22 13 7 13 33 13	21 29 20 26 15 8 14 33 14	23 34 26 28 16 7 14 32 13	28 2 30 32 18 7 14 32 13
23	31 31 30 28 32 3 12 32 13	34 36 31 33 34 4 12 33 13	1 1 1 1 1 4 12 33 13	4 6 6 4 3 6 12 33 13	7 10 6 7 6 6 12 33 13	10 14 7 11 7 6 12 33 13	13 18 13 15 9 7 13 33 13	15 22 18 19 11 7 13 33 13	18 27 18 22 13 7 13 33 13	21 30 20 26 15 8 14 33 14	25 36 26 28 15 7 14 32 13	28 4 30 32 18 7 14 32 13
24	31 33 30 29 32 3 12 32 13	34 2 33 33 34 4 12 33 13	1 3 1 1 1 4 12 33 13	4 8 6 4 3 6 12 33 13	7 11 6 7 6 6 12 33 13	10 15 7 11 7 6 12 33 13	13 19 15 15 9 7 13 33 13	16 24 18 19 11 7 13 33 13	19 28 18 22 13 7 13 33 13	22 32 20 26 15 8 14 33 13	25 1 26 28 16 7 14 32 13	28 5 30 32 18 7 14 32 13
25	31 34 30 29 32 3 12 32 13	34 3 33 33 34 4 12 33 13	1 4 1 1 1 4 12 33 13	4 9 6 4 3 5 12 33 13	7 12 6 7 6 6 12 33 13	10 16 7 11 7 6 12 33 13	13 20 15 15 9 7 13 33 13	16 25 18 19 11 7 13 33 13	19 30 18 22 13 7 13 33 13	22 33 21 26 15 8 14 33 13	25 2 26 28 16 7 14 32 13	28 6 30 32 18 7 14 32 13
26	32 36 30 29 32 3 12 32 13	34 5 33 33 34 4 12 33 13	1 6 1 1 1 4 12 33 13	4 10 6 4 3 5 12 33 13	7 13 6 7 6 6 12 33 13	10 18 7 11 7 6 12 33 12	13 21 15 15 9 7 13 33 13	16 25 18 19 11 7 13 33 13	19 31 16 22 13 7 13 33 13	22 35 21 26 15 8 14 33 13	25 4 26 28 16 7 14 32 13	28 7 30 32 18 7 14 32 13
27	32 1 30 29 32 3 12 32 13	34 6 33 33 34 4 12 33 13	1 7 1 1 1 4 12 33 13	5 12 6 5 3 5 12 33 13	7 15 6 7 6 6 12 33 13	10 19 9 12 7 6 12 33 12	13 22 15 15 9 7 13 33 13	16 27 19 19 11 7 13 33 13	19 33 16 22 13 7 13 33 13	23 36 23 27 15 8 14 33 14	25 5 26 28 16 7 14 32 13	28 8 30 32 18 7 14 32 13
28	32 3 30 29 32 3 12 32 13	34 7 33 33 34 4 12 33 13	1 8 1 1 1 4 12 33 13	5 13 6 5 3 5 12 33 13	7 16 6 9 6 6 12 33 13	10 20 9 12 7 6 12 33 12	13 24 15 15 9 7 13 33 13	16 28 19 19 12 7 13 33 13	19 34 16 22 13 7 13 33 13	23 2 23 27 15 8 14 33 14	25 7 26 28 16 7 14 32 13	28 10 30 32 18 7 14 32 13
29	32 4 30 30 32 3 12 32 13		1 9 1 1 1 4 12 33 13	5 14 6 5 3 5 12 33 13	7 17 6 9 6 6 12 33 13	10 21 9 12 8 6 12 33 13	13 25 15 16 10 7 13 33 13	16 30 19 19 12 7 13 33 13	19 36 16 23 13 7 13 33 13	23 3 23 27 15 8 14 33 14	25 8 26 28 16 7 14 32 13	28 12 30 32 18 7 14 32 13
30	32 5 30 30 32 3 12 32 13	**1917**	1 10 1 1 1 4 12 33 13	5 15 6 5 3 5 12 33 13	7 18 6 9 6 6 12 33 13	10 22 9 12 8 6 12 33 12	13 27 15 16 10 7 13 33 13	16 31 19 19 12 7 13 33 13	20 2 17 23 14 8 14 32 14	23 5 23 27 15 8 14 33 14	25 9 26 28 16 7 14 32 13	29 13 30 32 18 7 14 32 13
31	32 6 30 30 32 3 12 32 13		1 12 1 1 1 4 12 33 13		7 19 6 9 6 6 12 33 13		13 28 15 16 10 7 13 33 13	16 33 19 19 12 7 13 33 13		23 6 23 27 15 8 14 33 14		29 14 29 32 18 7 14 32 13

	JAN	FEB	MAR	APR	MAY	JUNE	JULY	AUG	SEPT	OCT	NOV	DEC
1	29 15 29 33 18 7 14 33 13	31 19 30 33 19 7 13 33 13	35 21 34 31 18 7 13 33 13	1 25 3 33 17 7 13 33 13	5 28 4 36 17 8 14 33 13	7 34 4 3 18 9 13 33 13	10 1 11 7 19 9 14 33 13	13 7 16 10 21 10 13 33 13	16 12 16 15 23 11 15 33 14	20 15 19 19 25 11 15 33 13	23 20 24 23 27 11 15 33 14	25 23 27 25 29 11 15 33 13
2	29 16 29 33 18 7 14 33 13	31 21 30 33 19 7 13 33 13	35 22 34 31 18 7 13 33 13	1 27 3 33 17 7 13 33 13	5 30 4 36 17 8 14 33 13	7 36 4 3 18 9 13 33 13	10 3 11 7 19 9 14 33 13	13 9 16 10 21 10 13 33 13	16 13 16 15 23 11 15 33 14	20 16 19 19 25 11 15 33 13	23 21 24 23 27 11 15 33 14	25 24 27 25 29 11 15 33 13
3	29 18 29 33 18 7 14 33 13	31 22 30 33 19 7 13 33 13	35 23 34 31 18 7 13 33 13	1 28 4 33 17 7 13 33 13	5 32 4 36 17 8 14 33 13	7 1 6 4 18 9 13 33 13	10 4 11 7 19 9 13 33 13	13 10 16 10 21 10 13 33 13	16 15 16 15 23 11 15 33 14	20 18 19 19 25 11 15 33 13	23 23 24 23 27 11 15 33 14	25 25 27 25 29 11 15 33 13
4	29 19 29 33 18 7 14 33 13	31 24 30 33 19 7 13 33 13	35 24 34 31 18 7 13 33 13	1 29 4 33 16 7 13 33 13	5 33 4 36 17 8 14 33 13	9 2 6 4 18 9 13 33 13	10 6 11 7 19 9 13 33 13	13 11 16 10 21 10 13 33 13	16 16 16 14 23 11 14 32 14	20 19 19 19 25 11 15 33 13	23 24 24 23 27 11 15 33 14	25 27 27 25 29 11 15 33 13
5	29 20 29 33 18 7 14 33 13	32 25 30 32 19 7 14 32 13	35 25 34 31 18 7 13 33 13	1 30 4 33 16 7 13 33 13	5 34 4 36 17 8 14 33 13	9 3 6 4 18 9 13 33 13	10 7 12 7 19 9 13 33 13	13 12 18 12 21 10 13 33 13	16 17 16 14 23 11 14 32 14	20 20 19 19 25 11 15 33 13	23 25 24 23 27 11 15 33 14	25 28 27 25 29 11 15 33 13
6	29 21 28 33 19 7 14 33 13	32 26 30 32 19 7 14 32 13	35 27 34 31 18 7 13 33 13	1 34 4 34 16 7 13 33 13	5 35 4 36 17 8 14 33 13	9 4 6 4 18 9 13 33 13	10 9 12 7 19 9 13 33 13	13 13 18 12 21 10 13 33 13	16 18 16 14 23 11 14 32 14	20 21 19 19 25 11 15 33 13	23 26 24 23 27 11 15 33 14	25 29 27 25 29 11 15 33 13
7	29 23 28 33 19 7 14 33 13	32 27 30 32 19 7 14 32 13	35 28 34 31 18 7 13 33 13	1 33 4 34 16 7 13 33 13	5 1 4 1 17 8 14 33 13	9 6 6 4 18 9 13 33 13	10 10 12 7 19 9 13 33 13	13 15 18 12 21 10 13 33 13	16 19 16 14 23 11 14 32 14	20 22 19 19 25 11 15 33 13	23 27 24 23 27 11 15 33 14	25 30 27 25 29 11 15 33 13
8	29 24 28 33 19 7 14 33 13	32 28 30 32 19 7 14 32 13	36 30 34 31 18 7 13 33 13	3 34 4 34 16 7 13 33 13	5 2 4 1 17 8 14 33 13	9 8 6 4 18 9 13 33 13	10 12 12 7 19 9 13 33 13	13 16 18 12 21 10 13 33 13	17 21 16 14 23 11 14 32 14	20 24 19 19 25 11 15 33 13	23 28 24 23 27 11 15 33 14	25 31 27 25 29 11 15 33 13
9	29 25 28 33 19 7 14 33 13	32 30 30 32 19 7 14 32 13	36 31 36 31 18 7 13 33 13	3 36 4 34 16 7 13 33 13	5 4 4 1 17 8 13 32 13	9 9 6 4 18 9 13 33 13	10 13 13 7 19 9 13 33 13	13 18 18 12 21 10 13 33 13	17 22 16 14 23 11 14 32 14	20 25 19 19 25 11 15 33 13	23 30 26 23 27 11 15 33 14	27 33 27 27 29 11 15 33 13
10	29 27 28 33 19 7 14 33 13	33 31 31 33 19 7 15 33 13	36 33 36 31 18 7 13 33 13	3 1 4 34 16 7 13 33 13	5 5 4 1 17 8 13 32 13	9 10 7 4 18 9 13 33 13	10 13 13 7 19 9 13 33 13	14 19 18 12 21 10 14 33 13	17 23 16 14 23 11 14 32 14	20 26 19 19 25 11 15 33 13	23 31 26 23 27 11 15 33 14	27 35 27 27 29 11 15 33 13
11	29 28 28 33 19 7 14 33 13	33 33 31 33 19 7 15 33 13	36 34 36 31 18 7 13 33 13	3 3 4 34 16 7 13 33 13	5 7 4 1 17 8 13 32 13	9 12 7 4 18 9 13 33 13	11 15 13 7 19 9 13 33 13	14 19 18 12 21 10 14 33 13	17 23 16 14 23 11 14 32 14	21 27 19 19 25 12 15 33 13	24 33 25 24 27 12 15 33 13	27 36 27 27 30 11 15 33 13
12	29 30 28 33 19 7 14 33 13	33 34 31 33 19 7 15 33 13	36 36 36 31 18 7 13 33 13	3 4 4 34 16 7 13 33 13	5 8 4 1 17 8 13 32 13	9 13 7 4 18 9 13 33 13	11 16 13 7 19 9 13 33 13	14 21 16 12 21 10 14 32 13	17 25 16 16 23 11 14 32 14	21 28 21 19 25 12 15 33 13	24 33 25 24 27 12 15 33 13	27 1 27 27 30 11 15 33 13
13	29 31 28 33 19 7 14 33 13	33 36 31 33 19 7 15 33 13	36 1 36 31 18 7 13 33 13	3 6 4 34 16 7 13 33 13	5 10 4 1 17 8 13 32 13	9 15 7 4 18 9 13 33 13	11 18 13 7 19 9 13 33 13	14 22 16 12 21 10 14 32 13	17 26 16 16 23 11 14 32 13	21 30 21 19 25 12 15 33 13	24 36 25 24 27 12 15 33 13	27 3 27 27 30 11 15 33 13
14	30 32 27 33 18 6 14 33 13	33 1 31 33 19 7 15 33 13	36 3 36 31 18 7 13 33 13	3 7 4 34 16 7 13 33 13	5 11 4 1 17 8 13 32 13	9 16 7 4 18 9 13 33 13	11 19 13 7 19 9 13 33 13	14 23 16 12 21 10 14 32 13	18 27 16 16 23 11 14 32 13	21 31 21 19 25 12 15 33 13	24 35 25 24 27 12 15 33 13	27 4 27 27 30 11 15 33 13
15	30 33 27 33 18 6 14 33 13	33 3 33 33 19 7 15 33 13	36 4 36 31 18 7 13 33 13	3 9 4 34 16 7 13 33 13	5 12 4 1 17 8 13 32 13	9 17 7 4 18 9 13 33 13	11 20 13 7 19 9 13 33 13	14 24 16 12 21 10 14 32 13	18 28 16 16 23 11 14 32 13	21 33 21 19 25 12 15 33 13	24 1 25 24 27 12 15 33 13	27 6 27 27 30 11 15 33 13
16	30 35 27 33 18 6 14 33 13	33 4 33 33 19 7 15 33 13	36 6 36 33 18 7 13 33 13	3 10 4 34 16 7 13 33 13	5 13 4 2 17 8 13 32 13	9 18 8 5 18 9 14 33 13	12 21 13 9 19 10 13 33 13	14 26 16 12 21 10 14 32 13	18 29 16 16 23 11 14 32 13	21 34 21 19 25 12 15 33 13	24 3 25 24 28 12 15 33 13	27 7 27 27 30 11 15 33 13
17	30 36 27 33 18 6 14 33 13	33 6 33 33 19 7 15 33 13	36 7 1 33 18 7 13 33 13	3 12 4 34 16 7 13 33 13	5 14 4 2 17 8 13 32 13	9 19 8 5 18 9 14 33 13	12 22 13 9 19 10 13 33 13	14 27 16 13 22 10 14 32 13	18 31 16 16 23 11 14 32 13	21 36 21 19 25 12 15 33 13	26 4 25 24 28 12 15 33 13	27 9 27 27 30 11 15 33 13
18	30 2 27 33 18 6 14 33 13	33 7 33 33 19 7 15 33 13	36 8 1 33 18 7 13 33 13	3 13 4 34 16 7 13 33 13	6 16 4 2 17 8 13 33 13	9 21 8 5 18 9 14 33 13	12 24 13 9 19 10 13 33 13	14 28 16 13 22 10 14 32 13	18 32 16 16 23 11 14 32 13	21 1 21 19 25 12 15 33 13	24 6 25 24 28 11 15 33 13	27 10 27 27 30 10 15 33 13
19	30 3 27 33 18 6 14 33 13	34 9 33 33 19 7 15 33 13	36 9 1 33 18 7 13 33 13	3 13 4 34 16 7 13 33 13	6 17 4 2 17 8 13 33 13	9 22 8 5 18 9 14 33 13	12 25 13 9 19 10 13 33 13	14 30 16 13 22 10 14 32 13	18 34 16 16 23 11 14 32 13	21 3 21 19 25 11 15 33 13	24 7 25 24 28 11 15 33 13	27 11 27 27 30 10 15 33 13
20	30 5 27 33 18 6 14 33 13	34 10 33 33 19 7 15 33 13	36 10 1 33 18 7 13 33 13	3 15 4 34 16 7 13 33 13	6 18 4 2 17 8 13 33 13	9 23 8 5 18 9 14 33 13	12 26 13 9 19 10 13 33 13	14 31 16 13 22 13 14 32 13	18 36 17 17 24 11 15 33 14	21 4 21 19 25 11 15 33 13	24 9 27 24 28 11 15 33 13	27 13 27 28 31 10 15 33 13
21	31 6 28 33 19 7 14 33 13	34 11 32 32 19 7 14 33 13	1 12 1 33 18 7 13 33 13	4 16 4 34 16 7 13 33 13	6 19 4 2 17 8 13 33 13	9 24 9 5 18 9 14 33 13	12 27 15 9 20 9 14 33 13	14 32 16 13 22 13 14 32 13	18 2 17 17 24 11 15 33 13	21 6 22 21 27 11 15 33 13	24 11 27 24 29 11 15 33 13	27 14 27 28 31 10 15 33 13
22	31 7 28 33 19 7 14 33 13	34 12 32 32 19 7 14 33 13	1 13 1 33 18 7 13 33 13	4 18 4 34 16 7 13 33 13	7 21 4 2 17 8 13 33 13	10 25 9 6 19 9 14 33 13	12 29 11 9 20 9 14 33 13	14 32 16 13 22 13 14 32 13	18 3 17 17 24 11 15 33 13	21 7 22 21 27 11 15 33 13	24 12 27 24 29 11 15 33 13	27 15 27 28 31 10 15 33 13
23	31 9 28 33 19 7 13 33 13	34 14 32 32 19 7 14 33 14	1 15 1 33 18 7 13 33 13	4 19 4 34 16 7 13 33 13	7 22 4 2 17 8 13 33 13	10 27 9 6 19 9 14 33 13	12 30 15 9 20 9 14 33 13	14 36 16 13 22 13 14 32 13	18 5 17 17 24 11 15 33 13	21 9 22 21 27 11 15 33 13	25 13 27 25 29 11 15 33 13	28 17 27 28 31 10 15 33 13
24	31 10 28 33 19 7 13 33 13	34 15 33 32 19 7 14 33 13	1 15 1 33 18 7 13 33 13	4 20 4 34 16 7 13 33 13	7 22 4 2 17 8 13 33 13	10 28 9 6 19 9 14 33 13	13 32 15 9 20 9 14 33 13	16 1 16 13 22 13 14 32 13	19 6 17 17 24 11 15 33 13	22 10 22 21 27 11 15 33 13	25 15 27 25 29 11 15 33 13	28 18 27 28 31 10 15 33 13
25	31 11 28 33 19 7 13 33 13	34 16 33 32 19 7 14 33 13	1 17 3 33 18 7 13 33 13	4 21 4 34 16 7 13 33 13	7 24 4 2 17 8 13 33 13	10 30 10 6 19 9 14 33 13	13 33 15 10 20 10 14 33 13	16 2 16 13 22 13 14 32 13	19 7 17 17 24 11 15 33 13	22 11 22 21 27 11 15 33 13	25 16 27 25 29 11 15 33 13	28 19 27 28 31 10 15 33 13
26	31 13 28 33 19 7 13 33 13	34 17 33 32 19 7 14 33 13	1 18 3 33 18 7 13 33 13	4 22 4 34 16 7 13 33 13	7 26 4 2 17 8 13 33 13	10 31 10 6 19 9 14 33 13	13 34 15 10 20 10 14 33 13	16 4 16 13 22 13 14 32 13	19 9 18 18 24 11 15 33 13	22 13 22 21 27 11 15 33 13	25 17 27 25 29 11 15 33 13	28 21 27 28 31 10 15 33 13
27	31 14 29 33 19 7 13 33 13	34 18 33 32 18 7 14 33 13	1 19 3 33 18 7 13 33 13	4 24 4 34 16 7 13 33 13	7 27 4 3 17 8 13 33 18	10 32 10 6 19 9 14 33 13	13 36 15 10 20 10 14 33 13	16 5 16 13 22 10 14 32 13	19 11 18 18 24 11 15 33 13	22 13 22 21 27 11 15 33 13	25 18 27 25 29 11 15 33 13	28 22 25 27 31 10 15 33 13
28	31 15 29 33 19 7 13 33 13	34 19 33 32 18 7 14 33 13	1 20 3 33 18 7 13 33 13	4 25 4 34 16 7 13 33 13	7 28 4 3 17 8 13 33 13	10 33 10 6 19 9 14 33 13	13 1 16 10 20 10 14 33 13	16 7 16 13 22 10 13 32 13	20 12 18 18 24 11 15 33 14	22 15 22 21 27 11 15 33 13	25 20 27 25 29 11 15 33 13	28 22 25 28 31 10 15 33 18
29	31 16 29 33 19 7 13 33 13	1918	1 22 3 33 18 7 13 33 13	4 25 4 34 16 7 13 33 13	7 29 4 3 17 8 13 33 13	10 35 10 7 19 9 14 33 13	13 3 16 10 20 10 14 33 13	16 7 16 13 22 10 13 32 13	20 13 18 18 24 11 15 33 14	22 16 22 21 27 11 15 33 13	25 21 27 25 29 11 15 33 13	28 24 25 28 31 10 15 33 18
30	31 17 29 33 19 7 13 33 13		1 22 3 33 18 7 13 33 13	4 27 4 34 16 7 13 33 13	7 31 4 3 17 8 13 33 13	10 36 10 7 19 9 14 33 13	13 4 16 10 20 10 14 33 13	16 8 16 13 22 10 13 32 13	20 14 18 18 24 11 15 33 14	22 18 24 22 27 10 15 33 13	25 22 27 25 29 11 15 33 13	28 25 25 28 31 10 15 33 18
31	31 19 29 33 19 7 13 33 13		1 24 3 33 18 7 13 33 13		7 33 4 3 17 8 13 33 13		13 5 16 10 21 10 13 33 13	16 10 16 13 22 10 13 32 13		22 19 24 22 27 10 15 33 13		28 27 25 28 31 10 15 33 18

	JAN	FEB	MAR	APR	MAY	JUNE	JULY	AUG	SEPT	OCT	NOV	DEC
1	28 27 27 28 31 10 15 33 13	31 33 30 33 34 10 15 33 13	34 33 35 1 36 10 15 33 13	1 3 3 4 3 10 15 34 13	5 6 3 9 5 11 14 34 13	7 11 6 11 7 11 15 34 13	10 15 12 15 9 12 15 33 13	13 20 15 18 11 12 15 33 13	16 24 15 18 13 13 16 33 13	20 27 20 16 15 14 16 33 14	22 32 24 18 16 14 16 33 14	25 36 26 21 19 14 17 33 13
2	28 28 27 29 31 10 15 33 13	31 34 30 33 34 10 15 33 13	34 35 35 1 36 10 15 33 13	1 4 3 4 3 10 15 34 13	5 9 3 9 5 11 14 34 13	7 13 7 11 7 11 15 34 13	10 16 13 15 9 12 15 33 13	13 21 15 18 11 12 15 33 13	16 25 15 18 13 13 16 33 13	20 28 20 16 15 14 16 33 14	22 33 24 18 16 14 16 33 14	25 1 26 21 19 14 17 33 13
3	28 29 27 29 31 10 15 33 13	31 36 30 34 34 10 15 33 13	34 36 35 1 36 10 15 33 13	3 6 3 6 3 10 15 34 13	5 9 3 9 5 11 14 34 13	8 15 7 11 7 11 15 34 13	10 18 13 15 9 12 15 33 13	13 22 15 18 11 12 15 33 13	16 27 15 18 13 13 16 33 13	20 30 20 16 15 14 16 33 14	22 34 25 18 16 14 16 33 14	25 2 26 21 19 14 17 33 13
4	28 31 27 29 31 10 15 33 13	31 1 31 34 34 10 15 33 13	34 1 35 1 36 10 15 33 13	3 7 3 6 3 10 15 34 13	5 11 3 9 5 11 14 34 13	8 16 7 11 7 11 15 34 13	10 19 13 15 9 12 15 33 13	13 24 15 18 11 12 15 33 13	16 28 15 18 13 13 16 33 13	20 32 20 16 15 14 16 33 14	22 36 25 18 16 14 16 33 14	25 4 26 21 19 14 17 33 13
5	28 33 27 29 31 10 15 33 13	31 3 31 34 34 10 15 33 13	34 3 35 1 1 10 15 33 13	3 9 3 6 3 10 15 33 13	5 12 3 9 5 11 14 34 13	9 17 7 11 7 11 15 34 13	10 20 13 15 9 12 15 33 13	13 25 15 18 11 12 15 33 13	16 29 15 18 13 13 16 33 13	20 33 20 16 15 14 16 33 14	22 2 25 18 16 14 16 33 14	26 5 26 21 19 14 17 33 13
6	28 34 27 29 31 10 15 33 13	33 4 31 34 34 10 15 33 13	34 4 36 1 1 10 15 33 13	3 10 3 6 3 10 15 33 13	5 13 3 9 5 11 14 34 13	9 18 7 12 7 11 15 34 13	10 21 13 15 9 12 15 33 13	13 26 15 18 11 12 15 33 13	16 30 15 18 13 13 16 33 13	20 34 20 16 15 14 16 33 14	22 3 25 18 16 14 16 33 14	26 7 26 21 19 14 17 33 13
7	28 35 27 29 31 10 15 33 13	33 4 31 34 34 10 15 33 13	35 6 36 1 1 10 15 33 13	3 11 3 6 3 10 15 33 13	5 14 3 9 5 11 14 34 13	9 19 7 12 7 11 15 34 13	10 22 13 15 9 12 15 33 13	13 27 15 18 11 12 15 33 13	17 31 15 17 13 13 16 33 13	20 35 21 16 15 14 16 33 14	22 4 25 18 16 14 16 33 14	26 8 26 21 19 14 17 33 13
8	28 1 27 29 31 10 15 33 13	33 6 31 34 34 10 15 33 13	35 7 36 1 1 10 15 33 13	3 12 3 6 3 10 15 33 13	5 16 3 9 5 11 14 34 13	9 20 7 13 7 11 14 34 13	12 24 13 15 9 12 15 33 13	13 28 15 18 11 12 15 33 13	17 33 15 17 13 13 16 33 13	20 1 21 16 15 14 16 33 14	22 6 25 18 16 14 16 33 14	26 10 26 21 19 14 17 33 13
9	28 3 27 29 31 10 15 33 13	33 7 31 34 34 10 15 33 13	35 9 1 1 1 10 15 33 13	3 13 3 6 3 10 15 33 13	5 17 3 9 5 11 14 34 13	9 22 9 13 7 11 15 34 13	12 25 13 16 10 12 15 34 13	13 30 15 18 11 12 15 33 13	17 34 16 17 13 13 16 33 13	20 2 21 16 16 14 16 33 14	22 7 25 19 16 14 16 33 14	26 12 26 22 19 14 17 33 13
10	29 4 27 31 31 10 15 33 13	33 9 31 34 34 10 15 33 13	35 10 1 1 1 10 15 33 13	3 15 3 6 3 10 15 33 13	5 19 3 9 5 11 14 34 13	9 23 9 13 7 11 15 34 13	12 26 13 16 10 12 15 34 13	13 31 15 18 11 12 15 33 13	17 36 16 17 13 13 16 33 13	20 4 21 16 16 14 16 33 14	23 8 26 19 17 14 17 32 14	26 13 26 22 19 14 17 33 13
11	29 6 27 31 33 10 15 33 13	33 10 31 34 34 10 15 33 13	36 12 1 3 1 10 15 33 13	3 16 3 6 3 10 15 33 13	5 20 3 9 5 11 14 34 13	9 24 9 14 8 11 15 34 14	12 27 13 16 10 12 15 34 13	13 32 15 18 12 12 15 33 13	17 1 16 17 13 13 16 33 13	20 5 21 16 16 14 16 33 14	23 11 26 19 17 14 17 32 14	26 14 26 22 11 14 17 33 13
12	29 7 27 31 33 10 15 33 13	33 12 31 34 34 10 15 33 13	36 13 1 3 1 10 15 33 13	3 18 1 6 3 10 15 33 13	5 21 3 9 5 11 14 34 13	9 26 9 14 8 11 15 34 14	12 28 13 16 10 12 15 34 13	14 33 15 18 12 12 15 33 13	17 3 16 17 13 13 16 33 13	20 6 21 16 16 14 16 33 14	23 12 26 20 17 14 17 32 14	26 15 25 22 19 14 17 33 13
13	30 9 27 31 33 10 15 33 13	33 13 33 34 34 10 15 33 13	36 15 1 3 1 10 15 33 13	3 19 1 6 3 10 15 33 13	5 22 3 10 5 11 14 34 13	9 27 9 14 8 11 15 34 14	12 30 13 16 10 12 15 34 13	14 35 15 18 12 12 15 33 13	17 4 16 17 13 13 16 33 13	20 7 22 16 16 14 16 33 14	24 13 26 20 18 14 17 32 14	26 17 25 22 19 14 17 32 13
14	30 9 28 31 33 10 15 33 13	33 15 33 34 34 10 15 33 13	36 15 1 3 1 10 15 33 13	3 20 1 6 3 10 15 33 13	5 24 3 10 5 11 14 34 13	9 28 9 14 8 11 15 33 14	12 31 15 16 10 12 15 34 13	14 36 15 18 12 12 15 33 13	17 6 16 17 13 13 16 33 13	20 9 22 16 16 14 16 33 14	24 14 26 20 18 14 17 32 14	26 18 25 22 19 14 17 32 13
15	30 10 28 31 33 10 15 33 13	33 16 33 34 34 10 15 33 13	36 16 1 3 1 10 15 33 13	3 21 1 6 3 10 15 33 13	5 25 3 10 5 10 14 34 13	9 29 9 14 8 11 15 33 14	12 33 15 16 10 12 15 34 13	15 1 15 18 12 12 15 33 13	17 7 16 17 13 13 16 33 13	21 11 22 16 16 14 16 33 14	24 16 26 20 18 14 17 32 14	26 20 25 23 20 14 17 32 14
16	30 12 28 31 33 10 15 33 13	33 17 33 34 34 10 15 33 13	36 18 1 3 1 10 15 33 13	3 22 1 6 3 10 15 33 13	5 26 4 10 5 10 14 34 13	9 30 10 14 8 11 15 33 14	12 34 15 16 10 12 15 34 13	15 3 13 18 12 12 15 33 13	18 9 16 18 13 13 16 33 13	21 12 22 16 16 14 16 33 14	24 17 26 20 18 14 17 32 14	26 21 25 23 20 14 17-33 14
17	30 13 28 31 33 10 15 33 13	33 18 33 35 35 10 15 33 13	36 19 1 3 1 10 15 33 13	3 24 1 7 4 10 15 34 13	6 27 4 11 6 11 15 33 13	9 32 10 14 8 11 15 33 14	12 36 15 16 10 12 15 34 13	15 5 13 18 12 12 15 33 13	18 10 18 18 13 13 16 33 13	21 14 22 16 16 14 16 33 14	24 18 26 20 18 14 17 32 14	26 22 25 23 20 14 17 32 14
18	30 15 28 31 33 10 15 33 13	33 19 33 35 35 10 15 33 13	36 21 1 3 1 10 15 33 13	3 25 1 7 4 10 15 34 13	6 28 4 11 6 11 15 33 13	9 33 10 14 8 11 15 33 14	12 1 15 16 10 12 15 34 13	15 6 13 18 12 12 15 33 13	18 11 18 18 13 13 16 33 13	21 15 22 16 16 14 16 33 14	24 19 26 20 18 14 17 32 14	26 23 26 23 20 14 17 32 14
19	30 16 28 31 33 10 15 33 13	33 21 33 35 35 10 15 33 13	36 22 1 3 1 10 15 33 13	3 26 1 7 4 10 15 34 13	6 29 4 11 6 11 15 33 13	9 34 10 14 8 11 15 33 14	12 1 15 16 10 12 15 34 13	15 7 13 18 12 12 15 33 13	18 12 18 17 13 13 16 33 13	21 16 22 16 16 14 16 33 14	24 20 26 20 18 14 17 32 14	26 24 26 23 20 14 17 33 14
20	30 18 28 31 33 10 15 33 13	34 22 33 35 35 10 15 33 13	36 22 1 3 1 10 15 33 13	3 27 1 7 4 10 15 34 13	6 31 4 11 6 11 15 33 13	9 35 10 14 8 11 15 33 14	12 3 15 16 10 12 15 34 13	15 9 13 18 12 12 15 33 13	18 14 18 17 14 14 16 33 14	21 18 22 16 16 14 16 33 14	24 22 26 20 18 14 17 32 14	27 25 26 23 20 14 17 33 14
21	31 19 28 31 33 10 15 33 13	34 24 33 35 35 10 15 33 13	36 24 1 3 1 10 15 33 13	4 28 1 7 4 10 15 34 13	6 31 4 11 6 11 15 33 13	9 1 10 14 8 11 15 33 14	12 4 15 16 10 12 15 34 13	15 10 13 18 12 12 15 33 13	18 15 18 16 14 14 16 33 14	21 19 22 16 16 14 16 33 14	24 23 26 20 18 14 17 32 14	27 26 26 23 20 14 17 33 14
22	31 19 28 31 33 10 15 33 13	34 24 34 36 36 10 15 33 13	1 25 1 3 1 10 15 33 13	4 30 1 7 4 10 15 34 13	7 33 5 11 6 11 15 34 13	10 3 12 15 9 12 15 34 14	12 6 15 17 11 12 15 34 13	15 12 13 18 12 12 15 33 13	18 16 18 16 14 14 16 33 14	21 20 22 16 16 14 16 33 14	24 24 26 20 18 14 17 33 14	27 28 26 23 20 14 17 33 14
23	31 21 28 31 33 10 15 33 13	34 25 34 36 36 10 15 33 13	1 26 1 4 1 10 15 33 13	4 31 1 7 4 10 15 34 13	7 35 5 11 7 11 16 34 13	10 5 12 15 9 12 15 34 14	12 7 15 17 11 12 15 34 13	15 13 14 19 13 13 15 33 13	18 18 18 16 14 14 16 33 14	21 21 22 16 16 14 16 33 14	25 26 26 20 18 14 17 33 14	28 29 26 23 20 14 17 33 14
24	31 22 28 33 33 10 15 33 13	34 27 34 36 36 10 15 33 13	1 27 2 4 2 10 14 33 13	4 33 1 7 4 10 15 34 13	7 36 5 11 7 11 16 34 13	10 6 12 15 9 12 15 34 14	13 9 15 17 11 12 15 34 13	16 14 14 19 13 13 16 34 13	19 19 19 16 15 14 16 33 14	22 23 23 17 16 14 16 33 14	25 27 26 20 18 14 17 33 14	28 30 26 23 20 14 17 33 14
25	31 24 28 33 33 10 15 33 13	34 28 34 36 36 10 15 33 13	1 28 2 4 2 10 14 33 13	4 34 1 7 4 10 15 34 13	7 1 5 11 7 11 16 34 13	10 7 12 15 9 12 15 34 14	13 11 15 17 11 12 15 34 13	16 16 14 19 13 13 16 34 13	19 20 19 16 15 14 16 33 14	22 24 23 17 16 14 16 33 14	26 28 26 20 18 14 17 33 14	29 31 26 23 20 14 17 33 14
26	31 25 29 33 33 10 15 33 13	34 30 34 36 36 10 15 33 13	1 30 2 4 2 10 14 33 13	4 35 1 7 4 10 15 34 13	7 2 6 11 7 11 15 34 13	10 9 12 15 9 12 15 34 13	13 12 15 17 11 12 15 34 13	16 17 14 19 13 13 16 34 13	19 21 19 16 15 14 16 33 14	22 25 23 17 16 14 16 33 14	26 29 26 20 18 14 17 33 14	29 32 26 23 20 14 17 32 14
27	31 26 29 33 34 10 15 33 13	34 31 34 1 36 10 15 33 13	1 31 2 4 2 10 14 33 13	4 36 1 9 4 10 15 34 13	7 4 6 11 7 11 15 34 13	10 10 12 15 9 12 15 34 13	13 13 15 17 11 12 15 34 13	16 18 14 19 13 13 16 34 13	20 23 20 16 15 14 16 33 14	22 26 23 17 16 14 16 33 14	26 30 26 20 18 14 17 33 14	29 34 26 23 20 14 17 33 14
28	31 27 30 33 34 10 15 33 13	34 31 34 1 36 10 15 33 13	1 32 2 4 2 10 14 32 13	4 1 1 9 4 10 15 34 13	7 6 6 11 7 11 15 34 13	10 11 12 15 9 12 15 34 13	13 15 15 17 11 12 15 34 13	16 19 14 18 13 13 16 34 13	20 24 20 16 15 14 16 33 14	22 27 23 18 16 14 16 33 14	26 32 26 20 18 14 17 33 14	29 35 26 24 20 14 17 33 14
29	31 28 30 33 34 10 15 33 13		1 34 2 4 2 10 14 33 13	4 3 1 9 4 10 15 34 13	7 7 6 11 7 11 15 34 13	10 12 12 15 9 12 15 34 13	13 16 15 17 11 12 15 34 13	16 21 14 18 13 13 16 34 13	20 25 20 16 15 14 16 33 14	22 28 23 18 16 14 16 33 14	26 33 26 20 18 14 17 33 14	29 36 26 24 20 14 17 33 14
30	31 30 30 33 34 10 15 33 13	**1919**	1 36 2 4 2 10 14 33 13	4 4 1 9 4 10 15 34 13	7 9 6 11 7 11 15 34 13	10 13 12 15 9 12 15 34 13	13 17 15 17 11 12 15 34 13	16 22 14 18 13 13 16 34 13	20 26 20 16 15 14 16 33 14	22 30 23 18 16 14 16 33 14	26 35 26 20 18 14 17 33 14	29 2 26 24 20 14 17 33 14
31	31 31 30 33 34 10 15 33 13		1 1 2 4 2 10 14 33 13		7 10 6 11 7 11 15 34 13		13 19 15 17 11 12 15 34 13	16 23 14 18 13 13 16 34 13		22 31 23 18 16 14 16 33 14		29 3 26 24 20 14 17 33 14

	JAN	FEB	MAR	APR	MAY	JUNE	JULY	AUG	SEPT	OCT	NOV	DEC
1	29 5 27 24 20 14 17 33 14	32 10 32 28 22 14 16 34 14	34 12 36 31 22 13 16 34 13	1 17 35 35 22 13 16 34 13	5 21 3 3 21 13 16 34 13	7 25 9 7 21 13 16 34 13	10 28 13 10 20 14 16 34 14	13 33 12 13 22 15 16 34 13	16 1 16 19 25 16 16 34 13	19 5 20 22 26 16 17 34 13	23 11 25 26 29 17 17 34 14	26 15 23 29 31 17 17 34 13
2	29 6 27 24 20 14 16 33 14	32 12 32 28 22 14 16 34 14	34 13 36 31 22 13 16 34 13	1 19 35 35 22 13 16 34 13	5 22 3 3 21 13 16 34 13	7 27 9 7 21 13 16 34 13	10 30 13 10 20 14 16 34 14	13 34 12 13 22 15 16 34 13	16 3 16 19 25 16 16 34 13	19 7 20 22 26 16 17 34 13	23 13 25 26 29 17 17 34 14	26 16 23 29 31 17 17 34 13
3	29 8 27 24 20 14 16 33 14	32 13 32 28 22 14 16 34 14	34 15 1 31 22 13 16 34 13	1 20 35 35 22 13 16 34 13	5 23 3 3 21 13 16 34 13	7 28 9 7 21 13 16 34 13	10 31 13 10 20 14 16 34 14	13 36 12 13 22 15 16 34 13	16 4 16 19 25 16 16 34 13	19 8 20 22 26 16 17 34 13	23 14 25 26 29 17 17 34 14	26 17 23 29 31 17 17 34 13
4	29 9 27 25 20 14 16 33 14	32 14 32 28 22 14 16 34 14	34 16 1 31 22 13 16 34 13	1 21 35 35 22 13 16 34 13	5 25 3 3 21 13 16 34 13	7 29 9 7 21 13 16 34 13	10 32 13 10 20 14 16 34 14	14 1 12 13 23 15 17 34 14	17 6 16 19 25 16 17 34 13	19 10 20 22 26 16 17 34 13	23 16 25 26 29 17 17 34 14	26 19 23 29 31 17 17 34 13
5	29 10 27 25 20 14 16 33 14	31 16 31 28 22 13 16 34 13	34 18 1 31 22 13 16 34 13	1 22 35 35 22 13 16 34 13	5 25 3 3 21 13 16 34 13	7 30 9 7 21 13 16 34 13	10 34 13 10 20 14 16 34 14	14 3 12 15 23 15 17 34 14	17 7 17 19 25 16 17 34 13	20 11 22 22 26 16 17 34 14	23 17 25 26 29 17 17 34 14	26 20 23 29 31 17 17 34 13
6	29 12 27 25 20 14 16 33 14	31 17 31 28 22 13 16 34 13	34 19 1 31 22 13 16 34 13	1 24 36 36 22 13 16 34 13	5 27 3 3 21 13 16 34 13	8 32 10 7 20 14 16 34 14	10 34 13 10 21 14 16 34 14	14 4 12 15 23 15 17 34 14	17 8 17 19 25 16 17 34 13	20 13 22 22 26 16 17 34 14	23 17 25 26 29 17 17 34 14	26 22 23 29 31 17 17 34 13
7	29 14 27 25 20 14 16 33 14	31 18 31 28 22 13 16 34 13	34 21 1 31 22 13 16 34 13	1 25 36 36 22 13 16 34 13	5 28 4 4 21 13 16 34 13	8 33 10 7 20 14 16 34 14	11 36 13 11 21 14 16 34 14	14 5 12 15 23 15 17 34 14	17 10 17 19 25 16 17 34 13	20 14 22 22 26 16 17 34 14	23 19 25 26 29 17 17 34 14	26 23 23 29 31 17 17 34 13
8	29 15 28 25 20 14 16 33 14	31 19 31 29 22 13 16 34 13	35 22 1 31 22 13 16 34 13	2 26 36 36 22 13 16 34 13	5 29 4 4 21 13 16 34 13	8 34 10 7 20 14 16 34 14	11 2 13 11 21 14 16 34 14	14 6 12 15 23 15 17 34 14	17 11 17 19 25 16 17 34 13	20 16 23 23 26 16 17 34 14	23 20 25 26 29 17 17 34 14	26 23 23 29 31 17 17 34 13
9	29 16 28 25 20 14 16 33 14	31 21 31 29 22 13 16 34 13	35 22 1 32 22 13 16 34 13	2 27 36 36 22 13 16 34 13	6 30 4 4 21 13 16 34 13	8 35 10 7 20 14 16 34 14	11 2 13 11 21 14 16 34 14	14 8 12 15 23 15 17 34 14	17 13 17 19 25 16 17 34 13	20 17 23 23 26 16 17 34 14	23 22 25 26 29 17 17 34 14	26 25 23 29 31 17 17 34 13
10	29 18 29 26 20 14 17 33 14	31 22 31 29 22 13 16 34 13	35 24 1 32 22 13 16 34 13	2 28 36 36 22 13 16 34 13	6 31 4 4 21 13 16 34 13	8 36 10 7 20 14 16 34 14	11 4 13 11 21 14 16 34 14	14 9 13 15 23 15 17 34 14	17 14 17 19 25 16 17 34 13	20 18 23 23 26 16 17 34 14	23 23 25 26 29 17 17 34 14	26 26 23 29 31 17 17 34 13
11	29 19 29 26 20 14 17 33 14	32 23 32 29 22 13 16 34 13	35 25 1 33 22 13 16 34 13	2 30 36 1 22 13 16 34 13	6 33 4 4 21 13 16 34 13	8 2 10 7 20 14 16 34 14	11 5 13 11 22 15 16 34 13	14 10 13 15 23 15 17 34 14	17 16 17 19 25 16 17 34 13	20 20 23 23 26 16 17 34 14	23 25 25 26 29 17 17 34 14	26 28 23 29 32 17 17 34 14
12	29 20 29 26 20 14 17 33 14	32 25 32 29 22 13 16 34 13	36 27 1 33 22 13 16 34 13	2 31 36 1 22 13 16 34 13	6 34 4 4 21 13 16 34 13	8 3 10 8 20 14 16 34 14	11 7 13 11 22 15 16 34 13	14 12 13 16 23 15 17 34 14	17 17 17 19 25 16 17 34 13	20 21 23 23 26 16 17 34 14	23 26 25 26 29 17 17 34 14	26 29 25 31 32 17 17 34 14
13	29 21 29 26 20 14 17 33 14	32 25 32 29 22 13 16 34 13	36 28 1 33 22 13 16 34 13	2 32 36 1 22 13 16 34 13	6 36 4 4 21 13 16 34 13	8 5 10 8 20 14 16 34 14	12 9 13 12 22 15 16 34 13	14 14 13 16 23 15 17 34 14	17 19 17 19 25 16 17 34 13	20 22 23 23 26 16 17 34 14	23 26 23 26 29 17 17 34 14	26 29 25 31 32 17 17 34 14
14	29 23 29 26 20 14 17 33 14	33 27 33 29 22 13 16 33 13	36 28 1 33 22 13 16 34 13	3 33 36 36 21 12 15 33 12	6 1 4 4 21 13 16 34 13	8 6 10 8 20 14 16 34 14	12 10 13 12 22 15 16 34 13	14 15 13 16 23 15 17 34 14	17 20 17 19 25 16 17 34 13	20 23 23 23 26 16 17 34 14	23 28 23 26 29 17 17 34 14	26 31 25 31 32 17 17 34 14
15	29 24 29 26 20 14 17 33 14	33 28 33 30 22 13 16 33 13	36 30 1 33 22 13 16 34 13	3 34 36 36 21 12 16 33 12	6 3 4 4 21 13 16 34 13	8 7 10 8 20 14 16 34 14	12 12 13 12 22 15 16 34 13	14 17 13 16 23 14 17 34 14	17 22 17 19 25 16 17 34 13	20 25 23 23 26 16 17 34 14	23 29 23 26 29 17 17 34 14	26 32 25 31 32 17 17 34 14
16	29 25 29 26 20 14 17 33 14	33 29 34 30 22 13 16 33 13	36 31 1 34 22 13 16 34 13	3 36 36 36 21 12 15 33 12	6 4 4 4 21 13 16 34 13	8 8 11 8 20 14 16 34 14	12 13 13 12 22 15 16 34 13	14 18 13 17 23 14 17 34 14	17 23 17 19 25 16 17 34 13	20 26 23 23 26 16 17 34 14	23 31 23 26 29 17 17 34 14	26 34 26 32 32 17 17 34 14
17	29 26 29 26 20 14 17 33 14	33 31 34 30 22 13 16 33 13	36 33 1 34 22 13 16 34 13	3 1 36 36 21 13 15 33 13	6 6 4 4 21 13 16 34 13	8 10 11 8 20 14 16 34 14	12 15 13 12 22 15 16 34 13	14 20 13 17 23 14 17 34 14	17 24 19 19 25 16 17 34 13	21 27 23 23 27 16 17 34 14	23 32 23 26 29 17 17 34 14	26 35 26 32 32 17 17 34 14
18	29 27 29 26 20 14 17 33 14	33 32 34 30 22 13 16 33 13	36 34 1 34 22 13 16 34 13	3 2 36 36 21 13 15 33 13	6 7 5 5 21 14 16 34 14	8 12 12 8 20 14 16 34 14	12 16 13 12 22 15 16 34 13	14 21 13 17 23 14 17 34 14	17 25 19 19 25 16 17 34 13	21 28 23 23 27 16 17 34 14	23 33 23 28 29 17 17 34 14	26 35 26 32 32 17 17 34 14
19	30 29 29 26 21 14 17 33 14	33 33 34 30 22 13 16 33 13	36 36 36 34 22 13 16 34 13	3 4 36 36 21 13 16 34 12	6 8 5 5 21 14 16 34 14	8 14 12 8 20 14 16 34 14	12 17 13 13 22 15 16 34 13	14 22 13 17 23 14 17 34 14	18 26 20 20 26 16 17 34 14	21 29 23 23 27 16 17 34 14	23 34 23 28 29 17 17 34 14	26 1 26 32 32 17 17 34 14
20	30 30 29 26 21 14 17 33 14	34 34 34 30 22 13 16 34 13	36 1 36 34 22 13 16 34 13	4 5 1 1 22 13 16 34 13	6 10 5 5 21 14 16 34 14	8 15 12 8 20 14 16 34 14	12 19 13 13 22 15 16 34 13	14 23 13 17 23 14 17 34 13	18 28 20 20 26 16 17 34 14	21 31 23 23 27 16 17 34 14	23 35 23 28 29 17 17 34 14	26 2 26 32 32 17 17 34 14
21	31 31 30 27 21 14 17 33 14	34 36 34 30 22 13 16 34 13	1 1 1 34 22 13 16 34 13	4 7 1 1 22 13 16 34 13	7 11 5 5 21 14 16 34 14	8 16 12 8 20 14 16 34 14	12 20 13 13 22 15 16 34 13	14 24 13 17 23 14 17 34 13	18 29 20 21 26 16 17 34 14	21 32 23 25 27 16 17 34 14	23 1 23 28 29 17 17 34 14	26 4 26 32 32 17 17 34 14
22	31 32 30 27 21 14 17 33 14	34 1 34 30 22 13 16 34 13	1 3 1 34 22 13 16 34 13	4 8 1 1 22 13 16 34 13	7 13 5 5 21 14 16 34 14	10 18 12 10 20 14 16 34 14	12 20 13 13 22 15 16 34 13	14 26 14 17 23 14 17 34 13	18 30 20 21 26 16 17 34 14	21 33 23 25 27 16 17 34 14	23 2 23 28 29 17 17 34 14	28 5 26 32 32 17 17 34 14
23	32 33 30 27 21 14 17 33 14	34 3 34 31 22 13 16 34 13	1 4 36 34 22 13 16 34 13	4 10 1 1 22 13 16 34 13	7 14 5 5 21 14 16 34 14	10 19 12 10 20 14 16 34 14	13 22 13 13 22 15 16 34 13	16 27 15 17 24 16 17 34 13	19 32 20 21 26 16 17 34 14	21 34 23 25 27 16 17 34 14	25 3 23 28 29 17 17 34 14	28 7 26 32 32 17 17 34 14
24	32 34 30 27 21 14 17 33 14	34 4 35 31 22 13 16 34 13	1 6 36 34 22 13 16 34 13	4 12 1 1 22 13 16 34 13	7 16 7 6 21 13 16 34 13	10 20 12 10 20 14 16 34 14	13 24 13 13 22 15 16 34 13	16 28 15 17 24 16 17 34 13	19 33 20 21 26 16 17 34 14	22 35 23 25 28 16 17 34 14	25 5 23 28 29 17 17 34 14	28 8 26 32 32 17 17 34 14
25	32 36 30 27 21 14 17 33 14	34 6 36 31 22 13 16 34 13	1 7 36 34 22 13 16 34 13	4 13 1 1 22 13 16 34 13	7 17 7 6 21 13 16 34 13	10 22 12 10 20 14 16 34 14	13 25 13 13 22 15 16 34 13	16 29 15 17 24 16 17 34 13	19 34 20 21 26 16 17 34 14	22 1 23 25 28 16 17 34 14	25 5 23 28 29 17 17 34 14	28 10 26 32 32 17 17 34 14
26	32 2 30 27 21 14 17 33 14	34 7 36 31 22 13 16 34 13	1 9 36 34 22 13 16 34 13	4 15 1 1 22 13 16 34 13	7 18 7 6 21 13 16 34 13	10 23 12 10 20 14 16 34 14	13 27 13 13 22 15 16 34 13	16 31 15 17 24 16 17 34 13	19 35 20 21 26 16 17 34 14	22 2 23 25 28 16 17 34 14	25 7 23 28 29 17 17 34 14	28 11 26 32 32 17 17 34 14
27	32 3 30 27 21 14 17 33 14	34 7 36 31 22 13 16 34 13	1 10 36 34 22 13 16 34 13	4 16 1 1 21 13 16 34 13	7 19 7 6 21 13 16 34 13	10 24 14 10 20 14 16 34 14	13 27 13 13 22 15 16 34 13	16 32 15 17 24 16 17 34 13	19 36 20 21 26 16 17 34 14	22 4 23 25 28 16 17 34 14	25 8 23 28 29 17 17 34 14	28 13 26 32 32 17 17 34 14
28	32 5 30 27 21 14 17 33 14	34 10 36 31 22 13 16 34 13	1 12 36 34 22 13 16 34 13	4 17 1 3 21 13 16 34 13	7 21 7 6 21 13 16 34 13	10 25 14 10 20 14 16 34 14	13 28 13 13 22 15 16 34 13	16 33 15 16 24 16 16 34 13	19 2 20 21 26 16 17 34 14	22 5 25 25 28 16 17 34 14	25 10 23 29 31 17 17 34 14	28 14 26 32 32 17 17 34 14
29	32 6 30 27 21 14 17 33 14	34 11 36 31 22 13 16 34 13	1 13 35 34 22 13 16 34 13	4 18 1 3 21 13 16 34 13	7 22 7 6 21 13 16 34 13	10 26 14 10 20 14 16 34 14	13 30 13 13 22 15 16 34 13	16 34 15 16 24 16 16 34 13	19 3 20 21 26 16 17 34 14	22 7 25 25 28 16 17 34 14	25 11 23 29 31 17 17 34 14	28 16 26 32 32 17 17 34 14
30	32 8 32 27 21 14 17 33 14	1920	1 15 35 35 22 13 16 34 13	4 19 1 3 21 13 16 34 13	7 22 7 6 21 13 16 34 13	10 27 14 10 20 14 16 34 14	13 31 13 13 22 15 16 34 13	16 36 15 16 24 16 16 34 13	20 4 20 22 26 16 17 34 13	22 8 25 25 28 16 17 34 14	25 14 23 29 31 17 17 34 14	28 17 26 32 32 17 17 34 14
31	32 8 32 27 21 14 17 33 14		1 16 35 35 22 13 16 34 13		7 24 7 6 21 13 16 34 13		13 33 13 13 22 15 16 34 13	16 1 15 16 24 16 16 34 13		22 10 25 25 28 16 17 34 14		28 19 28 32 32 17 17 34 14

	JAN	FEB	MAR	APR	MAY	JUNE	JULY	AUG	SEPT	OCT	NOV	DEC
1	28 20 28 33 33 17 17 34 14	32 25 33 35 35 17 17 34 14	34 25 35 3 2 17 17 34 14	1 30 36 4 4 16 18 34 13	4 33 4 3 6 16 18 34 13	8 1 10 3 8 17 17 35 14	11 5 11 6 11 17 17 35 14	14 10 11 8 11 17 17 34 14	16 16 18 13 14 18 18 34 14	19 19 22 16 16 19 19 34 14	22 25 22 19 18 19 19 34 13	26 28 24 24 20 20 19 35 14
2	29 21 28 33 33 17 17 34 14	32 26 33 35 35 17 17 34 14	34 26 35 3.2 17 17 34 14	1 31 36 4 4 16 18 34 13	4 34 4 3 6 16 18 34 13	8 3 10 4 8 17 17 35 14	11 6 11 6 11 17 17 35 14	14 11 11 8 11 17 17 34 14	16 18 18 13 14 18 18 34 14	19 21 22 16 16 19 19 34 14	22 25 22 19 18 19 19 34 13	26 29 24 24 20 20 19 35 14
3	29 22 28 33 33 17 17 34 14	32 26 34 1 35 17 17 34 14	35 28 34 3 2 17 17 34 14	1 31 36 4 4 16 18 34 13	4 36 4 3 5 16 18 34 13	8 4 10 4 8 17 17 35 14	11 8 11 6 11 17 17 35 14	14 13 11 8 13 17 17 34 14	16 19 18 13 14 18 18 34 14	19 22 22 16 16 19 19 34 14	22 27 22 20 18 19 19 34 13	26 30 24 24 20 20 19 35 14
4	29 23 28 34 34 17 17 34 14	32 28 34 1 35 17 17 34 14	35 29 34 3 2 17 17 34 14	1 34 36 4 4 16 18 34 13	4 1 4 3 5 16 18 34 13	8 5 10 4 8 17 17 35 14	11 9 11 6 11 17 17 35 14	14 14 11 8 13 17 17 34 14	16 20 18 13 14 18 18 34 14	20 23 22 16 16 19 19 34 14	22 28 22 20 18 19 19 34 13	26 31 24 24 20 20 19 35 14
5	29 25 28 34 34 17 17 34 14	32 29 34 1 35 17 17 34 14	35 30 34 3 2 17 17 34 14	1 36 36 4 4 16 18 34 13	4 2 4 3 5 16 18 34 13	8 7 11 5 8 17 17 35 14	11 11 11 6 11 17 17 35 14	14 16 11 8 13 17 17 34 14	16 21 18 14 14 18 18 34 14	20 25 22 16 16 19 19 34 14	22 30 23 20 18 19 19 34 13	26 34 24 24 20 20 19 35 14
6	29 26 28 34 34 17 17 34 14	32 31 34 2 35 17 17 34 14	35 32 34 3 2 17 17 34 14	1 36 36 4 4 16 18 34 13	6 3 4 3 7 16 18 34 13	8 8 11 5 8 17 17 35 14	11 12 11 6 11 17 17 35 14	14 17 11 10 13 17 17 34 14	16 22 18 14 14 18 18 34 14	20 26 22 16 16 19 19 34 14	22 31 23 20 18 19 19 34 13	26 34 24 24 20 20 19 35 14
7	29 26 28 34 34 17 17 34 14	32 32 34 2 35 17 17 34 14	35 33 34 4 2 17 17 34 14	1 1 36 4 4 16 18 34 13	6 4 4 3 7 16 18 34 13	8 10 11 5 8 17 17 35 14	11 14 11 6 11 17 17 35 14	14 19 11 10 13 17 17 34 14	16 24 18 14 14 18 18 34 14	20 28 22 16 16 19 19 34 14	22 32 23 21 19 19 19 34 13	26 35 24 24 20 20 19 35 14
8	29 28 29 34 34 17 17 34 14	32 33 34 2 35 17 17 34 14	35 34 34 4 2 17 17 34 14	1 3 36 4 4 16 18 34 13	6 6 6 3 7 16 18 34 13	9 12 10 4 9 16 18 34 13	11 15 11 7 11 17 17 34 14	14 20 13 10 13 17 17 34 14	16 25 18 14 14 18 18 34 14	20 29 22 16 16 19 19 34 14	23 33 22 21 19 19 19 34 14	26 36 25 25 20 20 19 35 14
9	29 29 29 34 34 17 17 34 14	32 34 34 2 35 17 17 34 14	35 35 34 4 2 17 17 34 14	1 4 36 4 4 16 18 34 13	6 7 6 3 7 16 18 34 13	9 13 10 4 9 16 18 34 13	11 17 11 7 11 17 17 34 14	14 22 13 10 13 17 17 34 14	16 27 19 14 14 18 18 34 14	20 30 22 16 16 19 19 34 14	23 34 22 21 19 19 19 34 14	26 1 25 25 20 20 19 34 14
10	29 31 29 34 34 17 17 34 14	32 35 34 2 35 17 17 34 14	35 35 34 4 2 17 17 34 14	3 5 36 5 5 17 17 35 14	6 9 6 3 7 16 18 34 13	9 15 10 4 9 16 18 34 13	11 18 11 7 11 17 17 34 14	14 23 14 10 14 17 17 34 14	18 28 19 14 15 18 18 34 14	20 31 22 16 16 19 19 34 14	23 36 22 21 19 19 19 34 14	26 2 25 25 20 20 19 34 14
11	29 32 29 34 34 17 17 34 14	33 1 34 2 35 17 17 34 14	35 2 34 4 2 17 17 34 14	3 7 36 5 5 17 17 35 14	6 10 6 3 7 16 18 34 13	9 16 10 4 9 16 18 34 13	11 20 11 7 11 17 17 34 13	14 24 14 10 14 17 17 34 14	18 29 19 14 15 18 18 34 14	20 32 22 16 16 19 19 34 14	23 1 22 21 19 19 19 34 14	26 4 25 25 20 20 19 34 14
12	29 33 29 34 34 17 17 34 14	33 2 34 2 35 17 17 34 14	35 3 34 4 2 17 17 34 14	3 8 36 5 5 17 17 35 14	6 12 6 3 7 16 18 34 13	9 18 10 4 9 16 18 34 13	11 21 11 7 11 17 17 34 13	14 25 14 10 14 17 17 34 14	18 30 19 14 15 18 18 34 14	20 33 22 16 16 19 19 34 14	23 2 22 21 19 19 19 34 14	26 5 26 26 20 20 19 34 14
13	29 34 29 34 34 17 17 34 14	33 3 34 2 1 17 17 34 14	36 4 34 4 3 16 18 34 13	3 9 36 5 5 17 17 35 14	6 13 6 3 7 16 18 34 13	9 19 10 4 9 16 18 34 13	11 22 11 7 11 17 17 34 13	14 26 14 10 14 17 17 34 14	18 32 20 14 15 18 18 34 14	20 34 22 16 16 19 19 34 14	23 3 22 21 19 19 19 34 14	26 7 26 26 20 20 19 34 14
14	29 35 29 34 34 17 17 34 14	33 5 34 2 1 17 17 34 14	36 6 34 4 3 16 18 34 13	3 11 2 5 5 17 17 35 14	6 15 6 3 7 16 18 34 13	9 19 10 4 9 16 18 34 13	11 23 11 7 11 17 17 34 13	14 28 14 10 14 17 17 34 14	18 33 20 14 15 18 18 34 14	20 34 22 16 16 19 19 34 14	23 4 22 22 19 19 19 34 14	26 8 26 26 20 20 19 34 14
15	29 1 29 34 34 17 17 34 14	33 5 35 2 1 17 17 34 14	36 7 34 4 3 16 18 34 13	3 12 2 5 5 17 17 35 14	6 16 7 3 7 16 18 34 13	9 21 10 4 9 16 18 34 13	11 25 11 7 11 17 17 34 13	14 29 14 10 14 17 17 34 14	18 34 20 14 15 18 18 34 14	20 1 23 17 17 19 19 34 14	23 6 22 22 19 19 19 34 14	26 10 26 26 20 20 19 34 14
16	29 2 29 34 34 17 17 34 14	33 7 35 2 2 17 17 34 14	36 9 34 4 3 16 18 34 13	3 14 2 5 5 17 17 35 14	6 18 7 3 7 16 18 34 13	9 22 10 4 9 16 18 34 13	11 26 11 7 11 17 17 34 13	15 31 14 11 14 17 17 34 14	18 35 20 14 15 18 18 34 14	20 2 23 17 17 19 19 34 14	23 7 22 22 19 19 19 34 14	26 11 26 26 20 20 19 34 14
17	29 4 29 34 34 17 17 34 14	33 8 35 2 2 17 17 34 14	36 10 34 4 3 16 18 34 13	3 15 2 5 5 17 17 35 14	6 19 7 3 7 16 18 34 13	9 24 10 4 9 16 18 34 13	11 26 11 7 11 17 17 34 13	15 32 14 11 14 17 17 34 14	18 36 20 14 15 18 18 34 14	20 4 23 17 17 19 19 34 14	24 9 22 22 19 19 19 34 13	26 12 26 26 20 20 19 34 14
18	29 5 29 35 35 17 17 34 14	33 10 35 2 2 17 17 34 14	36 12 34 4 3 16 18 34 13	3 17 2 5 5 17 17 35 14	6 20 7 3 7 16 18 34 13	9 25 10 4 9 16 18 34 13	11 28 11 7 11 17 17 34 13	15 33 14 11 14 17 17 34 14	18 1 20 14 15 18 18 34 14	20 5 23 17 17 19 19 34 14	24 10 22 22 19 19 19 34 13	26 14 26 26 20 20 19 34 14
19	29 5 31 35 35 17 17 34 14	34 11 35 2 2 17 17 34 14	36 13 34 4 3 16 18 34 13	3 17 2 5 5 17 17 35 14	5 22 8 3 8 17 37 35 14	9 27 10 4 9 16 18 34 13	11 29 11 8 11 17 17 35 14	15 34 14 11 14 17 17 34 14	18 3 20 14 15 18 18 34 14	21 6 23 17 17 19 19 34 14	24 12 22 22 19 19 19 34 13	26 15 26 26 20 20 19 34 14
20	29 8 31 35 35 17 17 34 14	34 14 35 2 2 17 17 34 14	36 14 34 4 3 16 18 34 13	3 19 2 5 5 17 17 35 14	5 23 8 3 8 17 37 35 14	8 28 10 4 8 16 18 34 13	11 31 11 8 11 17 17 35 14	15 35 14 11 14 17 17 34 14	18 4 20 14 16 18 18 34 14	21 7 23 17 17 19 19 34 14	24 13 22 22 19 19 19 34 13	27 16 27 27 21 20 19 34 14
21	32 8 32 35 35 17 17 34 14	34 15 35 2 2 17 17 34 14	1 15 34 4 3 16 18 34 13	4 20 1 4 6 16 18 34 13	5 24 8 3 8 17 37 35 14	8 29 10 4 8 16 18 34 13	11 32 11 8 11 17 17 35 14	15 1 15 11 14 17 17 34 14	18 6 21 15 16 18 18 34 14	21 9 23 19 17 19 19 34 14	24 13 22 22 19 19 19 34 13	27 18 27 27 21 20 19 34 14
22	32 11 32 35 35 17 17 34 14	34 16 35 2 2 17 17 34 14	1 16 34 4 3 16 18 34 13	4 22 1 4 6 16 18 34 13	8 26 8 3 8 17 37 35 14	10 30 12 6 10 16 18 34 13	11 33 11 8 11 17 17 35 14	15 2 15 11 14 17 17 34 14	18 7 21 15 16 18 18 34 14	21 10 23 19 17 19 19 34 14	24 16 22 22 19 19 19 34 13	28 19 28 28 22 20 19 34 14
23	32 11 32 35 35 17 17 34 14	34 17 35 2 2 17 17 34 14	1 18 34 4 3 16 18 34 13	4 24 1 4 6 16 18 34 13	8 26 8 3 8 17 37 35 14	10 31 12 6 10 16 18 34 13	13 35 11 8 11 17 17 35 14	15 3 15 11 14 17 17 34 14	18 8 22 16 16 18 18 34 14	21 12 23 19 17 19 19 34 14	25 17 22 22 19 19 19 34 13	28 20 28 28 20 20 19 34 14
24	32 14 32 35 35 17 17 34 14	34 19 35 3 2 17 17 34 14	1 19 34 4 3 16 18 34 13	4 25 1 4 6 16 18 34 13	8 28 8 3 8 17 37 35 14	10 33 12 6 10 16 18 34 13	13 35 11 8 11 17 17 35 14	16 4 16 11 14 17 17 34 14	19 9 22 16 16 19 19 34 14	22 13 23 19 18 19 19 34 13	25 18 22 22 19 19 19 34 13	28 22 28 28 21 20 19 34 14
25	32 15 32 35 35 17 17 34 14	34 20 35 3 2 17 17 34 14	1 21 34 4 4 16 18 34 13	4 26 1 3 6 16 18 34 13	8 29 8 3 8 17 37 35 14	10 34 12 6 10 16 18 34 13	13 1 11 8 11 17 17 34 14	16 5 16 11 14 17 17 34 14	19 10 22 16 16 19 19 34 14	22 14 22 19 18 19 19 34 13	25 19 22 22 19 19 19 34 13	28 24 28 28 22 20 19 34 14
26	32 17 32 35 35 17 17 34 14	34 22 35 3 2 17 17 34 14	1 22 34 4 4 16 18 34 13	4 27 3 3 6 16 18 34 13	8 30 8 3 8 17 37 35 14	10 34 12 6 10 16 18 34 13	14 2 11 8 11 17 17 34 14	16 7 16 11 14 17 17 34 14	19 12 22 16 16 19 19 34 14	22 16 22 19 18 19 19 34 13	25 21 22 22 19 19 19 34 13	28 25 28 28 22 20 19 34 14
27	32 17 32 35 35 17 17 34 14	34 23 35 3 2 17 17 34 14	1 24 34 4 4 16 18 34 13	4 28 3 3 6 16 18 34 13	8 32 8 3 8 17 37 35 14	10 36 12 6 10 16 18 34 13	14 3 11 8 11 17 17 34 14	16 8 16 11 14 17 17 34 14	19 13 22 16 16 19 19 34 14	22 18 22 19 18 19 19 34 13	25 22 22 22 19 19 19 34 13	28 26 28 28 22 20 19 34 14
28	32 19 32 35 35 17 17 34 14	34 24 35 3 2 17 17 34 14	1 25 34 4 4 16 18 34 13	4 30 3 3 6 16 18 34 13	8 33 8 3 8 17 37 35 14	10 1 12 6 10 16 18 34 13	14 4 11 8 11 17 17 34 14	16 10 16 11 14 17 17 34 14	19 15 22 16 16 19 19 34 14	22 19 22 19 18 19 19 34 13	25 24 22 22 19 19 19 34 13	28 27 28 27 22 20 19 34 14
29	32 20 32 35 35 17 17 34 14	1921	1 27 34 4 4 16 18 34 13	4 31 3 3 6 16 18 34 13	8 35 9 3 8 17 37 35 14	10 2 12 6 10 16 18 34 13	14 5 11 8 11 17 17 34 14	16 11 16 11 14 17 17 34 14	19 16 22 16 16 19 19 34 14	22 20 22 19 18 19 19 34 13	25 25 22 22 19 19 19 34 13	28 28 28 27 22 20 19 34 14
30	32 22 32 35 35 17 17 34 14		1 28 34 4 4 16 18 34 13	4 31 3 3 6 16 18 34 13	8 35 9 3 8 17 37 35 14	10 4 12 6 10 16 18 34 13	14 7 11 8 11 17 17 34 14	16 13 16 11 14 17 17 34 14	19 18 22 16 16 19 18 34 14	22 22 22 19 18 19 19 34 13	25 26 22 22 19 19 19 34 13	28 30 28 28 22 20 19 34 14
31	32 23 32 35 35 17 17 34 14		1 28 34 4 4 16 18 34 13		8 36 10 3 8 17 37 35 14		14 8 11 8 11 17 17 34 14	16 14 16 11 14 17 17 34 14		22 23 22 19 18 19 19 34 13		28 31 28 28 22 20 19 34 14

	JAN	FEB	MAR	APR	MAY	JUNE
1	28 32 28 28 22 20 19 34 14	32 1 34 32 23 20 19 34 14	34 1 32 34 32 20 19 34 14	1 6 34 2 26 20 19 35 14	5 10 5 7 27 19 19 35 14	8 14 10 10 26 19 19 35 14
2	28 33 28 28 22 20 19 34 14	32 2 34 32 23 20 19 34 14	34 2 32 34 32 20 19 34 14	2 8 34 2 26 20 19 35 14	5 11 5 7 27 19 19 35 14	8 17 10 10 26 19 19 35 14
3	28 34 28 28 22 20 19 34 14	32 2 34 32 23 20 19 34 14	34 4 32 34 32 20 19 34 14	2 8 34 2 26 20 19 35 14	5 13 5 7 27 19 19 35 14	8 18 10 11 26 19 19 35 14
4	28 36 28 28 22 20 19 34 14	32 4 34 32 23 20 19 34 14	34 5 32 34 32 20 19 34 14	2 10 34 2 26 20 19 35 14	5 14 6 7 27 19 19 35 14	8 19 10 11 26 19 19 35 14
5	28 1 28 28 22 20 19 34 14	32 5 34 32 23 20 19 34 14	34 7 32 34 32 20 19 34 14	2 11 35 2 26 20 19 35 14	5 15 6 8 27 19 19 35 14	8 20 10 11 26 19 19 35 14
6	29 2 29 28 22 20 19 34 14	32 7 34 32 23 20 19 34 14	34 9 32 34 32 20 19 34 14	2 13 36 3 26 20 19 35 14	5 17 6 8 27 19 19 35 14	8 23 10 11 26 19 19 35 14
7	29 3 29 28 22 20 19 34 14	32 8 34 32 23 20 19 34 14	34 9 32 34 32 20 19 34 14	2 14 1 4 26 20 19 35 14	5 18 7 8 27 19 19 35 14	8 23 10 11 26 19 19 35 14
8	29 4 29 28 22 20 19 34 14	32 10 34 32 23 20 19 34 14	34 10 32 36 32 20 19 34 14	2 17 1 4 26 20 19 35 14	5 19 7 8 27 19 19 35 14	8 25 10 11 26 19 19 35 14
9	29 6 30 28 22 20 19 34 14	32 11 32 32 23 20 19 34 14	34 11 32 36 32 20 19 34 14	2 17 1 4 26 20 19 35 14	5 21 7 8 27 19 19 35 14	8 26 10 11 26 19 19 35 14
10	29 7 30 28 22 20 19 34 14	32 13 32 32 23 20 19 34 14	34 13 32 36 32 20 19 34 14	2 19 1 4 26 20 19 35 14	5 23 7 8 27 19 19 35 14	8 28 10 11 26 19 19 35 14
11	29 9 30 28 22 20 19 34 14	32 14 32 32 23 20 19 34 14	36 14 32 36 32 20 19 34 14	2 20 1 4 26 20 19 35 14	5 24 7 8 27 19 19 35 14	8 28 8 11 26 19 19 35 14
12	29 10 31 28 22 20 19 34 14	32 16 32 32 23 20 19 34 14	36 16 32 36 32 20 19 34 14	2 22 1 4 26 20 19 35 14	5 26 7 8 27 19 19 35 14	8 30 8 11 26 19 19 35 14
13	29 12 31 28 22 20 19 34 14	32 17 32 32 23 20 19 34 14	36 18 32 1 32 20 19 34 14	3 23 2 4 27 20 19 35 14	6 27 8 8 27 19 19 35 14	8 31 8 11 26 19 19 35 14
14	29 13 31 29 22 20 19 34 14	32 19 32 32 23 20 19 34 14	36 19 33 1 32 20 19 34 14	3 25 2 4 27 20 19 35 14	6 28 8 8 27 19 19 35 14	8 32 8 12 26 19 19 35 14
15	29 15 31 29 22 20 19 34 14	32 20 32 32 23 20 19 34 14	36 20 33 1 33 20 19 34 14	3 26 2 4 27 20 19 35 14	6 30 8 9 27 19 19 35 14	8 34 8 12 26 19 19 35 14
16	30 16 31 30 22 20 19 34 14	33 22 32 33 23 20 19 34 14	36 22 33 1 33 20 19 34 14	3 27 2 4 27 20 19 35 14	6 32 8 9 27 19 19 35 14	8 35 8 12 26 19 19 35 14
17	30 18 31 30 22 20 19 34 14	33 23 32 34 23 20 19 34 14	36 23 33 1 33 20 19 34 14	3 28 2 4 27 20 19 35 14	6 32 8 9 27 19 19 35 14	8 36 8 12 26 19 19 35 14
18	30 19 32 30 23 20 19 34 14	33 24 32 34 25 20 19 34 14	36 25 34 1 34 20 19 34 14	3 29 3 4 27 20 19 35 14	6 33 8 9 27 19 19 35 14	9 1 8 12 26 19 19 35 14
19	30 20 32 30 23 20 19 34 14	34 25 32 34 25 20 19 34 14	36 26 34 1 34 20 19 34 14	3 31 3 4 27 20 19 35 14	6 35 9 9 27 19 19 35 14	9 2 8 12 26 19 19 35 14
20	30 22 32 30 23 20 19 34 14	34 25 32 34 25 20 19 34 14	36 28 34 1 34 20 19 34 14	3 32 3 4 27 20 19 35 14	6 35 9 9 27 19 19 35 14	9 4 8 13 26 19 19 35 14
21	31 23 32 31 23 20 19 34 14	34 26 32 34 25 20 19 34 14	1 29 34 1 34 20 19 34 14	4 33 3 4 27 20 19 35 14	6 1 9 9 27 19 19 35 14	9 5 8 13 26 19 19 35 14
22	31 25 32 31 23 20 19 34 14	34 28 32 34 25 20 19 34 14	1 30 34 1 34 20 19 34 14	4 35 3 4 27 20 19 35 14	7 1 9 9 27 19 19 35 14	10 6 8 13 26 19 19 35 14
23	31 26 32 21 23 20 19 34 14	34 29 32 34 25 20 19 34 14	1 32 34 1 34 20 19 34 14	4 36 3 5 27 20 19 35 14	7 3 9 9 27 19 19 35 14	10 8 8 13 26 19 19 35 14
24	31 27 32 31 23 20 19 34 14	34 31 32 34 25 20 19 34 14	1 32 34 1 34 20 19 34 14	4 1 4 5 27 20 19 35 14	7 5 9 9 27 19 19 35 14	10 8 8 13 26 19 19 35 14
25	31 28 32 31 23 20 19 34 14	34 32 32 34 25 20 19 34 14	1 34 34 2 34 20 19 34 14	5 2 5 5 27 20 19 35 14	7 6 9 9 27 19 19 35 14	10 10 8 13 26 19 19 35 13
26	31 29 32 31 23 20 19 34 14	34 33 32 34 25 20 19 34 14	1 34 34 2 34 20 19 34 14	5 3 5 5 27 20 19 35 14	7 7 9 10 27 19 19 34 14	10 12 8 13 26 19 19 35 13
27	31 31 32 31 23 20 19 34 14	34 34 32 34 25 20 19 34 14	1 36 34 2 34 20 19 34 14	5 5 5 5 27 20 19 35 14	7 7 9 10 27 19 19 34 14	10 13 8 13 26 19 19 35 13
28	31 32 32 31 23 20 19 34 14	34 36 32 34 25 20 19 34 14	1 1 34 2 34 20 19 34 14	5 6 5 5 27 20 19 35 14	7 10 9 10 27 19 19 34 14	10 14 8 13 26 19 19 35 13
29	31 33 32 31 23 20 19 34 14	**1922**	1 2 34 2 34 20 19 34 14	5 8 5 5 27 20 19 35 14	7 10 9 10 27 19 19 34 14	10 16 8 13 26 19 19 35 13
30	31 34 32 31 23 20 19 34 14		1 4 34 2 34 20 19 34 14	5 9 5 5 27 20 19 35 14	7 12 9 10 27 19 19 34 14	10 17 8 13 26 19 19 35 13
31	31 35 33 31 23 20 19 34 14		1 5 34 2 34 20 19 34 14		7 14 9 10 27 19 19 34 14	

	JULY	AUG	SEPT	OCT	NOV	DEC
1	10 19 9 14 26 20 19 35 14	14 24 13 17 26 20 19 35 14	17 29 19 20 26 20 19 35 14	19 33 21 24 28 21 19 34 13	22 1 20 25 31 22 20 34 14	25 4 25 24 33 22 20 34 14
2	10 20 9 14 26 20 19 35 14	14 26 13 17 26 20 19 35 14	17 30 19 20 26 20 19 35 14	19 34 21 24 28 21 19 34 13	22 2 20 25 31 22 20 34 14	25 5 25 24 33 22 20 34 14
3	11 22 9 14 26 20 19 35 14	14 27 13 18 26 20 19 35 14	17 32 19 20 26 20 19 35 14	19 34 21 24 28 21 19 34 13	23 3 20 25 31 22 20 34 14	25 7 25 24 33 22 20 34 14
4	11 23 9 14 26 20 19 35 14	14 28 14 18 26 20 19 35 14	17 33 19 20 26 20 19 35 14	19 36 21 24 28 21 19 34 13	23 5 20 25 31 22 20 34 14	25 8 25 24 33 22 20 34 14
5	11 25 9 14 26 20 19 35 14	14 29 14 18 26 20 19 35 14	17 35 19 20 26 20 19 35 14	19 1 21 24 28 21 19 34 13	23 5 20 25 31 22 20 34 14	25 9 25 24 33 22 20 34 14
6	11 26 9 14 26 20 19 35 14	14 31 14 18 26 20 19 35 14	17 35 19 20 26 20 19 35 14	19 2 21 24 28 21 19 34 13	23 7 22 25 31 22 20 34 14	25 11 25 24 33 22 20 34 14
7	11 26 9 14 26 20 19 35 14	14 32 14 18 26 20 19 35 14	17 35 19 21 26 20 19 35 14	19 4 21 24 28 21 19 34 13	23 8 22 25 31 22 20 34 14	25 11 25 24 33 22 20 34 14
8	11 27 9 14 26 20 19 35 14	14 33 14 18 26 20 19 35 14	17 1 19 22 26 20 19 35 14	19 5 21 24 28 21 19 34 13	23 9 22 25 31 22 20 34 14	25 13 26 24 33 22 20 34 14
9	11 28 9 14 26 20 19 35 14	14 35 14 18 26 20 19 35 14	17 2 19 22 26 20 19 35 14	19 6 21 24 28 21 19 34 13	23 11 22 25 31 22 20 34 14	25 14 26 24 33 22 20 34 14
10	11 29 9 15 26 20 19 35 14	14 35 14 19 26 20 19 35 14	17 4 19 23 26 20 19 35 14	19 7 21 24 28 21 19 34 13	23 12 22 25 31 22 20 34 14	25 16 26 24 33 22 20 34 14
11	11 31 9 15 26 20 19 35 14	14 1 14 19 26 20 19 35 14	17 5 19 23 26 20 19 35 14	19 9 21 25 28 21 19 34 13	23 13 22 25 31 22 20 34 14	25 17 26 24 33 22 20 34 14
12	11 32 9 15 26 20 19 35 14	14 2 14 19 26 20 19 35 14	17 6 19 23 26 20 19 35 14	19 10 21 25 28 21 19 34 13	23 14 22 25 31 22 20 34 14	26 19 26 24 34 22 20 34 14
13	11 33 9 15 26 20 19 35 14	14 3 14 19 26 20 19 35 14	17 8 19 23 28 20 19 35 14	19 10 21 25 28 21 19 34 13	23 16 22 25 31 22 20 34 14	26 20 26 24 34 22 20 34 14
14	11 35 9 15 26 20 19 35 14	14 4 14 19 26 20 19 35 14	17 9 20 23 28 20 19 35 14	19 12 21 25 28 21 19 34 13	23 17 22 25 31 22 20 34 14	26 22 26 24 34 22 20 34 14
15	12 36 10 16 26 20 19 35 14	14 5 16 19 26 20 19 35 14	18 10 20 23 28 20 19 35 14	21 14 21 25 30 21 19 34 13	23 19 22 25 31 22 20 34 14	26 23 26 24 34 22 20 34 14
16	12 1 10 16 26 20 19 35 14	14 7 16 19 26 20 19 35 14	18 11 20 23 28 20 19 35 14	21 15 21 25 30 21 19 34 13	23 20 22 25 31 22 20 34 14	26 24 26 24 34 22 20 34 14
17	12 2 10 16 26 20 19 35 14	14 8 16 19 26 20 19 35 14	18 13 20 23 28 20 19 35 14	21 16 21 25 30 21 19 34 13	23 22 22 25 31 22 20 34 14	26 25 28 24 34 22 20 34 14
18	12 3 10 16 26 20 19 35 14	14 9 17 19 26 20 19 35 14	18 14 20 23 28 20 19 35 14	21 18 20 25 30 21 19 34 13	23 23 22 25 31 22 20 34 14	26 27 28 24 34 22 20 34 14
19	12 5 10 17 26 20 19 35 14	14 10 17 19 26 20 19 35 14	18 16 20 23 28 20 19 35 14	21 19 20 25 30 21 19 34 13	23 25 22 25 31 22 20 34 14	26 29 28 24 34 22 20 34 14
20	12 8 10 17 26 20 19 35 14	14 12 17 19 26 20 19 35 14	18 17 20 23 28 20 19 35 14	21 21 20 25 30 21 19 34 13	23 26 22 25 31 22 20 34 14	26 29 28 24 34 22 20 34 14
21	12 8 11 17 26 20 19 35 14	14 14 17 19 26 20 19 35 14	18 19 20 23 28 20 19 35 14	21 22 20 25 30 21 19 34 13	23 28 23 25 32 22 20 34 14	27 31 28 24 34 22 20 34 14
22	12 10 11 17 26 20 19 35 14	14 15 17 19 26 20 19 35 14	18 20 20 23 28 20 19 35 14	21 24 20 25 30 21 19 34 14	23 29 23 25 32 22 20 34 14	27 32 28 24 34 22 20 34 14
23	12 11 11 17 26 20 19 35 14	14 17 17 20 26 20 19 35 14	18 22 20 23 28 20 19 35 14	21 25 20 25 30 21 19 34 13	25 30 23 25 32 22 20 34 14	28 34 29 24 34 22 20 34 14
24	13 13 11 17 26 20 19 35 14	15 18 17 20 26 20 19 35 14	19 23 20 23 28 20 19 35 14	22 27 20 25 31 22 19 34 13	25 32 23 25 32 22 20 34 14	28 35 29 24 34 22 20 34 14
25	13 14 11 17 26 20 19 35 14	15 19 17 20 26 20 19 35 14	19 25 20 23 28 20 19 35 14	22 28 20 25 31 22 19 34 13	25 33 23 25 32 22 20 34 14	28 36 29 24 34 22 20 34 14
26	13 16 11 17 26 20 19 35 14	15 20 17 20 26 20 19 35 14	19 26 20 23 28 20 19 35 14	22 30 20 25 31 22 19 34 13	25 34 23 25 32 22 20 34 14	28 1 29 24 34 22 20 34 14
27	13 17 11 17 26 20 19 35 14	15 23 17 20 26 20 19 35 14	19 27 20 24 28 20 19 35 14	22 31 20 25 31 22 19 34 13	25 35 23 25 32 22 20 34 14	28 2 29 24 34 22 20 34 14
28	13 19 12 17 26 20 19 35 14	15 24 18 20 27 20 19 35 14	19 28 20 24 28 20 19 35 14	22 32 20 25 31 22 19 34 13	25 36 25 25 32 22 20 34 14	28 4 29 24 34 22 20 34 14
29	13 20 12 17 26 20 19 35 14	15 25 18 20 27 20 19 35 14	19 29 20 24 28 20 19 35 14	22 33 20 25 31 22 19 34 13	25 2 25 24 32 22 20 34 14	28 5 29 24 34 22 20 34 14
30	14 20 12 17 26 20 19 35 14	15 26 18 20 27 20 19 35 14	19 30 20 24 28 20 19 35 14	22 34 20 25 31 22 19 34 13	25 3 25 24 32 22 20 34 14	28 6 29 24 34 22 20 34 14
31	14 23 12 17 26 20 19 35 14	17 28 18 20 27 20 19 35 14		22 36 20 25 31 22 19 34 13		28 7 29 24 34 22 20 34 14

	JAN	FEB	MAR	APR	MAY	JUNE	JULY	AUG	SEPT	OCT	NOV	DEC
1	29 8 30 24 34 23 20 34 14	32 14 31 26 2 23 20 34 14	35 14 32 30 3 23 20 35 14	2 20 1 34 5 23 20 35 14	5 23 7 2 8 23 20 35 14	8 29 7 5 10 22 20 35 14	11 32 8 8 11 22 20 35 14	14 1 14 12 14 23 20 35 14	17 5 19 16 16 23 20 35 14	19 8 19 20 17 23 20 35 14	23 13 21 24 19 24 21 35 15	25 16 26 27 21 25 21 35 15
2	29 10 30 25 34 23 20 34 14	32 15 31 26 2 23 20 34 14	35 16 32 30 3 23 20 35 14	2 21 1 34 5 23 20 35 14	5 26 7 2 8 23 20 35 14	8 30 7 5 10 22 20 35 14	11 33 8 8 11 22 20 35 14	14 2 14 12 14 23 20 35 14	17 6 19 16 16 23 20 35 14	19 10 19 20 17 23 20 35 14	23 14 21 24 19 24 21 35 15	26 17 26 27 21 25 21 35 15
3	29 11 30 25 34 23 20 34 14	32 16 31 26 2 23 20 34 14	35 17 32 30 3 23 20 35 14	2 23 1 34 5 23 20 35 14	5 26 7 2 8 23 20 35 14	8 32 7 5 10 22 20 35 14	11 35 8 8 11 22 20 35 14	14 3 14 12 14 23 20 35 14	17 8 19 17 16 23 20 35 14	19 11 19 20 17 23 20 35 14	23 16 21 24 19 24 21 35 15	26 18 26 27 21 25 21 35 15
4	29 13 30 25 34 23 20 34 14	32 17 31 26 2 23 20 34 14	35 19 32 31 4 23 20 35 14	2 24 2 34 5 23 20 35 14	5 28 7 2 8 23 20 35 14	8 32 7 5 10 22 20 35 14	11 36 8 8 14 22 20 35 14	14 5 14 13 14 23 20 35 14	17 9 19 17 16 23 20 35 14	19 11 19 20 17 23 20 35 14	23 17 21 24 19 24 21 35 15	26 21 26 27 21 25 21 35 15
5	29 14 31 25 34 23 20 34 14	32 19 31 26 2 23 20 34 14	35 20 32 31 4 23 20 35 14	2 26 2 34 5 23 20 35 14	5 29 7 2 8 23 20 35 14	8 34 7 5 10 22 20 35 14	11 1 8 8 12 22 20 35 14	14 5 15 13 14 23 20 35 14	17 10 19 17 16 23 20 35 14	20 13 18 17 16 23 20 35 14	23 18 22 24 19 24 21 35 15	26 21 26 27 21 25 21 35 15
6	29 15 31 25 34 23 20 34 14	32 20 31 26 2 23 20 34 14	35 22 32 31 4 23 20 35 14	2 27 2 35 5 23 20 35 14	5 31 7 2 8 23 20 35 14	8 35 7 5 11 22 20 35 14	11 2 8 8 12 22 20 35 14	14 7 15 13 14 23 20 35 14	17 11 20 17 16 23 20 35 14	20 14 18 20 17 23 20 35 14	23 19 22 24 19 24 21 35 15	26 24 27 27 21 25 21 35 15
7	29 16 31 25 34 23 20 34 14	32 22 29 28 2 23 20 34 14	32 23 32 31 4 23 20 35 14	2 28 2 35 5 23 20 35 14	5 32 7 2 8 23 20 35 14	8 36 7 5 11 22 20 35 14	11 4 9 9 12 22 20 35 14	14 8 15 13 14 23 20 35 14	17 13 20 17 16 23 20 35 14	20 16 18 20 17 23 20 35 14	23 21 22 24 19 24 21 35 15	26 25 27 27 21 25 21 35 15
8	29 17 31 25 34 23 20 34 14	32 23 29 28 2 23 20 34 14	35 25 32 31 4 23 20 35 14	2 29 5 35 5 23 20 35 14	5 33 8 2 8 23 20 35 14	8 2 7 5 11 22 20 35 14	11 5 9 9 12 22 20 35 14	14 9 16 14 14 23 20 35 14	17 14 20 17 16 23 20 35 14	20 17 18 20 17 23 20 35 14	23 23 22 25 19 24 21 35 15	26 26 27 27 21 25 21 35 15
9	29 20 32 25 34 23 20 34 14	32 25 29 28 2 23 20 34 14	35 26 32 31 4 23 20 35 14	2 31 5 35 5 23 20 35 14	5 34 8 2 8 23 20 35 14	8 3 7 5 11 22 20 35 14	11 6 10 10 12 22 20 35 14	14 11 16 14 14 23 20 35 14	17 15 20 17 16 23 20 35 14	20 19 18 20 17 23 20 35 14	24 24 22 25 19 24 21 35 15	26 28 27 27 21 25 21 35 15
10	29 20 32 25 34 23 20 34 14	32 26 29 28 2 23 20 34 14	35 28 34 31 4 23 20 35 14	2 32 5 35 5 23 20 35 14	5 35 8 2 8 23 20 35 14	8 4 7 5 11 22 20 35 14	11 7 10 10 12 22 20 35 14	14 12 16 14 14 23 20 35 14	17 17 20 17 17 23 20 35 14	20 20 18 20 18 23 20 35 14	24 26 22 25 19 24 21 35 15	26 30 28 28 21 25 21 35 15
11	29 23 32 25 35 23 20 34 14	32 28 29 28 2 23 20 34 14	35 29 34 31 4 23 20 35 14	2 33 5 35 6 23 20 35 14	5 1 8 2 8 23 20 35 14	8 5 7 5 11 22 20 35 14	11 8 10 10 12 22 20 35 14	14 13 17 14 14 23 20 35 14	17 18 20 17 17 23 20 35 14	20 22 18 20 18 23 20 35 14	24 27 24 26 19 24 21 35 15	26 31 28 28 22 25 21 35 15
12	29 24 32 25 35 23 20 34 14	32 29 29 28 2 23 20 34 14	35 30 34 31 4 23 20 35 14	2 35 5 35 6 23 20 35 14	5 2 8 2 8 23 20 35 14	8 6 7 5 11 22 20 35 14	11 10 11 11 12 22 20 35 14	14 14 17 14 14 23 20 35 14	17 20 20 17 17 23 20 35 14	20 23 19 20 18 23 20 35 14	24 29 24 26 21 24 21 35 15	26 33 28 28 22 25 21 35 15
13	29 25 32 25 35 23 20 34 14	32 30 29 28 2 23 20 34 14	35 31 34 31 4 23 20 35 14	2 35 5 35 6 23 20 35 14	5 3 8 2 8 23 20 35 14	8 7 7 7 11 22 20 35 14	11 11 11 11 12 22 20 35 14	14 16 17 14 14 23 20 35 14	17 21 20 17 17 23 20 35 14	20 25 19 20 18 23 20 35 14	24 30 24 26 21 24 21 35 15	26 34 29 28 22 25 21 35 15
14	29 26 32 25 35 23 20 34 14	32 31 31 28 2 23 20 34 14	35 32 34 31 4 23 20 35 14	2 1 5 35 6 23 20 35 14	6 4 8 2 8 23 20 35 14	8 8 7 7 11 22 20 35 14	11 12 11 11 12 22 20 35 14	14 17 17 14 14 23 20 35 14	17 23 20 17 17 23 20 35 14	20 26 19 20 18 23 20 35 14	24 32 24 26 21 24 21 35 15	26 35 29 28 22 25 21 35 15
15	29 28 32 25 35 23 20 34 14	32 32 31 28 2 23 20 34 14	35 34 34 32 5 23 20 35 14	2 2 4 35 6 23 20 35 14	6 5 9 2 8 23 20 35 14	8 11 7 7 11 22 20 35 14	11 14 11 11 12 22 20 35 14	14 19 17 14 14 23 20 35 14	17 24 20 17 17 23 20 35 14	21 28 21 22 18 24 21 35 15	24 33 24 26 21 24 21 35 15	26 36 29 28 22 25 21 35 15
16	29 29 32 25 35 23 20 34 14	32 34 31 29 2 23 20 34 14	35 35 35 32 5 23 20 35 14	2 3 4 35 7 23 20 35 14	6 7 8 2 8 23 20 35 14	8 11 7 7 11 22 20 35 14	11 15 11 11 12 22 20 35 14	14 20 17 14 14 23 20 35 14	17 26 20 17 17 23 20 35 14	21 30 21 22 18 24 21 35 15	24 34 24 26 21 24 21 35 15	27 1 29 28 22 25 21 35 15
17	29 31 32 25 35 23 20 34 14	32 35 31 29 2 23 20 34 14	36 36 35 32 5 23 20 35 14	2 5 4 35 7 23 20 35 14	6 8 8 3 8 23 20 35 14	8 13 8 8 11 22 20 35 14	11 16 11 11 12 22 20 35 14	14 22 17 14 14 23 20 35 14	17 27 20 18 17 23 20 35 14	21 31 21 22 18 24 21 35 15	24 35 24 26 21 24 21 35 15	27 3 29 28 22 25 21 35 15
18	29 32 32 25 35 23 20 34 14	32 36 31 29 2 23 20 34 14	36 1 35 32 5 23 20 35 14	3 5 4 35 7 23 20 35 14	6 8 8 3 8 23 20 35 14	8 14 8 8 11 22 20 35 14	12 17 11 11 12 22 20 35 14	14 23 17 14 14 23 20 35 14	17 28 20 18 17 23 20 35 14	21 32 21 22 19 24 21 35 15	24 1 24 26 21 24 21 35 15	27 4 29 29 22 25 21 35 15
19	29 33 32 25 35 23 20 34 14	32 2 31 29 2 23 20 34 14	36 2 35 32 5 23 20 35 14	3 7 4 35 7 23 20 35 14	6 10 8 3 8 23 20 35 14	9 15 8 8 11 22 20 35 14	12 19 11 11 12 22 20 35 14	14 24 17 14 14 23 20 35 14	18 29 20 18 17 23 20 35 14	21 33 21 22 19 24 21 35 15	24 3 24 26 21 24 21 35 15	27 5 29 29 22 25 21 35 15
20	29 34 32 25 35 23 20 34 14	34 2 31 29 2 23 20 34 14	36 4 35 32 5 23 20 35 14	3 8 4 35 7 23 20 35 14	6 11 8 3 8 23 20 35 14	9 17 8 8 11 22 20 35 14	12 19 11 11 12 22 20 35 14	14 26 17 14 14 23 20 35 14	18 31 20 18 17 23 20 35 14	21 34 21 22 19 24 21 35 15	24 3 24 26 21 24 21 35 15	27 6 31 31 22 25 22 35 15
21	31 35 32 25 1 23 20 34 14	34 4 31 29 2 23 20 34 14	36 5 35 32 5 23 20 35 14	4 9 4 35 7 23 20 35 14	6 13 8 3 8 23 20 35 14	9 18 8 8 11 22 20 35 14	12 22 11 11 12 22 20 35 14	14 27 17 14 14 23 20 35 14	18 32 20 18 17 23 20 35 14	21 35 21 22 19 24 21 35 15	24 4 24 26 21 24 21 35 15	27 8 31 31 22 25 22 35 15
22	31 1 32 25 1 23 20 34 14	34 5 31 29 2 23 20 34 14	1 6 35 32 5 23 20 35 14	4 11 4 35 7 23 20 35 14	7 14 7 4 8 23 20 35 14	10 19 8 8 11 22 20 35 14	12 23 11 11 12 22 20 35 14	14 29 17 14 14 23 20 35 14	18 34 20 18 17 23 20 35 14	21 1 21 22 19 24 21 35 15	24 5 24 26 21 24 21 35 15	27 9 31 31 22 25 22 35 15
23	31 2 32 25 1 23 20 34 14	34 6 32 29 2 23 20 34 14	1 7 35 32 5 23 20 35 14	4 12 4 36 7 23 20 35 14	7 16 7 4 8 23 20 35 14	10 20 8 8 11 22 20 35 14	12 25 11 11 12 22 20 35 14	15 29 17 14 14 23 20 35 14	18 35 20 18 17 23 20 35 14	21 3 21 22 19 24 21 35 15	25 7 24 26 21 25 21 35 15	28 10 31 31 22 25 22 35 15
24	31 3 32 25 1 23 20 34 14	34 7 32 29 2 23 20 34 14	1 8 35 32 5 23 20 35 14	4 13 4 36 7 23 20 35 14	7 17 7 4 8 23 20 35 14	10 22 8 8 11 22 20 35 14	13 26 13 11 13 22 20 35 14	16 31 17 14 14 23 20 35 14	19 36 19 19 17 23 20 35 14	22 3 21 22 19 24 21 35 15	25 8 26 26 21 25 21 35 15	28 11 31 31 22 25 22 35 15
25	31 4 32 25 1 23 20 34 14	34 8 32 29 2 23 20 34 14	1 10 35 32 5 23 20 35 14	4 14 4 36 7 23 20 35 14	7 18 7 4 9 23 20 35 14	10 23 8 8 11 22 20 35 14	13 28 13 11 13 22 20 35 14	16 32 18 14 14 23 20 35 14	19 1 19 19 17 23 20 35 14	22 4 21 22 19 24 21 35 15	25 9 26 26 21 25 21 35 15	28 12 31 31 22 25 22 35 15
26	31 5 32 25 1 23 20 34 14	34 10 32 29 2 23 20 34 14	1 11 35 32 5 23 20 35 14	4 16 4 36 7 23 20 35 14	7 20 7 4 9 23 20 35 14	10 25 8 8 11 22 20 35 14	13 29 13 11 13 22 20 35 14	16 34 18 14 14 23 20 35 14	19 2 19 19 17 23 20 35 14	22 6 21 24 19 24 21 35 15	25 10 26 30 21 25 21 35 15	28 14 31 31 22 25 22 35 15
27	31 7 32 26 1 23 20 34 14	34 11 32 29 2 23 20 34 14	1 12 35 32 5 23 20 35 14	5 17 4 1 8 23 20 35 14	7 21 7 4 9 23 20 35 14	10 26 8 8 11 22 20 35 14	13 31 13 11 13 22 20 35 14	16 35 18 14 16 23 20 35 14	19 4 19 19 17 23 20 35 14	22 7 21 24 19 24 21 35 15	25 12 26 30 21 25 21 35 15	28 15 31 31 22 25 22 35 15
28	31 8 31 26 1 23 20 34 14	34 13 32 29 2 23 20 34 14	1 14 35 32 5 23 20 35 14	5 19 6 1 8 23 20 35 14	7 23 7 5 9 23 20 35 14	10 28 8 8 11 22 20 35 14	13 31 13 11 13 22 20 35 14	16 36 19 16 16 23 20 35 14	19 5 19 19 17 23 20 35 14	22 8 21 24 19 24 21 35 15	25 13 26 30 21 25 21 35 15	28 16 31 31 22 25 22 35 15
29	31 9 31 26 1 23 20 34 14		2 15 35 32 5 23 20 35 14	5 20 6 1 8 23 20 35 14	7 24 7 5 9 23 20 35 14	10 29 8 8 11 22 20 35 14	13 33 13 11 13 22 20 35 14	16 2 19 16 16 23 20 35 14	19 6 19 19 17 23 20 35 14	22 9 21 24 19 24 21 35 15	25 14 26 30 21 25 21 35 15	28 17 31 31 22 25 22 35 15
30	31 11 31 26 1 23 20 34 14	**1923**	2 17 35 33 5 23 20 35 14	5 22 6 1 8 23 20 35 14	7 26 7 5 9 23 20 35 14	10 31 8 8 11 22 20 35 14	13 34 13 12 13 22 20 35 14	16 2 19 16 16 23 20 35 14	19 7 19 19 17 23 20 35 14	22 10 21 24 19 24 21 35 15	25 15 26 30 21 25 21 35 15	28 19 31 31 22 25 22 35 15
31	31 12 31 26 1 23 20 34 14		2 18 1 33 5 23 20 35 14		7 27 7 5 9 23 20 35 14		13 35 14 12 13 22 20 35 14	16 3 19 16 16 23 20 35 14		22 12 21 24 19 24 21 35 15		28 20 31 31 22 25 22 35 15

	JAN	FEB	MAR	APR	MAY	JUNE	JULY	AUG	SEPT	OCT	NOV	DEC
1	29 22 30 31 23 25 22 35 14	21 25 29 35 26 26 22 35 14	35 29 32 2 26 26 22 35 14	2 35 4 5 29 26 22 35 14	4 2 5 8 31 26 22 35 14	8 6 6 12 33 26 21 35 15	10 10 10 10 34 26 21 35 14	14 15 16 10 34 26 21 36 15	16 19 17 12 33 26 21 35 14	20 23 17 15 33 26 22 35 15	22 28 22 17 34 27 22 35 15	26 33 27 22 35 27 22 35 15
2	29 23 30 31 23 25 22 35 14	32 28 29 35 26 26 22 35 14	35 31 32 2 26 26 22 35 14	2 35 4 5 29 26 22 35 14	4 3 5 8 31 26 21 35 14	8 7 6 12 33 26 21 35 15	10 12 10 10 34 26 21 35 14	14 16 16 10 34 26 21 36 15	16 24 17 12 33 26 21 35 14	20 24 17 15 33 26 22 35 15	22 30 23 17 34 27 22 35 15	26 34 27 22 35 27 22 35 15
3	29 25 30 31 23 25 22 35 14	32 29 29 35 26 26 22 35 14	35 32 32 2 26 26 22 35 14	2 1 4 5 29 26 22 35 14	4 4 5 8 31 26 22 35 14	8 8 6 12 33 26 21 35 15	10 12 10 10 34 26 21 35 14	14 18 16 10 34 26,21 36 15	17 22 17 12 33 26 21 35 14	20 26 17 15 33 26 22 35 15	22 31 23 19 34 27 22 35 15	26 35 28 22 35 27 22 35 15
4	29 26 30 31 23 25 22 35 14	32 31 29 35 26 26 22 35 14	35 34 34 4 28 26 22 35 14	2 2 4 5 29 26 22 35 14	4 5 5 8 31 26 22 35 14	8 10 6 12 33 26 21 35 15	10 14 10 10 34 26 21 35 14	14 18 16 10 34 26 21 36 15	17 23 17 12 33 26 21 35 14	20 27 17 15 33 26 22 35 15	22 33 23 19 34 27 22 35 15	26 36 28 22 35 27 22 35 15
5	29 28 30 31 23 25 22 35 14	32 32 29 35 26 26 22 35 14	35 35 34 4 28 26 22 35 14	2 3 4 7 29 26 22 35 14	4 7 5 8 31 26 22 35 14	8 12 6 12 33 26 21 35 15	10 15 10 10 34 26 21 35 14	15 19 16 10 34 26 21 36 15	17 25 17 12 33 26 21 35 14	20 29 17 15 33 26 22 35 15	22 34 23 19 34 27 22 35 15	26 1 28 22 35 27 22 35 15
6	29 29 30 31 23 25 22 35 14	32 35 29 35 26 26 22 35 14	35 36 34 4 28 26 22 35 14	2 5 4 7 29 26 22 35 14	4 8 5 10 31 26 22 35 14	8 12 6 12 33 26 21 35 15	10 16 10 10 34 26 21 35 14	15 21 16 10 34 26 21 36 15	17 26 27 12 33 26 21 35 14	20 30 17 15 33 26 22 35 15	22 35 24 19 34 27 22 35 15	26 3 28 22 35 27 22 35 15
7	29 31 30 31 23 25 22 35 14	32 35 29 35 26 26 22 35 14	35 1 34 4 28 26 22 35 14	2 5 4 7 29 26 22 35 14	4 9 5 10 31 26 22 35 14	8 15 6 12 33 26 21 35 15	12 17 12 10 34 26 21 35 14	15 22 16 10 34 26 21 36 15	17 28 17 12 33 26 21 35 14	20 31 19 15 33 26 22 35 15	22 36 24 19 34 27 22 35 15	26 4 28 22 35 27 22 35 15
8	29 32 30 31 23 25 22 35 14	32 1 29 35 26 26 22 35 14	35 2 34 4 28 26 22 35 14	2 7 4 7 30 26 21 35 14	5 10 5 10 32 26 21 35 14	8 15 6 12 33 26 21 35 15	12 19 12 10 34 26 21 35 14	15 24 16 10 34 26 21 36 15	17 29 17 12 33 26 21 35 14	20 33 19 16 33 26 22 35 15	22 2 24 19 34 27 22 35 15	26 6 28 22 35 27 22 35 15
9	29 33 30 31 23 25 22 35 14	32 2 29 35 26 26 22 35 14	35 4 34 4 28 26 22 35 14	2 8 4 7 30 26 21 35 14	5 12 5 10 32 26 21 35 14	8 16 6 12 33 26 21 35 15	12 21 12 10 34 26 21 35 14	15 26 18 10 34 26 21 36 15	17 30 17 13 33 26 21 35 14	20 34 19 16 33 26 22 35 15	23 3 24 19 34 27 22 35 15	26 6 28 22 35 27 22 35 15
10	29 34 30 31 23 25 22 35 14	32 3 30 36 26 26 22 35 14	35 5 35 4 28 26 22 35 14	2 9 4 7 30 26 21 35 14	5 13 5 10 32 26 21 35 14	8 17 6 12 33 26 21 35 15	12 21 12 10 34 26 21 35 14	15 27 18 10 34 26 21 36 15	17 32 17 13 33 26 21 35 14	20 35 19 16 33 26 22 35 15	23 4 24 19 34 27 22 35 15	26 7 28 22 35 27 22 35 15
11	29 35 30 31 23 25 22 35 14	32 4 30 36 26 26 22 35 14	35 6 35 4 28 26 22 35 14	3 10 5 7 30 26 21 35 14	5 14 5 10 32 26 21 35 14	8 19 6 12 33 26 21 35 15	12 22 12 10 34 26 21 35 14	15 28 18 10 34 26 21 36 15	17 33 17 13 33 26 21 35 14	20 1 19 16 33 26 22 35 15	23 6 24 19 34 27 22 35 15	27 8 29 23 36 27 23 36 15
12	29 1 29 31 23 25 22 35 14	32 5 31 1 26 26 22 35 14	35 7 35 4 28 26 22 35 14	3 12 5 7 30 26 21 35 14	5 15 5 10 32 26 21 35 14	8 21 6 12 33 26 21 35 15	12 23 12 10 34 26 21 35 14	15 30 18 10 34 26 21 36 15	17 34 17 13 33 26 21 35 14	20 2 19 16 33 26 22 35 15	24 7 25 19 35 27 22 35 15	27 10 29 23 36 27 23 36 15
13	29 2 29 31 23 25 22 35 14	32 7 31 1 26 26 22 35 14	35 8 35 4 28 26 22 35 14	3 13 5 7 30 26 21 35 14	5 16 5 10 32 26 21 35 14	8 22 7 12 33 26 21 35 15	12 25 12 10 34 26 21 35 14	15 31 18 10 34 26 21 36 15	17 35 17 13 33 26 21 35 14	20 3 20 16 33 26 22 35 15	24 8 25 21 35 27 22 35 15	27 11 29 23 36 27 23 36 15
14	29 4 29 31 23 25 22 35 14	32 8 31 1 26 26 22 35 14	35 10 35 4 28 26 22 35 14	3 14 5 7 30 26 21 35 14	5 17 5 10 32 26 21 35 14	8 24 7 12 33 26 21 35 15	12 26 13 10 34 26 21 35 14	15 33 18 10 33 26 21 36 15	17 1 17 13 33 26 22 35 15	20 4 20 16 33 26 22 35 15	24 9 25 21 35 27 22 35 15	27 12 29 24 36 27 23 36 15
15	29 5 29 31 23 25 22 35 14	32 9 31 1 26 26 22 35 14	35 11 35 4 28 26 22 35 14	3 16 5 8 30 26 21 35 14	5 19 5 10 32 26 21 35 14	8 25 7 12 33 26 21 35 15	12 28 13 10 34 26 21 25 14	15 34 18 10 33 26 21 36 15	17 3 17 13 33 26 22 35 15	20 6 21 16 33 26 22 35 15	24 10 25 21 35 27 22 35 15	27 14 29 24 36 27 23 36 15
16	30 5 29 31 23 25 21 35 14	32 10 31 1 26 26 22 35 14	35 12 35 4 28 26 22 35 14	3 17 5 8 30 26 21 35 14	5 21 5 10 32 26 21 35 14	8 26 7 12 33 26 21 35 15	12 30 13 10 34 26 21 35 14	15 36 18 10 33 26 21 36 15	17 4 17 13 33 26 22 35 15	20 7 21 17 33 26 22 35 15	24 11 25 21 35 27 22 35 15	27 15 29 24 36 27 23 36 15
17	30 7 29 34 25 25 21 35 14	32 12 31 1 26 26 22 35 14	35 14 35 4 28 26 22 35 14	3 18 5 8 30 26 21 35 14	5 22 5 10 32 26 21 35 14	8 28 7 12 33 26 21 35 15	12 31 13 10 34 26 21 35 14	15 1 18 10 33 26 21 36 15	17 5 17 13 33 26 22 35 15	20 8 21 17 33 26 22 35 15	24 13 25 21 35 27 22 35 15	27 16 29 24 36 27 23 36 15
18	30 8 29 34 25 25 21 35 14	33 13 31 1 26 26 22 35 14	36 14 35 5 29 26 22 35 14	3 20 5 8 30 26 21 35 14	5 23 5 10 32 26 21 35 14	8 29 7 12 33 26 21 35 15	12 33 14 10 34 26 21 35 14	15 2 18 10 33 26 21 36 15	17 6 17 13 33 26 22 35 15	20 10 21 17 33 26 22 35 15	24 14 26 21 35 27 22 35 15	27 17 29 24 36 27 23 36 15
19	30 9 29 34 25 25 21 35 14	33 14 31 1 26 26 22 35 14	36 16 35 5 29 26 22 35 14	3 21 5 8 30 26 21 35 14	5 25 5 10 32 26 21 35 14	8 31 7 11 33 26 21 35 14	12 34 14 10 34 26 21 35 14	15 3 18 12 33 26 21 36 15	17 7 17 13 33 26 22 35 15	20 11 21 17 33 26 22 35 15	24 15 26 21 35 27 22 35 15	27 18 29 24 36 27 23 36 15
20	30 11 29 34 25 25 21 35 14	34 15 31 1 26 26 22 35 14	36 17 35 5 29 26 22 35 14	4 23 5 8 31 26 22 35 14	5 26 5 10 32 26 21 35 14	8 32 7 11 33 26 21 35 14	12 35 14 10 34 26 21 35 14	15 4 18 12 33 26.21 36 15	17 8 17 13 33 26 22 35 15	21 12 21 17 33 26 22 35 15	24 16 26 21 35 27 22 36 15	27 20 29 24 36 27 23 36 15
21	31 12 29 35 26 25 22 35 14	34 17 32 2 26 26 22 35 14	36 19 35 5 28 26 22 35 14	4 24 5 8 31 26 22 35 14	7 28 5 10 32 26 21 35 14	8 33 8 11 33 26 21 35 14	12 1 14 10 34 26 21 35 14	15 6 18 12 33 26 21 36 15	17 10 17 14 33 26 22 35 15	21 13 21 17 33 26 22 35 15	24 17 26 21 35 27 22 35 15	28 21 29 24 1 28 23 36 15
22	31 13 29 35 26 26 22 35 14	34 17 32 2 26 26 22 35 14	2 20 2 5 29 26 22 35 14	4 26 5 8 31 26 22 35 14	7 30 5 10 32 26 21 35 14	10 35 8 11 33 26 21 35 14	13 3 14 10 34 26 21 35 14	15 7 18 12 33 26 21 36 15	17 11 17 14 33 26 22 35 15	22 15 21 17 34 26 22 35 15	24 19 26 21 35 27 22 35 15	28 23 29 25 36 28 23 36 15
23	31 14 29 35 26 26 22 35 14	34 19 32 2 26 26 22 35 14	2 22 2 5 29 26 22 35 14	4 27 5 8 31 26 22 35 14	7 31 5 11 32 26 21 35 14	10 35 8 11 32 26 21 35 14	13 3 14 10 34 26 21 35 14	16 8 18 12 34 26 21 36 15	19 12 17 14 33 26 22 35 15	22 16 21 17 34 26 22 35 15	25 21 26 21 35 27 22 35 15	28 24 29 25 36 28 23 36 15
24	31 16 29 35 26 26 22 35 14	34 20 32 2 26 26 22 35 14	2 23 2 5 29 26 22 35 14	4 29 5 8 31 26 22 35 14	7 32 5 11 32 26 21 35 14	10 1 8 11 33 26 21 35 14	13 5 14 10 34 26 21 35 14	16 9 18 12 34 26 21 36 15	19 13 17 14 33 26 22 35 15	22 17 21 17 34 26 22 35 15	25 2 26 21 35 27 22 35 15	28 26 29 25 36 28 23 36 15
25	31 17 29 35 26 26 22 35 14	34 22 32 2 26 26 22 35 14	2 25 2 5 29 26 22 35 14	4 31 5 8 31 26 22 35 14	7 34 5 11 32 26 20 35 14	10 3 8 11 33 26 21 35 14	13 6 14 10 34 26 21 35 14	16 10 18 12 34 26 21 36 15	19 14 17 15 33 26 22 35 15	22 18 22 17 34 26 22 35 15	25 24 27 21 35 27 22 35 15	28 27 29 25 36 28 23 36 15
26	31 19 29 35 26 26 22 35 14	34 23 32 2 26 26 22 35 14	2 26 2 5 29 26 22 35 14	4 32 5 8 31 26 22 35 14	7 35 5 11 32 26 20 35 14	10 4 8 11 33 26 21 35 14	14 7 14 10 34 26 21 35 14	16 12 18 12 34 26 21 36 15	19 16 17 15 33 26 22 35 15	22 19 22 17 34 26 22 35 15	25 25 27 21 35 27 22 35 15	28 28 29 25 36 28 23 36 15
27	31 20 29 35 26 26 22 35 14	34 25 32 2 26 26 22 35 14	2 28 2 5 29 26 22 35 14	4 33 5 8 31 26 22 35 14	7 36 5 11 32 26 20 35 14	10 5 8 11 33 26 21 35 14	14 8 14 10 34 26 21 35 14	16 13 18 12 34 26 21 36 15	19 17 17 15 33 26 22 35 15	22 21 22 17 34 26 22 35 15	25 26 27 22 35 27 22 35 15	28 30 29 25 36 28 23 36 15
28	31 21 29 35 26 26 22 35 14	34 26 32 2 26 26 22 35 14	2 29 2 5 29 26 22 35 14	4 34 5 8 31 26 22 35 14	7 1 5 11 32 26 20 35 14	10 6 8 11 33 26 31 35 14	14 9 14 10 34 26 21 35 14	16 14 18 12 34 26 21 36 15	19 19 17 15 33 26 22 35 15	22 22 22 17 34 26 22 35 15	25 28 27 22 35 27 22 35 15	28 32 29 25 36 29 23 36 15
29	31 23 29 35 26 26 22 35 14	34 28 32 2 26 26 22 35 14	2 31 2 5 29 26 22 35 14	4 35 5 8 31 26 22 35 14	7 2 5 11 32 26 20 35 14	10 7 8 11 33 26 21 35 14	14 10 14 10 34 26 21 35 14	16 15 18 12 34 26 21 36 15	19 20 17 15 33 26 22 35 15	22 23 22 17 34 26 22 35 15	25 29 27 22 35 27 22 35 15	28 33 29 25 36 28 23 36 15
30	31 24 29 35 26 26 22 35 14	**1924**	2 32 2 5 29 26 22 35 14	4 1 5 8 31 26 22 35 14	7 4 5 11 32 26 20 35 14	10 8 10 11 33 26 21 35 14	14 12 14 10 34 26 21 35 14	16 16 18 12 34 26 21 36 15	19 22 17 15 33 26 22 35 15	22 25 22 17 34 26 22 35 15	25 31 27 22 35 27 22 35 15	28 34 28 26 36 28 23 36 15
31	31 25 29 35 26 26 22 35 14		2 33 2 5 29 26 22 35 14		8 5 5 11 32 26 20 35 14		14 14 16 10 34 26 21 35 14	16 18 18 12 33 26 21 36 15		22 26 22 17 34 26 22 35 15		28 35 28 26 36 28 23 36 15

	JAN	FEB	MAR	APR	MAY	JUNE	JULY	AUG	SEPT	OCT	NOV	DEC
1	28 1 27 27 1 28 22 35 15	32 6 29 29 3 28 23 35 15	35 7 34 32 5 29 23 35 14	2 11 3 2 8 29 23 36 15	4 13 3 4 9 30 22 36 15	9 19 6 9 12 30 22 36 15	10 22 12 13 13 30 22 36 15	13 27 16 16 15 29 22 36 15	16 33 15 19 16 28 22 36 15	19 1 19 23 19 29 23 36 15	23 6 24 27 20 29 23 36 15	25 9 27 30 24 30 24 36 15
2	28 3 27 27 1 28 22 35 15	32 7 29 29 3 28 23 35 15	35 8 34 32 5 29 23 35 14	2 12 4 2 6 29 23 36 15	4 15 3 4 9 30 22 36 15	9 20 6 9 12 30 22 36 15	10 24 12 13 13 30 22 36 15	13 29 16 16 15 29 22 36 15	16 34 15 19 16 28 22 36 15	19 2 19 23 19 29 23 36 15	23 7 24 27 20 29 23 36 15	25 10 27 30 24 30 24 36 15
3	23 4 27 27 1 28 22 35 15	32 8 29 29 3 28 23 35 15	35 9 34 32 5 29 23 35 14	2 14 4 2 8 29 23 36 15	4 16 3 4 9 30 22 36 15	9 21 6 9 12 30 22 36 15	10 25 12 13 13 30 22 36 15	13 30 16 16 15 29 22 36 15	16 36 15 19 16 28 22 36 15	19 3 19 23 19 29 23 36 15	23 9 24 27 20 29 23 36 15	25 12 27 30 24 30 24 36 15
4	28 4 27 27 1 28 22 35 15	32 9 29 29 3 29 23 35 15	35 10 35 34 5 29 23 35 14	2 15 4 2 8 29 23 36 15	4 18 3 4 9 30 22 36 15	9 22 6 9 12 30 22 36 15	10 27 13 13 13 30 22 36 15	13 32 16 16 15 29 22 36 15	16 1 15 19 16 28 22 36 15	19 5 19 23 19 29 23 36 15	23 9 24 27 20 29 23 36 15	25 13 27 30 24 30 24 36 15
5	28 6 27 27 1 28 22 35 15	32 10 29 29 4 28 23 35 15	35 11 35 34 5 29 23 35 14	2 16 4 2 8 29 23 36 15	4 19 3 4 9 30 22 36 15	9 24 6 9 12 30 22 36 15	10 28 13 13 13 30 22 36 15	13 33 16 17 15 29 22 36 15	16 3 15 19 16 28 22 36 15	20 6 20 23 20 29 23 36 15	23 10 24 27 20 29 23 36 15	27 15 27 30 24 30 24 36 15
6	29 7 27 27 1 28 23 35 15	32 11 29 29 4 28 23 35 15	35 12 35 34 5 29 23 35 14	2 17 4 2 8 29 23 36 15	4 21 3 4 9 30 22 36 15	9 25 6 9 12 30 22 36 15	10 30 13 13 13 30 22 36 15	13 35 16 17 15 29 22 36 15	16 4 15 19 16 28 22 36 15	20 7 20 24 20 29 23 36 15	23 12 24 27 20 29 23 36 15	27 15 27 31 24 30 24 36 15
7	29 8 27 27 1 28 23 35 15	31 13 31 31 4 28 23 35 15	35 15 35 34 5 29 23 35 14	2 18 4 2 8 29 23 36 15	4 22 3 4 9 30 22 36 15	9 27 7 9 12 30 22 36 15	10 31 13 13 13 30 22 36 15	13 36 16 17 15 29 22 36 15	18 6 15 19 16 28 22 36 15	20 9 20 24 20 29 23 36 15	23 13 25 28 30 29 23 36 15	27 16 27 31 24 30 24 36 15
8	29 10 27 27 1 28 23 35 15	32 14 31 31 4 28 23 35 15	35 15 35 34 5 29 23 35 14	2 19 4 2 8 29 23 36 15	4 24 3 4 9 30 22 36 15	9 28 7 9 12 30 22 36 15	10 33 13 13 13 30 22 36 15	13 1 16 17 15 29 22 36 15	18 7 15 19 16 28 22 36 15	20 10 20 24 20 29 23 36 15	23 14 25 28 30 29 23 36 15	27 18 27 31 24 30 24 36 15
9	29 11 27 27 1 28 23 35 15	32 15 31 31 4 28 23 35 15	35 16 35 34 5 29 23 35 14	2 21 4 2 8 29 23 36 15	4 25 3 4 9 30 22 36 15	9 30 7 9 12 30 22 36 15	10 34 13 13 13 30 22 36 15	13 3 16 17 15 29 22 36 15	18 8 15 21 16 28 22 36 15	20 11 20 24 20 29 23 36 15	23 15 25 28 30 29 23 36 15	27 19 27 31 24 30 24 36 15
10	29 12 27 27 1 28 23 35 15	32 16 31 31 4 28 23 35 15	35 17 35 34 5 29 23 35 14	2 23 4 2 8 29 23 36 15	6 27 4 6 10 30 22 36 15	9 31 7 10 12 30 22 36 15	12 36 13 13 13 30 22 36 15	13 4 16 18 15 29 22 36 15	18 9 15 21 16 28 22 36 15	20 12 20 24 20 29 23 36 15	23 16 25 28 30 29 23 36 15	27 21 27 31 24 30 24 26 15
11	29 13 27 27 1 28 23 35 15	32 17 31 31 4 28 23 35 15	35 19 35 34 5 29 23 35 14	2 24 4 2 8 29 23 36 15	6 28 4 6 10 30 22 36 15	9 33 7 10 12 30 22 36 15	12 1 13 13 13 30 22 36 15	15 6 16 18 15 29 22 36 15	18 10 16 21 18 28 22 36 15	20 14 20 24 20 29 23 36 15	23 18 25 28 21 29 23 36 15	27 21 27 31 24 30 24 36 15
12	29 15 27 27 1 28 23 35 15	33 19 31 31 4 28 23 35 15	35 20 35 34 5 29 23 35 14	2 25 4 2 8 29 23 36 15	6 30 4 6 10 30 22 36 15	9 34 7 10 12 30 22 36 15	12 2 13 13 13 30 22 36 15	15 7 16 18 15 29 22 36 15	18 11 16 21 18 28 22 36 15	20 15 20 26 20 29 23 36 15	23 19 25 28 21 29 23 36 15	27 22 27 31 24 30 24 36 15
13	29 16 27 27 1 28 23 35 15	33 21 32 32 5 28 23 35 15	35 21 35 34 5 29 23 35 14	2 27 4 2 8 29 23 36 15	6 31 4 6 10 30 22 36 15	9 36 7 10 12 30 22 36 15	12 3 13 13 13 30 22 36 15	15 8 16 18 16 28 22 36 15	18 13 16 21 18 28 22 36 15	20 16 21 26 20 29 23 36 15	23 20 25 28 21 29 23 36 15	27 24 27 31 24 30 24 36 15
14	29 17 28 28 3 28 23 35 15	33 22 32 32 5 28 23 35 15	35 23 1 35 6 29 23 35 15	2 28 4 2 8 29 23 36 15	6 32 4 6 10 30 22 36 15	9 1 7 10 12 30 22 36 15	12 4 13 13 13 30 22 36 15	15 9 16 18 16 28 22 36 15	18 13 16 21 18 28 22 36 15	20 17 21 26 20 29 23 36 15	23 22 27 28 22 29 23 36 15	27 25 27 31 24 30 24 36 15
15	29 18 28 28 3 28 23 35 15	33 23 32 32 5 28 23 35 15	35 24 1 35 6 29 23 35 15	3 30 3 3 9 30 23 36 15	6 33 4 6 10 30 22 36 15	9 3 9 10 12 30 22 36 15	12 6 13 13 13 30 22 36 15	15 10 16 18 16 28 22 36 15	18 15 16 21 18 28 22 36 15	21 18 21 26 20 29 23 36 15	23 23 27 28 22 29 23 36 15	27 27 27 31 24 30 24 36 15
16	29 19 28 28 3 28 23 35 15	33 24 32 32 5 28 23 35 15	35 25 1 35 6 29 23 35 15	3 31 3 3 9 30 23 36 15	6 34 4 6 10 30 22 36 15	9 4 9 10 12 30 22 36 15	12 7 15 15 13 30 22 36 15	15 12 16 18 16 28 22 36 15	18 16 16 22 18 28 22 36 15	21 20 21 26 20 29 23 36 15	23 24 27 29 22 29 23 36 15	27 28 27 31 24 30 24 36 15
17	29 21 28 28 3 28 23 35 15	33 26 32 32 5 28 23 35 14	35 26 1 35 6 29 23 35 15	3 33 3 3 9 30 23 36 15	6 36 4 6 10 30 22 36 15	9 4 9 10 12 30 22 36 15	12 9 15 15 13 30 22 36 15	15 13 16 18 16 28 22 36 15	18 18 16 22 18 28 22 36 15	21 21 22 26 20 29 23 36 15	23 27 27 29 22 29 23 36 15	27 30 27 31 24 30 24 36 15
18	29 23 28 28 3 28 23 35 15	33 27 32 32 5 28 23 35 14	35 28 1 35 6 29 23 35 15	3 34 3 3 9 30 23 36 15	6 1 4 6 10 30 22 36 15	9 6 9 10 12 30 22 36 15	12 10 15 15 13 30 22 36 15	15 14 16 18 16 28 22 36 15	18 19 16 22 18 28 22 36 15	21 22 22 26 20 29 23 36 15	23 27 27 29 22 29 23 36 15	27 31 27 31 24 30 24 36 15
19	29 23 28 28 3 28 23 35 15	34 28 32 32 5 28 23 35 14	35 29 3 35 6 29 23 35 15	3 35 2 3 9 30 23 36 15	6 3 4 6 10 30 22 36 15	9 7 9 10 12 30 22 36 15	12 11 15 15 13 30 22 36 15	15 15 16 18 16 28 22 36 15	18 20 16 22 18 28 22 36 15	21 23 22 26 20 29 23 36 15	23 29 27 29 22 29 23 36 15	27 33 27 33 24 30 24 36 15
20	29 25 28 28 3 28 23 35 15	34 30 32 32 5 28 23 35 14	35 30 3 35 6 29 23 35 15	3 36 2 3 9 30 23 36 15	6 4 4 6 10 30 22 36 15	9 9 9 10 12 30 22 36 15	12 12 15 15 13 30 22 36 15	15 16 16 18 16 28 22 36 15	18 21 16 22 18 28 22 36 15	21 25 23 26 20 29 23 36 15	23 29 27 29 22 29 23 36 15	27 34 27 33 24 30 24 36 15
21	31 26 28 28 3 28 23 35 15	34 32 32 32 5 28 23 35 14	1 31 3 1 6 29 23 35 15	4 2 2 4 9 30 23 36 15	6 6 4 6 10 30 22 36 15	9 10 10 10 12 30 22 36 15	12 13 15 15 13 30 22 36 15	15 18 16 18 16 28 22 36 15	18 22 18 22 18 28 22 36 15	21 27 23 26 20 29 23 36 15	24 31 27 29 22 29 23 36 15	27 36 27 33 24 30 24 36 15
22	31 28 28 28 3 28 23 35 15	34 32 32 32 5 28 23 35 14	1 33 3 1 6 29 23 35 15	4 3 2 4 9 30 23 36 15	7 7 4 7 10 30 22 36 15	10 11 10 10 12 30 22 36 15	12 15 15 15 15 30 22 36 15	15 19 16 19 16 28 22 36 15	18 24 18 22 18 28 22 36 15	21 28 23 26 20 29 23 36 15	24 32 27 29 22 29 23 36 15	28 1 27 33 24 30 24 36 15
23	31 29 28 29 3 28 23 35 15	34 35 32 32 5 28 23 35 14	1 34 3 1 6 29 23 35 15	5 5 2 5 9 30 23 36 15	7 8 4 7 10 30 22 36 15	10 12 10 10 12 30 22 36 15	13 16 15 15 15 30 22 36 15	15 20 16 19 16 28 22 36 15	18 25 18 22 18 28 22 36 15	21 29 23 26 20 29 23 36 15	25 34 27 29 22 29 23 36 15	28 2 27 33 24 30 24 36 15
24	31 32 28 28 3 28 23 35 15	34 35 32 32 5 28 23 35 14	1 35 3 1 7 29 23 35 15	5 6 2 5 9 30 23 36 15	7 9 4 7 10 30 22 36 15	10 13 10 12 12 30 22 36 15	13 17 15 15 15 30 22 36 15	16 21 16 19 16 28 22 36 15	19 27 18 22 18 28 22 36 15	22 30 23 26 20 29 23 36 15	25 36 27 29 22 29 23 36 15	28 3 27 33 24 30 24 36 15
25	32 32 28 28 3 28 23 35 15	34 1 32 32 5 28 23 35 14	1 1 3 1 7 29 23 35 15	5 7 2 5 9 30 23 36 15	7 10 4 7 10 30 22 36 15	10 15 10 12 12 30 22 36 15	13 18 15 15 15 30 22 36 15	16 22 16 19 16 28 22 36 15	19 28 18 22 18 28 22 36 15	22 32 23 26 20 29 23 36 15	25 1 27 29 22 29 23 36 15	28 4 27 33 24 30 24 36 15
26	32 34 28 28 3 28 33 35 15	34 2 34 32 5 28 23 35 14	1 3 3 1 7 29 23 35 15	5 9 2 5 9 30 23 36 15	7 12 4 7 10 30 22 36 15	10 16 12 12 13 30 22 36 15	13 19 16 15 15 30 22 36 15	16 24 16 19 16 28 22 36 15	19 28 18 22 18 28 22 36 15	22 33 24 27 20 29 23 36 15	25 3 27 29 22 29 23 36 15	28 5 27 33 24 30 24 36 15
27	32 35 28 28 3 28 23 35 15	34 4 34 32 5 28 23 35 14	1 4 3 1 7 29 23 35 15	5 9 2 5 9 30 23 36 15	7 13 4 7 10 30 22 36 15	10 17 12 12 13 30 22 36 15	13 21 16 16 15 30 22 36 15	16 25 15 19 16 28 22 36 15	19 31 18 22 18 28 22 36 15	22 34 24 27 20 29 23 36 15	25 4 27 29 22 29 23 36 15	28 7 27 33 24 30 24 36 15
28	32 1 28 28 3 28 23 35 15	34 5 34 32 5 28 23 35 14	1 5 3 1 7 29 23 35 15	5 10 2 5 9 30 23 36 15	7 14 4 7 10 30 22 36 15	10 18 12 12 13 30 22 36 15	13 22 16 16 15 30 22 36 15	16 27 15 19 16 28 22 36 15	19 33 18 22 18 28 22 36 15	22 36 24 27 20 29 23 36 15	25 5 27 29 22 29 23 36 15	28 9 27 33 25 30 24 36 15
29	32 2 28 28 3 28 23 35 15	**1925**	1 7 3 1 7 29 23 35 15	5 12 2 5 9 30 23 36 15	7 15 4 7 10 30 22 36 15	10 19 12 12 13 30 22 36 15	13 24 16 16 15 30 22 36 15	16 28 15 19 16 28 22 36 15	19 34 19 22 19 29 22 36 15	22 1 24 27 20 29 23 36 15	25 6 27 29 23 29 23 36 15	28 10 27 33 25 30 24 36 15
30	32 3 29 29 3 28 23 35 15		1 8 3 1 7 29 23 35 15	5 13 2 5 9 30 23 36 15	7 16 4 7 10 30 22 36 15	10 21 12 12 13 30 22 36 15	13 24 16 16 15 30 22 36 15	16 30 15 19 16 28 22 36 15	19 35 19 22 19 28 22 36 15	23 2 24 27 20 29 23 36 15	25 7 27 29 23 29 23 36 15	28 11 27 33 25 30 24 36 15
31	32 5 29 29 3 28 23 35 15		1 10 3 1 7 29 23 35 15		7 18 6 7 10 30 22 36 15		13 25 16 16 15 30 22 36 15	16 31 15 19 16 28 22 36 15		23 4 24 27 20 29 23 36 15		28 12 27 33 25 30 24 36 15

	JAN	FEB	MAR	APR	MAY	JUNE	JULY	AUG	SEPT	OCT	NOV	DEC
1	28 13 27 33 25 30 24 36 15	31 18 31 33 27 31 24 36 15	35 19 36 31 29 31 24 36 15	1 24 1 33 31 33 24 36 15	5 27 3 36 33 33 24 36 15	8 33 8 3 36 33 24 36 15	10 36 13 7 1 33 23 36 14	13 6 15 12 4 33 24 36 15	17 10 15 15 6 33 24 36 15	19 13 21 18 6 33 24 36 15	22 18 25 22 4 32 24 36 15	25 21 25 25 4 33 25 36 15
2	28 15 27 33 25 30 24 36 15	31 19 31 33 27 31 24 36 15	35 19 36 31 29 31 24 36 15	1 25 1 34 31 33 24 36 15	5 28 3 36 33 33 24 36 15	8 34 8 3 36 33 24 36 15	10 1 13 7 1 33 23 36 14	13 7 15 12 4 33 24 36 15	17 12 15 15 6 33 24 36 15	19 15 21 19 6 33 24 36 15	22 19 25 22 4 32 24 36 15	25 22 25 25 4 33 25 36 15
3	28 16 27 33 25 30 24 36 15	31 20 31 33 27 31 24 36 15	35 21 36 31 29 31 24 36 15	1 26 1 34 31 33 24 36 15	5 30 3 36 33 33 24 36 15	8 35 8 4 36 33 24 36 15	11 3 14 8 2 33 23 36 14	14 8 14 12 4 33 23 36 14	17 13 15 15 6 33 24 36 15	21 16 21 18 6 33 24 36 15	22 20 25 22 4 32 24 36 15	25 24 25 25 4 33 25 36 15
4	30 17 27 33 25 30 24 36 15	31 21 31 33 27 31 24 36 15	35 22 36 31 29 31 24 36 15	1 27 1 34 31 33 24 36 15	6 31 3 36 34 33 24 36 15	8 36 8 4 36 33 24 36 15	11 5 14 8 2 33 23 36 14	14 9 14 12 4 33 23 36 14	17 15 15 15 6 33 24 36 15	21 17 21 18 6 33 24 36 15	22 21 25 22 4 32 24 36 15	26 25 25 26 4 33 25 36 15
5	30 18 27 33 25 30 24 36 15	31 23 31 33 27 31 24 36 15	35 24 36 31 29 31 24 36 15	1 29 1 34 31 33 24 36 15	6 33 3 36 34 33 24 36 15	8 2 8 4 36 33 24 36 15	11 5 14 8 2 33 23 36 14	14 10 14 12 4 33 23 36 14	17 15 15 15 6 33 24 36 15	21 18 21 18 6 33 24 36 15	22 23 25 22 4 32 24 36 15	26 27 25 26 4 33 25 36 15
6	30 19 27 33 25 31 24 36 15	33 24 31 33 27 31 24 36 15	36 25 1 31 30 31 24 36 15	1 30 1 34 31 33 24 36 15	6 34 3 36 34 33 24 36 15	8 3 8 4 36 33 24 36 15	11 6 14 8 2 33 23 36 14	14 12 14 12 4 33 23 36 14	17 16 16 15 6 33 24 36 15	21 19 21 19 6 33 24 36 15	22 24 25 22 4 32 24 36 15	26 28 25 26 4 33 25 36 15
7	30 21 27 33 25 31 24 36 15	33 25 31 33 27 31 24 36 15	36 27 1 31 30 31 24 36 15	1 31 1 34 31 33 24 36 15	6 36 3 1 34 33 24 36 15	8 4 8 4 36 33 24 36 15	11 7 14 8 2 33 23 36 14	14 13 14 12 4 33 23 36 14	17 18 16 15 6 33 24 36 15	21 21 21 19 6 33 24 36 15	22 25 25 22 4 32 24 36 15	26 29 25 26 4 33 25 36 15
8	30 22 27 33 25 31 24 36 15	33 27 31 33 27 31 24 36 15	36 28 1 31 30 31 24 36 15	1 33 1 34 31 33 24 36 15	6 1 3 1 34 33 24 36 15	8 6 9 3 36 33 24 36 15	11 9 14 8 2 33 23 36 14	15 14 14 12 4 33 24 36 15	17 18 16 15 6 33 24 36 15	21 22 21 19 6 33 24 36 15	22 27 25 22 4 32 24 36 15	26 30 25 26 4 33 25 36 15
9	30 24 27 33 25 31 24 36 15	33 28 31 33 28 31 24 36 15	36 29 1 31 30 31 24 36 15	1 34 1 34 31 33 24 36 15	6 3 3 1 34 33 24 36 15	8 7 9 3 36 33 24 36 15	11 11 14 8 2 33 23 36 14	15 15 13 12 4 33 24 36 15	17 20 16 15 6 33 24 36 15	21 24 21 19 6 33 24 36 15	22 28 25 22 4 32 24 36 15	27 32 25 27 4 33 25 36 15
10	30 25 27 33 25 31 24 36 15	33 30 31 33 28 31 24 36 15	36 30 1 31 30 31 24 36 15	1 36 1 34 31 33 24 36 15	6 4 3 1 34 33 24 36 15	8 9 9 3 36 33 24 36 15	11 12 14 8 2 33 23 36 14	15 16 13 12 4 33 24 36 15	17 21 16 15 6 33 24 36 15	21 24 22 19 6 33 24 36 15	22 30 26 22 4 32 24 36 15	27 33 25 27 4 33 25 36 15
11	30 25 28 33 25 31 24 36 15	33 31 33 31 28 31 24 36 15	36 31 1 31 30 31 24 36 15	3 1 1 33 33 33 24 36 15	6 6 3 1 34 33 24 36 15	9 10 9 3 36 33 24 36 15	11 13 14 8 2 33 23 36 14	15 18 13 12 4 33 24 36 15	18 22 16 15 6 33 24 36 15	21 25 22 19 6 33 24 36 15	24 31 26 22 4 32 24 36 15	27 35 25 27 4 33 25 36 15
12	30 27 28 33 25 31 24 36 15	33 33 33 31 28 31 24 36 15	36 33 1 31 30 31 24 36 15	3 3 1 33 33 33 24 36 15	6 6 3 1 34 33 24 36 15	9 11 10 6 36 33 24 36 15	11 14 14 8 2 33 23 36 14	15 19 13 12 4 33 24 36 15	18 24 17 16 6 33 24 36 15	21 27 22 19 6 33 24 36 15	24 32 26 24 4 32 24 36 15	27 36 25 27 4 33 25 36 15
13	30 28 28 33 25 31 24 36 15	33 34 33 31 28 31 24 36 15	36 36 1 31 30 31 24 36 15	3 4 1 33 33 33 24 36 15	6 8 4 1 34 33 24 36 15	9 12 10 6 36 33 24 36 15	12 16 15 9 3 33 24 36 15	15 20 13 12 4 33 24 36 15	18 25 17 16 6 33 24 36 15	21 28 22 21 6 33 24 36 15	24 33 26 24 4 32 24 36 15	27 1 25 27 4 33 25 36 15
14	30 30 28 33 25 30 24 36 15	33 36 33 31 28 31 24 36 15	36 1 1 31 30 31 24 36 15	3 6 1 33 33 33 24 36 15	6 9 4 1 34 33 24 36 15	9 13 10 6 36 33 24 36 15	12 17 15 9 3 33 24 36 15	15 21 13 12 4 33 24 36 15	18 26 17 16 6 33 24 36 15	21 30 22 21 6 33 24 36 15	24 34 26 24 4 32 24 36 15	27 3 25 27 4 33 25 36 15
15	30 32 28 33 25 31 24 36 15	33 1 33 31 28 31 24 36 15	36 2 1 31 30 31 24 36 15	3 7 1 33 33 33 24 36 15	6 10 4 1 34 33 24 36 15	9 13 10 6 36 33 24 36 15	12 18 15 9 3 33 24 36 15	15 22 13 12 4 33 24 36 15	18 27 18 16 6 33 24 36 15	21 31 24 21 6 33 24 36 15	24 36 26 24 4 32 24 36 15	27 4 25 27 4 33 25 36 15
16	30 33 28 33 27 31 24 36 15	33 3 33 31 28 31 24 36 15	36 3 1 31 30 31 24 36 15	3 9 1 33 33 33 24 36 15	6 12 4 1 34 33 24 36 15	9 16 10 6 36 33 24 36 15	12 19 15 9 3 33 24 36 15	15 24 13 12 4 33 24 36 15	18 28 18 16 6 33 24 36 15	21 33 24 21 6 33 24 36 15	24 2 26 24 4 32 24 36 15	27 6 25 27 4 33 25 36 15
17	30 36 28 33 27 31 24 36 15	33 4 33 31 28 31 24 36 15	36 5 1 31 30 31 24 36 15	3 10 1 33 33 33 24 36 15	6 13 4 1 34 33 24 36 15	9 17 10 6 36 33 24 36 15	12 21 15 9 3 33 24 36 15	15 25 13 12 4 33 24 36 15	18 30 18 16 6 33 24 36 15	21 34 24 21 6 33 24 36 15	24 3 26 24 4 32 24 36 15	27 7 25 28 4 33 25 36 15
18	30 36 28 33 27 31 24 36 15	33 6 34 31 28 31 24 36 15	36 6 3 33 30 33 24 36 15	3 11 1 33 33 33 24 36 15	6 14 4 1 34 33 24 36 15	9 18 12 6 36 33 24 36 15	12 22 15 9 3 33 24 36 15	15'27 13 13 4 33 24 36 15	18 31 18 16 6 33 24 36 15	21 36 24 21 6 33 24 36 15	24 4 26 24 4 32 24 36 15	27 9 25 28 4 33 25 36 15
19	30 3 28 33 27 31 24 36 15	34 6 34 31 28 31 24 36 15	36 8 3 33 30 33 24 36 15	3 12 1 33 33 33 24 36 15	6 15 4 1 34 33 24 36 15	9 19 12 6 36 33 24 36 15	12 24 15 9 3 33 24 36 15	15 28 13 13 4 33 24 36 15	18 33 18 16 6 33 24 36 15	21 31 24 21 6 33 24 36 15	24 6 26 24 4 32 24 36 15	27 10 25 28 4 33 25 36 15
20	30 3 28 33 27 31 24 36 15	34 7 34 31 28 31 24 36 15	36 9 3 33 30 33 24 36 15	3 13 1 33 33 33 24 36 15	6 16 4 1 34 33 24 36 15	9 21 12 6 36 33 24 36 15	12 24 15 9 3 33 24 36 15	15 29 13 13 4 33 24 36 15	18 34 18 16 6 33 24 36 15	21 3 24 21 6 33 24 36 15	24 7 25 24 4 32 24 36 15	27 11 25 28 4 33 25 36 15
21	31 4 28 33 27 31 24 36 15	34 9 34 31 28 31 24 36 15	1 10 1 33 31 33 24 36 15	4 15 1 33 33 33 24 36 15	6 18 6 1 34 33 24 36 15	9 22 12 6 36 33 24 36 15	12 25 15 9 3 33 24 36 15	15 31 13 13 4 33 24 36 15	18 36 18 16 6 33 24 36 15	21 4 24 21 6 33 24 36 15	24 9 25 24 4 32 24 36 15	27 12 25 28 4 33 25 36 15
22	31 6 30 33 27 31 24 36 15	34 10 34 31 28 31 24 36 15	1 11 1 33 31 33 24 36 15	4 16 1 36 33 33 24 36 15	7 19 6 3 36 33 24 36 15	10 24 12 6 1 33 24 36 15	12 27 15 9 3 33 24 36 15	15 33 13 13 4 33 24 36 15	18 1 19 17 6 33 24 36 15	21 6 24 21 6 33 24 36 15	24 10 25 24 4 32 24 36 15	27 13 25 28 4 33 25 36 15
23	31 7 30 33 27 31 24 36 15	34 12 34 31 28 31 24 36 15	1 12 1 33 31 33 24 36 15	4 17 1 36 33 33 24 36 15	7 20 6 3 36 33 24 36 15	10 25 12 6 1 33 24 36 15	13 28 15 10 4 33 24 36 15	16 34 14 14 5 33 23 36 15	18 3 19 17 6 33 24 36 15	21 7 24 21 6 33 24 36 15	25 12 25 25 4 32 25 36 15	28 15 25 28 4 33 25 36 15
24	31 9 30 33 27 31 24 36 15	34 13 34 31 28 31 24 36 15	1 14 1 33 31 33 24 36 15	4 18 1 36 33 33 24 36 15	7 21 6 3 36 33 24 36 15	10 26 12 6 1 33 24 36 15	13 30 15 10 4 33 24 36 15	16 36 14 14 5 33 23 36 15	19 4 19 17 6 33 24 36 15	22 8 24 21 6 33 24 36 15	25 13 25 25 4 32 25 36 15	28 16 26 28 4 33 25 36 15
25	31 9 30 33 27 31 24 36 15	34 14 34 31 28 31 24 36 15	1 15 1 33 31 33 24 36 15	4 19 1 36 33 33 24 36 15	7 22 6 3 36 33 24 36 15	10 27 12 6 1 33 24 36 15	12 31 15 10 4 33 24 36 15	16 1 14 14 5 33 23 36 15	19 6 19 17 6 33 24 36 15	22 9 24 21 6 33 24 36 15	25 14 25 25 4 32 25 36 15	28 17 26 28 4 33 25 36 15
26	31 10 30 33 27 31 24 36 15	34 15 36 31 28 31 24 36 15	1 16 1 33 31 33 24 36 15	4 21 1 36 33 33 24 36 15	7 24 6 3 36 33 24 36 15	10 29 12 6 1 33 23 36 15	12 33 15 10 4 33 24 36 15	16 3 14 14 5 33 23 36 15	19 7 19 18 6 33 24 36 15	22 11 24 21 6 33 24 36 15	25 15 25 25 4 32 25 36 15	28 18 26 28 4 33 25 36 15
27	31 12 30 33 27 31 24 36 15	34 16 36 31 28 31 24 36 15	1 17 1 33 31 33 24 36 15	4 22 1 36 33 33 24 36 15	7 25 6 3 36 33 24 36 15	10 30 12 6 1 33 24 36 15	12 34 15 10 4 33 24 36 15	16 4 14 14 5 33 23 36 15	19 9 19 18 6 33 24 36 15	22 12 24 21 6 33 24 36 15	25 16 25 25 4 32 25 36 15	28 19 27 28 4 33 25 36 15
28	31 13 30 33 27 31 24 36 15	34 18 36 31 28 31 24 36 15	1 18 1 33 31 33 24 36 15	4 24 1 36 33 33 24 36 15	7 27 6 3 36 33 24 36 15	10 31 12 6 1 33 24 36 15	12 36 15 10 4 33 24 36 15	16 6 15 15 6 33 24 36 15	19 10 19 18 6 33 24 36 15	22 13 24 21 4 33 24 36 15	25 18 25 25 4 32 25 36 15	28 21 27 28 4 33 25 36 15
29	31 14 30 33 27 31 24 36 15	**1926**	1 19 1 33 31 33 24 36 15	4 24 1 36 33 33 24 36 15	7 28 6 3 36 33 24 36 15	10 33 13 7 36 33 24 36 15	13 1 15 10 4 33 24 36 15	16 6 15 15 6 33 24 36 15	19 11 19 18 6 33 24 36 15	22 15 24 31 4 33 24 36 15	25 19 25 25 4 32 25 36 15	28 22 27 28 4 33 25 36 15
30	31 15 30 33 27 31 24 36 15		1 21 1 33 31 33 24 36 15	4 25 1 36 33 33 24 36 15	7 30 7 1 34 33 24 36 15	10 34 13 7 36 33 24 36 15	13 3 15 10 4 33 24 36 15	16 7 15 15 6 36 24 36 15	19 12 21 18 6 33 24 36 15	22 16 24 22 4 33 24 36 15	25 20 25 25 4 32 25 36 15	28 23 27 28 4 33 25 36 15
31	31 16 30 33 27 31 24 36 15		1 22 1 33 31 33 24 36 15		7 31 7 1 34 33 24 36 15		13 4 15 10 4 33 24 36 15	16 9 15 15 6 33 24 36 15		22 17 25 22 4 33 24 36 15		28 24 27 28 4 33 25 36 15

	JAN	FEB	MAR	APR	MAY	JUNE	JULY	AUG	SEPT	OCT	NOV	DEC
1	29 25 27 30 5 33 25 36 15	33 31 33 33 6 34 25 36 15	34 31 36 1 7 34 25 36 15	1 1 36 6 9 36 25 36 15	4 4 3 9 10 36 25 1 15	7 10 10 13 13 1 25 1 15	10 15 13 15 15 1 25 1 15	13 18 12 18 16 1 25 1 15	16 22 16 18 18 36 25 36 15	20 25 21 16 20 36 25 36 15	22 30 24 18 22 36 25 36 15	26 34 24 21 24 36 26 36 15
2	29 27 27 30 5 33 25 36 15	33 33 33 34 6 34 25 36 15	34 33 36 1 7 34 25 36 15	1 3 36 6 9 36 25 36 15	4 6 3 9 10 36 25 1 15	7 11 10 13 13 1 25 1 15	10 15 13 15 15 1 25 1 15	13 19 12 18 16 1 25 1 15	16 24 16 18 18 36 35 36 15	20 27 21 16 20 36 25 36 15	22 31 24 18 22 36 25 36 15	26 35 24 21 24 36 26 36 15
3	29 28 27 30 5 33 25 36 15	33 34 33 34 6 34 25 36 15	34 34 36 1 7 34 25 36 15	1 4 36 6 9 36 25 36 15	4 7 3 9 10 36 25 1 15	7 12 10 13 13 1 25 1 15	10 16 13 15 15 1 25 1 15	13 20 12 18 16 1 25 1 15	16 25 16 18 18 36 25 36 15	20 28 22 16 20 36 25 36 15	22 33 24 18 22 36 25 36 15	26 36 24 21 24 36 26 36 15
4	29 30 28 30 5 33 25 36 15	33 36 33 34 6 34 25 36 15	34 36 36 1 7 34 25 36 15	1 6 36 6 9 36 25 36 15	4 9 3 9 10 36 25 1 15	7 14 10 13 13 1 25 1 15	10 17 13 15 15 1 25 1 15	13 21 12 18 16 1 25 1 15	17 26 18 18 18 36 24 36 15	20 29 22 16 20 36 25 36 15	22 34 24 18 22 36 25 36 15	26 2 24 21 24 36 26 36 15
5	29 32 28 30 5 33 25 36 15	33 1 33 34 6 34 25 36 15	34 1 36 1 7 34 25 36 15	1 7 36 6 9 36 25 36 15	4 10 3 9 10 36 25 1 15	8 15 10 13 13 1 25 1 15	10 18 13 16 15 1 25 1 15	13 22 12 18 16 1 25 1 15	17 27 18 18 18 36 24 36 15	20 30 22 16 20 36 25 36 15	22 36 24 18 22 36 25 36 15	26 3 24 21 24 36 26 36 15
6	29 33 28 30 5 33 25 36 15	33 2 33 34 6 34 25 36 15	34 3 36 1 7 34 25 36 15	1 8 36 6 9 36 25 36 15	4 12 4 9 10 36 25 1 15	8 16 10 13 13 1 25 1 15	11 19 13 16 15 1 25 1 15	14 24 12 18 16 1 25 1 15	17 28 18 18 18 36 24 36 15	20 32 22 16 20 36 25 36 15	22 1 24 18 22 36 25 36 15	26 4 24 21 24 36 26 36 15
7	30 34 28 30 5 33 25 36 15	33 3 33 34 6 34 25 36 15	34 4 36 1 7 34 25 36 15	3 9 36 6 9 36 25 36 15	6 13 4 9 12 36 25 1 15	8 17 10 13 13 1 25 1 15	11 21 13 16 15 1 25 1 15	14 25 12 18 16 1 25 1 15	17 30 18 17 18 36 24 36 15	20 33 22 16 20 36 25 36 15	22 3 24 18 22 36 25 36 15	26 6 24 21 24 36 26 36 15
8	30 36 28 30 5 33 25 36 15	33 5 33 34 6 34 25 36 15	34 6 36 1 7 34 25 36 15	3 11 36 6 9 36 25 36 15	6 14 4 9 12 36 25 1 15	8 19 10 13 13 1 25 1 15	11 22 13 16 15 1 25 1 15	14 26 12 18 16 1 25 1 15	17 31 18 17 18 36 24 36 15	20 34 22 16 20 36 25 36 15	22 4 22 18 22 36 25 36 15	26 8 24 21 25 36 26 36 15
9	30 1 28 31 4 33 25 36 15	33 6 33 34 6 34 25 36 15	35 7 36 1 7 34 25 36 15	3 12 36 6 9 36 25 36 15	6 15 4 9 12 36 25 1 15	9 20 10 13 13 1 25 1 15	11 23 13 16 15 1 25 1 15	14 27 12 18 16 1 25 1 15	17 33 18 17 18 36 24 36 15	20 36 22 16 20 36 25 36 15	24 6 22 18 24 36 25 36 15	26 9 25 22 25 36 26 36 15
10	30 3 28 31 4 33 25 36 15	33 7 34 34 6 34 25 36 15	35 9 36 1 7 34 25 36 15	3 13 36 6 9 36 25 36 15	6 16 4 10 12 36 25 1 15	9 21 10 13 13 1 25 1 15	11 24 13 16 15 1 25 1 15	14 28 12 18 16 1 25 1 15	17 34 18 17 18 36 24 36 15	20 2 22 16 20 36 25 36 15	24 7 24 19 24 36 25 36 15	26 11 25 22 25 36 26 36 15
11	30 4 28 31 4 33 25 36 15	33 9 34 34 6 34 25 36 15	36 10 36 1 7 34 25 36 15	3 15 36 6 9 36 25 36 15	6 18 4 10 12 36 25 1 15	9 22 10 13 13 1 25 1 15	11 25 13 16 15 1 25 1 15	15 30 13 18 17 1 25 1 15	17 36 18 17 18 36 24 36 15	20 3 22 16 20 36 25 36 15	24 9 24 19 24 36 25 36 15	26 12 26 22 26 36 26 36 15
12	30 4 28 31 4 33 25 36 15	33 10 34 34 6 34 25 36 15	36 11 36 2 7 34 25 36 15	3 16 36 6 9 36 25 36 15	6 19 4 10 12 36 25 1 15	9 24 11 13 13 1 25 1 15	11 27 13 16 15 1 25 1 15	15 31 13 18 17 1 25 1 15	17 1 18 17 18 36 24 36 15	21 4 22 16 21 36 25 36 15	24 10 24 19 24 36 25 36 15	26 13 26 22 26 36 26 36 15
13	30 7 28 31 4 33 25 36 15	33 12 34 34 6 34 25 36 15	36 12 36 2 7 34 25 36 15	3 18 36 6 9 36 25 36 15	6 20 4 10 12 36 25 1 15	9 25 11 13 13 1 25 1 15	12 28 13 16 15 1 25 1 15	15 33 13 18 17 1 25 1 15	17 3 18 17 18 36 24 36 15	21 6 22 16 21 36 25 36 15	24 12 24 19 24 36 25 36 15	26 15 26 22 26 36 26 36 15
14	30 8 28 31 4 33 25 36 15	33 13 34 35 6 34 25 36 15	35 13 36 2 7 34 25 36 15	3 18 36 6 9 36 25 36 15	6 21 6 10 12 36 25 1 15	9 26 11 13 13 1 25 1 15	12 30 13 16 15 1 25 1 15	15 34 13 18 17 1 25 1 15	17 4 18 17 18 36 24 36 15	21 7 22 16 21 36 25 36 15	24 13 24 19 24 36 25 36 15	27 17 26 22 26 36 26 36 15
15	30 9 28 31 4 33 25 36 15	33 14 34 35 6 34 25 36 15	36 15 36 2 7 34 25 36 15	3 19 36 6 9 36 25 36 15	6 22 6 10 12 36 25 1 15	9 27 11 13 13 1 25 1 15	12 31 13 16 15 1 25 1 15	15 36 13 18 17 1 25 1 15	17 6 18 17 18 36 25 36 15	21 9 22 16 21 36 25 36 15	24 15 24 19 24 36 25 36 15	27 18 26 22 26 36 26 36 15
16	30 10 29 31 4 33 25 36 15	33 15 34 35 6 34 25 36 15	36 16 36 2 7 34 25 36 15	3 21 36 6 9 36 25 36 15	6 24 6 10 12 36 25 1 15	9 28 11 13 13 1 25 1 15	12 33 13 16 15 1 25 1 15	15 1 13 18 17 1 25 1 15	17 7 18 17 18 36 25 36 15	21 10 22 16 21 36 25 36 15	24 15 24 19 24 36 25 36 15	27 18 26 22 26 36 26 36 15
17	30 12 29 31 4 33 25 36 15	33 16 34 36 6 34 25 36 15	36 17 36 2 7 34 25 36 15	3 22 1 7 10 36 25 1 15	6 25 6 10 12 36 25 1 15	9 30 11 13 13 1 25 1 15	12 34 13 16 15 1 25 1 15	15 3 13 18 17 1. 24 1 15	17 8 18 17 18 36 24 36 15	21 12 22 16 21 36 25 36 15	24 16 24 19 24 36 25 36 15	27 20 26 22 26 36 26 36 15
18	30 13 29 31 4 34 25 36 15	33 18 34 36 6 34 25 36 15	36 18 36 2 7 34 25 36 15	3 23 1 7 10 36 25 1 15	6 26 6 10 12 36 25 1 15	9 31 12 13 13 1 25 1 15	12 35 13 16 15 1 25 1 15	15 4 13 18 17 1 24 1 15	18 9 18 17 18 36 24 36 15	21 13 22 16 21 36 25 36 15	24 18 24 19 24 36 25 36 15	27 21 26 22 26 36 26 36 15
19	30 13 29 31 4 34 25 36 15	33 19 34 36 6 34 25 36 15	36 19 36 2 7 34 25 36 15	3 24 1 7 10 36 25 1 15	6 27 6 10 12 36 25 1 15	9 33 12 13 13 1 25 1 15	12 36 13 16 15 1 25 1 15	15 6 13 18 17 1 24 1 15	18 11 18 17 18 36 24 36 15	21 15 24 18 21 36 25 36 15	24 19 24 19 24 36 25 36 15	27 22 26 22 26 36 26 36 15
20	31 15 29 31 4 34 25 36 15	34 20 36 36 7 34 25 36 15	36 21 36 2 7 34 25 36 15	3 25 1 7 10 36 25 1 15	6 30 6 10 12 36 25 1 15	9 34 12 13 13 1 25 1 15	12 2 13 17 15 1 25 1 15	15 7 14 18 18 1 24 1 15	18 12 18 16 18 36 25 36 15	21 16 24 18 21 36 25 36 15	24 20 24 19 24 36 25 36 15	27 23 26 22 26 36 26 36 15
21	31 16 29 33 6 34 25 36 15	34 21 36 36 7 34 25 36 15	36 22 36 2 7 34 25 36 15	4 27 1 7 10 36 25 1 15	6 30 6 10 12 36 25 1 15	9 36 13 13 13 1 25 1 15	12 3 13 17 15 1 25 1 15	15 9 14 18 18 1 24 1 15	18 13 18 16 18 36 25 36 15	21 18 24 18 21 36 25 36 15	24 21 24 19 24 36 25 36 15	27 24 26 22 26 36 26 36 15
22	31 18 29 33 6 34 25 36 15	34 22 36 36 7 34 25 36 15	1 23 34 1 7 34 25 36 15	4 28 1 7 10 36 25 1 15	7 31 7 12 12 36 25 1 15	10 1 13 13 13 1 25 1 15	12 5 13 17 15 1 25 1 15	15 10 15 18 18 1 24 1 15	18 15 18 16 18 36 25 36 15	22 18 24 18 22 36 25 36 15	24 22 24 19 24 36 25 36 15	27 26 26 22 26 36 26 36 15
23	31 19 31 33 6 34 25 36 15	34 24 36 36 7 34 25 36 15	1 24 34 4 7 34 25 36 15	4 29 1 7 10 36 25 1 15	7 33 7 12 12 36 25 1 15	10 2 13 13 13 1 25 1 15	12 6 13 17 15 1 25 1 15	15 11 15 18 18 1 24 1 15	19 16 19 16 19 1 25 1 15	22 19 24 18 22 36 25 36 15	25 24 24 19 24 36 25 36 15	28 27 26 22 26 36 26 36 15
24	31 20 31 33 6 34 25 36 15	34 25 36 36 7 34 25 36 15	1 25 34 4 7 34 25 36 15	4 30 1 7 10 36 25 1 15	7 34 7 12 12 36 25 1 15	10 4 13 13 13 1 25 1 15	13 7 13 17 15 1 25 1 15	16 13 15 18 18 1 25 1 15	19 17 21 16 19 1 25 1 15	22 20 24 18 22 36 25 36 15	25 25 24 19 24 36 25 36 15	28 28 27 22 26 36 26 36 15
25	31 21 31 33 6 34 25 36 15	34 26 36 36 7 34 25 36 15	1 27 35 4 8 35 25 36 15	4 32 1 7 10 36 25 1 15	7 36 7 12 12 36 25 1 15	10 4 13 15 15 1 25 1 15	13 9 12 17 16 1 25 1 15	16 14 15 18 18 1 25 1 15	19 18 21 16 19 1 25 1 15	22 22 24 18 22 36 25 36 15	25 26 24 19 24 36 25 36 15	29 30 27 22 26 36 26 36 15
26	31 24 31 33 6 34 25 36 15	34 27 36 36 7 34 25 36 15	1 28 35 4 8 35 25 36 15	4 35 1 7 10 36 25 1 15	7 1 7 12 12 36 25 1 15	10 6 13 15 15 1 25 1 15	13 10 12 17 16 1 25 1 15	16 15 15 18 18 1 25 1 15	19 19 21 16 19 1 25 1 15	22 23 24 18 22 36 25 36 15	25 27 24 19 24 36 25 36 15	29 31 27 22 26 36 26 36 15
27	31 24 31 33 6 34 25 36 15	34 28 36 1 8 34 25 36 15	1 30 35 4 8 35 25 36 15	4 34 1 7 10 36 25 1 15	7 2 7 12 12 36 25 1 15	10 7 13 15 15 1 25 1 15	13 12 12 17 16 1 25 1 15	16 16 15 18 18 1 25 1 15	19 21 21 16 19 1 25 1 15	22 24 24 18 22 36 25 36 15	25 28 24 19 24 36 25 36 15	28 32 27 22 26 36 26 36 15
28	31 25 31 33 6 34 25 36 15	34 30 36 1 7 34 25 36 15	1 31 35 4 8 35 25 36 15	4 34 3 7 10 36 25 1 15	7 4 9 12 12 36 25 1 15	10 9 13 15 15 1 25 1 15	13 13 12 17 16 1 25 1 15	16 18 15 18 18 1 25 1 15	19 22 21 16 19 1 25 1 15	22 25 24 18 22 36 25 36 15	25 30 24 19 24 36 25 36 15	28 33 27 22 26 36 26 36 15
29	31 27 31 33 6 34 25 36 15		1 33 35 5 8 35 25 36 15	4 1 3 7 10 36 25 1 15	7 6 9 12 12 36 25 1 15	10 10 13 15 15 1 25 1 15	13 14 12 17 16 1 25 1 15	16 19 16 18 18 1 25 1 15	19 23 21 16 19 1 25 1 15	22 27 24 18 22 36 25 36 15	25 31 24 21 24 36 25 36 15	28 35 27 22 26 36 26 36 15
30	31 28 31 33 6 34 25 36 15	1927	1 34 35 5 8 35 25 36 15	4 3 3 9 10 36 25 1 15	7 7 9 12 12 36 25 1 15	10 12 13 15 15 1 25 1 15	13 15 12 17 16 1 25 1 15	16 20 16 18 18 1 25 1 15	19 24 21 16 19 1 25 1 15	22 29 24 18 22 36 25 36 15	25 33 24 21 24 36 25 36 15	28 36 27 22 26 36 26 36 15
31	33 29 33 33 6 34 25 36 15		1 36 35 5 8 35 25 36 15		7 8 9 12 12 36 25 1 15		13 16 12 17 16 1 25 1 15	16 21 16 18 18 1 25 1 15		22 29 24 18 22 36 25 36 15		28 2 27 22 26 36 26 36 15

	JAN	FEB	MAR	APR	MAY	JUNE	JULY	AUG	SEPT	OCT	NOV	DEC
1	28 3 28 24 26 36 26 36 15	32 8 33 28 28 1 26 1 15	35 11 33 31 31 1 26 1 15	2 16 35 35 33 1 26 2 15	4 19 4 3 36 3 27 1 15	8 24 11 8 2 3 26 2 15	10 26 10 10 4 4 26 1 15	14 31 12 15 6 4 26 1 15	17 36 18 18 8 5 26 1 15	19 4 22 22 10 4 26 1 16	22 10 21 26 10 4 26 1 16	26 13 25 29 10 4 26 1 16
2	29 4 29 24 26 36 26 36 15	32 10 33 28 28 1 26 1 15	35 12 33 31 31 1 26 1 15	2 17 35 35 33 1 26 2 15	5 20 5 3 36 3 27 1 15	8 25 11 8 2 3 26 2 15	10 28 10 10 4 4 26 1 15	14 33 12 15 6 4 26 1 15	17 1 18 18 8 5 26 1 15	19 6 22 22 10 4 26 1 16	22 11 22 26 10 4 26 1 16	26 14 25 29 10 4 26 1 16
3	29 6 29 24 26 36 26 36 15	32 11 33 28 28 1 26 1 15	35 13 33 31 31 1 26 1 15	2 18 35 35 33 1 26 2 15	5 21 5 3 36 3 27 1 15	8 26 11 8 2 3 26 2 15	10 29 10 10 4 4 26 1 15	14 34 12 15 6 4 26 1 15	17 3 18 18 8 5 26 1 15	20 8 22 22 10 4 26 1 16	22 12 22 26 10 4 26 1 16	26 16 25 29 10 4 26 1 16
4	29 8 29 25 26 36 26 36 15	32 12 33 28 28 1 26 1 15	35 15 33 31 31 1 26 1 15	2 19 35 35 33 1 26 2 15	5 23 5 3 36 3 27 1 15	8 27 11 8 2 4 26 2 15	10 31 10 10 4 4 26 1 15	14 36 13 15 6 4 26 1 15	17 5 18 18 8 5 26 1 15	20 8 22 22 10 4 26 1 16	22 14 22 26 10 4 26 1 16	26 17 25 30 10 4 26 1 16
5	29 9 29 25 26 36 26 36 15	32 14 33 29 29 1 26 1 15	35 16 33 32 31 1 26 1 15	2 20 35 35 33 1 26 2 15	5 24 5 3 36 3 27 1 15	8 28 10 8 2 4 26 1 15	10 31 10 10 4 4 26 1 15	14 1 13 15 6 4 26 1 15	17 6 19 19 8 5 26 1 15	20 10 22 22 10 4 26 1 16	22 15 22 26 10 4 26 1 16	26 19 25 30 10 4 26 1 16
6	29 10 29 26 27 36 26 36 15	32 15 33 29 29 1 26 1 15	35 17 33 32 31 1 26 1 15	2 22 35 35 33 1 26 2 15	6 25 6 4 36 3 27 1 15	8 30 10 8 2 4 26 1 15	10 33 10 10 4 4 26 1 15	14 2 13 15 6 4 26 1 15	17 8 19 19 8 5 26 1 15	20 11 22 22 10 4 26 1 16	22 16 22 26 10 4 26 1 16	26 20 25 30 10 4 26 1 16
7	29 12 29 26 27 36 26 36 15	32 17 34 28 28 1 26 1 15	35 18 33 32 31 1 26 1 15	2 23 35 35 33 1 26 2 15	6 27 6 4 36 3 27 1 15	8 31 10 8 2 4 26 1 15	10 35 10 10 4 4 26 1 15	14 3 13 15 6 4 26 1 15	17 8 19 19 8 5 26 1 15	20 13 22 22 10 4 26 1 16	22 17 22 26 10 4 26 1 16	26 21 25 30 10 4 26 1 16
8	29 13 29 26 27 36 26 36 15	32 18 34 28 28 1 26 1 15	35 20 33 32 31 1 26 1 15	2 24 35 35 33 1 26 2 15	6 27 6 4 36 3 27 1 15	8 32 10 8 2 4 26 1 15	10 36 10 10 4 4 26 1 15	14 4 13 15 6 4 26 1 15	17 10 19 19 8 5 26 1 15	20 14 22 22 10 4 26 1 16	23 19 22 26 10 4 26 1 16	26 22 25 31 10 4 26 1 16
9	29 14 29 26 27 36 26 36 15	33 19 34 28 28 1 26 1 15	35 21 33 33 31 1 26 1 15	2 25 35 35 33 1 26 2 15	6 29 6 4 36 3 27 1 15	8 33 10 8 2 4 26 1 15	10 1 10 10 4 4 26 1 15	14 6 13 16 7 4 26 1 15	17 12 19 19 8 5 26 1 15	20 15 22 22 10 4 26 1 16	23 20 22 26 10 4 26 1 16	26 24 26 31 10 4 26 1 16
10	30 16 30 26 27 36 26 36 15	33 20 35 28 28 1 26 1 15	35 22 33 33 31 1 26 1 15	2 26 35 35 33 1 26 2 15	6 30 7 4 36 3 27 1 15	8 36 10 8 2 4 26 1 15	11 2 10 11 4 4 26 1 15	14 8 13 16 7 4 26 1 15	17 13 19 19 8 5 26 1 15	20 17 22 22 10 4 26 1 16	23 21 22 26 10 4 26 1 16	26 25 26 31 10 4 26 1 16
11	30 17 30 26 27 36 26 36 15	33 21 35 28 28 1 26 1 15	35 23 33 33 31 1 26 1 15	2 28 1 1 33 1 26 2 15	6 31 7 4 36 3 27 1 15	8 36 10 8 2 4 26 1 15	11 4 10 11 4 4 26 1 15	14 9 13 16 7 4 26 1 15	17 15 19 19 8 5 26 1 15	20 18 22 22 10 4 26 1 16	23 22 22 26 10 4 26 1 16	26 26 26 31 10 4 26 1 16
12	30 18 30 26 27 36 26 36 15	33 22 35 28 28 1 26 1 15	35 24 33 33 31 1 26 1 15	2 29 1 1 33 1 26 2 15	6 33 7 4 36 3 27 1 15	8 1 10 8 2 4 26 1 15	11 6 10 11 4 4 26 1 15	14 11 13 16 7 4 26 1 15	17 16 19 19 8 5 26 1 15	20 19 22 22 10 4 26 1 16	23 24 22 26 10 4 26 1 16	27 27 27 31 9 4 27 1 16
13	30 19 30 26 27 36 26 36 15	33 24 35 28 28 1 26 1 15	35 26 33 33 31 1 26 1 15	2 30 1 1 33 1 26 2 15	6 34 7 4 36 3 27 1 15	8 3 10 8 2 4 26 1 15	11 7 10 11 4 4 26 1 15	14 12 13 16 7 4 26 1 15	17 17 19 19 8 5 26 1 15	20 20 22 22 10 4 26 1 16	23 25 22 26 10 4 26 1 16	27 28 27 31 9 4 27 1 16
14	30 21 30 26 27 36 26 36 15	33 25 35 28 28 1 26 1 15	35 26 33 33 31 1 26 1 15	2 31 1 1 34 1 26 2 15	6 36 7 4 36 3 27 1 15	8 4 10 8 2 4 26 1 15	11 8 10 11 4 4 26 1 15	15 13 13 17 8 4 26 1 15	17 17 19 19 8 5 26 1 15	20 22 22 22 10 4 26 1 16	23 26 22 26 10 4 26 1 16	27 29 27 31 9 4 27 1 16
15	30 22 30 26 27 36 26 36 15	33 26 35 30 30 1 26 1 15	35 28 33 33 31 1 26 1 15	2 32 1 1 34 1 26 2 15	6 36 7 4 34 3 27 1 15	8 6 10 8 2 4 26 1 15	11 10 10 11 4 4 26 1 15	15 15 15 17 8 4 26 1 15	17 19 19 19 8 5 26 1 15	20 23 22 23 10 4 26 1 16	23 27 22 26 10 4 26 1 16	27 31 27 31 9 4 27 1 16
16	30 23 30 26 27 36 26 36 15	33 27 35 30 30 1 26 1 15	35 29 33 33 31 1 26 1 15	2 34 1 1 34 1 26 2 15	6 1 9 4 36 3 27 1 15	9 8 10 8 2 4 26 1 15	12 11 10 12 4 4 26 1 15	15 17 15 17 8 4 26 1 15	17 21 19 19 8 5 26 1 15	20 24 22 23 10 4 26 1 16	24 28 22 26 10 4 26 1 16	27 32 27 31 9 4 27 1 16
17	30 24 31 26 27 36 26 36 15	33 28 35 30 30 1 26 1 15	35 31 33 33 31 1 26 1 15	2 35 1 1 34 1 26 2 15	6 3 9 4 1 3 27 1 15	9 8 10 8 2 4 26 1 15	12 12 10 12 4 4 26 1 15	15 18 15 17 8 4 26 1 15	17 22 20 20 8 4 26 1 15	20 26 22 23 10 4 26 1 16	24 30 22 28 10 4 26 1 16	27 33 27 31 9 4 27 1 16
18	30 26 31 26 27 36 26 36 15	33 30 35 30 30 1 26 1 15	35 32 33 33 31 1 26 1 15	2 1 1 1 34 1 26 2 15	6 5 9 4 1 3 27 1 15	9 10 10 8 3 4 26 1 15	12 14 10 12 4 4 26 1 15	15 19 15 17 8 4 26 1 15	17 23 20 20 8 4 26 1 15	20 26 22 23 10 4 26 1 16	24 31 22 28 10 4 26 1 16	27 34 27 31 9 4 27 1 16
19	30 27 31 26 27 36 26 36 15	33 31 35 31 31 1 26 1 15	35 33 33 33 32 1 26 2 15	2 2 1 1 35 1 26 2 15	6 6 9 4 1 3 27 1 15	9 12 10 9 3 4 26 1 15	12 15 10 12 4 4 26 1 15	15 20 15 17 8 4 26 1 15	18 24 20 20 9 4 26 1 15	20 28 22 23 10 4 26 1 16	24 32 22 28 10 4 26 1 16	27 36 27 31 9 4 27 1 16
20	30 28 32 26 27 36 26 36 15	34 33 34 31 31 1 26 1 15	35 35 33 33 32 1 26 2 15	4 4 2 2 35 1 26 2 15	6 9 9 6 1 3 27 1 15	9 13 10 9 3 4 26 1 15	12 17 10 12 6 4 26 1 15	15 21 17 17 8 4 26 1 15	18 26 20 20 9 4 26 1 16	20 29 22 23 10 4 26 1 16	24 33 23 28 10 4 26 1 16	27 1 27 32 9 4 27 1 16
21	31 29 32 26 28 1 26 1 15	34 34 34 31 31 1 26 1 15	1 36 34 34 32 1 26 2 15	4 6 2 2 35 1 26 2 15	7 9 9 6 1 3 27 1 15	9 15 10 9 3 4 26 1 15	12 18 10 12 6 4 26 1 15	15 22 17 17 8 4 26 1 15	18 27 20 20 9 4 26 1 16	20 30 22 23 10 4 26 1 16	24 35 23 28 10 4 26 1 16	27 3 27 32 9 4 27 1 16
22	31 30 32 26 28 1 26 1 15	34 35 34 31 31 1 26 1 15	1 2 34 34 32 1 26 2 15	4 7 2 2 35 1 26 2 15	7 11 9 6 1 3 27 1 15	10 16 10 10 4 4 26 1 15	12 19 10 12 6 4 26 1 15	15 24 17 17 8 4 26 1 15	18 28 21 21 9 4 26 1 16	20 31 22 23 10 4 26 1 16	24 35 23 28 10 4 26 1 16	28 4 28 32 9 4 27 1 16
23	31 32 32 26 28 1 26 1 15	34 1 34 31 31 1 26 1 15	1 3 34 34 32 1 26 2 15	4 8 2 2 35 1 26 2 15	7 12 9 6 1 3 27 1 15	10 17 10 10 4 4 26 1 15	13 21 10 13 6 4 26 1 15	17 25 17 17 8 5 26 1 15	19 29 22 22 10 4 26 1 16	20 32 22 23 10 4 26 1 16	25 1 23 28 10 4 26 1 16	28 5 28 32 9 4 27 1 16
24	31 33 32 26 29 1 26 1 15	34 2 34 31 31 1 26 1 15	1 5 34 34 33 1 26 2 15	4 10 2 2 35 1 26 2 15	7 13 9 6 1 3 27 1 15	10 18 10 10 4 4 26 1 15	13 22 10 13 6 4 26 1 15	17 26 17 17 8 5 26 1 15	19 30 22 22 10 4 26 1 16	22 33 22 25 10 4 26 1 16	25 3 23 28 10 4 26 1 16	28 7 28 32 9 4 27 1 16
25	31 35 32 26 28 1 26 1 15	34 4 34 31 31 1 26 1 15	1 6 34 34 33 1 26 2 15	4 12 2 2 35 1 26 2 15	7 15 9 6 1 3 27 1 15	10 20 10 10 4 4 26 1 15	13 23 10 13 6 4 26 1 15	17 27 17 17 8 5 26 1 15	19 31 22 22 10 4 26 1 16	22 34 21 25 10 4 26 1 16	25 4 23 28 10 4 26 1 16	28 9 28 32 9 4 27 1 16
26	31 36 32 27 28 1 26 1 15	34 6 33 31 31 1 26 1 15	1 7 35 35 32 1 26 2 15	4 13 2 2 35 1 26 2 15	7 16 9 6 2 3 26 2 15	10 21 10 10 4 4 26 1 15	13 24 10 13 6 4 26 1 15	17 28 17 17 8 5 26 1 15	19 33 22 22 10 4 26 1 16	22 1 21 25 10 4 26 1 16	25 6 23 28 10 4 26 1 16	28 10 28 32 9 4 27 1 16
27	31 1 32 27 28 1 26 1 15	34 7 33 31 31 1 26 1 15	1 8 35 35 32 1 26 2 15	4 14 4 2 35 1 26 2 15	7 18 9 6 2 3 26 2 15	10 22 10 10 4 4 26 1 15	13 26 10 13 6 4 26 1 15	17 30 17 17 8 5 26 1 15	19 34 22 22 10 4 26 1 16	22 2 21 25 10 4 26 1 16	25 7 23 28 10 4 26 1 16	28 12 28 32 9 4 27 1 16
28	31 3 33 27 28 1 26 1 15	34 8 33 31 31 1 26 1 15	1 10 35 35 32 1 26 2 15	4 15 4 2 35 1 26 2 15	7 19 9 6 2 3 26 2 15	10 23 10 10 4 4 26 1 15	13 27 10 13 6 4 26 1 15	17 31 17 17 8 5 26 1 15	19 36 22 22 10 4 26 1 16	22 4 21 25 10 4 26 1 16	25 8 24 29 10 4 26 1 16	28 13 29 33 9 4 27 1 16
29	31 4 33 28 28 1 26 1 15	34 9 33 31 31 1 26 1 15	1 11 35 35 32 1 26 2 15	4 16 4 2 35 1 26 2 15	8 20 11 6 2 3 26 2 15	10 24 10 10 4 4 26 1 15	13 28 10 13 6 4 26 1 15	17 32 17 17 8 5 26 1 15	19 1 22 22 10 4 26 1 16	22 5 21 26 10 4 26 1 16	25 9 24 29 10 4 26 1 16	28 14 29 33 9 4 27 1 16
30	31 6 33 28 28 1 26 1 15	**1928**	1 13 35 35 32 1 26 2 15	4 17 4 2 35 1 26 2 15	8 21 11 8 2 3 26 2 15	10 26 10 10 4 4 26 1 15	13 29 10 13 6 4 26 1 15	17 33 17 17 8 5 26 1 15	19 3 22 22 10 4 26 1 16	22 6 21 26 10 4 26 1 16	25 12 24 29 10 4 26 1 16	28 16 29 33 9 4 27 1 16
31	31 7 33 28 28 1 26 1 15		1 14 35 35 32 1 26 2 15		8 22 11 8 2 3 26 2 15		13 30 12 13 6 4 26 1 15	17 35 17 17 8 5 26 1 15		22 8 21 26 10 4 26 1 16		28 17 29 33 9 4 27 1 16

	JAN	FEB	MAR	APR	MAY	JUNE
1	28 18 28 33 9 4 27 1 16	33 23 33 36 9 4 27 1 16	34 24 32 3 9 4 27 1 16	1 28 36 4 10 4 28 1 15	5 31 6 3 11 6 27 1 15	8 36 9 3 14 6 27 2 15
2	29 19 29 33 9 4 27 1 16	33 24 33 36 9 4 27 1 16	34 25 32 3 9 4 27 1 16	1 29 36 4 10 4 28 1 15	5 32 6 3 11 6 27 1 15	8 2 9 3 14 6 27 2 15
3	29 21 29 33 9 4 27 1 16	33 25 33 31 9 4 27 1 16	34 26 32 3 9 4 27 1 16	1 30 36 4 10 4 28 1 15	5 33 6 3 11 6 27 1 15	8 3 9 4 14 6 27 2 15
4	29 22 29 33 9 4 27 1 16	33 27 33 1 9 4 27 1 16	34 27 32 3 9 4 27 1 16	1 31 1 4 10 4 28 1 15	5 35 7 3 11 6 27 1 15	8 4 9 4 14 6 27 2 15
5	29 23 30 33 9 4 27 1 16	33 27 33 1 9 4 27 1 16	34 28 33 3 9 4 27 1 16	1 33 1 4 10 4 28 1 15	5 36 7 3 11 6 27 1 15	8 6 9 4 14 6 27 2 15
6	29 24 30 34 9 4 27 1 16	33 28 33 1 9 4 27 1 16	34 30 33 3 9 4 27 1 16	1 34 1 4 10 4 28 1 15	5 1 7 3 11 6 27 1 15	8 7 9 4 14 6 27 2 15
7	29 25 30 34 9 4 27 1 16	33 30 33 1 9 4 27 1 16	35 31 33 3 9 4 27 1 16	1 36 1 4 10 4 28 1 15	5 3 7 3 11 6 27 1 15	8 9 9 4 14 6 27 2 15
8	29 27 31 34 9 4 27 1 16	33 31 33 1 9 4 27 1 16	35 32 33 4 9 4 27 1 16	1 1 1 4 10 4 28 1 15	5 4 7 3 11 6 27 1 15	8 10 9 4 14 6 27 2 15
9	29 28 31 34 9 4 27 1 16	33 33 33 1 9 4 27 1 16	35 33 33 4 9 4 27 1 16	1 2 1 4 10 5 28 1 15	5 5 7 3 11 6 27 1 15	8 12 9 4 14 6 27 2 15
10	29 29 31 34 9 4 27 1 16	33 34 33 1 9 4 27 1 16	35 34 33 4 9 4 27 1 16	3 4 1 4 10 5 27 1 15	5 7 7 3 11 6 27 1 15	8 13 8 4 14 6 27 2 15
11	30 30 31 34 9 4 27 1 16	33 36 33 1 9 4 27 1 16	36 36 33 4 9 4 27 1 16	3 5 1 4 10 5 27 1 15	5 9 7 3 11 6 27 1 15	9 15 8 4 15 6 27 2 15
12	30 31 31 34 9 4 27 1 16	33 36 33 1 9 4 27 1 16	36 1 33 4 9 4 27 1 16	3 6 1 4 10 5 27 1 15	5 10 7 3 11 6 27 1 15	9 16 8 4 15 7 27 2 15
13	30 33 31 34 9 4 27 1 16	33 1 31 1 9 4 27 1 16	36 3 33 4 9 4 27 1 16	3 7 3 4 10 5 27 1 15	5 12 7 3 12 6 27 1 15	9 17 8 4 15 7 27 2 15
14	30 34 32 35 9 4 27 1 16	33 3 31 1 9 4 27 1 16	36 4 33 4 9 4 27 1 16	3 9 3 3 10 5 27 1 15	5 13 7 3 12 6 27 1 15	9 18 8 4 15 7 27 2 15
15	30 36 32 35 9 4 27 1 16	33 4 31 1 9 4 27 1 16	36 6 33 4 9 4 27 1 16	3 10 3 3 10 5 27 1 15	5 15 7 3 13 6 27 1 15	9 20 8 4 15 7 27 2 15
16	30 1 32 35 9 4 27 1 16	33 6 31 1 9 4 27 1 16	36 7 34 4 9 4 27 1 16	3 12 3 3 10 5 27 1 15	5 16 7 3 13 6 27 1 15	9 21 8 4 15 7 27 2 15
17	30 2 33 36 9 4 27 1 16	33 7 31 1 9 4 27 1 16	36 8 34 4 9 4 27 1 16	3 13 3 3 10 5 27 1 15	5 17 7 3 13 6 27 1 15	9 22 8 5 15 7 27 2 15
18	30 3 33 36 9 4 27 1 16	33 9 31 3 9 4 27 1 16	36 9 34 4 9 4 27 1 16	3 15 3 3 10 5 27 1 15	5 18 7 3 13 6 27 1 15	9 24 8 5 15 7 27 2 15
19	30 6 33 36 9 4 27 1 15	34 10 31 3 9 4 27 1 16	36 10 34 4 9 4 27 1 16	3 16 3 3 10 5 27 1 15	5 21 7 3 13 6 27 1 15	9 24 8 6 15 7 27 2 15
20	31 6 33 36 9 4 27 1 15	34 12 31 3 9 4 27 1 16	36 12 34 4 9 4 27 1 16	4 18 4 4 11 5 27 1 15	5 21 9 3 13 6 27 1 15	9 26 8 6 15 7 27 2 15
21	31 7 33 36 9 4 27 1 15	34 13 31 3 9 4 27 1 16	1 13 34 4 10 4 28 1 15	4 19 4 4 11 5 27 1 15	5 22 9 3 13 6 27 1 15	9 27 8 6 15 7 27 2 15
22	31 9 33 36 9 4 27 1 15	34 15 31 3 9 4 27 1 16	1 15 34 4 10 4 28 1 15	4 20 4 4 11 5 27 1 15	7 24 9 3 13 6 27 1 15	10 28 8 6 15 7 27 2 15
23	31 10 33 36 9 4 27 1 15	34 16 31 3 9 4 27 1 16	1 16 34 4 10 4 28 1 15	4 21 4 4 11 5 27 1 15	7 25 9 3 13 6 27 1 15	10 29 8 6 15 7 27 2 15
24	31 12 33 36 9 4 27 1 15	34 18 31 3 9 4 27 1 16	1 18 34 4 10 4 28 1 15	4 23 4 4 11 5 27 1 15	7 26 9 3 13 6 27 1 15	10 30 8 6 15 7 27 2 15
25	31 13 33 36 9 4 27 1 15	34 18 31 3 9 4 27 1 16	1 19 34 4 10 4 28 1 15	4 24 4 4 11 5 27 1 15	7 27 9 3 13 6 27 1 15	10 32 8 6 15 7 27 2 15
26	31 15 33 36 9 4 27 1 15	34 19 31 3 9 4 27 1 16	1 21 34 4 10 4 28 1 15	4 25 4 4 11 5 27 1 15	7 28 9 3 13 6 27 1 15	10 33 8 6 15 7 27 2 15
27	31 16 33 36 9 4 27 1 15	34 21 31 3 9 4 27 1 16	1 22 35 4 10 4 28 1 15	4 26 4 4 11 5 27 1 15	7 30 9 3 13 6 27 1 15	10 34 8 6 15 7 27 2 15
28	31 18 33 36 9 4 27 1 15	34 22 31 3 9 4 27 1 16	1 23 35 4 10 4 28 1 15	4 27 4 4 11 5 27 1 15	7 31 9 3 13 6 27 1 15	10 36 8 6 15 7 27 2 15
29	31 19 33 36 9 4 27 1 15		1 24 35 4 10 4 28 1 15	4 28 4 4 11 5 27 1 15	7 32 9 3 13 6 27 1 15	10 1 8 6 15 7 27 2 15
30	31 21 33 36 9 4 27 1 15	**1929**	1 25 35 4 10 4 28 1 15	4 29 4 4 11 5 27 1 15	7 33 9 3 13 6 27 1 15	10 2 8 6 15 7 27 2 15
31	31 22 33 36 9 4 27 1 15		1 27 35 4 10 4 28 1 15		7 34 9 3 13 6 27 1 15	

	JULY	AUG	SEPT	OCT	NOV	DEC
1	10 3 9 6 15 7 27 1 15	14 9 14 9 18 8 27 2 16	16 14 20 14 20 8 27 2 16	19 18 21 16 21 8 27 2 16	23 22 21 19 23 8 27 1 16	26 26 26 24 26 8 28 1 16
2	10 4 9 6 15 7 27 1 15	14 10 14 9 18 8 27 2 16	16 15 20 14 20 8 27 2 16	19 19 21 16 21 8 27 1 16	23 23 21 19 23 8 27 1 16	26 27 26 24 26 8 27 1 16
3	10 6 9 6 15 7 27 1 15	14 11 14 9 18 8 27 2 16	16 16 20 14 20 8 27 2 16	19 21 21 16 21 8 27 1 16	23 25 21 19 23 8 27 1 16	26 28 26 24 26 8 28 1 16
4	10 7 9 6 15 7 27 1 15	14 13 14 9 18 8 27 2 16	17 18 20 14 20 8 27 2 16	19 22 21 16 21 8 27 1 16	23 26 21 21 23 8 27 1 16	26 30 26 24 26 8 28 1 16
5	10 9 9 6 15 7 27 1 15	14 15 14 10 18 8 27 2 16	17 20 20 14 20 8 27 2 16	19 23 21 17 21 8 27 1 16	23 27 21 21 23 8 27 1 16	26 31 26 24 26 8 28 1 16
6	10 10 9 6 15 7 27 1 15	14 16 14 10 18 8 27 2 16	17 21 20 14 20 8 27 2 16	19 24 19 17 22 8 27 1 16	23 28 22 21 23 8 27 1 16	26 32 26 24 26 8 28 1 16
7	10 12 9 6 15 7 27 1 15	14 18 14 10 18 8 27 2 16	18 22 20 14 20 8 27 2 16	19 26 19 17 22 8 27 1 16	23 29 22 21 23 8 27 1 16	27 33 27 25 27 7 28 1 16
8	10 13 9 7 16 7 27 1 15	14 19 14 11 18 8 27 2 16	18 24 20 14 20 8 27 2 16	19 27 19 17 22 8 27 1 16	23 31 22 21 23 8 27 1 16	27 35 27 25 27 7 28 1 16
9	10 15 9 7 16 7 27 1 15	14 20 14 11 18 8 27 2 16	18 25 20 14 20 8 27 2 16	19 28 19 18 22 8 27 1 16	23 32 22 21 23 8 27 1 16	27 36 27 25 27 7 28 1 16
10	10 16 9 7 16 7 27 1 15	14 21 14 11 18 8 27 2 16	18 26 20 14 20 8 27 2 16	19 29 19 18 22 8 27 1 16	23 32 22 21 23 8 27 1 16	27 1 27 25 27 7 28 1 16
11	10 18 10 7 16 7 27 1 15	14 22 14 11 18 8 27 2 16	18 27 20 14 20 8 27 2 16	19 30 19 18 22 8 27 1 16	23 34 22 21 23 8 27 1 16	27 3 27 25 27 7 28 1 16
12	10 19 10 7 16 7 27 1 15	14 24 16 11 18 8 27 2 16	18 28 20 14 20 8 27 2 16	19 31 19 18 22 8 27 1 16	23 36 23 22 23 8 27 1 16	27 3 27 25 27 7 28 1 16
13	10 21 10 7 16 7 27 1 15	14 25 16 11 18 8 27 2 16	18 30 20 14 20 8 27 2 16	21 33 19 18 22 8 27 1 16	24 1 23 22 24 8 27 1 16	27 5 27 25 27 7 28 1 16
14	12 22 10 7 16 7 27 1 15	15 27 16 11 18 8 27 2 16	18 31 21 15 21 8 27 2 16	21 34 19 18 22 8 27 1 16	24 2 23 22 24 8 27 1 16	27 7 28 25 27 7 28 1 16
15	12 23 10 7 16 7 27 1 15	15 27 16 11 18 8 27 2 16	18 32 21 15 21 8 27 2 16	21 35 19 18 22 8 27 1 16	24 4 23 22 24 8 27 1 16	27 8 28 25 27 7 28 1 16
16	12 24 10 7 16 7 27 1 15	15 29 16 11 18 8 27 2 16	18 33 21 15 21 8 27 2 16	21 36 19 18 22 8 27 1 16	24 5 23 22 24 8 27 1 16	27 9 27 25 27 7 27 1 16
17	12 25 10 7 16 7 27 1 15	15 30 17 11 18 8 27 2 15	18 34 21 15 21 8 27 2 16	21 1 19 18 22 8 27 1 16	24 7 23 22 24 8 27 1 16	27 10 27 25 27 7 27 1 16
18	12 27 10 7 16 7 27 1 15	15 31 17 11 18 8 27 2 15	18 36 21 15 21 8 27 2 16	21 3 19 18 22 8 27 1 16	24 8 24 22 23 8 27 1 16	27 12 27 25 27 7 27 1 16
19	12 28 10 7 16 7 27 1 15	15 32 17 11 18 8 27 2 15	18 2 21 15 21 8 27 2 16	21 4 19 19 22 8 27 1 16	24 10 24 22 23 8 27 1 16	27 13 27 27 27 7 27 1 16
20	12 29 10 7 16 7 27 1 15	15 33 18 11 18 8 27 2 15	18 3 21 15 21 8 27 2 16	21 6 19 19 22 8 27 1 16	24 12 24 22 23 8 27 1 16	27 15 27 27 27 7 27 1 16
21	12 30 10 7 16 7 27 1 15	15 35 18 11 18 8 27 2 15	18 4 21 15 21 8 27 2 16	21 8 19 19 22 8 27 1 16	24 13 24 22 23 8 27 1 16	27 16 27 27 27 7 27 1 16
22	12 31 10 7 16 7 27 1 15	15 36 18 11 19 9 27 2 15	18 5 21 15 21 8 27 2 16	21 9 19 19 22 8 27 1 16	24 14 24 22 23 8 27 1 16	28 18 27 28 28 7 28 1 16
23	13 33 12 9 16 7 27 1 15	15 2 18 12 20 8 27 2 15	18 6 21 15 21 8 27 2 16	21 10 19 19 22 8 27 1 16	25 15 25 22 25 8 27 1 16	28 19 27 28 28 7 28 1 16
24	13 34 12 9 16 7 27 1 16	16 3 18 12 20 8 27 2 16	19 8 21 15 21 8 27 1 16	22 12 19 19 22 8 27 1 16	25 17 25 23 25 8 27 1 16	28 21 29 28 28 7 28 1 16
25	13 35 12 9 16 7 27 1 16	16 4 18 12 20 8 27 2 16	19 9 21 15 21 8 27 1 16	22 13 19 19 23 8 27 1 16	25 18 25 23 25 8 27 1 16	28 22 29 28 28 7 28 1 16
26	13 36 12 9 16 7 27 1 16	16 5 18 12 20 8 27 2 16	19 10 21 16 21 8 27 1 16	22 15 19 19 23 8 27 1 16	25 19 25 23 25 8 27 1 16	28 23 29 28 28 7 28 1 16
27	13 1 12 9 16 7 27 1 16	16 7 18 12 20 8 27 2 16	19 12 21 16 21 8 27 1 16	22 16 19 19 23 8 27 1 16	25 21 25 23 25 8 27 1 16	28 24 29 28 28 7 28 1 16
28	13 3 13 9 16 7 27 1 16	16 8 18 12 20 8 27 2 16	19 13 21 16 21 8 27 1 16	22 18 19 19 23 8 27 1 16	25 22 25 23 25 8 27 1 16	28 25 29 28 28 7 28 1 16
29	13 4 13 9 18 7 27 1 16	16 9 18 12 20 8 27 2 16	19 15 21 16 21 8 27 1 16	22 19 21 19 23 8 27 1 16	25 23 25 23 25 8 27 1 16	28 26 29 28 28 7 28 1 16
30	13 6 13 9 18 7 27 1 16	16 11 19 12 20 8 27 2 16	19 16 21 16 21 8 27 1 16	22 20 21 19 23 8 27 1 16	25 25 25 23 25 8 27 1 16	28 28 29 28 28 7 28 1 16
31	13 7 13 9 18 7 27 1 16	16 12 19 12 20 8 27 2 16		22 21 21 19 23 8 27 1 16		28 29 29 28 28 7 28 1 16

	JAN	FEB	MAR	APR	MAY	JUNE	JULY	AUG	SEPT	OCT	NOV	DEC
1	28 30 30 28 28 7 28 1 16	31 35 30 31 30 7 28 1 16	34 36 32 34 32 7 28 1 16	2 5 2 3 35 8 29 2 16	4 8 7 7 1 8 28 1 16	7 13 6 10 3 9 28 1 16	10 18 9 15 6 10 28 1 16	14 22 15 17 8 10 28 2 16	16 27 19 21 10 11 28 2 16	19 30 18 23 11 11 28 1 16	22 35 22 25 13 12 28 1 16	26 2 26 23 14 11 29 2 16
2	28 31 31 28 28 7 28 1 16	31 36 30 31 30 7 28 1 16	34 1 32 34 32 7 28 1 16	2 6 2 3 35 8 29 2 16	4 9 7 7 1 8 28 1 16	7 15 6 10 3 9 28 1 16	10 19 9 15 6 10 28 1 16	14 23 16 17 8 10 28 2 16	16 28 19 21 10 11 28 2 16	19 31 18 23 11 11 28 1 16	22 36 22 25 13 12 28 1 16	26 3 26 23 14 11 29 2 16
3	28 33 31 28 28 7 28 1 16	31 1 30 31 30 7 28 1 16	34 2 32 35 32 7 28 1 16	2 8 2 3 35 8 29 2 16	4 10 7 7 1 8 28 1 16	7 16 6 10 4 9 28 1 16	10 20 10 15 6 10 28 1 16	14 25 16 17 8 10 28 2 16	17 29 19 21 10 11 28 2 16	19 33 18 23 11 11 28 1 16	22 1 22 25 13 12 28 1 16	26 5 26 23 14 11 29 2 16
4	28 34 31 28 28 7 28 1 16	31 3 30 31 30 7 28 1 16	34 3 32 35 32 7 28 1 16	2 8 2 4 35 8 29 2 16	4 12 7 7 1 8 28 1 16	7 18 6 10 4 9 28 1 16	10 21 10 15 6 10 28 1 16	14 26 16 17 8 10 28 2 16	17 31 19 21 10 11 28 2 16	19 34 18 23 11 11 28 1 16	22 3 22 25 13 12 28 1 16	26 5 26 23 14 11 29 2 16
5	28 35 31 28 28 7 28 1 16	31 4 30 31 30 7 28 1 16	34 4 32 35 32 7 28 1 16	2 11 2 4 35 8 29 2 16	4 13 7 7 1 8 28 1 16	7 19 6 10 4 9 28 1 16	10 23 10 15 6 10 28 1 16	14 27 16 17 8 10 28 2 16	17 32 19 21 10 11 28 2 16	19 35 18 23 11 11 29 1 16	22 4 22 25 13 12 28 1 16	26 7 27 23 14 11 29 2 16
6	29 36 31 28 28 7 28 1 16	32 5 30 32 30 7 28 1 16	34 5 33 36 33 7 28 1 16	2 11 3 4 35 8 29 2 16	4 15 7 8 1 8 28 1 16	7 21 6 10 4 9 28 1 16	11 24 11 15 6 10 28 2 16	14 28 16 18 8 10 28 2 16	17 33 19 21 10 11 28 2 16	19 36 18 23 11 11 28 1 16	22 5 22 25 13 12 28 1 16	26 8 27 23 14 11 29 2 16
7	29 1 31 28 28 7 28 1 16	32 6 30 32 31 7 28 1 16	34 7 33 36 33 7 28 1 16	2 13 3 4 35 8 29 2 16	4 16 7 8 1 8 28 1 16	7 22 7 10 4 9 28 1 16	11 25 11 15 6 10 28 2 16	14 29 16 18 8 10 28 2 16	17 34 19 22 10 11 28 2 16	19 1 18 23 11 11 28 1 16	22 6 22 25 13 12 28 1 16	26 11 28 23 14 11 29 2 16
8	29 3 31 28 28 7 28 1 16	32 7 30 32 31 7 28 1 16	34 9 33 36 33 7 28 1 16	2 14 3 4 35 8 29 2 16	4 18 7 8 1 8 28 1 16	7 23 7 10 4 9 28 1 16	11 27 11 16 7 10 28 2 16	14 31 16 18 8 10 28 2 16	17 35 19 22 10 11 28 2 16	19 2 18 23 11 11 28 1 16	22 7 22 25 13 12 28 1 16	26 11 28 23 14 11 29 2 16
9	29 4 31 28 28 7 28 1 16	32 8 30 32 31 7 28 1 16	34 10 33 36 33 7 28 1 16	2 16 3 4 35 8 29 2 16	5 20 7 8 2 8 29 2 16	9 24 7 10 4 9 28 1 16	11 28 11 16 7 10 28 2 16	14 32 16 19 8 10 28 2 16	17 1 19 22 10 11 28 2 16	20 4 18 23 11 12 28 2 16	22 9 22 25 13 12 28 1 16	26 13 28 23 14 11 29 2 16
10	29 6 31 28 28 7 28 1 16	32 10 30 32 31 7 28 1 16	34 12 34 36 33 7 28 1 16	2 17 5 5 35 8 29 2 16	5 21 7 8 2 8 29 2 16	9 25 7 10 4 9 28 1 16	11 29 11 16 7 10 28 2 16	14 33 16 19 8 10 28 2 16	17 2 19 22 10 11 28 2 16	21 6 18 23 12 12 28 3 16	22 10 22 25 13 12 28 1 16	26 14 28 23 14 11 29 2 16
11	30 7 31 28 28 7 28 1 16	32 12 30 32 31 7 28 1 16	36 13 34 36 33 7 28 1 16	2 18 5 5 35 8 29 2 16	5 22 7 8 2 8 29 2 16	9 27 7 12 4 9 28 1 16	11 30 11 16 7 10 28 2 16	14 35 16 19 8 10 28 2 16	17 3 19 22 10 11 28 2 16	21 7 19 35 12 12 28 3 16	22 12 22 25 13 12 28 1 16	26 16 28 23 14 11 29 2 16
12	30 8 31 28 28 7 28 1 16	32 13 30 32 31 7 28 1 16	36 15 34 36 33 7 28 1 16	3 20 5 5 35 8 29 2 16	6 23 7 8 2 8 29 2 16	9 28 7 12 4 9 28 1 16	11 31 11 16 7 10 28 2 16	14 36 16 19 8 10 28 2 16	17 4 19 22 10 11 28 2 16	21 8 19 25 12 12 28 3 16	23 13 23 25 13 12 28 1 16	26 17 28 23 14 11 29 2 16
13	30 10 31 28 28 7 28 1 16	32 14 30 32 31 7 28 1 16	36 16 34 1 33 7 28 1 16	3 21 5 5 35 8 29 2 16	6 25 7 8 2 8 29 2 16	9 29 7 12 4 9 28 1 16	11 33 11 15 6 10 28 2 16	14 1 16 19 8 10 28 2 16	17 5 19 22 10 11 28 2 16	21 9 19 25 12 12 28 3 16	23 15 23 25 13 12 28 1 16	26 19 28 23 14 11 29 2 16
14	30 12 31 28 28 7 28 1 16	32 16 30 32 31 7 28 1 16	36 18 34 1 33 7 28 1 16	3 22 5 5 35 8 29 2 16	6 26 7 8 2 8 29 2 16	9 30 7 12 4 9 28 1 16	11 34 11 16 7 10 28 2 16	14 2 17 19 8 10 28 2 16	17 7 19 23 11 11 28 2 16	21 12 19 25 12 12 28 3 16	23 16 23 25 13 12 28 1 16	26 20 28 23 14 11 29 2 16
15	30 13 31 28 28 7 28 1 16	32 18 30 32 31 7 28 1 16	36 19 34 1 33 7 28 1 16	3 23 5 5 35 8 29 2 16	6 27 7 8 2 8 29 2 16	9 31 7 12 4 9 28 1 16	11 35 11 16 7 10 28 2 16	14 3 18 20 9 11 29 2 16	17 8 19 23 11 11 28 2 16	21 12 19 25 12 12 28 3 16	24 18 24 25 13 12 28 1 16	27 21 28 23 14 11 29 2 16
16	30 15 31 28 28 7 28 1 16	32 19 31 32 31 7 28 1 16	36 21 34 1 33 7 28 1 16	3 25 5 5 35 8 29 1 16	6 29 7 8 2 8 29 2 16	9 33 7 12 4 9 28 1 16	11 36 11 16 7 10 28 2 16	15 5 18 20 9 11 29 2 16	17 10 19 23 11 11 28 2 16	21 13 19 25 12 12 28 2 16	24 19 24 25 13 12 28 1 16	27 23 28 23 14 11 29 2 16
17	30 16 31 28 28 7 28 1 16	32 20 31 32 31 7 28 1 16	36 22 34 1 34 7 28 1 16	3 26 5 5 35 8 29 2 16	6 30 6 8 2 8 29 2 16	9 34 7 12 4 9 28 1 16	11 1 12 16 7 10 28 1 16	15 6 18 20 9 11 29 2 16	17 11 19 23 11 11 28 2 16	21 15 19 25 12 12 28 2 16	24 21 25 25 13 12 28 1 16	27 24 28 23 14 11 29 2 16
18	30 18 31 28 28 7 28 1 16	32 22 31 32 31 7 28 1 16	36 23 34 1 34 7 28 1 16	3 28 5 5 35 8 29 2 16	6 31 6 8 2 8 29 2 16	9 36 7 12 4 9 28 1 16	12 3 12 16 7 10 28 2 16	15 8 18 20 9 11 29 2 16	18 12 19 23 11 11 28 2 16	21 16 19 25 12 12 28 2 16	24 22 25 25 13 12 28 1 16	27 25 28 23 14 11 29 2 16
19	30 19 31 29 29 7 28 1 16	34 24 31 34 31 7 28 1 16	36 24 34 1 34 7 28 1 16	3 29 5 5 36 8 29 2 16	6 32 6 8 2 8 29 2 16	9 1 7 13 4 9 28 1 16	12 4 13 16 7 10 28 2 16	15 9 18 20 9 11 29 2 16	18 14 18 23 11 11 28 2 16	21 18 19 25 12 12 28 2 16	24 23 25 25 13 12 28 1 16	27 26 28 23 14 11 29 2 16
20	30 20 31 29 29 7 28 1 16	34 25 31 34 31 7 28 1 16	36 25 34 1 34 7 28 1 16	3 30 5 5 36 8 29 2 16	6 33 6 8 2 8 29 2 16	9 2 7 13 4 9 28 1 16	12 5 13 16 7 10 28 2 16	15 10 18 20 9 11 29 2 16	18 15 18 23 11 11 28 2 16	21 19 19 25 12 12 28 2 16	24 24 25 25 13 12 28 1 16	27 28 28 23 14 11 29 2 16
21	31 21 31 31 29 7 28 1 16	34 26 31 34 31 7 28 1 16	1 27 34 1 34 7 28 1 16	4 31 5 5 36 8 29 1 16	6 34 6 8 2 8 29 2 16	9 3 7 13 4 9 28 1 16	12 6 13 16 7 9 28 1 16	15 11 18 20 9 11 29 2 16	18 17 18 23 11 11 28 2 16	21 20 21 25 12 12 28 2 16	24 25 25 25 13 12 28 1 16	27 29 28 23 14 11 29 2 16
22	31 23 31 31 29 7 28 1 16	34 27 31 34 31 7 28 1 16	1 28 36 1 34 7 28 1 16	4 32 5 5 36 8 29 2 16	7 35 6 8 2 8 28 2 16	10 4 7 13 4 9 28 1 16	12 7 14 16 7 10 28 2 16	15 13 18 20 9 11 29 2 16	18 19 18 23 11 11 28 2 16	21 22 21 25 12 12 28 2 16	24 27 25 24 13 12 28 1 16	27 30 28 23 14 11 29 2 16
23	31 24 31 31 29 7 28 1 16	34 28 31 34 31 7 28 1 16	1 29 36 1 34 7 28 1 16	5 34 6 6 36 8 29 2 16	7 1 6 8 2 8 28 2 16	10 5 7 13 4 9 28 1 16	12 9 14 16 7 10 28 2 16	15 15 18 20 9 11 29 2 16	18 20 18 23 11 11 28 2 16	21 23 21 25 12 12 28 2 16	25 28 25 24 13 12 28 1 16	28 33 28 23 14 11 29 2 16
24	31 25 31 31 29 7 28 1 16	34 30 31 34 31 7 28 1 16	1 30 36 1 34 7 28 1 16	5 35 6 6 36 9 29 2 16	7 2 6 8 2 8 28 2 16	10 7 7 13 4 9 28 1 16	13 10 14 17 8 10 28 1 16	16 16 18 20 9 11 29 2 16	19 21 18 23 11 11 28 2 16	22 25 21 25 13 12 28 2 16	25 30 25 24 13 12 28 1 16	28 33 28 23 14 11 29 2 16
25	31 26 30 31 29 7 28 1 16	34 31 31 34 31 7 28 1 16	1 31 36 1 34 7 28 1 16	5 36 6 6 36 8 29 2 16	7 3 6 10 2 9 28 1 16	10 9 7 13 4 9 29 1 16	13 12 14 17 8 10 28 2 16	16 18 18 20 9 11 29 2 16	19 23 18 23 11 11 28 2 16	22 26 21 25 13 12 28 2 16	25 31 25 24 13 12 28 1 16	28 34 28 23 14 11 29 2 16
26	31 28 30 31 30 7 28 1 16	34 31 31 34 31 7 28 1 16	1 33 36 1 34 7 28 1 16	5 1 6 6 1 8 28 1 16	7 5 6 10 3 9 28 1 16	10 10 7 13 4 9 28 1 16	13 14 14 17 8 10 28 2 16	16 19 18 20 9 11 28 2 16	19 24 18 23 11 11 28 2 16	22 28 21 25 13 12 28 2 16	25 32 25 24 13 12 28 1 16	29 35 30 23 14 11 29 2 16
27	31 29 30 31 30 7 28 1 16	34 33 31 34 31 7 28 1 16	2 35 2 2 35 8 29 2 16	5 2 6 6 1 8 28 1 16	7 6 6 10 3 9 28 1 16	10 11 7 13 4 10 28 1 16	13 15 14 17 8 10 28 2 16	16 20 19 20 10 11 28 2 16	19 26 18 23 11 11 28 2 16	22 29 21 25 13 12 28 2 16	25 33 25 24 13 12 28 1 16	29 36 30 23 14 11 29 2 16
28	31 30 30 31 30 7 28 1 16	34 34 31 34 31 7 28 1 16	2 36 2 2 35 8 29 2 16	5 4 6 6 1 8 29 2 16	7 7 6 10 3 9 28 1 16	10 13 7 14 5 10 28 1 16	13 17 14 17 8 10 28 2 16	16 22 19 20 10 11 28 2 16	19 27 18 23 11 11 28 2 16	22 30 21 25 13 12 28 2 16	25 34 25 24 13 12 28 1 16	29 2 30 24 14 11 29 2 16
29	31 31 30 31 30 7 28 1 16		2 1 2 2 35 8 29 2 16	5 6 6 6 1 8 29 2 16	7 9 6 10 3 9 28 1 16	10 14 7 14 5 10 28 1 16	13 18 14 17 8 10 28 2 16	16 24 19 20 10 11 28 2 16	19 28 18 23 11 11 28 2 16	22 31 21 25 13 12 28 2 16	25 36 25 24 13 12 28 1 16	29 3 30 24 14 11 29 2 16
30	31 32 30 31 30 7 28 1 16	**1930**	2 2 2 3 35 8 29 2 16	5 7 6 6 1 8 29 2 16	7 10 6 10 3 9 28 1 16	10 16 7 14 5 10 28 1 16	14 19 14 17 8 10 28 1 16	16 25 19 20 10 11 28 2 16	19 29 18 23 11 11 28 2 16	22 32 22 25 13 12 28 2 16	25 1 25 24 13 12 28 1 16	29 4 30 24 14 11 29 2 16
31	31 34 30 31 30 7 28 1 16		2 3 2 3 35 8 29 2 16		7 12 6 10 3 9 28 1 16		14 21 14 17 8 10 28 2 16	16 26 19 20 10 11 28 2 16		22 34 22 25 13 12 28 2 16		29 5 30 24 14 11 29 2 16

	JAN	FEB	MAR	APR	MAY	JUNE
1	29 7 29 24 14 11 29 2 16	31 12 29 27 13 11 29 2 16	35 12 33 30 12 11 30 3 16	2 19 2 34 13 11 29 2 16	5 22 4 1 14 11 29 2 16	7 27 5 5 15 12 30 3 16
2	29 8 29 24 14 11 29 2 16	31 13 29 27 13 11 29 2 16	35 14 33 30 12 11 30 3 16	2 19 2 34 13 11 29 2 16	5 23 4 2 14 11 29 2 16	7 28 5 5 15 12 30 3 16
3	29 9 29 24 14 11 29 2 16	31 14 29 27 13 11 29 2 16	35 15 34 30 12 11 30 3 16	2 20 2 34 13 11 29 2 16	5 24 4 2 14 11 29 2 16	9 30 5 5 15 12 30 3 16
4	29 11 29 25 14 11 29 2 16	31 16 29 28 13 11 29 2 16	35 17 34 30 12 11 30 3 16	2 22 4 34 13 11 29 2 16	5 26 4 2 14 11 29 2 16	9 31 5 5 15 12 30 3 16
5	29 12 29 25 14 11 29 2 16	32 17 29 28 13 11 29 2 16	35 18 34 30 12 11 30 3 16	2 24 4 34 13 11 29 2 16	5 27 4 2 14 11 29 2 16	9 32 5 5 15 12 30 3 16
6	29 14 29 25 14 11 29 2 16	32 19 29 28 13 11 29 2 16	35 21 34 31 12 11 30 3 16	2 25 4 34 13 11 29 2 16	5 28 4 2 14 11 29 2 16	9 33 6 6 15 12 30 3 16
7	29 15 29 25 14 11 29 2 16	32 20 29 29 13 11 29 2 16	35 21 34 31 12 11 30 3 16	2 26 4 34 13 11 29 2 16	5 29 4 2 14 11 29 2 16	9 34 7 7 16 12 30 3 16
8	29 17 29 25 14 11 29 2 16	32 22 31 28 13 11 29 2 16	35 23 34 31 12 11 30 3 16	2 28 4 34 13 11 29 2 16	5 31 4 2 14 11 29 2 16	9 36 7 7 16 12 30 3 16
9	29 18 29 25 14 11 29 2 16	32 23 31 28 13 11 29 2 16	35 24 36 31 12 11 30 3 16	2 29 5 35 13 11 29 2 16	5 32 4 2 14 11 29 2 16	9 1 7 7 16 12 30 3 16
10	29 20 29 25 14 11 29 2 16	32 25 31 28 13 11 29 2 16	35 25 36 33 12 11 30 3 16	2 30 5 35 13 11 29 2 16	5 34 4 2 14 11 29 2 16	9 2 7 7 16 12 30 3 16
11	29 21 29 25 14 11 29 2 16	33 26 31 28 13 11 29 2 16	35 27 36 33 12 11 30 3 16	2 31 5 35 13 11 29 2 16	5 35 4 2 14 11 29 2 16	9 3 7 7 16 12 30 3 16
12	29 23 29 26 14 11 29 2 16	33 27 31 28 13 11 29 2 16	36 28 36 33 12 11 30 3 16	2 33 5 35 13 11 29 2 16	5 36 4 2 14 11 29 2 16	9 5 7 7 16 12 30 3 16
13	29 24 29 26 14 11 29 2 16	33 29 31 28 13 11 29 2 16	36 30 36 33 12 11 30 3 16	2 34 5 35 13 11 29 2 16	5 1 4 2 14 11 29 2 16	9 6 7 7 16 12 30 3 16
14	29 25 29 26 14 11 29 2 16	33 30 31 28 13 11 29 2 16	36 31 36 33 12 11 30 3 16	2 35 5 35 13 11 29 2 16	5 2 4 2 14 11 29 2 16	9 7 7 7 16 12 30 3 16
15	29 27 29 26 14 11 29 2 16	33 31 31 29 13 11 29 2 16	36 32 36 33 12 11 30 3 16	2 36 5 35 13 11 29 2 16	5 3 4 2 14 11 29 2 16	9 8 7 7 16 12 30 3 16
16	29 28 29 26 14 11 29 2 16	33 32 31 29 12 11 29 2 16	36 33 36 33 12 11 30 3 16	3 2 5 36 13 11 30 2 16	5 5 4 2 14 11 29 2 16	9 9 7 7 16 12 30 3 16
17	30 29 29 26 14 11 29 2 16	33 33 31 29 12 11 29 2 16	36 34 36 33 12 11 30 3 16	3 3 5 36 13 11 30 2 16	5 6 4 2 14 11 29 2 16	9 11 7 7 16 12 30 3 16
18	30 30 29 26 14 11 29 2 16	33 34 32 29 12 11 29 2 16	36 35 36 33 12 11 30 3 16	3 4 5 36 13 11 30 2 16	5 7 4 2 14 11 29 2 16	9 12 7 7 16 12 30 3 16
19	30 32 29 26 14 11 29 2 16	34 36 32 29 12 11 29 2 16	36 1 1 33 12 11 30 3 16	3 5 5 36 13 11 30 2 16	5 8 4 2 14 11 29 2 16	9 14 7 7 16 12 30 3 16
20	30 33 29 26 14 11 29 2 16	34 1 32 29 12 11 29 2 16	36 2 1 33 12 11 30 3 16	3 6 5 36 13 11 30 2 16	5 10 4 2 14 11 29 2 16	9 15 9 7 16 12 30 3 16
21	31 34 29 26 13 11 29 2 16	34 2 32 29 12 11 29 2 16	36 3 1 33 12 11 30 3 16	4 8 5 36 13 11 29 2 16	5 11 4 4 14 11 29 2 16	9 17 9 7 16 12 30 3 16
22	31 35 29 26 13 11 29 2 16	35 3 32 29 12 11 29 2 16	1 4 3 33 12 11 30 3 16	4 9 5 36 13 11 29 2 16	5 13 4 4 14 11 29 2 16	10 18 9 7 16 12 30 3 16
23	31 36 29 26 13 11 29 2 16	35 5 32 29 12 11 29 2 16	1 6 3 33 12 11 30 3 16	4 11 5 36 14 11 29 2 16	7 14 4 4 15 11 29 2 16	10 20 9 7 16 12 30 3 16
24	31 2 29 26 13 11 29 2 16	35 6 32 29 12 11 29 2 16	1 7 3 33 12 11 30 3 16	4 12 5 36 14 11 29 2 16	7 15 4 4 15 11 29 2 16	10 21 9 7 16 12 30 3 16
25	31 3 29 26 13 11 29 2 16	35 7 32 30 12 11 30 3 16	1 8 3 33 12 11 30 3 16	4 14 5 36 14 11 29 2 16	7 17 4 4 15 11 29 2 16	10 22 9 7 16 12 30 3 16
26	31 4 29 26 13 11 29 2 16	35 8 32 30 12 11 30 3 16	1 9 3 33 12 11 30 3 16	4 15 5 36 14 11 29 2 16	7 18 4 4 15 11 29 2 16	10 24 10 7 16 12 30 3 16
27	31 5 29 26 13 11 29 2 16	35 10 33 30 12 11 30 3 16	2 10 2 33 12 11 30 2 16	5 16 5 1 14 11 29 2 16	7 19 4 4 15 11 29 2 16	10 25 10 7 16 12 30 3 16
28	31 6 29 26 13 11 29 2 16	35 12 33 30 12 11 30 3 16	2 12 2 33 12 11 30 2 16	5 17 5 1 14 11 29 2 16	7 20 4 4 15 11 29 2 16	10 26 10 7 16 12 30 3 16
29	31 8 29 26 13 11 29 2 16		2 13 2 33 12 11 30 2 16	5 19 5 1 14 11 29 2 16	7 22 4 4 15 11 29 2 16	10 28 10 7 16 12 30 3 16
30	31 9 29 27 14 11 29 2 16	1931	2 15 2 33 12 11 30 2 16	5 21 5 1 14 11 29 2 16	7 24 5 5 15 11 29 2 16	10 30 10 7 16 12 30 3 16
31	31 10 29 27 14 11 29 2 16		2 16 2 33 12 11 30 2 16		7 25 5 5 15 11 29 2 16	

	JULY	AUG	SEPT	OCT	NOV	DEC
1	10 30 12 9 18 12 30 3 16	13 35 16 12 19 13 29 2 16	16 3 17 16 20 14 29 2 16	20 6 17 20 23 14 29 2 16	22 11 23 23 25 14 29 2 16	25 14 26 26 26 14 29 2 16
2	10 32 12 9 18 12 30 3 16	13 36 16 13 19 13 29 2 16	16 5 17 16 20 14 29 2 16	20 8 17 20 23 14 29 2 16	22 12 23 23 25 14 29 2 16	25 16 28 28 26 14 29 2 16
3	10 33 12 9 18 12 30 3 16	13 1 16 13 19 13 29 2 16	16 6 17 17 20 14 29 2 16	20 9 18 20 23 14 29 2 16	22 14 23 23 25 14 29 2 16	25 17 28 28 26 14 29 2 16
4	12 34 12 9 18 12 30 3 16	13 2 16 13 19 13 29 2 16	16 7 17 17 20 1 4 29 2 16	20 10 18 20 23 14 29 2 16	22 15 23 23 25 14 29 2 16	25 19 28 28 26 14 29 2 16
5	12 36 12 9 18 12 30 3 16	13 3 16 13 19 13 29 2 16	16 8 17 17 20 14 29 2 16	20 11 19 20 23 14 29 2 16	22 16 23 23 25 14 29 2 16	25 20 28 28 26 14 29 2 16
6	12 36 12 9 18 12 30 3 16	13 5 16 13 19 13 29 2 16	16 9 17 17 20 14 29 2 16	20 13 19 20 23 14 29 2 16	22 18 23 23 25 14 29 2 16	26 22 28 28 26 14 29 2 14
7	12 2 12 9 18 12 30 3 16	13 6 16 13 19 13 29 2 16	17 11 17 17 20 14 29 2 16	20 14 19 20 23 14 29 2 16	23 19 24 26 26 14 29 2 17	26 23 28 28 26 14 29 2 16
8	12 3 12 10 18 12 30 3 16	13 7 16 13 19 13 29 2 16	17 12 17 17 20 14 29 2 16	20 16 19 20 23 14 29 2 16	23 20 24 26 26 14 29 2 17	26 25 28 28 26 14 29 2 16
9	12 4 12 10 18 12 30 3 16	14 8 16 13 19 13 29 2 16	17 14 16 17 20 14 29 2 16	20 17 20 20 23 14 29 2 16	23 22 24 26 26 14 29 2 17	26 26 28 28 26 14 29 2 16
10	12 5 12 10 18 12 30 3 16	14 10 16 13 19 13 29 2 16	17 15 16 17 20 14 29 2 16	20 19 20 20 23 14 29 2 16	23 24 24 26 26 14 29 2 17	26 28 28 29 28 14 29 2 16
11	12 6 13 10 18 12 30 3 16	14 12 17 13 19 13 29 2 16	17 16 16 17 20 14 29 2 16	20 20 20 20 23 14 29 2 16	23 26 25 26 26 14 29 2 17	26 29 28 29 28 14 29 2 16
12	12 8 13 10 18 12 30 3 16	14 13 17 13 19 13 29 2 16	17 18 16 17 20 14 29 2 16	20 22 20 20 23 14 29 2 16	23 27 25 26 26 14 29 2 17	26 30 28 29 28 14 29 2 16
13	12 9 13 10 18 12 30 3 16	14 14 17 13 19 13 29 2 16	17 19 16 17 20 14 29 2 16	20 23 20 20 23 14 29 2 16	23 28 25 26 26 14 29 2 17	26 32 28 29 28 14 29 2 16
14	12 10 13 10 18 12 30 3 16	14 15 17 13 19 13 29 2 16	17 20 16 17 20 14 29 2 16	20 25 20 20 23 14 29 2 16	23 29 25 26 26 14 29 2 17	26 33 28 29 28 14 29 2 16
15	12 12 13 10 18 12 30 3 16	14 17 17 13 19 13 29 2 16	17 22 16 17 22 14 29 2 16	20 26 20 22 23 14 29 2 16	23 31 26 26 26 14 29 2 17	26 34 28 29 28 14 29 2 16
16	12 13 13 10 18 12 30 3 16	14 18 17 13 19 13 29 2 16	17 24 16 17 22 14 29 2 16	20 27 20 22 23 14 29 2 16	23 32 26 26 26 14 29 2 17	26 35 28 29 28 14 29 2 16
17	11 15 14 11 17 11 29 2 16	15 20 17 14 20 13 29 2 16	17 25 16 17 22 14 29 2 16	20 29 20 22 23 14 29 2 16	23 33 26 26 26 14 29 2 17	26 1 28 29 28 14 29 2 16
18	11 16 14 11 17 11 29 2 16	15 21 17 14 20 13 29 2 16	18 26 16 18 22 14 29 2 16	20 30 20 22 23 14 29 2 16	23 35 26 26 26 14 29 2 17	26 2 28 29 28 14 29 2 16
19	11 17 14 11 17 11 29 2 16	15 23 17 14 20 13 29 2 16	18 28 16 18 22 14 29 2 16	20 32 20 22 23 14 29 2 16	23 36 26 26 26 14 29 2 17	26 3 28 29 28 14 29 2 16
20	11 19 14 11 17 11 29 2 16	15 24 17 14 20 13 29 2 16	18 29 16 18 22 14 29 2 16	20 33 20 22 23 14 29 2 16	23 1 26 26 26 14 29 2 17	26 4 28 29 28 14 29 2 16
21	11 20 14 11 17 11 29 2 16	15 26 17 14 20 13 29 2 16	18 30 16 18 22 14 29 2 16	20 34 21 22 23 14 29 2 16	23 2 26 26 26 14 29 2 17	26 5 26 29 29 14 29 2 16
22	11 22 14 11 17 11 29 2 16	15 27 17 14 20 13 29 2 16	18 32 16 18 22 14 29 2 16	21 35 21 22 23 14 29 2 16	23 3 26 26 26 14 29 2 17	26 7 26 29 29 14 29 2 16
23	11 23 14 11 17 11 29 2 16	15 28 17 14 20 13 29 2 16	18 33 16 18 22 14 29 2 16	21 36 21 22 23 14 29 2 16	25 5 26 26 26 14 29 2 16	28 8 26 29 29 14 29 2 16
24	13 24 14 11 17 13 29 2 16	16 29 17 14 20 13 29 2 16	19 34 16 19 22 14 29 2 16	22 1 22 23 23 14 29 2 16	25 6 26 26 26 14 29 2 16	29 9 26 29 29 14 29 2 16
25	13 25 14 11 17 13 29 2 16	16 31 17 14 20 13 29 2 16	19 35 16 19 22 14 29 2 16	22 2 22 23 23 14 29 2 16	25 7 26 26 26 14 29 2 16	28 10 26 31 29 14 29 2 16
26	13 26 14 11 17 13 29 2 16	16 32 17 14 20 13 29 2 16	19 1 17 19 22 14 29 2 16	22 4 22 23 23 14 29 2 16	25 8 26 26 26 14 29 2 16	28 11 26 31 29 14 29 2 16
27	13 29 14 11 17 13 29 2 16	16 33 17 16 20 13 29 2 16	19 2 17 20 22 14 29 2 16	22 5 22 23 23 14 29 2 16	25 9 26 26 26 14 29 2 16	28 13 26 31 29 14 29 2 16
28	13 30 14 11 17 13 29 2 16	16 34 17 16 20 13 29 2 16	19 3 17 20 22 14 29 2 16	22 6 22 23 23 14 29 2 16	25 11 26 26 26 14 29 2 16	28 14 26 31 29 14 29 2 16
29	13 31 16 11 17 13 29 2 16	16 36 17 16 20 13 29 2 16	19 4 17 20 22 14 29 2 16	22 7 22 23 23 14 29 2 16	25 12 26 26 26 14 29 2 16	28 16 26 31 29 14 29 2 16
30	13 32 16 11 18 13 29 2 16	16 1 17 16 20 13 29 2 16	19 5 17 20 22 14 29 2 16	22 8 22 23 23 14 29 2 16	25 13 26 26 26 14 29 2 16	28 17 26 31 29 14 29 2 16
31	13 33 16 11 18 13 29 2 16	16 2 17 16 20 13 29 2 16		22 10 22 23 23 14 29 2 16		28 19 26 31 29 14 29 2 16

	JAN	FEB	MAR	APR	MAY	JUNE	JULY	AUG	SEPT	OCT	NOV	DEC
1	30 21 27 31 30 15 30 3 16	32 25 30 34 32 14 30 2 16	34 28 34 2 34 14 30 2 16	2 32 2 6 36 14 31 2 16	4 36 2 8 2 14 31 2 16	7 4 6 12 6 15 31 3 16	10 7 12 10 7 15 31 3 16	13 12 16 9 9 15 31 3 16	16 18 15 12 12 16 30 3 16	19 21 19 15 13 16 30 3 16	23 27 24 18 15 17 30 3 17	25 30 27 22 16 17 30 3 16
2	30 21 27 31 30 15 30 3 16	32 27 30 34 32 14 30 2 16	34 29 35 2 34 14 30 2 16	2 34 2 6 36 14 31 2 16	4 1 2 8 2 14 31 2 16	7 6 6 12 6 15 31 3 16	10 9 12 10 7 15 31 3 16	13 13 16 9 9 15 31 3 16	16 19 15 12 12 16 30 3 16	19 22 19 15 13 16 30 3 16	23 28 24 18 15 17 30 3 17	25 33 27 22 16 17 31 3 16
3	30 23 27 31 30 15 30 3 16	32 28 30 36 32 14 30 2 16	34 30 35 2 34 14 30 2 16	2 35 2 6 36 14 31 2 16	4 2 2 8 2 14 31 2 16	7 7 7 12 6 15 31 3 16	10 10 13 10 7 15 31 3 16	14 15 16 9 9 15 30 3 16	16 20 15 12 12 16 30 3 16	19 24 19 15 13 16 30 3 16	23 29 25 19 15 17 30 3 17	25 33 27 22 16 17 31 3 16
4	30 24 27 31 30 15 30 3 16	32 30 30 36 32 14 30 2 16	34 32 35 2 34 14 30 2 16	2 36 2 6 36 14 31 2 16	4 4 2 8 2 14 31 2 16	7 8 7 12 6 15 31 3 16	10 11 13 10 7 15 31 3 16	14 16 16 9 9 15 30 3 16	16 21 15 12 12 16 30 3 16	19 25 19 15 13 16 30 3 16	23 30 25 19 15 17 30 3 17	25 34 27 22 16 17 31 3 16
5	30 26 27 32 30 15 30 3 16	32 31 30 36 32 14 30 2 16	34 33 35 2 34 14 30 2 16	2 2 2 7 1 14 31 2 16	5 5 2 8 2 14 31 2 16	9 9 7 12 6 15 31 3 16	10 13 13 10 7 15 31 3 16	14 18 16 10 10 15 30 3 16	16 23 15 12 12 16 30 3 16	19 27 19 15 13 16 30 3 16	23 32 25 19 15 17 30 3 17	26 36 27 23 16 17 31 3 16
6	30 27 27 32 30 15 30 3 16	32 32 31 36 32 14 30 2 16	34 34 35 2 34 14 30 2 16	2 2 2 7 1 14 31 2 16	5 6 2 8 2 14 31 2 16	9 12 7 12 6 15 31 3 16	10 14 13 10 7 15 31 3 16	14 19 16 10 10 15 30 3 16	16 24 15 12 12 16 30 3 16	19 28 19 15 13 16 30 3 16	23 33 25 19 15 17 30 3 17	26 1 27 23 16 17 31 3 16
7	30 28 27 32 30 15 30 3 16	32 33 31 36 32 14 30 2 16	35 35 36 3 34 14 30 2 16	2 4 2 7 1 14 31 2 16	5 7 2 8 2 14 31 2 16	9 12 7 12 6 15 31 3 16	12 15 13 10 7 15 31 3 16	15 21 16 10 10 15 30 3 16	16 25 15 12 12 16 30 3 16	20 30 20 16 13 16 30 2 16	23 35 25 19 15 17 30 3 17	26 2 25 22 16 17 31 3 16
8	30 30 27 32 30 15 30 3 16	32 34 31 36 32 14 30 2 16	35 1 36 3 34 14 30 2 16	2 5 2 7 1 14 31 2 16	5 8 2 8 2 14 31 2 16	9 13 7 12 6 15 31 3 16	12 16 13 10 7 15 31 3 16	15 22 16 10 10 15 30 3 16	16 27 15 12 12 16 30 3 16	20 31 20 16 13 16 30 2 16	23 36 25 19 15 17 30 3 17	26 3 25 22 16 17 31 3 16
9	30 31 27 32 30 15 30 3 16	32 36 31 36 32 14 30 2 16	35 2 36 3 34 14 30 2 16	2 6 2 7 1 14 31 2 16	5 10 2 8 2 14 31 2 16	9 15 7 12 6 15 31 3 16	12 18 13 10 7 15 31 3 16	15 24 16 10 10 15 30 3 16	17 28 16 13 12 16 30 3 16	20 32 20 16 13 16 30 2 16	23 1 25 19 15 17 30 3 17	26 4 25 22 16 17 31 3 16
10	30 33 27 32 30 15 30 3 16	32 1 31 36 32 14 30 2 16	35 3 1 4 34 14 31 2 16	2 7 2 7 1 14 31 2 16	5 11 2 8 2 14 31 2 16	9 16 7 12 6 15 31 3 16	12 19 13 10 7 15 31 3 16	15 25 16 10 10 15 30 3 16	17 30 16 13 12 16 30 3 16	20 34 20 16 13 16 30 2 16	23 2 25 19 15 17 30 3 17	26 6 25 22 16 17 31 3 16
11	30 34 27 32 30 15 30 3 16	32 2 32 36 32 14 30 2 16	36 4 1 4 34 14 31 2 16	2 8 2 7 1 14 31 2 16	5 12 2 8 2 14 31 2 16	9 17 9 12 6 15 31 3 16	12 21 13 10 8 15 31 3 17	15 26 16 10 10 15 30 3 16	17 31 16 13 12 16 30 3 16	20 35 20 16 13 16 30 2 16	23 3 25 19 15 17 30 3 17	27 7 25 22 16 17 31 3 16
12	30 35 27 32 30 14 30 2 16	32 3 32 36 32 14 30 2 16	36 5 1 4 34 14 31 2 16	2 10 2 7 1 14 31 2 16	5 13 2 8 2 14 31 2 16	9 18 9 12 6 15 31 3 16	12 22 15 10 7 15 31 3 17	15 27 15 10 10 16 30 3 16	18 33 16 13 12 16 30 3 16	20 36 20 16 13 16 30 3 16	23 5 27 21 15 17 31 3 17	27 8 25 22 16 17 31 3 16
13	30 36 27 32 30 14 30 2 16	32 5 32 1 32 14 30 2 16	36 7 1 4 34 14 31 2 16	2 11 2 7 1 14 31 2 16	5 15 2 10 4 14 31 2 16	9 20 9 10 6 15 31 3 16	12 24 15 10 9 15 31 3 16	15 29 15 10 10 16 30 3 16	18 34 16 13 12 16 30 3 16	21 2 22 16 14 16 30 3 16	23 6 27 21 15 17 31 3 17	27 9 25 22 16 17 31 3 16
14	30 2 28 32 30 14 30 2 16	32 6 32 1 32 14 30 2 16	36 8 1 4 34 14 31 2 16	2 12 2 7 1 14 31 2 16	5 16 2 10 4 14 31 2 16	9 21 9 10 6 15 31 3 16	12 25 15 9 9 15 31 3 16	15 30 15 10 10 16 30 3 16	18 35 16 13 12 16 30 3 16	21 3 23 17 15 17 30 3 17	23 7 27 21 16 17 31 3 16	27 11 25 22 16 17 31 3 16
15	30 3 28 32 30 14 30 2 16	32 7 32 1 32 14 30 2 16	36 9 2 4 34 14 31 2 16	2 13 2 8 2 14 31 2 16	5 17 2 10 4 14 31 2 16	9 22 9 10 6 15 31 3 16	12 27 15 9 9 15 31 3 16	15 31 15 10 10 16 30 3 16	18 36 16 13 12 16 30 3 16	21 4 23 17 15 17 30 3 17	23 8 27 21 16 17 31 3 16	27 12 26 22 17 17 31 3 17
16	30 4 28 32 30 14 30 2 16	32 8 32 1 32 14 30 2 16	36 10 2 4 34 14 31 2 16	2 15 2 8 2 14 31 2 16	6 19 4 10 4 14 31 2 16	9 24 9 10 6 15 31 3 16	12 28 15 9 9 15 31 3 16	15 33 15 10 10 16 30 3 16	18 2 16 13 12 16 30 3 16	21 5 23 17 15 17 30 3 17	23 9 27 21 16 17 31 3 16	27 13 26 22 17 17 31 3 17
17	30 5 28 32 30 14 30 2 16	32 9 32 1 32 14 30 2 16	36 11 2 4 35 14 31 2 16	2 16 2 8 2 14 31 2 16	6 20 4 10 4 14 31 2 16	9 26 10 10 6 15 31 3 16	12 29 15 9 9 15 30 3 16	15 34 15 10 10 16 30 3 16	18 3 16 13 12 16 30 3 16	21 6 23 17 15 17 30 3 17	23 11 27 21 16 17 31 3 16	27 14 26 22 17 17 31 3 17
18	30 6 28 32 30 14 30 2 16	32 11 32 1 32 14 30 2 16	36 13 2 4 35 14 31 2 16	2 18 2 8 2 14 31 2 16	6 22 4 10 4 14 31 2 16	9 27 10 10 6 15 31 3 16	12 30 15 9 9 15 30 3 16	15 36 15 10 10 16 30 3 16	18 4 16 13 12 16 30 3 16	21 8 23 17 15 17 30 3 17	23 12 27 21 16 17 31 3 16	27 15 26 22 17 17 31 3 17
19	30 8 28 32 30 14 30 2 16	32 12 32 2 32 14 30 2 16	36 14 2 4 35 14 31 2 16	2 19 2 8 2 14 31 2 16	6 24 4 10 4 14 31 2 16	9 29 10 10 6 15 31 3 16	12 32 15 9 9 15 30 3 16	15 1 15 10 10 16 30 3 16	18 5 16 14 12 16 30 3 16	21 9 23 17 15 17 30 3 17	23 13 27 21 16 17 31 3 16	27 17 26 22 17 17 31 3 17
20	30 9 28 34 30 14 30 2 16	34 14 34 2 34 14 30 2 16	36 16 2 5 35 14 31 2 16	2 20 2 8 2 14 31 2 16	6 25 4 10 4 14 31 2 16	9 30 10 10 6 15 31 3 16	12 33 15 9 9 15 30 3 16	15 2 15 10 10 16 30 3 16	18 6 16 14 13 16 30 3 16	21 10 23 17 15 17 30 3 17	23 15 27 21 16 17 30 3 16	27 18 26 22 17 17 31 3 17
21	31 10 28 34 31 14 31 2 16	34 15 34 2 34 14 30 2 16	1 17 2 5 35 14 31 2 16	4 22 2 8 2 14 31 2 16	7 26 4 10 4 14 31 2 16	9 31 10 10 6 15 31 3 16	12 35 15 9 9 15 30 3 16	15 3 15 10 10 16 30 3 16	18 7 18 14 13 16 30 3 16	21 11 23 17 15 17 30 3 17	23 16 27 21 16 17 30 3 16	27 19 26 22 17 17 31 3 17
22	31 11 28 34 31 14 31 2 16	34 16 34 2 34 14 30 2 16	1 19 2 5 35 14 31 2 16	4 23 2 8 2 14 31 2 16	7 28 4 10 4 14 31 2 16	10 33 10 10 6 15 31 3 16	12 36 15 9 9 15 30 3 16	15 4 15 10 10 16 30 3 16	18 9 18 15 13 16 30 3 16	21 12 23 17 15 17 30 3 17	25 17 27 21 16 17 30 3 16	28 21 26 26 17 17 31 3 17
23	31 13 28 34 31 14 31 2 16	34 18 34 2 34 14 30 2 16	1 20 2 5 35 14 31 2 16	4 26 2 8 2 14 31 2 16	7 29 4 10 4 14 31 2 16	10 34 10 10 7 15 31 3 16	13 2 15 9 9 15 30 3 16	16 6 15 10 10 16 30 3 16	19 10 18 15 13 16 30 3 16	21 14 23 17 15 17 30 3 16	25 18 27 21 16 17 30 3 16	28 22 26 26 17 17 31 3 17
24	31 14 28 34 31 14 31 2 16	34 19 34 2 34 14 30 2 16	1 22 2 5 35 14 31 2 16	4 27 2 8 2 14 31 2 16	7 31 4 10 4 14 31 2 16	10 35 10 10 7 15 31 3 16	13 3 15 9 9 15 30 3 16	16 7 15 10 10 16 30 3 16	19 12 18 15 13 16 30 3 16	22 15 23 17 15 17 30 3 16	25 20 27 21 16 17 30 3 16	28 23 26 26 17 17 31 3 17
25	31 15 28 34 31 14 31 2 16	34 21 34 2 34 14 30 2 16	1 23 2 5 35 14 31 2 16	4 28 2 8 2 14 31 2 16	7 32 4 10 4 14 31 2 16	10 36 10 10 7 15 31 3 16	13 4 15 9 9 15 30 3 16	16 8 15 12 12 16 30 3 16	19 13 18 15 13 16 30 3 16	22 16 23 17 15 17 30 3 16	25 21 27 21 16 17 30 3 16	28 25 26 26 17 17 31 3 17
26	31 16 28 34 31 14 30 2 16	34 22 34 2 34 14 30 2 16	1 25 2 5 35 14 31 2 16	4 29 2 8 2 14 31 2 16	7 33 4 10 4 14 31 2 16	10 2 10 10 7 15 31 3 16	13 5 15 9 9 15 30 3 16	16 9 15 12 12 16 30 3 16	19 14 19 15 13 16 30 3 16	22 17 23 17 15 17 30 3 16	25 22 27 22 16 17 31 3 16	28 27 26 26 17 17 31 3 17
27	31 18 28 34 31 14 30 2 16	34 23 34 2 34 14 30 2 16	1 26 2 5 35 14 31 2 16	4 31 2 8 2 14 31 2 16	7 34 4 10 4 14 31 2 16	10 3 12 10 7 15 31 3 16	13 6 15 9 9 15 30 3 16	16 11 15 12 12 16 30 3 16	19 15 19 15 13 16 30 3 16	22 19 23 17 15 17 30 3 16	25 24 27 22 16 17 31 3 16	28 28 26 26 17 17 31 3 17
28	31 20 30 34 31 14 30 2 16	34 25 34 2 34 14 30 2 16	1 27 2 5 35 14 31 2 16	4 32 2 8 2 14 31 2 16	7 36 4 10 4 14 31 2 16	10 4 12 10 7 15 31 3 16	13 8 16 9 9 15 30 3 16	16 12 15 12 12 16 30 3 16	19 16 19 15 13 16 30 3 16	22 21 23 17 15 17 30 3 16	25 26 27 22 16 17 31 3 16	28 30 26 26 17 17 31 3 17
29	32 21 30 34 32 14 30 2 16	34 26 34 2 34 14 30 2 16	1 29 2 6 36 14 31 2 16	4 34 2 8 2 14 31 2 16	7 1 5 10 4 14 31 2 16	10 5 12 10 7 15 31 3 16	13 9 16 9 9 15 30 3 16	16 13 15 12 12 16 30 3 16	19 18 19 15 13 16 30 3 16	22 22 23 17 15 17 30 3 16	25 27 27 22 16 17 31 3 16	28 31 26 26 17 17 31 3 17
30	32 23 30 34 32 14 30 2 16	**1932**	2 30 2 6 36 14 31 2 16	4 35 2 8 2 14 31 2 16	7 2 5 10 4 14 31 2 16	10 6 12 10 7 15 31 3 16	13 10 16 9 9 15 30 3 16	16 14 15 12 12 16 30 3 16	19 19 19 15 13 16 30 3 16	22 23 23 18 15 17 30 3 16	25 29 27 22 16 17 31 3 16	28 33 26 26 17 17 31 3 17
31	32 24 30 34 32 14 30 2 16		2 31 2 6 36 14 31 2 16		7 3 5 10 4 14 31 2 16		13 11 16 9 9 15 30 3 16	16 16 15 12 12 16 30 3 16		22 25 23 18 15 17 30 3 16		28 34 26 26 17 17 31 3 17

	JAN	FEB	MAR	APR	MAY	JUNE	JULY	AUG	SEPT	OCT	NOV	DEC
1	29 35 26 26 17 17 31 2 17	31 4 31 30 18 18 31 2 16	34 4 36 33 16 16 31 2 16	2 9 36 2 16 17 32 2 16	5 12 3 5 16 16 32 3 16	7 16 9 9 16 16 31 3 16	10 20 14 12 18 16 32 3 16	14 25 14 16 20 18 32 3 16	16 31 15 20 22 18 31 3 16	19 34 21 24 24 19 31 3 16	23 3 26 27 27 20 32 3 17	26 7 23 30 29 20 32 3 17
2	29 36 26 26 17 17 31 2 17	31 5 31 30 18 18 31 2 16	34 5 36 33 16 16 31 2 16	2 10 36 2 16 17 32 2 16	5 14 3 5 16 16 32 3 16	7 18 9 9 16 16 31 3 16	10 22 14 12 18 16 32 3 16	14 27 14 16 20 18 32 3 16	16 32 16 20 22 18 31 3 16	19 35 21 24 24 19 31 3 16	23 5 26 27 27 20 32 3 17	26 8 23 30 29 20 32 3 17
3	29 2 26 26 17 17 31 2 17	31 6 31 30 18 18 31 2 16	34 7 36 33 16 16 31 2 16	2 11 36 2 16 17 32 2 16	5 14 3 5 16 16 32 3 16	7 19 9 9 16 16 31 3 16	10 22 14 13 18 16 32 3 16	14 28 14 16 20 18 32 3 16	16 34 16 20 22 18 31 3 16	19 1 21 24 24 19 31 3 16	23 6 26 27 27 20 32 3 17	26 9 23 30 29 20 32 3 17
4	29 2 26 26 17 17 31 2 17	31 7 31 30 18 18 31 2 16	34 8 1 34 16 16 31 2 16	2 12 36 2 16 17 32 2 16	5 16 3 5 16 16 32 3 16	7 21 9 9 16 16 31 3 16	10 25 14 13 18 16 32 3 16	14 30 13 16 20 18 32 3 16	16 35 16 20 22 18 31 3 16	19 3 21 24 24 19 31 3 16	23 8 26 27 27 20 32 3 17	26 11 23 30 29 20 32 3 17
5	29 4 26 26 17 17 31 2 17	31 9 31 30 18 18 31 2 16	34 9 1 34 16 16 31 2 16	2 14 36 2 16 17 32 2 16	5 17 3 5 16 16 32 3 16	7 22 9 9 16 16 31 3 16	11 26 14 13 18 17 32 3 16	14 32 13 16 20 18 32 3 16	16 36 15 21 22 18 31 3 16	19 4 21 24 24 19 31 3 16	23 9 26 27 27 20 32 3 17	26 12 24 30 29 20 32 3 17
6	29 5 26 26 17 17 31 2 17	31 10 31 30 18 18 31 2 16	34 10 1 34 16 16 31 2 16	2 15 36 2 16 17 32 2 16	5 18 3 5 16 16 32 3 16	7 24 9 9 16 16 31 3 16	11 28 14 13 19 17 32 3 16	14 33 13 16 20 18 32 3 16	16 1 15 21 22 18 31 3 16	19 5 22 24 24 19 31 3 16	23 10 26 27 27 20 32 3 17	26 13 24 30 29 20 32 3 17
7	29 6 26 26 17 17 31 2 17	32 11 31 31 18 18 31 2 16	34 12 1 34 16 16 31 2 16	2 16 36 2 16 17 32 2 16	5 20 3 5 16 16 32 3 16	7 25 9 9 16 16 31 3 16	11 29 14 13 19 17 32 3 16	14 34 13 16 20 18 32 3 16	16 3 15 21 22 18 31 3 16	19 6 22 24 24 19 31 3 16	23 11 26 28 27 20 32 3 17	26 14 24 30 29 20 32 3 17
8	29 8 26 26 17 17 31 2 17	32 12 32 31 18 18 31 2 16	34 13 1 34 16 16 31 2 16	2 18 36 2 16 17 32 2 16	5 21 3 5 16 16 32 3 16	7 27 9 9 16 16 31 3 16	11 30 14 14 18 17 32 3 16	14 36 13 16 21 18 32 3 16	16 5 15 21 22 18 31 3 16	19 7 22 24 24 19 31 3 16	23 12 26 28 27 20 32 3 17	26 15 24 32 30 20 32 3 17
9	29 9 28 26 17 17 31 2 17	32 13 32 31 18 18 31 2 16	34 14 1 34 16 16 31 2 16	2 19 36 2 16 17 32 2 16	5 23 3 5 16 16 32 3 16	7 28 10 10 16 16 31 3 16	11 32 14 14 18 17 32 3 16	14 1 13 16 21 18 32 3 16	16 6 15 21 22 18 31 3 16	19 9 22 25 25 19 31 3 16	23 14 26 28 27 20 32 3 17	26 17 24 32 30 20 32 3 17
10	29 10 28 26 17 17 31 2 17	32 14 32 31 18 18 31 2 16	35 15 1 34 16 17 31 2 16	2 20 36 2 16 17 32 2 16	5 24 3 5 16 16 32 3 16	7 30 10 10 16 16 31 3 16	11 33 14 14 18 17 32 3 16	14 2 14 17 21 17 32 3 17	16 7 15 21 23 19 32 3 16	21 10 22 25 25 19 31 3 16	23 15 26 29 27 20 32 3 17	26 18 24 32 30 20 32 3 17
11	29 11 28 26 17 17 31 2 17	32 16 32 31 18 18 31 2 16	35 16 1 34 16 17 31 2 16	2 22 36 2 16 17 32 2 16	5 25 4 5 16 16 32 3 16	8 31 10 10 17 16 32 3 17	11 34 14 14 18 17 32 3 16	14 3 14 17 21 17 32 3 17	16 8 15 21 23 19 32 3 16	21 11 22 25 25 19 31 3 16	23 16 26 29 27 20 32 3 17	26 19 24 32 30 20 32 3 17
12	29 12 28 26 17 17 31 2 17	32 18 32 31 18 18 31 2 16	35 18 1 34 16 17 31 2 16	2 23 36 2 16 17 32 2 16	5 27 4 5 16 16 32 3 16	8 32 10 10 17 16 32 3 17	11 36 14 14 18 17 32 3 16	14 5 14 17 21 17 32 3 17	16 9 15 21 23 19 32 3 16	21 12 22 25 25 19 31 3 16	23 17 26 29 27 20 32 3 17	26 20 25 32 30 20 32 2 17
13	29 13 28 26 17 17 31 2 17	32 19 32 31 18 18 31 2 16	35 19 1 34 16 17 31 2 16	2 25 36 2 16 17 32 2 16	5 28 4 5 16 16 32 3 16	8 34 10 10 17 16 32 3 17	12 2 14 14 18 18 32 3 16	14 6 14 17 21 17 32 3 17	16 11 18 21 23 19 32 3 16	21 13 22 25 25 19 31 3 16	24 18 26 29 27 20 32 3 17	26 22 25 32 30 20 32 3 17
14	29 15 28 28 17 17 31 2 17	32 20 34 31 18 18 31 2 16	35 21 1 34 16 17 31 2 16	2 26 36 2 16 17 32 2 16	5 30 4 5 16 16 32 3 16	8 35 10 10 17 16 32 3 17	12 3 14 14 18 18 32 3 16	15 7 14 18 21 18 32 3 16	18 12 18 21 23 19 32 3 16	21 15 22 25 25 19 31 3 16	24 20 25 29 27 20 32 3 17	26 23 25 32 30 20 32 3 17
15	29 17 28 28 17 17 31 2 17	32 21 34 31 18 18 31 2 16	35 22 1 34 16 17 31 2 16	3 28 36 3 16 17 32 3 16	5 32 5 7 16 16 32 3 16	8 1 10 10 17 16 32 3 17	12 4 14 14 18 18 32 3 16	15 9 14 18 21 18 32 3 16	18 13 18 21 23 19 32 3 16	21 16 22 25 25 19 31 3 16	24 21 25 29 27 20 32 3 17	27 24 26 32 30 20 32 3 17
16	30 18 28 28 18 18 31 2 16	32 23 34 31 18 18 31 2 16	35 24 1 35 16 17 31 2 16	3 30 36 3 16 17 32 3 16	5 33 5 7 16 16 32 3 16	8 2 10 10 17 16 32 3 17	12 5 14 14 20 18 32 3 16	15 9 14 18 21 18 32 3 16	18 14 18 21 23 19 32 3 16	21 18 22 25 25 19 31 3 16	24 23 24 29 27 20 32 3 17	27 26 26 32 30 20 32 3 17
17	30 19 28 28 18 18 31 2 16	32 24 34 31 18 18 31 2 16	35 25 1 35 16 17 31 2 16	3 31 1 3 16 17 32 3 16	5 34 5 7 16 16 32 3 16	8 3 10 10 17 16 32 3 17	12 6 14 14 20 18 32 3 16	15 11 14 18 21 18 32 3 16	18 15 18 21 23 19 32 3 16	21 19 22 25 25 19 31 3 16	24 24 24 29 27 20 32 3 17	27 27 26 32 30 20 32 3 17
18	30 21 28 28 18 18 31 2 16	32 27 36 31 18 18 31 2 16	35 26 1 35 16 17 31 2 16	3 32 1 3 16 17 32 3 16	5 36 5 7 16 16 32 3 16	8 4 10 10 17 16 32 3 17	12 7 14 14 20 18 32 3 16	15 12 14 18 21 18 32 3 16	18 16 18 21 23 19 32 3 16	21 20 22 25 25 19 31 3 16	24 25 24 29 27 20 32 3 17	27 30 26 32 30 20 32 3 17
19	30 22 28 28 18 18 31 2 16	34 27 26 31 18 18 31 2 16	35 28 1 35 16 17 31 2 16	3 33 1 3 16 17 32 3 16	6 1 5 7 16 16 32 3 16	9 5 12 12 18 16 32 3 18	12 9 14 14 20 18 32 3 16	15 14 14 18 21 18 32 3 16	18 18 19 22 23 19 31 3 16	21 21 22 25 25 19 31 3 16	24 27 24 29 27 20 32 3 17	27 31 26 32 30 20 32 3 17
20	31 23 28 28 18 18 31 2 16	34 29 36 31 18 18 31 2 16	35 29 1 35 16 17 31 2 16	4 34 1 4 16 17 32 3 16	6 2 5 7 16 16 32 3 16	9 7 12 12 18 16 32 3 18	12 10 14 18 20 18 32 3 16	15 15 14 18 21 18 32 3 16	18 19 19 22 21 19 31 3 16	21 22 22 25 25 19 31 3 16	24 28 24 29 27 20 32 3 17	27 32 26 32 30 20 32 3 17
21	31 24 30 28 18 18 31 2 16	34 30 36 31 18 18 31 2 16	1 32 1 35 16 17 32 2 16	4 36 1 4 16 17 32 3 16	6 3 5 7 16 16 32 3 16	9 9 12 12 18 16 32 3 18	12 11 14 14 20 18 32 3 16	15 16 14 18 21 18 32 3 16	18 21 19 22 23 19 31 3 16	21 24 24 25 25 19 31 3 16	24 30 24 30 28 20 32 3 17	27 33 26 32 30 20 32 3 17
22	31 27 30 28 18 18 31 2 16	34 31 36 31 18 18 31 2 16	1 33 1 35 16 17 32 2 16	4 1 1 4 16 17 32 3 16	7 5 5 7 16 16 32 3 16	10 9 12 12 18 16 32 3 18	12 12 14 14 20 18 32 3 16	15 17 14 19 21 18 32 3 16	18 22 19 22 23 19 31 3 16	21 25 24 25 25 19 31 3 16	24 32 24 30 28 20 32 3 17	28 35 26 32 30 20 32 3 17
23	31 27 30 28 18 18 31 2 16	34 33 36 31 18 18 31 2 16	1 34 1 35 16 17 32 2 16	4 2 1 4 16 17 32 3 16	7 5 5 7 16 16 32 3 16	10 10 12 12 18 16 32 3 18	13 14 14 15 20 18 32 3 16	15 18 14 19 21 18 32 3 16	19 24 19 22 23 19 31 3 16	21 27 24 25 25 19 31 3 16	25 33 23 30 29 20 32 3 17	28 36 26 32 30 20 32 3 17
24	31 28 30 28 18 18 31 2 16	34 34 34 33 16 16 31 2 16	1 35 1 35 16 17 32 2 16	4 4 2 4 16 17 32 3 16	7 7 6 7 16 16 32 3 16	10 12 12 12 18 16 32 3 18	13 15 14 15 20 18 32 3 16	16 20 14 20 21 18 32 3 16	19 25 19 22 23 19 31 3 16	22 28 24 25 25 19 31 3 16	25 34 23 30 29 20 32 3 17	29 2 26 32 30 20 32 3 17
25	31 30 30 30 18 18 31 2 18	34 34 34 33 16 16 31 2 16	1 36 36 36 16 17 32 2 16	4 5 2 4 16 17 32 3 16	7 8 7 7 16 16 32 3 16	10 13 12 12 18 16 32 3 18	13 16 14 15 20 18 32 3 16	16 21 14 20 21 18 32 3 16	19 26 19 22 23 19 31 3 16	22 30 24 25 25 19 31 3 16	25 35 23 30 29 20 32 3 17	28 3 26 32 30 20 32 3 17
26	31 31 30 30 18 18 31 2 18	34 1 34 33 16 16 31 2 16	1 1 36 36 16 17 31 2 16	4 6 2 4 16 17 32 3 16	7 9 7 7 16 16 32 3 16	10 14 12 12 18 16 32 3 18	13 17 14 15 20 18 32 3 16	16 22 15 20 21 18 32 3 16	19 27 19 22 24 19 31 3 16	22 31 24 25 25 19 31 3 16	26 36 23 30 29 20 32 3 17	29 4 26 32 30 20 32 3 17
27	31 33 31 30 18 18 31 2 18	34 2 35 33 16 16 31 2 16	1 2 36 36 16 17 31 2 16	5 7 2 5 16 17 32 3 16	7 11 7 7 16 16 32 3 16	10 15 13 12 18 16 32 3 18	13 18 14 16 20 18 32 3 16	16 24 15 20 21 18 32 3 16	19 29 19 22 24 19 31 3 16	22 33 24 25 25 19 31 3 16	26 2 23 30 29 20 32 3 17	29 5 26 32 30 20 32 3 17
28	31 34 31 30 18 18 31 2 18	34 3 35 33 16 16 31 2 16	1 4 36 1 16 17 31 2 16	5 8 2 5 16 17 32 3 16	7 12 7 7 16 16 32 3 16	10 17 13 12 18 16 32 3 18	14 20 14 16 20 18 32 3 16	16 25 15 20 21 18 32 3 16	19 30 19 22 24 19 31 3 16	22 34 24 25 25 19 31 3 16	26 3 23 30 29 20 32 3 17	29 6 26 32 30 20 32 3 17
29	31 36 31 30 18 18 31 2 18	1933	1 5 36 1 16 17 31 2 16	5 10 2 5 16 17 32 3 16	7 13 7 7 16 16 31 3 16	10 18 13 12 18 16 32 3 18	14 21 14 16 20 18 32 3 16	16 27 15 20 21 18 32 3 16	19 31 19 22 24 19 31 3 16	22 36 24 25 25 19 31 3 16	26 5 23 30 29 20 32 3 17	29 8 26 32 30 20 32 3 17
30	31 1 31 30 18 18 31 2 18		1 7 36 1 16 17 31 2 16	5 11 2 5 16 17 32 3 16	7 13 7 7 16 16 31 3 16	10 19 13 12 18 16 32 3 18	14 23 14 16 20 18 32 3 16	16 28 15 20 21 18 32 3 16	19 33 20 22 24 19 31 3 16	22 1 25 27 27 19 31 3 16	26 6 23 30 29 20 32 3 17	29 9 26 32 30 20 32 3 17
31	31 2 31 30 18 18 31 2 18		1 8 36 1 16 17 31 2 16		7 15 7 7 16 16 31 3 16		14 24 14 16 20 18 32 3 16	16 30 15 20 21 18 32 3 16		22 2 25 27 27 19 31 3 16		29 10 26 32 30 20 32 3 17

	JAN	FEB	MAR	APR	MAY	JUNE	JULY	AUG	SEPT	OCT	NOV	DEC
1	29 12 27 32 31 21 32 3 17	33 16 33 33 33 21 33 3 17	35 17 35 32 35 21 33 3 17	3 21 35 33 3 21 33 3 17	4 26 3 36 4 20 33 3 16	7 30 9 3 6 20 33 3 16	11 35 12 8 8 20 33 3 17	13 3 11 11 11 20 33 4 17	17 8 17 15 13 21 33 4 17	19 12 22 18 15 21 33 3 17	22 16 24 22 17 22 33 3 17	26 19 24 26 18 23 34 3 17
2	29 13 28 32 31 21 32 3 17	33 17 33 33 33 21 33 3 17	35 18 35 32 35 21 33 3 17	3 23 35 33 3 21 33 3 17	4 27 3 36 4 20 33 3 16	7 32 10 3 6 20 33 3 16	11 36 12 8 9 20 33 3 17	13 5 11 11 11 20 33 4 17	17 9 17 15 13 21 33 4 17	19 13 22 18 15 21 33 3 17	22 17 22 22 17 22 33 3 17	26 20 24 26 18 23 34 3 17
3	29 14 28 32 31 21 32 3 17	33 18 33 33 33 21 33 3 17	35 19 35 32 35 21 33 3 17	3 24 35 33 3 21 33 3 17	4 28 4 36 4 20 33 3 16	7 33 10 3 7 20 33 3 16	11 1 12 8 9 20 33 3 17	13 6 11 11 11 20 33 4 17	17 11 17 15 13 21 33 4 17	19 14 22 18 15 21 33 3 17	22 18 22 22 17 22 33 3 17	26 21 24 26 18 23 34 3 17
4	29 15 29 32 32 21 32 3 17	33 20 33 33 34 21 33 3 17	35 21 35 32 35 21 33 3 17	3 26 35 33 3 21 33 3 17	4 30 4 36 4 20 33 3 16	7 35 10 3 7 20 33 3 16	11 3 12 8 9 20 33 3 17	14 8 11 11 11 20 33 4 17	17 12 17 15 13 21 33 4 17	19 15 22 18 15 21 33 3 17	22 19 22 22 17 22 33 3 17	26 22 24 26 18 23 34 3 17
5	29 17 29 32 32 21 32 3 17	33 21 33 33 34 21 33 3 17	35 22 35 32 35 21 33 3 17	3 27 35 33 3 21 33 3 17	4 31 4 36 4 20 33 3 16	7 36 10 3 7 20 32 3 16	11 4 12 8 9 20 33 3 17	14 9 11 11 11 20 33 4 17	17 13 17 15 13 21 33 4 17	19 16 22 19 15 21 33 3 17	22 21 22 22 17 22 33 3 17	26 24 24 26 18 23 34 3 17
6	30 18 29 32 32 21 32 3 17	33 22 33 33 34 21 33 3 17	35 24 35 32 36 21 33 3 17	3 29 35 34 3 21 33 3 17	4 33 4 36 4 20 33 3 16	7 2 10 3 7 20 33 3 16	11 5 12 8 9 20 33 3 17	14 10 11 11 11 20 33 4 17	17 14 17 15 13 21 33 4 17	19 17 22 19 15 21 33 3 17	24 22 22 22 17 22 33 3 17	26 25 25 26 18 23 34 3 17
7	30 19 29 32 32 21 32 3 17	33 24 35 33 35 21 33 3 17	35 25 35 32 36 21 33 3 17	3 30 35 34 3 21 33 3 17	4 34 4 36 4 20 33 3 16	7 3 10 3 7 20 33 3 16	11 6 12 8 9 20 33 3 17	14 11 11 11 11 20 33 4 17	17 15 18 15 13 21 33 4 17	19 19 22 19 15 21 33 3 17	24 24 22 22 17 22 33 3 17	26 27 25 26 18 23 34 3 17
8	30 20 29 32 32 21 32 3 17	33 25 35 33 35 21 33 3 17	35 26 35 32 36 21 33 3 17	3 31 36 34 3 21 33 3 16	4 35 4 36 4 20 33 3 16	7 4 10 3 7 20 33 3 16	11 8 11 8 9 20 33 3 17	14 12 12 11 11 20 33 4 17	17 17 18 15 13 21 33 4 17	19 20 22 19 15 21 33 3 17	24 25 22 24 17 22 33 3 17	26 29 25 26 18 23 34 3 17
9	30 21 29 32 32 21 32 3 17	33 27 35 33 35 21 33 3 17	35 27 35 32 36 21 33 3 17	3 33 36 34 3 21 33 3 16	4 36 4 36 4 20 33 3 16	7 6 10 3 7 20 33 3 16	11 9 11 8 9 20 33 3 17	14 13 12 11 11 20 33 4 17	17 18 18 15 13 21 33 4 17	19 21 22 19 15 21 33 3 17	24 26 22 24 17 22 33 3 17	26 30 25 26 18 23 34 3 17
10	30 23 29 32 32 21 32 3 17	33 28 35 33 35 21 33 3 17	35 29 35 32 36 21 33 3 17	3 34 36 34 3 21 33 3 16	6 2 6 36 6 20 33 3 16	7 7 10 3 7 20 33 3 16	11 10 11 8 9 20 33 3 17	14 15 13 11 11 20 33 4 17	17 19 18 15 13 21 33 4 17	19 23 22 19 15 21 33 3 17	24 27 22 24 17 22 33 3 17	26 33 25 26 18 23 34 3 17
11	30 24 30 32 32 21 32 3 17	33 30 35 33 35 21 33 3 17	35 30 35 32 36 21 33 3 17	3 35 36 34 3 21 33 3 16	6 3 6 36 6 20 33 3 16	9 8 10 3 7 20 33 3 16	11 11 11 8 9 20 33 3 17	15 16 13 12 12 21 33 4 16	17 21 19 16 13 21 33 4 17	20 24 22 20 15 21 33 3 17	24 29 22 24 17 22 33 3 17	27 33 26 27 18 23 34 3 17
12	30 26 30 32 32 21 32 3 17	33 31 35 33 35 21 33 3 17	36 32 35 32 36 21 33 3 17	3 1 36 34 3 21 33 3 16	6 5 6 36 6 20 33 3 16	9 9 10 4 7 20 33 3 16	11 12 11 8 9 20 33 3 17	15 17 13 12 12 21 33 4 16	17 22 19 16 13 21 33 4 17	20 25 24 20 15 21 33 3 17	24 30 22 24 17 22 33 3 17	27 35 26 27 18 23 34 3 17
13	30 27 30 32 32 21 32 3 17	33 33 35 33 35 21 33 3 17	36 33 35 32 36 21 33 3 17	3 3 36 34 3 21 33 3 16	6 6 6 36 6 20 33 3 16	9 11 10 4 7 20 33 3 16	11 14 11 8 9 20 33 3 17	15 18 13 12 12 21 33 4 16	17 23 19 16 13 21 33 4 17	20 27 24 20 15 21 33 3 17	24 32 22 24 17 22 33 3 17	27 36 26 27 18 23 34 3 17
14	30 29 30 32 32 21 32 3 17	33 34 35 33 35 21 33 3 17	36 35 35 33 36 21 33 3 17	3 4 36 34 3 21 33 3 16	6 7 6 36 6 20 33 3 16	9 12 10 4 7 20 33 3 16	11 15 11 8 9 20 33 3 17	15 19 13 12 12 21 33 4 16	17 24 19 16 13 21 33 4 17	20 28 24 20 15 21 33 3 17	24 33 22 24 17 22 33 3 17	27 1 26 27 18 23 34 3 17
15	30 30 30 33 33 21 33 3 17	33 35 35 33 35 21 33 3 17	36 36 35 33 36 21 33 3 17	3 5 1 34 3 21 33 3 16	6 8 6 36 6 20 33 3 16	9 13 10 4 7 20 33 3 16	11 16 11 8 9 20 33 3 17	15 20 13 12 12 21 33 4 16	17 26 19 17 13 21 33 4 17	21 29 24 21 15 21 33 3 17	24 35 22 24 17 22 33 3 17	27 3 26 27 18 23 34 3 17
16	30 33 30 33 33 21 33 3 17	33 1 35 32 35 21 33 3 17	36 2 35 33 36 21 33 3 17	3 6 1 34 3 21 33 3 16	6 9 6 36 6 20 33 3 16	9 14 10 4 7 20 33 3 16	12 17 11 9 10 20 33 3 16	15 22 14 12 12 21 33 4 16	18 27 20 17 13 21 33 4 17	21 30 24 21 15 21 33 3 17	24 36 22 24 17 22 33 3 17	27 4 26 28 19 23 34 3 17
17	30 33 30 33 33 21 33 3 17	33 2 35 32 35 21 33 3 17	36 3 35 33 36 21 33 3 17	3 8 1 34 3 21 33 3 16	6 11 7 36 6 20 33 3 16	9 15 11 4 7 20 33 3 16	12 18 11 9 10 20 33 3 16	15 23 14 12 12 21 33 4 16	18 28 20 17 13 21 33 4 17	21 33 24 21 15 21 33 3 17	24 2 22 24 17 22 33 3 17	27 5 26 28 19 23 34 3 17
18	30 35 30 33 33 21 33 3 17	33 3 35 32 35 21 33 3 17	36 5 35 33 36 21 33 3 17	3 9 1 34 3 21 33 3 16	6 12 7 36 6 20 33 3 16	9 16 11 4 7 20 33 3 16	12 20 11 9 10 20 33 3 16	15 24 15 13 12 21 33 4 16	18 30 20 17 13 21 33 4 17	21 33 24 21 15 21 33 3 17	24 3 22 24 17 22 33 3 17	27 6 26 28 19 23 34 3 17
19	30 36 30 33 33 21 33 3 17	33 5 35 32 35 21 33 3 17	36 6 35 33 36 21 33 3 17	3 10 1 34 3 21 33 3 16	6 13 7 36 6 20 33 3 16	9 18 12 6 7 20 33 3 16	12 21 11 9 10 20 33 3 16	15 26 15 13 12 21 33 4 16	18 31 20 17 13 21 33 4 17	21 35 24 21 16 21 33 3 17	24 4 22 24 17 22 33 3 17	27 8 26 28 19 23 34 3 17
20	30 2 30 33 33 21 33 3 17	34 6 35 32 35 21 33 3 17	36 7 35 33 36 21 33 3 17	3 11 1 34 3 21 33 3 16	6 14 7 36 6 20 33 3 16	9 19 12 6 7 20 33 3 16	12 22 11 9 10 20 33 3 16	15 27 15 13 12 21 33 4 16	18 33 20 17 13 21 33 4 17	21 36 24 21 16 21 33 3 17	24 6 22 24 17 22 33 3 17	27 9 26 28 19 23 34 3 17
21	31 3 31 33 33 21 33 3 17	34 7 35 32 35 21 35 3 17	1 8 35 33 1 21 33 3 17	4 12 2 34 4 20 33 3 16	6 15 7 36 6 20 33 3 16	9 20 12 6 7 20 33 3 16	12 24 11 9 10 20 33 3 16	15 29 15 13 12 21 33 4 16	18 35 21 17 15 21 33 4 17	21 2 24 21 16 21 33 3 17	24 7 22 24 17 22 33 3 17	27 10 26 28 19 23 34 3 17
22	31 4 31 33 33 21 33 3 17	35 8 35 32 35 21 33 3 17	1 9 35 33 1 21 33 3 17	4 14 2 34 4 20 33 3 16	7 16 7 36 6 20 33 3 16	9 21 12 6 7 20 33 3 16	12 25 11 9 10 20 33 3 16	15 30 15 13 12 21 33 4 16	18 36 21 17 15 21 33 4 17	22 3 24 21 17 22 33 4 17	24 8 24 24 17 22 33 3 17	27 12 26 28 19 23 34 3 17
23	31 6 31 33 33 21 33 3 17	35 9 35 32 35 21 33 3 17	1 10 35 33 1 21 33 3 17	4 15 2 34 4 20 33 3 16	7 18 7 36 6 20 33 3 16	10 23 12 6 7 20 33 3 16	13 27 11 9 10 20 33 3 16	15 31 15 13 12 21 33 4 16	18 1 21 17 15 21 33 4 17	22 4 24 21 17 22 33 4 17	25 9 24 25 17 22 33 3 17	28 13 27 28 19 23 34 3 17
24	31 6 31 33 33 21 33 3 17	35 11 35 32 35 21 33 3 17	1 12 35 33 1 21 33 3 17	4 16 2 34 4 20 33 3 16	7 20 7 36 6 20 33 3 16	10 24 12 6 7 20 33 3 16	13 28 11 10 10 20 33 4 16	16 33 16 13 13 21 33 4 16	19 3 21 17 15 21 33 4 17	22 6 24 21 17 22 33 4 17	25 11 24 25 17 22 33 3 17	28 14 27 28 19 23 34 3 17
25	31 8 31 33 33 21 33 3 17	35 12 35 32 35 21 33 3 17	1 13 35 33 1 21 33 3 17	4 17 2 34 4 20 33 3 16	7 21 7 36 6 20 33 3 16	10 25 12 6 7 20 33 3 16	13 29 11 10 10 20 33 4 16	16 35 16 13 13 21 33 4 16	19 4 21 17 15 21 33 4 17	22 7 24 21 17 22 33 4 17	25 12 24 25 17 22 33 3 17	28 15 27 28 19 23 34 3 17
26	31 9 31 33 33 21 33 3 17	35 13 35 32 35 21 33 3 17	1 15 35 33 1 21 33 3 17	4 18 2 36 4 20 33 3 16	7 22 7 36 6 20 33 3 16	10 27 12 6 7 20 33 3 16	13 31 11 10 10 20 33 4 16	16 36 16 13 13 21 33 4 16	19 6 21 17 15 21 33 4 17	22 9 24 21 17 22 33 4 17	25 13 24 25 17 22 33 3 17	28 16 27 28 19 23 34 3 17
27	31 10 31 33 33 21 33 3 17	35 14 35 32 35 21 33 3 17	1 15 35 33 1 21 33 3 17	4 20 3 36 4 20 33 3 16	7 23 9 36 6 20 33 3 16	10 29 12 6 7 20 33 3 16	13 33 11 10 10 20 33 4 16	16 2 16 14 11 20 33 4 16	19 7 21 17 15 21 33 4 17	22 10 24 21 17 22 33 4 17	25 14 24 25 17 22 33 3 17	28 17 27 28 19 23 34 3 17
28	31 11 31 33 33 21 33 3 17	35 15 35 32 35 21 33 3 17	1 17 35 33 1 21 33 3 17	4 21 3 36 4 20 33 3 16	7 25 9 36 6 20 33 3 16	10 30 12 6 7 20 33 3 16	13 34 11 10 10 20 33 4 16	16 3 16 14 11 20 33 4 16	19 8 21 17 15 21 33 4 17	22 11 24 21 17 22 33 4 17	26 15 24 26 17 22 33 3 17	29 19 28 28 19 23 34 3 17
29	33 12 33 33 33 21 33 3 17		1 18 35 33 1 21 33 3 17	4 22 3 36 4 20 33 3 16	7 26 9 36 6 20 33 3 16	10 32 12 6 7 20 33 3 16	13 35 11 10 10 20 33 4 16	16 4 16 14 11 20 33 4 16	19 9 21 17 15 21 33 4 17	22 12 24 21 17 22 33 4 17	26 17 24 26 17 22 33 3 17	29 19 28 28 19 23 34 3 17
30	33 15 33 33 33 21 33 3 17	**1934**	1 19 35 33 1 21 33 3 17	4 24 3 36 4 20 33 3 16	7 28 9 36 6 20 33 3 16	10 33 12 6 9 20 33 3 16	13 1 11 10 10 20 33 4 16	16 5 16 15 11 20 33 4 16	19 11 22 18 15 21 33 4 17	22 14 24 22 17 22 33 4 17	26 18 24 26 17 22 33 3 17	29 21 28 28 19 23 34 3 17
31	33 15 33 33 33 21 33 3 17		1 20 35 33 1 21 33 3 17		7 29 9 36 6 20 33 3 16		13 2 11 10 10 20 33 4 16	16 7 16 15 11 20 33 4 16		22 15 24 22 17 22 33 4 17		29 22 28 28 19 23 34 3 17

	JAN	FEB	MAR	APR	MAY	JUNE	JULY	AUG	SEPT	OCT	NOV	DEC
1	29 24 29 30 20 23 33 3 17	32 29 33 33 21 23 33 3 17	34 30 33 1 21 24 34 3 17	2 34 36 6 20 24 34 4 16	5 3 5 7 19 23 34 4 16	8 8 10 12 19 23 35 4 17	11 11 9 15 20 23 35 4 17	13 16 13 17 22 23 35 4 17	17 20 18 17 23 23 34 4 17	19 24 22 16 25 24 34 4 17	22 28 21 17 28 24 34 4 17	25 32 25 21 30 25 34 4 17
2	29 25 29 30 20 23 33 3 17	32 30 33 34 21 23 33 3 17	34 31 33 1 21 24 34 3 17	2 36 36 6 20 24 34 4 16	5 4 5 7 19 23 34 4 16	8 9 10 12 19 23 35 4 17	11 13 9 15 20 23 35 4 17	13 17 13 17 22 23 35 4 17	17 21 18 17 23 23 34 4 17	19 25 22 16 25 24 34 4 17	22 29 21 17 28 24 34 4 17	25 33 25 21 30 25 34 4 17
3	29 27 29 30 20 23 33 3 17	32 32 33 34 21 23 33 3 17	35 33 33 1 21 24 34 3 17	2 2 36 6 20 24 34 4 16	5 5 5 7 19 23 34 4 16	8 10 10 12 19 23 35 4 17	11 14 9 15 20 23 35 4 17	13 18 13 17 22 23 34 4 17	17 22 19 17 23 23 34 4 17	19 26 22 16 25 24 34 4 17	22 31 21 17 28 24 34 4 17	25 34 25 21 30 25 34 4 17
4	29 29 29 30 20 23 33 3 17	32 33 33 34 21 23 33 3 17	35 34 33 1 21 24 34 3 17	2 3 36 6 20 24 34 4 16	5 7 5 7 19 23 34 4 16	8 11 10 12 19 23 35 4 17	11 15 9 15 20 23 35 4 17	13 19 13 17 22 23 34 4 17	17 23 19 17 23 23 34 4 17	19 27 22 16 25 24 34 4 17	22 33 21 17 28 24 34 4 17	25 36 25 21 30 25 34 4 17
5	29 30 29 30 20 23 33 3 17	32 35 33 34 21 23 33 3 17	35 36 33 1 21 24 34 3 17	2 4 36 6 20 24 34 4 16	5 9 5 9 19 23 34 4 16	8 13 10 12 19 23 35 4 17	11 17 9 15 20 23 35 4 17	13 20 13 17 22 23 34 4 17	17 25 19 17 23 23 34 4 17	19 28 22 16 25 24 34 4 17	23 34 21 18 29 24 34 4 17	25 2 25 21 30 25 34 4 17
6	29 31 30 30 20 23 33 3 17	32 36 33 35 21 23 33 3 17	35 1 33 1 21 24 34 3 17	2 6 36 6 20 24 34 4 16	5 10 5 9 19 23 34 4 16	8 14 10 12 19 23 35 4 17	11 17 9 15 20 23 35 4 17	13 22 13 17 22 23 34 4 17	17 26 19 17 23 23 34 4 17	19 30 22 16 25 24 34 4 17	23 36 21 18 29 24 34 4 17	25 3 25 21 30 25 34 4 17
7	29 33 30 30 20 23 33 3 17	32 2 33 35 21 23 33 3 17	35 3 33 1 21 24 34 3 17	2 7 36 6 20 24 34 4 16	5 11 5 9 19 23 34 4 16	8 15 10 13 19 23 35 4 17	11 18 9 15 20 23 35 4 17	13 23 13 17 22 24 35 4 17	17 28 19 17 23 23 34 4 17	19 31 22 16 25 24 34 4 17	23 1 21 18 29 24 34 4 17	25 4 25 22 31 25 34 4 17
8	30 34 30 30 21 23 33 3 17	32 3 33 35 21 23 33 3 17	35 4 33 1 21 24 34 3 17	2 9 36 6 20 24 34 4 16	5 12 5 9 19 23 34 4 16	8 17 10 13 19 23 35 4 17	11 19 9 16 20 23 35 4 17	13 24 13 17 22 24 35 4 17	17 29 19 16 23 23 34 4 17	20 33 22 16 26 24 34 4 17	23 2 22 18 29 24 34 4 17	26 6 26 22 31 25 34 4 17
9	30 35 30 31 21 23 33 3 17	32 5 33 35 21 23 33 3 17	35 6 33 1 21 24 34 3 17	2 10 1 6 20 24 34 4 16	5 13 7 9 19 23 34 4 16	9 18 10 13 19 23 35 4 17	11 20 9 17 20 23 35 4 17	14 25 13 17 22 24 35 4 17	17 30 19 16 23 23 34 4 17	20 34 22 16 26 24 34 4 17	23 4 22 18 29 24 34 4 17	26 7 26 22 31 25 34 4 17
10	30 1 30 31 21 23 33 3 17	33 6 33 35 21 24 33 3 17	35 7 33 1 21 24 34 3 17	2 11 1 6 20 24 34 4 16	5 15 7 9 19 23 34 4 16	8 19 10 13 19 23 35 4 17	11 22 9 17 20 23 35 4 17	14 26 14 17 22 24 35 4 17	17 31 19 16 23 23 34 4 17	20 36 22 16 26 24 34 4 17	23 5 22 18 29 24 34 4 17	26 9 26 22 31 25 34 4 17
11	30 2 30 31 21 23 33 3 17	33 8 33 35 21 24 33 3 17	35 8 33 3 21 24 34 3 17	2 13 1 6 20 24 34 4 16	5 16 7 9 19 23 34 4 16	8 20 10 13 19 23 35 4 17	11 23 9 17 20 23 35 4 17	14 28 14 17 22 24 35 4 17	17 32 19 16 23 23 34 4 17	20 1 22 16 26 24 34 4 17	23 6 22 18 29 24 34 4 17	26 10 26 22 31 25 34 4 17
12	30 3 30 31 21 23 33 3 17	33 9 33 35 21 24 33 3 17	35 9 33 3 21 24 34 3 17	2 14 2 6 20 24 34 4 16	5 17 7 10 19 23 34 4 16	9 21 10 13 19 23 35 4 17	11 26 9 17 20 23 35 4 17	14 30 14 17 22 24 35 4 17	17 34 19 16 23 23 34 4 17	20 3 22 16 26 24 34 4 17	23 7 22 20 29 24 34 4 17	26 12 26 22 31 25 34 4 17
13	30 5 31 31 21 23 33 3 17	33 10 33 35 21 24 33 3 17	35 11 33 3 21 24 34 3 17	2 15 2 6 20 24 34 4 16	5 18 7 10 19 23 34 4 16	9 22 10 14 20 23 35 4 17	11 26 9 17 20 23 35 4 17	14 31 14 17 22 24 35 4 17	17 36 20 16 23 23 34 4 17	20 4 22 16 26 24 34 4 17	23 9 22 20 29 24 34 4 17	26 13 26 22 31 25 34 4 17
14	30 6 31 31 21 23 33 3 17	33 11 33 35 21 24 33 3 17	35 12 33 3 21 24 34 3 17	3 16 2 6 20 24 34 3 16	5 19 7 10 19 23 34 4 16	9 23 10 14 20 23 35 4 17	11 27 10 17 20 23 35 4 17	14 32 14 17 22 34 35 4 17	17 2 20 16 23 23 34 4 17	20 6 22 16 26 24 34 4 17	23 11 22 20 29 24 34 4 17	26 14 26 22 31 25 34 4 17
15	30 8 31 31 21 23 33 3 17	33 12 33 35 21 24 33 3 17	36 13 33 3 21 24 34 3 17	3 17 2 6 20 24 34 3 16	5 20 7 10 19 23 34 4 16	9 26 10 14 20 23 35 4 17	11 29 11 17 20 23 35 4 17	14 34 15 17 22 24 35 4 17	17 3 20 16 23 23 34 4 17	20 7 22 16 26 24 34 4 17	23 12 22 20 29 24 34 4 17	26 15 26 22 31 25 34 4 17
16	30 9 31 31 21 23 33 3 17	33 13 33 35 21 24 33 3 17	36 15 33 3 21 24 34 3 17	3 18 2 7 20 24 34 3 16	5 22 7 10 19 23 34 4 16	9 26 10 14 20 23 35 4 17	11 30 11 17 20 23 35 4 17	14 35 15 17 22 24 35 4 17	17 4 20 16 25 23 34 4 17	20 8 20 16 26 24 34 4 17	24 13 22 20 29 24 34 4 17	26 16 27 22 31 25 34 4 17
17	30 10 32 32 21 23 33 3 17	33 14 33 35 21 24 33 3 17	36 15 33 3 21 24 34 3 17	3 20 2 7 20 24 34 3 16	5 23 7 10 19 23 34 4 16	9 28 10 14 20 23 35 4 17	12 31 11 17 21 23 35 4 17	14 1 16 17 22 24 35 4 17	17 6 20 16 25 23 34 4 17	20 10 20 16 26 24 34 4 17	24 14 22 20 29 24 34 4 17	26 18 27 22 31 25 34 4 17
18	30 11 32 32 21 23 33 3 17	33 15 33 35 21 24 33 3 17	36 17 33 3 21 24 34 3 17	3 21 2 7 20 24 34 3 16	5 24 7 10 19 23 34 4 16	9 29 10 14 20 23 35 4 17	12 33 11 17 21 23 35 4 17	14 2 16 17 22 24 35 4 17	18 7 20 16 25 23 34 4 17	20 11 20 16 26 24 34 4 17	24 16 22 20 29 24 34 4 17	26 19 28 22 31 25 34 4 17
19	30 12 32 32 21 23 33 3 17	33 17 33 35 21 24 33 3 17	36 18 34 3 21 24 34 3 17	3 22 2 7 20 24 34 3 16	6 25 7 10 19 23 34 4 16	9 31 10 14 20 23 35 4 17	12 35 11 17 21 23 35 4 17	14 4 16 17 22 24 35 4 17	18 9 20 16 25 23 34 4 17	20 12 20 17 26 24 34 4 17	24 17 23 20 29 24 34 4 17	26 20 28 22 31 25 34 4 17
20	30 14 32 32 21 23 33 3 17	34 18 33 35 21 24 34 3 17	36 19 34 3 21 24 34 3 17	3 24 2 7 20 24 34 3 16	6 27 7 10 19 23 34 4 16	9 32 9 14 20 23 35 4 17	12 36 11 17 21 23 35 4 17	15 5 16 17 22 24 35 4 17	18 10 20 16 25 23 34 4 17	20 13 20 17 26 24 34 4 17	24 18 23 20 29 24 34 4 17	27 21 28 22 31 25 34 4 17
21	31 15 32 32 21 23 33 3 17	34 19 33 36 21 24 34 3 17	36 21 34 3 21 24 34 3 17	4 25 3 7 20 24 34 4 16	6 28 7 10 19 23 34 4 16	9 33 9 14 20 23 35 4 17	12 2 11 17 21 23 35 4 17	15 7 16 17 22 24 35 4 17	18 11 21 16 25 23 34 4 17	20 15 20 17 26 24 34 4 17	24 20 23 20 29 24 34 4 17	27 23 28 23 32 25 34 4 17
22	31 16 32 32 21 23 33 3 17	34 21 33 36 21 24 34 3 17	1 21 34 3 21 24 34 3 17	4 26 3 7 20 24 34 4 16	7 30 9 10 19 23 34 4 16	10 35 9 14 20 23 35 4 17	12 3 11 17 21 23 35 4 17	15 8 16 17 22 24 35 4 17	18 31 21 16 25 23 34 4 17	21 16 21 17 27 24 34 4 17	24 20 23 20 29 24 34 4 17	27 24 28 23 32 25 34 4 17
23	31 17 32 32 21 23 33 3 17	34 21 33 36 21 24 34 3 17	1 23 34 3 21 24 34 3 17	4 27 3 7 20 24 34 4 16	7 31 9 10 19 23 34 4 16	10 36 9 14 20 23 35 4 17	12 4 11 17 21 23 35 4 17	15 9 16 17 22 24 35 4 17	18 14 21 16 25 23 34 4 17	21 17 21 17 27 24 34 4 17	25 22 23 20 29 25 34 4 17	28 25 28 23 32 25 34 4 17
24	31 18 33 33 21 23 33 3 17	34 23 33 36 21 24 34 3 17	1 24 34 4 21 24 34 4 16	4 29 4 7 19 24 34 4 16	7 32 9 10 19 23 34 4 16	10 2 9 14 20 23 35 4 17	13 5 11 17 22 23 35 4 17	16 11 16 17 23 23 34 4 17	19 15 21 16 25 23 34 4 17	21 18 21 17 27 24 34 4 17	25 23 23 20 29 25 34 4 17	28 26 28 23 32 25 34 4 17
25	31 20 33 33 21 23 33 3 17	34 24 33 36 21 24 34 3 17	1 25 34 4 21 24 34 4 16	4 30 4 7 19 24 34 4 16	7 34 9 10 19 23 34 4 16	10 3 9 14 20 23 35 4 17	13 7 11 17 22 23 35 4 17	16 12 16 17 23 23 34 4 17	19 16 21 16 25 23 34 4 17	22 20 20 17 28 24 34 4 17	25 24 23 20 29 25 34 4 17	28 27 28 23 32 25 34 4 17
26	31 21 33 33 21 23 33 3 17	34 25 33 1 21 24 34 3 17	1 27 34 4 21 24 34 4 16	4 31 4 7 19 24 34 4 16	7 36 9 12 19 23 34 4 16	10 4 9 14 20 23 35 4 17	13 8 11 17 22 23 35 4 17	16 13 17 17 23 23 34 4 17	19 17 21 16 25 23 34 4 17	22 21 20 17 28 24 34 4 17	25 25 23 20 29 25 34 4 17	28 28 28 23 32 25 34 4 17
27	31 22 33 33 21 23 33 3 17	34 27 33 1 21 24 34 3 17	1 28 34 4 21 24 34 4 16	4 33 4 7 19 24 34 4 16	7 1 9 12 19 23 34 4 16	10 5 9 14 20 23 35 4 17	13 10 11 17 22 23 35 4 17	16 14 17 17 23 23 34 4 17	19 19 21 16 25 23 34 4 17	22 22 20 17 28 24 34 4 17	25 26 23 20 29 25 34 4 17	28 29 28 23 32 25 34 4 17
28	31 23 33 33 21 23 33 3 17	34 29 33 1 21 24 34 3 17	1 29 34 4 21 24 34 4 16	4 34 4 7 19 24 34 4 16	7 2 9 12 19 23 34 4 16	10 3 9 14 20 23 35 4 17	13 11 12 17 22 23 35 4 17	16 15 17 17 23 23 34 4 17	19 20 22 16 25 23 34 4 17	22 23 20 17 28 24 34 4 17	25 28 23 20 29 25 34 4 17	28 31 29 23 32 25 34 4 17
29	31 24 33 33 21 23 33 3 17	1935	1 30 34 4 21 24 34 4 16	4 36 4 7 19 24 34 4 16	7 4 9 12 19 23 34 4 16	10 9 9 14 20 23 35 4 17	13 12 12 17 22 23 35 4 17	16 16 17 17 23 23 34 4 17	19 21 22 16 25 23 34 4 17	22 24 20 17 28 24 34 4 17	25 29 23 20 29 25 34 4 17	28 32 29 23 32 25 34 4 17
30	31 26 33 33 21 23 33 3 17		1 31 34 4 21 24 34 4 16	4 1 4 7 19 24 34 4 16	7 5 10 12 19 23 34 4 16	10 10 9 14 20 23 35 4 17	13 13 12 17 22 23 35 4 17	16 17 17 17 23 23 34 4 17	19 22 22 16 25 23 34 4 17	22 25 20 17 28 24 34 4 17	25 31 25 20 29 25 34 4 17	28 34 29 23 32 25 34 4 17
31	31 27 33 33 21 23 33 3 17		1 33 34 4 21 24 34 4 16		7 6 10 12 19 23 34 4 16		14 14 12 17 22 23 35 4 17	16 19 17 17 23 23 34 4 17		22 27 20 17 28 24 34 4 17		28 35 29 23 32 25 34 4 17

	JAN	FEB	MAR	APR	MAY	JUNE	JULY	AUG	SEPT	OCT	NOV	DEC
1	29 36 30 24 33 26 35 4 17	32 7 31 28 35 26 35 4 17	35 9 32 32 1 27 35 4 17	2 14 1 35 4 27 35 4 17	5 17 7 3 6 27 35 4 17	8 22 7 7 8 27 36 4 17	10 25 8 11 10 26 36 4 17	13 30 14 14 12 26 35 4 17	16 35 19 18 14 26 35 4 17	19 3 19 22 16 26 35 4 17	22 8 21 26 18 27 35 4 17	25 12 26 29 20 27 35 4 17
2	29 2 30 24 33 26 35 4 17	32 8 31 28 25 26 35 4 17	35 10 32 32 1 27 35 4 17	2 15 1 35 4 27 35 4 17	5 18 7 3 6 27 35 4 17	8 23 7 7 8 27 36 4 17	11 26 9 11 10 26 36 4 17	14 31 15 14 12 26 35 4 17	16 36 19 18 14 26 35 4 17	19 4 19 22 16 26 35 4 17	23 9 22 26 18 27 35 4 17	26 13 26 29 20 28 35 4 17
3	29 3 30 25 33 26 35 4 17	32 10 31 28 35 26 35 4 17	35 12 32 32 1 27 35 4 17	2 16 1 36 4 27 35 4 17	5 20 7 3 6 27 35 4 17	8 24 7 7 8 27 36 4 17	11 27 9 11 10 26 36 4 17	14 32 15 15 12 26 35 4 17	17 2 19 18 14 26 35 4 17	20 6 19 22 16 26 35 4 17	23 11 22 26 18 27 35 4 17	26 14 26 30 20 28 35 4 17
4	29 4 30 25 33 26 35 4 17	32 11 31 28 35 26 35 4 17	35 13 32 32 1 27 35 4 17	2 17 1 36 4 27 35 4 17	5 21 7 3 6 27 35 4 17	8 25 7 7 8 27 36 4 17	11 28 9 11 10 26 36 4 17	14 34 15 15 12 26 35 4 17	17 3 19 19 14 26 35 4 17	20 7 19 22 16 26 35 4 17	23 12 22 26 18 27 35 4 17	26 15 27 30 20 28 35 4 17
5	29 6 30 25 33 26 35 4 17	32 12 31 29 35 26 35 4 17	35 14 32 32 1 27 35 4 17	2 19 2 36 4 27 35 4 17	5 22 7 4 6 27 35 4 17	8 26 7 7 8 27 36 4 17	11 30 9 11 10 26 36 4 17	14 35 15 15 12 26 35 4 17	17 5 19 19 14 26 35 4 17	20 8 19 22 16 26 35 4 17	23 13 22 26 18 27 35 4 17	26 17 27 30 20 28 35 4 17
6	29 7 31 25 33 26 35 4 17	32 13 31 29 35 26 35 4 17	35 15 33 32 2 27 35 4 17	2 20 2 36 4 27 35 4 17	5 23 7 4 6 27 35 4 17	8 28 7 7 8 27 36 4 17	11 31 9 11 10 26 36 4 17	14 1 15 15 12 26 35 4 17	17 6 20 19 14 26 35 4 17	20 10 19 23 16 26 35 4 17	23 15 22 26 18 27 35 4 17	26 18 27 30 20 28 35 4 17
7	29 9 31 25 33 26 35 4 17	32 15 31 29 35 26 35 4 17	35 17 33 32 2 27 35 4 17	2 21 2 36 4 27 35 4 17	5 24 7 4 6 27 35 4 17	8 29 7 8 8 27 36 4 17	11 33 10 11 10 26 36 4 17	14 2 16 15 12 26 35 4 17	17 7 20 19 14 26 35 4 17	20 11 19 23 16 26 35 4 17	23 16 22 26 18 27 35 4 17	26 19 27 30 20 28 35 4 17
8	29 10 31 25 33 26 35 4 17	32 16 31 29 35 26 35 4 17	35 18 33 32 2 27 35 4 17	2 22 2 36 4 27 35 4 17	5 25 7 4 6 27 35 4 17	8 30 7 8 8 26 36 4 17	11 34 10 11 10 26 36 4 17	14 4 16 15 12 26 35 4 17	17 9 20 19 14 26 35 4 17	20 12 19 23 16 26 35 4 17	23 17 23 27 18 27 35 4 17	26 20 27 30 20 28 35 4 17
9	29 11 31 25 33 26 35 4 17	32 17 31 29 36 26 35 4 17	35 19 33 33 2 27 35 4 17	2 23 2 36 4 27 35 4 17	5 27 7 4 6 27 35 4 17	8 32 7 8 8 26 36 4 17	11 35 10 12 10 26 36 4 17	14 5 16 15 12 26 35 4 17	17 10 20 19 14 26 35 4 17	20 14 19 23 16 26 35 4 17	23 18 23 27 18 27 35 4 17	26 22 27 30 20 28 35 4 17
10	29 12 31 25 33 26 35 4 17	33 19 31 29 36 26 35 4 17	35 20 33 33 2 27 35 4 17	3 25 3 36 4 27 35 4 17	5 28 8 4 6 27 35 4 17	8 33 7 8 8 26 36 4 17	11 1 10 12 11 26 36 4 17	14 6 16 15 13 26 35 4 17	17 11 20 19 15 26 35 4 17	20 15 19 23 16 26 35 4 17	23 19 23 27 18 27 35 4 17	26 23 28 31 20 28 35 4 17
11	30 14 31 26 33 26 35 4 17	33 20 31 29 36 26 35 4 17	36 21 33 33 2 27 35 4 17	3 26 3 1 4 27 35 4 17	6 29 8 4 6 27 35 4 17	9 34 7 8 9 26 36 4 17	11 2 10 12 11 26 36 4 17	14 8 16 16 13 26 35 4 17	17 13 20 19 15 26 35 4 17	20 16 19 23 16 26 35 4 17	23 21 23 27 18 27 35 4 17	26 24 28 31 20 28 35 4 17
12	30 16 31 26 33 26 35 4 17	33 21 31 29 36 26 35 4 17	36 23 33 33 2 27 35 4 17	3 27 3 1 4 27 35 4 17	6 31 8 4 6 27 35 4 17	9 36 7 8 9 26 36 4 17	12 4 10 12 11 26 36 4 17	14 9 16 16 13 26 35 4 17	17 14 20 20 15 26 35 4 17	20 17 19 23 17 27 35 4 17	24 22 23 27 18 27 35 4 17	27 25 28 31 20 28 35 4 17
13	30 17 32 26 33 26 35 4 17	33 22 31 29 36 26 35 4 17	36 24 34 33 2 27 35 4 17	3 28 3 1 4 27 35 4 17	6 32 7 5 7 27 35 4 17	9 1 7 8 9 26 36 4 17	12 5 10 12 11 26 36 4 17	15 10 17 16 13 26 35 4 17	18 15 20 20 15 26 35 4 17	21 18 19 23 17 27 35 4 17	24 23 23 27 18 27 35 4 17	27 26 28 31 20 28 35 4 17
14	30 19 32 26 34 26 35 4 17	33 23 31 30 36 26 35 4 17	36 25 34 33 2 27 35 4 17	3 30 3 1 4 27 35 4 17	6 33 7 5 7 27 35 4 17	9 3 7 8 9 26 36 4 17	12 7 11 12 11 26 36 4 17	15 12 17 16 13 26 35 4 17	18 16 20 20 15 26 35 4 17	21 20 19 23 17 27 35 4 17	24 24 24 27 19 27 35 4 17	27 28 28 31 20 28 35 4 17
15	30 20 32 26 34 26 35 4 17	33 24 31 30 36 26 35 4 17	36 26 34 33 2 27 35 4 17	3 31 4 1 5 27 35 4 17	6 35 7 5 7 27 35 4 17	9 4 7 9 9 26 36 4 17	12 8 11 12 11 26 36 4 17	15 13 17 16 13 26 35 4 17	18 18 20 20 15 26 35 4 17	21 21 19 24 17 27 35 4 17	24 25 24 27 19 27 35 4 17	27 29 28 31 20 28 35 4 17
16	30 21 32 26 34 26 35 4 17	33 25 31 30 36 27 35 4 17	36 27 34 33 2 27 35 4 17	3 32 4 1 5 27 35 4 17	6 36 7 5 7 27 35 4 17	9 6 7 9 9 26 36 4 17	12 9 11 12 11 26 36 4 17	15 14 17 16 13 26 35 4 17	18 19 20 20 15 26 35 4 17	21 22 19 23 17 27 35 4 17	24 27 24 28 19 27 35 4 17	27 30 29 31 20 28 35 4 17
17	30 22 32 26 34 26 35 4 17	33 27 31 30 36 27 35 4 17	36 29 34 34 2 27 35 4 17	3 34 4 1 5 27 35 4 17	6 2 7 5 7 27 35 4 17	9 7 7 9 9 26 36 4 17	12 11 11 13 11 26 36 4 17	15 16 17 16 13 26 35 4 17	18 20 20 20 15 26 35 4 17	21 23 19 23 17 27 35 4 17	24 28 24 28 19 27 35 4 17	27 31 29 31 20 28 35 4 17
18	30 23 32 26 34 26 35 4 17	33 28 31 30 36 27 35 4 17	36 30 34 34 2 27 35 4 17	3 35 4 1 5 27 35 4 17	6 3 7 5 7 27 35 4 17	9 8 7 9 9 26 36 4 17	12 12 11 13 11 26 36 4 17	15 17 17 16 13 26 35 4 17	18 21 20 20 15 26 35 4 17	21 25 19 23 17 27 35 4 17	24 29 24 28 19 27 35 4 17	27 33 29 31 21 28 35 4 17
19	30 25 32 26 34 26 35 4 17	33 29 31 30 36 27 35 4 17	36 31 35 34 3 27 35 4 17	3 1 5 2 5 27 35 4 17	6 5 7 5 7 27 35 4 17	9 10 7 9 9 26 36 4 17	12 13 12 13 11 26 36 4 17	15 18 17 17 13 26 35 4 17	18 22 20 20 15 26 35 4 17	21 26 19 23 17 27 35 4 17	24 30 24 28 19 27 35 4 17	27 34 29 31 21 28 35 4 17
20	30 26 32 27 34 26 35 4 17	34 31 31 30 36 27 35 4 17	36 32 35 34 3 27 35 4 17	4 2 5 2 5 27 35 4 17	6 6 7 5 7 27 35 4 17	9 11 7 9 9 26 36 4 17	12 15 12 13 11 26 36 4 17	15 19 18 17 13 26 35 4 17	18 24 20 21 15 26 35 4 17	21 27 20 24 17 27 35 4 17	24 32 24 28 19 27 35 4 17	27 35 29 31 21 28 35 4 17
21	31 27 32 27 34 26 35 4 17	34 32 31 30 1 27 35 4 17	1 34 35 34 3 27 35 4 17	4 4 5 2 5 27 35 4 17	7 8 7 6 7 27 36 4 17	9 12 7 9 9 26 36 4 17	12 16 12 13 11 26 36 4 17	15 20 18 17 13 26 35 4 17	18 25 20 21 15 26 35 4 17	21 28 20 24 17 27 35 4 17	24 33 24 28 19 27 35 4 17	27 1 29 31 21 28 35 4 17
22	31 28 32 27 34 26 35 4 17	34 34 31 30 1 27 35 4 17	1 36 35 34 3 27 35 4 17	4 5 5 2 5 27 35 4 17	7 9 7 6 7 27 36 4 17	10 14 7 9 9 26 36 4 17	12 17 12 13 11 26 36 4 17	15 22 18 17 13 26 35 4 17	18 26 20 21 15 26 35 4 17	21 29 20 24 17 27 35 4 17	25 34 25 28 19 27 35 4 17	28 2 29 32 21 28 35 4 17
23	31 29 32 27 34 26 35 4 17	34 35 31 31 1 27 35 4 17	1 2 35 34 3 27 35 4 17	4 7 5 2 5 27 35 4 17	7 10 7 6 7 27 36 4 17	10 15 8 10 9 26 36 4 17	13 18 13 13 11 26 36 4 17	16 23 18 17 13 26 35 4 17	19 27 20 21 15 26 35 4 17	22 31 20 25 17 27 35 4 17	25 36 25 28 19 27 35 4 17	28 4 30 31 21 28 35 4 17
24	31 31 32 27 34 26 35 4 17	34 1 31 31 1 27 35 4 17	1 3 35 34 3 27 35 4 17	4 8 5 2 5 27 35 4 17	7 12 7 6 7 27 36 4 17	10 16 8 10 9 26 36 4 17	13 20 13 13 11 26 36 4 17	16 24 18 17 13 26 35 4 17	19 29 20 21 15 26 35 4 17	22 32 20 25 17 27 35 4 17	25 1 25 28 19 27 35 4 17	28 5 30 31 21 28 35 4 17
25	31 33 32 27 34 26 35 4 17	34 2 31 31 1 27 35 4 17	1 5 36 35 3 27 35 4 17	4 10 6 2 5 27 35 4 17	7 13 7 6 7 27 36 4 17	10 17 8 10 10 26 36 4 17	13 21 13 13 11 26 36 4 17	16 25 18 17 14 26 35 4 17	19 30 20 21 15 26 35 4 17	22 33 20 25 17 27 35 4 17	25 3 25 29 19 27 35 4 17	28 7 30 31 21 28 35 4 17
26	31 34 32 27 34 26 35 4 17	34 4 32 31 1 27 35 4 17	1 6 36 35 3 27 35 4 17	4 11 6 2 5 27 35 4 17	7 14 7 6 7 27 36 4 17	10 19 8 10 10 26 36 4 17	13 22 13 14 12 26 36 4 17	16 26 18 17 14 26 35 4 17	19 31 20 21 15 26 35 4 17	22 35 20 25 17 27 35 4 17	25 4 25 29 19 27 35 4 17	28 8 30 31 21 28 35 4 17
27	31 36 32 27 35 26 35 4 17	34 5 32 31 1 27 35 4 17	1 7 36 35 3 27 35 4 17	4 12 6 3 5 27 35 4 17	7 16 7 6 8 27 36 4 17	10 20 8 10 10 26 36 4 17	13 23 13 14 12 26 36 4 17	16 28 19 18 14 26 35 4 17	19 33 20 21 16 26 35 4 17	22 36 21 25 17 27 35 4 17	25 6 26 29 19 27 35 4 17	28 9 30 31 21 28 35 4 17
28	31 1 32 28 35 26 35 4 17	34 7 32 31 1 27 35 4 17	1 9 36 35 3 27 35 4 17	4 13 6 3 5 27 35 4 17	7 17 7 6 8 27 36 4 17	10 21 8 10 10 26 36 4 17	13 24 14 14 12 26 36 4 17	16 29 19 18 14 26 35 4 17	19 34 19 22 16 26 35 4 17	22 2 21 25 17 27 35 4 17	25 7 26 29 19 27 35 4 17	28 11 30 31 21 28 35 4 17
29	31 3 32 28 35 26 35 4 17	34 8 32 31 1 27 35 4 17	1 10 36 35 3 27 35 4 17	4 15 6 3 6 27 35 4 17	7 18 7 6 8 27 36 4 17	10 22 8 10 10 26 36 4 17	13 26 14 14 12 26 36 4 17	16 30 19 18 14 26 35 4 17	19 35 19 22 16 26 35 4 17	22 3 21 25 18 27 35 4 17	25 9 26 29 19 27 35 4 17	28 12 30 33 21 28 35 4 17
30	31 4 32 28 35 26 35 4 17	**1936**	1 11 36 35 3 27 35 4 17	5 16 6 3 6 27 35 4 17	7 19 7 7 8 27 36 4 17	10 23 8 10 10 26 36 4 17	13 27 14 14 12 26 36 4 17	16 32 19 18 14 26 35 4 17	19 1 19 22 16 26 35 4 17	22 5 21 25 18 27 35 4 17	25 10 26 29 19 27 35 4 17	28 13 30 33 21 28 35 4 17
31	32 6 32 28 35 26 35 4 17		2 13 1 35 3 27 35 4 17		7 20 7 7 8 27 36 4 17		13 28 14 14 12 26 36 4 17	16 33 19 18 14 26 35 4 17		22 6 21 26 18 27 35 4 17		28 15 30 33 21 28 35 4 17

	JAN	FEB	MAR	APR	MAY	JUNE	JULY	AUG	SEPT	OCT	NOV	DEC
1	29 16 31 33 21 28 35 4 17	32 21 29 36 23 29 36 4 17	35 22 33 3 24 29 36 4 17	2 26 2 4 25 30 36 4 17	4 29 6 3 25 30 1 4 17	8 34 5 3 24 30 1 5 17	10 2 10 6 23 30 1 5 17	13 7 16 9 24 30 1 5 17	16 12 18 13 26 29 1 5 17	19 16 18 16 28 29 1 5 17	22 21 23 20 30 30 36 5 18	25 24 27 24 32 30 36 5 18
2	29 18 31 33 22 28 35 4 17	32 22 29 1 23 29 36 4 17	35 23 33 3 24 29 36 4 17	2 27 3 4 25 30 36 4 17	5 30 6 3 25 30 1 4 17	8 35 5 3 24 30 1 5 17	11 3 10 6 23 30 1 5 17	13 8 16 9 24 30 1 5 17	16 14 18 13 26 29 1 5 17	19 17 18 16 28 29 1 5 17	22 22 23 20 30 30 36 5 18	25 25 27 24 32 30 36 5 18
3	29 19 21 33 22 28 35 4 17	32 23 29 1 23 29 36 4 17	35 24 33 3 24 29 36 4 17	2 28 3 4 25 30 36 4 17	5 32 6 3 25 30 1 4 17	8 1 5 3 24 30 1 5 17	11 4 10 6 23 30 1 5 17	13 10 16 9 24 30 1 5 17	17 15 18 13 26 29 1 5 17	19 19 18 17 28 29 1 5 17	23 23 23 20 30 30 36 5 18	26 26 27 24 32 30 36 5 18
4	29 20 21 33 22 28 35 4 17	32 24 29 1 23 29 36 4 17	35 25 33 3 24 30 36 4 17	2 29 3 4 25 30 36 4 17	5 33 6 2 25 30 1 4 17	8 2 5 3 24 30 1 5 17	11 6 10 6 23 30 1 5 17	14 11 16 9 24 29 1 5 17	17 16 18 13 26 29 1 5 17	19 20 18 17 28 29 1 5 17	23 24 23 20 30 30 36 5 18	26 28 28 24 32 30 36 5 18
5	29 21 31 33 22 28 35 4 17	32 25 30 1 23 29 36 4 17	35 26 33 3 24 30 36 4 17	2 31 3 4 25 30 36 4 17	5 34 6 2 25 30 1 4 17	8 4 6 4 24 30 1 5 17	11 7 11 6 23 30 1 5 17	14 13 16 10 24 29 1 5 17	17 18 18 13 26 29 1 5 17	20 21 18 17 28 29 1 5 17	23 25 23 21 30 30 36 5 18	26 29 28 24 32 30 36 5 18
6	29 22 31 34 22 28 35 4 17	32 27 30 1 23 29 36 4 17	35 27 34 3 24 30 36 4 17	2 32 3 4 25 30 36 4 17	5 36 6 2 25 30 1 4 17	8 5 6 4 24 30 1 5 17	11 9 11 6 24 30 1 5 17	14 14 16 10 24 29 1 5 17	17 19 18 13 26 29 1 5 17	20 22 18 17 28 29 1 5 17	23 27 23 21 30 30 36 5 18	26 30 28 24 32 30 36 5 18
7	29 23 31 34 22 28 35 4 17	32 28 30 1 23 29 36 4 17	35 28 34 3 24 30 36 4 17	2 33 4 4 25 30 36 4 17	5 1 6 2 25 30 1 4 17	8 7 6 4 24 30 1 5 17	11 10 11 6 24 30 1 5 17	14 16 16 10 24 29 1 5 17	17 20 18 13 26 29 1 5 17	20 23 18 17 28 29 1 5 17	23 28 24 21 30 30 36 5 18	26 31 28 25 32 30 36 5 18
8	29 25 31 34 22 28 35 4 17	32 29 30 1 23 29 36 4 17	35 30 34 3 24 30 36 4 17	2 35 4 4 25 30 36 4 17	5 3 6 2 25 30 1 4 17	8 8 6 4 24 30 1 5 17	11 12 11 7 24 30 1 5 17	14 17 17 10 24 29 1 5 17	17 21 18 14 26 29 1 5 17	20 25 19 17 28 29 1 5 17	23 29 24 21 30 30 36 5 18	26 32 28 25 33 30 36 5 18
9	29 26 30 34 22 28 35 4 17	33 31 30 1 23 29 36 4 17	35 31 34 3 24 30 36 4 17	2 36 4 4 25 30 36 4 17	5 4 6 2 25 30 1 5 17	8 10 6 4 24 30 1 5 17	11 13 11 7 24 30 1 5 17	14 18 17 10 25 29 1 5 17	17 23 18 14 26 29 1 5 17	20 26 19 17 28 29 1 5 17	23 30 24 21 30 30 36 5 18	26 34 28 25 33 30 36 5 18
10	29 27 30 34 22 28 35 4 17	33 32 30 1 23 29 36 4 17	35 33 34 4 24 30 36 4 17	3 2 4 4 25 30 36 4 17	5 5 6 2 25 30 1 5 17	8 11 6 4 24 30 1 5 17	11 15 12 7 24 30 1 5 17	14 19 17 10 25 29 1 5 17	17 24 18 14 26 29 1 5 17	20 27 19 17 28 29 1 5 17	23 31 24 21 30 30 36 5 18	26 35 28 25 33 30 36 5 18
11	30 28 30 34 22 28 35 4 17	33 33 30 1 23 29 36 4 17	36 34 34 4 24 30 36 4 17	3 3 4 4 25 30 36 4 17	6 7 5 2 25 30 1 5 17	9 12 6 4 24 30 1 5 17	11 16 12 7 24 30 1 5 17	14 21 17 10 25 29 1 5 17	17 25 18 14 26 29 1 5 17	20 28 19 18 28 29 1 5 17	23 33 24 21 30 30 36 5 18	26 36 28 25 33 30 36 5 18
12	30 30 30 34 22 28 35 4 17	33 34 30 2 23 29 36 4 17	36 35 35 4 24 30 36 4 17	3 5 5 4 25 30 36 4 17	6 9 5 2 25 30 1 5 17	9 14 6 4 24 30 1 5 17	11 17 12 7 24 30 1 5 17	14 22 17 10 25 29 1 5 17	17 26 18 14 26 29 1 5 17	20 29 19 18 28 29 1 5 17	23 34 24 21 31 30 36 5 18	27 2 29 25 33 30 36 5 18
13	30 31 30 34 22 28 35 4 17	33 36 30 2 23 29 36 4 17	36 1 35 4 25 30 36 4 17	3 6 5 4 25 30 36 4 17	6 10 5 2 25 30 1 5 17	9 15 6 4 24 30 1 5 17	12 19 12 7 24 30 1 5 17	15 23 17 10 25 29 1 5 17	18 27 18 14 26 29 1 5 17	20 31 19 18 28 29 1 5 17	24 35 24 22 31 30 36 5 18	27 3 29 25 33 30 36 5 18
14	30 32 30 34 22 28 35 4 17	33 31 31 2 23 29 36 4 17	36 2 35 4 25 30 36 4 17	3 8 5 4 25 30 36 4 17	6 12 5 2 25 30 1 5 17	9 17 7 4 24 30 1 5 17	12 20 12 7 24 30 1 5 17	15 24 17 11 25 29 1 5 17	18 29 18 14 26 29 1 5 17	21 32 20 18 28 29 1 5 17	24 1 25 22 31 30 36 5 18	27 4 29 25 33 30 36 5 18
15	30 34 30 35 22 29 35 4 17	33 3 31 2 24 29 36 4 17	36 4 35 4 25 30 36 4 17	3 9 5 3 25 30 36 4 17	6 13 5 3 24 30 1 5 17	9 18 7 4 24 30 1 5 17	12 21 13 7 24 30 1 5 17	15 25 18 11 25 29 1 5 17	18 30 17 14 27 29 1 5 17	21 33 20 18 29 29 1 5 17	24 2 25 22 31 30 36 5 18	27 6 29 26 33 30 36 5 18
16	30 35 30 35 22 29 35 4 17	33 4 31 2 24 29 36 4 17	36 5 35 4 25 30 36 4 17	3 11 5 3 25 30 36 4 17	6 14 5 3 24 30 1 5 17	9 19 7 4 24 30 1 5 17	12 22 13 7 24 30 1 5 17	15 27 18 11 25 29 1 5 17	18 31 17 14 27 29 1 5 17	21 35 20 18 29 29 1 5 17	24 4 25 22 31 30 36 5 18	27 7 29 26 33 30 36 5 18
17	30 36 29 35 22 29 35 4 17	33 6 31 2 24 29 36 4 17	36 7 35 4 25 30 36 4 17	3 12 5 3 25 30 36 4 17	6 16 5 3 24 30 1 5 17	9 20 7 5 24 30 1 5 17	12 23 13 8 24 30 1 5 17	15 28 18 11 25 29 1 5 17	18 32 17 15 27 29 1 5 17	21 36 20 18 29 29 1 5 17	24 5 25 22 31 30 36 5 18	27 9 29 26 33 30 36 5 18
18	30 2 29 35 22 29 35 4 17	33 7 31 2 24 29 36 4 17	36 8 36 4 25 30 36 4 17	3 13 5 3 25 30 36 4 17	6 17 5 3 24 30 1 5 17	9 21 7 5 24 30 1 5 17	12 25 13 8 24 30 1 5 17	15 29 18 11 25 29 1 5 17	18 34 17 15 27 29 1 5 17	21 1 20 18 29 29 36 5 18	24 7 25 22 31 30 36 5 18	27 10 29 26 33 30 36 5 18
19	30 3 29 35 22 29 35 4 17	34 8 31 2 24 29 36 4 17	36 10 36 4 25 30 36 4 17	3 15 5 3 25 30 36 4 17	6 18 5 3 24 30 1 5 17	9 23 7 5 23 30 1 5 17	12 26 13 8 24 30 1 5 17	15 30 18 11 25 29 1 5 17	18 35 17 15 27 29 1 5 17	21 3 20 19 29 29 36 5 18	24 8 25 22 31 30 36 5 18	27 12 29 26 33 30 36 5 18
20	30 4 29 35 22 29 35 4 17	34 10 31 2 24 29 36 4 17	36 11 36 4 25 30 36 4 17	3 16 5 3 25 30 36 4 17	6 19 5 3 24 30 1 5 17	9 24 8 5 23 30 1 5 17	12 27 14 8 24 30 1 5 17	15 32 18 11 25 29 1 5 17	18 1 17 15 27 29 1 5 17	21 4 21 19 29 29 36 5 18	24 10 26 22 31 30 36 5 18	27 13 29 26 33 31 36 5 18
21	31 6 29 35 22 29 35 4 17	34 11 32 2 24 29 36 4 17	1 12 36 4 25 30 36 4 17	4 17 6 3 25 30 36 4 17	6 21 5 3 24 30 1 5 17	9 25 8 5 23 30 1 5 17	12 28 14 8 24 30 1 5 17	15 33 18 11 25 29 1 5 17	18 2 17 15 27 29 1 5 17	21 6 21 19 29 29 36 5 18	24 11 26 23 31 30 36 5 18	27 15 29 26 34 31 36 5 18
22	31 7 29 35 22 29 35 4 17	34 13 32 2 24 29 36 4 17	1 14 36 4 25 30 36 4 17	4 18 6 3 25 30 36 4 17	7 22 5 3 24 30 1 5 17	10 26 8 5 23 30 1 5 17	12 29 14 8 24 30 1 5 17	15 34 18 12 25 29 1 5 17	18 3 17 15 27 29 1 5 17	21 7 21 19 29 29 36 5 18	24 13 26 23 31 30 36 5 18	28 16 29 27 34 31 36 5 18
23	31 9 29 35 22 29 35 4 17	34 14 32 2 24 29 36 4 17	1 15 36 4 25 30 36 4 17	4 19 6 3 25 30 36 4 17	7 23 5 3 24 30 1 5 17	10 27 8 5 23 30 1 5 17	13 31 14 8 24 30 1 5 17	15 36 18 12 25 29 1 5 17	19 5 17 15 27 29 1 5 17	21 9 21 19 29 29 36 5 18	25 14 26 23 31 30 36 5 18	28 18 29 27 34 31 36 4 18
24	31 10 29 36 22 29 35 4 17	34 15 32 3 24 29 36 4 17	1 16 1 4 25 30 36 4 17	4 21 6 3 25 30 36 4 17	7 24 5 3 24 30 1 5 17	10 29 8 5 23 30 1 5 17	13 32 14 8 24 30 1 5 17	16 1 18 12 25 29 1 5 17	19 6 17 15 27 29 1 5 17	22 10 21 19 29 30 36 5 18	25 15 26 23 31 30 36 5 18	28 19 29 27 34 31 36 4 18
25	31 12 29 36 23 29 35 4 17	34 16 32 3 24 29 36 4 17	1 17 1 4 25 30 36 4 17	4 22 6 3 25 30 36 4 17	7 25 5 3 24 30 1 5 17	10 30 8 5 23 30 1 5 17	13 33 15 8 24 30 1 5 17	16 2 18 12 25 29 1 5 17	19 8 17 16 27 29 1 5 17	22 12 21 19 29 30 36 5 18	25 17 26 23 31 30 36 5 18	28 20 29 27 34 31 36 4 18
26	31 13 29 36 23 29 35 4 17	34 18 32 3 24 29 36 4 17	1 19 1 4 25 30 36 4 17	4 23 6 3 25 30 1 4 17	7 26 5 3 24 30 1 5 17	10 31 9 5 23 30 1 5 17	13 35 15 8 24 30 1 5 17	16 4 18 12 25 29 1 5 17	19 9 17 16 27 29 1 5 17	22 13 22 19 29 30 36 5 18	25 18 26 23 32 30 36 5 18	28 21 29 27 34 31 36 4 18
27	31 14 29 36 23 29 35 4 17	34 19 32 3 24 29 36 4 17	1 20 1 4 25 30 36 4 17	4 24 6 3 25 30 1 4 17	7 28 5 3 24 30 1 5 17	10 32 9 5 23 30 1 5 17	13 36 15 9 24 30 1 5 17	16 5 18 12 25 29 1 5 17	19 11 17 16 27 29 1 5 17	22 14 22 19 29 30 36 5 18	25 19 27 23 32 30 36 5 18	28 23 29 27 34 31 36 4 18
28	31 16 29 36 23 29 35 4 17	34 20 33 3 24 29 36 4 17	1 21 2 4 25 30 36 4 17	4 25 6 3 25 30 1 4 17	7 29 5 3 24 30 1 5 17	10 34 9 6 23 30 1 5 17	13 1 15 9 24 30 1 5 17	16 7 18 12 25 29 1 5 17	19 12 17 16 27 29 1 5 17	22 16 22 20 29 30 36 5 18	25 20 27 23 32 30 36 5 18	28 24 28 27 34 31 36 4 18
29	31 17 29 36 23 29 35 4 17		1 22 2 4 25 30 36 4 17	4 27 6 3 25 30 1 4 17	7 30 5 3 24 30 1 5 17	10 35 9 6 23 30 1 5 17	13 3 15 9 24 30 1 5 17	16 8 18 12 26 29 1 5 17	19 13 17 16 27 29 1 5 17	22 17 22 20 30 30 36 5 18	25 21 27 24 32 30 36 5 18	28 25 28 27 34 31 36 4 18
30	32 18 29 36 23 29 35 4 17	1937	1 23 2 4 25 30 36 4 17	4 28 6 3 25 30 1 4 17	7 31 5 3 24 30 1 5 17	10 36 9 6 23 30 1 5 17	13 4 15 9 24 30 1 5 17	16 9 18 12 26 29 1 5 17	19 14 17 16 28 29 1 5 17	22 18 22 20 30 30 36 5 18	25 23 27 24 32 30 36 5 18	28 26 28 28 34 31 36 4 18
31	32 18 29 36 23 29 36 4 17		2 25 2 4 25 30 36 4 17		7 33 5 3 24 30 1 5 17		13 6 15 9 24 30 1 5 17	16 11 18 13 26 29 1 5 17		22 19 22 20 30 30 36 5 18		28 27 28 28 34 31 36 4 18

	JAN	FEB	MAR	APR	MAY	JUNE	JULY	AUG	SEPT	OCT	NOV	DEC
1	29 28 28 28 34 31 36 4 18	32 33 30 32 1 32 1 4 18	35 34 34 35 3 32 1 5 18	2 3 4 3 5 33 1 5 17	5 7 3 7 7 33 2 5 17	8 12 5 10 9 34 2 5 17	10 16 11 14 11 34 2 5 17	13 21 16 18 13 33 2 5 17	16 25 16 21 15 33 2 5 18	19 29 19 24 17 33 2 5 18	22 33 24 25 19 33 2 5 18	25 36 27 24 21 33 2 5 18
2	29 30 28 28 34 31 36 4 18	32 34 30 32 1 32 1 4 18	35 35 34 35 3 32 1 5 18	2 4 4 3 5 33 1 5 17	5 8 3 7 7 33 2 5 17	8 13 6 11 9 34 2 5 17	10 17 12 14 11 34 2 5 17	13 22 16 18 13 33 2 5 17	16 27 16 21 15 33 2 5 18	19 30 19 24 17 33 2 5 18	22 34 24 25 19 33 2 5 18	25 1 27 24 21 33 2 5 18
3	29 31 28 28 34 31 36 4 18	32 36 30 32 1 32 1 4 18	35 1 34 35 3 32 1 5 17	2 6 4 3 5 33 1 5 17	5 10 3 7 7 33 2 5 17	8 15 6 11 9 34 2 5 17	11 19 12 14 11 34 2 5 17	14 23 16 18 13 33 2 5 17	17 28 15 21 15 33 2 5 18	19 31 19 24 17 33 2 5 18	23 35 24 25 19 33 2 5 18	26 3 27 24 21 33 2 5 18
4	29 32 28 28 35 31 36 4 18	32 1 30 32 1 32 1 4 18	35 2 34 36 3 32 1 5 17	2 7 4 3 5 33 1 5 17	5 11 3 7 7 33 2 5 17	8 16 6 11 9 34 2 5 17	11 20 12 14 11 34 2 5 17	14 25 16 18 13 33 2 5 17	17 29 15 21 15 33 2 5 18	20 32 19 24 17 33 2 5 18	23 1 24 25 19 33 2 5 18	26 4 27 24 21 33 2 5 18
5	29 33 28 28 35 31 36 4 18	32 2 30 32 1 32 1 4 18	35 3 35 36 3 32 1 5 17	2 9 4 4 5 33 1 5 17	5 12 3 7 7 33 2 5 17	8 18 6 11 9 34 2 5 17	11 21 12 14 11 34 2 5 17	14 26 16 18 13 33 2 5 17	17 30 15 21 15 33 2 5 18	20 33 19 24 17 33 2 5 18	23 2 24 25 19 33 2 5 18	26 6 27 24 21 33 2 5 18
6	29 35 28 28 35 31 36 4 18	32 4 30 32 1 32 1 4 18	35 5 35 36 3 32 1 5 17	2 10 4 4 5 33 1 5 17	5 14 3 7 7 33 2 5 17	8 19 6 11 9 34 2 5 17	11 22 12 15 11 34 2 5 17	14 27 16 18 13 33 2 5 17	17 31 15 21 15 33 2 5 18	20 35 20 24 17 33 2 5 18	23 3 24 25 19 33 2 5 18	26 7 27 23 21 33 2 5 18
7	29 36 27 29 35 31 36 4 18	32 5 30 32 1 32 1 4 18	35 6 35 36 3 32 1 5 17	2 11 4 4 5 33 1 5 17	5 15 3 7 7 33 2 5 17	8 20 6 11 10 34 2 5 17	11 24 13 15 12 34 2 5 17	14 28 17 18 14 33 2 5 17	17 33 15 22 15 33 2 5 18	20 36 20 24 17 33 2 5 18	23 5 25 25 19 33 2 5 18	26 9 27 23 21 33 2 5 18
8	29 1 27 29 35 31 36 4 18	32 6 31 33 1 32 1 4 18	35 7 35 36 3 32 1 5 17	2 13 4 4 5 33 1 5 17	5 17 3 8 8 33 2 5 17	8 21 7 11 10 34 2 5 17	11 25 13 15 12 34 2 5 17	14 29 17 18 14 33 2 5 17	17 34 15 22 16 33 2 5 18	20 1 20 24 17 33 2 5 18	23 6 25 25 19 33 2 5 18	26 10 27 23 21 33 2 5 18
9	29 3 27 29 35 31 36 4 18	33 8 31 33 1 32 1 4 18	35 9 35 36 3 32 1 5 17	2 14 4 4 6 33 1 5 17	5 18 3 8 8 33 2 5 17	8 23 7 11 10 34 2 5 17	11 26 13 15 12 34 2 5 17	14 30 17 18 14 33 2 5 17	17 35 15 22 16 33 2 5 18	20 3 20 24 18 33 2 5 18	23 8 25 25 19 33 2 5 18	26 12 27 23 21 33 2 5 18
10	29 4 27 29 35 31 36 4 18	33 9 31 33 1 32 1 4 18	35 10 36 36 3 32 1 5 17	2 16 4 4 6 33 1 5 17	5 19 3 8 8 33 2 5 17	8 24 7 12 10 34 2 5 17	11 27 13 15 12 34 2 5 17	14 32 17 19 14 33 2 5 17	17 36 16 22 16 33 2 5 18	20 4 20 24 18 33 2 5 18	23 9 25 25 20 33 2 5 18	26 13 27 23 21 33 2 5 18
11	30 5 27 29 35 31 36 4 18	33 11 31 33 1 32 1 5 18	36 12 36 36 3 32 1 5 17	3 17 4 4 6 33 1 5 17	6 20 3 8 8 33 2 5 17	9 25 7 12 10 34 2 5 17	11 28 13 15 12 34 2 5 17	14 33 17 19 14 33 2 5 17	17 2 16 22 16 33 2 5 18	20 5 20 24 18 33 2 5 18	23 11 25 25 20 33 2 5 18	26 14 27 23 21 33 2 5 18
12	30 7 27 29 35 31 36 4 18	33 12 31 33 1 32 1 5 18	36 13 36 1 4 32 1 5 17	3 18 4 4 6 33 1 5 17	6 22 3 8 8 33 2 5 17	9 26 7 12 10 34 2 5 17	11 30 13 15 12 34 2 5 17	14 34 17 19 14 33 2 5 17	17 3 16 22 16 33 2 5 18	20 7 21 24 18 33 2 5 18	23 12 25 25 20 33 2 5 18	26 16 27 23 22 33 2 5 18
13	30 8 28 29 35 31 36 4 18	33 14 31 33 2 32 1 5 18	36 14 36 1 4 32 1 5 17	3 20 4 5 6 33 1 5 17	6 23 3 8 8 33 2 5 17	9 27 8 12 10 34 2 5 17	12 31 14 15 12 34 2 5 17	15 35 17 19 14 33 2 5 17	18 4 16 22 16 33 2 5 18	20 8 21 24 18 33 2 5 18	24 13 25 25 20 33 2 5 18	27 17 27 23 22 33 2 5 18
14	30 10 28 29 35 31 1 4 18	33 15 31 33 2 32 1 5 18	36 16 36 1 4 32 1 5 17	3 21 4 5 6 33 1 5 17	6 24 3 8 8 34 2 5 17	9 29 8 12 10 34 2 5 17	12 32 14 16 12 34 2 5 17	15 1 17 19 14 33 2 5 17	18 6 16 22 16 33 2 5 18	21 9 21 25 18 33 2 5 18	24 15 26 25 20 33 2 5 18	27 19 27 23 22 33 2 5 18
15	30 11 28 30 35 31 1 4 18	33 16 32 33 2 32 1 5 18	36 17 1 1 4 32 1 5 17	3 22 4 5 6 33 2 5 17	6 25 3 8 8 34 2 5 17	9 30 8 12 10 34 2 5 17	12 33 14 16 12 34 2 5 17	15 2 17 19 14 33 2 5 17	18 7 16 22 16 33 2 5 18	21 11 21 25 18 33 2 5 18	24 16 26 24 20 33 2 5 18	27 20 26 24 22 33 2 5 18
16	30 13 28 30 35 31 1 4 18	33 18 32 34 2 32 1 5 18	36 19 1 1 4 32 1 5 17	3 23 4 5 6 33 2 5 17	6 27 3 9 8 34 2 5 17	9 31 8 12 10 34 2 5 17	12 34 14 16 12 34 2 5 17	15 3 17 19 14 33 2 5 17	18 8 16 22 16 33 2 5 18	21 12 21 25 18 33 2 5 18	24 18 26 24 20 33 2 5 18	27 21 26 24 22 33 2 5 18
17	30 14 28 30 36 31 1 4 18	33 19 32 34 2 32 1 5 18	36 20 1 1 4 33 1 5 17	3 25 4 5 6 33 2 5 17	6 28 4 9 8 34 2 5 17	9 32 8 12 10 34 2 5 17	12 36 14 16 12 34 2 5 17	15 5 17 19 14 33 2 5 17	18 10 16 23 16 33 2 5 18	21 14 21 25 18 33 2 5 18	24 19 26 24 20 33 2 5 18	27 23 26 24 22 33 2 5 18
18	30 16 28 30 36 31 1 4 18	33 21 32 34 2 32 1 5 18	36 21 1 1 4 33 1 5 17	3 26 4 5 6 33 2 5 17	6 29 4 9 8 34 2 5 17	9 33 9 12 10 34 2 5 17	12 1 14 16 12 34 2 5 17	15 6 17 19 14 33 2 5 17	18 11 16 23 16 33 2 5 18	21 15 22 25 18 33 2 5 18	24 20 26 24 20 33 2 5 18	27 24 26 24 22 33 2 5 18
19	30 17 28 30 36 31 1 4 18	34 22 32 34 2 32 1 5 18	36 23 1 1 4 33 1 5 17	3 27 4 5 6 33 2 5 17	6 30 4 9 8 34 2 5 17	9 35 9 13 10 34 2 5 17	12 2 15 16 12 34 2 5 17	15 7 17 20 14 33 2 5 17	18 13 17 23 16 33 2 5 18	21 16 22 25 18 33 2 5 18	24 22 26 24 20 33 2 5 18	27 25 26 24 22 33 2 5 18
20	30 18 28 30 36 31 1 4 18	34 23 32 34 2 32 1 5 18	36 24 2 2 4 33 1 5 17	3 28 4 5 6 33 2 5 17	6 31 4 9 8 34 2 5 17	9 36 9 13 10 34 2 5 17	12 4 15 16 12 34 2 5 17	15 9 17 20 14 33 2 5 17	18 14 17 23 16 33 2 5 18	21 18 22 25 18 33 2 5 18	24 23 26 24 20 33 2 5 18	27 26 26 24 22 33 2 5 18
21	31 20 28 30 36 31 1 4 18	34 24 33 34 2 32 1 5 18	1 25 2 2 4 33 1 5 17	4 29 4 5 6 33 2 5 17	6 33 4 9 8 34 2 5 17	9 1 9 13 10 34 2 5 17	12 5 15 16 12 34 2 5 17	15 10 16 20 14 33 2 5 18	18 16 17 23 16 33 2 5 18	21 19 22 25 18 33 2 5 18	24 24 27 24 20 33 2 5 18	27 27 26 24 22 33 2 5 18
22	31 21 28 30 36 31 1 4 18	34 25 33 34 2 32 1 5 18	1 26 2 2 4 33 1 5 17	4 31 4 6 6 33 2 5 17	7 34 4 9 8 34 2 5 17	10 3 10 13 11 34 2 5 17	12 6 15 16 12 34 2 5 17	15 12 16 20 14 33 2 5 18	18 17 17 23 16 33 2 5 18	21 20 22 25 18 33 2 5 18	24 25 27 24 20 33 2 5 18	28 29 26 24 22 33 2 5 18
23	31 22 28 31 36 31 1 4 18	34 27 33 34 2 32 1 5 18	1 27 2 2 4 33 1 5 17	4 32 3 6 6 33 2 5 17	7 35 4 9 9 34 2 5 17	10 4 10 13 11 34 2 5 17	13 8 15 17 13 34 2 5 17	15 13 16 20 15 33 2 5 18	18 18 17 23 16 33 2 5 18	21 22 22 25 18 33 2 5 18	25 27 27 24 20 33 2 5 18	28 30 26 24 22 33 2 5 18
24	31 23 29 31 36 31 1 4 18	34 28 33 35 2 32 1 5 18	1 29 2 2 4 33 1 5 17	4 33 3 6 6 33 2 5 17	7 36 4 9 9 34 2 5 17	10 5 10 13 11 34 2 5 17	13 9 15 17 13 34 2 5 17	16 15 16 20 15 33 2 5 18	19 20 17 23 17 33 2 5 18	22 23 22 25 18 33 2 5 18	25 28 27 24 20 33 2 5 18	28 31 26 24 22 33 2 5 18
25	31 25 29 31 36 31 1 4 18	34 29 33 35 2 32 1 5 18	1 30 3 2 4 33 1 5 17	4 34 3 6 6 33 2 5 17	7 2 4 10 9 34 2 5 17	10 7 10 13 11 34 2 5 17	13 11 15 17 13 34 2 5 17	16 16 16 20 15 33 2 5 18	19 21 18 23 17 33 2 5 18	22 25 23 25 19 33 2 5 18	25 29 27 24 20 33 2 5 18	28 32 26 24 22 33 2 5 18
26	31 26 29 31 36 31 1 4 18	34 30 33 35 3 32 1 5 18	1 31 3 2 5 33 1 5 17	4 36 3 6 6 33 2 5 17	7 3 5 10 9 34 2 5 17	10 8 10 13 11 34 2 5 17	13 12 15 17 13 34 2 5 17	16 18 16 20 15 33 2 5 18	19 22 18 23 17 33 2 5 18	22 26 23 25 19 33 2 5 18	25 30 27 24 21 33 2 5 18	28 33 26 24 22 33 2 5 18
27	31 27 29 31 36 31 1 4 18	34 31 34 35 3 32 1 5 18	1 32 3 2 5 33 1 5 17	4 1 3 6 7 33 2 5 17	7 5 5 10 9 34 2 5 17	10 10 11 14 11 34 2 5 17	13 14 16 17 13 34 2 5 17	16 19 16 20 15 33 2 5 18	19 24 18 23 17 33 2 5 18	22 27 23 25 19 33 2 5 18	25 31 27 24 21 33 2 5 18	28 35 26 24 22 33 2 5 18
28	31 28 29 31 36 31 1 4 18	34 33 34 35 3 32 1 5 18	1 33 3 3 5 33 1 5 17	4 2 3 6 7 33 2 5 17	7 6 5 10 9 34 2 5 17	10 11 11 14 11 34 2 5 17	13 15 16 17 13 34 2 5 17	16 20 16 21 15 33 2 5 18	19 25 18 23 17 33 2 5 18	22 28 23 25 19 33 2 5 18	25 33 27 24 21 33 2 5 18	28 36 26 24 23 33 2 5 18
29	31 29 29 31 36 31 1 4 18	**1938**	1 35 3 3 5 33 1 5 17	4 4 3 6 7 33 2 5 17	7 7 5 10 9 34 2 5 17	10 13 11 14 11 34 2 5 17	13 17 16 17 13 34 2 5 17	16 22 16 21 15 33 2 5 18	19 26 18 24 17 33 2 5 18	22 29 23 25 19 33 2 5 18	25 34 27 24 21 33 2 5 18	28 1 26 24 23 33 2 5 18
30	32 31 29 31 1 31 1 4 18		1 36 3 3 5 33 1 5 17	4 5 3 7 7 33 2 5 17	7 9 5 10 9 34 2 5 17	10 14 11 14 11 34 2 5 17	13 18 16 17 13 33 2 5 17	16 23 16 21 15 33 2 5 18	19 27 18 24 17 33 2 5 18	22 31 23 25 19 33 2 5 18	25 35 27 24 21 33 2 5 18	28 2 26 24 23 34 2 5 18
31	32 32 29 32 36 31 1 4 18		2 2 3 3 5 33 1 5 17		7 10 5 10 9 34 2 5 17		13 20 16 17 13 33 2 5 17			22 32 24 25 19 33 2 5 18		28 4 26 24 23 34 2 5 18

	JAN	FEB	MAR	APR	MAY	JUNE	JULY	AUG	SEPT	OCT	NOV	DEC
1	29 5 26 24 23 34 2 5 18	32 10 31 27 25 34 2 5 18	35 11 35 30 26 35 2 5 18	2 16 2 34 28 36 2 5 18	5 20 2 1 30 36 3 5 18	8 25 7 5 31 1 3 5 18	10 28 13 9 31 1 3 6 18	13 33 15 12 30 1 4 6 18	16 1 15 16 30 1 4 6 18	19 5 20 20 31 1 3 6 18	22 10 25 24 32 36 3 6 18	25 14 25 28 34 36 3 5 18
2	29 6 26 24 23 34 2 5 18	32 12 31 27 25 34 2 5 18	35 12 36 30 26 35 2 5 18	2 18 2 34 28 36 2 5 18	5 22 2 1 30 36 3 5 18	8 26 7 5 31 1 3 5 18	10 30 13 9 31 1 3 6 18	13 34 15 13 30 1 4 6 18	16 3 15 16 30 1 4 6 18	19 6 20 20 31 1 3 6 18	22 11 25 24 32 36 3 6 18	25 15 25 28 34 36 3 5 18
3	29 8 26 24 23 34 2 5 18	32 13 31 27 25 34 2 5 18	35 14 36 30 26 35 2 5 18	2 19 2 34 28 36 2 5 18	5 23 2 1 30 36 3 5 18	8 28 7 5 31 1 3 5 18	11 31 13 9 31 1 3 6 18	14 35 15 13 30 1 4 6 18	16 4 15 16 30 1 4 6 18	19 7 20 20 31 1 3 6 18	23 13 25 24 33 36 3 6 18	26 16 24 28 34 36 3 5 18
4	29 9 27 24 23 34 2 5 18	32 15 31 27 25 34 2 5 18	35 15 36 30 26 35 2 5 18	2 21 2 34 28 36 3 5 18	5 24 2 2 30 36 3 5 18	8 29 7 5 31 1 3 5 18	11 32 13 9 31 1 3 6 18	14 1 15 13 30 1 4 6 18	17 5 15 17 30 1 4 6 18	20 9 20 20 31 1 3 6 18	23 14 25 24 33 36 3 6 18	26 18 24 28 34 36 3 5 18
5	29 11 26 25 23 34 2 5 18	32 16 31 27 25 34 2 5 18	35 17 36 31 26 35 2 5 18	2 22 2 34 28 36 3 5 18	5 26 2 2 30 36 3 5 18	8 30 8 5 31 1 3 5 18	11 33 13 9 31 1 3 6 18	14 2 15 13 30 1 4 6 18	17 6 15 17 30 1 4 6 18	20 10 21 20 31 1 3 6 18	23 15 25 24 33 36 3 6 18	26 19 24 28 35 36 3 5 18
6	29 12 26 25 23 34 2 5 18	32 18 32 28 25 34 2 5 18	35 18 36 31 26 35 2 5 18	2 23 2 34 28 36 3 5 18	5 27 2 2 30 36 3 5 18	8 31 8 6 31 1 3 5 18	11 34 13 9 31 1 4 5 18	14 3 15 13 30 1 4 6 18	17 8 15 17 30 1 4 6 18	20 11 21 21 31 1 3 6 18	23 17 25 24 33 36 3 6 18	26 21 24 28 35 36 3 5 18
7	29 14 26 25 23 34 2 5 18	32 19 32 28 25 34 2 5 18	35 20 1 31 27 35 2 5 18	2 25 1 34 28 36 3 5 18	5 28 3 2 30 36 3 5 18	8 32 8 6 31 1 3 5 18	11 36 14 9 31 1 4 5 18	14 4 14 13 30 1 4 6 18	17 9 16 17 30 1 4 6 18	20 13 21 21 31 1 3 6 18	23 18 25 25 33 36 3 6 18	26 22 24 28 35 36 3 5 18
8	29 15 26 25 23 34 2 5 18	32 21 32 28 25 34 2 5 18	35 21 1 31 27 35 2 5 18	2 26 1 34 28 36 3 5 18	5 29 3 2 30 36 3 5 18	8 34 8 6 31 1 3 5 18	11 1 14 9 31 1 4 5 18	14 5 14 13 30 1 4 6 18	17 10 16 17 30 1 4 6 18	20 14 21 21 31 1 3 6 18	23 20 25 25 33 36 3 6 18	26 23 24 28 35 36 3 5 18
9	29 17 26 25 23 34 2 5 18	33 22 32 28 25 34 2 5 18	35 23 1 31 27 35 2 5 18	2 27 1 35 29 36 3 5 18	5 30 3 2 30 36 3 5 18	8 35 9 6 31 1 3 5 18	11 2 14 10 31 1 4 5 18	14 7 14 13 30 1 4 6 18	17 12 16 17 30 1 4 6 18	20 16 21 21 31 1 3 6 18	23 21 25 25 33 36 3 6 18	26 25 24 29 35 36 3 5 18
10	29 18 26 25 23 34 2 5 18	33 23 32 28 25 34 2 5 18	35 24 1 31 27 35 2 5 18	2 28 1 35 29 36 3 5 18	5 32 3 2 30 36 3 5 18	8 36 9 6 31 1 3 5 18	11 3 14 10 31 1 4 5 18	14 8 14 14 30 1 4 6 18	17 13 16 17 30 1 4 6 18	20 17 21 21 31 1 3 6 18	23 23 25 25 33 36 3 6 18	26 26 24 29 35 36 3 5 18
11	30 20 26 25 23 34 2 5 18	33 24 32 28 25 34 2 5 18	36 25 1 31 27 35 2 5 18	3 30 1 35 29 36 3 5 18	6 33 3 2 30 1 3 5 18	8 1 9 6 31 1 3 5 18	11 5 14 10 31 1 4 5 18	14 10 14 14 30 1 4 6 18	17 15 16 17 30 1 4 6 18	20 19 22 21 31 1 3 6 18	23 24 26 25 33 36 3 6 18	26 27 24 29 35 36 3 5 18
12	30 21 28 25 23 34 2 5 18	33 26 32 28 25 34 2 5 18	36 26 1 31 27 35 2 5 18	3 31 1 35 29 36 3 5 18	6 34 3 3 30 1 3 5 18	9 3 9 6 31 1 3 5 18	11 6 14 10 31 1 4 5 18	14 11 14 14 30 1 4 6 18	17 16 17 18 30 1 4 6 18	20 20 22 21 31 1 3 6 18	23 25 26 25 33 36 3 5 18	26 28 24 29 35 36 3 5 18
13	30 22 28 25 24 34 2 5 18	33 27 32 28 25 35 2 5 18	36 28 1 31 27 35 2 5 18	3 32 1 35 29 36 3 5 18	6 35 3 3 30 1 3 5 18	9 4 9 6 31 1 3 5 18	12 7 14 10 31 1 4 5 18	14 13 14 14 30 1 4 6 18	17 18 17 18 30 1 4 6 18	20 21 22 21 31 1 3 6 18	24 27 26 25 33 36 3 5 18	27 30 24 29 35 36 3 5 18
14	30 23 28 25 24 34 2 5 18	33 28 33 28 25 35 2 5 18	36 29 2 32 27 35 2 5 18	3 33 1 35 29 36 3 5 18	6 36 4 3 30 1 3 5 18	9 5 10 7 31 1 3 5 18	12 9 14 10 31 1 4 5 18	15 14 14 14 30 1 4 6 18	18 19 17 18 30 1 4 6 18	21 22 22 22 31 1 3 6 18	24 28 26 25 33 36 3 5 18	27 31 25 29 35 36 3 5 18
15	30 25 28 25 24 34 2 5 18	33 29 33 29 26 35 2 5 18	36 30 2 32 27 35 2 5 18	3 34 1 35 29 36 3 5 18	6 2 4 3 30 1 3 5 18	9 7 10 7 31 1 3 5 18	12 10 14 10 31 1 4 5 18	15 16 14 14 30 1 4 6 18	18 21 17 18 30 1 4 6 18	21 24 22 22 31 1 3 6 18	24 29 26 26 33 36 3 5 18	27 32 25 29 35 36 3 5 18
16	30 26 28 25 24 34 2 5 18	33 30 33 29 26 35 2 5 18	36 31 2 32 27 35 2 5 18	3 36 1 35 29 36 3 5 18	6 3 4 3 30 1 3 5 18	9 8 10 7 31 1 3 5 18	12 12 14 10 31 1 4 5 18	15 17 14 14 30 1 4 6 18	18 22 17 18 30 1 4 6 18	21 25 22 22 32 1 3 6 18	24 30 26 26 33 36 3 5 18	27 34 25 29 35 36 3 5 18
17	30 27 28 26 24 34 2 5 18	33 32 33 29 26 35 2 5 18	36 32 2 32 27 35 2 5 18	3 1 1 36 29 36 3 5 18	6 4 4 3 30 1 3 5 18	9 9 10 7 31 1 3 5 18	12 13 15 11 31 1 4 5 18	15 19 14 14 30 1 4 6 18	18 23 17 18 30 1 4 6 18	21 26 22 22 32 1 3 6 18	24 32 26 26 33 36 3 5 18	27 35 25 30 35 36 3 5 18
18	30 28 28 26 24 34 2 5 18	33 33 33 29 26 35 2 5 18	36 34 2 32 27 35 2 5 18	3 2 1 36 29 36 3 5 18	6 6 4 3 30 1 3 5 18	9 11 10 7 31 1 3 5 18	12 15 15 11 31 1 4 5 18	15 20 14 14 30 1 4 6 18	18 25 18 18 30 1 4 6 18	21 28 23 22 32 1 3 6 18	24 33 26 26 33 36 3 5 18	27 36 25 30 35 36 3 5 18
19	30 29 29 26 24 34 2 5 18	34 34 34 29 26 35 2 5 18	36 35 2 32 27 35 2 5 18	3 3 1 36 29 36 3 5 18	6 7 4 3 30 1 3 5 18	9 12 11 7 31 1 3 6 18	12 16 15 11 31 1 4 5 18	15 22 14 15 30 1 4 6 18	18 26 18 18 30 1 4 6 18	21 29 23 22 32 1 3 6 18	24 34 26 26 34 36 3 5 18	27 1 25 30 35 36 3 5 18
20	30 31 29 26 24 34 2 5 18	34 35 34 29 26 35 2 5 18	36 36 2 32 27 35 2 5 18	3 5 1 36 29 36 3 5 18	6 8 5 4 30 1 3 5 18	9 14 11 7 31 1 3 6 18	12 18 15 11 31 1 4 5 18	15 23 14 15 30 1 4 6 18	18 28 18 19 30 1 4 6 18	21 31 23 22 32 1 3 6 18	24 35 26 26 34 36 3 5 18	27 2 25 30 35 1 3 5 18
21	31 32 29 26 24 34 2 5 18	34 36 34 29 26 35 2 5 18	1 1 2 32 28 35 2 5 18	4 6 1 36 29 36 3 5 18	6 10 5 4 30 1 3 5 18	9 15 11 7 31 1 3 6 18	12 19 15 11 31 1 4 5 18	15 24 14 15 30 1 4 6 18	18 29 18 19 30 1 4 6 18	21 32 23 22 32 1 3 6 18	24 36 26 26 34 36 3 5 18	27 4 25 30 35 1 3 5 18
22	31 33 29 26 24 34 2 5 18	34 2 34 29 26 35 2 5 18	1 3 2 32 28 35 2 5 18	4 7 1 36 29 36 3 5 18	7 11 5 4 30 1 3 5 18	10 17 11 8 31 1 3 6 18	12 21 15 11 30 1 4 5 18	15 25 14 15 30 1 4 6 18	18 30 18 19 30 1 3 5 18	21 33 23 23 32 1 3 6 18	24 2 26 26 34 36 3 5 18	27 5 25 30 35 1 3 5 18
23	31 34 29 26 24 34 2 5 18	34 3 34 29 26 35 2 5 18	1 4 2 33 28 35 2 5 18	4 9 1 36 29 36 3 5 18	7 13 5 4 30 1 3 5 18	10 18 11 8 31 1 3 6 18	12 22 15 11 30 1 4 5 18	15 27 14 15 30 1 4 6 18	18 31 19 19 30 1 3 5 18	21 34 23 23 32 1 3 6 18	25 3 26 27 34 36 3 5 18	28 6 26 30 36 1 3 5 18
24	31 35 29 26 24 34 2 5 18	34 4 35 29 26 35 2 5 18	1 5 2 33 28 35 2 5 18	4 10 1 36 29 36 3 5 18	7 14 5 4 30 1 3 5 18	10 19 12 8 31 1 3 6 18	13 23 15 11 30 1 4 5 18	16 28 14 15 30 1 4 6 18	19 32 19 19 31 1 3 5 18	22 36 23 23 32 1 3 6 18	25 4 25 27 34 36 3 5 18	28 8 26 30 36 1 3 5 18
25	31 1 29 26 24 34 2 5 18	34 5 35 30 26 35 2 5 18	1 6 2 33 28 35 2 5 18	4 12 1 1 29 36 3 5 18	7 16 5 4 31 1 3 5 18	10 21 12 8 31 1 3 6 18	13 24 15 12 30 1 4 5 18	16 29 14 15 30 1 4 6 18	19 34 19 19 31 1 3 5 18	22 1 24 23 32 1 3 6 18	25 5 25 27 34 36 3 5 18	28 9 26 31 36 1 3 5 18
26	31 2 30 26 24 34 2 5 18	34 7 35 30 26 35 2 5 18	1 8 2 33 28 35 2 5 18	4 13 1 1 29 36 3 5 18	7 17 6 4 31 1 3 5 18	10 22 12 8 31 1 3 6 18	13 26 15 12 30 1 4 5 18	16 30 14 15 30 1 4 6 18	19 35 19 19 31 1 3 5 18	21 2 24 23 32 1 3 6 18	25 7 25 27 34 36 3 5 18	28 10 26 31 36 1 3 5 18
27	31 3 30 27 24 34 2 5 18	34 8 35 30 26 35 2 5 18	1 9 2 33 28 36 2 5 18	4 14 2 1 29 36 3 5 18	7 18 6 4 31 1 3 5 18	10 23 12 8 31 1 3 6 18	13 27 15 12 30 1 4 5 18	16 31 14 16 30 1 4 6 18	19 36 19 19 31 1 3 5 18	21 3 24 23 32 1 3 6 18	25 8 25 27 34 36 3 5 18	28 12 26 31 36 1 3 5 18
28	31 4 30 27 24 34 2 5 18	34 10 35 30 26 35 2 5 18	1 10 2 33 28 36 2 5 18	4 16 2 1 29 36 3 5 18	7 20 6 4 31 1 3 5 18	10 25 12 8 31 1 3 6 18	13 28 15 12 30 1 4 5 18	16 33 14 16 30 1 4 6 18	19 1 19 20 31 1 3 5 18	21 5 24 23 32 1 3 6 18	25 9 25 27 34 36 3 5 18	28 13 26 31 36 1 3 5 18
29	31 6 30 27 25 34 2 5 18	1939	1 12 2 33 28 36 2 5 18	4 17 2 1 30 36 3 5 18	7 21 6 5 31 1 3 5 18	10 26 12 8 31 1 3 6 18	13 29 15 12 30 1 4 5 18	16 34 14 16 30 1 4 6 18	19 2 20 20 31 1 3 5 18	21 6 24 23 32 1 3 6 18	25 11 25 27 34 36 3 5 18	28 15 26 31 36 1 3 5 18
30	31 7 30 27 25 34 2 5 18		1 13 2 33 28 36 2 5 18	4 19 2 1 30 36 3 5 18	7 22 6 5 31 1 3 5 18	10 27 13 8 31 1 3 6 18	13 31 15 12 30 1 4 5 18	16 35 14 16 30 1 4 6 18	19 4 20 20 31 1 3 5 18	21 7 24 24 32 36 3 6 18	25 12 25 27 34 36 3 5 18	28 16 27 31 36 1 3 5 18
31	32 9 30 27 25 34 2 5 18		2 15 2 34 28 36 2 5 18		7 24 7 5 31 1 3 5 18		13 32 15 12 30 1 4 5 18	16 36 14 16 30 1 4 6 18		21 8 24 24 32 36 3 6 18		28 18 27 31 36 1 3 5 18

	JAN	FEB	MAR	APR	MAY	JUNE	JULY	AUG	SEPT	OCT	NOV	DEC
1	29 19 27 31 36 1 3 5 18	32 24 32 35 2 1 3 5 18	35 26 36 3 4 2 3 5 18	2 31 35 6 6 2 4 5 18	5 34 3 9 8 3 4 6 18	8 3 9 11 10 4 4 6 18	10 6 13 10 12 4 5 6 18	13 11 12 10 14 5 5 6 18	16 16 16 12 16 5 5 6 18	19 21 21 15 18 5 5 6 18	22 25 24 18 20 5 5 6 18	25 29 23 22 22 4 4 6 18
2	29 20 27 32 36 1 3 5 18	32 25 32 35 3 1 3 5 18	35 28 36 3 4 2 3 5 18	2 32 35 6 7 2 4 5 18	5 35 3 9 9 3 4 6 18	8 4 9 11 11 4 4 6 18	11 7 13 10 12 4 5 6 18	14 12 12 10 14 5 5 6 18	16 17 16 12 16 5 5 6 18	19 22 21 15 18 5 5 6 18	23 26 24 19 20 5 5 6 18	26 30 24 22 22 4 4 6 18
3	29 22 27 32 36 1 3 5 18	32 27 32 35 3 1 3 5 18	35 29 36 3 5 2 3 5 18	2 33 35 6 7 2 4 5 18	5 1 3 9 9 3 4 6 18	8 5 9 11 11 4 4 6 18	11 9 13 10 13 4 5 6 18	14 14 12 10 14 5 5 6 18	17 19 16 12 16 5 5 6 18	20 23 22 15 18 5 5 6 18	23 28 24 19 20 5 5 6 18	26 31 24 22 22 4 4 6 18
4	29 23 27 32 1 1 3 5 18	32 28 32 36 3 1 3 5 18	35 30 36 3 5 2 3 5 18	2 35 35 6 7 2 4 5 18	5 2 3 9 9 3 4 6 18	8 6 9 11 11 4 4 6 18	11 10 13 10 13 4 5 6 18	14 15 12 10 15 5 5 6 18	17 20 17 12 17 5 5 6 18	20 24 22 15 18 5 5 6 18	23 29 24 19 20 5 5 6 18	26 33 24 22 22 4 4 6 18
5	29 24 27 32 1 1 3 5 18	32 29 32 36 3 1 3 5 18	35 31 1 3 5 2 3 5 18	2 36 35 7 7 3 4 5 18	5 3 3 9 9 3 4 6 18	8 8 10 11 11 4 4 6 18	11 11 13 10 13 5 5 6 18	14 16 12 10 15 5 5 6 18	17 22 17 12 17 5 5 6 18	20 26 22 15 18 5 5 6 18	23 31 24 19 21 5 5 6 18	26 34 24 23 22 4 4 6 18
6	29 26 28 32 1 1 3 5 18	32 30 33 36 3 1 3 5 18	35 33 1 3 5 2 3 5 18	2 1 35 7 7 3 4 5 18	5 4 3 9 9 3 4 6 18	8 9 10 11 11 4 4 6 18	11 13 13 9 13 5 5 6 18	14 18 12 10 15 5 5 6 18	17 23 17 12 17 5 5 6 18	20 27 22 15 19 5 5 6 18	23 32 24 19 21 5 5 6 18	26 35 24 23 23 4 4 6 18
7	29 27 28 32 1 1 3 5 18	32 32 33 36 3 1 3 5 18	35 34 1 3 5 2 3 5 18	2 2 36 7 7 3 4 6 18	5 5 4 10 9 3 4 6 18	8 10 10 11 11 4 4 6 18	11 14 13 9 13 5 5 6 18	14 19 12 10 15 5 5 6 18	17 25 17 12 17 5 5 6 18	20 28 22 16 19 5 5 6 18	23 33 24 19 21 5 5 6 18	26 36 24 23 23 4 4 6 18
8	29 28 28 32 1 1 3 5 18	32 33 33 36 3 1 3 5 18	35 35 36 4 5 2 3 5 18	2 3 36 7 7 3 4 6 18	5 7 4 10 9 3 4 6 18	8 12 10 11 11 4 4 6 18	11 16 13 9 13 5 5 6 18	14 21 12 10 15 5 5 6 18	17 26 17 12 17 5 5 6 18	20 30 22 16 19 5 5 6 18	23 34 24 19 21 4 5 6 18	26 1 24 23 23 4 4 6 18
9	29 30 28 32 1 1 3 5 18	32 34 33 36 3 1 3 5 18	35 36 36 4 5 2 3 5 18	2 5 36 7 7 3 4 6 18	5 8 4 10 9 3 4 6 18	8 13 10 11 11 4 4 6 18	11 17 13 9 13 5 5 6 18	14 22 12 10 15 5 5 6 18	17 27 18 13 17 5 5 6 18	20 31 22 16 19 5 5 6 18	23 35 24 19 21 4 5 6 18	26 3 25 23 23 4 4 6 18
10	29 31 28 33 1 1 3 5 18	33 35 33 36 3 1 3 5 18	35 1 36 4 5 2 3 5 18	3 6 36 7 7 3 4 6 18	5 9 4 10 9 3 4 6 18	8 15 11 11 11 4 5 6 18	11 18 13 9 13 5 5 6 18	14 24 12 10 15 5 5 6 18	17 29 18 13 17 5 5 6 18	20 32 22 16 19 5 5 6 18	23 1 24 20 21 4 5 6 18	26 4 25 23 23 4 4 6 18
11	30 32 28 33 1 1 3 5 18	33 36 34 36 3 1 3 5 18	36 2 36 4 5 2 3 5 18	3 7 36 7 7 3 4 6 18	6 11 4 10 9 3 4 6 18	9 16 11 11 11 4 5 6 18	11 20 13 9 13 5 5 6 18	14 25 12 10 15 5 5 6 18	17 30 18 13 17 5 5 6 18	20 33 23 16 19 5 5 6 18	23 2 23 20 21 4 5 6 18	26 5 25 23 23 4 4 6 18
12	30 33 28 33 1 1 3 5 18	33 2 34 1 3 1 3 5 18	36 4 36 4 5 2 3 5 18	3 8 36 7 7 3 4 6 18	6 12 5 10 9 3 4 6 18	9 17 11 11 11 4 5 6 18	11 21 13 9 13 5 5 6 18	14 26 13 10 15 5 5 6 18	17 31 18 13 17 5 5 6 18	20 35 23 16 19 5 5 6 18	24 3 23 20 21 4 5 6 18	27 6 25 23 23 4 4 6 18
13	30 34 29 33 1 1 3 5 18	33 3 34 1 3 1 3 5 18	36 5 36 4 5 2 3 5 18	3 10 36 7 7 3 4 6 18	6 13 5 10 9 3 4 6 18	9 19 11 11 11 4 5 6 18	12 23 13 9 13 5 5 6 18	15 28 13 10 15 5 5 6 18	18 32 18 13 17 5 5 6 18	20 36 23 16 19 5 5 6 18	24 4 23 20 21 4 5 6 18	27 7 25 24 23 4 4 6 18
14	30 36 29 33 1 1 3 5 18	33 4 34 1 3 1 3 5 18	36 6 36 4 5 2 3 5 18	3 11 36 8 7 3 4 6 18	6 15 5 10 9 3 4 6 18	9 20 11 11 11 4 5 6 18	12 24 13 9 13 5 5 6 18	15 29 13 10 15 5 5 6 18	18 34 19 13 17 5 5 6 18	21 1 23 16 19 5 5 6 18	24 5 23 20 21 4 5 6 18	27 9 25 24 23 4 4 6 18
15	30 1 29 33 1 1 3 5 18	33 5 34 1 3 1 3 5 18	36 7 36 4 5 2 3 5 18	3 12 36 8 7 3 4 6 18	6 16 5 10 9 3 4 6 18	9 22 11 11 11 4 5 6 18	12 25 13 9 13 5 5 6 18	15 30 13 10 15 5 5 6 18	18 35 19 13 17 5 5 6 18	21 2 23 16 19 5 5 6 18	24 7 23 20 21 4 5 6 18	27 10 25 24 23 4 4 6 18
16	30 2 29 33 1 1 3 5 18	33 6 34 1 3 1 3 5 18	36 9 36 4 5 2 3 5 18	3 14 36 8 7 3 4 6 18	6 18 5 10 9 4 4 6 18	9 23 11 11 11 4 5 6 18	12 27 13 9 13 5 5 6 18	15 32 13 10 15 5 5 6 18	18 36 19 13 17 5 5 6 18	21 3 23 17 19 5 5 6 18	24 8 23 20 21 4 5 6 18	27 11 26 24 23 4 4 6 18
17	30 3 29 33 1 1 3 5 18	33 8 35 1 4 1 3 5 18	36 10 36 5 5 2 3 5 18	3 15 1 8 8 3 4 6 18	6 19 6 10 9 4 4 6 18	9 24 11 11 11 4 5 6 18	12 28 13 9 13 5 5 6 18	15 33 13 11 15 5 5 6 18	18 1 19 13 17 5 5 6 18	21 4 23 17 19 5 5 6 18	24 9 23 20 21 4 5 6 18	27 13 26 24 23 4 4 6 18
18	30 4 29 34 1 1 3 5 18	33 9 35 1 4 1 3 5 18	36 11 36 5 6 2 3 5 18	3 17 1 8 8 3 4 6 18	6 21 6 10 10 4 4 6 18	9 26 12 10 12 4 5 6 18	12 29 13 9 13 5 5 6 18	15 34 13 11 15 5 5 6 18	18 2 19 14 17 5 5 6 18	21 6 23 17 19 5 5 6 18	24 10 23 21 21 4 5 6 18	27 14 26 24 23 4 4 6 18
19	30 6 30 34 2 1 3 5 18	33 10 35 1 4 1 3 5 18	36 13 36 5 6 2 3 5 18	3 18 1 8 8 3 4 6 18	6 22 6 10 10 4 4 6 18	9 27 12 10 12 4 5 6 18	12 31 13 9 14 5 5 6 18	15 35 14 11 15 5 5 6 18	18 4 19 14 17 5 5 6 18	21 7 24 17 19 5 5 6 18	24 12 23 21 21 4 5 6 18	27 15 26 24 23 4 4 6 18
20	30 7 30 34 2 1 3 5 18	34 12 35 2 4 1 3 5 18	36 14 35 5 6 2 4 5 18	4 20 1 8 8 3 4 6 18	6 24 6 10 10 4 4 6 18	9 28 12 10 12 4 5 6 18	12 32 13 9 14 5 5 6 18	15 36 14 11 16 5 5 6 18	18 5 20 14 18 5 5 6 18	21 8 24 17 19 5 5 6 18	24 13 23 21 21 4 4 6 18	27 17 26 24 23 4 4 6 18
21	31 8 30 34 2 1 3 5 18	34 13 35 2 4 2 3 5 18	1 16 35 5 6 2 4 5 18	4 21 1 8 8 3 4 6 18	7 25 7 10 10 4 4 6 18	9 30 12 10 12 4 5 6 18	12 33 12 9 14 5 5 6 18	15 2 14 11 16 5 5 6 18	18 6 20 14 18 5 5 6 18	21 9 24 17 20 5 5 6 18	24 14 23 21 22 4 4 6 18	27 18 26 25 24 4 4 6 18
22	31 10 30 34 2 1 3 5 18	34 15 35 2 4 2 3 5 18	1 17 35 5 6 2 4 5 18	4 23 1 8 8 3 4 6 18	7 26 7 10 10 4 4 6 18	10 31 12 10 12 4 5 6 18	12 34 12 9 14 5 5 6 18	15 3 14 11 16 5 5 6 18	18 7 20 14 18 5 5 6 18	21 11 24 17 20 5 5 6 18	25 16 23 21 22 4 4 6 18	28 19 26 25 24 4 4 6 18
23	31 11 30 34 2 1 3 5 18	34 16 36 2 4 2 3 5 18	1 19 35 5 6 2 4 5 18	4 24 1 8 8 3 4 6 18	7 28 7 11 10 4 4 6 18	10 32 12 10 12 4 5 6 18	13 36 12 9 14 5 5 6 18	16 4 14 11 16 5 5 6 18	19 8 20 14 18 5 5 6 18	22 12 24 17 20 5 5 6 18	25 17 23 21 22 4 4 6 18	28 21 27 25 24 4 4 6 18
24	31 13 30 34 2 1 3 5 18	34 18 36 2 4 2 3 5 18	1 20 35 5 6 2 4 5 18	4 25 1 8 8 3 4 6 18	7 29 7 11 10 4 4 6 18	10 34 12 10 12 4 5 6 18	13 1 12 9 14 5 5 6 18	16 5 14 11 16 5 5 6 18	19 10 20 14 18 5 5 6 18	22 13 24 18 20 5 5 6 18	25 18 23 21 22 4 4 6 18	28 22 27 25 24 4 4 6 18
25	31 14 31 34 2 1 3 5 18	34 19 36 2 4 2 3 5 18	1 22 35 5 6 2 4 5 18	4 27 2 9 8 3 4 6 18	7 30 7 11 10 4 4 6 18	10 35 12 10 12 4 5 6 18	13 2 12 9 14 5 5 6 18	16 6 15 11 16 5 5 6 18	19 11 20 14 18 5 5 6 18	22 15 24 18 20 5 5 6 18	25 20 23 21 22 4 4 6 18	28 24 27 25 24 4 4 6 18
26	31 16 31 34 2 1 3 5 18	34 21 36 2 4 2 3 5 18	1 23 35 6 6 2 4 5 18	4 28 2 9 8 3 4 6 18	7 31 8 11 10 4 4 6 18	10 36 12 10 12 4 5 6 18	13 3 12 9 14 5 5 6 18	16 8 15 11 16 5 5 6 18	19 12 20 14 18 5 5 6 18	22 16 24 18 20 5 5 6 18	25 21 23 21 22 4 4 6 18	28 25 27 25 24 4 4 6 18
27	31 17 31 35 2 1 3 5 18	34 22 36 2 4 2 3 5 18	1 25 35 6 6 2 4 5 18	4 29 2 9 8 3 4 6 18	7 33 8 11 10 4 4 6 18	10 1 13 10 12 4 5 6 18	13 4 12 9 14 5 5 6 18	16 9 15 11 16 5 5 6 18	19 14 21 14 18 5 5 6 18	22 18 24 18 20 5 5 6 18	25 23 23 22 22 4 4 6 18	28 27 27 25 24 4 4 6 18
28	31 19 31 35 2 1 3 5 18	34 24 36 3 4 2 3 5 18	1 26 35 6 6 2 4 5 18	4 31 2 9 8 3 4 6 18	7 34 8 11 10 4 4 6 18	10 2 13 10 12 4 5 6 18	13 5 12 9 14 5 5 6 18	16 10 15 11 16 5 5 6 18	19 15 21 15 18 5 5 6 18	22 19 24 18 20 5 5 6 18	25 24 23 22 22 4 4 6 18	28 28 27 25 24 4 4 6 18
29	31 20 31 35 2 1 3 5 18	34 25 36 3 4 2 3 5 18	1 27 35 6 6 2 4 5 18	4 32 2 9 8 3 4 6 18	7 35 8 11 10 4 4 6 18	10 3 13 10 12 4 5 6 18	13 7 12 9 14 5 5 6 18	16 12 16 12 16 5 5 6 18	19 17 21 15 18 5 5 6 18	22 21 24 18 20 5 5 6 18	25 26 23 22 22 4 4 6 18	28 29 28 26 24 4 4 6 18
30	31 21 31 35 2 1 3 5 18	**1940**	1 29 35 6 6 2 4 5 18	4 33 2 9 8 3 4 6 18	7 36 8 11 10 4 4 6 18	10 5 13 10 12 4 5 6 18	13 8 12 9 14 5 5 6 18	16 13 16 12 16 5 5 6 18	19 18 21 15 18 5 5 6 18	22 22 24 18 20 5 5 6 18	25 27 23 22 22 4 4 6 18	28 31 28 26 24 4 4 6 18
31	32 23 32 35 2 1 3 5 18		2 30 35 6 6 2 4 5 18		7 1 9 11 10 4 4 6 18		13 9 12 9 14 5 5 6 18	16 14 16 12 16 5 5 6 18		22 24 24 18 20 5 5 6 18		28 32 28 26 24 4 4 6 18

	JAN	FEB	MAR	APR	MAY	JUNE
1	29 33 28 26 24 4 4 6 18	32 2 33 30 26 4 4 6 18	35 3 34 33 28 5 5 6 18	2 7 35 1 30 5 5 6 18	5 10 4 5 33 6 5 6 18	8 15 10 9 35 7 6 6 18
2	29 35 28 26 24 4 4 6 18	32 3 33 30 26 4 4 6 18	35 4 34 33 28 5 5 6 18	2 8 35 1 31 5 5 6 18	5 12 4 5 33 6 5 6 18	8 17 10 9 35 7 6 6 18
3	29 36 28 26 24 4 4 6 18	32 4 34 30 27 4 4 6 18	35 5 34 34 28 5 5 6 18	2 9 35 1 31 5 5 6 18	5 13 4 5 33 6 5 6 18	8 18 10 9 35 7 6 6 18
4	29 1 28 26 24 4 4 6 18	32 5 34 30 27 4 4 6 18	35 6 34 34 29 5 5 6 18	2 11 35 2 31 5 5 6 18	5 14 5 5 33 6 5 6 18	8 19 10 9 35 7 6 6 18
5	29 2 29 26 24 4 4 6 18	32 7 34 30 27 4 4 6 18	35 7 34 34 29 5 5 6 18	2 12 36 2 31 5 5 6 18	5 16 5 5 33 6 5 6 18	8 21 10 9 35 7 6 6 18
6	29 3 29 27 25 4 4 6 18	32 8 34 30 27 4 4 6 18	35 9 34 34 29 5 5 6 18	2 13 36 2 31 5 5 6 18	5 17 5 6 33 6 5 6 18	8 22 10 9 35 7 6 6 18
7	29 5 29 27 25 4 4 6 18	32 9 34 31 27 4 4 6 18	35 10 33 34 29 5 5 6 18	2 15 36 2 31 5 5 6 18	5 18 5 6 33 6 5 6 18	8 24 10 9 35 7 6 6 18
8	29 6 29 27 25 4 4 6 18	32 10 34 31 27 4 4 6 18	35 11 33 34 29 5 5 6 18	2 16 36 2 31 5 5 6 18	5 20 6 6 33 6 5 6 18	8 25 11 10 35 7 6 6 18
9	29 7 29 27 25 4 4 6 18	33 12 34 31 27 4 4 6 18	35 12 33 34 29 5 5 6 18	2 18 36 2 31 5 5 6 18	5 21 6 6 33 6 5 6 18	8 27 11 10 35 7 6 6 18
10	29 8 29 27 25 4 4 6 18	33 13 34 31 27 4 4 6 18	35 14 33 34 29 5 5 6 18	3 19 36 2 31 5 5 6 18	5 23 6 6 33 6 5 6 18	8 28 11 10 35 7 6 6 18
11	30 10 30 27 25 4 4 6 18	33 14 35 31 27 4 4 6 18	36 15 33 35 29 5 5 6 18	3 21 36 2 31 5 5 6 18	6 24 6 6 33 6 5 6 18	9 30 11 10 35 7 6 6 18
12	30 11 30 27 25 4 4 6 18	33 16 35 31 27 4 4 6 18	36 17 33 35 29 5 5 6 18	3 22 1 3 31 5 5 6 18	6 26 6 6 33 6 5 6 18	9 31 11 10 35 7 6 6 18
13	30 12 30 28 25 4 4 6 18	33 17 35 31 27 4 4 6 18	36 18 33 35 29 5 5 6 18	3 24 1 3 31 6 5 6 18	6 27 7 6 33 6 5 6 18	9 32 11 10 35 7 6 6 18
14	30 14 30 28 25 4 4 6 18	33 19 35 31 27 4 4 6 18	36 20 33 35 29 5 5 6 18	3 25 1 3 31 6 5 6 18	6 29 7 6 33 6 5 6 18	9 34 11 10 35 7 6 6 18
15	30 15 30 28 25 4 4 6 18	33 20 35 31 27 4 4 6 18	36 21 33 35 29 5 5 6 18	3 27 1 3 31 6 5 6 18	6 30 7 7 33 6 5 6 18	9 35 11 10 35 7 6 6 18
16	30 16 30 28 25 4 4 6 18	33 22 35 32 27 4 4 6 18	36 23 33 35 29 5 5 6 18	3 28 1 3 31 6 5 6 18	6 32 7 7 34 6 5 6 18	9 36 11 11 36 7 6 6 18
17	30 18 31 28 25 4 4 6 18	33 23 35 32 27 4 4 6 18	36 24 34 35 29 5 5 6 18	3 29 1 3 32 6 5 6 18	6 33 7 7 34 6 5 6 18	9 1 11 11 36 7 6 6 18
18	30 19 31 28 25 4 4 6 18	33 25 35 32 28 4 4 6 18	36 26 34 35 29 5 5 6 18	3 31 2 3 32 6 5 6 18	6 34 8 7 34 6 5 6 18	9 3 11 11 36 7 6 6 18
19	30 21 31 28 25 4 4 6 18	34 26 35 32 28 4 4 6 18	36 27 34 36 30 5 5 6 18	3 32 2 3 32 6 5 6 18	6 35 8 7 34 6 5 6 18	9 4 11 11 36 7 6 6 18
20	31 22 31 28 26 4 4 6 18	34 27 35 32 28 4 4 6 18	36 28 34 36 30 5 5 6 18	3 33 2 4 32 6 5 6 18	6 36 8 7 34 6 5 6 18	9 5 11 11 36 7 6 6 18
21	31 23 31 28 26 4 4 6 18	34 29 35 32 28 5 4 6 18	1 30 34 36 30 5 5 6 18	4 34 2 4 32 6 5 6 18	7 2 8 7 34 6 5 6 18	9 6 11 11 36 7 6 6 18
22	31 25 31 29 26 4 4 6 18	34 30 35 32 28 5 4 6 18	1 31 34 36 30 5 5 6 18	4 36 2 4 32 6 5 6 18	7 3 8 7 34 6 5 6 18	10 7 11 11 36 7 6 6 18
23	31 26 32 29 26 4 4 6 18	34 31 35 33 28 5 4 6 18	1 32 34 36 30 5 5 6 18	4 1 2 4 32 6 5 6 18	7 4 9 8 34 6 5 6 18	10 8 11 11 36 7 6 6 18
24	31 28 32 29 26 4 4 6 18	34 33 34 33 28 5 4 6 18	1 33 34 36 30 5 5 6 18	4 2 3 4 32 6 5 6 18	7 5 9 8 34 6 6 6 18	10 10 11 12 36 7 6 6 18
25	31 29 32 29 26 4 4 6 18	34 34 34 33 28 5 4 6 18	1 35 34 36 30 5 5 6 18	4 3 3 4 32 6 5 6 18	7 6 9 8 34 6 6 6 18	10 11 11 12 36 7 6 6 18
26	31 30 32 29 26 4 4 6 18	34 35 34 33 28 5 4 6 18	1 36 34 36 30 5 5 6 18	4 4 3 4 32 6 5 6 18	7 8 9 8 34 6 6 6 18	10 12 11 12 36 7 6 6 18
27	31 32 32 29 26 4 4 6 18	34 36 34 33 28 5 5 6 18	1 1 34 1 30 5 5 6 18	4 5 3 4 32 6 5 6 18	7 9 9 8 34 7 6 6 18	10 14 11 12 36 7 6 6 18
28	31 33 33 29 26 4 4 6 18	34 1 34 33 28 5 5 6 18	1 2 34 1 30 5 5 6 18	4 7 3 5 32 6 5 6 18	7 10 9 8 34 7 6 6 18	10 15 11 12 36 7 6 6 18
29	31 34 33 29 26 4 4 6 18	1941	1 3 35 1 30 5 5 6 18	4 8 4 5 32 6 5 6 18	7 11 9 8 34 7 6 6 18	10 16 11 12 36 7 6 6 18
30	32 35 33 30 26 4 4 6 18		1 5 35 1 30 5 5 6 18	4 9 4 5 32 6 5 6 18	7 13 10 8 34 7 6 6 18	10 18 11 12 36 7 6 6 18
31	32 1 33 30 26 4 4 6 18		2 6 35 1 30 5 5 6 18		7 14 10 9 35 7 6 6 18	

	JULY	AUG	SEPT	OCT	NOV	DEC
1	10 19 11 12 36 7 6 6 18	13 24 12 16 2 8 6 6 18	16 30 18 20 3 8 6 7 18	19 33 22 23 2 9 6 7 18	22 2 21 27 2 9 6 6 18	25 5 24 30 2 8 6 6 18
2	11 20 10 12 1 7 6 6 18	13 26 12 16 2 8 6 6 18	16 31 18 20 3 8 6 7 18	19 34 22 24 2 9 6 7 18	22 3 21 27 2 9 6 6 18	25 6 24 30 2 8 6 6 18
3	11 22 10 13 1 7 6 6 18	14 27 12 16 2 8 6 6 18	17 32 18 20 3 8 6 7 18	19 36 22 24 2 9 6 7 18	23 4 21 27 2 9 6 6 18	26 7 25 30 2 8 6 6 18
4	11 23 10 13 1 7 6 6 18	14 29 12 17 2 8 6 6 18	17 34 18 20 3 8 6 7 18	20 1 22 23 2 9 6 7 18	22 5 21 27 2 9 6 6 18	26 9 25 30 2 8 6 6 18
5	11 25 10 13 1 7 6 6 18	14 30 12 17 2 8 6 6 18	17 35 18 20 3 8 6 7 18	20 2 22 23 2 9 6 7 18	22 7 21 27 2 9 6 6 18	26 10 25 30 2 8 6 6 18
6	11 26 10 13 1 7 6 6 18	14 31 13 17 2 8 6 6 18	17 36 18 20 3 8 6 7 18	20 3 22 23 2 9 6 7 18	22 8 21 28 2 9 6 6 18	26 11 25 31 2 8 6 6 18
7	11 28 10 13 1 7 6 6 18	14 33 13 17 2 8 6 6 18	17 1 19 21 3 8 6 7 18	20 5 22 23 2 9 6 7 18	22 9 21 28 2 9 6 6 18	26 12 25 31 2 8 6 6 18
8	11 29 10 13 1 7 6 6 18	14 34 13 17 2 8 6 7 18	17 3 19 21 3 8 6 7 18	20 6 22 23 2 9 6 7 18	22 10 21 28 2 9 6 6 18	26 14 25 31 2 8 6 6 18
9	11 30 10 13 1 7 6 6 18	14 35 13 17 2 8 6 7 18	17 4 19 21 3 8 6 7 18	20 7 23 24 2 9 6 7 18	22 11 21 28 2 8 6 6 18	26 15 26 31 2 8 6 6 18
10	11 32 10 13 1 8 6 6 18	14 36 13 7 2 8 6 7 18	17 5 19 21 3 9 6 7 18	20 8 23 24 2 9 6 7 18	22 13 21 28 2 8 6 6 18	26 16 26 31 2 8 6 6 18
11	11 33 10 14 1 8 6 6 18	14 2 14 17 2 8 6 7 18	17 6 19 21 3 9 6 7 18	20 9 23 25 2 9 6 7 18	22 14 21 28 2 8 6 6 18	26 17 26 31 2 8 6 6 18
12	11 34 10 14 1 8 6 6 18	14 3 14 17 2 8 6 7 18	17 7 19 21 3 9 6 7 18	20 11 23 25 2 9 6 7 18	22 15 22 28 2 8 6 6 18	27 19 26 31 2 8 6 6 18
13	12 36 10 14 1 8 6 6 18	15 4 14 18 2 8 6 7 18	18 8 20 21 3 9 6 7 18	20 12 23 25 2 9 6 7 18	24 17 22 28 2 8 6 6 18	27 20 26 31 2 8 6 6 18
14	12 1 10 14 1 8 6 6 18	15 5 14 18 2 8 6 7 18	18 10 20 21 3 9 6 7 18	21 13 23 25 2 9 6 7 18	24 18 22 28 2 8 6 6 18	27 22 26 31 2 8 6 6 18
15	12 2 10 14 1 8 6 6 18	15 6 14 18 2 8 6 7 18	18 11 20 22 3 9 6 7 18	21 14 23 25 2 9 6 7 18	24 19 22 28 2 8 6 6 18	27 23 26 31 2 8 6 6 18
16	12 3 10 14 1 8 6 6 18	15 8 15 18 3 8 6 7 18	18 12 20 22 3 9 6 7 18	21 16 23 25 2 9 6 7 18	24 21 22 29 2 8 6 6 18	27 25 27 31 2 8 6 6 18
17	12 5 10 14 1 8 6 6 18	15 9 15 18 3 8 6 7 18	18 14 20 22 3 9 6 7 18	21 17 23 25 2 9 6 7 18	24 22 22 29 2 8 6 6 18	27 26 27 31 2 8 6 6 18
18	12 6 10 14 1 8 6 6 18	15 10 15 18 3 8 6 7 18	18 15 20 22 3 9 6 7 18	21 19 23 25 2 9 6 7 18	24 24 22 29 2 8 6 6 18	27 28 27 32 2 8 6 6 18
19	12 7 10 15 1 8 6 6 18	15 11 15 18 3 8 6 7 18	18 16 20 22 3 9 6 7 18	21 20 23 26 2 9 6 7 18	24 25 22 29 2 8 6 6 18	27 29 27 32 2 8 6 6 18
20	12 8 10 15 1 8 6 6 18	15 13 15 18 3 8 6 7 18	18 18 21 22 3 9 6 7 18	21 21 23 26 2 9 6 7 18	24 27 23 29 2 8 6 6 18	27 31 27 32 2 8 6 6 18
21	12 9 10 15 2 8 6 6 18	15 14 16 19 3 8 6 7 18	18 19 21 22 3 9 6 7 18	21 23 22 26 2 9 6 7 18	24 28 23 29 2 8 6 6 18	27 32 27 32 3 8 6 6 18
22	12 11 10 15 2 8 6 6 18	15 15 16 19 3 8 6 7 18	18 21 21 22 3 9 6 7 18	21 25 22 26 2 9 6 7 18	24 30 23 29 2 8 6 6 18	28 33 28 32 3 8 6 6 18
23	13 12 11 15 2 8 6 6 18	15 17 16 19 3 8 6 7 18	19 22 21 22 3 9 6 7 18	21 26 22 26 2 9 6 7 18	25 31 23 29 2 8 6 6 18	28 35 28 32 3 8 6 6 18
24	13 13 11 15 2 8 6 6 18	16 18 16 19 3 8 6 7 18	19 24 21 23 3 9 6 7 18	22 27 22 26 2 9 6 7 18	25 33 23 29 2 8 6 6 18	28 36 28 32 3 8 6 6 18
25	13 15 11 15 2 8 6 6 18	16 20 16 19 3 8 6 7 18	19 25 21 23 3 9 6 7 18	22 29 22 26 2 9 6 7 18	25 34 23 30 2 8 6 6 18	28 1 28 32 3 8 6 6 18
26	13 16 11 15 2 8 6 6 18	16 21 17 19 3 8 6 7 18	19 26 21 23 3 9 6 7 18	22 30 22 26 2 9 6 7 18	25 35 24 30 2 8 6 6 18	28 2 28 32 3 8 6 6 18
27	13 17 11 16 2 8 6 6 18	16 23 17 19 3 8 6 7 18	19 28 21 23 3 9 6 7 18	22 32 22 26 2 9 6 7 18	25 36 24 30 2 8 6 6 18	28 4 28 32 3 8 6 6 18
28	13 19 11 16 2 8 6 6 18	16 24 17 19 3 8 6 7 18	19 29 22 23 3 9 6 7 18	22 33 22 27 2 9 6 7 18	25 2 24 30 2 8 6 6 18	28 5 29 32 3 8 6 6 18
29	13 20 11 16 2 8 6 6 18	16 25 17 20 3 8 6 7 18	19 31 22 23 3 9 6 7 18	22 34 22 27 2 9 6 7 18	25 3 24 30 2 8 6 6 18	28 6 29 32 3 8 6 6 18
30	13 21 11 16 2 8 6 6 18	16 27 17 20 3 8 6 7 18	19 32 22 23 2 9 6 7 18	22 35 21 27 2 9 6 7 18	25 4 24 30 2 8 6 6 18	28 7 29 32 3 8 6 6 18
31	13 23 12 16 2 8 6 6 18	16 28 17 20 3 8 6 7 18		22 1 21 27 2 9 6 7 18		28 8 29 32 3 8 6 6 18

	JAN	FEB	MAR	APR	MAY	JUNE	JULY	AUG	SEPT	OCT	NOV	DEC
1	29 10 29 32 3 8 6 6 18	32 14 33 32 5 8 6 6 18	35 15 32 31 6 8 6 6 18	2 20 36 33 8 8 6 6 18	5 24 6 36 10 9 6 6 18	8 29 9 3 12 9 7 7 18	10 33 8 7 14 10 7 7 18	13 2 13 11 16 11 7 7 18	16 6 19 14 17 11 8 7 18	19 9 21 18 19 12 8 7 18	22 14 21 22 21 12 8 7 19	25 18 25 26 24 12 8 7 19
2	29 11 29 32 3 8 6 6 18	32 15 33 32 5 8 6 6 18	35 16 32 31 6 8 6 6 18	2 22 36 33 8 8 6 6 18	5 25 6 36 10 9 6 6 18	8 31 9 4 12 9 7 7 18	10 34 8 7 14 10 7 7 18	13 3 13 11 16 11 7 7 18	16 8 19 14 18 11 8 7 18	19 10 21 18 19 12 8 7 18	22 15 21 22 22 12 8 7 19	25 19 26 26 24 12 8 7 19
3	29 12 30 32 3 8 6 6 18	32 17 33 32 5 8 6 6 18	35 18 32 31 6 8 6 6 18	2 23 36 33 8 8 6 6 18	5 27 6 36 10 9 6 6 18	8 32 9 4 12 9 7 7 18	11 36 8 7 14 10 7 7 18	14 4 14 11 16 11 7 7 18	16 9 19 15 18 11 8 7 18	19 11 21 18 20 12 8 7 19	23 16 21 22 22 12 8 7 19	26 20 26 26 24 12 8 7 19
4	29 13 30 32 3 8 6 6 18	32 18 33 32 5 8 6 6 18	35 19 32 31 6 8 6 6 18	2 24 36 33 8 8 6 6 18	5 28 6 36 10 9 6 6 18	8 33 9 4 12 9 7 7 18	11 1 9 7 14 10 7 7 18	14 6 14 11 16 11 8 7 18	17 10 19 15 18 11 8 7 18	20 12 21 18 20 12 8 7 19	23 18 21 22 22 12 8 7 19	25 21 26 26 24 12 8 7 19
5	29 15 30 33 3 8 6 6 18	32 19 33 32 5 8 6 6 18	35 21 32 31 6 8 6 6 18	2 26 1 33 8 8 6 6 18	5 30 7 36 10 9 6 6 18	8 35 9 4 12 9 7 7 18	11 2 9 7 14 10 7 7 18	14 7 14 11 16 11 8 7 18	17 11 19 15 18 11 8 7 18	20 13 21 19 20 12 8 7 19	23 19 21 22 22 12 8 7 19	25 23 26 26 24 12 8 7 19
6	29 16 30 33 3 8 6 6 18	32 21 33 32 5 8 6 6 18	35 22 32 31 6 8 6 6 18	2 27 1 34 8 8 6 6 18	5 31 7 1 10 9 6 6 18	8 36 9 4 12 9 7 7 18	11 3 9 8 14 10 7 7 18	14 8 14 11 16 11 8 7 18	17 12 19 15 18 11 8 7 18	20 14 21 19 20 12 8 7 19	23 20 21 23 22 12 8 7 19	25 24 26 26 24 12 8 7 19
7	29 17 30 33 3 8 6 6 18	32 22 33 32 5 8 6 6 18	35 23 32 31 7 8 6 6 18	2 29 1 34 8 8 6 6 18	5 32 7 1 10 9 6 6 18	8 1 9 4 12 9 7 7 18	11 5 9 8 14 10 7 7 18	14 9 14 11 16 11 8 7 18	17 14 19 15 18 11 8 7 18	20 16 21 19 20 12 8 7 19	23 22 22 23 22 12 8 7 19	25 26 26 26 24 12 8 7 19
8	29 18 30 33 3 8 6 6 18	32 24 33 31 5 8 6 6 18	35 25 32 31 7 8 6 6 18	2 30 1 34 8 8 6 6 18	5 34 7 1 10 9 6 6 18	8 3 9 4 12 9 7 7 18	11 6 9 8 14 10 7 7 18	14 10 15 11 16 11 8 7 18	17 15 20 15 18 11 8 7 18	20 17 20 19 20 12 8 7 19	23 23 22 23 22 12 8 7 19	25 27 27 27 24 12 8 7 19
9	29 20 30 33 3 8 6 6 18	33 25 33 31 5 8 6 6 18	35 26 33 31 7 8 6 6 18	2 31 1 34 8 8 6 6 18	5 35 7 1 10 9 7 6 18	8 4 9 4 12 9 7 7 18	11 7 9 8 14 10 7 7 18	14 11 15 12 16 11 8 7 18	17 16 20 15 18 11 8 7 18	20 18 20 19 20 12 8 7 19	23 25 22 23 22 12 8 7 19	25 29 27 27 24 12 8 7 19
10	29 21 31 33 3 8 6 6 18	33 27 32 31 5 8 6 6 18	35 28 33 31 7 8 6 6 18	2 33 1 34 9 8 6 6 18	5 36 7 1 10 9 7 6 18	8 5 9 4 12 10 7 7 18	11 8 9 8 14 10 7 7 18	14 13 15 12 16 11 8 7 18	17 17 20 16 18 11 8 7 18	20 20 20 19 20 12 8 7 19	23 26 22 23 22 12 8 7 19	25 30 27 27 24 12 8 7 19
11	30 23 31 33 3 8 6 6 18	33 28 32 31 5 8 6 6 18	36 29 33 32 7 8 6 6 18	3 34 2 34 9 8 6 6 18	6 2 8 1 10 9 7 6 18	8 6 9 5 12 10 7 7 18	11 9 9 8 14 10 7 7 18	14 14 15 12 16 11 8 7 18	17 19 20 16 18 11 8 7 18	20 21 20 19 20 12 8 7 19	23 28 22 23 22 12 8 7 19	25 32 27 27 24 12 8 7 19
12	30 24 31 33 4 8 6 6 18	33 29 32 31 5 8 6 6 18	36 30 33 32 7 8 6 6 18	3 35 2 34 9 8 6 6 18	6 3 8 1 11 9 7 6 18	9 7 9 5 12 10 7 7 18	11 11 9 8 14 10 7 7 18	14 15 15 12 16 11 8 7 18	17 20 20 16 18 11 8 7 18	20 22 20 19 20 12 8 7 19	23 29 22 23 22 12 8 7 19	25 33 27 27 24 12 8 7 19
13	30 26 31 33 4 8 6 6 18	33 31 32 31 5 8 6 6 18	36 32 33 32 7 8 6 6 18	3 1 2 34 9 8 6 6 18	6 4 8 1 11 9 7 6 18	9 9 8 5 12 10 7 7 18	12 12 10 8 14 10 7 7 18	15 16 16 12 16 11 8 7 18	18 21 20 16 18 11 8 7 18	20 24 20 20 20 12 8 7 19	24 31 23 23 22 12 8 7 19	27 34 27 27 24 12 8 7 19
14	30 27 31 33 4 8 6 6 18	33 32 32 31 5 8 6 6 18	36 33 33 32 7 8 6 6 18	3 2 2 34 9 8 6 6 18	6 5 8 1 11 9 7 6 18	9 10 8 5 13 10 7 7 18	12 13 10 8 14 10 7 7 18	15 18 16 12 16 11 8 7 18	18 22 20 16 18 12 8 7 18	20 25 20 20 20 12 8 7 19	24 32 23 24 22 12 8 7 19	27 36 27 27 24 12 8 7 19
15	30 28 31 33 4 8 6 6 18	33 34 32 31 5 8 6 6 18	36 34 33 32 7 8 6 6 18	3 3 2 34 9 8 6 6 18	6 6 8 2 11 9 7 7 18	9 11 8 5 13 10 7 7 18	12 14 10 9 14 10 7 7 18	15 19 16 12 16 11 8 7 18	18 24 20 16 18 12 8 7 18	21 27 20 20 20 12 8 7 19	24 33 23 24 22 12 8 7 19	27 1 28 27 24 12 8 7 19
16	30 30 32 33 4 8 6 6 18	33 35 32 31 5 8 6 6 18	36 36 33 32 7 8 6 6 18	3 4 3 34 9 8 6 6 18	6 8 8 2 11 9 7 7 18	9 12 8 5 13 10 7 7 18	12 16 10 9 15 10 7 7 18	15 20 16 12 16 11 8 7 18	18 26 20 16 18 12 8 7 18	21 28 20 20 20 12 8 7 19	24 35 23 24 22 12 8 7 19	27 2 28 28 25 12 8 7 19
17	30 31 32 33 4 8 6 6 18	33 36 32 31 5 8 6 6 18	36 1 34 32 7 8 6 6 18	3 6 3 35 9 8 6 6 18	6 9 8 2 11 9 7 7 18	9 13 8 5 13 10 7 7 18	12 17 10 9 15 10 7 7 18	15 22 16 13 17 11 8 7 18	18 27 21 16 19 12 8 7 18	21 29 20 20 20 12 8 7 19	24 36 23 24 23 12 8 7 19	27 4 28 28 25 12 8 7 19
18	30 33 32 33 4 8 6 6 18	33 2 32 31 6 8 6 6 18	36 2 34 32 7 8 6 6 18	3 7 3 35 9 8 6 6 18	6 10 8 2 11 9 7 7 18	9 15 8 5 13 10 7 7 18	12 18 10 9 15 10 7 7 18	15 23 16 13 17 11 8 7 18	18 28 21 16 19 12 8 7 18	20 31 20 20 21 12 8 7 19	24 1 23 24 23 12 8 7 19	27 5 28 28 25 12 8 7 19
19	30 34 32 33 4 8 6 6 18	34 3 32 31 6 8 6 6 18	36 4 34 32 7 8 6 6 18	3 8 3 35 9 8 6 6 18	6 11 8 2 11 9 7 7 18	9 15 8 6 13 10 7 7 18	12 19 11 9 15 10 7 7 18	15 25 17 13 17 11 8 7 18	18 30 21 17 19 12 8 7 18	21 32 20 20 21 12 8 7 19	24 3 24 24 23 12 8 7 19	27 6 28 28 25 12 8 7 19
20	30 35 32 32 4 8 6 6 18	34 4 32 31 6 8 6 6 18	36 5 34 32 7 8 6 6 18	3 9 4 35 9 8 6 6 18	6 12 9 2 11 9 7 7 18	9 17 8 6 13 10 7 7 18	12 21 11 9 15 10 7 7 18	15 26 17 13 17 11 8 7 18	18 31 21 17 19 12 8 7 18	21 34 20 20 21 12 8 7 19	24 4 24 24 23 12 8 7 19	27 7 28 28 25 12 7 7 18
21	31 1 32 32 4 8 6 6 18	34 5 32 31 6 8 6 6 18	1 6 34 32 7 8 6 6 18	4 10 4 35 9 8 6 6 18	6 14 9 2 11 9 7 7 18	9 18 8 6 13 10 7 7 18	12 22 11 9 15 10 7 7 18	15 27 17 13 17 11 8 7 18	18 33 21 17 19 12 8 7 18	21 35 20 21 21 12 8 7 19	24 5 24 24 23 12 8 7 19	27 8 29 27 25 12 7 7 18
22	31 2 32 32 4 8 6 6 18	34 6 32 31 6 8 6 6 18	1 7 34 32 7 8 6 6 18	4 12 4 35 9 8 6 6 18	7 15 9 2 11 9 7 7 18	10 20 8 6 13 10 7 7 18	12 23 11 9 15 10 7 7 18	15 29 17 13 17 11 8 7 18	18 34 21 17 19 12 8 7 18	21 36 20 21 21 12 8 7 19	24 6 24 25 23 12 8 7 19	28 10 29 27 25 12 7 7 18
23	31 3 33 32 4 8 6 6 18	34 8 32 31 6 8 6 6 18	1 8 34 32 7 8 6 6 18	4 13 4 35 9 8 6 6 18	7 16 9 2 11 9 7 7 18	10 21 8 6 13 10 7 7 18	12 25 11 10 15 10 7 7 18	15 30 17 13 17 11 8 7 18	18 35 21 17 19 12 8 7 18	21 2 20 21 21 12 8 7 19	25 8 24 25 23 12 8 7 19	28 11 29 29 25 12 7 7 18
24	31 4 33 32 4 8 6 6 18	34 9 32 31 6 8 6 6 18	1 10 35 32 8 8 6 6 18	4 14 4 35 9 9 6 6 18	7 17 9 3 11 9 7 7 18	10 22 8 6 13 10 7 7 18	13 26 12 10 15 10 7 7 18	15 32 17 13 17 11 8 7 18	19 1 21 17 19 12 8 7 18	22 3 20 21 21 12 8 7 19	25 9 24 25 23 12 8 7 19	28 12 29 29 25 12 7 7 18
25	31 6 33 32 4 8 6 6 18	34 10 32 31 6 8 6 6 18	1 11 35 32 8 8 6 6 18	4 35 5 35 9 9 6 6 18	7 19 9 3 11 9 7 7 18	10 24 8 6 13 10 7 7 18	13 28 12 10 15 11 7 7 18	16 33 18 14 17 11 8 7 18	19 2 21 17 19 12 8 7 18	22 4 20 21 21 12 8 7 19	25 10 24 25 23 12 8 7 19	28 13 29 29 25 12 7 7 18
26	31 7 33 32 4 8 6 6 18	34 11 32 31 6 8 6 6 18	1 12 35 33 8 8 6 6 18	4 17 5 35 10 9 6 6 18	7 20 9 3 11 9 7 7 18	10 26 8 6 13 10 7 7 18	13 29 12 10 15 11 7 7 18	16 35 18 14 17 11 8 7 18	19 3 21 17 19 12 8 7 18	22 6 20 21 21 12 8 7 19	25 11 25 25 23 12 8 7 19	28 14 29 29 25 12 7 7 18
27	31 8 33 32 4 8 6 6 18	34 12 32 31 6 8 6 6 18	1 13 35 33 8 8 6 6 18	4 18 5 36 10 9 6 6 18	7 22 9 3 11 9 7 7 18	10 27 8 6 13 10 7 7 18	13 31 12 10 15 11 7 7 18	16 36 18 14 17 11 8 7 18	19 5 21 18 19 12 8 7 18	22 7 20 21 21 12 8 7 19	25 12 25 25 23 12 8 7 19	28 16 29 29 25 12 7 7 18
28	31 9 33 32 4 8 6 6 18	34 14 32 31 6 8 6 6 18	1 15 35 33 8 8 6 6 18	4 19 5 36 10 9 6 6 18	7 23 9 3 11 9 7 7 18	10 29 8 7 13 10 7 7 18	13 32 12 10 15 11 7 7 18	16 1 18 14 17 11 8 7 18	19 6 21 18 19 12 8 7 18	22 9 20 21 21 12 8 7 19	25 14 25 25 23 12 8 7 19	28 17 30 29 25 12 7 7 18
29	31 10 33 32 4 8 6 6 18	**1942**	1 16 35 33 8 8 6 6 18	4 21 5 36 10 9 6 6 18	7 25 9 3 12 9 7 7 18	10 30 8 7 13 10 7 7 18	13 34 13 10 15 11 7 7 18	16 3 18 14 17 11 8 7 18	19 7 21 18 19 12 8 7 18	22 10 20 22 21 12 8 7 19	25 15 25 25 23 12 8 7 19	28 18 30 29 25 12 7 7 18
30	31 12 33 32 4 8 6 6 18		1 17 36 33 8 8 6 6 18	4 22 6 36 10 9 6 6 18	7 26 9 3 12 9 7 7 18	10 32 8 7 14 10 7 7 18	13 35 13 10 15 11 7 7 18	16 4 18 14 17 11 8 7 18	19 8 21 18 19 12 8 7 18	22 12 20 22 21 12 8 7 19	25 16 25 26 23 12 8 7 19	28 19 30 29 26 12 7 7 18
31	32 13 33 32 5 8 6 6 18		2 19 36 33 8 8 6 6 18		7 28 9 3 12 9 7 7 18		13 1 13 10 15 11 7 7 18	16 5 19 14 17 11 8 7 18		22 13 21 22 21 12 8 7 19		28 21 30 30 26 12 7 7 18

	JAN	FEB	MAR	APR	MAY	JUNE	JULY	AUG	SEPT	OCT	NOV	DEC
1	29 22 30 30 26 12 7 7 19	32 27 30 34 28 11 7 7 19	35 28 32 1 30 11 7 7 19	2 32 1 5 32 11 7 7 19	5 1 6 8 34 11 8 7 18	8 6 6 12 1 12 8 7 18	10 10 9 15 3 13 8 7 18	13 14 15 17 5 13 9 7 18	16 18 19 17 7 14 9 7 19	19 22 18 16 8 14 9 7 19	22 27 22 18 9 15 9 7 19	25 31 27 21 8 15 9 7 19
2	29 33 30 30 26 12 7 7 19	32 29 30 34 28 11 7 7 19	35 30 32 1 30 11 7 7 19	2 33 2 5 32 11 7 7 19	5 3 7 8 35 11 8 7 18	8 7 6 12 1 12 8 7 18	10 11 9 15 3 13 8 7 18	13 15 15 17 5 13 9 7 19	16 20 19 17 7 14 9 7 19	19 23 18 16 8 14 9 7 19	22 28 22 18 9 15 9 7 19	25 32 27 21 8 15 9 7 19
3	29 25 31 30 26 12 7 7 19	32 30 30 34 28 11 7 7 19	35 31 32 1 30 11 7 7 19	2 34 2 5 32 11 7 7 19	5 4 7 9 35 11 8 7 18	8 9 6 12 1 12 8 7 18	11 12 9 15 3 13 8 7 18	14 16 15 17 5 13 9 7 19	17 21 19 17 7 14 9 7 19	19 25 18 16 8 14 9 7 19	23 30 22 18 9 15 9 7 19	26 34 27 21 8 15 9 7 19
4	29 26 31 20 26 12 7 7 19	32 32 30 34 28 11 7 7 19	35 33 33 1 30 11 7 7 19	2 2 2 5 33 11 7 7 19	5 5 7 9 35 11 8 7 18	8 10 6 12 1 12 8 7 18	11 13 9 15 3 13 8 7 18	14 18 15 17 5 13 9 7 19	17 22 19 17 7 14 9 7 19	20 26 18 16 8 15 9 7 19	23 31 22 18 9 15 9 7 19	26 35 27 21 8 15 9 7 19
5	29 28 31 30 26 12 7 7 19	32 33 30 34 28 11 7 7 19	35 34 33 1 30 11 7 7 19	2 3 2 5 33 11 7 7 19	5 7 7 9 35 11 8 7 18	8 11 6 12 1 12 8 7 18	11 14 9 15 3 13 8 7 18	14 19 16 17 5 13 9 7 19	17 24 19 17 7 14 9 7 19	20 27 18 16 8 15 9 7 19	23 33 22 18 9 15 9 7 19	26 36 27 21 8 15 9 7 19
6	29 29 31 30 26 12 7 7 19	32 35 30 34 28 11 7 7 19	35 36 33 2 30 11 7 7 19	2 4 2 5 33 11 7 7 19	5 8 7 9 35 11 8 7 18	8 12 6 12 1 12 8 7 18	11 15 10 15 3 13 8 7 18	14 20 16 17 5 13 9 7 19	17 25 19 17 7 14 9 7 19	20 29 18 16 8 15 9 7 19	23 34 23 18 9 15 9 7 19	26 2 27 21 8 15 9 7 19
7	29 31 31 30 26 12 7 7 19	32 36 30 34 28 11 7 7 19	35 1 33 2 30 11 7 7 19	2 6 3 6 33 11 7 7 19	5 9 7 9 35 11 8 7 18	8 13 6 12 1 12 8 7 18	11 17 10 15 3 13 8 7 18	14 21 16 17 6 13 9 7 19	17 26 19 17 7 14 9 7 19	20 30 18 16 8 15 9 7 19	23 35 23 18 9 15 9 7 19	26 4 28 21 8 15 9 7 19
8	29 32 31 31 26 12 7 7 19	32 2 30 34 28 11 7 7 19	35 2 33 2 30 11 7 7 19	2 7 3 6 33 11 7 7 19	5 10 7 9 35 11 8 7 18	8 15 6 13 1 12 8 7 18	11 18 10 16 4 13 8 7 18	14 23 16 17 6 13 9 7 19	17 28 19 17 7 14 9 7 19	20 32 18 16 8 15 9 7 19	23 1 23 18 9 15 9 7 19	26 5 28 22 8 15 9 7 19
9	29 34 31 31 26 12 7 7 19	32 3 30 35 28 11 7 7 19	35 4 33 2 31 11 7 7 19	2 8 3 6 33 11 7 7 19	5 11 7 9 35 12 8 7 18	8 16 6 13 1 12 8 7 18	11 19 10 16 4 13 9 7 18	14 24 16 17 6 13 9 7 19	17 29 19 17 7 14 9 7 19	20 33 18 16 8 15 9 7 19	23 2 23 18 9 15 9 7 19	26 6 28 22 8 15 9 7 19
10	29 35 31 31 26 12 7 7 19	33 4 30 35 29 11 7 7 19	35 5 33 2 31 11 7 7 19	2 9 3 6 33 11 7 7 19	5 13 7 9 35 12 8 7 18	8 17 6 13 2 12 8 7 18	11 20 10 16 4 13 9 7 18	14 25 16 17 6 13 9 7 19	17 31 19 16 7 14 9 7 19	20 34 18 16 9 15 9 7 19	23 4 23 19 9 15 9 7 19	26 7 28 22 8 15 9 7 19
11	30 1 31 31 26 12 7 7 19	33 5 30 35 29 11 7 7 19	36 6 34 2 31 11 7 7 19	3 11 3 6 33 11 7 7 19	5 14 7 10 35 12 8 7 18	8 18 6 13 2 12 8 7 18	11 22 11 16 4 13 9 7 18	14 27 17 18 6 13 9 7 19	17 32 19 16 7 14 9 7 19	20 36 18 16 9 15 9 7 19	23 5 23 19 9 15 9 7 19	26 8 28 22 8 15 9 7 19
12	30 2 31 31 26 12 7 7 19	33 7 30 35 29 11 7 7 19	36 7 34 2 31 11 7 7 19	3 12 4 6 33 11 7 7 19	6 15 7 10 35 12 8 7 18	9 19 6 13 2 12 8 7 18	11 23 11 16 4 13 9 7 18	14 28 17 18 6 13 9 7 19	17 34 19 16 8 14 9 7 19	20 1 19 16 9 15 9 7 19	23 6 24 19 9 15 9 7 19	26 10 28 22 8 15 9 7 19
13	30 3 32 31 27 11 7 7 19	33 8 30 35 29 11 7 7 19	36 9 34 2 31 11 7 7 19	3 13 4 6 33 11 7 7 19	6 16 7 10 35 12 8 7 18	9 21 6 13 2 12 8 7 18	12 24 11 16 4 13 9 7 18	14 30 17 18 6 13 9 7 19	17 35 19 16 8 14 9 7 19	20 3 19 16 9 15 9 7 19	24 8 24 19 9 15 9 7 19	27 11 28 22 7 15 9 7 19
14	30 5 32 31 27 11 7 7 19	33 9 30 35 29 11 7 7 19	36 10 34 3 31 11 7 7 19	3 14 4 6 33 11 7 7 19	6 17 7 10 36 12 8 7 18	9 22 7 13 2 12 8 7 18	12 26 11 16 4 13 9 7 18	15 31 17 18 6 13 9 7 19	18 36 19 16 8 14 9 7 19	21 4 19 16 9 15 9 7 19	24 9 24 19 9 15 9 7 19	27 12 28 22 7 15 9 7 19
15	30 6 32 31 27 11 7 7 19	33 10 30 35 29 11 7 7 19	36 11 34 3 31 11 7 7 19	3 15 4 6 33 11 7 7 19	6 19 7 10 36 12 8 7 18	9 24 7 13 2 12 8 7 18	12 27 11 16 4 13 9 7 18	15 33 17 18 6 13 9 7 19	18 2 19 16 8 14 9 7 19	21 6 19 16 9 15 9 7 19	24 10 24 19 8 15 9 7 19	27 13 29 22 7 15 9 7 19
16	30 7 32 32 27 11 7 7 19	33 11 31 35 29 11 7 7 19	36 12 34 3 31 11 7 7 19	3 17 4 7 33 11 7 7 19	6 20 7 10 36 12 8 7 18	9 25 7 13 2 12 8 7 18	12 29 11 16 4 13 9 7 18	15 34 17 18 6 14 9 7 19	18 3 19 16 8 14 9 7 19	21 7 19 17 9 15 9 7 19	24 11 24 19 8 15 9 7 19	27 15 29 22 7 15 9 7 19
17	30 8 32 32 27 11 7 7 19	33 13 31 36 29 11 7 7 19	36 13 35 3 31 11 7 7 19	3 18 5 7 33 11 7 7 19	6 21 7 10 36 12 8 7 18	9 26 7 14 2 12 8 7 18	12 30 12 16 4 13 9 7 18	15 36 17 18 6 14 9 7 19	18 5 19 16 8 14 9 7 19	21 8 19 17 9 15 9 7 19	24 13 24 19 9 15 9 7 19	27 16 29 23 7 15 9 7 19
18	30 9 31 32 27 11 7 7 19	33 14 31 36 29 11 7 7 19	36 15 35 3 31 11 7 7 19	3 19 5 7 34 11 7 7 18	6 23 7 10 36 12 8 7 18	9 28 7 14 2 12 8 7 18	12 32 12 16 4 13 9 7 18	15 1 17 18 6 14 9 7 19	18 6 19 18 6 14 9 7 19	21 9 19 17 9 15 9 7 19	24 14 25 19 8 15 9 7 19	27 17 29 23 7 15 9 7 19
19	30 11 31 32 27 11 7 7 19	33 15 31 36 29 11 7 7 19	36 16 35 3 31 11 7 7 19	3 21 5 7 34 11 7 7 18	6 24 7 10 36 12 8 7 18	9 29 7 14 2 12 8 7 18	12 33 12 16 4 13 9 7 18	15 3 18 18 6 14 9 7 19	18 7 19 16 8 14 9 7 19	21 11 20 17 9 15 9 7 19	24 15 25 19 8 15 9 7 19	27 18 29 23 7 15 9 7 19
20	30 12 31 32 27 11 7 7 19	34 16 31 36 29 11 7 7 19	36 17 35 3 31 11 7 7 19	3 22 5 7 34 11 8 7 18	6 26 7 11 36 12 8 7 18	9 31 7 14 2 12 8 7 18	12 35 13 16 4 13 9 7 18	15 4 18 18 6 14 9 7 19	18 9 19 16 8 14 9 7 19	21 12 20 17 9 15 9 7 19	24 16 25 20 8 15 9 7 19	27 19 29 23 7 15 9 7 19
21	31 13 31 32 27 11 7 7 19	34 17 31 36 29 11 7 7 19	1 18 35 3 31 11 7 7 19	4 23 5 7 34 11 8 7 18	6 27 7 11 36 12 8 7 18	9 32 7 14 2 12 8 7 18	12 36 13 17 4 13 9 7 18	15 5 18 17 6 14 9 7 19	18 10 19 16 8 14 9 7 19	21 13 20 17 9 15 9 7 19	24 17 25 20 8 15 9 7 19	27 21 29 23 7 15 9 7 19
22	31 14 31 32 27 11 7 7 19	34 19 31 36 29 11 7 7 19	1 20 35 4 32 11 7 7 19	4 25 5 7 34 11 8 7 18	7 29 7 11 36 12 8 7 18	10 34 7 14 2 12 8 7 18	12 2 13 17 4 13 9 7 18	15 6 18 17 6 14 9 7 19	18 11 19 16 8 14 9 7 19	21 14 20 17 9 15 9 7 19	24 19 25 20 8 15 9 7 19	27 22 29 23 7 15 9 7 19
23	31 15 31 32 27 11 7 7 19	34 20 31 36 30 11 7 7 19	1 21 36 4 32 11 7 7 19	4 26 6 7 34 11 8 7 18	7 30 7 11 36 12 8 7 18	10 35 7 14 2 12 8 7 18	12 3 13 17 5 13 9 7 18	15 8 18 17 6 14 9 7 19	18 12 19 16 8 14 9 7 19	21 15 20 17 9 15 9 7 19	25 20 25 20 8 15 9 7 19	28 23 30 23 7 15 9 7 19
24	31 17 31 33 27 11 7 7 19	34 21 31 36 30 11 7 7 19	1 22 36 4 32 11 7 7 19	4 28 6 8 34 11 8 7 18	7 31 7 11 36 12 8 7 18	10 1 8 14 3 12 8 7 18	13 4 13 17 5 13 9 7 18	16 9 18 17 7 14 9 7 19	19 13 19 16 8 14 9 7 19	22 17 20 17 9 15 9 7 19	25 21 25 20 8 15 9 7 19	28 25 30 23 7 15 9 7 19
25	31 18 31 33 27 11 7 7 19	34 23 32 36 30 11 7 7 19	1 24 36 4 32 11 7 7 19	4 29 6 8 34 11 8 7 18	7 33 7 11 36 12 8 7 18	10 2 8 14 3 12 8 7 18	13 6 14 17 5 13 9 7 18	16 10 18 17 7 14 9 7 19	19 15 18 16 8 14 9 7 19	22 18 21 17 9 15 9 7 19	25 22 26 20 8 15 9 7 19	28 26 30 23 7 15 9 7 19
26	31 19 31 33 27 11 7 7 19	34 24 32 1 30 11 7 7 19	1 25 36 4 32 11 7 7 19	4 30 6 8 34 11 8 7 18	7 34 6 11 36 12 8 7 18	10 3 8 14 3 12 8 7 18	13 7 14 17 5 13 9 7 18	16 11 18 17 7 14 9 7 19	19 16 18 16 8 14 9 7 19	22 19 21 17 9 15 9 7 19	25 24 26 20 8 15 9 7 19	28 27 30 24 7 15 9 7 19
27	31 20 31 33 27 11 7 7 19	34 25 32 1 30 11 7 7 19	1 26 36 4 32 11 7 7 19	4 32 6 8 34 11 8 7 18	7 36 6 11 36 12 8 7 18	10 5 8 15 3 12 8 7 18	13 8 14 17 5 13 9 7 18	16 13 19 17 6 14 9 7 19	19 17 18 16 8 14 9 7 19	22 20 21 17 9 15 9 7 19	25 25 26 20 8 15 9 7 19	28 29 30 24 7 15 9 7 19
28	31 22 30 33 28 11 7 7 19	34 27 32 1 30 11 7 7 19	1 28 1 4 32 11 7 7 19	4 33 6 8 34 11 8 7 18	7 1 6 11 1 12 8 7 18	10 6 8 15 3 12 8 7 18	13 9 14 17 5 13 9 7 18	16 14 19 17 6 14 9 7 19	19 18 18 16 8 14 9 7 19	22 22 21 17 9 15 9 7 19	25 27 26 20 8 15 9 7 19	28 30 30 24 7 15 9 7 19
29	31 23 30 33 28 11 7 7 19		1 29 1 4 32 11 7 7 19	4 35 6 8 34 11 8 7 18	7 2 6 12 36 12 8 7 18	10 7 8 15 3 12 8 7 18	13 10 14 17 5 13 9 7 18	16 15 19 17 6 14 9 7 19	19 19 18 16 8 14 9 7 19	22 23 21 17 9 15 9 7 19	25 28 26 21 8 15 9 7 19	28 32 30 24 7 15 9 7 19
30	31 24 30 33 28 11 7 7 19	**1943**	1 30 1 5 32 11 7 7 19	4 36 6 8 34 11 8 7 18	7 4 6 12 36 12 8 7 18	10 8 8 15 3 12 8 7 18	13 12 14 17 5 13 9 7 18	16 16 19 17 6 14 9 7 19	19 21 18 16 8 14 9 7 19	22 24 21 18 9 15 9 7 19	25 29 26 21 8 15 9 7 19	28 33 30 24 7 15 9 7 19
31	32 26 30 33 28 11 7 7 19		1 31 1 5 32 11 7 7 19		7 5 6 12 36 12 8 7 18		13 13 15 17 5 13 9 7 18	16 17 19 17 6 14 9 7 19		22 26 22 17 9 15 9 7 19		28 35 30 24 7 15 9 7 19

	JAN	FEB	MAR	APR	MAY	JUNE	JULY	AUG	SEPT	OCT	NOV	DEC
1	29 36 30 24 7 15 9 7 19	32 5 29 28 7 15 9 7 19	35 6 33 32 8 14 8 7 19	2 12 3 35 10 14 9 7 19	5 15 5 3 11 14 9 7 19	8 20 5 7 13 15 9 7 19	10 23 11 11 15 15 10 8 19	13 28 16 14 17 16 10 8 19	16 33 17 18 19 16 10 8 19	19 1 18 22 21 17 11 8 19	22 6 23 26 23 18 11 8 19	25 10 27 29 25 18 10 8 19
2	29 2 30 24 7 15 9 7 19	32 7 29 28 7 15 8 7 19	35 8 33 32 8 14 8 7 19	2 13 3 35 10 14 9 7 19	5 16 5 3 11 14 9 7 19	8 21 5 7 13 15 9 7 19	11 24 11 11 15 15 10 8 19	14 30 16 15 17 16 10 8 19	16 34 17 18 19 16 10 8 19	19 2 18 22 21 17 11 8 19	22 8 23 26 23 18 11 8 19	26 11 28 29 25 18 10 8 19
3	29 3 30 25 7 15 9 7 19	32 8 29 28 7 15 8 7 19	35 10 34 32 8 14 8 7 19	2 14 4 36 10 14 9 7 19	5 18 5 3 11 14 9 7 19	8 22 5 7 13 15 9 7 19	11 26 11 11 15 15 10 8 19	14 31 16 15 17 16 10 8 19	17 36 17 18 19 16 10 8 19	20 4 18 22 21 17 11 8 19	23 9 23 26 23 18 11 8 19	26 12 28 30 25 18 10 8 19
4	29 4 30 25 7 15 9 7 19	32 9 29 28 7 15 8 7 19	35 11 34 32 8 14 8 7 19	2 16 4 36 10 14 9 7 19	5 19 5 3 11 14 9 7 19	8 23 6 7 13 15 9 7 19	11 27 11 11 15 15 10 8 19	14 32 16 15 17 16 10 8 19	17 1 17 19 19 16 10 8 19	20 5 18 22 21 17 11 8 19	23 10 24 26 23 18 11 8 19	26 14 28 30 25 18 10 8 19
5	29 6 30 25 7 15 9 7 19	32 10 30 29 7 15 8 7 19	35 12 34 32 8 14 8 7 19	2 17 4 36 10 14 9 7 19	5 20 5 4 12 14 9 7 19	8 25 6 7 13 15 9 7 19	11 28 11 11 15 15 10 8 19	14 34 16 15 17 16 10 8 19	17 3 17 19 19 16 10 8 19	20 7 19 22 21 17 11 8 19	23 12 24 26 23 18 11 8 19	26 15 28 30 25 18 10 8 19
6	29 7 29 25 7 15 9 7 19	32 11 30 29 7 15 8 7 19	35 14 34 32 8 14 8 7 19	2 18 4 36 10 14 9 7 19	5 21 4 4 12 14 9 7 19	8 26 6 8 13 15 9 7 19	11 30 12 11 15 15 10 8 19	14 35 17 15 17 16 10 8 19	17 4 17 19 19 16 10 8 19	20 8 19 23 21 17 11 8 19	23 13 24 26 23 18 11 8 19	26 16 28 30 25 18 10 8 19
7	29 8 29 25 7 15 9 7 19	32 13 30 29 7 15 8 7 19	35 15 34 32 9 14 8 7 19	2 19 4 36 10 14 9 7 19	5 23 4 4 12 14 9 7 19	8 27 6 8 13 15 9 7 19	11 31 12 11 15 15 10 8 19	14 1 17 15 17 16 10 8 19	17 6 17 19 19 16 10 8 19	20 9 19 23 21 17 11 8 19	23 14 24 26 23 18 11 8 19	26 17 28 30 25 18 10 8 19
8	29 9 29 25 7 15 9 7 19	32 14 30 29 7 15 8 7 19	35 16 34 32 9 14 8 7 19	2 20 4 36 10 14 9 7 19	5 24 4 4 12 14 9 7 19	8 29 6 8 13 15 9 7 19	11 33 12 11 15 15 10 8 19	14 2 17 15 17 16 10 8 19	17 7 17 19 19 16 10 8 19	20 11 19 23 21 17 11 8 19	23 15 24 27 23 18 11 8 19	26 18 28 30 25 18 10 8 19
9	29 11 29 25 7 15 9 7 19	32 15 30 29 7 15 8 7 19	35 17 35 33 9 14 8 7 19	2 22 4 36 10 14 9 7 19	5 25 4 4 12 14 9 7 19	8 30 6 8 14 15 9 7 19	11 34 12 12 15 15 10 8 19	14 3 17 15 17 16 10 8 19	17 9 17 19 19 16 10 8 19	20 12 19 23 21 17 11 8 19	23 16 24 27 23 18 11 8 19	26 20 28 30 25 18 10 8 19
10	29 12 29 25 7 15 9 7 19	33 16 30 29 8 15 8 7 19	35 18 35 33 9 14 9 7 19	3 23 4 1 10 14 9 7 19	5 26 4 4 12 14 9 7 19	8 32 6 8 14 15 9 7 19	11 36 12 12 15 15 10 8 19	14 5 17 15 17 16 10 8 19	17 10 17 19 19 16 10 8 19	20 13 19 23 21 17 11 8 19	23 18 25 27 23 18 11 8 19	26 21 28 30 26 18 10 8 19
11	30 13 29 26 7 15 9 7 19	33 17 30 29 8 15 8 7 19	36 20 35 33 9 14 9 7 19	3 24 5 1 10 14 9 7 19	6 28 4 4 12 14 9 7 19	9 33 7 8 14 15 9 7 19	11 1 13 12 15 15 10 8 19	14 6 17 16 17 16 10 8 19	17 11 17 19 19 17 10 8 19	20 14 20 23 21 17 11 8 19	23 19 25 27 23 18 11 8 19	26 22 28 31 26 18 10 8 19
12	30 14 29 26 7 15 9 7 19	33 19 30 29 8 15 8 7 19	36 21 35 33 9 14 9 7 19	3 25 5 1 10 14 9 7 19	6 29 4 4 12 14 9 7 19	9 35 7 8 14 15 9 7 19	11 2 13 12 16 15 10 8 19	14 8 17 16 17 16 10 8 19	17 12 16 20 19 17 10 8 19	20 16 20 23 21 17 11 8 19	24 20 25 27 24 18 11 8 19	27 23 28 31 26 18 10 8 19
13	30 15 29 26 7 15 9 7 19	33 20 31 30 8 15 8 7 19	36 22 35 33 9 14 9 7 19	3 27 5 1 10 14 9 7 19	6 31 4 5 12 14 9 7 19	9 36 7 8 14 15 9 7 19	12 4 13 12 16 15 10 8 19	15 9 17 16 18 16 10 8 19	18 13 16 20 20 17 10 8 19	21 17 20 23 22 17 11 8 19	24 21 25 27 24 18 11 8 19	27 24 28 31 26 18 10 8 19
14	30 17 29 26 7 15 9 7 19	33 21 31 30 8 15 8 7 19	36 23 36 33 9 14 9 7 19	3 28 5 1 10 14 9 7 19	6 32 4 5 12 14 9 7 19	9 1 7 8 14 15 9 7 19	12 5 13 12 16 15 10 8 19	15 10 17 16 18 16 10 8 19	18 15 16 20 20 17 10 8 19	21 18 20 23 22 17 11 8 19	24 22 25 27 24 18 11 8 19	27 26 28 31 26 18 10 8 19
15	30 18 29 26 7 15 9 7 19	33 22 31 30 8 15 8 7 19	36 24 36 33 9 14 9 7 19	3 30 5 1 10 14 9 7 19	6 33 4 5 12 14 9 7 19	9 3 7 9 14 15 9 7 19	12 7 13 12 16 15 10 8 19	15 11 17 16 18 16 10 8 19	18 16 16 20 20 17 10 8 19	21 19 20 24 22 17 11 8 19	24 24 25 27 24 18 11 8 19	27 27 28 31 26 18 10 8 19
16	30 19 28 25 7 15 9 7 19	33 24 31 30 8 15 8 7 19	36 26 36 33 9 14 9 7 19	3 31 5 1 10 14 9 7 19	6 35 4 5 12 14 9 7 19	9 4 7 9 14 15 9 7 19	12 8 14 12 16 15 10 8 19	15 13 17 16 18 16 10 8 19	18 17 16 20 20 17 10 8 19	21 20 21 24 22 17 11 8 19	24 25 25 28 24 18 11 8 19	27 28 28 31 26 18 10 8 19
17	30 20 28 25 7 15 9 7 19	33 25 31 30 8 15 8 7 19	36 27 36 34 9 14 9 7 19	3 32 5 1 11 14 9 7 19	6 36 4 5 12 14 9 7 19	9 6 7 9 14 15 9 7 19	12 9 14 13 16 15 10 8 19	15 14 18 16 18 16 10 8 19	18 18 16 20 20 17 10 8 19	21 22 21 24 22 17 11 8 19	24 26 26 28 24 18 11 8 19	27 30 28 31 26 18 10 8 19
18	30 21 28 25 7 15 9 7 19	33 26 31 30 8 15 8 7 19	36 29 36 34 9 14 9 7 19	3 34 5 1 11 14 9 7 19	6 2 4 5 12 14 9 7 19	9 7 8 9 14 15 9 8 19	12 10 14 13 16 15 10 8 19	15 15 18 16 18 16 10 8 19	18 19 16 20 20 17 10 8 19	21 23 21 24 22 17 11 8 19	24 27 26 28 24 18 11 8 19	27 31 28 31 26 18 10 8 19
19	30 23 28 25 7 15 9 7 19	33 28 31 30 8 15 8 7 19	36 30 1 34 9 14 9 7 19	3 35 5 2 11 14 9 7 19	6 3 4 5 12 14 9 7 19	9 8 8 9 14 15 9 8 19	12 12 14 13 16 15 10 8 19	15 16 18 17 18 16 10 8 19	18 21 16 20 20 17 10 8 19	21 24 21 24 22 17 11 8 19	24 29 26 28 24 18 11 8 19	27 33 28 31 26 18 10 8 19
20	30 24 28 27 7 15 9 7 19	34 29 32 30 8 15 8 7 19	36 31 1 34 9 14 9 7 19	4 1 5 2 11 14 9 7 19	6 5 4 5 12 14 9 7 19	9 9 8 9 14 15 10 8 19	12 13 14 13 16 15 10 8 19	15 17 18 17 18 16 10 8 19	18 22 16 21 20 17 10 8 19	21 25 21 24 22 17 11 8 19	24 30 26 28 24 18 11 8 19	27 34 28 32 26 18 10 8 19
21	31 25 28 27 7 15 9 7 19	34 30 32 30 8 15 8 7 19	1 33 1 34 9 14 9 7 19	4 2 5 2 11 14 9 7 19	7 6 4 6 12 14 9 7 19	9 11 8 9 14 15 10 8 19	12 14 14 13 16 15 10 8 19	15 19 18 17 18 16 10 8 19	18 23 16 21 20 17 10 8 19	21 26 21 24 22 17 11 8 19	24 31 26 28 24 18 11 8 19	27 35 28 32 26 18 10 8 19
22	31 27 28 27 7 15 9 7 19	34 32 32 31 8 15 8 7 19	1 34 1 34 9 14 9 7 19	4 4 5 2 11 14 9 7 19	7 7 4 6 12 14 9 7 19	10 12 9 9 14 15 10 8 19	12 15 15 13 16 15 10 8 19	15 20 18 17 18 16 10 8 19	18 24 17 21 20 17 10 8 19	21 28 22 24 22 17 11 8 19	25 33 26 28 24 18 10 8 19	28 1 28 32 26 18 10 8 19
23	31 28 28 27 7 15 9 7 19	34 34 32 31 8 15 8 7 19	1 36 1 34 9 14 9 7 19	4 5 5 2 11 14 9 7 19	7 9 4 6 13 14 9 7 19	10 13 9 10 14 15 10 8 19	13 16 15 13 16 15 10 8 19	16 21 18 17 18 16 10 8 19	19 25 17 21 20 17 10 8 19	21 29 22 25 22 17 11 8 19	25 34 26 28 24 18 10 8 19	28 2 28 32 27 18 10 8 19
24	31 30 28 27 7 15 9 7 19	34 35 32 31 8 15 8 7 19	1 1 2 34 9 14 9 7 19	4 6 5 2 11 14 9 7 19	7 10 4 6 13 14 9 7 19	10 14 9 10 14 15 10 8 19	13 18 15 13 16 15 10 8 19	16 22 18 17 18 16 10 8 19	19 27 17 21 20 17 10 8 19	22 30 22 25 22 17 11 8 19	25 36 27 28 24 18 10 8 19	28 4 27 32 27 18 10 8 19
25	31 31 29 27 7 15 9 7 19	34 1 32 31 8 15 8 7 19	1 3 2 35 9 14 9 7 19	4 8 5 2 11 14 9 7 19	7 11 5 6 13 14 9 7 19	10 16 9 10 14 15 10 8 19	13 19 15 14 16 15 10 8 19	16 23 18 17 18 16 10 8 19	19 28 17 21 20 17 11 8 19	22 32 22 25 22 17 11 8 19	25 1 27 29 24 18 10 8 19	28 5 27 32 27 18 10 8 19
26	31 33 29 27 7 15 9 7 19	34 2 33 31 8 15 8 7 19	1 4 2 35 9 14 9 7 19	4 9 5 2 11 14 9 7 19	7 12 5 6 13 14 9 7 19	10 17 9 10 15 15 10 8 19	13 20 15 14 16 16 10 8 19	16 25 18 17 18 16 10 8 19	19 29 17 21 20 17 11 8 19	22 33 22 25 22 17 11 8 19	25 3 27 29 25 18 10 8 19	28 6 27 32 27 18 10 8 19
27	31 34 29 27 7 15 9 7 19	34 3 33 31 8 15 8 7 19	1 6 2 35 9 14 9 7 19	4 10 5 3 11 14 9 7 19	7 14 5 6 13 14 9 7 19	10 18 10 9 14 15 10 8 19	13 21 15 14 16 16 10 8 19	16 26 18 18 18 16 10 8 19	19 31 17 21 20 17 11 8 19	22 35 22 25 22 17 11 8 19	25 4 27 29 25 18 10 8 19	28 8 27 32 27 18 10 8 19
28	31 36 29 28 7 15 9 7 19	34 5 33 31 8 14 8 7 19	1 7 2 35 10 14 9 7 19	4 12 5 3 11 14 9 7 19	7 15 5 6 13 15 9 7 19	10 19 10 9 14 15 10 8 19	13 22 15 14 17 16 10 8 19	16 27 18 18 18 16 10 8 19	19 32 17 22 20 17 11 8 19	22 36 22 25 22 17 11 8 19	25 5 27 29 25 18 10 8 19	28 9 27 33 27 18 10 8 19
29	31 1 29 28 7 15 9 7 19	34 6 33 31 8 14 8 7 19	1 8 3 35 10 14 9 7 19	4 13 5 3 11 14 9 7 19	7 16 5 7 13 15 9 7 19	10 20 10 9 14 15 10 8 19	13 24 16 14 17 16 10 8 19	16 29 18 18 19 16 10 8 19	19 34 18 22 21 17 11 8 19	22 2 23 25 23 17 11 8 19	25 7 27 29 25 18 10 8 19	28 10 27 33 27 18 10 8 19
30	31 3 29 28 7 15 9 7 19	**1944**	1 10 3 35 10 14 9 7 19	4 14 5 3 11 14 9 7 19	7 17 5 7 13 15 9 7 19	10 22 10 9 14 15 10 8 19	13 25 16 14 17 16 10 8 19	16 30 18 18 19 16 10 8 19	19 35 18 22 21 17 11 8 19	22 3 23 25 23 18 11 8 19	25 8 27 29 25 18 10 8 19	28 12 27 33 27 18 10 8 19
31	32 4 29 28 7 15 9 7 19		2 11 3 35 10 14 9 7 19		7 18 5 7 13 15 9 7 19		13 26 16 14 17 16 10 8 19	16 31 17 18 19 16 10 8 19		22 5 23 26 23 18 11 8 19		28 13 27 33 27 18 10 7 19

	JAN	FEB	MAR	APR	MAY	JUNE
1	29 14 27 33 27 18 10 7 19	32 19 30 36 30 18 10 7 19	35 20 35 3 32 18 10 7 19	2 24 3 4 34 18 10 7 19	5 27 2 2 36 17 10 8 19	8 32 6 3 3 17 10 8 19
2	29 16 27 33 27 18 10 7 19	32 20 30 1 30 18 10 7 19	35 21 35 3 32 18 10 7 19	2 25 3 4 34 18 10 8 19	5 29 2 2 36 17 10 8 19	8 34 6 3 3 17 11 8 19
3	29 17 27 33 27 18 10 7 19	32 21 30 1 30 18 10 7 19	35 22 35 3 32 18 10 7 19	2 26 3 4 34 17 10 8 19	5 30 2 2 1 17 10 8 19	8 35 6 3 3 17 11 8 19
4	29 18 27 33 27 18 10 7 19	32 22 30 1 30 18 10 7 19	35 23 35 3 32 18 10 7 19	2 28 3 4 34 17 10 8 19	5 31 2 2 1 17 10 8 19	8 1 7 3 3 17 11 8 19
5	29 19 27 33 28 18 10 7 19	32 24 31 36 30 18 10 7 19	35 24 35 3 32 18 10 7 19	2 29 3 4 34 17 10 8 19	5 33 2 2 1 17 10 8 19	8 2 7 4 3 17 11 8 19
6	29 20 27 34 28 18 10 7 19	32 25 31 36 30 18 10 7 19	35 26 36 3 32 18 10 7 19	2 30 3 4 34 17 10 8 19	5 34 3 2 1 17 10 8 19	8 3 7 4 3 17 11 8 19
7	29 22 27 34 28 18 10 7 19	32 26 31 36 30 18 10 7 19	35 27 36 3 32 18 10 7 19	2 32 3 4 35 17 10 8 19	5 36 3 2 1 17 10 8 19	8 5 7 4 3 17 11 8 19
8	29 23 27 34 28 18 10 7 19	32 27 31 36 30 18 10 7 19	35 28 36 3 32 18 10 7 19	2 33 3 3 35 17 10 8 19	5 1 3 2 1 17 10 8 19	8 6 7 4 3 17 11 8 19
9	29 24 27 34 28 18 10 7 19	33 29 31 36 30 18 10 7 19	35 29 36 3 32 18 10 7 19	2 35 3 3 35 17 10 8 19	5 2 3 2 1 17 10 8 19	8 8 8 4 3 17 11 8 19
10	29 25 27 34 28 18 10 7 19	33 30 31 36 30 18 10 7 19	35 31 36 3 32 18 10 7 19	3 36 3 3 35 17 10 8 19	5 4 3 2 1 17 10 8 19	8 9 8 4 3 17 11 8 19
11	30 27 27 34 28 18 10 7 19	33 31 31 36 30 18 10 7 19	36 32 1 4 32 18 10 7 19	3 2 3 3 35 17 10 8 19	6 6 3 2 1 17 10 8 19	9 11 8 4 3 17 11 8 19
12	30 28 27 34 28 18 10 7 19	33 33 32 36 30 18 10 7 19	36 34 1 4 33 18 10 7 19	3 3 3 3 35 17 10 8 19	6 7 3 2 1 17 10 8 19	9 12 8 4 4 17 11 8 19
13	30 29 27 34 28 18 10 7 19	33 34 32 2 30 18 10 7 19	36 35 1 4 33 18 10 7 19	3 5 3 3 35 17 10 8 19	6 8 3 2 1 17 10 8 19	9 13 8 4 4 17 11 8 19
14	30 31 28 34 28 18 10 7 19	33 36 32 2 31 18 10 7 19	36 1 1 4 33 18 10 7 19	3 6 3 3 35 17 10 8 19	6 10 3 2 1 17 10 8 19	9 15 9 4 4 17 11 8 19
15	30 32 28 35 28 18 10 7 19	33 1 32 2 31 18 10 7 19	36 2 1 4 33 18 10 7 19	3 8 3 3 35 17 10 8 19	6 11 3 2 1 17 10 8 19	9 16 9 4 4 17 11 8 19
16	30 34 28 35 28 18 10 7 19	33 3 32 2 31 18 10 7 19	36 4 1 4 33 18 10 7 19	3 9 3 3 35 17 10 8 19	6 13 3 2 2 17 10 8 19	9 17 9 4 4 17 11 8 19
17	30 35 28 35 28 18 10 7 19	33 4 32 2 31 18 10 7 19	36 5 2 4 33 18 10 7 19	3 10 3 3 35 17 10 8 19	6 14 4 2 2 17 10 8 19	9 18 9 5 4 17 11 8 19
18	30 36 28 35 28 18 10 7 19	33 6 33 2 31 18 10 7 19	36 7 2 4 33 18 10 7 19	3 12 2 3 35 17 10 8 19	6 15 4 2 2 17 10 8 19	9 19 10 5 4 17 11 8 19
19	30 2 28 35 29 18 10 7 19	34 7 33 2 31 18 10 7 19	36 8 2 4 33 18 10 7 19	3 13 2 3 35 17 10 8 19	6 16 4 3 2 17 10 8 19	9 21 10 5 4 17 11 8 19
20	31 3 28 35 29 18 10 7 19	34 8 33 2 31 18 10 7 19	36 9 2 4 33 18 10 7 19	4 14 2 3 36 17 10 8 19	6 17 4 3 2 17 10 8 19	9 22 10 5 4 17 11 8 19
21	31 5 28 35 29 18 10 7 19	34 10 33 2 31 18 10 7 19	1 11 2 4 33 18 10 7 19	4 15 2 3 36 17 10 8 19	7 19 4 3 2 17 10 8 19	9 23 10 5 4 17 11 8 19
22	31 6 29 35 29 18 10 7 19	34 11 33 2 31 18 10 7 19	1 12 2 4 33 18 10 7 19	4 17 2 3 36 17 10 8 19	7 20 4 3 2 17 10 8 19	10 24 10 5 4 17 11 8 19
23	31 8 29 35 29 18 10 7 19	34 12 34 2 31 18 10 7 19	1 13 3 4 33 18 10 7 19	4 18 2 3 36 17 10 8 19	7 21 4 3 2 17 10 8 19	10 26 11 5 4 17 11 8 19
24	31 9 29 36 29 18 10 7 19	34 14 34 3 31 18 10 7 19	1 14 3 4 33 18 10 7 19	4 19 2 3 36 17 10 8 19	7 22 5 3 2 17 10 8 19	10 27 11 5 4 17 11 8 19
25	31 10 29 36 29 18 10 7 19	34 15 34 3 31 18 10 7 19	1 16 3 4 34 18 10 7 19	4 20 2 2 36 17 10 8 19	7 23 5 3 2 17 10 8 19	10 28 11 5 5 18 11 8 19
26	31 11 29 36 29 18 10 7 19	34 16 34 3 31 18 10 7 19	1 17 3 4 34 18 10 7 19	4 21 2 2 36 17 10 8 19	7 25 5 3 2 17 10 8 19	10 29 11 5 5 18 11 8 19
27	31 13 29 36 29 18 10 7 19	34 17 34 3 32 18 10 7 19	1 18 3 4 34 18 10 7 19	4 23 2 2 36 17 10 8 19	7 26 5 3 2 17 10 8 19	10 31 11 5 5 18 11 8 19
28	31 14 29 36 29 18 10 7 19	34 18 34 3 32 18 10 7 19	1 19 3 4 34 18 10 7 19	4 24 2 2 36 17 10 8 19	7 27 5 3 2 17 10 8 19	10 32 12 5 5 18 11 8 19
29	31 15 29 36 29 18 10 7 19		1 20 3 4 34 18 10 7 19	4 25 2 2 36 17 10 8 19	7 28 5 3 3 17 10 8 19	10 33 12 6 5 18 11 8 19
30	32 16 30 36 29 18 10 7 19	**1945**	1 22 3 4 34 18 10 7 19	4 26 2 2 36 17 10 8 19	7 30 6 3 3 17 10 8 19	10 35 12 6 5 18 11 8 19
31	32 18 30 36 29 18 10 7 19		2 23 3 4 34 18 10 7 19		7 31 6 3 3 17 10 8 19	

	JULY	AUG	SEPT	OCT	NOV	DEC
1	10 36 12 6 5 18 11 8 19	13 6 16 9 7 18 11 8 19	16 11 15 13 9 19 12 8 19	19 14 19 16 11 19 12 8 19	22 19 24 20 12 20 12 8 19	25 22 27 24 13 21 12 8 19
2	11 2 12 6 5 18 11 8 19	13 7 16 9 7 18 11 8 19	16 12 15 13 9 19 12 8 19	19 16 19 16 11 19 12 8 19	22 20 24 20 12 20 12 8 19	25 23 27 24 13 21 12 8 19
3	11 3 12 6 5 18 11 8 19	14 8 16 9 7 18 11 8 19	17 13 15 13 9 19 12 8 19	19 17 19 17 11 19 12 8 19	23 21 24 20 12 20 12 8 19	26 25 26 24 13 21 12 8 19
4	11 4 13 6 5 18 11 8 19	14 10 16 10 7 18 11 8 19	17 15 15 13 9 19 12 8 19	20 18 20 17 11 19 12 8 19	23 22 25 21 12 20 12 8 19	26 26 26 24 13 21 12 8 19
5	11 6 13 6 5 18 11 8 19	14 11 16 10 7 18 11 8 19	17 16 15 13 9 19 12 8 19	20 19 20 17 11 19 12 8 19	23 24 25 21 12 20 12 8 19	26 27 26 24 13 21 12 8 19
6	11 7 13 6 5 18 11 8 19	14 12 16 10 7 18 11 8 19	17 17 15 13 9 19 12 8 19	20 20 20 17 11 19 12 8 19	23 25 25 21 12 20 12 8 19	26 28 26 25 13 21 12 8 19
7	11 9 13 7 5 18 11 8 19	14 14 16 10 8 18 11 8 19	17 18 15 13 9 19 12 8 19	20 22 20 17 11 19 12 8 19	23 26 25 21 12 20 12 8 19	26 29 26 25 13 21 12 8 19
8	11 10 13 7 5 18 11 8 19	14 15 16 10 8 18 11 8 19	17 20 15 14 10 19 12 8 19	20 23 20 17 11 19 12 8 19	23 27 25 21 12 20 12 8 19	26 31 26 25 13 21 12 8 19
9	11 11 13 7 6 18 11 8 19	14 16 16 10 8 18 11 8 19	17 21 15 14 10 19 12 8 19	20 24 21 17 11 19 12 8 19	23 28 25 21 12 20 12 8 19	26 32 26 25 13 21 12 8 19
10	11 13 14 7 6 18 11 8 19	14 17 16 10 8 18 11 8 19	17 22 16 14 10 19 12 8 19	20 25 21 17 11 19 12 8 19	23 30 25 21 12 20 12 8 19	26 33 26 25 13 21 12 8 19
11	11 14 14 7 6 18 11 8 19	14 19 16 10 8 18 11 8 19	17 23 16 14 10 19 12 8 19	20 26 21 18 11 20 12 8 19	23 31 26 21 12 20 12 8 19	26 35 25 25 13 21 12 8 19
12	11 15 14 7 6 18 11 8 19	14 20 16 10 8 18 11 8 19	17 24 16 14 10 19 12 8 19	20 28 21 18 11 20 12 8 19	23 32 26 22 13 20 12 8 19	27 36 25 25 13 21 12 8 19
13	12 17 14 7 6 18 11 8 19	15 21 16 11 8 18 11 8 19	18 25 16 14 10 19 12 8 19	20 29 21 18 11 20 12 8 19	24 34 26 22 13 20 12 8 19	27 1 25 25 13 21 12 8 19
14	12 18 14 7 6 18 11 8 19	15 22 16 11 8 18 11 8 19	18 27 16 14 10 19 12 8 19	21 30 21 18 11 20 12 8 19	24 35 26 22 13 20 12 8 19	27 3 25 26 13 21 12 8 19
15	12 19 14 7 6 18 11 8 19	15 23 16 11 8 18 11 8 19	18 28 16 14 10 19 12 8 19	21 31 22 18 11 20 12 8 19	24 36 26 22 13 20 12 8 19	27 4 25 26 13 21 12 8 19
16	12 20 14 7 6 18 11 8 19	15 25 16 11 8 18 11 8 19	18 29 17 15 10 19 12 8 19	21 32 22 18 12 20 12 8 19	24 2 26 22 13 20 12 8 19	27 6 25 26 13 21 12 8 19
17	12 21 15 8 6 18 11 8 19	15 26 15 11 8 18 11 8 19	18 31 17 15 10 19 12 8 19	21 34 22 18 12 20 12 8 19	24 3 26 22 13 20 12 8 19	27 7 25 26 13 21 12 8 19
18	12 23 15 8 6 18 11 8 19	15 27 15 11 8 18 11 8 19	18 32 17 15 10 19 12 8 19	21 36 22 18 12 20 12 8 19	24 5 26 22 13 20 12 8 19	27 9 25 26 13 21 12 8 19
19	12 24 15 8 6 18 11 8 19	15 28 15 11 8 18 11 8 19	18 33 17 15 10 19 12 8 19	21 1 22 19 12 20 12 8 19	24 6 26 22 13 20 12 8 19	27 10 25 26 13 21 12 8 19
20	12 25 15 8 6 18 11 8 19	15 30 15 11 8 18 11 8 19	18 35 17 15 10 19 12 8 19	21 3 22 19 12 20 12 8 19	24 8 26 23 13 20 12 8 19	27 12 25 26 13 21 12 8 19
21	12 26 15 8 6 18 11 8 19	15 31 15 11 8 18 12 8 19	18 36 17 15 10 19 12 8 19	21 4 23 19 12 20 12 8 19	24 9 27 23 13 20 12 8 19	27 13 25 26 13 21 12 8 19
22	12 28 15 8 6 18 11 8 19	15 32 15 12 8 18 12 8 19	18 2 18 15 10 19 12 8 19	21 6 23 19 12 20 12 8 19	24 11 27 23 13 20 12 8 19	28 14 25 27 13 21 12 8 19
23	13 29 15 8 7 18 11 8 19	15 34 15 12 9 18 12 8 19	19 3 18 15 10 19 12 8 19	21 7 23 19 12 20 12 8 19	25 12 27 23 13 20 12 8 19	28 16 25 27 13 21 12 8 19
24	13 30 15 8 7 18 11 8 19	16 35 15 12 9 18 12 8 19	19 5 18 15 10 19 12 8 19	22 9 23 19 12 20 12 8 19	25 14 27 23 13 20 12 8 19	28 17 26 27 13 21 12 8 19
25	13 32 15 8 7 18 11 8 19	16 1 15 12 9 19 12 8 19	19 6 18 16 11 19 12 8 19	22 10 23 19 12 20 12 8 19	25 15 27 23 13 20 12 8 19	28 18 26 27 13 21 12 8 19
26	13 33 15 9 7 18 11 8 19	16 2 15 12 9 19 12 8 19	19 8 18 16 11 19 12 8 19	22 11 23 19 12 20 12 8 19	25 16 27 23 13 20 12 8 19	28 19 26 27 12 21 12 8 19
27	13 34 16 9 7 18 11 8 19	16 4 15 12 9 19 12 8 19	19 9 19 16 11 19 12 8 19	22 13 23 20 12 20 12 8 19	25 17 27 23 13 20 12 8 19	28 21 26 27 12 21 12 8 19
28	13 36 16 9 7 18 11 8 19	16 5 15 12 9 19 12 8 19	19 10 19 16 11 19 12 8 19	22 14 24 20 12 20 12 8 19	25 19 27 24 13 20 12 8 19	28 22 26 27 12 21 12 8 19
29	13 1 16 9 7 18 11 8 19	16 7 15 12 9 19 12 8 19	19 12 19 16 11 19 12 8 19	22 15 24 20 12 20 12 8 19	25 20 27 24 13 20 12 8 19	28 23 26 27 12 21 12 8 19
30	13 3 16 9 7 18 11 8 19	16 8 15 13 9 19 12 8 19	19 13 19 16 11 19 12 8 19	22 16 24 20 12 20 12 8 19	25 21 27 24 13 21 12 8 19	28 24 26 28 12 21 12 8 19
31	13 4 16 9 7 18 11 8 19	16 9 15 13 9 19 12 8 19		22 18 24 20 12 20 12 8 19		28 25 26 28 12 21 12 8 19

	JAN	FEB	MAR	APR	MAY	JUNE	JULY	AUG	SEPT	OCT	NOV	DEC
1	29 27 26 28 12 21 12 8 19	32 31 31 32 11 21 11 8 19	35 32 36 35 11 21 11 8 19	2 1 1 3 12 21 11 8 19	5 5 2 7 13 21 11 8 19	8 10 8 11 14 20 12 8 19	10 14 13 14 16 20 12 8 19	13 19 14 18 18 21 12 9 19	16 23 15 21 20 21 13 9 19	19 26 21 24 22 22 13 9 19	22 31 25 25 24 22 13 9 19	25 34 24 23 26 23 13 9 20
2	29 28 27 28 12 21 12 8 19	32 33 31 32 11 21 11 8 19	35 33 36 35 11 21 11 8 19	2 3 36 3 12 21 11 8 19	5 6 2 7 13 21 11 8 19	8 12 8 11 15 20 12 8 19	10 15 13 14 16 20 12 9 19	13 20 14 18 18 21 12 9 19	16 25 15 21 20 21 13 9 19	19 28 21 24 22 22 13 9 19	22 32 25 25 24 22 13 9 19	25 36 24 23 26 23 13 9 20
3	29 29 27 28 12 21 12 8 19	32 34 31 32 11 21 11 8 19	35 35 36 35 11 21 11 8 19	2 4 36 3 12 21 11 8 19	5 8 2 7 13 20 11 8 19	8 13 8 11 14 20 12 8 19	11 17 13 14 16 20 12 8 19	14 21 14 18 18 21 13 9 19	17 26 15 21 20 21 13 9 19	19 29 21 24 22 22 13 9 19	23 33 25 25 24 22 13 9 19	26 1 24 23 26 23 13 9 20
4	29 30 27 28 12 21 12 8 19	32 35 32 32 11 21 11 8 19	35 36 1 36 11 21 11 8 19	2 6 36 3 12 21 11 8 19	5 9 2 7 13 20 11 8 19	8 15 8 11 15 20 12 8 19	11 18 13 14 16 20 12 8 19	14 23 14 18 18 21 13 9 19	17 27 16 21 20 21 13 9 19	20 30 21 24 22 22 13 9 19	23 35 25 25 24 22 13 9 19	26 2 24 23 27 23 13 9 20
5	29 32 27 28 12 21 12 8 19	32 1 32 32 11 21 11 8 19	35 2 1 36 11 21 11 8 19	2 7 36 4 12 21 11 8 19	5 11 3 7 13 20 11 8 19	8 16 9 11 14 20 12 8 19	11 19 13 15 16 20 12 8 19	14 24 14 18 18 21 13 9 19	17 28 16 21 20 21 13 9 19	20 31 21 24 22 22 13 9 19	23 36 25 25 24 22 13 9 19	26 4 24 23 27 23 13 9 20
6	29 33 27 28 12 21 12 8 19	32 2 32 32 11 21 11 8 19	35 3 1 36 11 21 11 8 19	2 8 36 4 12 21 11 8 19	5 12 3 7 13 20 11 8 19	8 17 9 11 14 20 12 8 19	11 21 13 15 16 20 12 8 19	14 25 14 18 18 21 13 9 19	17 29 16 21 20 21 13 9 19	20 33 21 24 22 22 13 9 19	23 1 25 25 24 22 13 9 19	26 5 24 23 27 23 13 9 20
7	29 34 27 29 12 21 12 8 19	32 4 32 32 11 21 11 8 19	35 5 1 36 11 21 11 8 19	2 10 36 4 12 21 11 8 19	5 14 3 7 13 20 11 8 19	8 18 9 11 14 20 12 8 19	11 22 14 15 16 20 12 8 19	14 26 14 18 18 21 13 9 19	17 31 16 22 20 21 13 9 19	20 34 21 24 22 22 13 9 19	23 3 25 25 25 22 13 9 19	26 7 24 23 27 23 13 8 20
8	29 36 27 29 12 21 12 8 19	32 5 32 33 11 21 11 8 19	35 6 1 36 11 21 11 8 19	2 11 36 4 12 21 11 8 19	5 15 3 8 13 20 12 8 19	8 20 9 11 14 20 12 8 19	11 23 14 15 17 20 12 8 19	14 27 14 18 18 21 13 9 19	17 32 16 22 20 21 13 9 19	20 35 22 24 22 22 13 9 19	23 4 25 25 25 22 13 9 19	26 8 24 23 27 23 13 8 20
9	29 1 27 29 12 21 12 8 19	33 6 32 33 11 21 11 8 19	35 7 1 36 11 21 11 8 19	2 13 36 4 12 21 11 8 19	5 16 3 8 13 20 12 8 19	8 21 9 11 14 20 12 8 19	11 24 14 15 17 20 12 8 19	14 28 14 19 18 21 13 9 19	17 33 17 22 20 21 13 9 19	20 1 22 24 23 22 13 9 19	23 6 25 24 25 22 13 9 19	26 10 24 23 27 23 13 8 20
10	29 2 28 29 12 21 12 8 19	33 8 33 33 11 21 11 8 19	35 9 1 36 11 21 11 8 19	3 14 36 4 12 21 11 8 19	5 17 3 8 13 20 12 8 19	8 22 10 12 15 20 12 8 19	11 25 14 15 17 20 12 8 19	14 30 14 19 19 21 13 9 19	17 34 17 22 21 21 13 9 19	20 2 22 24 23 22 13 9 19	23 7 25 24 25 22 13 9 19	26 11 24 23 27 23 13 8 20
11	30 4 28 29 12 21 12 8 19	33 9 33 33 11 21 11 8 19	36 10 1 1 11 21 11 8 19	3 15 36 4 12 21 11 8 19	6 1[illegible] 4 8 13 20 12 8 19	8 23 10 12 15 20 12 8 19	11 26 14 15 17 20 12 8 19	14 31 14 19 19 21 13 9 19	17 36 17 22 21 21 13 9 19	20 4 22 24 23 22 13 9 19	23 9 25 24 25 23 13 9 19	26 13 24 23 27 23 13 8 20
12	30 5 28 29 12 21 12 8 19	33 11 33 33 11 21 11 8 19	36 12 1 1 11 21 11 8 19	3 17 36 4 12 21 11 8 19	6 20 4 8 13 20 12 8 19	9 24 10 12 15 20 12 8 19	11 28 14 15 17 20 12 8 19	14 32 14 19 19 21 13 9 19	17 1 17 22 21 21 13 9 19	20 5 22 24 23 22 13 9 19	23 10 25 24 25 23 13 9 19	26 14 24 23 27 23 13 8 20
13	30 7 28 29 12 21 12 8 19	33 12 33 33 11 21 11 8 19	36 13 1 1 11 21 11 8 19	3 18 36 5 12 21 11 8 19	6 21 4 8 13 20 12 8 19	9 26 10 12 15 20 12 8 19	12 29 14 15 17 20 12 8 19	15 34 14 19 19 21 13 9 19	18 3 17 22 21 21 13 9 19	20 6 22 24 23 22 13 9 19	24 12 25 24 25 23 13 9 19	27 16 25 23 27 23 13 8 20
14	30 8 28 29 12 21 12 8 19	33 13 33 33 11 21 11 8 19	36 14 1 1 11 21 11 8 19	3 19 36 5 12 21 11 8 19	6 22 4 8 14 20 12 8 19	9 27 10 12 15 20 12 8 19	12 30 14 16 17 20 12 8 19	15 35 14 19 19 21 13 9 19	18 4 18 22 21 21 13 9 19	21 8 22 24 23 22 13 9 19	24 13 25 24 25 23 13 9 19	27 17 25 23 27 23 13 8 20
15	30 10 28 30 12 21 12 8 19	33 15 33 33 11 21 11 8 19	36 16 2 1 11 21 11 8 19	3 20 36 5 12 21 11 8 19	6 24 4 8 14 20 12 8 19	9 28 11 12 15 20 12 8 19	12 31 14 16 17 20 12 8 19	15 36 14 19 19 21 13 9 19	18 5 18 22 21 21 13 9 19	21 9 23 24 23 22 13 9 19	24 15 25 24 25 23 13 9 19	27 18 25 23 27 23 13 8 20
16	30 11 29 30 12 21 12 8 19	33 16 34 34 11 21 11 8 19	36 17 2 1 11 21 11 8 19	3 21 36 5 12 21 11 8 19	6 25 4 9 14 20 12 8 19	9 29 11 12 15 20 12 8 19	12 33 14 16 17 20 12 8 19	15 2 14 19 19 21 13 9 19	18 7 18 22 21 21 13 9 19	21 11 23 25 23 22 13 9 19	24 16 25 24 25 23 13 9 19	27 19 25 23 27 23 13 8 20
17	30 12 29 30 12 21 12 8 19	33 17 34 34 11 21 11 8 19	36 18 2 1 11 21 11 8 19	3 23 1 5 12 21 11 8 19	6 26 5 9 14 20 12 8 19	9 30 11 12 15 20 12 8 19	12 34 14 16 17 20 12 8 19	15 3 14 19 19 21 13 9 19	18 8 18 22 21 21 13 9 19	21 12 23 25 23 22 13 9 19	24 17 25 24 25 23 13 9 19	27 21 25 23 28 23 13 8 20
18	30 14 29 30 12 21 12 8 19	33 19 34 34 11 21 11 8 19	36 19 2 1 11 21 11 8 19	3 24 1 5 12 21 11 8 19	6 27 5 9 14 20 12 8 19	9 32 11 13 15 20 12 8 19	12 35 14 16 17 20 12 8 19	15 4 14 19 19 21 13 9 19	18 10 18 23 21 21 13 9 19	21 14 23 25 23 22 13 9 19	24 19 25 24 25 23 13 9 19	27 22 25 23 28 23 13 8 20
19	30 15 29 30 12 21 12 8 19	34 20 34 34 11 21 11 8 19	36 21 1 2 11 21 11 8 19	3 25 1 5 12 21 11 8 19	6 28 5 9 14 20 12 8 19	9 33 11 13 15 20 12 8 19	12 1 14 16 17 20 12 8 19	15 6 14 20 19 21 13 9 19	18 11 18 23 21 21 13 9 19	21 15 23 25 23 22 13 9 19	24 20 25 24 25 23 13 9 19	27 23 25 23 28 23 13 8 20
20	30 16 29 30 12 21 12 8 19	34 21 34 34 11 21 11 8 19	36 22 1 2 11 21 11 8 19	3 26 1 5 12 21 11 8 19	6 29 5 9 14 20 12 8 19	9 34 11 13 16 20 12 8 19	12 2 14 16 17 20 12 8 19	15 7 14 20 19 21 13 9 19	18 12 19 23 21 21 13 9 19	21 16 23 25 23 22 13 9 19	24 21 25 24 25 23 13 9 20	27 24 25 23 28 23 13 8 20
21	31 18 29 30 12 21 12 8 19	34 22 35 34 11 21 11 8 19	1 23 1 2 11 21 11 8 19	4 27 1 6 12 21 11 8 19	6 31 5 9 14 20 12 8 19	9 36 12 13 16 20 12 8 19	12 3 14 16 17 20 12 8 19	15 9 14 20 19 21 13 9 19	18 14 19 23 21 21 13 9 19	21 18 23 25 23 22 13 9 19	24 22 24 24 26 23 13 9 20	27 25 26 24 28 23 13 8 20
22	31 19 29 30 11 21 12 8 19	34 23 35 34 11 21 11 8 19	1 24 1 2 11 21 11 8 19	4 28 1 6 12 21 11 8 19	7 32 6 9 14 20 12 8 19	10 1 12 13 16 20 12 8 19	12 5 14 17 17 20 12 8 19	15 10 14 20 19 21 13 9 19	18 15 19 23 21 21 13 9 19	21 19 24 25 23 22 13 9 19	24 23 24 24 26 23 13 9 20	28 27 26 24 28 23 13 8 20
23	31 20 30 31 11 21 12 8 19	34 25 35 34 11 21 11 8 19	1 25 1 2 11 21 11 8 19	4 30 1 6 13 21 11 8 19	7 33 6 9 14 20 12 8 19	10 2 12 13 16 20 12 8 19	12 6 14 17 17 20 12 9 19	15 11 14 20 19 21 13 9 19	18 17 19 23 21 21 13 9 19	21 20 24 25 23 22 13 9 19	25 25 24 24 26 23 13 9 20	28 28 26 24 28 23 13 8 20
24	31 21 30 31 11 21 12 8 19	34 26 35 35 11 21 11 8 19	1 27 1 2 11 21 11 8 19	4 31 1 6 13 21 11 8 19	7 35 6 10 14 20 12 8 19	10 4 12 13 16 20 12 8 19	13 8 14 17 18 20 12 9 19	16 13 14 20 19 21 13 9 19	19 18 19 23 21 21 13 9 19	22 21 24 25 24 22 13 9 19	25 26 24 24 26 23 13 9 20	28 29 26 24 28 23 13 8 20
25	31 23 30 31 11 21 12 8 19	34 27 35 35 11 21 11 8 19	1 28 1 2 11 21 11 8 19	4 32 1 6 13 21 11 8 19	7 36 6 10 14 20 12 8 19	10 5 12 13 16 20 12 8 19	13 9 14 17 18 20 12 9 19	16 14 14 20 20 21 13 9 19	19 19 20 23 22 22 13 9 19	22 23 24 25 24 22 13 9 19	25 27 24 24 26 23 13 9 20	28 30 26 24 28 23 13 8 20
26	31 24 30 31 11 21 12 8 19	34 28 36 35 11 21 11 8 19	1 29 1 2 11 21 11 8 19	4 34 1 6 13 21 11 8 19	7 1 6 10 14 20 12 8 19	10 7 12 13 16 20 12 8 19	13 11 14 17 18 20 12 9 19	16 16 14 20 20 21 13 9 19	19 21 20 23 22 22 13 9 19	22 24 24 25 24 22 13 9 19	25 28 24 23 26 23 13 9 20	28 21 26 24 28 23 13 8 20
27	21 25 30 31 11 21 12 8 19	34 29 36 35 11 21 11 8 19	1 30 1 2 11 21 11 8 19	4 35 1 6 13 21 11 8 19	7 3 7 10 14 20 12 8 19	10 8 12 14 16 20 12 8 19	13 12 14 17 18 21 12 9 19	16 17 14 20 20 21 13 9 19	19 22 20 23 22 22 13 9 19	22 25 24 25 24 22 13 9 19	25 29 24 23 26 23 13 9 20	28 33 27 24 28 23 13 8 20
28	31 26 30 31 11 21 12 8 19	34 31 36 35 11 21 11 8 19	1 31 1 3 12 21 11 8 19	4 36 2 6 13 21 11 8 19	7 4 7 10 14 20 12 8 19	10 10 13 14 16 20 12 8 19	13 13 14 17 18 21 12 9 19	16 18 14 21 20 21 13 9 19	19 23 20 23 22 22 13 9 19	22 26 24 25 24 22 13 9 19	25 31 24 23 26 23 13 9 20	28 34 27 24 28 23 13 8 20
29	31 27 31 31 11 21 12 8 19	1946	1 33 1 3 12 21 11 8 19	4 2 2 7 13 21 11 8 19	7 6 7 10 14 20 12 8 19	10 11 13 14 16 20 12 8 19	13 15 14 17 18 21 12 9 19	15 20 15 21 20 21 13 9 19	19 24 20 23 22 22 13 9 19	22 27 24 25 24 22 13 9 19	25 32 24 23 26 23 13 9 20	28 35 27 24 28 23 13 8 20
30	32 29 31 31 11 21 12 8 19		1 34 1 3 12 21 11 8 19	4 3 2 7 13 21 11 8 19	7 7 7 10 14 20 12 8 19	10 13 13 14 16 20 12 8 19	13 16 14 17 18 21 12 9 19	16 21 15 21 20 21 13 9 19	19 25 20 24 22 22 13 9 19	22 28 25 25 24 22 13 9 19	25 33 24 23 26 23 13 9 20	28 36 27 24 28 24 13 8 20
31	32 30 31 32 11 21 11 8 19		2 36 1 3 12 21 11 8 19		7 9 7 10 14 20 12 8 19		13 18 14 18 18 21 12 9 19	16 22 15 21 20 21 13 9 19		22 30 25 25 24 22 13 9 19		28 2 27 24 29 24 13 8 20

	JAN	FEB	MAR	APR	MAY	JUNE	JULY	AUG	SEPT	OCT	NOV	DEC
1	29 3 27 24 29 24 13 8 20	32 8 32 27 31 24 13 8 20	35 9 36 30 33 24 13 8 20	2 15 35 34 36 24 13 8 19	5 18 3 1 2 24 13 8 19	8 23 9 5 4 24 13 9 19	10 27 12 9 7 23 13 9 19	13 31 11 12 9 23 14 9 19	16 36 17 16 11 24 14 9 19	19 3 22 20 13 24 14 9 20	22 8 23 24 14 25 15 9 20	25 12 24 28 15 25 15 9 20
2	29 5 27 24 29 24 13 8 20	32 10 33 27 31 24 13 8 20	35 11 36 30 33 24 13 8 20	2 16 35 34 36 24 13 8 19	5 20 3 1 2 24 13 8 19	8 24 10 5 4 24 13 9 19	10 28 12 9 7 23 13 9 19	13 32 11 13 9 23 14 9 19	16 1 17 16 11 24 14 9 19	19 4 22 20 13 24 14 9 20	22 10 23 24 14 25 15 9 20	25 14 24 28 16 25 15 9 20
3	29 6 28 24 29 24 13 8 20	32 11 33 27 31 24 13 8 20	35 12 36 30 33 24 13 8 20	2 17 35 34 36 24 13 8 19	5 21 3 2 2 24 13 8 19	8 26 10 5 4 24 13 9 19	11 29 12 9 7 23 13 9 19	14 33 12 13 9 23 14 9 19	17 2 17 17 11 24 14 9 19	19 6 22 20 13 24 14 9 20	23 11 23 24 14 25 15 9 20	26 15 24 28 16 25 15 9 20
4	29 7 28 24 29 24 13 8 20	32 13 33 27 31 24 13 8 20	35 14 36 30 34 24 13 8 20	2 19 35 34 36 24 13 8 19	5 22 4 2 2 24 13 8 19	8 27 10 5 5 24 13 9 19	11 30 12 9 7 23 13 9 19	14 35 12 13 9 23 14 9 19	17 3 17 17 11 24 14 9 19	20 7 22 20 13 24 14 9 20	23 12 23 24 14 25 15 9 20	26 16 24 28 16 25 15 9 20
5	29 9 28 25 29 24 13 8 20	32 14 33 27 31 24 13 8 20	35 15 35 31 34 24 13 8 20	2 20 35 34 36 24 13 8 19	5 24 4 2 2 24 13 8 19	8 28 10 5 5 24 13 9 19	11 31 12 9 7 23 13 9 19	14 36 12 13 9 23 14 9 19	17 5 17 17 11 24 14 9 19	20 9 22 21 13 24 14 9 20	23 14 23 24 14 25 15 9 20	26 18 24 28 16 25 15 9 20
6	29 11 28 25 29 24 13 8 20	32 16 33 28 31 24 13 8 20	35 17 35 31 34 24 13 8 20	2 21 35 34 36 24 13 8 19	5 25 4 2 2 24 13 8 19	8 29 10 6 5 23 13 9 19	11 32 12 9 7 23 13 9 19	14 1 12 13 9 23 14 9 19	17 6 18 17 11 24 14 9 19	20 10 22 21 13 24 14 9 20	23 15 23 24 14 25 15 9 20	26 19 24 28 16 25 15 9 20
7	29 12 28 25 29 24 13 8 20	32 17 33 28 32 24 13 8 20	35 18 35 31 34 24 13 8 20	2 23 35 34 36 24 13 8 19	5 26 4 2 2 24 13 8 19	8 30 10 6 5 23 13 9 19	11 34 12 9 7 23 13 9 19	14 2 12 13 9 23 14 9 19	17 7 18 17 11 24 14 9 19	20 11 22 21 13 24 14 9 20	23 17 23 25 14 25 15 9 20	26 20 25 28 15 25 15 9 20
8	29 14 28 25 29 24 13 8 20	32 19 34 28 32 24 13 8 20	35 19 35 31 34 24 13 8 20	2 24 36 35 36 24 13 8 19	5 27 4 2 3 24 13 8 19	8 32 10 6 5 23 13 9 19	11 35 12 10 7 23 13 9 19	14 4 12 13 9 23 14 9 19	17 9 18 17 11 24 14 9 19	20 13 22 21 13 24 14 9 20	23 18 22 25 15 25 15 9 20	26 22 25 28 15 25 15 9 20
9	29 15 29 25 29 24 13 8 20	32 20 34 28 32 24 13 8 20	35 21 35 31 34 24 13 8 20	2 25 36 35 36 24 13 8 19	5 28 5 2 3 24 13 8 19	8 33 11 6 5 23 13 9 19	11 36 12 10 7 23 13 9 19	14 5 12 13 9 23 14 9 19	17 10 18 17 11 24 14 9 19	20 14 22 21 13 24 14 9 20	23 19 22 25 15 25 15 9 20	26 23 25 29 16 26 15 9 20
10	29 16 29 25 29 24 13 8 20	33 21 34 28 32 24 13 8 20	35 22 35 31 34 24 13 8 19	2 26 36 35 36 24 13 8 19	5 30 5 2 3 24 13 9 19	8 34 11 6 5 23 13 9 19	11 1 12 10 7 23 13 9 19	14 6 12 14 9 23 14 9 19	17 12 18 17 11 24 14 9 19	20 16 23 21 13 24 15 9 20	23 21 22 25 15 25 15 9 20	26 24 25 29 16 26 15 9 20
11	30 18 29 25 29 24 13 8 20	33 22 34 28 32 24 13 8 20	36 23 35 31 34 24 13 8 19	3 28 36 35 36 24 13 8 19	5 31 5 2 3 24 13 9 19	8 35 11 6 5 23 13 9 19	11 3 12 10 7 23 13 9 19	14 8 13 14 9 23 14 9 19	17 13 18 18 11 24 14 9 19	20 17 23 21 13 24 15 9 20	23 22 22 25 15 25 15 9 20	26 26 25 29 16 26 15 9 20
12	30 19 29 25 29 24 13 8 20	33 24 34 28 32 24 13 8 20	36 24 35 31 34 24 13 8 19	3 29 36 35 1 24 13 8 19	6 32 5 3 3 24 13 9 19	9 1 11 6 5 23 13 9 19	11 4 12 10 7 23 13 9 19	14 9 13 14 9 23 14 9 19	17 15 19 18 11 24 14 9 19	20 18 23 21 13 24 15 9 20	23 23 22 25 15 25 15 9 20	26 27 25 29 16 26 15 9 20
13	30 20 29 25 30 24 13 8 20	33 25 34 28 32 24 13 8 20	36 26 35 31 34 24 13 8 19	3 30 36 35 1 24 13 8 19	6 33 5 3 3 24 13 9 19	9 2 11 6 5 23 13 9 19	12 5 12 10 7 23 13 9 19	14 11 13 14 9 23 14 9 19	17 16 19 18 11 24 14 9 19	20 20 23 21 13 24 15 9 20	24 25 22 25 15 25 15 9 20	27 28 25 29 16 26 15 9 20
14	30 22 29 25 30 24 13 8 20	33 26 35 28 32 24 13 8 20	36 27 35 32 34 24 13 8 19	3 31 36 35 1 24 13 8 19	6 34 6 3 3 24 13 9 19	9 3 11 7 5 23 13 9 19	12 7 12 10 7 23 13 9 19	15 12 13 14 10 23 14 9 19	18 18 19 18 12 24 14 9 19	21 21 23 22 13 24 15 9 20	24 26 22 25 15 25 15 9 20	27 29 26 29 16 26 15 9 20
15	30 23 29 25 30 24 13 8 20	33 27 35 29 32 24 13 8 20	36 28 35 32 34 24 13 8 19	3 32 36 35 1 24 13 8 19	6 36 6 3 3 24 13 9 19	9 5 11 7 5 23 13 9 19	12 8 12 10 8 23 13 9 19	15 14 13 14 10 23 14 9 19	18 19 19 18 12 24 14 9 19	21 23 23 22 13 24 15 9 20	24 27 22 26 15 25 15 9 20	27 30 26 29 16 26 15 9 20
16	30 24 30 25 30 24 13 8 20	33 28 35 29 32 24 13 8 20	36 29 35 32 34 24 13 8 19	3 34 1 35 1 24 13 8 19	6 1 6 3 3 24 13 9 19	9 6 11 7 5 23 13 9 19	12 10 12 10 8 23 13 9 19	15 15 14 14 10 23 14 9 19	18 20 19 18 12 24 14 9 19	21 24 23 22 13 24 15 9 20	24 28 22 26 15 25 15 9 20	27 32 26 29 16 26 15 9 20
17	30 25 30 26 30 24 13 8 20	33 30 35 29 32 24 13 8 20	36 30 35 32 34 24 13 8 19	3 35 1 36 1 24 13 8 19	6 2 6 3 3 24 13 9 19	9 8 12 7 6 23 13 9 19	12 11 11 11 8 23 13 9 19	15 17 14 14 10 23 14 9 19	18 22 19 18 12 24 14 9 19	21 25 23 22 13 24 15 9 20	24 30 22 26 15 25 15 9 20	27 33 26 30 16 26 15 9 20
18	30 26 30 26 30 24 13 8 20	33 31 35 29 32 24 13 8 20	36 32 34 32 35 24 13 8 19	3 36 1 36 1 24 13 8 19	6 4 7 3 3 24 13 9 19	9 9 12 7 6 23 13 9 19	12 13 11 11 8 23 14 9 19	15 18 14 15 10 23 14 9 19	18 23 20 18 12 24 14 9 19	21 26 23 22 13 24 15 9 20	24 31 22 26 15 25 15 9 20	27 34 26 30 16 26 15 9 20
19	30 28 30 26 30 24 13 8 20	34 32 35 29 32 24 13 8 20	36 33 34 32 35 24 13 8 19	3 2 1 36 1 24 13 8 19	6 5 7 3 3 24 13 9 19	9 11 12 7 6 23 13 9 19	12 14 11 11 8 23 14 9 19	15 20 14 15 10 23 14 9 19	18 24 20 19 12 24 14 9 19	21 28 23 22 14 24 15 9 20	24 32 22 26 15 25 15 9 20	27 35 26 30 16 26 15 9 20
20	30 29 30 26 30 24 13 8 20	34 33 36 29 33 24 13 8 20	36 34 34 32 35 24 13 8 19	3 3 1 36 1 24 13 8 19	6 7 7 4 3 24 13 9 19	9 12 12 7 6 23 13 9 19	12 16 11 11 8 23 14 9 19	15 21 14 15 10 23 14 9 19	18 26 20 19 12 24 14 9 20	21 29 23 22 14 24 15 9 20	24 33 22 26 15 25 15 9 20	27 36 27 30 16 26 15 9 20
21	31 30 30 26 30 24 13 8 20	34 35 36 29 33 24 13 8 20	1 35 34 32 35 24 13 8 19	4 4 1 36 1 24 13 8 19	6 8 7 4 4 24 13 9 19	9 14 12 7 6 23 13 9 19	12 17 11 11 8 23 14 9 19	15 22 15 15 10 23 14 9 19	18 27 20 19 12 24 14 9 20	21 30 24 22 14 24 15 9 20	24 34 22 26 15 25 15 9 20	27 2 27 30 16 26 15 9 20
22	31 31 31 26 30 24 13 8 20	34 36 36 29 33 24 13 8 20	1 1 34 33 35 24 13 8 19	4 6 1 36 1 24 13 8 19	7 10 7 4 4 24 13 9 19	10 15 12 8 6 23 13 9 19	12 19 11 11 8 23 14 9 19	15 24 15 15 10 23 14 9 19	18 28 20 19 12 24 14 9 20	21 31 24 23 14 24 15 9 20	25 36 22 26 15 25 15 9 20	27 3 27 30 16 26 15 9 20
23	31 32 31 26 30 24 13 8 20	34 1 36 29 33 24 13 8 20	1 2 34 33 35 24 13 8 19	4 7 2 36 1 24 13 8 19	7 11 8 4 4 24 13 9 19	10 16 12 8 6 23 13 9 19	12 20 11 11 8 23 14 9 19	15 25 15 15 10 23 14 9 19	18 29 20 19 12 24 14 9 20	21 32 24 23 14 24 15 9 20	25 1 23 27 15 25 15 9 20	28 4 27 30 16 26 15 9 20
24	31 34 31 26 30 24 13 8 20	34 2 36 30 33 24 13 8 20	1 3 34 33 35 24 13 8 19	4 9 2 36 1 24 13 8 19	7 13 8 4 4 24 13 9 19	10 18 12 8 6 23 13 9 19	13 21 11 11 8 23 14 9 19	16 26 15 15 10 23 14 9 19	19 30 21 19 12 24 14 9 20	22 34 24 23 14 25 15 9 20	25 2 23 27 15 25 15 9 20	28 6 27 30 16 26 15 9 20
25	31 35 31 26 30 24 13 8 20	34 4 36 30 33 24 13 8 20	1 5 34 33 35 24 13 8 19	4 10 2 1 2 24 13 8 19	7 14 8 4 4 24 13 9 19	10 19 12 8 6 23 13 9 19	13 23 11 12 8 23 14 9 19	16 27 15 15 10 24 14 9 19	19 32 21 19 12 24 14 9 20	22 35 24 23 14 25 15 9 20	25 3 23 27 15 25 15 9 20	28 7 27 31 16 26 15 9 20
26	31 36 31 26 31 24 13 8 20	34 5 36 30 33 24 13 8 20	1 6 35 33 35 24 13 8 19	4 12 2 1 2 24 13 8 19	7 15 8 4 4 24 13 9 19	10 20 12 8 6 23 13 9 19	13 24 11 12 8 23 14 9 19	16 28 16 16 10 24 14 9 19	19 33 21 19 12 24 14 9 20	22 36 24 23 14 25 15 9 20	25 5 23 27 15 25 15 9 20	28 8 27 31 16 26 15 9 20
27	31 1 31 26 31 24 13 8 20	34 7 36 30 33 24 13 8 20	1 8 35 33 35 24 13 8 19	4 13 2 1 2 24 13 8 19	7 17 8 4 4 24 13 9 19	10 22 12 8 6 23 13 9 19	13 25 11 12 8 23 14 9 19	16 29 16 16 10 24 14 9 19	19 34 21 20 12 24 14 9 20	22 1 24 23 14 25 15 9 20	25 6 23 27 15 25 15 9 20	28 10 28 31 16 26 15 9 20
28	31 3 32 27 31 24 13 8 20	34 8 36 30 33 24 13 8 20	1 9 35 33 35 24 13 8 19	4 14 2 1 2 24 13 8 19	7 18 9 5 4 24 13 9 19	10 23 12 8 6 23 13 9 19	13 26 11 12 8 23 14 9 19	16 31 16 16 10 24 14 9 19	19 35 21 20 12 24 14 9 20	22 3 24 23 14 25 15 9 20	25 8 23 27 15 25 15 9 20	28 11 28 31 16 26 15 9 20
29	31 4 32 27 31 24 13 8 20		1 10 35 33 35 24 13 8 19	4 16 3 1 2 24 13 8 19	7 19 9 5 4 24 13 9 19	10 24 12 8 6 23 13 9 19	13 27 11 12 8 23 14 9 19	16 32 16 16 11 24 14 9 19	19 36 21 20 12 24 14 9 20	22 4 24 23 14 25 15 9 20	25 9 23 27 15 25 15 9 20	25 13 28 31 16 26 15 9 20
30	31 6 32 27 31 24 13 8 20	**1947**	1 12 35 33 36 24 13 8 19	4 17 3 1 2 24 13 8 19	7 21 9 5 4 24 13 9 19	10 25 12 9 6 23 13 9 19	13 29 11 12 9 23 14 9 19	16 33 16 16 11 24 14 9 19	19 2 21 20 12 24 14 9 20	22 5 23 24 14 25 15 9 20	25 11 23 27 15 25 15 9 20	28 14 28 31 16 26 15 9 20
31	32 7 32 27 31 24 13 8 20		1 13 35 34 36 24 13 8 19		7 22 9 5 4 24 13 9 19		13 20 11 12 9 23 14 9 19	16 34 16 16 11 24 14 9 19		22 7 23 24 14 25 15 9 20		28 16 28 31 16 26 15 9 20

	JAN	FEB	MAR	APR	MAY	JUNE	JULY	AUG	SEPT	OCT	NOV	DEC
1	28 17 28 31 16 26 15 9 20	32 22 33 35 16 27 14 9 20	35 25 33 3 15 27 14 9 20	2 29 35 6 14 27 14 9 20	5 32 5 9 15 27 14 9 20	8 1 10 11 16 27 14 9 20	10 4 9 9 18 27 15 9 20	13 9 12 9 19 27 15 9 20	16 14 18 12 21 26 15 10 20	19 18 22 15 23 27 16 10 20	22 23 21 19 26 27 16 10 20	25 27 25 22 28 28 16 9 20
2	29 19 29 32 16 26 15 9 20	32 24 34 35 16 27 14 9 20	35 26 33 3 15 27 14 9 20	2 30 35 6 14 27 14 9 20	5 33 5 9 15 27 14 9 20	8 2 10 11 16 27 14 9 20	11 5 9 9 18 27 15 9 20	14 10 13 9 19 26 15 9 20	16 16 18 12 21 26 15 10 20	19 19 22 15 23 27 16 10 20	22 25 21 19 26 27 16 10 20	26 28 25 22 28 28 16 9 20
3	29 20 29 32 16 26 15 9 20	32 25 34 36 16 27 14 9 20	35 27 33 3 15 27 14 9 20	2 31 36 6 14 27 14 9 20	5 35 5 9 15 27 14 9 20	8 3 10 11 16 27 14 9 20	11 7 9 9 18 27 15 9 20	14 12 13 10 20 26 15 9 20	16 17 18 12 21 26 15 10 20	20 21 22 15 24 27 16 10 20	23 26 21 19 26 27 16 10 20	26 29 25 22 28 28 16 9 20
4	29 21 29 32 16 26 15 9 20	32 26 34 36 16 27 14 9 20	35 28 33 3 15 27 14 9 20	2 33 36 6 14 27 14 9 20	5 36 6 9 15 27 14 9 20	8 4 10 11 16 27 14 9 20	11 8 9 9 18 27 15 9 20	14 13 13 10 20 26 15 9 20	17 19 19 12 22 26 15 10 20	20 22 22 15 24 27 16 10 20	23 27 21 19 26 27 16 10 20	26 31 25 23 28 28 16 9 20
5	29 23 29 32 16 26 15 9 20	32 27 34 36 16 27 14 9 20	35 29 33 3 15 27 14 9 20	2 34 36 6 14 27 14 9 20	5 1 6 9 15 27 14 9 20	8 6 10 11 16 27 14 9 20	11 9 9 9 18 27 15 9 20	14 15 13 10 20 26 15 9 20	17 20 19 12 22 26 15 10 20	20 24 22 16 24 27 16 10 20	23 29 21 19 26 27 16 10 20	26 32 25 23 28 28 16 9 20
6	29 24 29 32 16 26 15 9 20	32 29 34 36 16 27 14 9 20	35 31 33 3 15 27 14 9 20	2 35 36 7 14 27 14 9 20	5 2 6 9 15 27 14 9 20	8 7 10 11 16 27 14 9 20	11 11 9 9 18 27 15 9 20	14 16 13 10 20 26 15 9 20	17 22 19 12 22 26 15 10 20	20 25 22 16 24 27 16 10 20	23 30 21 19 26 27 16 10 20	26 33 26 23 28 28 16 9 20
7	29 25 29 32 16 26 15 9 20	32 30 34 36 16 27 14 9 20	35 32 33 3 15 27 14 9 20	2 36 36 7 14 27 14 9 20	5 4 6 10 15 27 14 9 20	8 9 10 11 16 27 14 9 20	11 12 9 9 18 27 15 9 20	14 18 15 10 20 26 15 9 20	17 23 19 12 22 26 15 10 20	20 26 22 16 24 27 16 10 20	23 31 21 19 26 27 16 10 20	26 34 26 23 28 28 16 9 20
8	29 26 30 32 16 26 15 9 20	32 31 34 36 16 27 14 9 20	35 33 33 4 15 27 14 9 20	2 1 36 7 14 27 14 9 20	5 5 6 10 15 27 14 9 20	8 10 10 11 16 27 14 9 20	11 14 9 9 18 27 15 9 20	14 19 14 10 20 26 15 9 20	17 24 19 12 22 26 15 10 20	20 28 22 16 24 27 16 10 20	23 32 21 19 26 27 16 10 20	26 35 26 23 28 28 16 9 20
9	29 28 30 32 16 26 15 9 20	32 32 34 36 16 27 14 9 20	35 34 33 4 15 27 14 9 20	2 3 1 7 14 27 14 9 20	5 6 7 10 15 27 14 9 20	8 11 10 11 16 27 14 9 20	11 15 9 9 18 27 15 9 20	14 21 14 10 20 26 15 9 20	17 26 19 13 22 26 15 10 20	20 29 22 16 24 27 16 10 20	23 33 21 19 26 27 16 10 20	26 1 26 23 28 28 16 9 20
10	29 29 30 33 16 26 15 9 20	33 33 34 36 15 27 14 9 20	35 35 33 4 15 27 14 9 20	3 4 1 7 14 27 14 9 20	5 8 7 10 15 27 14 9 20	8 13 10 11 17 27 14 9 20	11 17 9 9 18 27 15 9 20	14 22 14 10 20 26 15 9 20	17 27 20 13 22 27 15 10 20	20 30 22 16 24 27 16 10 20	23 35 22 20 26 27 16 10 20	26 2 26 23 29 28 16 9 20
11	30 30 30 33 16 26 15 9 20	33 34 34 36 16 27 14 9 20	36 1 33 4 15 27 14 9 20	3 5 1 7 14 27 14 9 20	6 9 7 10 15 27 14 9 20	9 14 10 10 17 27 14 9 20	11 18 9 9 18 27 15 9 20	14 23 14 10 20 26 15 9 20	17 28 20 13 22 27 15 10 20	20 31 22 16 24 27 16 10 20	23 36 22 20 26 27 16 10 20	26 3 26 23 29 28 16 9 20
12	30 31 30 33 16 26 15 9 20	33 36 34 1 15 27 14 9 20	36 2 33 4 14 27 14 9 20	3 7 1 7 14 27 14 9 20	6 10 7 10 15 27 14 9 20	9 16 10 10 17 27 14 9 20	11 20 10 9 18 27 15 9 20	14 25 15 10 20 26 15 9 20	17 29 20 13 22 27 15 10 20	20 33 22 16 24 27 16 10 20	24 1 22 20 26 27 16 9 20	27 4 27 24 29 28 16 9 20
13	30 32 30 33 16 26 15 9 20	33 1 34 1 15 27 14 9 20	36 3 33 4 14 27 14 9 20	3 8 1 7 14 27 14 9 20	6 12 7 10 15 27 14 9 20	9 17 10 10 17 27 14 9 20	12 21 10 9 18 27 15 9 20	15 26 15 10 20 26 15 9 20	18 31 20 13 22 27 15 10 20	20 34 22 16 24 27 16 10 20	24 2 22 20 26 27 16 9 20	27 5 27 24 29 28 16 9 20
14	30 34 31 33 16 26 15 9 20	33 2 34 1 15 27 14 9 20	36 4 33 4 14 27 14 9 20	3 9 1 8 14 27 14 9 20	6 13 8 10 15 27 14 9 20	9 19 10 10 17 27 14 9 20	12 22 10 9 18 27 15 9 20	15 27 15 10 20 26 15 9 20	18 32 20 13 22 27 15 10 20	21 35 22 16 24 27 16 10 20	24 3 22 20 27 27 16 9 20	27 7 27 24 29 28 16 9 20
15	30 35 31 33 16 26 15 9 20	33 3 34 1 15 27 14 9 20	36 6 33 4 14 27 14 9 20	3 11 2 8 14 27 14 9 20	6 15 8 10 15 27 14 9 20	9 20 10 10 17 27 14 9 20	12 24 10 9 18 27 15 9 20	15 28 15 10 20 26 15 9 20	18 33 20 13 22 27 15 10 20	21 36 22 17 24 27 16 10 20	24 5 22 20 27 28 16 10 20	27 8 27 24 29 28 16 9 20
16	30 36 31 33 16 26 15 9 20	33 5 34 1 15 27 14 9 20	36 7 33 4 14 27 14 9 20	3 12 2 8 14 27 14 9 20	6 16 8 10 15 27 14 9 20	9 21 10 10 17 27 14 9 20	12 25 10 9 18 27 15 9 20	15 30 15 10 20 26 15 9 20	18 34 20 13 22 27 15 10 20	21 1 22 17 24 27 16 10 20	24 6 22 20 27 28 16 10 20	27 9 27 24 29 28 16 9 20
17	30 1 31 33 16 26 15 9 20	33 6 34 1 15 27 14 9 20	36 8 33 5 14 27 14 9 20	3 14 2 8 15 27 14 9 20	6 17 8 10 15 27 14 9 20	9 23 10 10 17 27 14 9 20	12 26 10 9 19 27 15 9 20	15 31 16 10 20 26 15 9 20	18 35 20 13 22 27 15 10 20	21 3 22 17 25 27 16 10 20	24 7 23 20 27 28 16 10 20	27 11 27 24 29 28 16 9 20
18	30 2 31 34 16 26 15 9 20	33 7 34 1 15 27 14 9 20	36 10 34 5 14 27 14 9 20	3 15 2 8 15 27 14 9 20	6 19 8 10 15 27 14 9 20	9 24 10 10 17 27 14 9 20	12 27 10 9 19 27 15 9 20	15 32 16 11 20 26 15 9 20	18 36 21 14 22 27 15 10 20	21 4 21 17 25 27 16 10 20	24 9 23 21 27 28 16 10 20	27 12 27 24 29 28 16 9 20
19	30 4 31 34 16 26 15 9 20	33 9 34 1 15 27 14 9 20	36 11 34 5 14 27 14 9 20	3 16 2 8 15 27 14 9 20	6 20 8 10 16 27 14 9 20	9 25 10 10 17 27 14 9 20	12 29 10 9 19 27 15 9 20	15 33 16 11 21 26 15 9 20	18 2 21 14 23 27 16 10 20	21 5 21 17 25 27 16 10 20	24 10 23 21 27 28 16 10 20	27 14 28 24 29 28 16 9 20
20	31 5 32 34 16 26 15 9 20	34 10 33 2 15 27 14 9 20	36 13 34 5 14 27 14 9 20	4 18 3 8 15 27 14 9 20	6 22 9 10 16 27 14 9 20	9 27 10 10 17 27 14 9 20	12 30 10 9 19 27 15 9 20	15 34 16 11 21 26 15 9 20	18 3 21 14 23 27 16 10 20	21 6 21 17 25 27 16 10 20	24 11 23 21 27 28 16 10 20	27 15 28 25 29 28 16 9 20
21	31 6 32 34 16 26 15 9 20	34 12 33 2 15 27 14 9 20	1 14 34 5 14 27 14 9 20	4 19 3 8 15 27 14 9 20	7 23 9 10 16 27 14 9 20	9 28 10 10 17 27 14 9 20	12 31 10 9 19 27 15 9 20	15 36 16 11 21 26 15 9 20	18 4 21 14 23 27 16 10 20	21 8 21 17 25 27 16 10 20	24 13 23 21 27 28 16 10 20	27 17 28 25 29 28 16 9 20
22	31 8 32 34 16 26 15 9 20	34 13 33 2 15 27 14 9 20	1 15 34 5 14 27 14 9 20	4 21 3 8 15 27 14 9 20	7 24 9 10 16 27 14 9 20	10 29 10 10 17 27 14 9 20	12 32 11 9 19 27 15 9 20	15 1 16 11 21 26 15 9 20	18 5 21 14 23 27 16 10 20	21 9 21 17 25 27 16 10 20	25 14 23 21 27 28 16 10 20	28 18 28 25 29 28 16 9 20
23	31 9 32 34 16 26 15 9 20	34 15 33 2 15 27 14 9 20	1 17 34 5 14 27 14 9 20	4 22 3 8 15 27 14 9 20	7 26 9 10 16 27 14 9 20	10 30 10 10 17 27 14 9 20	13 33 11 9 19 26 15 9 20	16 2 17 11 21 26 15 9 20	19 7 21 14 23 27 16 10 20	21 10 21 17 25 27 16 10 20	25 16 24 21 27 28 16 10 20	28 19 28 25 30 28 16 9 20
24	21 11 32 34 16 26 15 9 20	34 16 33 2 15 27 14 9 20	1 18 34 5 14 27 14 9 20	4 24 3 8 15 27 14 9 20	7 27 9 10 16 27 14 9 20	10 31 10 10 17 27 14 9 20	13 35 11 9 19 26 15 9 20	16 3 17 11 21 26 15 9 20	19 8 21 14 23 27 16 10 20	22 12 21 18 25 27 16 10 20	25 17 24 21 27 28 16 10 20	28 21 28 25 30 28 16 9 20
25	31 12 32 34 16 27 15 9 20	34 18 33 2 15 27 14 9 20	1 20 34 5 14 27 14 9 20	4 25 4 9 15 27 14 9 20	7 28 9 10 16 27 14 9 20	10 33 10 10 17 27 14 9 20	13 36 11 9 19 26 15 9 20	16 4 17 11 21 26 15 9 20	19 9 21 14 23 27 16 10 20	22 13 21 18 25 27 16 10 20	25 18 24 21 27 28 16 10 20	28 22 29 25 30 28 16 9 20
26	31 14 33 35 16 27 15 9 20	34 19 33 2 15 27 14 9 20	1 21 34 6 14 27 14 9 20	4 26 4 9 15 27 14 9 20	7 29 9 11 16 27 14 9 20	10 34 10 10 17 27 14 9 20	13 1 11 9 19 26 15 9 20	16 6 17 11 21 26 15 9 20	19 11 21 14 23 27 16 10 20	22 14 21 18 25 27 16 10 20	25 20 24 22 27 28 16 10 20	28 24 29 25 30 28 16 9 20
27	31 15 33 35 16 27 15 9 20	34 21 33 2 15 27 14 9 20	1 23 35 6 14 27 14 9 20	4 27 4 9 15 27 14 9 20	7 31 9 11 16 27 14 9 20	10 35 10 10 17 27 14 9 20	13 2 11 9 19 26 15 9 20	16 7 17 11 21 26 15 9 20	19 12 22 15 22 27 16 10 20	22 16 21 18 25 27 16 10 20	25 21 24 22 28 28 16 10 20	28 25 29 25 30 28 16 9 20
28	31 17 33 35 16 27 15 9 20	34 22 33 3 15 27 14 9 20	1 24 35 6 14 27 14 9 20	4 29 4 9 15 27 14 9 20	7 32 10 11 16 27 14 9 20	10 36 10 10 17 27 14 9 20	13 3 12 9 19 26 15 9 20	16 8 17 11 21 26 15 9 20	19 13 22 15 22 27 16 10 20	22 17 20 18 25 27 16 10 20	25 23 24 22 28 28 16 10 20	28 26 29 26 30 28 16 9 20
29	31 18 33 35 16 27 15 9 20	34 24 33 3 15 27 14 9 20	1 25 35 6 14 27 14 9 20	4 30 4 9 15 27 14 9 20	7 33 10 11 16 27 14 9 20	10 2 9 9 18 27 15 9 20	13 5 12 9 19 26 15 9 20	16 10 18 12 21 26 15 9 20	19 15 22 15 22 27 16 10 20	22 19 20 18 25 27 16 10 20	25 24 24 22 28 28 16 10 20	28 28 29 26 30 28 16 9 20
30	31 20 33 35 16 27 15 9 20	**1948**	1 27 35 6 14 27 14 9 20	5 31 5 9 15 27 14 9 20	7 34 10 11 16 27 14 9 20	10 3 9 9 18 27 15 9 20	13 6 12 9 19 26 15 9 20	16 11 18 12 21 26 15 9 20	19 16 22 15 22 27 16 10 20	22 20 20 18 25 27 16 10 20	25 25 25 22 28 28 16 10 20	28 29 29 26 30 29 16 9 20
31	32 21 33 35 16 27 14 9 20		2 28 35 6 14 27 14 9 20		7 35 10 11 16 27 14 9 20		13 7 12 9 19 26 15 9 20	16 13 18 12 21 26 15 10 20		22 21 20 19 26 27 16 10 20		28 30 29 26 30 29 16 9 20

	JAN	FEB	MAR	APR	MAY	JUNE	JULY	AUG	SEPT	OCT	NOV	DEC
1	29 31 30 26 30 29 16 9 20	32 36 32 30 33 29 16 9 20	35 1 32 33 35 30 16 9 20	2 5 36 1 1 30 16 9 20	5 9 6 5 4 31 15 9 20	8 13 8 9 6 31 16 9 20	10 17 8 12 8 30 16 10 20	13 23 14 16 10 30 16 10 20	16 28 19 20 12 30 16 10 20	19 31 20 23 14 30 17 10 20	22 36 21 27 16 30 17 10 20	25 3 26 30 17 31 17 10 20
2	29 33 30 26 30 29 16 9 20	32 1 32 30 33 29 16 9 20	35 2 32 34 35 30 16 9 20	2 6 1 1 1 30 16 9 20	5 10 7 5 4 31 15 9 20	8 15 8 9 6 31 16 9 20	11 19 8 13 8 30 16 10 20	13 24 14 16 10 30 16 10 20	16 29 19 20 12 30 16 10 20	19 33 20 24 14 30 17 10 20	22 1 21 27 16 30 17 10 20	25 4 26 30 17 31 17 10 20
3	29 34 30 26 30 29 16 9 20	32 2 32 30 33 29 16 9 20	35 3 32 34 35 30 16 9 20	2 8 1 2 1 30 15 9 20	5 11 7 5 4 31 15 9 30	8 16 8 9 6 31 16 9 20	11 20 9 13 8 30 16 10 20	13 25 14 16 10 30 16 10 20	17 30 19 20 12 30 16 10 20	20 34 20 24 14 30 17 10 20	23 2 21 27 16 30 17 10 20	26 6 26 30 17 31 17 10 20
4	29 35 30 26 30 29 16 9 20	32 3 32 30 33 29 16 9 20	35 4 32 34 35 30 16 9 20	2 9 1 2 2 30 15 9 20	5 12 7 5 4 31 15 9 20	8 18 8 9 6 31 16 9 20	11 22 9 13 8 30 16 10 20	14 27 15 17 10 30 16 10 20	17 32 19 20 12 30 16 10 20	20 35 19 24 14 30 17 10 20	23 3 22 27 16 30 17 10 20	26 7 26 30 18 31 17 10 20
5	29 36 30 27 31 29 16 9 20	32 5 32 30 33 29 16 9 20	35 5 32 34 35 30 16 9 20	2 10 1 2 2 30 15 9 20	5 14 7 5 4 31 15 9 20	8 19 8 9 6 31 16 9 20	11 23 9 13 8 30 16 10 20	14 28 15 17 10 30 16 10 20	17 33 19 20 12 30 16 10 20	20 36 19 24 14 30 17 10 20	23 5 22 27 16 30 17 10 20	26 8 27 30 18 31 17 10 20
6	29 1 31 27 31 29 16 9 20	32 6 31 31 33 29 16 9 20	35 7 32 34 35 30 16 9 20	2 11 1 2 2 30 15 9 20	5 15 7 6 4 31 15 9 20	8 21 8 9 6 31 16 9 20	11 24 9 13 8 30 16 10 20	14 29 15 17 10 30 16 10 20	17 34 20 21 12 30 17 10 20	20 1 19 24 14 30 17 10 20	23 6 22 28 16 30 17 10 20	26 9 27 31 18 31 17 10 20
7	29 2 31 27 31 29 16 9 20	32 7 31 31 33 29 16 9 20	35 8 33 34 35 30 16 9 20	2 13 2 2 2 30 15 9 20	5 17 7 6 4 31 15 9 20	8 22 8 10 6 31 16 9 20	11 26 9 13 8 30 16 10 20	14 31 15 17 10 30 16 10 20	17 35 20 21 13 30 17 10 20	20 3 19 24 14 30 17 10 20	23 7 22 28 16 30 17 10 20	26 11 27 31 18 31 17 10 20
8	29 4 31 27 31 29 16 9 20	32 8 31 31 33 29 16 9 20	35 9 33 34 35 30 16 9 20	2 14 2 2 2 30 15 9 20	5 18 7 6 4 31 15 9 20	8 23 8 10 6 31 16 9 20	11 27 9 13 8 30 16 10 20	14 32 15 17 10 30 16 10 20	17 1 20 21 13 30 17 10 20	20 4 19 24 14 30 17 10 20	23 8 22 28 16 30 17 10 20	26 12 27 31 18 31 17 10 20
9	29 5 31 27 31 29 16 9 20	33 10 31 31 33 29 16 9 20	35 11 33 34 36 30 16 9 20	2 16 2 2 2 30 15 9 20	5 20 7 6 4 31 15 9 20	8 25 8 10 6 31 16 9 20	11 29 9 13 9 30 16 10 20	14 33 16 17 11 30 16 10 20	17 2 20 21 13 30 17 10 20	20 5 19 24 14 30 17 10 20	23 10 22 28 16 30 17 10 20	26 13 27 31 18 31 17 10 20
10	29 6 31 27 31 29 16 9 20	33 11 31 31 33 29 16 9 20	35 12 33 35 36 30 16 9 20	3 17 2 2 2 30 15 9 20	5 21 8 6 4 31 15 9 20	8 26 7 10 7 31 16 10 20	11 30 10 14 9 30 16 10 20	14 34 16 17 11 30 16 10 20	17 3 20 21 13 30 17 10 20	20 6 19 25 15 30 17 10 20	23 11 23 28 16 30 17 10 20	26 14 27 31 18 31 17 10 20
11	30 8 31 27 31 29 16 9 20	33 13 31 31 33 29 16 9 20	36 13 33 35 36 30 16 9 20	3 19 2 2 2 30 15 9 20	6 23 8 6 4 31 15 9 20	9 28 7 10 7 31 16 10 20	11 31 10 14 9 30 16 10 20	14 36 16 17 11 30 16 10 20	17 4 20 21 13 30 17 10 20	20 7 19 25 15 30 17 10 20	23 12 23 28 16 30 17 10 20	26 16 28 31 18 31 17 10 20
12	30 9 31 27 31 29 16 9 20	33 14 31 31 34 29 16 9 20	36 15 33 35 36 30 16 9 20	3 20 3 3 2 30 15 9 20	6 24 8 6 4 31 15 9 20	9 29 7 10 7 31 16 10 20	11 32 10 14 9 30 16 10 20	14 1 16 18 11 30 16 10 20	17 5 20 21 13 30 17 10 20	20 9 19 25 15 30 17 10 20	23 13 23 28 16 30 17 10 20	27 17 28 31 18 31 17 10 20
13	30 10 32 28 31 29 16 9 20	33 16 31 31 34 30 16 9 20	36 16 33 35 36 30 16 9 20	3 22 3 3 2 31 15 9 20	6 25 8 6 4 31 15 9 20	9 30 7 10 7 31 16 10 20	12 34 10 14 9 30 16 10 20	15 2 16 18 11 30 16 10 20	18 6 20 21 13 30 17 10 20	20 10 19 25 15 30 17 10 20	24 15 23 28 16 30 17 10 20	27 19 28 31 18 31 17 10 20
14	30 12 32 28 31 29 16 9 20	33 17 31 32 34 30 16 9 20	36 18 34 35 36 30 16 9 20	3 23 3 3 2 31 15 9 20	6 27 8 7 5 31 15 9 20	9 32 7 10 7 31 16 10 20	12 35 10 14 9 30 16 10 20	15 3 16 18 11 30 16 10 20	18 8 20 21 13 30 17 10 20	21 11 19 25 15 30 17 10 20	24 16 23 28 17 30 17 10 20	27 20 28 31 18 31 17 10 20
15	30 13 32 28 31 29 16 9 20	33 19 31 32 34 30 16 9 20	36 19 34 35 36 30 16 9 20	3 25 3 3 2 31 15 9 20	6 28 8 7 5 31 15 9 20	9 33 7 10 7 31 16 10 20	12 36 11 14 9 30 16 10 20	15 4 17 18 11 30 16 10 20	18 9 20 22 13 30 17 10 20	21 12 19 25 15 30 17 10 20	24 18 23 28 17 30 17 10 20	27 21 28 31 18 31 17 10 20
16	30 15 32 28 31 29 16 9 20	33 20 31 32 34 30 16 9 20	36 21 34 35 36 30 16 9 20	3 26 4 3 2 31 15 9 20	6 30 8 7 5 31 15 9 20	9 34 7 11 7 31 16 10 20	12 1 11 14 9 30 16 10 20	15 6 17 18 11 30 16 10 20	18 10 20 22 13 30 17 10 20	21 14 19 25 15 30 17 10 20	24 19 24 29 17 30 17 10 20	27 23 28 31 18 31 17 10 20
17	30 16 32 28 32 29 16 9 20	33 22 31 32 34 30 16 9 20	36 22 34 35 36 30 16 9 20	3 27 4 3 3 31 15 9 20	6 31 8 7 5 31 15 9 20	9 35 7 11 7 31 16 10 20	12 2 11 14 9 30 16 10 20	15 7 17 18 11 30 16 10 20	18 12 20 22 13 30 17 10 20	21 15 19 25 15 30 17 10 20	24 20 24 29 17 30 17 10 20	27 24 28 31 18 31 17 10 20
18	30 18 32 28 32 29 16 9 20	33 23 31 32 34 30 16 9 20	36 24 34 36 36 30 16 9 20	3 29 4 3 3 31 15 9 20	6 32 8 7 5 31 15 9 20	9 36 7 11 7 31 16 10 20	12 4 11 15 9 30 16 10 20	15 8 17 18 11 30 16 10 20	18 13 20 22 13 30 17 10 20	21 17 19 25 15 30 17 10 20	24 22 24 29 17 30 17 10 20	27 26 29 31 18 31 17 10 20
19	30 19 32 28 32 29 16 9 20	34 24 31 32 34 30 16 9 20	36 25 34 36 36 30 16 9 20	3 30 4 3 3 31 15 9 20	6 33 8 7 5 31 15 9 20	9 2 7 11 7 31 16 10 20	12 5 11 15 9 30 16 10 20	15 9 17 18 11 30 16 10 20	18 14 20 22 13 30 17 10 20	21 18 19 26 15 30 17 10 20	24 23 24 29 17 30 17 10 20	27 27 29 32 18 31 17 10 20
20	31 21 32 28 32 29 16 9 20	34 26 31 32 34 30 16 9 20	36 27 34 36 36 30 16 9 20	4 31 4 4 3 31 15 9 20	6 34 8 7 5 31 15 9 20	9 3 7 11 7 31 16 10 20	12 6 12 15 9 30 16 10 20	15 11 17 18 11 30 16 10 20	18 16 20 22 13 30 17 10 20	21 20 20 26 15 30 17 10 20	24 25 24 29 17 30 17 10 20	27 29 29 32 18 31 17 10 20
21	31 22 32 29 32 29 16 9 20	34 27 31 32 34 30 16 9 20	1 28 35 36 36 30 16 9 20	4 32 5 4 3 31 15 9 20	7 36 8 7 5 31 15 9 20	9 4 7 11 7 31 16 10 20	12 7 12 15 9 30 16 10 20	15 12 18 19 11 30 16 10 20	18 17 20 22 13 30 17 10 20	21 21 20 26 15 30 17 10 20	24 26 24 29 17 30 17 10 20	27 30 29 32 18 31 17 10 20
22	31 23 32 29 32 29 16 9 20	34 28 31 33 34 30 16 9 20	1 29 35 36 1 30 16 9 20	4 34 5 4 3 31 15 9 20	7 1 8 8 5 31 15 9 20	10 5 8 11 7 31 16 10 20	12 9 12 15 9 30 16 10 20	15 14 18 19 11 30 16 10 20	18 19 20 22 13 30 17 10 20	21 23 20 26 15 30 17 10 20	24 28 25 29 17 30 17 10 20	28 31 29 32 18 31 17 10 20
23	31 25 33 29 32 29 16 9 20	34 29 31 33 34 30 16 9 20	1 30 35 36 1 30 16 9 20	4 35 5 4 3 31 15 9 20	7 2 8 8 5 31 15 9 20	10 6 8 11 7 31 16 10 20	13 10 12 15 10 30 16 10 20	15 15 18 19 12 30 16 10 20	19 20 20 23 14 30 17 10 20	21 24 20 26 15 30 17 10 20	25 30 25 29 17 30 17 10 20	28 33 29 32 18 31 17 10 20
24	31 26 33 29 32 29 16 9 20	34 31 31 33 34 30 16 9 20	1 32 35 36 1 30 16 9 20	4 36 5 4 3 31 15 9 20	7 3 8 8 5 31 15 9 20	10 8 8 12 8 31 16 10 20	13 11 12 15 10 30 16 10 20	16 17 18 19 12 30 16 10 20	19 22 20 23 14 30 17 10 20	22 26 20 26 15 30 17 10 20	25 31 25 29 17 30 17 10 20	28 34 29 32 18 31 17 10 20
25	31 27 33 29 32 29 16 9 20	34 32 31 33 35 30 16 9 20	1 33 35 36 1 30 16 9 20	4 1 5 4 3 31 15 9 20	7 4 8 8 5 31 15 9 20	10 9 8 12 8 31 16 10 20	13 13 13 15 10 30 16 10 20	16 18 18 19 12 30 16 10 20	19 23 20 23 14 30 17 10 20	22 27 20 26 15 30 17 10 20	25 32 25 29 17 30 17 10 20	28 35 30 32 18 31 17 10 20
26	31 28 32 29 32 29 16 9 20	34 33 32 33 35 30 16 9 20	1 34 35 1 1 30 16 9 20	4 2 6 4 3 31 15 9 20	7 6 8 8 5 31 15 9 20	10 10 8 12 8 31 16 10 20	13 14 13 15 10 30 16 10 20	16 19 18 19 12 30 16 10 20	19 25 20 23 14 30 17 10 20	22 28 20 26 15 30 17 10 20	25 33 25 30 17 30 17 10 20	25 36 30 32 19 31 17 10 20
27	31 30 32 29 32 29 16 9 20	34 34 32 33 35 30 16 9 20	1 35 36 1 1 30 16 9 20	4 4 6 4 3 31 15 9 20	7 7 8 8 6 31 15 9 20	10 12 8 12 8 31 16 10 20	13 16 13 16 10 30 16 10 20	16 21 18 19 12 30 16 10 20	19 26 20 23 14 30 17 10 20	22 30 20 26 16 30 17 10 20	25 34 25 30 17 30 17 10 20	28 1 30 32 19 31 17 10 20
28	31 31 32 29 32 29 16 9 20	34 35 32 33 35 30 16 9 20	1 36 36 1 1 30 16 9 20	4 5 6 5 3 31 15 9 20	7 8 8 8 6 31 15 9 20	10 13 8 12 8 30 16 10 20	13 17 13 16 10 30 16 10 20	15 22 19 19 12 30 16 10 20	19 28 20 23 14 30 17 10 20	22 31 20 27 16 30 17 10 20	25 36 25 30 17 30 17 10 20	28 3 30 32 19 31 17 10 20
29	31 32 32 30 32 29 16 9 20	1949	1 1 36 1 1 30 16 9 20	4 6 6 5 3 31 15 9 20	7 9 8 8 6 31 15 9 20	10 15 8 12 8 30 16 10 20	13 18 13 16 10 30 16 10 20	16 24 19 20 12 30 16 10 20	19 29 20 23 14 30 17 10 20	22 32 21 27 16 30 17 10 20	25 1 26 30 17 30 17 10 20	28 4 30 32 19 31 17 10 20
30	32 33 32 30 33 29 16 9 20		1 3 36 1 1 30 16 9 20	4 7 6 5 4 31 15 9 20	7 11 8 9 6 31 15 9 20	10 16 8 12 8 30 16 10 20	13 20 14 16 10 30 16 10 20	16 25 19 20 12 30 16 10 20	19 30 20 23 14 30 17 10 20	22 34 21 27 16 30 17 10 20	25 2 26 30 17 30 17 10 20	28 5 30 32 19 31 17 10 20
31	32 35 32 30 33 29 16 9 20		2 4 36 1 1 30 16 9 20		7 12 8 9 6 31 16 9 20		13 21 14 16 10 30 16 10 20	16 27 19 20 12 30 16 10 20		22 35 21 27 16 30 17 10 20		28 6 30 32 19 31 17 10 20

	JAN	FEB	MAR	APR	MAY	JUNE	JULY	AUG	SEPT	OCT	NOV	DEC
1	29 8 31 32 19 31 17 10 20	32 12 29 31 20 32 17 10 20	35 13 33 31 19 33 17 10 20	2 18 2 33 18 33 17 10 20	5 22 6 36 18 34 17 10 20	8 27 5 3 18 34 17 10 20	10 31 9 7 19 34 17 10 20	13 36 15 11 21 34 18 10 20	16 4 19 14 23 34 18 10 20	19 8 18 18 25 33 18 10 20	22 12 22 22 27 33 18 10 20	25 15 27 26 29 33 19 10 20
2	29 9 21 32 19 31 17 10 20	32 14 29 31 20 32 17 10 20	35 14 33 31 19 33 17 10 20	2 20 2 33 18 33 17 10 20	5 24 6 36 18 34 17 10 20	8 29 5 4 18 34 17 10 20	11 32 10 7 19 34 17 10 20	13 1 16 11 21 34 18 10 20	16 5 19 15 23 34 18 10 20	19 9 18 18 25 33 18 10 20	22 13 23 22 27 33 18 10 20	25 17 27 26 30 34 19 10 20
3	29 10 31 32 19 31 17 10 20	32 15 29 31 20 32 17 10 20	35 16 33 31 19 33 17 10 20	2 21 2 33 18 33 17 10 20	5 25 6 36 18 34 17 10 20	8 30 6 4 18 34 17 10 20	11 34 10 7 19 34 17 10 20	14 2 16 11 21 34 18 10 20	17 7 19 15 23 34 18 10 20	19 10 18 18 25 33 18 10 20	23 14 23 22 27 33 18 10 20	26 18 27 26 30 34 19 10 20
4	29 11 31 32 19 31 17 10 20	32 16 30 31 20 32 17 10 20	35 17 33 31 19 33 17 10 20	2 23 3 33 18 33 17 10 20	5 27 6 36 18 34 17 10 20	8 32 6 4 18 34 17 10 20	11 35 10 7 19 34 17 10 20	14 3 16 11 21 34 18 10 20	17 8 19 15 23 34 18 10 20	20 11 18 19 25 33 18 10 20	23 16 23 22 27 33 18 10 20	26 19 27 26 30 34 19 10 20
5	29 13 31 32 19 31 17 10 20	32 18 30 31 20 32 17 10 20	35 19 33 31 19 33 17 10 20	2 24 3 33 18 33 17 10 20	5 28 6 36 18 34 17 10 20	8 33 6 4 18 34 17 10 20	11 36 10 7 20 34 17 10 20	14 5 16 11 21 34 18 10 20	17 9 19 15 23 34 18 10 20	20 12 18 19 25 33 18 10 20	23 17 23 23 27 33 18 10 20	26 21 28 26 30 34 19 10 20
6	29 14 31 32 19 31 17 10 20	32 19 30 31 20 32 17 10 20	35 20 33 31 19 33 17 10 20	2 26 3 33 18 33 17 10 20	5 29 6 1 18 34 17 10 20	8 34 6 4 18 34 17 10 20	11 1 10 8 20 34 17 10 20	14 6 16 11 21 34 18 10 20	17 10 19 15 23 34 18 10 20	20 14 18 19 25 33 18 10 20	23 18 23 23 28 33 18 10 20	26 22 28 26 30 34 19 10 20
7	29 15 31 32 19 31 17 10 20	32 21 30 31 20 32 17 10 20	35 22 33 31 19 33 17 10 20	2 27 3 34 18 33 17 10 20	5 31 6 1 18 34 17 10 20	8 35 6 4 18 34 17 10 20	11 3 11 8 20 34 17 10 20	14 7 16 11 21 34 18 10 20	17 12 19 15 23 34 18 10 20	20 15 18 19 25 33 18 10 20	23 20 23 23 28 33 18 10 20	26 24 28 27 29 34 19 10 20
8	29 17 31 32 19 31 17 10 20	32 22 30 31 20 32 17 10 20	35 23 34 31 19 33 17 10 20	2 28 4 34 18 33 17 10 20	5 32 6 1 18 34 17 10 20	8 1 6 4 18 34 17 10 20	11 4 11 8 20 34 17 10 20	14 8 16 12 21 34 18 10 20	17 13 19 15 23 34 18 10 20	20 16 18 19 25 33 18 10 20	23 21 23 23 28 33 18 10 20	26 25 28 27 29 34 19 10 20
9	29 18 31 32 19 31 17 10 20	33 24 30 31 20 32 17 10 20	35 25 34 31 19 33 17 10 20	2 30 4 34 18 33 17 10 20	5 33 6 1 18 34 17 10 20	8 2 6 4 18 34 17 10 20	11 5 11 8 20 34 17 10 20	14 9 17 12 21 34 18 10 20	17 14 19 15 23 34 18 10 20	20 18 18 19 25 33 18 10 20	23 23 24 23 28 33 18 10 20	26 27 28 27 29 34 19 10 20
10	29 20 31 32 19 31 17 10 20	33 25 30 31 20 32 17 10 20	35 26 34 31 19 33 17 10 20	3 31 4 34 18 33 17 10 20	5 35 6 1 18 34 17 10 20	8 3 6 5 18 34 17 10 20	11 6 11 8 20 34 17 10 20	14 11 17 12 21 34 18 10 20	17 15 19 16 23 34 18 10 20	20 19 19 19 26 33 18 10 20	23 24 24 23 28 33 18 10 20	26 28 28 27 29 34 19 10 20
11	30 21 31 32 19 31 17 10 20	33 26 30 31 20 32 17 10 20	36 27 34 31 19 33 17 10 20	3 32 4 34 18 33 17 10 20	6 36 6 1 18 34 17 10 20	8 4 6 5 18 34 17 10 20	11 7 11 8 20 34 17 10 20	14 12 17 12 22 34 18 10 20	17 17 18 16 24 34 18 10 20	20 21 19 19 26 33 18 10 20	23 26 24 23 28 33 18 10 20	26 30 28 27 29 34 19 10 20
12	30 22 31 32 19 31 17 10 20	33 28 30 31 20 32 17 10 20	36 29 34 31 19 33 17 10 20	3 34 4 34 18 33 17 10 20	6 1 6 1 18 34 17 10 20	9 5 6 5 19 34 17 10 20	11 9 12 8 20 34 17 10 20	14 13 17 12 22 34 18 10 20	17 18 18 16 24 34 18 10 20	20 22 19 20 26 33 18 10 20	23 27 24 23 28 33 18 10 20	26 31 29 27 29 34 19 10 20
13	30 24 31 32 19 31 17 10 20	33 29 30 31 20 32 17 10 20	36 30 34 32 19 33 17 10 20	3 35 4 34 18 33 17 10 20	6 2 6 1 18 34 17 10 20	9 7 6 5 19 34 17 10 20	12 10 12 8 20 34 17 10 20	15 15 17 12 22 34 18 10 20	18 21 18 16 24 34 18 10 20	20 24 19 20 26 33 18 10 20	24 29 24 24 28 33 18 10 20	27 33 29 27 29 34 19 10 20
14	30 25 31 32 19 31 17 10 20	33 30 30 31 20 32 17 10 20	36 31 35 32 19 33 17 10 20	3 36 5 34 18 33 17 10 20	6 3 6 1 18 34 17 10 20	9 8 6 5 19 34 17 10 20	12 11 12 9 20 34 17 10 20	15 16 17 12 22 34 18 10 20	18 22 18 16 24 34 18 10 20	21 25 19 20 26 33 18 10 20	24 30 24 24 28 33 18 10 20	27 34 29 27 29 34 19 10 20
15	30 27 30 32 19 31 17 10 20	33 32 31 31 20 32 17 10 20	36 33 35 32 19 33 17 10 20	3 1 5 34 18 34 17 10 20	6 5 6 2 18 34 17 10 20	9 9 7 5 19 34 17 10 20	12 12 12 9 20 34 17 10 20	15 17 17 12 22 34 18 10 20	18 23 18 16 24 33 17 10 20	21 27 19 20 26 33 18 10 20	24 32 25 24 28 33 18 10 20	27 35 29 28 31 34 19 10 20
16	30 28 30 32 19 32 17 10 20	33 33 31 31 20 32 17 10 20	36 34 35 32 19 33 17 10 20	3 2 5 35 18 34 17 10 20	6 6 6 2 18 34 17 10 20	9 10 7 5 19 34 17 10 20	12 14 13 9 20 34 17 10 20	15 19 17 12 22 34 18 10 20	18 24 18 16 24 33 17 10 20	21 28 20 20 26 33 18 10 20	24 33 25 24 28 33 18 10 20	27 1 29 28 31 34 19 10 20
17	30 29 30 32 19 32 17 10 20	33 34 31 31 20 32 17 10 20	36 35 35 32 19 33 17 10 20	3 4 5 35 18 34 17 10 20	6 7 6 2 18 34 17 10 20	9 11 7 5 19 34 17 10 20	12 15 13 9 20 34 17 10 20	15 20 18 13 22 34 18 10 20	18 26 18 16 24 33 17 10 20	21 29 20 20 26 33 18 10 20	24 34 25 24 28 33 18 10 20	27 2 29 28 31 34 19 10 20
18	30 31 30 32 19 32 17 10 20	33 36 31 31 20 32 17 10 20	36 36 35 32 19 33 17 10 20	3 5 5 35 18 34 17 10 20	6 8 6 2 18 34 17 10 20	9 13 7 5 19 34 17 10 20	12 16 13 9 20 34 17 10 20	15 22 18 13 22 34 18 10 20	18 27 18 17 24 33 17 10 20	21 31 20 20 26 33 18 10 20	24 36 25 24 28 33 18 10 20	27 3 29 28 31 34 19 10 20
19	30 32 30 32 19 32 17 10 20	34 1 31 31 20 32 17 10 20	36 2 36 32 19 33 17 10 20	3 6 5 35 18 34 17 10 20	6 9 6 2 18 34 17 10 20	9 14 7 6 19 34 17 10 20	12 18 13 9 20 34 17 10 20	15 23 18 13 22 34 18 10 20	18 28 18 17 24 33 17 10 20	21 32 20 20 26 33 18 10 20	24 1 25 24 28 33 18 10 20	27 4 29 28 31 34 19 10 20
20	30 33 30 32 19 32 17 10 20	34 2 31 31 20 32 17 10 20	36 3 36 32 19 33 17 10 20	3 7 5 35 18 34 17 10 20	6 11 6 2 18 34 17 10 20	9 15 7 6 19 34 17 10 20	12 19 13 9 20 34 17 10 20	15 24 18 13 22 34 18 10 20	18 30 18 17 24 33 17 10 20	21 33 20 21 26 33 18 10 20	24 2 25 24 29 33 18 10 20	27 5 29 28 31 34 19 10 20
21	31 35 30 32 19 32 17 10 20	34 3 31 31 20 32 17 10 20	1 4 36 32 19 33 17 10 20	4 8 6 35 18 34 17 10 20	6 12 5 2 18 34 17 10 20	9 17 8 6 19 34 17 10 20	12 20 13 9 20 34 17 10 20	15 26 18 13 22 34 18 10 20	18 31 17 17 24 33 17 10 20	21 35 21 21 26 33 18 10 20	24 3 25 25 29 33 19 10 20	27 7 29 28 31 34 19 10 20
22	31 36 30 32 19 32 17 10 20	34 4 32 31 20 32 17 10 20	1 5 36 32 19 33 17 10 20	4 10 6 35 18 34 17 10 20	7 13 5 2 18 34 17 10 20	10 18 8 6 19 34 17 10 20	12 22 14 9 20 34 17 10 20	15 27 18 13 22 34 18 10 20	18 32 17 17 24 33 17 10 20	21 36 21 21 26 33 18 10 20	24 4 26 25 29 33 19 10 20	28 8 29 28 31 34 19 10 20
23	31 1 29 32 19 32 17 10 20	34 6 32 31 20 32 17 10 20	1 6 36 32 19 33 17 10 20	4 11 6 35 18 34 17 10 20	7 14 5 2 18 34 17 10 20	10 19 8 6 19 34 17 10 20	13 23 14 10 20 34 17 10 20	15 29 18 13 22 34 18 10 20	18 34 17 17 24 33 17 10 20	21 1 21 21 26 33 18 10 20	25 6 26 25 29 33 19 10 20	28 9 29 29 31 34 19 10 20
24	31 2 29 32 19 32 17 10 20	34 7 32 31 20 32 17 10 20	1 8 1 32 19 33 17 10 20	4 12 6 35 18 34 17 10 20	7 16 5 3 18 34 17 10 20	10 21 8 6 19 34 17 10 20	13 25 14 10 21 34 17 10 20	16 30 18 13 22 34 18 10 20	19 35 17 17 24 33 17 10 20	22 2 21 21 27 33 18 10 20	25 7 26 25 29 33 19 10 20	28 10 29 29 31 34 19 10 20
25	31 4 29 32 19 32 17 10 20	34 8 32 31 19 32 17 10 20	1 9 1 32 19 33 17 10 20	4 13 6 35 18 34 17 10 20	7 17 5 3 18 34 17 10 20	10 22 8 6 19 34 17 10 20	13 26 14 10 21 34 18 10 20	16 31 18 14 22 34 18 10 20	19 36 17 17 24 33 17 10 20	22 4 21 21 27 33 18 10 20	25 8 26 25 29 33 19 10 20	28 11 29 29 31 34 19 10 20
26	31 5 29 32 19 32 17 10 20	34 9 32 31 19 32 17 10 20	1 10 1 33 19 33 17 10 20	4 15 6 36 18 34 17 10 20	7 18 5 3 18 34 17 10 20	10 24 8 6 19 34 17 10 20	13 28 14 10 21 34 18 10 20	16 33 18 14 22 34 18 10 20	19 1 17 18 25 33 17 10 20	22 5 21 21 27 33 18 10 20	25 9 26 25 29 33 19 10 20	28 13 29 29 31 34 19 10 20
27	31 6 29 32 19 32 17 10 20	34 10 32 31 19 33 17 10 20	1 11 1 33 19 33 17 10 20	4 16 6 36 18 34 17 10 20	7 20 5 3 18 34 17 10 20	10 25 9 7 19 34 17 10 20	13 29 15 10 21 34 18 10 20	16 34 18 14 23 34 18 10 20	19 3 17 18 25 33 17 10 20	22 6 22 21 27 33 18 10 20	25 10 26 25 29 33 19 10 20	28 14 29 29 31 34 19 10 20
28	31 7 29 32 19 32 17 10 20	34 12 32 31 19 33 17 10 20	1 13 1 33 18 33 17 10 20	4 18 6 36 18 34 17 10 20	7 21 5 3 18 34 17 10 20	10 27 9 7 19 34 17 10 20	13 30 15 10 21 34 18 10 20	16 35 19 14 23 34 18 10 20	19 4 17 18 25 33 17 10 20	22 7 22 22 27 33 18 10 20	25 12 27 25 29 33 19 10 20	28 15 29 29 32 34 19 10 20
29	31 8 29 32 19 32 17 10 20		1 14 2 33 18 33 17 10 20	4 19 6 36 18 34 17 10 20	7 23 5 3 18 34 17 10 20	10 28 9 7 19 34 17 10 20	13 32 15 10 21 34 18 10 20	15 1 19 14 23 34 18 10 20	19 5 17 18 25 33 17 10 20	22 8 22 22 27 33 18 10 20	25 13 27 26 29 33 19 10 20	28 16 29 29 32 34 19 10 20
30	32 10 29 32 20 32 17 10 20	**1950**	1 15 2 33 18 33 17 10 20	4 20 6 36 18 34 17 10 20	7 24 5 3 18 34 17 10 20	10 30 9 7 19 34 17 10 20	13 33 15 10 21 34 18 10 20	16 2 19 14 23 34 18 10 20	19 6 17 18 25 33 17 10 20	22 9 22 22 27 33 18 10 20	25 14 27 26 29 33 19 10 20	28 15 29 29 32 34 19 10 20
31	32 11 29 32 20 32 17 10 20		2 17 2 33 18 33 17 10 20		7 26 5 3 18 34 17 10 20		13 35 15 11 21 34 18 10 20	16 3 19 14 23 34 18 10 20		22 11 22 22 27 33 18 10 20		28 19 29 30 32 34 19 10 20

	JAN	FEB	MAR	APR	MAY	JUNE	JULY	AUG	SEPT	OCT	NOV	DEC
1	29 21 29 30 32 34 19 10 20	32 26 29 34 34 35 19 10 20	35 27 34 1 36 35 19 10 20	2 32 3 5 3 36 18 10 20	5 36 4 8 5 1 18 10 20	8 4 5 12 7 1 18 10 20	10 8 11 15 9 2 18 10 20	13 12 16 17 11 2 18 11 20	16 17 16 17 13 2 19 11 20	19 20 18 16 15 1 19 11 20	22 25 23 18 17 1 19 11 20	25 29 27 21 19 1 20 11 21
2	29 22 29 30 32 34 19 10 20	32 27 29 34 34 35 19 10 20	35 28 34 1 1 35 19 10 20	2 33 4 5 3 36 18 10 20	5 1 3 9 5 1 18 10 20	8 5 5 12 7 1 18 10 20	10 9 11 15 9 2 18 10 20	13 13 16 17 11 2 18 11 20	16 18 16 17 13 2 19 11 20	19 22 19 16 15 1 19 11 20	22 27 24 18 17 1 19 11 21	25 31 28 21 19 1 20 11 21
3	29 23 28 30 32 34 19 10 20	32 28 30 34 34 35 19 10 20	35 29 34 1 1 35 19 10 20	2 35 4 5 3 36 18 10 20	5 2 3 9 5 1 18 10 20	8 7 6 12 7 1 18 10 20	11 10 12 15 9 2 18 10 20	14 14 16 17 12 2 18 11 20	17 19 16 17 14 2 19 11 20	19 23 19 16 15 1 19 11 20	23 28 24 18 17 1 19 11 21	26 32 28 21 19 1 20 11 21
4	29 25 28 30 32 34 19 10 20	32 30 30 34 35 35 19 10 20	35 31 34 1 1 35 19 10 20	2 36 4 5 3 36 18 10 20	5 3 3 9 5 1 18 10 20	8 8 6 12 7 1 18 10 20	11 11 12 15 10 2 18 10 20	14 16 16 17 12 2 18 11 20	17 21 16 16 14 2 19 11 20	20 24 19 16 15 1 19 11 20	23 30 24 18 17 1 19 11 21	26 34 28 21 19 1 20 11 21
5	29 26 28 30 32 34 19 10 20	32 31 30 34 35 35 19 10 20	35 32 34 2 1 35 19 10 20	2 1 4 5 3 36 18 10 20	5 5 3 9 5 1 18 10 20	8 9 6 12 8 1 18 10 20	11 12 12 15 10 2 18 10 20	14 17 16 17 12 2 18 11 20	17 22 16 16 14 2 19 11 20	20 25 19 16 16 1 19 11 20	23 31 24 18 17 1 19 11 21	26 35 28 21 19 1 20 11 21
6	29 28 28 30 32 34 19 10 20	32 33 30 34 35 35 19 10 20	35 34 35 2 1 35 19 10 20	2 2 4 5 3 36 18 10 20	5 6 3 9 5 1 18 10 20	8 10 6 12 8 1 18 10 20	11 14 12 15 10 2 18 10 20	14 18 17 17 12 2 18 11 20	17 23 16 16 14 2 19 11 20	20 27 19 16 16 1 19 11 20	23 32 24 18 17 1 20 11 21	26 36 28 21 19 1 20 11 21
7	29 29 28 30 32 34 19 10 20	32 34 30 34 35 35 19 10 20	35 35 35 2 1 35 19 10 20	2 4 4 6 3 36 18 10 20	5 7 3 9 5 1 18 10 20	8 11 6 13 8 1 18 10 20	11 15 12 15 10 2 18 11 20	14 20 17 17 12 2 18 11 20	17 25 16 16 14 2 19 11 20	20 29 19 16 16 1 19 11 20	23 34 24 18 18 1 20 11 21	26 2 28 21 19 1 20 11 21
8	29 31 28 31 32 34 19 10 20	32 36 30 34 35 35 19 10 20	35 36 35 2 1 35 18 10 20	2 5 4 6 3 36 18 10 20	5 8 3 9 6 1 18 10 20	8 13 6 13 8 1 18 10 20	11 16 12 16 10 2 18 11 20	14 21 17 17 12 2 18 11 20	17 26 16 16 14 2 19 11 20	20 30 20 16 16 1 19 11 20	23 35 25 18 18 1 20 11 21	26 3 28 22 19 1 20 11 21
9	29 32 28 31 32 34 19 10 20	32 1 30 35 35 35 19 10 20	35 2 35 2 1 35 18 10 20	2 6 4 6 3 36 18 10 20	5 9 3 9 6 1 18 10 20	8 14 7 13 8 1 18 10 20	11 17 13 16 10 2 18 11 20	14 22 17 17 12 2 18 11 20	17 27 16 16 14 2 19 11 20	20 31 20 16 16 1 19 11 20	23 1 25 18 18 1 20 11 21	26 4 28 22 19 1 20 11 21
10	29 33 28 31 33 34 19 10 20	33 2 31 35 35 35 19 10 20	35 3 35 2 1 36 18 10 20	2 7 4 6 4 36 18 10 20	5 11 3 9 6 1 18 10 20	8 15 7 13 8 1 18 10 20	11 19 13 16 10 2 18 11 20	14 24 17 17 12 2 18 11 20	17 29 16 16 14 2 19 11 20	20 33 20 16 16 1 19 11 20	23 2 25 19 18 1 20 11 21	26 6 28 22 19 1 20 11 21
11	30 34 28 31 33 34 19 10 20	33 3 31 35 35 35 19 10 20	36 4 36 2 1 36 18 10 20	3 9 4 6 4 36 18 10 20	5 12 3 10 6 1 18 10 20	8 16 7 13 8 1 18 10 20	11 20 13 16 10 2 18 11 20	14 25 17 17 12 2 18 11 20	17 30 16 16 14 2 19 11 20	20 34 20 16 16 1 19 11 20	23 3 25 19 18 1 20 11 21	26 7 28 22 19 1 20 11 21
12	30 36 28 31 33 34 19 10 20	33 5 31 35 35 35 19 10 20	36 5 36 2 1 36 18 10 20	3 10 4 6 4 36 18 10 20	6 13 3 10 6 1 18 10 20	9 18 7 13 8 1 18 10 20	11 21 13 16 10 2 18 11 20	14 26 17 17 12 2 18 11 20	17 32 16 16 14 2 19 11 20	20 36 20 16 16 1 19 11 20	23 4 25 19 18 1 20 11 21	27 8 27 22 20 1 20 11 21
13	30 1 28 31 33 34 19 10 20	33 6 31 35 35 35 19 10 20	36 7 36 3 1 36 18 10 20	3 11 4 6 4 36 18 10 20	6 14 3 10 6 1 18 10 20	9 19 7 13 8 2 18 10 20	12 23 13 16 10 2 18 11 20	14 28 17 17 12 2 18 11 20	17 33 16 16 14 2 19 11 20	20 1 20 16 16 1 19 11 20	24 6 25 19 18 1 20 11 21	27 9 27 22 20 1 20 11 21
14	30 3 28 31 33 34 19 10 20	33 7 31 35 35 35 19 10 20	36 8 36 3 1 36 18 10 20	3 12 4 6 4 36 18 10 20	6 15 3 10 6 1 18 10 20	9 20 7 13 8 2 18 10 20	12 24 14 16 10 2 18 11 20	15 29 17 17 12 2 19 11 20	18 35 16 16 14 2 19 11 20	21 2 21 16 16 1 19 11 20	24 7 25 19 18 1 20 11 21	27 10 27 22 20 1 20 11 21
15	30 4 28 31 33 34 19 10 20	33 8 31 35 35 35 19 10 20	36 9 36 3 2 36 18 10 20	3 13 4 7 4 36 18 10 20	6 17 4 10 6 1 18 10 20	9 21 8 13 8 2 18 10 20	12 25 14 16 10 2 18 11 20	15 31 17 17 12 2 19 11 20	18 36 16 16 14 2 19 11 20	21 4 21 16 16 1 19 11 20	24 8 26 19 18 1 20 11 21	27 11 27 22 20 1 20 11 21
16	30 5 28 32 33 34 19 10 20	33 9 32 35 35 35 19 10 20	36 10 1 3 2 36 18 10 20	3 15 4 7 4 36 18 10 20	6 18 4 10 6 1 18 10 20	9 22 8 13 8 2 18 10 20	12 27 14 16 10 2 18 11 20	15 32 17 17 12 2 19 11 20	18 1 16 16 14 2 19 11 20	21 5 21 16 16 1 19 11 20	24 9 26 19 18 1 20 11 21	27 13 27 22 20 1 20 11 21
17	30 6 28 32 33 34 19 10 20	33 11 32 36 36 35 19 10 20	36 11 1 3 2 36 18 10 20	3 16 4 7 4 36 18 10 20	6 19 4 10 6 1 18 10 20	9 24 8 14 8 2 18 10 20	12 29 14 16 10 2 18 11 20	15 34 17 17 12 2 19 11 20	18 3 16 16 14 2 19 11 20	21 6 21 17 16 1 19 11 20	24 11 26 19 18 1 20 11 21	27 14 27 23 20 1 20 11 21
18	30 7 28 32 33 34 19 10 20	33 12 32 36 36 35 19 10 20	36 13 1 3 2 36 18 10 20	3 17 4 7 4 36 18 10 20	6 21 4 10 6 1 18 10 20	9 25 8 14 8 2 18 10 20	12 30 14 16 10 2 18 11 20	15 35 17 17 12 2 19 11 20	18 4 16 16 14 2 19 11 20	21 7 21 17 16 1 19 11 20	24 12 26 19 18 1 20 11 21	27 15 27 23 20 1 20 11 21
19	30 9 28 32 33 34 19 10 20	34 13 32 36 36 35 19 10 20	36 14 1 3 2 36 18 10 20	3 19 4 7 4 36 18 10 20	6 22 4 10 6 1 18 10 20	9 27 9 14 9 2 18 10 20	12 32 14 16 11 2 18 11 20	15 1 17 17 13 2 19 11 20	18 5 16 16 15 2 19 11 20	21 9 21 17 16 1 19 11 20	24 13 26 19 18 1 20 11 21	27 16 27 23 20 1 20 11 21
20	30 10 28 32 33 34 19 10 20	34 14 32 36 36 35 19 10 20	36 15 1 3 2 36 18 10 20	3 20 4 7 4 36 18 10 20	6 24 4 11 6 1 18 10 20	9 28 9 14 9 2 18 10 20	12 33 15 16 11 2 18 11 20	15 2 17 17 13 2 19 11 20	18 7 16 16 15 2 19 11 20	21 10 22 17 16 1 19 11 20	24 14 26 20 18 1 20 11 21	27 17 26 23 20 1 20 11 21
21	31 11 28 32 33 34 19 10 20	34 16 32 36 36 35 19 10 20	1 16 2 4 2 36 18 10 20	4 21 4 7 4 36 18 10 20	6 25 4 11 6 1 18 10 20	9 31 9 14 9 2 18 10 20	12 34 15 16 11 2 18 11 20	15 4 17 17 13 2 19 11 20	18 8 17 16 15 2 19 11 20	21 11 22 17 17 1 19 11 20	24 15 26 20 18 1 20 11 21	27 19 26 23 20 1 20 11 21
22	31 12 28 32 33 34 19 10 20	34 17 32 36 36 35 19 10 20	1 18 2 4 2 36 18 10 20	4 23 4 7 4 1 18 10 20	7 27 4 11 7 1 18 10 20	10 32 9 14 9 2 18 10 20	12 36 15 17 11 2 18 11 20	15 5 17 17 13 2 19 11 20	18 9 17 16 15 2 19 11 20	21 12 22 17 17 1 19 11 20	24 17 27 20 18 1 20 11 21	27 20 26 23 20 1 20 11 21
23	31 13 28 32 34 34 19 10 20	34 18 33 36 36 35 19 10 20	1 19 2 4 2 36 18 10 20	4 24 4 7 4 1 18 10 20	7 28 4 11 7 1 18 10 20	10 34 9 14 9 2 18 10 20	12 1 15 17 11 2 18 11 20	15 6 17 17 13 2 19 11 20	18 10 17 16 15 2 19 11 20	21 13 22 17 17 1 19 11 20	25 18 27 20 18 1 20 11 21	28 21 26 23 20 1 20 11 21
24	31 15 28 33 34 34 19 10 20	34 20 33 36 36 35 19 10 20	1 21 2 4 2 36 18 10 20	4 26 4 8 5 1 18 10 20	7 30 4 11 7 1 18 10 20	10 35 10 14 9 2 18 10 20	13 2 15 17 11 2 18 11 20	16 7 17 17 13 2 19 11 20	19 11 17 16 15 2 19 11 20	22 14 22 17 17 1 19 11 20	25 19 27 20 19 1 20 11 21	28 23 26 23 20 1 20 11 21
25	31 16 29 33 34 34 19 10 20	34 21 33 1 36 35 19 10 20	1 22 2 4 2 36 18 10 20	4 27 4 8 5 1 18 10 20	7 31 4 11 7 1 18 10 20	10 36 10 14 9 2 18 10 20	13 4 15 17 11 2 18 11 20	16 8 17 17 13 2 19 11 20	19 12 17 16 15 2 19 11 20	22 16 22 17 17 1 19 11 20	25 20 27 20 19 1 20 11 21	28 24 26 24 20 1 20 11 21
26	31 17 29 33 34 34 19 10 20	34 22 33 1 36 35 19 10 20	1 23 2 4 2 36 18 10 20	4 29 4 8 5 1 18 10 20	7 33 4 11 7 1 18 10 20	10 2 10 14 9 2 18 10 20	13 5 15 17 11 2 18 11 20	16 9 17 17 13 2 19 11 20	19 14 17 16 15 2 19 11 20	22 17 23 17 17 1 19 11 20	25 22 27 20 19 1 20 11 21	28 26 26 24 20 1 20 11 21
27	31 19 29 33 34 35 19 10 20	34 24 33 1 36 35 19 10 20	1 25 3 4 2 36 18 10 20	4 30 4 8 5 1 18 10 20	7 34 5 11 7 1 18 10 20	10 3 10 15 9 2 18 10 20	13 6 15 17 11 2 18 11 20	16 10 17 17 13 2 19 11 20	19 15 18 16 15 1 19 11 20	22 18 23 17 17 1 19 11 20	25 23 27 20 19 1 20 11 21	28 27 26 24 20 1 20 11 21
28	31 20 29 33 34 35 19 10 20	34 25 34 1 36 35 19 10 20	1 26 3 4 3 36 18 10 20	4 32 4 8 5 1 18 10 20	7 35 5 11 7 1 18 10 20	10 4 10 15 9 2 18 10 20	13 7 16 17 11 2 18 11 20	16 12 17 17 13 2 19 11 20	19 16 18 16 15 1 19 11 20	22 20 23 17 17 1 19 11 20	25 25 27 20 19 1 20 11 21	28 29 26 24 20 1 20 11 21
29	31 21 29 33 34 35 19 10 20		1 28 3 4 3 36 18 10 20	4 33 4 8 5 1 18 10 20	7 1 5 12 7 1 18 10 20	10 5 11 15 9 2 18 10 20	13 8 16 17 11 2 18 11 20	16 13 16 17 13 2 19 11 20	19 17 18 16 15 1 19 11 20	22 21 23 17 17 1 19 11 20	25 26 27 21 19 1 20 11 21	28 30 26 24 20 1 20 11 21
30	31 23 29 33 34 35 19 10 20	1951	1 29 3 5 3 36 18 10 20	4 34 4 8 5 1 18 10 20	7 2 5 12 7 1 18 10 20	10 6 11 15 9 2 18 10 20	13 10 16 17 11 2 18 11 20	16 14 16 17 13 2 19 11 20	19 19 18 16 15 1 19 11 20	22 22 23 18 17 1 19 11 20	25 28 27 21 19 1 20 11 21	28 32 26 24 20 1 20 11 21
31	32 24 29 33 34 35 19 10 20		1 31 3 5 3 36 18 10 20		7 3 5 12 7 1 18 10 20		13 11 16 17 11 2 18 11 20	16 15 16 17 13 2 19 11 20		22 24 23 18 17 1 19 11 20		28 33 26 24 21 1 20 11 21

	JAN	FEB	MAR	APR	MAY	JUNE	JULY	AUG	SEPT	OCT	NOV	DEC
1	29 34 26 24 21 1 20 11 21	32 3 30 28 22 2 20 11 21	35 6 35 32 23 2 20 11 21	2 10 2 35 23 3 20 10 21	5 13 2 3 23 4 19 11 20	8 18 6 7 22 4 19 11 20	10 21 13 11 22 5 19 11 20	13 26 15 14 23 5 20 11 20	16 31 15 18 25 6 20 11 20	19 35 20 22 27 6 20 11 21	22 4 25 26 29 5 21 11 21	25 8 25 29 31 5 21 11 21
2	29 36 26 24 21 1 20 11 21	32 5 30 28 22 2 20 11 21	35 7 36 32 23 2 20 11 21	2 11 2 36 23 3 20 10 21	5 14 2 3 23 4 19 11 20	8 19 7 7 22 4 19 11 20	11 22 13 11 22 5 19 11 20	14 27 15 15 23 5 20 11 20	16 33 15 18 25 6 20 11 20	19 36 20 22 27 6 20 11 21	23 6 25 26 29 5 21 11 21	26 9 25 30 31 5 21 11 21
3	29 1 26 25 21 1 20 11 21	32 6 31 28 22 2 20 11 21	35 8 36 32 23 2 20 11 21	2 12 2 36 23 3 20 11 21	5 16 2 3 22 4 19 11 20	8 20 7 7 22 4 19 11 20	11 24 13 11 22 5 19 11 20	14 29 15 15 23 5 20 11 20	17 34 15 19 25 6 20 11 20	20 2 20 22 27 6 20 11 21	23 7 25 26 29 5 21 11 21	26 10 25 30 31 5 21 11 21
4	29 3 27 25 21 1 20 11 21	32 7 31 28 22 2 20 11 21	35 9 36 32 23 2 20 10 21	2 14 2 36 23 3 20 11 21	5 17 2 4 22 4 19 11 20	8 21 7 7 22 4 19 11 20	11 25 13 11 22 5 19 11 20	14 30 15 15 23 5 20 11 20	17 36 15 19 25 6 20 11 21	20 3 20 22 27 5 20 11 21	23 8 25 26 29 5 21 11 21	26 12 25 30 31 5 21 11 21
5	29 4 27 25 21 1 20 11 21	32 8 31 29 22 2 20 11 21	35 10 36 32 23 2 20 10 21	2 15 2 36 23 3 20 11 21	5 18 2 4 22 4 19 11 20	8 23 8 7 22 4 19 11 20	11 26 13 11 22 5 19 11 20	14 32 15 15 23 5 20 11 20	17 1 15 19 25 6 20 11 21	20 5 21 22 27 5 20 11 21	23 10 25 26 29 5 21 11 21	26 13 25 30 32 5 21 11 21
6	29 5 27 25 21 1 20 11 21	32 10 31 29 22 2 20 11 21	35 12 36 32 23 2 20 10 21	2 16 2 36 23 3 20 11 21	5 19 2 4 22 4 19 11 20	8 24 8 8 22 4 19 11 20	11 28 13 11 22 5 19 11 20	14 33 15 15 23 5 20 11 20	17 3 15 19 25 6 20 11 21	20 6 21 23 27 5 20 11 21	23 11 25 26 29 5 21 11 21	26 14 25 30 32 5 21 11 21
7	29 6 27 25 21 1 20 11 21	32 11 31 29 22 2 20 11 21	35 13 36 32 23 2 20 10 21	2 17 2 36 23 3 20 11 21	5 21 3 4 22 4 19 11 20	8 26 8 8 22 4 19 11 20	11 29 14 11 22 5 19 11 20	14 35 15 15 23 5 20 11 20	17 4 16 19 25 6 20 11 21	20 7 21 23 27 5 20 11 21	23 12 25 26 29 5 21 11 21	26 15 25 30 32 5 21 11 21
8	29 7 27 25 21 1 20 11 21	32 12 31 29 22 2 20 11 21	35 14 1 33 23 2 20 10 21	2 18 2 36 23 3 20 11 21	5 22 3 4 22 4 19 11 20	8 27 8 8 22 4 19 11 20	11 31 14 12 22 5 19 11 20	14 36 15 15 23 5 20 11 20	17 5 16 19 25 6 20 11 21	20 9 21 23 27 5 20 11 21	23 13 25 27 29 5 21 11 21	26 16 25 30 32 5 21 11 21
9	29 9 27 25 21 1 20 11 21	32 13 31 29 22 2 20 11 21	35 15 1 33 23 2 20 10 21	2 20 2 36 23 3 20 11 21	5 23 3 4 22 4 19 11 20	8 29 8 8 22 4 19 11 20	11 32 14 12 22 5 19 11 20	14 2 15 15 23 5 20 11 20	17 7 16 19 25 6 20 11 21	20 10 21 23 27 5 20 11 21	23 14 25 27 30 5 21 11 21	26 17 25 30 32 5 21 11 21
10	29 10 27 25 21 1 20 11 21	33 14 32 29 22 2 20 11 21	35 16 1 33 23 2 20 10 21	3 21 2 1 23 3 20 11 21	5 25 3 4 22 4 19 11 20	8 30 9 8 22 4 19 11 20	11 34 14 12 22 5 19 11 20	14 3 15 16 24 5 20 11 20	17 8 16 19 25 6 20 11 21	20 11 21 23 27 5 20 11 21	23 16 26 27 30 5 21 11 21	26 19 25 30 32 5 21 11 21
11	30 11 27 26 21 1 20 11 21	33 16 32 29 22 2 20 11 21	36 18 1 33 23 2 20 10 21	3 22 2 1 23 3 20 11 21	6 26 3 4 22 4 19 11 20	9 32 9 8 22 4 19 11 20	11 35 14 12 22 5 19 11 20	14 4 15 16 24 5 20 11 20	17 9 16 20 25 6 20 11 21	20 12 22 23 27 5 20 11 21	23 17 26 27 30 5 21 11 21	26 20 25 31 32 5 21 11 21
12	30 12 27 26 21 1 20 11 21	33 17 32 29 22 2 20 11 21	36 19 1 33 23 2 20 10 21	3 24 2 1 23 3 20 11 21	6 28 3 4 22 4 19 11 20	9 33 9 8 22 5 19 11 20	12 1 14 12 22 5 19 11 20	14 6 15 16 24 5 20 11 20	17 10 16 20 25 6 20 11 21	20 14 22 23 28 5 20 11 21	24 18 26 27 30 5 21 11 21	27 21 25 31 32 5 21 11 21
13	30 14 28 26 21 1 20 11 21	33 18 32 30 23 2 20 11 21	36 20 1 33 23 2 20 10 21	3 25 2 1 23 3 20 11 21	6 29 3 5 22 4 19 11 20	9 34 9 8 22 5 19 11 20	12 2 14 12 22 5 19 11 20	15 7 14 16 24 5 20 11 20	18 12 17 20 26 6 20 11 21	21 15 22 23 28 5 20 11 21	24 19 26 27 30 5 21 11 21	27 22 25 31 32 5 21 11 21
14	30 15 28 26 21 1 20 11 21	33 19 32 30 23 2 20 11 21	36 21 2 33 23 2 20 10 21	3 27 1 1 23 3 20 11 21	6 30 3 5 22 4 19 11 20	9 36 10 9 22 5 19 11 20	12 3 14 12 22 5 19 11 20	15 8 14 16 24 5 20 11 20	18 13 17 20 26 6 20 11 21	21 16 22 24 28 5 20 11 21	24 20 26 27 30 5 21 11 21	27 24 25 31 32 5 21 11 21
15	30 16 28 26 21 1 20 11 21	33 20 33 30 23 2 20 11 21	36 23 2 33 23 2 20 10 21	3 28 1 1 23 3 20 11 21	6 32 4 5 22 4 19 11 20	9 1 10 9 22 5 19 11 20	12 5 14 12 22 5 19 11 20	15 9 14 16 24 5 20 11 20	18 14 17 20 26 6 20 11 21	21 17 22 24 28 5 20 11 21	24 22 26 27 30 5 21 11 21	27 25 25 31 32 5 21 11 21
16	30 17 28 26 21 1 20 11 21	33 22 33 30 23 2 20 11 21	36 24 2 33 23 2 20 10 21	3 29 1 1 23 3 20 11 21	6 33 4 5 22 4 19 11 20	9 2 10 9 22 5 19 11 20	12 6 15 12 22 5 19 11 20	15 11 14 16 24 6 20 11 20	18 15 17 20 26 6 20 11 21	21 18 22 24 28 5 20 11 21	24 23 26 28 30 5 21 11 21	27 27 25 31 32 5 21 11 21
17	30 18 28 26 21 1 20 11 21	33 23 33 30 23 2 20 11 21	36 25 2 34 23 2 20 10 21	3 31 1 1 23 3 20 11 21	6 35 4 5 22 4 19 11 20	9 4 10 9 22 5 19 11 20	12 7 15 13 22 5 19 11 20	15 12 14 16 24 6 20 11 20	18 16 17 20 26 6 20 11 21	21 20 22 24 28 5 20 11 21	24 24 26 28 30 5 21 11 21	27 28 25 31 32 5 21 11 21
18	30 19 28 26 21 1 20 11 21	33 24 33 30 23 2 20 11 21	36 27 2 34 23 3 20 10 21	3 32 1 2 23 3 20 11 21	6 36 4 5 22 4 19 11 20	9 5 10 9 22 5 19 11 20	12 9 15 13 22 5 19 11 20	15 13 14 17 24 6 20 11 20	18 17 18 20 26 6 20 11 21	21 21 23 24 28 5 20 11 21	24 26 26 28 30 5 21 11 21	27 29 25 31 33 5 21 11 21
19	30 21 28 27 21 1 20 11 21	33 26 33 30 23 2 20 11 21	36 28 2 34 23 3 20 10 21	3 34 1 2 23 3 20 11 21	6 1 4 5 22 4 19 11 20	9 6 10 9 22 5 19 11 20	12 10 15 13 22 5 19 11 20	15 14 14 17 24 6 20 11 20	18 19 18 20 26 6 20 11 21	21 22 23 24 28 5 20 11 21	24 27 26 28 30 5 21 11 21	27 31 25 32 33 5 21 11 21
20	30 22 28 27 21 1 20 11 21	34 27 33 30 23 2 20 11 21	36 30 2 34 23 3 20 10 21	4 35 1 2 23 3 20 11 21	6 3 4 5 22 4 19 11 20	9 8 11 9 22 5 19 11 20	12 11 15 13 23 5 19 11 20	15 15 14 17 24 6 20 11 20	18 20 18 21 26 6 20 11 21	21 23 23 24 28 5 20 11 21	24 29 26 28 30 5 21 11 21	27 32 25 32 33 5 21 11 21
21	21 23 29 27 21 1 20 11 21	34 29 34 31 23 2 20 11 21	1 31 2 34 23 3 20 10 21	4 36 1 2 23 3 20 11 21	7 4 5 6 22 4 19 11 20	9 9 11 9 22 5 19 11 20	12 12 15 13 23 5 19 11 20	15 17 14 17 24 6 20 11 20	18 21 18 21 26 6 20 11 21	21 25 23 24 28 5 20 11 21	24 30 26 28 30 5 21 11 21	27 34 25 32 33 5 21 11 21
22	31 25 29 27 22 1 20 11 21	34 30 34 31 23 2 20 11 21	1 33 2 34 23 3 20 10 21	4 2 1 2 23 3 20 11 21	7 5 5 6 22 4 19 11 20	10 10 11 10 22 5 19 11 20	12 13 15 13 23 5 19 11 20	15 18 14 17 24 6 20 11 20	18 22 18 21 26 6 20 11 21	21 26 23 25 28 5 20 11 21	25 31 26 28 31 5 21 11 21	28 35 25 32 33 5 21 11 21
23	31 26 29 27 22 1 20 11 21	34 32 34 31 23 2 20 11 21	1 34 2 34 23 3 20 10 21	4 3 1 2 23 3 19 11 20	7 7 5 6 22 4 19 11 20	10 11 11 10 22 5 19 11 20	13 14 15 13 23 5 19 11 20	15 19 14 17 24 6 20 11 20	19 24 18 21 26 6 20 11 21	22 27 23 25 28 5 20 11 21	25 33 26 28 31 5 21 11 21	28 1 26 32 33 5 21 11 21
24	31 28 29 27 22 1 20 11 21	34 33 34 31 23 2 20 11 21	1 36 2 34 23 3 20 10 21	4 5 1 2 23 3 19 11 20	7 8 5 6 22 4 19 11 20	10 12 12 10 22 5 19 11 20	13 16 15 13 23 5 19 11 20	16 20 14 17 24 6 20 11 20	19 25 19 21 26 6 20 11 21	22 29 23 25 28 5 20 11 21	25 34 26 29 31 5 21 11 21	28 2 26 32 33 5 21 11 21
25	31 29 29 27 22 1 20 11 21	34 35 34 31 23 2 20 11 21	1 1 3 35 23 3 20 10 21	4 6 2 2 23 3 19 11 20	7 9 5 6 22 4 19 11 20	10 14 12 10 22 5 19 11 20	13 17 15 14 23 5 19 11 20	16 21 14 17 24 6 20 11 20	19 28 19 21 26 6 20 11 21	22 30 24 25 28 5 20 11 21	25 36 26 29 31 5 21 11 21	28 3 26 32 33 5 21 11 21
26	31 31 29 27 22 1 20 11 21	34 36 35 31 23 2 20 11 21	1 2 3 35 23 3 20 10 21	4 7 2 3 23 3 19 11 20	7 10 6 6 22 4 19 11 20	10 15 12 10 22 5 19 11 20	13 18 15 14 23 5 19 11 20	16 23 14 18 24 6 20 11 20	19 28 19 21 26 6 20 11 21	22 32 24 25 29 5 20 11 21	25 1 26 29 31 5 21 11 21	28 5 26 32 33 5 21 11 21
27	31 32 29 27 22 1 20 11 21	34 2 35 31 23 2 20 11 21	1 4 3 35 23 3 20 10 21	4 8 2 3 23 3 19 11 20	7 12 6 6 22 4 19 11 20	10 16 12 10 22 5 19 11 20	13 19 15 14 23 5 19 11 20	16 24 14 18 24 6 20 11 20	19 29 19 21 26 6 20 11 21	22 33 24 25 29 5 20 11 21	25 2 26 29 31 5 21 11 21	28 6 26 32 33 5 21 11 21
28	31 34 30 28 22 1 20 11 21	34 3 35 32 23 2 20 11 21	1 5 3 35 23 3 20 10 21	4 10 2 3 23 3 19 11 20	7 13 6 6 22 4 19 11 20	10 17 12 10 22 5 19 11 20	13 21 15 14 23 5 20 11 21	16 25 14 18 25 6 20 11 20	19 31 19 22 27 6 20 11 21	22 34 24 25 29 5 21 11 21	25 4 26 29 31 5 21 11 21	28 7 26 33 33 5 21 11 21
29	31 35 30 28 22 1 20 11 21	34 4 35 32 23 2 20 11 21	1 6 2 35 23 3 20 10 21	4 11 2 3 23 4 19 11 21	7 14 6 7 22 4 19 11 20	10 18 12 10 22 5 19 11 20	13 22 15 14 23 5 20 11 21	16 27 14 18 25 6 20 11 20	19 32 20 22 27 6 20 11 21	22 36 24 25 29 5 21 11 21	25 5 25 29 31 5 21 11 21	28 9 26 33 33 5 21 11 21
30	31 1 30 28 22 2 20 11 21	1952	1 8 2 35 23 3 20 10 21	5 12 2 3 23 4 19 11 21	7 15 6 7 22 4 19 11 20	10 20 13 11 22 5 19 11 20	13 23 15 14 23 5 20 11 21	16 28 14 18 25 6 20 11 20	19 34 20 22 27 6 20 11 21	22 1 24 26 29 5 21 11 21	25 6 25 29 31 5 21 11 21	28 10 26 33 33 5 21 11 21
31	32 2 30 28 22 2 20 11 21		2 9 2 35 23 3 20 10 21		7 16 6 7 22 4 19 11 20		13 24 15 14 23 5 20 11 21	15 30 14 18 25 6 20 11 20		22 3 24 26 29 5 21 11 21		28 11 27 33 34 5 21 11 21

	JAN	FEB	MAR	APR	MAY	JUNE	JULY	AUG	SEPT	OCT	NOV	DEC
1	29 12 27 33 34 5 21 11 21	32 17 32 36 36 5 21 11 21	35 18 36 3 2 5 21 11 21	2 22 35 3 4 6 21 11 21	5 26 2 2 7 6 21 11 21	8 31 9 3 9 7 21 11 21	10 35 13 6 11 8 21 11 21	13 4 12 9 13 8 21 12 21	16 9 16 13 15 9 21 12 21	19 12 21 16 17 9 21 12 21	22 17 25 20 18 9 22 12 21	25 20 23 24 20 9 22 12 21
2	29 14 27 33 34 5 21 11 21	32 18 32 1 36 5 21 11 21	35 19 36 3 2 5 21 11 21	2 23 35 3 4 6 21 11 21	5 27 3 2 7 6 21 11 21	8 32 9 3 9 7 21 11 21	11 36 13 6 11 8 21 11 21	13 5 12 9 13 8 21 12 21	16 10 16 13 15 9 21 12 21	19 14 21 17 17 9 21 12 21	22 18 25 20 19 9 22 12 21	26 21 23 24 20 9 22 12 21
3	29 15 27 33 34 5 21 11 21	32 19 32 1 36 5 21 11 21	35 20 1 3 21 5 21 11 21	2 25 36 3 5 6 21 11 21	5 28 3 2 7 6 21 11 21	8 34 9 3 9 7 21 11 21	11 1 13 6 11 8 21 11 21	14 7 12 9 13 8 21 12 21	17 12 16 13 15 9 21 12 21	19 15 21 17 17 9 21 12 21	23 19 25 20 19 9 22 12 21	26 23 24 24 20 9 22 12 21
4	29 16 27 33 34 5 21 11 21	32 20 32 1 36 5 21 11 21	35 21 1 3 21 5 21 11 21	2 26 36 3 5 6 21 11 21	5 30 3 2 7 6 21 11 21	8 35 9 3 9 7 21 11 21	11 3 13 6 11 8 21 11 21	14 8 12 10 13 8 21 12 21	17 13 16 13 15 9 21 12 21	20 16 21 17 17 9 21 12 21	23 20 25 21 18 9 22 12 21	26 24 24 24 21 9 22 12 21
5	29 17 27 34 34 5 21 11 21	32 22 32 1 36 5 21 11 21	35 22 1 3 21 5 21 11 21	2 27 36 3 5 6 21 11 21	5 31 3 2 7 6 21 11 21	8 36 9 3 9 7 21 11 21	11 4 13 6 11 8 21 11 21	14 9 12 10 13 8 21 12 21	17 14 17 13 15 9 21 12 21	20 17 22 17 17 9 21 12 21	23 22 25 21 18 9 22 12 21	26 25 24 24 21 9 22 12 21
6	29 18 28 34 34 5 21 11 21	32 23 33 1 36 5 21 11 21	35 24 1 3 21 5 21 11 21	2 29 36 3 5 6 21 11 21	5 32 3 2 7 6 21 11 21	8 2 10 4 9 7 21 11 21	11 6 13 6 11 8 21 11 21	14 11 12 10 13 8 21 12 21	17 15 17 13 15 9 21 12 21	20 18 22 17 17 9 21 12 21	23 23 25 21 18 9 22 12 21	26 26 24 25 21 9 22 12 21
7	29 19 28 34 34 5 21 11 21	32 24 33 1 36 5 21 11 21	35 25 1 3 3 5 21 11 21	2 30 36 3 5 6 21 11 21	5 34 3 2 7 6 21 11 21	8 3 10 4 9 7 21 11 21	11 7 13 7 11 8 21 11 21	14 12 12 10 13 8 21 12 21	17 16 17 14 15 9 21 12 21	20 20 22 17 17 9 21 12 21	23 24 24 21 18 9 22 12 21	26 28 24 25 21 9 22 12 21
8	29 21 28 34 34 5 21 11 21	32 25 33 1 1 5 21 11 21	35 26 1 3 3 5 21 11 21	2 31 36 3 5 6 21 11 21	5 35 4 2 7 6 21 11 21	8 5 10 4 9 7 21 11 21	11 8 13 7 11 8 21 11 21	14 13 12 10 13 8 21 12 21	17 18 17 14 15 9 21 12 21	20 21 22 17 17 9 21 12 21	23 25 24 21 18 9 22 12 21	26 29 24 25 21 9 22 12 21
9	29 22 28 34 34 5 21 11 21	33 27 33 1 1 5 21 11 21	35 28 1 3 3 5 21 11 21	2 33 36 3 5 6 21 11 21	5 1 4 2 7 6 21 11 21	8 6 10 4 9 7 21 11 21	11 10 13 7 11 8 21 11 21	14 14 12 10 13 9 21 12 21	17 19 17 14 15 9 21 12 21	20 22 22 17 17 9 21 12 21	23 27 24 21 18 9 22 12 21	26 30 24 25 21 9 22 12 21
10	29 23 28 34 34 5 21 11 21	33 28 33 1 1 5 21 11 21	35 29 1 3 3 5 21 11 21	3 34 36 3 5 6 21 11 21	5 2 4 2 7 7 21 11 21	8 7 10 4 9 7 21 11 21	11 11 13 7 11 8 21 11 21	14 15 12 10 13 9 21 12 21	17 20 18 14 15 9 21 12 21	20 23 22 18 17 9 21 12 21	23 28 24 21 18 9 22 12 21	26 32 24 25 21 9 22 12 21
11	30 25 28 34 34 5 21 11 21	33 30 33 1 1 5 21 11 21	36 30 1 3 3 5 21 11 21	3 36 36 3 5 6 21 11 21	6 4 4 2 7 7 21 11 21	9 9 10 4 9 7 21 11 21	11 12 13 7 11 8 21 11 21	14 17 12 10 13 9 21 12 21	17 21 18 14 15 9 21 12 21	20 24 22 18 17 9 21 12 21	23 29 24 21 18 9 22 12 21	26 33 25 25 21 9 22 12 21
12	30 26 28 34 34 5 21 11 21	33 31 34 1 1 5 21 11 21	36 32 1 3 3 5 21 11 21	3 1 36 3 5 6 21 11 21	6 5 4 2 7 7 21 11 21	9 10 11 4 9 7 21 11 21	11 13 13 7 11 8 21 11 21	14 18 13 10 13 9 21 12 21	17 22 18 14 15 9 21 12 21	20 26 23 18 17 9 21 12 21	23 31 24 22 18 9 22 12 21	27 34 25 25 21 9 22 12 21
13	30 27 29 34 35 5 21 11 21	33 33 34 2 1 5 21 11 21	36 33 1 3 3 5 21 11 21	3 3 36 3 5 6 21 11 21	6 7 5 2 7 7 21 11 21	9 11 11 4 9 7 21 11 21	12 15 13 7 11 8 21 11 21	15 19 13 11 13 9 21 12 21	18 23 18 14 15 9 21 12 21	20 27 23 18 17 9 21 12 21	24 32 24 22 18 9 22 12 21	27 36 25 25 21 9 22 12 21
14	30 29 29 35 35 5 21 11 21	33 34 34 2 1 5 21 11 21	36 35 1 3 3 5 21 11 21	3 4 36 3 5 6 21 11 21	6 8 5 2 7 7 21 11 21	9 13 11 4 10 7 21 11 21	12 16 13 7 12 8 21 11 21	15 20 13 11 14 9 21 12 21	18 25 18 14 15 9 21 12 21	21 28 23 18 17 9 21 12 21	24 33 24 22 18 9 22 12 21	27 1 25 26 21 9 22 12 21
15	30 30 29 35 35 5 21 11 21	33 36 34 2 1 5 21 11 21	36 36 1 4 3 5 21 11 21	3 6 36 3 5 6 21 11 21	6 9 5 2 7 7 21 11 21	9 14 11 4 10 7 21 11 21	12 17 13 7 12 8 21 11 21	15 21 13 11 14 9 21 12 21	18 26 18 14 16 9 21 12 21	21 30 23 18 17 9 21 12 21	24 35 24 22 18 9 22 12 21	27 3 25 26 21 9 22 12 21
16	30 32 29 35 35 5 21 11 21	33 1 34 2 1 5 21 11 21	36 2 36 4 3 5 21 11 21	3 7 36 3 5 6 21 11 21	6 11 5 2 8 7 21 11 21	9 15 11 4 10 7 21 11 21	12 18 13 7 12 8 21 11 21	15 23 13 11 14 9 21 12 21	18 27 19 15 16 9 21 12 21	21 31 23 18 18 9 21 12 21	24 36 23 22 18 9 22 12 21	27 4 25 26 21 9 22 12 21
17	30 33 29 35 35 5 21 11 21	33 3 35 2 1 5 21 11 21	36 3 36 4 3 5 21 11 21	3 8 36 3 6 6 21 11 21	6 12 5 2 8 7 21 11 21	9 16 11 5 10 7 21 11 21	12 19 13 8 12 8 21 11 21	15 24 13 11 14 9 21 12 21	18 29 19 15 16 9 21 12 21	21 32 23 18 18 9 21 12 21	24 2 23 22 18 9 22 12 21	27 6 26 26 21 9 22 12 21
18	30 35 29 35 35 5 21 11 21	33 4 35 2 1 5 21 11 21	36 5 36 4 3 5 21 11 21	3 10 1 2 6 6 21 11 21	6 13 6 2 8 7 21 11 21	9 17 12 5 10 7 21 11 21	12 21 13 8 12 8 21 11 21	15 25 13 11 14 9 21 12 21	18 30 19 15 16 9 21 12 21	21 34 23 18 18 9 21 12 21	24 3 23 22 20 9 22 12 21	27 7 26 26 21 9 22 12 21
19	30 36 30 35 35 5 21 11 21	34 5 35 2 1 5 21 11 21	36 6 36 4 3 5 21 11 21	3 11 1 2 6 6 21 11 21	6 14 6 2 8 7 21 11 21	9 19 12 5 10 7 21 11 21	12 22 13 8 12 8 21 11 21	15 26 13 11 14 9 21 12 21	18 31 19 15 16 9 21 12 21	21 35 23 19 18 9 21 12 21	24 5 23 22 20 9 22 12 21	27 8 26 26 21 9 22 12 21
20	31 2 30 35 35 5 21 11 21	34 7 35 2 1 5 21 11 21	36 8 36 4 4 5 21 11 21	4 12 1 2 6 6 21 11 21	6 15 6 2 8 7 21 11 21	9 20 12 5 10 7 21 11 21	12 23 13 8 12 8 21 11 21	15 28 14 11 14 9 21 12 21	18 33 19 15 16 9 21 12 21	21 1 24 19 18 9 21 12 21	24 6 23 23 20 9 22 12 21	27 10 26 27 22 9 22 12 21
21	31 3 30 35 35 5 21 11 21	34 8 35 2 2 5 21 11 21	1 9 36 4 4 5 21 11 21	4 13 1 2 6 6 21 11 21	7 17 6 2 8 7 21 11 21	9 21 12 5 10 7 21 11 21	12 24 13 8 12 8 21 11 21	15 29 14 12 14 9 21 12 21	18 34 19 15 16 9 21 12 21	21 2 24 19 18 9 21 12 21	24 8 23 23 20 9 22 12 21	27 11 26 27 22 9 22 12 21
22	31 4 30 35 35 5 21 11 21	34 9 35 2 2 5 21 11 21	1 10 36 4 4 5 21 11 21	4 15 1 2 6 6 21 11 21	7 18 6 3 8 7 21 11 21	10 22 12 5 10 8 21 11 21	12 26 13 8 12 8 21 11 21	15 31 14 12 14 9 21 12 21	18 36 20 15 16 9 21 12 21	21 4 24 19 18 9 21 12 21	24 9 23 23 20 9 22 12 21	28 12 26 27 22 9 22 12 21
23	31 6 30 35 35 5 21 11 21	34 10 36 2 2 5 21 11 21	1 11 36 4 4 5 21 11 21	4 16 1 2 6 6 21 11 21	7 19 7 3 8 7 21 11 21	10 24 12 5 10 8 21 11 21	13 27 13 8 12 8 21 11 21	16 32 14 12 14 9 21 12 21	19 1 20 15 16 9 21 12 21	21 5 24 19 18 9 22 12 21	25 10 23 23 20 9 22 12 21	28 14 26 27 22 9 22 12 21
24	31 7 30 36 35 5 21 11 21	34 12 36 2 2 5 21 11 21	1 13 36 4 4 5 21 11 21	4 17 1 2 6 6 21 11 21	7 20 7 3 8 7 21 11 21	10 25 12 5 10 8 21 11 21	13 28 13 8 12 8 21 11 21	15 34 14 12 14 9 21 12 21	19 3 20 16 16 9 21 12 21	22 7 24 19 18 9 22 12 21	25 12 23 23 20 9 22 12 21	28 15 27 27 22 8 22 12 21
25	31 8 30 36 35 5 21 11 21	34 13 36 3 2 5 21 11 21	1 14 36 4 4 6 21 11 21	4 18 1 2 6 6 21 11 21	7 21 7 3 8 7 21 11 21	10 26 12 5 10 8 21 11 21	13 30 13 8 12 8 21 11 21	16 35 14 12 14 9 21 12 21	19 4 20 16 16 9 21 12 21	22 8 24 19 18 9 22 12 21	25 13 23 23 20 9 22 12 21	28 16 27 27 22 8 22 12 21
26	31 10 31 36 36 5 21 11 21	34 14 36 3 2 5 21 11 21	1 15 36 4 4 6 21 11 21	4 19 2 2 6 6 21 11 21	7 23 7 3 8 7 21 11 21	10 28 13 5 10 8 21 11 21	13 31 13 9 12 8 21 11 21	16 1 15 12 14 9 21 12 21	19 6 20 16 16 9 21 12 21	22 10 24 19 18 9 22 12 21	25 14 23 23 20 9 22 12 21	28 17 27 27 22 8 22 12 21
27	31 11 31 36 36 5 21 11 21	34 15 36 3 2 5 21 11 21	1 16 36 4 4 6 21 11 21	4 21 2 2 6 6 21 11 21	7 24 8 3 8 7 21 11 21	10 29 13 5 10 8 21 11 21	13 33 13 9 12 8 21 11 21	16 2 15 12 14 9 21 12 21	19 7 20 16 16 9 21 12 21	22 11 24 20 18 9 22 12 21	25 15 23 23 20 9 22 12 21	28 19 27 27 22 8 22 12 21
28	31 12 31 36 36 5 21 11 21	34 16 36 3 2 5 21 11 21	1 17 36 4 4 6 21 11 21	4 22 2 2 6 6 21 11 21	7 25 8 3 8 7 21 11 21	10 30 13 6 10 8 21 11 21	13 34 12 9 12 8 21 11 21	16 4 15 12 14 9 21 12 21	19 9 21 16 16 9 21 12 21	22 12 24 20 18 9 22 12 21	25 17 23 24 20 9 22 12 21	28 20 27 27 22 8 22 12 21
29	31 13 31 36 36 5 21 11 21	**1953**	1 19 36 4 4 6 21 11 21	4 23 2 2 6 6 21 11 21	7 27 8 3 8 7 21 11 21	10 32 13 6 11 8 21 11 21	13 36 12 9 12 8 21 11 21	16 1 15 12 14 9 21 12 21	19 10 21 16 16 9 21 12 21	22 13 24 20 18 9 22 12 21	25 18 23 24 20 9 22 12 21	28 21 27 28 22 8 22 12 21
30	32 14 31 36 36 5 21 11 21		1 20 35 4 4 6 21 11 21	4 24 2 2 6 6 21 11 21	7 28 8 3 9 7 21 11 21	10 33 13 6 11 8 21 11 21	13 1 12 9 13 8 21 11 21	16 6 15 13 15 9 21 12 21	19 11 21 16 16 9 21 12 21	22 15 24 20 18 9 22 12 21	25 19 23 24 20 9 22 12 21	28 22 28 28 22 8 22 12 21
31	32 16 31 36 36 5 21 11 21		2 22 35 3 4 6 21 11 21		7 29 8 3 9 7 21 11 21		13 3 12 9 13 8 21 11 21	16 8 16 13 15 9 21 12 21		22 16 25 20 18 9 22 12 21		28 23 28 28 22 8 22 12 21

	JAN	FEB	MAR	APR	MAY	JUNE	JULY	AUG	SEPT	OCT	NOV	DEC
1	29 25 28 28 22 8 22 12 21	32 29 33 32 24 8 22 12 21	35 30 34 35 26 8 22 11 21	2 35 35 3 27 9 22 11 21	5 3 4 7 28 9 22 11 21	8 8 10 11 28 10 22 12 21	10 12 11 14 28 10 22 12 21	13 17 12 18 27 11 22 12 21	16 21 17 21 28 12 22 12 21	19 24 22 24 29 12 22 12 21	22 29 22 24 31 12 23 12 21	25 32 24 23 33 12 23 12 21
2	29 26 28 28 22 8 22 12 21	32 31 33 32 24 8 22 12 21	35 31 34 35 26 8 22 11 21	2 1 35 3 27 9 22 11 21	5 5 4 7 28 9 22 11 21	8 10 10 11 28 10 22 12 21	11 13 11 14 28 10 22 12 21	13 18 12 18 27 11 22 12 21	16 23 18 21 28 12 22 12 21	19 26 22 24 29 12 22 12 21	22 30 22 24 31 12 23 12 21	25 34 24 23 33 12 23 12 21
3	29 27 28 28 22 8 22 12 21	32 32 33 32 24 8 22 12 21	35 33 34 36 26 8 22 11 21	2 2 35 3 27 9 22 11 21	5 6 4 7 28 9 22 11 21	8 11 10 11 28 10 22 12 21	11 15 11 14 27 10 22 12 21	14 19 12 18 27 11 22 12 21	16 24 18 21 28 12 22 12 21	19 27 22 24 29 12 22 12 21	23 31 22 24 31 12 23 12 21	26 35 24 23 33 12 23 12 21
4	29 28 28 28 22 8 22 12 21	32 34 33 32 24 8 22 12 21	35 34 34 36 26 8 22 11 21	2 4 35 4 27 9 22 11 21	5 8 4 7 28 9 22 11 21	8 13 10 11 28 10 22 12 21	11 16 11 14 27 10 22 12 21	14 20 12 18 27 11 22 12 21	17 25 18 21 28 12 22 12 21	20 28 22 24 29 12 22 12 21	23 33 21 24 31 12 23 12 21	26 36 25 23 34 12 23 12 21
5	29 30 28 28 22 8 22 12 21	32 35 33 32 24 8 22 12 21	35 36 34 36 26 8 22 11 21	2 5 35 4 27 9 22 11 21	5 9 5 7 28 9 22 11 21	8 14 10 11 28 10 22 12 21	11 17 11 15 27 10 22 12 21	14 22 12 18 27 11 22 12 21	17 26 18 21 28 12 22 12 21	20 29 22 24 30 12 22 12 21	23 34 21 24 31 12 23 12 21	26 2 25 23 34 12 23 12 21
6	29 31 29 29 23 8 22 12 21	32 36 33 32 24 8 22 11 21	35 1 34 36 26 8 22 11 21	2 7 36 4 27 9 22 11 21	5 10 5 7 28 9 22 11 21	8 15 10 11 28 10 22 12 21	11 18 11 15 27 10 22 12 21	14 23 12 18 27 11 22 12 21	17 27 18 21 28 12 22 12 21	20 31 22 24 30 12 22 12 21	23 36 21 24 32 12 23 12 21	26 3 25 23 34 12 23 12 21
7	29 33 29 29 23 8 22 12 21	32 2 34 33 24 8 22 11 21	35 3 34 36 26 8 22 11 21	2 8 36 4 27 9 22 11 21	5 12 5 8 28 9 22 11 21	8 16 11 11 28 10 22 12 21	11 20 11 15 27 10 22 12 21	14 24 12 18 27 11 22 12 21	17 29 18 22 28 12 22 12 21	20 32 22 24 30 12 22 12 21	23 1 21 24 32 12 23 12 21	26 5 25 23 34 12 23 12 21
8	29 34 29 29 23 8 22 12 21	32 3 34 33 24 8 22 11 21	35 4 34 36 26 8 22 11 21	2 10 36 4 27 9 22 11 21	5 13 5 8 28 9 22 11 21	8 17 11 11 28 10 22 12 21	11 21 11 15 27 11 22 12 21	14 25 13 18 27 11 22 12 21	17 30 19 22 28 12 22 12 21	20 33 22 24 30 12 22 12 21	23 3 21 24 32 12 23 12 21	26 6 25 23 34 12 23 12 21
9	29 35 29 29 23 8 22 12 21	33 4 34 33 24 8 22 11 21	35 6 34 36 26 8 22 11 21	2 11 36 4 27 9 22 11 21	5 14 5 8 28 9 22 11 21	8 19 11 12 28 10 22 12 21	11 22 11 15 27 11 22 12 21	14 26 13 19 27 11 22 12 21	17 31 19 22 28 12 22 12 21	20 35 23 24 30 12 22 12 21	23 4 21 24 32 12 23 12 21	26 8 25 23 34 12 23 12 21
10	29 1 29 29 23 8 22 12 21	33 6 34 33 25 8 22 11 21	35 7 34 36 26 8 22 11 21	3 12 36 4 27 9 22 11 21	5 16 6 8 28 9 22 11 21	8 20 11 12 28 10 22 12 21	11 23 11 15 27 11 22 12 21	14 28 13 19 27 11 22 12 21	17 33 19 22 28 12 22 12 21	20 36 23 24 30 12 22 12 21	23 6 21 24 32 12 23 12 21	26 9 25 23 34 12 23 12 21
11	30 2 29 29 23 8 22 12 21	33 8 35 33 25 8 22 11 21	36 9 34 1 26 8 22 11 21	3 13 36 4 27 9 22 11 21	6 17 6 8 28 9 22 11 21	8 21 11 12 28 10 22 12 21	11 24 11 15 27 11 22 12 21	14 29 13 19 27 11 22 12 21	17 34 19 22 28 12 22 12 21	20 2 23 24 30 12 22 12 21	23 7 22 24 31 12 23 12 21	26 11 26 23 34 12 23 12 21
12	30 4 30 29 23 8 22 12 21	33 9 35 33 25 8 22 11 21	36 10 34 1 26 8 22 11 21	3 15 36 4 27 9 22 11 21	6 18 6 8 28 9 22 11 21	9 22 11 12 28 10 22 12 21	12 26 11 15 27 11 22 12 21	14 30 13 19 27 11 22 12 21	17 35 19 22 28 12 22 12 21	20 3 23 24 30 12 22 12 21	23 9 22 24 31 12 23 12 21	26 12 26 23 34 12 23 12 21
13	30 5 30 29 23 8 22 12 21	33 10 35 33 25 8 22 11 21	36 11 34 1 26 8 22 11 21	3 16 1 5 28 9 22 11 21	6 19 6 8 28 9 22 11 21	9 24 11 12 28 10 22 12 21	12 27 10 16 27 11 22 12 21	15 32 14 19 27 11 22 12 21	18 1 19 22 28 12 22 12 21	20 5 23 24 30 12 22 12 21	24 10 22 24 31 12 23 12 21	27 14 26 23 34 12 23 12 21
14	30 7 30 30 23 8 22 12 21	33 12 35 33 25 8 22 11 21	36 13 34 1 26 8 22 11 21	3 17 1 5 28 9 22 11 21	6 20 7 8 28 9 22 11 21	9 25 11 12 28 10 22 12 21	12 28 10 16 27 11 22 12 21	15 33 14 19 27 11 22 12 21	18 2 19 22 28 12 22 12 21	21 6 23 24 30 12 22 12 21	24 11 22 24 31 12 23 12 21	27 15 26 23 34 12 23 12 21
15	30 8 30 30 23 8 22 12 21	33 13 35 34 25 8 22 11 21	36 14 34 1 26 8 22 11 21	3 18 1 5 28 9 22 11 21	6 22 7 9 28 9 22 12 21	9 26 11 12 28 10 22 12 21	12 29 10 16 27 11 22 12 21	15 34 14 19 27 11 22 12 21	18 4 20 22 28 12 22 12 21	21 8 23 24 30 12 22 12 21	24 13 22 24 31 12 23 12 21	27 16 26 23 34 12 23 12 21
16	30 9 30 30 23 8 22 12 21	33 14 35 34 25 8 22 11 21	36 15 34 1 26 8 22 11 21	3 19 1 5 28 9 22 11 21	6 23 7 9 28 9 22 12 21	9 27 11 12 28 10 22 12 21	12 31 10 16 27 11 22 12 21	15 36 14 19 27 11 22 12 21	18 5 20 22 28 12 22 12 21	21 9 23 24 30 12 22 12 21	24 14 22 24 31 12 23 12 21	27 18 26 23 34 12 23 12 21
17	30 11 30 30 23 8 22 12 21	33 15 35 34 25 8 22 11 21	36 16 34 1 26 8 22 11 21	3 21 1 5 28 9 22 11 21	6 24 7 9 28 9 22 12 21	9 29 11 12 28 10 22 12 21	12 32 10 16 27 11 22 12 21	15 1 14 19 27 11 22 12 21	18 7 20 22 29 12 22 12 21	21 11 23 24 30 12 22 12 21	24 15 22 24 31 12 23 12 21	27 19 27 23 34 12 23 12 21
18	30 12 31 30 23 8 22 12 21	33 17 35 34 25 8 22 11 21	36 17 34 1 26 8 22 11 21	3 22 1 5 28 9 22 11 21	6 25 7 9 28 9 22 12 21	9 30 11 13 28 10 22 12 21	12 34 10 16 27 11 22 12 21	15 3 15 20 27 11 22 12 21	18 8 20 23 29 12 22 12 21	21 12 23 24 30 12 22 12 21	24 17 22 24 31 12 23 12 21	27 20 27 23 35 12 23 12 21
19	30 13 31 30 23 8 22 12 21	34 18 35 34 25 8 22 11 21	36 19 34 2 26 8 22 11 21	3 23 1 5 28 9 22 11 21	6 26 8 9 28 9 22 12 21	9 31 11 13 28 10 22 12 21	12 35 10 16 27 11 22 12 21	15 4 15 20 27 11 22 12 21	18 10 20 23 29 12 22 12 21	21 13 23 24 30 12 23 12 21	24 18 22 23 32 12 23 12 21	27 21 27 23 35 12 23 12 21
20	30 14 31 30 23 8 22 12 21	34 19 35 34 25 8 22 11 21	36 20 34 2 27 8 22 11 21	3 24 2 5 28 9 22 11 21	6 28 8 9 28 9 22 12 21	9 32 11 13 28 10 22 12 21	12 36 10 16 27 11 22 12 21	15 6 15 20 27 11 22 12 21	18 11 20 23 29 12 22 12 21	21 14 23 24 30 12 23 12 21	24 19 22 23 33 12 23 12 21	27 22 27 23 35 12 23 12 21
21	31 16 31 30 23 8 22 12 21	34 20 35 34 25 8 22 11 21	1 21 34 2 27 8 22 11 21	4 26 2 6 28 9 22 11 21	6 29 8 9 28 9 22 12 21	9 34 11 13 28 10 22 12 21	12 2 11 16 27 11 22 12 21	15 7 15 20 27 11 22 12 21	18 12 21 23 29 12 22 12 21	21 16 23 24 30 12 23 12 21	24 20 23 23 33 12 23 12 21	27 24 27 23 35 12 23 12 21
22	31 17 31 31 23 8 22 12 21	34 21 35 34 25 8 22 11 21	1 22 34 2 27 8 22 11 21	4 27 2 6 28 9 22 11 21	7 30 8 9 28 9 22 12 21	10 35 11 13 28 10 22 12 21	12 3 11 17 27 11 22 12 21	15 8 15 20 27 11 22 12 21	18 13 21 23 29 12 22 12 21	21 17 23 24 31 12 23 12 21	24 21 23 23 33 12 23 12 21	28 25 27 23 35 12 23 12 21
23	31 18 31 31 24 8 22 12 21	34 23 35 35 25 8 22 11 21	1 23 34 2 27 8 22 11 21	4 28 2 6 28 9 22 11 21	7 31 8 9 28 9 22 12 21	10 1 11 13 28 10 22 12 21	13 5 11 17 27 11 22 12 21	15 10 16 20 27 12 22 12 21	18 15 21 23 29 12 22 12 21	21 18 23 25 31 12 23 12 21	25 23 23 23 33 12 23 12 21	28 26 28 24 35 12 23 12 21
24	31 19 32 31 24 8 22 12 21	34 24 35 35 25 8 22 11 21	1 25 34 2 27 8 22 11 21	4 29 2 6 28 9 22 11 21	7 33 9 10 28 10 22 12 21	10 2 11 13 28 10 22 12 21	13 6 11 17 27 11 22 12 21	16 11 16 20 28 12 22 12 21	19 16 21 23 29 12 22 12 21	22 19 23 25 31 12 23 12 21	25 24 23 23 33 12 23 12 21	28 27 28 24 35 12 23 12 21
25	31 21 32 31 24 8 22 12 21	34 25 35 35 25 8 22 11 21	1 26 34 2 27 8 22 11 21	4 30 3 6 28 9 22 11 21	7 34 9 10 28 10 22 12 21	10 3 11 13 28 10 22 12 21	13 7 11 17 27 11 22 12 21	16 13 16 20 28 12 22 12 21	19 17 21 23 29 12 22 12 21	22 21 23 25 31 12 23 12 21	25 25 23 23 33 12 23 12 21	28 28 28 24 35 12 23 12 21
26	31 22 32 31 24 8 22 12 21	34 26 35 35 25 8 22 11 21	1 27 34 2 27 8 22 11 21	4 32 3 6 28 9 22 11 21	7 36 9 10 28 10 22 12 21	10 5 11 14 28 10 22 12 21	13 9 11 17 27 11 22 12 21	16 14 16 20 28 12 22 12 21	19 18 21 23 29 12 22 12 21	22 22 22 25 31 12 23 12 21	25 26 23 23 33 12 23 12 21	28 30 28 24 35 12 23 12 21
27	31 23 32 31 24 8 22 12 21	34 27 35 35 25 8 22 11 21	1 28 34 3 27 8 22 11 21	4 33 3 6 28 9 22 11 21	7 1 9 10 28 10 22 12 21	10 6 11 14 28 10 22 12 21	13 10 11 17 27 11 22 12 21	16 15 16 20 28 12 22 12 21	19 20 21 23 29 12 22 12 21	22 23 22 25 31 12 23 12 21	25 27 23 23 33 12 23 12 21	28 31 28 24 35 12 23 12 21
28	31 24 32 31 34 8 22 12 21	34 29 35 35 26 8 22 11 21	1 30 34 3 27 8 22 11 21	4 35 3 6 28 9 22 11 21	7 2 9 10 28 10 22 12 21	10 8 11 14 28 10 22 12 21	13 12 11 17 27 11 22 12 21	16 16 17 21 28 12 22 12 21	19 21 21 23 29 12 22 12 21	22 24 22 24 31 12 23 12 21	25 29 24 23 33 12 23 12 21	28 32 28 24 35 12 23 12 21
29	31 25 32 31 34 8 22 12 21		1 31 35 3 27 8 22 11 21	4 36 3 7 28 9 22 11 21	7 4 9 10 28 10 22 12 21	10 9 11 14 28 10 22 12 21	13 13 11 17 27 11 22 12 21	16 18 17 21 28 12 22 12 21	19 22 22 23 29 12 22 12 21	22 25 22 24 31 12 23 12 21	25 30 24 23 33 12 23 12 21	28 33 28 24 35 12 23 12 21
30	32 27 33 32 24 8 22 12 21	**1954**	1 32 35 3 27 8 22 11 21	4 2 4 7 28 9 22 11 21	7 5 9 10 28 10 22 12 21	10 11 11 14 28 10 22 12 21	13 14 11 17 27 11 22 12 21	16 19 17 21 28 12 22 12 21	19 23 22 24 29 12 22 12 21	22 27 22 24 31 12 23 12 21	25 31 24 23 33 12 23 12 21	28 35 29 24 35 12 23 12 21
31	32 28 33 32 24 8 22 12 21		2 34 35 3 27 9 22 11 21		7 7 10 10 28 10 22 12 21		13 16 11 18 27 11 22 12 21	16 20 17 21 28 12 22 12 21		22 28 22 24 31 12 23 12 21		28 36 29 24 35 12 23 12 21

	JAN	FEB	MAR	APR	MAY	JUNE	JULY	AUG	SEPT	OCT	NOV	DEC
1	29 1 29 24 36 12 23 12 21	32 7 33 27 2 12 24 12 21	35 8 32 30 4 12 24 12 21	2 13 36 34 6 12 24 12 21	5 17 6 1 8 12 23 12 21	8 21 9 5 10 12 23 12 21	10 25 9 9 12 13 23 12 21	13 29 13 13 14 13 23 12 21	16 34 19 16 16 14 23 13 21	19 1 21 20 18 15 23 13 21	22 6 21 24 20 15 24 13 21	25 10 25 28 22 16 24 13 22
2	29 3 29 24 36 12 23 12 21	32 8 33 27 2 12 24 12 21	35 9 32 30 4 12 24 12 21	2 14 36 34 6 12 24 12 21	5 18 6 1 8 12 23 12 21	8 23 9 5 10 12 23 12 21	10 26 9 9 12 13 23 12 21	13 30 13 13 14 13 23 12 21	16 35 19 16 16 14 23 13 21	19 3 21 20 18 15 23 12 21	22 8 21 24 20 15 24 13 21	25 12 25 28 22 16 24 13 22
3	29 4 29 24 36 12 23 12 21	32 10 33 27 2 12 24 12 21	35 11 32 30 4 12 24 12 21	2 16 36 34 6 12 24 12 21	5 19 6 2 8 12 23 12 21	8 24 9 5 10 12 23 12 21	11 27 9 9 12 13 23 12 21	14 32 13 13 14 13 23 12 21	16 36 19 17 16 14 23 13 21	19 4 21 20 18 15 23 13 21	23 9 21 24 20 15 24 13 21	26 13 25 28 22 16 24 13 22
4	29 6 29 24 36 12 23 12 21	32 11 33 27 2 12 24 12 21	35 12 32 30 4 12 24 12 21	2 17 36 34 6 12 24 12 21	5 20 6 2 8 12 23 12 21	8 25 9 5 10 12 23 12 21	11 28 9 9 12 13 23 12 21	14 33 14 13 14 13 23 12 21	17 2 19 17 16 14 23 13 21	20 6 21 20 18 15 23 13 21	23 11 21 24 20 15 24 13 21	26 15 26 28 22 16 24 13 22
5	29 7 30 24 36 12 23 12 21	32 12 33 27 2 12 24 12 21	35 13 32 31 4 12 24 12 21	2 18 36 34 6 12 24 12 21	5 22 6 2 8 12 23 12 21	8 26 9 6 10 12 23 12 21	11 29 9 9 12 13 23 12 21	14 34 14 13 14 13 23 12 21	17 3 19 17 16 14 23 13 21	20 7 21 21 18 15 23 13 21	23 12 21 24 20 15 24 13 21	26 16 26 28 22 16 24 13 22
6	29 9 30 25 36 12 23 12 21	32 14 33 28 2 12 24 12 21	35 15 32 31 4 12 24 12 21	2 20 36 34 6 12 24 12 21	5 23 7 2 8 12 23 12 21	8 27 9 6 10 12 23 12 21	11 31 9 9 12 13 23 12 21	14 35 14 13 14 13 23 12 21	17 5 19 17 16 14 23 13 21	20 8 21 21 18 15 23 13 21	23 14 21 25 20 15 24 13 21	26 17 26 28 22 16 24 13 22
7	29 10 30 25 36 12 23 12 21	32 15 33 28 2 12 24 12 21	35 16 32 31 4 12 24 12 21	2 21 1 34 6 12 24 12 21	5 24 7 2 8 12 23 12 21	8 28 9 6 10 12 23 12 21	11 32 9 9 12 13 23 12 21	14 1 14 13 14 13 23 12 21	17 6 19 17 16 14 23 13 21	20 10 21 21 18 15 23 13 21	23 15 21 25 20 15 24 13 21	26 19 26 28 22 16 24 13 22
8	29 12 30 25 36 12 23 12 21	32 17 33 28 2 12 24 12 21	35 17 32 31 4 11 24 12 21	2 22 1 35 6 12 23 12 21	5 25 7 2 8 12 23 12 21	8 30 9 6 10 12 23 12 21	11 33 9 10 12 13 23 12 21	14 2 14 13 14 13 23 12 21	17 7 19 17 16 14 23 13 21	20 11 21 21 18 15 23 13 21	23 16 22 25 20 15 24 13 21	26 20 26 29 22 16 24 13 22
9	29 13 30 25 36 12 23 12 21	32 18 33 28 2 12 24 12 21	35 19 33 31 4 11 24 12 21	2 23 1 35 6 12 23 12 21	5 26 7 2 8 12 23 12 21	8 31 9 6 10 12 23 12 21	11 34 9 10 12 13 23 12 21	14 3 15 13 14 13 23 12 21	17 9 20 17 16 14 23 13 21	20 13 21 21 18 15 23 13 21	23 18 22 25 20 15 24 13 21	26 21 26 29 22 16 24 13 22
10	29 14 30 25 36 12 23 12 21	33 19 33 28 2 12 24 12 21	35 20 33 31 4 11 24 12 21	2 24 1 35 6 12 23 12 21	5 28 7 2 8 12 23 12 21	8 32 9 6 11 12 23 12 21	11 36 9 10 12 13 23 12 21	14 5 15 14 14 13 23 12 21	17 10 20 17 16 14 23 13 21	20 14 21 21 18 15 23 13 21	23 19 22 25 20 15 24 13 21	26 22 27 29 22 16 24 13 22
11	30 16 31 25 36 12 23 12 21	33 20 33 28 2 12 24 12 21	36 21 33 31 4 11 24 12 21	3 26 1 35 7 12 23 12 21	6 29 7 3 9 12 23 12 21	8 33 9 6 11 12 23 12 21	11 1 9 10 13 13 23 12 21	14 6 15 14 14 13 23 12 21	17 12 20 18 16 14 23 13 21	20 15 21 21 18 15 23 13 21	23 20 22 25 20 15 24 13 21	26 24 27 29 22 16 24 13 22
12	30 17 31 25 36 12 23 12 21	33 22 33 28 3 12 24 12 21	36 22 33 31 4 11 24 12 21	3 27 2 35 7 12 23 12 21	6 30 8 3 9 12 23 12 21	9 35 9 6 11 12 23 12 21	11 2 9 10 13 13 23 12 21	14 8 15 14 15 13 23 12 21	17 13 20 18 17 14 23 13 21	20 17 21 21 18 15 23 13 21	23 22 22 25 20 15 24 13 21	26 25 27 29 22 16 24 13 22
13	30 18 31 25 36 12 23 12 21	33 23 33 28 3 12 24 12 21	36 24 33 32 5 11 24 12 21	3 28 2 35 7 12 23 12 21	6 31 8 3 9 12 23 12 21	9 36 9 7 11 13 23 12 21	12 4 9 10 13 13 23 12 21	14 9 15 14 15 13 23 12 21	17 14 20 18 17 14 23 13 21	20 18 21 22 19 15 23 13 21	24 23 22 25 20 15 24 13 21	27 26 27 29 22 16 24 13 22
14	30 20 31 25 36 12 23 12 21	33 24 33 28 3 12 24 12 21	36 25 33 32 5 11 24 12 21	3 29 2 35 7 12 23 12 21	6 32 8 3 9 12 23 12 21	9 1 9 7 11 13 23 12 21	12 5 10 10 13 13 23 12 21	15 11 15 14 15 13 23 12 21	18 16 20 18 17 14 23 13 21	21 19 20 22 19 15 23 13 21	24 24 22 26 21 15 24 13 21	27 27 27 29 23 16 24 13 22
15	30 21 31 25 1 12 23 12 21	33 25 32 29 3 12 24 12 21	36 26 33 32 5 11 24 12 21	3 30 2 35 7 12 23 12 21	6 34 8 3 9 12 23 12 21	9 3 9 7 11 13 23 12 21	12 7 10 10 13 13 23 12 21	15 12 16 14 15 13 23 12 21	18 17 20 18 17 15 23 13 21	21 21 20 22 19 15 24 13 21	24 25 23 26 21 15 24 13 21	27 28 27 29 23 16 24 13 22
16	30 22 31 25 1 12 23 12 21	33 26 32 29 3 12 24 12 21	36 27 33 32 5 11 24 12 21	3 32 2 36 7 12 23 12 21	6 35 8 3 9 12 23 12 21	9 4 9 7 11 13 23 12 21	12 8 10 11 13 13 23 12 21	15 13 16 14 15 13 23 12 21	18 18 20 18 17 15 23 13 21	21 22 20 22 19 15 24 13 21	24 26 23 26 21 15 24 13 21	27 30 28 30 23 16 24 13 22
17	30 23 32 26 1 12 23 12 21	33 28 32 29 3 12 24 12 21	36 28 33 32 5 11 24 12 21	3 33 3 36 7 12 23 12 21	6 36 8 3 9 12 23 12 21	9 6 9 7 11 13 23 12 21	12 10 10 11 13 13 23 12 21	15 15 16 14 15 13 23 12 21	18 20 21 18 17 15 23 13 21	21 23 20 22 19 15 24 13 21	24 27 23 26 21 16 24 13 21	27 31 28 30 23 16 24 13 22
18	30 24 32 26 1 12 23 12 21	33 29 32 29 3 12 24 12 21	36 30 34 32 5 11 24 12 21	3 34 3 36 7 12 23 12 21	6 2 8 3 9 12 23 12 21	9 7 9 7 11 13 23 12 21	12 11 10 11 13 13 23 12 21	15 16 16 15 15 13 23 12 21	18 21 21 18 17 15 23 13 21	21 24 20 22 19 15 24 13 21	24 29 23 26 21 16 24 13 21	27 32 28 30 23 16 24 13 22
19	30 26 32 26 1 12 23 12 21	34 30 32 29 3 12 24 12 21	36 31 34 32 5 11 24 12 21	3 36 3 36 7 12 23 12 21	6 3 8 3 9 12 23 12 21	9 9 9 7 11 13 23 12 21	12 13 10 11 13 13 23 12 21	15 18 16 15 15 13 23 12 21	18 22 21 19 17 15 23 13 21	21 25 20 22 19 15 24 13 21	24 30 23 26 21 16 24 13 21	27 33 28 30 23 16 24 13 22
20	30 27 32 26 1 12 23 12 21	34 31 32 29 3 12 24 12 21	36 32 34 32 5 11 24 12 21	3 1 3 36 7 12 23 12 21	6 5 9 4 9 12 23 12 21	9 10 9 7 11 13 23 12 21	12 14 11 11 13 13 23 12 21	15 19 17 15 15 13 23 12 21	18 23 21 19 17 15 23 13 21	21 27 20 22 19 15 24 13 21	24 31 23 26 21 16 24 13 21	27 34 28 30 23 16 24 13 22
21	31 28 32 26 1 12 23 12 21	34 33 32 29 3 12 24 12 21	1 33 34 32 5 11 24 12 21	4 3 3 36 7 12 23 12 21	6 6 9 4 9 12 23 12 21	9 12 9 7 11 13 23 12 21	12 15 11 11 13 13 23 12 21	15 20 17 15 15 13 23 12 21	18 25 21 19 17 15 23 13 21	21 28 20 23 19 15 24 13 21	24 32 24 26 21 16 24 13 21	27 36 28 30 23 16 24 13 22
22	31 29 32 26 1 12 23 12 21	34 34 32 29 3 12 24 12 21	1 36 34 33 5 11 24 12 21	4 4 4 36 7 12 23 12 21	7 8 9 4 9 12 23 12 21	10 13 9 8 11 13 23 12 21	12 17 11 11 13 13 23 12 21	15 21 17 15 15 13 23 12 21	18 26 21 19 17 15 23 13 21	21 29 20 23 19 15 24 13 21	24 34 24 27 21 16 24 13 21	27 1 28 30 23 16 24 13 22
23	31 30 33 26 1 12 24 12 21	34 35 32 29 3 12 24 12 21	1 36 34 33 5 11 24 12 21	4 6 4 36 7 12 23 12 21	7 9 9 4 9 12 23 12 21	10 15 9 8 11 13 23 12 21	12 18 11 11 13 13 23 12 21	15 23 17 15 15 13 23 12 21	18 27 21 19 17 15 23 13 21	21 30 20 23 19 15 24 13 21	25 35 24 27 21 16 24 13 21	28 2 29 30 23 16 24 13 22
24	31 32 33 26 1 12 24 12 21	34 1 32 30 3 12 24 12 21	1 2 34 33 5 11 24 12 21	4 7 4 36 7 12 23 12 21	7 11 9 4 9 12 23 12 21	10 16 9 8 11 13 23 12 21	13 19 11 12 13 13 23 12 21	16 24 17 15 15 13 23 12 21	19 28 21 19 17 15 23 13 21	22 32 20 23 19 15 24 13 21	25 36 24 27 21 16 24 13 22	28 4 29 31 23 16 24 13 22
25	31 33 33 26 1 12 24 12 21	34 2 32 30 3 12 24 12 21	1 3 35 33 5 12 24 12 21	4 9 4 1 7 12 23 12 21	7 12 9 4 9 12 23 12 21	10 17 9 8 11 13 23 12 21	13 21 11 12 13 13 23 12 21	16 25 17 15 15 13 23 13 21	19 29 21 19 17 15 23 13 21	22 33 20 23 19 15 24 13 21	25 1 24 27 21 16 24 13 22	28 5 29 31 23 16 24 13 22
26	31 34 33 26 1 12 24 12 21	34 4 32 30 4 12 24 12 21	1 5 35 33 5 12 24 12 21	4 10 4 1 8 12 23 12 21	7 14 9 4 10 12 23 12 21	10 19 9 8 12 13 23 12 21	13 22 12 12 13 13 23 12 21	16 26 18 16 15 13 23 13 21	19 31 21 19 17 15 23 13 21	22 34 20 23 19 15 24 13 21	25 3 24 27 21 16 24 13 22	28 7 29 31 23 16 24 13 22
27	31 36 33 26 1 12 24 12 21	34 5 32 30 4 12 24 12 21	1 6 35 33 6 12 24 12 21	4 11 5 1 8 12 23 12 21	7 15 9 4 10 12 23 12 21	10 20 9 8 12 13 23 12 21	13 23 12 12 14 13 23 12 21	16 27 18 16 16 13 23 13 21	19 32 21 20 17 15 23 13 21	22 35 20 23 19 15 24 13 21	25 4 25 27 21 16 24 13 22	28 8 29 31 23 16 24 13 22
28	31 1 33 27 1 12 24 12 21	34 6 32 30 4 12 24 12 21	1 8 35 33 6 12 24 12 21	4 13 5 1 8 12 23 12 21	7 16 9 5 10 12 23 12 21	10 21 9 8 12 13 23 12 21	13 24 12 12 14 13 23 12 21	16 29 18 16 16 13 23 13 21	19 33 21 20 18 15 23 13 21	22 1 20 23 19 15 24 13 21	25 6 25 27 21 16 24 13 22	28 10 29 31 23 16 24 13 22
29	31 3 33 27 2 12 24 12 21		1 9 35 33 6 12 24 12 21	4 14 5 1 8 12 23 12 21	7 18 9 5 10 12 23 12 21	10 22 9 8 12 13 23 12 21	13 26 12 12 14 13 23 12 21	16 30 18 16 16 13 23 13 21	19 35 21 20 18 15 23 13 21	22 2 20 24 20 15 24 13 21	25 7 25 27 22 16 24 13 22	28 11 30 31 23 16 24 13 22
30	31 4 33 27 2 12 24 12 21	1955	1 10 35 34 6 12 24 12 21	4 15 5 1 8 12 23 12 21	7 19 9 5 10 12 23 12 21	10 23 9 9 12 13 23 12 21	13 27 12 12 14 13 23 12 21	16 31 18 16 16 13 23 13 21	19 36 21 20 18 15 23 13 21	22 4 20 24 20 15 24 13 21	25 9 25 28 22 16 24 13 22	28 13 30 31 24 16 24 13 22
31	32 5 33 27 2 12 24 12 21		1 12 35 34 6 12 24 12 21		7 20 9 5 10 12 23 12 21		13 28 13 12 14 13 23 12 21	16 32 18 16 16 14 23 13 21		22 5 20 24 20 15 24 13 21		28 14 30 31 24 16 24 13 22

	JAN	FEB	MAR	APR	MAY	JUNE	JULY	AUG	SEPT	OCT	NOV	DEC
1	29 16 30 32 24 16 24 13 22	32 20 31 35 26 15 25 12 22	35 23 32 3 28 15 25 12 22	2 27 1 6 30 15 25 12 21	5 30 7 9 32 15 25 12 21	8 35 7 10 33 15 24 12 21	10 2 9 9 35 15 24 13 21	13 7 15 9 36 16 24 13 21	16 12 19 12 36 16 24 13 21	19 16 18 15 35 17 24 13 21	22 21 22 19 35 17 25 13 22	25 25 26 22 36 18 25 13 22
2	29 17 30 32 24 16 24 13 22	32 22 30 35 26 15 25 12 22	35 24 32 3 28 15 25 12 22	2 28 1 6 30 15 25 12 21	5 31 7 9 32 15 25 12 21	8 36 7 10 33 15 24 12 21	11 3 9 9 35 15 24 13 21	14 8 15 9 36 16 24 13 21	16 14 19 12 36 16 24 13 21	19 18 18 15 35 17 24 13 21	23 22 22 19 35 17 25 13 22	26 26 27 22 36 18 25 13 22
3	29 18 30 32 24 16 24 13 22	32 23 30 36 26 15 25 12 22	35 25 32 3 28 15 25 12 22	2 29 2 6 30 15 25 12 21	5 33 8 9 32 15 25 12 21	8 1 7 10 34 15 24 12 21	11 5 9 9 35 15 24 13 21	14 10 15 9 36 16 24 13 21	17 15 19 12 36 16 24 13 21	20 19 18 15 35 17 24 13 21	23 23 22 19 35 17 25 13 22	26 27 27 22 36 18 25 13 22
4	29 20 31 32 24 16 24 13 22	32 24 30 36 26 15 25 12 22	35 26 32 3 28 15 25 12 22	2 31 2 7 30 15 25 12 21	5 34 7 9 32 15 25 12 21	8 2 7 10 34 15 24 12 21	11 6 9 9 35 15 24 13 21	14 11 15 10 36 16 24 13 21	17 17 19 12 35 16 24 13 21	20 20 18 15 35 17 24 13 21	23 24 22 19 35 17 25 13 22	26 29 27 23 36 18 25 13 22
5	29 21 31 32 24 16 24 13 22	32 25 30 36 26 15 25 12 22	35 27 33 3 28 15 25 12 22	2 32 2 7 30 15 25 12 21	5 35 7 9 32 15 25 12 21	8 4 7 10 34 15 24 12 21	11 8 9 9 35 15 24 13 21	14 13 15 10 36 16 24 13 21	17 18 19 12 35 16 24 13 21	20 22 18 15 35 17 24 13 21	23 26 22 19 35 17 25 13 22	26 30 27 23 36 18 25 13 22
6	29 22 31 32 24 16 24 13 22	32 27 30 36 26 15 25 12 22	35 29 33 3 28 15 25 12 22	2 33 2 7 30 15 25 12 21	5 36 7 9 32 15 25 12 21	8 5 7 10 34 15 24 12 21	11 9 9 9 35 15 24 13 21	14 14 16 10 36 16 24 13 21	17 20 19 12 35 16 24 13 21	20 23 18 16 35 17 24 13 21	23 28 23 19 35 17 25 13 22	26 31 27 23 1 18 25 13 22
7	29 23 31 32 24 16 24 13 22	32 28 30 36 26 15 25 12 22	35 30 33 3 28 15 25 12 22	2 34 2 7 30 15 25 12 21	5 2 7 9 32 15 25 12 21	8 7 7 10 34 15 24 12 21	11 11 10 9 35 15 24 13 21	14 15 16 10 36 16 24 13 21	17 21 20 12 35 16 24 13 21	20 24 18 16 35 17 24 13 21	23 29 23 19 35 17 25 13 22	26 32 27 23 1 18 25 13 22
8	29 25 31 32 24 16 24 13 22	32 29 30 36 26 15 25 12 22	35 31 33 4 28 15 25 12 22	2 36 3 7 30 15 25 12 21	5 3 7 10 32 15 25 12 21	8 8 7 10 34 15 24 12 21	11 12 10 9 35 16 24 13 21	14 17 16 10 36 16 24 13 21	17 22 20 13 35 16 24 13 21	20 26 18 16 35 17 24 13 21	23 30 23 19 35 17 25 13 22	26 33 28 23 1 18 25 13 22
9	29 26 31 33 24 16 24 13 22	32 30 30 36 26 15 25 12 22	35 32 33 4 28 15 25 12 22	2 1 3 7 30 15 25 12 21	5 4 7 10 32 15 25 12 21	8 10 7 10 34 15 24 12 21	11 13 10 9 35 16 24 13 21	14 19 16 10 36 16 24 13 21	17 24 20 13 35 16 24 13 21	20 27 18 16 35 17 24 13 21	23 31 23 20 35 17 25 13 22	26 35 28 23 1 18 25 13 22
10	29 27 31 33 24 16 24 13 22	33 31 30 36 26 15 25 12 22	35 33 33 4 28 15 25 12 22	3 2 3 7 30 15 25 12 21	5 6 7 10 32 15 25 12 21	8 11 7 10 34 15 24 13 21	11 15 10 9 35 16 24 13 21	14 20 16 10 36 16 24 13 21	17 25 20 13 35 16 24 13 21	20 28 18 16 35 17 24 13 21	23 32 23 20 35 17 25 13 22	26 36 28 23 1 18 25 13 22
11	30 28 31 33 24 16 24 13 22	33 33 30 1 26 15 25 12 22	36 35 34 4 28 15 25 12 22	3 4 3 7 30 15 25 12 21	6 7 7 10 32 15 25 12 21	9 13 7 10 34 15 24 13 21	11 17 10 9 35 16 24 13 21	14 22 16 10 36 16 24 13 21	17 26 20 13 35 16 24 13 21	20 29 19 16 35 17 25 13 21	23 34 23 20 35 17 25 13 22	26 1 28 23 1 18 25 13 22
12	30 29 32 33 24 16 24 13 22	33 34 30 1 26 15 25 12 22	36 36 34 4 28 15 25 12 21	3 5 4 7 30 15 25 12 21	6 9 7 10 32 15 25 12 21	9 14 7 10 34 15 24 13 21	12 18 11 9 35 16 24 13 21	14 23 17 10 36 16 24 13 21	17 27 20 13 35 16 24 13 21	20 30 19 16 35 17 25 13 21	24 35 24 20 35 18 25 13 22	27 2 28 24 1 18 25 13 22
13	30 30 32 33 24 16 25 13 22	33 35 30 1 26 15 25 12 22	36 1 34 4 28 15 25 12 21	3 6 4 7 30 15 25 12 21	6 10 7 10 32 15 25 12 21	9 16 7 10 34 15 24 13 21	12 19 11 9 35 16 24 13 21	15 24 17 10 36 16 24 13 21	18 29 20 13 35 16 24 13 21	21 32 19 16 35 17 25 13 21	24 36 24 20 36 18 25 13 22	27 3 28 24 1 19 25 13 22
14	30 32 32 33 25 16 25 13 22	33 36 30 1 27 15 25 12 22	36 3 34 4 28 15 25 12 21	3 8 4 8 30 15 25 12 21	6 12 7 10 32 15 24 12 21	9 17 7 10 34 15 24 13 21	12 21 11 9 35 16 24 13 21	15 25 17 10 36 16 24 13 21	18 30 20 13 35 16 24 13 21	21 33 19 16 35 17 25 13 21	24 1 24 20 36 18 25 13 22	27 5 28 24 1 19 25 13 22
15	30 33 32 33 25 16 25 13 22	33 2 31 1 27 15 25 12 22	36 4 34 4 29 15 25 12 21	3 9 4 8 31 15 25 12 21	6 13 7 10 32 15 24 12 21	9 18 7 10 34 15 24 13 21	12 22 11 9 35 16 24 13 21	15 26 17 10 36 16 24 13 21	18 31 20 13 35 16 24 13 21	21 34 19 17 35 17 25 13 21	34 3 24 20 36 18 25 13 22	27 6 29 24 1 19 25 13 22
16	30 34 32 33 25 16 25 13 22	33 3 31 1 27 15 25 12 22	36 5 34 4 29 15 25 12 21	3 11 4 8 31 15 25 12 21	6 15 7 10 32 15 24 12 21	9 20 7 10 34 15 24 13 21	12 23 11 9 35 16 24 13 21	15 28 17 10 36 16 24 13 21	18 32 20 13 35 16 24 13 21	21 35 19 17 35 17 25 13 21	24 4 24 20 36 18 25 13 22	27 8 29 24 1 19 25 13 22
17	30 35 32 33 25 16 25 13 22	33 4 31 1 27 15 25 12 22	36 7 34 5 29 15 25 12 21	3 12 4 8 31 15 25 12 21	6 16 7 10 33 15 24 12 21	9 21 7 10 34 15 24 13 21	12 24 12 9 35 16 24 13 21	15 29 17 10 36 16 24 13 21	18 33 20 13 35 16 24 13 21	21 1 19 17 35 17 25 13 21	24 5 24 21 36 18 25 13 22	27 9 29 24 1 19 25 13 22
18	30 1 32 34 25 15 25 13 22	33 6 31 1 27 15 25 12 22	36 8 35 5 29 15 25 12 21	3 13 5 8 31 15 25 12 21	6 17 7 10 33 15 24 12 21	9 22 7 10 34 15 24 13 21	12 26 12 9 36 16 24 13 21	15 30 17 11 36 16 24 13 21	18 34 20 14 35 16 24 13 21	21 2 19 17 35 17 25 13 21	24 7 24 21 36 18 25 13 22	27 11 29 24 1 19 25 13 22
19	30 2 32 34 25 15 25 13 22	33 7 31 1 27 15 25 12 22	36 10 35 5 29 15 25 12 21	3 15 5 8 31 15 25 12 21	6 19 7 10 33 15 24 12 21	9 23 7 10 34 15 24 13 21	12 27 12 9 36 16 24 13 21	15 31 18 11 36 16 24 13 21	18 36 20 14 35 16 24 13 21	21 3 20 17 35 17 25 13 22	24 8 25 21 36 18 25 13 22	27 12 29 24 1 19 25 13 22
20	30 3 32 34·25 15 25 13 22	34 8 31 2 27 15 25 12 22	36 11 35 5 29 15 25 12 21	4 16 5 8 31 15 25 12 21	6 20 7 10 33 15 24 12 21	9 25 7 10 34 15 24 13 21	12 28 12 9 36 16 24 13 21	15 32 18 11 36 16 24 13 21	18 1 19 14 35 16 24 13 21	21 5 20 17 35 17 25 13 22	24 10 25 21 36 18 25 13 22	27 14 29 25 1 19 25 13 22
21	31 5 32 34 25 15 25 13 22	34 10 31 2 27 15 25 12 22	1 12 35 5 29 15 25 12 21	4 18 5 8 31 15 25 12 21	7 21 7 10 33 15 24 12 21	10 26 7 10 34 15 24 13 21	12 29 13 9 36 16 24 13 21	15 34 18 11 36 16 24 13 21	18 2 19 14 35 16 24 13 21	21 6 20 17 35 17 25 13 22	24 11 25 21 36 18 25 13 22	27 15 29 25 1 19 25 13 22
22	31 6 32 34 25 15 25 13 22	34 11 31 2 27 15 25 12 22	1 14 35 5 29 15 25 12 21	4 19 5 8 31 15 25 12 21	7 23 7 10 33 15 24 12 21	10 27 7 10 34 15 24 13 21	12 30 13 9 36 16 24 13 21	15 35 18 11 36 16 24 13 21	18 4 19 14 35 16 24 13 21	21 7 20 17 35 17 25 13 22	25 13 25 21 36 18 25 13 22	28 16 30 25 1 19 25 13 22
23	31 7 32 34 25 15 25 13 22	34 13 31 2 27 15 25 12 22	1 15 36 5 29 15 25 12 21	4 20 6 8 31 15 25 12 21	7 24 7 10 33 15 24 12 21	10 28 7 9 35 15 24 13 21	13 32 13 9 36 16 24 13 21	16 36 18 11 36 16 24 13 21	19 5 19 14 35 16 24 13 21	22 9 20 18 35 17 25 13 22	25 14 25 21 36 18 25 13 22	28 18 30 25 1 19 25 13 22
24	31 9 32 34 25 15 25 13 22	34 14 31 2 27 15 25 12 22	1 17 36 5 29 15 25 12 21	4 22 6 8 31 15 25 12 21	7 25 7 10 33 15 24 12 21	10 29 8 9 35 15 24 13 21	13 33 13 9 36 16 24 13 21	16 1 18 11 36 16 24 13 21	19 6 19 14 35 16 24 13 21	22 10 20 18 35 17 25 13 22	25 15 25 21 36 18 25 13 22	28 19 30 25 1 19 25 13 22
25	31 10 31 34 25 15 25 13 22	34 16 31 2 27 15 25 12 22	1 18 36 5 29 15 25 12 21	4 23 6 9 31 15 25 12 21	7 26 7 10 33 15 24 12 21	10 31 8 9 35 15 24 13 21	13 34 13 9 36 16 24 13 21	16 3 18 11 36 16 24 13 21	19 8 19 14 35 16 24 13 21	22 11 21 18 35 17 25 13 22	25 17 26 22 36 18 25 13 22	28 21 30 25 2 19 25 13 22
26	31 12 31 35 25 15 25 13 22	34 17 32 2 27 15 25 12 22	1 19 36 6 29 15 25 12 21	4 24 6 9 31 15 25 12 21	7 27 7 10 33 15 24 12 21	10 32 8 9 35 15 24 13 21	13 35 14 9 36 16 24 13 21	16 4 18 11 36 16 24 13 21	19 9 19 14 35 17 24 13 21	22 13 21 18 35 17 25 13 22	25 18 26 22 36 18 25 13 22	28 22 30 25 2 19 25 13 22
27	31 13 31 35 25 15 25 13 22	34 19 32 2 27 15 25 12 22	1 21 36 6 29 15 25 12 21	4 25 6 9 31 15 25 12 21	7 29 7 10 33 15 24 12 21	10 33 8 9 35 15 24 13 21	13 36 14 9 36 16 24 13 21	16 5 19 11 36 16 24 13 21	19 10 19 15 35 17 24 13 21	22 14 21 18 35 17 25 13 22	25 20 26 22 36 18 25 13 22	28 23 30 25 2 19 25 13 22
28	31 15 31 35 25 15 25 12 22	34 20 32 3 27 15 25 12 22	1 22 36 6 29 15 25 12 21	4 27 6 9 31 15 25 12 21	7 30 7 10 33 15 24 12 21	10 34 8 9 35 15 24 13 21	13 2 14 9 36 16 24 13 21	16 7 19 11 36 16 24 13 21	19 12 19 15 35 17 24 13 21	22 16 21 18 35 17 25 13 22	25 21 26 22 36 18 25 13 22	28 24 30 26 2 19 25 13 22
29	31 16 31 35 26 15 25 12 22	34 21 32 3 28 15 25 12 22	1 23 1 6 29 15 25 12 21	4 28 6 9 31 15 25 12 21	7 31 7 10 33 15 24 12 21	10 35 8 9 35 15 24 13 21	13 3 14 9 36 16 24 13 21	16 8 19 12 36 16 24 13 21	19 13 19 15 35 17 24 13 21	22 17 21 18 35 17 25 13 22	25 22 26 22 36 18 25 13 22	28 26 30 26 2 19 25 13 22
30	31 18 31 35 26 15 25 12 22	**1956**	1 25 1 6 30 15 25 12 21	5 29 7 9 31 15 25 12 21	7 32 7 10 33 15 24 12 21	10 1 8 9 35 15 24 13 21	13 4 14 9 36 16 24 13 21	16 9 19 12 36 16 24 13 21	19 15 18 15 35 17 24 13 21	22 19 21 18 35 17 25 13 22	25 24 26 22 36 18 25 13 22	28 27 30 26 2 19 25 13 22
31	32 19 31 35 26 15 25 12 22		2 26 1 6 30 15 25 12 21		7 33 7 10 33 15 24 12 21		13 6 15 9 36 16 24 13 21	16 11 19 12 36 16 24 13 21		22 20 22 18 35 17 25 13 22		28 28 30 26 2 19 25 13 22

	JAN	FEB	MAR	APR	MAY	JUNE	JULY	AUG	SEPT	OCT	NOV	DEC
1	29 29 30 26 2 19 25 13 22	32 34 29 30 4 19 26 13 22	35 35 33 33 5 18 26 13 22	2 3 3 1 7 18 26 13 22	5 7 5 5 9 18 26 13 22	8 12 5 9 11 18 26 13 22	10 16 10 13 13 18 25 13 21	13 21 16 16 15 18 25 13 21	16 26 18 20 17 19 25 13 22	19 29 18 24 19 20 25 14 22	22 34 23 27 21 20 26 14 22	25 1 27 30 23 21 26 14 22
2	29 31 30 26 2 19 25 13 22	32 35 29 30 4 19 26 13 22	35 36 33 34 6 18 26 13 22	2 5 3 1 7 18 26 13 22	5 8 5 5 9 18 26 13 22	8 13 5 9 11 18 26 13 22	11 17 10 13 13 18 25 13 21	13 23 16 16 15 18 25 13 21	16 27 18 20 17 19 25 13 22	19 31 18 24 19 20 25 14 22	22 35 23 27 21 20 26 14 22	26 2 28 30 23 21 26 14 22
3	29 32 30 26 2 19 25 13 22	32 36 29 30 4 19 26 13 22	35 1 33 34 6 18 26 13 22	2 6 3 2 8 18 26 13 22	5 9 5 5 9 18 26 13 22	8 15 5 9 11 18 26 13 22	11 19 11 13 13 18 25 13 21	14 24 16 17 15 18 25 13 21	17 29 18 20 17 19 25 13 22	20 32 18 24 19 20 25 14 22	23 36 23 27 21 20 26 14 22	26 4 28 30 23 21 26 14 22
4	29 33 30 26 2 19 25 13 22	32 1 30 30 4 19 26 13 22	35 2 34 33 5 18 26 13 22	2 7 3 2 8 18 26 13 22	5 11 5 5 9 18 26 13 22	8 16 5 9 11 18 26 13 22	11 20 11 13 13 18 25 13 21	14 25 16 17 15 18 25 13 21	17 30 18 20 17 19 25 13 22	20 33 18 24 19 20 25 14 22	23 2 23 27 21 20 26 14 22	26 5 28 30 23 21 26 14 22
5	29 34 30 27 2 19 25 13 22	32 3 30 30 4 19 26 13 22	35 4 34 33 5 18 26 13 22	2 8 4 2 8 18 26 13 22	5 12 5 6 10 18 26 13 22	8 18 6 9 11 18 26 13 22	11 21 11 13 13 18 25 13 21	14 26 16 17 15 18 25 13 21	17 31 18 20 17 19 25 13 22	20 34 18 24 19 20 25 14 22	23 3 24 27 21 20 26 14 22	26 6 28 30 23 21 26 14 22
6	29 35 30 27 2 19 25 13 22	32 4 30 31 4 19 26 13 22	35 5 34 33 5 18 26 13 22	2 10 4 2 8 18 26 13 22	5 14 5 6 10 18 26 13 22	8 19 6 9 12 18 26 13 22	11 22 11 13 13 18 25 13 21	14 28 17 17 15 18 25 13 22	17 32 18 21 17 19 25 13 22	20 35 19 24 19 20 26 14 22	23 4 24 28 21 20 26 14 22	26 7 28 30 23 21 26 14 22
7	29 36 30 27 2 19 26 13 22	32 5 30 31 4 19 26 13 22	35 6 34 33 5 18 26 13 22	2 11 4 2 8 18 26 13 22	5 15 5 6 10 18 26 13 22	8 20 6 10 12 18 26 13 22	11 23 11 13 14 18 25 13 21	14 29 17 17 15 19 25 13 22	17 33 17 21 17 19 25 13 22	20 1 19 24 19 20 26 14 22	23 5 24 28 21 20 26 14 22	26 9 28 31 23 21 26 14 22
8	29 2 30 27 2 19 26 13 22	32 6 30 31 4 19 26 13 22	35 7 34 33 5 18 26 13 22	2 13 4 2 8 18 26 13 22	5 17 5 6 10 18 26 13 22	8 22 6 10 12 18 26 13 22	11 25 12 13 14 18 25 13 21	14 30 17 17 16 19 25 13 22	17 35 17 21 17 19 25 13 22	20 2 19 24 19 20 26 14 22	23 6 24 28 21 20 26 14 22	26 10 28 31 24 21 26 14 22
9	29 3 29 27 2 19 26 13 22	33 8 30 31 4 19 26 13 22	35 9 34 33 5 18 26 13 22	2 14 4 2 8 18 26 13 22	5 18 5 6 10 18 26 13 22	8 23 6 10 12 18 26 13 22	11 27 12 13 14 18 25 13 21	14 31 17 17 16 19 25 13 22	17 36 17 21 18 19 25 13 22	20 3 19 24 19 20 26 14 22	23 8 24 28 22 20 26 14 22	26 11 28 31 24 21 26 14 22
10	30 4 29 27 2 19 26 13 22	33 9 30 31 4 19 26 13 22	35 10 35 35 6 18 26 13 22	3 15 4 2 8 18 26 13 22	5 19 5 6 10 18 26 13 22	8 24 6 10 12 18 26 13 22	11 28 12 14 14 18 25 13 21	14 33 17 17 16 19 25 13 22	17 1 17 21 18 19 25 13 22	20 4 19 25 20 20 26 14 22	23 9 24 28 22 20 26 14 22	26 13 28 31 24 21 26 14 22
11	30 6 29 27 2 19 26 13 22	33 11 30 31 4 19 26 13 22	36 12 35 35 6 18 26 13 22	3 17 5 3 8 18 26 13 22	6 21 5 6 10 18 26 13 22	9 26 6 10 12 18 26 13 22	11 29 12 14 14 18 25 13 21	14 34 17 17 16 19 25 13 22	17 2 17 21 18 19 25 13 22	20 6 19 25 20 20 26 14 22	23 10 24 28 22 20 26 14 22	26 14 28 31 24 21 26 14 22
12	30 7 29 27 3 19 26 13 22	33 12 30 31 4 19 26 13 22	36 13 35 35 6 18 26 13 22	3 18 5 3 8 18 26 13 22	6 22 5 6 10 18 26 13 22	9 27 7 10 12 18 26 13 22	11 30 12 14 14 18 25 13 21	14 35 17 18 16 19 25 13 22	17 3 17 21 18 19 25 13 22	20 7 20 25 20 20 26 14 22	23 12 25 28 22 21 26 14 22	27 16 29 31 24 21 26 14 22
13	30 8 29 28 3 19 26 13 22	33 14 31 31 4 19 26 13 22	36 15 35 35 6 18 26 13 22	3 20 5 3 8 18 26 13 22	6 24 5 7 10 18 26 13 22	9 28 7 10 12 18 26 13 22	12 32 13 14 14 18 25 13 21	15 36 17 18 16 19 25 13 22	18 5 17 21 18 19 25 13 22	20 8 20 25 20 20 26 14 22	24 13 25 28 22 21 26 14 22	27 17 29 31 24 21 26 14 22
14	30 10 29 28 3 19 26 13 22	33 15 31 32 5 19 26 13 22	36 16 35 35 6 18 26 13 22	3 21 5 3 8 18 26 13 22	6 25 5 7 10 18 26 13 22	9 30 7 10 12 18 26 13 22	12 33 13 14 14 18 25 13 21	15 1 17 18 16 19 25 13 22	18 6 17 22 18 19 25 13 22	21 9 20 25 20 20 26 14 22	24 15 25 28 22 21 26 14 22	27 18 29 31 24 21 26 14 22
15	30 11 29 28 3 19 26 13 22	33 17 31 32 5 19 26 13 22	36 18 35 35 6 18 26 13 22	3 23 5 3 8 18 26 13 22	6 26 5 7 10 18 26 13 22	9 31 7 11 12 18 26 13 22	12 34 13 14 14 18 25 13 21	15 2 17 18 16 19 25 13 22	18 7 17 22 18 19 25 13 22	21 11 20 25 20 20 26 14 22	24 16 25 29 22 21 26 14 22	27 20 29 31 24 21 26 14 22
16	30 13 29 28 3 19 26 13 22	33 18 31 32 5 19 26 13 22	36 19 36 35 6 18 26 13 22	3 24 5 3 8 18 26 13 22	6 28 5 7 10 18 26 13 22	9 32 7 11 12 18 25 13 22	12 35 13 14 14 18 25 13 21	15 4 18 18 16 19 25 13 22	18 8 17 22 18 19 25 13 22	21 12 20 25 20 20 26 14 22	24 17 25 29 22 21 26 14 22	27 21 29 31 24 21 26 14 22
17	30 14 29 28 3 19 26 13 22	33 20 31 32 5 19 26 13 22	36 21 36 35 6 18 26 13 22	3 25 5 3 8 18 26 13 22	6 29 5 7 10 18 26 13 22	9 33 7 11 12 18 25 13 21	12 36 13 14 14 18 25 13 21	15 5 18 18 16 19 25 13 22	18 10 17 22 18 19 25 14 22	21 13 20 25 20 20 26 14 22	24 19 25 29 22 21 26 14 22	27 23 29 31 24 21 26 14 22
18	30 16 29 28 3 19 26 13 22	33 21 31 32 5 19 26 13 22	36 22 36 36 7 18 26 13 22	3 27 5 3 8 18 26 13 22	6 30 5 7 10 18 26 13 22	9 34 7 11 12 18 25 13 21	12 2 14 15 14 18 25 13 21	15 6 18 18 16 19 25 13 22	18 11 17 22 18 19 25 14 22	21 15 21 25 20 20 26 14 22	24 20 26 29 22 21 26 14 22	27 24 29 31 24 21 26 14 22
19	30 17 29 28 3 19 26 13 22	34 22 31 32 5 19 26 13 22	36 23 36 36 7 18 26 13 22	3 28 5 4 9 18 26 13 22	6 31 5 7 10 18 26 13 22	9 36 8 11 12 18 25 13 21	12 3 14 15 14 18 25 13 21	15 7 18 18 16 19 25 13 22	18 13 17 22 18 19 25 14 22	21 16 21 26 20 20 26 14 22	24 22 26 29 22 21 26 14 22	27 25 29 31 24 21 26 14 22
20	31 19 29 28 3 19 26 13 22	34 24 32 32 5 18 26 13 22	36 25 36 36 7 18 26 13 22	4 29 5 4 9 18 26 13 22	6 32 5 7 10 18 26 13 22	9 1 8 11 12 18 25 13 21	12 4 14 15 14 18 25 13 21	15 9 18 19 16 19 25 13 22	18 14 17 22 18 19 25 14 22	21 18 21 26 20 20 26 14 22	24 23 26 29 22 21 26 14 22	27 27 28 32 24 21 26 14 22
21	31 20 29 29 3 19 26 13 22	34 25 32 32 5 18 26 13 22	1 26 1 36 7 18 26 13 22	4 30 5 4 9 18 26 13 22	7 34 5 7 11 18 26 13 22	9 2 8 11 13 18 25 13 21	12 5 14 15 14 18 25 13 21	15 10 18 19 16 19 25 13 22	18 16 17 22 18 19 25 14 22	21 19 21 26 20 20 26 14 22	24 25 26 29 22 21 26 14 22	27 28 28 32 24 21 26 14 22
22	31 22 29 29 3 19 26 13 22	34 26 32 33 5 18 26 13 22	1 27 1 36 7 18 26 13 22	4 32 5 4 9 18 26 13 22	7 35 5 8 11 18 26 13 22	10 3 8 11 13 18 25 13 21	12 7 14 15 14 18 25 13 21	15 12 18 19 16 19 25 13 22	18 17 17 22 18 19 25 14 22	21 21 21 26 20 20 26 14 22	24 26 26 29 22 21 26 14 22	28 29 28 32 24 21 26 14 22
23	31 23 29 29 3 19 26 13 22	34 28 32 33 5 18 26 13 22	1 28 1 36 7 18 26 13 22	4 33 5 4 9 18 26 13 22	7 36 5 8 11 18 26 13 22	10 4 8 12 13 18 25 13 21	13 8 14 15 15 18 25 13 21	16 13 18 19 16 19 25 13 22	19 19 17 23 18 19 25 14 22	21 22 21 26 20 20 26 14 22	25 27 26 29 22 21 26 14 22	28 31 28 32 25 21 26 14 22
24	31 24 29 29 3 19 26 13 22	34 29 32 33 5 18 26 13 22	1 30 1 36 7 18 26 13 22	4 34 5 4 9 18 26 13 22	7 1 5 8 11 18 26 13 22	10 6 9 12 13 18 25 13 21	13 9 15 15 15 18 25 13 21	16 15 18 19 17 19 25 13 22	19 20 17 23 19 19 25 14 22	22 24 22 26 20 20 26 14 22	25 29 26 29 23 21 26 14 22	28 32 28 32 25 21 26 14 22
25	31 25 29 29 3 19 26 13 22	34 30 32 33 5 18 26 13 22	1 31 1 36 7 18 26 13 22	4 35 5 4 9 18 26 13 22	7 2 5 8 11 18 26 13 22	10 7 9 12 13 18 25 13 21	13 11 15 15 15 18 25 13 21	16 16 18 19 17 19 25 13 22	19 22 17 23 19 19 25 14 22	22 25 22 26 21 20 26 14 22	25 30 27 29 23 21 26 14 22	28 33 28 32 25 21 26 14 22
26	31 27 29 29 3 19 26 13 22	34 31 33 33 5 18 26 13 22	1 32 2 1 7 18 26 13 22	4 36 5 4 9 18 26 13 22	7 4 5 8 11 18 26 13 22	10 9 9 12 13 18 25 13 21	13 12 15 16 15 18 25 13 21	16 18 18 19 17 19 25 13 22	19 23 17 23 19 20 25 14 22	22 27 22 26 21 20 26 14 22	25 31 27 30 23 21 26 14 22	28 34 28 32 25 21 26 14 22
27	31 28 29 29 3 19 26 13 22	34 32 33 33 5 18 26 13 22	1 33 2 1 7 18 26 13 22	4 2 5 5 9 18 26 13 22	7 5 5 8 11 18 26 13 22	10 10 9 12 13 18 25 13 21	13 14 15 16 15 18 25 13 21	16 19 18 19 17 19 25 13 22	19 24 17 23 19 20 25 14 22	22 28 22 26 21 20 26 14 22	25 32 27 30 23 21 26 14 22	28 36 28 32 25 21 26 14 22
28	31 29 29 29 3 19 26 13 22	34 33 33 33 5 18 26 13 22	1 34 2 1 7 18 26 13 22	4 3 5 5 9 18 26 13 22	7 6 5 8 11 18 26 13 22	10 11 9 12 13 18 25 13 21	13 15 15 16 15 18 25 13 21	16 21 18 20 17 19 25 13 22	19 26 17 23 19 20 25 14 22	22 29 22 27 21 20 26 14 22	25 34 27 30 23 21 26 14 22	28 1 28 32 25 21 26 14 22
29	31 30 29 30 4 19 26 13 22	**1957**	1 36 2 1 7 18 26 13 22	4 4 5 5 9 18 26 13 22	7 8 5 8 11 18 26 13 22	10 13 10 12 13 18 25 13 21	13 17 15 16 15 18 25 13 21	16 22 18 20 17 19 25 13 22	19 27 17 23 19 20 25 14 22	22 30 22 27 21 20 26 14 22	25 35 27 30 23 21 26 14 22	28 2 27 32 25 21 26 14 22
30	32 31 29 30 4 19 26 13 22		1 1 2 1 7 18 26 13 22	4 5 5 5 9 18 26 13 22	7 9 5 9 11 18 26 13 22	10 14 10 12 13 18 25 13 21	13 18 16 16 15 18 25 13 21	16 23 18 20 17 19 25 13 22	19 28 18 23 19 20 25 14 22	22 32 23 27 21 20 26 14 22	25 36 27 30 23 21 26 14 22	28 3 27 32 25 21 26 14 22
31	32 33 29 30 4 19 26 13 22		2 2 3 1 7 18 26 13 22		7 10 5 9 11 18 26 13 22		13 20 16 16 15 18 25 13 21	16 25 18 20 17 19 25 13 22		22 33 23 27 21 20 26 14 22		28 4 27 32 25 21 26 14 22

	JAN	FEB	MAR	APR	MAY	JUNE	JULY	AUG	SEPT	OCT	NOV	DEC
1	29 6 27 32 25 21 26 14 22	32 10 30 31 27 22 27 13 22	35 11 34 31 29 22 27 13 22	2 16 3 33 32 21 27 13 22	5 20 3 36 34 21 27 13 22	8 25 6 4 36 21 27 13 22	10 29 12 7 2 21 27 13 22	13 34 16 11 4 21 26 14 22	16 2 15 15 6 21 26 14 22	19 5 19 18 7 22 26 14 22	22 10 24 22 6 23 27 14 22	25 14 27 26 5 23 27 14 22
2	29 7 27 32 25 21 26 14 22	32 12 30 31 27 22 27 13 22	35 13 35 31 29 22 27 13 22	2 18 3 33 32 21 27 13 22	5 22 3 36 34 21 27 13 22	8 27 6 4 36 21 27 13 22	11 30 12 7 2 21 27 13 22	13 35 16 11 4 21 26 14 22	16 3 15 15 6 21 26 14 22	19 7 19 18 7 22 26 14 22	22 11 24 22 6 23 27 14 22	25 15 27 26 5 23 27 14 22
3	29 8 27 32 25 21 26 14 22	32 13 30 31 27 22 27 13 22	35 14 35 31 29 22 27 13 22	2 19 4 33 32 21 27 13 22	5 23 3 36 34 21 27 13 22	8 28 6 4 36 21 27 13 22	11 32 12 7 2 21 27 14 22	14 36 16 11 4 21 26 14 22	17 5 15 15 6 21 26 14 22	19 8 19 18 7 22 26 14 22	23 13 24 22 6 23 27 14 22	26 16 27 26 5 23 27 14 22
4	29 10 27 32 25 21 26 14 22	32 15 30 31 28 22 27 13 22	35 15 35 31 30 22 27 13 22	2 21 4 33 32 21 27 13 22	5 25 3 36 34 21 27 13 22	8 30 6 4 36 21 27 13 22	11 33 12 7 2 21 27 14 22	14 1 16 11 4 21 26 14 22	17 6 15 15 6 21 26 14 22	20 9 19 19 7 22 26 14 22	23 14 24 22 6 23 27 14 22	26 18 27 26 5 23 27 14 22
5	29 11 27 32 25 21 26 14 22	32 16 30 31 28 22 27 13 22	35 17 35 31 30 22 27 13 22	2 22 4 33 32 21 27 13 22	5 26 3 1 34 21 27 13 22	8 31 6 4 36 21 27 13 22	11 34 13 8 2 21 27 14 22	14 3 16 11 4 21 26 14 22	17 7 15 15 6 21 26 14 22	20 10 20 19 7 22 26 14 22	23 15 25 23 6 23 27 14 22	26 19 27 26 5 23 27 14 22
6	29 12 27 32 26 21 27 14 22	32 18 30 31 28 22 27 13 22	35 19 35 31 30 22 27 13 22	2 24 4 33 32 21 27 13 22	5 27 3 1 34 21 27 13 22	8 32 7 4 36 21 27 13 22	11 35 13 8 3 21 27 14 22	14 4 16 11 4 21 26 14 22	17 8 15 15 6 21 26 14 22	20 12 20 19 7 22 26 14 22	23 17 25 23 6 23 27 14 22	26 21 27 27 5 23 27 14 22
7	29 14 27 32 26 21 27 14 22	32 19 31 31 28 22 27 13 22	35 20 35 31 30 22 27 13 22	2 25 4 34 32 21 27 13 22	5 29 3 1 34 21 27 13 22	8 33 7 4 1 21 27 13 22	11 1 13 8 3 21 27 14 22	14 5 16 11 5 21 26 14 22	17 10 15 15 6 22 26 14 22	20 13 20 19 7 22 26 14 22	23 18 25 23 6 23 27 14 22	26 22 27 27 5 23 27 14 22
8	29 15 27 32 26 21 27 14 22	32 21 31 31 28 22 27 13 22	35 22 36 31 30 22 27 13 22	2 27 4 34 32 21 27 13 22	5 30 3 1 34 21 27 13 22	8 35 7 4 1 21 27 13 22	11 2 13 8 3 21 27 14 22	14 6 16 12 5 21 26 14 22	17 11 15 15 6 22 26 14 22	20 14 20 19 7 22 26 14 22	23 20 25 23 6 23 27 14 22	26 23 26 27 5 23 27 14 22
9	29 17 27 32 26 21 27 14 22	33 22 31 31 28 22 27 13 22	35 23 36 31 30 22 27 13 22	2 28 4 34 32 21 27 13 22	5 31 3 1 34 21 27 13 22	8 36 7 4 1 21 27 13 22	11 3 13 8 3 21 27 14 22	14 7 16 12 5 21 26 14 22	17 12 15 15 6 22 26 14 22	20 16 20 19 7 22 26 14 22	23 21 25 23 6 23 27 14 22	26 25 26 27 5 23 27 14 22
10	29 18 23 32 26 21 27 14 22	33 23 31 31 28 22 27 13 22	36 24 36 31 30 22 27 13 22	3 29 4 34 32 21 27 13 22	5 33 3 1 34 21 27 13 22	8 1 7 5 1 21 27 13 22	11 4 13 8 3 21 27 14 22	14 9 16 12 5 21 26 14 22	17 13 15 16 6 22 26 14 22	20 17 21 19 7 22 26 14 22	23 23 25 23 6 23 27 14 22	26 26 26 27 5 23 27 14 22
11	30 20 27 32 26 21 27 14 22	33 25 31 31 28 22 27 13 22	36 26 36 31 30 22 27 13 22	3 31 3 34 32 21 27 13 22	6 34 3 1 35 21 27 13 22	9 2 8 5 1 21 27 13 22	11 5 14 8 3 21 27 14 22	14 10 16 12 5 21 26 14 22	17 15 16 16 6 22 26 14 22	20 19 21 19 7 22 26 14 22	23 24 25 23 6 23 27 14 22	26 28 26 27 5 23 27 14 22
12	30 21 27 32 26 21 27 14 22	33 26 31 31 28 22 27 13 22	36 27 1 31 30 22 27 13 22	3 32 3 34 32 21 27 13 22	6 35 3 1 35 21 27 13 22	9 3 8 5 1 21 27 13 22	11 7 14 8 3 21 27 14 22	14 11 16 12 5 21 26 14 22	17 16 16 16 6 22 26 14 22	20 20 21 20 7 22 26 14 22	23 26 26 23 6 23 27 14 22	26 29 26 27 5 24 27 14 22
13	30 22 27 32 26 21 27 14 22	33 27 32 31 28 22 27 13 22	36 28 1 31 20 22 27 13 22	3 33 3 34 32 21 27 13 22	6 36 3 1 35 21 27 13 22	9 5 8 5 1 21 27 13 22	12 8 14 8 3 21 27 14 22	15 13 16 12 5 21 26 14 22	18 18 16 16 6 22 26 14 22	20 22 21 20 7 22 26 14 22	24 27 26 24 6 23 27 14 22	27 31 26 27 5 24 27 14 22
14	30 24 27 32 26 22 27 14 22	33 29 32 31 28 22 27 13 22	36 30 1 32 30 22 27 13 22	3 34 3 34 33 21 27 13 22	6 1 3 1 35 21 27 13 22	9 6 8 5 1 21 27 13 22	12 9 14 9 3 21 27 14 22	15 14 16 12 5 21 26 14 22	18 19 16 16 6 22 26 14 22	21 23 21 20 7 22 26 14 22	24 29 26 24 6 23 27 14 22	27 32 26 28 5 24 27 14 22
15	30 25 28 32 26 22 27 14 22	33 30 32 31 28 22 27 13 22	36 31 1 32 30 22 27 13 22	3 35 3 34 33 21 27 13 22	6 3 3 2 35 21 27 13 22	9 7 9 5 1 21 27 13 22	12 10 14 9 3 21 27 14 22	15 16 16 12 5 21 26 14 22	18 21 16 16 6 22 26 14 22	21 25 21 20 7 22 26 14 22	24 30 26 24 6 23 27 14 22	27 33 26 28 5 24 27 14 22
16	30 26 28 32 26 22 27 14 22	33 31 32 31 28 22 27 13 22	36 32 1 32 30 22 27 13 22	3 1 3 34 33 21 27 13 22	6 4 3 2 35 21 27 13 22	9 8 9 5 1 21 27 13 22	12 12 14 9 3 21 27 14 22	15 17 16 13 5 21 26 14 22	18 22 16 16 6 22 26 14 22	21 26 22 20 7 22 26 14 22	24 31 26 24 6 23 27 14 22	27 35 26 28 5 24 27 14 22
17	30 28 28 32 26 22 27 14 22	33 32 32 31 28 22 27 13 22	36 33 1 32 31 22 27 13 22	3 2 3 35 33 21 27 13 22	6 5 4 2 35 21 27 13 22	9 10 9 5 1 21 27 13 22	12 13 14 9 3 21 27 14 22	15 19 16 13 5 21 26 14 22	18 24 16 16 6 22 26 14 22	21 28 22 20 7 22 26 14 22	24 32 26 24 6 23 27 14 22	27 36 25 28 5 24 27 14 22
18	30 29 28 32 26 22 27 14 22	33 34 32 31 29 22 27 13 22	36 35 2 32 31 22 27 13 22	3 3 3 35 33 21 27 13 22	6 6 4 2 35 21 27 13 22	9 11 9 6 1 21 27 13 22	12 15 15 9 3 21 27 14 22	15 20 16 13 5 21 26 14 22	18 25 17 17 6 22 26 14 22	21 29 22 20 7 22 26 14 22	24 34 26 24 6 23 27 14 22	27 1 25 28 5 24 27 14 22
19	30 30 28 32 26 22 27 14 22	34 35 33 31 29 22 27 13 22	36 36 2 32 21 22 27 13 22	3 4 3 35 33 21 27 13 22	6 7 4 2 35 21 27 13 22	9 12 9 6 1 21 27 13 22	12 16 15 9 3 21 27 14 22	15 21 16 13 5 21 26 14 22	18 27 17 17 6 22 26 14 22	21 30 22 20 7 22 26 14 22	24 35 26 24 6 23 27 14 22	27 2 25 28 5 24 27 14 22
20	30 31 28 32 26 22 27 14 22	34 36 33 31 29 22 27 13 22	36 1 2 32 31 22 27 13 22	3 5 3 35 33 21 27 13 22	6 9 4 2 35 21 27 13 22	9 14 10 6 1 21 27 13 22	12 18 15 9 3 21 27 14 22	15 23 16 13 5 21 26 14 22	18 28 17 17 6 22 26 14 22	21 32 22 21 7 22 26 14 22	24 36 25 24 6 23 27 14 22	27 3 25 28 5 24 27 14 22
21	31 33 28 32 27 22 27 13 22	34 1 33 31 29 22 27 13 22	1 2 2 32 31 21 27 13 22	4 7 3 35 33 21 27 13 22	6 10 4 2 35 21 27 13 22	10 15 10 6 2 21 27 13 22	12 19 15 9 4 21 26 14 22	15 24 16 13 5 21 26 14 22	18 29 17 17 7 22 26 14 22	21 33 22 21 7 22 26 14 22	24 1 27 25 6 23 27 14 22	27 4 25 28 5 24 27 14 22
22	31 34 28 32 27 22 27 13 22	34 2 33 31 29 22 27 13 22	1 3 2 32 31 21 27 13 22	4 8 3 35 33 21 27 13 22	7 11 4 2 35 21 27 13 22	10 16 10 6 2 21 27 13 22	12 20 15 10 4 21 26 14 22	15 26 16 13 5 21 26 14 22	18 31 17 17 7 22 26 14 22	21 34 22 21 7 22 26 14 22	24 2 27 25 6 23 27 14 22	28 6 25 29 5 24 27 14 22
23	31 35 29 32 27 22 27 13 22	34 3 33 31 29 22 27 13 22	1 4 2 32 31 21 27 13 22	4 9 3 35 33 21 27 13 22	7 13 4 3 35 21 27 13 22	10 18 10 6 2 21 27 13 22	13 22 15 10 4 21 26 14 22	15 27 15 13 5 21 26 14 22	18 32 18 17 7 22 26 14 22	21 35 23 21 7 22 26 14 22	25 4 27 25 6 23 27 14 22	28 7 26 29 5 24 27 14 22
24	31 36 29 32 27 22 27 13 22	34 5 33 31 29 22 27 13 22	1 6 3 32 31 21 27 13 22	4 10 3 35 33 21 27 13 22	7 14 4 3 36 21 27 13 22	10 19 10 6 2 21 27 13 22	13 23 15 10 4 21 26 14 22	16 28 15 14 5 21 26 14 22	19 33 18 17 7 22 26 14 22	22 36 23 21 7 22 26 14 22	25 5 27 25 6 23 27 14 22	28 8 26 29 5 24 27 14 22
25	31 2 29 32 27 22 27 13 22	34 6 34 31 29 22 27 13 22	1 7 3 32 31 21 27 13 22	4 12 3 35 33 21 27 13 22	7 15 5 3 36 21 27 13 22	10 21 11 6 2 21 27 13 22	13 25 15 10 4 21 26 14 22	16 30 15 14 5 21 26 14 22	19 34 18 17 7 22 26 14 22	22 2 23 21 7 22 26 14 22	25 6 27 25 6 23 27 14 22	28 9 26 29 5 24 27 14 22
26	31 3 29 32 27 22 27 13 22	34 7 34 31 29 22 27 13 22	1 8 3 32 31 21 27 13 22	4 13 3 36 33 21 27 13 22	7 17 5 3 36 21 27 13 22	10 22 11 6 2 21 27 13 22	13 26 16 10 4 21 26 14 22	15 31 15 14 6 21 26 14 22	19 36 18 18 7 22 26 14 22	22 3 23 21 7 23 26 14 22	25 7 27 25 6 23 27 14 22	28 11 26 29 5 24 27 14 22
27	31 4 29 31 27 22 27 13 22	34 8 34 31 29 22 27 13 22	1 9 3 33 31 21 27 13 22	4 14 3 36 34 21 27 13 22	7 18 5 3 36 21 27 13 22	10 24 11 7 2 21 27 13 22	13 27 16 10 4 21 26 14 22	16 32 15 14 6 21 26 14 22	19 1 18 18 7 22 27 14 22	22 4 23 21 7 23 26 14 22	25 8 27 25 6 23 27 14 22	28 12 26 29 5 24 27 14 22
28	31 5 29 31 27 22 27 13 22	34 10 34 31 29 22 27 13 22	1 11 3 33 31 21 27 13 22	4 16 3 36 34 21 27 13 22	7 20 5 3 36 21 27 13 22	10 25 11 7 2 21 27 13 22	13 29 16 10 4 21 26 14 22	16 33 15 14 6 21 26 14 22	19 2 18 18 7 22 27 14 22	22 5 23 22 7 23 26 14 22	25 10 27 26 5 23 27 14 22	28 13 26 29 5 24 27 14 22
29	31 6 29 31 27 22 27 13 22	**1958**	1 12 3 33 31 21 27 13 22	4 17 3 36 34 21 27 13 22	7 21 5 3 36 21 27 13 22	10 26 11 7 2 21 27 13 22	13 30 16 10 4 21 26 14 22	16 35 15 14 6 21 26 14 22	19 3 19 18 7 22 27 14 22	22 6 24 26 6 23 26 14 22	25 11 27 26 5 23 27 14 22	28 15 26 29 5 24 27 14 22
30	32 8 29 31 27 22 27 13 22		1 13 3 33 31 21 27 13 22	4 19 3 36 34 21 27 13 22	7 23 5 3 36 21 27 13 22	10 28 12 7 2 21 27 13 22	13 31 16 11 4 21 26 14 22	16 36 15 14 6 21 26 14 22	19 4 19 18 7 22 27 14 22	22 8 24 26 6 23 26 14 22	25 13 27 26 5 23 27 14 22	28 16 26 30 5 24 27 14 22
31	32 9 30 31 27 22 27 13 22		2 15 3 33 32 21 27 13 22		7 24 6 3 36 21 27 13 22		13 33 16 11 4 21 26 14 22	16 1 15 14 6 21 26 14 22		22 9 24 26 6 23 26 14 22		28 17 26 30 5 24 27 14 22

	JAN	FEB	MAR	APR	MAY	JUNE	JULY	AUG	SEPT	OCT	NOV	DEC
1	29 19 26 30 5 24 27 14 22	32 24 31 34 6 24 28 14 22	35 25 36 1 7 25 28 14 22	2 30 1 5 9 25 28 14 22	5 34 2 8 11 24 28 14 22	8 2 7 12 13 24 28 14 22	10 6 13 15 14 24 28 14 22	13 10 14 17 16 24 28 14 22	16 15 15 16 18 24 28 14 22	19 18 20 16 20 24 28 14 22	22 24 25 18 22 25 28 15 22	25 27 24 21 24 26 28 15 22
2	29 20 26 30 5 24 27 14 22	32 25 31 34 6 24 28 14 22	35 27 36 1 7 25 28 14 22	2 32 1 5 9 25 28 14 22	5 35 2 9 11 24 28 14 22	8 4 8 12 13 24 28 14 22	10 7 13 15 14 24 28 14 22	13 11 14 17 16 24 28 14 22	16 16 15 16 18 24 28 14 22	19 20 20 16 20 24 28 14 22	22 25 25 18 22 25 28 15 22	25 29 24 21 24 26 28 15 22
3	29 22 27 30 5 24 27 14 22	32 27 31 34 6 24 28 14 22	35 28 36 1 7 25 28 14 22	2 33 1 5 9 25 28 14 22	5 36 2 9 11 24 28 14 22	8 5 8 12 13 24 28 14 22	11 8 13 15 14 24 28 14 22	13 13 14 17 16 24 28 14 22	17 17 15 16 18 24 28 14 22	19 21 21 16 20 24 28 14 22	23 27 25 18 22 25 28 15 22	26 30 24 21 24 26 28 15 22
4	29 23 27 30 5 24 27 14 22	32 28 31 34 6 24 28 14 22	35 29 36 1 8 25 28 14 22	2 34 1 5 9 25 28 14 22	5 2 2 9 11 24 28 14 22	8 6 8 12 13 24 28 14 22	11 9 13 15 15 24 28 14 22	14 14 14 17 16 24 28 14 22	17 19 15 16 18 24 28 14 22	20 23 21 16 20 24 28 14 22	23 28 25 18 22 25 28 15 22	26 32 24 21 25 26 28 15 22
5	29 25 27 30 5 24 28 14 22	32 29 31 34 6 24 28 14 22	35 31 1 2 8 25 28 14 22	2 35 1 5 9 25 28 14 22	5 3 2 9 11 24 28 14 22	8 7 8 12 13 24 28 14 22	11 10 13 15 15 24 28 14 22	14 15 14 17 16 24 28 14 22	17 20 16 16 18 24 28 14 22	20 24 21 16 20 24 28 14 22	23 29 25 18 23 25 28 15 22	26 33 24 21 25 26 28 15 22
6	29 26 27 30 5 24 28 14 22	32 31 32 34 6 24 28 14 22	35 32 1 2 8 25 28 14 22	2 1 1 6 9 25 28 14 22	5 4 3 8 11 24 28 14 22	8 8 8 12 13 24 28 14 22	11 12 13 15 15 24 28 14 22	14 17 14 17 17 24 28 14 22	17 22 16 16 19 24 28 14 22	20 26 21 16 21 25 28 14 22	23 31 25 18 23 25 28 15 22	26 34 24 21 25 26 28 15 22
7	29 27 27 31 5 24 28 14 22	32 32 32 34 6 24 28 14 22	35 33 1 2 8 25 28 14 22	2 2 1 6 9 25 28 14 22	5 5 3 8 11 24 28 14 22	8 10 9 13 13 24 28 14 22	11 13 14 15 14 24 28 14 22	14 18 14 17 17 24 28 14 22	17 23 16 16 19 24 28 14 22	20 27 21 16 21 25 28 14 22	23 32 25 18 23 25 28 15 22	26 36 24 21 25 26 28 15 22
8	29 29 27 31 5 24 28 14 22	32 34 32 35 6 24 28 14 22	35 34 1 2 8 25 28 14 22	2 3 1 6 9 25 28 14 22	5 6 3 8 11 24 28 14 22	8 11 9 13 13 24 28 14 22	11 14 14 15 14 24 28 14 22	14 19 14 17 17 24 28 14 22	17 25 16 16 19 24 28 14 22	20 28 21 16 21 25 28 14 22	23 34 25 18 23 25 28 15 22	26 1 24 22 25 26 28 15 22
9	29 30 27 31 5 24 28 14 22	32 35 32 35 6 24 28 14 22	35 36 1 2 8 25 28 14 22	2 4 1 6 9 25 28 14 22	5 7 3 8 11 24 28 14 22	8 12 9 13 13 24 28 14 22	11 16 14 16 15 24 28 14 22	14 21 13 17 17 24 28 14 22	17 26 16 16 19 24 28 14 22	20 30 22 16 21 25 28 15 22	23 35 25 18 23 25 28 15 22	26 2 24 22 25 26 28 15 22
10	29 31 27 31 5 24 28 14 22	33 36 32 35 6 24 28 14 22	35 1 1 2 8 25 28 14 22	2 5 1 6 10 25 28 14 22	5 9 3 8 11 24 28 14 22	8 13 9 13 13 24 28 14 22	11 17 14 16 15 24 28 14 22	14 22 13 17 17 24 28 14 22	17 27 17 16 19 24 28 14 22	20 31 22 16 21 25 28 15 22	23 36 25 19 23 25 28 15 22	26 3 24 22 25 26 28 15 22
11	30 33 28 31 5 24 28 14 22	33 1 33 35 7 24 28 14 22	36 2 1 2 8 25 28 14 22	3 7 1 6 10 25 28 14 22	6 10 3 8 11 24 28 14 22	8 15 9 13 13 24 28 14 22	11 18 14 16 15 24 28 14 22	14 23 13 17 17 24 28 14 22	17 29 17 16 19 24 28 14 22	20 33 22 16 21 25 28 15 22	23 1 25 19 23 25 28 15 22	26 5 24 22 25 26 28 15 22
12	30 34 28 31 5 24 28 14 22	33 3 33 35 7 25 28 14 22	36 3 1 2 8 25 28 14 22	3 8 1 6 10 25 28 14 22	6 11 3 10 11 24 28 14 22	9 16 10 13 13 24 28 14 22	11 20 14 16 15 24 28 14 22	14 25 13 17 17 24 28 14 22	17 30 17 16 19 24 28 14 22	20 34 22 16 21 25 28 15 22	23 3 25 19 23 25 28 15 22	26 6 24 22 25 26 28 15 22
13	30 35 28 31 5 24 28 14 22	33 4 33 35 7 25 28 14 22	36 5 2 3 8 25 28 14 22	3 9 1 6 10 25 28 14 22	6 12 4 10 11 24 28 14 22	9 17 10 13 13 24 28 14 22	12 21 14 16 15 24 28 14 22	14 26 13 17 17 24 28 14 22	17 32 17 16 19 24 28 14 22	20 35 22 16 21 25 28 15 22	24 4 25 19 23 25 28 15 22	27 7 24 22 25 26 28 15 22
14	30 1 28 31 6 24 28 14 22	33 5 33 35 7 25 28 14 22	36 6 2 3 8 25 28 14 22	3 10 1 6 10 25 28 14 22	6 14 4 10 11 24 28 14 22	9 19 10 13 13 24 28 14 22	12 22 14 16 15 24 28 14 22	15 28 13 17 17 24 28 14 22	18 33 17 16 19 24 28 14 22	21 36 22 16 21 25 28 15 22	24 5 25 19 23 25 28 15 22	27 8 25 22 25 26 28 15 22
15	30 2 28 32 6 24 28 14 22	33 6 33 35 7 25 28 14 22	36 7 2 3 8 25 28 14 22	3 11 1 7 10 25 28 14 22	6 15 4 10 12 24 28 14 22	9 20 10 13 13 24 28 14 22	12 24 14 16 15 24 28 14 22	15 29 13 17 17 24 28 14 22	18 34 17 16 19 24 28 14 22	21 2 22 16 21 25 28 15 22	24 6 25 19 23 25 28 15 22	27 9 25 22 25 26 28 15 22
16	30 3 28 32 6 24 28 14 22	33 7 33 36 7 25 28 14 22	36 8 2 3 8 25 28 14 22	3 13 1 7 10 25 28 14 22	6 16 4 10 12 24 28 14 22	9 21 10 13 13 24 28 14 22	12 25 14 16 15 24 28 14 22	15 31 13 17 17 24 28 14 22	18 35 18 16 19 24 28 14 22	21 3 23 16 21 25 28 15 22	24 7 25 19 23 25 28 15 22	27 11 25 23 25 26 28 15 22
17	30 4 28 32 6 24 28 14 22	33 8 34 36 7 25 28 14 22	36 9 2 3 8 25 28 14 22	3 14 1 7 10 25 28 14 22	6 18 4 10 12 24 28 14 22	9 23 11 14 13 24 28 14 22	12 27 14 16 15 24 28 14 22	15 32 13 17 17 24 28 14 22	18 1 18 16 19 24 28 14 22	21 4 23 16 21 25 28 15 22	24 9 25 19 23 25 28 15 22	27 12 25 23 25 26 28 15 22
18	30 5 29 32 6 24 28 14 22	33 10 34 36 7 25 28 14 22	36 11 2 3 8 25 28 14 22	3 15 1 7 10 25 28 14 22	6 19 4 10 12 24 28 14 22	9 24 11 14 14 24 28 14 22	12 28 14 16 15 24 28 14 22	15 33 13 17 17 24 28 14 22	18 2 18 16 19 24 28 14 22	21 5 23 17 21 25 28 15 22	24 10 25 19 23 25 28 15 22	27 13 25 23 26 26 28 15 22
19	30 6 29 32 6 24 28 14 22	34 11 34 36 7 25 28 14 22	36 12 2 3 8 25 28 14 22	3 17 1 7 10 25 28 14 22	6 20 5 10 13 24 28 14 22	9 26 11 14 14 24 28 14 22	12 30 14 16 15 24 28 14 22	15 35 13 17 17 24 28 14 22	18 3 18 16 19 24 28 14 22	21 6 23 17 21 25 28 15 22	24 11 25 20 23 25 28 15 22	27 14 25 23 26 26 28 15 22
20	30 8 29 32 6 24 28 14 22	34 11 34 36 7 25 28 14 22	36 13 2 3 8 25 28 14 22	3 18 1 7 10 25 28 14 22	6 22 5 11 12 24 28 14 22	9 27 11 14 14 24 28 14 22	12 31 14 16 16 24 28 14 22	15 36 13 17 17 24 28 14 22	18 4 18 15 19 24 28 14 22	21 8 23 17 21 25 28 15 22	24 12 25 20 24 25 28 15 22	27 15 25 23 26 26 28 15 22
21	31 9 29 32 6 24 28 14 22	34 14 34 36 7 25 28 14 22	1 14 2 4 8 25 28 14 22	4 20 1 7 10 25 28 14 22	6 23 5 11 12 24 28 14 22	9 29 11 14 14 24 28 14 22	12 32 14 16 16 24 28 14 22	15 1 13 17 18 24 28 14 22	18 6 19 15 20 24 28 14 22	21 9 23 17 22 25 28 15 22	24 13 25 20 24 25 28 15 22	27 17 25 23 26 26 28 15 22
22	31 10 29 32 6 24 28 14 22	34 15 35 36 7 25 28 14 22	1 16 2 4 8 25 28 14 22	4 21 1 7 10 25 28 14 22	7 25 5 11 12 24 28 14 22	10 30 12 14 14 24 28 14 22	12 34 14 16 16 24 28 14 22	15 2 14 17 18 24 28 14 22	18 7 19 15 20 24 28 14 22	21 10 23 17 22 25 28 15 22	24 15 25 20 24 25 28 15 22	27 18 26 23 26 26 28 15 22
23	31 12 29 33 6 24 28 14 22	34 16 35 36 7 25 28 14 22	1 17 2 4 9 25 28 14 22	4 23 1 8 10 25 28 14 22	7 26 5 11 12 24 28 14 22	10 32 12 14 14 24 28 14 22	12 35 14 17 16 24 28 14 22	15 4 14 17 18 24 28 14 22	18 8 19 15 20 24 28 14 22	21 11 24 17 22 25 28 15 22	25 16 25 20 24 26 28 15 22	28 19 26 23 26 26 28 15 22
24	31 13 30 33 6 24 28 14 22	34 18 35 1 7 25 28 14 22	1 19 2 4 9 25 28 14 22	4 24 1 8 10 24 28 14 22	7 28 6 11 13 24 28 14 22	10 33 12 14 14 24 28 14 22	13 1 14 17 16 24 28 14 22	16 5 14 17 18 24 28 14 22	19 9 19 15 20 24 28 14 22	22 12 24 17 22 25 28 15 22	25 17 25 20 24 26 28 15 22	28 21 26 23 26 26 28 15 22
25	31 14 30 33 6 24 28 14 22	34 19 35 1 7 25 28 14 22	1 20 2 4 9 25 28 14 22	4 26 1 8 10 24 28 14 22	7 29 6 11 12 24 28 14 22	10 34 12 14 14 24 28 14 22	13 2 14 17 16 24 28 14 22	16 6 14 17 18 24 28 14 22	19 10 19 16 19 24 28 14 22	22 14 24 17 22 25 28 15 22	25 19 24 20 24 26 28 15 22	28 22 26 24 26 26 28 15 22
26	31 16 30 33 6 24 28 14 22	34 21 35 1 7 25 28 14 22	1 22 2 4 9 25 28 14 22	4 27 1 8 10 24 28 14 22	7 31 6 11 13 24 28 14 22	10 36 12 14 14 24 28 14 22	13 3 14 17 16 24 28 14 22	16 7 14 17 18 24 28 14 22	19 12 19 16 19 24 28 14 22	22 15 24 17 22 25 28 15 22	25 20 24 20 24 26 28 15 22	28 24 26 24 26 26 28 15 22
27	31 17 30 33 6 24 28 14 22	34 22 35 1 7 25 28 14 22	1 23 1 4 9 25 28 14 22	4 29 1 8 10 24 28 14 22	7 32 6 11 12 24 28 14 22	10 1 12 15 14 24 28 14 22	13 4 14 17 16 24 28 14 22	16 8 14 17 18 24 28 14 22	19 13 20 16 19 24 28 14 22	22 16 24 17 22 25 28 15 22	25 21 24 20 24 26 28 15 22	28 25 26 24 26 26 28 15 22
28	31 18 30 33 6 24 28 14 22	34 24 36 1 7 25 28 14 22	1 25 1 4 9 25 28 14 22	4 30 2 8 11 24 28 14 22	7 33 6 11 12 24 28 14 22	10 2 12 15 14 24 28 14 22	13 5 14 17 16 24 28 14 22	16 10 14 17 18 24 28 14 22	19 14 20 16 19 24 28 14 22	22 18 24 17 22 25 28 15 22	25 23 24 20 24 26 28 15 22	28 27 26 24 26 26 28 15 22
29	31 20 30 33 6 24 28 14 22	**1959**	1 36 1 5 9 25 28 14 22	4 31 2 8 11 24 28 14 22	7 35 7 12 12 24 28 14 22	10 3 13 15 14 24 28 14 22	13 6 14 17 16 24 28 14 22	16 11 14 16 18 24 28 14 22	19 16 20 16 19 24 28 14 22	22 19 24 17 22 25 28 15 22	25 24 24 21 24 26 28 15 22	28 28 27 24 26 26 28 15 22
30	31 21 30 33 6 24 28 14 22		1 28 1 5 9 25 28 14 22	4 33 2 8 11 24 28 14 22	7 36 7 12 12 24 28 14 22	10 4 13 15 14 24 28 14 22	13 8 14 17 16 24 28 14 22	16 12 14 16 18 24 28 14 22	19 17 20 16 19 24 28 14 22	22 21 24 18 22 25 28 15 22	25 26 24 21 24 26 28 15 22	28 30 27 24 26 26 28 15 22
31	32 23 31 34 6 24 28 14 22		2 29 1 5 9 25 28 14 22		7 1 7 12 12 24 28 14 22		13 9 14 17 16 24 28 14 22	16 13 15 16 18 24 28 14 22		22 22 25 18 22 25 28 15 22		28 31 27 24 26 26 28 15 22

	JAN	FEB	MAR	APR	MAY	JUNE	JULY	AUG	SEPT	OCT	NOV	DEC
1	29 33 27 24 27 26 28 15 22	32 1 32 28 29 27 29 14 22	35 3 36 32 31 28 29 14 22	2 8 35 36 33 28 29 14 22	5 11 3 3 36 28 29 14 22	8 16 9 7 2 28 29 14 22	10 19 13 11 4 27 29 14 22	13 24 12 15 7 27 29 15 22	16 29 17 18 8 27 29 15 22	19 33 21 22 10 27 29 15 22	22 2 24 26 11 28 29 15 22	25 6 24 29 11 28 29 15 22
2	29 34 27 25 27 26 28 15 22	32 3 32 28 29 27 29 14 22	35 5 36 32 31 28 29 14 22	2 9 35 36 34 28 29 14 22	5 12 3 3 36 28 29 14 22	8 17 9 7 2 28 29 14 22	11 20 13 11 4 27 29 14 22	14 26 12 15 7 27 29 15 22	16 31 17 18 8 27 29 15 22	19 35 22 22 10 27 29 15 22	23 4 29 26 11 28 29 15 22	26 7 24 30 11 28 29 15 22
3	29 35 27 25 27 26 28 15 22	32 4 32 28 29 27 29 14 22	35 6 36 32 31 28 29 14 22	2 10 35 36 34 28 29 14 22	5 14 3 3 36 28 29 14 22	8 18 10 7 2 28 29 14 22	11 22 13 11 4 27 29 14 22	14 27 12 15 7 27 29 15 22	17 32 17 19 9 27 29 15 22	20 36 22 22 10 27 29 15 22	23 5 24 26 11 28 29 15 22	26 8 24 30 11 28 29 15 23
4	29 1 28 25 27 26 28 15 22	32 5 33 29 29 27 29 14 22	35 7 36 32 31 28 29 14 22	2 11 35 36 34 28 29 14 22	5 15 3 4 36 28 29 14 22	8 19 10 7 2 28 29 14 22	11 23 13 11 5 27 29 14 22	14 28 12 15 7 27 29 15 22	17 34 17 19 9 27 29 15 22	20 1 22 22 10 27 29 15 22	23 6 23 26 11 28 29 15 22	26 10 24 30 11 28 29 15 23
5	29 2 28 25 27 26 28 15 22	32 6 33 29 29 27 29 14 22	35 8 36 32 31 28 29 14 22	2 13 35 36 34 28 29 14 22	5 16 4 4 36 28 29 14 22	8 21 10 8 2 28 29 14 22	11 25 12 11 5 27 29 14 22	14 30 12 15 7 27 29 15 22	17 35 17 19 9 27 29 15 22	20 3 22 23 10 27 29 15 22	23 7 23 26 11 28 29 15 22	26 11 24 30 11 28 29 15 23
6	29 3 28 25 27 26 29 15 22	32 8 33 29 29 27 29 14 22	35 10 36 32 31 28 29 14 22	2 14 35 36 34 28 29 14 22	5 17 4 4 36 28 29 14 22	8 22 10 8 2 28 29 14 22	11 26 12 11 5 27 29 14 22	14 31 12 15 7 27 29 15 22	17 1 18 19 9 27 29 15 22	20 4 22 23 10 27 29 15 22	23 9 23 26 11 28 29 15 22	26 12 24 30 11 28 29 15 23
7	29 4 28 25 27 27 29 15 22	32 9 33 29 29 27 29 14 22	35 11 36 32 32 28 29 14 22	2 15 35 36 34 28 29 14 22	5 19 4 4 36 28 29 14 22	8 24 10 8 3 28 29 14 22	11 28 12 11 5 27 29 14 22	14 33 12 15 7 27 29 15 22	17 2 18 19 9 27 29 15 22	20 5 22 23 10 27 29 15 22	23 10 23 27 11 28 29 15 22	26 13 24 30 11 28 29 15 23
8	29 6 28 25 27 27 29 15 22	32 10 33 29 29 27 29 14 22	35 12 36 33 32 28 29 14 22	2 16 36 36 34 28 29 14 22	5 20 4 4 36 28 29 14 22	8 25 10 8 3 28 29 14 22	11 29 12 12 5 27 29 14 22	14 34 12 15 7 28 29 15 22	17 3 18 19 9 27 29 15 22	20 7 22 23 10 27 29 15 22	23 11 23 27 11 28 29 15 22	26 14 25 30 11 28 29 15 23
9	29 7 28 25 27 27 29 15 22	32 11 34 29 29 27 29 14 22	35 13 36 33 32 28 29 14 22	2 18 36 1 34 28 29 14 22	5 21 4 4 36 28 29 14 22	8 27 11 8 3 28 29 14 22	11 31 12 12 5 27 29 14 22	14 36 12 16 7 27 29 15 22	17 5 18 19 9 27 29 15 22	20 8 23 23 10 27 29 15 22	23 12 23 27 11 28 29 15 22	26 15 25 30 11 28 29 15 23
10	29 8 28 25 27 27 29 15 22	33 12 34 29 30 27 29 14 22	35 14 36 33 32 28 29 14 22	3 19 36 1 34 28 29 14 22	5 23 5 4 36 28 29 14 22	8 28 11 8 3 27 29 14 22	11 32 12 12 5 27 29 14 22	14 1 12 16 7 27 29 15 22	17 6 18 19 9 27 29 15 22	20 9 23 23 10 27 29 15 22	23 13 23 27 11 28 29 15 22	26 17 25 31 11 28 29 15 23
11	30 9 29 26 27 27 29 15 22	33 14 34 29 30 27 29 14 22	36 16 35 33 32 28 29 14 22	3 21 36 1 34 28 29 14 22	6 24 5 4 36 28 29 14 22	9 30 11 8 3 27 29 14 22	11 34 12 12 5 27 29 14 22	14 3 13 16 7 27 29 15 22	17 7 18 20 9 27 29 15 22	20 10 23 23 10 27 29 15 22	23 15 23 27 11 28 29 15 22	26 18 25 31 11 28 29 15 23
12	30 10 29 26 27 27 29 15 22	33 15 34 30 30 27 29 14 22	36 17 35 33 32 28 29 14 22	3 22 36 1 34 28 29 14 22	6 26 5 5 1 28 29 14 22	9 31 11 8 3 27 29 14 22	12 35 12 12 5 27 29 14 22	14 4 13 16 7 27 29 15 22	17 8 19 20 9 27 29 15 22	20 11 23 23 10 27 29 15 22	24 16 22 27 11 28 29 15 22	27 19 25 31 11 28 29 15 23
13	30 11 29 26 27 27 29 15 22	33 16 34 30 30 27 29 14 22	36 18 35 33 32 28 29 14 22	3 23 36 1 34 28 29 14 22	6 27 5 5 1 28 29 14 22	9 33 11 8 3 27 29 14 22	12 36 12 12 5 27 29 14 22	15 5 13 16 7 27 29 15 22	18 9 19 20 9 27 29 15 22	21 13 23 23 11 27 29 15 22	24 17 22 27 11 28 29 15 22	27 20 25 31 11 28 29 15 23
14	30 13 29 26 28 27 29 15 22	33 17 34 30 30 27 29 14 22	36 20 35 33 32 28 29 14 22	3 25 36 1 34 28 29 14 22	6 29 6 5 1 28 29 14 22	9 34 11 9 3 27 29 14 22	12 2 12 12 5 27 29 14 22	15 6 13 16 7 27 29 15 22	18 11 19 20 9 27 29 15 22	21 14 23 24 11 27 29 15 22	24 18 22 27 11 28 29 15 22	27 22 26 31 11 29 29 15 23
15	30 14 29 26 28 27 29 15 22	33 19 35 30 30 27 29 14 22	36 21 35 33 32 28 29 14 22	3 26 36 1 35 28 29 14 22	6 30 6 5 1 28 29 14 22	9 35 11 9 3 27 29 14 22	12 3 12 12 5 27 29 14 22	15 7 13 16 7 27 29 15 22	18 12 19 20 9 27 29 15 22	21 15 23 24 11 27 29 15 22	24 20 22 28 11 28 29 15 22	27 23 26 31 11 29 29 15 23
16	30 15 29 26 28 27 29 15 22	33 20 35 30 30 27 29 14 22	36 23 35 34 32 28 29 14 22	3 28 1 1 35 28 29 14 22	6 32 6 5 1 28 29 14 22	9 1 11 9 3 27 29 14 22	12 4 12 13 5 27 29 14 22	15 9 13 16 7 27 29 15 22	18 13 19 20 9 27 29 15 22	21 16 23 24 11 27 29 15 22	24 21 22 28 11 28 29 15 22	27 25 26 31 11 29 29 15 23
17	30 16 30 26 28 27 29 14 22	33 21 35 30 30 27 29 14 22	36 24 35 34 32 28 29 14 22	3 29 1 1 35 28 29 14 22	6 33 6 5 1 28 29 14 22	9 2 12 9 3 27 29 14 22	12 5 12 13 5 27 29 14 22	15 10 14 16 7 27 29 15 22	18 14 19 20 9 27 29 15 22	21 18 23 24 11 27 29 15 22	24 22 22 28 11 28 29 15 22	27 26 26 31 11 29 29 15 23
18	30 18 30 26 28 27 29 14 22	33 23 35 30 30 27 29 14 22	36 25 35 34 32 28 29 14 22	3 31 1 2 35 28 29 14 22	6 34 6 5 1 28 29 14 22	9 3 12 9 3 27 29 14 22	12 7 12 13 6 27 29 14 22	15 11 14 17 8 27 29 15 22	18 16 20 20 9 27 29 15 22	21 19 23 24 11 27 29 15 22	24 24 22 28 11 28 29 15 22	27 28 26 31 11 29 29 15 23
19	30 19 30 27 28 27 29 14 22	33 24 35 30 30 27 29 14 22	36 27 35 34 32 28 29 14 22	3 32 1 2 35 28 29 14 22	6 36 7 5 1 28 29 14 22	9 5 12 9 3 27 29 14 22	12 8 12 13 6 27 29 14 22	15 12 14 17 8 27 29 15 22	18 17 20 21 9 27 29 15 22	21 20 24 24 11 27 29 15 22	24 25 22 28 11 28 29 15 22	27 29 26 32 11 29 29 15 23
20	30 20 30 27 28 27 29 14 22	34 26 35 30 30 27 29 14 22	36 28 35 34 33 28 29 14 22	4 33 1 2 35 28 29 14 22	6 1 7 6 1 28 29 14 22	9 6 12 9 4 27 29 14 22	12 9 12 13 6 27 29 14 22	15 13 14 17 8 27 29 15 22	18 18 20 21 9 27 29 15 22	21 22 24 24 11 27 29 15 22	24 27 22 28 11 28 29 15 22	27 31 26 32 11 29 29 15 23
21	31 22 30 27 28 27 29 14 22	34 27 35 31 30 27 29 14 22	1 30 35 34 33 28 29 14 22	4 35 1 2 35 28 29 14 22	7 2 7 6 1 28 29 14 22	10 7 12 9 4 27 29 14 22	12 10 12 13 6 27 29 14 22	15 15 14 17 8 27 29 15 22	18 19 20 21 10 27 29 15 22	21 23 24 24 11 27 29 15 22	24 28 22 28 11 28 29 15 22	27 32 27 32 11 29 29 15 23
22	31 23 30 27 28 27 29 14 22	34 29 36 31 30 27 29 14 22	1 31 35 34 33 28 29 14 22	4 36 1 2 35 28 29 14 22	7 4 7 6 1 28 29 14 22	10 8 12 10 4 27 29 14 22	12 11 12 13 6 27 29 15 22	15 16 15 17 8 27 29 15 22	18 21 20 21 10 27 29 15 22	21 24 24 25 11 27 29 15 22	25 30 23 28 11 28 29 15 22	28 34 27 32 11 29 29 15 23
23	31 25 31 27 28 27 29 14 22	34 30 36 31 31 27 29 14 22	1 32 35 34 33 28 29 14 22	4 1 2 2 35 28 29 14 22	7 5 7 6 1 28 29 14 22	10 9 12 10 4 27 29 14 22	13 13 12 13 6 27 29 15 22	16 17 15 17 8 27 29 15 22	19 22 20 21 10 27 29 15 22	22 26 24 25 11 27 29 15 22	25 31 23 28 11 28 29 15 22	28 35 27 32 11 29 29 15 23
24	31 26 31 27 28 27 29 14 22	34 31 36 31 31 27 29 14 22	1 34 35 35 33 28 29 14 22	4 3 2 2 35 28 29 14 22	7 6 8 6 1 28 29 14 22	10 10 12 10 4 27 29 14 22	13 14 12 14 6 27 29 15 22	16 18 15 17 8 27 29 15 22	19 23 20 21 10 27 29 15 22	22 27 24 25 11 27 29 15 22	25 33 23 29 11 28 29 15 22	28 36 27 32 11 29 29 15 23
25	31 28 31 27 28 27 29 14 22	34 33 36 31 31 27 29 14 22	1 35 35 35 33 28 29 14 22	4 4 2 2 35 28 29 14 22	7 7 8 6 2 28 29 14 22	10 12 12 10 4 27 29 14 22	13 15 12 14 6 27 29 15 22	16 20 15 17 8 27 29 15 22	19 25 21 21 10 27 29 15 22	22 29 24 25 11 27 29 15 22	25 34 23 29 11 28 29 15 22	28 2 27 32 11 29 29 15 23
26	31 29 31 27 28 27 29 14 22	34 34 36 31 31 27 29 14 22	1 36 35 35 33 28 29 14 22	4 5 2 3 35 28 29 14 22	7 8 8 6 2 28 29 14 22	10 13 12 10 4 27 29 14 22	13 16 12 14 6 27 29 15 22	16 21 15 18 8 27 29 15 22	19 26 21 21 10 27 29 15 22	22 30 24 25 11 28 29 15 22	25 35 23 29 11 28 29 15 22	28 3 27 32 11 29 29 15 23
27	31 31 31 28 28 27 29 14 22	34 36 36 31 31 27 29 14 22	1 2 35 35 33 28 29 14 22	4 6 2 3 35 28 29 14 22	7 10 8 6 2 28 29 14 22	10 14 12 10 4 27 29 14 22	13 17 12 14 6 27 29 15 22	16 22 16 18 8 27 29 15 22	19 28 21 22 10 27 29 15 22	22 32 24 25 11 28 29 15 22	25 1 23 29 11 28 29 15 22	28 4 28 33 10 29 29 15 23
28	31 32 31 28 29 27 29 14 22	34 1 36 32 31 27 29 14 22	1 3 35 35 33 28 29 14 22	4 8 2 3 36 28 29 14 22	7 11 8 7 2 28 29 14 22	10 15 12 10 4 27 29 14 22	13 19 12 14 6 27 29 15 22	16 24 16 18 8 27 29 15 22	19 29 21 22 10 27 29 15 22	22 33 24 25 11 28 29 15 22	25 2 23 29 11 28 29 15 22	28 6 28 33 10 29 29 15 23
29	31 33 32 28 29 27 29 14 22	34 2 36 32 31 27 29 14 22	1 4 35 35 33 28 29 14 22	4 9 3 3 36 28 29 14 22	7 12 9 7 2 28 29 14 22	10 16 12 10 4 27 29 14 22	13 20 12 14 6 27 29 15 22	16 25 16 18 8 27 29 15 22	19 30 21 22 10 27 29 15 22	22 34 24 25 11 28 29 15 22	25 3 23 29 11 28 29 15 22	28 7 28 33 10 29 29 15 23
30	31 35 32 28 29 27 29 14 22	**1960**	1 6 35 35 33 28 29 14 22	5 10 3 3 36 28 29 14 22	7 13 9 7 2 28 29 14 22	10 18 12 11 4 27 29 14 22	13 21 12 14 6 27 29 15 22	16 27 16 18 8 27 29 15 22	19 32 21 22 10 27 29 15 22	22 36 24 26 11 28 29 15 22	25 5 23 29 11 28 29 15 22	28 8 28 33 10 29 29 15 23
31	32 36 32 28 29 27 29 14 22		2 7 35 35 33 28 29 14 22		7 14 9 7 2 28 29 14 22		13 23 12 14 6 27 29 15 22	16 28 16 18 8 27 29 15 22		22 1 24 26 11 28 29 15 22		28 9 28 33 10 29 29 15 23

	JAN	FEB	MAR	APR	MAY	JUNE	JULY	AUG	SEPT	OCT	NOV	DEC
1	29 10 28 33 10 29 29 15 23	32 15 33 36 10 30 30 15 23	35 15 33 3 10 30 30 15 23	2 20 35 3 11 31 30 15 23	5 24 5 2 12 31 30 15 22	8 29 10 3 14 31 30 15 22	10 33 10 6 16 31 30 15 22	13 2 12 9 18 31 30 15 22	16 7 18 13 19 30 30 15 22	19 10 22 16 21 30 30 15 22	22 15 21 20 24 30 30 15 23	25 18 25 24 26 31 30 16 23
2	29 11 28 33 10 29 29 15 23	32 16 34 1 10 30 30 15 23	35 17 33 3 10 30 30 15 23	2 21 35 3 11 31 30 15 23	5 25 5 2 12 31 30 15 22	8 30 10 3 14 31 30 15 22	11 34 10 6 16 31 30 15 22	13 3 12 9 18 31 30 15 22	16 8 18 13 20 30 30 15 22	19 11 22 17 22 30 30 15 22	22 16 21 20 24 30 30 16 23	26 19 25 24 26 31 30 16 23
3	29 12 29 33 10 29 29 15 23	32 17 34 1 10 30 30 15 23	35 18 33 3 10 30 30 15 23	2 23 35 3 11 31 30 15 23	5 26 5 2 12 31 30 15 22	8 32 10 3 14 31 30 15 22	11 35 10 6 16 31 30 15 22	14 5 12 9 18 31 30 15 22	17 9 18 13 20 30 30 15 22	20 13 22 17 22 30 30 15 22	23 17 21 21 24 30 30 16 23	26 20 25 24 26 31 30 16 23
4	29 14 29 33 10 29 30 15 23	32 18 34 1 10 30 30 15 23	35 19 33 3 10 30 30 15 23	2 24 36 3 11 31 30 15 23	5 28 5 2 12 31 30 15 22	8 33 10 3 14 31 30 15 22	11 1 10 6 16 31 30 15 22	14 6 13 10 18 31 30 15 22	17 11 18 13 20 30 30 15 22	30 14 22 17 22 30 30 15 22	23 18 21 21 24 30 30 16 23	26 21 25 24 26 31 30 16 23
5	29 15 29 34 10 29 30 15 23	32 19 34 1 10 30 30 15 23	35 20 33 3 10 30 30 15 23	2 25 36 3 11 31 30 15 23	5 29 5 2 12 31 30 15 22	8 34 10 3 14 31 30 15 22	11 2 10 6 16 31 30 15 22	14 7 13 10 18 31 30 15 22	17 12 19 13 19 30 30 15 22	20 15 22 17 22 30 30 15 22	23 19 21 21 24 31 30 16 23	26 23 25 25 26 31 30 16 23
6	29 16 29 34 10 29 30 15 23	32 21 34 1 10 30 30 15 23	35 22 33 3 10 30 30 15 23	2 27 36 3 11 31 30 15 23	5 31 6 2 13 31 30 15 22	8 36 10 4 14 31 30 15 22	11 4 10 6 16 31 30 15 22	14 8 13 10 18 31 30 15 22	17 13 19 13 19 30 30 15 22	20 16 22 17 22 30 30 15 23	23 21 21 21 24 31 30 16 23	26 24 25 25 26 31 30 16 23
7	29 17 29 34 10 29 30 15 23	32 22 34 1 10 30 30 15 23	35 23 33 3 10 30 30 15 23	2 28 36 3 11 31 30 15 23	5 32 6 2 13 31 30 15 22	8 1 10 4 14 31 30 15 22	11 5 10 7 16 31 30 15 22	14 10 13 10 18 31 30 15 22	17 14 19 14 20 30 30 15 22	20 17 22 17 22 30 30 15 23	23 22 21 21 24 31 30 16 23	26 25 26 25 26 31 30 16 23
8	29 18 29 34 10 29 30 15 23	32 23 34 1 10 30 30 15 23	35 24 33 3 10 30 30 15 23	2 29 36 3 11 31 30 15 23	5 33 6 2 13 31 30 15 22	8 3 10 4 14 31 30 15 22	11 6 10 7 16 31 30 15 22	14 11 13 10 18 31 30 15 22	17 15 19 14 20 30 30 15 22	20 19 22 17 22 30 30 15 23	23 23 21 21 24 31 30 16 23	26 27 26 25 26 31 30 16 23
9	29 20 30 34 10 29 30 15 23	33 25 34 1 10 30 30 15 23	35 26 33 3 10 30 30 15 23	2 31 36 3 11 31 30 15 23	5 35 6 2 13 31 30 15 22	8 4 10 4 14 31 30 15 22	11 7 10 7 16 31 30 15 22	14 12 14 10 18 31 30 15 22	17 16 19 14 20 30 30 15 22	20 20 22 17 22 30 30 15 23	23 25 21 21 24 31 30 16 23	26 28 26 25 26 31 30 16 23
10	30 21 30 34 10 29 30 15 23	33 26 34 1 10 30 30 15 23	35 27 33 3 10 30 30 15 23	3 32 1 3 11 31 30 15 23	5 36 6 2 13 31 30 15 22	8 5 10 4 14 31 30 15 22	11 9 10 7 16 31 30 15 22	14 13 14 10 18 31 30 15 22	17 18 19 14 20 30 30 15 22	20 21 22 18 22 30 30 15 23	23 26 21 21 24 31 30 16 23	26 30 26 25 26 31 30 16 23
11	30 22 30 34 10 29 30 15 23	33 27 34 1 10 30 30 15 23	36 28 33 3 10 30 30 15 23	3 34 1 3 11 31 30 15 23	6 2 7 2 13 31 30 15 22	9 6 10 4 14 31 30 15 22	11 10 10 7 16 31 30 15 22	14 14 14 10 18 31 30 15 22	17 19 20 14 20 30 30 15 22	20 22 22 18 22 30 30 15 23	23 27 22 22 24 31 30 16 23	26 31 26 25 27 31 30 16 23
12	30 24 30 34 10 29 30 15 23	33 29 34 1 10 30 30 15 23	36 30 33 3 10 30 30 15 23	3 35 1 2 11 31 30 15 23	6 3 7 2 13 31 30 15 22	9 8 10 4 15 31 30 15 22	11 11 10 7 16 31 30 15 22	14 16 14 11 18 30 30 15 22	17 20 20 14 20 30 30 15 22	20 24 22 18 22 30 30 15 23	23 29 22 22 24 31 30 16 23	27 32 26 25 27 31 30 16 23
13	30 25 30 34 10 29 30 15 23	33 30 34 2 10 30 30 15 23	36 31 33 3 10 30 30 15 23	3 1 1 2 11 31 30 15 23	6 4 7 2 13 31 30 15 22	9 9 11 4 15 31 30 15 22	12 12 10 7 16 31 30 15 22	15 17 14 11 18 30 30 15 22	18 21 20 14 20 30 30 15 22	20 25 22 18 22 30 30 15 23	24 30 22 22 24 31 30 16 23	27 34 26 26 27 31 30 16 23
14	30 27 30 35 10 29 30 15 23	33 32 34 2 10 30 30 15 23	36 33 33 3 10 30 30 15 23	3 2 1 2 11 31 30 15 23	6 6 7 2 13 31 30 15 22	9 10 11 4 15 31 30 15 22	12 13 10 7 16 31 30 15 22	15 18 15 11 18 30 30 15 22	18 22 30 14 20 30 30 15 22	21 26 22 18 22 30 30 15 23	24 31 22 22 25 31 30 16 23	27 35 27 26 27 31 30 16 23
15	30 28 31 35 10 29 30 15 23	33 33 34 2 10 30 30 15 23	36 34 33 3 10 30 30 15 23	3 3 1 2 11 31 30 15 23	6 7 7 2 13 31 30 15 22	9 11 11 4 15 31 30 15 22	12 15 10 7 16 31 30 15 22	15 19 15 11 18 30 30 15 22	18 24 20 15 20 30 30 15 22	21 28 22 18 22 30 30 15 23	24 33 22 22 25 31 30 16 23	27 1 27 26 27 31 30 16 23
16	30 30 31 35 10 29 30 15 23	33 35 34 2 10 30 30 15 23	36 36 33 3 10 31 30 15 23	3 5 2 2 12 31 30 15 23	6 8 8 2 13 31 30 15 22	9 13 11 4 15 31 30 15 22	12 16 10 8 17 31 30 15 22	15 20 15 11 18 30 30 15 22	18 25 20 15 20 30 30 15 22	21 29 22 18 23 30 30 15 23	24 34 22 22 25 31 30 16 23	27 2 27 26 27 31 30 16 23
17	30 31 31 35 10 29 30 15 23	33 36 34 2 10 30 30 15 23	36 1 33 3 10 31 30 15 23	3 6 2 2 12 31 30 15 23	6 9 8 2 13 31 30 15 22	9 14 11 5 15 31 30 15 22	12 17 10 8 17 31 30 15 22	15 22 15 11 19 30 30 15 22	18 27 20 15 21 30 30 15 22	21 30 22 18 23 30 30 15 23	24 36 22 22 25 31 30 16 23	27 3 27 26 27 31 30 16 23
18	30 33 31 35 10 29 30 15 23	33 2 34 2 10 30 30 15 23	36 3 34 3 10 31 30 15 23	3 7 2 2 12 31 30 15 23	6 11 8 2 13 31 30 15 22	9 15 11 5 15 31 30 15 22	12 18 10 8 17 31 30 15 22	15 23 15 11 19 30 30 15 22	18 28 20 15 21 30 30 15 22	21 32 22 19 23 30 30 15 23	24 1 23 22 25 31 30 16 23	27 5 27 26 27 31 30 16 23
19	30 34 31 35 10 29 30 15 23	34 3 34 2 10 30 30 15 23	36 4 34 3 10 31 30 15 23	3 9 2 2 12 31 30 15 23	6 12 8 2 13 31 30 15 22	9 16 10 5 15 31 30 15 22	12 19 10 8 17 31 30 15 22	15 24 16 11 19 30 30 15 22	18 29 21 15 21 30 30 15 22	21 33 22 19 23 30 30 15 23	24 2 23 23 25 31 30 16 23	27 6 27 26 27 31 30 16 23
20	31 35 31 35 10 29 30 15 23	34 4 34 2 10 30 30 15 23	36 5 34 3 10 31 30 15 23	4 10 2 2 12 31 30 15 23	6 13 8 2 13 31 30 15 22	9 17 10 5 15 31 30 15 22	12 21 10 8 17 31 30 15 22	15 26 16 11 19 30 30 15 22	18 32 21 15 21 30 30 15 22	21 35 22 19 23 30 30 15 23	24 4 23 23 25 31 30 16 23	27 8 28 26 27 31 30 16 23
21	31 1 32 35 10 29 30 15 23	34 6 34 2 10 30 30 15 23	1 7 34 3 10 31 30 15 23	4 11 2 2 12 31 30 15 23	7 14 8 2 13 31 30 15 22	9 19 10 5 15 31 30 15 22	12 22 10 8 17 31 30 15 22	15 27 16 12 19 30 30 15 22	18 34 21 15 21 30 30 15 22	21 36 22 19 23 30 30 15 23	24 5 23 23 25 31 30 16 23	27 9 28 27 27 31 30 16 23
22	31 2 32 35 10 29 30 15 23	34 7 34 2 10 30 30 15 23	1 8 34 3 10 31 30 15 23	4 12 3 2 12 31 30 15 23	7 15 9 2 13 31 30 15 22	10 20 10 5 15 31 30 15 22	12 23 10 8 17 31 30 15 22	15 28 16 12 19 30 30 15 22	19 35 21 15 21 30 30 15 22	21 1 21 19 23 30 30 15 23	24 7 23 23 25 31 30 16 23	28 10 28 27 27 31 30 16 23
23	31 4 32 35 10 29 30 15 23	34 8 34 2 10 30 30 15 23	1 9 34 3 11 31 30 15 23	4 13 3 2 12 31 30 15 23	7 17 9 2 13 31 30 15 22	10 21 10 5 15 31 30 15 22	13 25 11 8 17 31 30 15 22	16 30 16 12 19 30 30 15 22	19 1 21 16 21 30 30 15 22	21 3 21 19 23 30 30 15 23	25 8 23 23 25 31 30 16 23	28 11 28 27 27 31 30 16 23
24	31 5 32 36 10 29 30 15 23	34 9 33 2 10 30 30 15 23	1 10 34 3 11 31 30 15 23	4 15 3 2 12 31 30 15 23	7 18 9 2 13 31 30 15 22	10 22 10 5 15 31 30 15 22	13 26 11 8 17 31 30 15 22	16 31 17 12 19 30 30 15 22	19 2 21 16 21 30 30 15 22	22 4 21 19 23 30 30 15 23	25 9 23 23 25 31 30 16 23	28 13 28 27 27 31 30 16 23
25	31 6 32 36 10 29 30 15 23	34 11 33 2 10 30 30 15 23	1 11 34 3 11 31 30 15 23	4 16 3 2 12 31 30 15 23	7 19 9 3 14 31 30 15 22	10 24 10 5 15 31 30 15 22	13 28 11 8 17 31 30 15 22	16 33 17 12 19 30 30 15 22	19 4 21 16 21 30 30 15 22	22 6 21 19 23 30 30 15 23	25 10 24 23 25 31 30 16 23	28 14 28 27 28 31 30 16 23
26	31 7 32 36 10 29 30 15 23	34 12 33 3 10 30 30 15 23	1 13 34 3 11 31 30 15 23	4 17 3 2 12 31 30 15 23	7 20 9 3 14 31 30 15 22	10 25 10 5 15 31 30 15 22	13 29 11 9 17 31 30 15 22	16 34 17 12 19 30 30 15 22	19 5 21 16 21 30 30 15 22	22 7 21 20 23 30 30 15 23	25 12 24 23 25 31 30 16 23	28 15 29 27 28 31 30 16 23
27	31 9 33 36 10 30 30 15 23	34 13 33 3 10 30 30 15 23	1 14 34 3 11 31 30 15 23	4 18 4 2 12 31 30 15 23	7 22 9 3 14 31 30 15 22	10 27 10 6 15 31 30 15 22	13 30 11 9 17 31 30 15 22	16 36 17 12 19 30 30 15 22	19 6 22 16 21 30 30 15 22	22 8 21 20 23 30 30 15 23	25 13 24 24 25 31 30 16 23	28 16 29 27 28 31 30 16 23
28	31 10 33 36 10 30 30 15 23	34 14 33 3 10 30 30 15 23	1 15 35 3 11 31 30 15 23	4 19 4 2 12 31 30 15 23	7 23 9 3 14 31 30 15 22	10 28 10 6 15 31 30 15 22	13 32 11 9 17 31 30 15 22	16 1 17 12 19 30 30 15 22	19 8 22 16 21 30 30 15 22	22 10 21 20 23 30 30 15 23	25 14 24 24 26 31 30 16 23	28 17 29 27 28 31 30 16 23
29	31 11 33 36 10 30 30 15 23	1961	1 16 35 3 11 31 30 15 23	4 21 4 2 12 31 30 15 23	7 24 10 3 14 31 30 15 22	10 30 10 6 16 31 30 15 22	13 33 11 9 17 31 30 15 22	16 3 17 13 19 30 30 15 22	19 9 22 16 21 30 30 15 22	22 11 21 20 23 30 30 15 23	25 15 24 24 26 31 30 16 23	28 19 29 28 28 31 30 16 23
30	32 12 33 36 10 30 30 15 23		1 17 35 3 11 31 30 15 23	4 22 4 2 12 31 30 15 22	7 26 10 3 14 31 30 15 22	10 31 10 6 16 31 30 15 22	13 35 12 9 17 31 30 15 22	16 4 18 13 19 30 30 15 22		22 12 21 20 23 30 30 15 23	25 17 24 24 26 32 30 16 23	28 20 29 28 28 32 30 16 23
31	32 13 33 36 10 30 30 15 23		2 19 35 3 11 31 30 15 23		7 27 10 3 14 31 30 15 22		13 36 12 9 17 31 30 15 22	16 6 18 13 19 30 30 15 22		22 13 21 20 24 30 30 15 23		28 21 29 28 28 32 30 16 23

	JAN	FEB	MAR	APR	MAY	JUNE
1	29 22 30 28 28 32 30 16 23	32 27 33 32 30 32 31 15 23	35 28 32 35 33 33 31 15 23	2 34 36 3 35 34 31 15 23	5 2 6 7 1 34 32 15 23	8 7 8 11 4 35 32 15 23
2	29 23 30 28 28 32 30 16 23	32 28 32 32 31 32 31 15 23	35 29 32 35 33 33 31 15 23	2 35 36 3 35 34 31 15 23	5 3 6 7 1 34 32 15 23	8 8 8 11 4 35 32 15 23
3	29 25 30 28 28 32 30 16 23	32 30 32 32 31 32 31 15 23	35 31 32 36 33 33 31 15 23	2 1 1 3 35 34 31 15 23	5 5 7 7 2 34 32 15 23	8 10 8 11 4 35 32 15 23
4	29 26 30 28 28 32 31 16 23	32 31 32 32 31 32 31 15 23	35 32 32 36 33 33 31 15 23	2 2 1 4 35 34 31 15 23	5 6 7 7 2 34 32 15 23	8 11 8 11 4 35 32 15 23
5	29 28 30 28 28 32 31 16 23	32 33 32 32 31 32 31 15 23	35 34 32 36 33 33 31 15 23	2 4 1 4 35 34 31 15 23	5 7 7 7 2 34 32 15 23	8 12 8 11 4 35 32 15 23
6	29 29 30 29 28 32 31 16 23	32 34 32 32 31 32 31 15 23	35 35 32 36 33 33 31 15 23	2 5 1 4 35 34 31 15 23	5 9 7 7 2 34 32 15 23	8 13 8 11 4 35 32 15 23
7	29 31 31 29 29 32 31 16 23	32 36 32 33 31 32 31 15 23	35 1 33 36 33 33 31 15 23	2 7 1 4 36 34 31 15 23	5 10 7 8 2 34 32 15 23	8 15 8 11 4 35 32 15 23
8	29 32 31 29 29 32 31 16 23	32 1 32 33 31 32 31 15 23	35 2 33 36 33 33 31 15 23	2 8 2 4 36 34 31 15 23	5 11 7 8 2 34 32 15 23	8 16 8 11 4 35 32 15 23
9	29 33 31 29 29 32 31 15 23	33 3 32 33 31 32 31 15 23	35 4 33 36 33 33 31 15 23	2 9 2 4 36 34 31 15 23	5 13 7 8 2 34 32 15 23	8 17 8 12 4 35 32 15 23
10	29 35 31 29 29 32 31 15 23	33 4 32 33 31 32 31 15 23	35 5 33 36 33 33 31 15 23	3 11 2 4 36 34 32 15 23	5 14 8 8 2 34 32 15 23	8 18 8 12 4 35 32 15 23
11	30 36 31 29 29 32 31 15 23	33 5 32 33 31 33 31 15 23	36 6 33 1 33 33 31 15 23	3 12 2 4 36 34 32 15 23	6 15 8 8 2 34 32 15 23	9 19 8 12 5 35 32 15 23
12	30 2 31 29 29 32 31 15 23	33 7 31 33 31 33 31 15 23	36 8 33 1 34 33 31 15 23	3 13 2 5 36 34 32 15 23	6 16 8 8 2 34 32 15 23	9 21 8 12 5 35 32 15 23
13	30 3 31 29 29 32 31 15 23	33 8 31 33 31 33 31 15 23	36 9 33 1 34 33 31 15 23	3 14 3 5 36 34 32 15 23	6 17 8 8 2 34 32 15 23	9 22 8 12 5 35 32 15 23
14	30 4 32 30 29 32 31 15 23	33 9 31 33 31 33 31 15 23	36 10 33 1 34 33 31 15 23	3 15 3 5 36 34 32 15 23	6 19 8 8 2 34 32 15 23	9 23 8 12 5 35 32 15 23
15	30 6 32 30 29 32 31 15 23	33 11 31 34 32 33 31 15 23	36 12 34 1 34 33 31 15 23	3 17 3 5 36 34 32 15 23	6 20 8 9 2 34 32 15 23	9 24 8 12 5 35 32 15 23
16	30 7 32 30 29 32 31 15 23	33 12 31 34 32 33 31 15 23	36 13 34 1 34 33 31 15 23	3 18 3 5 36 34 32 15 23	6 21 8 9 3 34 32 15 23	9 26 8 12 5 35 32 15 23
17	30 8 32 30 29 32 31 15 23	33 13 31 34 32 33 31 15 23	36 14 34 1 34 33 31 15 23	3 19 3 5 36 34 32 15 23	6 22 8 9 3 34 32 15 23	9 27 8 13 5 35 32 15 23
18	30 10 32 30 29 32 31 15 23	33 14 31 34 32 33 31 15 23	36 15 34 1 34 33 31 15 23	3 20 4 5 36 34 32 15 23	6 24 8 9 3 34 32 15 23	9 28 8 13 5 35 32 15 23
19	30 11 32 30 29 32 31 15 23	34 15 31 34 32 33 31 15 23	36 16 34 2 34 33 31 15 23	3 21 4 5 36 34 32 15 23	6 25 8 9 3 34 32 15 23	9 30 8 13 5 35 32 15 23
20	31 12 32 30 30 32 31 15 23	34 17 31 34 32 33 31 15 23	36 18 34 2 34 33 31 15 23	4 23 4 6 1 34 32 15 23	6 26 8 9 3 34 32 15 23	9 31 8 13 5 35 32 15 23
21	31 13 32 30 30 32 31 15 23	34 18 31 34 32 33 31 15 23	1 19 34 2 34 33 31 15 23	4 24 4 6 1 34 32 15 23	7 27 8 9 3 35 32 15 23	9 33 8 13 5 35 32 15 23
22	31 14 32 31 30 32 31 15 23	34 19 31 34 32 33 31 15 23	1 20 35 2 34 33 31 15 23	4 25 4 6 1 34 32 15 23	7 29 8 9 3 35 32 15 23	10 34 8 13 5 35 32 15 23
23	31 16 33 31 30 32 31 15 23	34 20 31 35 32 33 31 15 23	1 21 35 2 34 33 31 15 23	4 26 5 6 1 34 32 15 23	7 30 8 10 3 35 32 15 23	10 35 8 13 5 35 32 15 23
24	31 17 33 31 30 32 31 15 23	34 21 31 35 32 33 31 15 23	1 22 35 2 34 33 31 15 23	4 28 5 6 1 34 32 15 23	7 32 8 10 3 35 32 15 23	10 1 8 13 5 35 32 15 23
25	31 18 33 31 30 32 31 15 23	34 23 32 35 32 33 31 15 23	1 24 35 2 35 33 31 15 23	4 29 5 6 1 34 32 15 23	7 33 8 10 3 35 32 15 23	10 2 8 13 6 35 32 15 23
26	31 19 33 31 30 32 31 15 23	34 24 32 35 32 33 31 15 23	1 25 35 2 35 34 31 15 23	4 30 5 6 1 34 32 15 23	7 34 9 10 3 35 32 15 23	10 4 8 14 6 35 32 15 23
27	31 20 33 31 30 32 31 15 23	34 25 32 35 32 33 31 15 23	1 26 35 3 35 34 31 15 23	4 32 5 6 1 34 32 15 23	7 36 9 10 3 35 32 15 23	10 5 8 14 6 35 32 15 23
28	31 22 33 31 30 32 31 15 23	34 26 32 35 33 33 31 15 23	1 27 36 3 35 34 31 15 23	4 33 6 7 1 34 32 15 23	7 1 9 10 3 35 32 15 23	10 6 8 14 6 35 32 15 23
29	31 23 33 31 30 32 31 15 23		1 29 36 3 35 34 31 15 23	4 34 6 7 1 34 32 15 23	7 3 8 10 4 35 32 15 23	10 8 8 14 6 35 32 15 23
30	32 24 33 32 30 32 31 15 23	1962	1 30 36 3 35 34 31 15 23	4 36 6 7 1 34 32 15 23	7 4 8 10 4 35 32 15 23	10 9 8 14 6 35 32 15 23
31	32 26 33 32 30 32 31 15 23		2 32 36 3 35 34 31 15 23		7 5 8 11 4 35 32 15 23	

	JULY	AUG	SEPT	OCT	NOV	DEC
1	10 10 8 14 6 35 32 15 23	13 14 14 18 8 35 31 15 23	16 19 19 21 10 34 31 16 23	19 22 20 23 12 34 31 16 23	22 27 21 24 14 34 31 16 23	25 30 26 23 15 34 31 16 23
2	11 11 8 14 6 35 32 15 23	13 16 14 18 8 35 31 15 23	16 20 19 21 10 34 31 16 23	19 23 20 24 12 34 31 16 23	22 28 21 24 14 34 31 16 23	25 32 26 23 15 34 31 16 23
3	11 12 8 14 6 35 32 15 23	14 17 14 18 8 35 31 15 23	17 21 19 21 10 34 31 16 23	19 25 20 24 12 34 31 16 23	23 29 21 24 14 34 31 16 23	26 33 26 23 15 34 31 16 23
4	11 14 9 15 6 35 32 15 23	14 18 14 18 8 35 31 15 23	17 22 19 21 10 34 31 16 23	20 26 20 24 12 34 31 16 23	23 31 21 24 14 34 31 16 23	26 34 26 23 15 34 31 16 23
5	11 15 9 15 6 35 31 15 23	14 19 14 18 8 35 31 15 23	17 24 19 21 10 34 31 16 23	20 27 20 24 12 34 31 16 23	23 32 22 24 14 34 31 16 23	26 36 26 23 15 34 31 16 23
6	11 16 9 15 6 35 31 15 23	14 20 15 18 8 35 31 15 23	17 25 19 21 10 34 31 16 23	20 28 20 24 12 34 31 16 23	23 33 22 24 14 34 31 16 23	26 1 27 23 15 34 31 16 23
7	11 17 9 15 6 35 31 15 23	14 22 15 18 9 35 31 15 23	17 26 20 22 11 34 31 16 23	20 30 20 24 12 34 31 16 23	23 35 22 24 14 34 31 16 23	26 3 27 23 15 34 31 16 23
8	11 18 9 15 6 35 31 15 23	14 23 15 18 9 35 31 15 23	17 28 20 22 11 34 31 16 23	20 31 20 24 12 34 31 16 23	23 36 22 24 14 34 31 16 23	26 4 27 23 15 34 31 16 23
9	11 20 9 15 7 35 31 15 23	14 24 15 19 9 35 31 15 23	17 29 20 22 11 34 31 16 23	20 33 20 24 12 34 31 16 23	23 2 22 24 14 34 31 16 23	26 6 27 23 15 34 31 16 23
10	11 21 9 15 7 35 31 15 23	14 25 15 19 9 35 31 16 23	17 30 20 22 11 34 31 16 23	20 34 20 24 12 34 31 16 23	23 3 22 24 14 34 31 16 23	26 7 27 23 15 34 31 16 23
11	11 22 10 15 7 35 31 15 23	14 27 16 19 9 35 31 16 23	17 32 20 22 11 34 31 16 23	20 35 19 24 12 34 31 16 23	23 5 23 24 14 34 31 16 23	26 8 27 23 15 34 31 16 23
12	11 23 10 15 7 35 31 15 23	14 28 16 19 9 35 31 16 23	17 33 20 22 11 34 31 16 23	20 1 19 24 13 34 31 16 23	23 6 23 24 14 34 31 16 23	27 10 27 23 15 34 31 16 23
13	12 25 10 16 7 35 31 15 23	15 29 16 19 9 35 31 16 23	18 35 20 22 11 34 31 16 23	20 2 19 24 13 34 31 16 23	24 8 23 23 14 34 31 16 23	27 11 28 23 15 34 31 16 23
14	12 26 10 16 7 35 31 15 23	15 31 16 19 9 34 31 16 23	18 36 20 22 11 34 31 16 23	21 4 19 24 13 34 31 16 23	24 9 23 23 14 34 31 16 23	27 13 28 23 15 34 31 16 23
15	12 27 10 16 7 35 31 15 23	15 32 16 19 9 34 31 16 23	18 2 20 22 11 34 31 16 23	21 5 19 24 13 34 31 16 23	24 11 23 23 14 34 31 16 23	27 14 28 23 15 34 31 16 23
16	12 29 10 16 7 35 31 15 23	15 34 16 19 9 34 31 16 23	18 3 20 22 11 34 31 16 23	21 7 19 24 13 34 31 16 23	24 12 23 23 14 34 31 16 23	27 15 28 23 15 34 31 16 23
17	12 30 11 16 7 35 31 15 23	15 35 17 19 9 34 31 16 23	18 5 20 22 11 34 31 16 23	21 8 19 24 13 34 31 16 23	24 13 24 23 14 34 31 16 23	27 16 28 23 15 34 31 16 23
18	12 31 11 16 7 35 31 15 23	15 1 17 20 9 34 31 16 23	18 6 21 23 11 34 31 16 23	21 10 19 24 13 34 31 16 23	24 14 24 23 14 34 31 16 23	27 18 28 23 15 34 31 16 23
19	12 33 11 16 7 35 31 15 23	15 2 17 20 9 34 31 16 23	18 7 21 23 11 34 31 16 23	21 11 19 24 13 34 31 16 23	24 16 24 23 14 34 31 16 23	27 19 29 23 15 34 31 16 23
20	12 34 11 16 7 35 31 15 23	15 4 17 20 9 34 31 16 23	18 9 21 23 11 34 31 16 23	21 12 19 24 13 34 31 16 23	24 17 24 23 14 34 31 16 23	27 20 29 23 15 34 31 16 23
21	12 36 11 16 7 35 31 15 23	15 5 17 20 9 34 31 16 23	18 10 21 23 11 34 31 16 23	21 14 19 24 13 34 31 16 23	24 18 24 23 14 34 31 16 23	27 21 29 23 15 34 31 16 23
22	12 1 12 17 7 35 31 15 23	15 6 17 20 10 34 31 16 23	18 11 21 23 11 34 31 16 23	21 15 20 24 13 34 31 16 23	24 19 24 23 14 34 31 16 23	28 22 29 23 15 34 31 16 23
23	13 3 12 17 8 35 31 15 23	16 8 18 20 10 34 31 16 23	19 13 21 23 11 34 31 16 23	21 16 20 24 13 34 31 16 23	25 20 24 23 14 34 31 16 23	28 24 29 23 15 34 31 16 23
24	13 4 12 17 8 35 31 15 23	16 9 18 20 10 34 31 16 23	19 14 21 23 12 34 31 16 23	22 17 20 24 13 34 31 16 23	25 22 25 23 14 34 31 16 23	28 25 29 23 15 34 31 16 23
25	13 5 12 17 8 35 31 15 23	16 10 18 20 10 34 31 16 23	19 15 21 23 12 34 31 16 23	22 18 20 24 13 34 31 16 23	25 23 25 23 14 34 31 16 23	28 26 29 24 15 34 31 16 23
26	13 7 12 17 8 35 31 15 23	16 12 18 20 10 34 31 16 23	19 16 21 23 12 34 31 16 23	22 20 20 24 13 34 31 16 23	25 24 25 23 14 34 31 16 23	28 27 30 24 15 34 31 16 23
27	13 8 13 17 8 35 31 15 23	16 13 18 20 10 34 31 16 23	19 17 21 23 12 34 31 16 23	22 21 20 24 13 34 31 16 23	25 25 25 23 15 34 31 16 23	28 29 30 24 15 34 31 16 23
28	13 9 13 17 8 35 31 15 23	16 14 18 21 10 34 31 16 23	19 19 21 23 12 34 31 16 23	22 22 20 24 13 34 31 16 23	25 26 25 23 15 34 31 16 23	28 30 30 24 15 34 31 16 23
29	13 11 13 17 8 35 31 15 23	16 15 18 21 10 34 31 16 23	19 20 21 23 12 34 31 16 23	22 23 20 24 13 34 31 16 23	25 28 25 23 15 34 31 16 23	28 31 30 24 15 34 31 16 23
30	13 12 13 17 8 35 31 15 23	16 17 19 21 10 34 31 16 23	19 21 20 23 12 34 31 16 23	22 24 21 24 13 34 31 16 23	25 29 26 23 14 34 31 16 23	28 33 30 24 15 34 31 16 23
31	13 13 14 18 8 35 31 15 23	16 18 19 21 10 34 31 16 23		22 26 21 24 13 34 31 16 23		28 34 30 24 15 34 31 16 23